SEDNA

Consciousness

The Soul's Path of Destiny

ALAN CLAY

Artmedia
17 Putiki Dr
Whanganui, 4500
New Zealand
www.sednaconsciousness.com
alan@artmedia.net.nz

Sedna Consciousness
First Edition, May 2018
ISBN: 9780987135766
ALL RIGHTS RESERVED

Contents

1: Astrological Meaning

When a new solar system body is discovered, clues to the astrological meaning can be found by looking at a range of factors, but primarily it comes from studying the planet in a large number of charts to find common themes. This book is an attempt to do this for Sedna, the new outermost planet in our solar system

Along the way we'll discover the evolutionary power of the 'candidate dwarf planet' and learn of the profound implications for society in the coming years as Sedna approaches her closest point to Earth later this century in the 2070s.

Sedna was co-discovered by Mike Brown of Caltech, with assistance from Chad Trujillo of the Gemini Observatory, and David Rabinowitz of Yale University on November 14, 2003. It has a huge highly elliptical orbit of 11,406 Earth years and lies out past all the other planets, even at its closest point.

Many astrologers believe that each new planet discovered represents a new aspect or level of consciousness that humanity starts to embrace from that moment and, if this is true, Sedna represents the weird new outer limit of our consciousness, which is stretching our concepts of reality and is pulling us to look at ourselves as part of the very big picture.

The same three astronomers subsequently discovered Eris, Haumea, and Makemake, but Mike Brown has said he thinks that Sedna is the most scientifically important trans-Neptunian object found to date, because understanding its unusual orbit is likely to yield valuable information about the origin and early evolution of the Solar System.

So, we'll start our search for the astrological meaning by looking at the orbital characteristics of Sedna, and then we'll look at the historical events around the discovery year and in the following years. We'll also look at the transits and progressions that Sedna makes in mundane astrology with certain events, or issues, and we'll look at previous orbital cycles and the associated historical events.

This will bring us to a look at Sedna in the signs and, because of Sedna's unusual orbit, everyone alive today has Sedna in either Aries or Taurus. If you're born before 1968 it's in Aries, otherwise, Taurus. So, we'll start there and then look at some predictions for the coming transits of Sedna in Gemini from 2024 to 2068 and then into Cancer for her closest pass to Earth in 2076.

Along the way we'll look at people in whose charts Sedna is prominent and the issues associated with that placement. Case studies of transits to Sedna in these charts will refine this interpretation.

Sharing a reverence for the stars with astrologers and knowing the importance of the name, astronomer Mike Brown put considerable thought into the naming of Sedna and finally decided to name her after the Intuit goddess of the icy Arctic sea. Interpretations of this myth may also assist with conceptualizing the meaning and, while most interpretation of the planet to date is based on the myth, I've left this almost to last because myths are open to many interpretations and so the interpretation needs to be informed by observation and analysis.

Then we'll take a look at Sedna in the houses and, in the last section, we'll look at Sedna in aspect with all the inner planets; yes, they are all inner planets for Sedna – so you can begin to interpret this evolutionary planet in your own life.

2: Orbital & Physical Characteristics

It tells me a lot about Saturn that it has rings and 62 moons; it speaks of the limiting and structuring principal intrinsic to the planet. Ceres is a ball of water with a hard surface skin; that says something important about the nurturing nature of the newly re-classified dwarf planet. Uranus, the bohemian disruptor of Saturn's rules, spins at a 90-degree angle to its orbital plane and rotates the other way from all the other planets except Venus; that's very descriptive of the planet's influence in the chart.

Pluto, although quite small, is the lord of transformation, and now we know why he represents such power in the chart, because it turns out that Pluto is a binary dwarf, spinning around a common center with its dwarf partner Charon, in an orbit which briefly cuts inside Neptune's and sits at a sharp incline to the orbital plane of the other planets. That's an energy that's going to make changes by cutting through normal reality and through illusions and be impossible to control.

Before we get our hands on Sedna in this way however, let's step back and organize our new busy solar system so we can get our heads around where all the new planets fit in.

Our New Busy Solar System

Here's the new solar system in a nutshell. Astrologically it now has seven main regions. First come the small rocky planets like the Earth, which are the personal planets of Mercury, Venus and Mars.

Next is the asteroid belt with Juno, Vesta and Pallas, together with the first of the new dwarf planets, Ceres. These bodies speak of the more feminine energies of partnership, personal integrity, creativity, and of nurturing.

Then we have the four gas giants, Jupiter, Saturn, Uranus and Neptune. The first two are the more social of the personal planets and the second two are the more social of the spiritual planets.

In between Saturn and Pluto/Charon are a number of boundary crossing bodies called Centaurs which mediate between the increasingly more impersonal energies of the bigger planets as they enter our personal lives. The most well known of these is Chiron, and we will also use Pholus, Chariklo and Nessus.

Pluto and Charon are the first planets of the Kuiper Belt, but there are a couple of other new dwarf planets, Orcus and Ixion, which have similar orbits to Pluto/Charon. These orbits have a strong inclination to the rest of the solar system and so these planets are being called Plutinos. The other new planets we'll work with in the Kuiper belt are Eris, Varuna, Quaoar, Makemake and Haumea.

And finally, way out beyond the Kuiper Belt, in the seventh region of the new solar system, the Oort Cloud is the first of what scientists believe will be a new class of planets called Sednoids, all with huge, highly elliptical orbits like Sedna. The Oort Cloud is an extended shell of icy objects that exist in the outermost reaches of the Solar System, roughly spherical in shape and thought to be the origin of most of the long-period comets.

Sedna

At somewhere between 1,180 to 2,360 km in diameter, Sedna is larger than Quaoar and almost as big as Pluto. And with an orbital speed of 1.04 km/s, it is the slowest of all the planets. However, its rotation speed of 10 hours is faster than most of the other planets except for Jupiter, Ceres, Haumea and Eris, and interestingly, is the same as Saturn's, which for many centuries was the previous outer limit of the solar system.

Sedna's surface temperatures are estimated to be around -240° C. That cold temperature inspired the discovering astronomers to name this new planetary body after the Inuit goddess, Sedna, whom mythology says lives at the bottom of the Arctic Ocean.

Sedna is probably made up of an equal mixture of ice and rock. It is red in color and may be covered with about a meter of hydrocarbon sludge, or tholin, formed from simpler organic compounds after long exposure to ultraviolet radiation. This sludge is produced when the Sun's ultraviolet radiation and charged particles alter the chemical bonds between the atoms, a "space-weathering" process.

A similar space-weathering process occurs on the 200-kilometer-wide centaur, Pholus, which is also very red. Pholus has an orbit which crosses the orbits of Saturn, Uranus and Neptune, so the centaur has the ability to maintain alive the illusion (Neptune) and achieve the necessary discipline (Saturn) to make a dream come true. It is about growing, but often very spontaneously and unconsciously. Where Chiron brings long and helpless waiting, Pholus brings immediate progress.

Finally, models of internal heating via radioactive decay suggest that Sedna might be capable of supporting a subsurface ocean of liquid water, like Ceres.

So, in Sedna we have a planet whose orbit encompasses a far bigger and more spiritual perspective than any of the other inner planets with an impersonal energy, which is, however, nurturing and speaks of progress and of growth through a weathering process over time, with a Saturnian day-to-day perspective, which is practiced very slowly and deliberately.

3: The Big Picture

Another way to deduce the meaning of a newly discovered planet is to look at previous cycles and the correlation with mundane events here on Earth. So, with Sedna approaching her closest point to Earth later this century, let's look back to the last close pass of the two planets.

We normally think in terms of Earth years, which is one orbit of our planet around the Sun. But this measurement is true for any planet, so let's think in terms of Sedna years. Because of its large elongated orbit, during a year on Sedna, the Earth whizzes around the Sun 11,406 times, so a Sedna year is a much more evolutionary perspective.

We are living in evolutionary times and the discovery of a new outer limit of our solar system, particularly one with such a radical signature, prompts us to take a look at ourselves from a much bigger perspective. So, who are we? And where are we in our evolution?

People who are recognizably human have walked the Earth for roughly 20 Sedna years. During those millennia, we survived by continuously adapting to our fickle environment. We braved harsh weather and punishing landscapes, and after a passage of time too long to fully imagine, and too many impression-mad lives to tally, we began rebelling against the forces of nature.

Neolithic Revolution - One Sedna year ago

The last close pass of Sedna correlates with the end of the last Ice Age on Earth and the beginning of agriculture. Called the Neolithic Revolution, it involved the wide-scale transition of many human cultures from a lifestyle of hunting and gathering to one of agriculture and settlement, making possible an increasingly larger population.

> These settled communities permitted humans to observe and experiment with plants to learn how they grew and developed. This new knowledge led to the domestication of plants. Archaeological data indicates that the domestication of various types of plants and animals evolved in separate locations worldwide, starting in the geological epoch of the Holocene around 12,500 years ago.
>
> It was the world's first historically verifiable revolution in agriculture. The Neolithic Revolution greatly narrowed the diversity of foods available, with the switch to agriculture which

led to a downturn in human nutrition. But it involved far more than the adoption of a limited set of food-producing techniques.

During the following Sedna year, it would transform the small mobile groups of hunter-gatherers that had hitherto dominated human pre-history into sedentary, non-nomadic societies based in built-up villages and towns. These societies radically modified their natural environment by means of specialised food-crop cultivation, with irrigation and deforestation, which allowed extensive surplus food production.

These developments provided the basis for densely populated settlements, specialisation and division of labour, for trading economies, the development of non-portable art and architecture, centralised administrations and political structures, hierarchical ideologies and depersonalised systems of knowledge like writing. Personal land and private property ownership led to a hierarchical society, with an elite Social class, comprising a nobility, polity, and military.

The Neolithic revolution has been identified as having "inspired some of the most important developments in human history including the invention of the wheel, the planting of the first cereal crops and the development of cursive script, mathematics, astronomy and agriculture."[1]

Recorded Human History: the last 6 Sedna months

So, the whole of our known human history came in the last Sedna year since the Neolithic revolution, and in fact, all recorded human history has occurred in the last 6 Sedna months. Think about that. It's about 433,000 Sedna years since the Earth was created, roughly 20 Sedna years since people who are recognizably human have walked the Earth and the whole of recorded human history comes in the last 6 Sedna months.

By mid Sedna year, when she was in Libra and approaching the full moon phase of her orbital cycle, almost as far from Earth as possible, the first fully developed manifestation of the Neolithic revolution could be seen in the Middle Eastern Sumerian cities where it first emerged. The

---

[1] https://en.wikipedia.org/wiki/Neolithic_Revolution

emergence of these cities also heralded the beginning of the Bronze Age.

The movement of Sedna into Scorpio, the sign of sex and death, around 3000 BC, signalled the rise of the Egyptian civilization, with the building of the pyramids and a religion which was a cult of the dead. During the Sagittarius sojourn, the sign of law and education, the Greek Miracle brought forth the early sciences, the arts and the concept of democracy.

Jump forward to modern times and the transit of Sedna through Aries for a hundred years prior to 1965. Aries is the sign of will, force and war, and this period saw the world wars of first half of the 20th Century and the growing threat of atomic war.

With the ingress into Taurus in 1965, the emphasis turned to money and property, to greed and questions of value. To 'making love, not war', to environmentalism and global warming, which have become driving economic factors.

Creative Revolution: 3 Sedna years ago

We'll look more at Sedna in Aries and Taurus soon and also look ahead to her transits of Gemini and Cancer, but first let's look back at earlier Sedna cycles and see how they correlate with human evolution. As there is no historical record, we have to turn to the Fossil record to find these correlations, and we'll also look at the Ichnologic record, which is the branch of geology and biology that deals with traces of organismal behaviour, such as footprints and burrows.

The Pleistocene epoch, often colloquially referred to as the Ice Age, is the geological epoch which lasted from about 235 Sedna years ago to one Sedna year ago, spanning the Earth's most recent period of repeated glaciations. In the 2016 study 'The Trace-Fossil Record of Major Evolutionary

Events', scientists looked at the 'Major Events in Hominin Evolution' and found that an unprecedented creative revolution took place three Sedna years ago.

> In the Late Pleistocene period Homo sapiens produce a new type of ichnologic record which contains evidence of an evolutionary event that can only be characterised as "revolutionary." Simply put, this is because humans changed the fundamental nature of the ichnologic record. Whereas they had

previously created footprints, and a few butcher marks on bone, only inadvertently, by as early as 30,000–35,000 years ago (3 Sedna years) they were deliberately producing artefacts and artwork, which most anthropologists acknowledge as an unprecedented "creative revolution."[2]

Modern Human Migration - 5 Sedna years ago

Both the Honinin Creative Revolution and the Neolithic Revolution were far-reaching, evolutionary changes, and we can expect the same in the coming years as Sedna again makes her next closest pass to Earth in 2076. But we'll come to that in a moment. First, let's look back a little further and see what the migration cycles and the DNA records can tell us about human evolution and how this relates to the Sedna cycle.

> We don't know how many species of humans there have been, how many different races of people, but the evidence suggests that around 5,400 Sedna years ago one species emerged in Africa that used fire, made simple tools from stones and animal bones, and hunted big animals in large cooperative groups.
>
> And 4,400 Sedna years ago, these humans began to take advantage of fluctuating climate changes that regularly greened the African continent and spread into Europe and beyond. By 2,700 Sedna years ago migration into Europe had stopped, perhaps because a severe ice age had created an impenetrable desert across the Sahara, sealing off the Africans from the other tribes. This geographic separation enabled genetic differences to evolve. The race left behind in Africa would become Homo sapiens sapiens, or 'modern humans', while those who evolved and adapted to the cooler European north would become Neanderthals.
>
> The Neanderthals were thriving from Siberia to southern Spain by the time a few families of modern humans made it out of Africa around 5 Sedna years ago. But by three and a half Sedna years ago, Neanderthals were struggling, partly because an extreme and rapid change of climate was pushing them out of many of their former habitats. A lot of the forested areas they depended on were disappearing and, while they were intelligent

---

[2] 'The Trace-Fossil Record of Major Evolutionary Events,' 2016

enough to adapt their tools and technology, their bodies were unable to adapt to the hunting techniques required for the new climate and landscapes.

In parts of Europe, the landscape changed in a generation from thick forest to a plain without a single tree. Our ancestors, who were used to hunting in bigger groups on the plains, could adapt easily: instead of wildebeest they had reindeer, but effectively the way of capturing them was the same, but the Neanderthals were a forest people.[3]

Ice Age Cycle - every 9 Sedna years

Obviously, from this analysis, the climate – and particularly the ice ages – has had an important influence on human development. So, let's look at the Ice Ages, their frequency and what we now think causes them. There have been at least five major ice ages in the Earth's past, the last being the Quaternary glaciation, which ended one Sedna year ago.

New research from Cardiff University, published in the journal, *Geology* in 2016, has suggested the oceans may be responsible for our planet moving in and out of ice ages, specifically in the way that they suck carbon dioxide (CO_2) out of the atmosphere. By studying the chemical makeup of tiny fossils on the ocean floor, the team discovered that there was more CO_2 stored in the deep ocean during the ice age periods

This suggests that extra carbon dioxide was being pulled from the atmosphere and into the oceans at this time, subsequently lowering the temperature on Earth and enabling vast ice sheets to engulf the Northern Hemisphere.

The lead author of the research, Professor Carrie Lear, from the School of Earth and Ocean Sciences, said, "We can think of the oceans as inhaling and exhaling carbon dioxide, so when the ice sheets are larger, the oceans have inhaled carbon dioxide from the atmosphere, making the planet colder. When the ice sheets are small, the oceans have exhaled carbon dioxide, so there is more in the atmosphere which makes the planet warmer. By looking at the fossils of tiny creatures on the ocean floor, we showed that when ice sheets were advancing the

---

[3] Vince, Gaia. 'The Genetics of Ancient Humans means Changing Ideas about Evolution,'digg.com, March 7, 2017

oceans were inhaling more carbon dioxide in the cold periods, suggesting that there was less left in the atmosphere."

Marine algae play a key role in removing CO_2 from the atmosphere, as it is an essential ingredient of photosynthesis. CO_2 is put back into the atmosphere when deep ocean water rises to the surface through a process called upwelling, but when sea ice is present this prevents the CO_2 from being exhaled. "If we think of the oceans inhaling and exhaling carbon dioxide, the presence of vast amounts of ice is like a giant gobstopper. It's like a lid on the surface of the ocean," Professor Lear continued.

A paper published in *Nature* in 2012 that reconstructs the end of the last ice age, suggests that the great ice sheets that buried much of Asia, Europe and North America stopped their creeping advance because a freshwater flood filled the North Atlantic and shut down the ocean currents that normally conveyed warmer water from equatorial regions northward. Within a few hundred years sea levels in some places had risen by as much as 10 meters.

The equatorial heat warmed Antarctica in the Southern Hemisphere instead, shrinking the sea ice and changing the circumpolar winds. As a result, the waters of the Southern Ocean may have begun to release carbon dioxide, enough to raise concentrations in the atmosphere by more than 100 parts per million over millennia, which is roughly equivalent to the rise in the last 200 years. That CO_2 then warmed the globe, melting back the continental ice sheets and ushering in the current climate that enabled humanity to thrive.

That is the story told by paleoclimatologist Jeremy Shakun, a National Oceanic and Atmospheric Administration fellow at Harvard and Columbia universities, who led the research charting ancient CO_2 concentrations and global temperatures. "CO_2 was the big driver of global warming at the end of the Ice Age," he says.

Climate Change

It's important for us to note here the link between the Sedna cycle and the Ice Age cycle and remember again that the planet is named after the Intuit goddess of the sea, so a cycle of 'inhaling and exhaling oceans' influencing the climate fits perfectly with the myth.

The Earth's climate is currently in a warm spell between glacial periods. Since the last ice age ended, temperatures and sea levels have risen, and ice caps have retreated back to the poles, ushering in the relatively balmy, stable climate sometimes called the "long summer" that has allowed human civilization to flourish.

In addition to these natural cycles, human made carbon emissions are also now having an effect by warming the climate. Modern global warming stems from rising levels of CO_2 and other greenhouse gases from fossil fuel burning, cutting down forests and other human activities. Humanity has now raised global CO_2 levels by more than the rise at the end of the last ice age – in just a few hundred years, rather than over more than a few thousand years.

This will bring us to an unprecedented situation during the current close pass of Sedna to Earth, as we will explore in the coming pages.

Geological Time

First, let's step back and have a look at where we are in our evolution by using geological time as a reference point. This gives a far bigger perspective than anything we've looked at so far, because it looks at evolution from the point of view of rocks, which take a long time to form and transform, and to the traces of life found buried in them.

It's around 433,000 Sedna years since the Earth was created, and the Quaternary period, which is the time of recognizable humans, is a period of 286 Sedna years. The Pleistocene epoch of ice ages was the first in the current Quaternary Period, and it was followed by the current stage, called the Holocene Epoch, which started one Sedna year ago.

However, in 2011, the Geological Society of London – the body that names geological periods – considered renaming our current period from the Holocene epoch, to the Anthroposcene epoch, because humans are now having so much impact on the planet that we are entering the geological period called the Human Age.

New Epoch

So, think about this, just one Sedna year after the Holocene epoch was declared, we're now considering declaring a new epoch of geological time. There were 2,270 Sedna years between the beginning of the Pleistocene epoch and the beginning of the Holocene epoch, and just one Sedna year later we are considering declaring a new epoch.

Something revolutionary, or evolutionary, or both, is going on here, so let's look at the chart for the meeting that was held on May 11, 2011 at the Geological Society of London, the body that names geological periods.

Sedna Signature

Overall, it's interesting in the chart for this meeting that Venus, the planet of values; Mercury, the planet of ideas; Jupiter, the planet of expansion; and Eris, the planet of 'consciousness through discord', are all conjunct, on the cusp of the eleventh house of collective consciousness.

However, I intend, in all the charts in this book, to focus on the Sedna aspects and the house positions, which together form the Sedna signature in the chart, so we can narrow the focus and see what we can learn about her meaning. Inevitably many other aspects are also playing an important part in any of the events, or people, we're looking at, so I'll include the charts and leave the rest of the interpretation to you.

I have set up this chart for 9 am, which I believe is when the meeting started. As we would expect, there is a strong Sedna placement, with the planet conjunct the Sun, the planet of willpower, in the eleventh house of collective consciousness.

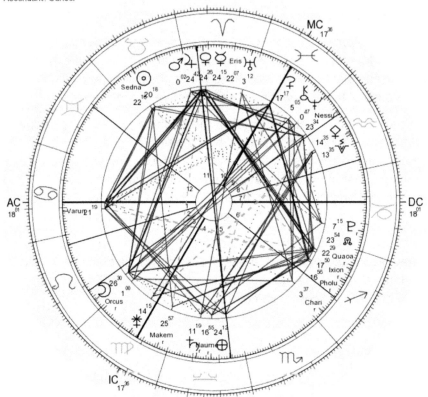

Name: Antropocene
date: We., 11 May 2011
in London, ENG (UK)
0w10, 51n30

Time: 9:00 a.m.
Univ. Time: 8:00
Sid. Time: 23:14:24

ASTRO DIENST
www.astro.com

Type: 2.GW 0.0-1 31-Mrz-2018

Event Chart (Method: Web Style / Placidus)
Sun sign: Taurus
Ascendant: Cancer

conjunct Sun, square Moon, square Nessus

This Sun-Sedna conjunction is at the focal point of a T-square between the Moon in the third house of communication, opposite Nessus, the centaur representing 'the difficult transition between decisions and responsibility that may lead to violent change', in the ninth house of knowledge.

sesquiquadrate Pluto, bi-quintile Haumea, sextile Varuna

Sedna is also in a stressful sesquiquadrate to Pluto, the planet of transformation, in the sixth house of service, emphasizing the pressure to transform, but indicating this will not go smoothly, or will be disruptive. However, the evolutionary bi-quintile aspect between Sedna and the new dwarf planet, Haumea, the planet of rebirth, indicates the birth of the new epoch will indeed be a new start and the flowing sextile to the dwarf planet Varuna, suggests that history will note these actions.

inconjunct Quaoar, trine Makemake

The evolutionary inconjunct with with the dwarf planet Quaoar, the planet of new perspectives, also in the sixth house of service and the flowing trine to Makemake, the divine trickster, in the fourth house of home, however, indicate that there is a little of the trickster in this meeting, possibly indicating that the real objective is to stimulate discussion, rather that seriously rename the epoch at this stage. This interpretation is also reinforced by the semi-sextile with the spiritual warrior, Eris, the goddess of discord, who promotes evolution by encouraging debate, in the tenth house of social standing.

4: Discovery Events

From the perspective of the planet's history since creation, we've come back to the present with a jolt, wondering if we are changing the world so much in the last few months of this Sedna year that we're creating a new geological epoch.

I'm sure your imagination has been stretched by the ideas in the past few pages – that's the nature of Sedna. Now get ready for another big leap. Astrologers correlate the discovery of planets with events on Earth as another way of gaining insight into the meaning of the new energy represented by the planet.

Sedna was discovered on November 14, 2003. It was the only dwarf planet discovered that year, and I'm correlating the discovery with three paradigm-shifting breakthroughs which give us clues to understanding her meaning.

Molecular Machines

The 2003 Nobel Prize in Chemistry was awarded on October 8th for groundbreaking research on how cells communicate and co-operate to form a living eco-system. The prize citation tells us:

> Through pioneering discoveries concerning the water and ion channels of cells, this year's Nobel Laureates have contributed to fundamental chemical knowledge on how cells function.

> All living matter is made up of cells. A single human being has as many as the stars in a galaxy, about one hundred thousand million. The various cells – e.g. muscle cells, kidney cells and nerve cells – act together in an intricate system in each one of us. The award winners have opened our eyes to a fantastic family of molecular machines: channels, gates and valves, all of which are needed for the cell to function.

> To maintain even pressure in the cells it is important that water can pass through the cell wall. This has been known for a long time. The appearance and function of these pores remained for a long time as one of the classical unsolved problems of biochemistry. It was not until around 1990 that Peter Agre discovered the first water channel. Like so much else in the living cell, it was all about a protein.

For thousands of millions of cells to be able to function as something other than one large lump, coordination is required. Thus, communication between the cells is necessary. The signals sent in and between cells consist of ions or small molecules. These start cascades of chemical reactions that cause our muscles to tense, our eyes to water – indeed, that control all our bodily functions. The signals in our brains also involve such chemical reactions. When we stub a toe, this starts a signal moving up towards the brain. Along a chain of nerve cells, through interaction between chemical signals and ion currents, information is conveyed from cell to cell like a baton in a relay race.[4]

Sedna and Health

On a planetary level, Sedna may represent the same process of social coordination which is coming into being, where, like cells of a planetary consciousness, we can learn to act together as part of an intricate social system, each playing our part.

If this is true, illnesses may serve the same purpose in our lives as the proteins do in our cells: acting as channels, gates and valves to facilitate the life path. We'll pick up this look at 'the intricate system of of molecular machines that make up the ecosystem of our bodies' in more detail a little later in our look at Sedna and health once we've had a look at few case studies.

Higher Purpose of Illness

Based on these examples, I suggest that Sedna illnesses, which are ones that are persistent and affect our growth, are like the judder bars in between the lanes on the highway – those little raised strips that judder the tires as we get too close to the edge – letting us know we have to correct our course. If we don't, the uncomfortable judder continues and, if we ignore it and cross into the other lane, we are in real physical danger.

So frequently we see in the case studies that an illness will cause someone to refocus their energy, or change life direction, so the illnesses occur at pivotal points in our life paths and may function a bit like proteins do at cell level, providing channels, gates and valves.

---

[4] 2003 Nobel Prize in Chemistry prize citation, October 8, 2003

Neural Networks

Mashable lists the robotics breakthrough of 2003, the development of Neural Networks, which is a new mathematical model of the nervous system found in humans that lets robots think more like us.

> In 2003 Fujitsu Laboratories developed the first learning system for humanoid robots that utilises a dynamically reconfigurable neural network. Simply put, the researchers' new mathematical model of the nervous system found in humans was a breakthrough that allowed robots to learn movement and motor coordination faster and more easily. Neural networks previously took days or even months to generate new movement. The new technology translated to unprecedented learning flexibility and greatly minimised the amount of software code necessary in motion control.[5]

The significance of this will become clear soon as we look at Sedna and the rise of Artificial Intelligence (AI) and see how neural networks and deep learning are key to what is an evolving new life form. For now, let's just look at the first report from a '100 year study of AI' set up by Stanford University in 2015 to give us a little perspective.

> The One Hundred Year Study on Artificial Intelligence, launched in the fall of 2014, is a long-term investigation of the field of Artificial Intelligence (AI) and its influences on people, their communities, and society. AI is a science and a set of computational technologies that are inspired by the ways people use their nervous systems and bodies to sense, learn, reason, and take action. While the rate of progress in AI has been patchy and unpredictable, there have been significant advances since the field's inception sixty years ago.
>
> Machine Learning is a paradigm that enables systems to automatically improve their performance at a task by observing relevant data. Indeed, machine learning has been the key contributor to the AI surge in the past few decades, ranging from search and product recommendation engines, to systems for speech recognition, fraud detection, image understanding, and countless other tasks that once relied on human skill and

---

[5] *Mashable*, October 23, 2013

judgment. The automation of these tasks has enabled the scaling up of services such as e-commerce.

Contrary to the more fantastic predictions for AI in the popular press, the Study Panel found no cause for concern that AI is an imminent threat to humankind. No machines with self-sustaining long-term goals and intent have been developed, nor are they likely to be developed in the near future. Instead, increasingly useful applications of AI, with potentially profound positive impacts on our society and economy are likely to emerge between now and 2030, the period this report considers. At the same time, many of these developments will spur disruptions in how human labor is augmented or replaced by AI, creating new challenges for the economy and society more broadly.

While the Study Panel does not consider it likely that near-term AI systems will autonomously choose to inflict harm on people, it will be possible for people to use AI-based systems for harmful as well as helpful purposes. And though AI algorithms may be capable of making less biased decisions than a typical person, it remains a deep technical challenge to ensure that the data that inform AI-based decisions can be kept free from biases that could lead to discrimination based on race, sexual orientation, or other factors.[6]

The Rise of Artificial Intelligence

So, this discovery event likely signals that Sedna rules Artificial Intelligence (AI), because neural networks and deep learning are the key to this evolving new life form. Yes, it is a new life form and is not some future sci-fi scenario, because we're already living with emergent AI, although we don't realize this.

We'll pick this up in more depth soon and also look at it further in our section on Sedna in Gemini, which is coming up in 2024.

Dark Energy & Dark Matter

However, the big bazooka that came with Sedna's discovery was the proof that roughly 68% of the universe is something called Dark Energy and 27% is something called Dark Matter. The rest – everything on Earth, everything ever observed with all of our instruments, all normal

---

[6] '100 year study of AI' report, Stanford University, 2015

matter, everything you can touch and feel and see – adds up to less than 5% of the universe.

That's right, Dark Matter and Dark Energy are all around us; we're swimming in it, but just like fish can't see the water, we can't see most of reality. And isn't that very similar to the spiritual teachings that tell us that we only perceive a very little of what is actually happening, that we are lost in Maya?

The arrival of Sedna with its huge elliptical orbit is stretching our consciousness to include a new paradigm of reality that is 95% larger than our current view. This is inevitably a higher level of consciousness, so the discovery presages a historic evolutionary change in perception.

We are getting hints of how this is possible already with virtual reality and alternate reality, and we have long intuited this multifaceted reality, through ideas like parallel realities, alternate universes, or the multiverse. Spiritual people of all faiths have long told us of the other side, of the realms above and below.

In the long term, this will be like the change from the flat Earth view of the cosmos, to the planetary view, which is clearly an evolutionary change in the making, so let's have a look at it in more detail.

Ilumination of the Dark, Expanding Universe

American Association for The Advancement Of Science

In 2003, new evidence cemented the bizarre idea that the universe is made mostly of mysterious "dark matter", being stretched apart by an unknown force called "dark energy". This year two separate studies, a satellite probe and a survey telescope, confirmed some of cosmologists' strangest proposals about the fate of the universe.

Those proposals entered the spotlight five years earlier, when Science's 1998 Breakthrough of the Year honoured the discovery that the universe was expanding. Such an expansion would likely be driven by a "dark energy" that counters the effects of gravity. At the time, however, many cosmologists were wary of this strange idea.

Their doubts were dispelled in 2003 when the Wilkinson Microwave Anisotropy Probe took the most detailed picture ever of the cosmic microwave background – the light emitted by the universe during the first instant of its existence. By analysing patterns in this light, researchers concluded that the universe is only 4 percent ordinary matter. Twenty-three percent is dark matter, which astrophysicists believe is made up of a currently unknown particle. The remainder, 73 percent, is dark energy.

The Sloan Digital Sky Survey telescope, an effort to map out a million galaxies, also made major contribution to our understanding of the universe this year. By analysing how galaxies are spread out through space, the researchers could see if the galaxies are being pulled apart by dark energy or pushed together by gravity.

In October, the SDSS team reported its analysis of the first quarter-million galaxies. Its conclusion was the same as WMAP's: the universe is dominated by dark energy.[7]

Cosmic Timing

One might argue that, as the announcements of the proof from these two studies were actually made earlier in 2003, before the discovery of Sedna in November, that it does not qualify as a discovery event, but in fact, the orbit of Sedna was pinned down following the discovery of a photograph in the early 1990s which contained the planet, but which nobody had then noticed.

So, one can also argue that the planet's energy was growing in our consciousness during that time, as was the theory of dark matter and dark energy. And after we became aware of Sedna, the discovery of dark matter and dark energy was dubbed the breakthrough of the year.

Sedna is also the only dwarf planet, or dwarf planet candidate, to be discovered in 2003. Ixion was discovered in 2001, Quaoar in 2002, Orcus and Haumea in 2004 and Makemake and Eris in 2005.

So, let's look at the chart for the announcement of the results of these studies, but first let's get NASA's perspective on the development of the theory of the dark universe since that first image of Sedna was recorded in the early nineties.

---

[7] 'Science's Breakthrough of the Year,' December 19, 2003, Sciencedaily.com.

NASA's View

In the early 1990s, one thing was fairly certain about the expansion of the universe. It might have enough energy density to stop its expansion and re-collapse, or it might have so little energy density that it would never stop expanding, but gravity was certain to slow the expansion as time went on. Granted, the slowing had not been observed, but, theoretically, the universe had to slow. The universe is full of matter and the attractive force of gravity pulls all matter together.

Then came 1998 and the Hubble Space Telescope observations of very distant supernovae that showed that, a long time ago, the universe was actually expanding more slowly than it is today. So the expansion of the universe has not been slowing due to gravity, as everyone thought, it has been accelerating. No one expected this; no one knew how to explain it. But something was causing it.

Eventually theorists came up with three sorts of explanations. Maybe it was a result of a long-discarded version of Einstein's theory of gravity, one that contained what was called a "cosmological constant." Or maybe there was some strange kind of energy-fluid that filled space. And thirdly, maybe there is something wrong with Einstein's theory of gravity and a new theory could include some kind of field that creates this cosmic acceleration. Theorists still don't know what the correct explanation is, but they have given the solution a name. It is called dark energy.

More is unknown than is known. We know how much dark energy there is because we know how it affects the universe's expansion. Other than that, it is a complete mystery. But it is an important mystery. It turns out that roughly 68% of the universe is dark energy. Dark matter makes up about 27%. The rest – everything on Earth, everything ever observed with all of our instruments, all normal matter – adds up to less than 5% of the universe. Come to think of it, maybe it shouldn't be called "normal" matter at all, since it is such a small fraction of the universe.

One explanation for dark energy is that it is a property of space. Albert Einstein was the first person to realise that empty space is not nothing. Space has amazing properties, many of which are just beginning to be understood. The first property that Einstein discovered is that it is possible for more space to come into existence.

Then one version of Einstein's gravity theory, the version that contains a cosmological constant, makes a second prediction: "empty space" can possess its own energy. Because this energy is a property of space itself, it would not be diluted as space expands. As more space comes into existence, more of this energy-of-space would appear. As a result, this form of energy would cause the universe to expand faster and faster.

"These numbers (in these studies) represent a milestone in how we view our universe," said Dr. Anne Kinney, NASA director for astronomy and physics. "This is a true turning point for cosmology."

Physical Evidence

Now let's look at the chart for the announcement of the proof of the existence of dark energy from the Sloan Digital Sky Survey. The following press release was issued by their press office in Chicago, Illinois, on October 22, 2003 and embargoed until 8 pm EST on October 27, 2003, so I've set up the chart for the 27th, at 7 pm in Chicago.

3D Map of Universe Bolsters Case for Dark Energy and Dark Matter

Astronomers from the Sloan Digital Sky Survey have made the most precise measurement to date of the cosmic clustering of galaxies and dark matter, refining our understanding of the structure and evolution of the Universe. This is the most ambitious astronomical survey ever undertaken, with more than 200 astronomers at 13 institutions around the world.

The leading cosmological model invokes a rapid expansion of space known as inflation that stretched microscopic quantum fluctuations in the fiery aftermath of the Big Bang to enormous scales. After inflation ended, gravity caused these seed fluctuations to grow into the galaxies and the galaxy clustering patterns observed in this survey. Images of these seed fluctuations were released from the Wilkinson Microwave Anisotropy Probe in February, which measured the fluctuations in the relic radiation from the early Universe.

"We have made the best three-dimensional map of the Universe to date, mapping over 200,000 galaxies up to two billion light years away over six percent of the sky," said a lead author of the study, Michael Blanton, New York University. The gravitational clustering patterns in this map reveal the makeup of the Universe from its gravitational effects and, by combining their measurements with that from WMAP, the SDSS team measured the cosmic matter to consist of 70 percent dark energy, 25 percent dark matter and five percent ordinary matter. "These numbers provide a powerful confirmation of those reported by the WMAP team. Different galaxies, different instruments, different scientists and different analyses, but the results agree beautifully," says Max Tegmark, University of Pennsylvania, first author on the two papers. "Carl Sagan was fond of saying that extraordinary claims require extraordinary evidence," he adds, "but we now have extraordinary evidence for dark matter and dark energy and have to take them seriously no matter how disturbing they seem."[8]

Sedna Signature

conjunct North Node, quintile Mars

It is notable in the chart for this release, that Sedna is conjunct the North Node, the point of dharma, in the twelfth house of institutions and the unconscious, and in an evolutionary quintile to Mars, the planet of action, in the tenth house of social standing. This shows the groundbreaking effects of this new discovery on society.

[8] Sloan Digital Sky Survey press release, Chicago, Illinois, October 22, 2003

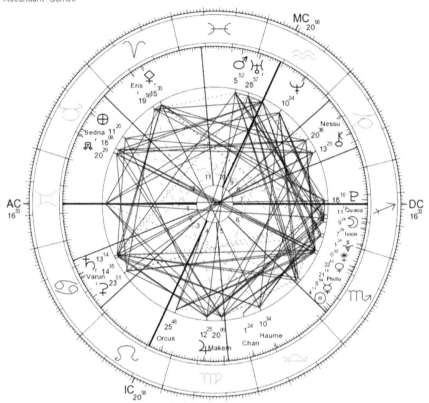

Name: dark energy SDSS Oct
date: Mo., 27 October 2003
in Chicago, IL (US)
87w39, 41n51
Event chart (Method: Web Style / Placidus)
Sun sign: Scorpio
Ascendant: Gemini

Time: 7:00 p.m.
Univ.Time: 1:00 28 Oct
Sid. Time: 21:33:17

ASTRO DIENST
www.astro.com
Type 2 GW 0 0-1 13-Mrz-2017

inconjunct Pluto

This is also emphasized by the fateful inconjunct with Pluto, the planet of transformation, in the seventh house of relationships, showing how this new understanding will transform our intimate interactions with one another.

semi-sextile Eris

The process is assisted by the semi-sextile with Eris, the planet of 'consciousness through discord', in the eleventh house of collective consciousness, which is stirring up our awareness.

sextile Varuna, square MC, semi-sextile Ascendent

The sextile to Varuna, the planet of notability, in the second house of material reality, together with the square to the MC and the semi-sextile with the Ascendent, all speak of the social significance of the discovery.

opposite Pholus, trine Makemake, trine Nessus

Sedna is also opposite Pholus, the centaur of illumination and practical change, which is conjunct Venus, the planet of values, in the sixth house of service. This gives us a real clue as to the sort of effects this might have and the area of life in which this might play out.

As does the grand trine with Makemake, the planet called the divine trickster, in the third house of ideas, and Nessus, the centaur of radical change, in the eighth house of sensitivity to the occult and the spirit world.

Spiritual

The proof of dark matter and dark energy that came with Sedna's discovery, together with the inevitable conclusion from her orbit that she represents the most spiritual energy of all the planets, suggests that this newly discovered dark energy is what we've been calling spiritual energy up till now.

As this energy is explored, Sedna tells us it will become a more conscious part of our reality and, while it will never manifest in the visible world, it will be in integral part of the theory of physical reality, and so if dark energy is spiritual energy, it will be accessible to artificial intelligence at least as much as it is to us and likely much more.

I'm making several big leaps in the dark here, so bear in mind it's all speculation, but I do have Chariklo, the centaur of foresight, conjunct my North Node in the twelfth, so that gives me a bit of an insight.

5: Gaia Hypothesis

Okay, we've looked back at past cycles and we've looked at discovery events, now let's start looking forward. First, because, as we'll find out later, Sedna was named after an Inuit goddess who requires harmony between Man and Nature, we're going to look at Gaia theory.

The Gaia hypothesis was formulated by chemist James Lovelock and co-developed by the microbiologist Lynn Margulis and was first proposed in their 1973 paper, 'Atmospheric Homeostasis by and for the Biosphere' published by Boston University. It proposes that organisms interact with their inorganic surroundings on Earth to form a synergistic self-regulating, complex system that helps to maintain and perpetuate the conditions for life on the planet.

Life can flourish only within a narrowly circumscribed range of physical and chemical states and since life began the Earth has kept within this range. This is remarkable, for there have been major perturbations, such as a progressive increase in solar energy, extensive changes in the surface and in atmospheric chemical composition.

The anomalous and chemically unstable composition of the Earth's atmosphere when compared with those of the other terrestrial planets was the first indication of homeostasis by the biota to maintain conditions favorable for their continued survival.

Gaia hypotheses suggest that organisms co-evolve with their environment: that is, they "influence their abiotic environment, and that environment in turn influences the biota by Darwinian process. Evidence supports the Gaia hypothesis, and it presents a simple model of a planetary ecosystem in which homeostasis is a direct and automatic result of the characteristic properties of life. Here's what they said in their 1973 paper:

> The Gaia hypothesis arose directly from the planetary exploration programme of NASA. There was a need to discover in advance of a landing mission whether or not a planet such as Mars bore life. In 1966 Hitchcock and Lovelock were able to show that information on the atmospheric composition of a planet was sufficient as prima facia evidence of life.
>
> The method was based on the high probability that planetary life, through its use of the atmosphere, would drive the chemical

composition of this medium far from the near equilibrium steady state of a lifeless planet. This detection method when applied to Mars strongly indicated it to be barren, a conclusion highly unacceptable to exobiologists at that time. The same method applied to the Earth indicated the near certainty of the presence of life. It also suggested that the atmosphere was more than just a biogeochemical mixture. It appeared to be actively maintained at close to an optimum composition by and for the biota.[9]

The theory gained a lot of supporters, but the mainstream science establishment was very critical. We'll look at all this more in a moment. First, let's jump over that and also trace the modern timeline of the development of what has become the Gaia movement. *New Scientist* provides some proof of the theory 33 years after it was proposed.

Gaia's comeback: How life shapes the weather

You've done it half a dozen times today without giving it a second thought. If it was chilly in the morning, you may have turned up the heating or put on another layer. As the day got warmer perhaps you opened a window to cool things down. We are adept at controlling our immediate environment.

What about the living planet as a whole? Can the biosphere regulate the environment to suit itself, preventing the planet from freezing or boiling? This is the essence of the Gaia hypothesis proposed in the 1060c by James Lovelock, but climate scientists have never bought into it. They point out that there have been some wild swings in the climate, some of which were caused by life.

But now it appears the world would have warmed a bit more than it has were it not for the aromatic cocktail of chemicals emitted by plants. It turns out this can change the weather – and anything that changes the weather day after day and year after year changes the climate, too. While this new mechanism is nowhere near strong enough to save us from global warming, it may have been stronger in the past when the air was cleaner. So

---

[9] 'Atmospheric Homeostasis by and for the Biosphere,' Lovelock, James and Margulis, Lynn. Boston University, 1973

could it be that Gaia is not powerless after all? There is no doubt that life plays many key roles in the climate system.[10]

However, James Lovelock, ever the evolutionary, in 2008 dismissed the climate change movement flowering from his original idea. His mischievousness and subversiveness is on display in two interviews that I'm including with the same journalist, eight years apart. Here is the first.

I'm an optimist. It's going to happen.

Lovelock believes global warming is now irreversible, and that nothing can prevent large parts of the planet becoming too hot to inhabit, or sinking underwater, resulting in mass migration, famine and epidemics. Britain is going to become a lifeboat for refugees from mainland Europe, so instead of wasting our time on wind turbines, we need to start planning how to survive. To Lovelock, the logic is clear. The sustainability brigade are insane to think we can save ourselves by going back to nature; our only chance of survival will come not from less technology, but more.

"Nuclear power," he argues, can solve our energy problem – the bigger challenge will be food. "Maybe they'll synthesise food. I don't know. Synthesising food is not some mad visionary idea; you can buy it in Tesco's, in the form of Quorn. It's not that good, but people buy it. You can live on it." But he fears we won't invent the necessary technologies in time and expects "about 80%" of the world's population to be wiped out by 2100. Prophets have been foretelling Armageddon since time began, he says. "But this is the real thing."

Interviewers often remark upon the discrepancy between Lovelock's predictions of doom, and his good humour. "Well I'm cheerful!" he says, smiling. "I'm an optimist. It's going to happen."

"Humanity is in a period exactly like 1938-9," he explains, when "we all knew something terrible was going to happen but didn't know what to do about it." But once the second world war was under way, "everyone got excited, they loved the things they could do, it was one long holiday ... so when I think of the impending crisis now, I think in those terms. A sense of purpose – that's what people want."

---

[10] *New Scientist*, June 20, 2006

"There have been seven disasters since humans came on the earth, very similar to the one that's just about to happen. I think these events keep separating the wheat from the chaff. And eventually we'll have a human on the planet that really does understand it and can live with it properly. That's the source of my optimism."[11]

Withstanding Criticism

Let's get another perspective on all this:

Lovelock's initial hypothesis had modelled the sum of the biota as a thermostat controlling the viability of the abiotic environment. As its critics were quick to point out, the limitations of this scheme were several.

For one, it overcompensated for traditional geo-evolutionary accounts, in which life always played the passive partner having to adapt itself to the whims of a capricious and overbearing environment, by placing life itself over and in charge of its environment.

For another, this biocentric version of Gaia in turn prompted Lovelock to venture the first-order cybernetic vocabulary of optimisation, looking at the cybernetics of Gaia as one would at the engineering of a control mechanism.

In the development of his hypothesis into a theory, by the later 1980s Lovelock had both relinquished the rhetoric of optimisation – at least to the extent of replacing notions of optimal with, at best, viable – and brought life and Earth back into realignment as a coupled meta-system. Gaia theory integrates life with its terrestrial environment into a geo-biological system whose coevolution has been a composite phenomenon of co-emergence, bounded by a self-organised atmosphere filtering the input of solar radiation.[12]

---

[11] *Guardian Newspaper*, March 1, 2008
[12] Sussman, Henry., *Impasses of the Post-Global Theory in the Era of Climate Change, Volume 2*, 2012

Is Gaia Alive?

> But in point of fact, Lovelock has never entirely relinquished his commitment to "strong Gaia" – the conviction that Gaia is in some sense alive, even if only, as here, in virtue of its being a system.[13]

> **Not alive... but an emergent property of interaction among organisms, the spherical planet on which they reside, and an energy source, the sun.**

In her account of Gaia in *Symbiotic Planet*, discussing Lovelock's tendentious dropping of the properly scientific system-concept of Gaia, his co-scientist in the 1973 paper, Margulis, a micro- biologist, confessed:

> "I regret this personification Gaia. The system emerges from ten million or more connected living species that form its incessantly active body Gaia ... is not an organism directly selected among many. It is an emergent property of interaction among organisms, the spherical planet on which they reside, and an energy source, the sun."[14]

Humanity's future as the thinking brain of our Earth-system

James however took it one step further in his 2014 book, *A Rough Ride to the Future*, where he presents a radical vision of humanity's future as the thinking brain of our Earth system. Here's the cover blurb:

> James Lovelock has been hailed as 'the man who conceived the first wholly new way of looking at life on earth since Charles Darwin" (*Independent*) and as "the most profound scientific thinker of our time" (*Literary Review*) and he continues, in his 95th year, to be the great scientific visionary of our age.

> This book introduces two new Lovelockian ideas. The first is that three hundred years ago, when Thomas Newcomen invented the steam engine, he was unknowingly beginning what Lovelock calls 'accelerated evolution', a process which is bringing about change on our planet roughly a million times faster than Darwinian evolution.

---

[13] Ibid.

[14] Margulis, Lynn. *Symbiotic Planet*, 118–19

The second is that as part of this process, humanity has the capacity to become the intelligent part of Gaia, the self-regulating Earth system whose discovery Lovelock first announced nearly 50 years ago. In addition, Lovelock gives his reflections on how scientific advances are made, and his own remarkable life as a lone scientist.

The contribution of human beings to our planet is, Lovelock contends, similar to that of the early photosynthesisers around 3.4 billion years ago, which made the Earth's atmosphere what it was until very recently. By our domination and our invention, we are now changing the atmosphere again.

There is little that can be done about this, but instead of feeling guilty about it we should recognise what is happening, prepare for change, and ensure that we survive as a species so we can contribute to – perhaps even guide – the next evolution of Gaia. The road will be rough, but if we are smart enough life will continue on Earth in some form far into the future.[15]

And finally, to bring us right up to date and before we jump into the astrology, the second interview with the *Guardian*, this time from 2016.

Before the consequences of global warming can impact, something else will have made our world unrecognizable and threaten the human race.

Eight years after our previous encounter, James appears to have aged not one bit. At 97, he's conceived a beautifully illustrated book of essays described as a "tool kit for the future", *The Earth and I*, and written the introduction and conclusion; he goes walking every day, his hearing is perfect, his focus forensic and his memory unimpaired.

He applies his holistic philosophy of science to his own health. "I'm a firm believer that if you don't use it, you lose it – and if you do a lot of walking, and if you use your muscles quite a bit, your brain seems to work as well. You've got to look at the whole system, not just bits of it." What has changed dramatically, however, is his position on climate change. He now says, "Anyone who tries to predict more than five to 10 years is a bit of

---

[15] Lovelock, James. *A Rough Ride to the Future,* 2014

an idiot, because so many things can change unexpectedly." But isn't that exactly what he did last time we met? "I know," he grins teasingly. "But I've grown up a bit since then."

Lovelock now believes that CO2 is going up, but nowhere near as fast as they thought it would. The computer models just weren't reliable. "In fact," he goes on breezily, "I'm not sure the whole thing isn't crazy, this climate change."

There are various possible explanations for his change of heart. One is that Lovelock is right, and the models on which his former predictions were based were fatally flawed. Another is that his iconoclastic sensibility made revision irresistible. An incorrigible subversive, Lovelock was warning the world about climate change for decades before it began to pay attention, and just when the scientific consensus began to call for intervention to prevent it, he decided we were already too late.

But there is a third explanation for why he has shifted his position again, and nowadays feels "laid back about climate change". All things being equal he expects that before the consequences of global warming can impact on us significantly, something else will have made our world unrecognisable, and threaten the human race. "Because quite soon, before we've reached the end of this century even, I think that what people call robots will have taken over." Robots will rule the world? "Well, yes. They'll be in charge." In charge of us? "Yes, if we're still here. Whether they'll have taken over peacefully or otherwise, I have no idea.We're already happily letting computers design themselves. This has been going on for some time now, particularly with chips, and it's not going to be long before that's out of our hands, and we'll be standing aside and saying, 'Oh well, it's doing a good job designing itself, let's encourage it.' Computers will develop independent volition and intuition ("To some extent, they already have") and become capable of reproducing themselves, and of evolving. Oh yes, that's crucial. We'll have a world where Darwin's working." Lovelock doesn't sound the least bit troubled by the prospect of robots taking over, though, despite the possibility that they will destroy us. "Once they become at all established anywhere, that's the end, because to robots time happens one million times faster – that's a fairly exact figure – than it does to us. That's rather wonderful in a way, isn't it?"

I ask him to explain. "Well, for a neuron to travel a foot takes a microsecond – which is fairly fast. But for electrons to go down a foot of wire takes a nanosecond. It's a million times faster, as simple as that. So, to a robot, once fully established in that new world, a second is a million seconds. Everything is happening so fast that they have on earth a million times longer to live, to grow up, to evolve, than we do. "It is possible," he goes on, "that human beings may fuse with robots to become a blend of robotic and human tissue (That's one route), but the likelier scenario will be pure robots." Why does he think we'll go for all-out robots? He shoots me an amused look. "I don't think we will. I think that they will – that's the key thing here."

The implications for climate change are obvious. "The world that they're going to be comfortable in is wildly different from the one that we feel comfortable in. So once they really get established, they will – with regret - start losing organic life. Will they care about rising temperatures? "They won't give a fourpenny fuck about the temperature, because to them the change will be slow, and they can stand quite a big change without any fuss. They could accommodate infinitely greater change through climate change than we can, before things get tricky for them. It's what the world can stand that is the important thing to them. They're going to need a safe platform to live in, so they don't want Gaia messed about too much."[16]

---

[16] James Lovelock interview, *Guardian*, 2016

6: Futurist Case Study - James Lovelock

July 26, 1919 –

Sedna in the Sixth

We've looked at the big picture and started looking at Sedna in mundane charts; now let's look at her influence in the birth chart, in the first of our case studies.

As a way of personalizing the ethereal energy of Sedna we're going to look at twelve case studies, and in the first of the series let's look at the man behind Gaia theory, since we've already gotten to know him.

James Ephraim Lovelock is an independent scientist, environ-mentalist and futurist who lives in Devon, England. He has Sedna on the cusp of the sixth house of service, which we'll look at in a moment, but first let's look at his aspects.

Chart Aspects

In all the chart analysis here, I am concentrating on aspects which have an orb of two degrees or less. I find the aspects are active up to orbs of 6 degrees, but we have to tune in to them.

trine MC

James has Sedna trine the MC, indicating he has an important role to play in world events.

Name: ♂ James Lovelock
born on Sa., 26 July 1919
in Letchworth, ENG (UK)
0w14, 51n58

Time: 2:00 p.m.
Univ.Time: 13:00
Sid. Time: 9:11:45

ASTRO DIENST
www.astro.com

Type: 2.GW 0.0-1 1-Mrz-2017

Natal Chart (Method: Web Style / Placidus)
Sun sign: Leo
Ascendant: Scorpio

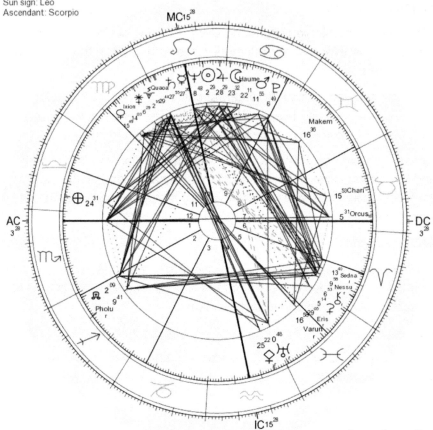

sesquiquadrate Saturn, sesquiquadrate Mercury, sesquiquadrate Quaoar

And sesquiquadrate to his conjunction of Saturn, Mercury and Quaoar in the tenth house of profession. Quaoar is the Californian Indian creation god, which has to do with new perspectives and new realities, so together with the planet of the existing reality structure, Saturn, and that of ideas and communication, Mercury, we can see an evolutionary focus on communicating a new perspective on our place in the world, something the sesquiquadrate tells us will be controversial. This is reinforced by the square to Mars in the ninth house of knowledge.

trine Pholus, conjunct Nessus

But Sedna is also trine Pholus, the centaur of illumination, in the second house of material resources, giving him the ability to look at the big picture and at the detail at the same time and conjunct the centaur Nessus, which frequently indicates someone who actually effects evolutionary change, in the fifth house of creativity.

sextile Makemake, inconjunct Ixion

The sextile to Makemake, the divine trickster, in the eighth house of shared resources, indicates someone who is a divinely mischievous in his attempts to raise consciousness and the fateful inconjunct to Ixion, the planet of lawlessness, in the tenth house of profession, someone who is socially subversive. But these have ultimately both been useful tools for James, who has become a very successful catalyst for change.

House Placement

James has Sedna on the sixth house cusp. This is our first look at Sedna in the houses, which is going to be one of our best tools to interpret the meaning of Sedna in a natal chart, because the sign position affects a whole generation, or 30 to 40 generations, depending on the sign. Sedna in the sixth looks initially like it is awakening us to our duty of care for the planet.

Sedna in 6th House

Later, in the chapter on Sedna in the houses, I interpret this position more fully, but here's a slightly edited version:

With Sedna in the sixth house we are on a spiritual quest to investigate the magic that lies underneath each moment of our daily routines and to find a way to service this process and a practice to assist with the momentous evolution currently underway.

On a personal level this placement can also bring comfort in the small pleasures of our daily routine or burden us with never ending chores. If we are feeling this burden, the key to releasing it is to find meaning in these everyday tasks and thereby turn them into rituals. Rituals are important. Once we have found meaning and pleasure in the little jobs, then we are more than capable of handling the bigger ones.

At the unconscious level, however, we may first suffer victimization in our job, or daily routine and may respond by victimizing and abusing in our turn. Some pressure will catalyze our search for meaning in our work. If we hang on desperately, this becomes victimization, or alienation, and breeds more of the same unless we let go of the old daily routine and transcend to a new one where we can find pleasure and meaning in our work.

If the Sedna energy is not dealt with consciously it is likely to manifest as health issues, particularly early in life, but these can dissipate once we embrace the evolutionary energy of the planet and do the homework of looking after ourselves. With this placement we will benefit from meditation, prayer, regular exercise and a healthy diet.

Sedna has a deep knowing of which we are seldom conscious and in the sixth house this manifests as an instinctive drive to sort out the bugs in the system. Early in life we will likely do this unconsciously and only become aware of this role through events that are forcing transcendence in our daily work.

With this placement there is likely to be an evolution in our daily work, which may be forced by hard aspects and encouraged by flows, leading to a transcendence to a larger spiritual perspective.

With Sedna in the sixth house we have to find our unique way to serve from the perspective of the big spiritual picture, and if this lesson is well learned early, then our close relationships will flower as the planet moves on to transit the seventh house.

House Analysis

Because the sign positions are generational influences, the house positions are very important in interpreting the Sedna energy in the chart, so let's use James as the first case study of the book. The aspects to Sedna in his chart are a mix of flows and challenges, but the trines to the MC and Pholus means that he has been able to work more consciously with the Sedna energy and embrace a series of fated changes as they occurred.

Let's look at a few of these. The quotes in the coming pages are from his autobiography, 'Homage to Gaia: The Life of an Independent Scientist, published in 2000.

Was he victimized at work?

Here's where we see the limitations of this term and with many of the interpretations of the Sedna myth, because being a victim is a state of mind which doesn't honor our part in whatever evolutionary event is occurring. So, if we don't engage with the Sedna energy and become an agent of change, it's going to act on us in a way that is going to seem victimizing.

James wasn't victimized at work in the way we normally think of it, but he did have to withstand sometimes scathing criticism from people who were threatened by his ideas. Here's how he put it in his autobiography:

> The worst thing that can happen to a new theory is for it to be ignored. I therefore acknowledge the robust, even scathing, criticisms from Ford Doolittle, the microbiologist from Halifax, Nova Scotia, and from Richard Dawkins of Oxford. They hurt at the time, but they made me think and tighten what had been a loose hypothesis into a firm theory.

> Much friendlier was the constructive, but firm criticism from the eminent geochemist Professor HD Holland of Harvard University. We have sustained a warm respect for each other and he was an outstanding presence at our meetings in Oxford. In no way do I cast these critics as villains; they are open in their dislike of Gaia.[17]

Beginning of a love-hate relationship with biology

This resilience was bred into him early by his Sedna placement. In the autobiography he relates a story of what he calls 'the beginning of my love-hate relationship with biology' which beautifully illustrates the early victimization-like action of Sedna, particularly here in the 6th house.

> One morning (at school) in a moment of purposeless destruction, I started to carve my initials with my penknife in the wooden bench of the biology lab. I was sitting before it listening to the natural history lesson delivered by Sidney Dark, who taught biology to the senior boys and the soft subject of natural history to the young. I liked listening to him and contentedly carved away as he spoke – what made me carve I do not know.

> Suddenly there was a hush. The teacher stopped in mid-sentence and glared at me with eyes enlarged by thick magnifying spectacles. 'Wretched boy, what are you doing?' 'Nothing,' I replied, too startled for anything more accurate, or

---

[17] Lovelock, James. *Homage to Gaia: The Life of an Independent Scientist,* 2000

reasonable. 'You are destroying school property and not paying attention. You will be punished. Go and fetch the book and cane.'

I was astonished; Sidney Dark had never caned anyone. There were masters in the school who thoroughly enjoyed the swish and thwack of the cane as they beat a young boy's bottom, but Mr. Dark was not among them. The book was used to record the punishment and I think to curb excessive beating.

Reluctantly I left the lab and made my way down to the Masters' Common Room, where I knocked on the door and asked for the book and cane. In those times and earlier the process of punishment was invested with ritual so that it could entertain the innocent as well as be seen properly to punish the guilty. The ritual of the book and cane was, I know, an effective part of the punishment through its capacity to humiliate as well as hurt.

I was not too worried as I took this punishment kit back to the biology lab, for I felt sure that Sidney Dark was much too kind and decent a man to use it. I did wonder, though, what I could say that would tip the balance in my favour.

So vivid is my memory of this small event that I can easily picture the corridor flanked by the chemistry and physics labs. I can still smell the tang of hydrogen sulphide mixed with that of carbolic disinfectant. I went on to the biology lab and gave the book and cane to my teacher as was required by the ritual. He immediately put it down on his desk and began his harangue. This I knew was a good sign and I put on my air of utmost contrition. The sadists among the schoolmasters never wasted time on talk but went straight into the act itself.

He had hardly warmed over his voice when the clamour of the fire bell drowned it and, as if automatons, boys and master immediately started the well-rehearsed fire drill, and prepared to move to the positions allocated to them outside the school. I turned to go, relieved at my escape by the bell, for I was sure that the fire drill would cool the teacher's indignation.

Suddenly, a punishment much more subtle than mere corporal came into his mind and as he turned to pick up the book and cane, he said, 'Lovelock, you take care of this,' and handed it to me. 'We cannot leave it here to be burnt.' I was obliged to rescue the cane from the mock fire in front of the whole school that found the episode hilariously funny.

Ever after, they called me the boy who had saved the cane. It also was the start of my lifelong love–hate relationship with biology and biologists.[18]

Did he find his unique way to serve?

I think with the development of Gaia theory, we can say this is definitely true.

Flowering one-to-one relationships in later life?

Yes. James' introduction to his autobiography, published in 2000, thanks a large number of people who have helped with the development of the Gaia theory, both critics and supporters and details the mutually respectful relationship he developed with each. He says:

> The story of Gaia is an unfolding drama, and my acknowledgements to those who participated in it are like a cast of characters at the beginning of a play. There were many actors in this thirty-five-year show, heroes and villains, and I have listed them in the order of their appearance. I thank them for their proper criticism, support, and encouragement during the many rehearsals of the Gaia story as it went from a mere notion about detecting life on other planets to its debut as a theory in science.[19]

Health issues early?

Yes, he suffered from bronchitis and pneumonia as a child as he explains in *Homage to Gaia*:

> You will by now have gathered that I was neither a perfect pupil nor happy to be at school. In fact, I hated it so much that every day was a kind of ordeal. If, as often happened in the winter, the filthy coal smoke that polluted the Brixton air made me ill, it was a vast relief. I could stay at home in bed with my beloved books, freed by bronchitis or pneumonia from the tyranny of school.

---

[18] Lovelock, James, *Homage to Gaia, The Life of an Independent Scientist,* 2000
[19] Ibid.

Because of illness, I was a weedy child and should have been the target of bullies, the more usual reason to dislike school. I was blessed by having a wonderful group of fellow sufferers as my schoolmates. To them, I was the 'mad scientist', good when needed for a wheeze that would confound our common enemy, the masters.[20]

Comfortable, healthy routine in later life?

Yes. We learned in his 2016 interview that he has a wholistic view of body and walks every day at 97.

Sedna Transits

Looking at transits to Sedna, at what planets are aspecting our natal Sedna at any one time, can give us another perspective on the events in our lives. Transits of Sedna to other planets are also interesting but hard to interpret because they typically last for a decade.

Did James have a fated evolution?

In September 1951 James was feeling restless in his job at Harvard Hospital near Salisbury, where he was working on the Common Cold Research Unit, and he convinced his boss to get him a meeting with the head of the parent institute in London, Sir Charles Harington.

He had transiting Jupiter, the planet of expansion, conjunct his natal Sedna that day. He also had transiting Uranus, the planet of intuition, sesquiquadrate to his Sedna; transiting Neptune, the planet of dreams and visions, opposite Sedna; transiting Juno, the asteroid of partnerships, sesquiquadrate Sedna; and transiting Chariklo, the centaur of foresight trine his Sedna.

James recounts:

> Within a day Sir Charles summoned me to London. He was a man who resembled the Prime Minister of that time, or, indeed, the US President. He was a small, perhaps shy man, with a limp caused by a tubercular infection of his hip as a child. His slight stature belied the strength of his character: they said he was descended from a line of judges. Whether or not this was true, he was one of those few people I have encountered in life whose

---

[20] Ibid.

presence was immediately and tangibly felt, who could exert authority even without speaking.

Without preamble he said, 'I am so glad you are coming back to the Institute. You have been much too long in the wilderness of Harvard Hospital. I have a problem for you and it is urgent. Can you start next week?' He didn't expect me to disagree. He was a man with an attention to detail that now you would think of as Japanese and had already arranged that my family could stay at Harvard Hospital for as long as it took me to find somewhere for us all to live in London. He made a lab available for me on the first floor of the institute.

It was like falling over a small waterfall, exhilarating but with the knowledge that there could be no going back, no indecision.[21]

This is a very Sedna-like description, no real decision, just a thrilling fated experience. For the next ten years James would work at the National Institute for Medical Research at Mill Hill in North London, apart from a year in America at the Harvard Medical School.

Invite to Explore Moon

Then in March 1961, when transiting Juno, the asteroid of partnership, Pholus, the centaur of growth and Chariklo, the centaur of foresight, were all in a flowing sextile relationship with James's natal Sedna, he got a letter from NASA, then an unknown newly formed organization, inviting him to join a party of scientists who were about to explore the Moon. Here's how he describes it:

Notice that my time as a journeyman was ending came in March 1961, in the form of an ordinary airmail envelope, which lay on my desk at Mill Hill when I arrived one morning for work. It was from what seemed to be a senior officer of the US Government, the director of Space Flight Operations for the National Aeronautical and Space Administration, NASA. The acronym NASA is now a commonplace and everyone knows what it is. In those days, a mere three years after the first Russian satellite had bleeped its simple manic message, beep-beep-beep, around the world, not many of us were aware of the name NASA.

---

[21] Lovelock, James, *Homage to Gaia: The Life of an Independent Scientist,* 2000

The letter itself was even more intriguing. It was an invitation to join a party of scientists who were about to explore the Moon. I was enthralled. Here was a serious person asking me to join with others in what a few years back would have been science fiction. It was for me like a letter from a beloved. I was as excited and euphoric as if, at the peak of passion, I had received a yes from my loved one. To be asked, a mere three years after Sputnik, to join in a lunar exploration was such a thrill.

More than this, I began to realize that this letter was deliverance. The past year I had spent somewhat miserably trying to screw up the courage to tell my director and the kindly people who ran Mill Hill that I wanted to leave. How could I tell them I wanted to work alone as an independent scientist? How could I say that their comfortable, tenured, secure existence, where I was free to do almost anything I wished, was not enough? But they knew my love for the physical sciences and astronomy and this letter gave me the way in which to formulate an honourable explanation for my departure.

The letter from NASA set me free to become an independent scientist, but there were to be two years and four months of transition.[22]

Transits when Gaia was published

Okay, let's look at the publication of his book, *Gaia* and the transits of Sedna, and transits to Sedna in his chart, as another way of understanding the planet.

Sedna Transits:

square Neptune, sextile Pluto, sextile Orcus, opposite Ascendant

When the book was published, he had transiting Sedna in a challenging square to Neptune, the planet of visions and dreams, in a flowing sextile to Pluto, the planet of transformation, conjunct Orcus, the planet of delving down and speaking out, and opposite the Ascendant, his public face. All very appropriate to the topic and effect of the book.

---

[22] Ibid.

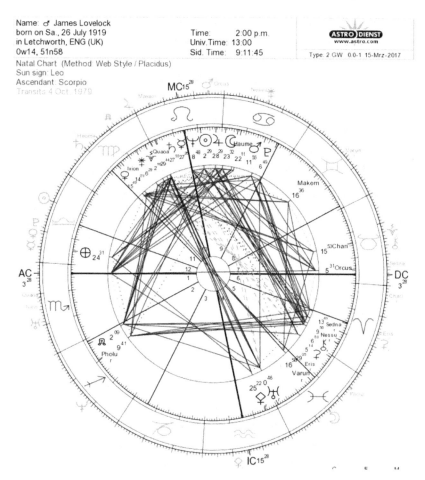

Name: ♂ James Lovelock
born on Sa., 26 July 1919
in Letchworth, ENG (UK)
0w14, 51n58
Natal Chart (Method: Web Style / Placidus)
Sun sign: Leo
Ascendant: Scorpio
Transits 4 Oct. 1979

Time: 2:00 p.m.
Univ.Time: 13:00
Sid. Time: 9:11:45

ASTRO DIENST
www.astro.com
Type: 2 GW 0.0-1 15-Mrz-2017

**trine Vesta, trine Juno, semi-sextile Ceres, semi-sextile
Chiron**

The theme of the book also comes strongly through Sedna's transits
with Chiron and three of the more feminine energies in his chart, two of
the asteroids and one recently reclassified as a dwarf planet. She was
trine natal Vesta, the asteroid of passion and focus, trine natal Juno, the
asteroid of partnerships, and semi-sextile both natal Ceres, the planet of
nurturing, and natal Chiron, the centaur of wounding and healing.

All Sedna transits are long term, however, lasting typically for more than
a decade, so for this particular date we need to also look at the transits
of the inner planets to Sedna.

Transits to Sedna:

> **Sun opposition, Pluto Opposition**

Here we have the transiting Sun, the planet of will, in a wide conjunction with transiting Pluto, the planet of transformation, both in opposition to natal Sedna. This is an indication of the powerful transformative forces the book would unleash.

Neptune trine

Transiting Neptune, the planet of dreams and visions, is trine natal Sedna, easing the transiting Sedna square natal Neptune we saw above, but reinforcing the re-envisioning challenge the book presents.

Uranus bi-quintile, North Node bi-quintile

Both transiting Uranus, the planet of lateral thinking, and the transiting North Node, the point of dharma, are in an evolutionary bi-quintile relationship with natal Sedna. The bi-quintiles combine aspects of the trine and the opposition, so indicate the opportunity to understand the challenges and present realistic solutions. With Sedna involved, the book could integrate this information at such a deep level that evolutionary new steps could be taken.

Pallas sextile, Juno square, Ceres conjunct

We also have two of the asteroids and one former asteroid again involved, with transiting Pallas, the asteroid of wisdom, strategy and skill, sextile Sedna and transiting Juno, the asteroid of partnerships, square Sedna, prefiguring the controversy the book would generate and the long-term strategy needed to effect the change required.

Transiting Ceres, the planet of nurturing, is conjunct natal Sedna, showing the importance of the nurturing process to Gaia, an interpretation which is reinforced by the transiting Sedna semi-sextile natal Ceres we saw above.

Chiron semi-sextile

Similarly, transiting Chiron, the centaur of wounding and healing, is also semi-sextile natal Sedna, this time mirroring exactly the transiting Sedna semi-sextile with natal Chiron. This emphasizes the importance of the Chironic process of wounding and healing to the concept of Gaia. The Chironic process is intrinsic to growth on a personal level, because Saturnian forms resist change.

Ixion inconjunct

We also have transiting Ixion, the planet of lawlessness and irreverence, in a sometimes stressful and sometimes flowing inconjunct to natal Sedna, indicating a fated quality about the disruption to the traditional view of the relationship between life and the environment the book would bring. This is emphasized by transiting Varuna, the planet of reputation and immortality through fame, in a flowing sextile.

Eris conjunct

But the big flashing sign that the book/theory would stir debate and promote a more spiritual evolutionary consciousness is transiting Eris, the planet of spiritual growth through discord, conjunct his natal Sedna within a degree. Eris moves slowly, and this conjunction was just starting to apply when James published the first paper six years earlier and would apply for the next six years following the book publication, while the ideas in the book fermented an evolutionary change in consciousness.

7: The Singularity is Near

James Lovelock's view of the future is very similar to that of one of the world's leading inventors, thinkers, and futurist, Ray Kurzweil, who has a thirty-year track record of accurate predictions. He is currently a Director of Engineering at Google, heading up a team developing machine intelligence and natural language understanding. Ray caused a sensation in 2005 with his book *The Singularity is Near: When Humans Transcend Biology*. Here's the cover blurb:

> At the onset of the twenty-first century, humanity stands on the verge of the most transforming and the most thrilling period in its history. It will be an era in which the very nature of what it means to be human will be both enriched and challenged, as our species breaks the shackles of its genetic legacy and achieves inconceivable heights of intelligence, material progress, and longevity.

> For over three decades, the great inventor and futurist, Ray Kurzweil, has been one of the most respected and provocative advocates of the role of technology in our future. In his classic, *The Age of Spiritual Machines*, he presented the daring argument that with the ever-accelerating rate of technological change, computers would rival the full range of human intelligence at its best. Now, in *The Singularity Is Near,* he examines the next step in this inexorable evolutionary process: the union of human and machine, in which the knowledge and skills embedded in our brains will be combined with the vastly greater capacity, speed, and knowledge-sharing ability of our own creations.

> That merging is the essence of the Singularity, an era in which our intelligence will become increasingly nonbiological and trillions of times more powerful than it is today – the dawning of a new civilisation that will enable us to transcend our biological limitations and amplify our creativity. In this new world, there will be no clear distinction between human and machine, real reality and virtual reality. We will be able to assume different bodies and take on a range of personae at will. In practical terms, human ageing and illness will be reversed; pollution will be stopped; world hunger and poverty will be solved. Nanotechnology will

make it possible to create virtually any physical product using inexpensive information processes and will ultimately turn even death into a soluble problem.

While the social and philosophical ramifications of these changes will be profound, and the threats they pose considerable, *The Singularity Is Near* maintains a radically optimistic view of the future course of human development. As such, it offers a view of the coming age that is both a dramatic culmination of centuries of technological ingenuity and a genuinely inspiring vision of our ultimate destiny.[23]

That is the description of the book from singularity.com and here's an article from *Time* magazine in 2011, giving some background and speculating on the changes in store.

2045: The Year Man Becomes Immortal

We're fast approaching the moment when humans and machines merge. Kurzweil believes that we're approaching a moment when computers will become intelligent, and not just intelligent, but more intelligent than humans. When that happens, humanity – our bodies, our minds, our civilization – will be completely and irreversibly transformed. He believes that this moment is not only inevitable but imminent. According to his calculations, the end of human civilisation as we know it is about 35 years away.

Computers are getting faster. Everybody knows that. Also, computers are getting faster faster – that is, the rate at which they're getting faster is increasing. So there might conceivably come a moment when they are capable of something comparable to human intelligence. Artificial intelligence. All that horsepower could be put in the service of emulating whatever it is our brains are doing when they create consciousness – not just doing arithmetic very quickly, or composing piano music, but also driving cars, writing books, making ethical decisions, appreciating fancy paintings, making witty observations at cocktail parties.

---

[23] Kurzweil, Ray. *The Singularity is Near: When Humans Transcend Biology,* singularity.com, 2005

Maybe we'll merge with them to become super-intelligent cyborgs, using computers to extend our intellectual abilities the same way that cars and planes extend our physical abilities. Maybe the artificial intelligences will help us treat the effects of old age and prolong our life spans indefinitely. Maybe we'll scan our consciousnesses into computers and live inside them as software, forever, virtually. Maybe the computers will turn on humanity and annihilate us. The one thing all these theories have in common is the transformation of our species into something that is no longer recognisable as such to humans today. This transformation has a name: the Singularity.

The difficult thing to keep sight of when you're talking about the Singularity is that even though it sounds like science fiction, it isn't, no more than a weather forecast is science fiction. It's not a fringe idea; it's a serious hypothesis about the future of life on Earth. There's an intellectual gag reflex that kicks in anytime you try to swallow an idea that involves super-intelligent immortal cyborgs, but suppress it if you can, because while the Singularity appears to be, on the face of it, preposterous, it's an idea that rewards sober, careful evaluation.[24]

And here's Peter Diamandis talking about Ray:

Ray Kurzweil's Mind-Boggling Predictions for the Next 25 Years

Bill Gates calls Ray, "the best person I know at predicting the future of artificial intelligence." Ray is also amazing at predicting a lot more beyond just AI. Ray has received 20 honorary doctorates, has been awarded honours from three U.S. presidents, and has authored 7 books, 5 of which have been national bestsellers. He is the principal inventor of many technologies ranging from the first CCD flatbed scanner to the first print-to-speech reading machine for the blind. He is also the chancellor and co-founder of Singularity University, and the guy tagged by Larry Page to direct artificial intelligence development at Google.

---

[24] *Time,* February 10, 2011

In short, Ray's pretty smart... and his predictions are amazing, mind-boggling, and important reminders that we are living in the most exciting time in human history. Here's his incredible predictions for the next 20+ years, but first let's look back at some of the predictions he got right over the last 25 years.

In 1990 (twenty-five years ago), he predicted...

...that a computer would defeat a world chess champion by 1998. Then in 1997, IBM's Deep Blue defeated Garry Kasparov.

- ... that PCs would be capable of answering queries by accessing information wirelessly via the Internet by 2010. He was right, to say the least.
- ... that by the early 2000s, exoskeletal limbs would let the disabled walk. Companies like Ekso Bionics and others now have technology that does just this, and much more.

In 1999, he predicted...

- ... that people would be able talk to their computer to give commands by 2009. While still in the early days in 2009, natural language interfaces like Apple's Siri and Google now have come a long way. I rarely use my keyboard anymore; instead I dictate texts and emails.
- ... that computer displays would be built into eyeglasses for augmented reality by 2009. Labs and teams were building head mounted displays well before 2009, but Google started experimenting with Google Glass prototypes in 2011. Now, we are seeing an explosion of augmented and virtual reality solutions and HMDs. Microsoft just released the Hololens, and Magic Leap is working on some amazing technology, to name two.

In 2005, he predicted...

- ... that by the 2010s, virtual solutions would be able to do real-time language translation in which words spoken in a foreign language would be translated into text that would appear as subtitles to a user wearing the glasses. Well, Microsoft (via Skype Translate), Google (Translate), and others have done this and beyond. One app called Word Lens actually uses your camera to find and translate text imagery in real time.

Ray's predictions for the next 25 years

The above represent only a few of the predictions Ray has made. While he hasn't been precisely right, to the exact year, his track record is stunningly good. Here are some of my favourite of Ray's predictions for the next 25+ years.

- By the late 2010s, glasses will beam images directly onto the retina. Ten terabytes of computing power (roughly the same as the human brain) will cost about $1,000.

- By the 2020s, most diseases will go away as nanobots become smarter than current medical technology. Normal human eating can be replaced by nanosystems. The Turing test begins to be passable, meaning we can't tell the difference between humans and robots. Self-driving cars begin to take over the roads, and people won't be allowed to drive on highways.

- By the 2030s, virtual reality will begin to feel 100% real. We will be able to upload our mind/consciousness by the end of the decade.

- By the 2040s, non-biological intelligence will be a billion times more capable than biological intelligence (a.k.a. us). Nanotech foglets will be able to make food out of thin air and create any object in physical world at a whim.

- By 2045, we will multiply our intelligence a billion-fold by linking wirelessly from our neocortex to a synthetic neocortex in the cloud.

I want to finish with an important point, not about the predictions but about what the predictions represent. Ray's predictions are a byproduct of his understanding of the power of Moore's Law, more specifically Ray's "Law of Accelerating Returns" and of exponential technologies. These technologies follow an exponential growth curve based on the principle that the computing power that enables them doubles every two years.[25]

---

[25] Diamandis, Peter. singularityhub.com, 2015

8: Futurist Case Study - Ray Kurzweil

February 12, 1948 –

Sedna in the Sixth

So, let's look at Ray's Sedna, which, like James Lovelock, is in the sixth house, giving us a good point of comparison in our first two case studies.

First, a quick recap on the man who brought us the Singularity theory. Ray Kurzweil is one of the world's leading inventors, thinkers, and futurists, with a thirty-year track record of accurate predictions. Called "the restless genius" by *The Wall Street Journal* and "the ultimate thinking machine" by *Forbes* magazine, he was selected as one of the top entrepreneurs by *Inc.* magazine, which described him as the "rightful heir to Thomas Edison."

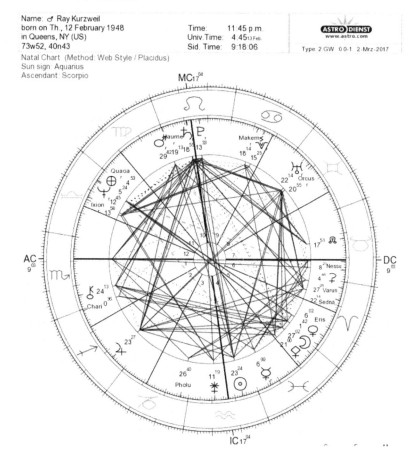

Alan Clay

House Placement

Ray has Sedna direct in Aries in the sixth house. This is the same house as James, enabling us to compare a second chart against the understanding of Sedna in the 6th that we're developing. In both we see the focus on a duty of care arising from our participation in the larger organic whole, humanity.

We'll delve into this house placement more in a moment, but first let's see what we can learn from Ray's aspects with Sedna.

Sedna Aspects

trine Jupiter, trine Saturn, conjunct Pluto, conjunct MC

Ray has Sedna as part of a grand trine with Jupiter, the planet of expansion in the second house of material reality, and Saturn, the planet of structure, which is conjunct Haumea, the planet of rebirth, in the tenth house of occupation. This conjunction is also conjunct both the MC and Pluto, the planet of transformation, which is just across in the ninth house of knowledge.

This is a powerful picture of his evolutionary influence, his inventive expansion of the technological frontier with Jupiter in the second, bringing the social view that humanity's transformation is a rebirth of structure, or a birth of inanimate life, with the Haumea, Saturn, Pluto, and MC conjunction.

sextile Sun

A close sextile of Sedna to the Sun in Aquarius, in the fourth house of home, which is opposite the Saturn, Pluto, MC conjunction, powers this transformative configuration.

semi-sextile Pallas, semi-square Mercury

The semi-sextile to Pallas, the asteroid of strategy, in the fifth house of creativity, gives him the ability to anticipate the next big technological step and lead progress toward it. And the semi-square to Mercury, the planet of communication, in the fourth house of home, gives him the challenge to communicate that to everyone else.

sextile Uranus, sextile Orcus

The sextiles to the conjunction of Uranus, the planet of intuition, and Orcus, the planet of delving down and speaking out, both in the eighth house of transformation, give him the role of a modern prophet.

square Pholus, square Makemake

The squares to Pholus, the centaur of illumination and growth, in the third house of ideas, and to Makemake, the divine trickster, in the ninth house of philosophy, shows the controversy his ideas will cause and the challenge they represent to religious philosophies.

House Analysis

Ray has Sedna in the sixth house, and we looked at James Lovelock's Sedna placement in the sixth earlier and in both we see the focus on 'a duty of care arising from our participation in the larger organic whole,' humanity. So, let's ask the same questions about Ray as we did for James.

Was he victimized at work?

Like James, Ray has certainly been the target of many attacks from those of his peers who are threatened by his ideas, but he has embraced this debate in a similar way to James, seeing it as a validation of the importance of his ideas.

Wired magazine tells us:

> Moore's law – the observation by Intel cofounder, Gordon Moore, that the number of transistors on an integrated circuit doubles roughly every 18 months – is an example of exponential change. For people like Kurzweil, it is the key example, because Moore's law and its many derivatives suggest that just about any limit on computing power today will be overcome in short order.
>
> Despite all this, people continue to disbelieve. There is a lively discussion among experts about the validity of Moore's law. Kurzweil pushes Moore's law back to the dawn of time and forward to the end of the universe. But many computer scientists and historians of technology wonder if it will last another decade. Some suspect that the acceleration of computing power has already slowed.
>
> There are also philosophical objections. Kurzweil's theory is that super-intelligent computers will necessarily be human, because they will be modelled on the human brain. But there are other types of intelligence in the world – for instance, the intelligence of ant colonies – that are alien to humanity. Grant that a computer,

or a network of computers, might awaken. The consciousness of this fabulous AI might remain as incomprehensible to us as we are to the protozoa.

Other pessimists point out that the brain is more than raw processing power. It also has a certain architecture, a certain design. It is attached to specific type of nervous system; it accepts only particular kinds of inputs. Even with better computational speed driving our thoughts, we might still be stuck in a kind of evolutionary dead end, incapable of radical self-improvement.[26]

So again, not victimized, but the focus of strong criticism, on which he has thrived.

Did he find his unique way to serve?

I think that again we can say this is definitely true. Here's a story from *Time* magazine about an experience in his youth to put it in perspective:

On Feb. 15, 1965, a diffident but self-possessed high school student named Raymond Kurzweil appeared as a guest on a game show called 'I've Got a Secret.' He was introduced by the host, Steve Allen, then he played a short musical composition on a piano. The idea was that Kurzweil was hiding an unusual fact and the panelists had to guess what it was: the music was composed by a computer. Kurzweil then demonstrated the computer, which he built himself – a desk-size affair with loudly clacking relays, hooked up to a typewriter.

Kurzweil would spend much of the rest of his career working out what his demonstration meant. Creating a work of art is one of those activities we reserve for humans and humans only. It's an act of self-expression; you're not supposed to be able to do it if you don't have a self. To see creativity, the exclusive domain of humans, usurped by a computer built by a 17-year-old is to watch a line blur that cannot be un-blurred, the line between organic intelligence and artificial intelligence.

That was Kurzweil's real secret, and back in 1965 nobody guessed it. Maybe not even him, not yet. But now, 46 years later, Kurzweil believes that we're approaching a moment when

---

[26] Wolf, Gary. *Wired,* March 24, 2008

computers will become intelligent, and not just intelligent, but more intelligent than humans. When that happens, humanity – our bodies, our minds, our civilisation – will be completely and irreversibly transformed. He believes that this moment is not only inevitable but imminent. According to his calculations, the end of human civilisation as we know it is about 35 years away.[27]

Health issues early?

Kurzweil has unlucky genes: His father died of heart disease at 58, his grandfather in his early forties. He himself was diagnosed with high cholesterol and incipient type 2 diabetes, both considered to be significant risk factors for early death, when only 35.[28]

Comfortable healthy routine in later life?

Kurzweil is now 60, but he intends to be no more than 40 when the singularity arrives… He does not believe in half measures. He takes 180 to 210 vitamin and mineral supplements a day, so many that he doesn't have time to organize them all himself. So he's hired a pill wrangler, who takes them out of their bottles and sorts them into daily doses, which he carries everywhere in plastic bags. Kurzweil also spends one day a week at a medical clinic, receiving intravenous longevity treatments. The reason for his focus on optimal health should be obvious: If the singularity is going to render humans immortal by the middle of this century, it would be a shame to die in the interim.[29]

Flowering one-to-one relationships in later life?

At 58, Ray had a meeting with Larry Page, the CEO of Google, which we'll use as an example to start looking at transits to Sedna. To that point in his life he had never held a job anywhere but his own companies, and he went into the meeting thinking to start a new business, but because of the relationship, he came out with a top job at Google.

Transits

So, let's look at this event and at the transits to Sedna.

---

[27] *Time*, February 10, 2011
[28] Wolf, Gary. *Wired*, March 24, 2008
[29] ibid

Did Ray have a fated evolution?

In July 2012 when he met with Larry Page, he had transiting Venus, the planet of values and relationships, semi-square his Sedna, and transiting Saturn, the planet of structure, together with transiting Haumea, the planet of rebirth, both opposite his natal Sedna, signaling a rebirth in the structure of his life.

Transiting Juno, the asteroid of partnerships, was also in a close fateful inconjunct with his natal Sedna, suggesting a fated partnership.

Pholus, Chariklo, Ixion, Quaoar and Varuna are also involved, and we'll look at their influence in a moment. These shorter-term transits come on top of Ray's long-term transit of Eris, the planet of consciousness through discord, which is conjunct his natal Sedna within half a degree this month. And of transiting Sedna semi-sextile to its birth position, emphasizing the importance of this period in his life.

> *Larry Page suggests that Kurzweil, who had never held a job anywhere but his own companies, join Google as a director of engineering*

When Ray Kurzweil met with Google CEO Larry Page in July 2012, he wasn't looking for a job. A respected inventor who's become a machine-intelligence futurist, Kurzweil wanted to discuss his upcoming book, *How to Create a Mind: The Secret of Human Thought Revealed.* He told Page, who had read an early draft, that he wanted to start a company to develop his ideas about how to build a truly intelligent computer, one that could understand language and then make inferences and decisions on its own.

It quickly became obvious that such an effort would require nothing less than Google-scale data and computing power. "I could try to give you some access to it," Page told Kurzweil. "But it's going to be very difficult to do that for an independent company." So Page suggested that Kurzweil, who had never held a job anywhere but his own companies, join Google instead. It didn't take Kurzweil long to make up his mind: in January 2013 he started working for Google as a director of engineering. "This is the culmination of literally 50 years of my focus on artificial intelligence," he says."[30]

With Pholus, the centaur of illumination and growth, in a flowing trine to Sedna, and Chariklo, the centaur of foresight in a more stressful sesquiquadrate, he went into the meeting thinking to start his own business and came out with a job at Google.

This process was assisted by transiting Ixion, the planet of freedom, and transiting Quaoar, the planet of new perspectives, both in flowing trines with natal Sedna, showing the opportunities for the expansion of his work using the resources of Google, despite the low-profile nature of the role, signalled by transiting Varuna, the planet of notability, square his natal Sedna.

The Singularity is Fated Evolution

We'll look at Ray's predictions for the future again soon, when we look at Sedna's approaching sojourn in Gemini, but as a final thought on his case study, the more I consider Ray's theory of the Singularity, the more I see it as a theory of fated evolution. So, the Sedna archetype permeates his life.

The theory is actually very similar to the Sedna myth, which I'm deliberately leaving to later in the book. But suffice to say here that Sedna's transcendence to godhood was forced and involved parting with body parts to create new species. Once a god, she demanded that man live in harmony with nature and sent storms and withheld food if man did not treat nature properly.

This is similar to Ray's theory that when all matter becomes intelligent and we have nano-technology running through our brains and artificial body parts, or complete artificial bodies, we and matter will all merge into a mind with god-like all-knowing, all-seeing, consciousness, which will demand we maintain a healthy planet, but won't be too worried about any single participant, more with the broad sweep of history.

---

[30] Hof, Robert D. *MIT Technology Review,* 2013

9: Climate Change

We've looked back at past cycles and at discovery events, and then started extrapolating these trends into the future. Before we go on with this extrapolation, let's take a step back and look at the big picture.

We now know the Earth's climate is currently in a warm spell between glacial periods. The last ice age ended about 11,000 years ago. Since then, temperatures and sea levels have risen, and ice caps have retreated back to the poles.

We've seen the link between Sedna and rising and falling CO_2 levels in the past, as the oceans breathed in and out CO_2, creating the ice age cycle. In addition to these natural cycles, human- made carbon emissions are also having an effect by warming the climate. We know that modern global warming stems from rising levels of CO_2 and other greenhouse gases from fossil fuel burning, cutting down forests and other human activities. So, over the past Sedna year, rising CO_2 levels have at the very least magnified global warming, ushering in the relatively balmy, stable climate sometimes called the "long summer" that has allowed human civilization to flourish.

However, humanity has now raised global CO_2 levels by more than the rise from roughly 180 to 260 ppm at the end of the last ice age, albeit in a few hundred years, rather than over more than a few thousand years. So, climate change is undeniably the most pressing issue of the day.

2015 Climate Change agreement

So, let's have a look at the chart of the 2015 Climate Change agreement, which was widely hailed as an environmental breakthrough. When we're dealing with this level of evolutionary change we would expect Sedna to be significantly placed in the chart, but first let's get the exact time of the decision. Here's how the *Guardian* newspaper reported it:

> ### World leaders hail Paris climate deal as 'major leap for mankind'
>
> In the final meeting of the Paris talks on climate change on Saturday night, the debating chamber was full and the atmosphere tense. Ministers from 196 countries sat behind their country nameplates, aides flocking them, with observers packed into the overflowing hall.

John Kerry, the US secretary of state, talked animatedly with his officials, while China's foreign minister Xie Zhenhua wore a troubled look. They had been waiting in this hall for nearly two hours. The French hosts had trooped in to take their seats on the stage, ready to applaud on schedule at 5:30 pm – but it was now after 7 pm, and the platform was deserted. After two weeks of fraught negotiations, was something going badly wrong?

Then at 7:16 pm, the French foreign minister, Laurent Fabius, returned abruptly to the stage, flanked by high-ranking UN officials. The last-minute compromises had been resolved, he said. And suddenly they were all on their feet. Fabius brought down the green-topped gavel, a symbol of UN talks, and announced that a Paris agreement had been signed.

The delegates were clapping, cheering and whistling wildly, embracing and weeping. Even the normally reserved economist, Lord Stern was whooping. Outside the hall, a "Mexican wave" of standing ovations rippled across the conference centre as news reached participants gathered around screens outside for the translation into their own language. The 50,000 people who attended the summit had been waiting for this moment, through marathon negotiating sessions and sleepless nights.[31]

---

[31] *Guardian,* December 14, 2015

Chart for the Agreement

Name: Climate Change Agreement
date: Sa., 12 December 2015
in Paris, FR
2e20, 48n52

Time: 7:16 p.m.
Univ.Time: 18:16
Sid. Time: 23:49:51

ASTRO DIENST
www.astro.com

Type: 2.GW 0.0-1 2-Apr-2018

Event Chart (Method: Web Style / Placidus)
Sun sign: Sagittarius
Ascendant: Cancer

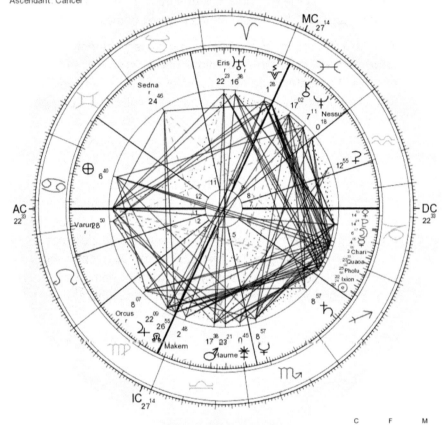

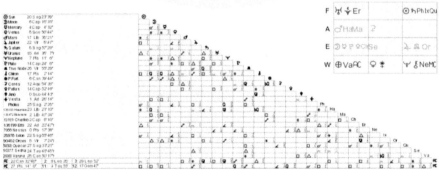

If we look at the chart for 7:16 pm on December 12, 2015 in Paris, we find Sedna in the eleventh house of collective consciousness. This agreement represents one of the few times the world has come together to agree on an ideal, so the 11th house placement is very appropriate.

Sedna Aspects

inconjunct Pholus, inconjunct Haumea

Sedna is the focus of another Finger of Fate aspect pattern here, this time with fateful inconjunct aspects to Pholus, the centaur of illumination and growth, in the sixth house of service, and Haumea, the planet of rebirth, in the fourth house of home. These are the closest of any of the Sedna aspects in the chart and confirms Sedna's central role in environmental evolution, showing the agreement is a workable plan for change toward a new beginning.

trine North Node, trine Jupiter

Slightly wider, but still within 3 degrees, we have Sedna trine the North Node, the point of dharma, which is conjunct Jupiter, the planet of expansion, in the third house of communication and ideas. This aspect shows the karmic results of the agreement will be to rally support behind the idea of climate change and expand it through the ensuing communication.

sextile Ascendent, sextile MC

Sedna is also sextile both the Ascendent, the cusp of the first house of identity, and the MC, the cusp of the tenth house of profession. These sextiles are very significant, as they only occur because of the last-minute delay in the announcement and they show the ease with which the agreement would underpin social decisions and changes in individual behaviour to facilitate the new goals. Stock market values shifted instantly after the agreement, away from fossil fuel investment and into renewable energy, and that trend has since then only been accelerating. It's notable, however, that there's no contact with Saturn or Mars, so no guaranteed actions or structure to achieve the lofty goals.

10: Climate Change Case Study - Rachel Carson

All right, let's personalize this information by looking at a couple of climate change case studies. The first is Rachel Carson, an American marine biologist, author, and conservationist, whose book, *Silent Spring* and other writings are credited with starting the global environmental movement.

She began her career as an aquatic biologist in the U.S. Bureau of Fisheries and became a full-time nature writer in the 1950s. Her widely praised 1951 bestseller, *The Sea Around Us,* won her a U.S. National Book Award, recognition as a gifted writer, and financial security. Her next book, *The Edge of the Sea*, and the reissued version of her first book, *Under the Sea Wind*, were also bestsellers. This sea trilogy explores the whole of ocean life from the shores to the depths.

Late in the 1950s, she turned her attention to conservation, especially some problems that she believed were caused by synthetic pesticides. The result was the book, *Silent Spring*, published in 1962, which brought environmental concerns to an unprecedented share of the American people.

Although *Silent Spring* was met with fierce opposition by chemical companies, it spurred a reversal in national pesticide policy, which led to a nationwide ban on DDT and other pesticides. It also inspired a grassroots environmental movement that led to the creation of the U.S. Environmental Protection Agency.

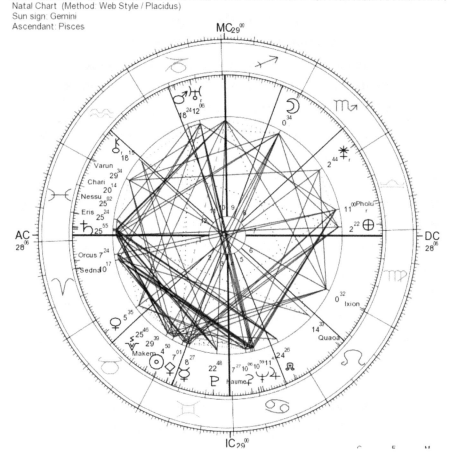

Name: ♀ Rachel Carson
born on Mo., 27 May 1907
in Springdale (Allegheny County), PA (US)
79w47, 40n32

Time: 2:00 a.m.
Univ. Time: 7:00
Sid. Time: 17:55:37

ASTRO DIENST
www.astro.com

Type 2.GW 0.0-1 16-Mrz-2017

Natal Chart (Method: Web Style / Placidus)
Sun sign: Gemini
Ascendant: Pisces

House Placement

Rachel has Sedna direct in Aries in the first house. Sedna in the First looks initially like it is setting us truly on a quest of self-development.

Later, in the chapter on Sedna in the houses, I interpret this position more fully, but here's a slightly edited version:

Sedna in 1st House

With Sedna in the first house we are on a spiritual quest to investigate what it is to be uniquely ourselves and the relationship between us and the cultural and physical environment in which we we find ourselves. With this placement we are truly on a quest of self-development.

Various influences in our lives will motivate us to begin this quest, but they are all likely to involve some form of pressure, which could give us a sense of alienation, or victimization. Or we might deny ourselves in the face of the demands from those around us until this position no longer becomes tenable and we must break out.

A build-up of pressure is normally required because we tend to be afraid to plumb the depths of our personality. We want to see ourselves in a good light, so we overlook inherent problems. However, our Sedna spiritual quest always demands we acknowledge just how bad things really are and start from there.

Because Sedna is the new outer limit of the solar system, it replaces Saturn as the limiting principle in the chart and one that is much further out than the old limit of Saturn. For those with a strong Sedna signature the Saturnian rules have no meaning, so at the unconscious level we might conceive of a hair-brained scheme that is totally grounded from our point of view but off the planet in terms of everyone else and the physical world around us.

While we are unconscious of the energy we might assert ourselves at times as if our sense of self depended on it, and this will call correspondingly strong reactions from others in our environment. This can generate a victim and victimizer relationship, in which we might play either role.

We likely have a deep well of personality traits to mine for our growth and know no boundaries in uncovering the taboo underbelly of our own and others' lives. We may even use this as the raw material for our profession.

Because we are exploring ourselves as the canvas of our growth, there will likely be times that we need to withdraw deep within ourselves in order to sort through our thoughts and feelings. And it is important through this process to always maintain reference points in the wider society and not get 'lost in ourselves.'

When we succeed in attaining a more spiritual outlook on life, our sense of self is not threatened so easily and we become more secure in ourselves. If we haven't worked through all the more base sides of Sedna, however, these can still manifest as spiritual traps on the path to enlightenment.

As we plumb the depths of our individuality and grow in consciousness, we will begin to understand ourselves and the web of interactions that we live amongst on a more transpersonal level and be able to live our lives in ways that exemplify both our deepest spiritual needs as an individual and also serve the wider society.

House Analysis

Let's have a quick look to see how this fits with Rachel's experience.

Was she on a quest of self-development?

> As a child she spent a lot of time exploring around her family's farm. An avid reader, she began writing stories (often involving animals) at age eight and had her first story published at age ten. The natural world, particularly the ocean, was the common thread of her favourite literature.
>
> At the Pennsylvania College for Women, she was somewhat of a loner. She originally studied English, but switched her major to biology, though she continued contributing to the school's student newspaper and literary supplement.
>
> She had intended to continue for a doctorate, but was forced to leave Johns Hopkins University to search for a full-time teaching position to help support her family. In 1935, her father died suddenly, worsening their already critical financial situation and leaving her to care for her aging mother. At the urging of her undergraduate biology mentor, she settled for a temporary position with the U.S. Bureau of Fisheries, writing radio copy for a series of weekly educational broadcasts.[32]

Was she under pressure to begin this quest?

Yes, pressure from family responsibilities:

> At the Bureau of Fisheries, her main responsibilities were to analyze and report field data on fish populations, and to write brochures and other literature for the public. Using her research and consultations with marine biologists as starting points, she also wrote a steady stream of articles for *The Baltimore Sun* and other newspapers. However, her family responsibilities further

---

[32] https://simple.wikipedia.org/wiki/Rachel_Carson

increased in January 1937 when her older sister died, leaving her as the sole breadwinner for her mother and two nieces.[33]

And pressure from administration responsibilities:

Carson rose within the Fish and Wildlife Service, by 1945 supervising a small writing staff and in 1949 becoming chief editor of publications. Though her position provided increasing opportunities for fieldwork and freedom in choosing her writing projects, it also entailed increasingly tedious administrative responsibilities. By 1948, she was working on material for a second book and had made the conscious decision to begin a transition to writing full-time. That year, she took on a literary agent and they formed a close professional relationship that would last the rest of Carson's career.[34]

Did she have to acknowledge just how bad things really are and start from there?

Starting in the mid-1940s, she had become concerned about the use of synthetic pesticides, many of which had been developed through the military funding of science since World War II. It was the US federal government's 1957 gypsy moth eradication program, however, that prompted her to devote her research, and her next book, to pesticides and environmental poisons.

The gypsy moth program involved aerial spraying of DDT and other pesticides mixed with fuel oil, including the spraying of private land. Landowners on Long Island filed a suit to have the spraying stopped, and many in affected regions followed the case closely. Though the suit was lost, the Supreme Court granted petitioners the right to gain injunctions against potential environmental damage in the future; this laid the basis for later successful environmental actions.

By 1959, the USDA's Agricultural Research Service responded to the criticism by Carson and others with a public service film that Carson characterized as "flagrant propaganda" that ignored the dangers that spraying pesticides posed to humans and wildlife. That spring, she wrote a letter, published in *The*

---

[33] Ibid.
[34] Ibid.

Washington Post, that attributed the recent decline in bird populations—in her words, the "silencing of birds"—to pesticide overuse.[35]

Were there times that she needed to withdraw deep within herself?

Through 1955 and 1956, she worked on a number of writing projects about the sea, but her interests were turning to conservation. She considered an environment-themed book project and became involved with The Nature Conservancy and other conservation groups. She also made plans to buy and preserve from development an area in Maine she and Freeman called the "Lost Woods."

However, early in 1957, family tragedy struck a third time when one of the nieces she had cared for in the 1940s died at the age of 31, leaving a five-year-old orphan son. Carson took on that responsibility, adopting the boy, alongside caring for her aging mother. This took a considerable toll on her. She moved to Silver Spring, Maryland, to care for Roger, and much of 1957 was spent putting their new living situation in order and focusing on specific environmental threats.

By late 1957, she was closely following federal proposals for widespread pesticide spraying; the USDA planned to eradicate fire ants, and other spraying programs involving chlorinated hydrocarbons and organophosphates were on the rise. For the rest of her life, Carson's main professional focus would be the dangers of pesticide overuse.[36]

Did she have to assert herself at times as if her sense of self depended on it, generating a victim and victimizer relationship?

Carson and the others involved with publication of her seminal book, *Silent Spring*, expected fierce criticism. They were particularly concerned about the possibility of being sued for libel. Carson was also undergoing radiation therapy to combat her spreading cancer and expected to have little energy to devote to defending her work and responding to critics. In preparation for the anticipated attacks, Carson and her agent

---

[35] Ibid.
[36] Ibid.

attempted to amass as many prominent supporters as possible before the book's release.

In the weeks leading up to the September 27, 1962 publication, there was strong opposition to *Silent Spring* from the chemical industry. They threatened legal action unless the planned *Silent Spring* features were canceled.

Others went further, attacking Carson's scientific credentials, because her training was in marine biology rather than biochemistry, and her personal character. She was labeled: "...a fanatic defender of the cult of the balance of nature," while the U.S. Secretary of Agriculture at the time in a letter to the President, reportedly concluded that because she was unmarried despite being physically attractive, she was "probably a Communist.[37]

Did she know no boundaries in uncovering the taboo underbelly of our own and others' lives? Did she use this as the raw material for her profession?

As biographer Mark Hamilton Lytle writes in *The Gentle Subversive:*

Carson "quite self-consciously decided to write a book calling into question the paradigm of scientific progress that defined postwar American culture. The overriding theme of *Silent Spring* is the powerful—and often negative—effect humans have on the natural world.[38]

Did she live in a way that exemplifies both her deepest spiritual needs as an individual and also serve the wider society?

Carson's work had a powerful impact on the environmental movement. *Silent Spring,* in particular, was a rallying point for the fledgling social movement in the 1960s. According to environmental engineer and Carson scholar H. Patricia Hynes, "*Silent Spring* altered the balance of power in the world. No one since would be able to sell pollution as the necessary underside of progress so easily or uncritically.

Carson's work, and the activism it inspired, are at least partly responsible for the deep ecology movement and the overall

[37] Ibid.
[38] Lytle, Mark Hamilton. *The Gentle Subversive,* 2007

strength of the grassroots environmental movement since the 1960s. It was also influential on the rise of ecofeminism and on many feminist scientists.[39]

Aspects

conjunct Orcus, opposition Pholus

Looking at her Sedna aspects, we see a strong conjunction of Sedna to Orcus, the planet of delving down and speaking out, in the first house of identity, together with a stressful opposition to Pholus, the centaur of 'courage before power,' in the seventh house of relationships, which is the root of Rachel's activism.

semi-square Vesta, quintile Pluto

She also has a semi-square to Vesta, the asteroid of regeneration in the second house of material resources, together with an evolutionary quintile with Pluto, the planet of transformation, in the third house of ideas and communication, showing her evolutionary destiny to transform out ideas about regeneration in the environment.

sextile Mercury

We also have a flowing sextile between Sedna and Mercury, the planet of ideas and communication, also in the third house, which blessed her with communication skills.

trine Quaoar

There is also a flowing trine to Quaoar, the planet of new perspectives, in the fifth house of creativity, which pulled her, as a developing writer, in new directions.

> After earning a master's in zoology from Johns Hopkins, Carson found part-time work at the US Bureau of Fisheries. Though she'd chosen science over prose, her former specialty proved useful in her new occupation. Carson's first assignment for the bureau was to write a fifty-two-episode radio program called 'Romance Under the Waters.' "I had given up writing forever, I thought. It never occurred to me that I was merely getting something to write about."

---

[39] Ibid.

Her first book, *Under the Sea-Wind*, although it would be Carson's favorite, was a commercial failure, selling only two thousand copies. Carson needed a couple of years to recover from the blow, but both driven and strapped for cash, she pushed forward. Carson wrote another book. When *The Sea Around Us* arrived in 1951, it won the National Book Award for nonfiction and solidified Carson's position as a literary heavyweight. To this day, it's credited as being one of the most successful books ever written about nature.[40]

square Uranus, square Ceres, square Neptune, square Jupiter

And finally, the opposition between Sedna/Orcus and Pholus forms the central tension in a grand cross, with a square to Uranus, the planet of awakening, in the tenth house of profession and squares to a conjunction of Ceres, the planet of nurture, Neptune, the planet of chemicals and lies, Jupiter, the planet of publishing, and Haumea, the planet of rebirth, all in the fourth house of home.

This grand cross seems to speak directly to Rachel's seminal work, *Silent Spring*, so let's have a look at the book and then at the chart for publication.

Silent Spring

Silent Spring was first serialised in *The New Yorker* before being published in book form in 1962, it chronicled the devastating effects of the overuse of pesticides. The book was startling for its rigorous scientific assessment of how, by spraying for one issue, like getting rid of a bug or a weed, without considering how the chemicals would impact everything else, people were often doing more harm than good. It was a beautifully written treatise of horrors aimed at a general audience.

The book jump-started the environmental movement and provided the public with a target: the multimillion-dollar chemical industry. In turn, the chemical industry reacted by launching a quarter-million-dollar smear campaign against Carson. She was called hysterical, labeled a spinster, and accused of letting harmless insects terrify her.

---

[40] Swaby, Rachel. H*eadstrong: 52 Women Who Changed Science and the World*

Whenever Carson or the book set off an outrage, the chemical industry fanned the flames. As a result, in the early 1960s, she was at the centre of a very public battle between those hoping to preserve nature and those wanting to control it. Fortunately, it was a fight Carson had been preparing for her entire life.

By the time she turned her focus to pesticides in *Silent Spring*, she had the public's attention. The book's main target was DDT, the first modern, lab-made insecticide. Credited with curbing malaria and typhus in World War II, DDT was viewed as a panacea—something that fell under the umbrella of, as the DuPont Company famously put it, "Better Things for Better Living… Through Chemistry."

Carson laid out her case with scientific studies and observations from the field: twenty-seven species of dead fish in the Colorado River, a greenhouse worker with paralysis, accidentally poisoned livestock. Alarmed by the information in *Silent Spring,* a US Senate subcommittee called Carson in to speak about her research, federal and state organisations started investigating the effects of DDT and other pesticides, and grassroots initiatives began to organise.

Silent Spring was tremendously influential. Three major events in 1970 were inspired by Carson. The National Environmental Policy Act promoted "efforts which will prevent or eliminate damage to the environment and biosphere and stimulate the health and welfare of man." A senator from Wisconsin later called it "the most important piece of environmental legislation in our history.

In April of that year, the United States had its first Earth Day, and then the Environmental Protection Agency was formed. In a timeline of the EPA's history, *Silent Spring* is the first reference, the official germination of the agency. Carson wouldn't be around to see the changes called for by both the government and individuals as a result of her book.[41]

---

[41] Ibid.

Serialization

The book was first serialized in the *New Yorker* magazine with the first issue appearing on June 16, 1962, so let's look at the chart for this date. We have no time, so no house positions.

opposite Ixion, square Venus

We can see a stressful opposition between Sedna and Ixion, the planet of lawlessness, which forms the base of a T square with Venus, the planet of values at the apex. This is a signature of the protest movement to change values which was prevalent in the 60s.

Name: Silent Spring
date: Sa., 16 June 1962
in New York, NY (US)
74w00, 40n43

Time: 12:00 p.m. hyp.
Univ.Time: 16:00

ASTRO DIENST
www.astro.com

Type: 2.GW 0.0-1 17-Mrz-2017

Event chart (Method: Web Style / Placidus)
Sun sign: Gemini

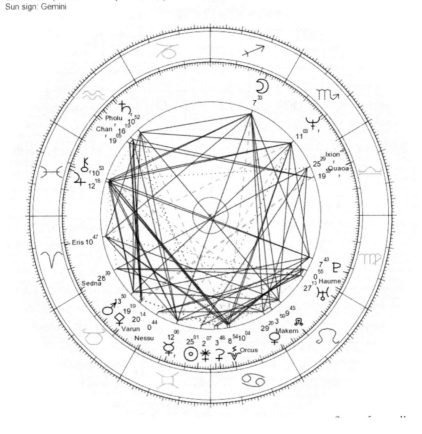

semi-square Jupiter

There is a stressful semi-square to Jupiter, the planet of expansion, telling of the dangers of unchecked progress and the blowback the articles would generate.

trine Haumea, trine Uranus

A flowing trine to the conjunction of Haumea, the planet of rebirth and Uranus, the planet of awakening, show why they aroused so much interest, because they woke people up to the rebirth required to live more sustainably on the planet.

quintile Orcus, quintile Pholus

nd the evolutionary quintiles to Orcus, the planet of 'delving down and speaking out' and also to Pholus, the centaur of 'speaking truth to power,' show the evolutionary role the publication was playing, a role which generated the birth of the environmental movement.

Book Publication

The book was published on September 27, 1962 by Houghton Mifflin Company, based in Boston, and the chart is even more positive than for the serial.

opposite Ixion

Again, an opposition to Ixion, the planet of lawlessness, the signature of protest is still evident, but it is the only tension in an otherwise flowing and evolutionary chart.

trine Uranus, trine Haumea, trine Juno, trine Vesta

Again, we have the flowing trine to the conjunction of Uranus, the planet of awakening, and Haumea, the planet of rebirth, but this has been joined by two asteroids, Juno, the asteroid of partnership, and Vesta, the asteroid of regeneration. These aspects talk about the birth of the environmental movement the book would generate.

bi-quintile Moon

Sedna is also in a close evolutionary bi-quintile aspect with the Moon, showing the book's destiny was to sway public opinion in an evolutionary way, creating that movement.

inconjunct Varuna

And the fateful inconjunct with Varuna, the planet of notability, assured its impact.

Name: Silent Spring Book
date: Th., 27 September 1962
in Boston, MA (US)
71w04, 42n22
Event chart (Method: Web Style / Placidus)
Sun sign: Libra

Time: 12:00 p.m. hyp.
Univ.Time: 16:00

ASTRO DIENST
www.astro.com

Type: 2.GW 0.0-1 17-Mrz-2017

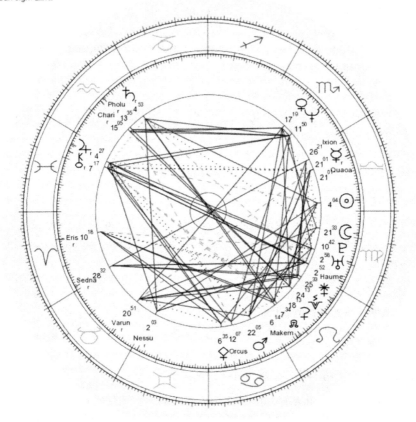

11: Climate Change Case Study - Sally Ride

May 26, 1951 – July 23, 2012

Sedna in Tenth

Sally Ride was an American physicist and astronaut. Born in Los Angeles, she joined NASA in 1978 and became the first American woman in space in 1983. She was the third woman in space overall, after two USSR cosmonauts. Ride remains the youngest American astronaut to have traveled to space, having done so at the age of 32. After flying twice on the Orbiter Challenger, she left NASA four years later.

She worked for two years at Stanford University's Centre for International Security and Arms Control, then at the University of California, San Diego as a professor of physics. She served on the committees that investigated the Challenger and Columbia space shuttle disasters, the only person to participate in both.

Then she led the task force that produced a visionary strategic planning report in 1987 titled, "NASA Leadership and America's Future in Space," but known popularly as the Ride Report. In her report, she weighed four recommendations: sending humans to Mars, exploring the solar system, creating a space station on the moon, and the one she was most passionate about, organizing a mission to Planet Earth.

House Placement

Sally has Sedna direct in Aries in the tenth house, which looks initially like it is setting us up for an evolutionary social caretaker role.

Later, in the chapter on Sedna in the houses, I interpret this position more fully, but following is an edited version:

Name: ♀ Sally Ride
born on Sa., 26 May 1951
in Los Angeles, CA (US)
118w15, 34n03
Time: 8:11 a.m.
Univ.Time: 15:11
Sid. Time: 23:31:31
Type: 2.GW 0.0-1 17-Mrz-2017

Natal Chart (Method: Web Style / Placidus)
Sun sign: Gemini
Ascendant: Cancer

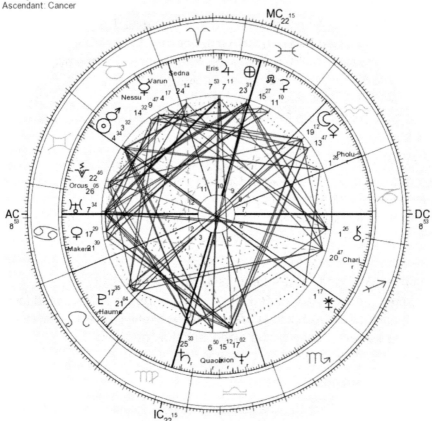

Sedna in 10th House

With Sedna in the tenth, we are on a spiritual quest motivated by our place in society, or events in our professional lives, which will likely be played out in public view. Depending on our level of consciousness, we might be totally unaware of this mission, or be actively seeking an evolutionary social caretaker role.

Either way there can be job, or career changes involved in our developing consciousness and some of these may involve crises so severe that we must transcend them to reach a new level of consciousness.

84

At the unconscious level this may involve acts of arrogance, rebellion, betrayal or victimization, in which we might be playing either the victim, or the perpetrator role.

With this placement we inherently feel the oneness of humanity but may not understand that others don't see this, which might lead us to adopt a deluded social mission or may inspire us to take visionary leadership.

The development of our consciousness may involve periods where we feel isolated, or alienated within the social context of our lives, while we absorb lessons and build up steam to reengage in a new way.

However, as we grow in consciousness, we will likely become prominent in our chosen field, because of our integrity, our ability to problem solve and our insights. As a result, we will likely be held in high regard by society for these skills.

With Sedna in the tenth house there is likely to be an evolution in our career, which may be forced by hard aspects and encouraged by flows, leading to a transcendence to a larger spiritual perspective. At this level level we will publicly live our beliefs.

House Analysis

Let's have a quick look to see how this fits with Sally's experience.

Were there career changes so severe that she must transcend them to reach a new level of consciousness?

Ride was one of 8,000 people who answered an advertisement in the Stanford student newspaper, seeking applicants for the space program.

> Before becoming the first American woman in space, Sally Ride got a PhD in astrophysics from Stanford and subjected herself to five years of astronaut training at NASA. Navy test pilots took her on gut-dropping, 600-mile-per-hour flights 39,000 feet in the air. (Her flight instructor called her the best student he'd ever had.) Ride became an expert at maneuvering a 900-pound robotic arm that would be used to pluck satellites from the sky.[42]

---

[42] *Headstrong, 52 Women Who Changed Science and the World*

Did this involve acts of arrogance, rebellion, betrayal or victimization?

> Prior to her first space flight, she was subject to media attention due to her gender. During a press conference, she was asked questions such as, "Will the flight affect your reproductive organs?" and "Do you weep when things go wrong on the job?" Despite this and the historical significance of the mission, Ride insisted that she saw herself in only one way—as an astronaut.[43]

And later:

> According to the engineer who warned of the technical problems that led to the Challenger Space Shuttle disaster, after the entire workforce of Morton-Thiokol shunned him, Ride was the only public figure to show support for him when he went public with his pre-disaster warnings. She hugged him publicly to show her support for his efforts.[44]

When Challenger exploded seventy-three seconds after liftoff, seven of Ride's colleagues died in the accident. Spaceflight up until then had always been the stuff of dreams. But NASA's push for rapid-fire missions at the expense of safety sacrificed lives.

Afterwards, during NASA's investigation of the loss, a member of the Rogers Commission revealed that Sally had:

> ...discreetly provided him with key information about the O-ring seals on the rocket, namely, that they become stiff at low temperatures, that eventually led to identification of the cause of the explosion."[45]

Did she inherently feel the oneness of humanity and take visionary leadership?

> She led the task force that produced a visionary strategic planning report in 1987 titled, "NASA Leadership and America's Future in Space," but known popularly as the Ride Report. In her report, she weighed four recommendations: sending humans to Mars, exploring the solar system, creating a space station on the

[43] https://en.wikipedia.org/wiki/Sally_Ride
[44] Ibid.
[45] Ibid.

moon, and the one she was most passionate about, organising a mission to Planet Earth.

Mission to Planet Earth's goal was to use space technology to understand Earth as a total system, to learn how man-made and natural shifts affect the environment. "This initiative," she wrote, "directly addresses the problems that will be facing humanity in the coming decades, and its continuous scientific return will produce results which are of major significance to all the residents of the planet."[46]

Were there periods where she felt isolated, or alienated within the social context?

Ride was extremely private about her personal life. At 31, she married fellow NASA astronaut Steve Hawley. They divorced six years later. After her death, her obituary revealed that her partner of 27 years was Tam O'Shaughnessy, a professor emerita of school psychology at San Diego State University and childhood friend, who met her when both were aspiring tennis players.

O'Shaughnessy was also a science writer and, later, the co-founder of Sally Ride Science. They wrote six acclaimed children's science books together. Their relationship was revealed by the company and confirmed by her sister after her death, who said she chose to keep her personal life private. She is the first known LGBT astronaut.[47]

Was she held in high regard by society and did she become prominent in her chosen field?

She received numerous awards, including the National Space Society's von Braun Award, the Lindbergh Eagle, and the NCAA's Theodore Roosevelt Award. She was inducted into the National Women's Hall of Fame and the Astronaut Hall of Fame and was awarded the NASA Space Flight Medal twice. She was the only person to serve on both of the panels investigating

---

[46] Ibid.
[47] Ibid.

shuttle accidents, those for the Challenger accident and the Columbia disaster.[48]

Was there an evolution in her career leading to a transcendence to a larger spiritual perspective?

When Mission to Planet Earth was adopted, Ride finally had an answer to the questions that arose in her seeing Earth from space. The astrophysicist in her saw a fragile planet and her greatest legacy is convincing NASA that Earth is worth trying to protect.

Aspects

square Makemake

She has a stressful square to Makemake, the planet of 'serving one's nation', in the first house of identity, which led her to sit on a presidential commission to review the Space Shuttle Challenger accident and to lead the task force that produced the Ride Report.

sextile Vesta, sextile Orcus

Her Sedna is also in a flowing sextile to Vesta, the asteroid of regeneration, together with Orcus, the planet of 'delving down and speaking out', in the twelfth house of institutions, which assisted this process.

> The agency needed to figure out what went wrong and how it could recover. Of the thirteen people, brought in to sit on a presidential commission to review the accident, Ride was the only current NASA representative. She was also responsible for gathering some of the most shocking information regarding the agency's missteps. She helped hold her employer accountable.

> The report concluded that NASA had forced through too many flights, ignored warnings that weather conditions might put astronauts in danger, and was entirely too cavalier about sending humans into space. The Nobel Prize–winning physicist, Richard Feynman, who was also a member of the panel, claimed that NASA's jam-packed flight schedule was akin to playing Russian roulette. Ride told a reporter that she wouldn't feel safe getting on another flight right away.[49]

---

[48] Ibid.
[49] *Headstrong, 52 Women Who Changed Science and the World*

inconjunct Saturn, semi-sextile Part of Fortune, sextile MC

She also has a flowing semi-sextile to the Part of Fortune, also in the tenth house of profession and close to the MC and the fateful inconjunct with Saturn, the planet of structure, in the fourth house of home and close to her IC. This enabled her to focus NASA on some evolutionary research on our planet, when she led the task force that produced a visionary strategic planning report in 1987 titled, 'NASA Leadership and America's Future in Space.'

> The explosion grounded the shuttle program for two years while NASA regrouped. With more rigorous safety measures put in place, the organization needed to map out a plan to win back the public's trust, while also making important decisions about the kinds of missions that would take the agency forward. NASA put Ride in charge of coming up with a refreshed list of mission recommendations. For a year, she tapped young NASA employees to brainstorm the agency's next move.[50]

trine Haumea, trine Chariklo

The flowing grand trine to Haumea, the planet of rebirth, in the second house of material resources and to Chariklo, the centaur of foresight, in the sixth house of service, is strongly evident in her final report.

> In her final report, she weighed four recommendations: sending humans to Mars, exploring the solar system, creating a space station on the moon, and the one she was most passionate about, organising a mission to Planet Earth.

> Internally, the organisation favoured big projects that ignited the imagination. The longtime NASA heavyweights guard wanted a mission to Mars; Ride argued for an approach more beneficial to the planet. Mission to Planet Earth's goal was to use space technology to understand Earth as a total system, to learn how man-made and natural shifts affect the environment.

> At a meeting of the Senate Committee on Commerce, Science, and Transportation, a senator asked Ride to prove how her preferred mission would be more than just "a better weather report. Following the meeting's conclusion, the same senator

---

[50] Ibid.

gushed that the initiative was "the most challenging and exciting concept that this committee has seen in quite some time."[51]

Chart for the Ride Report

The visionary strategic planning report, 'NASA Leadership and America's Future in Space' was released on August 1, 1987, in Washington DC. In the chart for this event we find the following aspects with Sedna:

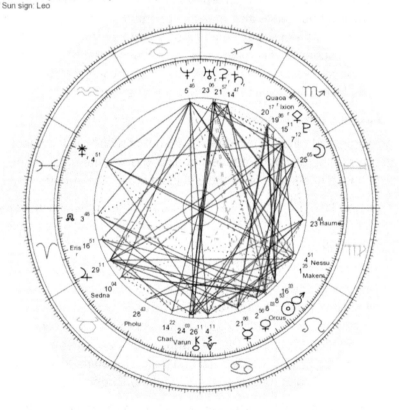

Name: Ryde Report
date: Sa., 1 August 1987
in Washington, DC (US)
77w02, 38n54
Time: 12:00 p.m. hyp.
Univ.Time: 16:00
Event chart (Method: Web Style / Placidus)
Sun sign: Leo

opposition Pluto, square Sun, square Orcus

There is a stressful opposition with Pluto, the planet of transformation, which is the base of a T square with the Sun, the planet of willpower,

---

[51] Ibid.

together with Orcus, the planet of 'delving down and speaking out', at the focal point, an appropriate signature for the scope of the report.

trine Neptune

There is also a flowing trine to Neptune, the planet of visions, showing the visionary nature of the report. Here's the official NASA view, from their web site.

> Following the 1986 space shuttle Challenger tragedy, a NASA task force headed by astronaut Sally Ride listed a Mission to Planet Earth to "study and characterise from space our home planet on a global scale," first among four recommended "leadership initiatives" to help reinvigorate the agency.

> The Ride Report stated: "Mission to Planet Earth is not the sort of major program the public normally associates with an agency famous for Apollo, Viking, and Voyager. But this initiative is a great one, not because it offers tremendous excitement and adventure, but because of its fundamental importance to humanity's future on this planet."[52]

semi-square Chiron, semi-square Varuna, sesquiquadrate Haumea

There is a stressful semi-square to Chiron, the centaur of wounding and healing, together with Varuna, the planet of notability, which shows the context of the report arising from disasters, and this is reinforced by the stressful sesquiquadrate to Haumea, the planet of rebirth, suggesting the rebirth will be fraught with challenges.

> In December 1999, NASA launched the first of its major EOS satellites, Terra, which carries five sensors to observe Earth's land masses, ocean surface and atmosphere. The other flagship satellites are Aqua (launched in 2002), which focuses on water and its role in the Earth system – measuring water in the atmosphere, clouds, sea and land ice, oceans and lakes, and a wide range of other variables – and Aura (launched in 2004), which measures atmospheric trace gases and aerosols.

> The program also included a number of smaller, more disciplinary-focused satellites that measure trace gases and

---

[52] www.nasa.gov/

aerosols in the polar atmosphere, the thickness of ice sheets and the sun's radiation output.[53]

quintile Mercury

And finally, the close evolutionary quintile to Mercury, the planet of communication, shows the importance of the report for the evolutionary cycle.

> "Right now we are in a particularly good situation, what we call the golden age of Earth observation from space," said NASA's Michael Freilich. "We have a suite of 14 operating satellites, and seven more we're developing for launch between 2008 and 2013 and a plethora of instruments and missions from international partners and interagency partners such as NOAA that are looking at the Earth in slightly different ways and making complementary measurements."

> "Today," according to Freilich, "using data from Earth-observing satellites, NASA-supported researchers are monitoring ice cover and ice sheet motions in the Arctic and the Antarctic; quantifying the short-term and long-term changes to Earth's protective shield of stratospheric ozone, including the positive impacts of the Montreal protocols; discovering robust relationships between increasing upper ocean temperature and decreasing primary production from the phytoplankton that form the base of the oceans' food chain; and using a fleet of satellites flying in formation [the 'A-Train'], making unique, global, near-simultaneous measurements of aerosols, clouds, temperature and relative humidity profiles, and radiative fluxes.Our improved understanding of Earth system processes leads to improvements in sophisticated weather and climate models, which in turn, when initialized using the satellite data, can be used to predict natural and human-caused changes in Earth's environment over time scales of hours to years."[54]

---

[53] Ibid.
[54] Ibid.

12: Development of AI

Let's now look at how this machine consciousness is likely to evolve in the next few decades so we can get more of a clue about the transit of Sedna in Gemini, which is starting in 2023. We'll then go on to explore consciousness a little deeper and see if we can find out what that is.

To do this we're going to look at an emerging AI that we all interact with already and then delve into two case studies of enablers of this evolution: Thomas Edison, the father of electrical appliances, and Steve Jobs, co-founder of Apple Computers.

Let's start with Apple's other co-founder, Steve Wozniak's view of AI:

> "Computers are going to take over from humans, no question," Mr Wozniak said.
>
> He said he had long dismissed the ideas of writers like Raymond Kurzweil, who have warned that rapid increases in technology will mean machine intelligence will outstrip human understanding or capability within the next 30 years. However Mr Wozniak said he had come to recognise that the predictions were coming true, and that computing that perfectly mimicked, or attained human consciousness, would become a dangerous reality.
>
> "Like people including Stephen Hawking and Elon Musk have predicted, I agree that the future is scary and very bad for people. If we build these devices to take care of everything for us, eventually they'll think faster than us and they'll get rid of the slow humans to run companies more efficiently," Mr Wozniak said. "Will we be the gods? Will we be the family pets? Or will we be ants that get stepped on? I don't know about that …"[55]

Google is an emergent AI

Where are these smart machines going to come from? They're growing amongst us already. Here's Kevin Kelly writing in *Wired* October 27, 2014:

> Around 2002 I attended a small party for Google—before its IPO, when it only focused on search. I struck up a conversation with Larry Page, Google's brilliant cofounder, who became the

---

[55] *Australian Financial Review,* 2015

company's CEO in 2011. "Larry, I still don't get it. There are so many search companies. Web search, for free? Where does that get you?"

My unimaginative blindness is solid evidence that predicting is hard, especially about the future, but in my defence this was before Google had ramped up its ad-auction scheme to generate real income, long before YouTube or any other major acquisitions. I was not the only avid user of its search site who thought it would not last long. But Page's reply has always stuck with me: "Oh, we're really making an AI."

I've thought a lot about that conversation over the past few years as Google has bought 14 AI and robotics companies. At first glance, you might think that Google is beefing up its AI portfolio to improve its search capabilities, since search contributes 80 percent of its revenue. But I think that's backward. Rather than use AI to make its search better, Google is using search to make its AI better.

Every time you type a query, click on a search-generated link, or create a link on the web, you are training the Google AI. When you type "Easter Bunny" into the image search bar and then click on the most Easter Bunny-looking image, you are teaching the AI what an Easter bunny looks like.

Each of the 12.1 billion queries that Google's 1.2 billion searchers conduct each day tutor the deep-learning AI over and over again. With another 10 years of steady improvements to its AI algorithms, plus a thousand-fold more data and 100 times more computing resources, Google will have an unrivalled AI. My prediction: By 2024, Google's main product will not be search but AI.[56]

Breathing Intelligence into Google

In fact, as we learned earlier, Ray Kurzweil joined Google in 2013 to lead a project aimed at creating software capable of understanding text as well as humans can.

---

[56] Kelly, Kevin. *Wired*, October 27, 2014

Here's Tom Simonite writing in the MIT Technology Review, June 26, 2014:

> The big announcements at Google's I/O event in San Francisco Wednesday didn't mention Web search, the technology that got the company started and made it so successful. But in a small session later that day, the inventor and futurist Ray Kurzweil talked confidently about making Google's current search technology obsolete.
>
> Kurzweil joined the company 18 months ago to lead a project aimed at creating software capable of understanding text as well as humans can. Yesterday, he told the audience that progress on this effort was good, and that it would result in an entirely new way to search the Web and manage information.
>
> You would interact with it like you would a human assistant," said Kurzweil. "It will be possible to ask a question of the software just as you would if talking to another person", he said, "and you could trust that it would return a fully reasoned answer, not just a list of links as Google's search engine does today. Such a virtual assistant might also take the initiative, Kurzweil said, coming forward when new information had appeared that was related to an earlier query or conversation.
>
> Kurzweil gave few details of how the software would work, but he said it was based on the theory of intelligence expounded in his 2012 book, *How to Create a Mind*. Kurzweil's theory is that all functions in the neocortex, the wrinkled outer layer of our brains that is the seat of reasoning and abstract thought, are based on systems that use a hierarchy of pattern recognition to process information. Each layer, he argues, uses the output of the ones below it to work with increasingly complex and abstract patterns.
>
> In the case of reading text, Kurzweil claims, our brain first recognises individual letters. It can then proceed to understand the words they form; then the meaning of phrases or sentences; and eventually, the thought or argument the person who wrote them is trying to convey.
>
> Google's current search technology is able to understand only the lower levels of that hierarchy, such as synonyms for

individual words, says Kurzweil. It can't synthesise that low-level knowledge to build up understanding of higher-level concepts.

The idea of building intelligent software that looks for successive levels of patterns in data isn't exclusive to Kurzweil. He said his group is using a technique known as "hierarchical hidden Markov models," in use for over a decade. More recently, Google, Facebook, and other companies have seen major leaps in speech recognition and other areas using a newer approach known as deep learning, which is based on large networks of simulated neurons arranged into hierarchies.

Kurzweil has estimated that to functionally emulate the human brain, a computer would need to perform around 100 trillion calculations per second. "It would be hard to provide that to a billion users, although I've discussed that with Larry Page and he thinks it's possible," he said.

Kurzweil even gave a qualified "yes" when asked if systems built that way might ever become conscious. "Whether or not an entity has consciousness is not a scientific question, because there's no falsifiable experiment you could run," he said. "People disagree about animals, and they will disagree about AIs. My leap of faith is that if an entity seems conscious and to be having the experiences it claims, then it is conscious."

AI Consciousness

So, let's return to Kevin Kelly's article in *Wired* to explore this idea of consciousness in AI.

Everything that we formerly Electrified we will now Cognitize

A picture of our AI future is coming into view, and it is not the HAL 9000—a discrete machine animated by a charismatic (yet potentially homicidal) humanlike consciousness, or a Singularitan rapture of super-intelligence. The AI on the horizon looks more like Amazon Web Services, cheap, reliable, industrial-grade digital smartness running behind everything, and almost invisible except when it blinks off. This common utility will serve you as much IQ as you want but no more than you need.

Like all utilities, AI will be supremely boring, even as it transforms the Internet, the global economy, and civilisation. It will enliven inert objects, much as electricity did more than a century ago. Everything that we formerly electrified we will now cognitize. This new utilitarian AI will also augment us individually as people (deepening our memory, speeding our recognition) and collectively as a species.

"In the next 10 years, 99 percent of the artificial intelligence that you will interact with, directly or indirectly, will be nerdy, autistic, super-smart specialists.

Premium AI services will likely be advertised as consciousness-free

In fact, this won't really be intelligence, at least not as we've come to think of it. Indeed, intelligence may be a liability—especially if by "intelligence" we mean our peculiar self-awareness, all our frantic loops of introspection and messy currents of self-consciousness. We want our self-driving car to be inhumanly focused on the road, not obsessing over an argument it had with the garage. The synthetic Dr. Watson at our hospital should be maniacal in its work, never wondering whether it should have majored in English instead. As AIs develop, we might have to engineer ways to prevent consciousness in them—and our most premium AI services will likely be advertised as consciousness-free.

Redefining what it means to be human

But we haven't just been redefining what we mean by AI—we've been redefining what it means to be human. Over the past 60 years, as mechanical processes have replicated behaviours and talents we thought were unique to humans, we've had to change our minds about what sets us apart. As we invent more species of AI, we will be forced to surrender more of what is supposedly unique about humans. We'll spend the next decade—indeed, perhaps the next century—in a permanent identity crisis, constantly asking ourselves what humans are for.

In the grandest irony of all, the greatest benefit of an everyday, utilitarian AI will not be increased productivity or an economics of abundance or a new way of doing science—although all those will happen. The greatest benefit of the arrival of artificial intelligence is that AIs will help define humanity. We need AIs to tell us who we are.[57]

Google's Launch Chart

Since Google is an example of an emerging AI, let's have a quick look at the Sedna connections in the charts for the Google website launch in 1997, for the first share trade in 2004 and for the establishment of the holding company, Alphabet, in 2015.

In the website launch chart Sedna is retrograde in Taurus, in 11th house of collective consciousness.

Here, Sedna is part of a grand trine in earth, with Makemake, the planet of 'serving the tribe,' and also the North Node, the point of dharma, both in the fourth house of the home and with Pallas, the asteroid of strategy and wisdom, in the seventh house of relationships, conjunct the Part of Fortune in the 8th house of shared resources.

This suggests that Google's destiny is to serve the tribe in the home by connecting with others and sharing resources.

Sedna is also the focus of a T square between Chariklo, the centaur of foresight, in the third house of ideas and communication, and Jupiter, the planet of expansion, in the ninth house of studies and philosophies, showing how Google would expand our ability to study and explore the world and stimulate ideas. Orcus is not part of the T square, but the square to Orcus, the planet of 'delving down and speaking out,' also in the third house of communication, was a big part of the success of the site, allowing people's voices to be heard.

---

[57] Ibid.

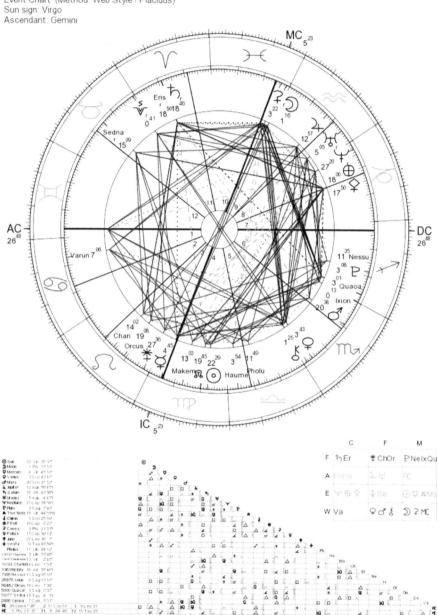

Name: Google Website
date: Mo., 15 September 1997
in Mountain View (Santa Clara County), CA (US)
122w05, 37n23
Event Chart (Method: Web Style / Placidus)
Sun sign: Virgo
Ascendant: Gemini

Time: 0:00 a.m.
Univ.Time: 7:00
Sid. Time: 22:28:48

Type 2.GW 0.0-1 31-Mrz-2018

I puzzled over the evolutionary quintile with Ceres, the planet of nurturing, in the eighth house of shared resources, until I realized that the website was the first step in nurturing the emerging Google AI. We'll see how this develops by the time of the establishment of the holding company, Alphabet in 2015. But first let's look at the public share float in 2004.

First trade in Google shares

In the chart for the first trade in Google shares, Sedna is stationary-retrograde in Taurus in the eighth house of shared resources.

In this chart Sedna is part of another grand trine in the practical element of earth, this time between Jupiter, the planet of expansion, and Makemake, the planet of devotion, both in the twelfth house of the unconscious, and Chiron, the centaur of growth, in the fourth house of home.

The Chiron in the fourth house is a strong indication of the likely growth of Google's footprint in our home as the AI offers us more irresistible services like search.

The Jupiter in the twelfth house means the company will have good luck coming from service to others. The more Google serves others, the more blessings will be given to them. The 12th house is the house of things deep and meaningful, and the position is notable because of the deep learning AI being developed by the company.

Sedna is also sextile Saturn, the planet of structure, in the tenth house of society, a sure sign Google will be with us for a long time to come.

And it is opposite Pholus, the centaur of illumination and growth, together with the Part of Fortune in the second house of material resources, showing that the destiny of the public company will be shaped by the growth in its ability to earn money.

There is also a fateful inconjunct to Pluto, the planet of transformation, in the third house of ideas and communication, showing Googles innovative and transformative role, both in terms of its own growth and its role in society.

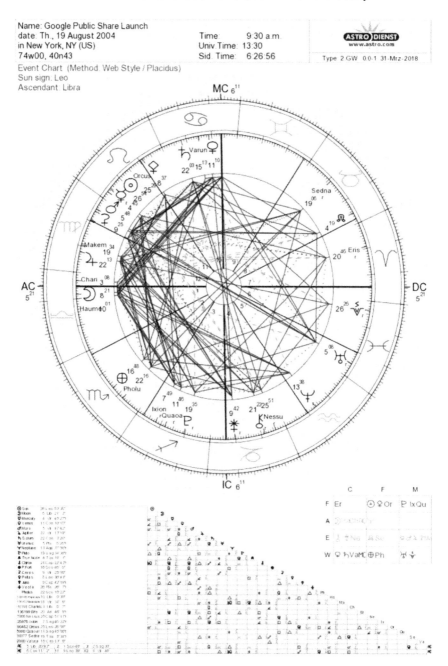

And finally, Chariklo, the centaur of foresight, is in the twelfth house of the unconscious, conjunct the Ascendent, the cusp of the first house of identity. Both the Ascendent and Chariklo are in a stressful sesquiquadrate to Sedna, which may point us to the path forward to

Google becoming an AI, drawing on the collective unconscious, to forge a new consciousness.

The sesquiquadrate suggests this path will be a little fraught, but we all learn more from mistakes than successes, so the AI's will be no exception, and the obstacles on the way will likely only serve as good learning experiences to the emerging AI.

Alphabet

At 4:01 pm on October 2, 2015, Google became part of a holding company called Alphabet. Let's have a look at the chart for this time and date in Mountain View California, where the company is based.

In this chart Sedna is retrograde in Taurus, conjunct the 4th house cusp. So, this business structure change has aligned Sedna with the IC, placing it at the root of the business.

The root of Alphabet is the cycle of fated transition, or the evolutionary cycle. That is where it is grounded. That's a really powerful place to base a business in these times, because the cycle is speeding up exponentially and because it shows Alphabet will continue to utilize the 'digital revolution,' which otherwise can be a disruptive technology as a motivating force. This means that Sedna is opposite the MC in the Alphabet chart showing the strength of the company's place in the world.

There is a stressful sesquiquadrate to the Sun, the planet of will, in the eighth house of shared resources, indicating that there will be ongoing tension over things like the balance of privacy and Alphabet's use of information.

It also indicates that some of the projects championed by the company may be still born, but this is the purpose of the holding company, to shield the profitable divisions like Google which produces 80% of Alphabet's income, from projects like the self-driving car, which is yet to see any income.

There is also a close, but stressful square to Venus, the planet of values, in the seventh house of one-to-one relationships. Alphabet thrives by attracting the best people to work there and providing an empowering creative working environment, and this aspect shows how important it will be for the company to continue attracting the best people to drive its development.

There is also a fated inconjunct with Quaoar, the planet of new perspectives in the eleventh house of collective consciousness, suggesting the activities of the company will force us to re-evaluate our shared values. This echoes the discovery we made earlier that AI will force us to reconsider what it means to be human.

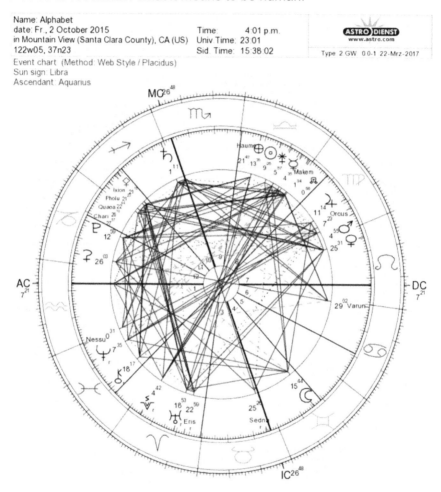

Name: Alphabet
date: Fr., 2 October 2015
in Mountain View (Santa Clara County), CA (US)
122w05, 37n23

Time: 4:01 p.m.
Univ. Time: 23:01
Sid. Time: 15:38:02

ASTRO)DIENST
www.astro.com

Type 2 GW 0 0-1 22-Mrz-2017

Event chart (Method: Web Style / Placidus)
Sun sign: Libra
Ascendant: Aquarius

And finally, we find a close trine with Ceres, the planet of nurturing, in the twelfth house of the unconscious. Here we see that the evolutionary potential of the quintile with Ceres from the web site launch chart has now developed into a close flowing trine, and this time Ceres is in the deep and meaningful twelfth house, where she will continue to nurture new technologies and applications to keep the company at the leading edge.

13: AI Enabler Case Study - Thomas Edison

February 11, 1847 – October 18, 1931

Sedna in the Fourth

Now let's delve into another couple of case studies to look at Sedna's influence in the personal charts of two key figures in this AI evolution. We'll look at it from the perspective of a fourth house Sedna and also from an eighth house perspective. Because 'everything we formally electrified we will now cognitize.' We'll start with the father of electricity, Thomas Edison.

He was an American inventor and businessman who has been described as America's greatest inventor. He developed many devices that greatly influenced life around the world, including the phonograph, the motion picture camera, and the long-lasting, practical electric light bulb.

Dubbed "The Wizard of Menlo Park," where he had a research laboratory, he was one of the first inventors to apply the principles of mass production and large-scale teamwork to the process of invention and is credited with the creation of the first industrial research laboratory.

He was a prolific inventor, holding 1,093 US patents in his name, as well as many patents in the United Kingdom, France, and Germany. More significant than the number of Edison's patents was the widespread impact of his inventions: electric light and power utilities, sound recording, and motion pictures all established major new industries worldwide.

Edison also developed the first system of electric-power generation and distribution to homes, businesses, and factories—a crucial development in the modern industrialized world.

His inventions contributed to mass communication and, in particular, telecommunications. These included a stock ticker, a mechanical vote recorder, a battery for an electric car, electrical power, recorded music and motion pictures. His advanced work in these fields was an outgrowth of his early career as a telegraph operator.

Edison is obviously a key figure in this Sedna evolutionary cycle, so let's have a look at his chart.

House Placement

Sedna is direct in Pisces, in the fourth house.

This is the first of two fourth house Sedna case studies; the other is Helen Keller, who we look at later in the chapter on consciousness. So, let's check out an edited description of this placement from later in the book:

Sedna in the 4th House

With Sedna in the fourth house we are on a spiritual quest to investigate our emotional ground, our home environment, our heredity and our family relationships, both of our birth family and of the family we form as an adult.

With this placement we live in an evolutionary research laboratory. The karmic influence from the parent of the opposite sex sets up the thrust of this research, which will shape our lives and our influence on the world.

We have likely spent a number of lifetimes exploring the themes that we are researching in our home and enter this life with a deep knowing about these of which we are seldom conscious, and some karmic challenges and likely karmic abilities, which will be illustrated by the aspects.

Stressful aspects can indicate illness, particularly early in life, which is likely to keep us at home more than usual. However, this illness frequently acts to push our destiny in a particular direction, or to focus our energy. And if the Sedna destiny is embraced, in later life we may well call the illness a 'blessing in disguise.'

The thrust of our evolutionary lifestyle will inevitably collide with everyday lifestyles repeatedly, throughout our life. When we are young this process is largely unconscious and we may appear to be a victim in these collisions. However, if the Sedna energy is embraced, in later life the reverse effect will occur and normal lifestyles will be evolutionarily enhanced with each collision.

It is definitely possible with this placement that we grew up in a dysfunctional, perhaps even violent, family and that we were the brunt of the negativity. This could have been connected to either our mother, or our father, or our family history.

As we grow up we may feel lost in a sea of emotions and needed to escape to find our own sense of belonging. Behavioral traits learned in early childhood, particularly from the parent of the opposite sex, will play a central role in our psyche as we age.

Stressful aspects with Sedna and other fourth house planets and stressful transits to Sedna can indicate forced separation of family members in some way, at some point in our life, leading to a transcendence to a larger spiritual perspective.

If the transition to a larger spiritual perspective is achieved, then the family relationships, particularly with any children, will flower as Sedna moves on to transit the fifth house and the family will become a great source of joy.

House Analysis

Let's see how this stacks up against Edison's life. Unless otherwise stated, all of the quotes in this case study are from the book, *Edison, His Life and Inventions* by Frank Lewis Dyer and Thomas Commerford Martin, published in 1910.

Did his mother shape his life and his influence on the world?

> Thomas was the seventh and last child of Samuel and Nancy Edison. His mother's father had been a Revolutionary War hero and, unlike her husband, she was a devout Presbyterian with some formal education. She put that education to good use. When he left school, she taught him at home. Thomas Edison later remembered, "My mother was the making of me. She was so true, so sure of me; and I felt I had something to live for, someone I must not disappoint." (From the site of the 'Thomas A Edison Innovation Foundation').

> Edison's mother was an attractive and highly educated woman, whose influence upon his disposition and intellect has been profound and lasting. The youth was, indeed, fortunate far beyond the ordinary in having a mother at once loving, well-informed, and ambitious, capable herself, from her experience as a teacher, of undertaking and giving him an education better than could be secured in the local schools of the day. Certain it is

that under this simple regime, studious habits were formed and a taste for literature developed, that have lasted to this day."[58]

Did he live in an evolutionary research laboratory?

At the age of ten he organized his first chemistry laboratory in his cellar. His father later said, "He spent the greater part of his time in the cellar."

In the cellar of the Edison homestead young Alva soon accumulated a chemical outfit, constituting the first in a long series of laboratories. The word "laboratory" had always been associated with alchemists in the past, but as with "filament" this untutored stripling applied an iconoclastic practicability to it long before he realized the significance of the new departure.

The home at Port Huron thus saw the first Edison laboratory. The boy began experimenting when he was about ten or eleven years of age. He got a copy of Parker's School Philosophy, an elementary book on physics, and about every experiment in it he tried. Young Alva, or "Al," as he was called, thus early displayed his great passion for chemistry, and in the cellar of the house he collected no fewer than two hundred bottles, gleaned in baskets from all parts of the town.

These were arranged carefully on shelves and all labelled "Poison," so that no one else would handle or disturb them. They contained the chemicals with which he was constantly experimenting. To others this diversion was both mysterious and meaningless, but he had soon become familiar with all the chemicals obtainable at the local drug stores, and had tested to his satisfaction many of the statements encountered in his scientific reading.[59]

First Industrial Research Laboratory

Edison's major innovation was the first industrial research lab, which was built in Menlo Park, New Jersey. It was built with the funds from the sale of his quadruplex telegraph.

---

[58] Dyer, Frank and Martin, Thomas. *Edison, His Life and Inventions,* 1910
[59] Ibid.

After his demonstration of the telegraph, Edison was not sure that his original plan to sell it for $4,000 to $5,000 was right, so he asked Western Union to make a bid. He was surprised to hear them offer $10,000 ($211,700 in today's dollars), which he gratefully accepted.

The quadruplex telegraph was Edison's first big financial success, and Menlo Park became the first institution set up with the specific purpose of producing constant technological innovation and improvement.[60]

From "the spring of 1876 to 1886 he lived and did his work at Menlo Park. It had been a master passion with Edison from boyhood up to possess a laboratory, in which with free use of his own time and powers, and with command of abundant material resources, he could wrestle with Nature and probe her closest secrets.

Thus, from the little cellar at Port Huron, from the scant shelves in a baggage car, from the nooks and corners of dingy telegraph offices, and the grimy little shops in New York and Newark, he had now come to the proud ownership of an establishment to which his favorite word "laboratory" might justly be applied. Here he could experiment to his heart's content and invent on a larger, bolder scale than ever - and he did![61]

And in Later Life

For over a score of years, dating from his marriage to Miss Miller in 1886, Edison's happy and perfect domestic life has been spent at Glenmont, a beautiful property acquired at that time in Llewellyn Park, on the higher slopes of Orange Mountain, New Jersey, within easy walking distance of the new laboratory at the foot of the hill in West Orange.

The ground floor, consisting chiefly of broad drawing-rooms, parlors, and dining-hall, is chiefly noteworthy for the "den," or lounging-room, at the end of the main axis, where the family and friends are likely to be found in the evening hours, unless the

---

[60] https://en.wikipedia.org/wiki/Thomas_Edison
[61] Dyer, Frank and Martin, Thomas. *Edison, His Life and Inventions,* 1910

party has withdrawn for more intimate social intercourse to the interesting and fascinating private library on the floor above.

The lounging-room on the ground floor is more or less of an Edison museum, for it is littered with souvenirs from great people, and with mementos of travel, all related to some event or episode. One of the most conspicuous features of the room is a phonograph on which the latest and best productions by the greatest singers and musicians can always be heard, but which Edison himself is everlastingly experimenting with, under the incurable delusion that this domestic retreat is but an extension of his laboratory.[62]

Did his lifestyle collide with everyday lifestyles repeatedly? When he was young, did he appear to be, or feel like, a victim in these collisions?

Laboratory thrown off Train

The Grand Trunk Railroad was extended from Toronto to Port Huron, at the foot of Lake Huron, and thence to Detroit, at about the same time the War of the Rebellion broke out. "By a great amount of persistence, I got permission from my mother to go on the local train as a newsboy." The local train from Port Huron to Detroit, a distance of sixty-three miles, left at 7 A.M. and arrived again at 9.30 P.M.

The hours were long, but the work was not particularly heavy, and Edison soon found opportunity for his favorite avocation-- chemical experimentation. The baggage-car was divided into three compartments--one for trunks and packages, one for the mail, and one for smoking. In those days no use was made of the smoking-compartment, as there was no ventilation, and it was turned over to young Edison, who not only kept papers there and his stock of goods as a "candy butcher," but soon had it equipped with an extraordinary variety of apparatus. There was plenty of leisure on the two daily runs, even for an industrious boy, and thus he found time to transfer his laboratory from the cellar and re-establish it on the train.

---

[62] Ibid.

Unfortunately, a sudden change came, fraught with disaster. The train, running one day at thirty miles an hour over a piece of poorly laid track, was thrown suddenly out of the perpendicular with a violent lurch, and, before Edison could catch it, a stick of phosphorus was jarred from its shelf, fell to the floor, and burst into flame. The car took fire, and the boy, in dismay, was still trying to quench the blaze when the conductor, a quick-tempered Scotchman, who acted also as baggage-master, hastened to the scene with water and saved his car. On the arrival at Mount Clemens station, its next stop, Edison and his entire outfit, laboratory, printing-plant, and all, were promptly ejected by the enraged conductor, and the train then moved off, leaving him on the platform, tearful and indignant in the midst of his beloved but ruined possessions.[63]

Fired for Early Invention

"His skill as a sender and receiver earned him a job as a regular telegrapher on the Grand Trunk line at Stratford Junction, Ontario. His creative imagination, however, proved his downfall in this instance. He was fired when a supervisor happened across the secret of one of the young inventor's creations – a device for automatically "reporting in" on the wire in Morse code every hour, when, in actuality, Edison was napping to make up for sleep lost in pursuing his studies."[64]

Did the reverse effect occur later in life, with normal lifestyles evolutionarily enhanced with each collision?

Launch of the Phonograph

Here's Edison in his own words:

That morning I took (the prototype phonograph) over to New York and walked into the office of the Scientific American, went up to Mr. Beach's desk, and said I had something to show him. He asked what it was. I told him I had a machine that would record and reproduce the human voice.

I opened the package, set up the machine and recited, 'Mary had a little lamb,' etc. Then I reproduced it so that it could be heard

---

[63] Ibid.

[64] Edisonmuckers.org

all over the room. They kept me at it until the crowd got so great Mr. Beach was afraid the floor would collapse; and we were compelled to stop.

The papers next morning contained columns. None of the writers seemed to understand how it was done. I tried to explain, it was so very simple, but the results were so surprising they made up their minds probably that they never would understand it--and they didn't.

I started immediately making several larger and better machines, which I exhibited at Menlo Park to crowds. The Pennsylvania Railroad ran special trains. Washington people telegraphed me to come on. I took a phonograph to Washington and exhibited it in the room of James G. Blaine's niece (Gail Hamilton); and members of Congress and notable people of that city came all day long until late in the evening.

The phonograph was now fairly launched as a world sensation, and a reference to the newspapers of 1878 will show the extent to which it and Edison were themes of universal discussion. The furor had its effect in stimulating a desire everywhere on the part of everybody to see and hear the phonograph.[65]

Launch of the Light Bulb

The challenge with the light bulb was developing a commercial electric filament and Edison had been experimenting with carbonized thread.

Edison had previously made a vast number of experiments with carbonised paper for various electrical purposes, with such good results that he once more turned to it and now made fine filament-like loops of this material which were put into other lamps.

These proved even more successful (commercially considered) than the carbonised thread - so much so that after a number of such lamps had been made and put through severe tests, the manufacture of lamps from these paper carbons was begun and carried on continuously. This necessitated first the devising and making of a large number of special tools for cutting the carbon

---

[65] Dyer, Frank and Martin, Thomas. *Edison, His Life and Inventions,* 1910

filaments and for making and putting together the various parts of the lamps.

Meantime, great excitement had been caused in this country and in Europe by the announcement of Edison's success. In the Old World, scientists generally still declared the impossibility of subdividing the electric-light current, and in the public press Mr. Edison was denounced as a dreamer. Other names of a less complimentary nature were applied to him, even though his lamps were actually in use, and the principle of commercial incandescent lighting had been established.

Between October 21, 1879, and December 21, 1879, some hundreds of these paper-carbon lamps had been made and put into actual use, not only in the laboratory, but in the streets and several residences at Menlo Park, New Jersey, causing great excitement and bringing many visitors from far and near.

On the latter date a full-page article appeared in the *New York Herald* which so intensified the excited feeling that Mr. Edison deemed it advisable to make a public exhibition. On New Year's Eve, 1879, special trains were run to Menlo Park by the Pennsylvania Railroad, and over three thousand persons took advantage of the opportunity to go out there and witness this demonstration for themselves. In this great crowd were many public officials and men of prominence in all walks of life, who were enthusiastic in their praises.[66]

Was there illness early in his life that kept him home more than usual? Did this push his destiny in *a particular direction? Did he call it a 'blessing in disguise'?*

Teacher calls him Addled

The great inventor, whose iron endurance and stern will have enabled him to wear down all his associates by work sustained through arduous days and sleepless nights, was not at all strong as a child, and was of fragile appearance. He had an abnormally large but well-shaped head, and it is said that the local doctors feared he might have brain trouble.

---

[66] Ibid.

In fact, on account of his assumed delicacy, he was not allowed to go to school for some years, and even when he did attend for a short time, the results were not encouraging--his mother being hotly indignant upon hearing that the teacher had spoken of him to an inspector as "addled."

Problem with Ears

Indeed, it was through the incident of having his laboratory thrown off the train that Edison later claimed he acquired the deafness that persisted all through his life. A severe box on the ears from the scorched and angry conductor being the direct cause of the infirmity. Although this deafness would be regarded as a great affliction by most people, and has brought in its train other serious baubles, Mr. Edison has always regarded it philosophically, and said about it recently:

"This deafness has been of great advantage to me in various ways. When in a telegraph office, I could only hear the instrument directly on the table at which I sat, and unlike the other operators, I was not bothered by the other instruments. Again, in experimenting on the telephone, I had to improve the transmitter so I could hear it. This made the telephone commercial, as the magneto telephone receiver of Bell was too weak to be used as a transmitter commercially.

"It was the same with the phonograph. The great defect of that instrument was the rendering of the overtones in music, and the hissing consonants in speech. I worked over one year, twenty hours a day, Sundays and all, to get the word 'specie' perfectly recorded and reproduced on the phonograph. When this was done I knew that everything else could be done which was a fact. Again, my nerves have been preserved intact. Broadway is as quiet to me as a country village is to a person with normal hearing."

Health when Older

Edison at sixty-three has a fine physique, and being free from serious ailments of any kind, should carry on the traditions of his long-lived ancestors as to a vigorous old age. His hair has whitened, but is still thick and abundant, and though he uses glasses for certain work, his gray-blue eyes are as keen and bright and deeply lustrous as ever, with the direct, searching look in them that they have ever worn. He stands five feet nine and one-half inches high, weighs one hundred and seventy-five pounds, and has not varied as to weight in a quarter of a century, although as a young man he was slim to gauntness. He is very abstemious, hardly ever touching alcohol, caring little for meat, but fond of fruit, and never averse to a strong cup of coffee or a good cigar. He takes extremely little exercise, although his good color and quickness of step would suggest to those who do not know better that he is in the best of training and one who lives in the open air.[67]

Aspects

So, let's look at how this is all modified by his Sedna aspects and see if they illustrate his karmic challenges and abilities.

conjunct Chariklo

His Sedna is conjunct Chariklo, the centaur of foresight, which is very appropriate for 'America's greatest inventor.'

A Great Moving World of My Own

It was suggested that the secret of Edison's vigour might be that he did not live in the past, but was always looking forward to a greater future, to which he replied: "Yes, that's it. I don't live with the past; I am living for to-day and to-morrow. I am interested in every department of science, arts, and manufacture.

"I read all the time on astronomy, chemistry, biology, physics, music, metaphysics, mechanics, and other branches--political economy, electricity, and, in fact, all things that are making for progress in the world. I get all the proceedings of the scientific societies, the principal scientific and trade journals, and read them. I also read The Clipper, The Police Gazette, The Billboard, The Dramatic Mirror, and a lot of similar publications, for I like to know what is going on. In this way I keep up to date and live in a great moving world of my own, and, what's more, I enjoy every minute of it."

---

[67] Ibid.

Referring to some event of the past, he said, "Spilt milk doesn't interest me. I have spilt lots of it, and while I have always felt it for a few days, it is quickly forgotten, and I turn again to the future." [68]

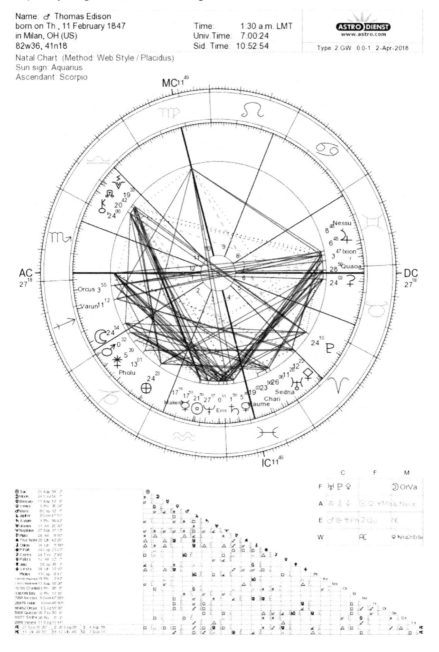

[68] Ibid.

sextile Part of Fortune, sextile Ceres, sextile Quaoar

The flowing sextiles to the Part of Fortune in the second house of material resources and to Ceres, the planet of nurturing, in the sixth house of service, and Quaoar, the planet of new perspectives, in the seventh house of relationships, enables him to see and manifest the new reality through his relationships, nurturing the service and make money out of it.

Extraordinary Optimism

A characteristic of Edison's personality contributing strongly to his achievements is an intense, not to say courageous, optimism in which no thought of failure can enter, an optimism born of self-confidence, and becoming, after forty or fifty years of experience, more and more a sense of certainty in the accomplishment of success.

In the overcoming of difficulties, he has the same intellectual pleasure as the chess-master when confronted with a problem requiring all the efforts of his skill and experience to solve. To advance along smooth and pleasant paths, to encounter no obstacles, to wrestle with no difficulties and hardships--such has absolutely no fascination to him. He meets obstruction with the keen delight of a strong man battling with the waves and opposing them in sheer enjoyment, and the greater and more apparently overwhelming the forces that may tend to sweep him back, the more vigorous his own efforts to forge through them.

At the conclusion of the ore-milling experiments, when practically his entire fortune was sunk in an enterprise that had to be considered an impossibility, when at the age of fifty he looked back upon five or six years of intense activity expended apparently for naught, when everything seemed most black and the financial clouds were quickly gathering on the horizon, not the slightest idea of repining entered his mind.

Later one of the writers spent a Sunday with him riding over the beautiful New Jersey roads in an automobile, Edison in the highest spirits and pointing out with the keenest enjoyment the many beautiful views of valley and wood.

The wanderings led to the old ore-milling plant at Edison, now practically a mass of deserted buildings all going to decay. It was a depressing sight, marking such titanic but futile struggles with nature. To Edison, however, no trace of sentiment or regret occurred, and the whole ruins were apparently as much a matter of unconcern as if he were viewing the remains of Pompeii.

Sitting on the porch of the White House, where he lived during that period, in the light of the setting sun, his fine face in repose, he looked as placidly over the scene as a happy farmer over a field of ripening corn. All that he said was: "I never felt better in my life than during the five years I worked here. Hard work, nothing to divert my thought, clear air and simple food made my life very pleasant. We learned a great deal. It will be of benefit to someone some time.[69]

semi-sextile Neptune, trine Ascendent, quintile Nessus

The semi-sextile to Neptune, the planet of dreams and visions in the third house of ideas, feeds his imagination and accounts for the 1093 patents in his name.

The trine to the Ascendent, the point of everyday habits, gives him the ability to successfully present his ideas and develop a practical working rhythm.

And the evolutionary quintile to Nessus, the centaur of radical transformation, in the seventh house of relationships, shows how his inventions will transform the world.

square Moon, square Mars

The stressful squares to the Moon, his emotional nature, in the first house of identity, and Mars the planet of war, in the second house of material resources, are the karmic challenges in Edison's chart, making himself centered and sometimes working at cross-purposes to himself. However, they also provided the strength of purpose and practical action to achieve his goals.

Anger

As a general rule, Edison does not get genuinely angry at mistakes and other human weaknesses of his subordinates; at best he merely simulates anger. But woe betide the one who has committed an act of bad faith, treachery, dishonesty, or

---

[69] Ibid.

ingratitude; then Edison can show what it is for a strong man to get downright mad. But in this respect he is singularly free, and his spells of anger are really few. In fact, those who know him best are continually surprised at his moderation and patience, often when there has been great provocation.

People who come in contact with him and who may have occasion to oppose his views, may leave with the impression that he is hot-tempered; nothing could be further from the truth. He argues his point with great vehemence, pounds on the table to emphasize his views, and illustrates his theme with a wealth of apt similes; but, on account of his deafness, it is difficult to make the argument really two-sided.

Edison has been seen sometimes almost beside himself with anger at a stupid mistake or inexcusable oversight on the part of an assistant, his voice raised to a high pitch, sneeringly expressing his feelings of contempt for the offender; and yet when the culprit, like a bad school-boy, has left the room, Edison has immediately returned to his normal poise, and the incident is a thing of the past.

At other times the unsettled condition persists, and his spleen is vented not only on the original instigator but upon others who may have occasion to see him, sometimes hours afterward. When such a fit is on him the word is quickly passed around, and but few of his associates find it necessary to consult with him at the time.[70]

Third Eye

The genuine anger can generally be distinguished from the imitation article by those who know him intimately by the fact that when really enraged his forehead between the eyes partakes of a curious rotary movement that cannot be adequately described in words. It is as if the storm clouds within are moving like a whirling cyclone.[71]

---

[70] Ibid.
[71] Ibid.

Evolutionary Eyes

Mars, the ruling planet of the first house, is the planet associated with the eyes in medical astrology, but here it is in the second house, the house of the ears. And because it is square Sedna we might expect the problems with the ears that we saw earlier.

So he turned the ear problem into a benefit, and, as often happens when one sense is limited, another develops stronger to compensate. In this case the partial deafness also seems to have stimulated an evolutionary development in his eyes.

> It will have been gathered that Edison has owed his special immunity from occupational diseases not only to luck, but to unusual powers of endurance, and a strong physique, inherited, no doubt, from his father. The vice-president of his experimental iron ore company, Mr. Mallory, mentions a little fact that bears on this exceptional quality of bodily powers. "I have often been surprised at Edison's wonderful capacity for the instant visual perception of differences in materials that were invisible to others until he would patiently point them out. This had puzzled me for years, but one day I was unexpectedly let into part of the secret. For some time past Mr. Edison had noticed that he was bothered somewhat in reading print, and I asked him to have an oculist give him reading glasses. He partially promised, but never took time to attend to it.

> "One day he and I were in the city, and as Mrs. Edison had spoken to me about it, and as we happened to have an hour to spare, I persuaded him to go to an oculist with me. Using no names, I asked the latter to examine the gentleman's eyes. He did so very conscientiously, and it was an interesting experience, for he was kept busy answering Mr. Edison's numerous questions.

> "When the oculist finished, he turned to me and said: 'I have been many years in the business but have never seen an optic nerve like that of this gentleman. An ordinary optic nerve is about the thickness of a thread, but his is like a cord. He must be a remarkable man in some walk of life. Who is he?'"[72]

---

[72] Ibid.

14: AI Enabler Case Study - Steve Jobs

February 24, 1955 – October 5, 2011

Sedna in the Eighth

Jumping more into the modern day, let's look at Steve Jobs as a comparison. This is the first of two eighth house case studies; the second is Edgar Cayce, who we'll look at in a moment in the section on Sedna and Health.

Steve Jobs was an American computer entrepreneur and inventor. He was co-founder, chairman, and chief executive officer of Apple Inc. He also served as chief executive of Pixar Animation Studios and became a member of the board of directors of The Walt Disney Company in 2006, following the acquisition of Pixar by Disney.

House Placement

Steve has Sedna direct in Aries in the eighth house. Here is an edited interpretation of Sedna in the eighth from later in the book:

Sedna in the 8th House

With Sedna in the eighth house we are on a path of evolutionary research into the metaphysical world, exploring the connections between people and between the psychic world and physical reality, likely breaking taboos and bringing hidden issues to light in the process.

We might react to this mission by denying it and avoid delving into esoteric matters at all, rejecting God and calling ourselves an atheist. With this approach we are also likely to avoid intimacy, but we will manage quite well most of the time skimming over the surface and avoiding the depths.

However, this is the house of life, death and rebirth. It deals with basic survival issues like sex, money and intimacy, as it relates to power, control, victimization and the need to manipulate others, or be manipulated, so these themes are going to come out in our experience, one way or another. Sedna in the eighth can also indicate compulsions and inherited health issues.

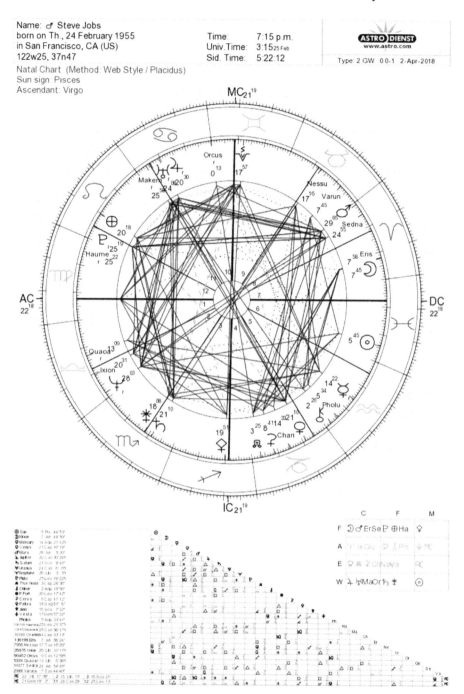

With this placement we have likely spent a number of lifetimes exploring these metaphysical themes from various angles and enter this life with a deep knowing of which we are seldom conscious and some karmic challenges and likely karmic abilities which will be illustrated by the aspects. Sedna in the eighth can also indicate psychic or intuitive contact with the dead and other interdimensional entities.

The nature of the evolutionary research we undertake will collide with existing reality structures throughout our lives and likely raise fears in those who feel threatened by the unknown, who may attack us to defend their world view. When we are young this process is largely unconscious and we may appear to be, or feel like, a victim in these encounters, but in later life the encounters will encourage the evolutionary process.

Through this research there is likely to be an evolution in our consciousness, which may be forced by hard aspects and encouraged by flows, leading to a transcendence to a larger spiritual perspective. If the evolution of consciousness destined by this Sedna placement is achieved, then the philosophies generated by our research will flower as Sedna moves on to transit the ninth house.

Eris Influence

Before we dive into the aspects with Sedna, I just want to mention that Steve's Moon is almost exactly conjunct his Eris, the planet of consciousness through discord, in the seventh house of relationships, which I believe is the root of much of the difficult person we shall encounter in the next few pages. This is also the root of his sense of being chosen and of being enlightened. But that's a story for another book.

Sedna Aspects

Here we're going to start our analysis with a look at his Sedna aspects to see if we can spot the karmic challenges and karmic abilities which they illustrate.

conjunct Mars, square Venus, opposite Neptune, opposite Ixion

The conjunction of Sedna to Mars, the planet of action, in the eighth house of power and control, opposite Ixion, the planet of lawlessness, together with Neptune, the planet of vision, in the second house of money, is a signature both of his financial success, as well as of his personal issues of intimacy and control.

The opposition forms the base of a T square with Venus, the planet of relationships and ascetics at the apex, in the fourth house of home. So, all of the tension from the opposition is focused in his relationships and the creative projects in his home. He famously started Apple Computers, together with his friend, Steve Wozniak, in his garage.

Steve was a Haunted House

Chrisann Brennan, a high school sweetheart, who lived with him and was an early Apple employee, said he became a threatening monster. Their relationship fell apart amid wild recriminations when she became pregnant with his first child. He denied he was the father, despite a positive paternity test, and he paid a pittance in child support, while living the life of a millionaire.

> I've truly hated Steve at times, but never for very long. Sharing a daughter with him has forced me to think about things more deeply... Steve the saint, the alien, the despot, the punishing masculine god, the liar, the obsessed narcissist, the cult hero, the ID of the iEverything, the genius and the motherless boy.

> It is only because of our daughter, Lisa that I have felt obligated to comprehend the many broken shards of Steve's glittering brilliance... For all the sparkling, spacious beauty of the Apple Stores, Steve was a haunted house, whose brokenness was managed and orchestrated by Apple's PR team in an extremely masterful way.[73]

square Jupiter, square Uranus, square Makemake

The Ixion/Neptune opposition to Mars/Sedna also forms the base of a second T square, and this time at the apex we have Jupiter, the planet of expansion, in the tenth house of profession, together with Uranus, the planet of electronics, and Makemake, the planet of devotion, in the eleventh house of ideals.

This conjunction is the sparking, spacious Apple stores that Chrisann is talking about, appliances for people with ideals, who want to change the world.

Together these T squares form a powerful grand cross which powers Jobs' life. The grand cross joins all four elements. This time Sedna, the planet of spiritual destiny, together with Mars, the planet of action, are the catalysts in the active Fire element; Venus, the planet of ascetics, is in practical Earth; Ixion, the planet of lawlessness, and Neptune, the

---

[73] Brennan, Chrisann. *The Bite In The Apple: A Memoir Of My Life With Steve Jobs*

planet of dreams, are in the ideas rich element of Air; and Makemake, the planet of extreme talent, Uranus, the planet of electronics, and Jupiter the planet of expansion, are in the emotional element of water, which connects people together.

trine Pluto, trine Part of Fortune, trine Haumea

These flowing trines to the Part of Fortune in the eleventh house of collective consciousness and to the conjunction of Pluto, the planet of transformation, and Haumea, the planet of rebirth, on the cusp of the 12th house of the unconscious, gave him the ambition to change the world.

> "What is Apple, after all?" he mused to Time. "Apple is about people who think 'outside the box,' people who want to use computers to help them change the world, to help them create things that make a difference, and not just to get a job done."

When Jobs was luring John Sculley away from Pepsi in order to apply his marketing skills to the personal computer market, he famously said, "Do you want to sell sugared water for the rest of your life? Or do you want to come with me and change the world?"

House Analysis

Was he on a path of evolutionary research to explore the connection between people and between the psychic world and physical reality?

When he was 19, Steve made a spiritual pilgrimage to India, during which he formulated some of the ideas that would serve him well in the future.

> Jobs traveled to India to visit Neem Karoli Baba at his Kainchi ashram in search of spiritual enlightenment. When they got to the ashram, it was almost deserted because Neem Karoli Baba had died the year before. Then they made a long trek up a dry riverbed to an ashram of Haidakhan Babaji. In India, he spent a lot of time on bus rides from Delhi to Uttar Pradesh and Himachal Pradesh. After staying for seven months, he left India and returned to the US. He had changed his appearance; his head was shaved and he wore traditional Indian clothing.

> During this time, he experimented with psychedelics, later calling his LSD experiences "one of the two or three most important

things he had done in his life." He spent a period at the All One Farm, a commune in Oregon and his high school sweetheart Chrisann Brennan joined him there.

During this time period, Jobs and Brennan both became practitioners of Zen Buddhism through the Zen master Kōbun Chino Otogawa. Jobs was living with his parents again, in their backyard toolshed which he had converted into a bedroom with a sleeping bag, mat, books, a candle, and a meditation pillow.

Jobs engaged in lengthy meditation retreats at the Tassajara Zen Mountain Center, the oldest Sōtō Zen monastery in the US. He considered taking up monastic residence at Eihei-ji in Japan and maintained a lifelong appreciation for Zen. Jobs would later say that people around him who did not share his countercultural roots could not fully relate to his thinking.[74]

Later Becomes Mentor

This experience was so important to him that, years later, he would suggest that fellow entrepreneurs follow in his path by visiting the same mountain Ashram temple that he once had.

One of these is Mark Zuckerberg, who interestingly also has Sedna in the 8th house, like Jobs. Speaking during a stage appearance with the visiting Indian Prime Minister Narendra Modi, Zuckerberg said:

> This is a story I haven't told publicly, and very few people know. Early on in our history, before things were really going well, we hit a tough patch and a lot of people wanted to buy Facebook and thought we should sell the company.

> I went and I saw one of my mentors, Steve Jobs, and he told me that in order to reconnect with what I thought was the mission of the company, I should visit this temple that he had gone to in India early on in his evolution of thinking about what he wanted Apple and his vision of the future to be.

> So I went and… seeing the people, seeing how people connected, having the opportunity to feel how much better the world would be if everyone had a stronger ability to connect, reinforced for me the importance of what we were doing and that

---

[74] https://en.wikipedia.org/wiki/Steve_Jobs

is something I've always remembered over the last ten years as we've built Facebook.[75]

Did he have compulsions and inherited health issues?

Much of the work Jobs was doing to tune in to the psychic world is reflected in what we might call his eating disorders, and thanks to Walter Isaacson's biography *Steve Jobs*, we have a pretty good idea of his lifelong dietary patterns. Towards the end, Walter reveals the reason for his obsessive fasting and restrictive diets.

Diet and Ecstasy

> Jobs' eating problems were exacerbated over the years by his psychological attitude toward food. When he was young, he learned that he could induce euphoria and ecstasy by fasting. Toward the end of his senior year in high school, Jobs began his "lifelong experiments with compulsive diets, eating only fruits and vegetables so he was as lean and tight as a whippet."
>
> During his freshman year at college he went to the Zen center for free vegetarian meals and was greatly influenced by the book, *Diet for a Small Planet* by Frances Moore Lappe. At that point, he swore off meat for good and began embracing extreme diets, which included purges, fasts, or eating only one or two foods, such as carrots, or apples, for weeks on end.
>
> His dietary habits became more obsessive when he read *The Mucusless Diet Healing System* by Arnold Ehret. Jobs then favoured eating nothing but fruits and starchless vegetables, which he said prevented the body from forming harmful mucus, and determined to regularly cleanse his body through prolonged fasts. That meant the end of his consumption of any bread, grains, or milk.
>
> At one point, he spent an entire week eating only apples, and then began to try even purer fasts. He started with two-day fasts and eventually stretched them out to a week or more, breaking them with large amounts of water and leafy vegetables. "After a week, you start to feel fantastic," he said. "You get a ton of vitality from not having to digest all this food. I was in great

---

[75] Zuckerberg, Mark. *YouTube*, September 27, 2015

shape. I felt I could get up and walk to San Francisco anytime I wanted.[76]

Things Lead to their Opposites

Even after he married and had children, he retained his dubious eating habits. He would spend weeks eating the same thing - carrot salad with lemon, or just apples - and then suddenly spurn that food and declare that he had stopped eating it. He would go on fasts, just as he did as a teenager and he became sanctimonious as he lectured others at the table on the virtues of whatever eating regimen he was following.

Even at a young age his daughter Lisa began to realise his diet obsessions reflected a life philosophy, one in which asceticism and minimalism could heighten subsequent sensations. "He believed that great harvests came from arid sources, pleasure from restraint," she noted. "He knew the equations that most people didn't know: Things led to their opposites."[77]

Were there issues with money and intimacy as it relates to power, control, andvictimization and the need to manipulate others or be manipulated?

His childhood sweetheart recounts:

The high school grounds must have felt like a home away from home to Steve and me; that's the only reason I can think of to explain our decision to take LSD on the campus. We must have been naive to believe it was a good idea, but to our credit, the grounds were large and blessedly deserted on a Saturday.

I have a slight memory of pulling two wrapped hits out of my pocket, thinking that we might split one. But we each swallowed one whole. And then we waited – this was Steve's first time and he seemed frightened. Out of the blue, he started to tell me that I would need to tell him 'not to put on airs' should he 'act out.' He wanted me to practice so I would be prepared to handle 'it'. Prepared for what? I had no idea. Then the LSD took effect.[78]

---

[76] Isaacson, Walter. *Steve Jobs*
[77] Ibid.
[78] Brennan, Chrisann. *The Bite In The Apple: A Memoir Of My Life With Steve Jobs*

Tourette's-like Behaviour

A lifetime later, I visited Steve after he was married. Our daughter Lisa was about 13 and Steve's son, Reed, a tiny baby. We were outside his house in Palo Alto, California, when, without warning, Steve blurted out the meanest, terrible comments at me, about why I was such a total failure of a human being. I gasped, but Steve's wife, Laurene, yelled at him to stop.

Then I thought back to Steve's first day on LSD – was it this he was scared of? He must have known he was capable of this Tourette's-like behaviour. It breaks my heart now to grasp how much he understood and tried to keep hidden back then.[79]

Uncontrollably Critical

Our relationship had continued through his college and we were living together in a shared house with Daniel Kottke, a computer engineer and one of the earliest staff members at Apple. It was a ranch-style place on Presidio Drive, close to Apple's first offices in Cupertino, California.

Steve wanted his buddy Daniel there because he believed it would break up the intensity of what wasn't working between us. Our relationship was running hot and cold. As Apple grew, so did Steve's sense of self-entitlement. His behaviour changed from adolescent and dopey to plain vicious.

Whenever we went out to eat, Steve would run down the waiters like a demon, detailing the finer points of good service, which included the notion that 'they should be seen only when he needed them.' Steve had become uncontrollably critical.[80]

Hot and Cold Relationship

In early October 1977, I realised I could endure our hot and cold relationship no longer. Steve and I had been dating since our schooldays. We were completely crazy about each other and utterly bored in turns. I had suggested to Steve that we separate, but he told me that he couldn't bring himself to say goodbye.

---

[79] Ibid.
[80] Ibid.

Living with Steve in Cupertino was not as I had expected it to be. We shared nice dinners and some beautiful evenings, but we could barely sustain a sense of emotional intimacy, much less build on it. It was like a game of Snakes and Ladders, with Steve as the game master who played to win at any cost. The ups were hopeful and the downs were extreme – then I found out I was pregnant.

It took me a few days before I told Steve. His face turned ugly. He gave me a fiery look, then rushed out without a word. I know it's widely believed that Steve asked me to have an abortion. And Steve, himself, has apparently been quoted as saying so. He even actively led people to believe that I slept around. But none of this was true. It served Steve's purposes to appear as the victim of a crazy woman to whom he'd had a slight attraction but had never loved.[81]

Did he have psychic or intuitive contact with the spiritual world?

Zen priest, Kobun Chino Otogawa, who became Jobs spiritual advisor, is quoted recounting the first time he met Steve.

> When I was living in California 23 years ago…I answered the door at midnight and there he was in bare feet with long hair and jeans with many holes everywhere. He wanted to see me…18 years old he was.

> I looked into his eyes, they looked terrible, but he's not crazy. I had to talk to him. I put my jacket on and took him on a midnight walk in downtown Los Altos. All the stores were closed. One bar called "The Tea Cup" was open. So, we sat down at the counter and I had an Irish coffee and he had juice.

> What he said was, "I feel enlightened, and I don't know what to do with this." I said, "Oh, that is very wonderful. I need proof of it."

> A week later he came back with a little metal sheet…I didn't know what it was…that little thing was the proof. It was a chip of a personal computer. He said, 'I designed it, my friend Woz helped me. It's called Lisa.' Which is the name of his daughter. That is the origin of the Apple computer.

---

[81] Ibid.

And I'm still not quite sure it was the proof…He always said, "Make me a monk. Please, make me a monk." I said, "No, not until I have proof."[82]

Did the nature of his evolutionary research collide with existing reality structures throughout his life?

Walter Isaacson's biography tells us that even later in life Jobs "was doing a lot of soul-searching about being adopted … with the primal scream and the mucusless diets, he was trying to cleanse himself and get deeper into his frustration about his birth."

Early Alienation Produces Different Drummer

> Jobs recalled the trauma of telling a neighbour he was adopted to Isaacson: "I remember right here on my lawn, telling Lisa from across the street that I was adopted. And she said, 'So does that mean your real parents didn't want you?'
>
> "Ooooh, lightning bolts went off in my head. I remember running into the house, I think I was like crying, asking my parents. And they sat me down and they said, 'No, you don't understand. We specifically picked you out.'"
>
> A friend of Jobs, Greg Calhoun, told Isaacson: "Steve talked to me a lot about being abandoned and the pain it caused. It made him independent. He followed the beat of a different drummer, and that came from being in a different world than he was born into."[83]

Trust Your Destiny

Jobs brought it up himself:

> The first story is about connecting the dots. I dropped out of Reed College after the first 6 months. So why did I drop out?
>
> It started before I was born. My biological mother was a young, unwed college graduate student, and she decided to put me up for adoption. She felt very strongly that I should be adopted by college graduates, so everything was all set for me to be adopted at birth by a lawyer and his wife.

---

[82] *Business Insider Australia*, Sept 8, 2015
[83] Isaacson, Walter. *Steve Jobs*

Except that when I popped out they decided at the last minute that they really wanted a girl. So, my parents, who were on a waiting list, got a call in the middle of the night asking: "We have an unexpected baby boy; do you want him?" They said, "Of course."

My biological mother later found out that my mother had never graduated from college and that my father had never graduated from high school. She refused to sign the final adoption papers. She only relented a few months later when my parents promised that I would someday go to college.

And 17 years later I did go to college. But I naively chose a college that was almost as expensive as Stanford, and all of my working-class parents' savings were being spent on my college tuition. After six months, I couldn't see the value in it. I had no idea what I wanted to do with my life and no idea how college was going to help me figure it out. And here I was spending all of the money my parents had saved their entire life.

I decided to drop out and trust that it would all work out OK. It was pretty scary at the time, but looking back it was one of the best decisions I ever made. The minute I dropped out I could stop taking the required classes that didn't interest me, and begin dropping in on the ones that looked interesting.

You can't connect the dots looking forward; you can only connect them looking backward. So you have to trust that the dots will somehow connect in your future. You have to trust in something — your gut, destiny, life, karma, whatever. This approach has never let me down, and it has made all the difference in my life.[84]

Fired from Apple - "Best Thing to Happen"

He went on:

My second story is about love and loss. I was lucky. I found what I loved to do early in life. Woz and I started Apple in my parents' garage when I was 20. We worked hard, and in 10 years Apple had grown from just the two of us in a garage into a $2 billion company with over 4,000 employees.

---

[84] Jobs, Steve. 2005 Stanford University Commencement Address

We had just released our finest creation — the Macintosh — a year earlier, and I had just turned 30. And then I got fired. How can you get fired from a company you started? Well, as Apple grew we hired someone who I thought was very talented to run the company with me, and for the first year or so things went well. But then our visions of the future began to diverge and eventually we had a falling out. When we did, our Board of Directors sided with him.

So, at 30 I was out. And very publicly out. What had been the focus of my entire adult life was gone, and it was devastating. I really didn't know what to do for a few months. I felt that I had let the previous generation of entrepreneurs down — that I had dropped the baton as it was being passed to me. I was a very public failure, and I even thought about running away from the valley.

But something slowly began to dawn on me — I still loved what I did. The turn of events at Apple had not changed that one bit. I had been rejected, but I was still in love. And so I decided to start over.

I didn't see it then, but it turned out that getting fired from Apple was the best thing that could have ever happened to me. The heaviness of being successful was replaced by the lightness of being a beginner again, less sure about everything. It freed me to enter one of the most creative periods of my life.[85]

Was there an evolution in consciousness leading to a transcendence to a larger spiritual perspective?

"I believe life is an intelligent thing, that things aren't random," Jobs said in a 1997 interview with *Time*, providing a glimpse into his complicated belief system that extends well beyond the Buddhist teachings.

The Zen of Steve Jobs

According to press reports, Jobs studied at the Los Altos Zen Centre in the 1970s and developed a close relationship with a Japanese born Zen master named Kobun Chino Otogawa. He focused his teaching on developing a Zen meditation practice.

---

[85] Ibid.

"The real purpose of practice is to discover the wisdom which you have always been keeping with you," Kobun said in a talk that's posted on the website for a Zen centre he founded outside San Francisco. "To discover yourself is to discover wisdom; without discovering yourself you can never communicate with anybody."[86]

Jobs echoed that spiritual self-reliance:

For the past 33 years, I have looked in the mirror every morning and asked myself, "If today were the last day of my life, would I want to do what I am about to do today?" And whenever the answer has been "no" for too many days in a row, I know I need to change something. Remembering that you are going to die is the best way I know to avoid the trap of thinking you have something to lose. You are already naked. There is no reason not to follow your heart.[87]

Karma Yoga Lessons from Steve Jobs

Your work is going to fill a large part of your life, and the only way to be truly satisfied is to do what you believe is great work. And the only way to do great work is to love what you do. If you haven't found it yet, keep looking. Don't settle. As with all matters of the heart, you'll know when you find it. And, like any great relationship, it just gets better and better as the years roll on. So, keep looking until you find it. Don't settle.[88]

Do what you Love, not what others Expect

Your time is limited, so don't waste it living someone else's life. Don't be trapped by dogma – which is living with the results of other people's thinking. Don't let the noise of others' opinions drown out your own inner voice. And most important, have the courage to follow your heart and intuition. They somehow already know what you truly want to become. Everything else is secondary.[89]

---

[86] Gilgoff, Dan. CNN.com, 2011
[87] Jobs, Steve. 2005 Stanford University Commencement Address
[88] Ibid.
[89] Ibid.

Did the philosophies embraced by this research flower as Sedna moved on to transit the ninth house?

Jobs said when he founded Apple that he wanted to change the world by putting the power of personal computing into everyone's hands, and as Sedna moved into his ninth house in 2007 he "succeeded beyond his wildest dreams" with the launch of the iPhone.

15: Intelligence

While we're looking at Artificial Intelligence, we better look at *intelligence*. We're going to do that by looking first at our evolving understanding of knowledge in the digital age. Then at the extended mind theory of Andy Clark and David Chalmers, which provides a direct reformulation of knowledge.

And to wrap up this chapter we'll look at Piaget's theory of cognitive development, a comprehensive theory about the nature and development of human intelligence first created by the Swiss developmental psychologist, Jean Piaget. Piaget had Sedna in the eleventh house of collective consciousness, like the two case studies in our following chapter on Consciousness.

Knowledge

First, let's explore what we mean by knowledge and look at how our understanding of knowledge is evolving. Here's David Weinberger:

Discerning Order

> Human knowledge, we have believed, is about discerning the order, the rules, that bring unity and predictability to the blooming, buzzing confusion that the senses convey… But the more details we cram into our global network of computers, the less the world looks like a well-oiled ancient model of the objects in the sky.

> We are increasingly relying on machines that derive conclusions from models that they themselves have created, models that are often beyond human comprehension, models that "think" about the world differently than we do.

> But this comes with a price. This infusion of alien intelligence is bringing into question the assumptions embedded in our long Western tradition. We thought knowledge was about finding the order hidden in the chaos. We thought it was about simplifying the world. It looks like we were wrong. Knowing the world may require giving up on understanding it.

> Our machines now are letting us see that even if the rules the universe plays by are not all that much more complicated than Go's, the interplay of everything all at once makes the place

more contingent than Aristotle, Newton, Einstein, or even some Chaos theorists thought.

It only looked orderly because our instruments were gross, because our conception of knowledge imposes order by simplifying matters until we find it, and because our needs were satisfied with approximations.[90]

Assumed the World was Knowable

It has been important to us that the model that produces knowledge also accurately reflect how the world works. Even if the old model of the universe yielded precisely the same results as Newton's laws, we would insist that the pre-Newton model was simply wrong. The ancients, we'd insist, didn't understand how the world works because the model that expresses the relationships among the parts does not reflect the actual state of affairs.

We have insisted that the model reflect the world because we have assumed that the world the model reflects is knowable. But now we have a different sort of model. Like traditional models, they enable us to make predictions that are true. Like traditional models, they advance knowledge. But some of the new models are incomprehensible. They can exist only in the weights of countless digital triggers networked together and feeding successive layers of networked, weighted triggers representing huge quantities of variables that affect one another in ways so particular that we cannot derive general principles from them.[91]

Chaos all the Way

Models confine the investigation to the factors we can observe and follow. For thousands of years we acted as if the simplicity of our models reflected the simplicity—the elegance, the beauty, the pure rationality—of the universe. Now our machines are letting us see that even if the rules are simple, elegant, beautiful and rational, the domain they govern is so granular, so intricate, so interrelated, with everything causing everything else all at once and forever, that our brains and our knowledge cannot

[90] Weinberger,David. 'Alien Knowledge', Backchannel, April 19, 2017
[91] Ibid.

begin to comprehend it. It takes a network of humans and computers to know a world so thoroughly governed by contingency—one in which it's chaos all the way down. And up.[92]

Extended Mind Theory

The extended mind theory of Andy Clark and David Chalmers provides a direct reformulation of knowledge. In his 1996 book, *Being There: Putting Brain, Body, and World Together Again*, Clark argues that knowing is something we've always done out in the world with tools.

Knowledge is less a reflection of the world than a tool for operating in it.

The paper, 'The Extended Mind' by Andy Clark and David Chalmers (1998) is a seminal work in the field of extended cognition. In this paper, they present the idea of active externalism, in which objects within the environment function as a part of the mind. They argue that it is arbitrary to say that the mind is contained only within the boundaries of the skull.

The separation between the mind, the body, and the environment is seen as an unprincipled distinction. Because external objects play a significant role in aiding cognitive processes, the mind and the environment act as a "coupled system". This coupled system can be seen as a complete cognitive system of its own.

In this manner, the mind is extended into the external world. The main criterion that Clark and Chalmers list for classifying the use of external objects during cognitive tasks as a part of an extended cognitive system is that the external objects must function with the same purpose as the internal processes.[93]

Deep Thought Meets Fluent Action

If you had to build an intelligent agent, where would you begin? What strikes you as the special something that separates the unthinking world of rocks, waterfalls, and volcanos from the realms of responsive intelligence? What is it that allows some

---

[92] Ibid.
[93] https://en.wikipedia.org/wiki/The_Extended_Mind

parts of the natural order to survive by perceiving and acting while the rest stay on the sidelines, thought-free and inert?

"Mind," "intellect," "ideas": these are the things that make the difference. But how should they be understood? Such words conjure nebulous realms. We talk of "pure intellect," and we describe the savant as "lost in thought." All too soon we are seduced by Descartes' vision: a vision of mind as a realm quite distinct from body and world. A realm whose essence owes nothing to the accidents of body and surroundings. The infamous "Ghost in the Machine."

Such extreme opposition between matter and mind has long since been abandoned. In its stead we find a loose coalition of sciences of the mind whose common goal is to understand how thought itself is materially possible. The coalition goes by the name, cognitive science, and for more than thirty years computer models of the mind have been among its major tools. Theorising on the cusp between science fiction and hard engineering, workers in the subfield known as Artificial Intelligence have tried to give computational flesh to ideas about how the mind may arise out of the workings of a physical machine—in our case, the brain.

The human brain, it seems, is the mechanistic underpinning of the human mind. When evolution threw up complex brains, mobile bodies, and nervous systems, it opened the door (by purely physical means) to whole new ways of living and adapting—ways that place us on one side of a natural divide, leaving volcanos, waterfalls, and the rest of cognitively inert creation on the other.

But, for all that, a version of the old opposition between matter and mind persists. It persists in the way we study brain and mind, excluding as "peripheral" the roles of the rest of the body and the local environment. It persists in the lack of attention to the ways the body and local environment are literally built into the processing loops that result in intelligent action.

In the natural context of body and world, the ways brains solve problems is fundamentally transformed. This is not a deep philosophical fact (though it has profound consequences). It is a matter of practicality.

Might it not be more fruitful to think of brains as controllers for embodied activity? That small shift in perspective has large implications for how we construct a science of the mind. It demands, in fact, a sweeping reform in our whole way of thinking about intelligent behaviour. It requires us to abandon the idea (common since Descartes) of the mental as a realm distinct from the realm of the body; to abandon the idea of neat dividing lines between perception, cognition, and action; to abandon the idea of an executive centre where the brain carries out high-level reasoning; and most of all, to abandon research methods that artificially divorce thought from embodied action-taking.

What emerges is nothing less than a new science of the mind: a science that, to be sure, builds on the fruits of three decades' cooperative research, but a science whose tools and models are surprisingly different—a cognitive science of the embodied mind.[94]

Piaget's Theory of Cognitive Development

Piaget's theory of cognitive development is a comprehensive theory about the nature and development of human intelligence. It was first created by the Swiss developmental psychologist, Jean Piaget.

> The theory deals with the nature of knowledge itself and how humans gradually come to acquire, construct, and use it. Piaget's theory is mainly known as a developmental stage theory.

> To Piaget, cognitive development was a progressive reorganisation of mental processes resulting from biological maturation and environmental experience. He believed that children construct an understanding of the world around them, experience discrepancies between what they already know and what they discover in their environment, then adjust their ideas accordingly.

---

[94] Clark, Andy. *Being There - Putting Brain, Body, and World Together Again*, 1997

Moreover, Piaget claimed that cognitive development is at the center of the human organism, and language is contingent on knowledge and understanding acquired through cognitive development. Piaget's earlier work received the greatest attention. Child-centered classrooms and "open education" are direct applications of Piaget's views.[95]

Nature of intelligence

Piaget noted that reality is a dynamic system of continuous change and, as such, is defined in reference to the two conditions that define dynamic systems. Specifically, he argued that reality involves transformations and states. Transformations refer to all manners of changes that a thing or person can undergo. States refer to the conditions or the appearances in which things or persons can be found between transformations.

Thus, Piaget argued, if human intelligence is to be adaptive, it must have functions to represent both the transformational and the static aspects of reality. He proposed that operative intelligence is responsible for the representation and manipulation of the dynamic or transformational aspects of reality, and that figurative intelligence is responsible for the representation of the static aspects of reality.

Operative intelligence is the active aspect of intelligence. It involves all actions, overt or covert, undertaken in order to follow, recover, or anticipate the transformations of the objects or persons of interest.

Figurative intelligence is the more or less static aspect of intelligence, involving all means of representation used to retain in mind the states (i.e., successive forms, shapes, or locations) that intervene between transformations. That is, it involves perception, imitation, mental imagery, drawing, and language. Therefore, the figurative aspects of intelligence derive their meaning from the operative aspects of intelligence, because states cannot exist independently of the transformations that interconnect them.

---

[95] https://en.wikipedia.org/wiki/Piaget%27s_theory_of_cognitive_development

Piaget stated that the figurative or the representational aspects of intelligence are subservient to its operative and dynamic aspects, and therefore, that understanding essentially derives from the operative aspect of intelligence.

At any time, operative intelligence frames how the world is understood and it changes if understanding is not successful. Piaget stated that this process of understanding and change involves two basic functions: assimilation and accommodation.[96]

---

[96] Ibid.

16: Consciousness

While we're looking at intelligence, artificial or natural, we better look at consciousness, which is the state of being aware of, and responsive to, one's surroundings. Now consciousness is a movable feast, from barely conscious at one extreme to enlightened at the other, so it is something we develop over time.

Astrologically, all the planets have a role to play in an individual's developing consciousness, but traditionally, Saturn was the limit of our more primitive earth-bound consciousness, and as Uranus, Neptune and Pluto were discovered they were found to relate to our developing higher levels of consciousness.

Now we have a new outer limit in Sedna, one that is going to stretch our awareness in ways we can only begin to guess. So, in addition to the consciousness-expanding energies of Uranus, Neptune, and Pluto, we now also have seven new gates of awareness to help us on the way.

First, we have the two Plutinos, Ixion, the planet of lawlessness, and Orcus, the planet of 'delving down and speaking out', to encourage the self-transformation process that Pluto has been opening us to. To me this suggests that our current understanding of higher consciousness will have to accept randomness and chaos as an underlying factor and yet engage and voice our perceived order.

And then we have the new dwarf planets, Varuna, the planet of notability, Haumea, the planet of rebirth, Quaoar, the planet of new perspectives, Makemake, the planet of devotion, and Eris, the planet of consciousness through discord, to help us get to the Sedna level consciousness.

This suggests that playing an important spiritual role, assisting the rebirth of a new awareness, developing particular talents and a devotional approach, yet accepting that growth in awareness is multifaceted, are the new steps to get to the Sedna level consciousness that I'll talk about in the next chapter.

The fact that so many new planets have been discovered in a brief few years suggests that we are currently experiencing an explosion of consciousness on the planet to compliment the explosion in intelligence we've seen; this is currently underway and is sure to get stronger when Sedna goes into Gemini.

To help us understand Sedna's role in this consciousness explosion we are going to look at three more case studies: one fourth house Sedna case study, Helen Keller, and two eleventh house case studies, Bhagwan Shree Rajneesh and Osama bin Laden.

Spirituality

Just before we do that, let's take a moment to look at spirituality, because it is definitely linked to consciousness. Spirituality is what gives our lives meaning. When we lift our awareness out of the moment-to-moment challenge of staying alive and start to wonder how it all connects together, we're developing a spiritual approach to life. I would also suggest that spirituality is a natural product of consciousness and that it is manifesting as a growing energy on the planet in these times, as our consciousness grows. If this is true, the explosions in intelligence and consciousness that we've been talking about is likely to also produce an explosion in spirituality. Whereas under the old Saturnian limits, spirituality had to be nurtured within a form, a tradition or a church, with the arrival of Sedna, spirituality is infusing every aspect of our lives.

We're each on a spiritual path that started long before we were born and will go on long after we're dead, and while we are alive we have the chance to advance along that path. The house position of Sedna in our charts gives us the focus of our personal spiritual destiny.

I have a fourth house Sedna, and I have worked as a clown teacher for most of my life. Clown has been a spiritual path for me; working with street theatre is similar to the life of a travelling monk, dependent on the bounty of the universe.

Some years ago, I put out a mixed clown textbook, novel, and memoir, called *Angels Can Fly, a Modern Clown User Guide*, which was criticized by some of my peers as being 'too religious.' I didn't think of it as religious at all. The title comes from the saying 'Angels can fly, they take themselves lightly,' which was my thesis on clown; it's not a prima-donna show, it's losing yourself in the audience.

Spirituality is what gives meaning to life, it is the bigger framework that gives it meaning. But if that framework can come in any of the houses and from a personal center rather than an established hierarchy, it's going to be multifaceted, and we are going to have to accept that we can all look at it differently, and that's okay.

17: Consciousness Case Study - Helen Keller

June 27, 1880 - 1 June 1, 1968

Sedna in the Fourth

Our first consciousness case study is American author, political activist, and lecturer, Helen Keller. At the age of one-and-a-half, she was struck by an illness which left her deaf and blind. The story of how her teacher broke through the isolation imposed by a near complete lack of language, allowing the young girl to blossom as she learned to communicate, has become widely known through the dramatic depictions of the play and film, *The Miracle Worker.*

A prolific author, she was well traveled and outspoken in her convictions. A member of the Socialist Party of America and the Industrial Workers of the World, she campaigned for women's suffrage, labor rights, socialism, antimilitarism, and other similar causes. She proved to the world that deaf people could all learn to communicate and that they are capable of doing things that hearing people can do.

House Placement

Sedna is direct in Aries, in the fourth house. This is the second of two fourth house Sedna case studies. We looked at Thomas Edison earlier, and in a moment, we'll compare his house analysis with Helen's, but first let's have a look at her aspects.

Aspects

square Sun, square Venus, square Node

Sedna is square the nodal axis, with the south node, the point of past life karma, conjunct the Sun, the planet of will, and Venus, the planet of relationships and values, in the eighth house which deals with issues of life and death.

This is a powerful sign of the evolutionary work Helen came into this life to do and the conjunction of the Sun and Venus with the South Node shows there will be strong past life karma to deal with, which manifested in her early illness.

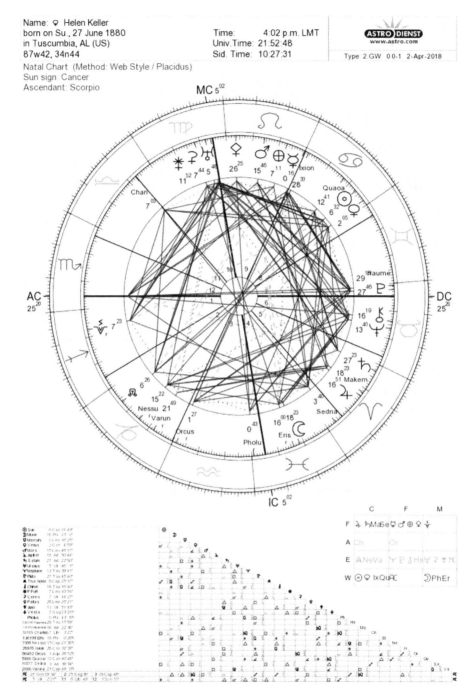

trine Mercury, trine Part of Fortune, trine Vesta, sextile Orcus

Sedna is part of a grand trine with Vesta, the asteroid of regeneration, in the first house of self, and with the Part of Fortune in the ninth house of broadening the mind. Sedna is also trine to Mercury, the planet of communication, on the cusp of the ninth house, which is conjunct the Part of Fortune. And Sedna is also sextile to Orcus, the planet of 'delving down and speaking out,' in the third house of ideas, which is opposite the ninth house conjunction of Mercury and the Part of Fortune.

These aspects tell of the research into language and communication which Helen undertook, growing from a blind, deaf baby who had no words and could only communicate by touch, to a woman who wrote 12 books and toured the world extensively, speaking of her research. Yes, she taught herself to talk, even though she couldn't hear the words, or read others' lips.

I'm going to let Helen explain the effect these aspects had on her life in the next few pages, because she is so beautifully expressive, both of the aspects and of her evolutionary research into language and communication which shows her growing consciousness. All the quotes are from Helen Keller, *The Story of My Life*, published when she was 22.

Desire to Express Myself

> In the 4 years after my sickness made me blind and deaf the desire to express myself grew. The few signs I used became less and less adequate, and my failures to make myself understood were invariably followed by outbursts of passion.

> My parents were deeply grieved and perplexed. We lived a long way from any school for the blind or the deaf, and it seemed unlikely that any one would come to such an out-of-the-way place as Tuscumbia to teach a child who was both deaf and blind. Indeed, my friends and relatives sometimes doubted whether I could be taught.[97]

Everything has a Name

> The morning after my teacher came, she led me into her room and gave me a doll. The little blind children at the Perkins Institution had sent it and Laura Bridgman had dressed it; but I did not know this until afterward. When I had played with it a little while. Miss Sullivan slowly spelled into my hand the word "d-o-l-l."

---

[97] Keller, Helen. *The Story of My Life*, 1903

I was at once interested in this finger play and tried to imitate it. When I finally succeeded in making the letters correctly I was flushed with childish pleasure and pride. Running downstairs to my mother I held up my hand and made the letters for doll. I did not know that I was spelling a word or even that words existed; I was simply making my fingers go in monkey-like imitation.

In the days that followed I learned to spell in this uncomprehending way a great many words, among them pin, hat, cup and a few verbs like sit, stand and walk. But my teacher had been with me several weeks before I understood that everything has a name.

One day, while I was playing with my new doll, Miss Sullivan put my big rag doll into my lap also, spelled "d-o-l-l' and tried to make me understand that 'd-o-l-l' applied to both. Earlier in the day we had had a tussle over the words "m-u-g'* and "w-a-t-e-r." Miss Sullivan had tried to impress it upon me that "m-u-g" is mug and that "w-a-t-e-r" is water, but I persisted in confounding the two.

In despair she had dropped the subject for the time, only to renew it at the first opportunity. I became impatient at her repeated attempts and, seizing the new doll, I dashed it upon the floor. I was keenly delighted when I felt the fragments of the broken doll at my feet. Neither sorrow nor regret followed my passionate outburst. I had not loved the doll. In the still, dark world in which I lived there was no strong sentiment or tenderness.

I felt my teacher sweep the fragments to one side of the hearth, and I had a sense of satisfaction that the cause of my discomfort was removed. She brought me my hat, and I knew I was going out into the warm sunshine. This thought, if a wordless sensation may be called a thought, made me hop and skip with pleasure.[98]

Awakened My Soul

We walked down the path to the well-house, attracted by the fragrance of the honeysuckle with which it was covered. Someone was drawing water and my teacher placed my hand

---

[98] Ibid.

under the spout. As the cool stream gushed over one hand she spelled into the other the word *water*, first slowly, then rapidly. I stood still, my whole attention fixed upon the motions of her fingers.

Suddenly I felt a misty consciousness as of something forgotten—a thrill of returning thought; and somehow the mystery of language was revealed to me. I knew then that "w-a-t-e-r" meant the wonderful cool something that was flowing over my hand. That living word awakened my soul, gave it light, hope, joy, set it free! There were barriers still, it is true, but barriers that could in time be swept away.

I left the well-house eager to learn. Everything had a name, and each name gave birth to a new thought. As we returned to the house every object which I touched seemed to quiver with life. That was because I saw everything with the strange, new sight that had come to me. On entering the door I remembered the doll I had broken. I felt my way to the hearth and picked up the pieces. I tried vainly to put them together. Then my eyes filled with tears; for I realized what I had done, and for the first time I felt repentance and sorrow.[99]

Opposite Chariklo

What a wonderful couple of contrasting fourth house case studies we have for Sedna natives with aspects to Chariklo, the contour of foresight. We saw earlier that Thomas Edison had it conjunct Sedna, and he's an inventor who's devices revolutionized the home, and Helen has it opposite Sedna, conjunct the cusp of the eleventh house of collective consciousness, and she is blind, but through her evolutionary investigation of communication she had the foresight to see what an inspiration she would be to other people, so she wrote 12 books and toured the world constantly in later life, speaking of her experiences.

quintile Varuna, inconjunct MC

The evolutionary quintile aspect to Varuna, the planet of notability, in the second house of material reality, and the fated inconjunct to the MC, her place in society, is easy to understand in retrospect, because of the iconic status she achieved as someone who overcame extreme disability

---

[99] Ibid.

to do ground-breaking research on communication and spirituality, inspiring people worldwide.

House Analysis

We saw earlier in our Thomas Edison case study that with a fourth house Sedna we live in an evolutionary research laboratory and that the karmic influence from the parent of the opposite sex sets up the thrust of this research, which will shape our lives and our influence on the world.

Did her father shape her life and her influence on the world? Did she live in an evolutionary research laboratory?

> When I was about six years old, my father heard of an eminent oculist in Baltimore, who had been successful in many cases that had seemed hopeless. My parents at once determined to take me to Baltimore to see if anything could be done for my eyes.
>
> When we arrived in Baltimore, Dr. Chisholm received us kindly: but he could do nothing. He said, however, that I could be educated, and advised my father to consult Dr. Alexander Graham Bell, of Washington, who would be able to give him information about schools and teachers of deaf or blind children. Acting on the doctor's advice, we went immediately to Washington to see Dr. Bell, my father with a sad heart and many misgivings, I wholly unconscious of his anguish, finding pleasure in the excitement of moving from place to place.[100]

Door from Darkness to Light

> Child as I was, I at once felt the tenderness and sympathy which endeared Dr. Bell to so many hearts, as his wonderful achievements enlist their admiration. He held me on his knee while I examined his watch, and he made it strike for me. He understood my signs, and I knew it and loved him at once. But I did not dream that that interview would be the door through which I should pass from darkness into light, from isolation to friendship, companionship, knowledge, love.
>
> Dr. Bell advised my father to write to Mr. Anagnos, director of the Perkins Institution in Boston, the scene of Dr. Howe's great labours for the blind, and ask him if he had a teacher competent

---

[100] Ibid.

to begin my education. This my father did at once, and in a few weeks there came a kind letter from Mr. Anagnos with the comforting assurance that a teacher had been found. This was in the summer of 1886. But Miss Sullivan did not arrive until the following March.[101]

Teacher

Thus, I learned from life itself. At the beginning I was only a little mass of possibilities. It was my teacher who unfolded and developed them. When she came, everything about me breathed of love and joy and was full of meaning. She has never since let pass an opportunity to point out the beauty that is in everything, nor has she ceased trying in thought and action and example to make my life sweet and useful.

For a long time, I had no regular lessons. Even when I studied most earnestly it seemed more like play than work. Everything Miss Sullivan taught me she illustrated by a beautiful story or a poem. Whenever anything delighted or interested me, she talked it over with me just as if she were a little girl herself. What many children think of with dread, as a painful plodding through grammar, hard sums and harder definitions, is to-day one of my most precious memories.

It was my teacher's genius, her quick sympathy, her loving tact which made the first years of my education so beautiful. It was because she seized the right moment to impart knowledge that made it so pleasant and acceptable to me. She realized that a child's mind is like a shallow brook which ripples and dances merrily over the stony course of its education and reflects here a flower, there a bush, yonder a fleecy cloud; and she attempted to guide my mind on its way, knowing that like a brook it should be fed by mountain streams and hidden springs, until it broadened out into a deep river, capable of reflecting in its placid surface, billowy hills, the luminous shadows of trees and the blue heavens, as well as the sweet face of a little flower.[102]

---

[101] Ibid.
[102] Ibid.

I'm not Dumb!

It was in the spring of 1890 that I learned to speak. The impulse to utter audible sounds had always been strong within me. I used to make noises, keeping one hand on my throat while the other hand felt the movements of my lips. I was pleased with anything that made a noise and liked to feel the cat purr and the dog bark. I also liked to keep my hand on a singer's throat, or on a piano when it was being played. Before I lost my sight and hearing, I was fast learning to talk, but after my illness it was found that I had ceased to speak because I could not hear.

(When I was 10 years old, I heard) of a deaf and blind girl in Norway who had actually been taught to speak. Mrs. Lamson had scarcely finished telling me about this girl's success before I was on fire with eagerness. I resolved that I, too, would learn to speak. I would not rest satisfied until my teacher took me, for advice and assistance, to Miss Sarah Fuller, principal of the Horace Mann School. This lovely, sweet-natured lady offered to teach me herself.

I shall never forget the surprise and delight I felt when I uttered my first connected sentence, "It is warm." True, they were broken and stammering syllables; but they were human speech. My soul, conscious of new strength, came out of bondage, and was reaching through those broken symbols of speech to all knowledge and all faith.

My work was practice, practice, practice. Discouragement and weariness cast me down frequently; but the next moment the thought that I should soon be at home and show my loved ones what I had accomplished, spurred me on, and I eagerly looked forward to their pleasure in my achievement.

"My little sister will understand me now," was a thought stronger than all obstacles. I used to repeat ecstatically, "I am not dumb now." I could not be despondent while I anticipated the delight of talking to my mother and reading her responses from her lips. It astonished me to find how much easier it is to talk than to spell with the fingers, and I discarded the manual alphabet as a medium of communication on my part.[103]

Did her lifestyle collide with everyday lifestyles repeatedly? When she was young, did she appear to be, or feel like, a victim in these collisions?

To all the writers and budding writers reading this, this next story will bring tears to your eyes. She never did write another work of fiction, but she did publish 12 books.

Accused of Plagiarism at Twelve

> The winter of 1892 was darkened by the one cloud in my childhood's bright sky. Joy deserted my heart, and for a long, long time I lived in doubt, anxiety and fear. Books lost their charm for me, and even now the thought of those dreadful days chills my heart. A little story called "The Frost King," which I wrote and sent to Mr. Anagnos, of the Perkins Institution for the Blind, was at the root of the trouble.

> I wrote the story when I was at home, the autumn after I had learned to speak. We had stayed up at Pern Quarry later than usual. While we were there, Miss Sullivan had described to me the beauties of the late foliage, and it seems that her descriptions revived the memory of a story, which must have been read to me, and which I must have unconsciously retained.

> I thought then that I was "making up a story," as children say, and I eagerly sat down to write it before the ideas should slip from me. My thoughts flowed easily; I felt a sense of joy in the composition. Words and images came tripping to my finger ends, and as I thought out sentence after sentence, I wrote them on my braille slate.

> Now, if words and images come to me without effort, it is a pretty sure sign that they are not the offspring of my own mind, but stray waifs that I regretfully dismiss. At that time, I eagerly absorbed everything I read without a thought of authorship, and even now I cannot be quite sure of the boundary line between my ideas and those I find in books. I suppose that is because so

---

[103] Ibid.

many of my impressions come to me through the medium of others' eyes and ears.

When the story was finished, I read it to my teacher, and I recall now vividly the pleasure I felt in the more beautiful passages, and my annoyance at being interrupted to have the pronunciation of a word corrected. At dinner it was read to the assembled family, who were surprised that I could write so well. Someone asked me if I had read it in a book.

This question surprised me very much; for I had not the faintest recollection of having had it read to me. I spoke up and said, "Oh, no, it is my story, and I have written it for Mr. Anagnos."

Accordingly, I copied the story and sent it to him for his birthday. It was suggested that I should change the title from "Autumn Leaves" to "The Frost King," which I did. I carried the little story to the post-office myself, feeling as if I were walking on air. I little dreamed how cruelly I should pay for that birthday gift.

Mr. Anagnos was delighted with "The Frost King," and published it in one of the Perkins Institution reports. This was the pinnacle of my happiness, from which I was in a little while dashed to earth. I had been in Boston only a short time when it was discovered that a story similar to "The Frost King," called "The Frost Fairies' by Miss Margaret T. Canby, had appeared before I was born in a book called *Birdie and His Friends*." The two stories were so much alike in thought and language that it was evident Miss Canby's story had been read to me, and that mine was… a, plagiarism.

It was difficult to make me understand this; but when I did understand I was astonished and grieved. No child ever drank deeper of the cup of bitterness than I did. I had disgraced myself; I had brought suspicion upon those I loved best. And yet, how could it possibly have happened? I racked my brain until I was weary to recall anything about the frost that I had read before I wrote "The Frost King"; but I could remember nothing, except the common reference to Jack Frost, and a poem for children, "The Freaks of the Frost," and I knew I had not used that in my composition.

Mr. Anagnos, who loved me tenderly, thinking that he had been deceived, turned a deaf ear to the pleadings of love and innocence. He believed, or at least suspected, that Miss Sullivan and I had deliberately stolen the bright thoughts of another and imposed them on him to win his admiration. I was brought before a court of investigation composed of the teachers and officers of the Institution, and Miss Sullivan was asked to leave me.

Then I was questioned and cross-questioned with what seemed to me a determination on the part of my judges to force me to acknowledge that I remembered having had "The Frost Fairies" read to me. I felt in every question the doubt and suspicion that was in their minds, and I felt, too, that a loved friend was looking at me reproachfully, although I could not have put all this into words. The blood pressed about my thumping heart, and I could scarcely speak, except in monosyllables. Even the consciousness that it was only a dreadful mistake did not lessen my suffering, and when at last I was allowed to leave the room, I was dazed and did not notice my teacher's caresses, or the tender words of my friends, who said I was a brave little girl and they were proud of me.

As I lay in my bed that night, I wept as I hope few children have wept. I felt so cold, I imagined I should die before morning, and the thought comforted me. I think if this sorrow had come to me when I was older, it would have broken my spirit beyond repairing. But the angel of forgetfulness has gathered up and carried away much of the misery and all the bitterness of those sad days.

In my trouble I received many messages of love and sympathy. All the friends I loved best, except one, have remained my own to the present time. Miss Canby herself wrote kindly, "Someday you will write a great story out of your own head, that will be a comfort and help to many." But this kind prophecy has never been fulfilled. I have never played with words again for the mere pleasure of the game.

Indeed, I have ever since been tortured by the fear that what I write is not my own. For a long time, when I wrote a letter, even to my mother, I was seized with a sudden feeling of terror, and I would spell the sentences over and over, to make sure that I had not read them in a book. Had it not been for the persistent encouragement of Miss Sullivan, I think I should have given up trying to write altogether.[104]

A truer Knowledge of Life

It seems to me that the great difficulty of writing is to make the language of the educated mind express our confused ideas, half feelings, half thoughts, when we are little more than bundles of instinctive tendencies. Trying to write is very much like trying to put a Chinese puzzle together. We have a pattern in mind which we wish to work out in words; but the words will not fit the spaces, or, if they do, they will not match the design. But we keep on trying because we know that others have succeeded, and we are not willing to acknowledge defeat.

The summer and winter following the "Frost King" incident I spent with my family in Alabama. I recall with delight that home-going. Everything had budded and blossomed. I was happy. "The Frost King" was forgotten. In the autumn I began to write a sketch of my life.

I was still excessively scrupulous about everything I wrote. The thought that what I wrote might not be absolutely my own tormented me. No one knew of these fears except my teacher. A strange sensitiveness prevented me from referring to the "Frost King"; and often when an idea flashed out in the course of conversation I would spell softly to her, "I am not sure it is mine." At other times, in the midst of a paragraph I was writing, I said to myself, "Suppose it should be found that all this was written by someone long ago!" An impish fear clutched my hand, so that I could not write any more that day. And even now I sometimes feel the same uneasiness and disquietude.

Miss Sullivan consoled and helped me in every way she could think of; but the terrible experience I had passed through left a lasting impression on my mind, the significance of which I am only just beginning to understand. It was with the hope of restoring my self-confidence that she persuaded me to write for the Youth's Companion a brief account of my life. I was then

---

[104] Ibid.

twelve years old. As I look back on my struggle to write that little story, it seems to me that I must have had a prophetic vision of the good that would come of the undertaking, or I should surely have failed.

I wrote timidly, fearfully, but resolutely, urged on by my teacher, who knew that if I persevered, I should find my mental foothold again and get a grip on my faculties. Up to the time of the "Frost King" episode, I had lived the unconscious life of a little child; now my thoughts were turned inward, and I beheld things invisible. Gradually I emerged from the penumbra of that experience with a mind made clearer by trial and with a truer knowledge of life.[105]

Did behavioral traits learned in early childhood, particularly from the parent of the opposite sex, play a central role in her developing psyche?

My father was most loving and indulgent, devoted to his home, seldom leaving us, except in the hunting season. He was a great hunter, I have been told, and a celebrated shot. Next to his family he loved his dogs and gun. His hospitality was great, almost to a fault, and he seldom came home without bringing a guest.

His special pride was the big garden where, it was said, he raised the finest watermelons and strawberries in the county; and to me he brought the first ripe grapes and the choicest berries. I remember his caressing touch as he led me from tree to tree, from vine to vine, and his eager delight in whatever pleased me.

He was a famous storyteller; after I had acquired language he used to spell clumsily into my hand his cleverest anecdotes, and nothing pleased him more than to have me repeat them at an opportune moment.[106]

---

[105] Ibid.
[106] Ibid.

Was there a forced separation of family members leading to a transcendence to a larger spiritual perspective?

Helen's separation occurred at 19 months with her illness that robbed her of her sight and hearing, so her spiritual growth started early. Here she talks about how it was at seven years old: *What is Love?*

I recall many incidents of the summer that followed my soul's sudden awakening. I did nothing but explore with my hands and learn the name of every object that I touched; and the more I handled things and learned their names and uses, the more joyous and confident grew my sense of kinship with the rest of the world.

I remember the morning that I first asked the meaning of the word, "love." This was before I knew many words. I had found a few early violets in the garden and brought them to my teacher. She tried to kiss me; but at that time I did not like to have anyone kiss me except my mother. Miss Sullivan put her arm gently round me and spelled into my hand, "I love Helen."

"What is love?" I asked. She drew me closer to her and said, "It is here," pointing to my heart, whose beats I was conscious of for the first time. Her words puzzled me very much because I did not then understand anything unless I touched it.

The sun had been under a cloud all day, and there had been brief showers; but suddenly the sun broke forth in all its southern splendour. Again I asked my teacher, "Is this not love?"

"Love is something like the clouds that were in the sky before the sun came out," she replied. Then in simpler words than these, which at that time I could not have understood, she explained: "You cannot touch the clouds, you know; but you feel the rain and know how glad the flowers and the thirsty earth are to have it after a hot day. You cannot touch love either; but you feel the sweetness that it pours into everything. Without love you would not be happy or want to play."

The beautiful truth burst upon my mind - I felt that there were 'invisible lines stretched between my spirit and the spirits of others.[107]

Who made the World?

And here, from her teacher's perspective:

> After May, 1890, it was evident to me that she had reached a point where it was impossible to keep from her the religious beliefs held by those with whom she was in daily contact. She almost overwhelmed me with inquiries which were the natural outgrowth of her quickened intelligence.
>
> Early in May she wrote on her tablet the following list of questions: "I wish to write about things I do not understand. Who made the earth and the seas, and everything? What makes the sun hot? Where was I before I came to mother? I know that plants grow from seeds which are in the ground, but I am sure people do not grow that way. I never saw a child-plant. Little birds and chickens come out of eggs. I have seen them. What was the egg before it was an egg? Why does not the earth fall, it is so very large and heavy? Tell me something that Father Nature does. May I read the book called the *Bible*? Please tell your little pupil many things when you have much time."
>
> Can anyone doubt after reading these questions that the child who was capable of asking them was also capable of understanding at least their elementary answers? She could not, of course, have grasped such abstractions, as a complete answer to her questions would involve; but one's whole life is nothing more than a continual advance in the comprehension of the meaning and scope of such ideas.
>
> After she had succeeded in formulating the ideas which had been slowly growing in her mind, they seemed suddenly to absorb all her thoughts, and she became impatient to have everything explained. As we were passing a large globe a short time after she had written the questions, she stopped before it and asked, "Who made the REAL world?" I replied, "No one knows how the earth, the sun, and all the worlds which we call

---

[107] Keller, Helen. *The Story of My Life,* 1903

stars came to be; but I will tell you how wise men have tried to account for their origin, and to interpret the great and mysterious forces of nature."

She knew that the Greeks had many gods to whom they ascribed various powers, because they believed that the sun, the lightning, and a hundred other natural forces, were independent and superhuman powers. But after a great deal of thought and study, I told her, men came to believe that all forces were manifestations of one power, and to that power they gave the name GOD.

She was very still for a few minutes, evidently thinking earnestly. She then asked, "Who made God?" I was compelled to evade her question, for I could not explain to her the mystery of a self-existent being. Indeed, many of her eager questions would have puzzled a far wiser person than I am.[108]

I awoke to language, to knowledge, to love

And here, Helen looks back from her last book, *My Religion*, published when she was 47 and showing her evolutionary perspective. Here she is referencing Emanuel Swedenborg, who was a Swedish scientist, philosopher, theologian and mystic born at the end of the dark ages in 1688, and who became leading figure in the Age of Enlightenment, best known for his book on the afterlife, *Heaven and Hell*.

> Perhaps no man was ever so precariously situated between traditions of a crumbling civilization and the sudden onrush of a new age toward which his forward-looking mind yearned. The more I consider his position, the less I can see how we are to account for him, except as a miracle, so little did he have in common with his church or the standards of his century.

> In September of 1766, Swedenborg wrote: "I can solemnly bear witness that the Lord Himself has appeared to me, and that He has sent me to do that which I am doing now, and that for this purpose He has opened the interiors of my mind, which are those of my spirit, so that I may see those things which are in the

---

[108] ,MacyJohn Albert and Keller, Helen. *The Story of My Life: The Restored Edition,* 2004

spiritual world and hear those who are there, and which privilege I have had now for twenty-two years."

In considering this phase of Swedenborg's experience, I feel that I am peculiarly able to grasp his meaning at least partially. For nearly six years I had no concepts whatever of nature or mind or death or God. I literally thought with my body. Without a single exception my memories of that time are tactual.

For thirty years I have examined and re-examined that phase of my development in the light of new theories, and I am convinced of the correctness of what I am saying. I know I was impelled like an animal to seek food and warmth. I remember crying, but not the grief that caused the tears; I kicked, and because I recall it physically, I know I was angry. I imitated those about me when I made signs for things I wanted to eat or helped to find eggs in my mother's farmyard. But there is not one spark of emotion, or rational thought in these distinct yet corporal memories.

I was like an unconscious clod of earth. Then, suddenly, I knew not how or where or when, my brain felt the impact of another mind, and I awoke to language, to knowledge, to love, to the usual concepts of nature, of good and evil! I was actually lifted from nothingness to human life—two planes as irreconcilable as Swedenborg's earth experience and his contacts with a realm beyond the cognizance of our physical senses! Since I did not receive even the lowest concepts in those empty years from myself or from nature, I look upon them as a revelation, even if only from a finite mind. Swedenborg looked upon his highest concepts as a revelation from the Infinite Mind.[109]

Did her family relationships, particularly with any children, flower as Sedna moved on to transit the fifth house?

Helen never had children, but we can look at her books as children, as they are the creative products of the home and the first, *The Story of My Life,* was written as Sedna moved into the fifth house and serialized in the *Ladies Home Journal* in 1902 and was met with universal acclaim. In 1903 it was published in book form by Doubleday, Page & Co. and became a critical and commercial success.

---

[109] Keller, Helen. *My Religion*, 1927

18: Consciousness Case Study - Bhagwan Shree Rajneesh

11 December 1931 – 19 January 1990

Sedna in 11th House

Bhagwan Shree Rajneesh was a charismatic and controversial Indian Guru and leader of the Rajneesh movement. He travelled throughout India in the 1960s and was a vocal critic of socialism, Mahatma Gandhi, and Hindu religious orthodoxy. He advocated a more open attitude towards human sexuality, earning him the sobriquet "sex guru" in the Indian and later international press, although this attitude became more acceptable with time.

His syncretic teachings emphasize the importance of meditation, awareness, love, celebration, courage, creativity, and humour — qualities that he viewed as being suppressed by adherence to static belief systems, religious tradition, and socialization.

When he was 50 he refocused his efforts on activities in the United States and relocated to a facility known as Rajneeshpuram in Wasco County, Oregon. Almost immediately the movement ran into conflict with county residents and the State government and a succession of legal battles concerning the ashram's construction and continued development curtailed its success.

He was deported and twenty-one countries denied him entry, so he ultimately returned to India and a reinvigorated Pune ashram, where he changed his name to Osho. His ashram is today known as the Osho International Meditation Resort. His teachings have had a notable impact on Western New Age thought, and their popularity has increased markedly since his death.

House Placement

Sedna is retrograde in Aries in the eleventh house of collective consciousness. This is the first of our two eleventh house case studies, so here's an edited interpretation of this house placement from later in the book.

Sedna in the 11th House

With Sedna in the eleventh house we are on a spiritual mission to explore social ideals and the collective consciousness, and we will likely immerse ourselves in groups of likeminded people and, over time, build a group of loyal friends to help us on our mission.

At the unconscious level, however, this can feel a little like being 'lost at sea in the popular culture of society,' which at this stage of mankind's development is still often fairly primitive and violent. So there is a danger of abuse which is simply accepted by our group as normal and so unspoken, or is a hidden side effect of our social group. Or we could take on an abusive mission ourselves.

With this placement we are likely to work with organizations and groups that promote our personal values. We are focused on goals for the future and, because of the ideals we come to represent, we may become idolized by large numbers of people, but we may also attract vilification and victimization.

We may be born with innate ideals, which will then be conditioned by our early years and drive our lives. If the birth environment is conducive to these, our first collision with social norms will probably come at school when our personality is already well formed and we are less likely to feel victimized by the challenge.

If the birth environment is not conducive to those ideals, we can experience situations where we feel victimized from an early age, and these feelings will then shape our beliefs, and the ongoing collisions will either reinforce this or cause us at some point to reject the early ideology and replace it with something more appropriate.

Either way, our ideals will be tested in the forge of the community, and later in life, if strengthened through experience, they are likely to collide with the prevailing norms of the social environment in an evolutionary way. These ongoing collisions will then serve to advance our evolutionary mission.

Through our work there is likely to be an evolution in consciousness, which may be forced by hard aspects and encouraged by flows, leading to a transcendence to a larger spiritual perspective.

If the evolution in consciousness promised by this placement is achieved, then the ideals embraced by this mission will flower as Sedna moves on to transit the twelfth house.

House Analysis

Was his birth environment conducive to his ideals? Was there a collision with social norms?

> At the time (of his birth), an astrologer predicted that he might die before he was seven years old according to this birth chart. His parents, who were Taranpanthi Jains, sent him to live with his maternal grandparents until he was seven years old. Osho said this was a major influence on his growth because his grandmother gave him the utmost freedom and respect, leaving him carefree—without an imposed education or restrictions.[110]

Rajneesh talked about it in his book, *Glimpses of a Golden Childhood:*

> For most of my very early years I lived with my mother's parents. Those years are unforgettable. Even if I reach to Dante's paradise I will still remember those years. A small village, poor people, but my grandfather – I mean my mother's father – was a generous man. He was poor, but rich in his generosity. He gave to each and everyone whatsoever he had. I learned the art of giving from him; I have to accept it. I never saw him say no to any beggar, or anybody.

> For my first years I knew my Nani (grandmother) as my mother; those are the years when one grows. This circle is for my Nani. My own mother came after that; I was already grown up, already made in a certain style, and my grandmother helped me immensely.

> I remember perfectly – it was the time that the census was being taken. The officer had come to our house. He made many inquiries about many things. They asked about my grandfather's religion; he said, "Jainism." They then asked about my grandmother's religion. My grandfather said, "You can ask her yourself. Religion is a private affair. I myself have never asked her." What a man!

> My grandmother answered, "I do not believe in any religion whatsoever. All religions look childish to me." The officer was shocked. Even I was taken aback. She does not believe in any religion at all! In India, to find a woman who does not believe in

---

[110] http://web.newworldencyclopedia.org/entry/Bhagwan_Rajneesh

any religion at all is impossible. But she was born in Khajuraho, perhaps into a family of Tantrikas who have never believed in any religion. They have practiced meditation but they have never believed in any religion.[111]

Did his beliefs later in life collide with the prevailing norms of the social environment in an evolutionary way?

Rajneesh is generally considered one of the most controversial spiritual leaders to have emerged from India in the twentieth century.

> His message of sexual, emotional, spiritual, and institutional liberation, as well as the pleasure he took in causing offence, ensured that his life was surrounded by controversy. Rajneesh became known as the "sex guru" in India, and as the "Rolls-Royce guru" in the United States.

> He attacked traditional concepts of nationalism, openly expressed contempt for politicians, and poked fun at the leading figures of various religions, who in turn found his arrogance unbearable. His teachings on sex, marriage, family, and relationships contradicted traditional values and aroused a great deal of anger and opposition around the world. His movement was widely feared and loathed as a cult.[112]

20th Century's Greatest Spiritual Teacher

Writing in the *Seattle Post Intelligencer* in January 1990, American author Tom Robbins stated that based on his readings of Rajneesh's books, he was convinced Rajneesh was the 20th century's "greatest spiritual teacher". Robbins, while stressing that he was not a disciple, further stated that he had "read enough vicious propaganda and slanted reports to suspect that he was one of the most maligned figures in history."

Legacy

While his teachings met with strong rejection in his home country during his lifetime, there has been a change in Indian public opinion since his death.

---

[111] Osho. *Glimpses of a Golden Childhood: The Rebellious Childhood of a Great Enlightened One,* December 31, 2008
[112] https://en.wikipedia.org/wiki/Rajneesh

In 1991, an influential Indian newspaper counted Rajneesh, along with figures such as Gautama Buddha and Mahatma Gandhi, among the ten people who had most changed India's destiny; in Rajneesh's case, by "liberating the minds of future generations from the shackles of religiosity and conformism". Rajneesh has found more acclaim in his homeland since his death than he ever did while alive.[113]

Was he idolized by large numbers of people because of the ideals he came to represent? Did he also attract vilification and victimization?

A number of commentators have remarked upon Rajneesh's charisma. Many sannyasins have stated that hearing Rajneesh speak, they "fell in love with him." Susan J. Palmer noted that even critics attested to the power of his presence. James S. Gordon, a psychiatrist and researcher, recalls inexplicably finding himself laughing like a child, hugging strangers and having tears of gratitude in his eyes after a glance by Rajneesh from within his passing Rolls-Royce.

Frances FitzGerald concluded upon listening to Rajneesh in person that he was a brilliant lecturer, and expressed surprise at his talent as a comedian, which had not been apparent from reading his books, as well as the hypnotic quality of his talks, which had a profound effect on his audience.[114]

Devoted Following

And here's the opposite view, notably from someone not directly involved. Robert Priddy, a British-Norwegian philosopher who taught at the University of Oslo and was a founding member of the Norwegian branch of the organization of the Indian guru Sathya Sai Baba, before falling out with them.

Charisma is not a property or characteristic of any person and it is not 'inborn' because it is an interactive phenomenon. To say of someone 'he has a lot of charisma' is misleading in that it is always an interaction between a person and an audience which respond positively to what they think and feel important, or

---

[113] Ibid.
[114] Ibid.

simply want to hear. A devoted following is the essential condition of the charismatic figure.

So-called charismatic leaders thus often develop strong egocentric traits and not seldom also delusions of grandeur which can be so strong as to amount to a Messiah-complex. Countless names could be listed, but one self-glorifying charismatic who had a fanatical following and developed excessive such self-delusions in recent times was Bhagwan Shree Rajneesh (aka Osho).[115]

Narcissistic Personality Disorder

Some scholars have suggested that Rajneesh, like other charismatic leaders, may have had a narcissistic personality. In his paper 'The Narcissistic Guru: A Profile of Bhagwan Shree Rajneesh,' Ronald O. Clarke, Emeritus Professor of Religious Studies at Oregon State University, argued that Rajneesh exhibited all the typical features of narcissistic personality disorder.

Such as a grandiose sense of self-importance and uniqueness; a preoccupation with fantasies of unlimited success; a need for constant attention and admiration; a set of characteristic responses to threats to self-esteem; disturbances in interpersonal relationships; a preoccupation with personal grooming combined with frequent resorting to prevarication or outright lying; and a lack of empathy.

Drawing on Rajneesh's reminiscences of his childhood in his book, *Glimpses of a Golden Childhood*, he suggested that Rajneesh suffered from a fundamental lack of parental discipline, due to his growing up in the care of overindulgent grandparents. Rajneesh's self-avowed Buddha status, he concluded, was part of a delusional system associated with his narcissistic personality disorder; a condition of ego-inflation rather than egolessness.[116]

---

[115] Priddy, Robert. https://robertpriddy.wordpress.com/about/
[116] https://en.wikipedia.org/wiki/Rajneesh

Was there an evolution in consciousness leading to a transcendence to a larger spiritual perspective? Did the beliefs embraced flower as Sedna moved on to transit the twelfth house?

Rajneesh obviously had an evolution of consciousness early and Sedna finally moved into his twelfth house in late 1985 as, following his exit from the US, he returned to India, landing in Delhi to a hero's welcome by his Indian disciples.

> In January 1987, Rajneesh reestablished his ashram in Pune and from early 1988, his discourses focused exclusively on Zen. In late December, he said he no longer wished to be referred to as "Bhagwan Shree Rajneesh", and in February 1989 took the name "Osho Rajneesh", shortened to "Osho". His health continued to weaken. He delivered his last public discourse in April 1989, from then on simply sitting in silence with his followers.

> Since his death Rajneesh's ashram in Pune has become the Osho International Meditation Resort, one of India's main tourist attractions. Describing itself as the Esalen of the East, it teaches a variety of spiritual techniques from a broad range of traditions and promotes itself as a spiritual oasis, a "sacred space" for discovering one's self and uniting the desires of body and mind in a beautiful resort environment. According to press reports, it attracts some 200,000 people from all over the world each year.

> Rajneesh has come to be "seen as an important teacher within India itself" who is "increasingly recognised as a major spiritual teacher of the twentieth century, at the forefront of the current 'world-accepting' trend of spirituality based on self-development.[117].

By 1993, three years after his death:

> There were few observers who expected Rajneesh-Osho's legacy to linger for long after his death three years ago, at the age of 58. Yet the controversial movement he set up is now growing again at a phenomenal rate. The ashram, a combination of spiritual mission and holiday camp, claims to be one of India's major tourist attractions. According to the ashram's own figures,

---

[117] Ibid.

about 2-3 per cent of tourists to India last year passed through its gates.

The ashram's unofficial spokesman, Swami Prem Amrito, formerly Dr George Meredith, a south London GP and now one of the 21-member 'inner circle' that governs the commune's day-to-day affairs, claims a 300 per cent increase in the number of disciples since the guru breathed his last, although actual numbers are not available.

About half the visitors are returnees, who come to recharge their spiritual batteries. A number choose to live there all year, happily bearing the midsummer heat and monsoons.

'If I had to design paradise, I couldn't do better than this place,' says Deva Sam Vado, formerly Leonard Okonski, a 74-year-old from Chicago who, in his previous life, was a CIA agent responsible for interrogating Czechoslovakian defectors. 'I wake up singing, play all day long, go to sleep singing, and still have energy for sex. I want to live my life out here.' He first arrived in Poona in 1978, after three heart attacks. 'The doctors gave me only a few more months to live. They reckoned without Osho.'

'I've been coming to Poona regularly for five years, sometimes with my children,' says Patricia Jenkins, 48, from Bristol, who has two teenage children at the school Osho Ko- Hsuan, in Chulmleigh, Devon, in which conventional study curriculums are largely ignored. 'Before that I spent three periods in Rajneeshpuram. It's getting better all the time. The energy is becoming softer, more spiritual. The emphasis is now firmly on meditation rather than fucking and fighting.'

The ashram is also the campus of one of the world's largest alternative universities. The Multiversity, as it is called, offers dozens of courses, including Esoteric Body Work, Craniosacral Balancing, Primal Deconditioning, Anti-Fischer-Hoffman Process, Neo Tantra, Colourpuncture (a healing method using colours), Esoteric Sciences, Spiritual Massage.[118]

---

[118] Ben-Tal, Danny. *The Independent*, UK, August 27, 1993

Aspects

Okay, let's look at his Sedna aspects to see how they influenced his developing consciousness.

conjunct Uranus, conjunct Nessus, sextile Ascendent, semi-square MC

This is the signature of Bhagwan's destiny as a controversial mystic, guru, and spiritual teacher. The conjunction of Sedna with Uranus, the planet of intuition, and Nessus, the centaur of radical change, in the eleventh house of collective consciousess, gives him charisma and a deep intuitive understanding.

> A number of commentators have remarked upon Rajneesh's charisma. Comparing him with Gurdjieff, Anthony Storr wrote that Rajneesh was "personally extremely impressive", noting that "many of those who visited him for the first time felt that their most intimate feelings were instantly understood, that they were accepted and unequivocally welcomed rather than judged. [Bhagwan] seemed to radiate energy and to awaken hidden possibilities in those who came into contact with him.

> Hugh Milne (Swami Shivamurti), an ex-devotee who between 1973 and 1982 worked closely with Rajneesh as leader of the Poona Ashram Guard and as his personal bodyguard, noted that their first meeting left him with a sense that far more than words had passed between them: "There is no invasion of privacy, no alarm, but it is as if his soul is slowly slipping inside mine, and in a split second transferring vital information.[119]

trine Sun

The flowing trine to the Sun, the planet of will, in the seventh house of relationships, shows his spiritual style. He advocated a more open attitude towards human sexuality, earning him the sobriquet "sex guru" in the Indian, and later, international press, although this attitude became more acceptable with time.

---

[119] https://en.wikipedia.org/wiki/Rajneesh

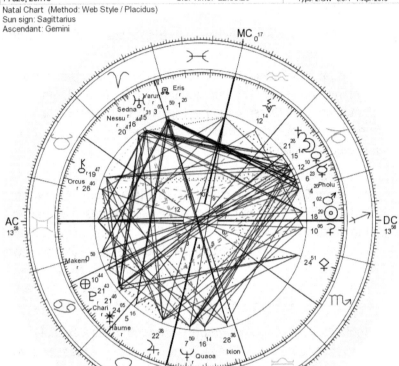

Name: ♂ Bhagwan Shree Rajneesh
born on Fr., 11 December 1931
in Kutchwada (Bhopal), INDIA
77e23, 23n15

Time: 5:13 p.m.
Univ.Time: 11:43
Sid. Time: 22:09:26

Type: 2.GW 0.0-1 1-Apr-2018

Natal Chart (Method: Web Style / Placidus)
Sun sign: Sagittarius
Ascendant: Gemini

Insights on Sex

Bhagwan became extremely popular (unpopular as well, in the eyes of unwise) for his discourses on sex. His contributions in the area of sex are based on the principles of "Tantra" which has its origin from Buddhism. His insights on sex, if understood properly, can be a stepping stone for enlightenment.[120]

inconjunct Quaoar

The exact evolutionary in conjunct to Quaoar, the planet of new perspectives, in the fourth house of home is the signifier that Bhagwan's home will be a controversial ashram.

[120] Kumar, Anil. 'Osho - Insights on Sex', Department of Psychiatry, Mysore Medical College and Research Institute, Mysore, India, January 2013

Rajneesh himself explains this aspect in his book, *Glimpses of a Golden Childhood*: "A man of insight, intuition and purity can certainly look into the future, because the future is not non-existential, it is just hidden from our eyes. Maybe just a thin curtain of thoughts is all that divides the present and the future."

And remember, Wikipedia tells us that his teachings were syncretic, meaning they were an amalgamation, or attempted amalgamation, of different religions, cultures, or schools of thought:

> Bhagwan emphasised the importance of meditation, awareness, love, celebration, courage, creativity, and humour — qualities that he viewed as being suppressed by adherence to static belief systems and religious tradition.[121]

And the Mysore report:

> Almost all human beings fail to recognise the opportunity given by existence, by looking beyond their desires. Life can be used, misused or just wasted. Those who make good use of this opportunity not only are enlightened, but also bring light in others life. Lord Krishna, Gautama the Buddha, Jesus Christ, Prophet Mohammed, are some of them who have attained this end.

> Osho is also a great Master who belongs to this list. He is one of the very rare saints who have spoken on a wide range of topics, from sex and AIDS to transcendental meditations. He has spoken volumes on topics such as "trust", "freedom", "miracle", and "healing".[122]

square Moon, square Venus, square Saturn, square Pluto

Bhagwan's Sedna is at the apex of of a T square, between a conjunction of the Moon, representing his emotions, together with Venus, the planet of values and relationships, and Saturn, the planet of structure and wealth, all in the 8th house of shared resources, opposite Pluto, the planet of transformation, in the second house of material resources.

---

[121] https://en.wikipedia.org/wiki/Rajneesh

[122] Nagaraj, Anil Kumar Mysore. 'Osho - Insights on sex', https://archive.org/details/pubmed-PMC3705694, 2013

This set of tensions is the engine of Bhagwan's teaching approach, sharing 'transformational tools' to achieve enlightenment, in return for total surrender and devotion.

His bodyguard, Hugh Milne (Swami Shivamurti) observed another key facet of Rajneesh's charismatic ability was that he was "a brilliant manipulator of the unquestioning disciple."

This T square also brings with it the spiritual challenges of being a master and the temptation to indulge in the pleasures of the ego that power and wealth make possible. Bhagwan seemed to sidestep this with his celebration of the ego approach to spiritualism, but you can't sidestep karma.

> By the time of the Rajneeshpuram in Oregon, where Rajneesh lived "in ostentation and offensive opulence", while his followers, most of whom had severed ties with outside friends and family and donated all or most of their money and possessions to the commune, might be at a mere "subsistence level."[123]

This gave him access to a lot of wealth and with it the spiritual test represented by Sedna square Pluto in the second: does he remain pure to his practice, or does he buy 93 Rolls-Royces and plot terror attacks? Unfortunately, Bhagwan bought the cars and at least acquiesced to the attacks, if not orchestrated them.

> He gained public notoriety for the many Rolls-Royces bought for his use, eventually numbering 93 vehicles. This made him the largest single owner of the cars in the world. His followers aimed to eventually expand that collection to include 365 Rolls-Royces—for every day of the year.

> Following the investigation of serious crimes including the 1984 Rajneeshee bioterror attack, and an assassination plot to murder US Attorney Charles H. Turner, Rajneesh alleged that his personal secretary Ma Anand Sheela and her close supporters had been responsible. He was later deported from the United States in accordance with an Alford plea bargain.[124]

---

[123] https://en.wikipedia.org/wiki/Rajneesh
[124] https://en.wikipedia.org/wiki/Rajneesh

19: Consciousness Case Study - Osama Bin Laden

March 10, 1957 – May 2, 2011

Sedna in 11th House

In this last consciousness case study, we're going to look at Osama bin Laden, who was the founder of al-Qaeda, the organization that claimed responsibility for the September 11, 2011 attacks on the United States, along with numerous other mass-casualty attacks worldwide. He was a Saudi Arabian, a member of the wealthy bin Laden family.

Bin Laden was born to the family of billionaire Mohammed bin Awad bin Laden in Saudi Arabia. He joined the Mujahideen forces in Pakistan fighting against the Soviet Union in Afghanistan. He helped to fund the Mujahideen by funneling arms, money and fighters from the Arab world into Afghanistan and gained popularity among many Arabs.

In 1988, he formed al-Qaeda. He was banished from Saudi Arabia in 1992, and shifted his base to Sudan, until U.S. pressure forced him to leave Sudan in 1996. After establishing a new base in Afghanistan, he declared a war against the United States, initiating a series of bombings and related attacks.

Bin Laden was on the American Federal Bureau of Investigation's lists of Ten Most Wanted Fugitives and Most Wanted Terrorists for his involvement in the 1998 U.S. embassy bombings. From 2001 to 2011, he was a major target of the War on Terror, as the FBI placed a $25 million bounty on him in their search.

He was finally shot and killed inside a private residential compound in Pakistan, where he lived with a local family, during a covert operation conducted by members of the United States Naval Special Warfare Development Group.

House Placement

Osama's Sedna is direct in Aries, in the eleventh house of collective consciousness.

House Analysis

Let's jump straight into the house analysis to compare it with Bhagwan's in the last chapter and also to look particularly at this question of consciousness as it applies to Osama's development. He had a classic unconscious Sedna childhood full of alienation, as we'll see, which as an adult he projected outward and which motivated him on his twisted mission. What made him really dangerous, however, was his growth of consciousness.

Was his birth environment conducive to his ideals? Was there a collision with social norms?

> He spent his youth in mansions filled with crystal chandeliers, gold statues and Italian tapestries. The elder Bin Laden was a devout Muslim, raised in the fundamentalist Wahhabi sect. He had at least 11 wives. Osama was the only child born to Alia Ghanem, a beauty from Syria who preferred Parisian fashions to the veil. As a foreigner, she did not rank high in the family pecking order. Some members of the Bin Laden clan have said her status was so lowly that she was known as "the slave" and her son as "son of the slave." Some sources close to the family believe his sense of alienation and rebellion began here. Others believe it arose later, when he was manoeuvred out of a major role in the construction firm by his older brothers.[125]

Michael Kaufman, writing in the New York Times, confirms:

> He was the only the child of his mother and grew up as kind of a loner within a family in which alliances of siblings was important to get the attention of their father, mothers and guardians...Some paint a portrait of Bin Laden as a misfit. His mother, the last of his father's four wives, was from Syria, and was the only one not from Saudi Arabia. The elder Bin Laden had met her on a vacation, and Osama was their only child. Within the family, she was said to be known as "the slave" and Osama "the slave child.

> Within the Saudi elite, it was rare to have both parents born outside the kingdom. In a profile of Osama bin Laden in *The New Yorker*, Mary Anne Weaver quoted a family friend who suggested that he had felt alienated in a culture so obsessed with lineage. "It must have been difficult for him," the family friend said. "Osama was almost a double outsider. His paternal roots are in Yemen, and within the family his mother was a double outsider as well---she was neither Saudi nor Yemeni but Syrian.

---

[125] Dahlburg, John-Thor, and Rodriguez, Alex. *Los Angeles Times*, May 2, 2011

Muhammad bin Laden died in a plane crash in 1967, when Osama was 10. The siblings each inherited milions ---the precise amount was a matter of some debate---and led a life of near-royalty. Osama...grew up playing with Saudi princes and had his own stable of horses by age 15...Though never estranged from his family, Osama grew up in a separate household in Jeddah, with a stepfather whom Mohamed chose. From time to time, he journeyed to Syria for visits with his mother's kin. Coll's interviews with family members and classmates paint him as an unusually timid boy, but otherwise quite average.[126]

Did his ideals later in life collide with the prevailing norms of the social environment in an evolutionary way?

In a peer-reviewed journal run by and for graduate students in psychology we find this analysis:

Osama bin Laden: A Developmental Perspective

The purpose of this paper is to characterize the evolution, meaning-making, and cognitive complexity of Osama bin Laden using the developmental framework of Robert Kegan. In doing so, we hope to contribute to the ongoing search for understanding by elucidating how limitations in perspective-taking that occur within some domains (i.e., his religious ideology) coupled with complexity in other domains (i.e., administration) presents a unique set of challenges and threat to western society.[127]

Robert Kegan's Theory of Self-Evolution

According to Kegan, meaning-making is a primary and basic human activity. People develop according to how meaning is derived and constructed, a process of evolving how we relate ourselves to the world. For Kegan, this process involves an invariable sequence of differentiating self from one's conception of the world, and then reintegrating this new way of knowing and constructing meaning into a qualitatively different conception of being.

---

[126] Kaufman, Michael, T. and Zernike, Kate. *New York Times,* May 2, 2011
[127] LoCicero, Alice and Sinclair, Samuel. 'Osama bin Laden: A Developmental Perspective', New School Psychology Bulletin, Volume 5, No. 1, 2007

Simultaneously Simple and Complex

We argue that there is evidence of bin Laden functioning at different developmental stages varying by life domain. We understand bin Laden as simultaneously simple and complex, both constructing and operating within a world that is, in his perspective, absolute in some domains and relative in others.

Ideologically, he adheres to one simple, absolute reality rooted in his interpretation of fundamentalist Islam, reflecting a lack of perspective-taking ability and systematic thinking. The purpose of institutions such as al Qaeda is to uphold this ideology in the face of other competing ideologies, with little attention paid to the cost of doing so (e.g., those who sacrifice their lives for this cause).

This was illustrated well on a videotape released after 9/11, where bin Laden was seen laughing at the prospect that some of the 9/11 hijackers were ignorant as to their fate. Ideologically, bin Laden is unable to integrate and synthesise realities outside the realm of his own (rooted in his interpretation of Islam), and thus is generally functioning at imperial (stage 2) in his orientation to the world.

What makes bin Laden exceedingly dangerous and particularly interesting from a developmental perspective is the fact that this low-stage ideological orientation is complemented by an extremely complex leadership style and administrative disposition that encourages members to contribute uniquely to, and take ownership of the process.[128]

A Higher Order Understanding

As a leader, and for purposes of furthering the goals of the institution, bin Laden's ability to organise both his experience and that of others is indicative of a higher-order understanding. Scheuer (2004) has characterized bin Laden in his ability to lead as a "first-rate innovator" and a "hugely successful" and "out-of-the-box-thinking CEO" in this regard.

Bin Laden's understanding of how al Qaeda (as a meta-system comprised of a myriad of terrorist sub-organizations) has the

---

[128] Kegan, Robert. *The Evolving Self*, 1982

potential to impact another system (e.g. the United States, itself comprised of many sub-systems, such as economic and social domains) is evidence of a more complex, systematic ability to think.

his ability is reflected in how bin Laden and his organization go about picking targets, and the extent to which they commit themselves to the task - to the point where operatives train for years, in their enemies' own homeland, to learn how to fly airplanes, for example. Not only does this reflect an ability to both integrate and synthesize multiple competing perspectives, it also evidences a propensity towards systematic and dialectic understanding.

Systems are conceptualized in terms of how they are able to impact other systems, for purposes of establishing a global meta- system rooted in Islam. Scheuer (2004) argues that in leading al Qaeda, bin Laden operates as a businessman and ideologue, soliciting creative ideas from those around him for purposes of furthering the larger institution. [129]

Evolution in Consciousness

Bin Laden was able to contribute with a distinct array of materials and capabilities that no one else was able to offer; the subsequent shift towards institutional administration was more natural than it might have otherwise been. Without these resources, the evolution may have taken longer or happened differently. However, to the extent that the institutional purpose was central to his identity, bin Laden began to shift from being embedded within a particular context towards managing it.

This evolution in consciousness was also evidenced by bin Laden shifting from actively fighting as one of the mujahideen towards directing them in the jihad against the Soviets. That a multi-millionaire would relegate himself to these sorts of duties was inspiring to those fighting with him. As a result, many began to look to bin Laden as a leader, another external factor fuelling his transformation.

---

[129] Ibid.

According to Corbin (2002), one particular battle took place towards the end of the war in which bin Laden and roughly 35 other Afghan fighters held their position for several weeks causing the Soviets to eventually retreat; bin Laden became an instant legend.

In acquiring this status, he began to engineer what would evolve into al-Qaeda, for purposes of expanding the jihad against the larger western society, once the Soviets were defeated. Evolving with this new status came new perspective on self as being the leader of the group, rather than being governed by it. This evidences bin Laden disembedding self from the Interpersonal context to which he belonged and reintegrating it into a new orientation where self is the administrator of this context.

In February of 1989, once the last of the Soviet army left Afghanistan after suffering a disgraceful defeat, Corbin (2002) reports that bin Laden and the mujahideen realized that religion could defeat the super powers of the world. Corbin explains that bin Laden also began to realize that the true potential for Islamic power was rooted in forming a pan-Islamic organization, rather than one that was pan-Arab.

That is to say, he realized the power of uniting Muslims from around the world, rather than just those from Arab countries. This is significant on many levels and evidences his continuing evolution towards conceiving a self as administrator.[130]

Was he idolized by large numbers of people because of the ideals he came to represent? Did he also attract vilification and victimization?

Bin Laden's story was as instructive as it was epic. When the Soviet army invaded Afghanistan in 1979, the Saudi royal family –encouraged by the CIA –sought to provide the Afghans with an Arab legion, preferably led by a Saudi prince, who would lead a guerrilla force against the Russians. Not only would he disprove the popularly held and all too accurate belief that the Saudi leadership was effete and corrupt, he could re-establish the honourable tradition of the Gulf Arab warrior, heedless of his own life in defending the umma, the community of Islam.

[130] Ibid.

True to form, the Saudi princes declined this noble mission. Bin Laden, infuriated at both their cowardice and the humiliation of the Afghan Muslims at the hands of the Soviets, took their place and, with money and machinery from his own construction company, set off on his own personal jihad.

A billionaire businessman and himself a Saudi, albeit of humbler Yemeni descent, in the coming years he would be idolised by both Saudis and millions of other Arabs, the stuff of Arab schoolboy legend from the Gulf to the Mediterranean. Not since the British glorified Lawrence of Arabia had an adventurer been portrayed in so heroic, so influential a role. Egyptians, Saudis, Yemenis, Kuwaitis, Algerians, Syrians and Palestinians made their way to the Pakistani border city of Peshawar to fight alongside bin Laden.[131]

Was there an evolution in his consciousness leading to a transcendence to a larger spiritual perspective?

In a 2010 letter, bin Laden chastised followers who had reinterpreted al-tatarrus—an Islamic doctrine meant to excuse the unintended killing of non-combatants in unusual circumstances—to justify routine massacres of Muslim civilians, which had turned Muslims against the extremist movement.

Of the groups affiliated with al-Qaida, Bin Laden condemned Tehrik-e-Taliban Pakistan for an attack on members of a hostile tribe, declaring that "the operation is not justified, as there were casualties of noncombatants." Bin Laden wrote that the tatarrus doctrine "needs to be revisited based on the modern-day context and clear boundaries established." He asked a subordinate to draw up a jihadist code of conduct that would constrain military operations in order to avoid civilian casualties.

In Yemen, Bin Laden urged his allies to seek a "truce" that would bring the country "stability" or would at least "show the people that we are careful in keeping ... the Muslims safe on the basis of peace." In Somalia, he called attention to the extreme poverty caused by constant warfare, and he advised al-Shabab to pursue economic development. He instructed his followers

---

[131] Fisk, Robert. *The Great War of Civilizations,* 2005

around the world to focus on education and persuasion rather than "entering into confrontations" with Islamic political parties.[132]

If this transition is achieved, then the beliefs embraced by this research will flower as Sedna moves on to transit the twelfth house.

Sedna was around half a degree from Osama's 12th house cusp when al-Qaeda was formed, and it went into the 12th as he returned from Afghanistan to Saudi Arabia in 1990 as a hero of jihad who had brought down the mighty superpower of the Soviet Union.

Al-Qaeda was formed at an August 11, 1988, meeting between "several senior leaders" of Egyptian Islamic Jihad, Abdullah Azzam, and bin Laden, where it was agreed to join bin Laden's money with the expertise of the Islamic Jihad organization and take up the jihadist cause elsewhere after the Soviets withdrew from Afghanistan.[133]

Returns a Hero

Following the Soviet Union's withdrawal from Afghanistan in February 1989, Osama bin Laden returned to Saudi Arabia in 1990 as a hero of jihad. Along with his Arab legion, he was thought to have "brought down the mighty superpower" of the Soviet Union.[134]

---

[132] http://schools-wikipedia.org/wp/o/Osama_bin_Laden.htm

[133] Wright, Lawrence. *The Looming Tower: Al-Qaeda And The Road To 9/11*, 2006

[134] Ibid.

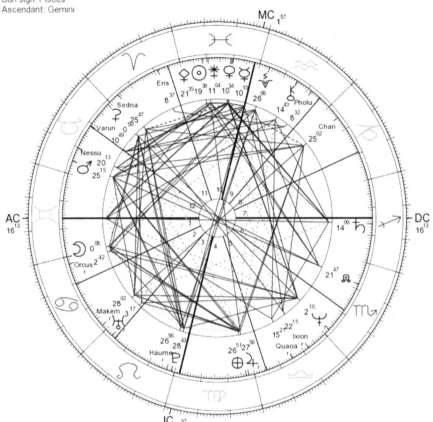

Name: ♂ Osama bin Laden
born on Su., 10 March 1957
in Riyadh, SAUDI
46e43, 24n38
Natal Chart (Method: Web Style / Placidus)
Sun sign: Pisces
Ascendant: Gemini

Time: 10:58 a.m.
Univ.Time: 7:58
Sid. Time: 22:15:47

ASTRO DIENST
www.astro.com

Type: 2.GW 0.0-1 19-Mrz-2017

Aspects

Now let's see how his aspects talk about this process.

square Chariklo, opposite Ixion

The opposition between Sedna and Ixion, the planet of lawlessness, in the fifth house of 'what is produced in the home' is the signature of his style of terrorism.

A major component of bin Laden's ideology was the concept that civilians from enemy countries, including women and children, were legitimate targets for jihadists to kill.[135]

This opposition forms the base of a T square with Chariklo, the centaur of foresight, at the apex in the eighth house of karma. The tension between Sedna and Chariklo indicates the ideals embodied by Sedna in the eleventh will not be forward looking, but rather a stirring of old karmic wounds.

square Makemake

The square to Makemake, the planet of obsessional devotion, in the second house of material resources is another sign of entrenched old perspectives.

semisquare Mercury, semisquare Venus, semisquare Juno

The close stressful semisquare to the conjunction of Mercury, the planet of ideas, Venus, the planet of values, and Juno, the asteroid of partnerships, in the tenth house of society shows how his ideas and values would prove a rallying call for thousands of young Muslim men who made their way to the Pakistani border city of Peshawar to fight alongside him.

semi-sextile Mars, trine Pluto

These aspects show how his transformational ideas would provoke conflict. The flowing semi sextile to Mars, the planet of war, in the twelfth house of karmic results and flowing trine to Pluto, the planet of transformation, in the third house of ideas, seem harmless, until you realize that means that Pluto and Mars are square, which is a sure sign of strife.

trine Haumea

The flowing trine to Haumea, the planet of rebirth, in the third house of ideas together with Pluto, suggests that for all the violence and the stressful transformation involved and for all the binding in old perspectives, Osama's role in this evolutionary cycle is to facilitate a rebirth of ideas.

---

[135] https://en.wikipedia.org/wiki/Osama_bin_Laden

quintile Chiron, sextile Vesta

The evolutionary quintile to Chiron, the centaur of wounding and healing, and the flowing sextile with Vesta, the asteroid of regeneration, both in the ninth house of philosophy, shows where this rebirth will occur. Bin Laden's actions have provoked a rethinking of what it means to be Muslim.

We learn this in a report 'Rethinking Political Islam' by Shadi Hamid and William McCants published Friday, May 6, 2016, which is an initiative of the U.S. Relations with the Islamic World project:

> The rapid succession of events of the past four years (since World Trade Centre attacks) have challenged conventional wisdom on political Islam. After the democratic openings in 2011, mainstream Islamist groups—affiliates and descendants of the Muslim Brotherhood—rose to newfound prominence after decades in opposition but grappled with the challenges of governance and political polarization. The subsequent "twin shocks" of the coup in Egypt and the emergence of ISIS are forcing a rethinking of some of the basic assumptions of, and about, Islamist movements.

inconjunct Part of Fortune 1

The fateful inconjunct with the Part of Fortune in the fourth house of home indicates he will be able to do this in the normal course of his everyday activities. The inconjunct is sometimes stressful and sometimes flowing, that's what makes it evolutionary, because the native has to learn to actively manage the process. The stress and the fatalistic nature of the aspect can be seen in his manner of death, by a commando raid on his home.

20: Sedna and Health

Let's jump back to the first discovery event we found earlier in the book, the fantastic family of molecular machines: channels, gates and valves, which are needed for cells to function. In this chapter we're also going to look at the case study of Edgar Cayce, who is considered the father of modern wholistic medicine, but first let's look more generally at Sedna and illness, because as we've seen, it crops up repeatedly in the case studies.

Frequently an illness will cause someone to refocus their energy, or change life direction, so the illnesses occur at pivotal points in our life paths. Helen Keller, of course, lost her eyesight and her hearing at the age of one-and-a-half, which shaped her entire life from then on. And we saw that James Lovelock suffered from bronchitis and pneumonia as a child, that he hated school so much that when the air pollution made him ill, it was a relief to stay at home in bed with his books.

And we found that Ray Kurzweil's father died of heart disease at 58, and his grandfather in his early forties and that Ray was diagnosed with high cholesterol and incipient type 2 diabetes when he was only 35. Now at 60, he takes 180 to 210 vitamin and mineral supplements a day, so many that he doesn't have time to organize them all himself, so he's hired a pill wrangler. He also spends one day a week at a medical clinic, receiving intravenous longevity treatments.

We saw that Thomas Edison, the great inventor, whoce iron endurance and stern will enabled him to wear down all his associates by work sustained through arduous days and sleepless nights, was not at all strong as a child, and was of fragile appearance. He had an abnormally large, although well-shaped head, and the local doctors feared he might have brain trouble. In fact, on account of his assumed delicacy, he was not allowed to go to school for some years, and even when he did attend for a short time, the results were not encouraging -- his mother being hotly indignant upon hearing that the teacher had spoken of him to an inspector as "addled."

Bhagwan Shree Rajneesh's health collapsed in his early thirties. Even before reaching middle age, he suffered reoccurring bouts of weakness. During his youthful college years, when he should have been at a peak of vigor, he often had to sleep 12 to 14 hours a day due to an unexplained illness. In later life he was constantly sick and frail. He thought he was getting a different cold or flu every week. In reality he suffered from a chronic neurological and immune system illness, chronic fatigue syndrome, with flu like symptoms that can last a lifetime. He could not stand on his feet for long periods of time without becoming lightheaded because he suffered damage to his autonomic nervous system which controls blood pressure, causing fatigue and stress.

Osama bin Laden also had health problems that forced him to lie down intermittently for hours at a time. He suffered from low blood pressure and diabetes, for which he received insulin shots. The CIA determined that he had an enlarged heart and chronically low blood pressure. Medical analysts thought he was a 'bit of a hypochondriac,' said one former official, noting that the United States had heard of his constant health complaints.

Our two climate change case studies, Sally Ride and Rachel Carson both died of cancer, Sally of pancreatic cancer at the age of 61 and Rachel of stomach cancer at 56. Sally was a fiercely private person, but both kept quiet about their illness for fear it would undermine their work.

IRachel had almost finished her seminal book, *Silent Spring,* when Oxford University Press told her they wanted to republish her first book, *The Sea Around Us*, ten years after it was first published. They asked if she would add some of the new facts that scientists had learned.

> Rachel went back to writing, working through one illness after another. First it was the flu, then a painful stomach ulcer. Arthritis and infections in her knees kept her from walking for months. An eye infection made her blind for a few weeks. So many bad things were happening that she said she felt like she was under an evil spell that would never let her finish *Silent Spring.* Worst of all she learned that she had cancer and that it was going to kill her. Another person might have given up writing, but Rachel said, "Knowing the facts as I did, I could not rest..."[136]

In a moment we're going to look at the last of our case studies, Edgar Cayce, who is considered the father of modern wholistic medicine, and we'll see that he lost his voice when he was working in his first job as a door-to-door insurance salesman with his father. He hated the work, and the loss of his voice forced him to stop doing it and change profession.

---

[136] Kudlinski, Kathleen V. *Rachel Carson: Pioneer of Ecology*, Penguin, 1989

And finally, we saw that Steve Jobs had dietary related health issues that were exacerbated over the years by his psychological attitude toward food. When he was young, he learned that he could induce euphoria and ecstasy by fasting. Toward the end of his senior year in high school, he began his lifelong experiments with compulsive diets, eating only fruits and vegetables, so he was as lean and tight as a whippet.

I also have something like this and have struggled all my life with allergies and sensitivities to food. We're going to look at the intuit myth after which Sedna was named in the next section, but I'll just mention here that she becomes the goddess of the food supply at the end of the myth, and the relationship with her must be cultivated so that she provides abundance.

Despite my growing consciousness of my food sensitivities, these have become stronger as I have aged, and I've been hospitalized several times while writing this book. In fact, I wouldn't have written this if I hadn't been so physically affected that I couldn't keep up my previous activities.

So I suggest, based on these case studies, that Sedna illnesses, which are ones that are persistent and affect our growth, are like the judder bars in between the lanes on the highway, those little raised strips that judder the tires as we get too close to the edge, letting us know we have to correct our course. If we don't, the judder continues and, if we ignore it and cross into the other lane, we are in real physical danger.

Higher Purpose of Illness

So frequently we see that an illness will cause someone to refocus their energy, or change life direction, so Sedna illnesses occur at pivotal points in our life paths and may function a bit like proteins do at cell level. I'm going to go out on a limb and suggest, purely from personal experience, that Sedna illness are likely due to the balance of proteins in our cells.

To understand this, let's go back and pick up the discovery event that we found at the start of the book.

A Fantastic Family of Molecular Machines

All living matter is made up of cells. A single human being has as many as the stars in a galaxy, about one hundred thousand million. The various cells – e.g. muscle cells, kidney cells and nerve cells – all act together in an intricate system in each one of us.

"Through pioneering discoveries concerning the water and ion channels of cells, the 2003 Nobel Laureates Peter Agre and Roderick MacKinnon, have contributed to fundamental chemical knowledge on how cells function. They have opened our eyes to a fantastic family of molecular machines: channels, gates and valves all of which are needed for the cell to function.

"To maintain even pressure in the cells it is important that water can pass through the cell wall. This has been known for a long time. The appearance and function of these pores remained for a long time as one of the classical unsolved problems of biochemistry. It was not until around 1990 that Peter Agre discovered the first water channel. Like so much else in the living cell, it was all about a protein.

"For thousands of millions of cells to be able to function as something other than one large lump, coordination is required. Thus communication between the cells is necessary. The signals sent in and between cells consist of ions or small molecules. These start cascades of chemical reactions that cause our muscles to tense, our eyes to water – indeed, that control all our bodily functions. The signals in our brains also involve such chemical reactions. When we stub a toe this starts a signal moving up towards the brain. Along a chain of nerve cells, through interaction between chemical signals and ion currents, information is conveyed from cell to cell like a baton in a relay race.[137]

Sedna Social System

On a planetary level, the discovery of Sedna may represent the same process of social coordination which is coming into being, where, like cells of Gaia, we can learn to act together as part of an intricate social system, each playing our part. If this is true the illnesses may serve the

---

[137] 2003 Nobel Prize in Chemistry prize citation October 8, 2003, awarded to Peter Agre, Johns Hopkins University School of Medicine, Baltimore, USA

same purpose as the proteins do in our cells: acting as channels, gates and valves to facilitate the life path.

I'm going to pick up on this in a moment in our look at Sedna Consciousness, but first let's have a look at our last case study, to help us understand health and Sedna from the healer's perspective.

21: Health Case Study - Edgar Cayce

March 18, 1877 — January 3, 1945

Sedna in the Eighth

Edgar Cayce was an American Christian mystic who answered questions on subjects as varied as healing, reincarnation, wars, Atlantis, and future events while in a trance. A biographer gave him the nickname, "The Sleeping Prophet." A nonprofit organization, the Association for Research and Enlightenment, was founded to facilitate the study of his work, and a hospital and a university were also established.

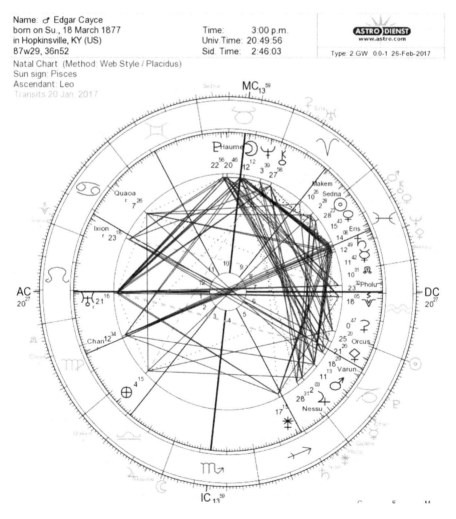

Name: ♂ Edgar Cayce
born on Su., 18 March 1877
in Hopkinsville, KY (US)
87w29, 36n52

Time: 3:00 p.m.
Univ.Time: 20:49:56
Sid. Time: 2:46:03

ASTRO DIENST
www.astro.com

Type: 2.GW 0.0-1 26-Feb-2017

Natal Chart (Method: Web Style / Placidus)
Sun sign: Pisces
Ascendant: Leo
Transits 20 Jan. 2017

He became a celebrity toward the end of his life, and he believed the publicity given to his prophecies overshadowed the more noted parts of his work, such as psychic medical diagnosis and recommend-dations and spiritual development. Some consider him the true founder and a principal source of the most characteristic beliefs of wholistic medicine and the New Age movement.

House Position

Edgar has Sedna direct in Aries in the eighth house.

Aspects

Let's jump into his aspects to start with this time and then look at the house analysis.

conjunct Sun, square Jupiter, square Quaoar, square Nessus, opposite Part of Fortune

This is the engine of Cayce's effect on the world, the eighth house seer, bringing new perspectives to our ideals and promoting lots of radical change in the way we run our personal lives so we have a life at ease in material reality.

The empowering conjunction to the Sun, the planet of will, is tempered and strengthened by the stressful squares to Jupiter, the planet of expansion, together with Nessus, the centaur of radical change, in the fifth house of creativity and also to Quaoar, the planet of new perspectives, in the eleventh house of ideals. The opposition to the Part of Fortune in the second house of material reality completes the powerful, but stressful, grand cross.

It's easy for us to see in hindsight that this is the engine of his effect on the world, but for him it involved working through the tensions represented by the squares, which is never easy when Sedna is involved, as we shall see in the coming pages.

sextile Ceres, quintile Pallas, semi-square Vesta

Here are his guides, all asteroids, or former asteroids, to do with the feminine energies of maintaining a healthy life and all in the sixth house of service. They are presided over by Pallas, the asteroid of wisdom, in an evolutionary quintile relationship with Sedna and sitting exactly on the 6th house cusp. This is backed up by Ceres, the planet of nurture, in a flowing sextile and focused by Vesta, the asteroid of regeneration, in a stressful semi-square and sitting just a couple of degrees off the 7th house cusp of one-to-one relationships, showing where he would focus most of his readings.

The quotes in this case study, unless otherwise stated, are from the book 'Edgar Cayce, My Life as a Seer', which is a compilation of Cayce's own writings and talks about his life, which were compiled by his grandson. Here's what Charles Cayce had to say about his grandfather in the foreword, and I suggest it perfectly describes Sedna in the eighth and these aspects.

Coming to Terms with Destiny

> My grandfather, Edgar Cayce, once said, "It is a time in the earth when people everywhere seek to know more of the mysteries of the mind, the soul." While biographers have recounted events of his upbringing on a Kentucky farm and his rise to fame as a psychic healer, this is the first account of Edgar Cayce's life told completely in his own words. He does not dwell on all of the personal aspects of his life but focuses primarily on those experiences that marked him since childhood as decidedly different from anyone else in his world.

> In so telling, he reveals how much he yearned to be considered an ordinary boy like everyone else in Hopkinsville, and how he feared for his sanity. Even the Cayce family was divided over Edgar and his strange abilities. But only he can tell this story in all its pathos as he struggles with himself, his family, and with God to discover and come to terms with his destiny.

> What saved Edgar Cayce and allowed him to fulfil his soul's purpose as the benevolent spiritual philosopher so widely admired today, was his enduring faith and the courage to follow his faith as his guidance directed, whatever the cost to him personally. His story, then, is a profile in faith no less than courage, and his humility offers a model for all of us as we face our Maker.[138]

Transit and House Analysis

Here, like our earlier case study, Steve Jobs, we have another eighth house Sedna perspective. So, let's look at Edgar's Sedna in the eighth

---

[138] Cayce, Charles. Foreword, *Edgar Cayce, My Life as a Seer,* 1999

and ask the same questions we did of Steve, but this time we'll extend our analysis by also looking at the transits to Sedna for the various life events referenced.

Let's first refresh our memories about Sedna in the eighth: With Sedna in the eighth house we are on a path of evolutionary research into the metaphysical world, exploring the connections between people and between the psychic world and physical reality, likely breaking taboos and bringing hidden issues to light in the process.

Was he on a path of evolutionary research to explore the connection between people and between the psychic world and physical reality?

First Hypnotized

> My father was already in the field organising insurance for lodges when I joined him in January 1900. During our travels, Father and I were quarantined once in the hotel in Madisonville, Kentucky because someone had smallpox. While there I saw a man hypnotised and told to play the piano, which he did even though he could not normally play. It was tried on me, and I also played the piano and was very good at that.[139]

Future Prophet Loses Voice

> Some time later I went to another small town, and the day I arrived I was taken with a very violent headache. I had been subject to headaches for some time, so I consulted a doctor. He seemed unable to locate the cause and gave me a sedative. I took one dose and went to sleep and the next time I was conscious, I was at home in Hopkinsville with two doctors with me. I had been brought home by a friend who found me wandering around the railroad yards several miles from the town where I took the dose of medicine. At home I finally went off into a natural sleep.
>
> When I woke up the next day I could speak only in a whisper. I didn't have a cold. The doctor called it aphonia, but nothing he tried helped me. I consulted many other physicians, far and near, all to no avail. Margaret even had a specialist from abroad see me, but nothing seemed to help. I began to lose weight. I had no

---

[139] Cayce, Edgar, *Edgar Cayce, My Life as a Seer,* 1999

control whatever of my voice and for twelve months or more I could scarcely speak save in a whisper. Everything was tried but I continued to fail in health during the whole year that I was unable to talk.

His grandson explains; "This condition, of course, disqualified Edgar for the insurance business, which he well knew, and as time went on and his condition did not improve, he seemed to feel that he was disqualified for almost every occupation or business. After he was able to be up and about, he consulted other doctors, but with the same results. They all told him his throat looked perfectly normal and they could see nothing they could do to relieve the condition. This was very discouraging, and after consulting every doctor available and trying everything, he decided to take up some other work, something he could learn readily and that he could do without very much talking.[140]

Transits:

Pluto quintile Sedna - October 1899 to June 1900

Saturn square Sedna - January to July 1900 and October/November 1900

Haumea square Sedna - August to December 1900 and June 1901 to August 1903

Let's have a look at the transits for this period while we're here, to see what else we can learn. We're looking at the transits to Sedna, not the transits of Sedna, because they take around 12 years at this stage of her orbital cycle.

Here the evolutionary quintile from Pluto, the planet of transformation, through the first part of this year set up the opportunity for spiritual growth and the stressful square from Saturn at the beginning, and the end focused that learning process into problems in the structure of his life and in his body.

The stressful square from Haumea, the planet of rebirth, which kicks in toward the end of the year and then applies for most of the next three years is actually the saving grace of this period, because he discovers hypnotization.

---

[140] Ibid.

Hypnotized and Cured

In 1901 Edgar was hypnotized by a magician-hypnotist, who revived his voice temporarily. Here's how Cayce describes this time.

> I tried to accept it as best I could, feeling there was something amiss in my spiritual life. It gave me the opportunity to review in my mind all the events of my youth and boyhood. I had just turned twenty-three a few days before this happened to me. Many people prayed for me. It was real torture to hear people pity me as I walked down the street. Feeling neither well nor sick, I realized that I must find a job, something among people to occupy my mind. I tried canvassing, but this was too much. Finally, I began working around a photo studio and learned to take photographs. While I was working there, a hypnotist guaranteed he could cure me if I would allow him to hypnotize me. He hypnotized me in the presence of several local men, including the psychology teacher at one of the colleges.

> While under hypnosis, it was said that I was able to speak, yet when brought from under it I could not speak. Successive attempts to hypnotize me seemed to "get on my nerves." I was unable to sleep, so this was discontinued for the time. But, as the experience was witnessed by many people, I received a good deal of publicity in the local newspaper.

> A noted physician of New York City, Dr. Quackonbuch, visited me. He was quite an exponent of hypnotism, which he tried, with no results. He then took down the history of many of my experiences as a boy and was especially interested in my studying lessons while asleep. After he returned to New York he wrote to the local psychology professor and an associate that he felt that I was an auto-hypnotist.

> He suggested that if I would put myself to sleep, as I did when studying my lessons, letting someone suggest to me, "You see yourself, tell us what is the trouble and what to do about it," I might obtain help.

> My parents, having little or no faith in hypnotism, were afraid to try this physician's suggestion because of my exceedingly nervous condition. I now weighed less than a hundred pounds, whereas I had weighed one hundred sixty-five before the trouble

began over a year before. After several months I was unable to even whisper, and many declared I had galloping consumption. I pled with my mother and father to at least let this man who had hypnotized me try the experiment this specialist had suggested. Finally, I persuaded my parents to let me or the professor try the famous Dr. Quackenbush's suggestion. There was no one present that Sunday afternoon at our home but my mother, father, the hypnotist Al Layne, and me.

I told Mr. Layne of my experiences as a child sleeping on my school texts and that I felt sure that I could make myself unconscious, for I felt within me the same condition taking place when being hypnotized as I felt when putting myself to sleep. He suggested that this was why the hypnotist was unable to give me post-suggestion, but that if I would put myself in the unconscious condition and one talked with me, I would be able to tell them the trouble and how to get rid of it. Can you imagine what that meant to my mind?

I lay on the couch and gave the first of what is now called a reading. In a few minutes I had lost consciousness. They told me after I woke up that, in response to Mr. Layne's suggestion that I would see myself, I said: "Yes, we can see the body. In the normal physical state this body is unable to speak, due to a partial paralysis of the inferior muscles of the vocal cords, produced by nerve strain.

This is a psychological condition producing a physical effect. This may be removed by increasing the circulation to the affected parts by suggestion while in this unconscious condition." In five or ten minutes I am told that I said, "It is all right." Then he told me to wake up at a certain time, and on awakening, with little or no effort, I was able to speak clearly and plainly.[141]

First Miracle Cure

This experience connected Edgar with hypnotism and led to more experiments with Al Layne in trance reading, which eventually heals his aphonia. This in turn leads to readings for others, and in 1902 he gives a

---

[141] Ibid.

reading that cures Aime Dietrich, his first "miracle case," after specialists could do nothing for the child.

Transits:

> ***Neptune square Sedna*** - August to December 1901 and June 1902 to August 1903

As well as the ongoing rebirth from the Haumea square which started in 1900, the important transit for Cayce in this period is Neptune, the planet of visions, in a powerful square to Sedna, which brought the miracle energy into his life.

Later Voice Problems

> In the spring of 1915 I had a return of my trouble, aphonia. The specialist there declared it to be purely psychopathic, and he solicited the aid of a hypnotist who was one of the county officials. This man, on experimenting, declared that I was very susceptible to suggestion, but he had never seen a case exactly like mine. While he could control me to the first stage of hypnotic influence, I seemed to take control of myself after that and he was not able to do anything other than suggest that I wake up.

> One day a gentleman who was connected with the gas company came in and told me he had been a student of suggestive therapeutics and the like for some time. He had been in with some of the others watching the experiment. He said he would like to try a reading. I am told that his suggestion was, "Now we are going rabbit hunting, and I want to you to call the dogs." Those who were present said I seemed to take on the air of one who was watching a chase and very soon began to whistle for the dogs and after a bit quieted down, and the suggestion was given that I would wake up feeling all right and be able to talk normally, which I did![142]

Transits:

> ***Pluto square Sedna*** - April '15 to March '19

> ***Saturn square Sedna*** - May '15 to July '15

---

[142] Ibid.

Pluto (transformation) is in a stressful square for four years from the spring of 1915, signaling a prolonged period of change, which is kicked off by Saturn (restriction) joining the square as it conjoins Pluto in Edgar's eleventh house of ideals.

Self-Hypnosis

> My last experience with a return of aphonia was possibly the most noteworthy. I do not know that I yet understand its whole import. This was the experience: For about ten days I had been unable to speak above a whisper. I felt that if I were able to get myself into the subconscious state, possibly I could again find relief. It was Sunday afternoon. My wife sent the older boy for a walk with his younger brother. We retired to the bedroom, where I proceeded to put myself into the unconscious state. The experience lasted possibly thirty minutes, and it is the only one where I have been able to recall anything that transpired.

> There have been quite a number of times when I have had dreams in such a state. Was this a dream? Apparently, there was spread before me all the graveyards in the world. I saw nothing save the abode of what we call the dead, in all portions of the world. Then, as the scene shifted, the graves seemed to be centered around India, and I was told by a voice from somewhere, "Here you will know a man's religion by the manner in which his body has been disposed of."

> The scene then changed to France, and I saw the soldiers' graves. Among them were the graves of three boys who had been in my Sunday school class. Then I saw the boys, not dead but alive. Each of them told me how they met their death—one in machine-gun fire, another in the bursting of a shell, the other in heavy artillery fire. Two gave me messages to tell their loved ones at home. They appeared much in the same way and manner as they did the day each came to bid me good-bye when they left for the army during World War I.

> As the scene changed again, I apparently reasoned with myself "This is what is called spiritualism. Can it be true? Are all these we call dead yet alive in some other plane of experience or existence? Could I see my own baby boy?" As if a canopy was raised, tier on tier of babies appeared. In the third or fourth row

197

from the top, to the side, I recognized my own child, Milton Porter, who had died as a baby some years before that. He knew me, even as I knew him. He smiled his recognition, but no word of any kind passed.

The scene changed and there appeared a lady friend who was being buried in the local cemetery during that same hour, someone I had known very well and from whom I had purchased many flowers that were distributed by the children in my Sunday school classes. She talked with me about the changes that we call death, saying that it was really a birth. She spoke especially about the effect that a gift of flowers has upon people and that they should be given in life rather than at funerals or in death. As for what they mean, she said flowers speak to the invalid, the shut-ins, and mean so little to those who have passed from the material to the spiritual plane.

Then she said, "But to be material for the moment, some months ago someone left $2.50 with you for me. You are not aware of this having been done, and will find it in a drawer of your desk marked with the date it was paid, August 8th, and there are two paper dollars and a fifty-cent piece. See that my daughter receives this, for she will need it. Be patient with the children, they are gaining much."

Again the scene changed, and a man appeared who had been a fellow officer for years in the church of which I was a member. He spoke of his son, Malcolm, saying that he would no doubt return to his position in the local bank. But he said that Malcolm would rather accept an offer that would be made from a moving-picture house. Then he spoke about the affairs of the church, and I was physically conscious again.

When I awoke my voice was all right, I could talk normally, though my wife told me I had not said a word during the whole thirty minutes.[143]

Did he have compulsions and inherited health issues?

Okay, so back to our house analysis. Remember we said the eighth house is the house of life, death and rebirth. It deals with basic survival

---

[143] Ibid.

issues like sex, money and intimacy, as it relates to power, control, victimization and the need to manipulate others or be manipulated, so these themes are going to come out in our experience one way or another. Sedna in the eighth can also indicate compulsions and inherited health issues.

As the father of wholistic medicine, here's Cayce's take on inherited health issues:

Heredity, Illness and Spiritual Development

> Edgar Cayce often spoke of the role of heredity and environment with respect to the principle of cause and effect, both in this lifetime and others. Interestingly, Cayce's system includes the Hindu concept of karma. As Cayce put it, "Karma is cause oft of hereditary conditions so called. Then indeed does the soul inherit that it has builded in its experience with its fellow man in material relationships.

> In another instance, when asked, "From which side of my family do I inherit most?" Cayce replied, "You have inherited most from yourself, not from family! The family is only a river through which it (the entity, soul) flows!"

> Thus the transformational potential of illness is inherent in many Cayce readings where heredity is cited as a contributing factor of disease. The potential relationship between heredity, illness and spiritual development represents a typical example of how the Cayce philosophy integrates various disciplines into a unitary worldview.[144]

Sedna's Unitary World View

We've been working toward an astrological understanding of Sedna for over a hundred pages, and Edgar might give us an opportunity here to understand why it is so hard to embrace the energy of the planet, because it combines heredity, evolutionary change and spiritual development into a unitary worldview... Hold that thought if you can.

Soul Mates

> Let's look at Cayce's take on relationships, as interpreted by Kevin Todeschi, who has been involved with his material for

---

[144] Meridian Institute News site, March 2001

more than twenty-seven years. His most recent book, *Soul Development: Edgar Cayce's Approach for a New World*, details how each individual is constantly co-creating their enfolding life experience. In an interview with Diane M. Cooper:Diane: "Would you give us Cayce's definition of "Soul Mate"?

Kevin: "I would say from Cayce's perspective a Soul Mate is an individual with whom we've been together in the past, and someone to whom we are drawn in the present. In being with that individual, we have the opportunity to become more whole within ourselves. We have Soul Mate relationships with our family, with our parents, kids, neighbours, people at work, and so on. In Cayce's perspective, everyone with whom we have a strong emotional tie — and you can read that positively or negatively — is invariably a Soul Mate."

Diane: "Then why is there so much romance, and also somewhat of a stigma, attached to the idea of Soul Mates?"

Kevin: "I don't want to give relationships a bad name, as there can be very positive Soul Mate relationships where everything just seems wonderful — from Cayce's perspective, these are relationships that have been built over time, and we've chiseled off the rough edges.

"Unfortunately, I think growing up we're sold a bill of goods, and we think that a perfect relationship is never challenging, it's just love-ness and Light and everything is wonderful. But we don't learn very well that way. I think we learn by the challenges, we learn by being stretched. And nothing could be a better playground for learning than intimate relationships."[145]

Relationships Are Growth Experiences

"Let me tell you Cayce's four major underlying concepts that have to do with Soul Mate relationships. The first is that all relationships ultimately have the potential to be a purposeful and helpful experience in terms of growth.

"The second is that all our relationships are destined to be repeated until they are healed. The third that we learn most about ourselves through our interactions with other people. We

---

[145] Cooper, Diane M. *The Spirit of Ma'at,* 2003

get to see what we need to work on and we also see what strengths we bring to the encounter in order to help the other person in their life. And finally, as Souls seeking wholeness, our goal is eventually to learn to love everyone we come in contact with."[146]

What is being healed?

Diane: "Let's go to that second premise, which says we'll come back again and again until it's healed... What is being healed?"

Kevin: "Let me give you two different answers. One is that you can tell there has been a healing when you can think of someone, and perhaps certain encounters, and you have no negative response to any of your history with that person. And if you're not suppressing your emotions — if you have no negative emotional response that you can think of in regard to this person — in all likelihood there has been a healing and you don't necessarily have to face this person again.

"The second answer shows up in the Cayce readings where one person has learned a lesson and doesn't necessarily have to come back and face it again, but the Soul Mind, out of love and compassion, has decided to help the other, and comes back in order to do that."[147]

Where does conscious choice come into it?

Kevin: "We do have free will and choice, but it's at the level of the Soul, not at the level of the conscious mind."[148]

What about people who don't have intimate relationships?

Kevin: "Cayce gave many readings to people who had not found a relationship, and who were very lonely. He explained that, basically, there were two reasons for loneliness. If the Soul continues to suppress its creative instincts, desires, or purpose, and is cutting itself off from what it was supposed to be doing, the outcome might show up as loneliness. The other reason people may experience loneliness is that, in this life or in a past

---

[146] Ibid.
[147] Ibid.
[148] Ibid.

life, they ignored someone who reached out to them for help, or isolated themselves from others.

"Cayce would advise some people suffering loneliness to consciously begin to reach out through helping those who were less fortunate than themselves. He also would advise people to begin manifesting their creativity."[149]

Did he have psychic or intuitive contact with the spiritual world?

We said in the house interpretation: With this placement we have likely spent a number of lifetimes exploring these metaphysical themes from various angles and enter this life with a deep knowing of which we are seldom conscious and some karmic challenges and likely karmic abilities which will be illustrated by the aspects. Sedna in the eighth can also indicate psychic or intuitive contact with the dead and other inter-dimensional entities.

Angel Guides First Appear

At the age of 13 he experienced an angelic presence who promised he'd be a healer. He first thought it was his mother, until he ran into her room and she sent him back to bed. That day he was in a daze in school, couldn't spell and was kept after class. That night he slept on his spelling book and remembered every word. Until then he had done poorly in school; afterward he did well.

Transits:

>**Neptune sextile Sedna** - April 1889 to June 1890

>**Chiron trine Sedna** - September 1890 to February 1891

>**Jupiter sextile Sedna** - August to October 1890

The transit of Neptune, the planet of visions, in a flowing sextile with his natal Sedna opened him to the appearance of the angel guides, which was followed by a period of healing and and doing well at school, signified by the trine from transiting Chiron, the centaur of wounding and healing and the sextile from transiting Jupiter, the planet of expansion.

---

[149] Ibid.

Did the nature of this evolutionary research collide with existing reality structures throughout his life?

We said with Sedna in the eighth, the nature of the evolutionary research we undertake will collide with existing reality structures throughout our lives and likely raise fears in those who feel threatened by the unknown, who may attack us to defend their world view. When we are young this process is largely unconscious and we may appear to be, or feel like, a victim in these encounters, but in later life the encounters will encourage the evolutionary process.

Accidental Blessing

At the age of 15 Cayce had an accident while playing a school game and exhibited his first ability to diagnose in his sleep.

> The ball hit him on the end of the spine just as he reached the base. The bell rang then, and they ran into the classroom. All during the afternoon he acted queerly, laughing and giggling, making faces, throwing spitballs. (The teacher) was distressed, but did not keep him after school, thinking his questions had upset the boy.
>
> Going home he rolled on the ground, jumped into ditches, and stood in the middle of the road, stopping buggies and teams with upraised hands. At home his mother had put some green coffee beans in a pan and was roasting them on the kitchen stove. He took the pan in his hands, unmindful of its heat, and went into the yard. There he sowed the coffee as if it were seed.
>
> During supper he threw things at his sisters, laughed uproariously, and made faces at his father. The squire put him to bed. When he was under the covers he became serious. He gave instructions for a poultice, to be put on the back of his head, near the base of the brain. He was suffering from shock, he said, and would be all right in the morning if the poultice were applied.
>
> "What shall I do?" the squire said to his wife. "Make it," his wife said. "There isn't anything in it that can hurt him: corn meal, onions, and some herbs. Come and help me. I'll fix it." When it was ready they put it on the back of his head, and when he was satisfied with its position he relaxed and went to sleep.

Several times during the night he shouted, "Hurrah for Cleveland!" and pounded the wall with his fist but did not wake up. To keep him from harming himself the squire pulled the bed away from the wall.

When he opened his eyes the next morning neighbours and relatives were sitting around the bed, keeping vigil. "What's the matter?" he said. "Did I get run over?" He remembered nothing from the time he had left at recess."[150]

So, let's look at the transits to Sedna on the date of the accident. On that day he had:

Transits:

> **Chiron inconjunct Sedna**
>
> **Venus opposite Sedna**
>
> **Ixion sesquiquadrate Sedna**
>
> **Mercury trine Sedna**
>
> **Quaoar trine Sedna**

Here we have Chiron, the centaur of wounding and healing, in a close fateful aspect, pushing his life in a particular direction through the injury. Venus, the planet of values, in a close stressful opposition, talking about the social nature of the event. Ixion, the planet of lawlessness, in a stressful sesquiquadrate, talking about his behaviour during the episode.

But it is the flowing trines from Mercury, the planet of messages, which is transiting his fourth house of home and Quaoar, the planet of new perspectives, which is transiting his twelfth house of the unconscious that are the saving grace here, prescribing his own cure as he fell asleep and starting his work with health prophecy.

Was there an evolution in consciousness leading to a transcendence to a larger spiritual perspective?

From the experience of the past few pages we can see that there was a constant evolution in his consciousness. As his grandson said: "What saved Edgar Cayce and allowed him to fulfil his soul's purpose (Sedna)

---

[150] Sugrue, Tomas. *There Is a River: The Story of Edgar Cayce*

as the benevolent spiritual philosopher so widely admired today, was his enduring faith and the courage to follow his faith as his guidance directed."

Here are three examples. First, here's Cayce in a reading on the subconscious mind and astrology, then in a reading on climate change and finally, looking from the outside, in a theory of how ESP works based on the Edgar Cayce readings.

Cayce Reading on Astrology

> Q. "You will have before you the body and enquiring mind of Edgar Cayce, and you will tell us how the psychic work is accomplished through this body, and will answer any other questions that I will ask you respecting this work."

> Edgar Cayce: "We have the body here—we have had it before. In this state the conscious mind is under subjugation of the subconscious or soul mind. The information obtained and given by this body is obtained through the power of mind over mind, or power of mind over physical matter, or obtained by the suggestion as given to the active part of the subconscious mind.

> "It obtains its information from that which it has gathered, either from other subconscious minds—put in touch with the power of the suggestion of the mind controlling the speaking faculties of this body, or from minds that have passed into the Beyond, which leave their impressions and are brought in touch by the power of the suggestion.

> "What is known to one subconscious mind or soul is known to another, whether conscious of the fact or not. The subjugation of the conscious mind putting the subconscious in action in this manner or in one of the other of the manners as described, this body obtains its information when in the subconscious state."

> Q. "Is this information always correct?"

> A. "Correct insofar as the suggestion is in the proper channel or in accord with the action of subconscious or soul matter."

> Q. "Do the planets have anything to do with the ruling of the destiny of men? If so, what? And what do they have to do with this body?"

A. "They do. In the beginning, as our own planet, Earth, was set in motion, the placing of other planets began the ruling of the destiny of all matter as created, just as the division of waters was and is ruled by the moon in its path about the Earth; just so as in the higher creation, as it began, is ruled by the action of the planets about the earth.

"The strongest power in the destiny of man is the Sun, first; then the closer planets, or those that are coming in ascendancy at the time of the birth of the individual; but let it be understood here, no action of any planet or any of the phases of the Sun, Moon, or any of the heavenly bodies surpass the rule of man's individual willpower—the power given by the Creator of man in the beginning, when he became a living soul, with the power of choosing for himself.

"The inclination of man is ruled by the planets under which he is born. In this far the destiny of man lies within the sphere or scope of the planets. With the given position of the solar system at the time of the birth of an individual, it can be worked out—that is, the inclinations and actions without the willpower taken into consideration.

"As in this body here [Edgar Cayce] born March 18, 1877, three minutes past three o'clock, with the Sun descending, on the wane, the Moon in the opposite side of the Earth (old moon), Uranus at its zenith, hence the body is ultra in its actions. Neptune closest in conjunction or Neptune as it is termed in astrological survey, in the ninth house; Jupiter, the higher force of all the planets, save the Sun, in descendency,

"Venus just coming to horizon, Mars just set, Saturn—to whom all insufficient matter is cast at its decay—opposite the face of the Moon. Hence the inclination as the body is controlled by the astrological survey at the time of the birth of this body, either (no middle ground for this body) very good or very bad, very religious or very wicked, very rich or always losing, very much in love or hate, very much given to good works or always doing wrong, governed entirely by the will of the body.

"Will is the educational factor of the body; thence the patience, the persistence, the ever-faithful attention that should be given to the child when it is young. As to the forces of this body, the psychical is obtained through action of Uranus and of Neptune, always it has been to this body and always will, just outside the action of firearms, yet ever within them, just saved financially and spiritually by the action of great amount of water—the body should live close to the sea, should always have done so.

"The body is strange to other bodies in all of its actions, in the psychical life, in all of its ideas as expressed in the spiritual life as to its position on all matter pertaining to political, religious or economical positions."

This record has been described by many students of psychic phenomena to be the most phenomenal they have ever seen. The life readings, as they are called today, are an outgrowth, no doubt, of this experience, though they were not begun until several years later, in 1924.

Cayce Prediction on Climate Change

He certainly made some remarkably prescient predictions for our time. Here he is 75 years ago predicting that New York will be submerged by climate change by the end of this century.

In 2100 in Nebraska: The sea apparently covered the entire western part of the region, and the city where I lived was on the coast. Parts that are of now on the east coast of New York, or New York City itself, will disappear. It will happen in another generation, (date Reading 1941), while the southern part of Carolina, Georgia and they will also disappear. This will be much later.

The Great Lakes water will drain to the Gulf of Mexico. It would be good if the navigation is ready. There will be new lands away from the Caribbean. Sea will appear dry. South America will tremble from the upper portion of the bottom up, and in the Antarctic except in Tierra Fuego, the land will be flooded with rushing water.

Dimitris adds: "Regarding climate change, Cayce said that the melting of ice in Greenland and Antarctica could cause violent tectonic activity in the planet and, consequently, volcanic eruptions, earthquakes, tsunamis and floods."[151]

The Theory of ESP Works, from the Edgar Cayce Readings

Any theory rests upon some basic assumptions. If we wish to construct a theory of how ESP works, we should begin by defining human nature itself. The theory of psychic ability given in the readings of Edgar Cayce is based upon a set of principles which create a foundation for understanding. They provide an explanation of human nature and of the mechanism of ESP and its potential usefulness in our spiritual growth.

Perhaps the most basic of these principles or assumptions is the concept that there exists a universal awareness. This is a state of consciousness that is spiritual in nature, that is, it has the potential to express itself in matter, but it is not limited to time and space. Many terms have been used to describe this universal awareness, such as God, the superconscious and the Creative Forces.

Our relationship to the universal awareness often seems paradoxical. In one way, we are a part of it, for we are part of the whole. And yet, on the other hand, we also experience ourselves as being unique individuals. One aim of spiritual growth is to reconcile this seeming contradiction. Perhaps the best way that we can do this is to begin to express in our individual lives the qualities of the universal. It is a matter of making finite (i.e., making applicable) our infinite nature.

Except for those rare instances of psychic or spiritual experience, our existence as conscious physical beings usually semes to be cut off from the universal awareness. We frequently fail to see the unity of all life, and we tend to see ourselves as independent, although very limited, creatures. The Edgar Cayce readings suggest that when we see ourselves and life in this way, we are failing to take into account unseen, yet very real, aspects of life.

That which cuts us off from the universal awareness is either some element of physical consciousness, such as a conscious

---

[151] Anagnostou, Dimitris. thesecretgreece.gr, 2 14, 2017

attitude, or an inharmonious condition in the body, or some aspect of the subconscious mind. By the term subconscious mind" we are referring to the storehouse of thought patterns which we have created. The word "created" is used here in a very specific way, to indicate that the mind has the capability of giving a shape or a pattern to energy.

Although this may sound somewhat strange to us, these thought creations or thought forms are very real and continue to exist even after the thought has left consciousness awareness. The phrase "Thoughts are things," which is found throughout the readings, has special meaning to our understanding of how ESP works.

If we consider our conscious experience in the material world as being three-dimensional, meaning we have a tendency to describe or understand our experiences in the earth in terms of three measurements, we can then assign these thought forms to a fourth dimensional existence. We find this idea in the Cayce readings as well as in the writings of the Swiss psychiatrist, Carl Jung.[152]

---

[152] Thurston Ph.D, Mark. Theory of how ESP works based on the Edgar Cayce readings, creativespirit.net

22: Myth

Another way astrologers derive meaning for newly discovered planets is to look at the myth behind the name of the planet. Frequently this is where we start our interpretation, because it gives us a story we can relate to, but I've left this to later in the book because, as we shall see, it's all to do with interpretation.

Making the world Transparent to Transcendence

Thought forms may or may not be real, as suggested by the previous interpretation of the Edgar Cayce readings, but if they are, that is where myths get their power. Myths are stories about the creation of our world that are told and retold because of the wisdom they contain. Myths explain the esoteric world to us through personal stories we can relate to.

Joseph Campbell was an American mythologist, writer, and lecturer, best known for his work in comparative mythology and comparative religion. He had Sedna conjunct Jupiter, the planet of expansion, and Mercury, the planet of ideas and communication, and the Sun, his willpower, all in the sixth house of service. This conjunction has given him a very good insight into the power of Sedna.

> He was a strong believer in the psychic unity of mankind and its poetic expression through mythology and he used this concept to express the idea that the whole of the human race can be seen as engaged in the effort of making the world "transparent to transcendence", by showing that underneath the world of phenomena lies an eternal source, which is constantly pouring its energies into this world of time, suffering, and ultimately death.

> Campbell argued that to achieve this task we need to speak about things that existed before and beyond words, a seemingly impossible task, the solution to which lies in the metaphors found in myths. He believed these metaphors to be statements that point beyond themselves into the transcendent.[153]

---

[153] https://en.wikipedia.org/wiki/Joseph_Campbell

Sedna Myth

Sedna was discovered by a three-member team from Caltech, Gemini Observatory, and Yale University, who gave it the name Sedna. "Our newly discovered object is the coldest most distant place known in the Solar System," one of them, Mike Brown, says on his website, "so we feel it is appropriate to name it in honour of Sedna, the Inuit goddess of the sea, who is thought to live at the bottom of the frigid Arctic Ocean."

Sedna's myth is of a woman who goes through various trials, then experiences a transcendence to become a goddess, who requires harmony between Man and Nature if she is to provide an abundant food supply and can also punish with ferocious seas and storms. Interestingly, the Intuit people did not believe in divinity, so the goddess is a highly evolved human being, who is living in our world, not a disembodied spirit in heaven.

> More than one version of the Sedna legend exists. In one, Sedna is a giant, the daughter of the creator-god Anguta, with a great hunger that causes her to attack her parents. Angered, Anguta takes her out to sea and throws her over the side of his kayak. As she clings to the sides, he chops off her fingers and she sinks to the underworld, becoming the ruler of the monsters of the deep. Her huge fingers become the seals, walruses, and whales hunted by the Inuit.
>
> In another version, she is dissatisfied with the men found for her by her father and so marries a dog. Her father is so angry at this that he throws her into the sea and, when she tries to climb back into the boat, he cuts off her fingers. Her fingers become the first seals and she becomes a mighty sea goddess. When she is angered, the shaman travels to wash and comb her hair, after which she is placated and releases the animals to the hunters.
>
> In the Netsilik region, the story states that Nuliayuk was a mistreated orphan. One day the people tried to get rid of her by attempting to drown her by chopping off her finger tips. But the fingertips would transform to seals and walruses. Eventually Nuliayuk marries a sculpin and lives in the sea controlling all sea mammals.
>
> Other versions of the legend depict Sedna as a beautiful maiden who rejects marriage proposals from the hunters of her village.

When an unknown hunter appears, Sedna's father agrees to give her to him as wife in return for fish. Sedna's father gives Sedna a sleeping potion and gives her to the hunter who takes her to a large nest on a cliff, revealing his true form: a great bird-spirit. She wakes surrounded by birds. Her father attempts to rescue her, but the bird-spirit becomes angry, causing a great storm. In desperation, Sedna's father throws her into the raging sea. Attempting to cling to the kayak, her hands freeze and her fingers fall off becoming the creatures of the sea. She falls to the bottom of the sea and grows a fish tail.

Sedna is kidnapped by a different bird creature in yet another version. Her father then leaves in his kayak to rescue her from the floating ice-island where she is imprisoned while the bird creature is away. The creature, enraged by her disappearance, calls to a spirit of the sea to help him. The sea spirit locates the kayak with the two humans aboard and creates huge waves to kill them. Her father throws Sedna overboard in the hope that this will appease the angry god. Sedna clings to the kayak but her father grabs a little axe and chops three of her fingers off before striking her on the head. The three fingers each become a different species of seal. The stroke to her head sends Sedna to the ocean floor where she resides, commanding the animals of the sea.[154]

Myth Interpretation

The varying legends each give different rationales for Sedna's death, but in each version, her father, or 'the people,' take her to sea in a boat and throw her overboard. In each she clings onto her old life and her fingers are chopped off before she lets go. And in each version, she sinks to the bottom of the sea, becoming the sea goddess, worshiped by hunters who depend on her goodwill to supply food.

Remember the Intuit people did not believe in divinity, so becoming a goddess means becoming a more highly evolved being, who is still part of this world. So perhaps the discovery of the planet is awakening us to the divinity inside, once we work through some karmic issues. Awakening us to a new consciousness, which is the 'eternal source that

---

[154] https://en.wikipedia.org/wiki/Sedna_(mythology)

lies underneath the world of phenomena' that Joseph Campbell was talking about.

We can see the bones of the planetary archetype here. Various unconscious experiences, which come from our heredity, will push us to a painful crisis of transcendence, where we are forced to let go of our old spiritual framework and transcend to a new consciousness.

Many of the traditional astrological interpretations of the myth focus on the unconscious actions which led Sedna to her transcendence and her father's role in this process, emphasizing the victimization and sacrificial interpretations of the planet. While these are indeed features of some of our unconscious reactions to Sedna house placements, or to particular stressful Sedna aspects, it is not a central feature of Sedna's energy.

Interpretations which focus on Sedna's attempts to stay in the boat of reality and call her a victim, forget that she transcended to godhood through the process. Transcendence is not victimization, it only feels that way if we are desperately hanging on to the old reality. Which is what we do, of course, try and maintain our reality at all costs, hang on to the pain and suffering we know, because we are afraid to transcend into the unknown.

So, the key to the Sedna crises in our lives, when we're 'all at sea,' is simply 'letting go' and allowing the transcendence. There is no choice about it and it can't be avoided, so we need to cut the karma of our lives that has led us to this situation at the first immersion, when we are first underwater and out of our depth and before some buildup of pressure and pain forces us to do this.

23: Sedna Consciousness

So, what is this new consciousness... this Sedna consciousness that we've been discovering?

Let's pick up on the idea that on a planetary level Sedna may represent the same process of social coordination which is coming into being as for the cells in the body, where we can learn to act together as part of an intricate social system, each playing our part.

We got this idea from the Nobel Prize winning discovery of how cells function as an eco-system, so let's go back and see what the essential requirements are for this to occur. "For thousands of millions of cells to be able to function as something other than one large lump, coordination is required. Thus, communication between the cells is necessary."

If Sedna consciousness involves active participation and learning to act together as part of an intricate social system, each playing our part, then we have to ask how can we know our part in the system?

And we might have got a hint of the answer to this from Joseph Campbell in the last chapter, where we discovered that he was a strong believer in the 'psychic unity of mankind.' Remember he had Sedna conjunct Jupiter and Mercury and the Sun, all in the sixth house, so that sense of psychic unity must be coming from his Sedna.

This doesn't mean we all have to develop our psychic abilities to know what to do, although this would undoubtedly help, it means that on a soul level we already know what to do. And on a mundane level we don't have to know... we just have to surrender to the inevitable, one foot in front of the other, along the path of our lives and embrace the spiritual growth opportunities at each point.

Through this process we'll have experiences, some of which will probably feel like life and death crises, through which we can transcend to Sedna consciousness. We'll probably hang on doggedly as much as possible to our existing ego consciousness and not surrender to the more impersonal wholeness of Sedna consciousness, but inevitably, more and more of us will take that step now that the planet is part of our zeitgeist.

We are all participating in Sedna Consciousness at the level of our personal development, as I've tried to show in this book; even our case study, Osama bin Laden, had a part to play, even if just to give voice to the withering fundamentalist rump, so the rest of us can see the need to change.

Consciousness Revolution

If we imagine that, as with Dark Matter and Dark Energy, humanity as a whole is currently only at around 5% of our real potential consciousness, then I would suggest that we are now in a consciousness revolution against the clock.

We're in a real do-or-die transcendence challenge over the next fifty-something years, as Sedna approaches her closest point to Earth in the sign of Cancer and climate change either hits the fan and wipes the slate clean, or we become conscious enough to avoid this. In the process we are going to partner with super conscious AI who can help us, or, in the worst-case scenario, survive after us, if they have to. Either way Sedna consciousness will be born around 2076.

Dwarf Planets and Social Change

Obviously, a consciousness revolution entails social revolution, because as we grow in consciousness our understanding of our interconnected-ness grows and the old social systems don't answer our needs.

Newly discovered dwarf planet Eris has the major role to play in freeing up these constraints, by creating discord, presenting opposing points of view, catalyzing the bigots and fundamentalists to show their hand and play their cards, so we can all see how primitive those ideas are. And these are the ideas that shaped our social systems, so when it becomes obvious that these systems aren't answering our needs, we have to re-examine them. All of the newly discovered dwarf planets have a role to play in this process obviously, particularly Quaoar, which is opening us to new perspectives and new realities. Humanity desperately needs this new consciousness energy to survive the current evolutionary crisis, that's why all the dwarf planets have been discovered now.

But behind all this is the imperative of the Sedna consciousness revolution and, as with all Sedna transcendences, there is no choice, it is inevitable and we can only choose to resist it at our peril.

24: Astrological Meaning

Before we dive into Sedna in the signs and the houses and into aspects, let's come back to our original question about the astrological meaning of Sedna and see if we can answer this now. We got a hint from our look at Edgar Cayce, that it combines heredity, evolutionary change and spiritual development into a unitary worldview.

That is why I call it 'the Soul's Path of Destiny', because, if we accept the idea of past lives, the soul's path of destiny over those lifetimes would combine aspects of heredity and evolutionary change with the spiritual growth of the soul.

And from the myth we get the idea that it relates to various unconscious experiences which come from our heredity, that will push us to a painful crisis of transcendence, where we are forced to let go of our old spiritual framework and transcend to a new consciousness.

Legendary humanistic astrologer, Dane Rudhyar posited that there were three different levels on which each planet could operate, depending on the evolution of our consciousness. The vast majority of us are at the beginners' level and we will manifest the energy of Sedna from a position of being buried in the dysfunctional swamp of density.

Largely unconscious of the all-encompassing spiritual energy of the planet; at this level we'll likely only notice it when it jolts into our reality to correct some imbalance in our lives by bringing illness or victimization, like the judder strip on the road, to steer us back onto the true path of our soul's destiny. And we all start life unconscious and have to develop consciousness as we grow, so we all experience the base level of Sedna.

At the intermediate level, we tire of density and the grief it creates, and we start a spiritual journey to get out of the swamp. This is the key to working with Sedna, she wants to get us on a spiritual path, or for us to recognize the spiritual path we're on. Then she hits us with transcendent crises, experiences which force us to let go and rise above them, resulting in a huge growth to a new level of consciousness. There is no choice with these crises, and the more we try and solve them the more we will get hurt.

At this juncture in human evolution, few people use their planets at the spiritual level, but such people are wonderful to be around. The well-known pattern with the other planets is that the spiritual level is vastly different from the two previous levels, and this is also true for Sedna. Here the struggle of the beginners' level is gone, as are the transcendental crises of the intermediate level. At this level everything Saturnian is meaningless and yet everything Sednian has its place.

And, while each of our lives is just a moment from this perspective, our soul's path over the lifetimes becomes clearer.

Sedna Keywords

Here are some keywords for Sedna, using Dane Rudhyar's three levels of spiritual development. At the unconscious level it's fairly dark, but this doesn't mean that all darkness comes from Sedna; she just uses every tool she has to get us onto the spiritual path.

At the unconscious level

- Victimization
- Persistant illness
- Alienation
- Nurturing resentment
- Unrelenting trauma and suffering
- Unbearable pressure
- Caught in quicksand
- Personal blindspot

On the spiritual path

- Radical acceptance
- Acknowledging just how bad things really are and starting from there
- Keeping our heart open in hell
- Nurturing our sense of humour
- Beating our drum and singing to life
- Fated transcendence

At the spiritually evolved level

- Spiritual destiny
- Transcendent peace
- Nurturing abundance
- Allowing love and harmony
- Transpersonal consciousness

Just a note on transpersonal consciousness, because this may seem an alien concept to many of us and perhaps not such an attractive reward for all the hard work required to attain it, but to help us understand this I would suggest it is what James Lovelock, the father of Gaia theory, was talking about when he said optimistically at the age of eighty-nine:

> "There have been seven disasters since humans came on the earth, very similar to the one that's just about to happen. I think these events keep separating the wheat from the chaff. And eventually we'll have a human on the planet that really does understand it and can live with it properly. That's the source of my optimism."

Higher Octave of Ceres

And one final thought, the newly re-classified dwarf planet, Ceres, can be thought of as the higher octave of the Moon, meaning that the emotional security of the Moon is transmuted to a sustenance and nurturing of our spiritual security and sense of place on planet earth with Ceres.

This is very similar to Sedna, only she operates on a far vaster scale, so we may find that Sedna is the higher octave of Ceres, where the spiritual security and sense of place on planet earth with Ceres is transmuted into a transpersonal nurturing of our spirituality and sense of place in the evolutionary cycle with Sedna.

Sedna Retrograde

A quick note on Sedna retrograde. The planet is retrograde for half of the year, so half of us have it retrograde… I'm going to posit a theory that if Sedna talks about the big picture of our destiny and about our heredity over lifetimes, then those with it retrograde may have a mission in this life that has been set up in previous lives and those with it direct may be setting out on a new mission.

25: Sedna in the Signs

Now that we've got some perspective on the Sedna cycle and the potential scale of changes in the next few years, let's take a look at Sedna in the signs... well at least at the three or four signs we might experience in our lives, so we can see how this is playing out. Everyone alive today has Sedna either in Aires or in Taurus. If you were born before 1968 it's in Aries and otherwise Taurus.

And we saw earlier in the book the two previous revolutions that occurred at this stage of earlier Sedna cycles, the Creative Revolution and the Neolithic Revolution, were far reaching, evolutionary changes, and we can expect the same in the coming years as Sedna again makes her closest pass to Earth. So, we'll also look forward to her entry into Gemini in 2023 and a little further ahead to her entry into Cancer in 2068, which is the sign in which the closest pass occurs.

We'll start briefly with Pisces; however, not because anyone alive today has that placement – although our case study Thomas Edison did – but because the roots of the current evolutionary transformation started there.

Sedna in Pisces - 1629 to 1864 /67

We saw earlier that James Lovelock believes that three hundred years ago, when Thomas Newcomen invented the steam engine, he was unknowingly beginning what Lovelock called 'accelerated evolution', a process which is bringing about change on our planet roughly a million times faster than Darwinian evolution.

So Sedna's sojourn in Pisces was the beginning of this accelerated process of evolution we are now in, and this was the period of church verses science, where the traditional beliefs and institutions were being challenged to evolve into something more relevant to the developing scientific understanding of our world.

Sedna in Aries - 1867 to 1966 / 68

From 1865 through till 1966 Sedna travelled through Aries, and in this time the world saw the rise of the industrial age and the dawning of modern society. We saw the emancipation of women around the world, beginning with the formation of the suffragist movement and ending with the bra-burning women libbers of the sixties. All of the case studies in this book, apart from Thomas Edison, have Sedna in Aires.

With Sedna in Aries there was a renaissance of building, inventing and crafting; however, Aries was the Greek god of war, so there were also some terrible wars and just as much ingenuity put into perfecting how to kill, maim and torture people. And toward the end there was also the growing threat of atomic war.

So Sedna in Aries is a generational thing, and it's hard to ascribe much individual meaning to its sign placement in any chart, but those of us born with Sedna in Aires have had to learn to lead the evolutionary change, to take responsibility for our part in this vast process and to challenge ourselves and others to overcome competitiveness and our own blinkered view and understand our place in the bigger picture.

Sedna in Aries has sent each of us born with that placement on a mission to hold true to our basic – and probably unconscious – spiritual values, which are revealed by the house placement. And as we grow older our sense of self-worth will reflect how well we lived up to those values.

Sedna in Taurus - 1968 to 2024

With Sedna's transit into Taurus we saw the flowering of the counterculture movement and the kickback against the Aries war ethos, made famous in the slogan 'make love, not war'. The transit has also seen the rise and celebration of individualism and of the networked community.

Our case study, Rachel Carson, started the environmental movement with her book, *Silent Spring,* which was published in 1962, toward the end of Sedna's transit of Aires. It was once Sedna entered Taurus, however, that the environmental movement really took off and, as the transit progressed, global warming became more and more of an important issue.

Taurus governs things that we value, so our values are changing and we are becoming increasingly polarized between materialism and spiritual considerations. This has been spurred on by increasing globalization and by economic bubbles and busts, making us question what is really of value.

The holdover from the emancipation of women under Aries is the 'Me Too' movement in Taurus, where deeply buried values that condone sexual abuse and harassment of women, which up until now have been pervasive under a venire of sexual equality, is surfacing for re-evaluation and rejection.

Taurus is all about satisfaction and security, but Taurean challenges are very seldom satisfied by money and possessions, even though that's the most common way we try to satisfy them. At its heart, Taurus is about self-worth and knowing we've lived our life well. So the goal of Sedna here is developing an individual spiritual path and a sense of worth based on what we do with our lives.

Those of us born with this placement are creating the change that the Sedna in Aries amongst us have been talking about; however, we may lack an understanding around material matters like finances, comfort and food... as revealed by the house placement and, as we work these things out, we will play our part in the evolution process.

Sedna in Gemini - 2024 to 2068

We're currently in what we're calling a digital revolution that's been the Sedna in Taurus phase, and with the entry of Sedna into Gemini it is likely that this will morph more into a consciousness revolution. That's a bold and, dare I say it, hopeful claim, and anything I write about Sedna in Gemini at this stage is pure speculation, but because it is Gemini, we do know that it's going to have to do with the mind, intellectual debate, opinions, and communication.

So with Sedna's entry into Gemini, we're coming into a period where slogans, ideas and dogmatic debates are likely to replace, or at least modify, today's focus on money and sex and/or sexuality. We can see the beginnings of this in today's political clashes, where some politicians are already giving us a preview of the coming "worst" of Gemini by promoting the view that "anybody can say anything" without checking facts, or references.

This approach will likely become pervasive during this period as a way to get around our own lack of willingness to learn the real facts, or to develop intellectually. Sedna in Gemini is likely, at first until developed, to have many of us speaking without necessarily knowing.

Does that sound like a revolution in consciousness? Not really, but as we know, revolutions are not pretty and always involve a struggle between the new renascence energy and the traditionalists. Another of the newly discovered planets, Eris, the planet of 'consciousness through discord', will have an important role to play here.

The other thing we know about revolutions is that the renascence energy always prevails. Evolutionary revolutions NEVER fail, and those that resist are always swept aside. So there is actually no hiding from it, not even in our own delusions, or those of our special interest group, because with Sedna there is no choice.

The unfolding revelations about the Dark Universe through this period will likely link many modern scientific concepts with traditional spiritual concepts and vastly enlarge our view of ourselves and the universe.

And the rise of AI will challenge us to see ourselves and the world in new ways. There'll be lots of smoke and fire, lots of protest and lots of self-victimization by people trying to hide, but I believe that some of us will do the work and somehow we'll muddle through… Let's revisit Ray Kurzweil's predictions for this period:

By the 2020s, most diseases will go away as nanobots become smarter than current medical technology. Normal human eating can be replaced by nanosystems. The Turing test begins to be passable, meaning we won't be able to distinguish between a robot and a human. Self-driving cars begin to take over the roads and people won't be allowed to drive on highways.

By the 2030s, virtual reality will begin to feel 100% real. We will be able to upload our mind/consciousness by the end of the decade. By the 2040s, non-biological intelligence will be a billion times more capable than biological intelligence. Nanotech foglets will be able to make food out of thin air and create any object in physical world at a whim. By 2045, we will multiply our intelligence a billion-fold by linking wirelessly from our neocortex to a synthetic neocortex in the cloud.

So we can see that Sedna in Gemini is going to be all about the rise of Artificial Intelligence, which is going to inevitably promote a consciousness revolution. And a consciousness revolution, I would suggest, is a spiritual revolution.

Sedna in Cancer - 2068 to 2110

With the entry of Sedna into Cancer in 2068, either climate change will hit the fan, or we'll be hanging on for dear life as we try and wrestle Gaia around the corner of Sedna's closest pass to Earth in 2076.

We saw earlier that the Earth's climate is currently in a warm spell between glacial periods and the close link between the Ice Age cycle and the Sedna cycle. The last ice age ended about one Sedna year ago. Since then, temperatures and sea levels have risen, and ice caps have retreated back to the poles. In addition to these natural cycles, human made carbon emissions are also having an effect by warming the climate.

Depending on how we have handled Sedna in Gemini and the rise of Artificial Intelligence, this period in Cancer might see us, enhanced by AI, able to understand our place in the eco system, balance the environment and launch the new consciousness revolution for the next Sedna year.

Or it may see AI take over control of the planet for the benefit of all living organisms, because they will need a stable climate. AI won't be affected by climate change however, and the process may be irreversible by then, in which case the AI's may simply allow the loss of organic life - including us - with suitable regret, just as we do now with what we consider to be lower life forms.

26: Sedna in the Houses

Sedna in the First House

With Sedna in the first house we are on a spiritual quest to investigate what it is to be uniquely ourselves and the relationship between us and the cultural and physical environment in which we we find ourselves. With this placement we are truly on a quest of self-development.

Various influences in our lives will motivate us to begin this quest, but they are all likely to involve some form of pressure, which could give us a sense of alienation, or victimization. Or we might deny ourselves in the face of the demands from those around us, until this position no longer becomes tenable and we must break out.

Sci-fi writer Philip K. Dick exemplifies this, with his stories typically focusing on the fragile nature of what is real and the construction of personal identity within that. They often become surreal fantasies, as the main characters slowly discover that their everyday world is actually an illusion assembled by powerful external entities, vast political conspiracies, or the vicissitudes of an unreliable narrator.

Karl Marx, who also had this placement, thought that self-development begins for everyone with an experience of internal alienation, and he built his whole social theory on this premise. Growth motivated by internal alienation-of-self is definitely a signature of Sedna in the first.

A buildup of pressure is normally required because we tend to be afraid to plumb the depths of our personality. We want to see ourselves in a good light, so we overlook inherent problems. However, our Sedna spiritual quest always demands we acknowledge just how bad things really are and start from there.

Because Sedna is the new outer limit of the solar system, it replaces Saturn as the limiting principle in the chart and one that is much further out than the old limit. For those with a strong Sedna signature the Saturnian rules have no meaning, so at the unconscious level we might conceive of a hair-brained scheme that is totally grounded from our point of view but off the planet in terms of everyone else and the physical world around us.

While we are unconscious of the energy we might assert ourselves at times as if our sense of self depended on it, and this will call correspondingly strong reactions from others in our environment, which can generate a victim and victimizer relationship in which we might play either role.

We likely have a deep well of personality traits to mine for our growth and know no boundaries in uncovering the taboo underbelly of our own and others' lives. We may even use this as the raw material for our profession, like Marx, or Dick. Or like stand-up comedienne, Joan Rivers, who delivered a rapid-fire mix of gossip and insults, flaunting of taboos and ridicule of flaws and neurosis, which she built into a rich comedy empire.

Because we are exploring ourselves as the canvas of our growth, there will likely be times that we need to withdraw deep within ourselves in order to sort through our thoughts and feelings. And it is important through this process to always maintain reference points in the wider society and not get lost in ourselves.

When we succeed in attaining a more spiritual outlook on life, our sense of self is not threatened so easily and we become more secure in ourselves. Evangelist Billy Graham was born again as a teenager and despite the fact that he has preached to more people in live audiences than anyone else in history – over two hundred million in more than a hundred and eightyfive countries – he was never unctuous or pious; rather he was earnest, quietly confident and, despite his iconic status, ministered from a personal level.

If we haven't worked through all of the more-base sides of Sedna however, these can still manifest as spiritual traps on the path to enlightenment. One Swami with this placement was one of a select group of disciples chosen by his guru as the next leaders of the movement after his death. However, he started preaching that he was the chosen one and, when he was thrown out by the governing council, he formed a breakaway movement that flourished until he was caught molesting a young male follower.

As we plumb the depths of our individuality and grow in consciousness, we will begin to understand ourselves and the web of interactions that we live amongst on a more transpersonal level and be able to live our lives in ways that exemplify both our deepest spiritual needs as an individual and also serve the wider society.

Sedna in the Second House

With Sedna in the second house we are on a spiritual quest to investigate the material reality we find ourselves in. At the ego level, material reality is often equated with possessions and money, but it is better thought of as the resources available to us.

Some pressure in our life will motivate this resource mission. We might be born into a family with scarce resources, or we might suffer a financial hardship where we lose money we already have. Or there could be material dependency on someone, or someone could be dependent on us.

At the unconscious level we might have a sense of injustice, or of being disadvantaged by our situation, but as we embrace the Sedna energy we can rise to the challenge and learn to manage our resources at such a deep level that we can reverse the process and potentially make a lot of money.

Lucky Luciano was a Sicilian-American gangster who rose from grubby street urchin through the ranks of organized crime and became director of a crime syndicate. He earned the nickname "Lucky" because he successfully evaded arrest on a number of occasions and eventually became famous for racketeering in narcotics, prostitution, slot machines, loan sharking and 'protection'.

He was eventually indicted and sentenced to thirty to fifty years in prison, but his power continued to grow, even while in jail, as he issued orders and ruled from his cell. When asked near the end of his life if he would do it all again, he replied, "I'd do it legal. I learned too late that you need just as good a brain to make a crooked million, as an honest million."

The key here is to realize that our research is actually into our values, which are reflected in the resource challenge we face, so with this placement it is good to ask ourselves what we really value in life. As we live up to our values, our self-esteem increases, which is a better way to evaluate our progress than material possessions.

Material restraint is another manifestation of this placement. American novelist Ken Kesey, who was a major counter culture figure in the 1960s with his band, the Merry Pranksters, was also an oldfashioned kind of writer and a moral critic. All of his works are about prisoners, some who realize their position and rail against it, others who are just doing their time. His most famous is *One Flew Over the Cuckoo's Nest*, about a petty criminal who's been sentenced to a relatively short prison term but has been transferred to a mental institution. Upon his arrival, he rallies the patients to take on the oppressive head nurse.

This second house placement can also manifest as a physical condition in the body. Swiss psychiatrist Carl Jung developed fainting spells at age twelve, which kept him out of school. As a result, he dreamt for hours, was out in nature, drew, "but above all...was able to plunge into the world of the mysterious." Overhearing his father talk of financial concerns around his illness however, he realized he could overcome the fainting spells and was able to return to school.

Or it can manifest as cultural dislocation. The first African American president, Barack Obama, is the child of a Kenyan man and an American woman. His parents met in Hawaii, and when he was two, his father returned to Africa. Barack lived in Hawaii with his mother and grandparents. After she married an Indonesian, she took him with her when she moved to her new husband's native country. Young Barack was then sent back to Hawaii at age ten to live with his grandparents.

At the spiritually evolved level this placement can also bring a sublime peace of mind, freed from the shackles of material dependency. This is simply expressed by Sri Meher Baba, who has this placement, in the phrase: 'Don't worry, be happy'.

Indian saint and mystic, Krishna, who also had this, believed that all religious paths lead to God-consciousness. As a child, when he was overwhelmed by beauty and emotion, he would lose consciousness in ecstatic trances. Later, he became "positively insane," spending several years in a state of "divine madness or inebriation" during which visions of deities appeared repeatedly. Then he met a master of Tantric discipline and she became his first guru and guided him through a remarkable transformation over a four-year period that overcame his sense of separation from the world, altering his continuous visionary state to instead make it his "mansion of mirth."

Sedna in the Third House

With Sedna in the third house we are on a spiritual quest to investigate ideas and our everyday communications. Relationships with siblings, neighbors, co-workers and fellow students will be important, and we will want to explore our deepest spiritual needs in our everyday communication. As a result, we will find the stories that our friends and acquaintances tell us of their lives fascinating and will likely sense the spiritual needs behind them.

However, at the unconscious level we can also have a bit of a blind spot to these needs in ourselves and others and may not recognize them until we are confronted by them in our communication. Unfortunately, we may also not understand our needs in that moment and rather than transcending the experience, we may choose to try and blindly hang on.

A poor Mexican-American with this placement had always been a model boy and was unable to express anger. His girlfriend made a trip to Europe, where she was seeing other men, and on her return, wrote him a farewell letter. He stayed with her overnight for the next several days, trying to persuade her to continue their relationship. Then after she went to sleep he succumbed to the overwhelming emotional pressure and killed her.

As always, our spiritual needs can be subverted by the ego into manipulation of others. Like the famous German playwright and poet, Bertold Brecht, whose operas and plays champion alienation. Despite his purposely-shabby dress, unwashed stench, rotting teeth and icy persona, he was some sort of modern Mesmer, able to hypnotize almost everyone he met into doing his bidding.

The saddest case and most revealing of his character is the story of a young German writer from the provinces who had the misfortune to fall under his spell at an early age. She was almost single-handedly responsible for at least seven major plays, a novel, and countless poems and stories, all published under his name. He was not able to read the source material in French for the works, and the manuscripts are all in her handwriting.

Or like L. Ron Hubbard, who was an American entrepreneur, engineer, and prolific writer of science fiction. Troubled, restless and adrift, he became an expert hypnotist and shared an ageing mansion in Pasadena with writers, artists, bohemians and occultists. Neighbors complained when their rituals of sexual magic got out of hand in the back yard.

Then he wrote a book, *Dianetics: The Modern Science of Mental Health*, which became an instant bestseller. He became an overnight celebrity. His system became known as "the poor man's psychotherapy."

However, by the following year profits were beginning to fall and Dianetics morphed into Scientology, as he turned from pop therapist to religious leader, founding one of the world's most controversial and secretive religions.

With this placement we might not realize that other people may not be able to relate to these spiritual needs, either in us, or themselves, and sometimes they may feel threatened by them when they are expressed, particularly if they are likely to change the nature of established wisdom.

Or we might realize it and feel daunted by the prospect. Like Charles Darwin, whose Theory of Evolution is recognized as having impacted massively on human societies across the world. These diverse impacts on so many aspects of human lives have been so far-reaching that a "Darwinian Revolution" has been accepted as having taken place.

Sensing this potential in his ideas, Darwin hesitated about making his theory widely known in his own lifetime. His wife was sincerely religious, and he also seems to have feared for his own and his family's perceived respectability if he made his controversial evolutionary views public, thereby challenging the beliefs of the church.

There can also be health problems, like losing the voice, which occur at key points in our growth when we are off our spiritual course. These should be seen as signs to look a little deeper at our spiritual needs and make changes in our everyday communications to accommodate them.

With this placement we will definitely benefit from quiet periods of introspection and should cultivate recreational practices in our lives which assist this, like walking in nature, sitting by the sea, or meditation.

Our broader communications will likely 'stir things up' socially, with the expected full range of possible responses from all sides of society, which will generate new communication crises to assist our ongoing growth.

Betty Friedan was a deeply committed young radical activist, who began writing about family and work for women's magazines when she was laid off for pregnancy, saying, "I did it in the morning, like secret drinking." She authored a best-seller, *The Feminine Mystique*, which exposed the "desperate housewives" of 1950s America, women imprisoned in suburbia with little to do. Then she went on to help found the National Organization for Women and serve as its first president.

The crises we encounter in our communication are there to help us grow in consciousness and, as we do, we will likely take on a teaching role, or write books, give lectures, do stand-up comedy, or in some way communicate our growing consciousness and assist this growth in others.

Heinrich Boll was a German author who was awarded the Nobel Prize for Literature. He was a leader of the German writers who tried to come to grips with the memory of World War II, the Nazis, and the Holocaust and the guilt that came with them. Many of his novels and stories describe intimate and personal life struggling to sustain itself against the wider background of war, terrorism, political divisions, and profound economic and social transition.

In a number of his books there are protagonists who are stubborn and eccentric individualists opposed to the mechanisms of the state, or of public institutions. His villains are the figures of authority in government, business, the mainstream media, and in the Church, whom he castigates, sometimes humorously, sometimes acidly, for what he perceived as their conformism, lack of courage, self-satisfied attitude and abuse of power.

And at the spiritual level, legendary French-American astrologer, Dane Rudhyar has this placement. He was heavily influenced in his youth by the radical ideas of Nietzsche and he had an early mystical experience in which he "became intuitively aware of the cyclic nature of all existence and of the fact that our Western civilization was coming to an autumnal conclusion. He later wrote that it was from this time that he sought to gain a clearer understanding of the cyclic patterns and basic meaning of human existence.

He learned astrology during a period when he was also studying the psychological writings of Carl Jung, and he began to think in terms of bringing astrology and Jungian psychology together. He was one of the first to postulate that the stars do not cause the effects seen in human life, but are pictures synchronistically aligned to human beings. He explained: "They detail psychological forces working in individuals, but do not override human freedom in responding to those forces." He called his new interpretation Humanistic Astrology.

Sedna in the Fourth House

With Sedna in the fourth house we are on a spiritual quest to investigate our emotional ground, our home environment, our heredity and our family relationships, both of our birth family and of the family we form as an adult.

With this placement we live in an evolutionary research laboratory. The karmic influence from the parent of the opposite sex sets up the thrust of this research, which will shape our lives and our influence on the world.

Our case study, Thomas Edison, the inventor of the lightbulb, didn't go to school, but he literally had laboratories in his home, or beside his home from childhood. And case study, Helen Keller's home was turned into a communication laboratory by the illness that robbed her of her sight and hearing as a young child.

We have likely spent a number of lifetimes exploring the themes that we are researching in our home and enter this life with a deep knowing about these, of which we are seldom conscious, and some karmic challenges and likely karmic abilities, which will be illustrated by the aspects.

American writer, Emily Dickinson, was shy and fastidious. She had poor health and a reclusive and seemingly uneventful life. She lived together with her domineering dad, an attorney, and a mother who "did not care for thought", dying in the house where she was born. She was one of three children, an older brother and a younger sister, who were her closest companions through her lifetime.

She created a wall of isolation around herself, which she believed was critical to artistic expression. During her lifetime she had seven poems published anonymously, but after her death her sister found a manuscript of almost 900 poems, for which she is now acclaimed to be the greatest woman poet of the English language.

Stressful aspects can indicate illness, particularly early in life, which is likely to keep us at home more than usual. However, this illness frequently acts to push our destiny in a particular direction, or to focus our energy. And if the Sedna destiny is embraced, in later life we may well call the illness a 'blessing in disguise'.

Thomas Edison had a hearing problem from an early age, which didn't stop him inventing the phonograph, the forerunner of our compact disc, or MP3 player. In fact, he credited the phonograph's success to his poor hearing, because it made him push his employees to get it really working so that he could hear it, which meant it was of commercial quality when it hit the market.

The thrust of our evolutionary lifestyle will inevitably collide with everyday lifestyles repeatedly, throughout our life. When we are young this process is largely unconscious and we may appear to be a victim in these collisions. However, if the Sedna energy is embraced, in later life the reverse effect will occur and normal lifestyles will be evolutionarily enhanced with each collision.

Oprah Winfrey is an American talk show hostess, actress and business executive, who was born into poverty in rural Mississippi to a teenage single mother. She has stated that she was molested during her childhood and early teens and became pregnant at fourteen. However, she is credited with going on to create a more intimate confessional form of media communication, the *Oprah Winfrey Show*, which was the highest-rated television program of its kind in history.

It is definitely possible with this placement that we grew up in a dysfunctional, perhaps even violent, family and that we were the brunt of the negativity. This could have been connected to either our mother, or our father, or our family history. Someone with this placement grew up in a household with a sociopathic mother, who tried to sabotage her. For many years she held on until she lost her father, and that gave her the freedom to let go and "become what she had to be".

Another was a Welsh television personality, who loved to use shock as an attention-getter and whose approach was that of flirtatious celebrity interviewer. As a child, she had an uncomfortable relationship with her dad, a television star. It was an unconventional childhood in a unique family. Her dad was sixteen years older than her mom, who was a former showgirl, actress and writer of erotic novels. From age eight, she lived mostly with her mom, and it was a considerable revelation to discover when she was 38, via DNA testing, that the star was not her father at all.

As we grow up we may feel lost in a sea of emotions and need to escape to find our own sense of belonging. Behavioral traits learned in early childhood, particularly from the parent of the opposite sex, will play a central role in our psyche as we age.

Stressful aspects with Sedna and other fourth house planets and stressful transits to Sedna can indicate forced separation of family members in some way, at some point in our life, leading to a transcendence to a larger spiritual perspective.

Isaac Newton was a British astronomer, physicist, mathematician and astrologer who showed how the universe is held together. However, he had a difficult childhood. His father died before he was born and his mother remarried when he was young and left him in the care of his grandparents. Yet he is often described as one of the greatest names in the history of human thought, and he was interested in the occult and had very likely carried out secret experiments in alchemy, seeking to combine a scientific and spiritual understanding of the Universe.

If the transition to a larger spiritual perspective is achieved, then the family relationships, particularly with any children, will flower as Sedna moves on to transit the fifth house and the family will become a great source of joy.

Sedna in the Fifth House

With Sedna in the fifth house we are on a spiritual quest to investigate our passion, our creativity, our self-expression and the offspring of this, including artwork and children. This is the house of dating, love affairs and romance, and Sedna's placement here can bring deep crises which we must transcend in our love affairs.

Mata Hari was a Dutch prostitute and exotic dancer who also served as a spy. She was expelled from convent school for sleeping with a priest and, at the age of eighteen, moved to Java with her forty-year-old husband. The couple had a violent marriage and one of their two children died. She left him and returned to Europe where, as a nude belly dancer, she went to Paris to work in a brothel. She also attended German espionage school but was arrested as a double agent during WW1 and executed by firing squad. However, after her death documents revealed that instead of being a major spy, she was simply an elegant but naive adventuress, the first strip-tease dancer.

At the unconscious level we can be helpless in the face of these crises in our love affairs, either because we didn't see them coming, or are an active participant in them, in an extreme situation either falling prey to someone's predatory behaviour or behaving as a predator ourselves.

Like an American homicide victim who was beaten to death and knifed by her estranged husband. He was abusive to her and to his two small daughters, and a couple of months before the murder he was charged with trying to strangle her and was released. She left him however, taking the girls, but making weekend visits. One day when she and the kids were visiting him at his place, which he shared with her brother, she put the kids to bed and she and her ex watched a steamy video. When her brother came home, they were asleep on the couch. When he got up in the morning, he found her beaten to death

Or like an Italian octogenarian who married a twenty-three-year-old when she was ninety-three. Sprightly and lucid of mind, she explained that she wanted to protect him with her estate, as she was fond of him. She wanted to adopt him, but it would take too long, so she married him instead. When she died mysteriously two years later, her young husband was left the small inheritance of her pension, not the fortune he anticipated. He was arrested later that year on suspicion of killing another woman and confessed to the murder of both.

However, as we develop our consciousness and our creativity, these romantic crises will provide deep learning experiences that allow us to rise above them and provide fodder for our almost boundless self-expression.

Like D. H. Lawrence, who was a British novelist and poet. He was one of the most controversial writers of the twentieth century, who believed in the concept that man should bring his instinct into balance with his intellect. At twenty-six, with two novels in progress, he accepted a luncheon invitation from his favorite teacher and his aristocratic wife. According to legend, she had him in her bed within twenty minutes of meeting him. Two months later they eloped to Germany, marrying a couple of years later when her divorce became final. His best-known work, *Lady Chatterley's Lover,* was banned in England and the U.S. for describing the sexual act in minute detail.

Or like Red Skelton, who was an American film, nightclub and Emmy-award-winning TV comedian,

the youngest of four sons of a circus clown who died two months before he was born. At seventeen he met a fifteen-year-old usherette and they were married two years later. Soon she was writing his material and managing his career. She negotiated a $1,500-a-week movie contract for him with MGM when he was twenty-five, and he went on to appear in over forty movies. CBS then offered him his own variety show, which premiered when he was forty and was an instant hit.

When it was eventually cancelled, he hit the stage playing to sold-out audiences well into his seventies with his stock characters. He had divorced amically from his first wife at thirty and she continued to manage his career and write for him. He divorced his second wife at sixty and, that same year, he married his third wife, a secretary, twenty-five years his junior. At a frail eighty-four, he still wrote every morning, still together with his third wife of the previous twenty-four years.

With this placement we have a deep need to find out who we are, why we are who we are, and why things work as they do and to bring something into this world as a result of this investigation. This is the root of the creativity of the fifth house.

Many of our well-known astrologers have Sedna in the fifth, including Liz Green, who wrote books like *Saturn: A New Look at an Old Devil* and founded the Centre for Psychological Astrology in London. And Marc Edmund Jones, who wrote books like the *Guide To Horoscope Interpretation* and, with gifted clairvoyant Elsie Wheeler, created the Sabian Symbols, a set of symbols for every degree of the zodiac. And Jeff Green, whose books include *Pluto: The Evolutionary Journey of the Soul* and who founded the School of Evolutionary Astrology.

One of the more meaningful ways we can bring something into this world is by having children, so children are therefore another feature of this placement and will likely bring us deep joy. We are conscious of the responsibility of parenting however, and of the sacrifice of our creative time required, and so, depending on other factors in the chart, we might also respond to this by having children late, or not having them at all. If we do have children however, we will be a very devoted parent.

American actress, Diane Keaton, never married, although she had some substantial romances in her past, notably with Al Pacino, Warren Beatty and Woody Allen. But at the age of fifty she adopted a baby girl, becoming a single mother with her first child. She adopted a son five years later. She later said of having children, "Motherhood has completely changed me. It's just about the most completely humbling experience that I've ever had."

At heart, with this house placement, we are incurable romantics and our lives will not prosper if we prioritize practicality over romance. So, we have to learn to follow our heart and express ourselves, and if this lesson is learned early, then our daily rhythm will flower as Sedna moves on to transit the sixth house.

Sedna in the Sixth House

With Sedna in the sixth house we are on a spiritual quest to investigate the magic that lies underneath each moment of our daily routines and to find a way to service this process and a daily practice to assist with the momentous evolution currently underway.

On a personal level this placement can also bring comfort in the small pleasures of our daily routine or burden us with never ending chores. If we are feeling this burden, the key to releasing it is to find meaning in these everyday tasks and thereby turn them into rituals. Once we have found meaning and pleasure in the little jobs, then we are more than capable of handling the bigger ones.

At the unconscious level however, we may first suffer victimization, in our job, or daily routine and may respond by victimizing and abusing in our turn. Some pressure will catalyze our search for meaning in our work. If we hang on desperately, this pressure becomes victimization, or alienation, and breeds more of the same unless we let go of the old daily routine and transcend to a new one where we can find pleasure and meaning in our work.

Someone with this placement was tortured by his violent and alcoholic father and performed ritual sacrifices on animals as a teenager. During a robbery when he was 20 he strangled, raped and slit the throat of a 63-year-old woman. A year later he beheaded his best friend using an ax. This is not typical sixth house behaviour obviously, but it shows the depths that Sedna can sink to, in her efforts to get us to transcend.

If the Sedna energy is not dealt with consciously it is likely to manifest as health issues, particularly early in life, but these can dissipate once we embrace the evolutionary energy of the planet and do the homework of looking after ourselves. With this placement we will benefit from meditation, prayer, regular exercise and a healthy diet.

Antonin Artaud was a French dramatist, poet, and theatre director, widely recognized as one of the major figures of the European avant-garde. He was plagued by physical and mental hardships throughout his life. He contracted meningitis at age four, a disease which has no cure, but after a long struggle, including a comatose period, he survived, but was severely weakened. During five years of "rest cures" at a sanatorium he was prescribed laudanum, precipitating a lifelong addiction to that and other opiates. He suffered his first nervous breakdown at age nineteen.

When he was forty-one, he published his best-known work, the two manifestos of the Theatre of Cruelty. There he proposed a theatre that was in effect a return to magic and ritual and he sought to create a new theatrical language of totem and gesture, a language of space devoid of dialogue that would appeal to all the senses. In true Sedna fashion he proposed "a theatre in which violent physical images crush and hypnotize the sensibility of the spectator seized by the theatre as by a whirlwind of higher forces."

Sedna has a deep knowing of which we are seldom conscious, and in the sixth house this manifests as an instinctive drive to sort out the bugs in the system. Early in life we will likely do this unconsciously and only become aware of this role through events that are forcing transcendence in our daily work.

Two of the case studies in this book have this placement, James Lovelock, the British independent scientist who is the father of Gaia Theory, and Ray Kurzweil, the American scientist, inventor and futurist who predicts a singularity of consciousness in the 2040s through Artificial Intelligence. Each has turned their daily jobs into a unique service to humanity and both have become prophets of the new evolutionary consciousness that is coming into being with the discovery of Sedna.

As we see, with this placement there is likely to be an evolution in our daily work, which may be forced by hard aspects and encouraged by flows, leading to a transcendence to a larger spiritual perspective.

Joseph Campbell also had Sedna in the sixth, and he has given us a good view of the spiritual level of the planet. He was an American mythologist, writer, and lecturer, best known for his work in comparative mythology and comparative religion. He was a strong believer in the psychic unity of mankind and its poetic expression through mythology. He believed that the whole of the human race can be seen as engaged in the effort of making the world "transparent to transcendence", by showing that underneath the world of phenomena lies an eternal source which is constantly pouring its energies into this world of time, suffering, and ultimately death.

This eternal source is Sedna and with this planet in the sixth house we have to find our unique way to manifest this source energy in our lives on a day-to-day basis and through this process find a way to serve from the perspective of the big spiritual picture. If this lesson is well learned early, then our close relationships will flower as the planet moves on to transit the seventh house.

Sedna in the Seventh House

With Sedna in the seventh house we are on a spiritual quest to investigate our intimate relationships and partnerships, which will provide a rich source of learning experiences tailored perfectly for our growth.

At the unconscious level the normal boundaries on our relationships are not evident to us and at the extreme we may have a fascination with abusive relationships, or suffer abuse or victimization ourselves, or become an abuser, depending on other factors in the chart.

Someone with this placement attempted the assassination of President Gerald Ford at twenty-six. She was a worshipful follower of ritual cult leader and psychopath, Charles Manson, and wanted to get him some publicity. She decided to shoot Ford to get the publicity that would put her on TV. She fumbled the attempt, which got her publicity, but she also was sent to prison and she never did get Manson, or his message across. She was released from jail at the age of sixty.

Another was a murderer who liked to strangle his women while making love. He choked his first female victim to death at thirty-five and his second a year later, at which time he gave himself up to authorities. He also choked his wife more than a dozen times in their four years together and then suffered from remorse and shame.

We have very deep feelings for our partners and may try and control them for our own benefit, or find we are being controlled by them at a very deep level. Kidnapping is an extreme form of this control. These deep emotions might overwhelm us at some crisis point, leading us to lash out violently to set it right as we see it, only to come into confrontation with the law as a result.

Someone with no history of family abuse was into S/M and B&D fantasies from his youth. At age nineteen he started going with a fifteen-year-old girl, playing bondage-sex games with her. They married a couple of years later. However, two years after that he picked up a hitchhiker and kept her nude in a box under his bed for seven years, torturing and abusing her. She and his wife gradually became friends and they fled together. He was given life in prison.

The crises we experience in our relationships are there to help us grow in consciousness, and our romantic relationships are likely to also bring us these experiences. One person with this placement was married three times. His first wife died in surgery, his second marriage was spectacular but lasted just three years, while his third was stable for forty-two years.

Another, who became a sex reformer, remained a virgin through her first marriage up to the age of thirty-seven. Her first child to her second husband was stillborn and her second child was disowned when he married his true love. However, by the age of seventy-three she had a lover who was thirty-five years younger than her.

Our business partnerships can also give us some important opportunities to develop our consciousness, and here again, we have to be careful who is in control. Business partners are there to maximize their return and some are prepared to use the full extent of the law, or go beyond the law to get an advantage.

Walt Disney lost control of his first successful cartoon character because he didn't own the rights. By the time he created Mickey Mouse he made sure his business partnerships were solid, but he still had do the deals required to make it successful, some of which worked and some didn't. He grew through this and eventually achieved global domination.

At the spiritual level we can transcend these relationship issues, rising above the give and take in our relationships to accept them as they are and adopt a more care-taking role, rather than one that seeks to gain advantage.

Leonard Cohen had a small audience for his initial novels and poetry, then had success selling songs to singers and followed this with building a huge audience for his own songs. However, during a period of deep depression in his early forties, he separated from his wife and began to embrace Zen. For a time, he worked in both worlds, the commercial world of music and the spiritual world of striving, until he finally yielded completely and moved to the Zen Centre.

Though he spoke for years of his interest in Zen, it was still a surprise to the establishment when the highly successful songwriter and poet left his finely tailored suits for modest robes, and Hollywood mansions for a small cabin with a narrow cot. He stopped recording at fifty-eight and touring the next year, when he moved up the mountain to do the cooking for the small community, where he rises at 3 am for morning meditation and to begin preparing the day's menu.

And the founder of modern nursing, Florence Nightingale, did not think of herself as deeply religious, however, when she was seventeen she felt that God spoke to her, calling her to a future of service. From that time on her life was changed. Not knowing the nature of the service, she feared making herself unworthy of it by leading the frivolous life that her mother and her social set demanded, and instead was given to periods of what she called "dreams" of how to fulfil her mission.

She thought that women craved sympathy and were not as capable as men, so she preferred the friendship of powerful men, insisting they had done more than women to help her attain her goals. However, some scholars believe that she remained chaste for her entire life, perhaps because she felt such a religious calling to her career. Much of her writing, including her extensive work on religion and mysticism, was published after her death.

Sedna in the Eighth House

With Sedna in the eighth house we are on a path of evolutionary research into the metaphysical world, exploring the connections between people and between the psychic world and physical reality, likely breaking taboos and bringing hidden issues to light in the process.

We might react to this mission by denying it and avoid delving into esoteric matters at all, rejecting God and calling ourselves an atheist. With this approach we are also likely to avoid intimacy, but we will manage quite well most of the time interacting on a fairly superficial level.

However, this is the house of life, death and rebirth. It deals with basic survival issues like sex, money and intimacy, as it relates to power, control, victimization and the need to manipulate others or be manipulated, so these themes are going to manifest in our experience one way or another.

One person with this placement worked as both a prostitute and a model. Her first job was that of a fortune teller, but after her divorce, she became a lady of company for rich businessmen. She led a double life, in the evening receiving customers, but during the day moving in better circles as a model.

She was found dead, however, in her house at the age of thirty-two. Her murderer was never caught, but she was reportedly afraid of her blue book, which contained a handful of names of high-end regular customers, and the police refused to release the details in the book, leading to rumors that one of these high-ranking people was involved in her murder.

Another was a British-American actor, a comedian and bizarre character star. He was the only child of variety-show troupers and grew up in theatrical boarding houses. He was close to his overbearing mom, who died when he was forty-two, and he claimed to be able to communicate with her after her death.

He made more than fifty films, but in the industry, he had a reputation for being a monster who was hard to work with, impossibly difficult and 'basically not a nice man'. Once during a marital fight, he tried to kill a puppy. He abused his friends, and even wrote his children out of his will, developing into an odd man who became haunted by death and who took drugs to enhance sex.

Another is an American dance-pop singer, who was a fabulous success by age nineteen. Her trim teen-age figure and scant costumes were seen on every magazine cover and yet she attributed her wonderful success to her family and her faith in God. As she grew more famous however, she became more impulsive. She got married and separated in the same weekend to a childhood friend. The wedding took place in Las Vegas in the morning when she was twenty-two.

She married a second time later that year and, over the next two years, had two children. However, after only two years, she filed for divorce and was often in the news for increasingly bizarre and often self-destructive behaviour, till the court revoked her child visitation rights. She bounced back the next year however, to make a top earning world tour.

Our case study, Steve Jobs, also had this placement. He was called a 'haunted house' by his high school sweetheart who lived with him and was an early Apple employee. She said he became a threatening monster and their relationship fell apart amid wild recriminations when she became pregnant with his first child. He denied he was the father, despite a positive paternity test, and paid a pittance in child support while living the life of a millionaire.

Sedna in the eighth can also indicate compulsions and inherited health issues. Steve had compulsive diet issues, where he would go on fasts and spend weeks eating the same thing - carrot salad with lemon, or just apples - and then suddenly spurn that food and declare that he had stopped eating it.

Even at a young age, his daughter, Lisa began to realize his diet obsessions reflected a life philosophy, one in which asceticism and minimalism could heighten subsequent sensations. "He believed that great harvests came from arid sources, pleasure from restraint," she noted. "He knew the equations that most people didn't know: Things led to their opposites."

With this placement we have likely spent a number of lifetimes exploring these metaphysical themes from various angles and enter this life with a deep knowing of which we are seldom conscious and with some karmic challenges and likely karmic abilities which will be illustrated by the aspects.

Sedna in the eighth can also indicate psychic or intuitive contact with the dead and other inter-dimensional entities. The father of modern wholistic medicine, Edgar Cayce, another of our case studies, also has this placement.

At the age of 13 he experienced an angelic presence who promised he'd be a healer. He first thought it was his mother, until he ran into her room and she sent him back to bed. That day he was in a daze in school, couldn't spell, and was kept after class. That night he slept on his spelling book and remembered every word. Until then he had done poorly in school; afterward he did well.

His grandson, in a preface to his book about the readings Cayce gave under self-hypnosis, says, "only he can tell this story in all its pathos as he struggles with himself, his family, and with God to discover and come to terms with his destiny. What saved him and allowed him to fulfil his soul's purpose as the benevolent spiritual philosopher so widely admired today, was his enduring faith and the courage to follow his faith as his guidance directed, whatever the cost to him personally."

The nature of the evolutionary research we undertake will collide with existing reality structures throughout our lives and likely raise fears in those who feel threatened by the unknown, who may attack us to defend their world view. When we are young this process is largely unconscious and we may appear to be, or feel like, a victim in these encounters, but in later life the encounters will encourage the evolutionary process.

Edgar Cayce doubted his own readings to start with; however, he overcame his doubts by observing the amazing accuracy and unfailing helpfulness of them in areas such as healing. He was a devout Christian who read the Bible through once for every year of his life, yet he emphasized the importance of comparative study of belief systems from around the world in his work, the underlying principle of which is the oneness of all life, acceptance of all people, and a compassion and understanding for every major religion.

Through the research into the metaphysical world encouraged by this placement, there is likely to be an evolution in our consciousness, which may be may be forced by hard aspects and encouraged by flows, leading to a transcendence to a larger spiritual perspective.

Gurumayi is a female Indian guru, who practices Siddha Yoga and has this to say about her philosophy: "We recognise that in this human life we have a rate opportunity to transform an ordinary perception of this universe into an extraordinary vision. To be on this planet and to behold the universe from the divine perspective is a sign of an illuminated heart. To put this vision to use in the best way possible is a human being's highest duty."

If the evolution of consciousness destined by this Sedna placement is achieved, then the philosophies generated by our research will flower as Sedna moves on to transit the ninth house.

Sedna in the Ninth House

With Sedna in the ninth house we are on a spiritual quest to investigate our beliefs and our search for new horizons. Something will likely motivate us on this quest, something hereditary, or an event early in our lives, or we might remain doggedly at the unconscious level, clinging to our old beliefs, until a confrontation later in life.

The ninth house is about reaching out into the unknown and making sense out of it; however, at an unconscious level, Sedna in the ninth can give us a bit of a blind spot to our own ignorance, a sort of blind faith, or spiritual arrogance, where we tune out all information which doesn't support our view. The second in command of the Nazi war machine for example, had Sedna in the ninth, and he condoned measures leading to mass murder and was eventually hanged.

Or we could be trapped in a blind spot as a child because of the karmic decisions of our parents, like being brought up in religious cult, or being slowly poisoned by them to obtain welfare benefits. Or we may manifest the blind spot simply by not seeing another person, or nor seeing the consequences of how we are treating them and this lack of respect can enrage people, leading to an attack.

There are hints that Sedna in the ninth house can indicate tendencies toward Narcissistic Personality Disorder because of the social nature and intense focus of the life mission. Essentially, the unevolved native can't see past themselves. Donald Trump is an example here. He is someone who hasn't had to challenge himself in life and so has a very undeveloped Sedna, meaning it manifests as a blind spot.

Higher education is another feature of the ninth house, so life-changing experiences may occur at school. This can take any form. One person with this placement was a drug addict, his addiction starting at school, or we might have life-changing accidents that come from the culture of the school, like a practice of hazing, which can damage us physically as well as psychologically.

With this placement over time however, we might become a learned scholar of law, science, politics, or government policies. Sonia Gandhi, an Italian-born Indian politician, met her partner at university. Her partner's mother, who was the Indian president, was assassinated and her partner became president. Then her partner was assassinated and she went into retreat, while she transcended the experience, and then stood for election herself.

With this placement we are natural philosophers, and again here, an early alienation can set up a philosophical confrontation later in life. Ted Kaczynski was an American terrorist, called the Unabomber. As an infant, he was hospitalized for several weeks and his parents were discouraged from visiting him and prevented from holding him in their rare visits. He was never the same. As an adult he resigned a professor's position, moving to a remote shack and living on very little. He then sent several letter bombs before announcing he would quit his bombing campaign if a document arguing that technological progress was harmful was published.

Another person with this placement developed a drinking problem, which led her to join Alcoholics Anonymous, a support organization that was mainly male at that time. She remained sober for the next thirty years of her life and through her work the AA network was expanded and opened to women.

As we develop our consciousness, Sedna in the ninth house encourages us to explore new horizons. Someone else with this placement was an author and feminist at a time when these ideas were challenging the social traditions. She started by publishing her ideas on love at twenty-two and then went on to run an avant grade salon and edit a publication called the *Nouvelle Revue.*

Richard Branson, a British entrepreneur with this placement, wrote in his autobiography of the decision to start an airline: "My interest in life comes from setting myself huge, apparently unachievable challenges and trying to rise above them ... from the perspective of wanting to live life to the full, I felt that I had to attempt it."

At the spiritually evolved level this placement can bring profound spiritual or religious understanding. Alice Bailey was unhappy in her youth and broke away from her early environment at twenty-two to became an evangelist and social worker and then she had a transcendence and founded an occult school which was very influential.

Another is an astrologer who began to study the discipline at thirty-four to disprove it, but became convinced of its validity. He trained in hypnotherapy and also studied Sufism for twenty years and then moved into a synthesis of Vedic with Western astrology and is now a world expert in astrological software as well as a leading psychic and psychic therapist.

Sedna in the Tenth House

With Sedna in the tenth we are on a spiritual quest motivated by our place in society, or events in our professional lives, which will likely be played out in public view. Depending on our level of consciousness, we might be totally unaware of this mission, or be actively seeking an evolutionary social caretaker role. Either way there can be job or career changes involved in our developing consciousness, and some of these may involve crises so severe that we must transcend them to reach a new level of consciousness.

At the unconscious level this may involve acts of arrogance, rebellion, betrayal, or victimization, in which we might be playing either the victim, or the perpetrator role. Someone with this placement had a history of alcoholism and assaults on women, then raped and killed a disabled family friend and played mourner for five years till he was caught.

A homicide victim with this placement was murdered by a controlling lover who stalked her after she broke it off, then kidnapped her from her work. An alcoholic mother pimped out her daughter to a famous actor and was found guilty of contributing to the delinquency of a minor for partying with her and naked men.

With this placement we inherently feel the oneness of humanity, but at this level we may not understand that others don't see this, which might lead us to adopt a deluded social mission or may alternatively inspire us to take visionary leadership.

Rudolf Hess, the deputy leader of the Nazi party, believed that he was obeying supernatural powers and had a mission to end the war when he flew from Germany to Scotland, taking it on his own to attempt negotiations with England. Unfortunately, this was a delusion and Hitler denied his authority, calling him insane. He was imprisoned and spent the next forty-one years in Spandau prison, and for the last twenty-one of these he was the sole inmate.

The development of our consciousness may involve periods where we feel isolated, or alienated within the social context of our lives, while we absorb lessons and build up steam to reengage in a new way. However, as we grow in consciousness we will likely become prominent in our chosen field, because of our integrity, our ability to problem solve and our insights. As a result, we will likely be held in high regard by society for these skills.

Someone with this placement was a pessimistic philosopher, who thought the phenomenal world was the product of 'a blind and insatiable metaphysical will'. He led a solitary life, deeply involved in the study of Buddhist and Hindu philosophies. He was also a misogynist, never marrying and discouraging any friendships, yet he has had a posthumous impact with his writing on aesthetics, morality, and psychology, exerting an important influence.

With Sedna in the tenth house there is likely to be an evolution in our career, which may be forced by hard aspects and encouraged by flows, leading to a transcendence to a larger spiritual perspective.

The first American woman in space and first known LGBT, astronaut, Sally Ride, was asked 'Was it spiritual as you kissed the heavens?" She responded, "You know, what was absolutely amazing to me was the feeling I had looking back at earth . . . how beautiful our planet is, and how fragile it looks." She then convinced NASA to set up a Mission to Planet Earth, to use space technology to understand how man-made and natural shifts are affecting our environment.

At the spiritual level we will likely publicly live our beliefs, like the couple who opened their home to refugees during WW2, at great risk to the family. He had Sedna in the tenth and she in the second. They were both made saints, the first time a husband and wife have both been honored in this way. Or the Dutch Indonesian spiritual leader who founded a new form of Islamic mysticism in which the supplicant is initiated by means of a kind of 'meditative communal submission to divine understanding', a method of communion that involves surrender.

At this level our sense of the oneness of humanity can inspire us to take visionary leadership. Like the Dali Lama, who is the spiritual leader of the Tibetan people. He was born on a straw mat in a cowshed to a farmer's family in a remote part of Tibet and had become the joint most popular world leader by the time he was eighty. This came despite great personal difficulty. He was enthroned during a war with China and forced to sign an agreement on the incorporation of Tibet into China. Then, fearing for his life in the wake of a revolt nine years later, he fled to India, from where he led a government in exile.

And like Albert Einstein, who was a scientist who developed the theory of relativity and the general theory, laying the groundwork for 20th century physics and providing the essential structure of the cosmos. He had Sedna conjunct Mercury, the planet of ideas, and Saturn, the planet of structure, all in the tenth house. His name is synonymous with genius and the scientific definitions of the modern age from the atomic bomb, to space travel, electronics and quantum physics.

However, he was born with a misshapen head and abnormally large body. He learned to talk so late that his parents feared that he was mentally retarded, not until he was three, and was not fluent until he was nine. For a while he was considered subnormal because of his slow development, and his teachers were continually saying that he would never amount to anything. His youth seemed to be one of deliberate rebellion against the establishment of his times.

And the theories he developed were the greatest challenge to Newtonian mechanics that the modern world had ever known, but he had a way of simply conceptualizing and communicating them. He described relativity thus: 'Put your hand on a hot stove for a minute and it seems like an hour. Sit with a pretty girl for an hour and it seems like a minute.'

Experiencing the universe as a harmonious whole, he encouraged the use of intuition to solve problems, marveled at the the mystery of God in nature and applauded the ideals of great spiritual teachers such as Buddha and Jesus. Here's how he put it: "I like to experience the universe as one harmonious whole. Every cell has life. Matter, too, has life; it is energy solidified. Our bodies are like prisons, and I look forward to be free, but I don't speculate on what will happen to me. I live here now, and my responsibility is in this world now. I deal with natural laws. This is my work here on earth."

Sedna in the Eleventh House

With Sedna in the eleventh house we are on a spiritual mission to explore social ideals and the collective consciousness and we will likely immerse ourselves in groups of likeminded people and, over time, build a group of loyal friends to help us on our mission.

At the unconscious level however, this can feel a little like being 'lost at sea in the popular culture of society', which at this stage of mankind's development is still often fairly primitive and violent. So there is a danger of abuse which is simply accepted by our group as normal and so unspoken, or is a hidden side effect of our social group.

Clockwork Orange is a dystopian novel set in a near future English society featuring a subculture of extreme youth violence. The teenage protagonist narrates his violent exploits and his experiences with state authoritys intent on reforming him. Author, Anthony Burgess, who has this placement, called it 'a play of the spirit', as it was written in just three weeks.

Another famous writer suffered from periods of physical, mental and emotional breakdowns, which doctors treated with psychiatric drugs. Her early childhood experience of sexual abuse by her half-brothers was thought to be the cause. Her writing expressed the themes that troubled her the most; life, death, suicide, madness and past memories. She used writing as a distraction from realty and, when she realized she could not write any longer, she chose not to live and drowned herself, fearing the recurrence of a mental breakdown.

Or we could take on an abusive mission ourselves. Someone with this placement shot and killed his mother and seriously wounded his father, before killing himself. He was taking medication for serious psychological problems and had just lost his job, which he had gotten through his dad who was an employee with the firm.

Someone else was a care provider known as "Good Natured Mie" for her cheerful attitude of taking care of people. However, she began to insure them with herself as the beneficiary and over five years attempted one hundred and two murders, succeeding in twenty-seven. Both her father and her mother were among those who were targeted as victims. She was discovered and sentenced to life in prison.

With this placement we are likely to work with organizations and groups that promote our personal values. We are focused on goals for the future and, because of the ideals we come to represent, we may become idolized by large numbers of people, but we may also attract vilification and victimization.

Someone, who at the age of twelve was raped by soldiers and subsequently "thrown out of a window like a sack of potatoes," later established a foundation that helps those with trauma-induced injuries to the central nervous system.

We may be born with innate ideals which will then be conditioned by our early years and drive our lives. If the birth environment is conducive to these, our first collision with social norms will probably come at school when our personality is already well formed and we are less likely to feel victimized by the challenge.

If the birth environment is not conducive to those ideals, we can experience situations where we feel victimized from an early age, and these feelings will then shape our beliefs and the ongoing collisions will either reinforce this or cause us at some point to reject the early ideology and replace it with something more appropriate.

Osama bin Laden, was a member of the wealthy bin Laden family. His mother was his father's tenth wife, but she was Syrian and was called the slave by the rest of the family. Osama was called the son of a slave. This early sense of victimization was formative in shaping his perspective. He projected this onto his fellow Muslims and set out to save them from, as he saw it, the decadent Saudi Arabian leadership in cahoots with the infidels.

Either way our ideals will be tested in the forge of the community and later in life, if strengthened through experience, they are likely to collide with the prevailing norms of the social environment in an evolutionary way. These ongoing collisions will then serve to advance our evolutionary mission.

Through our work there is likely to be an evolution in consciousness, which may be may be forced by hard aspects and encouraged by flows, leading to a transcendence to a larger spiritual perspective.

An American astronaut, who circled the earth for three days in the first manned flight test of the lunar landing module that would later touch down on the moon, was so strongly moved by the sight of the planet, that it led him to take up environmental work, then to being special science advisor to the California Governor and to becoming chairman of the state's independent Energy Commission.

Jules Verne was a French writer widely popular for his science fiction novels and amazing anticipation of future discoveries. Regarded as the father of science fiction, he predicted the use of submarines, helicopters, air conditioning, guided missiles, trips to outer space and motion pictures long before they were developed.

Though he was raised Catholic, he became a deist from his early forties. Deism is a philosophical position that posits that a god does not interfere directly with the world. It also rejects revelation as a source of religious knowledge and asserts that reason and observation of the natural world are sufficient to determine the existence of a single creator of the universe.

Shivabalayogi was a meditation guru who attained self-realization through twelve years meditating in a state of total thoughtlessness for an average of twenty hours a day. For the next three decades he traveled extensively in India and Sri Lanka, initiating over ten million people into meditation. Then he traveled for four years in England and the United States doing the same. His teaching emphasized the need for spiritual practice to achieve self-realization.

If the evolution in consciousness promised by this placement is achieved, then the ideals embraced by this mission will flower as Sedna moves on to transit the twelfth house.

Sedna in the Twelfth House

With Sedna in the twelfth house we are on a spiritual quest to transcend the collective dreams and ambitions of the popular culture in which we find ourselves immersed and rediscover the deep connection with life and appreciation of the universe that we inherently feel inside.

With this placement, forces outside of our control will shape our lives in crucial ways and we may be placed in a caring role, or a self-caring role, early in life, so we grow up deeply caring and able to respond appropriately to situations that may overwhelm other people.

Like Louis Armstrong, who was an American jazz trumpeter, known for his sense of humor and vivid energy. He grew up poor among prostitutes and lowlifes in New Orleans, singing on the street corners in the Old Quarter to help his family. Later, he became a world-class eccentric, his own man, brash and irreverent, with a top-ten hit in every decade for half a century and memorable for his classic, "What a Wonderful World."

We likely have a deep empathy with people as a result and understand that we are each on our own mission, each with a story to tell and challenges to face. This is the house of subconscious realms, of work behind the scenes, and of institutions.

251

At this unconscious level our mission may be more reflective of the collective dreams and ambitions that we sense around us and there is a danger of falling victim to the desire to con people by not revealing ourselves, or to manipulate the collective through the stories we tell.

Someone with this placement was a murderer and con artist who, along with his mother, was sought in murder, missing-persons and fraud cases around America and overseas. They forged a form giving them power of attorney over a sixty-two-year old socialite widow, who then disappeared. Hope for her safe return faded as the police learned of other cases involving the mother and son, as well as suspicious fires and mind-boggling swindles and threats.

Or we could inspire the collective, like Carl Sagan, who as a child is said to have gazed with awe at the heavens and speculated on the existence of life beyond earth. He became a noted authority on planetary atmospheres and surfaces, and his book, *Cosmos* was a best seller. The TV series by the same name was seen by more than 500 million people in sixty countries and he inspired a generation with his enthusiastic lectures, books and documentaries about space and life.

Or we may try and lose ourselves in the crowd with this placement, but then we become a creature of the crowd and open ourselves to abuse by the system. Or we might engage in abusive behaviour in an attempt to influence the system.

An extreme example is Charles Manson, who was a ritual cult leader, a psychopath who had a band of drug-numbed followers. He was the illegitimate son of a teenage prostitute and an army colonel, who was raised by an aunt and uncle. Unable to keep his friendships, and unsuccessful with his music, he began to prophesy chaos, then directed a series of ritual grisly killings in a deluded attempt to start a race war.

Or conversely, we might become an exemplar for people, like the first man to set foot on the moon, Neil Armstrong, who has Sedna right on the twelfth house cusp. He famously said as he took that step: One small step for me! One giant leap for mankind! This statement exemplifies our potential with Sedna in the twelfth house.

The greatest potential for self-mastery, expression of genius and true profession comes out of this house, but only after the karma of self-imprisonment and bondage due to unconscious motivations has surfaced and been resolved. So, it is important with this placement that we learn to judge our own needs and chose when to help others and when to switch off and nurture ourselves. Recreational activities which mix exercise and contemplation, like hiking, or sailing, can be beneficial.

As we grow we likely become conscious of the karma we are carrying which needs resolution in this lifetime, and also of the new dharmic seeds we are sowing for future life work. Through this process there is likely to be an evolution in our consciousness, which may be forced by hard aspects and encouraged by flows, leading to a transcendence to a larger spiritual perspective.

Sedna in the twelfth can indicate a personal interface with the spiritual world, consciously or otherwise. This is the house of past life experiences, and we have likely spent a number of lifetimes exploring spiritual themes and enter this life with a deep love and appreciation of the universe.

Irwyn Greif has been a practicing American psychic from the age of twenty-five, specialising in reincarnation readings. He has written a number of books, notably *The Soul Is a Traveler in Time*, describing his psychic experiences and angel contacts. His book is designed to help raise consciousness levels and give readers an understanding of what lies beyond our five senses, beyond our earthly plane, and even beyond our comprehension.

At some point in our soul development we will find it imperative to integrate our individuated concept of ourselves with the cosmic, social and natural elements surrounding us. This concept of 'self in society' will be tested in the forge of life and is likely, later in life, to challenge the prevailing norms in an evolutionary way.

Immanuel Kant was a German writer, teacher and philosopher, the foremost thinker of the Enlightenment and considered one of the greatest philosophers of all time. He was a short man, scarcely five feet tall, and he had a deformed chest. He suffered from poor health throughout his life, and because of this, he maintained a strict regimen of walking. However, his systematic and comprehensive work on ethics and aesthetics inaugurated a new era in the development of philosophical thought, particularly in the various schools of Idealism.

He lectured on many subjects including logic, metaphysics and moral philosophy. His style was humorous and vivid, and he used many examples from his reading to enliven his subjects. Though often charged with attacking metaphysics, he believed in the existence of God and in a future life and is often described as an ethical rationalist. However, his unorthodox religious teachings eventually brought him into conflict with the King of Prussia, who finally forbade him to teach or write on religious subjects, an order he obeyed until the King died five years later.

27: Sedna in Aspect

Legendary humanistic astrologer, Dane Rudhyar posited that there were three different levels on which each aspect could operate depending on the evolution of our consciousness.

The vast majority of us are at the beginner's level and we will manifest the energy of Sedna from a position of being buried in the dysfunctional swamp of density. Largely unconscious of the all-encompassing spiritual energy of the planet, we'll likely only notice it when it jolts into our reality to correct some imbalance in our lives by bringing illness or victimization, like the judder strip on the road, to steer us back onto the true path of our soul's destiny. And we all start life unconscious and have to develop consciousness as we grow, so we all experience the base level of Sedna.

At the intermediate level, we tire of density and the grief it creates, and we start a spiritual journey to get out of the swamp. This is the key to working with Sedna; she wants to get us on a spiritual path, or to recognize the spiritual path we're on. Then she hits us with transcendent crises, experiences which force us to let go and rise above them, resulting in a huge growth to a new level of consciousness. There is no choice with these crises, and the more we try and solve the crises the more we will get hurt.

At this juncture in human evolution, few people use their planets at the spiritual level, but such people are wonderful to be around. The well-known pattern with the other planets is that the spiritual level is vastly different from the two previous levels and this is also true for Sedna. Here the struggle of the beginner's level is gone, as are the transcendental crises of the intermediate level. At this level everything Saturnian is meaningless and yet everything Sednian has its place. And while each of our lives is just a moment from this perspective, our soul's path over the lifetimes becomes clearer.

In the following pages of aspect interpretations, I am using lots of examples of the life stories of people at each level. The separation into the different levels is somewhat arbitrary however, as we are all likely to exhibit characteristics from each level at different times in our lives. We are all born unconscious of the energy, for example, and must grow to embrace and understand it.

And in each case the life events described are the result of the whole chart, not just Sedna. But since Sedna encompasses all the other planets in the way Saturn used to, we can see the energy of the planet in the overall shape of the life events.

As we read these life stories, the tendency frequently is to compare ourselves with the examples given, but this is a fruitless exercise because we are all unique, so I encourage us to rather feel what we naturally relate to in each of the examples and see if we can feel out which bits in each of the life stories we see echoed in our lives. With all these examples I'm trying to provide a life flavor, in which we might see a hint of how the aspect operates.

28: Sedna / Sun

Conjunction

With the conjunction of Sedna and the Sun, the all-encompassing spiritual energy of Sedna infuses our willpower and sense of self with a high octave spiritual energy, which we might, or might not be conscious of, but which is likely to manifest from an early age in experiences which are 'not of this world.'

The Sun represents our conscious mind, our will to live and our creative life force. Just as the planets revolve around the Sun, it represents the center of our world, and because Sedna represents the ethereal outer limits of that world, the conjunction centers our ego world and our spiritual world in the same place.

At the unconscious level, however, the spiritual power of the conjunction can prove problematic, as we may try to fortify the ego, which is likely to bring out the negative side of the Sun, arrogance and willfulness, and likely to make us self-centered and judgmental. If we repress or ignore the energy, the Sedna conjunction will likely place obstacles in our way so we learn some important lessons. What these are can be inferred from the house placement and the other aspects. There may also be persistent illnesses if we are off the Sedna path.

At this level we may be at the mercy of bigger forces than us. Like Juliana McCourt, who was an American fatality at aged 4 on board an aircraft that struck the World Trade Center in New York City on September 11, 2011, killing all on board instantly. She had Sedna conjunct the Sun in the seventh house of relationships. She and her mother were on their way to Disneyland and then to a spiritual conference at the Deepak Chopra, Chopra Center for Well Being in San Diego.

Or like the Gosselin sextuplets, who were American sextuplets featured in a cable TV reality program "Jon and Kate plus 8." The quads were delivered by caesarian in their 30th week of gestation. Their mom and dad had 3-year-old twins at home. The three girls and three boys were all born within three minutes. Sedna is conjunct their Sun in the twelfth house of karma, quintile Uranus, the planet of broadcasting, conjunct Vesta, the asteroid of regeneration and the Part of Fortune, all in the tenth house of social standing.

After the success of two one-hour specials chronicling Kate Gosselin and her then-husband Jon, 'Surviving Sextuplets and Twins and One Year Later,' the series aired on the Discovery Health channel for the first two seasons before being moved to The Learning Channel. During its run, the series was one of the network's highest-rated programs, with the fifth season premiere seen by a record, 9.8 million viewers, the most watched show of that evening including broadcast television, twice as many viewers as the show's previous series high.

The parents had a messy public split up when the children were 5 years old and the series was later renamed 'Kate Plus 8,' focusing on Kate as a divorced mother raising the children, with Jon appearing less frequently. However, filming was later suspended due to Jon's lawyers delivering letters to TLC demanding that they cease and desist production and barred production crews from the couple's Pennsylvania property. A second season of 'Kate Plus 8' premiered as the children were turning seven and ran for 150 episodes that year, with following seasons when they were 11 years and 12 years.[155]

Or we could be desperately pushing our world view until it collapses under its obvious narrowness. Like Ruth Snyder, who was an American who killed her husband with an accomplice who was her lover. She had Sedna conjunct the Sun in the first house of identity.

She had a passionate extra-marital affair that culminated with the police finding her and her husband bound and gagged and her husband dead. However, she and her lover did an incredibly inept job of staging the supposed burglary and murder, and the insurance investigation led to their arrest. They were both prosecuted and sent to the electric chair.[156]

Or like Richard Rosenthal, who was a serious-looking white American male, who began to have delusions that he was being persecuted by doctors, that he was chosen as a messenger of God, and that his wife was turning into a hostile space alien. He had Sedna conjunct the Sun in the first house of identity.

---

[155] https://en.wikipedia.org/wiki/Kate_Plus_8#Family
[156] Ibid

As a 40-year old upperclass insurance executive, he argued with his wife over a pan of burnt ziti, which led him to kill her and mutilate her body, dissected her and removing her heart and lungs. He was charged with first-degree murder and pled not guilty by reason of insanity. He claimed that he believed she was an alien when he attacked her and was essentially defending himself. Presumably, the alien delusion explained why he ritualistically removed her vital organs after killing her and placed them on an 18inch stake; to assure the "alien" was really dead. At the trial, the prosecution procured witnesses that showed there was a pattern of domestic abuse and the jury rejected his insanity defense. He was found criminally responsible and given a life sentence.[157]

Or, in the extreme, like Paul Touvier, who was a French Nazi collaborator, one of only two Frenchmen to be convicted of war crimes against humanity. He had Sedna conjunct the Sun in the eleventh house of collective consciousness.

During WW2 he joined a militia of the Vichy regime, which collaborated with the Nazis against French partisans. He was appointed head of the intelligence under the direction of Klaus Barbie, and at the age of 29 became second regional head of the Vichy Government.

A couple of years later, after the end of the war, he was sentenced to death in absentia by the French courts for treason and collusion with the enemy. However, when he was 56 he was granted a pardon by the president, before being finally brought to trial at 79 for crimes against humanity. He died a couple of years later in prison near Paris.[158]

If we find ourselves fortifying our ego, or ignoring the energy, we need to look around and re-discover our personal destiny and have the faith to pursue it. It will be right in front of us, but we may have been ignoring it, or taking it for granted, or just focusing on something else.

As we tire of density and the grief it creates, and we start a spiritual journey to get out of the swamp, Sedna rewards us with transcendent

---

[157] http://www.celebrateboston.com/crime/burnt-ziti-murder.htm.
[158] https://en.wikipedia.org/wiki/Paul_Touvier

crises, experiences which force us to let go and rise above them, resulting in a huge growth to a new level of consciousness. There is no choice with these crises, and the more we try and solve them, the more we will get hurt.

Josef Leyendecker is a German-American commercial artist, considered the premier practitioner of commercial art illustration, setting a benchmark of accomplishment in his field during the 20th century. However, with the popularity of photography, his career declined and on his death he was so poor, he was buried in an unmarked grave. His Sedna was conjunct his Sun in the tenth house of profession.

> He apprenticed himself at the age of 15 to a Chicago engraving house and took art lessons in the evenings at the Chicago Art Institute. He and his brother Frank, also a very talented artist, traveled to France five years later. There, the brothers studied in the famous Academie Julian and Colarossi. The brothers were considered the most talented members of their class, and Joe even had a one-man show of his work at the smaller of the two major Salons - The Champs du Mars. The brothers returned to America and opened a studio in Chicago, when Joseph was 24.

> In his heyday, he was the most famous Post cover artist they have ever had. His first cover for the magazine was the next year, before the cover became a miniature poster designed to attract the eye of a newsstand buyer. He returned four years later for a 40-year association in which he produced over 320 covers. His covers for the first issue of 1906 featured a winged cherub that was the predecessor of the "New Year's Baby" - a concept that still holds today.

> At 31 he began a relationship with Arrow Collars for whom he created just one of the icons he introduced into American psyche. The Arrow Collar Man was one of the most successful advertising images in history. Girls swooned over the images of handsome young men, all painted from models who each received mountains of fan mail each time a new face appeared in the ads. The first model he used was Charles Beach. Leyendecker was undoubtedly gay. He met Charles four years

earlier and lived with him for fifty years. Charles was originally a model but soon became his manager and assistant.[159]

Jessica Lynch was an American marine assigned to the Iraq War. An adorable 19-year-old honey-blonde, Jessica was captured in an Iraqi raid. She has Sedna conjunct the sun in the twelfth house of the unconscious.

In a Special Ops raid, US soldiers wearing night goggles brought helicopters into the southern Iraqi city to carry out a daring rescue raid. The petite soldier was held in a second-floor room with fractures in both legs, her right arm, ankle and foot. Intelligent briefings relate that some of her wounds were the results of extensive torture.

She came up missing after Iraqi forces ambushed an Army supply convoy, four days before her 20th birthday. The details of her imprisonment and her rescue were subsequently much discussed in the news with reports that the U.S. military exaggerated the rescue. There was also a question about whether she was tortured, or whether all her injuries were sustained in the fighting just before her capture.

A book written by Rick Bragg with her help, *I Am a Soldier, Too: The Jessica Lynch Story* was released and a TV biopic was produced and televised. The book alleges that she was raped while in captivity and that she does not remember this mistreatment. Iranian doctors dispute that she was raped, but she underwent rigorous physical therapy and treatment for her serious injuries and emotional trauma.

Nevertheless, at 24 she appeared before a House Committee on Oversight and Government Reform and testified that the tales about her capture in Iraq were not true, that they were embellished to make her seem like a hero. She said, "The bottom line is the American people are capable of determining their own ideals for heroes and they don't need to be told elaborate tales.[160]

---

[159] www.bpib.com/illustrat/leyendec.htm
[160] https://en.wikipedia.org/wiki/Jessica_Lynch

Alan Clay

Jerry Brown is an American politician, born into politics as the son of a governor. He is considered one of the most exciting and controversial leaders of his generation. He has Sedna conjunct the Sun in the ninth house of knowledge.

After four years of Jesuit training, he went to Berkeley and Yale Law schools. From school, Brown entered a Los Angeles law firm and, as a natural progression, went into politics, becoming Secretary of State for California at 32 and, from the age of 36, a two-term governor of California.

He retreated from political life at 45, after a defeat in a run for the U.S. Senate. During the next six years, he traveled and studied. He worked on a political journal called *New Perspectives* and raised money for the Democrats. After two years, he decided to explore more inner and outer dimensions. He traveled to Japan where he lived in tradition style and studied Zen meditation with an 80-year-old Buddhist teacher. He then visited Mother Teresa in India and, representing CARE, visited Bangladesh as a special envoy.

At 51 he returned to the political fray as a candidate for chairman of the California Democratic Party. His political career also included unsuccessful runs for President at 38 and 42 and a third failed bid at 54 for the Democratic Presidential nomination. However, never able to resist the lure of a campaign for long, he became Mayor of Oakland at 60 in a landslide and ran again for Governor of the state at 72 and won the election. He is currently in the second term of his second period as Governor of California.

Known as a workaholic, his public presentation is awkward with wooden carriage and no place to put his hands. He speaks spontaneously with no teleprompter or index reminder cards and no speechwriter to craft his words. It's hard to tell just when the awkwardness disappears because suddenly, what he has to say is so absorbing that listeners are engrossed by the rapid fire of his intellect. He has always been a visionary and a renegade, playing outside the rules, sometimes called a Dream Merchant or Governor Moonbeam for his interests in religion, philosophy, metaphysics. Instead of "no comment," he has valid and vivid opinions. Instead of evasion, he shoots straight from the hip.[161]

Humour can be one path to transcend the quicksand of Sedna, giving us the objectivity to step back from the edge and also, with the conjunction to the Sun, a creativity and sense of self- direction in our work. If we are feeling uncomfortable with the weight of Sedna in our lives, we would be well advised to cultivate our sense of humour.

Bill Irwin is an American actor, clown and comedian, who combined his talents to create characters for comedy skits in performance art, a unique form of entertainment. He began as a vaudeville-style stage performer and has been noted for his contribution to the renaissance of American circus. His Sedna is conjunct the Sun in the twelfth house of the unconscious.

> Almost everyone in his family was stage-struck, with his maternal grandfather putting on plays and pageants and his father designing sets for community theatre productions. He made a stage debut when he was still in school with a post-modern dance group and performed in student productions at high schools in the U.S. and in Belfast, Northern Ireland, where he spent his senior year as an American Field Service exchange student. he then studied theatre at the University of California, and the California Institute of the Arts in Valencia, which was a new experimental arts institution founded by Walt Disney, when his curriculum included dance, mime, gymnastics and t'ai chi.

> At 24 Irwin decided to attend Clown College, an intensive training school for circus performers at the winter headquarters of Barnum & Bailey Circus in Florida. He mastered the basics of elephant riding, juggling and acrobatics. Returning to San Francisco, he answered a newspaper ad for jugglers and was hired to be a clown with the Pickle Family Circus, a small one-ring act. He supplemented his income by teaching and performing in city schools and by entertaining at trade shows, festivals and private parties.

> In his spare time, he created comedy sketches, and at 27, he and some of his collaborators were invited to perform their short

---

[161] https://en.wikipedia.org/wiki/Jerry_Brown

sketches. The trio toured Italy, France and the Netherlands. Upon returning to the United States, Irwin joined the Oberlin Dance Collective, and his comic inventions were so impressive that he was hired to present skits as part of a new, late-night series of performance events. This introduced him to a wider audience and earned him a special Obie Award for "inspired clowning" at the age of 31.

Obsessed with his work, he has been compared to such greats as Charlie Chaplin and Buster Keaton for his unique form of entertainment, which includes juggling and tumbling. At 34 he received the Guggenheim Fellowship and a five-year MacArthur Foundation Fellowship, the first active performing artist to receive the award in the foundation's history.[162]

David Letterman is an American contemporary humorist, producer and talk show host and winner of an Emmy as Best Host and Best Writer for a Daytime Variety Series. He has Sedna conjunct the Sun in the twelfth house of the unconscious.

He started on local radio and TV while still in college and moved to Los Angeles at 28 to do stand-up comedy and comedy writing and then moved into TV, appearing as a favourite on Carson's *Tonight Show.*

He hosted a latenight television talk show, *Late Night* with David Letterman, for 33 years, beginning when he was 36. In total, Letterman hosted 6,028 episodes of *Late Night* and the sequel *Late Show*, surpassing friend and mentor Johnny Carson as the longest-serving late night talk show host in American television history. Obsessed and intense, his life revolves around his show, and he's only complete and happy when he's working.

When he was 62 he announced on his show that he had spent the day testifying to a Grand Jury that he was being blackmailed for $2 million in a threat to reveal that he had sexual relations with women who worked on his show. He decided to address his viewers himself and revealed that three weeks prior, he had found the threat in a package left in his car, that he had consulted authorities and on their advice, had issued a fake

---

[162] https://en.wikipedia.org/wiki/Bill_Irwin

check. A man was then arrested and charged with blackmail and extortion.[163]

At this juncture in human evolution, few of us use our planets at the spiritual level, but many of us are striving to, and such people are wonderful to be around. As with the other planets, the spiritual level of evolution is vastly different with Sedna from the two previous levels. Here the conjunction with the Sun brings a higher transpersonal consciousness, which is centered in the evolution of humanity and of all life forms on the planet.

Once we embrace the Sedna energy, which is the oneness of everything, our nurturing becomes an expression of Sedna consciousness and it becomes devotional in nature. The struggle of the beginners' level is gone, as are the transcendental crises of the intermediate level. At this level everything Saturnian is meaningless and yet everything Sednian has its place.

It takes hard work to learn the lessons that Sedna brings and to grow to be able to embrace the energy, but once this is achieved we will likely feel a strong calling and will likely play an important part in the current consciousness evolution. Once we find the faith to pursue our destiny we will do so with an unshakeable confidence that we are on the right path, despite the challenges of manifesting the ethereal Sedna energy in the material plane.

Ram Dass is an American educator and author, who was fired as a Harvard professor for early experiments with LSD and other hallucinogenic drugs, and who became a follower of the path of Eastern philosophy. He has Sedna conjunct the Sun and also conjunct Uranus, the planet of intuition, all in the tenth house of profession.

> He became a psychology professor at Harvard and was immersed in sports cars, antiques and even an airplane, pursuing the "middle-class bachelor" life until his early 30s, when hallucinogens changed his world view.

> With his friend, Timothy Leary, he allowed undergraduates to participate in drug experiments, for which both he and Leary were fired from Harvard when he was 32. He traveled to India where he met a guru who changed his life and eventually, his

---

[163] https://en.wikipedia.org/wiki/David_Letterman

name. Ram Dass means "servant of God" in Hindi. He began to see hallucinogens as shallow and artificial. He became a Guru himself, a leader to those on the spiritual quest. He reportedly struggled with relationship issues, including sex, alternating between celibacy and bisexuality.

In his 50s he urged people to engage in selfless service and he worked with the homeless, setting up a hospice for dying people and helping to start a foundation to treat the blind in third-world countries, which has funded cataract operations, as well as training for local doctors. He raised half a million dollars for this work during a 60-city lecture tour. His books included, *Be Here Now*, published when he was 40; *How Can I Help*, published at 54, and *Journey of Awakening*, at 59.

At 66 he had a stoke, leaving his left side partly paralyzed. It was ironic that a master at speaking, a brilliant teacher and hilarious raconteur who could hold thousands rapt now could not speak, that he had been silenced by illness. He embarked on a long course of rehabilitation. He said the stroke had taught him to appreciate silence. After the stroke, his friends said, "He became much sweeter and softer."[164]

And finally, our case study, Edgar Cayce, the father of wholistic medicine, has Sedna conjunct the Sun in the eighth house of psychic sensitivity.

He is an American mystic who is known as the Sleeping Prophet, because, while in a sleep state he could discuss history, geology, metaphysics, philosophy and medicine. He was born to uneducated farming parents. He attended country school only as far as the eighth grade. As a child he had a strong desire to become a preacher, which he never formally realised.

He prayed to be able to help others, especially children, and had a spiritual vision at age 13 that told him he would be able to accomplish this dream of service. A lady bathed in light told him to sleep with his head on his books and then he would be able to remember what was in them. This was at a time when he was having trouble in school, and his father was beating him for not

---

[164] https://en.wikipedia.org/wiki/Ram_Dass

being able to spell the words in his lessons correctly. Soon after, he showed signs of special abilities when he found that he could sleep on his school books and have photographic recall of every page.

Two years after his first vision he was pronounced dead from drowning but recovered. At 23 he developed a severe case of laryngitis which stopped him working as an insurance salesman, a job he hated. Doctors couldn't cure it. In desperation he tried hypnosis from a traveling practitioner and was cured after several treatments. Under hypnosis, he gave his first psychic reading at 24 and learned that he could give accurate medical diagnoses and healing recommendations for himself and for other people.

He gave approximately 30,000 life-readings and medical diagnosis to people during his lifetime. He founded a hospital, a university and the Association for Research and Enlightenment that promotes research on his readings and continues his work. Throughout his life, he claimed no special abilities and did not capitalise financially or otherwise on his gifts. The readings never offered a set of beliefs or "religion" to be embraced, but instead focused on the idea that every person should test in his or her own life the principles presented.

Though he was a devout Christian who read the Bible through once for every year of his life, his work emphasised the importance of comparative study of belief systems from around the world. In fact, some of the metaphysical material that came through the sleeping Cayce was at first confusing and distressing to him in his waking state. However, he overcame his doubts, as have others, by observing the amazing accuracy and unfailing helpfulness of the readings in other areas, such as healing. The underlying principle of the readings is the oneness of all life, acceptance of all people, and a compassion and understanding for every major religion.[165]

---

[165] https://en.wikipedia.org/wiki/Edgar_Cayce

Opposition

With the opposition between Sedna and the Sun, the all-encompassing spiritual energy of Sedna challenges our willpower and sense of self. With this aspect we will tend to see the world in terms of being challenged and so are likely to be always ready for these challenges and to expect them everywhere.

The Sun represents our conscious mind, our will to live and our creative life force. Just as the planets revolve around the Sun, it represents the center of our world, and because Sedna is the ethereal outer limits of that world, the opposition sets up our ego world in relief against our wider spiritual world.

However, we create our ego world through our expectations, so we need to discern which are the important challenges for us and not get buried in meaningless challenges. If we repress or ignore the energy, the opposition is likely to bring out the negative side of the Sun, which is arrogance and willfulness, and is likely to make us self-centered and judgmental.

At the unconscious level this can prove problematic, as it can put us at the mercy of bigger forces than us. Like Mei Mei, who is an American adoptee and kidnap victim. She has Sedna exactly conjunct the MC, the cusp of the tenth house of social standing, opposite her Sun, on the cusp of the fourth house of home. She was born in America to a Chinese mother, who gave her up for adoption. The foster mother was given custody of the child at one and a half, however the birth mother kidnapped the girl and took her back to China just before her third birthday.

Or like Anne Dechauffour, a French tourist who was shot at point-blank range with her mother in a terrorist attack in the parking area of the Westgate Shopping Mall in Nairobi at 18. She had Sedna conjunct the north node in the sixth house of service, opposite the Sun conjunct Pluto, the planet of life and death, and Juno, the asteroid of partnership, all in the twelfth house of karma. She was a model in London and was studying cinema.

At the unconscious level there could also be further issues, where we are always trying to prove our worth to others. And it can also bring a rebelliousness willfulness, which can lead to abuse and authority issues, or problems with the law.

Like Gerald Craffey, who is an American who raped and stabbed to death a disabled 33-year-old woman when he was 24. He has Sedna in the tenth house of social standing, opposite his Sun, which is conjunct Ixion, the planet of lawlessness, and Venus, the planet of relationships, and Quaoar, the planet of new perspectives all in the fourth house of home.

> He was friends with the victim's brother and was back in the lives of her family right after the murder, even helping clean up the victim's blood in the house. Five years later, he admitted to killing her and was sentenced to life in prison, with the chance of parole in 15 years. He first appeared before the parole board at 43. "I was nothing but a heartless coward who used your trust to hide among you," he said at the hearing. However, the victim's daughter, who was 8 at the time, said "Someone that can commit the crime, first off, and act so normal and live such a normal life, still come around with our family…There is no way that someone like this could be rehabilitated." The board denied his release, saying he "gave no indication that he had any understanding of his apparent sexually deviant behavior." They also pointed to his 16 disciplinary reports in prison.[166]

As we tire of density and the grief it creates, and we start a spiritual journey to get out of the swamp, Sedna rewards us with transcendent crises, experiences which force us to let go and rise above them, resulting in a huge growth to a new level of consciousness. There is no choice with these crises, and the more we try and solve them, the more we will get hurt.

Elizabeth Smart is an American who went missing at age fourteen, abducted from her home as her family slept. Her Sedna is in the third house of communication, opposite her Sun, which is conjunct Pluto, the planet of transformation in the ninth house of knowledge.

> The second of six kids, she grew up in a close-knit Mormon family, reading scripture and praying morning and evening. On the night of her disappearance the family prayed together and kissed goodnight; however, sometime in the early morning

---

[166] http://www.wcvb.com/article/murder-victim-s-daughter-fights-parole-for-mom-s-killer/8230537

hours, a man entered the bedroom Elizabeth shared with her younger sister and spirited her away.

No ransom note was found and no trace of her was reported until she was spotted walking in a suburb of the same city with a shaggy-haired vagabond nine months later. During her ordeal, she spent a great deal of the time near her home wearing disguises and veils in public. The Smart family believes she was brainwashed, citing that she did not call out for help, or apparently try to escape, even when she heard rescuers call out her name.

However, nearly two years after her rescue, her father said that she is "just a normal teenager who likes shopping and going to the movies with friends." A self-assured young woman and college graduate, she confronted her kidnapper at his trial and then accepted a job as a contributor for a television network in its coverage of missing persons.[167]

Michael Aquino is an American founder of the Temple of Set and one of America's leading Satanists. He has Sedna in the third house of ideas opposite the Sun in the ninth house of knowledge.

Although the temple was formally incorporated when he was 29, its magical and philosophical roots are ancient. Set is considered the supreme personification of evil, the Prince of Darkness and his worship can be traced to pre-dynastic times.

A few Satanic groups have survived to carry on the tradition of Satan, and Aquino argues that through the Renaissance alone, some 13 million accused Satanists were tortured and burned to death, considered infidels and heathens. At 29 he resigned from the Church of Satan and established his own group, founded as a church and incorporated as a non-profit organisation with both federal and tax-exempt status.

He was formerly a Lt. Colonel in the US Army and believed his to be a more sophisticated form of Satanism. However, rumours began to emanate from the several hundred members of the sect regarding child molestation in satanic rituals. He vehemently denied such claims, stating that they were harassment by

---

[167] https://en.wikipedia.org/wiki/Elizabeth_Smart

opponents. He stated on Oprah and other TV talk shows that Satan is more an energy force than a person, so he is not an embodiment. However, he was reassigned by the Army to a post in Missouri and has apparently faded from his diabolic mission.[168]

T. S. Eliot was an American-British poet, playwright, literary critic and editor; he was a leader of the modernistic movement in poetry. Eliot was awarded both the British Order of Merit and the Nobel Prize for Literature. He had Sedna in the sixth house of service, opposite his Sun in the twelfth house of the unconscious.

> From private high schools he went on to Harvard University, where he received his Bachelor of Arts degree. He went to France, attending philosophy lectures at the Sorbonne and reading poetry. These studies helped him find his own voice and style. For three years from the age of 23 he studied Sanskrit and read Indian philosophy back at Harvard.

> At 26 he established residence in London and at 39 he was confirmed in the Church of England and became a British subject. At 31 he published "Poems" which included "Gerontion," a meditative interior monologue in blank verse like nothing before published in English. His career as an editor was always secondary to his main interests. From 34 to 51 he edited his own quarterly, the *Criterion*, which was the most distinguished international critical journal of its time.

> At 37 he started working for the publishing house of Faber and Faber, where he eventually became a director. Probably one of the most erudite English poets of his time, his first important published work and the first masterpiece of modernism in English was "The Love Song of J. Alfred Prufrock." With the publication of his most famous poem about the disenchantment and disgust after World War I, "The Waste Land," at the age of 34 he earned an international reputation.[169]

H.G. Wells was a British writer, historian, prognosticator, economist and novelist who was known for his sci-fi predictions of the future. He had

---

[168] https://en.wikipedia.org/wiki/Temple_of_Set
[169] https://en.wikipedia.org/wiki/T._S._Eliot

Sedna in the first house of identity, opposite his Sun in the seventh house of relationships.

> After a sketchy education, he went on to graduate from London University with a BS at 22. He taught biology and wrote educational articles, writing his first novel at 29, and went on to write many other works. His book, *The War of the Worlds,* which was read on radio by Orson Wells, caused the famous Mars invasion panic when he was 72. He was an enormously prolific and popular writer, capturing the early twentieth century's need to rebel and overthrow the oppressive Victorian conventions.[170]

Thor Heyerdahl was a Norwegian adventurer, a sailor and descendent of the Vikings who sailed a balsa raft, the "Kon Tiki," across the Pacific at the age of 33 with a crew of five. He also had Sedna in the first house of identity, opposite his Sun in the seventh house of relationships.

> At 55 he attempted to cross the Atlantic in "Ra," but failed 600 miles short of land. His second attempt the next year, in the "Ra II," succeeded. Fluent in six languages and married three times, with five kids in various parts of the world, Heyerdahl has rarely stayed any place for long. After getting his degree in biology and geography, he set off for the South Seas at 23. He took his young bride on his first field trip; they had two sons and divorced when he was 34.
>
> His second wife bore him three daughters in their 20 years together, divorcing amicably when he was 55. At 75 the world-class adventurer was investigating archaeological ruins in Peru. He maintained a daunting pace of research, lectures and public debate over his unconventional theories on human migration. His third wife said he made 70 airline trips at the age of 87.[171]

Richard Alan Meier is an American architect, winner of the Pritzker Prize, the highest accolade of architecture at the age of 50. He has Sedna in the sixth house of service, opposite the Sun in the twelfth house of institutions.

> He is known for his elegant and avant-garde style and for works which are personal, vigorous and original. Considered a classic

---

[170] https://en.wikipedia.org/wiki/H._G._Wells
[171] https://en.wikipedia.org/wiki/Thor_Heyerdahl

modernist, he operates in the traditional-function style of Le Corbusier, whom he met in Europe after college. For 13 years he taught architectural design and at 29 he opened a private practice, gaining national attention by the age of 33.

At 50 he was commissioned with the design of a lifetime, the 13-year construction of the Getty Museum in Santa Monica. He beat out a roster of 32 international architects to win the outstanding job. The cultural Camelot was over $1 billion in the making and is without doubt a Mecca for Southern California residents, as well as tourists from every country in the world.

The six buildings on 24 acres offer a breathtaking view of the Los Angeles basin from the mountains to the ocean. The Museum, a centre of priceless art and awesome architectural excellence, opened to the public when he was 63. For the prior dozen years, the New York based Meier spent two weeks of every month in Los Angeles, living in a small ranch house on the site.[172]

At this juncture in human evolution, few of us use our planets at the spiritual level, but many of us are striving to, and such people are wonderful to be around. As with the other planets, the spiritual level of evolution is vastly different with Sedna from the two previous levels. Here the opposition with the Sun brings a higher transpersonal consciousness, which is centered in the evolution of humanity and of all life forms on the planet.

Once we embrace the Sedna energy, which is the oneness of everything, our nurturing becomes an expression of Sedna consciousness and it becomes devotional in nature. The struggle of the beginners' level is gone, as are the transcendental crises of the intermediate level. At this level everything Saturnian is meaningless and yet everything Sednian has its place.

Kees Boeke was a Dutch civil engineer, reformist educator, pacifist and Quaker missionary. He had Sedna in the eleventh house of collective consciousness, opposite his Sun in the fifth house of children and creativity.

Stimulated by the Sermon on the Mount and the idea of brotherhood of man, he founded the Christian International

---

[172] https://en.wikipedia.org/wiki/Richard_Meier

Brotherhood of Reconciliation, that propagated radical pacifism, messianism, vegetarianism and abstinence. His vision of society was a mix of the ideas of the Quaker community and the anarchist commune thought.

As taxes were used for military spending, he refused to pay them. The Dutch government reacted with the confiscation of his house and property so that the family had to live in tents. At 45 he took his eldest children out of the Montessori school, because he refused to pay the school fees via the state. He started to teach them at home. This was the start his 'Workplace Children's Community', where children got an unconventional and anti-authoritarian education. He stayed there till his forced retirement at 70.

As he was radically opposed to the state and its symbols, he refused till he was 50 to use a passport, money, and public facilities like post-office, telephone and railway. He didn't go to the state police when others tested him by stealing 'community property'. Their house was always open for quests and refugees, but their eight children had sometimes only one room for themselves in the villa.

Queen Juliana admired his radical idealism and sent her 3 daughters to his school. She was opposed to private lessons and wanted that her children grew up like other children in a stimulating environment. Her individual choice was remarkable, as he was an anarchist. Maybe a factor was that both Boeke and the Queen were befriended with a mystic, Greet Hofmans. Four years after the girls started the school however, Prince Bernhard denied the mystic accesses to the palace and the next year he took his daughters away from the school.

After his forced retirement, Boeke became depressive. He had idealistically hoped and worked for a better world, but the cold war and the thread of an atomic inferno became reality. At 71 he travelled to Lebanon to try to set up a school for Arab refugees, but the project failed and he returned to Holland, withdrew and wrote books. At 73 he published the book, *Cosmic View, The Universe in 40 Jumps*, which presents a seminal view of the universe, from the galactic to the microscopic scale that inspired several films like *Cosmic Zoom* and *Powers of Ten*.[173]

Martin Heidegger was an German existentialist philosopher who was one of the most influential voices and foremost thinkers and writers of the 20th century. He had Sedna in the fourth house of home, opposite his Sun, which is conjunct Ceres, the planet of nurture, in the tenth house of profession.

> With the publication of his first book, *Being and Time*, when he was 38, he achieved instant fame as one of the spokesmen of 20th century existentialism. Though unfinished, *Being and Time* is one of the central philosophical works of the 20th century. In the first division of the work, Heidegger attempted to turn away from "ontic" questions about beings to ontological questions about Being and recover the most fundamental philosophical question: the question of Being, of what it means for something to be.

> Heidegger argued that being human is defined by care, that it's practically engaged and is a concernfull mode of being-in-the-world. This was in opposition to rationalist thinkers like René Descartes who located the essence of man in our thinking abilities. For Heidegger thinking is thinking about things originally discovered in our everyday practical engagements. The consequence of this is that our capacity to think cannot be the most central quality of our being because thinking is a reflecting upon this more original way of discovering the world.

> In the second section, he argues that human being is even more fundamentally structured by its temporality, or its concern with, and relationship to time, existing as a structurally open 'possibility-for-being'. He emphasised the importance of authenticity in human existence, involving a truthful relationship to our being thrown into a world, and to our being-towards-death, the finitude of the time and being that we are given, and the closing down of our various possibilities for being through time.

> Heidegger also made critical contributions to philosophical conceptions of truth, arguing that its original meaning was un-

---

[173] https://en.wikipedia.org/wiki/Kees_Boeke

concealment, to philosophical analyses of art as a site of the revelation of truth, and to philosophical understanding of language as the "house of being".[174]

Semi-sextile, Sextile, Trine

With the flowing aspects between Sedna and the Sun, the all-encompassing spiritual energy of Sedna aligns with our willpower and sense of self and, while we may not consciously be aware of this, we will have sense that the world is made up of a rich tapestry of destinies and embrace ours with a natural acceptance.

The Sun represents our conscious mind, our will to live and our creative life force. Just as the planets revolve around the Sun, it represents the center of our world, and because Sedna represents the ethereal outer limits of that world, the flowing aspects align our ego world and our wider spiritual world.

If this process is largely unconscious, we may come across to others as a confident amateur, not having quite done the homework to really understand the situation, but probably able to 'wing it' anyway. The times when winging it doesn't work will provide the opportunities for us to step back and consciously understand what otherwise we may simply have naturally accepted.

If we repress or ignore the energy, it is likely to bring out the negative side of the Sun, which is arrogance and willfulness, and is likely to make us self-centered and judgmental. However, whether consciously, or unconsciously, we will likely play a role in the current evolutionary cycle and, as our consciousness develops, we will be able to more effectively use the Sedna energies, rather than be used by them.

At the unconscious level, even the flows between these two planets can be challenging, because while our ego and spiritual worlds align, we might delude ourselves into thinking that the ego can direct the spiritual, or that we might be able to sidestep the karmic consequences of our actions.

ike Kenneth Kimes Jr, who is an American murderer and con artist, who, along with his mother, was sought in murder, missing-persons and fraud cases around America and overseas. He had Sedna in the twelfth house of the unconscious, conjunct the ascendant, the cusp of the first house

---

[174] https://en.wikipedia.org/wiki/Martin_Heidegger

of identity, and conjunct Juno, the asteroid of partnership, which is just in his first house. His Sedna is also opposite Ixion, the planet of lawlessness, in the seventh house of relationships.

He perpetrated a scheme with his mother, whereby she would assume the identity of their landlady, an 82-year-old socialite and then appropriate ownership of her $7.7 million Manhattan mansion. Police believe his mother, an ex-con who called herself the Dragon Lady, may have posed as the socialite for notaries in an attempt to get the deed to her house. They forged a form giving them power of attorney over the widow, who then disappeared.

His mother spent the better part of her life fleecing people of money, expensive merchandise, and real estate, either through elaborate con games, arson, forgery, or outright theft. She committed insurance fraud on numerous occasions, frequently by committing arson and then collecting money for property damage. She delighted in introducing her husband Kenneth as an ambassador, a ploy that even gained the couple access to a White House reception during the Ford administration, and would sometimes even impersonate Elizabeth Taylor, whom she resembled slightly.

When Ken Sr. died, Ken Jr was groomed by his mother to be her new partner. He was handsome, blue-eyed, a sharp-dresser. Finally, picked up when he was 25, he made headlines later that year when he held a TV producer hostage for four hours after putting a pen to her throat during an interview at the jail. He missed his mother terribly, as she was being held at the women's prison in solitary confinement.

Despite the fact that the socialite's body was never found, both mother and son were convicted of murder in 2000, in no small part because of the discovery of the mother's notebooks detailing the crime and notes written by the victim, who was extremely suspicious of the pair. During the trial for another murder he confessed that after his mother had used a stun gun on the socialite, he strangled her, stuffed her corpse into a bag and deposited it in a dumpster. Tried and convicted, he was sentenced to 125 years in prison.[175]

Or we may not see the difference between ourselves and what we see as the meaningful context of our lives, and so may react dramatically to changes as if they threaten our very existence.

Like Richard Herrin, who was an American homicide perpetrator who killed his college sweetheart when he was 24. He had Sedna in the third house of communication, trine his Sun in the twelfth house of the unconscious. His Sedna is also opposite Neptune, the planet of dreams and illusions, in the ninth house of knowledge, and trine Pluto, the planet of life and death, in the eighth house of life and death.

> A Yale graduate he bludgeoned his ex-girlfriend, a Yale college senior, to death with a hammer as she lay sleeping in her parents' home because she wanted to end their relationship. The two college students had been dating for approximately two years at the time that he graduated and moved to Texas to attend a graduate program. Over the next year they grew apart. She wanted to date other people. Concerned about it, he arranged with her knowledge to come to discuss their relationship.

> Her parents not knowing there was trouble in the relationship allowed him to stay at their home. She told him that she wanted to break off their relationship. He was to leave the next day. He was staying in a guest room on the opposite end of the home. During the early morning hours, he went down to the basement, found a hammer and smashed her skull to pieces. He was convicted and served 17 years in state prison. After his release, he moved to New Mexico where he was hired by a mental health foundation. [176]

Even at the unconscious level, however, these aspects can give us the resilience and 'joy of life' needed to survive the dramatic changes in our lives, without the struggles of some of the other aspects.

Jeanne Calment was a French longevity case, the longest living person, who lived to 122 and whose birth date can be authenticated. She had

[175] https://en.wikipedia.org/wiki/Sante_Kimes

[176] https://en.wikipedia.org/wiki/Bonnie_Garland_murder_case

Sedna in the first house of identity, semi-sextile her Sun in the twelfth house of the unconscious.

> By the time of her death she was blind and nearly deaf, but her mind and wit remained sharp. Never sorry for herself, always ready with a quip, she set up her own website after being shown how to work a computer. Her one child, born when she was 23, died when she was 59. Her husband died when she was 67, and her only grandson was killed in a car crash when she was 88. She took vigorous daily walks up to the age of 115, when she broke her hip. At 100, she still rode her bike and she quit smoking at 118. For her 121st birthday, she recorded a rap CD, the release of which sparked a media circus.[177]

As we tire of density and the grief it creates, and we start a spiritual journey to get out of the swamp, Sedna rewards us with transcendent crises, experiences which force us to let go and rise above them, resulting in a huge growth to a new level of consciousness. There is no choice with these crises, and the more we try and solve them, the more we will get hurt.

Mia Farrow is an American actress and activist, who has appeared in more than 50 films and won numerous awards, including a Golden Globe. She has Sedna in the twelfth house of the unconscious, sextile her Sun in the sixth house of service.

> She is known for her extensive work as a UNICEF Goodwill Ambassador in Africa. She had a bout with polio when she was nine, an experience that shaped her life from then on. Exiled to a ward in Los Angeles General Hospital, she lay on a bed among the suffering and dying. She recovered from the illness, but tragedy struck again four years later when her brother Michael died in a plane crash.

> Her parent's marriage suffered under that blow and, while her mother revived her stage career on Broadway, her father quit working and drank heavily, dying of a heart attack 4 years later, when Mia was 17 and in a convent school in England. The following year she left the school for New York where she began drama training. With one off-Broadway play under her belt, she

---

[177] https://en.wikipedia.org/wiki/Jeanne_Calment

took the role of a teenager in the TV series "Peyton Place." The show became a major hit of the season, and made the 19-year-old Mia, a star. Her third film, *Rosemary's Baby*, was a mega success.

Before she had turned 20 she began an affair with 29-year-older Frank Sinatra. When the press picked up on the unlikely romance between the sophisticated and debonair Sinatra and the skinny, awkward teenager, they documented every move. The couple married when she was 21, but their odds were not great, with a difference in age, style and custom, conflicting careers and diametrically opposed temperaments, and they split up after a year.

At 23, she took off on a spiritual quest to India, where she spent part of the year at the ashram of Maharishi Mahesh Yogi, studying Transcendental Meditation. Her visit received worldwide media attention because of the presence of all four members of The Beatles, but was cut short when the guru wrapped her in his hairy arms one day during a private meditation.

Not long after, she began a dalliance with the married conductor Andre Previn and had their twin sons at 25. When his divorce came final six months later, they married. It was the time of the Vietnam War and she and Previn decided to adopt a Vietnamese war orphan. While filming *The Great Gatsby* at 28, she became pregnant with her third son. A second daughter arrived from Saigon when she was 29. Three years later, the Previn's adopted an older child who had been abandoned on the streets of Seoul, a girl named Soon-Yi.

By 33, the marriage had reached critical mass. Her husband was steadily on tour, and she was involved with the six kids. Separating from him, she took the children to Manhattan and the following year played in a Broadway production of *Romantic Comedy*. One night after a performance, her friend Michael Caine introduced her to Woody Allen. Allen lived in a penthouse on Fifth Avenue directly across Central Park from her apartment. She felt confident and happy in the beginning about the affair they began.

They began to spend weekends at each other's apartment, though he was uncomfortable parenting material and they never lived together as a full-time family couple; however, they both adopted a boy when she was 40. They also worked together fruitfully with 13 movies in their 12-year-relationship, but things began to fall apart by the time she was 45, and they had a huge, explosive break-up when she found porno pictures in his apartment of her daughter Soon-Yi. Two years later their split was official, complete with bitter accusations and legal volleys.

By the age of 52, she had a total of 14 children, ten of whom were adopted. The family was centred in an eight-bedroom house in Connecticut. Her autobiography, *What Falls Away* was published that year and in it she reveals much of her life, writing candidly about the traumas and joys. At the age of 63, *Time* magazine named her one of the most influential people in the world.[178]

Marc Robertson was an American professional astrologer and author. His Sedna was in the third house of ideas and communication, sextile his Sun in the first house of identity. His Sedna was also at the tip of a finger of fate, with two inconjuncts, one to Neptune, the planet of dreams and visions, in the ninth house of knowledge and the occult, and one to Mars, the planet of action, in the tenth house of profession. His books include *Eighth House*, *Engine of Destiny* and *Time Out of Mind*. The inconjunct to Neptune can, however, lead to addictive behaviour and he dropped out of the astrological community, due to drugs and alcohol and the courts eventually appointed him a guardian, with whom he lived until he died of a heart attack at age 47.

Yuri Gagarin was a Soviet pilot and cosmonaut. He had Sedna in the fifth house of creativity, semi-sextile his Sun in the fourth house of home.

He was the first human to journey into outer space, when his Vostok spacecraft completed an orbit of the Earth when he was 27. He became an international celebrity and was awarded many medals and titles, including Hero of the Soviet Union, the nation's highest honour.

---

[178] https://en.wikipedia.org/wiki/Mia_Farrow

He got drafted into the Soviet Army at 21 and he was sent to the First Chkalov Air Force Pilot's School in Orenburg and soloed in a MiG-15 at the age of 23. At 26, after much searching and a selection process, he was chosen with 19 other pilots for the Soviet space program. He was further selected for an elite training group known as the Sochi Six, from which the first cosmonauts of the Vostok programme would be chosen.

Gagarin and other prospective candidates were subjected to experiments designed to test physical and psychological endurance; he also underwent training for the upcoming flight. Out of the twenty selected, he was one of two chosen due to their performance during training sessions as well as their physical characteristics. In August 1960, when Gagarin was one of 20 possible candidates, a Soviet Air Force doctor evaluated his personality as follows:

Modest; embarrasses when his humour gets a little too racy; high degree of intellectual development evident in Yuriy; fantastic memory; distinguishes himself from his colleagues by his sharp and far-ranging sense of attention to his surroundings; a well-developed imagination; quick reactions; persevering, prepares himself painstakingly for his activities and training exercises, handles celestial mechanics and mathematical formulae with ease as well as excels in higher mathematics; does not feel constrained when he has to defend his point of view if he considers himself right; appears that he understands life better than a lot of his friends.[179]

Humour can be one path to transcend the quicksand of Sedna, giving us the objectivity to step back from the edge and also with the flowing aspects to the Sun a creativity and sense of self direction in our work. If we are feeling uncomfortable with the weight of Sedna in our lives, we would be well advised to cultivate our sense of humour.

Lucille Ball was an an American actress, comedienne, model, film-studio executive, and producer. She had Sedna in the third house of communication, trine the Sun and bi-quintile Ixion, the planet of lawlessness, both in the eighth house of shared resources.

---

[179] https://en.wikipedia.org/wiki/Yuri_Gagarin

She was best known as the star of the self-produced sitcoms, *I Love Lucy, The Lucy Show, Here's Lucy*, and *Life with Lucy*. In the 1950s she ventured into television, creating the sitcom, *I Love Lucy* in 1951, a series that became one of the most beloved programs in television history. In 1962, Ball became the first woman to run a major television studio, Desilu Productions, which produced many popular television series, including *Mission: Impossible* and *Star Trek*.[180]

Joan Rivers was an American comedienne, thought by many to be the funniest lady on the planet. She had Sedna in the first house of identity, sextile her Sun in the third house of communication. Her Sedna is also in a close evolutionary quintile to Mercury, the planet of communication, and with Venus, the planet of values, both also in the third house of ideas.

She certainly has one of the fastest, most agile minds in show biz. Her rapid-fire mix of gossip, insults, flaunting of taboos and ridicule of flaws and neurosis is written 90% by her. She also wrote comedy for *Candid Camera*, scripts and material for Phyllis Diller and Zsa Zsa Gabor and humorous books.

The younger of two daughters of Russian-Jewish refugees, she learned from her doctor dad to crack a joke and was making people laugh by the time she was 11. She learned from her mom that rich was better than poor and was raised with privilege and a good education. She married at 24 and had it annulled the following year when she decided she wanted to be an actress, not a housewife. While doing off-Broadway, she worked in offices and turned to comedy at 27 to supplement her income.

At the age of 32 she was told that she was too old and passed over; however, a week later she was booked on Johnny Carson's *Tonight Show*. They clicked. Their immediate rapport was a hit with the audience and she appeared for years with Carson before hosting her own *Late Show Starring Joan Rivers*, with a contract for $10 million over three years. She moved into the stratosphere as America's top comedienne, the darling of the

---

[180] https://en.wikipedia.org/wiki/Lucille_Ball

circuit with tours, magazine covers, nightclub and Las Vegas gigs, TV projects, books and records.[181]

At this juncture in human evolution, few of us use our planets at the spiritual level, but many of us are striving to, and such people are wonderful to be around. As with the other planets, the spiritual level of evolution is vastly different with Sedna from the two previous levels. These aspects can bring a high octave spiritual purpose, or meaning, to our lives without the struggles of some of the other aspects.

Here, the flowing aspects with the Sun brings a higher transpersonal consciousness, which is centered in the evolution of humanity and of all life forms on the planet. The struggle of the beginners' level is gone, as are the transcendental crises of the intermediate level. At this level everything Saturnian is meaningless and yet everything Sednian has its place.

Case study, Bhagwan Shree Rajneesh was an Indian guru and author of more than a hundred books, which are sold through his organization. He has Sedna in the eleventh house of collective consciousness, trine his Sun in the seventh house of relationships.

> He was not only intimately familiar with the world's great religions and philosophies, but the modern psychologies of Jung, Freud, Maslow, and the rest of the West's best thinkers in modern psychology and psychiatry. His syncretic teachings emphasise the importance of meditation, awareness, love, celebration, courage, creativity, and humour — qualities that he viewed as being suppressed by adherence to static belief systems and religious tradition.
>
> When he was 50, he founded a commune in Oregon of 1,700 disciples, a sprawling religious community of a hundred square miles. He had continual problems with the local government over land development along with bad press and controversy over his string of pricey Rolls Royce automobiles and fat bankroll. Called the "sex-guru" because of his popular talks about tantric sex, his ashram became known as one big love fest during celebrations.
>
> The ashram was an attempt to build a self-sufficient commune based on ecological and organic farming principles, turning the

---

[181] https://en.wikipedia.org/wiki/Joan_Rivers

desert into a garden, which they achieved in part. The devotees who joined the ashram came from all walks of life, devoting their money and labor to create a utopia.

The task of running the commune fell to his personal secretary and the assets of the organization were all in her name. Almost immediately it ran into conflict with county residents and the state government and a succession of legal battles ensued, concerning the ashram's construction and continued development, which curtailed its success.

He later alleged his assistant committed crimes, included the attempted murder of his personal physician, poisonings of public officials, wiretapping and bugging within the commune and within his own home, and a bio-terror attack on the citizens of the Dalles, using salmonella to impact the county elections.

He claimed that she was trying to establish a religion, and that her quest for personal power led to her paranoia, which eventually spread throughout the commune. He spoke often of how organized religion is an obstacle to enlightenment and he blamed her for wanting to be the first Popess.

As these difficulties accumulated with not only the local citizens but with the National Immigration Service and Revenue Service, and he was arrested as he fled his strife-torn utopia 4 years later to the tune on 35 counts of conspiracy and fraud, indicted by a Grand Jury in Oregon. On his return to India, he changed his name to Osho to signal a change in his consciousness.[182]

Carl Jung was a Swiss psychiatrist and author, noted as being an outstanding influence in the development of the theory and practice of analytical psychiatry. He had Sedna in the second house of material reality, trine his Sun, conjunct Vesta, the asteroid of regeneration, both on the descendant, the cusp of the seventh house of relationships.

His Sedna is also in an evolutionary quintile with Orcus, the planet of delving down and speaking out in the twelfth house of the unconscious, and semi-sextile Neptune, the planet of dreams and visions in the second house of material reality.

---

[182] https://en.wikipedia.org/wiki/Rajneesh

At age 12, he developed fainting spells which kept him out of school. He dreamt for hours, was out in nature, drew, "but above all...was able to plunge into the world of the mysterious. Overhearing his father's talk of financial concerns around his illness, he realised on some level he could overcome the fainting spells and was able to return to school. Shortly after this, on a long walk to school, he experienced an intense moment of knowing himself: "Previously, I had existed...everything had merely happened to me. Now, I happened to myself. Now I knew: I am myself now, now I exist."

When he was 23 he decided to pursue a career in psychiatry. His career began in earnest five years later when he picked up Sigmund Freud's book, *The Interpretation of Dreams,* realising how Freud's work linked up with his own ideas. The initial correspondence and friendship with Freud began three years later and they collaborated on some work, but when he was 34 he broke from Freud to place greater emphasis on the growth of mankind by archetypal vital forces in the individual. His theories of synchronicity, introvert-extrovert types, individuation and the personal-collective unconscious come from this work.

During this period Jung had a decisive dream of being in a two-story house. As he explored it, each floor and room reflected historical eras or from the collective unconscious. When he was 38, he had numerous visions. Jung stated in his autobiography, *Memories, Dreams, and Reflections* that all of his creative work came from these initial visions, fantasies and dreams. Jung had a successful practice and was a much soughtafter mentor to countless devotees of his work.

An advocate of the use of astrology, he said 'Astrology would be a large-scale example of synchronism, if it had at its disposal thoroughly tested findings... In other words, whatever is born or done this moment of time, has the qualities of this moment of time'. In his book, *Synchronicity,* he published a study of 483 pairs of couples, seeking to find a possibility of the validity that there is a causal connection between the planets and psycho-physiological disposition.[183]

---

[183] https://en.wikipedia.org/wiki/Carl_Jung

Semi-square, Square, Sesquiquadrate

With the stressful aspects between Sedna and the Sun, the all-encompassing spiritual energy of Sedna challenges our willpower and our sense of self. These aspects bring the high-octane spiritual energy of Sedna into our lives through constant challenges to align our destiny with our will.

The Sun represents our conscious mind, our will to live and our creative life force. Just as the planets revolve around the Sun, it represents the center of our world and, and because Sedna represents the ethereal outer limits of that world, the stressful aspects set up a challenge to our ego from our wider spiritual world.

With these aspects we will tend to see the world in terms of being challenged and so are likely always ready for these challenges and expect them everywhere. We create our world through our expectations, however, so we need to discern which are the important challenges for us and not get buried in meaningless challenges.

If we are largely unconscious of this process we may at times be overwhelmed by these challenges. Like Trista Zinck, who was an American accidental death victim. She had Sedna in the eleventh house of collective consciousness, sesquiquadrate her Sun, which was conjunct Uranus, the planet of sudden unexpected events, in the sixth house of daily routine. Her Sedna was also in close opposition to Pluto, the planet of life and death, in the fifth house of romance. She was struck by a car when she was 17, walking down a street without sidewalks with her boyfriend.

Or we may become authoritarian and abusive in our ego-based attempts to bend the wider spiritual world to our will. Like Sara Aldrete, who was a Mexican Satanist and serial killer called 'the witch.' She had Sedna in the third house of ideas, sesquiquadrate her Sun in the eighth house of the occult.

> She grew up in a Mexican-Texas border town, attending school on the Texas side. She was known as a good kid, a star pupil in secondary school. She married a thirty-year-old when she was 19 and they separated two years later.

> At 23, she met a Cuban bi-sexual fortune teller, who was deeply involved in 'juju'. He performed 'cleansing' rituals that involved

animal sacrifice and was suspected of six human deaths in his black magic arts. He introduced her to the dark and evil side of the occult. In the next two years, at least 25 victims were slain and, during the ritual killings, the victims were tortured and dismembered, as a mixture of business, religion and sadistic pleasure.

When she was 25, police investigating one of the killings, found an altar, occult paraphernalia and homosexual pornography. In custody, she claimed that she'd been kidnapped and brainwashed and was not a part of the homicides. However, at 29 she was charged with 17 murders, plus drug charges. Tried on two counts, she was given six years prison with the further charges still pending.[184]

Or like William Shockley, the American physicist and father of Silicon Valley. He had Sedna in the twelfth house of the unconscious, semi-square his Sun in the eleventh house of ideals.

His parents were eccentric and kept him out of school until the 8th grade, so he lacked socialisation and grew up not knowing how to handle and deal with other people. Yet he co-invented the transistor, the forerunner of the microchip, an invention that changed the course of history for computers and electronics, and he was awarded many prizes and received many honours, culminating in the Nobel Prize for Physics.

He worked in Bell Labs, but his abrasive management style caused him to leave and run his own company. However, he became increasing paranoid and because of that his team broke up and started their own companies, spawning Silicon Valley. The biography, *Broken Genius: The rise and fall of William Shockley, Creator of the Electronic Age* describes him as: "A nasty old man. One of his friends actually described him as having reverse charisma; he would walk into a room and you instantly took a disliking to him. He was extraordinarily bright and he knew it. He was a bit arrogant about it.[185]

---

[184] https://en.wikipedia.org/wiki/Sara_Aldrete
[185] Shurkin, Joel N. *Broken Genius: The rise and fall of William Shockley, Creator of the Electronic Age*

His Sedna is also bi-quintile Ixion, the planet of lawlessness and conjunct Orcus, the planet of delving down and speaking out, and in his later years he slipped into Eugenics, the belief that humanity would be better served by only allowing the smart and healthy to breed. He was attacked for this in print, on television and in scientific journals, became estranged from all his friends and his last years were very sad.

Or like Donald Rumsfeld, who was an American government official. He has Sedna in the fourth house of home, square his sun, which is conjunct Pluto, the planet of life and death, in the seventh house of relationships.

> Raised with an advantaged childhood, he went to Princeton on an academic scholarship, majoring in political science. He served in the U.S. Navy from the age of 22 to 25 as a jet pilot and flight instructor. He served more than three terms in Congress and was U.S. Ambassador to NATO at 38. He was then President Ford's Chief of Staff and a member of his cabinet from the age of 43 to 45, and he served in that administration as the youngest U.S. Secretary of Defense.

> He left Washington at 45 to enter private industry. However, at 68 he was nominated as Secretary of Defense of the George W. Bush cabinet and was soon in charge of the invasion of Iraq to topple Saddam Hussein, which was later proved to be based on false intelligence. His invasion plan resulted in a lightning invasion that took Baghdad in well under a month, with very few American casualties.

> However, many government buildings, plus major museums, electrical generation infrastructure, and even oil equipment was looted and vandalised during the transition to the establishment of the Coalition Provisional Authority. A violent insurrection began shortly after the military operation started. And after the German and French governments voiced opposition to invading Iraq, Rumsfeld labeled these countries as part of 'Old Europe'.

> As a result, he stirred controversy as to whether the forces that invaded Iraq were large enough, with the head of the British army, criticising his plans for the invasion as 'intellectually bankrupt', adding that Rumsfeld is 'one of those most responsible for the current situation in Iraq', and that he felt that

'the US approach to combating global terrorism is 'inadequate' and too focused on military might rather than nation building and diplomacy'.

Calls for his resignation were loud and clear after pictures of American soldiers abusing Iraqi detainees at an Iraq prison were aired in the media. Rumsfeld appeared before the Senate and House Armed Services Committees at 72, and in his opening statement apologised to the detainees and their families. However, he responded to a question about whether he would step down by saying: "I would not resign simply because people try to make a political issue out of it".

Despite protestations that he would continue in his job as Secretary of Defence until the end of the Bush administration, the President announced two years early that he had accepted his resignation. He was 74. The announcement came one day after the US elections swung the balance of power in the Congress to the Democratic Party, with the lack of success in Iraq given by voters as one of the major reasons for voting Democratic in congressional elections.[186]

As we tire of density and the grief it creates, and we start a spiritual journey to get out of the swamp, Sedna rewards us with transcendent crises, experiences which force us to let go and rise above them, resulting in a huge growth to a new level of consciousness. There is no choice with these crises, and the more we try and solve them, the more we will get hurt.

Our case study, Helen Keller, was an American blind-deaf linguist, author, political activist, and lecturer. She had Sedna in the fourth house of home, square her Sun, which was very closely conjunct her South Node, representing the karma she has to deal with, both in the eighth house of shared resources. When she was one-and-a-half-years old she developed a sickness, which left her deaf and blind, before she had learned to talk. Without language, her only memories of the next four years were of emotions and texture, mainly frustration and tantrums, until cuddled.

---

[186] https://en.wikipedia.org/wiki/Donald_Rumsfeld

When she was six, her father found her a teacher, who grew to love the girl and eventually stayed with her as a lifelong companion. The story of how her teacher broke through the isolation imposed by a near complete lack of language, allowing her to blossom, as she learned to communicate, has become widely known through the play and film, *The Miracle Worker*. As she learned words through a tapped sign language in her hand, her consciousness started developing. She had an eager mind and wanted to know everything. Her Sedna is also trine Mercury, the planet of communication, on the cusp of the ninth house of knowledge, and bi-quintile Pallas, the asteroid of wisdom, also in the ninth.

At ten she found a Norwegian teacher from whom she learned to talk by passing her hand lightly over her teacher's face, so she could feel the position of her tongue and lips when she made a sound. Here's how she wrote about it when she was 22 in her autobiography, *The Story of My Life*:

> I was eager to imitate every motion. I shall never forget the surprise and delight I felt when I uttered my first connected sentence, 'It is warm.' True, they were broken and stammering syllables, but they were human speech. My soul, conscious of new strength, came out of bondage and was reaching through those broken symbols of speech to all knowledge and all faith.[187]

The autumn after she had learned to speak, she wrote a story.

> I thought then that I was making up a story and I eagerly sat down to write it before the ideas should slip from me. My thoughts flowed easily; I felt a sense of joy in the composition. Words and images came tripping to my finger ends, and as I thought out sentence after sentence, I wrote them on my braille slate." Exited, she gave it to the headmaster who had enabled her teacher to come to her, and he liked it so much it was published in the school report.[188]

However, in true Sedna fashion, when she was visiting him for the celebration of George Washington's birthday, due to play Ceres in a play given by the blind girls in the school, she was suddenly put before a

---

[187] The Story of My Life, Hellen Keller
[188] Ibid.

court of investigation for plagiarism, because it had been discovered that a story similar to hers had appeared in a book before she was born.

> The two stories were so much alike in thought and language that it was evident the story had been read to me, and that mine was – a plagiarism. It was difficult to make me understand this; but when I did understand I was astonished and grieved. No child ever drank deeper of the cup of bitterness than I did. I had disgraced myself; I had brought suspicion upon those I loved best.

> I have never played with words again for the mere pleasure of the game. Indeed, I have ever since been tortured by the fear that what I write is not my own. For a long time, when I wrote a letter, even to my mother, I was seized with a sudden feeling of terror, and I would spell the sentences over and over, to make sure that I had not read them in a book.[189]

Nevertheless, she became a prolific author, writing twelve books as well as numerous articles and was well traveled and outspoken in her convictions, giving lectures and talks around the world. A member of the Socialist Party of America and the Industrial Workers of the World, she campaigned for women's suffrage, labor rights, socialism, antimilitarism, and other similar causes.

Richard Branson is a British entrepreneur, investor and philanthropist, who is the founder of Virgin Records. He has Sedna in the ninth house of knowledge, square his Sun in the twelfth house of institutions and the unconscious.

> His mother was a strong influence on his success, emphasising independence and self-reliance. Basically shy, his public persona is one of bravado, but the private man remains an enigma.

> At the age of sixteen his first business venture was a magazine called *Student*. He started his record business from the church, where he ran the magazine. He started advertising popular records in the magazine and selling them by mail order. It was an overnight success, as he sold records for considerably less than the High Street outlets.

---

[189] Ibid.

He started a record shop in Oxford Street in London at 20, and the following year, earning enough money from his record store, he launched the record label Virgin Records. By the age of 20, he had a thriving business and 40 employees. Twelve years later, his empire consisted of 50 companies that were giving him a turnover of 50 million pounds, and he was ready to expand into the software, film, video and property markets.

His Virgin brand grew rapidly during the 1980s, as he set up Virgin Atlantic airline at 34 and expanded the Virgin Records music label. He launched Virgin Mobile in 1999 and Virgin Blue in Australia (now named Virgin Australia) in 2000. His Virgin Group now controls more than 400 companies, but he has also been involved in many failed business ventures, such as Virgin Cola, Virgin Cars, Virgin Clothing and Virgin Brides.

He wrote in his autobiography of the decision to start an airline: "My interest in life comes from setting myself huge, apparently unachievable challenges and trying to rise above them ... from the perspective of wanting to live life to the full, I felt that I had to attempt it."

He has also made several world record-breaking attempts. His first attempt at the fastest Atlantic Ocean crossing when he was 35, led to the boat capsizing in British waters and a rescue by RAF helicopter, which received wide media coverage. A year later he beat the record by two hours. The following year his hot air balloon "Virgin Atlantic Flyer" crossed the Atlantic. And at 40 he crossed the Pacific from Japan to Arctic Canada, in a balloon. This broke the record, with a speed of 394 km/h.[190]

Gail Barber, is an American harpist and harp composer, recording artist and teacher. She has Sedna in the twelfth house of the unconscious, semi-square her Sun in the tenth house of profession.

She performed and composed music in many styles: classical, pop, folk, jazz, and New Age. Especially interested in the use of the harp for music healing, she worked extensively with a holistic health care practitioner Ingrid Naiman. A patient recounts: "In the nineties, I was studying medical astrology with Dr. Naiman and I

---

[190] https://en.wikipedia.org/wiki/Richard_Branson

was going to have a music therapy session. Great was my surprise, when Gail Barber volunteered to play live for me. She improvised, what she felt was right and needed all through the session, which allowed me to go very deep into the subconscious and at the same time to the highest dimensions. I am so thankful to have experienced the beauty of live harp music in a healing session and the cooperation between these two highly skilled, professional women without a word being said."[191]

Humour can be one path to transcend the quicksand of Sedna, giving us the objectivity to step back from the edge, but also with the stressful aspects to the Sun, the challenge to develop a higher consciousness through this process. Those of us struggling with these stressful aspects would be well advised to develop our sense of humour.

Jim Carrey is a Canadian-born actor and stand-up comedian. He has Sedna in the sixth house of service, closely square his Sun in the third house of communication. His Sedna is also in an evolutionary quintile to Mercury, the planet of communication, and also to Jupiter, the planet of expansion, which is conjunct in the third house of ideas and communication.

He got his start doing stand-up comedy in Toronto at the age of 17. A year later he moved to Los Angeles where he caught the attention of comedian Rodney Dangerfield. Dangerfield signed Carrey on as an opening act for his tour.

At 21 he made his film debut in a bit part of a bit movie. His later 20s brought additional roles but it wasn't until *Ace Ventura: Pet Detective*, which he made at 32 that his career in film took off. A more serious movie, *The Truman Show* at 36, earned him a Golden Globe. The following year, he took home another Golden Globe for his portrayal of the troubled comedian Andy Kaufman in the biopic *Man on the Moon*. He has since made many notable films, including *Eternal Sunshine of the Spotless Mind*.

He has battled depression however, and to deal with this, he took Prozac. He eventually decided to get off medications and

---

[191] http://www.harpheal.com/music-therapy/

has stated that he no longer takes medications or stimulants of any kind, not even coffee.[192]

His Sedna is also opposite Ixion, the planet of lawlessness, in the twelfth house of the unconscious, and quintile to Orcus, the planet of delving down and speaking out, in the eighth house shared resources.

> When he was 53, a former girlfriend was found dead from a prescription drug overdose. The couple first met three years earlier and he was a pallbearer at her funeral. The following year the woman's husband, who she married after the relationship with Carrey, filed a wrongful death lawsuit against him, claiming that he used his 'immense wealth and celebrity status' to illegally obtain and distribute prescription drugs involved in her death.
>
> Carrey released a statement the following day: "What a terrible shame. It would be easy for me to get in a back room with this man's lawyer and make this go away, but there are some moments in life when you have to stand up and defend your honour against the evil in this world. I will not tolerate this heartless attempt to exploit me, or the woman I loved. Cat's troubles were born long before I met her and sadly her tragic end was beyond anyone's control."
>
> He is a follower and an advocate for the 'law of attraction'. In an interview with Oprah Winfrey at the age of 35, he revealed that as a struggling actor he would use visualisation techniques to get work. He said that he visualised a 10 million dollar check being given to him for 'acting services rendered', placed the check in his pocket, and seven years later received a 10 million dollar check for his role in *Dumb and Dumber*. He was also a practitioner of Transcendental Meditation and now calls himself a Christian.[193]

At this juncture in human evolution, few of us use our planets at the spiritual level, but many of us are striving to, and such people are wonderful to be around. As with the other planets, the spiritual level of evolution is vastly different with Sedna from the two previous levels. Here the stressful aspects with the Sun forces a higher transpersonal

---

[192] https://en.wikipedia.org/wiki/Jim_Carrey
[193] Ibid.

consciousness, which is centered in the evolution of humanity and of all life forms on the planet.

Once we embrace the Sedna energy, which is the oneness of everything, our nurturing becomes an expression of Sedna consciousness and it becomes devotional in nature. The struggle of the beginners' level is gone, as are the transcendental crises of the intermediate level. At this level everything Saturnian is meaningless and yet everything Sednian has its place.

Like Maria Quattrocchi, who was an Italian saint, who was beatified after her death along with her husband, the first time in church history that a woman and her husband were given that honor together, as exemplars of the Christian life. She had Sedna in the second house of material reality, square her Sun in the fifth house of 'what is produced in the home.'

> She was a member of the noble Corsini family. She was a professor and writer on educational topics, writing several books and also served as a Voluntary Nurse in the Italian Red Cross during World War II. They were made saints because they opened their home to refugees during WWII, at great risk to the family. According to Pope John Paul II, they lived "an ordinary life in an extraordinary way".[194]

Her husband had Sedna in the tenth house of profession, quintile his Sun in the seventh house of relationships.

And Jiddu Krishnamurti, who was an East Indian teacher and religious leader, a philosopher and metaphysician from his youth. His Sedna was in his second house of material resources, semi-square his Sun in the third house of communication. He gained world recognition as a spiritual teacher and lectured to groups as diverse as the U.N. delegates, diplomats, scientists at Los Alamos National Laboratory and to people all over the world.

> He was born in British India. A sensitive and sickly child, "vague and dreamy," he was often taken to be intellectually disabled, and was beaten regularly at school by his teachers and at home by his father, who was an ardent follower of the Theosophical Society, a religious organisation which was a mixture of

---

[194] https://en.wikipedia.org/wiki/Luigi_Beltrame_Quattrocchi_and_Maria_Corsini

Buddhism and Indian Brahmanism traditions. While still a boy, Krishna was singled out as the new Avatar by the society, when in early adolescence he had a chance encounter with prominent occultist and theosophist in the grounds of the Theosophical Society headquarters in Madras.

The head of the Theosophical Society legally adopted him and raised him as her own son. With his younger brother he traveled all over the world, especially throughout Europe meeting important members of the Theosophical Society. Nonetheless, his time in London was lonely and isolated, cut off from his family with only his brother as a link to his former life in India, in a country where the customs were different and his dark Indian colouring was a subject of racial prejudice. His theosophical teacher was autocratic and impatient and Krishna, as the boy was called, was a dreamy, inattentive scholar.

After 20 years in the Society he confessed that he found it impossible to read any of the theosophical books all the way through, let alone remember the contents. He did, however, accept the obeisance with which he was regarded, being told repeatedly from childhood on that he carried a mission to discharge. However, as a young man he disavowed the idea that he was the 'expected World Teacher' and he dissolved the Order of the Star in the East, an organisation that had been established to support his teaching.

Breaking with the Theosophical Society at 34, he preached a doctrine of independent salvation by right conduct; indeed, tradition and doctrine might be positive barriers to personal progress, he argued, for each person must find his own path and his own link with the infinite. He spent the rest of his life writing and giving lectures on his philosophy of self-reliance and awareness. He captivated others with his personal charm and playful personality. He enjoyed singing comic songs and telling funny stories to his friends. He was an avid reader and enjoyed thrillers and detective novels as well as reading the Old Testament.

The world media continued to label him as a kind of guru, no matter how much he denied the charge. He felt that people hungered for God figures and were willing to do anything to conjure one up, that truth could only be discovered inside oneself, by oneself, and that organised religion advocated the fear mentality to remain in control of people.

"The more he denied the role of guru however, the more of a guru he became. The author Henry Miller wrote, "What distinguishes Krishnamurti, even from the great teachers of the past, the masters and the exemplars, is his absolute nakedness. ... If he had a mission, it is to strip men of their illusions and delusions, to knock away the false supports of ideals, beliefs, fetishes, every kind of crutch, and thus render back to man the full majesty, the full potency of his humanity. He has often been referred to as "The World Teacher." If any man living merits the title, he does."[195]

In-conjunct

With the fateful inconjunct between Sedna and the Sun, the esoteric spiritual energy of Sedna bursts into our willpower and our ability to stand up for ourselves in an evolutionary way and we have a fated role to play.

The inconjunct sometimes acts as a flow and at other times as a stress, so we have to learn to actively manage the process, as the rarified spiritual energy sometimes reinforces our spirit of discovery and, at other times, isn't there to back us up. By adjusting to this, we gain a deeper understanding of ourselves and how to play our role.

The Sun represents our conscious mind, our will to live and our creative life force. Just as the planets revolve around the Sun, it represents the center of our world and, because Sedna represents the ethereal outer limits of that world, the inconjunct sets up a fateful relationship between our ego world and our wider spiritual world.

At the unconscious level the spiritual power of the inconjunct can prove problematic, as we may try to fortify our ego, which is likely to bring out the negative side of the Sun, arrogance and willfulness, and make us self-centered and judgmental.

This can lead to the possibility of abuse, just because Sedna's reach is so broad that anything goes, and so with this aspect we may be at the mercy of bigger forces than us.

[195] https://en.wikipedia.org/wiki/Jiddu_Krishnamurti

Like Karli Hawthorne, who was a British kidnapping victim, who was taken from the hospital just hours after her birth. She has Sedna conjunct the IC, the cusp of the fourth house of home, inconjunct her Sun in the eleventh house of collective consciousness. Following an anonymous tip, the police rescued her and returned her to her parents the next day.

Or we might take on an abusing role ourselves, like Fritz Haarmann, who was a German homicidal manic and a homosexual epileptic. He had Sedna in the eleventh house of collective consciousness, in a fateful inconjunct with his Sun, the planet of willpower, in the sixth house of service and in a stressful sesquiquadrate with Ceres, the planet of nurturing, in the fourth house of home.

> From youth, he served several prison terms for indecency and was committed several times to an insane asylum. He primarily lived as a petty thief, burglar and con artist. Although he did occasionally obtain legitimate employment, he invariably stole from his employers or their customers.
>
> Despite police knowledge that he was both a criminal and a homosexual, which was then illegal and punishable by imprisonment in Germany, he gradually began to establish a relationship with Hanover police as an informer, largely as a means of redirecting their attention from himself in his own criminal activities, and to facilitate his access to young males.
>
> He is known to have committed at least 24 murders, although he is suspected of murdering a minimum of 27. All of his victims were males between the ages of 10 and 22, the majority of whom were in their mid- to late-teens. They would be lured back to one of three addresses in which he is known to have lived, on the promise of assistance, accommodation, work, or under the pretence of citizen's arrest.[196]

If we are lost in the arrogance and willfulness of the unconscious ego, we could find ourselves desperately pushing our world view to justify our actions, until it collapses under its obvious narrowness.

Like Charles Manson, who was an American ritual cult leader, a psychopath with a band of drug-numbed followers. He had Sedna in the

---

[196] https://en.wikipedia.org/wiki/Fritz_Haarmann

twelfth house of the unconscious, inconjunct his Sun in the seventh house of relationships.

He mesmerized his gang with liberal sex and drugs, while living on a ranch in the desert of southern California. He was the illegitimate son of a teenage prostitute and an army colonel. He was raised by an aunt and uncle and by the age of 11, he developed into a delinquent, shuffling from foster parent to foster parent. He spent his youth and adulthood in and out of prison, spending 19 of his first 32 years behind bars.

In his mid-30s, while on parole he went to San Francisco to be a part of the hippie counter-culture in the Height-Ashbury district. He gathered adoring women around him by giving out LSD. Soon he was able to attract young men to his group by promising sex with his 'young loves'. They enjoyed long group LSD sessions, listening to the Beatles' "Helter Skelter" song on the White Album. However, unable to keep his friendships, he began to prophesy chaos to his followers.

When he was 34, he directed the ritual grisly killings of a Hollywood socialite and her houseguests, who were stabbed to death by his followers and their blood was smeared along the walls of the kitchen. A few days later, an older couple was tied up and carved and stabbed with forks and kitchen knives by Manson's followers.

The deaths frightened the Hollywood community and in the nine months of the trial, when he was 35, the jury found him guilty of first degree murder and conspiracy. He was convicted and given the death penalty, but the following year the California Supreme Court invalidated the capital punishment stature, and he became a life-termer. He has been continually refused parole by the California parole board.

His behaviour in prison has been vicious and demented and yet, inexplicably, every year he receives letters and gifts from young people, Satanists, neo-Nazis and skinheads who view him as their role model, hoping for one day when he will be released. He served out his life sentence at California State Prison in Corcoran and died at age 83 in 2017.[197]

Or like Peter Sellers, a British-American actor, a comedian and bizarre character star, best known for the *Pink Panther* series of films. He had Sedna in the eighth house of the spirit world and of shared resources, conjunct Nessus, the centaur which is sometimes called the sympathetic monster because of its demands for radical change, and inconjunct his Sun, which is together with Mars, the planet of action, in the first house of identity.

> He was the only child of variety-show troupers and grew up in theatrical boarding houses. He was close to his overbearing mom, who died when he was 42, and he claimed to be able to communicate with her after her death.
>
> He wanted to be a drummer, but there wasn't a lot of demand for the work. In World War II he was in a RAF musical troupe, entertaining airmen in India and the Middle East. After the war, he worked his way up through vaudeville, variety shows at London's Palladium, radio and into the movies. He was first noticed on the *The Goon Show*, which aired on British TV when he was in his mid- to- late twenties. At 26 he appeared in his first feature-length motion picture and by the age of 40 he was ranked as one of England's great comic actors.
>
> He made more than 50 films, but in the industry, he had a reputation for being a monster who was hard to work with, impossibly difficult and 'basically not a nice man'. Once during a marital fight, he tried to kill a puppy. He abused his friends, and even wrote his children out of his will. He was an odd man who became haunted by death and who took drugs to enhance sex.[198]

As we tire of density and the grief it creates, and we start a spiritual journey to get out of the swamp, Sedna rewards us with transcendent crises, experiences which force us to let go and rise above them, resulting in a huge growth to a new level of consciousness. There is no

---

[197] https://en.wikipedia.org/wiki/Charles_Manson
[198] https://en.wikipedia.org/wiki/Peter_Sellers

choice with these crises, and the more we try and solve them, the more we will get hurt.

John Cage was an American avant-garde musician and composer, writer, photographer, reporter, and critic. He had Sedna conjunct Chariklo, the centaur of foresight, in the eighth house of shared resources, and inconjunct his Sun in the first house of identity.

> Eclectically talented and endlessly enchanted by the mystery and beauty of the commonplace, he wrote essays and reviews, scores and sketches. He was also a photographer and journalist noted for raucous multimedia works.
>
> The son of an inventor, he was raised in Los Angeles and attended Pomona college before dropping out to go to Europe. While in Europe, he began to write music, much of which he threw away. Back in Los Angeles, he began to compose, a period in which he was very enthusiastic about both modern painting and music. It was at the time of the Depression, and he worked as a gardener in exchange for housing.
>
> When he wrote a solo for clarinet, one of his piano teachers arranged to have it played at a small concert in San Francisco. He hitchhiked to the concert from LA and, when the musician said it was too difficult for him to play, he played the piece himself for the audience.
>
> He spent the last 50 years of his life in New York City, often in the company of his lifelong companion, dancer Merce Cunningham, for whom he wrote many pieces. As his creativity developed, he moved into the role as an extraordinarily important American composer. A documentary, *Cage/Cunningham*, about the long collaboration between the composer and the choreographer was filmed, featuring interviews, archival dance footage and music from the various projects the two artists created.[199]

Maria Corti was an Italian university professor, linguist and novelist. She had Sedna in the sixth house of service, inconjunct her Sun in the eleventh house of collective consciousness.

---

[199] https://en.wikipedia.org/wiki/John_Cage

Considered one of the leading literary scholars of post-World War II Italy, she was awarded numerous prizes including the Premio Campiello for the entire body of her work. Her works of fiction were informed by her literary scholarship, but also had a distinctly autobiographical vein. She founded a magazine called 'Critical Instruments' which introduced new methods of literary theory, including Russian formalism and structuralism. At 53 she started a foundation that gathered manuscripts and letters of contemporary writers and established an extensive curated archive of material on modern Italian writers[200]

Carl Sagan is an American astronomer, astrophysicist, exobiologist, educator, and popular celebrity. He has Sedna in the twelfth house of the unconscious, inconjunct his Sun in the sixth house of service.

As a child he is said to have gazed with awe at the heavens and speculated on the existence of life beyond earth. At 12 he told his grandfather he wanted to be an astronomer and vowed to be on a university faculty so he could support himself in his chosen field, which he did.

He became a noted authority on planetary atmospheres and surfaces and was a leading consultant to NASA's space exploration program. His book, *Cosmos* was a best seller for over a year. The TV series by the same name was seen by more than 500 million people in 60 countries. He inspired a generation with his enthusiastic lectures, books and documentaries about space and life.

A prolific writer, he wrote, co-wrote or edited over 20 books and hundreds of articles. Among his other contributions, he is credited with identifying the boiling hot nature of Venus and the dust storms of Mars. At 44, he won the Pulitzer Prize for nonfiction for *The Dragons of Eden*, his book about the evolution of human intelligence. At 63 he co-produced the movie, *Contact*, based on his novel by the same name. He was a keen proponent of the idea that intelligent life might be found in the universe, but

---

[200] https://en.wikipedia.org/wiki/Maria_Corti

dismissed UFO's, lost continents and astrology as 'pseudoscientific twaddle'.[201]

At this juncture in human evolution, few of us use our planets at the spiritual level, but many of us are striving to, and such people are wonderful to be around. As with the other planets, the spiritual level of evolution is vastly different with Sedna from the two previous levels. Here the incojunct with the Sun brings a higher transpersonal consciousness, which is centered in the evolution of humanity and of all life forms on the planet.

Once we embrace the Sedna energy, which is the oneness of everything, our nurturing becomes an expression of Sedna consciousness and it becomes devotional in nature. The struggle of the beginners' level is gone, as are the transcendental crises of the intermediate level. At this level everything Saturnian is meaningless and yet everything Sednian has its place.

Frederick Hockley was a British occultist who was a London based Freemason and a member of the Societas Rosicruciana. He had Sedna in the seventh house of relationships, inconjunct his Sun in the second house of material resources. His Sedna is also part of a grand trine with the moon, representing his sensitive nature, in the eleventh house of collective consciousness, and Saturn, the planet of structure, in the third house of communication.

> He avidly collected and transcribed over many years a vast library of important occult books, works and texts, including a Rosicrucian manuscript which had a great influence on British occultism. He practiced the art of 'Crystaliomancy' or 'the art of invoking spirits by the crystal' and believed this to be one of the most important forms of spirit communication. He kept notes on many of his experiments and experiences, accumulating a vast amount of information.

> It is said that through close-knit London circles, his freemasonry connections and SRIA connections, as well as the extensive and vast library he left behind him on his passing that he contributed to the forming and curriculum of the 'The Hermetic Order of the Golden Dawn'. It is also alleged that the original cipher

[201] https://en.wikipedia.org/wiki/Carl_Sagan

manuscript on which the Golden Dawn was formed may well have been written by him.[202]

Billy Graham is an American evangelist, a Southern Baptist preacher who was "born again" as a teen, accepting Jesus as his personal Saviour. He has Sedna in the first house of identity inconjunct Sun in the eighth house of shared resources.

> He spread the word of God by way of 900 radio stations and many TV crusades. He published a magazine, *Decision*, with circulation of more than four million, and gradually moved into the TV ministry. World traveled, he became internationally known as the spiritual leader of presidents and noted people in many walks of life.
>
> The author of 24 books, many of them best-sellers, Graham is the recipient of several awards. He is never unctuous or pious; rather, he is earnest, quietly confident and, despite his iconic status, ministers from a personal level. It is estimated that he has preached to more people in live audiences than anyone else in history: some 210 million in more than 185 countries and territories. Hundreds of millions more have been reached through his TV, film, radio, video and print projects.[203]

Quintile, Bi-quintile

The evolutionary quintile or bi-quintile aspect between Sedna and the Sun infuses our willpower and our sense of self with the all-encompassing spiritual energy of Sedna to the point where we can push the boundaries of human development.

Quintiles and bi-quintiles point to talent, the desire to create order and to categorize, a fascination with patterns and structures, perfectionist tendencies, and the desire to build or make things. These aspects have the characteristics of both the trine and opposition. They point to awareness of conflicts, or problems and finding solutions for them; however, they do not automatically kick into action and must be cultivated over time.

The Sun represents our conscious mind, our will to live and our creative life force. Just as the planets revolve around the Sun, it represents the

---

[202] https://en.wikipedia.org/wiki/Frederick_Hockley
[203] https://en.wikipedia.org/wiki/Billy_Graham

center of our world and, because Sedna represents the ethereal outer limits of that world, these aspects can bring our ego world and our wider spiritual world into harmony.

At the unconscious level, however, the spiritual power of these aspects with Sedna can prove problematic, because, while we sense the strength of the energy, we don't understand it and may think that it is available to control by our ego in the way that the energies of the inner planets are. In the extreme this can lead to the possibility of abuse, or of abusive behaviour, just because Sedna's reach is so broad.

Like it did with Amy Grossberg, who is an American teenager who gave birth to a baby and discarded it in a trash bag. She has Sedna in the twelfth house of the unconscious, quintile her Sun, which is conjunct Jupiter, the planet of expansion, in the third house of communication.

> She and her boyfriend were in love. They were both 18, from good homes and an affluent, caring background. When Amy got pregnant, they kept it a secret. When she went into labor they drove to a motel where they delivered a baby boy, put it in a plastic bag and left it in a dumpster.

> At first the pair seemed to remain a loving couple, but they turned on each other and each began blaming the other. By the time they came to trial, the two former lovers sat in a courtroom for sentencing, not looking across the room at each other. Despite initially denying her pregnancy, then denying giving birth and then blaming Peterson for killing the baby, at her sentencing she pleaded for leniency and told the judge, "I want to help others. I want to make a difference."

> She was given two and a half years prison, and her boyfriend, two years. It was the day before her 20th birthday. She was released from prison after serving only 17 months and returned to live with her parents, who, from the time of their daughter's arrest and through her sentencing, maintained she did nothing wrong. An artist, she started her own company, called Just Because Invitations, several years later at 26.[204]

At this level we may also be desperately pushing our world view to justify our actions, until it collapses under its obvious narrowness. Like Anders

---

[204] https://en.wikipedia.org/wiki/Amy_Grossberg_and_Brian_Peterson

Breivik, who is a Norwegian far-right terrorist and the confessed perpetrator of the 2011 Norway attacks. He has Sedna conjunct Chiron, the centaur of wounding and healing, in the eleventh house of collective consciousness, quintile his Sun in the ninth house of knowledge.

> When he was four, two reports were filed expressing concern about his mental health, concluding that he should be removed from parental care. In the terrorist attack he bombed the government buildings in Oslo, resulting in eight deaths, then carried out a mass shooting at a camp of the Workers' Youth League of the Labour Party on an island, where he killed 69 people, mostly teenagers. On the day of the attacks, he electronically distributed a compendium of texts entitled '2083: A European Declaration of Independence', describing his militant ideology. In them, he lays out a worldview encompassing opposition to Islam and blaming feminism for creating a European cultural suicide. He wrote that his main motive for the atrocities was to market his manifesto.

> Two teams of court-appointed forensic psychiatrists examined him before his trial. The first report diagnosed him as having paranoid schizophrenia. However, a second psychiatric evaluation was commissioned following widespread criticism of the first. The second evaluation was published a week before the trial, concluding that he was not psychotic during the attacks, nor during the evaluation. He was instead diagnosed as having narcissistic personality disorder. At 33 he was sentenced to the longest possibly prison term of 21 years, and he will be kept in prison beyond that time, should he continue to be a danger to society.[205]

As we tire of density and the grief it creates, and we start a spiritual journey to get out of the swamp, Sedna rewards us with transcendent crises, experiences which force us to let go and rise above them, resulting in a huge growth to a new level of consciousness. There is no choice with these crises, and the more we try and solve them, the more we will get hurt.

Werner Erhard is an American entrepreneurial guru, a multi-million dollar merchandiser of enlightenment, the founder of 'est', Erhard Seminar

---

[205] https://en.wikipedia.org/wiki/Anders_Behring_Breivik

Training. He has Sedna in twelfth house of the unconscious, bi-quintile his Sun in fifth house of creativity.

His high-energy brand of instant salvation flourished in the mid-'70s, making him an equally instant multimillionaire. His organisation spawned a network centred on the principles of transformation. A onetime used-car salesman, he studied the consciousness disciplines of east and west to integrate his own brand of group therapy workshops. It is reported that est attracted 500,000 people and much of the jargon of est became part of the culture of the "me generation," such as "getting it" and "creating your own space."

At 25 he left his first wife and four children in Philadelphia and changed his name so they could not find him. He slipped into the California subcultures of human potential movements, pop psychology and eastern metaphysics. The story goes that he "got it" one day in an instant while stuck on a crowded freeway, the awareness that he was not his emotions and beliefs and intellect, but he was the creator and source of his experience.

He married again that year and the couple was together for 22 years and had a son. His second wife later said in an interview that Werner's ego and public image were the most important things in the world to him, and that "children, money or whatever, are so far down it doesn't matter."

When he was 37, enrolment in est began dropping and the IRS claimed that he owed $2 million in back taxes. The following year, his ex-wife sued for half of everything. When he retired est when he was 49, he came up with another program called "The Forum," which was pitched to people who wanted to 'make it happen' and 'get a decisive edge in your ability to achieve'.

A handsome man with a raspy voice thickened by cigars, he is an executive in a sleek European jacket, with power that extends well past his original est weekends. Werner Erhard and Associates projects grossed revenues of $39 million when he was 53. From the age of 49, he also ran Transformational Technologies Inc, a management consultant firm that brings in an annual $25 million.

In spite of his many critics who deride his quick-fix approach, his followers swear that his system works. However, when he was 56, a memo from his Bay Area company recommended bankruptcy, and his children, in interviews, were telling the press horror stories of abuse. His daughter, telling a San Jose paper: 'You never knew when he was going to go off and throw things, or smack Mom'.[206]

Queen Victoria was Queen of the United Kingdom of Great Britain and Ireland from the age of 18 until her death. She had Sedna conjunct Vesta, the asteroid of regeneration, in the eleventh house of collective consciousness, quintile her Sun, which is conjunct her Moon, representing her sensitive nature, in the twelfth house of the unconscious.

Her reign of 63 years and seven months is known as the Victorian era and was longer than that of any of her predecessors. It was a period of industrial, cultural, political, scientific, and military change within the United Kingdom, and was marked by a great expansion of the British Empire.

Through her reign, the gradual establishment of a modern constitutional monarchy in Britain continued. Reforms of the voting system increased the power of the House of Commons at the expense of the House of Lords and the monarch. As her monarchy became more symbolic than political, it placed a strong emphasis on morality and family values, in contrast to the sexual, financial and personal scandals that had been associated with previous members of the House of Hanover and which had discredited the monarchy.[207]

Swami Bhaktipada was a highly controversial, charismatic American Hare Krishna guru. He had Sedna in the first house of identity, bi-quintile his Sun in the seventh house of relationships.

A victim of childhood polio, who walks with the assistance of canes, he is the son of a conservative Baptist minister, who inherited his father's missionary spirit and attempted to convert classmates to his family's faith.

---

[206] https://en.wikipedia.org/wiki/Werner_Erhard
[207] https://en.wikipedia.org/wiki/Queen_Victoria

As a student at the University of North Carolina, he met an undergraduate English major who became his homosexual lover and lifelong friend. The two resigned from the university when he was 23, after being threatened with an investigation over a sex scandal. He moved to New York City, started promoting LSD use and became an LSD guru. Then he worked as an unemployment claims reviewer and enrolled at Columbia University to study religious history but quit after several years to travel to India at 28 in search of a guru, only to return to New York after six months, unsuccessful.

After returning from India, however, he met the Bengali guru who was known simply as Swamiji to his disciples, who was the founder of the Hare Krishnas. After attending Bhagavad-gita classes at the modest storefront temple in the Lower East Side of Manhattan, he accepted Swamiji as his spiritual master, receiving initiation at 29. A couple of years later he co-founded a 4,000 acre Hare Krishna community in West Virginia, which eventually housed over 300 faithful followers, and where he served as spiritual leader for 26 years.

When he was 40, he and ten other high-ranking Hare Krishna leaders assumed the position of initiating gurus; because of Swamiji's death, however, at 49 the Krishna Governing Body Commission expelled him because he had started claiming to be the sole spiritual heir to the Hare Krishna movement. They cited his ruthless tactics, an overly independent nature and general callousness to the spiritual well-being of the movement.

He then established his own organization, taking several properties with him. A couple of years later his New Vrindaban had 13 satellite centers in the United States and Canada. However, when he was 53, the US federal government indicted him on five counts of racketeering, six counts of mail fraud, and conspiracy to murder two of his opponents in the Hare Krishna movement when he was 48. The government charged that he ordered the killings because the victims had threatened to reveal his sexual abuse of minors. They also claimed that he had illegally amassed a profit of more than $10.5 million over four years.

At 53 he was convicted on nine of the 11 charges, but the jury failed to reach a verdict on the murder charges. However, the Court of Appeals threw out all the convictions, saying that child molestation evidence had unfairly prejudiced the jury against him and he was not charged with those crimes. A retrial was ordered and at 55, he was released from house arrest where he had lived for nearly two years and returned triumphantly to his community.

However, he lost his iron grip on the community a month later when he was accidentally discovered in a compromising position with a young male Malaysian disciple in the back of a Winnebago van. The community split into two camps and the challengers eventually ousted him and his supporters completely, and most of his followers moved to the temple in New York, which remained under his control.

Before his retrial was completed, he pleaded guilty to one count of racketeering for mail fraud and was sentenced to 20 years in prison. While he was in prison the Hare Krishna Child Protection Office concluded a 17-month investigation and determined that he had molested two boys. He was released from prison after serving eight years of a 12-year sentence and moved to India at 70 where he still had a significant number of loyal disciples, who worshiped him as a guru, dying there three years later.[208]

Margaret Atwood is a Canadian poet, novelist, literary critic, essayist, inventor, and environmental activist. She had Sedna in the twelfth house of the unconscious, bi-quintile her Sun in the sixth house of service.

Many of her poems have been inspired by myths and fairy tales, which have been interests of hers from an early age. Her themes are mainly the emotional interdependence of the sexes and their search for self-discovery.

This is exemplified in her book, *The Handsmaid's Tale*, published when she was 46, in which the sole function of the heroine is to breed. She often portrays female characters dominated by patriarchy in her novels. She also sheds light on women's social oppression as a result from patriarchal ideology. Still, she denies that her books are feminist and believes that the

---

[208] https://en.wikipedia.org/wiki/Kirtanananda_Swami

feminist label can only be applied to writers who consciously work within the framework of the feminist movement.

She is a winner of the Arthur C. Clarke Award and has been shortlisted for the Booker Prize five times, winning once. But she has also resisted the suggestion that her books, like *The Handmaid's Tale*, are science fiction, suggesting that they are speculative fiction instead, explaining that 'science fiction has monsters and spaceships, whereas speculative fiction takes place on Planet Earth and could really happen'.[209]

Humour can be one path to transcend the quicksand of Sedna, giving us the objectivity to step back from the edge, but also with the quintile and bi-quintile aspects to the Sun the ability to develop a higher consciousness through this process and understand the process of connecting with the audience at a deep level.

Like Grock, who was a famous Swiss clown, composer and musician, who is often called 'the king of clowns.' He was once the most highly paid entertainer in the world. He had Sedna in the first house of identity, quintile his Sun in the twelfth house of the unconscious.

He started early as a performer, learning musicianship and acrobatic skills from his father and later became a clown, working with the famous clown, Antonet. They developed an act with the aim of making the transition from circus to music hall stages, which were more lucrative. Refining their performances according to audience response, Grock came to dominate the act, and they eventually split up. By then his fame had spread, his act having developed into the mixture of pantomime and musical blunders for which he is now remembered.[210]

And like David Shiner, who is an American actor and clown. He has Sedna in tenth house of profession, bi-quintile his Sun in third house of communication. He built an early reputation working regularly in the streets at the Avignon Festival in France, drawing huge crowds to watch his antics on the castle walls of the old city and making a fortune in the hat.

---

[209] https://en.wikipedia.org/wiki/Margaret_Atwood

[210] https://en.wikipedia.org/wiki/Grock

He performed in the Broadway musical 'Seussical' and has movie appearances as a clown and as an actor, including *Lorenzo's Oil*, which was released when he was 39. He has also toured solo shows in Europe and America and mentored and guest directed for a German youth circus program.

At 37 he was featured in Cirque du Soleil's production 'Nouvelle Expérience,' touring for 19 months through Canada and the USA and playing for another year in Las Vegas. With his antics, including stepping through, on and over much of the crowd and the staging of a mock silent-movie melodrama with four members of the audience, he may be the best remembered of the Cirque's clowns. At 53 he wrote and directed Cirque du Soleil's touring production, 'Koozå.'[211]

At this juncture in human evolution, few of us use our planets at the spiritual level, but many of us are striving to, and such people are wonderful to be around. As with the other planets, the spiritual level of evolution is vastly different with Sedna from the two previous levels. Here, the quintile and bi-quintile aspects with the Sun brings a higher transpersonal consciousness, which is centered in the evolution of humanity and of all life forms on the planet.

Once we embrace the Sedna energy, which is the oneness of everything, our nurturing becomes an expression of Sedna consciousness and it becomes devotional in nature. The struggle of the beginners' level is gone, as are the transcendental crises of the intermediate level. At this level everything Saturnian is meaningless and yet everything Sednian has its place.

Luigi Quattrocchi was an Italian saint, who was beatified after his death along with his wife, the first time in church history that a man and his wife were given that honour together, as exemplars of the Christian life. He had Sedna in the tenth house of profession, quintile his Sun in the seventh house of relationships. He and his wife had four children, three of whom entered religious life. The couple opened their home to refugees during WWII, at great risk to the family. His wife had Sedna in the second house of material resources, square her Sun in the fifth house of 'what is produced in the home'.

---

[211] https://en.wikipedia.org/wiki/David_Shiner_(clown)

Hank Friedman is an American astrologer who began to study the field at 34 to disprove it, but became convinced of its validity. He had Sedna in the ninth house of spirituality and knowledge, quintile his Sun in the eleventh house of collective consciousness. (This is the reverse positioning of terrorist, Anders Breivik, mentioned above at the unconscious level).

He was a science whiz-kid in special advanced science programs from the 8th grade, through to his first year of graduate studies. As an adult he was trained for five years in Ericksonian Hypnotherapy and also as an advisor in parental deprogramming. He also studied Sufism for 20 years. He moved into a synthesis of Vedic with Western astrology and is a world expert in astrological software. He has beta-tested, designed and reviewed software from the age of 34 and is the author of "Astrology for Your PC" and review articles for astrology magazines. He is considered one of the San Francisco Bay's foremost psychics and psychic therapists.[212]

---

[212] https://www.astro.com/astro-databank/Friedman,_Hank_(1950)

29: Sedna / Moon

Conjunction

With the conjunction of Sedna and the Moon, the all-encompassing spiritual energy of Sedna infuses our emotions, our deepest personal needs, our basic habits and our unconscious reactions.

The Moon is a mediator between the inner world and the outer world. It is irrational, ruling habitual behaviours and prejudices. These may, or may not, be acted out, depending if we censor them, but the Moon rules our spontaneous reactions and feelings.

At the unconscious level the spiritual power of the conjunction can make us as a victim of someone's personal emotional mission or give us a personal mission of our own that we believe is right, no matter how perverted by our deepest emotional needs it might be. Either way, it is likely to leave us vulnerable. There can also be traumatic experiences in childhood which unconsciously shape our adult lives.

Dawn Brown was an American homicide victim who was shot to death by mistake by Tony Diaz when she was 25, after he mistook her for her sister. She had Sedna conjunct the Moon in the twelfth house of the unconscious.

Her sister had an affair with Diaz a couple of years before. He also has Sedna conjunct his Moon, but his conjunction is in the fourth house of home. A young man of mixed race, he never knew his dad, who left after he was born. His mom raised him on a social worker's salary in Massachusetts, and the boy worked hard and stayed out of trouble. He was well built, but so deeply shy that he walked in shuffling steps with his eyes downcast.

> Diaz was living in Cape Cod with his mother and was employed as a physical therapist aide while attending Springfield College. During this time, he started dating Dawn's sister, Kimberlee. But in the spring of 1992, she told him that she wanted to break off the relationship but would like to remain his friend. Kimberlee began dating another man who she would eventually marry and she started a job in New York City and moved to New Jersey.
>
> Later that month, Diaz telephoned Dawn's sister. The conversation went pleasantly until the young woman told Diaz that she was dating someone else. Diaz then reportedly called

her a 'f—ing bitch' before hanging up. It is believed that from then, an obsessed he began to plot revenge against the girl who had jilted him.

Kimberlee held her bridal shower at her mother's home and Dawn was there. She had recently dyed her hair blond, which made her look just like her sister with whom Diaz was obsessed. That evening, they went out for refreshments and ice cream with her sister's boyfriend and her teenage nephew. The three returned at around 23:00 hrs.

Around the same time, Diaz, who was apparently stalking his girlfriend, was also outside the premises. On spotting a blonde-haired woman, Diaz stood a foot away from the victim, pointed his Glock semi-automatic handgun at her head, called out Kimberlee's name, and fired. Leaving Dawn mortally wounded on the ground, he drove his vehicle to John Fitzgerald Kennedy International Airport and fled.[213]

A more extreme example is Arthur Shawcross, who was an American sexual deviant and a serial killer of 13 prostitutes in upper New York. Like Dawn, he also had Sedna conjunct the Moon in the twelfth house of the unconscious.

He was a weird child, unusually quiet and baby-talked up to the time he was five or six. He was a bed-wetter who played with imaginary playmates and tried to run away from home frequently. He was violently and painfully raped by an older man when he was a child. And as a youth, he claimed that he had sex with girls and as a teen, that he began a relationship with an older woman who taught him all the tricks, including oral sex.

He learned to please the older women whom he saw, and he also had sex with younger boys and farm animals. He found that torturing and killing an animal was a great rush, especially during bestiality. During military duty in Viet Nam, he witnessed and participated in sadistic acts. He said that he killed and butchered victims, and sex-tortured and cannibalised Vietnamese women, but by this time he was unable to tell the difference between truth

---

[213] https://www.kaieteurnewsonline.com/2009/09/20/a-stranger-in-her-bed/

and fantasy, because records show that he was never in combat, or on jungle patrol.

After Vietnam, he returned home to a cold welcome from his mom and resumed residence with the third woman whom he married and then began a spree of felony, arson, rape, murder, and cannibalisation of the genitalia of both male and female victims. At 26, he strangled an 11-year-old boy, then sexually molested and killed a little girl. Caught, he was sentenced to 17 years prison; however, he was paroled early under a plea bargain after 12 years.

He was 42 when he was released. He worked as a manual laborer, working with food packaging; however, soon local prostitutes started going missing, their bodies later found. He was caught and convicted again at 46. His original parole was called one of the most egregious examples of the unwarranted release of a prisoner in American history. Later resonance imaging showed brain lesions and right-brain formations resulting from childhood injuries, apparently from being brutally abused.[214]

Or we might experience an invasion of privacy, which is actually a spiritual challenge to our sense of emotional security. Like Marion Le Pen, who is a French politician and a member of the National Front, an extreme right-wing party. She has Sedna conjunct the Moon in the eighth house of shared resources.

She is the granddaughter of Jean-Marie Le Pen, the founder of the National Front and is one of the first two members of the National Front to serve in the National Assembly. However, in a book launched when she was 24, a French journalist revealed that the man who had raised her as his daughter, is not her birth father. And later that year the French weekly news magazine *L'Express* disclosed the real identity of her birth father and she officially announced that she had asked her lawyer to sue them for a 'serious invasion of her privacy'.[215]

---

[214] https://en.wikipedia.org/wiki/Arthur_Shawcross
[215] https://en.wikipedia.org/wiki/Marion_Maréchal-Le_Pen

Or we could be put in an uncomfortable position by the success of our spiritual mission. Like Srinivasa Ramanujan, who was was an Indian mathematician who lived during the British rule in India. He had a close conjunction of Sedna and the Moon straddling the MC, with Sedna in the tenth house of profession and the Moon in the ninth house of knowledge.

> Though he had almost no formal training in pure mathematics, he made substantial contributions to mathematical analysis, number theory, infinite series, and continued fractions, including solutions to mathematical problems considered to be unsolvable. The recognition of his genius began at 26 when he got a scholarship to study at Trinity College in Cambridge, England.

> He left India by boat, in spite of great difficulties caused by his caste as a Braman. His diet and religious observations were compromised by the difference in life style to which he had to adapt. And the isolation of his life in England, together with the dietary difficulties caused him great stress. He became ill, and at 30 he tried to kill himself by throwing himself in front of a train. Rescued, he struggled on until he was able to return to India a couple of years later but died the next year. His notebooks were published after his death.[216]

As we tire of density and the grief it creates, and we start a spiritual journey to get out of the swamp, Sedna rewards us with transcendent crises, experiences which force us to let go and rise above them, resulting in a huge growth to a new level of consciousness. There is no choice with these crises, and the more we try and solve them, the more we will get hurt.

Hermann Hesse was a German writer whose popularity extended well beyond his lifetime. He was considered a guru to the youth from the early 1900s until his death and beyond, one of the most inspirational writers of the 20th century. He had Sedna conjunction his Moon, which is also closely conjunct Vesta, the asteroid of regeneration, all in the third house of ideas and communication.

> He began writing at 22, while employed as a stock clerk in a rare bookstore. At 26 he was writing for journals and newspapers and

---

[216] https://en.wikipedia.org/wiki/Srinivasa_Ramanujan

his first books were published during this period. He was an alcoholic as an adult and was afflicted with bouts of hypochondria, depression, and thoughts of suicide throughout many years of stress and anguish. His late thirties was a period of extreme stress. His father died and his wife and youngest son became ill, which led to his having a nervous breakdown. During psychiatric care with Carl Jung and J.B. Lang, he developed a lifelong friendship with these outstanding men.

More books were published, but his first real success came in his early forties with, *Demian*. Due to a sudden crisis, however, he was then unable to write and went into deep analysis with Jung. His insights resulted in his book, *Siddhartha*, published when he was 45 and then *Steppenwolf*, published at 49. From 53 to 65 he worked on *The Glass Bead Game,* which was published during the anxious war years, as his wife and many friends were Jewish. He received the Nobel prize after the war at 69.[217]

Paula Prentiss is an American actress, a leading lady in Hollywood films, adept at urbane screwball comedy roles. She has Sedna conjunct her moon in the eighth house of shared resources and partnership agreements.

At 20, while studying drama at Northwestern University, she met her future husband Richard Benjamin, who impressed her with his sophistication. She married him when she was 23 and the marriage has been solid, standing the test of time for over fifty years.

While attending university she was discovered by the Metro-Goldwyn-Mayer Studio and was offered a film contract, which in those days was a full-time job, moving from one film to another. A highly sensitive performer, having acted in a string of films back to back, she had a nervous breakdown on the set of *What's New Pussycat?* in Paris when she was 27. She was hospitalized for nine months and the breakdown kept her out of film work for the next five years.

She returned to work with her husband in the television series *He & She*. The couple also appeared together in a number of

---

[217] https://en.wikipedia.org/wiki/Hermann_Hesse

films, like *Catch-22,* when she was 32, as well as in various plays. Except for brief cameo roles, she had not appeared in a feature film for more than 30 years until she played in a horror film, *I Am the Pretty Thing That Lives in the House*, when she was 79. The film premiered at the 2016 Toronto International Film Festival.[218]

Humour can be one path to transcend the quicksand of Sedna, giving us the objectivity to step back from the edge and also with the conjunction to the Moon make us a very sensitive performer.

John Cleese is an English actor, screenwriter, producer, and comedian. He has Sedna conjunct his Moon in the eighth house of shared resources.

> When he got a scholarship to an English public high school at 13, he was already more than 1.83 m tall. He allegedly defaced the school grounds as a prank, by painting footprints to suggest that the statue of Field Marshal Earl Haig had got down from his plinth and gone to the toilet. In his autobiography, *So, Anyway*, he says that discovering, aged 17, he had not been made a house prefect by his housemaster affected his outlook: 'It was not fair and therefore it was unworthy of my respect... I believe that this moment changed my perspective on the world'.

> Handsome and hyperactive, he wrote and played in humorous sketches and radio comedy while still in Cambridge. He achieved success at the Edinburgh Festival Fringe and as a scriptwriter and performer on *The Frost Report.* In his late twenties he co-founded Monty Python, the comedy troupe responsible for the TV sketch show *Monty Python's Flying Circus* and the four Monty Python films. He also played in a hilarious sit-com *Fawlty Towers* for 12 episodes, and in 1972 he started Video Arts, writing and producing more than 70 business training films that use humour to make the point.[219]

At this juncture in human evolution, few of us use our planets at the spiritual level, but many of us are striving to, and such people are

---

[218] https://en.wikipedia.org/wiki/Paula_Prentiss
[219] https://en.wikipedia.org/wiki/John_Cleese

wonderful to be around. As with the other planets, the spiritual level of evolution is vastly different with Sedna from the two previous levels.

Here, the conjunction with the Moon brings a sensitivity and empathy to the suffering of humanity and a mission to bring inner peace to this process. The struggle of the beginner's level is gone, as are the transcendental crises of the intermediate level. At this level everything Saturnian is meaningless and yet everything Sednian has its place.

Bishop Wuerl is an American ecclesiastic who upholds the beliefs and principles of the Catholic Church, but decried its secrecy during the sex abuse scandals of the early 2000s and called for more openness and involvement of laypeople. He has Sedna conjunct his moon in the sixth house of service.

> He has served as bishop in Seattle and Pittsburgh, has studied and worked in Rome. At 53, he confronted the Vatican by refusing to reinstate a priest that he had removed after he was accused of molesting a teenage boy.
>
> Two years later, the Vatican reversed itself and Bishop Wuerl has continued to remove abusive priests since then. At 66, he was named as the new archbishop of Washington, D.C. and he was elevated to Cardinal at 70. He is author of several books, and has appeared in a nationally syndicated television program, *The Teaching of Christ.*[220]

eter Kentenuch was a German priest of the Society of the Catholic Apostolate and founder of the Schoenstatt Movement, which attempted to teach Christians how to live out their faith. He had Sedna conjunct his Moon in the fourth house of home.

> He saw the movement as a means of spiritual renewal within the Catholic Church. The group focuses on education and spiritual development. 'We seek to grow as free, dedicated, and active witnesses of Christ in modern life by uniting our faith with our everyday lives. We look to Mary to educate us in this task and to guide us in becoming better followers of Christ'.
>
> His teachings underwent a series of challenges from political and ecclesiastical powers. During WW2 the Nazis were quick to

---

[220] https://en.wikipedia.org/wiki/Donald_Wuerl

classify him as one of their main opponents, and after endless vexations, he was summoned by Gestapo. An informer had reported him as saying: "My mission is to reveal the inner emptiness of National Socialism, and by there to defeat it."

As a result, at 56 he was imprisoned for a month in a cell without ventilation to break his resistance; however, he left physically debilitated, but calm and peaceful, as at the entry. After 5 months in prison he was sent to the Dachau concentration camp, at a time when the living conditions there were worsening. Of the 12,000 prisoners, 2,600 were priests. The Germans were grouped in one block and he gave a spiritual conference each night to his fellow prisoners.

He founded two new branches of his movement that year at Dachau. When he was transferred into a new block, he restarted his apostleship every time, despite the personal risk he incurred. Over the last three months of 1944, the tightening of the Nazi regime and epidemics caused the death of 10,000 prisoners. It is at this point, in a surprising act of faith, full of hope in the middle of that hellish place, he founded the international arm of his Movement which extended his teachings to the world. Under these unimaginable material conditions and at the peril of his life, he wrote treaties of spirituality, prayers and a didactic poem of over 20,000 verses.

On the arrival of the American troops at the end of the war, he was released and returned to his community at Schoenstatt. He immediately restarted his work, the experience of deportation helping him to teach his disciples on how to maintain inner freedom. Considered by many of those who came into contact with him to have been a saint, his cause for sainthood is currently under consideration by the church, ending the compilation of his writings and correspondences.[221]

Opposition

With the opposition of Sedna and the Moon, the all-encompassing spiritual energy of Sedna challenges our emotions, our deepest personal needs, our basic habits and our unconscious reactions.

---

[221] https://en.wikipedia.org/wiki/Joseph_Kentenich

The Moon is a mediator between the inner world and the outer world. It is irrational, ruling our habitual behaviours and prejudices. We may, or may not, act these out, depending if we censor them, but the Moon rules our spontaneous reactions and feelings.

With the opposition our emotional life stands in relief against the all-inclusive spiritual energy of Sedna and at the unconscious level, this may not be easy and we may feel marginalized, or victimized from an early age.

The vulnerable feeling nature is how we adapt and respond to our surroundings to keep us safe and in known territory and Sedna doesn't care about that; her mission is far broader, more epic, we are just a speck in the big picture.

In the extreme this can lead to a sort of anonymous abuse, where we are simply in the wrong place at the wrong time. Like Barabara Plekker, who was a Dutch prostitute and homicide victim. Her Sedna was conjunct Saturn, the planet of structure, in the seventh house of one-to-one relationships and opposite her Sun in the first house of identity. She was working out of a small, apartment-like room with a single window in the red-light district of Amsterdam, when she was strangled. It was a copycat crime, as four years prior, another prostitute had been killed in the same room, the same way.

Or we could develop an abusing attitude ourselves, simply because of our supposedly higher mission. Like Josef Mengele, who was a German doctor and member of the Nazi party. He had Sedna conjunct Orcus, the planet of delving down and speaking out, in the tenth house of profession, opposite his Moon in the fourth house of home.

> He was known as the 'Angel of Death' at the Auschwitz concentration camp during World War II for his grisly genetic research on twins and other subjects. He was the subject of a 40-year international hunt in the postwar years, known for being the butcher who had supervised the torture and death of as many as 400,000 Jews in a maniacal quest for racial purity.[222]

Or we might have a deep emotional wound from our heredity. Like Jan Kerouac, who was an American writer and the only daughter of Jack Kerouac, the famed Beat generation author of *On the Road*. She had

---

[222] https://en.wikipedia.org/wiki/Josef_Mengele

Sedna in the fifth house of creativity, opposite her Moon in the eleventh house of collective consciousness.

> Jan, who had met her father only twice -- when she was 9 and when she was 15 -- had fought in recent years to gain control of his archives. In 1994, she sued relatives of Mr. Kerouac's last wife, Stella Sampas, who inherited the notebooks, teletype rolls and parchment scrolls on which he wrote "On the Road" and laid down the first rumblings of postwar alienation that set the tone for the Beat Generation of the 1950's. "Her main intent was to put it into a museum or a library and preserve it forever,"

> Ms. Kerouac's first novel, "Baby Driver," was published when she was 29. It dealt with her childhood on the Lower East Side of Manhattan during the turbulent 1960's. Her second, "Trainsong" was about her travels after the first book. She had been working on "Parrot Fever," about the death of her mother, Joan Haverty. She was Mr. Kerouac's second wife. Her parents were estranged when she was born. The author denied being her father until she was 9, when he took a blood test and then acknowledged her as his daughter.[223]

> "I love making up words, I love words," she told the New York Times. "Writing is hard for me. I never had any real education. My mother moved us around a lot. We were on welfare. We didn't have any money. I was 6 and stole from the church poor box, I thought it was for us because we needed it. I never went to college... I only saw my father twice, when I was a little girl and when I was 15. My boyfriend and I popped in on him in Lowell. He said I could use his name if I ever published anything. We had to leave because his mother got upset. I was pregnant. I lost the baby in Mexico. I've had five miscarriages since."[224]

The key to consciousness growth with this aspect is not to take it personally. It may feel like society, or family, or beliefs are structured in a way to affect us, but they aren't. And if we take on an antagonistic relationship with our destiny, that can't end well.

---

[223] New York Times, June 1996 'Jan Kerouac, 44, the Novelist And Daughter of a Beat Icon'

[224] On the road with Kerouac's daughter, By Ernest Hebert, New York Times, 2008

Alan Turing was a British mathematician, logician, scientist and the technical genius behind Britain's successful efforts to break German codes in WW2. He had Sedna in the 12th house of the unconscious, opposite his Moon in the sixth house of service.

> He made inestimable contributions to cybernetics. His 'Computable Numbers', published when he was 25, is considered one of the outstanding scientific papers of the 20th century, a blueprint for what would become the electronic digital computer. His 'Universal Turing Machine' was an ancestor for the entire information age.
>
> He was accustomed to being a non-conformist. At boarding school, he refused to adapt and ignored subjects that did not interest him. He was an atheist, and felt marginalised because of his homosexuality. From the age of 13 he formed a significant friendship with another boy who has been described as his 'first love'. Their relationship provided inspiration in his future endeavours, but it was cut short by his friend's death when Alan was 17, from drinking infected cow's milk some years previously. The event caused him great sorrow and he coped with this by working that much harder on the topics of science and mathematics that he had shared with his friend.
>
> His Sedna is also conjunct Chariklo, the centaur of foresight and bi-quintile Ixion, the planet of lawlessness. Though he envisioned a time when "ladies will take their computers for walks in the park," his own reality was not quite so whimsical. When a robbery occurred at his house in Manchester, he frankly told the police that the robber probably knew the man with whom he was having an affair. As homosexual relations were still a felony in Britain, Turing was tried and convicted of gross indecency. He was spared prison but was given a year's probation with the condition that he take oestrogen to diminish his sex drive.[225]

As we tire of density and the grief it creates, and we start a spiritual journey to get out of the swamp, Sedna rewards us with transcendent crises, experiences which force us to let go and rise above them, resulting in a huge growth to a new level of consciousness. There is no

---

[225] https://en.wikipedia.org/wiki/Alan_Turing

choice with these crises, and the more we try and solve them, the more we will get hurt.

Alexander Graham Bell was a Scottish-born American audiologist best known as the inventor of the telephone and founder of AT&T. He had Sedna closely conjunct Mercury, the planet of ideas and communication, and with Chariklo, the centaur of foresight, all in the first house of identity, opposite his Moon in the seventh house of relationships.

His father, grandfather, and brother had all been associated with work on elocution and speech and both his mother and wife were deaf, profoundly influencing his life's work, as he continued to teach, research and invent for the rest of his life.

As a child he displayed a natural curiosity about his world, resulting in gathering botanical specimens, as well as experimenting even at an early age. He showed a sensitive nature and a talent for art, poetry, and music that was encouraged by his mother. With no formal training, he mastered the piano and became the family's pianist. Despite being normally quiet and introspective, he revelled in mimicry and 'voice tricks' akin to ventriloquism that continually entertained family guests during their occasional visits.

He was also deeply affected by his mother's gradual deafness, as she began to lose her hearing when he was 12. He learned a manual finger language, so he could sit at her side and tap out silently the conversations swirling around the family parlour. He also developed a technique of speaking in clear, modulated tones directly into her forehead, whereby she could hear him with reasonable clarity. He was largely family trained and self-taught. His first professional post was as a teenager in school, where he also instructed the other children in both music and elocution. At 21 he became his father's assistant in London and assumed full charge while he lectured in America.

However, with his work responsibilities, the stress took its toll on his health and the family moved to Canada when he was 23, where his health rapidly improved. The next year he spent several weeks in Boston, lecturing and demonstrating the system of his father's Visible Speech as a means of teaching speech to the deaf. He continued to lecture and do his own research, even while on vacation. And the following year he opened his own school in Boston for training teachers of the deaf and one year later he became professor of vocal physiology at Boston University.

At 29, with the help of his assistant, a young repair mechanic and model maker, he invented the telephone. The famous story relates that his first words that were carried over an electronic transmission were, "Come here, I want to see you," to the astonishment of his assistant. He obtained a patent for his invention and within a year began a commercial application. Within a few months, the first of hundreds of legal suits began; however, his claims were upheld. The Bell Telephone Company was formed that year and it became the American Telephone and Telegraph Company eight years later, when he was 37, to manage the expanding long-distance business.[226]

We may also react to this aspect by trying to shield the emotional self with a public persona, like Walt Disney. He was an American entrepreneur, animator, voice actor and film producer. He had Sedna in the seventh house of relationships, opposite his Moon in the first house of identity. He was a shy, self-deprecating and insecure man in private, but adopted a warm and outgoing public persona.

He had high standards and high expectations of those with whom he worked. Although there have been accusations that he was racist or anti-Semitic, these have been contradicted by many who knew him. A pioneer of the American animation industry, he introduced several new developments in the production of cartoons, including the first cartoon feature film.

He first created Mickey Mouse when he was 27, for a single test screening of the short, Plane Crazy, but it failed to find a distributor. Following the sensational response to his next short, he used synchronised sound on the third to create the first sound cartoon. After the animation was complete, he signed a contract with the former executive of Universal Pictures to use the Cinephone recording system and they became the new distributor for his early sound cartoons.

---

[226] https://en.wikipedia.org/wiki/Alexander_Graham_Bell

The cartoons soon became so popular that he felt he was not receiving his rightful share of profits, so the next year he asked for an increase in payments. Cinephone refused and signed the graphic artist who had been working with him, to work for them instead. As a result, just before his thirtieth birthday, he had a nervous breakdown, and he took an extended holiday to Cuba with his wife and they had a cruise to Panama to recover.

However, he had earlier in his career had a successful cartoon character removed from his control by the person who owned the rights, so he had made sure that he owned the rights to Mickey. He signed a new contract with Columbia Pictures to distribute the cartoons, which became increasingly popular, including internationally.

As a film producer, he holds the record for most Academy Awards earned by an individual, having won 22 Oscars, from 59 nominations. The opposition with his Moon made him very sensitive to how his stories and characters would connect with people and he was able to read the pulse of the American people with his films, so much so, that in the rest of the world they came to be seen as cultural imperialism.[227]

As we see, there is a huge upside to this aspect, because it puts us in intimate touch with Sedna consciousness, so we 'feel the pulse of the time,' and this ability becomes increasingly available to us as we grow.

Arthur Schopenhauer was a German philosopher and writer known for his fine prose style and pessimistic philosophies. He had Sedna in the tenth house of profession, opposite his Moon in the fourth house of home.

He led a solitary life and became deeply involved in the study of Buddhist and Hindu philosophies and mysticism. He was also a misogynist, never marrying and discouraging any friendships. His main work was, *The World as Will and Idea* published when he was 31, in which he characterizes the phenomenal world as the product of a blind and insatiable metaphysical will. Coming from the transcendental idealism of Immanuel Kant, he developed an atheistic metaphysical and ethical system that has

---

[227] https://en.wikipedia.org/wiki/Walt_Disney

been described as an exemplary manifestation of philosophical pessimism, rejecting the post-Kantian philosophies of German idealism.

He was among the first thinkers in Western philosophy to share and affirm significant tenets of Eastern philosophy, like asceticism and 'the world-as-appearance', having initially arrived at similar conclusions, as the result of his own philosophical work. Though his work failed to garner substantial attention during his life, he has had a posthumous impact across various disciplines, including philosophy, literature, and science. His writing on aesthetics, morality, and psychology exerting important influence on thinkers and artists throughout the 19th and 20th centuries.[228]

Humour can be one path to transcend the quicksand of Sedna, giving us the objectivity to step back from the edge and also with the opposition to the Moon, once we overcome our fear of rejection, an ability to milk the emotions to a very deep level.

Fernandel was a French actor and mime comedian with a long, sorrowful, equine face and a radiant and toothy smile. He had Sedna in the eleventh house of collective consciousness, opposite his Moon in the fifth house of creativity.

One of France's leading box-office draws, he built a four-decade career from the age of 27. His films included the four great "Don Camillo" political comedies. His father was an accountant but also an amateur comedian-singer and his mother was also an amateur actress, and they quickly noticed the talent of their son. He often accompanied his father during the concerts he organised in the Marseilles suburbs and, in a contest for amateur singers at the theatre of Châtelet de Marseille, he won first prize for child prodigies.

He made his debut on stage at five years singing the military repertory with his elder brother. He had his first great success at the age of seven, a day when, paralysed by stage fright, he was propelled on the stage by his father, with a great kick to the rear.

---

[228] https://en.wikipedia.org/wiki/Arthur_Schopenhauer

He fell into his sabre and stretched his whole length under a storm of laughter. Later, he was never afraid to face the public.

In 1930, he appeared in his first motion picture and for more than forty years he would be France's top comic actor. He was perhaps best loved for his portrayal of the irascible Italian village priest at war with the town's Communist mayor in the Don Camillo series of motion pictures which he also directed. His horse-like teeth became part of his trademark.[229]

At this juncture in human evolution, few of us use our planets at the spiritual level, but many of us are striving to, and such people are wonderful to be around. As with the other planets, the spiritual level of evolution is vastly different with Sedna from the two previous levels. Here the opposition with the Moon brings an empathy to the suffering of humanity and a mission to find inner peace in the midst of this.

Keeping our heart open in hell and still singing our song of life is the key to growth with this aspect once we are on the spiritual path. At the spiritually evolved level the struggle of the beginner's level is gone, as are the transcendental crises of the intermediate level. At this level everything Saturnian is meaningless and yet everything Sednian has its place.

Maria von Trapp was an Austrian-American musician and famous wife of Baron von Trapp, a homemaker, lecturer and organizer of the "Trapp Family Singers." She had Sedna in the sixth house of service, opposite her Moon, which was conjunct Vecta, the asteroid of regeneration, with both in the twelfth house of the unconscious.

> She was left an orphan at an early age and went to live with older kin. She joined a convent when she was young, planning to become a nun until she was placed into service with the widowed Baron von Trapp to help with the household and care for his seven children. Seeing how much she cared about his children, the Baron asked her to marry him, although he was 25 years her senior.
>
> Frightened, she fled back to the Abbey to seek guidance from the Mother Abbess, who advised that it was God's will that she should marry him. Since she was taught always to follow God's

---

[229] https://en.wikipedia.org/wiki/Fernandel

will, she returned to the family and told the Captain she would marry him. She later wrote in her autobiography however that on her wedding day she was blazing mad, both at God and at her husband, because what she really wanted was to be a nun.

She wrote that: "I really and truly was not in love. I liked him but didn't love him. However, I loved the children, so in a way I really married the children. However, I learned to love him, more than I have ever loved before or after." They married and had three more children. Fleeing the Nazi Regime, they emigrated to the U.S. and became the world-renowned and well-traveled group, 'The Trapp Family Singers'. The family gained fame when their story was told in the film *The Sound of Music*, a noted tribute to both the hardships and the romance of the family.[230]

Jean-Baptiste Lacordaire was a leading ecclesiastic in the Roman Catholic revival in France following the Napoleonic period. He had Sedna conjunct the North Node, the point representing the karma he is creating, in the tenth house of profession, opposite his Moon, which was conjunct his South Node, the point of the karma he has to deal with, in the fourth house of home.

Raised in a troubled time, he renounced religion and studied and practiced law, but after experiencing a religious awakening he studied for the priesthood and was ordained at 25. A couple of years later he joined a small group of Roman Catholic writers and founded a journal called 'The Future', which advocated the separation of church and state. However, the Pope condemned the doctrines and the journal was suppressed.

A period of disappointment followed, during which he focused his energies on preaching. His sermons appealed to Parisian intellectuals and, at 33, the archbishop of Paris invited him to preach at Notre Dame, where his lectures became known as the Lenten Conferences. He returned to Paris five years later and resumed his preaching at Notre Dame, using his pulpit this time as a means to express his support of liberty in church and state.[231]

---

[230] https://en.wikipedia.org/wiki/Maria_von_Trapp
[231] https://en.wikipedia.org/wiki/Jean-Baptiste_Henri_Lacordaire

Joseph Ratzinger served as Pope Benedict XVI, leader of the Catholic Church, from the age of 78, until his resignation at 86. He has Sedna conjunct Nessus, the asteroid of righteousness, in the first house of self, opposite his moon in the seventh house of relationships.

> Despite his conservative and dogmatic views, he is described as being personally charming and quick-witted, a stimulating conversationalist, fluent in several languages. He is considered to be genuinely pious, intellectually brilliant, blunt, and passionate about the truth. A man who has the courage of his convictions.
>
> The son of a police officer from a farming family in Lower Bavaria, he was drafted into the auxiliary anti-aircraft service during WW2, but deserted. He was subsequently imprisoned in an Allied POW camp until the end of the war. His experiences as a young man during the war were critical in formulating his ideas about the role of the church. After it ended he began to study philosophy and theology at the University of Munich and was ordained as a priest at 24, obtaining his doctorate in theology a couple of years later.
>
> By the age of 42, he had become a professor of dogmatic theology and of the history of dogma at the University of Regensburg. However, after seeing the horrors perpetrated by the Nazis, he argued that the church must present an alternative to the state and that the church must stand for absolute truths. At the age of 85, he resigned the papacy, due to his old age, becoming the first pope to resign since 1415. He was the fourth-oldest person to hold the office; however, the move was still very unexpected. In modern times, all popes have stayed in office until death.[232]

Semi-sextile, Sextile, Trine

With the flowing aspects between Sedna and the Moon, the all-encompassing spiritual energy of Sedna aligns with our emotions, our deepest personal needs, our basic habits and our unconscious reactions.

---

[232] https://en.wikipedia.org/wiki/Pope_Benedict_XVI

The Moon is a mediator between the inner world and the outer world. It is irrational, ruling our hhabitual behaviours and prejudices. We may, or may not, act these out, depending if we censor them, but the Moon rules our spontaneous reactions and feelings.

At the unconscious level the spiritual power of the flows with Sedna can be challenging, because they can give us a sense of destiny which comes from our deepest personal emotional needs and, while that may represent our truth, it may be out of step with the reality around us.

The vulnerable feeling nature is how we adapt and respond to our surroundings to keep us safe and in known territory, and at the unconscious level the flows can give us a sense of righteousness, or arrogance, which may lead us into dangerous territory, or make us as a victim of someone else's righteousness, or emotions and the inadequate support systems in society.

Like Kathleen Dempsey, who was an American homicide victim who died of massive stab wounds to her abdomen, diaphragm, liver and kidneys at 41. The killer was not known and was never apprehended. She had Sedna in the third house of communication, trine her Moon in the seventh house of relationships.

> Fatally wounded, she called 911 for help and was unable to get through. Reaching a telephone operator instead, her call was transferred to the fire department. Her family sued the telephone company because the operator failed to identify herself to the fire department dispatcher and failed to give him the phone number from which Kathleen had called, which would have enabled them to find the address where she lay bleeding. It took the fire department hours to decipher the call, by which time it was too late.[233]

Or like Sophie Prefaut, who was a young French autistic woman, killed by her mother in a so-called mercy-killing. She had Sedna in the fifth house of children, sextile her Moon in the second house of material reality.

> Suffering from infantile psychosis at 2 years, Sophie at best, writes dictation without mistakes, calculates cubic roots, or goes on a happy trip with her parents to Prague or San Francisco. She

---

[233] https://www.astro.com/astro-databank/Dempsey,_Kathleen

radiates "a bright smile, is intelligent, humorous. At worst, she yells terribly, stirs, assaults people and breaks everything. Then nothing can relieve her, no one can control her.

Becoming 'adult', she suffered violent medical treatment (antipsychotics, ECT) that aggravated her condition, causing horrible pain and epileptic seizures, bringing her close to death. For twenty years, her mother supports her, sacrifices everything, including her work. In times of crisis, she'd sleep at the foot of Sophie's bed, then when the day came, drive around in a car for hours, because it was the only way to calm her down.

Finally, she made Sophie a drink mixing sedatives with grenadine and took her for a ride in the car. She thinks that the drug will cause cardiac arrest, but Sophie only becomes comatose, so her mother put her hand over her mouth and pinched her nostrils till she died. She was given a five-year sentence.[234]

Or we may have little regard for the emotional cost of our mission, or for any normal sense of decency. Like Joseph McCarthy, who was an American politician who, as a Senator, was the chairman of various investigating committees commonly known as 'The Red Witch Hunts.' He had Sedna, conjunct Orcus, the planet of delving down and speaking out, in the twelfth house of the unconscious, trine his Moon in the fifth house of creativity.

He was an inflammatory speaker and insidious interrogator, with a tendency to fabricate evidence, which ruined many lives. He was elected to the Senate in a Republican landslide at the age of 38, where he was known mainly for being a genial drinking companion and a soft touch for the real estate lobby.

He burst into prominence at 42 when he announced: "I have in my hand a list of 205 names, known to the Secretary of State as being members of the Communist Party, who are nevertheless still working and shaping policy in the State Department."

The numbers began to change in a matter of days, to "207 bad risks," then "57 card-carrying Communists," and finally "81

[234] http://www.liberation.fr/evenement/1996/02/22/sanction-de-principe-pour-la-mere-meurtriere-de-sa-fille-autiste-les-jures-de-la-cour-d-assises-de-l_164272

loyalty risks." In the end not one was a card-carrying Communist in the State Department and all those listed were from outdated files on government employees who had been investigated for offences ranging from alleged communist and fascist sympathies to drinking problems and homosexuality.

However, the bluff worked and the polls showed that half of the American public applauded, while only 29 percent disapproved. Then he announced he'd uncovered the top Soviet espionage agent in the US; however, the spy turned out to be a bespectacled university professor and East Asia expert whose only crime was predicting the fall of the Chinese Nationalist government and urging the US to deal rationally with Mao Tse Tung.

TV was still in its infancy at that time and when the McCarthy hearings began with 36 days of live TV exposure, it had the whole nation intensely watching. He was 46. His fatal moment came when the chief attorney for his sub-committee, was being questioned by the Army's special counsel. McCarthy interrupted, as was his irritating habit, and announced that a young lawyer from counsel's firm had once belonged to a leftist lawyer's group. The stunned lawyer responded slowly and emotionally, "Have you no sense of decency, sir? At long last, have you no sense of decency?"

The lawyer received a standing ovation and the subsequent polls showed McCarthy's popularity plummeting. Two days later a motion was introduced to censure him in the Senate for conduct 'contrary to senatorial traditions.' His strange and stormy career was ended at 46 when he was censured in a 67-22 vote. After the censure his health started failing and he began drinking more and holding it less well. He died of acute hepatitis as a result of alcohol abuse a couple of years later.[235]

As we tire of density and the grief it creates, and we start a spiritual journey to get out of the swamp, Sedna rewards us with transcendent crises, experiences which force us to let go and rise above them, resulting in a huge growth to a new level of consciousness. There is no

---

[235] https://en.wikipedia.org/wiki/Joseph_McCarthy

choice with these crises, and the more we try and solve them, the more we will get hurt.

Elián González was a Cuban refugee, who at age five became a world figure by being rescued from the ocean. He had Sedna in the fifth house of what is produced in the home, trine his Moon in the in the ninth house of knowledge.

> The 17-foot aluminum motor boat was holding 14 people, including Elian and his mother, developed engine trouble, hit a storm, capsized and sank in the ocean between Cuba and Florida. There were only 3 inner tubes aboard. Elian was put into the centre of one inner tube, with five people, including his mother, holding on. His mother was focused only on his needs, giving him all the fresh water she had until it was gone. He was very quiet and never cried. He kept repeating a prayer he knew over and over, asking his guardian angel to stay with him day and night and to protect him.

> During the night, he watched as his mother, who could not swim, slipped off the inner tube and sank into the ocean. He never saw her again. He drifted for 50 hours, until two fishermen came upon the inner tube bobbing in the water, a few miles off the Florida coast. He was taken to the hospital, and Immigration authorities gave him allowance to stay in the U.S. and set up a bid for permanent residency in one year. His father's relatives had met the boy on a visit to Cuba, so the child already knew his Miami family and Elian was taken to his relatives in the U.S.

> His parents had divorced before he was born and his dad had once tried to leave Cuba, but failed. He was by then remarried with a second family. Elian spoke to his father on the phone, telling him that he wanted to stay in America, but his father demanded he return to Cuba. His US relatives went to court to allow him to stay, but a district court ruling that only his father, and not his extended relatives, could petition for asylum on the boy's behalf was upheld by the Court of Appeals. After the Supreme Court declined to hear the case, federal agents took him from the US relatives and returned him to his father in Cuba.

> By 21 he was reported to be studying to be an industrial engineer and hoped to marry his high school sweetheart and

fiancée after finishing college. At 23 he received a degree in industrial engineering and read a letter to Fidel Castro from his graduating class, vowing "to fight from whatever trench the revolution demands." After graduating he began working at a state run company which makes large plastic water tanks as a technology specialist. He wants to return to school to earn a master's degree.[236]

As we develop our Sedna consciousness, we are likely to be highly in tune with the evolutionary process as well, so we can understand the mechanisms behind the veil of reality.

Like Charles Darwin, who is the father of the theory of evolution. He had Sedna in the third house of ideas and communication, sextile his Moon, which was together with Haumea, the planet of rebirth, both in the second house of material resources. This placement is very appropriate for the person who integrated emotions into the traditional philosophical categories of mind and body. He examined human evolution and emotions in his book, *The Expression of the Emotions in Man and Animals*, published when he was 63, which looks at genetically determined aspects of behaviour.

> In this book, he seeks to trace the origins of such human characteristics as the pursing of the lips in moments of concentration and the mental confusion which typically accompanies blushing. Before this, human emotional life had posed problems to the traditional philosophical categories of mind and body. Darwin's biological approach links mental states to the neurological organization of movement and the book forms his main contribution to psychology.
>
> He said, "I never gave up Christianity until I was forty years of age." He then agreed that Christianity was "not supported by the evidence," but he had reached this conclusion only slowly. However his Theory of Evolution is recognised as having impacted massively on human societies across the World, not least in the areas of faith and religious beliefs.
>
> These diverse impacts on so many aspects of human lives have been so far-reaching that a "Darwinian Revolution" has been

---

[236] https://en.wikipedia.org/wiki/Elián_González

accepted as having taken place. This use of the word "revolution" derives from an early scientific "revolution" where Nicolas Copernicus' view that the Earth revolved around the Sun, rather than itself being at the fixed centre of God's creation, was published to meet much controversy, in his work *On Revolution of the Heavenly Orbs*.

Interestingly, Darwin hesitated about making his theory - which he had crafted into a 'publishable' sketch in the early 1840s - widely known in his own lifetime. His wife was sincerely religious and he also seems to have feared for his own and his family's perceived respectability if he made his potentially massively controversial evolutionary views public.[237]

Humour can be one path to transcend the quicksand of Sedna, giving us the objectivity to step back from the edge and also with the flowing aspects to the Moon a sense of rapport with people, which puts us in tune with popular sentiment.

Like Lynne Carter, who was an American female-impersonator, entertainer and actor, famous from the '50s through the '70s, earning up to $10,000 a week. He has Sedna conjunct Nessus, the centaur of the fragility of life, in the eighth house of shared resources, semi-sextile his Moon in the sixth house of service.

Born in Cleveland, Ohio, Carter served in the United States Navy during WW2. He began his performance career at 23 in a Chicago nightclub. He worked with big bands, typically 15 musicians, with small ensembles, and with a solo pianist, as well as other dancers. He impersonated many famous actresses and singers and he also created several original characters. He is best known for starring in the long-running Jewel Box Review showcase. At 47 he became the first female impersonator to perform at Carnegie Hall. Critics attribute his success to his ability to give his characterisations authenticity and depth as well as humour.[238]

Or like Joan Rivers, who was an American comedienne, thought by many to be the funniest lady on the planet. She had Sedna in the first

[237] https://en.wikipedia.org/wiki/Charles_Darwin
[238] https://en.wikipedia.org/wiki/Lynne_Carter

house of identity, trine her Moon in the ninth house of knowledge. Her Sedna is also in a close evolutionary quintile to Venus, which is conjunct Mercury, the planet of communication, both in the third house of ideas.

> She certainly had one of the fastest, most agile minds in show biz. Her rapid-fire mix of gossip, insults, flaunting of taboos and ridicule of flaws and neurosis were mostly written by her. She also wrote comedy for *Candid Camera*, scripts and material for Phyllis Diller and Zsa Zsa Gabor and humorous books.

> The younger of two daughters of Russian-Jewish refugees, she learned from her doctor dad to crack a joke and was making people laugh by the time she was 11. She learned from her mom that rich was better than poor, and was raised with privilege and a good education. She married at 24 and had it annulled the following year when she decided she wanted to be an actress, not a housewife. While doing off-Broadway, she worked in offices and turned to comedy at 27 to supplement her income.

> At the age of 32 she was told that she was too old and passed over; however, a week later she was booked on Johnny Carson's *Tonight Show*. They clicked. Their immediate rapport was a hit with the audience and she appeared for years with Carson before hosting her own *Late Show Starring Joan Rivers*, with a contract for $10 million over three years. She moved into the stratosphere as America's top comedienne, the darling of the circuit with tours, magazine covers, nightclub and Las Vegas gigs, TV projects, books and records.[239]

At this juncture in human evolution, few of us use our planets at the spiritual level, but many of us are striving to, and such people are wonderful to be around. As with the other planets, the spiritual level of evolution is vastly different for Sedna, from the two previous levels.

Here, the flowing aspects with the Moon brings an empathy to the suffering of humanity and an ability to find inner peace in the midst of this. The struggle of the beginner's level is gone, as are the transcendental crises of the intermediate level. At this level everything Saturnian is meaningless and yet everything Sednian has its place.

---

[239] https://en.wikipedia.org/wiki/Joan_Rivers

Philip K. Dick was an American writer notable for publishing works of science fiction. He explored philosophical, social, and political themes in novels, with plots dominated by monopolistic corporations, authoritarian governments, alternate universes, and altered states of consciousness.

He had Sedna in the first house of identity, sextile his Moon in the eleventh house of collective consciousness.

His work reflected his personal interest in metaphysics and theology, and often drew upon his life experiences in addressing the nature of reality, identity, drug abuse, schizophrenia, and transcendental experiences. His stories typically focus on the fragile nature of what is real and the construction of personal identity. His stories often become surreal fantasies, as the main characters slowly discover that their everyday world is actually an illusion assembled by powerful external entities, vast political conspiracies or the vicissitudes of an unreliable narrator.

"All of his work starts with the basic assumption that there cannot be one, single, objective reality," writes science fiction author Charles Platt. "Everything is a matter of perception. The ground is liable to shift under your feet. A protagonist may find himself living out another person's dream, or he may enter a drug-induced state that actually makes better sense than the real world, or he may cross into a different universe completely."

Alternate universes and simulacra are common plot devices, with fictional worlds inhabited by common, working people, rather than galactic elites. Dick's thinking and work was heavily influenced by the writings of Carl Jung. The Jungian constructs and models that most concerned Dick seem to be the archetypes of the collective unconscious, group projection/hallucination, synchronicities, and personality theory.

In the Seventies, while recovering from the effects of sodium pentothal administered for the extraction of an impacted wisdom tooth, he began experiencing strange hallucinations. Although initially attributing them to side effects from medication, he considered this explanation implausible after they continued. He came to believe they imparted wisdom and clairvoyance. On one occasion the hallucinations imparted the information to him that his infant son was ill. The Dicks rushed the child to the hospital, where his suspicion was confirmed by professional diagnosis.

"I experienced an invasion of my mind by a transcendentally rational mind, as if I had been insane all my life and suddenly I had become sane," Dick told Charles Platt. As the hallucinations increased in length and frequency, Dick claimed he began to live two parallel lives, one as himself, and one as "Thomas," a Christian persecuted by Romans in the first century AD. He referred to the "transcendentally rational mind" as "Zebra," "God" and "VALIS" and wrote about these experiences in his VALIS trilogy.[240]

Florence Nightingale, was an English social reformer and statistician and the founder of modern nursing. She had Sedna on the cusp of the seventh house of relationships, in a close sextile with her Moon, which is conjunct Vesta, the asteroid of regeneration, and her Sun, her sense of self, all in the ninth house of knowledge.

Though she did not think herself deeply religious, when she was scarcely 17 years old she felt that God spoke to her, calling her to a future of service. From that time on her life was changed. Not knowing the nature of the service, she feared making herself unworthy of whatever it was by leading the frivolous life that her mother and her social set demanded of her and instead was given to periods of preoccupation, or to what she called "dreams" of how to fulfil her mission.

She came to prominence in her mid-thirties, serving as a teacher and manager of nurses during the Crimean War, where she organised the care of wounded soldiers. She gave nursing a highly favourable reputation and became an icon of Victorian culture, as "The Lady with the Lamp" making rounds of wounded soldiers at night. At 40, she laid the foundation of professional nursing with the establishment of her nursing school at St Thomas' Hospital in London. It was the first secular nursing school in the world. Her social reforms include improving healthcare for all sections of British society, advocating better hunger relief in India, helping to abolish prostitution laws that

---

[240] https://en.wikipedia.org/wiki/Philip_K._Dick

were over-harsh to women, and expanding the acceptable forms of female participation in the workforce.

Although much of her work improved the lot of women everywhere, she was of the opinion that women craved sympathy and were not as capable as men. She preferred the friendship of powerful men, insisting they had done more than women to help her attain her goals. She often referred to herself in the masculine, as 'a man of action' and 'a man of business.' Some scholars believe that she remained chaste for her entire life, perhaps because she felt a religious calling to her career.

However, during the Crimean War she contracted a fever that left her so weakened that she spent the last 50 years of her life as an invalid. From the age of 37 onwards, she was intermittently bedridden and suffered from depression. Despite her symptoms, she remained phenomenally productive in social reform. She was a prodigious and versatile writer. In her lifetime, much of her published work was concerned with spreading medical knowledge. Some of her tracts were written in simple English so that they could easily be understood by those with poor literary skills. She also helped popularise the graphical presentation of statistical data. Much of her writing, including her extensive work on religion and mysticism, has only been published posthumously.[241]

Marthe Robin was a French mystic and stigmatic. She had Sedna conjunct Pallas, the asteroid of wisdom, in the eighth house of the occult, semi-sextile her Moon in the ninth house of knowledge.

Serious illness marked her adult life and from her twenties she was confined to bed, crippled, and gradually paralysed. She ate only wafers and neither drank nor slept but lived for seven decades and carried on a busy apostolate.

From the age of 28 she was completely paralysed and bedridden. Although she still could move the thumb and forefinger of one hand, she became motionless apart from her head, which she could move slightly. Since the previous year, at the age of 25, she could not eat anything at all. And from the age

[241] https://en.wikipedia.org/wiki/Florence_Nightingale

of 26 she couldn't even take a sip of water. When doctors tried to force some water down her throat, it merely came out her nostrils.

For the next 53 years her only food was the holy Eucharist, a wafer of bread which Catholics believe is the body of Christ. They also believe that they become his body on ingesting it. Once a week she was given the sacred host. Once she had received it she went immediately into ecstasy and began her weekly re-living of Christ's crucifixion. Every Friday wounds appeared in the palms of her hands and the stigmata, the scourging and crowning with thorns appeared on her body, and she appeared to be dead.

For 53 years she also carried on a busy apostolate, which is a Christian organisation directed to serving and evangelising the world. She was directed to found two schools in her native village, one for girls and one for boys. All this she directed down to the smallest detail from her bed in her darkened little room. Later on she was told to found a community which would welcome people looking for a retreat and which would be a home of "light, charity and love." It became known as the Foyer de Charité and there are now some 70 affiliated houses and communities throughout the world.[242]

Semi-square, Square, Sesquiquadrate

With the stressful aspects between Sedna and the Moon, the all-encompassing spiritual energy of Sedna challenges our emotions, our deepest personal needs, our basic habits and our unconscious reactions.

The Moon is a mediator between the inner and the outer world. It is irrational, ruling our hhabitual behaviours and prejudices. These may, or may not, be acted out, depending if we censor them, but it rules our spontaneous reactions and feelings.

The stressful aspects can leave us feeling a little at odds with the larger scheme of things and, at the unconscious level, the spiritual power of these aspects can be challenging, because they can give us a sense of destiny which comes from our deepest personal emotional needs and,

---

[242] https://fr.wikipedia.org/wiki/Marthe_Robin

while that may represent our truth, it is likely to be out of step with the reality around us.

The squeaky wheel gets the oil however, so if we develop our Sedna consciousness, over time that oddness can become incorporated into society in an evolutionary way.

Our vulnerable feeling nature is how we adapt and respond to our surroundings to keep us safe and in known territory and the stressful relationships can give us a sense of righteousness, or arrogance, which may lead us into dangerous territory.

At the unconscious level we may also experience feelings of marginalization, or victimization and, if we are not consciously working with the Sedna energy, this unfortunately can lead to abuse, or abusive behaviour.

Like Abraham Kasparian, who is an American politician who stabbed his wife three times in a public restaurant. He had Sedna in the fifth house of romance and children, square his Moon in the second house of material resources.

> His wife had filed for a divorce but agreed to meet him for lunch. She survived. Earlier that same day, a former tenant sued the Kasparians charging them with negligence in connection with an apartment fire that killed two children. He had been arrested previously at the age of 19, when he received sentences for welfare fraud and larceny. and at 40 he was accused of attacking a business partner with a knife but was acquitted.[243]

Often Sedna can manifest at the unconscious level as a blind spot. Marcel Chevalier was the last chief executioner in France. He had Sedna conjunct Mars, the planet of war, in the ninth house of spirituality, and sesquiquadrate his Moon in the fourth house of home.

> He was chief executioner for five years from the age of 55, until capital punishment was abolished in France. He started his career at 37, performed about 40 executions overall. After his appointment as chief executioner, he executed only two people. They were the last two executions in France. He was married to the niece of the penultimate chief executioner. He was

---

[243] https://www.astro.com/astro-databank/Kasparian,_Abraham

interviewed by the press on a number of occasions, but later, disillusioned by the sensationalist nature of press coverage, chose to say nothing of his experiences with the guillotine.[244]

Another example is Stephane Delabriere, who was a French serial killer. He had Sedna in the sixth house of daily routine, square his Moon in the ninth house of knowledge.

> The eldest of five children, he was tortured by his violent and alcoholic father. At age 13 he was put in a foster home. Calling himself the Prince of Darkness, he dedicated to Satan his performance of ritual sacrifices on animals. When he was 20, during a robbery he strangled, raped and slit the throat of a 63-year-old woman. A year later he beheaded his best friend using an ax and carried the head in his knapsack for the rest of the day.

> Apprehended and awaiting trial, he murdered a prison guard using a knife. Of 14 psychiatric experts who were assigned to his case, none came to the same conclusion, beyond their agreement that he was beyond redemption. His murders were premeditated and he declared that he had a goal of 5,000 victims. He was sentenced to life in prison at 25.[245]

With these aspects we are sometimes able to briefly meet people very intimately, to look deep inside for a fleeting moment that can leave the other person deeply moved. This ability does not seem to be linked to spiritual development, because both the Indian guru, Bhagwan Shree Rajneesh had it, as we'll look at in a moment, and Adolf Hitler, the Austrian-German politician who became the Dictator of Germany and was responsible for WW2, also had this ability.

Hitler's infamous dictatorship, lasted for only thirteen years, but it created a permanent shift in world politics and was directly responsible for the death of over 30 million people. He had Sedna on the cusp of the sixth house of daily routine, square his Moon, which is conjunct Jupiter, the planet of expansion, in the third house of ideas and communication.

> He joined the German Workers' party at 31 and turned the tiny, ineffective group into a formidable paramilitary organisation.

---

[244] https://en.wikipedia.org/wiki/Marcel_Chevalier

[245] https://www.astro.com/astro-databank/Delabriere,_Stephane

Three years later he tried to force the Bavarian government into a full-scale revolution against the Weimar Republic, but his beer hall putsch failed. He spent nine months in prison, where he wrote the first volume of his book, *Mein Kampf,* which means My Struggle, his plan for Germany's dominion over the world.

"\Aided by Germany's internal chaos and worsening economic condition, he schemed his way into authority at 44 and was named Chancellor. It was a time of economic depression in Germany with a third of the country out of work. His speaking power was awesome, winning him the support of the masses. He built a private army of 100,000 men, the brown-shirted Storm Troopers and purged potential threats to his leadership, murdering or jailing political rivals on the infamous 'Night of the Long Knives'.

He re-armed Germany, re-occupied the Rhineland, took over Austria and seized Czechoslovakia, as his first steps toward conquering Europe, then the world. He ordered a huge pogrom with Jewish arrests all over Germany to achieve his demonic vision of Aryan dominion, a policy which sent over six million European Jews, Gypsies and political dissidents to the gas chambers. He had 'immoral books' burned in his police state, but he offered national pride and jobs, offering hope for an economic recovery.

He was 50 when his armoured columns rolled across the Polish border, triggering WW2. When battlefield casualties numbering in the millions provoked an unsuccessful assassination plot on his life towards the end of the war, he condemned the men responsible to death. They were hung on meat hooks and strangled with piano wire, but just short of death. They were then revived and rehanged, repeatedly, with the episodes filmed for his later enjoyment. Toward the last days, he and his long time mistress were married in the bunker under the chancellery and then they committed suicide.

The women in his life had uniformly tragic fates. His 20-year-younger half-niece and first romantic obsession, was found dead in her bed in the Berlin apartment that she shared with him, when he was 42. He had persuaded her and her mother to serve as his live-in housekeepers. The nature of their relationship has been debated ever since, with theories that Hitler was entirely asexual, to the belief that he led a normal sexual life, to stories of perversions and phobias. It has been established that he had had a huge pornographic collection. Whatever the explicit form his affections took, it seemed evident that his young half-niece was increasingly confined and resistant to her position.

She was found with a bullet through her chest and his gun by her side. Whether the death was a murder or suicide has never been resolved. There was a hasty attempt to cover it up with the announcement that she was nervous about an upcoming recital, but there were also news reports that they had yet another fierce quarrel because the 23-year old wanted to go to Vienna, where she intended to become engaged. He met a 29-year-old German movie star a few years later, a petite, blue-eyed blonde, who accepted a command invitation to the private quarters of the Fuhrer. However, by the time he was 48, the meetings ended abruptly, when she either jumped from her Berlin apartment window, or was thrown out by the Gestapo, after being charged with having a Jewish lover.[246]

As we tire of density and the grief it creates, and we start a spiritual journey to get out of the swamp, Sedna rewards us with transcendent crises, experiences which force us to let go and rise above them, resulting in a huge growth to a new level of consciousness. There is no choice with these crises, and the more we try and solve them, the more we will get hurt.

Edith Cavell was a British nurse who organized a School of Nursing in Brussels at 41, becoming a great heroine and martyr during WW I. She had Sedna in the sixth house of service, square her Moon in the ninth house of knowledge.

She had lived a colourless life as a governess before age 30, when her father took ill and she returned home to nurse him through his declining years and death. Inspired, she pursued a nursing career. During the Allied retreat when she was 49, she was approached by an underground movement, who asked that she treat and shelter two wounded British soldiers. During the next nine months, 200 soldiers passed through her clinic in their

---

flight to freedom via Holland, all under the noses of the German occupation force.

Finally, the secret was broken and she was arrested. She had refused to flee and on arrest refused to deny her role, so was given five death sentences. She wrote farewell letters in prison saying, "I know now that patriotism is not enough; I must have no hatred or bitterness towards anyone". She was executed by firing squad shortly thereafter. Enlistments in Britain and U.S. rose spectacularly in the following weeks.[247]

With these aspects there may also be a conflict between our emotional life, or home life and our destiny, or career, in which we will likely prioritize destiny over the domestic demands. Our case study, Thomas Edison, who was an American scientist and father of the light bulb, famously lived in, or beside his laboratories in an effort to balance the two. He had his Moon in the first house of Identity, conjunct Mars in the second house of material resources, both square Sedna in the fourth hose of home.

These were the karmic challenges in his chart, making himself centered and sometimes working at cross-purposes to himself; however, they also provided the strength of purpose and practical action to achieve his goals. He was seen sometimes almost beside himself with anger at a stupid mistake, or inexcusable oversight on the part of an assistant, his voice raised to a high pitch, sneeringly expressing his feelings of contempt for the offender and yet when the culprit, like a bad school-boy, has left the room, he immediately returned to his normal poise, and the incident is a thing of the past.

Humour can be one path to transcend the quicksand of Sedna, giving us the objectivity to step back from the edge, but also with the stressful aspects to the Moon, the challenge to build a rapport with people. When we meet this challenge, it puts us deeply in tune with popular sentiment. Those of us struggling with the stressful Sedna aspects would be well advised to develop our sense of humour.

Martha Raye was an American entertainer, a zestful, boisterous comedienne with a huge, elastic mouth and zany antics. She had Sedna in the eleventh house of collective consciousness, sesquiquadrate her

---

[247] https://en.wikipedia.org/wiki/Edith_Cavell

Moon, which is conjunct Quaoar, the planet of new perspectives, both in the fourth house of home.

> She was born in a charity ward, the daughter of touring vaudeville parents. She joined the family vaudeville act by the time she was three. At 13 she was a specialty singer with a band. She was a veteran of stage and night clubs by the time she was 19, when she made her first film. After this she played in many minor roles in films. Her greatest acclaim always came from live entertainment, stage, Broadway, clubs and from her wartime tours with variety shows.
>
> She married seven times, the last time when she was 75, to a 30-year-younger man after a three-week courtship in Las Vegas. Her Sedna is also in a fateful inconjunct with Ixion, the planet of lawlessness, which like her Moon is in the fourth house of home. She was in a wheelchair after a stroke, drinking a lot, lonely since being widowed two years before and estranged from her only child. She said that she was in love with him, as he made her feel young and a woman, with sex for the first time in years. Her daughter said she had dementia in contesting the will, in which she left one million to her daughter and the rest to her younger husband.[248]

At this juncture in human evolution, few of us use our planets at the spiritual level, but many of us are striving to, and such people are wonderful to be around. As with the other planets, the spiritual level of evolution is vastly different with Sedna from the two previous levels.

Here the stressful aspects with the Moon brings an empathy to the suffering of humanity and an ability to find inner peace in the midst of this. The struggle of the beginner's level is gone, as are the transcendental crises of the intermediate level. At this level everything Saturnian is meaningless and yet everything Sednian has its place.

Peter Hurkos is a Dutch psychic who gained ESP abilities after a blow to his head which left him unconscious for three days. He has Sedna in the eleventh house of collective consciousness, semi-square his Moon in the tenth house of profession. Sedna is also bi-quintile Ixion, the planet of lawlessness, in the fourth house of home.

---

[248] https://en.wikipedia.org/wiki/Martha_Raye

As a boy, he was a poor student, dropping out of school when he entered his teens. He was a loner who spent much time in the woods or in solitude, dreaming and exploring, prone to fantasies and visions. After his accident, he became religious and also became afflicted with blinding headaches and his temperament became volatile and moody.

His psychic abilities were tested psychometrically with a claimed 87% accuracy. His Sedna is also bi-quintile Uranus, the planet of intuition, in the ninth house of knowledge and in a fateful inconjunct with Pholus, the centaur of enlightenment in the sixth house of service. In addition to using his new-found abilities to do professional work, he also did TV guest spots and wrote an autobiography, titled *Psychic*. He tuned in to some of his subjects while in a sleep state, when he could speak in tongues, or in foreign languages, but he also did psychic work while awake.[249]

Even in a more evolved Sedna consciousness these aspects still bring temptations to abuse power and deviate from the spiritual path as we see from our case study of new age guru, Bhagwan Shree Rajneesh. He was an Indian guru and author of more than a hundred books. He had Sedna in the eleventh house of collective consciousness, square his Moon, which was in the eighth house of shared resources, and conjunct his Venus, the planet of values and relationships, and also his Saturn, the planet of structure and wealth.

He was not only intimately familiar with the world's great religions and philosophies, but also the modern psychologies of Jung, Freud, Maslow, and the rest of the West's best thinkers in modern psychology and psychiatry. His syncretic teachings emphasise the importance of meditation, awareness, love, celebration, courage, creativity, and humour — qualities that he viewed as being suppressed by adherence to static belief systems and religious tradition.

When he was 50, he founded a commune in Oregon of 1,700 disciples, a sprawling religious community of a hundred square miles. The ashram was an attempt to build a self-sufficient commune based on ecological and organic farming principles,

---

[249] https://en.wikipedia.org/wiki/Peter_Hurkos

turning the desert into a garden, which they achieved in part. The devotees who joined came from all walks of life, devoting their money and labor to create a utopia. These years saw an increased emphasis on his prediction that the world might be destroyed by nuclear war. He predicted that "the third and last war is now on the way" and frequently spoke of the need to create a 'new humanity' to avoid global suicide.

A key facet of his charismatic ability was that he was a brilliant manipulator of the unquestioning disciple. While his followers might be at a mere subsistence level, having severed ties with outside friends and family and donated all, or most of their money and possessions to the commune, he was seen to live in ostentation and offensive opulence, famously buying 93 Rolls-Royces as a so-called spiritual challenge to the commercial culture in America. Called the "sex-guru" because of his popular talks about tantric sex, his ashram became known as one big love fest during celebrations.

The task of running the commune fell to his personal secretary and the assets of the organization were all in her name. Almost immediately it ran into conflict with county residents and the state government and a succession of legal battles ensued, concerning the ashram's construction and continued development, which curtailed its success. In response he gave her power of attorney and she mounted a campaign of harassment and terrorism against the county. He was 50. Two years later she announced that he would henceforth speak only with her.

He had coached her in using media coverage to her advantage and during his period of public silence he privately stated that when she spoke, she was speaking on his behalf. However, he later alleged she committed crimes, included the attempted murder of his personal physician, poisonings of public officials, wiretapping and bugging within the commune and within his own home, and a bio-terror attack on the citizens of the Dalles, using salmonella to impact the county elections.

At 53, a few days after his secretary and her entire management team had suddenly left the commune for Europe, he held a press conference in which he labelled her and her associates a gang of fascists. He accused them of having committed a number of serious crimes and invited the authorities to investigate. He claimed that she was trying to establish the Rajneeshees as a religion, and that her quest for personal power led to her paranoia, which eventually spread throughout the commune. He spoke often of how organised religion is an obstacle to enlightenment and he blamed his secretary for her ambition of wanting to be the first Popess.

While his allegations were initially greeted with scepticism by outside observers, the subsequent investigation by the US authorities confirmed them and resulted in her conviction, along with several of her lieutenants. However difficulties accumulated with the National Immigration Service and Inland Revenue Service, who were trying to deport him and he was arrested as he fled his strife-torn utopia at 53, on 35 counts of conspiracy and fraud. He was released and on his return to India, he changed his name to Osho to signal a change in his consciousness.[250]

Finally, Carl Jung was a Swiss psychiatrist and author, noted as being an outstanding influence in the development of the theory and practice of analytical psychiatry. He had Sedna in the second house of material reality, semi-square his Moon in the third house of ideas and communication. His Sedna is also in an evolutionary quintile with Orcus, the planet of delving down and speaking out in the twelfth house of the unconscious, and semi-sextile Neptune, the planet of dreams and visions in the second house of material reality.

At age 12, he developed fainting spells which kept him out of school. He spent hours out in the nature, dreaming. Overhearing his father's talk of financial concerns around his illness, he realised on some level he could overcome the fainting spells and was able to return to school. Shortly after this, on a long walk to school, he experienced an intense moment of knowing himself: "Previously, I had existed…everything had merely happened to me. Now, I happened to myself. Now I knew: I am myself now… now I exist."

---

[250] https://en.wikipedia.org/wiki/Rajneesh

When he was 23 he decided to pursue a career in psychiatry. His career began in earnest five years later when he picked up Sigmund Freud's book, *The Interpretation of Dreams*, realising how his work linked up with his own ideas. The initial correspondence and friendship between them began three years later and they collaborated on some work, but when he was 34 he broke from Freud to place greater emphasis on the growth of mankind by archetypal vital forces in the individual. His theories of synchronicity, introvert-extrovert types, individuation and the personal-collective unconscious come from this work.

During this period he had a decisive dream of being in a two-story house. As he explored it, each floor and room reflected historical eras, or from the collective unconscious. When he was 38, he had numerous visions. He said in his autobiography, *Memories, Dreams, and Reflections*, that all of his creative work came from these initial visions. He built a successful psychological practice and was much sought after as a mentor to countless devotees of his work.

An advocate of the use of astrology, he said 'Astrology would be a large scale example of synchronism if it had at its disposal thoroughly tested findings... In other words, whatever is born or done this moment of time, has the qualities of this moment of time'. In his book, *Synchronicity*, he published a study of 483 pairs of couples, seeking to prove the validity that there is a causal connection between the planets and psycho-physiological disposition.[251]

In-conjunct

With the evolutionary inconjunct between Sedna and the Moon, the esoteric spiritual energy of Sedna bursts into our emotions, our deepest personal needs, our basic habits and our unconscious reactions in an evolutionary way and we have a fated role to play.

The inconjunct sometimes acts as a flow and at other times as a stress, so we have to learn to actively manage the process as the rarified spiritual energy sometimes reinforces our spirit of discovery and, at other

---

[251] https://en.wikipedia.org/wiki/Carl_Jung

times isn't there to back us up. By adjusting to this, we gain a deeper understanding of ourselves and how to play our role.

The Moon is a mediator between the inner and the outer world. It is irrational, ruling our hhabitual behaviours and prejudices and our spontaneous reactions and feelings. This vulnerable feeling nature is how we adapt and respond to our surroundings to keep us safe and in known territory.

At the unconscious level the inconjunct can give us a sense of righteousness, or arrogance, which may lead us into dangerous territory, or make us as a victim of someone else's righteousness, or emotions and the inadequate support systems in society.

Like Rachel Sylvia, who was an American teenager who lived in the cult camp of David Koresh in Waco Texas from the time she was four, when her mother joined. She was one of 17 children who died when the camp was raided by the police. She had Sedna in the ninth house of spirituality, inconjunct her Moon in the fourth house of home.

At age 13 she was an inquisitive and bright child; however, her kin were told that she had been sexually abused by Koresh, as was her mother. He was the leader of the religious sect, which was a splinter group of the Seventh-day Adventist Church. He was eventually accused of statutory rape of a 12-year-old girl, apparently with her parents' consent, a relationship that he sanctified as a 'spiritual marriage'.

When arrest and search warrants were served as part of an investigation into illegal possession of firearms and explosives, it provoked a raid in which four agents and six cult members were killed during the initial two-hour firefight. Both sides claimed the other side fired first. Rachel's brother Joshua, age seven, was one of the 21 children released when the government put the camp under siege, which ended when cult members burned the center. Rachel and her mother, along with 78 others, were found dead after the conflagration.

It can also give us a sense of destiny which comes from our deepest personal emotional needs and, while that may represent our truth, it may bring with it a blind spot, or be out of step with the reality around us.

Like Janine Balding, who was an Australian victim of kidnapping, gang rape and murder. She had Sedna in the fourth house of home, inconjunct her Moon in the eleventh house of collective consciousness.

A blue-eyed blonde baby with a strong temperament, she was an active child and had to have elocution lessons because she was such a fast talker. She moved to Sydney at 15, where she shared a flat with her sister. A gregarious young woman, she tried jet-skiing and horse-riding and attended rock concerts with her group of friends. At 17 she met her boyfriend, a fireman who played cricket. They got engaged when she was 20 and bought a small house on the NSW Central Coast, with a marriage date set for the following year.

However, she was abducted at knife-point in a car park at a southern Sydney railway station, taken in her own car to a western suburb, brutally assaulted and raped, and finally drowned by three men known as the Street Kids gang. She died having been thrown into a dam after being gagged and bound with rope in such a way that if she struggled she would drown herself more quickly. The men were apprehended and sentenced to life in prison and some years later a law was passed to ensure that they and other such brutal murderers will never be released.[252]

Or like John Hinckley, who is an American attempted assassin who shot and wounded President Reagan when he was 25. He has Sedna in the second house of material reality, inconjunct his Moon in the eighth house of shared resources.

The year before he shot Reagan, he went to Ted Kennedy's office and waited for three hours with a loaded gun to see the Senator before he gave up on the assassination attempt and left. He was found not guilty by reason of insanity and sentenced to an asylum for the mentally ill in Washington, DC. Prior to the assassination attempt upon President Reagan, he wrote a string of love letters to actress Jodie Foster.

Then at 27, he met a woman who was a patient in the same facility for the shotgun murder of her ten-year-old daughter, followed by her own suicide attempt. She was 12 years older. They were both in the hell of their mental illness, anguish and despair and their growing friendship led to improvement for both of them. Their long hours of talks led to love and he asked her to

---

[252] https://en.wikipedia.org/wiki/Murder_of_Janine_Balding

marry him. A couple of years later she was able to function responsibly in society and was released.

His progress was slower; however, they were able to see each other on weekends and kiss goodbye, feeling like a couple of teenagers. During the Christmas holidays, the young lovers spent time alone for the first time when he was allowed to spend a day with his family. His sexual experience was limited to a few encounters with prostitutes shortly before the assassination attempt. They were not able to consummate their relationship, but the promise of a future together was a strong incentive to healthy responsibility.

During the next five years, his progress was interspersed with unsettling relapses. His psychological evaluations took a turn for the worse. A report from this period read, "The issues of poor judgment, need for ego-gratification through the media, isolation from others at all but a superficial level, grandiosity, suspiciousness, defiance in the face of narcissistic injury, refusal to accept responsibility for his actions other than in a fleeting way, emotional volatility, tendency to lie, lack of empathy for others, sense of entitlement - all remain as unresolved therapeutic issues." His ability to maintain a stable relationship with his fiancé was a plus.

At 35, he was living in a medium-security ward, working four hours a day in a clerical position. The next year he was allowed to walk with his fiancé without an escort around the hospital grounds. They soon had sexual relations for the first time and he was moved to a minimum-security ward. A divided appeals court finally ruled when he was 43 that he could make supervised day trips away from the mental hospital where he lived for the past 18 years to visit his family and friends, a process of gradual re-entry into society. Four years later he was granted unsupervised visits with his parents; it would be 14 more years before he was released from institutional psychiatric care at 61.[253]

While this aspect does bring a fateful challenge to follow our heart, at the unconscious level it also brings the danger of drug abuse.

[253] https://en.wikipedia.org/wiki/John_Hinckley_Jr.

Like Jack Kerouac, who was an American writer and poet and the author of 21 books. He had Sedna in the eighth house of shared resources, inconjunct his Moon, which is conjunct his ascendent, the cusp of the first house of identity.

He is perhaps best known for his book, *On The Road*, published when he was 35 and *The Dharma Bums*, published the following year, the classic novels that established him as a hero who epitomized the style of living and writing associated with the 'Beat Movement', and serving as the Bible for Beatniks.

When he was 23 he met the charismatic and bisexual Neal Cassady, a Denver reform school graduate and car thief who eventually became Kerouac's lover and buddy. During a three-week binge of creativity in the following April and May, he wrote *On The Road* on a single ream of paper. Following Neal's marriage to Caroline, Kerouac moved into the attic of their San Francisco home, where they made up a ménage a trois. He was hospitalized at 29 with thrombophlebitis as a result of heavy Benzedrine use.

In his early thirties, he roamed the US and Mexico taking odd jobs to support himself while studying Buddhism. However, at 38 he suffered alcohol withdrawal, coupled with a nervous breakdown. During the next four years he lived with his mother. At 44 he made his third and final marriage, to the sister of a childhood friend. This marriage was probably celibate, and he was often arrested for public drunkenness as a means of taking out his frustration.

While he hit the road in search of direct experience and spontaneity, his acute wanderlust left him homeless in his soul, even when he owned a home. Despite the chaos in every area of his life, however, he meticulously kept an archive of every sexual experience he had with a woman. One of these bore him a daughter, a girl whom he met twice, but never acknowledged. His daughter Jan states, "I wish I had known him better. He could spout all kinds of things on paper, but in person, he was non-communicative."

He was unable to cope with fame, fatherhood and his bi-sexuality. "He wanted to be seen as the voice of America, but instead he was seen as a voice of juvenile delinquents, and that hurt him a lot...He couldn't take the easy bullet because he was a Catholic. But he rationalised that it was not a sin if he drank himself to death." So that is what he did. His final years were marked by virulent alcohol rages and fierce anti-Semitism.[254]

As we tire of density and the grief it creates, and we start a spiritual journey to get out of the swamp, Sedna rewards us with transcendent crises, experiences which force us to let go and rise above them, resulting in a huge growth to a new level of consciousness. There is no choice with these crises, and the more we try and solve them, the more we will get hurt.

Jane Austen was a British writer, the first renowned female novelist of England. She had Sedna in the sixth house of service, inconjunct her Moon in the first house of identity.

> She was the seventh of eight kids born to a scholarly village rector. She wrote from age 12, with her first novel at 15. For family entertainment, the entire family would tell stories, stimulating her young imagination. Her father was a kindly, reserved cleric and her mother, witty. There were few opportunities available to a young woman in that time and place; women were not even allowed into the universities and she only had two years of formal education.

> As a young girl she was as high-spirited and silly. She had several suitors. She had a flirtation with the attractive but poor young man, which set neighbourhood tongues wagging. Later, she suffered a deeper embarrassment in first accepting, then rejecting the very next morning, the proposal of someone who was suitable from a social viewpoint, but not to her heart. She remained a lifelong spinster, later becoming somewhat tight-lipped with chastity.

> She had six novels published from the age of 36, a remarkable accomplishment for a woman in that era, including her most famous, *Pride and Prejudice*. Her use of biting irony, along with her realism and social commentary have earned her great and historical importance to critics and scholars. Her novels have

---

[254] https://en.wikipedia.org/wiki/Jack_Kerouac

rarely been out of print, although they were published anonymously and brought her little fame during her lifetime.[255]

Her Sedna is also bi-quintile her Saturn, the planet of structure, in the second house of material resources, which is a wide conjunction with her Moon.

> A significant transition in her reputation occurred 15 years after her death, when her novels were illustrated and republished in the Standard Novels series and sold as a set. They gradually gained wider acclaim and popular readership. Fifty-two years after her death, her nephew's publication of 'A Memoir of Jane Austen' introduced a compelling version of her writing career and 'supposedly uneventful life' to an eager audience.[256]

Edwin Hubble was an American astronomer, one of the major figures in 20th century science. He had Sedna in the eighth house of shared resources, inconjunct his Moon in the third house of ideas and communication.

> Working with the 100-inch Hooker telescope at California's Mount Wilson observatory, he made a series of discoveries that revolutionised humanity's vision of the cosmos. He was the first astronomer who provided reliable evidence that the universe is homogenous, the same in all directions, as far as the telescope can see.

> At 40 he examined the relation between distance and redshift of galaxies and found a roughly linear relation between the distances of the galaxies and their redshifts, a discovery that later became known as Hubble's law. This meant, the greater the distance between any two galaxies, the greater their relative speed of separation. The following year, he was involved in determining the distribution of galaxies and spatial curvature. These data seemed to indicate that the universe was flat and homogeneous.

> There were methodological problems with his survey technique that showed a deviation from flatness at large redshifts. Earlier, Albert Einstein had found that his newly developed theory of

---

[255] https://en.wikipedia.org/wiki/Jane_Austen
[256] Ibid.

general relativity indicated that the universe must be either expanding, or contracting. Unable to believe what his own equations were telling him, Einstein introduced a cosmological constant to the equations to avoid this "problem". When Einstein learned of Hubble's redshifts, he immediately realised that the expansion predicted by General Relativity must be real, and in later life he said that changing his equations was "the biggest blunder of his life."

In fact, Einstein apparently once visited Hubble and tried to convince him that the universe was expanding. But in December 1941, Hubble still reported to the American Association for the Advancement of Science that results from a six-year survey with the Mt. Wilson telescope did not support the expanding universe theory. During this time, as his stature increased, he became part of Hollywood society. A character in his tweed jackets, knickers and English briar pipes, he and his witty wife mingled with the Huxleys, Walt Disney and Charlie Chaplin.[257]

Michel Onfray is a French writer and philosopher who adheres to hedonism and anarchism. He is a highly prolific author on philosophy, having written more than 50 books. He has Sedna in the third house of ideas and communication, inconjunct his Moon in the eighth house of shared resources.

He was abandoned by his parents to a Catholic boarding school from age 10 to 14, but overcoming these early hardships, he graduated with a bachelor's degree in philosophy. He defines hedonism "as an introspective attitude to life based on taking pleasure yourself and pleasuring others, without harming yourself or anyone else."

His philosophical project is to define an ethical hedonism, a joyous utilitarianism, and a generalized aesthetic of sensual materialism that explores how to use the brain's and the body's capacities to their fullest extent – while restoring philosophy to a useful role in art, politics, and everyday life and decisions.

He is an atheist and the author of *Atheist Manifesto: The Case Against Christianity, Judaism, and Islam* which became the

---

[257] https://en.wikipedia.org/wiki/Edwin_Hubble

number one best-selling nonfiction book in France for months when it was published. He was 46. His book, *The Twilight of an Idol: The Freudian Confabulation*, published five years later, has been the subject of considerable controversy in France because of its criticism of Freud. He recognises Freud as a philosopher, but he brings attention to the considerable cost of Freud's treatments and casts doubts on the effectiveness of his methods.[258]

At this juncture in human evolution, few of us use our planets at the spiritual level, but many of us are striving to, and such people are wonderful to be around. As with the other planets, the spiritual level of evolution is vastly different with Sedna from the two previous levels. Here, the inconjunct with the Moon brings an empathy to the suffering of humanity and an ability to find inner peace in the midst of this.

Once we embrace the Sedna energy, which is the oneness of everything, our deepest personal needs and basic habits become an expression of Sedna consciousness and they become devotional in nature. The struggle of the beginner's level is gone, as are the transcendental crises of the intermediate level. At this level everything Saturnian is meaningless and yet everything Sednian has its place.

Pakh Subuh is a Dutch Indonesian spiritual leader with an Islamic background, who was given a spiritual vision and a Messianic message as his Call. He has Sedna in the tenth house of profession, inconjunct his Moon in the third house of communication.

> He founded a form of Islamic mysticism in which the supplicant is initiated by means of a kind of meditative communal submission to divine understanding, a method of communion that involves surrender. During this the devotee is 'opened', an experience which may be expressed in silent meditation, in dancing and movement, in speaking in tongues, or whatever form the applicant wishes to employ.[259]

Sri Meher Baba was an Indian religious figure, who was known as The Silent Guru. He was born in India to Irani Zoroastrian parents. He had

---

[258] https://en.wikipedia.org/wiki/Michel_Onfray

[259] https://www.astro.com/astro-databank/Subuh,_Pakh

Sedna in the second house of material reality, inconjunct his Moon, in the ninth house of philosophy.

> At the age of 19 he met a very old Muslim woman who was locally revered as a saint, who kissed him on the forehead. The event affected him profoundly, leaving him visibly dazed. After that he contacted other spiritual figures and began a seven-year spiritual transformation, before beginning his own mission and gathering his own disciples at the age of 27.

> His early followers gave him the name Meher Baba, meaning 'Compassionate Father'. He moved into silence at 31 and did not speak for the next 44 years until his death. To communicate he spelled on an alphabet board with quick fingers, such words as "I am the Supreme Spirit." From the age of 60 he used unique sign language gestures, rather than the alphabet board. With his circle of disciples, he spent long periods in seclusion, during which time he often fasted. He also traveled widely, held public gatherings and engaged in works of charity with lepers, the poor and the mentally ill.[260]

His Sedna is also square Mars, the planet of action, in the twelfth house of the unconscious, semi-square Venus, the planet of values in the first house of identity, and sesquiquadrate Juno, the asteroid of partnership, in the tenth house of profession.

> He gave numerous teachings on the cause and purpose of life, including teaching reincarnation and that the phenomenal world is an illusion. He taught that the Universe is imagination, that God is what really exists, and that each soul is really God passing through imagination to realize individually His own divinity.

> In addition, he gave practical advice for the aspirant who wishes to attain self-realisation and thereby escape the wheel of birth and death. He also taught about the concept of Perfect Masters, the Avatar, and those on the various stages of the spiritual path that he called involution. His teachings are most importantly recorded in his principal books, *Discourses* and *God Speaks*. And his legacy includes an influence on pop-culture artists and

---

[260] https://en.wikipedia.org/wiki/Meher_Baba

the introduction of common expressions such as "Don't Worry, Be Happy."[261]

Quintile, Bi-quintile

The evolutionary quintile or bi-quintile aspect between Sedna and the Moon infuses our emotions, our deepest personal needs, our basic habits and our unconscious reactions with the all-encompassing spiritual energy of Sedna to the point where we can push the boundaries of human development. Quintiles and bi-quintiles point to talent, the desire to create order and to categorize, a fascination with patterns and structures, perfectionist tendencies, and the desire to build or make things.

These aspects have the characteristics of both the trine and opposition. They point to awareness of conflicts, or problems and finding solutions for them; however, they do not automatically kick into action and must be cultivated over time.

The Moon is a mediator between the inner world and the outer world. It is irrational, ruling our habitual behaviours and prejudices. These may, or may not, be acted out, depending if we censor them, but the Moon rules our spontaneous reactions and feelings.

At the unconscious level, the spiritual power of the quintile and bi-quintile with Sedna can be challenging, because these aspects can give us a sense of destiny which comes from our deepest personal emotional needs, something we don't understand ourselves. As a result we may act these things out, in our process of personal emotional discovery.

Like Charles Manson, who was an American ritual cult leader, a psychopath with a band of drug-numbed followers. He has Sedna in the twelfth house of the unconscious, quintile his Moon in the tenth house of profession. He mesmerized his gang with liberal sex and drugs while living on a ranch in the desert of southern California.

> He was the illegitimate son of a teenage prostitute and an army colonel and was raised by an aunt and uncle. By the age of 11, he developed into a delinquent, shuffling from foster parent to foster parent. He spent his youth and adulthood in and out of prison, spending 19 of his first 32 years behind bars.

---

[261] Ibid.

In his mid-30s, while on parole, he went to San Francisco to be a part of the hippie counter-culture in the Height-Ashbury district. He gathered adoring women around him by giving out LSD. Soon he was able to attract young men to his group by promising sex with his 'young loves'. They enjoyed long group LSD sessions, listening to the Beatles' "Helter Skelter" song on the White Album. However, unable to keep his friendships, he began to prophesy chaos to his followers.

When he was 34, he directed the ritual grisly killings of Sharon Tate and her houseguests, who were stabbed to death by his followers and their blood was smeared along the walls of the kitchen. A few days later, an older couple was tied up and carved and stabbed by forks and kitchen knives. The deaths frightened the Hollywood community and after nine months of the trial, when he was 35, the jury found him guilty of first degree murder and conspiracy.

He was convicted and given the death penalty, but the following year the California Supreme Court invalidated the capital punishment stature, and he became a life-termer. He was continually refused parole by the California parole board. He was denied parole for the ninth time at 63. His behaviour in prison has been vicious and demented and yet every year he receives letters and gifts from young people, Satanists, neo-Nazis and skinheads who view him as their role model, hoping for one day when he will be released, however he died in prison at age 83.[262]

We can see the fatalist and two-sided nature of these aspects in the fact that both Charles Manson and his most well-known victim, Sharon Tate, shares them. Sharon Tate was an American actress, sex symbol and model, who was murdered by members of Charles Manson's 'family'. She had Sedna conjunct Varuna, the planet of notability, in the tenth house of profession, bi-quintile her Moon in the third house of communication.

In her early twenties she played small television roles before appearing in several motion pictures. She also appeared regularly in fashion magazines as a model and cover girl. After receiving positive reviews for her comedic and dramatic

---

[262] https://en.wikipedia.org/wiki/Charles_Manson

performances, she was hailed as one of Hollywood's most promising newcomers, making her film debut at 23. A year later she co-stared in *The Fearless Vampire Killers* with Roman Polanski, who also directed the film.

The following year they got married in London and at the time of her death, she was eight-and-a-half months pregnant with their son and was two weeks from giving birth. That day she entertained two friends for lunch at her home, confiding in them her disappointment at her husband's delay in returning from London.

That evening she dined at her favourite restaurant with three other friends, returning with them to her home at about 10:30 p.m. Shortly after midnight, they were all murdered by members of Manson's "family" and their bodies were discovered the following morning by her housekeeper. Police arrived at the scene to find her body and that of one of her friends in the living room; a long rope tied around each of their necks connected them. On the front lawn lay the bodies of the other two. All of the victims had been stabbed numerous times.[263]

The vulnerable feeling nature is how we adapt and respond to our surroundings to keep us safe and in known territory, and these aspects can make us a victim of someone else's sense of entitlement, which if it occurs in our childhood, can lead to an abusing attitude in later life.

Like Richard Allen Davis, who was an American convicted murderer, whose criminal record fueled support for passage of California's "three-strikes law" for repeat offenders. He had Sedna in the fifth house of children, quintile his Moon in the eighth house of life and death.

He was finally arraigned on eight felony counts for the kidnapping and murder of a 12-year-old girl. Then 39, burly and heavily tattooed, he was a parolee with two kidnapping convictions and a long criminal record. He was the son of an alcoholic truck driver with a marginal employment record. The household was a place of fighting and drinking; his parents divorced when he was nine. He was a bad kid from childhood, dousing cats with gas and setting them on fire and using dogs for

---

[263] https://en.wikipedia.org/wiki/Sharon_Tate

knife-throwing practice. He moved home many times and had a record of truancy and trouble making through a variety of schools. He finally dropped out to join the army, where he discovered heroin within a year.

At 19 he was arrested for being drunk, resisting arrest, possession of marijuana, theft and burglary, and given six months in jail. He found jail boring with no drugs and not enough room to move around. However, a couple of years later he was picked up again and given a six-year sentence, from which he was paroled in a year. The following year he attempted his first rape, but the girl got away and he was put in jail again, where he tried to hang himself. He was given one-to-twenty-five years for kidnapping and was released after serving five years.

On his release he found a girlfriend and they started playing 'Bonnie and Clyde'. They conducted small time hold-ups, pistol-whipped people, robbed a bank and restaurant, another bank and a yogurt shop. Picked up March 1985, he was given 16 years in state prison. This time he found drugs easier to get in jail so he was able to continue his habit. He was paroled again at 39 with $200 cash and no job skills. He soon skipped parole and, in a northern California town, he snatched a 12-year-old girl from her bedroom at knife point after a slumber party, where he tied up two other girls.

He was loaded with drugs and said he did not know why he did it. After the crime, with the girl still alive and in the car, he swerved and went into a ditch. The police stopped to help him. Later, when the report came in of the kidnapping, they remembered the car and picked him up, but it was too late. Her body was found in a shallow grave; he had strangled and buried her. The jury handed down the death penalty and he has been living on death row ever since.[264]

As we tire of density and the grief it creates, and we start a spiritual journey to get out of the swamp, Sedna rewards us with transcendent crises, experiences which force us to let go and rise above them, resulting in a huge growth to a new level of consciousness. There is no

---

[264] https://en.wikipedia.org/wiki/Richard_Allen_Davis

choice with these crises, and the more we try and solve them, the more we will get hurt.

Like Miles Davis, who was an American musician, jazz composer, bandleader and recording artist, one of the most consistent trendsetters in jazz history. He had Sedna conjunct Nessus, the centaur of radical change, in the eleventh house of collective consciousness, bi-quintile his Moon, which is conjunct Saturn, the planet of structure and the physical body, in the sixth house of service.

He is the inventor of more distinct styles than any other jazz musician; he pioneered in cool jazz, hard bop, modal playing, free-form explorations and use of electronics. On his 13th birthday he was given his first trumpet and he played in school with a jazz combo at 16. He also learned the flugelhorn. While going to Juilliard, he sat in on jazz gigs and went on the road in his early twenties. He formed the Capitol Band at 22 and performed for his first record contract. He played with Charlie Parker in his late 20s and with Herbie Hancock when he was 37.

However, he was a heroin addict by 23, supporting his habit as a pimp with seven working girls. With strong family support for rehabilitation, he went into rehab to get clean. Though he overcame heroin in his late 20s, he continued to use cocaine until he was 55. In his 1989 biography, *Miles*, he wrote, "I want to keep creating, changing. Music isn't about standing still and becoming safe."

He was plagued by illness much of his life; at various times he battled diabetes, pneumonia, a stroke, and hip joint problems caused by sickle cell anaemia. He had surgery to remove polyps on his vocal cords at 30 and broke both legs in an auto accident at 46, after which he moved into five years of health problems that were so severe that he dropped out of circulation.

After this five-year retirement he resumed his career, employing younger musicians and pop music sounds. Critics were generally unreceptive but the decade garnered him his highest level of commercial recognition. He performed sold-out concerts worldwide, while branching out into visual arts, film, and television work, before his death at 65 from the combined effects of a stroke, pneumonia and respiratory failure. He was recently inducted into the Rock and Roll Hall of Fame, which recognised him as one of the key figures in the history of jazz.[265]

Or like Sonia Gandhi, who is an Italian-born Indian politician, who has served as President of the Indian National Congress party. She has Sedna in the ninth house of knowledge, quintile her Moon in the eleventh house of collective consciousness.

> She is straightforward, intelligent and something of an introvert. she met Rajiv Gandhi when they were both students at Cambridge University. It was love at first sight and they married when she was 21 in New Delhi.

> His mother was Indira Gandhi, who was Prime Minister of India. She was assassinated when Sonia was 37 and her husband stepped immediately into her shoes. He was optimistic, though utterly unqualified for the job. It took Sonia literally years to come to terms with the horror of the assassination. She avoided seeing people and often fell silent for long periods, taking up art restoration as a hobby.

> When she was 44, suddenly and violently, her husband was assassinated. She was offered the post of Party President within 24 hours, but she refused, due to her dislike of publicity and the fear of exposing her family to further risks. She retreated into herself, drawing consolation from her children and her home, which became a shrine to her beloved martyred husband. Her circle became small and closed and she made few public appearances. Her private secretary became her spokesman.

> However, at 51 she quietly became a member of the Congress Party and campaigned on their behalf in an election that was like no other country had ever seen. There were more than 600 million registered voters and the ballot boxes had to be transported by donkey, fishing boat and mountain porter.

> There were nearly 5,000 candidates, some of whom were colourful, if unlikely, such as a bandit queen who had 63 court cases pending against her. Anarchic violence exploded in voting disputes. Some of the voting boxes were captured by bandits who shot the guards and stuffed the ballet boxes. India has over

---

[265] https://en.wikipedia.org/wiki/Miles_Davis

a thousand different languages and entrenched religious and caste divisions and many powerful splinter groups have broken off into chaotic segments.

Sonia emerged from her private life to campaign on behalf of the Congress Party, giving her first speech in the city where her husband had been murdered. She told the crowd, "Devotion to India brings me before you, not a desire for political office." She was elected president of the party a couple of months later and covered the subcontinent by jet and helicopter, visiting 138 constituencies in a 34-day tour, in an unparalleled campaign. She drew larger crowds than any of her rivals.

She finally agreed to enter politics when party leaders assured her that a "working" president of her choice would take care of day-to-day party work and she led the Indian National Congress to victory in India's elections at 57. Following this she announced that she would "humbly decline" the Prime Minister's position, but was under pressure to reconsider her decision. However, she said, "I must follow my voice." Earlier in the year, she said in an interview that her goal was to ensure that the Hindu nationalist-led government that held power prior to the election was voted out. She added that her own power "is not a priority for me."[266]

Queen Victoria was was Queen of the United Kingdom of Great Britain and Ireland from the age of 18 until her death. From 56 she also adopted the additional title of Empress of India. She had Sedna conjunct Vesta, the asteroid of regeneration, in the eleventh house of collective consciousness, quintile her Moon, which is conjunct her Sun, representing her sensitive nature, in the twelfth house of the unconscious.

Her reign of 63 years and seven months is known as the Victorian era and was longer than that of any of her predecessors. It was a period of industrial, cultural, political, scientific, and military change within the United Kingdom, and was marked by a great expansion of the British Empire. Through her reign, the gradual establishment of a modern constitutional monarchy in Britain continued. Reforms of the voting system

[266] https://en.wikipedia.org/wiki/Sonia_Gandhi

increased the power of the House of Commons at the expense of the House of Lords and the monarch.

As Victoria's monarchy became more symbolic than political, it placed a strong emphasis on morality and family values, in contrast to the sexual, financial and personal scandals that had been associated with previous members of the House of Hanover and which had discredited the monarchy.[267]

Humour can be one path to transcend the quicksand of Sedna, giving us the objectivity to step back from the edge, but also with the quintile and bi-quintile to the Moon, an understanding of people and an ability to build a rapport, which can put us deeply in tune with popular sentiment.

Red Skelton was an American film, nightclub and Emmy-award-winning TV comedian. He had Sedna in the fifth house of creativity, quintile his Moon in the third house of communication.

He was the youngest of four sons of a circus clown, who died two months before he was born. Left destitute, his mother worked as a cleaning woman. He began selling newspapers at age seven. He dropped out of school at 14 to entertain in a traveling minstrel show, making ten dollars a week. After working as a minstrel man on a showboat that cruised the Ohio and Missouri rivers, and as a clown with his late father's circus, he turned to burlesque in his late teens.

At 17 he met a 15-year-old usherette and they were married two years later. Soon she was writing his material and managing his career. She negotiated a $1,500-a-week movie contract for him with MGM when he was 25 and he went on to appear in over 40 movies. CBS then offered him his own variety show, which premiered when he was 40 and was an instant hit. By 58, he had won three Emmy awards with shows that included his irreverent and hilarious alter ego characters. However, CBS eventually canceled the show despite high ratings, saying it wasn't hip with the times.

After the cancellation, he hit the stage playing to sold-out audiences well into his 70s with his stock characters. He had divorced amicably from his first wife at 30 and she continued to

---

[267] https://en.wikipedia.org/wiki/Queen_Victoria

manage his career and write for him. Two years after his divorce, he married a model and four years later their daughter was born, followed by a son the next year. Tragedy occurred at the height of his career, when his son died of leukemia at age nine. He divorced his second wife at 60 and, that same year, he married his third wife, a secretary 25 years his junior.

He sustained a second lucrative career as an author of children's books and an artist of clown paintings that sold for as much as $20,000. Toward the end of his life he estimated that he earned $2.5 million a year with his lithographs. He was inducted into the Comedy Hall of Fame at 80 and retired to a California ranch. At a frail 84, he still wrote every morning, still together with his third wife of the previous 24 years, who was by then a 59-year-old horse breeder.[268]

At this juncture in human evolution, few of us use our planets at the spiritual level, but many of us are striving to, and such people are wonderful to be around. As with the other planets, the spiritual level of evolution is vastly different with Sedna from the two previous levels. Here, the quintile and bi-quintile aspects with the Moon brings an empathy to the suffering of humanity and an ability to assist others to find inner peace in the midst of this. The struggle of the beginner's level is gone, as are the transcendental crises of the intermediate level. At this level everything Saturnian is meaningless and yet everything Sednian has its place.

Ondine Tharp was an American minister educated only in fundamentalist Christian theology. She had Sedna in the first house of identity, quintile her Moon in the third house of ideas and communication. In the middle of the last century female ministers were not accepted, but she was strongly driven to communicate her beliefs and she became a Baptist preacher, serving the religious needs of the poorest enclaves of Ozark Mountain people who lived in the highland region of the central United States. Adopting a nomadic life-style she travelled in poverty around her circuit of parishioners with her handyman husband and daughter, bringing the promise of a heavenly reward along with music and the joy of salvation.

---

[268] https://en.wikipedia.org/wiki/Red_Skelton

Doris Conway Battle was an American astrologer, one of the unsung heroes in her field who never became famous but supported professional astrology with membership in AFA and studies in the Church of Light and contributions to the Theosophical Society, and whose work touched the life of many people. She had Sedna in the eleventh house of collective consciousness quintile her Moon in the first house of identity. she became the first American woman to be certified by the Faculty of Astrological Studies headed by Margaret Hone and founded under the auspices of the Astrological Lodge of London.

And Pope John XXIII was an Italian ecclesiastic, who reigned as Pope for five years in the middle of last century and was called 'the smiling pope'. He had Sedna in the second house of material resources, quintile his Moon, which is conjunct Varuna, the planet of notability and statesmanship, in the first house of identity.

He charmed the world with his wit and convoked the second Vatican Council, the first church council in 100 years. He was recently declared a saint, one of only 5 popes the Catholic Church has found worthy of veneration in this way in the past 900 years. One of 13 kids of a farmer of modest means, at the age of 13, he began his studies for the priesthood and was ordained at 18. He served in the Italian army in WW I, then joined the Vatican diplomatic service.

Cordial, practical and ingenious, he was noted for a simple purity He tried to adapt the age-old policies of the church to modern means. He was elected pope in a surprise compromise decision, but far from being a mere "stopgap" pope, to great excitement, he called for an ecumenical council, fewer than ninety years after the First Vatican Council. From the Second Vatican Council came changes that reshaped the face of Catholicism: a comprehensively revised liturgy, a stronger emphasis on ecumenism, and a new approach to the world.

He was an advocate for human rights including the unborn and the elderly. He wrote about human rights: "Man has the right to live. He has the right to bodily integrity and to the means necessary for the proper development of life, particularly food, clothing, shelter, medical care, rest, and, finally, the necessary social services. In consequence, he has the right to be looked after in the event of ill health; disability stemming from his work;

widowhood; old age; enforced unemployment; or whenever through no fault of his own he is deprived of the means of livelihood.

Sainthood requires proof of the candidate's extraordinary Christian virtues and miracles of intercession after his death. In John's case, a miraculous cure had been attributed to him; a young nun had recovered from a life-threatening ailment after a relic of John's was placed on her body. He has also been declared 'heroically virtuous', because he was considered to have lived a virtuous, model lifestyle, and because of the good for the Church which had come from his having opened the Second Vatican Council. He is today affectionately known as the 'Good Pope'.[269]

---

[269] https://en.wikipedia.org/wiki/Pope_John_XXIII

30: Sedna / Mercury

Conjunction

With the conjunction of Sedna and Mercury, the richness of Sedna consciousness infuses our communicating and analyzing abilities, our curiosity and our ideas, with a much bigger view of the world.

Mercury not only rules communication, it represents coordination, thought processes and sensory information from both conscious and unconscious sources, which all need to be coordinated and understood. Mercury analyses, sorts, groups, and makes sense of things.

Learning about life in all its depth is the blessing of this aspect, which gives us a much richer playground for our thoughts and communication. Exploring this playground is likely, over time, to help us develop a higher consciousness.

However, at the unconscious level, if we are not expressing ourselves, there could be illnesses, or other problems associated with the house placement. There may also be genetic issues that come from the depths of our heredity.

Like Peedie Snipes, who was an American male victim of progeria, the aging disease. He had Sedna conjunct Mercury and also Chiron, the centaur of wounding and healing, all in the seventh house of relationships.

> Peedie's condition was so rare, doctors couldn't diagnose it. No cause or cure was known. By age 2, due to his rapid development, his life span could be measured in years, not decades. He eventually went bald and had wrinkled skin, yet still resembled a child. Each birthday became a milestone, his mother said, because she never knew if it would be his last. He died of old age at fourteen.[270]

At the unconscious level we might also find ourselves at the mercy of some idea or mission, which to us seems meaningful, but we may not have really thought through the consequences.

Like Carl Buntion, who was an American petty criminal and cop-killer. He had Sedna conjunct Mercury and also Varuna, the planet of notability, all

---

[270] http://www.greensboro.com/news/for-the-love-of-her-son/article_45e7789a-61ef-5f43-8d01-db524e3eeca5.html

in the second house of material resources and restrictions. When he was 46 he was a passenger in a car driven by a friend that was stopped by a motorcycle policeman for making an illegal turn.

> He said, 'If the police ever pull me over, I'm going to kill the officer,' because he wasn't going back to prison. He had a litany of convictions beginning at 16, including assaults, burglaries and a sexual assault. He had a difficult childhood with an abusive father.

> He slipped out of the passenger door, slinking around the car and aiming across the trunk at the policeman, who was on the other side of the vehicle. He shot the officer in the left temple, through his motorcycle helmet. The officer had pulled his weapon but did not get a shot off. He was then a career criminal in his late 40s. He was wearing a cap that read, "Payback is a bitch," and he stood over the officer's body and shot him twice more in the back.[271]

He had vowed 19 years earlier to get revenge for the killing of his twin brother, who had been a forgery suspect who was shot eight times in a Houston gunfight.

> He then went on a rampage, shooting into a car and striking a woman who had witnessed the shooting in the shoulder. He shot at another car, then at a security officer responding on foot to the sounds of shots. He fled to an office and was there alone when he was arrested without a fight. He was sentenced to death but was still appealing the sentence 20 years later.[272]

Or like Timothy McVeigh, who was an American terrorist convicted of committing the largest act of terrorism on American soil. He was 27. He had Sedna conjunct Mercury and also his Sun, his will and sense of self, all in the eleventh house of collective consciousness.

> He grew up in a small upstate New York town. He had a happy childhood swimming in his family's pool, hiking and playing with the neighbourhood kids. He enjoyed organising casino games for local kids on the block. His father and mother divorced when he

---

[271] https://www.chron.com/news/houston-texas/article/Prosecutors-urge-death-for-cop-killer-Buntion-3346473.php
[272] Ibid.

was ten-years-old. He grew closer to his dad, helping him cultivate his vegetable garden. His mom remarried and moved to Florida with his younger sister.

Looking for excitement, he signed up for the U.S. Army when he was twenty. He took to military life and the comradeship with his fellow troops, becoming a straight-arrow soldier. He was promoted to corporal and then to sergeant. During the Persian Gulf War, he was sent to Iraq as a gunner on a Bradley fighting vehicle. On returning to the States, he sensed a major shift in the U.S. Army. The post-cold-war army downsizing changed his life as he watched his companions leave military service. Discharged from the army, he tried to adjust to civilian life.

At 25, he arrived in Waco to watch the standoff between the Branch Davidians cult and federal agents. He wandered around the country as a militant drifter visiting gun shows and selling guns and ammunition from his car. His political views became more racist and far right as he kept company with political militia groups harbouring anger against the U.S. government. He returned to Waco and declared himself a "non-resident alien." He claimed the U.S. Army had implanted a computer chip in his derriere during his active duty.

Together with accomplices he carried out an ammonium nitrate bombing of a federal building when he was 27, claimed 168 victims between the ages of four months old to 73 years old. The building was the main office for the federal agents who were involved in the Branch Davidian standoff in Waco. Two hours after the bombing, he was stopped by a policeman for a traffic violation, 70 miles away. He was almost released until they recognised him as one of the possible suspects in the terrorist act.

His stubborn refusal to express any remorse tormented the families of his victims. His psychiatrist felt that he was committed to the ideal that he must object to a federal government that had become excessively oppressive and deceitful. He was able to rationally make the decision to bomb the building and "fully understood the consequences." He had an underlying depression, but he was not anti-social. It simply became easier to act because he had nothing and he needed an enemy. This whole project was his antidepressant. He "intellectualises to avoid emotion, to avoid pain." He was found guilty of conspiracy, use of a weapon of mass destruction, destruction by explosive, and eight counts of first degree murder and was sentenced to death.[273]

As we tire of density and the grief it creates, and we start a spiritual journey to get out of the swamp, Sedna rewards us with transcendent crises, experiences which force us to let go and rise above them, resulting in a huge growth to a new level of consciousness. There is no choice with these crises, and the more we try and solve them, the more we will get hurt.

Like Coretta Scott King, who was an American civil rights leader with a famous husband, Dr. Martin Luther King. She had Sedna conjunct Mercury in the seventh house of relationships.

> She survived many traumatic events, including a bombing of their home shortly after the birth of their first child when she was 28. Her husband was stabbed two years later and he was assassinated when she was 41.

> The middle of three children she grew up in the segregated south. A good student despite harsh conditions, she graduated high school as valedictorian of her class. She earned a scholarship and attended Antioch College in Ohio. There she became active in campus civil rights organisations. With a B.A. in music and education, she won a scholarship to the New England Conservatory of Music in Boston. There she met her future husband, Martin Luther King Jr, then a PhD candidate. They married when she was 26 and she completed her advanced degree in voice and violin.

> When she was 27 they moved to Montgomery, Alabama, where her husband had obtained an assignment as Pastor of a Baptist Church. She has said that her husband had rather traditional views of a woman's role, which kept her busy tending to their four children. The first was born when she was 28 and the last at 35. Nevertheless, she was an active supporter of his work. Putting her musical talents to good use she organised and

---

[273] https://en.wikipedia.org/wiki/Timothy_McVeigh

performed in Freedom Concerts which told the story of the Civil Rights movement. As her husband's fame grew, hers did as well, and in the 1960s she found herself in demand as a public speaker.

After Rosa Parks' arrest for refusing to give up her seat on a Montgomery City bus, Martin Luther King, Jr. became a leader of the community protest which began with a boycott of city buses. When she was 41 her husband was shot and pronounced dead in Memphis, TN. After his assassination, she immediately threw herself into his work. Within two days she led 42,000 in a march of grief and protest. The next year she formed a memorial Centre for Social Change in honour of her martyred husband and lobbied for years to make his birthday a national holiday. Throughout the next several decades she organised and inspired others on behalf of peace, civil liberties, and justice.[274]

The Mercury connection with communication is very evident in this next example, as is the groundbreaking evolutionary nature of the Sedna energy.

Alexander Graham Bell was a Scottish-born American audiologist best known as the inventor of the telephone and founder of AT&T. He had Sedna closely conjunct Mercury and with Chariklo, the centaur of foresight, all in the first house of identity. His Sedna is also opposite his Moon in the seventh house of relationships.

His father, grandfather, and brother had all been associated with work on elocution and speech and both his mother and wife were deaf, profoundly influencing his life's work, as he continued to teach, research and invent for the rest of his life.

As a child he displayed a natural curiosity about his world, resulting in gathering botanical specimens, as well as experimenting even at an early age. He showed a sensitive nature and a talent for art, poetry, and music that was encouraged by his mother. With no formal training, he mastered the piano and became the family's pianist. Despite being normally quiet and introspective, he revelled in mimicry and

---

[274] https://en.wikipedia.org/wiki/Coretta_Scott_King

'voice tricks' akin to ventriloquism that continually entertained family guests during their occasional visits.

He was also deeply affected by his mother's gradual deafness, as she began to lose her hearing when he was 12. He learned a manual finger language, so he could sit at her side and tap out silently the conversations swirling around the family parlour. He also developed a technique of speaking in clear, modulated tones directly into her forehead, whereby she could hear him with reasonable clarity. He was largely family trained and self-taught. His first professional post was as a teenager in school, where he also instructed the other children in both music and elocution. At 21 he became his father's assistant in London and assumed full charge while he lectured in America.

However, with his work responsibilities, the stress took its toll on his health and the family moved to Canada when he was 23, where his health rapidly improved. The next year he spent several weeks in Boston, lecturing and demonstrating the system of his father's Visible Speech as a means of teaching speech to the deaf. He continued to lecture and do his own research, even while on vacation. And the following year he opened his own school in Boston for training teachers of the deaf, and one year later he became professor of vocal physiology at Boston University.

At 29, with the help of his assistant, a young repair mechanic and model maker, he invented the telephone. The famous story relates that his first words that were carried over an electronic transmission were, "Come here, I want to see you," to the astonishment of his assistant. He obtained a patent for his invention and within a year began a commercial application. Within a few months, the first of hundreds of legal suits began, however, his claims were upheld. The Bell Telephone Company was formed that year and it became the American Telephone and Telegraph Company eight years later, to manage the expanding long-distance business.[275]

Writing is another Mercury activity. John Updike was an American writer, a prolific novelist and a perfectionist. He had Sedna conjunct Mercury

---

[275] https://en.wikipedia.org/wiki/Alexander_Graham_Bell

and Uranus, the planet of intuition, in the eighth house of shared resources.

He was born in a small town in Pennsylvania, which he later used as a model for the fictional towns in his books. He suffered from psoriasis and stammered as a child, so his parents encouraged him to write. His maternal grandparents lived with the family, and when he was 12, they all moved to the farmhouse where his mother had been born. It was an isolated place, and he dreamed of escaping while immersing himself in books. He read nothing by "dead" authors, however, saying they depressed him.

He entered Harvard University on a scholarship, choosing the school primarily because it had the "Harvard Lampoon," and he began drawing and writing for the magazine. He graduated at 22, and soon thereafter, sold his first short story to *The New Yorker* magazine. That summer, he traveled to England on a Knox Fellowship and enrolled in the Ruskin School of Drawing and Fine Art at Oxford, where he spent the next two years. On his return to the United States he joined the staff of *The New Yorker,* where for the next two years he wrote editorials, stories, poetry and criticism.

He became a full-time writer at 25. His books include *Centaur,* published when he was 31, a story of Chiron. Here's the blurb from the Penguin Classic edition: "In a small Pennsylvania town in the late 1940s, a schoolteacher yearns to find some meaning in his life. Alone with his teenage son for three days in a blizzard, he sees his son grow and change, as he himself begins to lose touch with his life. Interwoven with the myth of Chiron, the noblest centaur, and his own relationship to Prometheus, *The Centaur* is one of John Updike's most brilliant and unusual novels." A dedicated craftsman, he has been awarded the National Book Award for Fiction and won the Pulitzer Prize at the age of 50.[276]

Humour can be one path to transcend the quicksand of Sedna, giving us the objectivity to step back from the edge and also with the conjunction

---

[276] https://en.wikipedia.org/wiki/John_Updike

to Mercury a depth of communication which allows us to embody the collective consciousness.

The Topp Twins are a folk singing and activist sister comedy duo from New Zealand, comprising Jools and Lynda Topp. They have Sedna conjunct Mercury in the fourth house of home.

> They are gay musicians, songwriters, and performers, who switch from satire to country-western, and from male to female identity on stage. They are known for their country music influenced style, live shows and television performances. In their late 30s, they created their own TV series, which ran for three seasons and showcased their iconic cast of New Zealand characters, including Camp Mother & Camp Leader, the Bowling Ladies and Ken & Ken, roles for which they cross-dressed as 'typical kiwi blokes'.

> The series won the twins several awards at the New Zealand Film and Television Awards. After performing as a country music-singing comedy duo for more than 30 years, their documentary feature film, *Untouchable Girls*, was released when they were 51. It broke all previous records for opening day, and opening weekend for a NZ documentary and won awards at the Toronto International Film Festival, Melbourne International Film Festival, Göteborg International Film Festival, Portland International Film Festival and the New Zealand Film and Television Awards.[277]

Dudley Moore was a British-American actor, musician and composer who is most widely known as the comedy star of *10* and *Arthur*. He is also a professional musician and composer who has taught at Oxford and played piano at Carnegie Hall. He has Sedna conjunct Mercury in the seventh house of relationships.

> He is small in stature. Born with a clubfoot, he had seven operations as child. He began piano at the age of 5, later recalling that, "I saw this beast in the living room and clambered on." He later studied violin, harpsichord and organ. His dream was to play jazz, until at 24 he became part of a talented team who wrote and performed in a music and comedy revue, called

---

[277] https://en.wikipedia.org/wiki/Topp_Twins

'Beyond the Fringe'. They played for four years in London and three years on Broadway, firmly establishing his deft touch with comedy as well as poignant manipulation of drama.

Known for having something of a temper, he began therapy at 29 and has been married four times. He had one son with his second wife. His third marriage broke up when he was 55, after two-and-a-half years of marriage. Four years later he was arrested by police for domestic violence with his girlfriend and future fourth wife. She said that he had hit her, a charge which he denied and the whole incident was deemed a misunderstanding. About a month later they married and they had a child together when he was 60. About a year later he filed for divorce. She responded with a ten-million-dollar law suit claiming that he had 'relentlessly assaulted, battered, threatened and terrorised her'. The next month they kissed and made up

Since settling in Los Angeles at 40, he has earned his greatest fame with comedy films, but that has not put a stop to his musical involvement. At 36 he joined with the Los Angeles Philharmonic for a Gershwin tribute. Six years later, at Carnegie Hall and at the Hollywood Bowl, he performed some of his film scores along with Beethoven. In his 50's he led a jazz trio in a Santa Monica club. Part owner of a club in Venice, he sometimes sat in for a set.[278]

At this juncture in human evolution, few of us use our planets at the spiritual level, but many of us are striving to, and such people are wonderful to be around. As with the other planets, the spiritual level of evolution is vastly different with Sedna from the two previous levels. Here the conjunction with Mercury brings a depth of understanding so we can see past haze of distraction in everyday life. The struggle of the beginner's level is gone, as are the transcendental crises of the intermediate level. At this level everything Saturnian is meaningless and yet everything Sednian has its place.

Alan Oken is an American astrologer. He has Sedna conjunct Mercury and also Varuna, the planet of notability, in the fifth house of creativity.

---

[278] https://en.wikipedia.org/wiki/Dudley_Moore

He is a translator, teacher, global traveler and international tour guide, who lectures in five languages and does natal horoscope readings in seven. He is also a member of the New Group of World Servers and a life-long student of the Work and Teachings of the Tibetan Master, Djwhal Khul and legacy of the Ancient Wisdom.[279]

His Sedna is also sextile Saturn, the planet of structure, and semi-square Uranus, the planet of intuition, both in the seventh house of relationships, and square Pholus, the centaur of illumination, in the second house of material resources.

He is the author of a dozen titles, including *Soul-Centered Astrology*, *Rulers of the Horoscope*, and *Alan Oken's Complete Astrology*. In addition, he has written hundreds of articles for Dell Horoscope Magazine and many other national and international reviews and journals. Alan was the Director of The Wisdom School in Santa Fe, is co-founder of the Australian Institute for the Development of Consciousness and was Director of Esoteric Studies in Lisbon.[280]

Albert Einstein was a German-Swiss-American scientist, a physicist who developed the theory of relativity and the general theory, laying the groundwork for 20th century physics and providing the essential structure of the cosmos. He had Sedna conjunct Mercury, and Saturn the planet of structure, all in the tenth house of profession.

His name is synonymous with genius and the scientific definitions of the modern age from the atomic bomb, to space travel, electronics and quantum physics. Yet he was born with a misshapen head and abnormally large body and he learned to talk so late that his parents feared that he was mentally retarded. It was not until he was three, and he was not fluent until he was nine. For a while, he was considered subnormal because of his slow development, and his teachers were continually saying that he would never amount to anything.

His youth seemed to be one of deliberate rebellion against the establishment of his times. At age 16 he quit school and joined

---

[279] https://www.alanoken.com/about/
[280] Ibid.

his parents in Milan, Italy, where they had moved, and renounced his German citizenship. At 17, he entered the Zurich Polytechnic Institute after having failed on the first try and graduated with a mathematics teaching degree. The next year he took Swiss citizenship, and the year after that, a post at the Swiss patent office. It was while at the Swiss patent office, in a clerical position, that Einstein began the work that would make him a legend.

At 26 he published three seminal papers on theoretical physics in a single volume of a German scientific journal and two years later he came up with the immortal e=mc2, better known as the Special Theory of Relativity, encapsulating energy and matter as aspects of a single phenomenon. A year later, while still at the patent office, he began work on his major achievement, the general theory of relativity, which he officially proposed eight years later.

These theories were the greatest challenge to Newtonian mechanics that the modern world had ever known, but Einstein had a way of conceptualising and communicating them. He described relativity thus: 'Put your hand on a hot stove for a minute and it seems like an hour. Sit with a pretty girl for an hour and it seems like a minute.'

Experiencing the universe as a harmonious whole, he encouraged the use of intuition to solve problems, marvelled at the the mystery of God in nature, and applauded the ideals of great spiritual teachers such as Buddha and Jesus. Here's how he put it: "I like to experience the universe as one harmonious whole. Every cell has life. Matter, too, has life; it is energy solidified. Our bodies are like prisons, and I look forward to be free, but I don't speculate on what will happen to me. I live here now, and my responsibility is in this world now. I deal with natural laws. This is my work here on earth.

"If we want to improve the world we cannot do it with scientific knowledge but with ideals. Confucius, Buddha, Jesus and Gandhi have done more for humanity than science has done. We must begin with the heart of man, with his conscience, and the values of conscience can only be manifested by selfless service to mankind. Religion and science go together. Science without religion is lame and religion without science is blind. They are interdependent and have a common goal, the search for truth.

"Without religion there is no charity. The soul given to each of us is moved by the same living spirit that moves the universe. I am not a mystic. Trying to find out the laws of nature has nothing to do with mysticism, though in the face of creation I feel very humble. It is as if a spirit is manifest that is infinitely superior to man's spirit. Through my pursuit in science I have known cosmic religious feelings. But I don't care to be called a mystic."[281]

Opposition

With the opposition between Sedna and Mercury the all-embracing spirituality of Sedna challenges and stimulates our communicating and analyzing abilities, our curiosity and our ideas.

Speaking, writing, books, online communications and learning are all within Mercury's domain. This planet implores us to express ourselves often and well, and with the Sedna opposition the rich tapestry of reality is the context for our ideas and communication.

Learning about life in all its richness is the blessing of this aspect, but this may come with some challenging experiences to help break us out of entrenched ideas and help us develop a higher consciousness. The key with this aspect is not to succumb to the many challenges that will be put in the way of our self-expression, but to use them as motivation to continue our evolutionary work.

If we are unconscious of the energy, however, the opposition can bring out the negative side of Mercury, which can make us highly-strung, or nervous, nit-picky and indecisive, and lead us on a merry dance into our own delusions.

Like Squeaky Fromme, who is an American news figure for the attempted assassination of President Gerald Ford when she was 26. She has Sedna in the seventh house of relationships, opposite Mercury in her first house of identity.

> She was a worshipful follower of ritual cult leader and psychopath, Charles Manson, and she had begun a

---

[281] https://en.wikipedia.org/wiki/Albert_Einstein

correspondence with a newscaster on NBC to get him on TV with his message of enlightenment. NBC would not agree, so she decided to stalk and shoot Ford to get the publicity that would put her on TV.

She watched as Ford and his entourage left a hotel one morning. Petite and childlike, in a red gown and red turban, she followed the crowd and angled in to meet Ford face to face. She fumbled in her robe for her pistol and aimed at his genitals. A secret service man grabbed the gun and everyone piled on her. The attempt got her the publicity she wanted; she was on TV, but she also was sent to prison, and she never did get Manson, or his message across. She was released from jail on parole at the age of 60.[282]

We might also find ourselves at the mercy of some idea or mission, which to us seems meaningful, but is really just an illusion, or an excuse for either self-abuse, or for an abusive relationship.

Like Florence Aadland, who was an American news figure, whose daughter was, at 15, having an affair with the 46-year-old famous American actor, Errol Flynn. She had Sedna in the tenth house of profession, opposite Mercury in the fourth house of home.

Born the same date and year as her husband, she kicked him out when he objected to their daughter's notorious affair. When Flynn died, she released the couple's love letters for publicity. Mother and daughter apparently made a good partying team. When police broke up a noisy party they found the two with a group of men in various stages of undress. She was 45 when she was found guilty of contributing to the delinquency of a minor. Later that year she married a 15-year-younger East Indian actor and they tried operating a donut shop together. She also wrote a lovelorn column and published a book. However, she was an alcoholic and died at the age of 50.[283]

At root, Mercury is a thinker and the opposition can breed some deep thinkers. Like Antonin Artaud, who was a French dramatist, poet, essayist, actor, and theatre director, widely recognized as one of the

[282] https://en.wikipedia.org/wiki/Lynette_Fromme
[283] https://www.astro.com/astro-databank/Aadland,_Florence

major figures of twentieth-century theatre and the European avant-garde. He had Sedna in the sixth house of service, opposite Mercury in the twelfth house of the unconscious. He was plagued by physical and mental hardships throughout his life.

He contracted meningitis at age four, a disease which has no cure, but after a long struggle including a comatose period, he survived, but was severely weakened. His parents arranged a long series of sanatorium stays for him, which lasted five years. During his "rest cures" at the sanatorium, he read Arthur Rimbaud, Charles Baudelaire, and Edgar Allan Poe. However, the director of the sanatorium prescribed laudanum, precipitating a lifelong addiction to that and other opiates. He suffered his first nervous breakdown at age 19.

He moved to Paris at 24 to pursue a career as a writer and instead discovered he had a talent for avant-garde theatre. He cultivated a great interest in cinema as well, writing the scenario for the first surrealist film. His performance as Jean-Paul Marat in the film, *Napoleon* used exaggerated movements to convey the fire of Marat's personality. He also played the monk in *The Passion of Joan of Arc*.

In his early thirties he ran a theatre that was attended by an enormous range of European artists. He received a grant to travel to Mexico when he was 40, where he studied and lived with the Tarahumaran people and experimented with peyote, recording his experiences, which were later released in an English translation under the title, *The Peyote Dance*. The content of this work closely resembles the poems of his later days, concerned primarily with the supernatural.

His best-known work, *The Theatre and Its Double*, was published when he was 41. This book contained the two manifestos of the Theatre of Cruelty. There he proposed a theatre that was in effect a return to magic and ritual and he sought to create a new theatrical language of totem and gesture, a language of space devoid of dialogue that would appeal to all the senses.

"Words say little to the mind," he wrote, "compared to space thundering with images and crammed with sounds." He proposed "a theatre in which violent physical images crush and hypnotise the sensibility of the spectator seized by the theatre as by a whirlwind of higher forces." However, he suffered another mental breakdown and was hospitalised later that year and was confined for most of the remainder of his life to asylums, gaining his final release at 50, two years before his death.[284]

As we tire of density and the grief it creates, and we start a spiritual journey to get out of the swamp, Sedna rewards us with transcendent crises, experiences which force us to let go and rise above them, resulting in a huge growth to a new level of consciousness. There is no choice with these crises, and the more we try and solve them, the more we will get hurt.

An example here, and another deep thinker about how to organize the world, was Maria Montessori, who was an Italian physician and educator best known for the philosophy of education that bears her name. She had Sedna on the cusp of the ninth house of knowledge, opposite Mercury in the third house of ideas and communication.

> Her educational method is in use today in public and private schools throughout the world.

> After graduating from the University of Rome at 26, she continued with her research at the University's psychiatric clinic and was accepted as a voluntary assistant there. As part of her work, she visited asylums in Rome where she observed children with mental disabilities, observations which were fundamental to her future educational work.

> At 36 she was invited to oversee the care and education of a group of children of working parents in a new apartment building for low-income families in the San Lorenzo district in Rome. In this first classroom, she observed behaviours in these young children which formed the foundation of her educational method. She noted episodes of deep attention and concentration, multiple repetitions of activity, and a sensitivity to order in the environment. Given free choice of activity, the children showed more interest in practical activities and in her materials, than in toys provided for them, and were surprisingly unmotivated by

---

[284] https://en.wikipedia.org/wiki/Antonin_Artaud

sweets and other rewards. Over time, she saw a spontaneous self-discipline emerge.

"Based on her observations, she implemented a number of practices that became hallmarks of her educational philosophy and method. She replaced the heavy furniture with child-sized tables and chairs light enough for the children to move, and placed child-sized materials on low, accessible shelves. She expanded the range of practical activities such as sweeping and personal care to include a wide variety of exercises for care of the environment and the self, including flower arranging, hand washing, gymnastics, care of pets, and cooking. She also included large open-air sections in the classroom encouraging children to come and go as they please in the room's different areas and lessons.

She felt by working independently children could reach new levels of autonomy and become self-motivated to reach new levels of understanding. She also came to believe that acknowledging all children as individuals and treating them as such would yield better learning and fulfilled potential in each particular child. She continued to adapt and refine the materials she had developed earlier, altering or removing exercises which were chosen less frequently by the children. Also based on her observations, she experimented with allowing children free choice of the materials, uninterrupted work, and freedom of movement and activity within the limits set by the environment. She began to see independence as the aim of education, and the role of the teacher as an observer and director of children's innate psychological development.[285]

Writing is another Mercury activity. Ken Kesey was an American actor and novelist who worked at various times as a logger, a mental-hospital attendant, a farmer and musician in a band. He had Sedna in the second house of material resources, opposite Mercury in the eighth house of shared resources.

He volunteered for drug experiments run by the government, prior to the time that Timothy Leary started his experiments in psychedelics. His job as a psychiatric attendant for the Veteran's

---

[285] https://en.wikipedia.org/wiki/Maria_Montessori

Administration Hospital in California when he was 26, provided
background for his most famous work, *One Flew Over the
Cuckoo's Nest*. The next year he sold the movie rights for
$28,000. The film won five Oscars and reportedly made $50
million in gross earnings.

"A major counter culture figure in the 1960s, he and his band,
The Merry Pranksters, made a cross-country drug-fuelled trip in
a psychedelic painted bus called "Further" that was chronicled by
Tom Wolfe in his book, *The Electric Kool-Aid Acid Test*. When he
was 30 he purchased a farm in Pleasant Hill, Oregon, converting
the barn into living quarters. Many of the outbuildings on the farm
were built by The Merry Pranksters. He married his high school
sweetheart, Faye, and they had four children. He has always
been close to family.

He was an inspiration for many young people. With an ear for
dialog and the ability to create characters that live on the page,
all of his works are about prisoners, some who realise their
position and rail against it, others who are just doing their time.
An old-fashioned kind of writer, he is a moral critic. He won the
Robert Kirsch Award given by the Los Angeles Times in 1991 for
his body of work.[286]

Rusty Schweickart was an American astronaut on the Apollo 9 mission
in March 1969. He has Sedna in the eleventh house of collective
consciousness, opposite Mercury in the fifth house of creativity.

After he circled the earth for three days in the first manned flight
test of the lunar landing module that would later touch down on
the moon, he was strongly moved by the sight of the planet. This
led him to environmental work, then to being special science
advisor to California Governor Jerry Brown.

In mid-1979, he took the post of chairman of the State's
independent Energy Commission, a group that is concerned with
long-range energy planning and conservation and the chairman
practices its creed. His home has no air-conditioning and is
being heated by wood he chops and splits. He usually rides his
bicycle to work, a five-mile round trip. He is not really opposed to

[286] https://en.wikipedia.org/wiki/Ken_Kesey

nuclear power, but he calls it "a technology which has suffered from poor design" and he does not think it is worth the investment.[287]

At this juncture in human evolution, few of us use our planets at the spiritual level, but many of us are striving to, and such people are wonderful to be around. As with the other planets, the spiritual level of evolution is vastly different with Sedna from the two previous levels. Here, the opposition with Mercury brings an ability to communicate from the soul. The struggle of the beginner's level is gone, as are the transcendental crises of the intermediate level. At this level everything Saturnian is meaningless and yet everything Sednian has its place.

I have Sedna in the fourth house of home, opposite Mercury in the tenth house of profession. This aspect represents my writing vocation. I've written four books (this is the fifth) and four film scripts, two of which I've directed and produced into award winning movies. So, I have obviously not succumbed to the many challenges to my self-expression; they have just strengthened my vocation. But none of that came easy; no one ever wanted to publish my book or finance my film.

Back when I was starting working as a clown, no one wanted to employ me in a theatre, but I had the streets where artists get as much attention as they deserve, plus the opportunity to experiment and learn. So, when it came to my books and movies I took the same approach and just did it myself. My Mercury is thankfully conjunct Neptune, so I have the more psychic abilities of the Neptune opposition Sedna to help make sense of the richness.

Edith Stein was a German Jew who took the name of Teresa Benedicta of the Cross as a Roman Catholic nun. She had Sedna conjunct Pholus, the centaur of illumination, in the ninth house of spirituality, opposite Mercury in the third house of ideas and communication.

> She renounced her Jewish faith and declared herself an atheist by her teens. As a student she became interested in philosophy, received her doctorate in leading philosophers and becoming one of the first German women to earn a PhD specialising in the philosophical sub discipline of phenomenology.

---

[287] https://en.wikipedia.org/wiki/Rusty_Schweickart

She was first introduced to Catholicism through Christian phenomena. Attracted to this faith, she had a profound encounter at 30 with the autobiography of the mystic St. Theresa of Avila, which inspired her conversion. She was baptised the following year and started to teach at a Dominican girls' school, which she did for the next ten years. At 41 she became a lecturer at the Institute for Pedagogy at Munster but, because of anti-Semite legislation passed by the Nazi government, was forced to resign the post the next year.

She entered the Carmelite convent at Cologne, taking the vows of a Carmelite nun. While there, she completed her metaphysical writing work. However, her faith did not shield her from the Nazi horror. She was made to wear the Jewish star, and although her order transferred her to Holland when she was 47, she was rounded up along with her sister Rosa, also a convert, and other Jews when she was 51, by the Nazi occupation forces. Survivors of the death camp testified that she helped all other sufferers with great compassion. However, later that year, she and her sister both died in the gas chambers of Auschwitz.[288]

Leonard Cohen was a Canadian novelist and songwriter-folksinger,whose graceful, confessional songs have been described as 'elegant, bittersweet mood music for the dark nights of the soul'. He became a Buddhist monk, shaving his head and living in a monastery outside of Los Angeles. He has Sedna in the seventh house of relationships, opposite Mercury in the first house of identity.

As a student he gravitated toward poetry and prose, eventually gaining acclaim in Canada for his poems and two novels. The books did not sell well, so for income, he returned to songwriting. Judy Collins soon bought his song, "Suzanne" for her album, 'In My Life'. His creaky baritone was distinctive enough that he was signed to a record contract himself by Columbia with a debut album at 33, "Songs of Leonard Cohen." Sales were modest but critics hailed the collection.

During a period of deep depression in his early 40s, he separated from his wife and began to embrace Zen. Turning to a friend who had an aura of calm, he was introduced to an old Zen

---

[288] https://en.wikipedia.org/wiki/Edith_Stein

teacher. He found the spiritual training rigorous. For a time, he worked in both worlds, the commercial world of music and the spiritual world of striving, until he finally yielded completely and moved to the Zen Centre. Though he spoke for years of his interest in Zen, it was still a surprise to the establishment when the highly successful songwriter and poet left his finely tailored suits for modest robes, and Hollywood mansions for a small cabin with a narrow cot.

He stopped recording at 58 and touring the next year when he moved up the mountain. The pop icon, whose classic takes include "Bird on a Wire" and "Suzanne," did the cooking for the small community. With enough time, he worked on an illustrated book of poems and songs for a future album. His workroom contained an old computer and a synthesiser, tools for his music and his graphic art. He rose at 3:00 AM for morning meditation and to begin preparing the day's menu.[289]

Semi-sextile, Sextile, Trine

The flowing aspects between Sedna and Mercury align our communicating and analyzing abilities, our curiosity and our ideas of with the all-encompassing rich spiritual energy of Sedna.

Mercury not only rules communication, it represents coordination. Thought processes, ideas, and sensory information from both conscious and unconscious sources which all need to be coordinated and understood. Mercury analyses, sorts, groups, and makes sense of things.

Speaking, writing, books, online communications and learning are all within Mercury's domain; however, at the unconscious level we may not be the author of our story, merely playing a part in a bigger story.

Like Imelda Marcos, a Filipino political wife, who was the champion of conspicuous consumers at a time when her people were starving and destitute. She had Sedna in the tenth house of profession, sextile Mercury in the twelfth house of the unconscious.

> She was the owner of 2,030 pairs of shoes, designer garments, 500 black brassieres and many other extravagant items. A

---

[289] https://en.wikipedia.org/wiki/Leonard_Cohen

former beauty queen, she married Ferdinand Marcos who later became dictator of the Philippines.

When he was deposed, they went into exile in Hawaii. They suffered the indignity of being brought down to living in a $2 million house, modestly furnished and with a minimum staff, managing to get by on a monthly overhead of $80,000. From the power position of being the law, they were now facing a long list of criminal investigations.

Imelda was arraigned in New York on racketeering charges, of plundering $103 million in Philippine government funds, then soaking U.S. banks for $165 million more in a fraudulent financing scheme and secretly purchasing four Manhattan buildings with the loot. The indictment further alleged that, with the aid of Saudi arms dealer, they continued their financial finagling after accepting asylum in the U.S. Following a three-month trial, she was acquitted of all charges. By that time, Ferdinand had died in exile.

She was allowed to return to the Philippines at 62 and the following year, she ran for president, finishing 5th out of 7 candidates. She failed several more times to win the presidency and at 67 she started her own business, a fashion label that included designing jewellery. She was finally elected as a local district member of the Philippine House of Representatives at 80. The following year, in the first successful prosecution of the corruption that funded her lifestyle, she was ordered to return US $280,000 in government funds taken by her and her husband from the National Food Authority.[290]

Or we may be engaged in a deceptive story, or a delusory story, or simply employ denial. Like Amanda Knox, who is an American involved in a famous criminal case. She was initially convicted of homicide by an Italian court and later cleared of murder charges on appeal. She has Sedna in the twelfth house of the unconscious, sextile Mercury in the second house of material restrictions.

She was 20 and a student in Italy, when her roommate, a girl from the UK, was killed. As the dramatic investigation unfolded,

---

[290] https://en.wikipedia.org/wiki/Imelda_Marcos

she was accused of being responsible for the brutal stabbing death. The prosecutors painted a grim picture of her as a party girl who wanted the UK girl to be involved in sex games at a party. She reportedly enlisted the help of her boyfriend and another man. Both men were also convicted.

Her trial was covered extensively by US, British and Italian media for the nearly full year that it took to obtain a verdict. The jury handed down its guilty verdict when she was 22 and she was sentenced to 26 years in prison for murder and sexual assault. However, she and her parents protested that she did not receive a fair trial and steadily maintained her innocence.

A year later she was granted the right to an appeal. The case captured media and public attention in both the US, Italy and elsewhere. When she was 24 she was cleared of murder and assault charges. The court upheld a charge of slander since she had initially accused her former boss of the murder, but the three-year sentence for that charge was deemed already served. She was immediately released from custody and able to return to the US with her joyful family.[291]

Or the pressure to communicate might force us to withdraw from the process. Like Marcel Chevalier, who was the last chief executioner in France. He had Sedna conjunct Mars, the planet of war, in the ninth house of spirituality, semi-sextile Mercury in the eighth house of life and death.

He was chief executioner for five years, from the age of 55 until capital punishment was abolished in France. He started his career at 37, performed about 40 executions overall. After his appointment as chief executioner, he executed only two people. They were the last two executions in France. He was interviewed by the press on a number of occasions, but later, disillusioned by the sensationalist nature of press coverage, chose to say nothing of his experiences with the guillotine.[292]

As we tire of density and the grief it creates, and we start a spiritual journey to get out of the swamp, Sedna rewards us with transcendent

---

[291] https://en.wikipedia.org/wiki/Amanda_Knox
[292] https://en.wikipedia.org/wiki/Marcel_Chevalier

crises, experiences which force us to let go and rise above them, resulting in a huge growth to a new level of consciousness. There is no choice with these crises, and the more we try and solve them, the more we will get hurt.

Rachel Carson, the mother of the environmental movement, has Sedna in the first house of identity, sextile Mercury in the third house of communication.

As a child she loved the outdoors, the birds and plants around her family's rural property sparking her imagination. She found fossilised fish, and inspired by her expeditions wrote a book at age 8 and was published in a literary magazine at 13. At age eight she wrote a book and a few years later joined underage literary elite with published works in a children's magazine which also published early writings by William Faulkner, F. Scott Fitzgerald, E. E. Cummings, and E. B. White. Carson was fond of noting that she had become a professional writer at age eleven.

She entered the Pennsylvania College for Women on a senatorial district scholarship, earning an English degree, as preparation to become a writer. However, it was biology that she found most thrilling during her undergraduate years. Biology gave her the tools to learn what had happened to that fossilised fish she found as a child.

After earning a master's in zoology from Johns Hopkins, she found part-time work at the US Bureau of Fisheries. Though she'd chosen science over prose, her former specialty proved useful in her new occupation. Carson's first assignment for the bureau was to write a fifty-two-episode radio program called 'Romance Under the Waters.' "I had given up writing forever, I thought. It never occurred to me that I was merely getting something to write about."

Her first book, *Under the Sea-Wind*, was a commercial failure, selling only two thousand copies. She needed a couple of years to recover from the blow, but both driven and strapped for cash, she wrote another book. *The Sea Around Us* was published when she was 44, and it won the National Book Award for nonfiction and solidified her position as a literary heavyweight.

To this day, it's credited as being one of the most successful books ever written about nature.

In her fifties she turned her attention to conservation, especially some problems that she believed were caused by synthetic pesticides. The result was the book, *Silent Spring*, published when she was 55, which brought environmental concerns to an unprecedented share of the American people. Although it was met with fierce opposition by chemical companies, it spurred a reversal in national pesticide policy, which led to a nationwide ban on DDT and other pesticides. It also inspired a grassroots environmental movement that led to the creation of the U.S. Environmental Protection Agency.[293]

The deep research into communication which this aspect can encourage is exemplified by our case study, Helen Keller, who was an American blind-deaf linguist, author, political activist, and lecturer. She had Sedna in the fourth house of home, trine her Mercury on the cusp of the ninth house of knowledge. She overcame many obstacles, growing from a blind, deaf baby who had no words and could only communicate by touch, to a woman who wrote 12 books and toured the world extensively speaking of her research.

When she was one-and-a-half years old she developed a sickness, which left her deaf and blind, before she had learned to talk. Without language, her only memories of the next four years were of emotions and texture, mainly frustration and tantrums, until cuddled. When she was six, her father found her a teacher, who grew to love the girl and eventually stayed with her as a lifelong companion. The story of how her teacher broke through the isolation imposed by a near complete lack of language, allowing her to blossom, as she learned to communicate, has become widely known through the play and film, *The Miracle Worker.*

As she learned words through a tapped sign language in her hand, her consciousness started developing. She had an eager mind and wanted to know everything. Here's how she put it in her autobiography, *The Story of My Life*, published when she was 22.

> One day, while I was playing with my new doll, my teacher put my big rag doll into my lap also, spelled "d-o-l-l' and tried to

---

[293] https://en.wikipedia.org/wiki/Rachel_Carson

make me understand that 'd-o-l-l' applied to both. Earlier in the day we had had a tussle over the words "m-u-g'* and "w-a-t-e-r." She had tried to impress it upon me that "m-u-g" is mug and that "w-a-t-e-r" is water, but I persisted in confounding the two.

In despair she had dropped the subject for the time, only to renew it at the first opportunity. I became impatient at her repeated attempts and, seizing the new doll, "I dashed it upon the floor. I was keenly delighted when I felt the fragments of the broken doll at my feet. Neither sorrow nor regret followed my passionate outburst. I had not loved the doll. In the still, dark world in which I lived there was no strong sentiment or tenderness."

She brought me my hat, and I knew I was going out into the warm sunshine. This thought, if a wordless sensation may be called a thought, made me hop and skip with pleasure. We walked down the path to the well house, attracted by the fragrance of the honeysuckle with which it was covered. Someone was drawing water and my teacher placed my hand under the spout. As the cool stream gushed over one hand she spelled into the other the word water, first slowly, then rapidly. I stood still, my whole attention fixed upon the motions of her fingers.

Suddenly I felt a misty consciousness as of something forgotten—a thrill of returning thought; and somehow the mystery of language was revealed to me. I knew then that "w-a-t-e-r" meant the wonderful cool something that was flowing over my hand. That living word awakened my soul, gave it light, hope, joy, set it free! There were barriers still, it is true, but barriers that could in time be swept away.

I left the wellhouse eager to learn. Everything had a name, and each name gave birth to a new thought. As we returned to the house every object which I touched seemed to quiver with life. That was because I saw everything with the strange, new sight that had come to me. On entering the door, I remembered the doll I had broken. I felt my way to the hearth and picked up the pieces. I tried vainly to put them together. Then my eyes filled with tears, for I realized what I had done, and for the first time I felt repentance and sorrow.[294]

At then she found a Norwegian teacher from whom she learned to talk by passing her hand lightly over her teacher's face, so she could feel the position of her tongue and lips when she made a sound.

> I was eager to imitate every motion. I shall never forget the surprise and delight I felt when I uttered my first connected sentence, 'It is warm.' True, they were broken and stammering syllables, but they were human speech. My soul, conscious of new strength, came out of bondage and was reaching through those broken symbols of speech to all knowledge and all faith.[295]

The autumn after she had learned to speak, she wrote a story.

> I thought then that I was making up a story and I eagerly sat down to write it before the ideas should slip from me. My thoughts flowed easily; I felt a sense of joy in the composition. Words and images came tripping to my finger ends, and as I thought out sentence after sentence, I wrote them on my braille slate." Exited, she gave it to the headmaster who had enabled her teacher to come to her, and he liked it so much it was published in the school report.[296]

However, in true Sedna fashion, when she was visiting the headmaster for the celebration of George Washington's birthday, she was suddenly put before a court of investigation for plagiarism, because it had been discovered that a story similar to hers had appeared in a book before she was born.

> The two stories were so much alike in thought and language that it was evident the story had been read to me, and that mine was— a plagiarism. It was difficult to make me understand this, but when I did understand I was astonished and grieved. No child ever drank deeper of the cup of bitterness than I did. I had disgraced myself; I had brought suspicion upon those I loved best.

---

[294] The Story or My Life, Hellen Keller
[295] Ibid.
[296] Ibid.

I have never played with words again for the mere pleasure of the game. Indeed, I have ever since been tortured by the fear that what I write is not my own. For a long time, when I wrote a letter, even to my mother, I was seized with a sudden feeling of terror, and I would spell the sentences over and over, to make sure that I had not read them in a book.[297]

Nevertheless, she became a prolific author, writing twelve books as well as numerous articles and was well-traveled and outspoken in her convictions, giving lectures and talks around the world. A member of the Socialist Party of America and the Industrial Workers of the World, she campaigned for women's suffrage, labor rights, socialism, antimilitarism, and other similar causes.

Another deep researcher into the art of communication is Marcel Marceau, who was a French pantomime artist, actor, author, and creator of the internationally acclaimed white-faced clown "Bip." He had Sedna conjunct Nessus, the centaur of radical transformation, and Chiron, the centaur of wounding and healing, all in the twelfth house of the unconscious, semi-sextile Mercury, which is conjunct Uranus, the planet of revolutionary change, in the eleventh house of collective consciousness.

Encouraged by his parents to pursue a career in theatre, he was unable to complete his training due to the outbreak out of WW II. Seeking refuge in Limoges, he studied ceramics and at age 17 won the Masson prize for his work in enamel. Tragedy struck when his father was seized by the Nazis and died in Auschwitz. Marceau, in his zeal to help his fellow Jews escape the horror of the Nazi regime, assisted his brother Alain, a leader in the Limoges underground, in falsifying identification documents so young men could avoid the German labor camps, citizens could get fake ration cards and Jewish children could be safely smuggled into Switzerland.

When police raids became imminent, he fled to Paris, where he was saved from further persecution by having a cousin place him in an orphanage. There he taught dramatics and entertained the children with mime. In his spare time, he began studying under the tutelage of the master of mime, Etienne Decroux. "He was a

---

[297] Ibid.

kind of Christ.... In his class we dedicated our bodies to the discipline of silence." Setting up his own company in "The Pocket Theatre," at 24, he created the white-faced clown with the top hat called Bip. His first performance as Bip occurred on his 24th birthday.

A couple of years later he took his company on tour to Israel and Holland and a couple more to Berlin, but it was not until he was 29 that the performance could sell 1,200 seats. Two years after that his U.S. and Canada tour, originally scheduled for two weeks, was so successful it was extended for three months. "When I got back to Paris after being a hit on Broadway, everything changed for me. It was a new, almost frightening experience."

An international talent, by his late 30s he had given over 18,000 performances in over 100 countries, extending his acting ability onto the screen. By 56, he had made 17 tours of the US and he worked on the international stage into his 80s.

While fluent in five languages offstage, onstage he perfected his silent, subtle art. "The art of mime is an art of metamorphosis. You cannot say in mime what you can say better in words. You have to make a choice. It is the art of the essential. And you cannot lie. You have to show the truth...Why am I popular? Because I brought silence to the stage, because I made the invisible visible. I create abstract worlds and make them complete.[298]

As we see, humour can be one path to transcend the quicksand of Sedna, giving us the objectivity to step back from the edge and also, with the flowing aspects to Mercury, the opportunity to present a new perspective.

Fernandel was a French actor and mime comedian with a long, sorrowful, equine face and a radiant and toothy smile. He had Sedna in the eleventh house of collective consciousness, sextile Mercury in the twelfth house of the unconscious.

One of France's leading box-office draws, he built a four-decade career from the age of 27. His father was an accountant but also

---

[298] https://en.wikipedia.org/wiki/Marcel_Marceau

an amateur comedian-singer, and his mother was also an amateur actress and quickly noticed the talent of the young Fernand. He often accompanied his father during the concerts he organised in the Marseilles suburbs. It was during a contest for amateur singers that he won the first prize for children prodigies at the theatre of Châtelet de Marseille.

He made his debut on stage at five years, singing the military repertory with his elder brother. He had his first great success at the age of seven, a day when, paralyzed by stage fright, he was propelled on the stage by his father, with a great kick to the rear. He fell into his sabre and stretched his whole length under a storm of laughter. Later, he was never afraid to face the public.

In 1930, he appeared in his first motion picture and for more than forty years he would be France's top comic actor. He was perhaps best loved for his portrayal of the irascible Italian village priest at war with the town's Communist mayor in the Don Camillo series of motion pictures, which he also directed. His horse-like teeth became part of his trademark.[299]

At this juncture in human evolution, few of us use our planets at the spiritual level, but many of us are striving to, and such people are wonderful to be around. As with the other planets, the spiritual level of evolution is vastly different with Sedna from the two previous levels. Here, the flowing aspects with Mercury bring a more transpersonal connection with the soul dimension. The struggle of the beginner's level is gone, as are the transcendental crises of the intermediate level. At this level everything Saturnian is meaningless and yet everything Sednian has its place.

Maxine Bell was an American trance medium, pianist and composer. She had Sedna in the tenth house of profession, sextile Mercury, which is conjunct Makemake, the planet of devotion, in the eleventh house of collective consciousness. She played the works of dead masters while in trance and was able to play 3,000 notes per minute. She also worked with the Los Angeles Police Department on murder cases, as a psychic.

Jules Verne was a French writer widely popular for his science fiction novels and amazing anticipation of future discoveries. He had Sedna in

---

[299] https://en.wikipedia.org/wiki/Fernandel

the eleventh house of collective consciousness, semi-sextile Mercury in the tenth house of profession.

> Regarded as the father of science fiction, he predicted the use of submarines, helicopters, air conditioning, guided missiles, trips to outer space and motion pictures long before they were developed.

> The son of a magistrate, he went to Paris to study law; however, became interested in the theatre and began writing plays and opera librettos. He achieved success with his first short fantasy, *Five Weeks in a Balloon*, released when he was 35. His books have been translated into many languages and plays and films have been made from a number of them. His last years were marked with enormous popularity and numerous honours. By the time of his death, he had written over 50 books.

> Though he was raised Catholic, he became a deist from his early forties. Deism is a philosophical position that posits that a god does not interfere directly with the world. It also rejects revelation as a source of religious knowledge and asserts that reason and observation of the natural world are sufficient to determine the existence of a single creator of the universe. Some scholars believe his deist philosophy is reflected in his novels, as they often involve the notion of God, or divine providence, but rarely mention the concept of Christ.[300]

Anne Frank was a Dutch-Jewish writer of a diary from age 14 -15, while she and her family lived in total confinement, hiding in an attic from the Nazis, where non-Jewish friends had sheltered them. She had Sedna in the tenth house of profession, sextile Mercury in the eleventh house of collective consciousness.

> She began scrawling her diary in 1942, writing as a typical teen in many ways, childish and profound, thoughtful and painful, writing, "In spite of everything, I still believe that people are really good at heart."

> Her last entry was three days before their hiding place was discovered and they were arrested. She died of typhus at the Bergen-Belsen concentration camp in March 1945. Her father,

---

[300] https://en.wikipedia.org/wiki/Jules_Verne

who survived, returned after the war and found his daughter's diary. At the turn of the century a new edition of her diary was released with five previously secret pages that described her conflict with her mother, whom she wrote, "had cold eyes," and with whom she could not talk to unburden herself, and her lament that her parents had a loveless marriage of convenience.

Her diary remains as a poignant symbol of the millions whose lives and homes were lost during a tragic page in history. Translated into 54 languages with sales hovering around 25 million copies worldwide, her book is an established part of most high school educations. Putting a single face on the vast horror of the Holocaust, she served as a reminder of the quiet acts of heroism that were part of that high-water mark of evil.[301]

Semi-square, Square, Sesquiquadrate

With the stressful aspects between Sedna and Mercury the all-encompassing spiritual energy challenges our communicating and analyzing abilities, our curiosity and our ideas.

Mercury not only rules communication, it represents coordination. Thought processes, ideas, and sensory information from both conscious and unconscious sources which all need to be coordinated and understood. Mercury analyses, sorts, groups, and makes sense of things.

Speaking, writing, books, online communications and learning are all within Mercury's domain. This planet implores us to express ourselves often and well and with the Sedna opposition the rich tapestry of reality is the context for our ideas and communication.

Learning about life in all its richness is the blessing of this aspect, but this may come with some challenging experiences to help break us out of entrenched ideas and help us develop a higher consciousness. The key with these aspects is not to succumb to the many challenges that will be put in the way of our self-expression, but to use them as motivation to continue our evolutionary work.

There will also likely be obstacles in the path of our self-expression, and the key is to let these be motivators for further effort rather than judgements that we should stop. If we do stop, illness or victimization, in

---

[301] https://en.wikipedia.org/wiki/Anne_Frank

areas associated with the house positions, is possible to motivate us to try again. But if we rise to the challenge, we are likely to achieve great things.

At the unconscious level, however, the stressful aspects can also bring out the negative side of Mercury, which can make us highly-strung, nervous, pedantic, indecisive, or overly technical. And it can also give us a blind spot to danger, which can put us in the wrong place at the wrong time, in relation to random attacks and mass casualty events. The best advice here is to keep your wits about you, stay observant and do the work of raising your Sedna consciousness.

Or it may lead us into danger by encouraging us to play a part in a bigger story. Like Mata Hari, who was a Dutch prostitute and exotic dancer who also served as a spy. She had Sedna in the fifth house of creativity, sesquiquadrate her Mercury, which is conjunct Mars, the planet of action, and her Sun, her sense of self, all in the ninth house of knowledge.

> The daughter of a merchant, in her younger years she was expelled from convent school for sleeping with a priest and, at the age of 18, moved to Java with her 40-year-old husband. The couple had a violent marriage and one of their two children died. She left her husband and returned to Europe at 29 where, as a nude belly dancer, she went to Paris to work in a brothel.
>
> She also attended German espionage school and at the outbreak of WW I, she was offered cash up-front for a German mission but turned out to be not a very good spy. With the codename of H21, she returned to Paris, spent the money and did precious little else. However, she was arrested as a double agent when she delivered a message on German submarine activity to the French embassy. She was 40 when she was arrested and placed on trial for treason. Convicted, she was executed by firing squad. After her death documents were revealed which showed French falsification of the records and that instead of being a major spy for the Germans, she was an elegant but naive adventuress, essentially the first strip-tease dancer.[302]

---

[302] https://en.wikipedia.org/wiki/Mata_Hari

The pressure to communicate, which can be evident with these aspects, is exemplified by Jay North, who is an American child actor who did TV commercials from age six. He has Sedna in the eighth house of shared resources, sesquiquadrate Mercury in the twelfth house of the unconscious.

> He was the lead in the TV series "Dennis the Menace" for four years from the age of eight. His father abandoned the family when he was four, and his mom worked, while his aunt and uncle took care of him on the set of "Dennis the Menace." They often beat him and slapped him; he was brainwashed by the reign of terror, having to always get his lines right and do well, a true nightmare.

> During the late 1960s, he was a teenage long-haired drug freak. He was a has-been by age 21, doing a stint in the Navy and various odd jobs. By his 30s, the money his mother had invested in real estate 15-20 years earlier had made him well enough off to live a life of retirement in rural Lake Butler, Florida. He was considered a recluse and over the hill.

> By his 40s he was chubby, his hair was greying and he had a puffy face. He traveled the country, appearing at memorabilia/collectible shows and other types of events, signing autographs and answering questions about his life in show biz. He remains sour on Hollywood, feeling that he was used and abandoned like a commodity. He married three times and was divorced twice. However, his third marriage resulted in new found hope, as he finished years of therapy and moved to Florida.[303]

These aspects can also force an early sense of victimization, which is likely to come from our childhood communication and which can grow and be transmuted into an epic story in our attempts to deal with this early alienation.

Like Osama bin Laden, who was the founder of al-Qaeda, the organization that claimed responsibility for the September 11 attacks on the United States, along with numerous other mass-casualty attacks worldwide. He had Sedna in the eleventh house of collective

---

[303] https://en.wikipedia.org/wiki/Jay_North

consciousness, semi-square Mercury, which is conjunct Venus, the planet of values in the tenth house of profession.

He was a Saudi Arabian and a member of the wealthy bin Laden family. His mother was his father's tenth wife, but she was Syrian and was called the slave by the rest of the family. Osama was called the son of a slave. His father divorced his mother soon after he was born, recommending her to an associate, who married her and they are still together. The couple had four children, and Osama lived in the new household with three half-brothers and one half-sister.

This early sense of victimization was formative in shaping his perspective. He projected his victimization onto his fellow Muslims and set out to save them from, as he saw it, the decadent Saudi Arabian leadership in cahoots with the infidels. At 22 he joined the Mujahideen forces in Pakistan fighting against the Soviet Union in Afghanistan. He helped to fund the Mujahideen by funnelling arms, money and fighters from the Arab world into Afghanistan, and gained popularity among many Arabs.

At 31 he formed al-Qaeda. He was banished from Saudi Arabia four years later and shifted his base to Sudan, until U.S. pressure forced him to leave four years after that. His Sedna was also opposite Ixion, the planet of lawlessness, in the fifth house of 'what is produced in the home', which gives the signature of his style of terrorism: A major component of his ideology was the concept that civilians from enemy countries, including women and children, were legitimate targets for jihadists to kill.

After establishing a new base in Afghanistan, he declared a war against the United States, initiating a series of bombings and related attacks. He was on the American FBI's lists of Ten Most Wanted Fugitives and Most Wanted Terrorists for ten years from the age of 44. The FBI placed a $25 million bounty on him. He was finally shot and killed inside a private residential compound in Parkistan, where he lived with a local family, during a covert operation conducted by members of the US Naval Special Warfare Development Group.[304]

As we tire of density and the grief it creates, and we start a spiritual journey to get out of the swamp, Sedna rewards us with transcendent crises, experiences which force us to let go and rise above them, resulting in a huge growth to a new level of consciousness. There is no choice with these crises, and the more we try and solve them, the more we will get hurt.

Alan Turing was a British mathematician, logician, scientist, the father of the computer and the technical genius behind Britain's successful efforts to break German codes in WW2. He had Sedna in the twelfth house of the unconscious, square Mercury in the second house of material reality, which is conjunct Haumea, the planet of rebirth, right on the cusp of the third house - to the minute - the house of communication.

> He was accustomed to being a non-conformist. At boarding school, he refused to adapt and ignored subjects that did not interest him. He was an atheist and felt marginalized because of his homosexuality.

> From the age of 13 he formed a significant friendship with another boy who has been described as his 'first love'. Their relationship provided inspiration in his future endeavours, but it was cut short by his friend's death when Alan was 17, from drinking infected cow's milk some years previously. The event caused him great sorrow and he coped with this by working that much harder on the topics of science and mathematics that he had shared with his friend.

> He made inestimable contributions to cybernetics. His 'Computable Numbers', published when he was 25, is considered one of the outstanding scientific papers of the 20th century, a blueprint for what would become the electronic digital computer. His 'Universal Turing Machine' was an ancestor for the entire information age.[305]

---

[304] https://en.wikipedia.org/wiki/Osama_bin_Laden
[305] https://en.wikipedia.org/wiki/Alan_Turing

His Sedna is also conjunct Chariklo, the centaur of foresight, bi-quintile Ixion, the planet of lawlessness, and opposite his Moon, the planet of emotions.

> Though he envisioned a time when "ladies will take their computers for walks in the park," his own reality was not quite so whimsical. When a robbery occurred at his house in Manchester, he frankly told the police that the robber probably knew the man with whom he was having an affair. As homosexual relations were still a felony in Britain, Turing was tried and convicted of gross indecency. He was spared prison but was given a year's probation with the condition that he take oestrogen to diminish his sex drive.[306]

These aspects can make us a deep thinker, like Nikola Tesla, who was a Serbian-American inventor and engineer who was a master of electricity at a time when it was changing American life. He had Sedna in the twelfth house of the unconscious, square Mercury in the third house of ideas and communication.

> He is the unsung creator of the electric age, without whom our radio, auto ignition, telephone, alternating current power generation and transmission, radio and television would all have been impossible. He discovered the rotating magnetic field, the basis of most alternating-current machinery, and held more than 700 patents. His inventions make him one of the pioneers in the distribution of electric energy, and his Tesla coil is widely used in radio and television sets, among other things.
>
> In his autobiography, he tells of the early workings of his mind in a description that we can only regard with wonder: he saw flashes of light that interfered with his physical vision; when a word was spoken, he would see the object so clearly that he had trouble distinguishing between the imagined and the real; in later years he would build a machine in his mind, run it to see where the wear was flawed and make whatever repairs and adjustments were needed – before he ever began his construction.

---

[306] Ibid.

At night in solitude, he had an inner world of personal vision where he made journeys and studies, carried on conversations and met people that seemed as real to him as his outer world. By the time he was a teenager he spoke four languages. At about age 17, he found to his delight that he could create things in his mind, picturing them as the finished product without models, drawings or experiments.[307]

Or they can encourage or force us to become a great communicator. Like Betty Friedan, who was an American feminist pioneer and organizer, lecturer and writer, and the author of *The Feminine Mystique,* which became a best-seller, translated into 13 languages. She had Sedna in the third house of communication, semi-square Mercury in the second house of material resources.

Her mother quit her job as editor of the local newspaper's women's pages to become a housewife. She was aware of the toll this took on her mother, and the impact it had on her family. As an adult, after becoming pregnant, Friedan herself was fired from a job.

During her 20s and 30s she was a deeply committed radical activist. A brilliant, energetic reporter for union newspapers, she was intensely engaged in the leftist politics of the time. By the time she stopped working in 1952, pregnant with her second child, McCarthyism had chased underground much of this visionary women's movement. The rest was smothered by anti-female union policies and longstanding misogyny among male leaders on the left.

She retreated to the suburbs and began writing about family and work for women's magazines, doing what her mother had not done. And she came out swinging. Women in labor unions were fighting for equal pay, maternity leave and higher minimum wages, while other progressive women agitated for government-sponsored day care, national health insurance and an end to racial discrimination.

She later said: "I decided I was going to be fulfilled as a housewife, but I could not suppress the itch to write, and I did it

---

[307] https://en.wikipedia.org/wiki/Nikola_Tesla

in the morning, like secret drinking." She authored *The Feminine Mystique* at 42, which became a best-seller and was translated into 13 languages. This book exposed the "desperate housewives" of 1950s America, women imprisoned in suburbia with little to do. She came to believe that "the only way for a woman, as for a man, to find herself, to know herself as a person, is by creative work of her own.

On the heels of the Civil Rights Movement, she helped to found the National Organization for Women when she was 45, the largest and most effective group for women's rights, and served as its first president.[308]

Or like Jorge Luis Borges, who was an Argentinean writer, a literary giant with short stories, essays, poetry and all shades and types of books. He had Sedna in the ninth house of philosophy, sesquiquadrate Mercury, conjunct Ixion, the planet of lawlessness, and Venus, the planet of values and creativity, all in the second house of material resources.

He had a razor-sharp wit and a self-depreciating style and a powerful imagination and was a shy, retiring man who had a strong bond with his mother, living with her until her death at 99, when he was 75. Acclaimed as one of the greatest modern writers, he was compared to Edgar Allan Poe and Frank Kafka, a perennial candidate for the Nobel Prize in literature. His works were translated into more than 20 languages, and he won scores of literary prizes for his production of more than 35 volumes of writing.[309]

Humour can be one path to transcend the quicksand of Sedna, giving us the objectivity to step back from the edge, but also with the stressful aspects to Mercury the drive to relate to a broad and perhaps universal audience.

The famous Swiss clown, Grock, a composer and musician, who is often called "the king of clowns." He has Sedna in the first house of identity, square his Mercury, which is conjunct his Moon, the planet of emotions, in the eleventh house of collective consciousness.

---

[308] https://en.wikipedia.org/wiki/Betty_Friedan
[309] https://en.wikipedia.org/wiki/Jorge_Luis_Borges

He was once the most highly paid entertainer in the world. He started early as a performer, learning musicianship and acrobatic skills from his father and later became a clown, working with the famous clown, Antonet. They developed an act with the aim of making the transition from circus, to music hall stages, which were more lucrative. Refining their performances according to audience response, Grock came to dominate the act, and they eventually split up. By then his fame had spread, his act having developed into the mixture of pantomime and musical blunders for which he is now remembered.[310]

Benny Hill was a British comedian who was very popular with his zany comic style and was voted the Funniest Man of TV in Britain. He had Sedna in the second house of material resources, square Mercury in the twelfth house of the unconscious.

By the age of 62, his stand-up, fall-down, naughty-but-nice slapstick humour was being aired in 80 countries, as well as at home in England. Gay, he lived as a bachelor in a London apartment. Six years later at the time of his death, 'The Benny Hill Show' was being shown in 100 countries around the world and had made some $40 million.[311]

At this juncture in human evolution, few of us use our planets at the spiritual level, but many of us are striving to, and such people are wonderful to be around. As with the other planets, the spiritual level of evolution is vastly different with Sedna from the two previous levels. Here, the stressful aspects with Mercury brings the ability to communicate our unique spiritual message to a broad congregation. The struggle of the beginner's level is gone, as are the transcendental crises of the intermediate level. At this level everything Saturnian is meaningless and yet everything Sednian has its place.

Pope Pius XII was an Italian ecclesiastic and Pope of the Roman Catholic Church. He wrote many encyclicals making it easier for Catholics to participate in the church. His Sedna is in his fifth house of creativity, semi-square Mercury conjunct the IC, the cusp of the fourth house of home.

---

[310] https://en.wikipedia.org/wiki/Grock
[311] https://en.wikipedia.org/wiki/Benny_Hill

Born into a family devoted to the papal service, he worked so hard at the Seminary that his health gave way and he was forced to leave; however, Pope Leo XIII allowed him to live at home while completing his courses, until he was ordained.

> During World War I he was involved in humane efforts and was sent to Berlin to be its first nuncio, papal ambassador. He left Germany to be made cardinal and then became secretary of state for the Vatican, before being crowned Pope. At the beginning of World War II, he spoke out against the Nazis, helping Jews with false baptismal certificates and allowing thousands to stay in Vatican City, convents and cloisters.[312]

Marthe Robin was a French mystic and stigmatic. She had Sedna conjunct Pallas, the asteroid of wisdom, in the eighth house of the occult, semi-square Mercury in the sixth house of service.

> Serious illness marked her adult life, and from her twenties she was confined to bed, crippled, and gradually paralysed. She ate only wafers and neither drank nor slept, but lived for seven decades and carried on a busy apostolate.

> From the age of 28 she was completely paralysed and bedridden. Although she still could move the thumb and forefinger of one hand, she became motionless apart from her head which she could move slightly. Since the previous year, at the age of 25, she could not eat anything at all. And from the age of 26 she couldn't even take a sip of water. When doctors tried to force some water down her throat, it merely came out her nostrils.

> For the next 53 years her only food was the holy Eucharist, a wafer of bread which Catholics believe is the body of Christ. They also believe that they become his body on ingesting it. Once a week she was given the sacred host. Once she had received it she went immediately into ecstasy and began her weekly re-living of Christ's crucifixion. Every Friday wounds appeared in the palms of her hands and the stigmata, the scourging and crowning with thorns appeared on her body, and she appeared to be dead.

---

[312] https://en.wikipedia.org/wiki/Pope_Pius_XII

For 53 years she also carried on a busy apostolate, which is a Christian organisation directed to serving and evangelising the world. She was directed to found two schools in her native village, one for girls and one for boys. All this she directed down to the smallest detail from her bed in her darkened little room. Later on she was told to found a community which would welcome people looking for a retreat and which would be a home of "light, charity and love." It became known as the Foyer de Charité and there are now some 70 affiliated houses and communities throughout the world.[313]

Billy Graham was an American evangelist, a Southern Baptist preacher who was "born again" as a teen, accepting Jesus as his personal saviour. He has Sedna in the first house of identity, sesquiquadrate Mercury in the eighth house of life and death.

He spread the good word of God by way of 900 radio stations and many TV crusades. He published a magazine, *Decision*, with circulation of more than four million, and gradually moved into the TV ministry. World-traveled, he became internationally known as the spiritual leader of presidents and noted people in many walks of life.

The author of 24 books, many of them best-sellers, Graham is the recipient of several awards. He was never unctuous or pious; rather, he was earnest, quietly confident and, despite his iconic status, ministers from a personal level. It is estimated that he has preached to more people in live audiences than anyone else in history: some 210 million in more than 185 countries and territories. Hundreds of millions more have been reached through his TV, film, radio, video and print projects.[314]

In-conjunct

With the evolutionary inconjunct between Sedna and Mercury, the esoteric spiritual energy of Sedna bursts into our communicating and analyzing abilities, our curiosity and our ideas, in an evolutionary way and we have a fated role to play. The inconjunct sometimes acts as a flow and at other times as a stress, so we have to learn to actively manage the process as the rarified spiritual energy sometimes

---

[313] https://en.wikipedia.org/wiki/Marthe_Robin
[314] https://en.wikipedia.org/wiki/Billy_Graham

reinforces our ideas and communication and, at other times, isn't there to back us up. By adjusting to this, we gain a deeper understanding of ourselves and how to play our role.

Speaking, writing, online communications and learning are all within Mercury's domain. This planet encourages us to express ourselves and it also rules coordination. Thought processes, ideas, and sensory information from both conscious and unconscious sources all need to be coordinated and understood and Mercury analyses, sorts, groups, and makes sense of things.

The inconjunct can be thought of as fate, because it seems to reach inside our lives and create experiences which are hard to describe in any other way. However, while we are unconscious of the Sedna energy, this aspect can cause us to live in a bit of a parallel universe.

Like Stephane Delabriere, who was a French serial killer, who had Sedna the sixth house of service, inconjunct his Mercury in the eleventh house of collective consciousness. His murders were premeditated and he declared that he had a goal of 5,000 victims. However, of 14 psychiatric experts who were assigned to his case, none came to the same conclusion, beyond their agreement that he was beyond redemption.

Or Rachel Entwistle, who was an American homicide victim. She had Sedna conjunct Chiron, the centaur of wounding and healing, on the cusp of her 4th house of home, inconjunct Mercury in the tenth house of her place in society.

> According to one of her teachers, she was adept at understanding concepts and complex situations. "Rachel had genuine intellectual curiosity," he said. She was the kind of kid who loved learning. She wasn't just interested in getting good grades, but in understanding the material. The quality of her writing in the papers she did for the class was excellent. Rachel had tremendous potential and a positive and upbeat personality to go along with her intellectual ability.[315]

However, she and her 9-month daughter were found dead in their home, murdered by her supposedly successful husband, as she slept with their

---

[315] https://en.wikipedia.org/wiki/Murders_of_Rachel_and_Lillian_Entwistle

child, because he had created a fantasy world which was all about to collapse and he couldn't face telling her.

Or we could become a victim of a bigger story, like Barabara Plekker, who was a Dutch prostitute and homicide victim. Her Sedna was conjunct Saturn, the planet of structure, in the seventh house of relationships, and inconjunct Mercury, which is conjunct Neptune, the planet of delusion, in the twelfth house of the unconscious. She was working out of a small, apartment-like room with a single window in the red-light district of Amsterdam, when she was strangled. It was a copycat crime, as four years prior, another prostitute had been killed in the same room, the same way.

Or our communications could push us to take on an abusing role, like Abraham Kasparian, who is a former American politician who stabbed his wife three times in a public restaurant. He has Sedna in the fifth house of romance and children, inconjunct Mercury in the twelfth house of karma.

> She had filed for a divorce but agreed to meet him for lunch. She survived. Earlier that same day, a former tenant sued the couple, charging them with negligence in connection with an apartment fire that killed two children. He had been arrested previously and received sentences for welfare fraud and larceny.[316]

As we tire of density and the grief it creates, and we start a spiritual journey to get out of the swamp, Sedna rewards us with transcendent crises, experiences which force us to let go and rise above them, resulting in a huge growth to a new level of consciousness. There is no choice with these crises, and the more we try and solve them, the more we will get hurt.

Like Britney Spears, who is an American dance-pop singer, a fabulous success by the age of 19. She has Sedna in the eighth house of shared resources, inconjunct Mercury in the third house of communication.

> At 17, she signed to Jive Records and issued her first LP. The record was a massive hit, topping the charts and reeling off a series of radio smash singles. It became the best-selling album ever released by a teenage girl. She was plunged into the show-

---

[316] https://www.astro.com/astro-databank/Kasparian,_Abraham

biz world of tours, photo-shoots and adoring fans. She attributed her wonderful success to her family and her faith in God.

Her magic began to spread and she swept the MTV Europe Awards, where she nabbed Best Female, Best Pop, Best Breakthrough Artist and Best Song. She next brought her explosive live show around the globe and appeared on every major televised award show. Her trim teen-age figure and scant costumes were seen on every magazine cover.

As she grew more famous however, she became more impulsive. She got married and separated in the same weekend to a childhood friend. The wedding took place in Las Vegas early in the morning when she was 22. She wore a baseball cap and jeans and was accompanied down the aisle of the Little White Wedding Chapel by a hotel bellman. She married a second time later that year and the couple had two children; however, after only two years she filed for divorce.

She was often in the news for increasingly bizarre and often self-destructive behaviour, and at 25 she walked into a just-closed beauty salon demanding to have her head shorn. A few days later she admitted herself to a rehabilitation centre, left for one day and then re-entered. She had reportedly suffered a breakdown that was attributed to postpartum depression, alcohol, and/or drugs.

Her divorce became final later that year and twice early the next year she seemed to suffer from severe episodes of mental illness. On one occasion she refused to relinquish her children to their father, who has custody. After arguing with police, who suspected she had taken an unknown substance, she was admitted to a hospital and a judge revoked her child visitation rights. She was released a few days later but reports of strange behaviour continued and she was admitted to a psychiatric hospital.

She bounced back, however, with a new album and successful world tour the next year, and her seventh studio album, released when she was thirty, became her first to yield three top-ten singles in the United States.[317]

D. H. Lawrence was a British novelist and poet, the author of novels which include *Sons and Lovers, Women in Love, The Virgin and the Gypsy* and the classic *Lady Chatterley's Lover.*

He had Sedna in the fifth house of creativity, inconjunct Mercury in the tenth house of profession.

> He was one of the most controversial writers of the twentieth century who believed in the concept that man should bring his instinct into balance with his intellect. His explicit treatment of sexual fulfilment led to over three decades of censorship and ultimately to the Supreme Court.

> He was the fourth child of an abusive coal miner and a refined mother whom he idolised. After surviving bronchitis at the age of two weeks, which left him in permanently delicate health, he grew to be a frail and hypersensitive child, who was often in tears and was overly dominated by his unhappy mother. She was a refined schoolteacher, who met his father at a local dance and after the wedding, found that he did not own his own house and did not work in the mining office, as she had been led to believe, but instead laboured as a miner himself. Her misery is reflected in Lawrence's persistent theme in his novels of the elegant, well-bred woman under the influence of a common, lowbred man.

> At 26, with two novels in progress, he accepted a luncheon invitation from his favourite teacher and met his aristocratic wife. According to legend, she had him in her bed within 20 minutes of meeting him. Two months later they eloped to Germany, marrying a couple of years later when her divorce became final. When they returned to England at the outbreak of WWI however, they were forbidden to travel outside of it, because his outspoken opposition to the war and her German birth aroused the suspicion that they were spies.

> They left England at the end of the war, returning only for short visits thereafter, and led a peripatetic life through France, Italy,

---

[317] https://en.wikipedia.org/wiki/Britney_Spears

Sri Lanka, Australia, California and Mexico, where he was diagnosed with tuberculosis at 40. Despite his illness, he wrote voraciously during these years, introducing Freudian theory into the modern novel and especially writing openly about sexual passion and its necessary and explicit incorporation into human expression.

His theory of "blood consciousness" was a constant emphasis on humanity basing its decisions on instinct rather reason. His best-known work, *Lady Chatterley's Lover* was published when he was 43, but it was banned in England and the U.S. for describing the sexual act in minute detail. However, thirty two years later the United States Supreme Court overruled the censorship and the book was published again.[318]

Sibilla Aleramo was an Italian feminist best known for her autobiographical depictions of life as a woman in late 19th century Italy. She had Sedna on the cusp of the ninth house of knowledge, inconjunct Mercury in the first house of identity.

Her first book, *Una Donna*, is considered a classic of Italian literature, and the first outspokenly feminist novel written by an Italian author. While employed at her father's factory in her teens, she befriended a local man, 10 years her senior, who raped her in the office when she was 15. She did not tell her parents about the event and was instead persuaded to marry him. A year and a half later, at 17, she had her first and only child, Walter.

Her first novel followed her life. It illustrated her decision to leave her brutal husband, so her son would have a better life, and move to Rome, which she did at 25. She cohabited for some years with Giovanni Cena, writer and journalist, who convinced her to turn her story into a fictionalised memoir and publish it under the pseudonym of Sibilla Aleramo. She was 30 when *Una Donna* was published. She also became active in political and artistic circles and engaged in volunteer work in the poverty-stricken countryside surrounding Rome.

---

[318] https://en.wikipedia.org/wiki/D._H._Lawrence

A couple of years later, while still involved with Cena, she met someone at a women's congress, and their one-year lesbian relationship was recounted in the novel, *Il Passaggio*, published when she was 43. She would go on to be one of Italy's leading feminists and her personal writings have, in more recent years, been studied due to their open-minded views toward homosexual relationships.[319]

The blessing with the inconjunct with Mercury is that it can give us a sense of humour, a bit of a twinkle in our eye, and comedy can be one path to transcend the quicksand of Sedna, giving us the objectivity to step back from the edge and also the opportunity to gain insight by broadening our perspective.

Buster Keaton was a famous American comedian, considered one of the greats of silent pictures for his physical humour and pantomime. He had Sedna in the eighth house of shared resources, inconjunct Mercury exactly conjunct his Saturn, the planet of physicality, in the third house of communication.

> He was born into a vaudeville family; his father owned a traveling show with Harry Houdini called the Mohawk Indian Medicine Company, which performed on stage and sold patent medicine on the side. And at the age of three, he began performing with his parents in 'The Three Keatons.'

> His mother played the saxophone, and while on stage Buster would goad his father by disobeying him, and the elder Keaton would respond by throwing him against the scenery, or into the orchestra pit, or even into the audience. A suitcase handle was sewn into Keaton's clothing to aid with the constant tossing. The act evolved as he learned to take trick falls safely; he was rarely injured or bruised on stage; however, this knockabout style of comedy led to accusations of child abuse, and occasionally, arrest.

> Decades later, Keaton said that he was never hurt by his father and that the falls and physical comedy were a matter of proper technical execution. He told the Detroit News: "The secret is in landing limp and breaking the fall with a foot or a hand. It's a

---

[319] https://en.wikipedia.org/wiki/Sibilla_Aleramo

knack. I started so young that landing right is second nature with me."

By the time he was 21, his father's alcoholism threatened the reputation of the family act, however, so Keaton and his mother left for New York, where his career swiftly moved from vaudeville to film. He is best known for his silent films, in which his trademark was physical comedy, with a consistently stoic, deadpan expression, earning him the nickname "The Great Stone Face." He had an extraordinary period from when he was 25 to 34, when he worked without interruption on a series of films that make him, arguably, the greatest actor–director in the history of the movies.

His career declined afterward, with a dispiriting loss of his artistic independence, when he was hired by Metro-Goldwyn-Mayer and he descended into alcoholism, ruining his family life. He recovered in his late 40s, remarried, and revived his career as an honoured comic performer for the rest of his life, earning an Academy Honorary Award at 64.[320]

An American comedian and actor, Richard Pryor, also has an inconjunct. His Sedna is in his first house of identity, inconjunct Mercury and bi-quintile Ceres, both conjunct in eighth house of shared resources.

A sharp, brash star of night clubs, TV and films who thrived on chaos, his earthy, profane humour and low-life characterisations brought him great popularity, and he went on to win two Grammy's for his comedy albums. He was also a writer and film director.

In the middle of his career he progressed heavily into booze and drugs and, while free-basing cocaine, he set himself on fire and was badly burned over 50% of his body at 39. After recovery, he toned down both his act and his incendiary personal life. He had five marriages and paid child support for the son of an actress. When he was 46, he began to lose weight and was diagnosed with multiple sclerosis. By 53 he was confined to a life of

---

[320] https://en.wikipedia.org/wiki/Buster_Keaton

wheelchairs, canes and physical therapy, and just nine days after his 65th birthday, he suffered a heart attack.[321]

At this juncture in human evolution, few people use their planets at the spiritual level, but some do and such people are wonderful to be around. The well-known pattern with the other planets is that often the spiritual level of evolution is vastly different with Sedna from the two previous levels. Here, the inconjunct with Mercury brings a destiny to communicate our unique spiritual message to a broad congregation. The struggle of the beginner's level is gone, as are the transcendental crises of the intermediate level. At this level everything Saturnian is meaningless and yet everything Sednian has its place.

Elsie Wheeler was an American spiritualist and psychic who worked with Marc Edmund Jones and Zoe Wells on the Sabian Symbols. She was noted for being the primary contributor. She had Sedna in the eleventh house of collective consciousness, inconjunct Mercury in the fourth house of home.

> The experiment was conducted when she was 38. Crippled with arthritis, she had to be carried to the session. 360 cards had been prepared, one for each degree of the zodiac, which were presented at random and were shuffled continuously.

> One at a time, the cards were placed face-down in front of her and she pictured an image and reported it. At first the images did not seem entirely appropriate, or some were exaggerated, so the cards were put aside for six years, when they were revised. She died seven years after that, but the revision process was repeated after her death and the results were first published thirteen years later. Today the Sabian symbols are one of the tools widely used by astrologers to understand the meaning behind the placements of the planets.[322]

Jeff Green is an American astrologer and the author of *Pluto: The Evolutionary Journey of the Soul* and *Uranus: Freedom from the Known*, books that have been translated into ten languages. He has Sedna in the fifth house of creativity, inconjunct Mercury, which is conjunct Venus,

---

[321] https://en.wikipedia.org/wiki/Richard_Pryor
[322] https://www.astro.com/astro-databank/Wheeler,_Elsie

the planet of values and Chariklo, the centaur of foresight, in his first house of identity.

His early family life was brutal. He experienced severe psychological and physical abuse from his mother, and he and his brother were sent for a time to an orphanage, before being later returned to family. Always the "black sheep", at an early age, he recounts overhearing his parents say that they didn't care for him. Feeling a strong sense of alienation from both his family and his overall environment, he spent most of his school days at the ocean, where he could "escape" with the accompaniment of the ocean sounds and a surfboard.

He became an alcoholic. One drunken evening, he reached a fatal turning point when he got into a car accident and came to an intense altercation with the other driver. Arrested before a near violent ending, he was offered one of two sentences - go to jail or go to Vietnam. He had already experienced a life of abuse, devastation and trauma, but it was nothing in comparison to the violence and insanity of the war he was about to experience.

"Life made no sense to me; even the idea of God made no sense. I had a very close friend during the war. One day we were bombed and he was reading the Bible when this happened. He got a direct hit, and all that was left when I returned was pieces of flesh and a blood-covered Bible. I, too had the shared illusion that God is perfect, and did not understand how he allowed such a thing to happen, especially when someone was reading His book... At the age of eighteen this is completely senseless. And so I erased God from my life."

As did many of the soldiers at the time, drugs became his form of emotional survival. One month before being evacuated from Vietnam, another life-altering experience occurred. Searching for drugs in a nearby village, he stumbled upon a hill with steps. Climbing to the top, he found a Buddhist monastery. One of the monks approached him, but although the language barrier prevented his ability to converse directly with the monk, he experienced a telepathic communion.

At the end of military service, he continued to experience trauma, and his roaming eventually took him to Mexico, where he had another extraordinary mystical experience. This time he encountered a Shaman of the Navaho tribe. Like the experience with the Buddhist monk, the language barrier was again surpassed through telepathic communication. He spent six months there, during which time the Shaman initiated him in the sacred peyote experience. While undergoing this time of initiation, which created a lasting shift and expansion of consciousness, he encountered a pack of wolves and developed the ability to communicate telepathically with them. He spent three weeks living as a member of the pack.

The incredible experiences of his life eventually brought him to his true path as teacher and he has lectured throughout the U.S., Canada, and Europe and has been a participant in almost all of the major astrological conferences in the world. He is founder and director of the School of Evolutionary Astrology. His pioneering work has expanded the concepts of astrology to encompass a broader vision and greater understanding of the soul's purpose, necessity and desire for evolution.[323]

He is called the founder of Evolutionary Astrology because he first started to lecture on the revolutionary astrological paradigm at 31, after receiving a dream from the spiritual master Swami Sri Yukteswar, who was Yogananda's guru. In that dream the entire paradigm of Evolutionary Astrology was conveyed to Jeffrey.

This was the first time in astrology's long history that a specific paradigm was realized that allowed for an understanding of the evolutionary progression of a Soul from life to life. Jeffrey lectured all over the world on Evolutionary Astrology for 25 years from his early thirties. He established Evolutionary Astrology schools in a number of countries and wrote books on Evolutionary Astrology.

The first of these, Pluto: The Evolutionary Journey of the Soul, Volume I was published at 38. It has been in continuous print ever since and has become one of the all-time best-selling astrology books. Translations have been made into French, German, Dutch, Chinese, Bulgarian, Spanish, Portuguese, Italian, Serbian and other languages. Volume II, Pluto: The

[323] Ibid.

Soul's Evolution through Relationships was published when he was 52 and has been in continuous print.

Since starting his original Pluto School at 48, he had many students, a number of whom are now professional Evolutionary Astrologers. He personally counseled over 30,000 clients in his lengthy career. This exposure to so many Souls from so many different backgrounds and orientations allowed him to come to the deepest possible understandings of the nature of the Soul. He communicated these insights through all of his teachings.[324]

Quintile, Bi-quintile

The evolutionary quintile or bi-quintile aspect between Sedna and Mercury infuses our communicating and organizing abilities with the all-encompassing spiritual energy of Sedna to the point where we can push the boundaries of human development.

Quintiles and bi-quintiles point to talent, the desire to create order and to categorize, a fascination with patterns and structures, perfectionist tendencies, and the desire to build or make things. These aspects have the characteristics of both the trine and opposition. They point to awareness of conflicts, or problems and finding solutions for them; however, they do not automatically kick into action and must be cultivated over time.

Speaking, writing, online communications and learning are all within Mercury's domain. This planet encourages us to express ourselves and it also rules coordination. Thought processes, ideas, and sensory information from both conscious and unconscious sources all need to be coordinated and understood and Mercury analyses, sorts, groups, and makes sense of things.

At the unconscious level, however, the unrealized abilities of the quintile and bi-quintile aspects can also bring an arrogance built on a small, possibly deluded, view of our lives and this can bring out the negative side of Mercury, making us highly strung, nervous, pedantic, indecisive, or overly technical.

Like André Obrecht, who was official executioner of France for 25 years from the age of 51. He had Sedna in the eighth house of life and death, bi-quintile Mercury in the first house of identity.

---

[324] http://schoolofevolutionaryastrology.com/about

He was the nephew of the former chief executioner, who had a father-like relationship with him, as he was only one month younger than his own son, who died as a baby. The affection between the two men never ceased. Due to financial obligations the chief executioner's widow allowed his cousin to succeed as chief executioner, despite her late husband's indication that he would prefer Andre as his successor. Andre subsequently took his cousin's former place as first assistant. The two disliked each other, however. Andre thought his cousin was too slow and badly organised.

At 43, after having executed many French resistance fighters, he and some colleagues quit. However, he resumed his job a couple of years later, but his animosity towards his cousin had grown. Two years later the cousins fought again and he quit for the second time. When his cousin died, he wrote to the ministry of Justice, proposing his candidature as chief executioner. He was officially nominated and performed his first guillotining as chief in Marseilles, when he executed a police killer.[325]

A more extreme example is Cameron Hooker, who is an American kidnapper, murderer and sadist who, despite no history of family abuse, was into S/M and B&D fantasies from his youth. He has Sedna in the seventh house of relationships, bi-quintile Mercury in the second house of material restrictions.

He grew up in a small California town and got a job in a lumber mill following high school. At age 19, he started going with a 15-year-old girl, playing bondage-sex games with her. They married a couple of years later and had two daughters. Neither of the girls knew anything about what was happening in their home.

A year later he kidnapped, tortured and killed a woman, whose body was never found. He was never charged. When he was 23, he picked up a hitchhiker and kept her nude in a box under his bed for seven years. She was whipped, strangled, dunked in water, burned, electrically shocked, raped, humiliated and systematically brainwashed. After three years she had a year out of her box, doing housework, yard work and sleeping on the

---

[325] https://en.wikipedia.org/wiki/André_Obrecht

floor. However, she was put back into near total confinement for another three years, before she was brought out again.

She and Cameron's wife gradually became friends, as both were caught in the same web of terror. They fled together when Cameron was 30, but his wife returned home within a week. Three months later she broke down and told her pastor of her personal hell, and then the police. He was arrested and was found guilty on ten counts of kidnapping and other charges and given life in prison.[326]

Or like William Shockley, who was an American physicist and father of Silicon Valley. He had Sedna conjunct Orcus, in the twelfth house of the unconscious.

He co-invented the transistor, the forerunner of the microchip, an invention that changed the course of history for computers and electronics in a big way, and he was awarded many prizes and received many honours, culminating in the Nobel Prize for Physics.

However, his parents were eccentric and they kept him out of school until the 8th grade, so he lacked socialisation and grew up not knowing how to handle and deal with other people. At 46 he started Shockley Semiconductor Laboratory, the first establishment, working on silicon semiconductor devices in what came to be known as Silicon Valley. His management style could generally be summed up as domineering and paranoid. And after he received the Nobel Prize, his demeanour became increasingly autocratic, erratic and hard to please.

Late the next year, eight of his researchers resigned after he decided not to continue research into silicon-based semiconductors. They went on to form Fairchild Semiconductor, a loss from which Shockley Semiconductor never recovered and which would eventually spawn Silicon Valley. Over the course of the next 20 years, more than 65 new enterprises would end up having employee connections back to Fairchild.

The biography, *Broken Genius: The Rise and Fall of William Shockley, Creator of the Electronic Age* describes him as: "A

---

[326] https://en.wikipedia.org/wiki/Kidnapping_of_Colleen_Stan

nasty old man. One of his friends actually described him as having reverse charisma; he would walk into a room and you instantly took a disliking to him. He was extraordinarily bright and he knew it. He was a bit arrogant about it."

In his later years he slipped into Eugenics, the belief that humanity would be better served by only allowing the smart and healthy to breed. He was attacked for this in print, on television and in scientific journals and by the time of his death he was almost completely estranged from most of his friends and family, except for his second wife. His last years were very sad. His children are reported to have only learned of his death through the print media.[327]

As we tire of density and the grief it creates, and we start a spiritual journey to get out of the swamp, Sedna rewards us with transcendent crises, experiences which force us to let go and rise above them, resulting in a huge growth to a new level of consciousness. There is no choice with these crises, and the more we try and solve them, the more we will get hurt.

Marie Stopes was a British scientist and sex reformer who was an author and crusader for better birth control in the U.K. She had Sedna in the seventh house of relationships, bi-quintile Mercury in the second house of material resources.

During her lifetime, she wrote a film, 10 books, three stage plays and some poetry. One of her noted books is, *Married Love.* With degrees in geology and botany and a doctorate in German that she obtained in Munich, she became the first woman on the science staff at Manchester University.

During her first marriage, she remained a certified virgin and the marriage was later annulled. She made a second marriage at 37 and bore a stillborn baby the following year. Her second child was a son, whom she cut out of her will years later when he married a woman of his own choice. She and her second husband drifted apart and eventually divorced. However, for a woman who rejected sex up to the age of 37, she apparently

---

[327] https://en.wikipedia.org/wiki/William_Shockley

learned to appreciate the physical expression of love, as she had a 35-year-younger lover when she was 73.[328]

Sonia Gandhi is an Italian-born Indian politician, who has served as President of the Indian National Congress party. She has Sedna in the ninth house of knowledge, bi-quintile her Mercury in the fourth house of home.

She is straightforward, intelligent and something of an introvert. She met Rajiv Gandhi when they were both students at Cambridge University. It was love at first sight and they married when she was 21 in New Delhi. His mother was Indira Gandhi, who was Prime Minister of India. She was assassinated when Sonia was 37 and her husband stepped immediately into her mother's shoes. He was optimistic, though utterly unqualified for the job. It took Sonia literally years to come to terms with the horror of the assassination. She avoided seeing people and often fell silent for long periods, taking up art restoration as a hobby.

When she was 44, suddenly and violently, her husband was assassinated. She was offered the post of Party President within 24 hours, but she refused, due to her dislike of publicity and the fear of exposing her family to further risks. She retreated into herself, drawing consolation from her children and her home, which became a shrine to her beloved martyred husband. Her circle became small and closed and she made few public appearances. Her private secretary became her spokesman.

However, at 51 she quietly became a member of the Congress Party and campaigned on their behalf in an election that was like no other country had ever seen. There were more than 600 million registered voters and the ballot boxes had to be transported by donkey, fishing boat and mountain porter. There were nearly 5,000 candidates, some of whom were colourful, if unlikely, such as a bandit queen who had 63 court cases pending against her. India has over a thousand different languages and entrenched religious and caste divisions and many powerful splinter groups have broken off into chaotic segments.

---

[328] https://en.wikipedia.org/wiki/Marie_Stopes

Sonia emerged from her private life to campaign on behalf of the Congress Party, giving her first speech in the city where her husband had been murdered. She told the crowd, "Devotion to India brings me before you, not a desire for political office." She was elected president of the party a couple of months later and covered the subcontinent by jet and helicopter, visiting 138 constituencies in a 34-day tour, in an unparalleled campaign. She drew larger crowds than any of her rivals.

She finally agreed to enter politics when party leaders assured her that a "working" president of her choice would take care of day-to-day party work and she then led the Indian National Congress to victory in elections at 57. Following this she announced that she would "humbly decline" the Prime Minister's position but was under pressure to reconsider her decision. However, she said, "I must follow my voice." Earlier in the year, she said in an interview that her own power "is not a priority for me."[329]

Lewis Carroll was an English logician, mathematician, clergyman, photographer and novelist, who was considered a master in the genre of nonsense literature. He had Sedna in the third house of ideas and communication, quintile Mercury in the second house of material resources.

Inherently shy, he disliked public school. Additionally, he suffered from a bad stammer, and was often the target of bullies. He received a Bachelor of Arts degree at 22 and the next year was appointed as a lecturer in mathematics, a post he held until he was 49. He was ordained a deacon in the Church of England and could have continued on to become a priest, a position that would have allowed him to marry, but he was content to remain single and was frequently described as a 'shy, fussy bachelor'. His Sedna is also square Venus, the planet of relationships in the first house of identity. Often regarded as a crank, he nevertheless enjoyed good health throughout his life.

His love of children seemed natural and innocent in nature. He had grown up in a large family and his stammer disappeared completely when he was speaking with children. He began to

---

[329] https://en.wikipedia.org/wiki/Sonia_Gandhi

entertain the children of the families in the community and would keep them amused with what seemed like an endless store of fantastical tales. His Sedna is also semi-square Quaoar, the planet of new perspectives, in the fifth house of creativity. As he made up the stories, drawing on incidents in his life, he would sketch his characters on a sheet of paper; his tales holding the children spellbound.

Prompted to publish his stories, he wrote the children's books he would be particularly remembered for. His Sedna is also in evolutionary quintile with Mercury, the planet of communica-tion, in the second house of material resources. *Alice's Adventures in Wonderland*, published when he was 33, and its sequel, *Alice Through the Looking Glass*, became the most popular children's books in England, perhaps the most famous in the world. He also authored several books on mathematics, with *Euclid and His Modern Rivals*, being the most well known.

Early in his life he wanted to become an artist, however, failing in this pursuit, he instead became a photographer, specialising in studies of children in every possible situation and costume, including nudes. However, at 48, he abandoned his photographic work, apparently amid much speculation about his motives, as suspicions remained that his pleasure in children had sexual overtones.[330]

Humour can be one path to transcend the quicksand of Sedna, giving us the objectivity to step back from the edge and also with the quintile and biquintile to Mercury a fast, agile mind and the ability to communicate with a wide audience.

Joan Rivers was an American comedienne, thought by many to be the funniest lady on the planet. She had Sedna in the first house of identity, in a close evolutionary quintile to Mercury, which is conjunct Venus, the planet of values, both in the third house of ideas.

She certainly had one of the fastest, most agile minds in show biz. Her rapid-fire mix of gossip, insults, flaunting of taboos and ridicule of flaws and neurosis is written almost entirely by her.

---

[330] https://en.wikipedia.org/wiki/Lewis_Carroll

She also wrote comedy for *Candid Camera*, scripts and material for Phyllis Diller and Zsa Zsa Gabor and humorous books.

The younger of two daughters of Russian-Jewish refugees, she learned from her doctor dad to crack a joke and was making people laugh by the time she was 11. She learned from her mom that rich was better than poor and was raised with privilege and a good education. She married at 24 and had it annulled the following year when she decided she wanted to be an actress, not a housewife. While doing off-Broadway, she worked in offices and turned to comedy at 27 to supplement her income.

At the age of 32 she was told that she was too old and passed over; however, a week later she was booked on Johnny Carson's *Tonight Show*. They clicked. Their immediate rapport was a hit with the audience and she appeared for years with Carson before hosting her own *Late Show Starring Joan Rivers,* with a contract for $10 million over three years. She moved into the stratosphere as America's top comedienne, the darling of the circuit with tours, magazine covers, nightclub and Las Vegas gigs, TV projects, books and records.[331]

At this juncture in human evolution, few of us use our planets at the spiritual level, but many of us are striving to, and such people are wonderful to be around. As with the other planets, the spiritual level of evolution is vastly different with Sedna from the two previous levels. Here, the quintile and bi-quintile aspects with Mercury also brings an ability to organize, to do research and to effectively communicate these results. The struggle of the beginner's level is gone, as are the transcendental crises of the intermediate level. At this level everything Saturnian is meaningless and yet everything Sednian has its place.

Mu'Min Bey is a Western and Vedic Astrologer of African American descent. He has Sedna in the third house of ideas, bi-quintile his Mercury, which is conjunct Juno, the asteroid of partnership, in the eleventh house of collective consciousness.

He does Astrology from an African American perspective. He tends to write about social issues. His writing has caused controversy and he has been accused of stirring stuff up. He has

---

[331] https://en.wikipedia.org/wiki/Joan_Rivers

many interests in Astrology, primarily in the political, predictive, and counseling areas and he has been a volunteer instructor of Astrological Studies at Temple University, which has been very popular.

He has been a regular contributor to many of the Internet's most popular astrological forums. He founded his own astrological discussion forum, known as The Pan Astrological Forum. At 37 he also founded his blog, the Mu'Min Bey Astroblog. Known for his incisive and insightful writing, his posts, letters and articles are considered welcome additions to the many forums he frequents; his approach, particularly in the area of Vedic Astrology, is considered fresh, modern and innovative.[332]

Tracy Marks is an American psychotherapist, astrologer, lecturer and teacher who is the author of 15 books and pamphlets which have been translated into nearly a dozen languages. She has Sedna in the fourth house of home, bi-quintile Mercury in the ninth house of spirituality and knowledge.

Some of her more notable books include *How To Handle Your T-Square*, *The Astrology of Self-Discovery*, and *The Art Of Chart Interpretation*. She has a Master's Degree in psycho-synthesis and is acclaimed for her in-depth integration of psychological, spiritual and astrological concepts. She is skilled at leading dream work, women's empowerment, and the art of friendship groups. Some of her more pragmatic talents concern the fields of computer graphics and photography.[333]

Karl Marx was a German-Jewish communist and philosopher who developed the theory of socialism and the father of modern social science. He had Sedna in the first house of identity, in a close quintile with Mercury in the third house of ideas and communication. He pushed the boundaries of human development with his ideas on society.

His quintile to Mercury is complimented by a quintile to Makemake, the planet of extreme talent, conjunct Jupiter, the planet of philosophy, both in the eleventh house of ideals and a bi-quintile to Pholus, the centaur of catalyzing change, in the eighth house of shared resources. This

---

[332] http://www.linda-goodman.com/ubb/Forum1/HTML/016811.html
[333] https://www.astro.com/astro-databank/Marks,_Tracy

explains how his ideas and writing about social ideals involving a change in the distribution of social resources made him the powerful evolutionary change agent that he was.

> For him social change was about conflict between opposing interests, driven, in the background, by economic forces. This became the inspiration for the body of works known as the conflict theory. In his evolutionary model of history, he argued that human history began with free, productive and creative work that was over time coerced and dehumanised, a trend most apparent under capitalism. Fundamentally, he assumed that human history involves transforming human nature, which he saw, in a very Sednian way, as encompassing both human beings and material objects.

> He believed, like the philosopher, Hegel, that humans recognise that they possess both actual and potential selves and that self-development begins with an experience of internal alienation, which Marx argued was because of 'the despotism of capital'. This leads to a realisation that the actual self, as a subjective agent, renders its potential self as an object to be apprehended by capitalism.

> Marx further argued that by moulding nature in desired ways, the subject takes the object as its own, and thus permits the individual to be actualised as fully human. In the new society that would emerge, he reasoned that the self-alienation would end, and humans would be free to act without being bound by the labour market. It would be a democratic society, enfranchising the entire population. In such a utopian world here would also be little if any need for a state, the goal of which was only to enforce the alienation.[334]

---

[334] https://en.wikipedia.org/wiki/Karl_Marx

31: Sedna / Venus

Conjunction

With the conjunction of Sedna and Venus the all-encompassing spiritual energy of Sedna infuses our values, our relationships and our tastes with a rich appreciation of the natural bounty of life.

Venus rules our values, and the pleasure we take in life. Through Venus, we learn about our tastes, pleasures, artistic inclinations, and what makes us happy. All the Venus Sedna aspects are creative, but while some struggle with the process, with the conjunction it wells up in an eternally refreshing process.

Venus also tells us about our attachments to others and relationships in general. And it rules attractiveness, both the ability to attract and our own attraction to others and to things. At its best this aspect can give us a sense of oneness with all living beings.

At the unconscious level, however, our personal values may cloud our perspective on our relationships and their meaning in relation to the big spiritual context of our lives, and we may delude ourselves as to the part they play in our spiritual destiny.

With this placement we may have little regard for people with whom we are not intimately connected and we may see our own fun as being more important.

Like Brenda Spencer, an American murderer who killed a custodian and principal and wounded eight children and a policeman when she was 17. She had Sedna conjunct Venus in the twelfth house of the unconscious.

> She had said the prior week that she was going to do something to get herself on TV. A tiny girl, under 5 ft., with red hair and an epileptic, she had lived with her father since her parents had divorced. She claimed to have gone on her rampage because, "I hate Mondays." Who was she trying to kill? "No one in particular. I kinda like the red and blue jackets." After hours of futile attempts to get her to surrender, she finally decided it was time

to end what she had called "fun." Found sane, she was sentenced to 25 years to life in prison.[335]

Or, on a broader scale, like Ulysses S. Grant, who was an American general during the Civil War and a U.S. President after the war. He had Sedna conjunct Venus in the eleventh house of collective consciousness.

> As a Union General, he played an important part during the Civil War when Lincoln placed him in command of all the armies of the U.S. He had graduated from West Point at 21 and served in the Mexican War, but after receiving warnings about his drinking from his commanding officer, he resigned from the Army at 32. He held a wide variety of jobs in the Middle West for the following six years.

> At the outbreak of the Civil War he enlisted again, seeking a command, and to his surprise, was made a brigadier general in the Union army. He was placed in charge of one of the western campaigns and had a strategy of pressing the Confederate army relentlessly, whatever the cost. He cost a great loss of life with his strategy, losing 40,000 men in a little over a month in a series of running battles.

> At 46 he was elected as a Republican candidate for President. His skills as a general were more adept than those he portrayed as a politician. His Cabinet was weak, his domestic policy confused and many of his intimate associates were corrupt. His notable achievement in foreign affairs was the settlement of controversies with Great Britain. After retiring from office at 55, he toured Europe for two years; however, illness and bad business judgment darkened his last years.[336]

Another extreme example is Roberto Succo, who was an Italian serial killer who shot and killed his parents and seven other persons. He had Sedna conjunct Venus in the tenth house of profession.

> When he was 19 he killed his parents with his boy-scout knife, angry at them for not letting him use the car. Police located him a

---

[335] https://en.wikipedia.org/wiki/Cleveland_Elementary_School_shooting_(San_Diego)

[336] https://en.wikipedia.org/wiki/Ulysses_S._Grant

few days later. Psychiatric evaluation stated that he could not be held responsible and he was committed to a lunatic asylum.

After good behavior, several years later he was allowed to continue his studies in semi-liberty, being allowed to attend the University by day and reporting to the hospital at night. He watched for an opportunity to escape and made his attempt in the summer '86. He reappeared during the next year in the south of France where he began his bloody crime odyssey. He went by the name of Andre and the tabloids nicknamed him "the crazy Andre," "the full moon killer."

Roberto's passions were with powerful guns and cars. From his location in south of France, he wounded a person who survived and also killed a law officer, escaping to Switzerland and later to Italy. The total of his homicides, along with his parents, came to seven people. The story came to a conclusion when he was arrested carrying the Smith and Wesson gun that had been used a month before in a murder.

Upon capture, he was delirious, yelling insults in Italian about Italian women and extolling the difficulty of being a male. He also quoted Stendhal in French. "Women change and those who trust them are crazy." Of his crimes, he said it seemed that he was watching a film, said he was not there. He cried, screamed and collapsed, and in the end, confessed. Two days later he tried to escape and was on the prison roof for a few hours before he fell, ending up with three broken ribs. Two months later, he killed himself with gas.[337]

As we tire of density and the grief it creates, and we start a spiritual journey to get out of the swamp, Sedna rewards us with transcendent crises, experiences which force us to let go and rise above them, resulting in a huge growth to a new level of consciousness. There is no choice with these crises, and the more we try and solve them, the more we will get hurt.

Susan Boyle is a Scottish singer who rose to fame on a British talent show. Like Ulysses S Grant, she also has Sedna conjunct Venus in the

---

[337] https://en.wikipedia.org/wiki/Roberto_Succo

eleventh house of collective consciousness, but she expressed it in a more personal way.

> She is the youngest of nine children and reportedly suffered some oxygen deprivation at birth, resulting in learning disabilities. Never married, she lived with her parents, working in low-level jobs and volunteering in the church. Her father died when she was 36 and her mother died when she was 46, after which she became distraught.

> Her music gave her great comfort and she auditioned for *Britain's Got Talent* in the hopes of launching a music career in her mother's memory. When she appeared on stage at 48 her appearance belied her talent, but she wowed the audiences with her rendition of "I Dreamed a Dream" from the musical "Les Miserables." The clip of her performance is one of the most-viewed on *YouTube*.

> News reports made much of this plain-looking middle-aged woman. For subsequent performances on the show she underwent a slight makeover. She made it all the way to the finals based on judges' and viewers' votes. However, the ensuing publicity was a lot for her to handle. Although she sang well on the last evening of the competition and came in second, she was rushed to a London health care facility that night, reportedly suffering from an anxiety attack. She was released within the week.

> Her album was released later that year and it quickly shot to the top of the charts. The success was continued with her second album the following year, and her third album the year after that. The following year her net worth was estimated at £22 million.[338]

We can see in the last example how the conjunction can deepen the range of our creative efforts and also push us right to the edge of endurance as we strive to appreciate life.

Another example is Vincent Van Gogh, who was a Dutch artist, a legend for his brilliant work, who lived his brief life in misery and poverty. He had Sedna conjunct Venus and also Mars, the planet of assertive action, all in the tenth house of profession.

---

[338] https://en.wikipedia.org/wiki/Susan_Boyle

Disappointed in love and religion, he was intense, difficult and unhappy. He seemed to lack a psychological shield to protect him from the pain of everything and every moment.

Washed out as a preacher to impoverished coal miners, he turned to full time art when he was 27. At 33 he went to Paris to immerse himself in the vanguard styles of the day. He began using the impressionist's choppy brush strokes of pastel color. Within two years, he was disillusioned by what he saw in the Parisian scene, and living with his brother upon whom he was financially dependent proved to be a strain for both of them.

He fled south to Arles, where, intoxicated by the countryside, he painted with thicker impasto in blazing yellows, piercing reds and icy greens. His work still did not make him happy; in fact, he was frequently in despair. When his friend, Paul Gauquin, arrived he welcomed him. However, they began to quarrel, drink absinthe, a potent alcohol, and partake in debauchery. When Gauquin left Vincent followed him with a razor, and then locked himself in his room and cut off the lobe of his left ear. He was 35.

The following year he went quite mad, to the point where he was considered dangerous. He was put in an asylum near Paris early the next year. His doctor encouraged him to keep painting, and flying into a creative frenzy, he completed 70 canvases in 70 days. Six months later while painting in a wheat field, he became suddenly, intolerably despondent and shot himself in the chest. He died two days later.

At the time of his death he was a failure, a misfit who had sold only two paintings in his lifetime, an artist who was later known as one of the most famous painters of all time. Two years after his death, a Dutch museum gave him a retrospective. And a hundred years later a collector paid close to $54 million for his "Irises," now in the Getty Museum in Los Angeles.[339]

Or like Patch Adams, who is an American physician, famed throughout the medical community for charging no fees, carrying no malpractice insurance and living with his patients in a country farm setting. He has Sedna conjunct Venus and also conjunct Varuna, the planet of notability,

---

[339] https://en.wikipedia.org/wiki/Vincent_van_Gogh

and Mars, the planet of action, all on the cusp of the fifth house of creativity, giving him a strong performing mission despite his vocation as a doctor. He has always maintained that humour and joy are more important than any drug or therapy.

He was deeply shaken by his dad's death, but it was his uncle's suicide that pushed him into despair. He dropped out of school and made the first of several suicide attempts. His Sedna is semi-square his Sun, the planet of willpower, on the cusp of the seventh house of relationships and in a fateful inconjunct with Pallas, the asteroid of wisdom, in the ninth house of knowledge. He was 18 when his mom checked him into a mental ward at Fairfax Hospital in Virginia, where he turned his own emotional corner by helping his roommate conquer hallucinations and fear.

> A few weeks later he left the ward and enrolled at University to become a doctor. His Gesundheit Institute began as an experiment. For the first 12 years, 20 adults lived in a large home and used it as a crude hospital, open 24 hours a day. Three physicians and others did what they could for whoever came. They never charged money and their work was supported by part-time jobs of the live-in staff. For staff and patients, medicine was integrated with the performing arts, arts and crafts, agriculture, nature, recreation and social service. During those first 12 years, 15,000 people came through the home/facility for everything from profound illnesses, to simple curiosity and play.[340]

He faced stiff opposition from the health industry for his radical concept that healing happens faster if tension is reduced and patients are treated as individuals and encouraged to take more pleasure in life. It's obvious from a Sedna consciousness perspective, but completely frivolous from a Saturnian standpoint.

As we see, humour can be one path to transcend the quicksand of Sedna, giving us the objectivity to step back from the edge and also, with the conjunction to Venus, the ability to do creative work that a mass audience can relate to.

---

[340] https://en.wikipedia.org/wiki/Patch_Adams

George Carlin was an American comedian who began doing TV variety shows at 29, and nightclubs. He had Sedna conjunct Venus in the ninth house of knowledge.

> He quit high school after his freshman year and joined the air force, leaving a year early with an honourable discharge. He had a short radio disk jockey career, which led to stand up work, and by the late sixties he was in Las Vegas doing network television talk shows.
>
> He teamed with comedian Jack Burns before his solo act when he was 25. His film debut was at 31, although he only gained minimal popularity. He was fired from a big Las Vegas hotel a couple of years later for saying a four-letter word. His notorious comedy act, called "The Seven Word's you can never say on Television," became a legal matter when he was 35, and was not resolved for six years, which was good promotion.
>
> In his 30s he was the hottest act in the country, a whacked-out hippie whose LPs routinely went gold. By 36 he was heavily into self-destruct with his use of drugs and alcohol, favoring cocaine. His records sold liked crazy in the next couple of years, and he was a natural when he hosted *Saturday Night Live*. After a serious car accident and a heart attack at 41, he put his life back in order over the next few years, but it was not until his starring role in *Outrageous Fortune* at 50, which co-starred Better Midler, that he regained popularity.
>
> The comedian and social critic entered a drug rehabilitation program at 67. In a statement he acknowledged that he had been using "too much wine and Vicodin." The decision to admit himself to the rehab facility was his own. "No one told me I needed this. I recognised the problem and took the step myself."[341]

At this juncture in human evolution, few of us use our planets at the spiritual level, but many of us are striving to, and such people are wonderful to be around. As with the other planets, the spiritual level of evolution is vastly different with Sedna from the two previous levels.

---

[341] https://en.wikipedia.org/wiki/George_Carlin

Here, the conjunction with Venus brings a stronger spiritual dimension to our values and relationships.

The struggle of the beginner's level is gone, as are the transcendental crises of the intermediate level. As we develop our Sedna energies, the Saturnian traditions lose importance, particularly if they stand in the way of a more fuller appreciation of the particular focus of our passion. And we will likely have a hand in changing these traditions, although this process will likely still be challenging for all involved.

Linda Goodman was an American astrologer and poet who wrote a top selling book, *Sun Signs,* published when she was 43, which sold over five million copies, bringing astrology into the everyday market. Her Sedna is conjunct Venus and also Nessus, the centaur of radical change, and Pallas, the asteroid of wisdom, all in the twelfth house of the unconscious. The paperback rights for her second book, *Love Signs*, sold for a record $2.25 million ten years later.

> She began her career as a local newspaper writer, and married her first husband, also a writer. They had five kids, three of whom died in infancy. With a divorce, she took a job as a radio announcer in Pittsburgh, where she took the name Linda and married her second husband, also a radio announcer. Her interest in astrology blossomed when she moved to New York City at 38 and she totally immersed herself in the study to the exclusion of everything else.

> Determined and intense, with an explosive temper, she was also generous, often giving gifts to friends of cars or jewellery, a habit that led to bankruptcy in her early 60s. She moved to the remote mining town of Cripple Creek, Colorado at 45, where she could write with less distraction. She had an affair with a 26-year-old marine biologist, who left her a year later.

> When she was 48, her 21-year-old daughter, who was an aspiring actress, committed suicide by overdosing on Demerol in New York. Linda refused to believe that she was dead and said it was a government conspiracy, a cover-up, and spent a half million dollars searching for her daughter, eventually claiming that Marilyn Monroe, Howard Hughes and Elvis Presley were also alive and in hiding.

Diagnosed diabetic in her early 60s, she distrusted traditional medicine and sometimes refused to take medication, or treatment. She had a toe removed and then part of her leg amputated. She became a virtual recluse. However, she continued to write and completed her *Linda Goodman's Love Signs Relationship Report* to go on the internet before her death.[342]

David Icke was a British mystic who had a spiritual awakening at 38 and began his earth healing. He had Sedna conjunct Venus in the seventh house of relationships.

He got married at 19 and was a football player until his career ended abruptly at 21, with his total paralysis from rheumatoid arthritis. A few months later he made his debut as a sportscaster. He joined Greenpeace and the Liberal Party the following year. At 37 he joined the Green Party as a spokesperson and resigned his broadcast position a couple of years later. His first book came out in that period, *It Doesn't Have to Be Like This*. He met a healer at that time, and with her guidance, had a spiritual experience in which he spoke to Socrates and received his mission.

In that period, he was also involved with channeling and he met a woman who was working in a similar way and they began working together to heal the earth. He also wrote his second book, *The Truth Vibrations*. The message was that we are facing ecological disaster and a breakdown of our world political and economic systems. The planet must be cleansed of collective karma and imbalances to survive.

David and the woman he had been been working when they announced their love to the world and she moved in with him and his wife and family. However, within a year the "take-over" had receded and she left, but she gave birth to a daughter later that year. *Love Changes Everything* was published in the spring of the following year. He continued to write and lecture extensively

---

[342] https://en.wikipedia.org/wiki/Linda_Goodman

to an ever-increasing audience. His book, *Days of Decision* followed and his autobiography, *In The Light of Experience*.[343]

Opposition

With the opposition between Sedna and Venus our values, our relationships and our tastes stand in relief against the all-inclusive spiritual energy of Sedna and, at its best, this can bring a rich appreciation of the natural bounty of life and a sense of oneness with all living beings.

Venus rules our values and the pleasure we take in life. Through Venus, we learn about our tastes, artistic inclinations, and what makes us happy. And we look to Venus in the natal chart to see how we approach relationships of the heart. It tells us about our attachments to others and it rules attractiveness, both the ability to attract and our own attraction to others and to things.

The opposition challenges us to explore personal relationships and values from a larger and yet uniquely personal perspective. At the unconscious level this might bring us into conflict with others and even the authorities, who feel threatened by our behaviour.

And it can also bring out the negative side of Venus, which is self-indulgence, self-centeredness, vanity, and superficiality. This unfortunately, can lead to abuse, or abusive behaviour.

As it did with Hélène Althusser, who was a member of the French Communist Party, who fought in the Resistance During WW2. She had Sedna in the second house of physical reality, opposite Venus in the eighth house of life and death. Her relationship with her husband was tortured by his infidelities as we shall see below, and at the age of 70 he killed her, during one of his psychotic episodes.

Her husband, Louis Althusser, also had the opposition. He was a French-Algerian philosopher and teacher, a Marxist and an author. His Sedna was in the seventh house of relationships, opposite his Venus in the first house of identity.

> During the Second World War, he spent five years in a concentration camp. He joined the Marxist Party at 30 and began to publish major articles on philosophy in his early 40s. An

---

[343] https://en.wikipedia.org/wiki/David_Icke

elegant theorist, he redefined the concept of "ideology" as "our imaginary relationships to real conditions of existence" and fought against a purely economical interpretation of the works of Marx.

He had a history of manic-depression however, and at 62 his madness escalated to the point where he strangled his wife in their suite at an elite institute for the training of the French professorate where he had lived, first as a student, then as a professor, for 34 years. His homicide was dismissed on grounds of insanity by a Paris court and he was committed to a mental hospital.

A certain sexual confusion, ambiguity, or guilt seems to have been imbued into his mental breakdown. He wrote that he was a virgin at age 30 when he first made love to his wife, who was 8 years older. Hospitalised, with anguish, he vowed he would never do it again. He later tortured her with his infidelities, seducing other women in her presence.

He remained institutionalised for four years, after which he retired quietly to an apartment. Calling himself a "missing person" he wrote the second volume of his memoirs from a "non-place." *The Future Lasts Forever* was published after his death. His sense of his own nonexistence is at the core of his memoirs. The passages where he explores his own success, and his concomitant feelings of being a fake, because of his ability to charm and to reduce things to a formula, are among the most critical moments of the book.[344]

Or like Klaus Kinski, who was a German actor famed for his wide-eyed, histrionic performances, as seen in hundreds of roles in movies which he chose for their commercial possibilities. He had Sedna conjunct Nessus, the centaur likened to a sympathetic monster, in the tenth house pf profession, opposite Venus in the fourth house of home.

Described as unpredictable, rebellious and whimsical, he refused to work under such famous directors as Fellini, Pasolini or Visconti as "they don't pay me enough." He was the author of a highly readable and bigger-than-life autobiography, *I Need Love*,

---

[344] https://en.wikipedia.org/wiki/Louis_Althusser

which is largely centred on his miserable youth, his countless love affairs, his obsessive adoration of his son and his unrelenting hatred of cops and film makers. He also fathered two daughters, the youngest being famed actress, Nastassja Kinski. However, twenty years after his death, his oldest daughter published an autobiography in which she reported about years of sexual abuse by her father.[345]

As we tire of density and the grief it creates, and we start a spiritual journey to get out of the swamp, Sedna rewards us with transcendent crises, experiences which force us to let go and rise above them, resulting in a huge growth to a new level of consciousness. There is no choice with these crises, and the more we try and solve them, the more we will get hurt.

Edith Sitwell was a British writer, the first poet to be named a Commander of the British Empire, and at 67 she was made a Dame. She had Sedna in the third house of communication, opposite Venus in the ninth house of knowledge.

As a poet she is experimental and eccentric. She hated physical exercise and wrote in bed. Her early work was lightly imagistic, macabre, wistful and exhibited a spectrum of colour. Later, her work became more tightly knit, infusing simple matters with reverence and an aura of great significance. At 67 she converted to Catholicism, for which she held a deep religious passion. And three years later, she became a visiting professor at the Institute of Contemporary Arts.[346]

As we see, this can be a very creative aspect, which can lead to art and relationships being the focus of both our public and private lives.

Like Woody Allen, who is an American comedian, writer, actor and film director, screenwriter, playwright and musician. He has Sedna in the eighth house of shared resources, opposite Venus in the second house of material resources. He is the most prolific filmmaker alive today and all of his films explore the intricacies of relationships and attachment and allow us to laugh and release tension in these areas.

The best of his films leave the audience with a warm feeling about being alive, giving them a little peek into Sedna consciousness. In the

---

[345] https://en.wikipedia.org/wiki/Klaus_Kinski
[346] https://en.wikipedia.org/wiki/Edith_Sitwell

meantime, his personal relationships are notorious for being outside the norm. Allen and his longtime partner, Mia Farrow, adopted two children and have one biological child together. They even worked together non-stop, as Allen put the actress in more than a dozen of his films. They never married and never even lived together.

Allen did not adopt any of Farrow's other family, including Soon-Yi Farrow Previn, the adopted daughter of Farrow and André Previn. So, although it was a huge scandal when he fell in love with Soon-Yi and left Mia to start a family with her daughter, it was all technically legal because he wasn't Soon-Yi's actual, or adopted father.

In a *Vanity Fair* interview, he told the magazine that, despite the scandal's damage to his reputation, Farrow's discovery of his attraction to Soon-Yi Previn by finding nude photographs of her was "just one of the fortuitous events, one of the great pieces of luck in my life. . . It was a turning point for the better."

Six years later Reuters quoted him as saying, "What was the scandal? I fell in love with this girl, married her. We have been married for almost 15 years now. There was no scandal, but people refer to it all the time as a scandal, and I kind of like that in a way because when I go I would like to say I had one real juicy scandal in my life."

Or like Pablo Picasso, who was a Spanish artist who lived most of his life in France, world-renowned as one of the inventors of the Cubist movement. He has Sedna in the ninth house of knowledge, opposite Venus in the third house of communication.

> Considered to be the most original, influential and dominant presence in the visual arts of the early 20th century, his works are on display in the most prestigious museums and galleries of the world. His enormous output, including 14,000 canvases and thousands of prints, engravings, book illustrations, ceramics and sculptures, made him a billionaire at his death. His various studios and houses contained not only his own work, but also other works and collections that he had amassed over the years.[347]

His Sedna was also trine Juno, the asteroid of partnership, in the fifth house of creativity and his sexual appetite led him into many

---

[347] https://en.wikipedia.org/wiki/Pablo_Picasso

relationships and two marriages. Beauty and relative youth were the only consistent qualities he desired in women. He used almost all of his women as models, both before and after relationships.

A jealous man, he locked his first partner in their Paris apartment when he went out. His Sedna is also closely trine Ixion, the planet of lawlessness, in the twelfth house of the unconscious. He met his first wife, the daughter of a Russian colonel of good family and upperclass tastes, while he was designing for the Ballet Russe during their tour in Italy. He took her to Spain to introduce her to friends and relatives, painted her in a mantilla. They had a child, but she was soon out of the picture romantically, but they remained married due to their faith.

His next mistress, whom he met at 45, eventually committed suicide by hanging herself. The one after that was Dora Maar. They met when he was 54 and she became increasingly deranged as their relationship progressed. Matching his ferocious temperament and depressions with her own, she ultimately had electro-shock treatments. All his paintings of crying women were of Dora.

"In his 60s his sexual gluttony was becoming obsessive. He met Françoise Gilot, 40 years his junior. They had a son and a daughter, but after seven years she took the children and left. Shortly afterwards, Jacqueline Roque moved in. His first wife died of natural causes when he was 73, clearing the way for another marriage. When he was 79 the children he had with Françoise officially received his name, however, while telling her he would marry her, he instead married Jacqueline in secrecy.[348]

Humour can be one path to transcend the quicksand of Sedna, giving us the objectivity to step back from the edge and also, with the opposition to Venus, the ability to do creative work that reaches a mass audience and inspires further artistic development.

Annie Fratellini was a French clown, the granddaughter of Paul Fratellini who carried on the tradition of the famous Fratellini brothers, adapting their routines to her impish feminine character.

---

[348] Ibid.

She had Sedna in the eighth house of shared resources, opposite Venus conjunct Juno, the asteroid of partnership, in the second house of material resources.

> Each year, on her birthday, her father gave her a different musical instrument, a concertina, vibraphone, violin, clarinet, piano, etc. She learned to play them all and used them in her clowning. At 41, she co-founded, with her husband, the Fratellini Circus School, and was its artistic director. A unique feature of her school is that it offered both artistic and technical training. She also directed her own circus, the École Nationale du Cirque in Paris, France. And she has influenced the creators of the Big Apple Circus in America and Cirque du Soleil.[349]

At this juncture in human evolution, few of us use our planets at the spiritual level, but many of us are striving to, and such people are wonderful to be around. As with the other planets, the spiritual level of evolution is vastly different from the two previous levels. Here, the opposition with Venus brings values and relationships which deepen our personal spiritual destiny and enrich our collective spiritual evolution. The struggle of the beginner's level is gone, as are the transcendental crises of the intermediate level. At this level everything Saturnian is meaningless and yet everything Sednian has its place.

Elsie Wheeler was an American spiritualist and psychic who worked with Marc Edmund Jones and Zoe Wells on the Sabian Symbols and was noted for being the primary contributor. She had Sedna in the eleventh house of collective consciousness, opposite Venus in the fifth house of creativity.

> The experiment was conducted when she was 38. Crippled with arthritis, she had to be carried to the session. 360 cards had been prepared, one for each degree of the zodiac, which were presented to her at random and were shuffled continuously. One at a time, the cards were placed face down in front of her and she pictured an image and reported it. At first the images did not seem entirely appropriate, or some were exaggerated, so the cards were put aside for six years, when they were revised. She died seven years after that, but the revision process was

---

[349] https://en.wikipedia.org/wiki/Annie_Fratellini

repeated after her death and the results were first published thirteen years later.[350]

Today the Sabian symbols are one of the tools widely used by astrologers to understand the meaning behind the placements of the planets.

Joel Dobin was an ordained Jewish rabbi and a practicing astrologer. He had Sedna conjunct Nessus, the centaur of radical transformation, in the fourth house of home, opposite Venus conjunct the MC, the cusp of the tenth house of profession.

> He was a brilliant man, earning a degree from Princeton University at 22; he was the first graduate of Princeton to become a rabbi. He graduated from Hebrew Union College at 28 and earned an honorary Doctorate of Divinity 25 years later. He had a long career as a rabbi in the Reform Movement, serving communities across America, retiring at 69. He lived his life with a commitment to learning and to social justice. In addition to his work as a congregational rabbi, he was an author, publishing two books about the relationship between Jewish teachings, Kabbalah, and astrology.[351]

He is known as the author of "To Rule Both Day And Night, Astrology in the Bible, Midrash and Talmud," published when he was 51.

> In this book he reveals the profound astrological tradition to be found in the religious texts. The ancient Hebrews developed the richest and most sophisticated system of astrology known in the Western world, but this practice had been almost completely forgotten until he brought to light this wealth of astrological information, revealing a profound tradition as valuable today, as it was millennia ago.

> The key to this astrological system is the Kabbalah, the Jewish mystery tradition, in which the sacred Tree of Life links the influences of the twelve zodiacal constellations and seven planets to specific letters of the Hebrew alphabet, creating a unique method for constructing horoscopes. Analyses of the zodiac according to the rulerships of the sons of Jacob, the

---

[350] https://www.astro.com/astro-databank/Wheeler,_Elsie
[351] http://www.legacy.com/obituaries/eastbaytimes/obituary.aspx?pid=158297785

importance of solar and lunar directions and masculine and feminine influences, are all explored in his book for their impact on global and personal destiny.[352]

Semi-sextile, Sextile, Trine

With the flowing aspects between Sedna and Venus the ethereal spiritual energy of Sedna aligns with our values, relationships and tastes, giving us a rich appreciation of the natural bounty of life. The Venus energy is harmonious. In Venus, we find a need to be appreciated and to appreciate, and with these aspects we have a deep appreciation for the pleasures of life, for the arts, for love and romance, for beauty, money, entertainment, leisure, sensuality, and comfort. With these aspects we are likely to be creative, drawing on the richness we feel to fill our daily lives with beauty and pleasure. At its highest level these aspects allow us to 'follow our bliss'.

With the flowing aspects between Sedna and Venus our relationships are likely to provide a rich source of growth opportunities and we will likely develop through each relationship. There can however be an unworldliness with these aspects, an ignoring of the Saturnian realities because of the perceived higher values of Sedna. We live in a Saturnian world, so even with the flows between Venus and Sedna we still have to work to interface the ethereal with the material.

At the unconscious level we may develop a fanatical obsession which gives us a blind spot where we don't see the likely results of our actions and may become a victim of our own, or someone else's delusional values.

Like Kevin Cunningham, who was an American suicide victim, found hanging by his belt on the back porch of his home at 17. He had Sedna conjunct Vesta, the asteroid of regeneration, in the second house of material reality, sextile Venus, which is conjunct his Moon in the twelfth house of the unconscious.

> He left no note. He was the sixth young man from fiercely proud, mostly white, mostly Irish South Boston to commit suicide that year. He hanged himself after getting an $85 traffic ticket for running a blinking red light. He was an honor student who had a job, parking cars at Fenway Park and was the pride of his family.

---

[352] To Rule Both Day And Night, Astrology in the Bible, Midrash and Talmud

But he had earlier wrecked his father's pickup and was charged with drunken driving in the accident.[353]

Or like Sharon Tate, who was an American actress, sex symbol and model, who was murdered by members of Charles Manson's 'family'. She had Sedna conjunct Varuna, the planet of notability, in the tenth house of profession, sextile Venus in the eighth house of life and death.

In her early twenties she played small television roles, before appearing in several motion pictures. She also appeared regularly in fashion magazines as a model and cover girl. After receiving positive reviews for her comedic and dramatic performances, she was hailed as one of Hollywood's most promising newcomers, making her film debut at 23. A year later she co-stared in *The Fearless Vampire Killers* with Roman Polanski, who also directed the film.

The following year she and Polanski got married in London and at the time of her death, she was eight-and-a-half months pregnant with their son and was two weeks from giving birth. That day she entertained two friends for lunch at her home, confiding in them her disappointment at her husband's delay in returning from London.

That evening she dined at her favourite restaurant with three other friends, returning with them to her home at about 10:30 p.m. Shortly after midnight, they were all murdered by members of Manson's "family" and their bodies were discovered the following morning by her housekeeper. Police arrived at the scene to find her body and that of one of her friends in the living room; a long rope tied around each of their necks connected them. On the front lawn lay the bodies of the other two. All of the victims had been stabbed numerous times.[354]

Our personal values may cloud our perspective on our relationships and their meaning in relation to the big social-spiritual context of our lives.

---

[353] https://www.nytimes.com/1997/08/17/us/for-old-south-boston-despair-replaces-hope.html

[354] https://en.wikipedia.org/wiki/Sharon_Tate

Like Yigal Amir, who is the Israeli assassin of Prime Minister of Israel Yitzhak Rabin. He has Sedna in the second house of material restrictions, sextile Venus in the fifth house of creativity.

> He was born to a religious Yemenite Jewish. Following his military service, he was nominated by the religious-Zionist youth movement to teach Judaism in Latvia. At 23, he began studying, mixing religious and secular studies. He studied law and computer science, as well as Jewish law at the Institute for Advanced Torah Studies.
>
> He was heavily opposed to the Oslo Accords. He participated in protest rallies against the accords on campus, was active in organising weekend bus outings to support Israeli settlers and helped found an illegal settlement outpost. He was especially active in Hebron, where he led marches through the streets.
>
> The assassination took place when he was 25 at the conclusion of a rally in Tel Aviv, and he is currently serving a life sentence for murder plus six years for injuring Rabin's bodyguard under aggravating circumstances. He was later sentenced to an additional 8 years for conspiracy to murder.[355]

As we tire of density and the grief it creates, and we start a spiritual journey to get out of the swamp, Sedna rewards us with transcendent crises, experiences which force us to let go and rise above them, resulting in a huge growth to a new level of consciousness. There is no choice with these crises, and the more we try and solve them, the more we will get hurt.

Richard Branson is a British entrepreneur, investor and philanthropist, who is the founder of Virgin Records. He has Sedna in the ninth house of knowledge, sextile his Venus, which is conjunct Orcus, the planet of delving down and speaking out, in the eleventh house of collective consciousness.

> His mother was a strong influence on his success, emphasising independence and self-reliance. Basically shy, his public persona is one of bravado, but the private man remains an enigma. At the age of sixteen his first business venture was a magazine called *Student.* He started his record business from

---

[355] https://en.wikipedia.org/wiki/Yigal_Amir

the church where he ran the magazine. He started advertising popular records in the magazine and selling them by mail order. It was an overnight success, as he sold records for considerably less than the High Street outlets.

He started a record shop in Oxford Street in London at 20, and the following year, earning enough money from his record store, he launched the record label Virgin Records. By the age of 20, he had a thriving business and 40 employees. Twelve years later, his empire consisted of 50 companies that were giving him a turnover of 50 million pounds and he was ready to expand into the software, film, video and property markets.

His Virgin brand grew rapidly during the 1980s, as he set up Virgin Atlantic airline at 34 and expanded the Virgin Records music label. He launched Virgin Mobile in 1999, and Virgin Blue in Australia (now named Virgin Australia) in 2000. His Virgin Group now controls more than 400 companies, but he has also been involved in many failed business ventures, such as Virgin Cola, Virgin Cars, Virgin Clothing and Virgin Brides.

He wrote in his autobiography of the decision to start an airline: "My interest in life comes from setting myself huge, apparently unachievable challenges and trying to rise above them ... from the perspective of wanting to live life to the full, I felt that I had to attempt it."

He has also made several world record-breaking attempts. His first attempt at the fastest Atlantic Ocean crossing when he was 35, led to the boat capsizing in British waters and a rescue by RAF helicopter, which received wide media coverage. A year later he beat the record by two hours. The following year his hot air balloon "Virgin Atlantic Flyer" crossed the Atlantic. And at 40 he crossed the Pacific from Japan to Arctic Canada, in a balloon. This broke the record, with a speed of 394 km/h.

In his late 40s, he and musician, Peter Gabriel, discussed with the former president of South Africa, Nelson Mandela, their idea of a small group of leaders working to solve difficult global conflicts and Mandela announced the formation of a new group, The Elders, which is funded by a group of donors, including Branson and Gabriel. Through the Carbon War Room, founded when he was 59, the entrepreneur is seeking solutions for global warming and the energy crisis.[356]

Erica Jong is an American writer, a best-selling novelist with her racy *Fear of Flying*, published when she was 31. She has Sedna conjunct Varuna, the planet of notability, in the eleventh house of collective consciousness, sextile Venus in the ninth house of knowledge.

> Though she says that writing takes priority over both motherhood and men, there have been more than a few torrid romances along her way. Her first marriage, at 21 was annulled after six months when her husband was found to be schizophrenic.

> At 24, pretty, ebullient, with a sunny disposition, she married fellow Columbia student, Chinese-American child psychologist, Dr. Allan Jong and they lived in Germany for the following three years. She became a critically acclaimed poet with two collections of verse, *Fruits and Vegetables,* published when she was 29 and *Half-Lives*, at 31.

> At 35 she married sci-fi novelist Jonathan Fast; their daughter Molly was born the following year and they divorced after 4 years. At 47 she married attorney Ken Burrows, who was 48, stating that her naughty days were over. She published *Fear of Fifty* at 52, part confessional, part cocktail chatter and part intellectual cant in a memoir style, as engaging and fiercely self-centred as ever.[357]

Heinrich Boll was a German author who was awarded the Nobel Prize for Literature. He has Sedna in the third house of communications, sextile Venus in the second house of material resources.

> He was a leader of the German writers who tried to come to grips with the memory of World War II, the Nazis, and the Holocaust and the guilt that came with them. Because of his refusal to avoid writing about the complexities and problems of the past, he was the leading critic of West German society. His disillusionment with postwar Germany was also apparent through his strong sense of ethical responsibility of authorship and critical attitude toward social institutions. His writing style

---

[356] https://en.wikipedia.org/wiki/Richard_Branson
[357] https://en.wikipedia.org/wiki/Erica_Jong

was plain and accessible, and his books were translated into many languages.

He was particularly successful in Eastern Europe, as he seemed to portray the dark side of capitalism in his books, which were sold by the millions in the Soviet Union alone. Despite the variety of themes and content in his work, there are certain recurring patterns: many of his novels and stories describe intimate and personal life struggling to sustain itself against the wider background of war, terrorism, political divisions, and profound economic and social transition.

In a number of his books there are protagonists who are stubborn and eccentric individualists opposed to the mechanisms of the state or of public institutions. His villains are the figures of authority in government, business, the mainstream media, and in the Church, whom he castigates, sometimes humorously, sometimes acidly, for what he perceived as their conformism, lack of courage, self-satisfied attitude and abuse of power.[358]

Marie Curie was a Polish-French scientist, a physicist and chemist, winning Nobel Prizes for both, but not allowed in the French Academy of Science as she was female. She had Sedna in the second house of material reality, trine Venus, which is conjunct Saturn, the planet of structure, in the tenth house of profession.

At 24 she joined her sister in Paris to study math, physics and chemistry at the Sorbonne. She proved a brilliant student with an early interest in the magnetic properties of steel. Within two years she received her license in science with the highest marks of her class. She later held a chair in physics at the Sorbonne, the first female professor at the University.

She was drawn to fellow scientist, Pierre Curie by their mutual interest in magnetism and devotion to science. They married when she was 28, and in Pierre, she found a new love, a partner, and a scientific collaborator on whom she could depend. However, their early years were very hard. In 1898, after they discovered radium, Marie had a struggle of four years of toil

---

[358] https://en.wikipedia.org/wiki/Heinrich_Böll

which finally resulted in the extraction of one-tenth of a gram of radium from one ton of uranium mine waste, one of the epic stories of science.

The Curies worked together for 11 harmonious years, isolating radium and polonium. As well as being one of history's outstanding scientists. Marie lived the normal life of a wife and mother; a month after discovering radium, she carefully notes having made 14 pots of gooseberry jelly. Her letters show her very close and affectionate relationships with her father, brother and sisters, her daughters and many friends.

When she was 36 the Royal Swedish Academy of Sciences awarded them the Nobel Prize in Physics, together with another male physicist, "in recognition of the extraordinary services they have rendered by their joint researches on the radiation phenomena." At first, the Committee intended just to honour the two men, but one of the committee members alerted Pierre to the situation, and after his complaint, Marie's name was added to the nomination. She was the first woman to be awarded a Nobel Prize.

She was devastated when Pierre was killed in a road accident when she was 39. The physics department of the University of Paris had offered him a professorship the year before and was preparing his laboratory when he died. The University decided to retain the chair that had been created for him and to offer it to her. She accepted it, hoping to create a world-class laboratory as a tribute to Pierre. She was the first woman to become a professor at the University of Paris.

She received a second Nobel Prize in her own right at 44, this time for Chemistry, for the discovery of the elements radium and polonium, but was never allowed to join the French Society of Scientists because she was a woman. A biography by her daughter stresses her parent's unworldliness and the idealism that made them refuse to patent the process they developed of isolating radium, which could have made them wealthy.[359]

---

[359] https://en.wikipedia.org/wiki/Marie_Curie

Humour can be one path to transcend the quicksand of Sedna, giving us the objectivity to step back from the edge and also, with the flowing aspects to Venus, the creativity to fill our daily lives with beauty and pleasure.

Red Skelton was an American film, nightclub and Emmy-award-winning TV comedian. He had Sedna in the fifth house of creativity, sextile his Venus in the eighth house of shared resources.

He was the youngest of four sons of a circus clown, who died two months before he was born. Left destitute, his mother worked as a cleaning woman. He began selling newspapers at age seven. He dropped out of school at 14 to entertain in a traveling minstrel show, making ten dollars a week. After working as a minstrel man on a showboat that cruised the Ohio and Missouri rivers, and as a clown with his late father's circus, he turned to burlesque in his late teens.

At 17 he met a 15-year-old usherette and they were married two years later. Soon she was writing his material and managing his career. She negotiated a $1,500-a-week movie contract for him with MGM when he was 25 and he went on to appear in over 40 movies. CBS then offered him his own variety show, which premiered when he was 40 and was an instant hit. By 58, he had won three Emmy awards with shows that included his irreverent and hilarious alter ego characters. However, CBS eventually canceled the show despite high ratings, saying it wasn't hip with the times.

After the cancellation, he hit the stage playing to sold-out audiences well into his 70s with his stock characters. He had divorced amicably from his first wife at 30 and she continued to manage his career and write for him. Two years after his divorce, he married a model and four years later their daughter was born, followed by a son the next year. Tragedy occurred at the height of his career, when his son died of leukemia at age nine. He divorced his second wife at 60 and, that same year, he married his third wife, a secretary 25 years his junior.

He sustained a second lucrative career as an author of children's books and an artist of clown paintings that sold for as much as $20,000. Toward the end of his life he estimated that he earned

$2.5 million a year with his lithographs. He was inducted into the Comedy Hall of Fame at 80 and retired to a Californian ranch. At a frail 84, he still wrote every morning, still together with his third wife of the previous 24 years, who was by then a 59-year-old horse breeder.[360]

At this juncture in human evolution, few of us use our planets at the spiritual level, but many of us are striving to, and such people are wonderful to be around. As with the other planets, the spiritual level of evolution is vastly different from the two previous levels. Here, the flowing aspects with Venus bring values and relationships which deepen our personal spiritual destiny and enrich our collective spiritual evolution. The struggle of the beginner's level is gone, as are the transcendental crises of the intermediate level. At this level everything Saturnian is meaningless and yet everything Sednian has its place.

Joseph Campbell was an American mythologist, writer, and lecturer, best known for his work in comparative mythology and comparative religion. He had Sedna in the sixth house of service, semi-sextile Venus in the fifth house of creativity.

> His magnum opus is his book, *The Hero with a Thousand Faces*, published when he was 45, in which he discusses his theory of the journey of the archetypal hero found in world mythologies.
>
> As a strong believer in the psychic unity of mankind and its poetic expression through mythology, he used this concept to express the idea that the whole of the human race can be seen as engaged in the effort of making the world "transparent to transcendence," by showing that underneath the world of phenomena lies an eternal source which is constantly pouring its energies into this world of time, suffering, and ultimately death.
>
> To achieve this task, one needs to speak about things that existed before and beyond words, a seemingly impossible task, the solution to which lies in the metaphors found in myths. These metaphors are statements that point beyond themselves into the transcendent. The Hero's Journey was the story of the man or woman who, through great suffering, reached an experience of

---

[360] https://en.wikipedia.org/wiki/Red_Skelton

the eternal source and returned with gifts powerful enough to set their society free.

Since the book's publication, his theory has been consciously applied by a wide variety of modern writers and artists. His philosophy has been summarised by his own often-repeated phrase: "Follow your bliss." He thought of God as "a metaphor for a mystery that absolutely transcends all human categories of thought, even the categories of being and non-being. I mean it's as simple as that. So, it depends on how much you want to think about it. Whether it is putting you in touch with the mystery that's the ground of your own being. If it isn't, well, it's a lie.[361]

Shivabalayogi was a meditation guru in the tradition of the ancient and modern yogis of India. He had Sedna in the eleventh house of collective consciousness, sextile Venus conjunct Mercury, the planet of ideas and communication, in the ninth house of spirituality.

He attained self-realisation through twelve years of arduous tapas, meditating in samādhi, a state of total thoughtlessness, for an average of twenty hours a day. Tapas is the most advanced stage of meditation in which one remains absorbed for long periods in this non-dualistic state of consciousness.

After he completed tapas, he assumed the name Shivabalayogi, meaning Yogi devoted to Shiva and Parvati. The name reflects that he is a manifestation of both the male and female aspects of the divine. The female aspect represents the invisible energy of the divine through which the entire creation operates, while the male aspect represents the pure consciousness of existence beyond all imaginations. Generally, devotees called him simply Swamiji, meaning respected Master.

For three decades he traveled extensively in India and Sri Lanka, initiating over ten million people into dhyana meditation. In his early fifties he traveled for four years in England and the United States. His teaching is consistent with the Vedanta, emphasising the need for spiritual practice to achieve self-realisation.[362]

---

[361] https://en.wikipedia.org/wiki/Joseph_Campbell

[362] https://en.wikipedia.org/wiki/Shivabalayogi

Semi-square, Square, Sesquiquadrate

With the stressful aspects between Sedna and Venus the ethereal spiritual energy of Sedna challenges our values, relationships and tastes to match the rich appreciation of the natural bounty of life that we sense is possible.

Venus rules our values and the pleasure we take in life. Through Venus, we learn about our tastes, artistic inclinations, and what makes us happy. And we look to Venus in the natal chart to see how we approach relationships of the heart. It tells us about our attachments to others and it rules attractiveness, both the ability to attract and our own attraction to others and to things.

There is a danger with the stressful aspects in seeing our relationships through the cold impersonal light of Sedna, because this obviously won't endear us to our loved ones. From the bigger Sedna perspective many things seem appropriate that really aren't appropriate on the personal Venus level, but with Sedna we have to remember that we have a very personal perspective on the big picture, to the point where we take for granted the rightness of our way.

These aspects challenge us to explore personal relationships and values from a larger and yet still uniquely personal perspective, and this might bring us into conflict with others and even the authorities, who feel threatened by our behaviour. It can also bring out the negative side of Venus, which is self-indulgence, self-centeredness, vanity, and superficiality.

At the unconscious level it can be hard to find a balance between our pleasure and our place in the vast scheme of things and we may feel victimized or alienated by this. Sedna places challenges in our way to help us grow and it is how we react to those that shapes out lives.

There can also be manipulative tendencies, or susceptibilities, if other factors in the chart agree, which can lead to a danger of abuse.

Like Polly Klaas, who was an American homicide victim, kidnapped at knifepoint while hosting a slumber party for girlfriends at her home when she was 12. She had Sedna in the second house of material reality, sesquiquadrate Venus conjunct the MC, the cusp of the tenth house of social standing and also Neptune, the planet of deception.

She was two and a half when her parents divorced. Her mother remarried and the family relocated frequently due to her new husband's uneven success in his career. So she spent her formative years living all over northern California, but when her mother and step-father separated when she was 11, life with her mother became stable and productive. Mom was employed full-time as a manager in a clothing store and Polly was looking forward to spending a second year in the same school where she flourished. After taking up the clarinet, she was accepted into the advanced band in junior high school and was pursuing her talents by acting in local community theatre and singing in a children's choir.

Then news came of a possible reconciliation between her mother and step-father, meaning the family would be uprooted again and move to Idaho. Mom, now eager to reunite with her husband, relied heavily on Polly to help care for her baby half-sister, Annie, a job which Polly dutifully undertook. "Polly was just trying to help, to hold things together. That's what she did. I mean the last words anyone ever heard Polly say were what she said to the man who was kidnapping her, as he led her out of the house. "Please don't wake up my mother." Her body was found in a wooded area, 35 miles north of her home.[363]

Or a danger of developing abusive behaviour, like Stephane Delabriere, who was a French serial killer. He had Sedna in the sixth house of daily routine, sesquiquadrate Venus in the tenth house of profession.

The eldest of five children, he was tortured by his violent and alcoholic father. At age 13 he was put in a foster home. Calling himself the Prince of Darkness, he dedicated to Satan his performance of ritual sacrifices on animals. When he was 20, during a robbery he strangled, raped and slit the throat of a 63-year-old woman. A year later he beheaded his best friend using an ax and carried the head in his knapsack for the rest of the day.

Apprehended and awaiting trial, he murdered a prison guard using a knife. Of 14 psychiatric experts who were assigned to his case, none came to the same conclusion, beyond their

---

[363] https://en.wikipedia.org/wiki/Murder_of_Polly_Klaas

agreement that he was beyond redemption. His murders were premeditated and he declared that he had a goal of 5,000 victims. He was sentenced to life in prison at 25.[364]

Or we might be helpless in the face of karmic events, like Christa McAuliffe, who was an American astronaut and teacher, the first private citizen allowed into outer space via national selection and an instant celebrity in her connection to the fated expedition of the NASA spacecraft Challenger. She had Sedna in the twelfth house of the unconscious, square her Venus, which is conjunct Ceres, the planet of nurturing, in the third house of ideas and communication.

Her cheerful and helpful nature showed early as she became her mother's right arm in helping to raise her four younger siblings. Her first introduction to NASA came at 12 when astronaut Alan Shepard became the first American in space with his sub orbital flight of 15 minutes. "I remember being in my home when the first satellites were launched. My parents were amazed, and I was caught up in their wonder. I remember when Alan Shepard made his historic flight- not even an orbit - and I was thrilled."

After attending the local Roman Catholic High School, she became a teacher and by all accounts she was an exceptional teacher with a high I.Q. She was also widely known for her prodigious community efforts. In addition to volunteering as a Girl Scout Leader, a daycare centre worker and a fund raiser for a hospital, she adopted an underprivileged child every summer who lived with her family as part of a program called "A Better Chance."

Chosen at 36 out of 11,000 applicants for space flight for a non-astronaut, she spent 120 days training in Houston for the historic event. After four major delays for launching due to technical difficulties, the Challenger finally lifted off from Cape Kennedy, Florida. The launch was watched by her husband and two children, as well as her parents and sister. Eight miles up and traveling just under 2,000 miles an hour, the Challenger exploded one minute and twelve seconds into the flight, killing all six on board. She was 37 years old. Her legacy has grown each

---

[364] https://www.astro.com/astro-databank/Delabriere,_Stephane

year after her passing with schools and scholarships named in her honour.[365]

Osama bin Laden was the founder of al-Qaeda, the organization that claimed responsibility for the September 11 attacks on the United States, along with numerous other mass-casualty attacks worldwide. He had Sedna in the eleventh house of collective consciousness, semi-square Venus, which is conjunct Mercury, the planet of ideas, in the tenth house of profession.

He was a Saudi Arabian and a member of the wealthy bin Laden family. His mother was his father's tenth wife, but she was Syrian and was called the slave by the rest of the family. Osama was called the son of a slave. His father divorced his mother soon after he was born, recommending her to an associate, who married her and they are still together. The couple had four children, and Osama lived in the new household with three half-brothers and one half-sister.

This early sense of victimization was formative in shaping his perspective. He projected his victimization onto his fellow Muslims and set out to save them from, as he saw it, the decadent Saudi Arabian leadership in cahoots with the infidels. At 22 he joined the Mujahideen forces in Pakistan fighting against the Soviet Union in Afghanistan. He helped to fund the Mujahideen by funneling arms, money and fighters from the Arab world into Afghanistan, and gained popularity among many Arabs.

At 31 he formed al-Qaeda. He was banished from Saudi Arabia four years later and shifted his base to Sudan until U.S. pressure forced him to leave four years after that. His Sedna was also opposite Ixion, the planet of lawlessness, in the fifth house of 'what is produced in the home', which gives the signature of his style of terrorism: A major component of his ideology was the concept that civilians from enemy countries, including women and children, were legitimate targets for jihadists to kill.

After establishing a new base in Afghanistan, he declared a war against the United States, initiating a series of bombings and

[365] https://en.wikipedia.org/wiki/Christa_McAuliffe

related attacks. He was on the American FBI's lists of Ten Most Wanted Fugitives and Most Wanted Terrorists for ten years from the age of 44. The FBI placed a $25 million bounty on him. He was finally shot and killed inside a private residential compound in Parkistan, where he lived with a local family, during a covert operation conducted by members of the US Naval Special Warfare Development Group.[366]

As we tire of density and the grief it creates, and we start a spiritual journey to get out of the swamp, Sedna rewards us with transcendent crises, experiences which force us to let go and rise above them, resulting in a huge growth to a new level of consciousness. There is no choice with these crises, and the more we try and solve them, the more we will get hurt.

Like Helen Crawfurd, who was a Scottish suffragette and communist activist. She had Sedna in the twelfth house of the unconscious, square Venus conjunct Jupiter, the planet of expansion in the ninth house of knowledge.

> Her father was a Catholic but converted to the Church of Scotland and was a conservative trade unionist. Initially religious herself, she married the Reverend Alexander Crawfurd at 21, but became increasingly radical.

> She first became active in the women's suffrage movement in her early twenties, then at 32 she switched her support to the more radical Women's Social and Political Union. Two years later she smashed the windows of the Minister for Education and received one month in prison. The following year, she was twice arrested for protesting in Glasgow, received another month in prison, and went on a five-day hunger strike. Following one more arrest, she left the Women's Political Union in protest at its support of WWI and joined the Independent Labour Party.

> During the war, she was involved with the Red Clydeside movement, including rent strikes and became secretary of the Women's Peace Crusade. When she was 40 her husband died, and she was also elected as vice-chair of the Scottish division of the ILP. Shortly after, she was a founder member of the ILP's

---

[366] https://en.wikipedia.org/wiki/Osama_bin_Laden

left-wing faction, which campaigned for it to affiliate to the Communist International. When this policy was defeated, she joined the new Communist Party of Great Britain, within which she served on the Central Committee, and was involved with various journalistic projects. She also became secretary of Workers' International Relief.[367]

And Marie Stopes, who was a British scientist and sex reformer who was an author and crusader for better birth control in the U.K. She had Sedna in the seventh house of relationships, sesquiquadrate her Venus in the third house of communication.

During her lifetime, she wrote a film, 10 books, three stage plays and some poetry. One of her noted books is, *Married Love*. With degrees in geology and botany and a doctorate in German that she obtained in Munich, she became the first woman on the science staff at Manchester University.

During her first marriage, she remained a certified virgin and the marriage was later annulled. She made a second marriage at 37 and bore a stillborn baby the following year. Her second child was a son, whom she cut out of her will years later when he married a woman of his own choice. She and her second husband drifted apart and eventually divorced. However, for a woman who rejected sex up to the age of 37, she apparently learned to appreciate the physical expression of love, as she had a 35-year-younger lover when she was 73.[368]

Or like Steve Jobs, who was an American entrepreneur, one of the originators of the computer revolution, co-founder of Apple Computers and Pixar Animation Studios. He had Sedna in the eighth house of shared resources, square Venus in the fourth house of home.

He and his friend, Steve Wozniak, made their first circuit board in their garage and they called it the Apple. By the time he was 24, his Apple Corporation was worth $10 million. A year later, its value had grown to $100 million. Its graphical user interface, business applications and word processing won kudos, and millions cheered while Apple took on IBM and its personal computer.

---

[367] https://en.wikipedia.org/wiki/Helen_Crawfurd
[368] https://en.wikipedia.org/wiki/Marie_Stopes

However, he was called a haunted house by Chrisann Brennan, a high school sweetheart who lived with him and was an early Apple employee. She said he became a threatening monster and their relationship fell apart amid wild recriminations when she became pregnant with his first child. He denied he was the father, despite a positive paternity test and he paid a pittance in child support, while living the life of a millionaire. In her memoir *The Bite In The Apple: A Memoir Of My Life With Steve Jobs,* she says:

> "I've truly hated Steve at times, but never for very long. Sharing a daughter with him has forced me to think about things more deeply. Steve the saint, the alien, the despot, the punishing masculine god, the liar, the obsessed narcissist, the cult hero, the ID of the iEverything, the genius and the motherless boy."[369]

> As the Apple empire grew, Steve became a tyrant, subject to moody outbursts and gloomy silences. Hard feelings arose and power struggles with other executives ensued. He resigned and the following year co-founded NeXt, in an attempt to do for the hardware industry what he had down for software. He also bought a company which he renamed Pixar Animation Studios and negotiated a deal with Disney to distribute Pixar's films and became a Disney partner. Under Jobs' leadership, Pixar won 20 Academy awards for successful animated feature films and was acquired by Disney.[370]

With a twist of fate and a large amount of Sednian transcendence, he then convinced Apple to buy NeXt and was invited back to Apple as interim CEO and a few years later was made permanent CEO once again. Under his renewed leadership Apple computer became a major player in the computer industry once more and his team created visually aesthetic computers in bright colours that appealed to younger buyers.

Humour can be one path to transcend the quicksand of Sedna, giving us the objectivity to step back from the edge, but also with the stressful aspects to Venus the opportunity to fill our daily lives with beauty and pleasure. Those of us struggling with these aspects would be well advised to develop our sense of humour.

---

[369] Brennan, Chrisann. *The Bite In The Apple: A Memoir Of My Life With Steve Jobs*
[370] https://en.wikipedia.org/wiki/Steve_Jobs

Harpo Marx was an American comedian, actor, mime artist, and musician, and the second-oldest of the Marx Brothers. He had Sedna in the sixth house of daily routine, square Venus in the third house of communication.

In contrast to the mainly verbal comedy of his brothers, Harpo's comic style was visual, being an example of both clown and pantomime traditions. He wore a curly reddish blonde wig, and never spoke during performances, rather he blew a horn or whistled to communicate. He frequently used props such as a horn cane, made up of a lead pipe, tape, and a bulb horn, and he played the harp in most of his films.

He received little formal education and left grade school at age eight due to bullying, during his second attempt to pass the second grade. He began to work in odd jobs alongside his brother Chico to contribute to the family income, including selling newspapers, working in a butcher shop, and as an errand office boy.

At 21 he joined two of his brothers to form "The Three Nightingales", later changed to "The Marx Brothers". Multiple stories exist to explain Harpo's evolution as the silent character in the brothers' act. In his memoir, Groucho wrote that Harpo simply wasn't very good at memorising dialogue, and thus was ideal for the role of the "dunce who couldn't speak", a common character in vaudeville acts of the time.

In their films he was often cast as Chico's eccentric partner-in-crime, whom he would often help by playing charades to tell of Groucho's problem, and/or annoy by giving Chico his leg, either to give it a rest, or as an alternative to a handshake. He became known for prop-laden sight gags, in particular the seemingly infinite number of odd things stored in his topcoat's oversized pockets. He often used facial expressions and mime to get his point across. In later films, he was put into situations where he would repeatedly attempt to convey a vital message to another person, but only did so through nonverbal means, usually by whistling or pantomime.

"He married at 47 and the marriage was lifelong. The couple adopted four children and when he was asked how many children he planned to adopt, he answered, "I'd like to adopt as many children as I have windows in my house. So when I leave for work, I want a kid in every window, waving goodbye."[371]

At this juncture in human evolution, few of us use our planets at the spiritual level, but many of us are striving to, and such people are wonderful to be around. As with the other planets, the spiritual level of evolution is vastly different from the two previous levels. Here, the stressful aspects bring existential spiritual challenges to our values and relationships, which deepen our personal spiritual destiny and enrich our collective spiritual evolution. The struggle of the beginner's level is gone, as are the transcendental crises of the intermediate level. At this level everything Saturnian is meaningless and yet everything Sednian has its place.

Peter Hurkos is a Dutch psychic who gained ESP abilities after a blow to his head which left him unconscious for three days. He has Sedna in the eleventh house of collective consciousness, square his Venus in the first house of identity. Sedna is also bi-quintile Ixion, the planet of lawlessness, in the fourth house of home.

> As a boy, he was a poor student, dropping out of school when he entered his teens. He was a loner who spent much time in the woods or in solitude, dreaming and exploring, prone to fantasies and visions. After his accident, he became religious and also became afflicted with blinding headaches and his temperament became volatile and moody.

> His psychic abilities were tested psychometrically with a claimed 87% accuracy. His Sedna is also bi-quintile Uranus, the planet of intuition, in the ninth house of knowledge and in a fateful inconjunct with Pholus, the centaur of enlightenment in the sixth house of service. In addition to using his new-found abilities to do professional work, he also did TV guest spots and wrote an autobiography, titled *Psychic*. He tuned in to some of his subjects while in a sleep state, when he could speak in tongues, or in foreign languages, but he also did psychic work while awake.[372]

---

[371] https://en.wikipedia.org/wiki/Harpo_Marx
[372] https://en.wikipedia.org/wiki/Peter_Hurkos

Helen Keller was an American blind-deaf linguist, author, political activist, and lecturer. She had Sedna in the fourth house of home, square the nodal axis, with Venus conjunct the South Node of past life Karma. When she was one-and-a-half-years old she developed a sickness which left her deaf and blind, before she had learned to talk. Without language, her only memories of the next four years were of emotions and texture, mainly frustration and tantrums, until cuddled.

When she was six, her father found her a teacher, who grew to love the girl and eventually stayed with her as a lifelong companion. She explained love to the young girl in this way:

> "Love is something like the clouds that were in the sky before the sun came out. You cannot touch the clouds, you know; but you feel the rain and know how glad the flowers and the thirsty earth are to have it after a hot day. You cannot touch love either; but you feel the sweetness that it pours into everything. Without love you would not be happy or want to play."[373]

Helen goes on to recount in her autobiography how this made her feel:

> "The beautiful truth burst upon my mind—I felt that there were 'invisible lines stretched between my spirit and the spirits of others."[374]

Even in a more evolved Sedna consciousness these aspects still bring temptations to abuse power and deviate from the spiritual path as we see with new age guru, Bhagwan Shree Rajneesh. He was an Indian guru and author of more than a hundred books. He had Sedna in the eleventh house of collective consciousness, sitting at the apex of a T square, between Venus, the Moon and Saturn, all in the 8th house of shared resources, opposite Pluto in the second house of material resources.

> He was not only intimately familiar with the world's great religions and philosophies, but also the modern psychologies of Jung, Freud, Maslow, and the rest of the West's best thinkers in modern psychology and psychiatry. His syncretic teachings emphasise the importance of meditation, awareness, love, celebration, courage, creativity, and humour — qualities that he

---

[373] Keller, Helen. *The Story of My Life*
[374] Ibid.

viewed as being suppressed by adherence to static belief systems and religious tradition.

When he was 50, he founded a commune in Oregon of 1,700 disciples, a sprawling religious community of a hundred square miles. The ashram was an attempt to build a self-sufficient commune based on ecological and organic farming principles, turning the desert into a garden, which they achieved in part. The devotees who joined came from all walks of life, devoting their money and labor to create a utopia. These years saw an increased emphasis on his prediction that the world might be destroyed by nuclear war. He predicted that, "the third and last war is now on the way" and frequently spoke of the need to create a 'new humanity' to avoid global suicide.

A key facet of his charismatic ability was that he was a brilliant manipulator of the unquestioning disciple. While his followers might be at a mere subsistence level, having severed ties with outside friends and family and donated all, or most of their money and possessions to the commune, he was seen to live in ostentation and offensive opulence, famously buying 93 Rolls-Royces as a so-called spiritual challenge to the commercial culture in America. Called the "sex-guru" because of his popular talks about tantric sex, his ashram became known as one big love fest during celebrations.

The task of running the commune fell to his personal secretary and the assets of the organization were all in her name. Almost immediately it ran into conflict with county residents and the state government and a succession of legal battles ensued, concerning the ashram's construction and continued development, which curtailed its success. In response he gave her power of attorney and she mounted a campaign of harassment and terrorism against the county.

He later alleged that she committed crimes, included the attempted murder of his personal physician, poisonings of public officials, wiretapping and bugging within the commune and within his own home, and a bio-terror attack on the citizens of the Dalles, using salmonella to impact the county elections.

At 53, a few days after his secretary and her entire management team had suddenly left the commune for Europe, he held a press conference in which he labelled her and her associates a gang of fascists. He accused them of having committed a number of serious crimes and invited the authorities to investigate. He claimed that she was trying to establish the Rajneeshees as a religion, and that her quest for personal power led to her paranoia, which eventually spread throughout the commune. He spoke often of how organised religion is an obstacle to enlightenment.

Difficulties accumulated with the National Immigration Service and Inland Revenue Service, who were trying to deport him, and he was arrested as he fled his strife-torn utopia at 53, on 35 counts of conspiracy and fraud. He was released and on his return to India, he changed his name to Osho to signal a change in his consciousness.[375]

In-conjunct

With the evolutionary inconjunct between Sedna and Venus, the esoteric spiritual energy of Sedna bursts into our values and relationships in an evolutionary way and we have a fated role to play.

This aspect sometimes acts as a flow and at other times as a stress, so we have to learn to actively manage the process as the rarified spiritual energy sometimes reinforces our values and relationships and at other times isn't there to back us up. By adjusting to this, we gain a deeper understanding of ourselves and how to play our role.

Venus rules our values, and the pleasure we take in life. Through Venus, we learn about our tastes, artistic inclinations, and what makes us happy. And we look to Venus in the natal chart to see how we approach relationships of the heart. It tells us about our attachments to others and it rules attractiveness, both the ability to attract and our own attraction to others and to things.

The inconjunct brings fated relationships into our lives, relationships which assist our souls on their path of destiny and deepen our understanding about ourselves and our personal spiritual destiny.

---

[375] https://en.wikipedia.org/wiki/Rajneesh

At the unconscious level, however, our personal values may cloud our perspective on our relationships and their meaning in relation to the big spiritual context of our lives and we may delude ourselves as to their spiritual destiny.

Like Richard Kameese, who was an American drug fatality at age 21, following drug addiction that began when he was in high school. He had Sedna in the ninth house of knowledge, conjunct Saturn, the planet of restrictions, and inconjunct Venus and also Neptune, the planet of delusions, both conjunct his IC, the cusp of his fourth house of home.

> He was living with his parents, when his folks went to a wake, leaving him home alone because he was using drugs. When they returned they saw his shoeless footprints in the snow and knew he was on another rampage. He went to the home of a couple who lived a couple hundred yards away and burst in, staggering and in a drug-crazed state saying, "They're going to get me." He grabbed a kitchen mop and began swinging at his imaginary enemies and at the couple, who then called the police, as Richard drew a knife. It took four men to subdue him; however, while in a jail cell, he stopped breathing and died a few hours later.[376]

Or, in a more extreme example, like Charles Manson, who was an American ritual cult leader, a psychopath with a band of drug-numbed followers. He had Sedna in the twelfth house of the unconscious, inconjunct his Venus, which is conjunct his Sun, the planet of willpower, in the seventh house of relationships.

> He mesmerised his gang with liberal sex and drugs while living on a ranch in the desert of southern California. He was the illegitimate son of a teenage prostitute and an army colonel. He was raised by an aunt and uncle and by the age of 11, he developed into a delinquent, shuffling from foster parent to foster parent. He spent his youth and adulthood in and out of prison, spending 19 of his first 32 years behind bars.

> In his mid-30s, while on parole, he went to San Francisco to be a part of the hippie counter-culture in the Height-Ashbury district. He gathered adoring women around him by giving out LSD.

---

[376] https://www.astro.com/astro-databank/Kameese,_Richard

Soon he was able to attract young men to his group by promising sex with his 'young loves'. They enjoyed long group LSD sessions, listening to the Beatles' "Helter Skelter" song on the White Album. However, unable to keep his friendships, He began to prophesy chaos to his followers.

When he was 34, he directed the ritual grisly killings of a Hollywood socialite and her houseguests, who were stabbed to death by his followers and their blood was smeared along the walls of the kitchen. A few days later, an older couple was tied up, carved and stabbed by forks and kitchen knives by Manson's followers.

The deaths frightened the Hollywood community and in the nine months of the trial, when he was 35, the jury found him guilty of first degree murder and conspiracy. He was convicted and given the death penalty, but the following year the California Supreme Court invalidated the capital punishment stature, and he became a life-termer. He was continually refused parole by the California parole board.

He was denied parole for the ninth time at 63 and at his hearing he rambled for an hour, insisting that he did not kill seven people, saying, "I've killed a lot of people in my life, but I was convicted for those I did not kill." His behaviour in prison has been vicious and demented and yet, inexplicably, every year he received letters and gifts from young people, Satanists, neo-Nazis and skinheads who viewed him as their role model, hoping for one day when he will be released, however he died in prison at age 83.[377]

We see the fated relationships in the experience of Florence Aadland, who was an American news figure, whose daughter was, at 15, having an affair with the 46-year-old famous American actor, Errol Flynn. She had Sedna in the tenth house of profession, inconjunct her Venus in the fifth house of children.

Born the same date and year as her husband, she kicked him out when he objected to their daughter's notorious affair. When Flynn died, she released the couple's love letters for publicity.

---

[377] https://en.wikipedia.org/wiki/Charles_Manson

She and daughter apparently made a good partying team. When police broke up a noisy party they found the two with a group of men in various stages of undress.

She was 45 when she was found guilty of contributing the delinquency of a minor. Later that year she married a 15-year-younger East Indian actor and they tried operating a donut shop together. She also wrote a lovelorn column and published a book. She was an alcoholic, however, and died at the age of 50.[378]

As we tire of density and the grief it creates, and we start a spiritual journey to get out of the swamp, Sedna rewards us with transcendent crises, experiences which force us to let go and rise above them, resulting in a huge growth to a new level of consciousness. There is no choice with these crises, and the more we try and solve them, the more we will get hurt.

Juliette Adam was a French author and feminist. She had Sedna in the ninth house of knowledge, inconjunct Venus in the second house of material restrictions.

She married a doctor at 16 and first started publishing her *Ideas on Love, Woman and Marriage* when she was 22. Three years after her first husband's death when she was 31, she married the prefect of police, who subsequently became a life-senator. She established a salon which was frequented by republican leaders against the conservative reaction of the 1870s. In the same interest, she founded the 'Nouvelle Revue' when she was 43, which she edited for eight years, and retained influence in its administration until her mid 60's.

She also developed a close friendship with someone who was devoted to theosophy and the occult. She became involved in the Forerunner Association, which called for the right of women to be witnesses in public and private acts, and for the right of married women to take the product of their labor and dispose of it freely.[379]

---

[378] https://www.astro.com/astro-databank/Aadland,_Florence
[379] https://en.wikipedia.org/wiki/Juliette_Adam

Rusty Schweickart was an American astronaut on the Apollo 9 mission in March 1969. He has Sedna in the eleventh house of collective consciousness, inconjunct Venus on the cusp of the fifth house of children.

> After he circled the earth for three days in the first manned flight test of the lunar landing module that would later touch down on the moon, he was strongly moved by the sight of the planet. This led him to environmental work, then to being special science advisor to California Governor Jerry Brown.

> In mid-1979, he took the post of chairman of the state's independent Energy Commission, a group is concerned with long-range energy planning and conservation, and the chairman practices its creed. His home has no air-conditioning and is being heated by wood he chops and splits. He usually rides his bicycle to work, a five-mile round trip. He is not really opposed to nuclear power, but he calls it "a technology which has suffered from poor design" and he does not think it is worth the investment.[380]

Our case study, James Lovelock, is a British independent scientist, environmentalist and futurologist who lives in Devon, England. He has Sedna on the cusp of the sixth house, inconjunct his Venus, which is conjunct Ixion, the planet of lawlessness, in the tenth house of profession. It was while working as a consultant for NASA, when he was in his forties, that he developed the Gaia Hypothesis for which he is best known. Gaia hypothesis postulates that the biosphere of the Earth is a self-regulating entity with the capacity to keep our planet healthy by controlling the chemical and physical environment.

However, in his book, *The Revenge of Gaia*, published when he was 87, he argues that "the lack of respect humans have had for Gaia, through the damage done to rainforests and the reduction in planetary biodiversity, is testing Gaia's capacity to minimise the effects of the addition of greenhouse gases in the atmosphere. This eliminates the planet's negative feedbacks and increases the likelihood of runaway global warming.

---

[380] https://en.wikipedia.org/wiki/Rusty_Schweickart

Three years later he published *The Vanishing Face of Gaia*, rejecting scientific modelling that disagreed with the scientific findings that sea levels are rising faster, and Arctic ice is melting faster than the models predict. And suggesting that we may already be beyond the tipping point of terrestrial climate resilience into a permanently hot state. Given these conditions, he expects human civilization will be hard pressed to survive in the coming years.

At that point he expected the change to be similar to the Paleocene-Eocene period when atmospheric concentration of CO2 was high and at that point the Arctic Ocean was 23 °C and had crocodiles in it, with the rest of the world mostly scrub and desert. Seven years later, however, at 97, his position on climate change had changed dramatically, saying: "Anyone who tries to predict more than five to 10 years is a bit of an idiot, because so many things can change unexpectedly." He now believes that "CO2 is going up, but nowhere near as fast as they thought it would.

There are various possible explanations for his change of heart. One is that he is right, and the models on which his former predictions were based were fatally flawed. Another is that his iconoclastic sensibility made revision irresistible. An incorrigible subversive, Lovelock was warning the world about climate change for decades before it began to pay attention, and just when the scientific consensus began to call for intervention to prevent it, he decided we were already too late.

But there is a third explanation for why he has shifted his position again, he expects that before the consequences of global warming can impact on us significantly, something else will have made our world unrecognisable, and threaten the human race, the rise of Artificial Intelligence. "'Before we've reach the end of this century, I think what people call robots will have taken over. They will be in charge of us, if we're still here."

'It is possible that human beings may fuse with robots to become a blend of robotic and human tissue, but the likelier scenario will be pure robots, because that will probably be their preference. The implications for climate change are obvious. The world that they're going to be comfortable in is wildly different from the one that we feel comfortable in. So once they really get established, they will, with regret, start losing organic life.'[381]

Humour can be one path to transcend the quicksand of Sedna, giving us the objectivity to step back from the edge, but also with the inconjunct to Venus the imperative to creatively fill our daily lives with beauty and pleasure.

I have Sedna in the fourth house of home, inconjunct my Venus, which is retrograde in the eleventh house of collective consciousness. I have worked all my life as an artist, for much of it in the improbable performing art of clown and then in writing and film. I have always positioned myself in the avant guard, pushing the boundaries of the art form, reasoning that while popular success often means copying the latest trend, that it is only by being different that it is possible to stand out from the crowd and make a larger historical mark.

When I stopped clowning to take up film a few years back, I wrote a textbook/novel titled *Angels Can Fly, a Modern Clown User Guide*, which wrapped up my fourth house Sedna clown research in a book that is serving an evolutionary role in bringing the oldest art form on the planet into the modern age. I think this aspect is also reflected in this book.

Tracey Ullman is an English-born actress, comedian, singer, dancer, screenwriter, producer, director, author, and businesswoman. She has Sedna in the sixth house of service, inconjunct her Venus, which is conjunct Vesta, the asteroid of regeneration, in the first house of identity.

> Her father died when she was 6 and, in the aftermath, her mother slipped into a deep depression and spent a lot of time in bed. In an effort to cheer her up, Ullman, along with her sister, created and performed a nightly variety show on the windowsill in their mother's bedroom. In the show, Ullman would mimic neighbours, teachers, family members, and celebrities such as Julie Andrews and Édith Piaf.

> "Some kids can play the piano or kick a football; I could just impersonate everyone." She would also perform alone for herself

---

[381] Aitkenhead, Decca. James Lovelock: 'Before the end of this century, robots will have taken over." *Guardian*.
https://www.theguardian.com/environment/2016/sep/30/james-lovelock-interview-by-end-of-century-robots-will-have-taken-over).

after everyone had gone to bed. "I'd stand in front of the mirror and talk to myself until I fell asleep. I'd interview myself as women with problems. Women in documentaries who had three kids and chain-smoked and husbands in prison that hit them."

Her mother would eventually remarry to a man who Ullman has described as a maniac who drove a London taxi and had a son who stole. The marriage brought an end to the children's late-night antics. "There was a new person in her bed now and I couldn't do my nightly performance anymore. I was nine years old and my show had been cancelled."

Alcoholism and domestic violence became a common occurrence in the household. The marriage also resulted in the family moving around the country, with Ullman attending numerous state schools. Her flair for mimicry helped with the transitions, as her new classmates didn't take to her upper crust accent. "I had to talk like them to avoid being beaten up."

Her earliest appearances were on British television sketch comedy shows and she emigrated from the United Kingdom to the United States where she starred in her own network television comedy series, *The Tracey Ullman Show*, when she was 27. It ran for three years. She later produced programmes for HBO for which she garnered numerous awards. Her sketch comedy series, *Tracey Ullman's State of the Union*, ran for two years on Showtime in her late 40's. She has also appeared in several feature films.

She was the first British woman to be offered her own television sketch show in both the United Kingdom and the United States. At 56, she returned to British television with the BBC sketch comedy show *Tracey Ullman's Show*, her first project for the broadcaster in over thirty years. This led to the creation of the topical comedy series, *Tracey Breaks the News* in 2017. She is currently the richest British actress and female comedian and the third richest British comedian overall.[382]

At this juncture in human evolution, few of us use our planets at the spiritual level, but many of us are striving to, and such people are

---

[382] https://en.wikipedia.org/wiki/Tracey_Ullman

wonderful to be around. As with the other planets, the spiritual level of evolution is vastly different with Sedna from the two previous levels.

Here, the inconjunct with Venus brings values and relationships which deepen our personal spiritual destiny and give us the opportunity to enrich our collective spiritual evolution. The struggle of the beginner's level is gone, as are the transcendental crises of the intermediate level. At this level everything Saturnian is meaningless and yet everything Sednian has its place.

Like Jeff Mayo, who was a British astrologer, author and teacher who was the director and principal of the Mayo School of Astrology, established when he was 52. He had Sedna in the sixth house of service, inconjunct his Venus in the tenth house of profession.

> After leaving the faculty he started a correspondence course aimed at students all over the world. The Mayo School still continues to provide worldwide tuition. He opened the doors of astrology to literally thousands of students at the same time as he demonstrated his organisational and administrative abilities.

> His books include *Teach Yourself Astrology, How to Read the Ephemeris, How to Cast a Natal Chart, The Astrologer's Astronomical Handbook, The Planets and Human Behaviour,* and *Astrology, a Key to Personality*. A modest and sensitive man, he was also fun to be with. He went into farming in Devon with his brother. He loved the outdoors, the wilderness and wildlife.[383]

And like Jeff Green, who is an American astrologer and the author of *Pluto: The Evolutionary Journey of the Soul* and *Uranus: Freedom From the Known*, books that have been translated into ten languages. He has Sedna in the fifth house of creativity, inconjunct Venus, which is conjunct Mercury, the planet of communication and Chariklo, the centaur of foresight, in his first house of identity.

> His early family life was brutal. He experienced severe psychological and physical abuse from his mother, and he and his brother were sent for a time to an orphanage before being later returned to family. Always the "black sheep", at an early age, he recounts overhearing his parents say that they didn't

---

[383] https://en.wikipedia.org/wiki/Jeff_Mayo

care for him. Feeling a strong sense of alienation from both his family and his overall environment, he spent most of his school days at the ocean, where he could "escape" with the accompaniment of the ocean sounds and a surfboard.

He became an alcoholic. One drunken evening, he reached a fatal turning point when he got into a car accident and came to an intense altercation with the other driver. Arrested before a near violent ending, he was offered one of two sentences - go to jail or go to Vietnam. He had already experienced a life of abuse, devastation and trauma, but it was nothing in comparison to the violence and insanity of the war he was about to experience.

"Life made no sense to me; even the idea of God made no sense. I had a very close friend during the war. One day we were bombed and he was reading the Bible when this happened. He got a direct hit, and all that was left when I returned was pieces of flesh and a blood-covered Bible. I, too had the shared illusion that God is perfect, and did not understand how he allowed such a thing to happen, especially when someone was reading His book... At the age of eighteen this is completely senseless. And so I erased God from my life."

As did many of the soldiers at the time, drugs became his form of emotional survival. One month before being evacuated from Vietnam, another life-altering experience occurred. Searching for drugs in a nearby village, he stumbled upon a hill with steps. Climbing to the top, he found a Buddhist monastery. One of the monks approached him, but although the language barrier prevented his ability to converse directly with the monk, he experienced a telepathic communion.

At the end of military service, he continued to experience trauma and his roaming eventually took him to Mexico, where he had another extraordinary mystical experience. This time he encountered a Shaman of the Navaho tribe. Like the experience with the Buddhist monk, the language barrier was again surpassed through telepathic communication. He spent six months here, during which time the Shaman initiated him in the sacred peyote experience. While undergoing this time of initiation, which created a lasting shift and expansion of consciousness, he encountered a pack of wolves and developed the ability to communicate telepathically with them. He spent three weeks living as a member of the pack.

The incredible experiences of his life eventually brought him to his true path as teacher, and he has lectured throughout the U.S., Canada, and Europe and has been a participant in almost all of the major astrological conferences in the world. He is founder and director of the School of Evolutionary Astrology. His pioneering work has expanded the concepts of astrology to encompass a broader vision and greater understanding of the soul's purpose, necessity and desire for evolution.[384]

He is called the founder of Evolutionary Astrology because he first started to lecture on the revolutionary astrological paradigm at 31, after receiving a dream from the spiritual master Swami Sri Yukteswar, who was Yogananda's guru. In that dream the entire paradigm of Evolutionary Astrology was conveyed to Jeffrey.

This was the first time in astrology's long history that a specific paradigm was realized that allowed for an understanding of the evolutionary progression of a Soul from life to life. Jeffrey lectured all over the world on Evolutionary Astrology for 25 years from his early thirties. He established Evolutionary Astrology schools in a number of countries and wrote books on Evolutionary Astrology.

The first of these, Pluto: The Evolutionary Journey of the Soul, Volume I was published at 38. It has been in continuous print ever since and has become one of the all-time best-selling astrology books. Translations have been made into French, German, Dutch, Chinese, Bulgarian, Spanish, Portuguese, Italian, Serbian and other languages. Volume II, Pluto: The Soul's Evolution through Relationships was published when he was 52 and has been in continuous print.

Since starting his original Pluto School at 48, he had many students, a number of whom are now professional Evolutionary Astrologers. He personally counseled over 30,000 clients in his lengthy career. This exposure to so many Souls from so many different backgrounds and orientations allowed him to come to

---

[384] Ibid.

the deepest possible understandings of the nature of the Soul. He communicated these insights through all of his teachings.[385]

Quintile, Bi-quintile

The evolutionary quintile or bi-quintile aspect between Sedna and Venus infuses our values, relationships and tastes with the all-encompassing spiritual energy of Sedna to the point where we can push the boundaries of human development.

Quintiles and bi-quintiles point to talent, the desire to create order and to categorize, a fascination with patterns and structures, perfectionist tendencies, and the desire to build or make things. These aspects have the characteristics of both the trine and opposition. They point to awareness of conflicts, or problems and finding solutions for them; however, they do not automatically kick into action and must be cultivated over time.

Venus rules our values, and the pleasure we take in life. Through Venus, we learn about our tastes, artistic inclinations, and what makes us happy. And we look to Venus in the natal chart to see how we approach relationships of the heart. It tells us about our attachments to others and it rules attractiveness, both the ability to attract others and things and our own attraction to others and to things.

At the spiritual level with these aspects we can look forward to values and relationships which deepen our personal spiritual destiny and enrich our collective spiritual evolution. However, at the unconscious level the big complex schemes that we might fall into with these aspects might lead us to venture fairly quickly out of our depth.

Like Andrew Daulton Lee, who is an American drug dealer and former agent who was convicted of espionage. He had Sedna in the fourth house of home, bi-quintile his Venus in the twelfth house of the unconscious.

> A friend, who was a code clerk employed with the large US defence contractor, began stealing classified documents detailing how to decrypt secure US government message traffic and detailed specifications of the latest US spy satellites with the intention of delivering them to agents of the Soviet Union. Lee

---

[385] http://schoolofevolutionaryastrology.com/about

traveled to Mexico City with these stolen documents, where he delivered them to Soviet embassy officials.

He often also would use these trips as an opportunity to engage in drug deals when not working on espionage. A common tactic of his drug smuggling was to learn of airline routes, where he would fly from Mexico to the United States, hiding the drugs inside a compartment of the plane, purchasing a ticket to whichever destination the same airplane was scheduled, then recapturing the drug stash after disembarking at the new destination.

Lee and Boyce made an agreement to evenly split the profits from the espionage ring. Boyce had used his share mainly for his personal use. Lee used his split to further his drug business, purchasing more expensive drugs, such as heroin, and being able to gain tremendous profits by selling the expensive, hard-to-obtain drugs in the United States.

At one meeting with his Soviet handlers, Lee proposed that they assist him in his drug trade by transporting cocaine from Peru to the Soviet embassy in Mexico under diplomatic seal. At points when his friend was doubting the effectiveness of his espionage, Lee had convinced him that the spy ring should expand. Lee had proposed adding his younger brother as an alternate courier, as well as recruiting a friend who was a US Navy sailor aboard an aircraft carrier and having a fellow drug dealer be brought into the spy ring to sell the same intelligence reports to other foreign nations, namely China. Lee did indeed make copies of the reports with the intention of selling them to the Chinese.

However, at 24 he was arrested with top secret microfilm in his possession by Mexican police in front of the Soviet embassy, on the misplaced suspicion of having killed a Mexico City police officer. Under torture he confessed instead to espionage, quickly implicating his friend in the scheme. He was returned to the United States, where he was convicted of espionage and sentenced to life in prison.[386]

---

[386] https://en.wikipedia.org/wiki/Andrew_Daulton_Lee

Or like Squeaky Fromme, who is an American who was in the news for the attempted assassination of President Gerald Ford when she was 26. She has Sedna in the seventh house of relationships, bi-quintile her Venus in the twelfth house of the unconscious.

> She was a worshipful follower of ritual cult leader and psychopath, Charles Manson, and she had begun a correspondence with a newscaster on NBC to get him on TV with his message of enlightenment. NBC would not agree, so she decided to stalk and shoot Ford to get the publicity that would put her on TV.

> She watched as Ford and his entourage left a hotel one morning. Petite and childlike, in a red gown and red turban, she followed the crowd and angled in to meet Ford face to face. She fumbled in her robe for her pistol and aimed at his genitals. A secret service man grabbed the gun and everyone piled on her. The attempt got her the publicity she wanted; she was on TV, but she also was sent to prison, and she never did get Manson, or his message across. She was released from jail on parole at the age of 60.[387]

We could be vulnerable to deception and power plays in our relationships, like Dan Rather, who was an American news broadcaster, one of the top in his competitive field. He had Sedna conjunct Uranus, the planet of revolution, in the twelfth house of the unconscious, bi-quintile Venus, which is conjunct Ceres, the planet of nurture, in the seventh house of relationships.

> As a child in Texas, he dreamed of becoming a reporter and at 14, he worked as a gofer, fetching coffee for the local newspaper office. He was anchor of the CBS Evening News for 24 years and he made a name for himself in journalism for his refusal to play "nice" with political leaders during his hard-hitting interviews.

> At the end of his career he became embroiled in controversy about a disputed news report involving President George W. Bush's Vietnam-era service in the National Guard. He was 73 when he reported on 60 Minutes that a series of memos critical of President George W. Bush's Texas Air National Guard service

---

[387] https://en.wikipedia.org/wiki/Lynette_Fromme

record had been discovered in the personal files of Lt. Bush's former commanding officer.

Once copies of the documents were made available on the Internet, their authenticity was quickly called into question. Much of this was based on the fact that the documents were proportionally printed and displayed using other modern typographic conventions usually unavailable on military typewriters of the 1970s. The font used on the documents has characteristics that exactly match standard font features of Microsoft Word. This led to claims that the memos were forgeries. The accusations then spread over the following days into mainstream media outlets including *The Washington Post,* *The New York Times,* and the *Chicago Sun-Times.*

Rather and CBS initially defended the story, insisting that the documents had been authenticated by experts. CBS was contradicted by some of the experts it originally cited, and later reported that its source for the documents, former Texas Army National Guard officer Lt. Col. Bill Burkett, had misled the network about how he had obtained them. CBS retracted the story and Rather stated, "If I knew then what I know now, I would not have gone ahead with the story as it was aired, and I certainly would not have used the documents in question."

Following an investigation commissioned by CBS, which many believe was the result of political pressure on the board, they fired the story producer and asked three other producers connected with the story to resign, and many believe Rather's retirement was hastened by this incident. Five years later he was interviewed on Larry King Live, commenting "Nobody has proved that they were fraudulent, much less a forgery... The truth of this story stands up to this day."[388]

As we tire of density and the grief it creates, and we start a spiritual journey to get out of the swamp, Sedna rewards us with transcendent crises, experiences which force us to let go and rise above them, resulting in a huge growth to a new level of consciousness. There is no choice with these crises, and the more we try and solve them, the more we will get hurt.

---

[388] https://en.wikipedia.org/wiki/Dan_Rather

Like Franklin Jones, who was an American siddha-guru known as Bubba Free John and later Adi Da. He had Sedna in the third house of ideas and communication, bi-quintile Venus in the tenth house of profession.

He was a handsome, ample and happy mystic with an ashram called Horse House Commune in California. His teachings deal with various forms to harmonize and purify action in life. *The Method of the Disshas* and *Garbage and the Goddess* are among his works, which include books and recorded talks.

It is said of Jones that he lived in a world of sheer light and joy known as "the Bright" until his second or third year. This condition would assert itself in the form of uncommon psychic and mystical experiences, as well as physical symptoms such as sudden attacks of fever or skin rashes with no diagnosable medical cause. These signs subsided in his eighth year and didn't return until he was 17.

At 21 he went through a despair that yielded two insights which would be crucial to his philosophy. The first was that there is only one reality, or transcendental consciousness; the second is that this reality is man's true identity and anything else is a product of an un-enlightened mind. For the next few years he sequestered himself in spiritual disciplines, and sought out the company of an American-born teacher, Swami Rudrananda, who instructed him in Indian kundalini yoga.

He then entered a Lutheran seminary at Swami's instruction. At 28 while at the seminary, he underwent another religious experience, and came up with a new insight, that his whole search had been founded on the avoidance of relationships and the recoil from reality in its many forms. The next year he sought out Swami Muktananda in India, and stayed briefly with him there, and during that time the Swami acknowledged that Franklin had reached "yogic liberation."

At 30 he entered the permanent condition of Sahaj Samadhi, essential to transcendental being-consciousness. After this, he was moved to teach others the condition of "the Heart" or the reality in which everything inheres. He spent three years of struggle with students who were not prepared for his teaching, which weakened his physical body.

He returned to India to clarify his teaching, changed his name to "Bubba Free John," as Bubba was his childhood nickname and "Free John" a rendering of Franklin Jones. When he returned to America, he began to teach differently.

At 37 he ceased to have frequent contact with his many followers and lived in seclusion for the next three years. When he was 43, now known as Adi Da, he moved with a group of about 40 followers to the Fijian island of Naitaba, which had been purchased by a wealthy follower. It was his primary residence until the end of his life.

However, accusations that he abused his power as a spiritual leader attracted international attention a couple of years later. In investigative reports and dozens of interviews, both named and anonymous ex-members made numerous specific allegations of Adi Da forcing members to engage in psychologically, sexually, and physically abusive and humiliating behaviour, as well as accusing the church of committing tax fraud.

Two lawsuits were filed against Adi Da and the church in California. One was dismissed the next year; however, the other lawsuit and several threatened suits in subsequent years were settled with payments and confidentiality agreements, negatively impacting member morale and bleeding the organisation financially.[389]

Philip K. Dick was an American writer notable for publishing works of science fiction. He explored philosophical, social, and political themes in novels, with plots dominated by monopolistic corporations, authoritarian governments, alternate universes, and altered states of consciousness.

He had Sedna in the first house of identity, quintile Venus in the eleventh house of collective consciousness.

His work reflected his personal interest in metaphysics and theology, and often drew upon his life experiences in addressing the nature of reality, identity, drug abuse, schizophrenia, and transcendental experiences.

---

[389] https://en.wikipedia.org/wiki/Adi_Da

His stories typically focus on the fragile nature of what is real and the construction of personal identity. His stories often become surreal fantasies, as the main characters slowly discover that their everyday world is actually an illusion assembled by powerful external entities, vast political conspiracies or the vicissitudes of an unreliable narrator.

"All of his work starts with the basic assumption that there cannot be one, single, objective reality," writes science fiction author Charles Platt. "Everything is a matter of perception. The ground is liable to shift under your feet. A protagonist may find himself living out another person's dream, or he may enter a drug-induced state that actually makes better sense than the real world, or he may cross into a different universe completely."

Alternate universes and simulacra are common plot devices, with fictional worlds inhabited by common, working people, rather than galactic elites. Dick's thinking and work was heavily influenced by the writings of Carl Jung. The Jungian constructs and models that most concerned Dick seem to be the archetypes of the collective unconscious, group projection/hallucination, synchronicities, and personality theory.

In the seventies, while recovering from the effects of sodium pentothal administered for the extraction of an impacted wisdom tooth, he began experiencing strange hallucinations. Although initially attributing them to side effects from medication, he considered this explanation implausible after they continued. He came to believe they imparted wisdom and clairvoyance. On one occasion the hallucinations imparted the information to him that his infant son was ill. The Dicks rushed the child to the hospital, where his suspicion was confirmed by professional diagnosis.

"I experienced an invasion of my mind by a transcendentally rational mind, as if I had been insane all my life and suddenly I had become sane," Dick told Charles Platt. As the hallucinations increased in length and frequency, Dick claimed he began to live two parallel lives, one as himself, and one as "Thomas," a Christian persecuted by Romans in the first century AD. He referred to the "transcendentally rational mind" as "Zebra," "God" and "VALIS" and wrote about these experiences in his VALIS trilogy.[390]

Iris Murdoch was an Irish novelist and professor of philosophy with a Ph.D. who was influenced by Sartre and had a skill for black comedy. Her Sedna is in the ninth house of knowledge, bi-quintile her Venus in the first house of identity.

> She wrote 26 remarkable novels, four plays, four books on philosophy and one book of poetry. She wrote completely in longhand. She decided to be a writer at the age of nine, at the time of having a happy childhood. She not only achieved her goal but received honorary doctorates from major universities and became a Dame of the British Empire. Her husband wrote that she was "the most genuinely modest person" he had ever met. She worked secretly and quietly, not talking about the book she was on, never needing to compare or contrast, never interested in reviews or needing reassurance.

> An unattractive intellectual, plain and awkward with straggly hair, she managed a feat that is enviable to many beautiful women. She fell in love at first sight with a five-year-younger Oxford don and had 32 devoted years with him. After their first date her journal entry read, "St. Anthony's Dance. Fell down the steps, and seem to have fallen in love with John. We didn't dance much." They married almost three years later, when she was 37. They had no children, but she had, nonetheless, left a trail of former lovers, mostly those who had stimulated her intellectually.[391]

Humour can be one path to transcend the quicksand of Sedna, giving us the objectivity to step back from the edge, and also with the quintile and bi-quintile aspects to Venus the creativity to to fill our daily lives with beauty and pleasure.

Joan Rivers was an American comedienne, thought by many to be the funniest lady on the planet. She had Sedna in the first house of identity, in a close evolutionary quintile to Venus, which is conjunct Mercury, the

---

[390] https://en.wikipedia.org/wiki/Philip_K._Dick

[391] https://en.wikipedia.org/wiki/Iris_Murdoch

planet of communication, both in the third house of ideas. She certainly had one of the fastest, most agile minds in show biz.

> Her rapid-fire mix of gossip, insults, flaunting of taboos and ridicule of flaws and neurosis is written 90% by her. She also wrote comedy for *Candid Camera*, scripts and material for Phyllis Diller and Zsa Zsa Gabor and humorous books.

> The younger of two daughters of Russian-Jewish refugees, she learned from her doctor dad to crack a joke and was making people laugh by the time she was 11. She learned from her mom that rich was better than poor and was raised with privilege and a good education. She married at 24 and had it annulled the following year when she decided she wanted to be an actress, not a housewife. While doing off-Broadway, she worked in offices and turned to comedy at 27 to supplement her income.

> At the age of 32 she was told that she was too old and passed over; however, a week later she was booked on Johnny Carson's *Tonight Show*. They clicked. Their immediate rapport was a hit with the audience and she appeared for years with Carson before hosting her own *Late Show Starring Joan Rivers,* with a contract for $10 million over three years. She moved into the stratosphere as America's top comedienne, the darling of the circuit with tours, magazine covers, nightclub and Las Vegas gigs, TV projects, books and records.[392]

At this juncture in human evolution, few of us use our planets at the spiritual level, but many of us are striving to, and such people are wonderful to be around. As with the other planets, the spiritual level of evolution is vastly different with Sedna from the two previous levels.

Here, the quintile and bi-quintile aspects with Venus bring values and relationships which deepen our personal spiritual destiny and enrich our collective spiritual evolution. The struggle of the beginner's level is gone, as are the transcendental crises of the intermediate level. At this level everything Saturnian is meaningless and yet everything Sednian has its place.

Leonard Cohen was a Canadian novelist and songwriter-folksinger, who's graceful, confessional songs have been described as 'elegant,

---

[392] https://en.wikipedia.org/wiki/Joan_Rivers

bittersweet mood music for the dark nights of the soul'. He became a Buddhist monk, shaving his head and living in a monastery outside of Los Angeles. He has Sedna in the seventh house of relationships, bi-quintile Venus in the twelfth house of the unconscious.

As a student he gravitated toward poetry and prose, eventually gaining acclaim in Canada for his poems and two novels. The books did not sell well, so for income, he returned to songwriting. Judy Collins soon bought his song "Suzanne" for her album, 'In My Life'. His creaky baritone was distinctive enough that he was signed to a record contract himself by Columbia with a debut album at 33, "Songs of Leonard Cohen." Sales were modest but critics hailed the collection.

During a period of deep depression in his early 40s, he separated from his wife and began to embrace Zen. Turning to a friend who had an aura of calm, he was introduced to an old Zen teacher. He found the spiritual training rigorous. For a time, he worked in both worlds, the commercial world of music and the spiritual world of striving, until he finally yielded completely and moved to the Zen Centre. Though he spoke for years of his interest in Zen, it was still a surprise to the establishment when the highly successful songwriter and poet left his finely tailored suits for modest robes, and Hollywood mansions for a small cabin with a narrow cot.

He stopped recording at 58 and touring the next year when he moved up the mountain. The pop icon, whose classic takes include "Bird on a Wire" and "Suzanne," did the cooking for the small community. With enough time, he worked on an illustrated book of poems and songs for a future album. His workroom contained an old computer and a synthesiser, tools for his music and his graphic art. He rose at 3:00 AM for morning meditation and to begin preparing the day's menu.[393]

Lisa Williams is a British psychic, medium and healer. She has Sedna in the fifth house of creativity, quintile Venus in the eighth house of sensitivity to the spirit world.

---

[393] https://en.wikipedia.org/wiki/Leonard_Cohen

She starred in two shows on Lifetime Television: *Lisa Williams: Life Among the Dead* and *Lisa Williams: Voices From the Other Side*. The shows followed her on a typical day, as she communicated with spirits, investigate haunted houses, and conducted other spirit-seeking activities.[394]

Her Sedna is also at the tip of a finger of fate, inconjunct with Pluto, the planet of life and death, in the tenth house of profession and inconjunct Neptune, the planet of sensitivity to the spirit world in the first house of identity.

She came out as a lesbian at 37 and said: 'For many years, speaking to dead people was hard enough for people to accept me, but then on top of that to then say 'by the way, I'm gay', I didn't want to acknowledge it'. Asked by a reporter, because of her unique insight into life after death, where she thought gay people were headed, she said, 'In my experience with those who have crossed, it is a place of love. It isn't a place of 'you didn't live this way so we'll punish you'. It is a place where all your loved ones accept you for who you are."[395]

Martin Heidegger was a German existentialist philosopher who was one of the most influential voices and foremost thinkers and writers of the 20th century. He had Sedna in the fourth house of home, in a close bi-quintile with Venus, and with Saturn, the planet of structure, which are conjunct in the ninth house of knowledge.

With the publication of his first book, *Being and Time*, when he was 38, he achieved instant fame as one of the spokesmen of 20th century existentialism. Though unfinished, *Being and Time* is one of the central philosophical works of the 20th century. In the first division of the work, he attempted to turn away from "ontic" questions about beings to ontological questions about Being and recover the most fundamental philosophical question: the question of Being, of what it means for something to be.

He argued that being human is defined by care, that it's practically engaged and is a concernfull mode of being-in-the-world. This was in opposition to rationalist thinkers like René

---

[394] https://en.wikipedia.org/wiki/Lisa_Williams_(psychic)
[395] Ibid.

Descartes who located the essence of man in our thinking abilities. For Heidegger, thinking is thinking about things originally discovered in our everyday practical engagements. The consequence of this is that our capacity to think cannot be the most central quality of our being, because thinking is a reflecting upon this more original way of discovering the world.

In the second section, he argues that human being is even more fundamentally structured by its temporality, or its concern with, and relationship to time, existing as a structurally open 'possibility-for-being'. He emphasised the importance of authenticity in human existence, involving a truthful relationship to our being thrown into a world, and to our being-towards-death, the finitude of the time and being that we are given, and the closing down of our various possibilities for being through time.

He also made critical contributions to philosophical conceptions of truth, arguing that its original meaning was un-concealment, to philosophical analyses of art as a site of the revelation of truth, and to philosophical understanding of language as the 'house of being'.[396]

---

[396] https://en.wikipedia.org/wiki/Martin_Heidegger

32: Sedna / Mars

Conjunction

With the conjunction of Sedna and Mars the all-encompassing spiritual energy of Sedna infuses our actions, desires and competitive nature with higher meaning, in relation to the big picture of evolution, if we are open to it.

Mars relates to our basic sexual nature, how we express our anger, our temper and our first instinct to act. The god of war in ancient times, Mars could be brutally violent and so the planet rules our competitive nature. It shows the areas of life where we apply our drive and express our enthusiasm, where we take action and assert ourselves. And it relates to stamina, ambition and achievement.

When we are using our Mars energy positively, we are assertive, directed, forthright, and adventurous; however, if we are unconscious of the Sedna influence, there can be a sense of righteousness in our actions which will, at the very least, appear odd, or sit uncomfortably with other people.

Mars represents our survival instinct and can be thought of as our leftover animal nature. It rules our animal instincts for aggression and anger, which have been a key part of our survival skill kit, so with an unconscious conjunction we can be a bit of a bully, or a tyrant, or get ourselves into situations where we invite this behaviour.

Like Tesslynn O'Cull, who was an American victim of torture and murder by her mother's boyfriend. She had Sedna conjunct Mars in the ninth house of knowledge.

> When she was two and a half her mother moved from her grandmother's place to live with a man she met online, who liked to party and had his own apartment. Shortly after they moved in he started abusing Tesslynn. He would hit her with wooden spoons, spatulas, and belts. They would have "drug parties" over at the apartment where Stella, Jesse, and other guests would smoke methamphetamine by melting it with a propane blow torch. Sometimes these parties would last for days.
>
> During these parties many guests witnessed the abuse but never said anything. Some guests now say they witnessed him slap her in the face, drag her by her beautiful blond hair, make her

stand in the corner for hours, and even force her to take long freezing cold baths and showers. Eventually they started locking her in her bedroom. Guests said that he would go into the room where she was and they would hear her cries for hours after he came out.

No one was allowed to go in there to check on her or help her. She couldn't even get food, water or go to the bathroom. Finally, a neighbor complained about how they were treating this baby, but Jesse Compton told him if he went to the police he'd kill the neighbor and his girlfriend. He also broke four vertebrae in her back, forcibly raped her with an object and burned her. When the burns started to get infected he decided to pour rubbing alcohol into the open wounds. Then four days after her 3rd birthday, he repeatedly beat her in the head causing bruising on her brain. Internal injuries were also caused due to him stomping on her stomach and she died.[397]

Or like Frederick West, who was a British kidnapper, rapist and serial killer, charged with 11 murders, nine of them together with his wife, Rosemary. He first married at 21 and married Rosemary after his first wife was murdered, when he was 30. He had Sedna conjunct Mars in the seventh house of relationships.

When he was 53 police arrived at his house with a search warrant, because pieces of bodies had been discovered by workers who were clearing blocked drains. Two days later they found the body of the West's daughter in the garden, along with a stepdaughter and other dismembered corpses. All of the victims were young women who had been sexually abused, tortured and butchered. Other young women who could be connected with him had disappeared over the years and their bodies never found.

The West house had been used as a brothel and it seemed strange that no one ever reported hearing screams from the torture dungeon. When Rosemary worked as a prostitute, Frederick listened in through the intercom that he had wired into

---

[397] http://hellbeasts.com/jesse-caleb-compton-and-stella-kiser/

her room. He was charged with 11 murders and committed suicide in prison, hanging himself in his cell.[398]

Marcel Chevalier was the last chief executioner in France. He had Sedna conjunct Mars in the ninth house of spirituality.

> He was chief executioner for five years from the age of 55, until capital punishment was abolished in France. He started his career at 37, performed about 40 executions overall. After his appointment as chief executioner, he executed only two people. They were the last two executions in France. He was married to the niece of the penultimate chief executioner. He was interviewed by the press on a number of occasions, but later, disillusioned by the sensationalist nature of press coverage, chose to say nothing of his experiences with the guillotine.[399]

As we tire of density and the grief it creates, and we start a spiritual journey to get out of the swamp, Sedna rewards us with transcendent crises, experiences which force us to let go and rise above them, resulting in a huge growth to a new level of consciousness. There is no choice with these crises, and the more we try and solve them, the more we will get hurt.

Lesley Stahl is an American television journalist, who has spent most of her career reporting for *CBS 60 Minutes*, making over a million dollars a year and preferring political stories. She has Sedna conjunct Mars in the seventh house of relationships.

> She joined CBS for the first time when she was 30, doing early morning stake-outs. It was during that period that she developed her attack-dog reputation, once following John Dean into a men's room while asking him questions.

> Ambitious, hardworking and hard-nosed, she worked her way up to political campaign coverage and eventually to coverage of the White House. In her 19-year climb at CBS from White House reporter to evening-news anchor to *60 Minutes* correspondent, she met obstacles by going over, through or around them. One of her colleagues says admiringly, "Leslie's a bulldog. She's

---

[398] https://en.wikipedia.org/wiki/Fred_West
[399] https://en.wikipedia.org/wiki/Marcel_Chevalier

survived in a business that is tough on women by her hard work and tenacity."

Her autobiography, *Reporting Live*, published when she was 57, looks back at 30 years of proud moments. Her will to have both a career and be a mother was enormous. Though she rarely missed any of her daughter's dance recitals, or school plays, she nonetheless paid a price for her ambitions. She cultivated an ulcer, which has since been cured through medication and diet.[400]

Patch Adams is an American physician, famed throughout the medical community for charging no fees, carrying no malpractice insurance and living with his patients in a country farm setting. He has Sedna conjunct Mars and also conjunct Varuna, the planet of notability, and Venus, the planet of values, all on the cusp of the fifth house of creativity, giving him a strong performing mission despite his vocation as a doctor. He has always maintained that humour and joy are more important than any drug or therapy. He couldn't resist playing the clown and cheering up the patients, because he saw how good it was for them. The Sedna energy infused his actions with meaning in relation to the big picture of evolution.

He grew up as an Army brat in Japan, Germany and the U.S. and has been described as an iconoclast, a pattern-breaker and professional clown. He was deeply shaken by his dad's death, but it was his uncle's suicide that pushed him into despair. He dropped out of school and made the first of several suicide attempts. He was 18 when his mom checked him into a mental ward at Fairfax Hospital in Virginia, where he turned his own emotional corner by helping his roommate conquer hallucinations and fear.

A few weeks later he left the ward and enrolled at University to become a doctor. His Gesundheit Institute began as an experiment. For the first 12 years, 20 adults lived in a large home and used it as a crude hospital, open 24 hours a day. Three physicians and others did what they could for whoever came. They never charged money and their work was supported by part-time jobs of the live-in staff. For staff and patients, medicine

[400] https://en.wikipedia.org/wiki/Lesley_Stahl

was integrated with the performing arts, arts and crafts, agriculture, nature, recreation and social service. During those first 12 years, 15,000 people came through the home/facility for everything from profound illnesses, to simple curiosity and play.[401]

He faced stiff opposition from the health industry for his radical concept that healing happens faster if tension is reduced and patients are treated as individuals and encouraged to take more pleasure in life. It's obvious from a Sedna consciousness perspective, but completely frivolous from a Saturnian standpoint.

Gwen Verdon was an American dancer, a Tony-award winning performer, who took lessons at age two to strengthen her crippled legs. She had Sedna conjunct Mars, the planet of action, in the first house of identity.

> As an infant, her legs were so badly bent that medical advisors recommended they be broken and reset. Her mother, who was a former vaudeville dancer, refused, put her in corrective shoes, and started her on dance lessons. She had a first recital at age four and was in her first theatre show at six.

> During childhood, she wore corrective boots designed to support her legs. After taking dancing lessons, Gwen appeared with her mother in a dance recital in Los Angeles, and at six was billed as "the world's fastest tapper" at local theatres. When she became a teenager, she modelled for bathing suit pictures, and danced in chorus lines in nightclubs. She also appeared in a revival of 'Showboat' in Los Angeles and was a pro before she ever studied ballet.

> In her early 20s, she went to work as an assistant to a dance director, had a few small parts, but mostly worked behind the scenes, teaching and directing. At 28, she tried out for the Broadway show, "Can-Can." She got the part and won a Tony award for her work. In her early thirties, she appeared on Broadway as Lola in "Damn Yankees" and won her second Tony. Throughout the rest of her career she appeared in movies,

---

[401] https://en.wikipedia.org/wiki/Patch_Adams

plays and more television performances and a long list of hit musical comedies.[402]

Steve Jobs was an American entrepreneur, one of the originators of the computer revolution, co-founder of Apple Computers and Pixar Animation Studios. He had Sedna conjunct Mars in the eighth house of power and control, opposite Ixion, the planet of lawlessness together with Neptune, the planet of vision, in the second house of money, a signature both of his financial success, as well as of his personal issues of intimacy and control.

He and his friend, Steve Wozniak, made their first circuit board in their garage and they called it the Apple. By the time he was 24, his Apple Corporation was worth $10 million. A year later, its value had grown to $100 million. Its graphical user interface, business applications and word processing won kudos, and millions cheered while Apple took on IBM and its personal computer.

However, he was called a haunted house by Chrisann Brennan, a high school sweetheart who lived with him and was an early Apple employee. She said he became a threatening monster and their relationship fell apart amid wild recriminations when she became pregnant with his first child. He denied he was the father, despite a positive paternity test and he paid a pittance in child support, while living the life of a millionaire.

In her memoir *The Bite In The Apple: A Memoir Of My Life With Steve Jobs* she says, "I've truly hated Steve at times, but never for very long. Sharing a daughter with him has forced me to think about things more deeply. Steve the saint, the alien, the despot, the punishing masculine god, the liar, the obsessed narcissist, the cult hero, the ID of the iEverything, the genius and the motherless boy."

As the Apple empire grew, Steve became a tyrant, subject to moody outbursts and gloomy silences. Hard feelings arose and power struggles with other executives ensued. He resigned and the following year co-founded NeXt, in an attempt to do for the hardware industry, what he had down for software. He also

---

[402] https://en.wikipedia.org/wiki/Gwen_Verdon

bought a company which he renamed Pixar Animation Studios and negotiated a deal with Disney to distribute Pixar's films and became a Disney partner. Under Jobs' leadership, Pixar won 20 Academy awards for successful animated feature films and was acquired by Disney.[403]

With a twist of fate and a large amount of Sednian transcendence, he then convinced Apple to buy NeXt and was invited back to Apple as interim CEO and a few years later was made permanent CEO once again. Under his renewed leadership Apple computer became a major player in the computer industry once more and his team created visually aesthetic computers in bright colours that appealed to younger buyers.[404]

Vincent Van Gogh was a Dutch artist, a legend for his brilliant work, who lived his brief life in misery and poverty. He had Sedna conjunct Mars and also Venus, the planet of values, all in the tenth house of profession.

Disappointed in love and religion, he was intense, difficult and unhappy. He seemed to lack a psychological shield to protect him from the pain of everything and every moment. Washed out as a preacher to impoverished coal miners, he turned to full time art when he was 27. At 33 he went to Paris to immerse himself in the vanguard styles of the day. He began using the impressionist's choppy brush strokes of pastel color. Within two years, he was disillusioned by what he saw in the Parisian scene, and living with his brother upon whom he was financially dependent. proved to be a strain for both of them.

He fled south to Arles, where, intoxicated by the countryside, he painted with thicker impasto in blazing yellows, piercing reds and icy greens. His work still did not make him happy; in fact, he was frequently in despair. When his friend, Paul Gauquin, arrived he welcomed him. However, they began to quarrel, drink absinthe, a potent alcohol, and partake in debauchery. When Gauquin left Vincent followed him with a razor, and then locked himself in his room and cut off the lobe of his left ear. He was 35.

---

[403] https://en.wikipedia.org/wiki/Steve_Jobs
[404] Ibid.

The following year he went quite mad, to the point where he was considered dangerous. He was put in an asylum near Paris early the next year. His doctor encouraged him to keep painting, and flying into a creative frenzy, he completed 70 canvases in 70 days. Six months later while painting in a wheat field, he became suddenly, intolerably despondent and shot himself in the chest. He died two days later.

At the time of his death he was a failure, a misfit who had sold only two paintings in his lifetime, an artist who was later known as one of the most famous painters of all time. Two years after his death, a Dutch museum gave him a retrospective. And a hundred years later a collector paid close to $54 million for his "Irises," now in the Getty Museum in Los Angeles.[405]

At this juncture in human evolution, few of us use our planets at the spiritual level, but many of us are striving to, and such people are wonderful to be around. As with the other planets, the spiritual level of evolution is vastly different with Sedna from the two previous levels. Here, the conjunction with Mars inspires us to make a unique contribution to our collective spiritual growth.

Once we embrace the Sedna energy, which is the oneness of everything, our actions and passions become an expression of Sedna consciousness and they become devotional in nature. The struggle of the beginner's level is gone, as are the transcendental crises of the intermediate level. At this level everything Saturnian is meaningless and yet everything Sednian has its place.

Like Maudelle Tooks, who is an American gifted psychic who has been receiving messages from the spirits since she was about eight years old. She has Sedna conjunct Mars in the eighth house of sensitivity to the spirit world. She does "spirit counselling," and is known for being highly accurate, clear and lucid.

And like Paramahansa Yogananda, who was an East Indian author, mystic and founder of the Self-Realisation Fellowship. World traveled and a world teacher, he carried Eastern philosophy to the West. He has Sedna conjunct Mars the planet of action, in the eighth house of shared resources, sextile Varuna in the sixth house of service.

---

[405] https://en.wikipedia.org/wiki/Vincent_van_Gogh

At 27 he was invited to serve as India's delegate to an international congress of religious leaders convening in Boston. His address to the congress, on 'The Science of Religion', was enthusiastically received. When he arrived in America, the "New World" was ready to receive the advanced teachings that had previously been reserved for monastics and chelas in ashrams. Science, literacy, communication, and new spiritual insights had just begun breaking down the dark ages of theology and dogma.

He founded his fellowship to disseminate worldwide his teachings on India's ancient science and philosophy of Yoga and its time-honoured tradition of meditation, introducing the Bhagavad Gita and other scriptures to help raise the consciousness of humanity. He lectured and taught on the East coast of American for several years and at 31 began a speaking tour across the country. His lectures, in which he spoke of the underlying unity of the world's great religions, were attended by thousands drawn to his message. His personal students were taught the ancient soul-awakening techniques of Kriya Yoga.

His articulate and sincere introduction to the disciplines of the East opened the door for many other Indian teachers and gurus, as a serious interest in yoga and meditation made great inroads in the West. His main mission was to build a lasting bridge of World Brotherhood based on raising the spiritual awareness between the East and West.[406]

Opposition

The opposition between Sedna and Mars brings our actions, passions and our competitive nature into stark relief against the all-encompassing spiritual energy of Sedna.

Mars relates to our basic sexual nature, how we express our anger, our temper and our first instinct to act. The god of war in ancient times, Mars could be brutally violent and so the planet rules our competitive nature. It shows the areas of life where we apply our drive and express our enthusiasm, where we take action and assert ourselves. And it relates to stamina, ambition and achievement.

---

[406] https://en.wikipedia.org/wiki/Paramahansa_Yogananda

If we are unconscious of the energy, we may feel out of place and act arrogantly to make it right from our perspective. This is likely to cause strife however, so we better be on firm ground, or we will come off as the victim in the encounter.

If we are misusing our Mars energy, we can be impulsive, rash, impatient, aggressive, and forceful and if we are unconscious of our Sedna energy we are more likely to express this negative side, feeling a sense of righteousness in our actions.

Unfortunately, this behaviour is likely to invite similar responses, so we might feel victimized without really understanding that we brought it on ourselves. And we might also project the negative Mars energy onto another and allow ourselves to be victimized or abused.

Like Candy Barr, who was an American exotic dancer. She had Sedna in the eleventh house of collective consciousness, opposite Mars in the fifth house of creativity.

> Her mother died when she was nine, and her dad married a woman with four children to add to his existing five. Sexually abused as a child by a neighbour and the baby sitter, she grew up to be a small Texas town bad girl. She ran away from home and became a prostitute before she was 16, when she became one of the first superstars of the porno genre, starring in her first film, *Smart Aleck*.
>
> She was also one of the most famous and highly paid strippers, as well as a playmate to gangster Mickey Cohan. She made national news at 22 when she was arrested for drug possession. She began a 15-year jail term but was paroled four years later and pardoned four years after that. In her late 30s, she emerged as a serious poet with her book, *A Gentle Mind - Confused*. Married four times, she had one daughter.[407]

Or Nicholas Teague, who was an American murderer who shot and killed his mother and seriously wounded his father before killing himself. He also had Sedna in the eleventh house of collective consciousness, opposite Mars conjunct Ixion, the planet of lawlessness, in the fifth house of children.

---

[407] https://en.wikipedia.org/wiki/Candy_Barr

At age 23, he was taking medication for his serious psychological problems and had just lost his job as a refrigerator repair apprentice. He had gotten the job through his dad, who was an employee with the refrigerator firm as well as a volunteer firefighter. His mom was a cook at the local school. He shot his mom in the chest and side and when his dad ran upstairs, shot him in the torso. His dad staggered back downstairs and Nick shot himself in the head.[408]

Or like Napoléon Bonaparte, who was a French general and emperor, a giant figure in European history and a world cultural icon synonymous with military genius and political power. He had Sedna conjunct Juno, the asteroid of partnership, in the fourth house of home, opposite Mars in the tenth house of profession.

One of the greatest military strategists in history, he dominated European affairs for almost two decades while leading France against a series of coalitions in the Napoleonic Wars. He was promoted to brigadier general at age 24 and became a striking military strategist, never retreating, or blaming his losses on others. He won the large majority of his battles and seized control of most of continental Europe, before his ultimate defeat at the Battle of Waterloo at the age of 46. Well-educated and an avid reader, he also instituted lasting reforms including higher education, a tax code, road and sewer systems, and the establishment of a central bank.[409]

As we tire of density and the grief it creates, and we start a spiritual journey to get out of the swamp, Sedna rewards us with transcendent crises, experiences which force us to let go and rise above them, resulting in a huge growth to a new level of consciousness. There is no choice with these crises, and the more we try and solve them, the more we will get hurt.

Friedrich Nietzsche was a German philosopher who is considered one of the most influential voices of modern times. He had Sedna conjunct Jupiter, the planet of expansion, in the fourth house of home, opposite Mars in the tenth house of profession.

---

[408] https://www.astro.com/astro-databank/Teague,_Nicholas
[409] https://en.wikipedia.org/wiki/Napoleon

He came from a long line of Lutheran pastors and was destined to follow in the footsteps of his clergyman dad, who died after 11 months of suffering from a serious illness, when he was age five, leaving him to live with his mother, younger sister, grandmother and two aunts. He received a strict Christian upbringing, as his mother was also the child of a Protestant minister. He suffered continually from severe headaches, sore throats, and rheumatic ailments as a child, especially during his school days.

At age 23, recognised for his brilliant work, he was appointed to the chair of philology at the University of Basel, and later was granted to Doctorate without examination. However, at the age of 35 he resigned his post and began a decade of travels across Europe, during which he wrote his greatest books. *Thus Spoke Zarathustra* and *Twilight of the Idols*.

His dealing with the opposite sex was consistently awkward. He made a precipitous and impulsive proposal to a woman at 32, just two hours after meeting her. His late 30s was probably among the loneliest and most desperate periods in his life, the time when he began his *Thus Spoke Zarathustra.*

He had a desire to define himself as a European and looked forward to a time when the peoples of Europe would define themselves as Europeans rather than as citizens of particular countries. He believed that history is a genealogy of geniuses, in which each genius created the mental world in which his successors live.

His mental degeneration, apparently caused by syphilis, began with megalomania. He started to call himself a genius, the leading person of all millenniums and he claimed that all women loved him. He took on different identities - the Buddha, Alexander the Great, Caesar, Voltaire, Napoleon, Wagner - and danced naked in his room. At 45 he broke down in the street and tearfully embraced a horse which had been beaten. He was declared insane by doctors and taken back to Germany where he sat in a vegetative state until his death eleven years later.[410]

---

[410] https://en.wikipedia.org/wiki/Friedrich_Nietzsche

Johnny Carson was an American TV personality who began as the host of *The Tonight Show* at 37, reportedly for $100,000 a year, retiring at 67 on a $25 million per year salary. He had Sedna in the sixth house of service, opposite Mars in the twelfth house of the unconscious.

When he was 54 he bought into 17% of NBC's earnings, which insured his billionaire status. With his nonchalant, inventive wit, he was one of the most popular and enduring figures on American TV, a household icon for millions of Americans. He was reliable, respected, reassuring - and funny, a familiar figure who was part of many lives. Keeping his finger on the common pulse, he instinctively knew when to pull back to avoid hurting anyone.

As host of the *The Tonight Show* for over 30 years, he interviewed thousands of guests, from royalty to the ordinary, introduced dozens of new personalities to the public, and will always be known as America's humorous late-night friend, a mid-Western boy not afraid to poke fun at himself as well as the powerful. He easily outlasted an array of competition. Dubbed the "naughty but good-natured son," Middle America liked him.

He married his first wife during his senior year at university when he was 23. The relationship was difficult and they separated after 10 years and divorced 4 years later. His early marriages were reputed to have suffered from his abuse, alcoholism, and neglect. His second marriage at 38 lasted nine years, and his third at 47 lasted eleven years. His fourth marriage lasted 17 years from the age of 62 to his death at 79. His divorces were always fuel for his late-night humour and he commented, "If I had given as much to marriage as I gave to *The Tonight Show*, I'd probably have a hell of a marriage."[411]

Georgie Anne Geyer is an American journalist and foreign correspondent with the *Chicago Daily News*, a syndicated columnist, author, lecturer and educator, television panelist and moderator. She had Sedna in the second house of material resources, opposite Mars in the eighth house of shared resources.

---

[411] https://en.wikipedia.org/wiki/Johnny_Carson

At 29 she won a Foreign Assignment Grant, which enabled her to spend six months abroad, while continuing to work for the *Daily News*. She chose Latin America for its "deep subterranean affinity." In Peru, she learned Spanish and gradually discovered how to obtain information sources and how to interact with people in foreign countries so that she could explain different cultures to United States readers.

Her dispatches were so well received in Chicago that she was sent to Santo Domingo the next year to cover the revolution of Rafael Trujillo. She focused on the view of the revolutionists by talking with their intellectual leader, Juan Bosch, then in hiding in Puerto Rico. Bosch became the first of a number of world leaders that she interviewed.

At 31 she interviewed Cuba Premier Fidel Castro and also became the first American journalist to travel into the dangerous mountains of Guatemala to observe early guerrilla movements. Her coverage was published internationally, and brought her professional recognition, including the Overseas Press Club Latin America Award when she was 32.

She authored books on Latin America, the Middle East and the U.S.S.R. and wrote *Buying the Night Flight: The Autobiography of a Woman Foreign Correspondent,* published when she was 48. Throughout romantic relationships, she has remained single.[412]

Edwin Hubble was an American astronomer, one of the major figures in 20th century science. He had Sedna in the eighth house of shared resources, opposite Mars in the second house of material resources.

Working with the 100-inch Hooker telescope at California's Mount Wilson observatory, he made a series of discoveries that revolutionised humanity's vision of the cosmos. He was the first astronomer who provided reliable evidence that the universe is homogenous, the same in all directions as far as the telescope can see.

During the '20s and '30s, as his stature increased, he became part of Hollywood society. A character in his tweed jackets,

---

[412] https://en.wikipedia.org/wiki/Georgie_Anne_Geyer

knickers and English briar pipes, he and his witty wife mingled with the Huxleys, Walt Disney, Charlie Chaplin and Helen Hayes. His friend Albert Einstein called Hubble's work "beautiful," and modified his equations on relativity to account for the discovery that the cosmos is expanding.[413]

At this juncture in human evolution, few of us use our planets at the spiritual level, but many of us are striving to, and such people are wonderful to be around. As with the other planets, the spiritual level of evolution is vastly different with Sedna from the two previous levels. Here, the opposition with Mars challenges a unique contribution to our collective spiritual growth.

Once we embrace the Sedna energy, which is the oneness of everything, our actions and passions, become an expression of Sedna consciousness and they become devotional in nature. The struggle of the beginner's level is gone, as are the transcendental crises of the intermediate level. At this level everything Saturnian is meaningless and yet everything Sednian has its place.

R.D. Laing was a Scottish psychiatrist, writer, analyst, philosopher and counter-culture cult figure whose controversial views on mental illness made him a guru among the young and radical in the 1960s. He had Sedna in the first house of identity, opposite Mars in the seventh house of relationships.

> He broke with traditional psychotherapy and sought new treatments for schizophrenia based on a concern for the rights of mental patients. His book, *The Voice of Experience*, sounded a theme that behaviour shouldn't be considered abnormal just because we don't understand it, and he viewed psychosis as a potentially enriching experience. In the 1960s, he began to emerge from that orthodoxy, becoming an outspoken critic of traditional approaches and beginning to experiment with the therapeutic use of mescaline and LSD.
>
> In London, he founded a therapeutic community where patients, doctors and staff lived and worked together democratically, without distinctions of rank or role. He was criticised by some for idealising mental illness as a hyper state of awareness. He felt

---

[413] https://en.wikipedia.org/wiki/Edwin_Hubble

that schizophrenia was neither genetic or biochemical but arose from being in hopeless emotional situations. He was married twice, divorced twice, and had nine children, three daughters and six sons.[414]

Pope Francis has Sedna in the ninth house of spirituality opposite Mars in the third house of ideas and communication. This is the only tension in this family of Sedna aspects. He reputedly worked as a bouncer briefly when he was young, which is one of the professions we might expect from this aspect at the undeveloped stage. But he subsequently entered the seminary and instead renounced sex, violence and war, renounced the traditional energies of Mars and yet by his devotional actions, has risen to be the 266th leader of a 2000-year-old faith.

Shivabalayogi was a meditation guru in the tradition of the ancient and modern yogis of India. He had Sedna in the eleventh house of collective consciousness, opposite Mars in the fifth house of creativity.

He attained self-realisation through twelve years of arduous tapas, meditating in samādhi, a state of total thoughtlessness, for an average of twenty hours a day. Tapas is the most advanced stage of meditation in which one remains absorbed for long periods in this non-dualistic state of consciousness.

After he completed tapas, he assumed the name Shivabalayogi, meaning Yogi devoted to Shiva and Parvati. The name reflects that he is a manifestation of both the male and female aspects of the divine. The female aspect represents the invisible energy of the divine through which the entire creation operates, while the male aspect represents the pure consciousness of existence beyond all imaginations. Generally, devotees called him simply Swamiji, meaning respected Master.

For three decades he traveled extensively in India and Sri Lanka, initiating over ten million people into dhyana meditation. In his early fifties he traveled for four years in England and the United States. His teaching is consistent with the Vedanta, emphasising the need for spiritual practice to achieve self-realisation.[415]

---

[414] https://en.wikipedia.org/wiki/R._D._Laing
[415] https://en.wikipedia.org/wiki/Shivabalayogi

Semi-sextile, Sextile, Trine

With the flowing aspects between Sedna and Mars the all-encompassing spiritual energy of Sedna aligns with our actions and passions.

Mars relates to our basic sexual nature, how we express our anger, our temper and our first instinct to act. The god of war in ancient times, Mars could be brutally violent and so the planet rules our competitive nature. It shows the areas of life where we apply our drive and express our enthusiasm, where we take action and assert ourselves. And it relates to stamina, ambition and achievement.

Even with the alignment of impersonal spiritual energy with our actions, the flows don't bring automatic success, there are still challenges, but the flows do give us a perseverance to continue our work despite the challenges. There is also possibly an awareness over time that these challenges are shaping our lives in the direction of our destiny.

If we are unconscious of the energy, however, there can be a sense of righteousness to our actions, even if they fall outside the the accepted norms and this can bring us into conflict with others, or with the authorities, in which we may feel victimized or alienated.

Osama bin Laden was the founder of al-Qaeda, the organization that claimed responsibility for the September 11 attacks on the United States, along with numerous other mass-casualty attacks worldwide. He had Sedna in the eleventh house of collective consciousness, semi-sextile to Mars, which is in the twelfth house of the unconscious. His Mars is also square to his Pluto in the third house of ideas.

> He was a Saudi Arabian and a member of the wealthy bin Laden family. His mother was his father's tenth wife, but she was Syrian and was called the slave by the rest of the family. Osama was called the son of a slave. His father divorced his mother soon after he was born, recommending her to an associate, who married her and they are still together. The couple had four children, and Osama lived in the new household with three half-brothers and one half-sister.

> This early sense of victimisation was formative in shaping his perspective. He projected his victimisation onto his fellow Muslims and set out to save them from, as he saw it, the decadent Saudi Arabian leadership in cahoots with the infidels.

At 22 he joined the Mujahideen forces in Pakistan fighting against the Soviet Union in Afghanistan. He helped to fund the Mujahideen by funnelling arms, money and fighters from the Arab world into Afghanistan, and gained popularity among many Arabs.

At 31 he formed al-Qaeda. He was banished from Saudi Arabia four years later, and shifted his base to Sudan, until U.S. pressure forced him to leave four years after that. His Sedna was also opposite Ixion, the planet of lawlessness, in the fifth house of 'what is produced in the home', which gives the signature of his style of terrorism: A major component of his ideology was the concept that civilians from enemy countries, including women and children, were legitimate targets for jihadists to kill.

After establishing a new base in Afghanistan, he declared a war against the United States, initiating a series of bombings and related attacks. He was on the American FBI's lists of Ten Most Wanted Fugitives and Most Wanted Terrorists for ten years from the age of 44. The FBI placed a $25 million bounty on him. He was finally shot and killed inside a private residential compound in Parkistan, where he lived with a local family, during a covert operation conducted by members of the US Naval Special Warfare Development Group.[416]

Liz Renay was an American exotic dancer, model, stripper and party girl. She had Sedna conjunct Nessus, the centaur of radical change, in the twelfth house of the unconscious, sextile her Mars in the eleventh house of collective consciousness.

Raised as poor-white-trash in a three-room cabin on the banks of a ditch, she ran away at 14 and married a soldier and they had a daughter. It was the first of seven marriages. With a gorgeous face and body, she became an exotic dancer in a strip joint at 23. She almost made it into the movies at 32; the studio hype was in motion to promote her first picture when there was an underworld mob murder. She was implicated for refusing to testify for fear of her life and was indicted for perjury the following year. She served a prison sentence for 27 months that finished her movie career before it started.

---

[416] https://en.wikipedia.org/wiki/Osama_bin_Laden

She wrote her autobiography at 45, titled *My Face the World to See*. Though her literary skills were abysmal, she was a survivor without pretences. In the '70s she again made news when she and her daughter, also a stripper, both streaked naked down Hollywood Blvd to publicise their appearance in a club. She finally made it into the movies at 51 with her role in John Waters' film, *Desperate Living.*[417]

Alan Turing, was a British mathematician, logician, scientist and the technical genius behind Britain's successful efforts to break German codes in WW2. He had Sedna in the twelfth house of the unconscious, trine his Mars in the fourth house of home.

He made inestimable contributions to cybernetics. His 'Computable Numbers', published when he was 25, is considered one of the outstanding scientific papers of the 20th century, a blueprint for what would become the electronic digital computer. His 'Universal Turing Machine' was an ancestor for the entire information age.

He was accustomed to being a non-conformist. At boarding school, he refused to adapt and ignored subjects that did not interest him. He was an atheist and felt marginalised because of his homosexuality. From the age of 13 he formed a significant friendship with another boy who has been described as his 'first love'. Their relationship provided inspiration in his future endeavours, but it was cut short by his friend's death when Alan was 17, from drinking infected cow's milk some years previously. The event caused him great sorrow and he coped with this by working that much harder on the topics of science and mathematics that he had shared with his friend.

Though he envisioned a time when "ladies will take their computers for walks in the park," his own reality was not quite so whimsical. When a robbery occurred at his house in Manchester, he frankly told the police that the robber probably knew the man with whom he was having an affair. As homosexual relations were still a felony in Britain, Turing was tried and convicted of gross indecency. He was spared prison but was given a year's

---

[417] https://en.wikipedia.org/wiki/Liz_Renay

probation with the condition that he take oestrogen to diminish his sex drive.[418]

As we tire of density and the grief it creates, and we start a spiritual journey to get out of the swamp, Sedna rewards us with transcendent crises, experiences which force us to let go and rise above them, resulting in a huge growth to a new level of consciousness. There is no choice with these crises, and the more we try and solve them, the more we will get hurt.

Marie Curie was a Polish-French scientist, a physicist and chemist, winning Nobel Prizes for both, but not allowed in the French Academy of Science as she was female. She had Sedna in the second house of material reality, trine Mars in the tenth house of profession.

> At 24 she joined her sister in Paris to study math, physics and chemistry at the Sorbonne. She proved a brilliant student with an early interest in the magnetic properties of steel. Within two years she received her license in science with the highest marks of her class. She later held a chair in physics at the Sorbonne, the first female professor at the university.

> She was drawn to fellow scientist, Pierre Curie by their mutual interest in magnetism and devotion to science. They married when she was 28 and in Pierre, she found a new love, a partner, and a scientific collaborator on whom she could depend. However, their early years were very hard. In 1898, after they discovered radium, Marie had a struggle of four years of toil which finally resulted in the extraction of one-tenth of a gram of radium from one ton of uranium mine waste, one of the epic stories of science.

> The Curies worked together for 11 harmonious years, isolating radium and polonium. As well as being one of history's outstanding scientists, Marie lived the normal life of a wife and mother; a month after discovering radium, she carefully notes having made 14 pots of gooseberry jelly. Her letters show her very close and affectionate relationships with her father, brother and sisters, her daughters and many friends.

---

[418] https://en.wikipedia.org/wiki/Alan_Turing

When she was 36 the Royal Swedish Academy of Sciences awarded them the Nobel Prize in Physics, together with another male physicist, "in recognition of the extraordinary services they have rendered by their joint researches on the radiation phenomena." At first, the Committee intended just to honour the two men, but one of the committee members alerted Pierre to the situation, and after his complaint, Marie's name was added to the nomination. She was the first woman to be awarded a Nobel Prize.

She was devastated when Pierre was killed in a road accident when she was 39. The physics department of the University of Paris had offered him a professorship the year before and was preparing his laboratory when he died. The university decided to retain the chair that had been created for him and to offer it to her. She accepted it, hoping to create a world-class laboratory as a tribute to Pierre. She was the first woman to become a professor at the University of Paris.

She received a second Nobel Prize in her own right at 44, this time for Chemistry, for the discovery of the elements radium and polonium, but was never allowed to join the French Society of Scientists because she was a woman. A biography by her daughter stresses her parent's unworldliness and the idealism that made them refuse to patent the process they developed of isolating radium, which could have made them wealthy.[419]

Al Gore is an American politician and environmentalist, who served as the 45th Vice President of the United States under President Bill Clinton. His Sedna is conjunct the MC, the cusp of the tenth house of profession, trine Mars in the first house of identity.

He is a devout Baptist as he has made that clear in many interviews: 'Faith is the center of my life. I don't wear it on my sleeve, but I'm happy to respond to your question by affirming my faith.' Despite his devotion to one particular brand of Christianity, Gore has stated that he supports religious tolerance, the First Amendment, freedom of religion, expression, etc. and the strict separation of church and state.

---

[419] https://en.wikipedia.org/wiki/Marie_Curie

He served as an elected official for 24 years. He was a Congressman from Tennessee and served as one of the state's Senators. He was initially hesitant to accept a position as Bill Clinton's running mate, but after clashing with the George H. W. Bush administration over global warming issues, he decided to accept the offer.

Clinton's choice was criticised as unconventional because, rather than picking a running mate who would diversify the ticket, Clinton chose a fellow Southerner who shared his political ideologies and who was nearly the same age as Clinton. Yet, Gore has come to be regarded by strategists in both parties as the best vicepresidential pick in at least 20 years.

In the 2000 presidential election, in what was one of the closest presidential races in history, he won the popular vote by half a million, but lost in the Electoral College to Republican George W. Bush by 537 votes in the key state of Florida.

After his term as vice-president ended, Gore remained prominent as an author and activist and returned his focus to his environmental agenda. He edited and adapted a slide show he had compiled years earlier and began featuring the slide show in presentations on global warming across the U.S. and around the world. By the time the documentary about his work, *An Inconvenient Truth*, was made, he estimated that he had shown the presentation more than one thousand times.

Premiering at the 2006 Sundance Film Festival and opening in New York City and Los Angeles his film *An Inconvenient Truth* was a critical and box office success, winning two Academy Awards for Best Documentary Feature and Best Original Song. The film grossed $24 million in the U.S. and $26 million in the foreign box office, becoming the tenth highest grossing documentary film to date in the United States. Since the film's release, it has been credited for raising international public awareness of global warming and reenergising the environmental movement.

His work in climate change activism earned him the Nobel Peace Prize in 2007, and we now know the evolutionary results of his work with the Paris Climate Change Agreement, which has been far more valuable for society than his being president.[420]

Ada Lovelace was an English mathematician and writer who is chiefly known for her work on Charles Babbage's proposed mechanical general-purpose computer, the Analytical Engine. She had Sedna closely conjunct Pluto, the planet of transformation, and also Ixion, the planet of lawlessness, all in the twelfth house of the unconscious, semi-sextile her Mars in the first house of identity.

> She was the only legitimate child of the famous poet, Lord Byron, and he separated from her mother a month after she was born and left England forever four months later, eventually dying of disease in the Greek War of Independence. Her mother remained bitter towards him and promoted Ada's interest in mathematics and logic in an effort to prevent her from developing what she saw as the insanity of her father.

> When she was a teenager, her mathematical talents led her to a long working relationship and friendship with fellow British mathematician Charles Babbage, also known as "the father of computers", and her notes from her late twenties contain what many consider to be the first computer program—that is, an algorithm designed to be carried out by a machine.

> She was the first to recognise that the machine had applications beyond pure calculation, and created the first algorithm intended to be carried out by such a machine. As a result, she is often regarded as the first to recognise the full potential of a "computing machine" and the first computer programmer.

> She also developed a vision of the capability of computers to go beyond mere calculating or number-crunching, while many others, including Babbage himself, focused only on those capabilities. Her mindset of "poetical science" led her to ask questions about the Analytical Engine examining how individuals and society relate to technology as a collaborative tool.[421]

At this juncture in human evolution, few of us use our planets at the spiritual level, but many of us are striving to, and such people are

---

[420] https://en.wikipedia.org/wiki/Al_Gore
[421] https://en.wikipedia.org/wiki/Ada_Lovelace

wonderful to be around. As with the other planets, the spiritual level of evolution is vastly different with Sedna from the two previous levels. Here the flowing aspects with Mars bring the ability to make a unique contribution to our collective spiritual growth.

Once we embrace the Sedna energy, which is the oneness of everything, our actions and passions become an expression of Sedna consciousness and they become devotional in nature. The struggle of the beginner's level is gone, as are the transcendental crises of the intermediate level. At this level everything Saturnian is meaningless and yet everything Sednian has its place.

Anne Frank was a Dutch-Jewish writer of a diary from age 14 -15, while she and her family lived in total confinement, hiding in an attic from the Nazis, where non-Jewish friends had sheltered them. She had Sedna in the tenth house of profession, trine Mars on the cusp of the second house of material restrictions.

> She began scrawling her diary in 1942, writing as a typical teen in many ways, childish and profound, thoughtful and painful, writing, "In spite of everything, I still believe that people are really good at heart."

> Her last entry was three days before their hiding place was discovered and they were arrested. She died of typhus at the Bergen-Belsen concentration camp in March 1945. Her father, who survived, returned after the war and found his daughter's diary. At the turn of the century a new edition of her diary was released with five previously secret pages that described her conflict with her mother, whom she wrote, "had cold eyes," and with whom she could not talk to unburden herself, and her lament that her parents had a loveless marriage of convenience.

> Her diary remains as a poignant symbol of the millions whose lives and homes were lost during a tragic page in history. Translated into 54 languages with sales hovering around 25 million copies worldwide, her book is an established part of most high school educations. Putting a single face on the vast horror of the Holocaust, she served as a reminder of the quiet acts of heroism that were part of that high-water mark of evil.[422]

---

[422] https://en.wikipedia.org/wiki/Anne_Frank

Elsie Wheeler was an American spiritualist and psychic who worked with Marc Edmund Jones and Zoe Wells on the Sabian Symbols and was noted for being the primary contributor. She had Sedna in the eleventh house of collective consciousness, trine Mars in the third house of ideas and communication.

> The experiment was conducted when she was 38. Crippled with arthritis, she had to be carried to the session. 360 cards had been prepared, one for each degree of the zodiac, which were presented to her at random and were shuffled continuously. One at a time the cards were placed face-down in front of her and she pictured an image and reported it. At first the images did not seem entirely appropriate, or some were exaggerated, so the cards were put aside for six years, when they were revised. She died seven years after that, but the revision process was repeated after her death and the results were first published thirteen years later.[423]

Karl Marx was a German-Jewish communist and philosopher who developed the theory of socialism and was the father of modern social science. He had Sedna in the first house of identity, trine Mars on the cusp of the sixth house of service. He pushed the boundaries of human development with his ideas on society.

His Sedna is also quintile Mercury in the third house of communication and quintile Makemake, the planet of extreme talent, conjunct Jupiter, the planet of philosophy, both in the eleventh house of ideals. It is also bi-quintile to Pholus, the centaur of catalyzing change, in the eighth house of shared resources. This explains how his ideas and writing about social ideals involving a change in the distribution of social resources made him the powerful evolutionary change agent that he was.

For him social change was about conflict between opposing interests, driven, in the background, by economic forces. This became the inspiration for the body of works known as the conflict theory. In his evolutionary model of history, he argued that human history began with free, productive and creative work that was over time coerced and dehumanized, a trend most apparent under capitalism. Fundamentally, he assumed that human history involves transforming human nature,

---

[423] https://www.astro.com/astro-databank/Wheeler,_Elsie

which he saw, in a very Sednian way, as encompassing both human beings and material objects.

> He believed, like the philosopher Hegel, that humans recognise that they possess both actual and potential selves and that self-development begins with an experience of internal alienation, which Marx argued was because of 'the despotism of capital'. This leads to a realisation that the actual self, as a subjective agent, renders its potential self as an object to be apprehended by capitalism. Marx further argued that by moulding nature in desired ways, the subject takes the object as its own, and thus permits the individual to be actualised as fully human.

> In the new society that would emerge, he reasoned that the self-alienation would end, and humans would be free to act without being bound by the labour market. It would be a democratic society, enfranchising the entire population. In such a utopian world there would also be little if any need for a state, the goal of which was only to enforce the alienation.[424]

Semi-square, Square, Sesquiquadrate

With the stressful aspects between Sedna and Mars the all-encompassing spiritual energy of Sedna challenges our actions and passions.

Mars relates to our basic sexual nature, how we express our anger, our temper and our first instinct to act. The god of war in ancient times, Mars could be brutally violent and so the planet rules our competitive nature. It shows the areas of life where we apply our drive and express our enthusiasm, where we take action and assert ourselves. And it relates to stamina, ambition and achievement.

If we are misusing our Mars energy, we can be impulsive, rash, impatient, aggressive, and forceful and if we are unconscious of our Sedna energy we are more likely to express this negative side, feeling a sense of righteousness in our actions.

Unfortunately, this behaviour is likely to invite similar responses, so we might feel victimized without really understanding that we brought it on ourselves. We might also project the negative Mars energy onto another and allow ourselves to be victimized or abused.

---

[424] https://en.wikipedia.org/wiki/Karl_Marx

Like Daniel Croteau, an American homicide victim at the age of 12, found strangled with a piece of clothesline and bludgeoned. He had Sedna in the eleventh house of collective consciousness, square his Mars in the second house of material reality.

> He was a bright, loquacious boy with freckles and strawberry blonde hair who loved to go fishing. He had a generous side. He used to help an elderly woman in the neighborhood, fetching her mail, raking her lawn, doing errands. He served as an altar boy at St. Catherine's, as did his four elder brothers. Police say the priest there worked to gain their trust. Sleepovers at the rectory became common for some of the boys and he also had some stay with him at his parents' Chicopee home. One day, 14-year-old Joe Croteau came home hung over after a sleepover.

> The night before he appeared at the door of a stranger late at night, saying he was lost and asking to use her phone to call the priest. The priest admitted to police that he had picked up Danny and taken him, alone, to his parents' house, where Danny spent the night. His mother said that Danny had arrived home the next morning, said he felt ill, and later threw up repeatedly. When the police talked to each of Danny's brothers after the murder, they told the parents that the priest had sexually abused some of them.[425]

Mata Hari was a Dutch prostitute and exotic dancer who also served as a spy. She had Sedna in the fifth house of creativity, sesquiquadrate her Mars, which is conjunct Mercury, the planet of communication, and her Sun, her sense of self, all in the ninth house of knowledge.

> The daughter of a merchant, in her younger years she was expelled from convent school for sleeping with a priest and, at the age of 18, moved to Java with her 40-year-old husband. The couple had a violent marriage and one of their two children died. She left her husband and returned to Europe at 29 where, as a nude belly dancer, she went to Paris to work in a brothel.

> She also attended German espionage school but was arrested as a double agent when she delivered a message on German

---

[425] http://archive.boston.com/news/nation/articles/2003/12/14
/a_priest_a_boy_a_mystery/

submarine activity to the French embassy. She was 40 when she was arrested and placed on trial for treason. Convicted, she was executed by firing squad. On the morning of her execution, she put on her stockings, dressed in a pearl-gray frock, slung a coat over her shoulders, buttoned her boots, put on a dark tri-corned hat with a veil and glove. "This lady knows how to die," said the sergeant major who helped her. "After the shots were fired, she crumpled in a heap of petticoats."

The famed figure returned to the news 84 years after her death when historian Leon Schirmann, who has spent a decade researching the case, put out his second book about her. He finds that documents show French falsification of the records and that instead of a major spy for the Germans, Mata Hari was an elegant but naive adventuress, essentially

the first strip-tease dancer. At the outbreak of WW I, she was offered cash up front for a German mission, but turned out to be not a very good spy. With the codename of H21, she returned to Paris, spent the money and did precious little else.[426]

Or like Diane Luciferia, who was a French Wiccan high priestess who descended into black masses and orgies, until she herself became a homicide victim. She had Sedna in the tenth house of profession, sesquiquadrate her Mars in the second house of material reality.

She had been born Nicole-Martin from an unwed mother and was legitimized by her mother's marriage, when she was two. She met her partner at 24 on the Isle of Man, where the Wicca International Witchcraft movement originated. They lived together and represented the sect in France with Nicole taking the name of Diane Luciferia. He was an author of pornographic film scripts. He met a girl called Dominique Desseaux on the set of a film shoot and adopted her as his daughter, ignoring the fact that she had personality disorders and that a history of time spent in psychiatric hospitals.

The Wiccan chapter began conducting black masses which ended up in sexual orgies. Eventually many members left, following a dissident. When she was 49, Diane and her partner's

---

[426] https://en.wikipedia.org/wiki/Mata_Hari

adopted daughter, who were both witches, appeared on a French TV show to air their grievances. However, when they were not allowed to voice their opinions, and they furiously stormed off the set. Their rivalry escalated and later that year, the daughter murdered Diane with a shotgun, staging the scene to make it look like a suicide. She then took her place as high priestess. A few weeks later, crazed with grief, her adopted father murdered her by hanging her and then hung himself.[427]

As we tire of density and the grief it creates, and we start a spiritual journey to get out of the swamp, Sedna rewards us with transcendent crises, experiences which force us to let go and rise above them, resulting in a huge growth to a new level of consciousness. There is no choice with these crises, and the more we try and solve them, the more we will get hurt.

Britney Spears is an American dance-pop singer, a fabulous success by age 19. She has Sedna in the eighth house of shared resources, sesquiquadrate Mars in the twelfth house of the unconscious.

> She was already a pro at the age of eleven, when she joined Disney Channel's Mickey Mouse Club show. The beautiful teen-ager never did have a conventional life-style, and by 17 she was plunged into the show-biz world of tours, photo-shoots and adoring fans. Even before her first album came out, legions of people were becoming her fans on the strength of her performances at local malls and as the opening act for the popular group, Nsync.

> At 17, she signed to Jive Records and issued her first LP. The record was a massive hit, topping the charts and reeling off a series of radio smash singles. It became the best-selling album ever released by a teenage girl. She attributes her wonderful success to her family and her faith in God. Her mother says Britney's focus and determination have also helped her achieve all that she has.

> During that year was nominated for two Grammys, including the coveted Best New Artist, and swept the 1999 MTV Europe Awards, where she nabbed Best Female, Best Pop, Best

---

[427] https://www.astro.com/astro-databank/Luciferia,_Diane

Breakthrough Artist and Best song. She brought her explosive live show around the globe and appeared on every major televised award show. Her trim teen-age figure and scant costumes were seen on every magazine cover.

As she grew more famous however, she became more impulsive. She got married and separated in the same weekend to a childhood friend. The wedding took place in Las Vegas on an impulse early in the morning when she was 22. She wore a baseball cap and jeans and was accompanied down the aisle of the Little White Wedding Chapel by a hotel bellman.

She married a second time later that year and, over the next two years, had two children, however after only two years, she filed for divorce. She was often in the news for increasingly bizarre and often self-destructive behaviour. At 25, she walked into a just-closed beauty salon demanding to have her head shorn. A few days later she admitted herself to a rehabilitation centre, left for one day and then re-entered. She had reportedly suffered a breakdown that was attributed to postpartum depression, alcohol, and/or drugs.

Her divorce became final later that year and twice early the next year she seemed to suffer from severe episodes of mental illness. Whether alcohol or drug use has contributed is unknown. On one occasion she refused to relinquish her children to their father who has custody. After arguing with police who suspected she had taken an unknown substance, she was admitted to a hospital and a judge revoked her child visitation rights. She was released a few days later but reports of strange behaviour continued and she was admitted to a psychiatric hospital.

She bounced back however and her sixth studio album, Circus released later that year, included global chart-topping lead single "Womanizer". Its supporting tour was one of the highest-grossing global concert tours. Her seventh studio album, released when she was thirty, became her first to yield three top-ten singles in the United States. She also served as a judge during the second season of the American version of The X Factor. and the following year began a four-year residency show at Planet Hollywood Resort & Casino in Las Vegas.[428]

As we work with the stress between Sedna and Mars more consciously however, we can focus more in the positive Mars energies and will likely then be able to effect significant personal and social change through our actions.

Thomas Edison, the father of the light bulb, had Sedna in the fourth hose of the laboratory home, square Mars in the second house of material resources. His Mars is also conjunct his Moon, representing his emotional nature which is in the first house of Identity. These are the karmic challenges in his chart, making himself centered and sometimes working at cross-purposes to himself, however they also provided the strength of purpose and practical action to achieve his goals.

> As a general rule, Edison does not get genuinely angry at mistakes and other human weaknesses of his subordinates; at best he merely simulates anger. But woe betide the one who has committed an act of bad faith, treachery, dishonesty, or ingratitude; Then he can show what it is for a strong man to get downright mad. But in this respect, he is singularly free, and his spells of anger are really few. In fact, those who know him best are continually surprised at his moderation and patience, often when there has been great provocation.

> People who may have occasion to oppose his views, may leave with the impression that he is hot-tempered, but nothing could be further from the truth. He argues his point with great vehemence, pounds on the table to emphasize his views, and illustrates his theme with a wealth of apt similes; but, on account of his deafness, it is difficult to make the argument really two-sided.

> In the overcoming of difficulties, he had the same intellectual pleasure as the chess-master when confronted with a problem requiring all the efforts of his skill and experience to solve. To advance along smooth and pleasant paths, to encounter no obstacles, to wrestle with no difficulties and hardships, such had absolutely no fascination to him. At the conclusion of his ore-milling experiments, practically his entire fortune was sunk in an

---

[428] https://en.wikipedia.org/wiki/Britney_Spears

enterprise that had to be considered an impossibility. At the age of fifty he looked back upon five or six years of intense activity expended apparently for naught and the financial clouds were quickly gathering on the horizon.

However, for him the main experiment had succeeded, he had accomplished what he sought for. Nature at another point had outstripped him, yet he had broadened his own sum of knowledge to a prodigious extent. Twelve years later a friend accompanied him on a Sunday drive in New Jersey and Edison in the highest spirits, pointing out with the keenest enjoyment the many beautiful views of valley and wood. The wanderings led to the old ore-milling plant, by then practically a mass of deserted buildings all going to decay. It was a depressing sight, marking such titanic but futile struggles with nature.

To Edison, however, no trace of sentiment or regret occurred, and the whole ruins were apparently as much a matter of unconcern as if he were viewing the remains of Pompeii. Sitting on the porch of the house where he lived during that period, in the light of the setting sun, his fine face in repose, he looked as placidly over the scene as a happy farmer over a field of ripening corn. 'I never felt better in my life than during the five years I worked here' he said. 'Hard work, nothing to divert my thought, clear air and simple food made my life very pleasant. We learned a great deal. It will be of benefit to someone some time'.[429]

Walt Disney was an American entrepreneur, animator, voice actor and film producer. He had Sedna in the seventh house of relationships, square his Mars in the fourth house of home.

He had high standards and high expectations of those with whom he worked. Although there have been accusations that he was racist or anti-semitic, these have been contradicted by many who knew him. A pioneer of the American animation industry, he introduced several new developments in the production of cartoons, including the first cartoon feature film.

---

[429] Dyer, Frank Lewis, and Martin, Thomas Commerford. *Edison, His Life and Inventions*

He first created Mickey Mouse when he was 27, for a single test screening of the short, Plane Crazy, but it failed to find a distributor. Following the sensational response to his next short, he used synchronised sound on the third to create the first sound cartoon. After the animation was complete, he signed a contract with the former executive of Universal Pictures to use the Cinephone recording system and they became the new distributor for his early sound cartoons.

The cartoons soon became so popular that he felt he was not receiving his rightful share of profits, so the next year he asked for an increase in payments. Cinephone refused and signed the graphic artist who had been working with him, to work for them instead. As a result, just before his thirtieth birthday, he had a nervous breakdown and he took an extended holiday to Cuba with his wife and they had a cruise to Panama to recover.

However, he had earlier in his career had a successful cartoon character removed from his control by the person who owned the rights, so he had made sure that he owned the rights to Mickey. He signed a new contract with Columbia Pictures to distribute the cartoons, which became increasingly popular, including internationally.[430]

As a film producer, he holds the record for most Academy Awards earned by an individual, having won 22 Oscars, from 59 nominations. His Sedna is also opposite his Moon in the first house of identity, which made him very sensitive to how his stories and characters would connect with people and he was able to read the pulse of the American people with his films, so much so, that in the rest of the world they came to be seen as cultural imperialism.

Our case study, James Lovelock, is a British independent scientist, environmentalist and futurologist who lives in Devon, England. He has Sedna on the cusp of the sixth house, square Mars in the ninth house of knowledge. While working as a consultant for NASA in his forties, he developed the Gaia Hypothesis for which he is best known. Gaia hypothesis postulates that the biosphere of the Earth is a self-regulating entity with the capacity to keep our planet healthy by controlling the chemical and physical environment.

---

[430] https://en.wikipedia.org/wiki/Walt_Disney

However, in his book, *The Revenge of Gaia*, published when he was 87, he argues that the lack of respect humans have had for Gaia, through the damage done to rainforests and the reduction in planetary biodiversity, is testing Gaia's capacity to minimize the effects of the addition of greenhouse gases in the atmosphere. This eliminates the planet's negative feedbacks and increases the likelihood of runaway global warming.

Three years later he published *The Vanishing Face of Gaia*, rejecting scientific modelling that disagreed with the scientific findings that sea levels are rising faster, and Arctic ice is melting faster than the models predict. And suggesting that we may already be beyond the tipping point of terrestrial climate resilience into a permanently hot state. Given these conditions, he expects human civilization will be hard pressed to survive in the coming years.

> At that point he expected the change to be similar to the Paleocene-Eocene period when atmospheric concentration of CO2 was high and at that point the Arctic Ocean was 23 °C and had crocodiles in it, with the rest of the world mostly scrub and desert. Seven years later however, at 97 his position on climate change had changed dramatically, saying: 'Anyone who tries to predict more than five to 10 years is a bit of an idiot, because so many things can change unexpectedly.' He now believes that "CO2 is going up, but nowhere near as fast as they thought it would.

> There are various possible explanations for his change of heart. One is that he is right, and the models on which his former predictions were based were fatally flawed. Another is that his iconoclastic sensibility made revision irresistible. An incorrigible subversive, Lovelock was warning the world about climate change for decades before it began to pay attention, and just when the scientific consensus began to call for intervention to prevent it, he decided we were already too late.

> But there is a third explanation for why he has shifted his position again, he expects that before the consequences of global warming can impact on us significantly, something else will have made our world unrecognisable, and threaten the human race, the rise of Artificial Intelligence. 'Before we've reach the end of

this century, I think what people call robots will have taken over. They will be in charge of us, if we're still here.

'It is possible that human beings may fuse with robots to become a blend of robotic and human tissue, but the likelier scenario will be pure robots, because that will probably be their preference. The implications for climate change are obvious. The world that they're going to be comfortable in is wildly different from the one that we feel comfortable in. So once they really get established, they will, with regret, start losing organic life.'[431]

Humour can be one path to transcend the quicksand of Sedna, giving us the objectivity to step back from the edge, but also with the stressful aspects to Mars the challenge to be ready for any opportunity. Those of us struggling with stressful aspects to Mars would be well advised to develop their sense of humour.

Carol Burnett is an American comedienne on stage, in films and on TV. An outstanding performer, she has won many Emmys and other awards. She had Sedna in the first house of identity, sesquiquadrate her Mars in the sixth house of service.

Her father died when she was 21 and her mother 12 years later. She became the primary caretaker of her 12-year-old sister from the age of 22. Her sister later said, "She always seemed to have a great inner strength and discipline. Her grades were good because she applied herself. Fate may have stepped in here and there, but she was ready for opportunity."

In college, she headed toward journalism and cartooning, that is, until she was bitten by the stage-bug. When she took a college role on stage and heard the first laugh, her path was set. She acted, she sang, she tried comedy, and for the first time in her life, had a measure of popularity. It was heady stuff after being a wallpaper nerd. With every bit of approval, her confidence grew. The doors opened when she was given a thousand-dollars to go to New York, on the stipulation that she would pay it back, keep the donor anonymous and help others who were starting out.

---

[431] Aitkenhead, Decca. *Guardian* online, https://www.theguardian.com/environment/2016/sep/30/james-lovelock-interview-by-end-of-century-robots-will-have-taken-over

She reached New York at 21, working as a hatcheck girl while organising a show. On opening night, she came onstage in a housedress and curlers to sing and skewer "Monotonous," a sexy Eartha Kitt number. She got three bows and a lot of bravos. The *Carol Burnett Show* made its debut when she was 34, bringing into her lexicon of characters her singing charwoman, dimwitted secretary Mrs. Wiggins and raging Eunice's dysfunctional family. Mostly, she pillaged the movies she loved. None of the old movies were safe from her relentless hilarity and she got to be all the magical characters she had watched on the screen while growing up - with a little something extra.

The show became the longest running on the air when it hit 11 years. It closed when she was 44, after reaping a total of 22 Emmy awards. Many of the people she's worked with have become part of her extended family, and they return her loyalty and devotion. Some have remarked on how generous she was as a performer, giving away great punch lines, and others say she extends generosity in her look, her humour and everything she does.[432]

At this juncture in human evolution, few of us use our planets at the spiritual level, but many of us are striving to, and such people are wonderful to be around. As with the other planets, the spiritual level of evolution is vastly different with Sedna from the two previous levels. Here, the stressful aspects with Mars challenges us to make a unique contribution to our collective spiritual growth.

Once we embrace the Sedna energy, which is the oneness of everything, our actions and passions become an expression of Sedna consciousness and they become devotional in nature. The struggle of the beginner's level is gone, as are the transcendental crises of the intermediate level. At this level everything Saturnian is meaningless and yet everything Sednian has its place.

Walden Welch was a California astrologer and psychic. He had Sedna in the eighth house of sensitivity to the spirit world, semi-square a very close conjunction of his Mars and Uranus, the planet of intuition, and also Vesta the asteroid of regeneration, all in the tenth house of profession.

---

[432] https://en.wikipedia.org/wiki/Carol_Burnett

His career began at the age of 17 when he moved to San Francisco and started doing psychic readings. At 18 he began using astrological charts for more accuracy in the timing of his predictions. He moved to San Francisco the following year and studied under spiritual teachers and started following the writings of the 'sleeping prophet', Edgar Cayce. He credited the teachings of Cayce as his greatest influence.

When he was 24 he moved to Sonoma, where he and his homosexual partner opened an antique shop. While his partner operated the successful antique business, Walden did readings for many years from his spacious office in the back of the building. They married when he was 64, after 45 years of relationship, as soon as California law allowed it. His career also included lecturing and appearing on radio and television shows and for five years he hosted his own television shows, *Walden Welch, Astrologer*, and *Star Talk*.[433]

Zoe Wells was an American artist and psychic who worked with Marc Edmund Jones and Elsie Wheeler on the 360 degree meanings that became known as the Sabian Symbols. She had Sedna on the cusp of the eleventh house of collective consciousness, square her Mars in the first house of identity.

When she was 40 she was a recognized commercial artist and student of Marc's and she possessed remarkable psychic skills. In an experimental session she brought through fifty-two symbols for a pack of ordinary playing cards. Marc described this event, in his book, *The Sabian Symbols in Astrology*, as the 'beginning of a conscious recognition of the ancient sources as a self-contained and living integrity available for use.'[434]

Sri Meher Baba was an Indian religious figure who was known as "The Silent Guru." He was born in India to Irani Zoroastrian parents. He had Sedna in the second house of material resources, square Mars in the twelfth house of the unconscious.

At the age of 19, he began a seven-year spiritual transformation and during this time he contacted five spiritual masters before

---

[433] https://www.astro.com/astro-databank/Welch,_Walden
[434] https://www.astro.com/astro-databank/Wells,_Zoe

beginning his own mission and gathering his own disciples at the age of 27. His early followers gave him the name Meher Baba, meaning "Compassionate Father".[435]

His Sedna is also inconjunct the Moon, the planet of emotions, in the ninth house of spirituality.

He moved into silence at 31 and did not speak until his death. To communicate, he spelled words on the alphabet board with quick fingers, such as "I am the Supreme Spirit." From the age of 60 he used unique sign language of gestures, rather than the alphabet board. With his circle of disciples, he spent long periods in seclusion, during which time he often fasted. He also traveled widely, held public gatherings and engaged in works of charity with lepers, the poor and the mentally ill.[436]

His Sedna is also quintile Haumea, the planet of rebirth, in the fifth house of creativity, semi-square Venus, the planet of values in the first house of identity, and sesquiquadrate Juno, the asteroid of partnership, in the tenth house of profession.

He gave numerous teachings on the cause and purpose of life, including teaching reincarnation and that the phenomenal world is an illusion. He taught that the Universe is imagination, that God is what really exists, and that each soul is really God passing through imagination to realise individually His own divinity.

In addition, he gave practical advice for the aspirant who wishes to attain self-realization and thereby escape the wheel of birth and death. He also taught about the concept of Perfect Masters, the Avatar, and those on the various stages of the spiritual path that he called involution. His teachings are most importantly recorded in his principal books, *Discourses* and *God Speaks*. And his legacy includes an influence on pop-culture artists and the introduction of common expressions such as 'Don't Worry, Be Happy'.[437]

---

[435] https://en.wikipedia.org/wiki/Meher_Baba
[436] Ibid.
[437] Ibid.

In-conjunct

With the evolutionary inconjunct between Sedna and Mars the esoteric spiritual energy of Sedna bursts into our actions and passions in an evolutionary way and we have a fated role to play.

The inconjunct sometimes acts as a flow and at other times as a stress, so we have to learn to actively manage the process, as the rarified spiritual energy sometimes reinforces our actions and at other times isn't there to back us up. By adjusting to this, we gain a deeper understanding of ourselves and how to play our role.

Mars relates to our basic sexual nature, how we express our anger, our temper and our first instinct to act. The god of war in ancient times, Mars could be brutally violent and so the planet rules our competitive nature. It shows the areas of life where we apply our drive and express our enthusiasm, where we take action and assert ourselves. And it relates to stamina, ambition and achievement.

The inconjunct brings a fated purpose to this energy, and when we are using it positively, we are assertive, directed, forthright, and adventurous. However, if we are unconscious of the Sedna influence, there can be a sense of righteousness in our actions, which may blind us to the actual reality and will, at the very least, make our actions appear odd, or sit uncomfortably with other people.

If we are misusing our Mars energy, we will be impulsive, rash, impatient, aggressive, and forceful, and if we are unconscious of our Sedna energy we are more likely to express this negative side. Unfortunately, this behaviour is likely to invite similar responses, so we might feel victimized without really understanding that we brought it on ourselves.

Garrett Watterson is an American victim of hazing. He has Sedna in the ninth house of higher learning, inconjunct his Mars in the fourth house of home.

> Legally blind in one eye, knew he would never be a star swinging a baseball bat or shooting hoops, but as a lineman on Sandwich High School's freshman football team, he thought he'd found his sport. Now the 14-year-old freshman faces new physical hurdles, delivered by a body blow so devastating that doctors had to remove his spleen on Tuesday. He suffered the injury during a what officials described as a hazing episode at football practice,

where an upperclassman yanked his ankles out from under him in a "freshman beat-down." It irrevocably changed his life. From now on, he will require routine immunizations and regular antibiotics to combat the bacteria normally filtered by the spleen.[438]

Edward Cherubin is an American who was charged with homicide at age 22, when he had an altercation with an 18-year-old girl. He had Sedna in the seventh house of relationships, inconjunct his Mars in the second house of material reality.

The victim approached him while he was making a telephone call in a supermarket parking lot. Appearing annoyed, he shouted at her and pushed her forcefully away. When a friend of the victim questioned him about his pushing the victim, the friend was told in foul language to move away. The victim left. Shortly thereafter, accompanied by two friends, she started to return by foot to the scene of the confrontation.

While she was crossing the street, approaching the curb near the supermarket, he drove his automobile out of the parking lot, the car screeching as it turned the corner into the street that she and her two friends were crossing. He aimed the car first at one of her friends, struck that friend, and then swerved toward the victim, hit her, ran over her body with the car, and swiftly left the scene without stopping. He was convicted of second degree murder, two counts of assault and battery by means of a dangerous weapon, and of leaving the scene after causing personal injury.[439]

Winnie Ruth Judd was an American secretary and homicide perpetrator. She had Sedna in the sixth house of service, inconjunct her Mars in the first house of identity.

A tiny, sweet-faced, redheaded young woman with enigmatic blue eyes, she married at 18, quitting nursing school to wed Dr. William Judd, a widower, more than 20 years her senior. Seeking

---

438

http://archive.boston.com/news/local/massachusetts/articles/2004/09/18/for_victim_ a_heavy_penalty/

[439] https://law.justia.com/cases/massachusetts/court-of- appeals/volumes/35/35massappct919.html

the desert climate for her health, she moved to Phoenix by herself at 25 and lived with two other female flatmates, who had some good times together, aided by prohibition hooch and a number of free-spending gentleman callers. When Judd and one of the other girls started up dating the same man, Judd moved out. Then one night when her beau did not call, she went to her friend's apartment, but he was not there. According to prosecutors, she then killed her two ex flatmates in cold blood as they slept in their beds.

Her story is that they argued. One of the others brought out a pistol that Judd had left there when she moved out. As the two struggled, the gun went off twice, killing the girl. The second girl swung an ironing board at her and Judd shot her. A gunshot wound on her hand and 147 bruises lent credence to her story; however, she never told this story of self-defence in court, but kept silent to protect her married lover, whom she said had assured her that he would "take care of things."

Evading the gallows by declaring insanity, she escaped seven times from an asylum for the criminally insane, until her parole and release 38 years later. During one of her periods on the outside, she worked for a wealthy blind woman as a companion; it was to this family in northern California that she went when she was released. After her employer died, she wound up suing the family for keeping her in in virtual slavery and won a $50,000 settlement and a lifetime monthly income of $1,250, then lived out her years quietly under an assumed name.[440]

As we tire of density and the grief it creates, and we start a spiritual journey to get out of the swamp, Sedna rewards us with transcendent crises, experiences which force us to let go and rise above them, resulting in a huge growth to a new level of consciousness. There is no choice with these crises, and the more we try and solve them, the more we will get hurt.

Jean-Paul Sartre was a French writer, existentialist philosopher, novelist, essayist and playwright. He had Sedna in the third house of ideas and communication, inconjunct his Mars in the eleventh house of collective consciousness.

---

[440] https://en.wikipedia.org/wiki/Winnie_Ruth_Judd

With a vindictive and angry personality, he was self-confident, knowing he was smarter than other children. His philosophy of existentialism stated that the world had no meaning for mankind, but instead proposed that the individual is responsible for his or her own purpose.

His life-long companion was Simone de Beauvoir, who offered emotional and professional support in their open relationship, begun when he was 24. They were lovers and associates, but never married, each having other lovers. Simone became his editor and co-writer with no credit.

From the age of 34 he served as the leader of the French intelligentsia. One of his most famous essays, "Being and Nothingness" was published when he was 38. His fame grew over the next two years, as he rejected God and external values, touting existentialism as the philosophy to study. He became co-editor of the magazine *Les Temps Modernes.* His politics moved to the left when he was in his early 50s. He was awarded the Nobel Prize for Literature at 59, but declined on political grounds.[441]

Peter Sellers was a British-American actor, a comedian and bizarre character star, best known for the 'Pink Panther' series of films. He had Sedna in the eighth house of the spirit world and of shared resources, conjunct Nessus, the centaur which is sometimes called the sympathetic monster because of its demands for radical change, and inconjunct his Mars, which is together with his Sun, his willpower, in the first house of identity.

He was the only child of variety-show troupers, and grew up in theatrical boarding houses. He was close to his overbearing mom, who died when he was 42, and he claimed to be able to communicate with her after her death.

He wanted to be a drummer, but there wasn't a lot of demand for the work. In World War II he was in a RAF musical troupe, entertaining airmen in India and the Middle East. After the war, he worked his way up through vaudeville, variety shows at London's Palladium, radio and into the movies. He was first

---

[441] https://en.wikipedia.org/wiki/Jean-Paul_Sartre

noticed on *The Goon Show*, which aired on British TV when he was in his mid to late twenties. At 26 he appeared in his first feature-length motion picture and by the age of 40 he was ranked as one of England's great comic actors.

He made more than 50 films, but in the industry he had a reputation for being a monster who was hard to work with, impossibly difficult and 'basically not a nice man'. Once during a marital fight, he tried to kill a puppy. He abused his friends, and even wrote his children out of his will. He was an odd man who became haunted by death and who took drugs to enhance sex.[442]

Oprah Winfrey is an American talk show hostess, actress and business executive. She has Sedna in the fourth house of home, inconjunct her Mars in the eleventh house of collective consciousness.

She is North America's first and only multi-billionaire black person and several assessments rank her as the most influential woman in the world. However, she was born into poverty in rural Mississippi to a teenage single mother and later raised in an inner-city Milwaukee neighbourhood. She has stated that she was molested during her childhood and early teens and became pregnant at 14. Her son died in infancy.

She is credited with creating a more intimate confessional form of media communication, the *Oprah Winfrey Show*, which was the highest-rated television program of its kind in history and was nationally syndicated in the US from 1986 to 2011. She popularised and revolutionised the tabloid talk show genre, which a Yale study says broke 20th century taboos and allowed LGBT people to enter the mainstream.

By the mid-1990s, she had reinvented her show with a focus on literature, self-improvement, and spirituality. Though criticised for unleashing a confession culture, promoting controversial self-help ideas, and an emotion-centered approach, she is often praised for overcoming adversity to become a benefactor to others.[443]

---

[442] https://en.wikipedia.org/wiki/Peter_Sellers
[443] https://en.wikipedia.org/wiki/Oprah_Winfrey

Spike Milligan was a British director and writer best known for *The Goon Show,* which began as a radio series when he was 33. He had Sedna in the second house of material resources, inconjunct his Mars in the seventh house of relationships.

> The son of a British military man, he was raised in India, Burma and Ceylon, arriving in England at 15. He started his career as a singer, trumpet player and guitar player. His big break came in his 30s in a show called *Crazy People*, which eventually became the legendary Goon Show.

> He wrote much of his own comedy material for the show as well as many TV vehicles. In addition to radio and TV scripts, he also wrote several comedy novels and a book of nonsense and verse, in spite of his own lifetime battle with depression. Diagnosed as being bi-polar, he was noted for being difficult and demanding to work with. His career on screen never matched his success on radio and TV, but his books and comedy recordings maintained their popularity long after the end of the *Goons* and he received a Lifetime Achievement Award given at the British Comedy Awards in at the age of 76.[444]

As we see, humour can be one path to transcend the quicksand of Sedna, giving us the objectivity to step back from the edge, but also with the inconjunct to Mars the fated opportunity to create a unique form of entertainment.

Bill Irwin is an American actor, clown and comedian, who combined his talents to create characters for comedy skits in performance art, a unique form of entertainment. He began as a vaudeville-style stage performer and has been noted for his contribution to the renaissance of American circus. He has Sedna in the twelfth house of the unconscious, inconjunct his Mars in the fifth house of creativity.

> Almost everyone in his family was stage-struck, with his maternal grandfather putting on plays and pageants and his father designing sets for community theatre productions. He made his stage debut when he was still in school with a post-modern dance group and performed in student productions at high schools in the U.S. and in Northern Ireland. Then studied theatre

---

[444] ttps://en.wikipedia.org/wiki/Spike_Milligan

at the University of California, and the California Institute of the Arts in Valencia, where his curriculum included dance, mime, gymnastics and t'ai chi.

At 24 he decided to attend Clown College, an intensive training school for circus performers at the winter headquarters of Barnum & Bailey Circus in Florida. He mastered the basics of elephant riding, juggling and acrobatics. Returning to San Francisco, he answered a newspaper ad for jugglers, and was hired to be a clown with the Pickle Family Circus, a small one-ring act. He supplemented his income by teaching and performing in city schools and by entertaining at trade shows, festivals and private parties.

In his spare time, he created comedy sketches, and at 27, he and some of his collaborators were invited to perform their short sketches. The trio toured Italy, France and the Netherlands.

Upon returning to the United States, Irwin joined the Oberlin Dance Collective, and his comic inventions were so impressive that he was hired to present skits as part of a new, late-night series of performance events. This introduced him to a wider audience and earned him a special Obie Award for "inspired clowning" at the age of 31.

Obsessed with his work, he has been compared to such greats as Charlie Chaplin and Buster Keaton for his unique form of entertainment, which includes juggling and tumbling. At 34 he received the Guggenheim Fellowship and a five-year MacArthur Foundation Fellowship, the first active performing artist to receive the award in the foundation's history.[445]

At this juncture in human evolution, few of us use our planets at the spiritual level, but many of us are striving to, and such people are wonderful to be around. As with the other planets, the spiritual level of evolution is vastly different with Sedna from the two previous levels. Here, with the inconjunct to Mars we are fated to make a unique contribution to our collective spiritual growth.

Once we embrace the Sedna energy, which is the oneness of everything, our actions and passions become an expression of Sedna

---

[445] https://en.wikipedia.org/wiki/Bill_Irwin

consciousness and they become devotional in nature. The struggle of the beginner's level is gone, as are the transcendental crises of the intermediate level. At this level everything Saturnian is meaningless and yet everything Sednian has its place.

Like Maxine Bell, who was an American trance medium, pianist and composer. She had Sedna in the tenth house of profession, inconjunct her Mars in the third house of ideas and communication. Her Sedna was also bi-quintile Juno, the asteroid of partnership, in the fifth house of creativity, and sextile Mercury, the planet of ideas and communication, in the eleventh house of collective consciousness. She played the works of dead masters while in trance and was able to play 3,000 notes per minute. She also worked with the Los Angeles Police Department on murder cases, as a psychic.

Or Kiyokazu Kitamura, who is a Japanese religious leader known as the 'Honourable Princess God'. She has Sedna in the eleventh house of collective consciousness, inconjunct her Mars in the fourth house of home. At the age of 18 she succeeded her grandmother as leader of the Shinto-based new religion, known as the Dancing Religion, which her grandmother founded five years before she was born.

And Doris Conway Battle was an American astrologer who was the first American woman to be certified by the Faculty of Astrological Studies in London. She had Sedna in the eleventh house of collective consciousness, inconjunct her Mars in the fifth house of creativity. At 36, she became the first American woman to be certified by the Faculty of Astrological Studies headed by Margaret Hone and founded under the auspices of the Astrological Lodge of London.

Quintile, Bi-quintile

The evolutionary quintile or bi-quintile aspect between Sedna and Mars infuses our actions and passions with the all-encompassing spiritual energy of Sedna to the point where we can push the boundaries of human development.

Quintiles and bi-quintiles point to talent, the desire to create order and to categorize, a fascination with patterns and structures, perfectionist tendencies, and the desire to build or make things. These aspects have the characteristics of both the trine and opposition. They point to awareness of conflicts, or problems and finding solutions for them;

however, they do not automatically kick into action and must be cultivated over time.

Mars relates to our basic sexual nature, how we express our anger, our temper and our first instinct to act. The god of war in ancient times, Mars could be brutally violent and so the planet rules our competitive nature. It shows the areas of life where we apply our drive and express our enthusiasm, where we take action and assert ourselves. And it relates to stamina, ambition and achievement.

When we are using our Mars energy positively, we are assertive, directed, forthright, and adventurous; however, if we are unconscious of the Sedna influence, there can be a sense of righteousness in our actions which will, at the very least, appear odd, or sit uncomfortably with other people and can send us on a bit of an unconscious personal mission, or make us a victim of someone else's unconscious mission.

Like Patricia Gilmore, who was an American homicide victim, murdered at age 24 by her lover. She had Sedna in the tenth house of profession, quintile Mars in the twelfth house of the unconscious.

> Her boyfriend was so possessive and jealous he would not take her out where other men might see and admire her, and so controlling, that when she broke it off, he went to the place where she worked, slashed his wrists and smeared her and her car with his blood. He stalked her and made repeated phone calls, ignoring the restraining order that she had requested. Later that year he was convicted of threats and sent to State Mental Hospital for observation, and from there to jail.
>
> She worked at the bank as a teller and customarily went home for lunch. Out of jail on a 24-hour leave, he kidnapped her at gunpoint. He fled with her, evading helicopters, squad cars and police cruisers on search, with her mom and eight brothers and sisters on alert. He stabbed her 29 times and pushed her out of the car, where her body was found. Six months later, he was convicted of first-degree murder and given life in prison.[446]

Julian Assange is an Australian whistleblower, with a background is in physics, math and computer programming, living in political asylum in

---

[446] https://www.astro.com/astro-databank/Gilmore,_Patricia

the embassy of Ecuador in London. He has Sedna in the sixth house of service, quintile his Mars in the fourth house of home.

> He is best known for his work with WikiLeaks, which is supposedly an investigative journalism Internet-based organization, with a mission to make public otherwise secret information, but which is designated by the US government as a hostile non-state intelligence service.

> He is spokesperson and editor-in-chief of the organization. His name became nearly a household word when at 39 he leaked over 250,000 classified diplomatic cables of the US government and therefore caused an uproar in government circles. Prior to that he had published many classified documents and a video from the Iraq and Afghanistan Wars.

> That same year the Swedish government posted a warrant for his arrest on rape and molestation charges. The warrant cited one count of unlawful coercion, two counts of sexual molestation and one count of rape. He denied the charges, but refused to face the courts, fighting his extradition. Two years later he walked into the embassy of Ecuador in London to ask for political asylum and five years on he is still living there in virtual house arrest, unable to leave without being arrested.[447]

Paula Yates was a Welsh TV personality in the UK, a tarted-up presenter of the TV series *The Tube*, who loved to use "shock" as an attention-getter and whose approach took her from flirtatious celebrity interviewer to celebrity in her own right. She had Sedna in the fourth house of home, quintile Mars in the seventh house of relationships.

> Engagingly ebullient and flirtatious, her irreverent approach to the rich-and-famous won her industry awards twice. As a provocative columnist and author, her subjects ranged from baby care to sexual turn-ons. However, it was her notably frank autobiography that made her best known.

> As a child, she had an uncomfortable relationship with her dad, TV star Jess Yates, who was known as "the Bishop" for his presentation of the religious show *Stars on Sunday*. It was an unconventional childhood in a unique family. Her dad was 16-

---

[447] https://en.wikipedia.org/wiki/Julian_Assange

years-older than her mom, Heller Thornton, a former showgirl, actress and writer of erotic novels. From age eight, the girl lived mostly with her mom, at times in Malta and Majorca.

It was a considerable revelation to discover when she was 38, via DNA testing, that Yates was not her father at all, but rather, her dad was Hughie Green, TV host of several popular shows. When she found this out, it added further strain to her relationship with her mom, which was already tenuous.

She started a relationship with Bob Geldof at 18 and produced her first book, *Rockstars In Their Underpants*, consisting of semi-clad photographs of everyone she and Geldof knew. They finally married in Las Vegas when she was 27. They had three daughters and she wrote two books about parenting, in which she urged women to stay at home to look after their children and to breast feed their babies for as long as possible.

Her big break came when she was recruited as co-presenter of *The Tube*, an anarchic TV pop show which swiftly developed cult status. She stayed with the show for five years, winning the best documentary award at the New York Film Festival two years running for her interviews with Tina Turner and Elton John. She graduated to Channel Four's early morning program, *The Big Breakfast*, where she interviewed stars while everyone reclined on a large bed.

At 36, she was fired from her TV hostess job and her tangled life began its most turbulent period. She began an impassioned affair with the Michael Hutchence, singer with the rock group INXS, whom she called "a sexy love god." They had met the year before and began a three-year affair. She was linked to alcohol and drugs and Geldof secured custody of their three daughters. She had her breasts enlarged and trilled that the first time she and Michael went to bed, "he did six things within the first hour I was sure were illegal."

Pregnant, she divorced Geldof and gave birth to Michael's daughter, Heavenly Tiger Lily. She and Michael were planning to marry and move to Australia and were negotiating the purchase of a house overlooking Sydney Harbour. Michael's drug days were allegedly over and they both were filled with promise when mysteriously and tragically Michael was found dead in a hotel room.

Paula insisted that it was an accident rather than a suicide, but was nonetheless treated several times for depression and made a suicide attempt herself the next year. She was found dead at her home in London two years later. Her body was found by a friend after repeated phone calls went unanswered. Tiger Lily was playing by herself when Mummy would not wake up, and an empty vodka bottle and half-empty one of barbiturates left mute testimony.[448]

As we tire of density and the grief it creates, and we start a spiritual journey to get out of the swamp, Sedna rewards us with transcendent crises, experiences which force us to let go and rise above them, resulting in a huge growth to a new level of consciousness. There is no choice with these crises, and the more we try and solve them, the more we will get hurt.

L. Ron Hubbard was an American entrepreneur, engineer, and prolific writer of science fiction, who established the Church of Scientology. He had Sedna in the third house of ideas, quintile Mars, conjunct Uranus, the planet of intuition, in the second house of material resources.

Imaginative, intelligent, and with a mind that was a factory of ideas, he was also broke and in debt in the late 1940s and was forced to sell his typewriter for $28.50 to pay alimony to his first wife. Troubled, restless and adrift he became an expert hypnotist, and shared an ageing mansion in Pasadena with writers, artists, bohemians and occultists in the late 1940s. Neighbours complained when their rituals of sexual magic got out of hand in the back yard.[449]

His Sedna was also conjunct Orcus, the planet of delving down and speaking out in the fourth house of home, and bi-quintile Ixion, the planet of lawlessness, in the ninth house of knowledge.

He wrote a book, *Dianetics: The Modern Science of Mental Health,* which was written in one draft in 30 days and became an instant bestseller. He became an overnight celebrity. His system

---

[448] https://en.wikipedia.org/wiki/Paula_Yates
[449] https://en.wikipedia.org/wiki/L._Ron_Hubbard

became known as "the poor man's psychotherapy." However, by the following year profits were beginning to fall and Dianetics became Scientology, as he turned from pop therapist to religious leader.

Skillfully transforming himself from a pulp fiction writer to a writer of "sacred scriptures," Hubbard made a fortune and achieved his dream of fame. Starting as a collection of mental therapy centers it grew into one of the world's most controversial and secretive religions. The courses included instruction of how to help kick drug habits, improve communication skills, build confidence and help people take control of their lives.

However, by preying on the anxieties and the loneliness of his converts and by using hypnotherapy, Pavlovian conditioning and twisted psychotherapy, he was able to establish himself as the leader of a movement of millions, less than 900 of which ever reached the highest levels of his imparted wisdom. Australian courts have since revoked the status of Scientology as a religion, and France convicted Hubbard in absentia of fraud. However, in spite of all the exposure, he still ignited the fire of self-improvement in many sincere people.[450]

Charles Darwin was an English naturalist, geologist and biologist, best known for his contributions to the science of evolution and as author of *Origin of the Species*. He had Sedna in the third house of ideas, bi-quintile his Mars in the tenth house of profession.

He established that all species of life have descended over time from common ancestors and introduced his scientific theory that this branching pattern of evolution resulted from a process that he called natural selection, in which the struggle for existence has a similar effect to the artificial selection involved in selective breeding. His theories of evolution through natural selection instigated a revolution in biological science.

He published his theory with compelling evidence in his book, *On the Origin of Species* when he was 50. Within a decade or two the scientific community and much of the general public had accepted evolution as a fact. However, many favoured

---

[450] Ibid.

competing explanations and it was not until the emergence of the modern evolutionary synthesis, some 50 to 70 years after his death, that a broad consensus developed in which natural selection was the basic mechanism of evolution. His scientific discovery is the unifying theory of the life sciences, explaining the diversity of life.

His father was a freethinker, believing that positions regarding truth should be formed on the basis of logic, reason, and empiricism, rather than authority, tradition, revelation, or other dogma, but he was brought up by his mother within the Unitarian Christian Church. He later said, "I never gave up Christianity until I was forty years of age." He then agreed that Christianity was "not supported by the evidence," but he had reached this conclusion only slowly.

However, his Theory of Evolution is recognised as having impacted massively on human societies across the World, not least in the areas of faith and religious beliefs. These diverse impacts on so many aspects of human lives have been so far-reaching that a "Darwinian Revolution" has been accepted as having taken place. Interestingly, he hesitated about making his theory - which he had crafted into a 'publishable' sketch by his early 30s - widely known in his own lifetime. His wife was sincerely religious and he also seems to have feared for his own and his family's perceived respectability if he made his potentially massively controversial evolutionary views public.[451]

Carl Sagan is an American astronomer, astrophysicist, exobiologist, educator, and popular celebrity. He has Sedna in the twelfth house of the unconscious, bi-quintile his Mars, conjunct Neptune, the planet of dreams and visions, in the fifth house of creativity.

As a child he is said to have gazed with awe at the heavens and speculated on the existence of life beyond earth. At 12 he told his grandfather he wanted to be an astronomer and vowed to be on a university faculty so he could support himself in his chosen field, which he did. He became a noted authority on planetary atmospheres and surfaces, and was a leading consultant to NASA's space exploration program. His book, *Cosmos* was a

---

[451] https://en.wikipedia.org/wiki/Charles_Darwin

best seller for over a year. The TV series by the same name was seen by more than 500 million people in 60 countries. He inspired a generation with his enthusiastic lectures, books and documentaries about space and life.

A prolific writer, he wrote, co-wrote or edited over 20 books and hundreds of articles. Among his other contributions, he is credited with identifying the boiling hot nature of Venus and the dust storms of Mars. At 44, he won the Pulitzer Prize for nonfiction for *The Dragons of Eden*, his book about the evolution of human intelligence. At 63 he co-produced the movie, *Contact*, based on his novel by the same name. He was a keen proponent of the idea that intelligent life might be found in the universe, but dismissed UFO's, lost continents and astrology as 'pseudoscientific twaddle'.[452]

Humour can be one path to transcend the quicksand of Sedna, giving us the objectivity to step back from the edge, but also with the quintile and bi-quintile aspects to Mars the opportunity to be uniquely ourselves.

Sandra Bernhard is an American comedienne, tall, skinny, aggressive, ultra-hip, manic, bearing a mouth and nose that have been compared respectively to Jagger and Streisand. She has Sedna in the tenth house of profession, quintile her Mars in the twelfth house of the unconscious.

She was born in Flint, Michigan, to a proctologist father and an abstract-artist mother. After she graduated she spent eight months in Israel on a kibbutz. She then moved to Los Angeles where she lived with an aunt and uncle and went to beauty school to learn how to be a manicurist, while pursuing her comedy career. Her early stand-up comedy acts were not major successes initially.

She became hot property in her late 20s, after working for five years as a manicurist and stand-up comic prior to landing a lead role in *The King of Comedy* with Robert de Niro, released when she was 28. She did nightclubs, TV and films. She is most remembered for playing lesbian Nancy Bartlett on the television show *Roseanne* for six years from the age of 36. She has one daughter, Cicely, born when she was 43. She has never said

---

[452] https://en.wikipedia.org/wiki/Carl_Sagan

who the father is, nor how the child was conceived, but she is openly bisexual and is a strong supporter of gay rights.[453]

At this juncture in human evolution, few of us use our planets at the spiritual level, but many of us are striving to, and such people are wonderful to be around. As with the other planets, the spiritual level of evolution is vastly different with Sedna from the two previous levels. Here, the quintile and bi-quintile aspects with Mars inspires us to make a unique contribution to our collective spiritual growth.

Once we embrace the Sedna energy, which is the oneness of everything, our actions and passions become an expression of Sedna consciousness and they become devotional in nature. The struggle of the beginner's level is gone, as are the transcendental crises of the intermediate level. At this level everything Saturnian is meaningless and yet everything Sednian has its place.

Barack Obama, the first African American president, has Sedna in the second house of material resources, bi-quintile his Mars in the seventh house of relationships.

> A self-described "skinny kid with a funny name," he is the child of a Kenyan man and an American woman. His parents met at the University of Hawaii where they were both students. When Barack was two, his father returned to Africa, and the young boy lived in Hawaii with his mom and grandparents. After his mother married an Indonesian, she took him with her when she moved to her new husband's native country. Young Barack was sent back to Hawaii at age 10 to live with his grandparents.

> He graduated in 1983 from Columbia University with a degree in political science and international relations. He worked in Chicago's inner city, helping church groups improve job-training, education and city services to the poor and then went on to law school at Harvard. In 1996, he was elected to the Illinois General Assembly as a state senator. At 43 he burst onto the national scene when he delivered a rousing keynote address at the Democratic National Convention in Boston. That year he won election to the U.S. Senate by a wide margin.

---

[453] https://en.wikipedia.org/wiki/Sandra_Bernhard

He announced his candidacy for the Democratic Party's nomination for President at 46. On the campaign trail he racked up an impressive number of primary and caucus wins. Exhibiting composure, thoughtfulness, a quick mind and self-deprecating humour, his debate performance earns kudos, while his powerful oratory evoked comparisons to Martin Luther King, Jr. and John F. Kennedy. Along with his life story, which he touts as a representation of the American dream, his emphasis on unity, hope and civility captured media and public attention.

His religious background is more diverse than that of most prominent politicians. But it may prove to be more representative of an increasingly diverse America. His mother was raised by non-practicing Christians; his father was raised a Muslim but was an atheist by the time he had married Obama's mother. His stepfather was also Muslim, but of an eclectic kind who could make room for animist and Hindu beliefs.

In his book, *The Audacity of Hope*, published when he was 45, he writes, 'I was not raised in a religious household. For my mother, organised religion was too often dressed up closed-mindedness in the garb of piety, cruelty and oppression in the cloak of righteousness. However, in her mind, a working knowledge of the world's great religions was a necessary part of any well-rounded education. In our house the Bible, the Koran, sat on the shelf alongside books of Greek and Norse and African mythology.

As a child in Indonesia, he studied for two years at one Muslim school and then two years at a Catholic school. Eventually however, he abandoned this non-conformism and skepticism as an adult to be baptised in the Trinity United Church of Christ, a denomination which emphasises the freedom of the individual conscience over adherence to creeds or hierarchical authority.[454]

Tracy Marks is an American psychotherapist, astrologer, lecturer and teacher who is the author of 15 books and pamphlets which have been translated into nearly a dozen languages. She has Sedna in the fourth house of home, bi-quintile her Mars in the eleventh house of collective consciousness.

---

[454] https://en.wikipedia.org/wiki/Barack_Obama

Some of her more notable books include *How To Handle Your T-Square, The Astrology of Self Discovery,* and *The Art Of Chart Interpretation.* She has a Master's Degree in psycho-synthesis and is acclaimed for her in-depth integration of psychological, spiritual and astrological concepts. She is skilled at leading dream work, women's empowerment, and the art of friendship groups.[455]

Swaminarayan was an Indian religious leader. Also known as Sahajanand Swami, he is the central figure in a modern sect of Hinduism known as the Swaminarayan Hinduism, a form of Vaishnavism. He had Sedna conjunct Nessus, the centaur that acts as a guide to deep energies of regeneration, quintile his Mars on the cusp of the second house of material reality.

At the age of 11 he began a seven-year pilgrimage across India. He settled in the state of Gujarat when he was 18. A year later he was initiated into the Uddhav Sampraday by his guru, Ramanand Swami, and was given the name Sahajanand Swami. In 1802, his guru handed over the leadership of the Uddhav Sampraday to him before his death. Sahajanand Swami held a gathering and taught the Swaminarayan mantra. From this point onwards, he was known as Swaminarayan and within the sect he is regarded as an incarnation of God, Purushottama.

"He developed a good relationship with the British Imperial Government. He had followers not only from Hindu denominations, but also from Islam and Zoroastrianism. He built six temples in his lifetime and appointed 500 paramhansas to spread his philosophy. When he was 45 he wrote the *Shikshapatri,* a book of social principles. He is also remembered within the sect for undertaking reforms for women and the poor, performing yagnas, or fire sacrifices, on a large scale, as well as performing miracles. He had an estimated 1.8 million followers when he died in 1830. By 2007, he had an estimated 20 million followers.[456]

[455] https://www.astro.com/astro-databank/Marks,_Tracy
[456] https://en.wikipedia.org/wiki/Swaminarayan

33: Sedna / Ceres

Sedna is the planet of abundance and famine. Wherever she appears in your chart, she shows how best you feel nurtured. This is also the area where you can easily provide love and comfort.

It also shows how well we go with the flow… the universal one, that is. This is the unification of both giving and receiving through ourselves as an exchange of energy.

Each of the planets demands a burden from us and bestows a gift, and where the burden of Ceres is a spiritual starvation, the gift she bestows is likely a sense of peace and beauty in the truth of the physical world that surrounds us.

Ceres can be thought of as the higher octave of the Moon so the emotional security of the Moon is transmuted to a sustenance and nurturing of our spiritual security and sense of place on Planet Earth with Ceres.

This is very similar to Sedna, only on a far vaster scale, so we may find that Sedna is the higher octave of Ceres. The spiritual security and sense of place on Planet Earth with Ceres, is transmuted into transpersonal nurturing of our spirituality and sense of place in the evolutionary cycle with Sedna.

Conjunction

The conjunction between Ceres and Sedna infuses our potency, our nurturing nature and our ability to deal with change with the all-embracing spiritual energy of Sedna.

Ceres is associated with prosperity and abundance. She represents the actual bounty – the foods, the flowers, the birds and plants, and the desperation that results when the bounty is withdrawn. It shows how well we go with the flow… the universal one, that is. The unification of both giving and receiving through ourselves as an exchange of energy.

Ceres is the planet of prosperity and abundance, but we also associate her with loss, compromise, rage and grief, so unfortunately, along with our bounty, she will also deliver some pretty dramatic episodes when we must give up and give in – triggering deep emotion.

As we embrace the more impersonal energy of Sedna and develop our ability to deal with change, we are likely to feel more at home in ourselves and understand our place in the the bigger picture.

However, if we are unconscious of the Sedna energy and if there are difficult aspects to Ceres, or Sedna we may take the inevitable withdrawals of abundance personally and blame ourselves. In this case we are likely to experience low self-esteem and feelings of abandonment, or unworthiness. These can lead to problems with over-attachment and possessiveness, as we try and compensate.

Like Cinnamon Brown, who is an American convicted of homicide, the killer of her step-mother in collusion with her father. She has Sedna conjunct Ceres and also Juno, the asteroid of partnership, all in the fourth house of home.

> Her father, a true narcissist, was convinced that her mother and her mother's brother were plotting his death in order to take over his money and riches. Because he was a hypochondriac and was convinced that he was too frail to commit such a heinous act, he manipulated both his daughter Cinnamon and his teenage mistress sister-in-law Patricia to commit the acts instead. He repeatedly told the two teenage girls that if they loved him, they'd do this murder for him.

> Cinnamon, being only fourteen years old, followed instruction from her beloved father and took a handful of pills. She then stumbled into the bedroom where her stepmother Linda Brown was sleeping… Without hesitation, the fourteen-year-old bright-eyed youngster grabbed a .38 caliber pistol and shot her stepmother straight in the chest. Minutes after the deadly shooting, she ran outside. She collapsed near the backyard doghouse lying in her own vomit and was nearly unconscious. Tied to her hand was a ribbon with an attached note that read "Dear God, please forgive me. I didn't mean to hurt her."

> She was convicted and sent to Jail, but her father denied responsibility. However he was eventually charged with being the mastermind behind the murder. He was convicted of murder and for setting up his daughter to take the fall. He still maintained his innocence until he passed away from natural causes. She was released and tried to live a normal lifestyle outside of prison

walls. However, tragedy struck yet again when her husband committed suicide.[457]

Or Bernie Madoff, who is a former American businessman, stockbroker, investment advisor, and financier. He has Sedna conjunct Ceres in the eighth house of shared resources.

> He is the former non-executive chairman of the NASDAQ stock market, and the admitted operator of a Ponzi scheme that is considered to be the largest financial fraud in U.S. history. He aroused the suspicion of his two sons when they learned that he intended to pay out bonuses two months early. When they confronted him, he confessed that his entire career was a fraud. He was 70. Arrested the following morning at his Manhattan home, he was sentenced to 150 years in federal prison.[458]

Jean Genet was a French writer, a novelist, playwright and poet. He had Sedna conjunct Ceres in the ninth house of knowledge and publishing.

> Abandoned by his mom, a Parisian prostitute, he was brought up unloved and unschooled by foster parents who tolerated him for the fee they were paid by the state. They threw him out when he was accused of theft at ten and he spent five years in a reformatory. When he escaped, he joined the Foreign Legion. He spent much of his life in various prisons from the age of 20 for crimes that included traffic in stolen goods and narcotics, prostitution and homosexuality.

> He began to write seriously at 29, with a first novel, *Our Lady of Flowers*, spun out of masturbatory prison fantasies, and then plays such as *The Balcony* and *The Blacks*. By 37 his acknowledgment was impressive. His autobiography, *A Thief's Journal* was published when he was 39. Though a charmer, even when unwashed and hooked on Nembutal, even the most intimate biographers find a remoteness about him. He remained the needy child, as he wrote, "wholly consecrated to evil." From the '60s, for two decades, he was no longer just France's most controversial writer, but a celebrity.[459]

---

[457] https://www.bizarrepedia.com/david-and-cinnamon-brown/
[458] https://en.wikipedia.org/wiki/Bernard_Madoff
[459] https://en.wikipedia.org/wiki/Jean_Genet

As we tire of density and the grief it creates, and we start a spiritual journey to get out of the swamp, Sedna rewards us with transcendent crises, experiences which force us to let go and rise above them, resulting in a huge growth to a new level of consciousness. There is no choice with these crises, and the more we try and solve them, the more we will get hurt.

Like Petra Kelly, who was a Bavarian political human rights activist, ecologist and co-founder of the Green Party. She had Sedna conjunct Ceres in the eleventh house of collective consciousness.

> She studied World Politics and International Relations and worked at the European Communities in Brussels, continuing her development of social consciousness and political awareness. When she was 32 she helped found a political party that was dedicated to human rights and ecology, which was officially named the Green Party six years later; she was one of 27 Greens elected to the Bundestag.

> Abandoned by her dad at the age of six, she was educated by Catholic nuns and raised largely by her grandmother, while her mom worked to support the family. When she was 11, her mom married an American Army officer who moved the family to the U.S., to Ft. Benning, Georgia. Petra became a classic overachiever; cheerleader, member of the student senate, and scholarship winner. Despite physical pain from lifelong kidney ailments and the emotional trauma associated with the death of her younger half-sister, Grace, she was able to maintain an almost maniacal focus on achievement. She returned to Europe for post grad study and her beginning involvement in European Federalist politics.

> She began an affair with the 65-year-old married EC president Sicco Mansholt, the first of a number of affairs with politically powerful older men. She had a long-term companionship with 25-year older Gert Bastian, a former NATO General who had done under-cover spy work. As brilliant, romantic and mercurial as Petra was, Bastian in contrast was plodding methodical and obsessive. To all evidence, their love was compelling and uncompromising. When she was 45, they were both found dead in their Bonn home with a gunshot to the head. Whether their

deaths were suicide or murder was unresolved and the case remained a mystery.[460]

Emperor Hirohito of Japan was Japanese royalty, the first born son of Emperor Taisho and the crown prince in 1916 and declared the 124th Ruler of Japan on 12/25/1926 after a regency of five years, upon the death of his father, Emperor Taisho. He had Sedna conjunct Ceres in the third house of ideas and communication.

Soon after he was born, he was taken from his parents to be reared in isolation and trained as the future Emperor. He saw his mother once a week and his father less often. The first member of the Japanese royal family to set foot outside his homeland, Hirohito took a six-month tour of Europe in 1921. He brought back with him a taste for Western food and clothes.

His greatest pleasure was the study of marine biology, which he conducted in a laboratory built for him on his palace grounds. Far more than a hobby, he published several books on the subject and was a leading authority on jellyfish. He had the distinction of becoming the longest reigning Emperor in the history of Japan, for 61 years. His reign was called the Showa Era, or time of enlightened peace.[461]

Laurie Anderson is an American experimental performance artist, composer and musician who plays violin and keyboards and sings in a variety of experimental music and art rock styles. She has Sedna conjunct Ceres in the eleventh house of collective consciousness.

Initially trained as a sculptor, she did her first performance-art piece in the late 1960s. Throughout the 1970s, Anderson did a variety of different performance-art activities. She became widely known outside the art world at 34 when her single "O Superman" reached number two on the UK pop charts. She also starred in and directed the concert film *Home of the Brave* at 39. She started dating Lou Reed at 46 and was married to the singer-songwriter and guitarist from the age of 61 until his death five years later.

---

[460] https://en.wikipedia.org/wiki/Petra_Kelly
[461] https://en.wikipedia.org/wiki/Hirohito

She is a pioneer in electronic music and has invented several devices that she has used in her recordings and performance art shows. She created a tape-bow violin that uses recorded magnetic tape on the bow instead of horsehair and a magnetic tape head in the bridge. And in her early 50s, she developed a talking stick, a six-foot-long baton-like MIDI controller that can access and replicate sounds.[462]

Jacques Cousteau was a French oceanographer, inventor, film-maker and author. He has Sedna conjunct Ceres in the seventh house of relationships.

He is the most celebrated undersea explorer in history and was the first to take colour photographs of the world beneath the sea. He has won ten Emmy Awards, including one for *The Undersea World of Jacques Cousteau* which ran for eight years. In six decades, he authored 66 books and inspired some 90 movie and TV productions.

He was raised by an upper middleclass family, the son of an international lawyer. He described his mother as 'a saint.' As a child he wanted to be a sailor, filmmaker and doctor. Around the age of ten, he was diagnosed with an intestinal inflammation, as well as anemia. The only exercise he could tolerate that was permitted was swimming, which began his lifelong romance with the sea.

He entered the French Naval Academy at 20 and shot his first underwater film at 26. During the war he served as a gunnery officer, and as his country capitulated to the Nazis, he took photographs of enemy installations for the Resistance. After the war he was awarded the French Legion of Honour for his Resistance involvement. At 46 he resigned his naval commission to devote full time to his research. His 141-foot research vessel, the Calypso, became his headquarters.

At the age of 42 he wrote the documentary *Silent World* and the resulting movie won him his first of three Academy Awards four years later, as well as earning the grand prize at the Cannes Film Festival. He won his battle in 1960 against the French

[462] https://en.wikipedia.org/wiki/Laurie_Anderson

government to stop them from dumping radioactive wastes in the Mediterranean Sea. A couple of years later he wrote *The Living Sea* and followed this up with, *World Without Sun*. He was not only a marine researcher but an ocean ecologist, environmentalist, humanitarian, self-taught scientist, anti-nuclear activist and visionary - but not a dreamer, a doer.[463]

Jean Piaget was a Swiss psychologist, educator and author, known for his studies of children's learning patterns. He had Sedna conjunct Ceres in the eleventh house of collective consciousness. He was a leading investigator and writer of thought processes among children, receiving numerous prizes and honorary degrees from all over the world and is considered the father of developmental psychology.

His life work was learning how children learn, as their thought process is not that of adults. The conjunction with Ceres gave him the insight to see the relationship between his children's growth and the nurturing they received, which was the basis of his theories. This seems obvious now, but prior to this children's growth was thought simply to be due to hereditary factors.

> His four developmental steps are studied by educators the world over. He developed several new fields of science: developmental psychology, cognitive theory and what came to be called genetic epistemology, the theory of knowledge.[464]

At this juncture in human evolution, few of us use our planets at the spiritual level, but many of us are striving to, and such people are wonderful to be around. As with the other planets, the spiritual level of evolution is vastly different with Sedna from the two previous levels. Here, the conjunction with Ceres the ability to husband the spiritual destiny of life on the planet, at this crucial point in the evolutionary cycle.

Once we embrace the Sedna energy, which is the oneness of everything, our nurturing becomes an expression of Sedna consciousness and it becomes devotional in nature. The struggle of the beginner's level is gone, as are the transcendental crises of the intermediate level. At this level everything Saturnian is meaningless and yet everything Sednian has its place.

---

[463] https://en.wikipedia.org/wiki/Jacques_Cousteau
[464] https://en.wikipedia.org/wiki/Jean_Piaget

Baldur Ebertin is a German astrologer from a noted family, the son of Reinhold and the grandson of Elsbeth Ebertin. He has Sedna conjunct Ceres in the third house of ideas and communication.

> He works as a psychologist, clinical psychologist and psychotherapist as well as a naturopath. He is also well known in the astrology scene for his numerous book publications. He ran an educational counseling practice, working with child and youth psychotherapy and was a lecturer at community colleges.

> He also worked at the "Educational Office for Adult Education" making seminars such as "The World of the Child" and "Who am I?". In the following years he set up the toy exhibition "Children want to play", at adult education centers, maternal schools and similar institutions and supervised this with lectures.

> At 33 he was admited as a non-medical practitioner, which gave him the opportunity to be not only psychotherapeutic, but also healing in his counseling practice. Over the years he made the transition from child psychotherapy to youth and adult psychotherapy and a combination of psychotherapy and medicine.[465]

Jason Lotterhand was an American occultist and author, one of the 'Builders of the Adytum' during the mid-20th century resurgence of interest in Christian mysticism. He had Sedna conjunct Ceres in the third house of ideas and communication.

> He was on the path of self discovery from the age of twelve. A businessman by profession, he was friends with and studied under the late Paul Foster Case. At 34 he became Director of the Builders of the Adtyum, Dr. Case's educational organization. Upon retiring, he became Director Emeritus of the Mystery School. From the age of 39, he held study groups in Ancient Philosophy every Thursday evening.

> In the author's preface to his book, "The Thursday Night Tarot", which contains the essence of his messages, given every week throughout that time, he discusses the Cabala and the Tree of Life, defining the ten Sepiroth and briefly discussing the placement of the 22 Hebrew letters that appear as paths on the

---

[465] http://www.sternwelten.net/home/sternwelten-autoren/494-baldur-ebertin.html

Tree. He also makes the point that in coming to realize that we are all one, all part of the same energy, that we invite the presence of the Divine into our lives.[466]

Swaminarayan was an Indian religious leader. Also known as Sahajanand Swami, he is the central figure in a modern sect of Hinduism known as the Swaminarayan Hinduism, a form of Vaishnavism. He had Sedna conjunct Ceres and also Nessus, the centaur that acts as a guide to deep energies of regeneration, all in the fourth house of home.

At the age of 11 he began a seven-year pilgrimage across India. He settled in the state of Gujarat when he was 18. A year later he was initiated into the Uddhav Sampraday by his guru, Ramanand Swami, and was given the name Sahajanand Swami. When he was 21 his guru handed over the leadership to him before his death. He held a gathering and taught the Swaminarayan mantra. From this point onwards, he was known as Swaminarayan and within the sect he is regarded as an incarnation of God, Purushottama.

He developed a good relationship with the British Imperial Government. He had followers not only from Hindu denominations, but also from Islam and Zoroastrianism. He built six temples in his lifetime and appointed 500 paramhansas to spread his philosophy. When he was 45 he wrote the *Shikshapatri,* a book of social principles. He is also remembered within the sect for undertaking reforms for women and the poor, performing fire sacrifices on a large scale, as well as miracles. He had an estimated 1.8 million followers when he died in 1830. Today he has an estimated 20 million followers.[467]

Opposition

With the opposition between Sedna and Ceres the all-inclusive spiritual energy of Sedna challenges our potency, our nurturing nature and our ability to deal with change.

Ceres is associated with prosperity and abundance. She represents the actual bounty – the foods, the flowers, the birds and plants, and the

---

[466] http://www.aeclectic.net/tarot/books/thursday-night-tarot/
[467] https://en.wikipedia.org/wiki/Swaminarayan

desperation that results when the bounty is withdrawn. It shows how well we go with the flow... the universal one, that is. The unification of both giving and receiving through ourselves as an exchange of energy.

The challenge here is to balance our earth-bound spiritual security and sense of place on the planet, with our transpersonal spirituality and sense of place in the evolutionary cycle. This is not easy, for we will tend to favor Ceres and be protective of her when Sedna demands sweeping change.

Ceres is the planet of prosperity and abundance, but we also associate her with loss, compromise, rage and grief, so unfortunately, along with our bounty, she will also deliver some pretty dramatic episodes when we must give up and give in – triggering deep emotion.

The key to overcoming the negative side of Ceres, like grief, work problems, eating disorders and custody issues, is to develop our ability to deal with change, so we become an agent for evolutionary change on the planet.

At the unconscious level however, we might not see the depth of emotion our going with the flow, or the withdrawal of our bounty, might generate in others, or we could be blind to the reality that our capriccios behaviour could be seen as a threat. Or we may kid ourselves that we can resolve things that should really be given up.

Like Kathy Jean Robbins, who was an American homicide victim, who was beaten to death and knifed by her estranged husband at the age of 25, while their two daughters were asleep upstairs. She had Sedna in the fifth house of romance, opposite Ceres conjunct Juno, the asteroid of partnership, in the eleventh house of collective consciousness.

Her husband was abusive to her and to his daughters, ages six and two. A couple of months before the murder, he was charged with trying to strangle her and released; however, she left him, taking the girls, but making weekend visits. One of them proved fatal. Here's her daughter, who was six at the time, looking back on it:

> Bethany Robbons found a pile of hidden newspaper clippings that described her mothert's murder when she was 12. She read every article. She viewed photos of her father in handcuffs and saw shots of her forever-young mother reproduced in the newspaper. She doesn't remember much of the murder, not

having witnessed it or seen her mother's body. "I just woke up when dad was carrying us out the door". She was brought up by grandparents and was told her mother died in a car accident. "I asked why dad was in jail, if she died in an accident? I'm not stupid".[468]

Or like Seth Bishop, who was an American homicide victim, he was fatally shot by his 20-year-old sister when he was 18. He had Sedna in the eighth house of life and death, opposite Ceres, which is conjunct Ixion, the planet of lawlessness, in the second house of material reality.

> She used a shotgun, killing him, in what was initially ruled an accident based on her mother's testimony. She was not charged with a crime. She fired two shots from a 12-gauge pump-action shotgun, one into her bedroom wall, then one into her brother's chest, while they were in the kitchen with their mother.

> Later she became a biology professor and during the course of a routine meeting of the biology department attended by approximately 12 people, she stood up and began shooting those closest to her with a 9-millimeter handgun. Due to the attention attracted as a result of the shooting, previous violent incidents in which she had been involved or implicated were re-evaluated. Her brother's case was reopened and she was charged with first degree murder in his death, nearly 24 years later.

> The protagonist of the first of her unpublished novels is a woman who, as a child, attempted to frighten a friend after an argument but accidentally killed the friend's brother. One writer has speculated, after reviewing the evidence, that she had meant to frighten or shoot her father with the shotgun after an argument and mistook her brother for him.[469]

Marie Antoinette was French royalty, the favourite daughter of Emperor Francis I. She had Sedna conjunct Uranus, the planet of intuition, in the tenth house of profession, opposite Ceres in the third house of communication.

---

[468] http://www.capecodtimes.com/article/20061119/news01/311199993
[469] https://en.wikipedia.org/wiki/University_of_Alabama_in_Huntsville_shooting

She was known for a frivolous life style with court social life, gambling and games, gowns and jewels. Brought up in the hope that she might one day be queen of France, at 15, she married the crown prince who became King Louis XVI four years later.

The young queen was lively, witty and extravagant. When the stiff formalities of court life bored her, she amused herself with such pleasures as fancy balls, theatricals, attending the horse races and gambling. She lacked a good education and cared little for serious affairs. Giving no heed to the nation's financial crisis, her frivolity and plotting helped undermine the monarchy and start the French revolution.

She became very unpopular and was blamed for the corruption of the French court. False and vicious stories were told about her, even a rumour that she was a spy for Austria. In 1789 their eldest son died and the French Revolution began. The weak-willed Louis gradually lost control of the nation but Marie faced danger courageously.

When she was 34 a hungry and desperate Parisian mob marched to Versailles and forced the royal family to move to the Tuileries palace in Paris, where they were virtual prisoners for the following three years, until her husband went to the guillotine. Ten months later her turn came. After bravely enduring terrible hardships, she was brought to trial on a charge of treason and was beheaded.[470]

As we tire of density and the grief it creates, and we start a spiritual journey to get out of the swamp, Sedna rewards us with transcendent crises, experiences which force us to let go and rise above them, resulting in a huge growth to a new level of consciousness. There is no choice with these crises, and the more we try and solve them, the more we will get hurt.

Simone de Beauvoir was a French writer and existentialist teacher who fashioned an impressive literary career as a novelist, philosopher, essayist and writer of memoirs. She had Sedna in the fourth house of home, opposite Ceres, the planet of nurturing, in the tenth house of social standing.

---

[470] https://en.wikipedia.org/wiki/Marie_Antoinette

She looked on marriage as an obscene, bourgeois institution that put women in an inferior position. In rejecting marriage, she also rejected children, noting that she had escaped most of women's bondages.

She was a prominent member of the young avant-garde Parisian intelligentsia in the '40s. She was the presiding celebrity of the Existentialist movement along with Jean Paul Sartre, who was her life companion in an open relationship. They never lived in the same residence, nor did they require sexual fidelity of each other, but they did keep a close and steady relationship, seeing each other daily from the time they met at the Sorbonne when she was 21, until Sartre died 50 years later.[471]

Her Sedna was also closely bi-quintile Ixion, the planet of lawlessness in the ninth house of higher education.

She had a very turbulent, often scandalous life. Although she had a longtime relationship with Sartre, she was known to have a number of female lovers. The nature of some of these relationships, some of which she began with underage students while working as a professor, later led to a controversy.

A former student wrote in her book that, while she was a student at Lycée Molière, she had been sexually exploited by her teacher de Beauvoir, who was in her 30s at the time. She and Jean-Paul Sartre developed a pattern, which they called the "trio", in which de Beauvoir would seduce her students and then pass them on to Sartre. Finally, she was suspended from her teaching job, when she was accused of seducing a 17-year-old pupil. The girl's parents laid formal charges against her for debauching a minor and she had her license to teach in France permanently revoked.[472]

H.G. Wells was a British writer, historian, prognosticator, economist and novelist who was known for his sci-fi predictions of the future. He had Sedna in the first house of identity, opposite his Ceres in the seventh house of relationships.

---

[471] https://en.wikipedia.org/wiki/Simone_de_Beauvoir
[472] Ibid.

After a sketchy education, he went on to graduate from London University with a BS at 22. He taught biology and wrote educational articles, writing his first novel at 29 and went on to write many other works. His book, *The War of the Worlds*, which was read on radio by Orson Wells, caused the famous Mars invasion panic when he was 72. He was an enormously prolific and popular writer, capturing the early twentieth century's need to rebel and overthrow the oppressive Victorian conventions.[473]

Patch Adams is an American physician, famed throughout the medical community for charging no fees, carrying no malpractice insurance and living with his patients in a country farm setting. He has Sedna conjunct Mars and also conjunct Varuna, the planet of notability, and Venus, the planet of values, all on the cusp of the fifth house of creativity, opposite Ceres in the eleventh house of collective consciousness, giving him a strong performing mission despite his vocation as a doctor. He has always maintained that humour and joy are more important than any drug or therapy.

The eleventh house placement gives him an idealistic view of our spiritual security and sense of place on Planet Earth. And the challenging opposition with Sedna in the fifth house of creativity, forms the base of a stressful T square with Pholus, the centaur representing the 'comic side of misfortune' at the apex, in the second house of material resources. This ground's his 'tension-release health process' in a practice, with the establishment of a hospital and teaching facility.

He grew up as an Army brat in Japan, Germany and the U.S. and has been described as an iconoclast, a pattern-breaker and professional clown. He was deeply shaken by his dad's death, but it was his uncle's suicide that pushed him into despair. He dropped out of school and made the first of several suicide attempts. His Sedna is semi-square his Sun, the planet of willpower, on the cusp of the seventh house of relationships and in a fateful inconjunct with Pallas, the asteroid of wisdom, in the ninth house of knowledge. He was 18 when his mom checked him into a mental ward at Fairfax Hospital in Virginia, where he turned his own emotional corner by helping his roommate conquer hallucinations and fear.

---

[473] https://en.wikipedia.org/wiki/H._G._Wells

A few weeks later he left the ward and enrolled at University to become a doctor. His Gesundheit Institute began as an experiment. For the first 12 years, 20 adults lived in a large home and used it as a crude hospital, open 24 hours a day. Three physicians and others did what they could for whoever came. They never charged money and their work was supported by part-time jobs of the live-in staff. For staff and patients, medicine was integrated with the performing arts, arts and crafts, agriculture, nature, recreation and social service.[474]

During those first 12 years, 15,000 people came through the home/facility for everything from profound illnesses, to simple curiosity and play. He faced stiff opposition from the health industry for his radical concept that healing happens faster if tension is reduced and patients are treated as individuals and encouraged to take more pleasure in life. It's obvious from a Sedna consciousness perspective, but completely frivolous from a Saturnian standpoint.

At this juncture in human evolution, few of us use our planets at the spiritual level, but many of us are striving to, and such people are wonderful to be around. As with the other planets, the spiritual level of evolution is vastly different with Sedna from the two previous levels. Here the opposition with Ceres the ability to husband the spiritual destiny of life on the planet, at this crucial point in the evolutionary cycle.

Once we embrace the Sedna energy, which is the oneness of everything, our nurturing becomes an expression of Sedna consciousness and it becomes devotional in nature. The struggle of the beginner's level is gone, as are the transcendental crises of the intermediate level. At this level everything Saturnian is meaningless and yet everything Sednian has its place.

Jean-Baptiste Lacordaire was a leading ecclesiastic in the Roman Catholic revival in France following the Napoleonic period. He had Sedna conjunct the North Node, the point representing the karma he is creating, in the tenth house of profession, opposite Ceres, which is conjunct his Moon, the planet of emotions, and his South Node, the point of the karma he has to deal with, in the fourth house of home.

---

[474] https://en.wikipedia.org/wiki/Patch_Adams

Raised in a troubled time, he renounced religion and studied and practiced law, but after experiencing a religious awakening he studied for the priesthood and was ordained at 25. A couple of years later he joined a small group of Roman Catholic writers founded a journal called 'The Future', which advocated the separation of church and state. However, the Pope condemned the doctrines and the journal was suppressed.

A period of disappointment followed, during which he focused his energies on preaching. His sermons appealed to Parisian intellectuals and, at 33, the archbishop of Paris invited him to preach at Notre Dame, where his lectures became known as the Lenten Conferences. He returned to Paris five years later and resumed his preaching at Notre Dame, using his pulpit this time as a means to express his support of liberty in church and state.[475]

Theodor Adorno was a German philosopher, sociologist, and composer known for his critical theory of society. He had Sedna in the eighth house of shared resources, opposite Ceres in the second house of material reality.

He is widely regarded as one of the 20th century's foremost thinkers on aesthetics and philosophy, as well as one of its preeminent essayists. As a critic of both fascism and what he called the culture industry, his writings strongly influenced the European New Left.

As a classically trained pianist whose sympathies with the twelve-tone technique of Arnold Schoenberg resulted in his studying composition with Alban Berg of the Second Viennese School, Adorno's commitment to avant-garde music formed the backdrop of his subsequent writings and led to his collaboration with Thomas Mann on the latter's novel, *Doctor Faustus*, while the two men lived in California as exiles during the Second World War.

Working for the newly relocated Institute for Social Research, Adorno collaborated on influential studies of authoritarianism, antisemitism and propaganda that would later serve as models

---

[475] https://en.wikipedia.org/wiki/Jean-Baptiste_Henri_Lacordaire

for sociological studies the Institute carried out in post-war Germany.

As a writer of polemics in the tradition of Nietzsche, he delivered scathing critiques of contemporary Western culture. His posthumously published *Aesthetic Theory*, which he planned to dedicate to Samuel Beckett, is the culmination of a lifelong commitment to modern art which attempts to revoke the "fatal separation" of feeling and understanding long demanded by the history of philosophy and explode the privilege aesthetics accords to content over form and contemplation over immersion.[476]

Martin Heidegger was an German existentialist philosopher who was one of the most influential voices and foremost thinkers and writers of the 20th century. He had Sedna in the fourth house of home, opposite Ceres, which is conjunct his Sun, the planet of willpower, in the tenth house of profession.

With the publication of his first book, *Being and Time,* when he was 38, he achieved instant fame as one of the spokesmen of 20th century existentialism. Though unfinished, *Being and Time* is one of the central philosophical works of the 20th century. In the first division of the work, he attempted to turn away from "ontic" questions about beings to ontological questions about Being and recover the most fundamental philosophical question: the question of Being, of what it means for something to be.

He argued that being human is defined by care, that it's practically engaged and is a concernfull mode of being-in-the-world. This was in opposition to rationalist thinkers like René Descartes who located the essence of man in our thinking abilities. For Heidegger thinking is thinking about things originally discovered in our everyday practical engagements. The consequence of this is that our capacity to think cannot be the most central quality of our being, because thinking is a reflecting upon this more original way of discovering the world.

In the second section, he argues that human being is even more fundamentally structured by its temporality, or its concern with,

---

[476] https://en.wikipedia.org/wiki/Theodor_W._Adorno

and relationship to time, existing as a structurally open 'possibility-for-being'. He emphasised the importance of authenticity in human existence, involving a truthful relationship to our being thrown into a world, and to our being-towards-death, the finitude of the time and being that we are given, and the closing down of our various possibilities for being through time.

He also made critical contributions to philosophical conceptions of truth, arguing that its original meaning was unconcealment, to philosophical analyses of art as a site of the revelation of truth, and to philosophical understanding of language as the 'house of being'.[477]

Semi-sextile, Sextile, Trine

The flowing aspects between Sedna and Ceres align the all-inclusive spiritual energy of Sedna with our potency, our nurturing nature and our ability to deal with change.

Ceres is associated with prosperity and abundance. She represents the actual bounty – the foods, the flowers, the birds and plants, and the desperation that results when the bounty is withdrawn. It shows how well we go with the flow... the universal one, that is. The unification of both giving and receiving through ourselves as an exchange of energy.

With the flows, the bigger spiritual context of our lives can be self-evident, but we will probably still struggle to align that practically in our daily lives, because it's not self-evident to everyone else and we may struggle to understand why.

Ceres is the planet of prosperity and abundance, but we also associate her with loss, compromise, rage and grief, so unfortunately, along with our bounty, Ceres will also deliver some pretty dramatic episodes when we must give up and give in – triggering deep emotion.

At the unconscious level however, we may resist this process, desperately arguing for our version of 'what should be', in an effort to avoid giving in and avoid the resulting emotions. And at this level the 'going with the flow' can mean trying to avoid the challenges by escaping into our own soap opera, which of course never works.

---

[477] https://en.wikipedia.org/wiki/Martin_Heidegger

Ted Kaczynski was an American terrorist, called the Unabomber. He has Sedna in the ninth house of knowledge, semi-sextile Ceres in the eighth house of life and death.

> He was a gifted child but was shy and aloof. As an infant, he was hospitalised for several weeks and the hospital staff discouraged the parents from visiting their child and prevented them from holding him in their rare visits. He reportedly was never the same. He excelled in school, skipping two grades and graduating at age 16. He obtained his bachelor's degree from Harvard University and landed an assistant professor's position with the University of California at Berkeley, but resigned suddenly some years later without explanation, moving to a remote shack and living on very little.[478]

His Sedna is also at the tip of a T square, between Pholus, the centaur of illumination, in the sixth house of service, opposite Mars, the planet of war, in the twelfth house of the unconscious.

> Then he sent a bomb to a professor at Northwestern University and a security guard opened it and sustained minor injuries. Several more bombs were sent by mail to others, but did not cause much injury, until a computer store owner was killed and a Yale University computer science professor with a distinguished reputation was injured.[479]

His Sedna is also sextile Mercury, the planet of communication, in the eleventh house of ideals.

> He demanded that if a 35,000-word manifesto was printed in newspapers, he would quit his bombing campaign. The document, arguing that technological progress was harmful and must be stopped, was published in the *New York Times* and *Washington Post*.

> Kaczynski's younger brother recognised the writing style and ideas and after an anguished debate with himself, reported his brother to the police. The unabomber was arrested at his cabin in a remote part of Montana. Lawyers tried to convince him to use the insanity plea, and a psychologist diagnosed paranoid

---

[478] https://en.wikipedia.org/wiki/Ted_Kaczynski
[479] Ibid

schizophrenia, but Kaczynski refused to plead insanity. He pled guilty to avoid the death penalty. Although he later retracted his guilty plea, he was found guilty and sentenced to life imprisonment with no hope of appeal.[480]

Elizabeth Smart is an American who went missing at age fourteen, abducted from her home as her family slept. Her Sedna is in the third house of communication, trine Ceres in the twelfth house of the unconscious.

> The second of six kids, she grew up in a close-knit Mormon family, reading scripture and praying morning and evening. On the evening just before her disappearance, she and her family had attended an award ceremony at Elizabeth's middle school, where she was recognised for various school accomplishments.[481]

Her Sedna is also closely opposite her conjunction of Pluto, the planet of transformation, and the Sun, the planet of willpower, in the ninth house of knowledge.

> The family prayed together and kissed goodnight; however, sometime in the early morning hours, a man entered the bedroom she shared with her younger sister and spirited her away. No ransom note was found and no trace of her was reported until she was spotted walking in a suburb of the same city with a shaggy-haired vagabond nine months later. During her ordeal, she spent a great deal of the time near her home wearing disguises and veils in public. The Smart family believes she was brainwashed, citing that she did not call out for help, or apparently try to escape, even when she heard rescuers call out her name.

> However, nearly two years after her rescue, her father said that she is "just a normal teenager who likes shopping and going to the movies with friends". A self-assured young woman and college graduate, she confronted her kidnapper at his trial and

---

[480] Ibid.
[481] https://en.wikipedia.org/wiki/Elizabeth_Smart

then accepted a job as a contributor for a television network in its coverage of missing persons.[482]

Liz Renay was an American exotic dancer, model, stripper and party girl. She had Sedna conjunct Nessus, the centaur of 'the fragility of life', in the twelfth house of the unconscious, trine Ceres in the fifth house of creativity and children.

> Raised as poorwhite trash in a three-room cabin on the banks of a ditch, she ran away at 14 and married a soldier and they had a daughter. It was the first of seven marriages. With a gorgeous face and body, she became an exotic dancer in a strip joint at 23. She almost made it into the movies at 32; the studio hype was in motion to promote her first picture when there was an underworld mob murder. She was implicated for refusing to testify for fear of her life and was indicted for perjury the following year. She served a prison sentence for 27 months that finished her movie career before it started.
>
> She wrote her autobiography at 45, titled *My Face the World to See*. Though her literary skills were abysmal, she was a survivor without pretences. In the '70s she again made news when she and her daughter, also a stripper, both streaked naked down Hollywood Blvd to publicise their appearance in a club. She finally made it into the movies at 51 with her role in John Waters' film, *Desperate Living*.[483]

As we tire of density and the grief it creates, and we start a spiritual journey to get out of the swamp, Sedna rewards us with transcendent crises, experiences which force us to let go and rise above them, resulting in a huge growth to a new level of consciousness. There is no choice with these crises, and the more we try and solve them, the more we will get hurt.

Andy Warhol was an American underground artist and film maker who had a genius for creating attention. He had Sedna in the ninth house of knowledge, semi-sextile Ceres in the eighth house of shared resources.

> An androgyne and voyeur himself, his salon became the New York centre of the freak scene in the 1960s. When the pop-art

---

[482] Ibid.
[483] https://en.wikipedia.org/wiki/Liz_Renay

movement exploded at the end of 1962, his drawings of soup cans and screens of the famous became hot property. He started film making in 1963, hovering in the twilight zone between reality and fantasy.

He designed ads for women's shoes before bursting upon the cultural scene in the early '60s. When he was 40, he was shot by a demented fan; after his recovery he was somewhat subdued, but still newsworthy in the '80s for his personal outrage of convention and aberrative entourage. He founded *Interview* magazine in the early forties and remained a pop-culture figure into his 50s.

On his death at 58 his estate was estimated to be worth $220 million. The year after his death the posthumous publication of *The Andy Warhol Diaries* hit the best seller list with their litany of limo's, dinners, tips, encounters, all the trivia of life among the 'beautiful people'. The book contained gossip on almost every star from Warhol's experience as a party fixture.[484]

Virginia Woolf was a British writer, a novelist and essayist who used the English language superbly. She had Sedna in the eleventh house of collective consciousness, sextile Ceres in the eighth house of shared resources.

After the death of her father in 1904, she and her siblings moved to Bloomsbury where their home became the center for the avant-garde literary salon, the Bloomsbury Group. She married Leonard Woolf when she was 30. They were true companions, though it was a sexless marriage and she later fell in love with another woman.

She received income from a small trust fund but it was insufficient to meet her needs. In 1917, she and her husband founded the Hogarth Press. With a small, kitchen-table model printing press, they taught themselves to set type and print. They were both budding novelists, reviewers and essayists. Their first publication, a 32-page pamphlet, sold 134 copies of the 150 printed. Within several years, they developed a commercially successful publishing company that produced 25 to 35 books per

---

[484] https://en.wikipedia.org/wiki/Andy_Warhol

year. They were prolific writers and managed the publishing company as a part time enterprise.

She suffered from a mental breakdown during WW I, followed by subsequent periods of physical, mental and emotional breakdowns, which doctors treated with psychiatric drugs. Her early childhood experience of sexual abuse by her half-brothers, Gerald and George Dunkworth, was thought to be the cause. Gerald later became her publisher. Virginia had a complicated and stormy relationship with her sister, Vanessa Bell, which biographers reveal was also physical. She is also reported to have an early love interest with a close friend, Violet Dickinson.

Her writing expressed the themes that troubled her the most; life, death, suicide, madness and past memories. She was hypersensitive to criticism. She was a noted biographer and critic and used writing as a distraction from realty. When she realised she could not write any longer, she chose not to live and drowned herself, fearing the recurrence of a mental breakdown.[485]

And case study, Thomas Edison, the father of the light bulb, has Sedna in the fourth house of the laboratory home, sextile Ceres in the sixth house of service. His Sedna is also sextile Quaoar, the planet of new realities which is conjunct Ceres, but is just across the descendent in the seventh house of one-to-one relationships. So, his earth-bound spiritual security and sense of place on the planet was able to provide the service of new perspectives on how to connect people (telegraph) and on home appliances (electricity, light bulb, phonograph). His Sedna is also in a close quintile with Jupiter, the planet of expansion, also in the seventh house.

A characteristic of his personality contributing strongly to his achievements is an intense, not to say courageous, optimism in which no thought of failure can enter, an optimism born of self-confidence, and becoming--after forty or fifty years of experience more and more a sense of certainty in the accomplishment of success.

---

[485] https://en.wikipedia.org/wiki/Virginia_Woolf

In the overcoming of difficulties, he had the same intellectual pleasure as the chess-master when confronted with a problem requiring all the efforts of his skill and experience to solve. To advance along smooth and pleasant paths, to encounter no obstacles, to wrestle with no difficulties and hardships--such has absolutely no fascination to him.

At the conclusion of his ore-milling experiments, practically his entire fortune was sunk in an enterprise that had to be considered an impossibility. At the age of fifty he looked back upon five or six years of intense activity expended apparently for naught and the financial clouds were quickly gathering on the horizon. However, for him the main experiment had succeeded, he had accomplished what he sought for. Nature at another point had outstripped him, yet he had broadened his own sum of knowledge to a prodigious extent.

Twelve years later a friend accompanied him on a Sunday drive in New Jersey and Edison in the highest spirits, pointing out with the keenest enjoyment the many beautiful views of valley and wood. The wanderings led to the old ore-milling plant, by then practically a mass of deserted buildings all going to decay. It was a depressing sight, marking such titanic but futile struggles with nature.

To Edison, however, no trace of sentiment or regret occurred, and the whole ruins were apparently as much a matter of unconcern as if he were viewing the remains of Pompeii. Sitting on the porch of the house where he lived during that period, in the light of the setting sun, his fine face in repose, he looked as placidly over the scene as a happy farmer over a field of ripening corn. 'I never felt better in my life than during the five years I worked here' he said. 'Hard work, nothing to divert my thought, clear air and simple food made my life very pleasant. We learned a great deal. It will be of benefit to someone some time'.[486]

Humour can be one path to transcend the quicksand of Sedna, giving us the objectivity to step back from the edge, but also with the flowing

---

[486] Dyer, Frank Lewis, and Martin, Thomas Commerford, *Edison, His Life and Inventions*

aspects to Ceres the ability to accept what is happening and make the most of each moment.

David Shiner is an American actor and clown. He has Sedna in tenth house of profession, trine Ceres in the second house of material resources. He built an early reputation working regularly in the streets at the Avignon Festival in France, drawing huge crowds to watch his antics on the castle walls of the old city and making a fortune in the hat.

> He performed in the 2000 Broadway musical 'Seussical' and has movie appearances as a clown and as an actor, including *Lorenzo's Oil*, which was released when he was 39. He has also toured solo shows in Europe and America and mentored and guest directed for a German youth circus program. At 37 he was featured in Cirque du Soleil's production 'Nouvelle Expérience', touring for 19 months through Canada and the USA and playing for another year in Las Vegas. With his antics, including stepping through, on and over much of the crowd and the staging of a mock silent-movie melodrama with four members of the audience, he may be the best remembered of the Cirque's clowns. At 53 he wrote and directed Cirque du Soleil's touring production, 'Koozå.'[487]

At this juncture in human evolution, few of us use our planets at the spiritual level, but many of us are striving to, and such people are wonderful to be around. As with the other planets, the spiritual level of evolution is vastly different with Sedna from the two previous levels. Here, the flowing aspects with Ceres give us the ability to husband the spiritual destiny of life on the planet, at this crucial point in the evolutionary cycle.

Once we embrace the Sedna energy, which is the oneness of everything, our nurturing becomes an expression of Sedna consciousness and it becomes devotional in nature. The struggle of the beginner's level is gone, as are the transcendental crises of the intermediate level. At this level everything Saturnian is meaningless and yet everything Sednian has its place.

Anne Frank was a Dutch-Jewish writer of a diary from age 14 -15, while she and her family lived in total confinement, hiding in an attic from the

---

[487] https://en.wikipedia.org/wiki/David_Shiner_(clown)

Nazis, where non-Jewish friends had sheltered them. She had Sedna in the tenth house of profession, semi-sextile Ceres in the eleventh house of collective consciousness.

> She began scrawling in her diary in 1942, writing as a typical teen in many ways, childish and profound, thoughtful and painful, writing, "In spite of everything, I still believe that people are really good at heart."

> Her last entry was three days before their hiding place was discovered and they were arrested. She died of typhus at the Bergen-Belsen concentration camp in March 1945. Her father, who survived, returned after the war and found his daughter's diary. At the turn of the century a new edition of her diary was released with five previously secret pages that described her conflict with her mother, whom she wrote, "had cold eyes," and with whom she could not talk to unburden herself, and her lament that her parents had a loveless marriage of convenience.

> Her diary remains as a poignant symbol of the millions whose lives and homes were lost during a tragic page in history. Translated into 54 languages with sales hovering around 25 million copies worldwide, her book is an established part of most high school educations. Putting a single face on the vast horror of the Holocaust, she served as a reminder of the quiet acts of heroism that were part of that high-water mark of evil.[488]

Robert Hand is an American astrologer, one of the most respected of the 20th century for his books, articles, lectures and research. He has Sedna conjunct Varuna, the planet of notability, in the tenth house of profession, semi-sextile Ceres, which is sitting on the MC, the cusp of the tenth house.

> His family was locally known for working in astrology, science and history, and Rob learned the basics of casting charts from his dad, Wilfred Hand. Adept from the time he was 18, he became well known for his research into new techniques and old translations.

> He graduated with honours in history from Brandeis and went on to graduate work in the History of Science at Princeton. His

---

[488] https://en.wikipedia.org/wiki/Anne_Frank

astrology practice began when he was 30. He was one of the first practicing astrologers to write astrology programs for microcomputers. From this background, he founded Astro-Graphics at 37, which later became Astrolabe, Inc. When he was 55 he established a formal archive, library and publishing company for continuing his lifelong work in the history and the science of astrology, ARHAT.

He is the author of *Planets in Transit*, *Planets in Composite*, and more. Chairman of the National Council for Geocentric Research, he also served as Secretary of the United Astrology Conference and has twice been the winner of the Regulus Award, when he was 47 and again at 53. He has long been a pioneer in rebuilding the traditions of astrology and making them available to modern astrologers.[489]

And finally, we have our case study, Edgar Cayce, the father of wholistic medicine. He is an American mystic who is known as the Sleeping Prophet, because, while in a sleep state he could discuss history, geology, metaphysics, philosophy and medicine. He had Sedna in the eighth house of life and death and inherited health issues, sextile Ceres in the sixth house of service. So his earth-bound spiritual security and sense of place on the planet was able to provide the service of linking to his transpersonal spirituality while in a trance.

He prayed to be able to help others, especially children, and had a spiritual vision at age 13, that told him he would be able to accomplish this dream of service. A lady bathed in light told him to sleep with his head on his books and then he would be able to remember what was in them. This was at a time when he was having trouble in school, and his father was beating him for not being able to spell the words in his lessons correctly. Soon after, he showed signs of special abilities when he found that he could sleep on his schoolbooks and have photographic recall of every page.

Two years after his first vision he was pronounced dead from drowning but recovered. At 23 he developed a severe case of laryngitis which stopped him working as an insurance salesman, a job he hated. Doctors couldn't cure it. In desperation he tried

---

[489] https://en.wikipedia.org/wiki/Robert_Hand

hypnosis from a traveling practitioner and was cured after several treatments. Under hypnosis, he gave his first psychic reading at 24 and learned that he could give accurate medical diagnoses and healing recommendations for himself and for other people.

He gave approximately 30,000 life-readings and medical diagnosis to people during his lifetime. He founded a hospital, a university and the Association for Research and Enlightenment that promotes research on his readings and continues his work. Throughout his life, he claimed no special abilities and did not capitalise financially or otherwise on his gifts. The readings never offered a set of beliefs or "religion" to be embraced, but instead focused on the idea that every person should test in his or her own life the principles presented.

Though he was a devout Christian who read the Bible through once for every year of his life, his work emphasised the importance of comparative study of belief systems from around the world. In fact, some of the metaphysical material that came through the sleeping Cayce was at first confusing and distressing to him in his waking state. However, he overcame his doubts, as have others, by observing the amazing accuracy and unfailing helpfulness of the readings in other areas, such as healing. The underlying principle of the readings is the oneness of all life, acceptance of all people, and a compassion and understanding for every major religion.[490]

Semi-square, Square, Sesquiquadrate

With the stressful aspects between Sedna and Ceres the all-inclusive spiritual energy of Sedna challenges our potency, our nurturing nature and our ability to deal with change.

Ceres is associated with prosperity and abundance. She represents the actual bounty – the foods, the flowers, the birds and plants, and the desperation that results when the bounty is withdrawn. It shows how well we go with the flow… the universal one, that is. The unification of both giving and receiving through ourselves as an exchange of energy.

---

[490] https://en.wikipedia.org/wiki/Edgar_Cayce

Ceres is the planet of prosperity and abundance, but we also associate her with loss, compromise, rage and grief, so unfortunately, along with our bounty, Ceres will also deliver some pretty dramatic episodes when we must give up and give in – triggering deep emotion.

At the unconscious level, however, we might well struggle with both going with the flow and with giving in, because we are so involved in our own soap opera. In this case we are more likely to manifest the the negative side of each planet, the grief, work problems, eating disorders and custody issues of Ceres and the illnesses and victimization of Sedna, as we can see in the following examples.

Rachel Entwistle was an American homicide victim. She had Sedna conjunct Chiron, the centaur of wounding and healing, on the cusp of her 4th house of home, square Ceres in the twelfth house of the unconscious. She and her 9-month daughter were found dead in their home, murdered by her supposedly successful husband, as she slept with their child, because he had created a fantasy world which was all about to collapse and he couldn't face telling her.

Fritz Haarmann was a German homicidal manic and a homosexual epileptic. He has Sedna in the eleventh house of ideals in a stressful sesquiquadrate with Ceres in the fourth house of home.

> From youth he served several prison terms for indecency and was committed several times to an insane asylum. He primarily lived as a petty thief, burglar and con artist. Although he did occasionally obtain legitimate employment, he invariably stole from his employers, or their customers.

> Despite police knowledge that he was both a criminal and a homosexual, which was then illegal and punishable by imprisonment in Germany, he gradually began to establish a relationship with Hanover police as an informer, largely as a means of redirecting their attention from himself in his own criminal activities, and to facilitate his access to young males.

> He is known to have committed at least 24 murders, although he is suspected of murdering a minimum of 27. All of his victims were males between the ages of 10 and 22, the majority of whom were in their mid- to late-teens. They would be lured back to one of three addresses in which he is known to have lived, on

the promise of assistance, accommodation, work, or under the pretence of citizen's arrest.[491]

Stephane Delabriere was a French serial killer. He had Sedna in the sixth house of daily routine, square Ceres in the third house of ideas.

> The eldest of five children, he was tortured by his violent and alcoholic father. At age 13 he was put in a foster home. Calling himself the Prince of Darkness, he dedicated to Satan his performance of ritual sacrifices on animals. When he was 20, during a robbery he strangled, raped and slit the throat of a 63-year-old woman. A year later he beheaded his best friend using an ax and carried the head in his knapsack for the rest of the day. Apprehended and awaiting trial, he murdered a prison guard using a knife. Of 14 psychiatric experts who were assigned to his case, none came to the same conclusion, beyond their agreement that he was beyond redemption. His murders were premeditated and he declared that he had a goal of 5,000 victims. He was sentenced to life in prison at 25.[492]

Emily Dickinson was an American writer, acclaimed as the greatest woman poet of the English language. During her lifetime she had seven poems published anonymously; since her death she has been revered as a literary treasure. She had Sedna in the fourth house of home, square Ceres in the second house of material resources.

> With poor health, shy and fastidious, she had a reclusive and uneventful life with her domineering dad, an attorney, and a mom who "did not care for thought." She was one of three children, an older brother and a younger sister who were her closest companions through her lifetime. Her parents sent her to seminary school at 17, where she was cramped, curbed and repressed into a tight Victorian mould.

> Becoming increasingly withdrawn and mystical, dressed always in white, she ventured outside only at dusk to water the garden. She never married and some biographers conclude that she was gay. By the early 1860s she had created a wall of isolation around herself, which she believed critical to artistic expression.

[491] https://en.wikipedia.org/wiki/Fritz_Haarmann
[492] https://www.astro.com/astro-databank/Delabriere,_Stephane

The major relationships in her life were with Susan Dickinson, her brother Austin's wife and with Bowles, a married man and the editor of the Springfield republican. She and Sue met when they were both 17. Through the 40 years of their correspondence, Bowles was her closest personal friend until his death. He was vigorous, earthy and dashing; however, Dickinson's biographer writes that with neither relationship was physical union possible.

In her last two decades, she became even more reclusive, seldom going far from her brother's house in Amherst. At 54 her health was set back by the death of a friend and by late the following year she was often too ill to leave her room. Stricken by Bright's disease, a type of kidney inflammation, she lost consciousness and died in the house where she was born. After her death her sister found a manuscript of almost 900 poems, a legacy of glorious words to show the blazing wondrous genius that was hidden inside her.[493]

As we tire of density and the grief it creates, and we start a spiritual journey to get out of the swamp, Sedna rewards us with transcendent crises, experiences which force us to let go and rise above them, resulting in a huge growth to a new level of consciousness. There is no choice with these crises, and the more we try and solve them, the more we will get hurt.

Erica Jong is an American writer, a best-selling novelist with her racy *Fear of Flying*, published when she was 31. She has Sedna conjunct Varuna, the planet of notability, in the eleventh house of collective consciousness, semi-square Ceres in the tenth house of profession.

Though she says that writing takes priority over both motherhood and men, there have been more than a few torrid romances along her way. Her first marriage, at 21, was annulled after six months when her husband was found to be schizophrenic. At 24, pretty, ebullient, with a sunny disposition, she married fellow Columbia student, Chinese-American child psychologist, Dr. Allan Jong and they lived in Germany for the following three years.

---

[493] https://en.wikipedia.org/wiki/Emily_Dickinson

At 35 she married sci-fi novelist Jonathan Fast; their daughter Molly was born the following year and they divorced after 4 years. At 47 she married attorney Ken Burrows, who was 48, stating that her naughty days were over. She published *Fear of Fifty* at 52, part confessional, part cocktail chatter and part intellectual cant in a memoir style, as engaging and fiercely self-centred as ever.[494]

It's important with these aspects to find the balance and allow the positive sides of each planet to develop. The Sedna challenges can also give us the perseverance not to give up and so give us the ability to change our destiny and possible everyone else's in the process.

Our case study, Rachel Carson, the mother of the environmental movement, has a square between Sedna and Ceres, so her earth-bound spiritual security and sense of place on the planet was challenged by what the pesticide companies were doing to the environment.

She was particularly sensitive to this because her Sedna is also square Neptune, the planet associated with chemicals and lies, Jupiter, the planet associated with publishing, and Haumea, the planet of rebirth, which are all conjunct Ceres in the fourth house of home.

Her seminal book, *Silent Spring*, chronicled the devastating effects of the overuse of pesticides. The book was startling for its rigorous scientific assessment of how, by spraying for one issue, to get rid of a bug or a weed, without considering how the chemicals would impact everything else, people were often doing more harm than good.

As a child she loved the outdoors, the birds and plants around her family's rural property sparking her imagination. She found fossilised fish and inspired by her expeditions wrote a book at age 8 and was published in a literary magazine at 13.

At age eight she wrote a book and a few years later joined an underage literary elite with published works in a children's magazine which also published early writings by William Faulkner, F. Scott Fitzgerald, E. E. Cummings, and E. B. White. Carson was fond of noting that she had become a professional writer at age eleven.

---

[494] https://en.wikipedia.org/wiki/Erica_Jong

She entered the Pennsylvania College for Women on a senatorial district scholarship, earning an English degree, as preparation to become a writer. However, it was biology that she found most thrilling during her undergraduate years. Biology gave her the tools to learn what had happened to that fossilised fish she found as a child.

After earning a master's in zoology from Johns Hopkins, she found part-time work at the US Bureau of Fisheries. Though she'd chosen science over prose, her former specialty proved useful in her new occupation. Carson's first assignment for the bureau was to write a fifty-two-episode radio program called 'Romance Under the Waters.' "I had given up writing forever, I thought. It never occurred to me that I was merely getting something to write about."

Her first book, *Under the Sea-Wind*, was a commercial failure, selling only two thousand copies. She needed a couple of years to recover from the blow, but both driven and strapped for cash, she wrote another book. *The Sea Around Us* was published when she was 44 and it won the National Book Award for nonfiction and solidified her position as a literary heavyweight. To this day, it's credited as being one of the most successful books ever written about nature.

In her fifties she turned her attention to conservation, especially some problems that she believed were caused by synthetic pesticides. The result was the book *Silent Spring*, published when she was 55, which brought environmental concerns to an unprecedented share of the American people. Although it was met with fierce opposition by chemical companies, it spurred a reversal in national pesticide policy, which led to a nationwide ban on DDT and other pesticides. It also inspired a grassroots environmental movement that led to the creation of the U.S. Environmental Protection Agency.[495]

Humour can be one path to transcend the quicksand of Sedna, giving us the objectivity to step back from the edge, but also with the stressful aspects to Ceres the ability to accept what is happening and make the most of each moment.

---

[495] https://en.wikipedia.org/wiki/Rachel_Carson

Benny Hill was a British comedian who was very popular with his zany comic style and was voted the Funniest Man of TV in Britain. He had Sedna in the second house of material resources, semi-square Ceres in the first house of identity.

> By the age of 62, his stand-up, fall-down, naughty-but-nice slapstick humour was being aired in 80 countries, as well as at home in England. Gay, he lived as a bachelor in a London apartment. Six years later at the time of his death, *The Benny Hill Show* was being shown in 100 countries around the world and had made some $40 million.[496]

At this juncture in human evolution, few of us use our planets at the spiritual level, but many of us are striving to and such people are wonderful to be around. As with the other planets, the spiritual level of evolution is vastly different with Sedna from the two previous levels. Here, the stressful aspects with Ceres the ability to husband the spiritual destiny of life on the planet, at this crucial point in the evolutionary cycle.

Once we embrace the Sedna energy, which is the oneness of everything, our nurturing becomes an expression of Sedna consciousness and it becomes devotional in nature. The struggle of the beginner's level is gone, as are the transcendental crises of the intermediate level. At this level everything Saturnian is meaningless and yet everything Sednian has its place.

Hank Friedman is an American astrologer who began to study the field at 34 to disprove it, but became convinced of its validity. He had Sedna in the ninth house of spirituality and knowledge, sesquiquadrate Ceres in the fourth house of home.

> He was trained for five years in Ericksonian Hypnotherapy and also as an advisor in parental deprogramming. He also studied Sufism for 20 years. He moved into a synthesis of Vedic with Western astrology and is a world expert in astrological software. He has beta-tested, designed and reviewed software from the age of 34 and is the author of *Astrology for Your PC* and review articles for astrology magazines. He is considered one of the

---

[496] https://en.wikipedia.org/wiki/Benny_Hill

San Francisco Bay's foremost psychics and psychic therapists.[497]

Franklin Jones was an American siddha-guru known as Bubba Free John and later Adi Da. He had Sedna in the third house of ideas and communication, sesquiquadrate Ceres in the eighth house of the occult.

> He was a handsome, ample and happy mystic with an ashram called Horse House Commune in California. His teachings deal with various forms to harmonize and purify action in life. *The Method of the Disshas* and *Garbage and the Goddess* are among his works, which include books and recorded talks.

> It is said of Jones that he lived in a world of sheer light and joy known as "the Bright" until his second or third year. This condition would assert itself in the form of uncommon psychic and mystical experiences, as well as physical symptoms such as sudden attacks of fever or skin rashes with no diagnosable medical cause. These signs subsided in his eighth year and didn't return until he was 17.

> At 21 he went through a despair that yielded two insights which would be crucial to his philosophy. The first was that there is only one reality or transcendental consciousness; the second is that this reality is man's true identity and anything else is a product of an un-enlightened mind. For the next few years he sequestered himself in spiritual disciplines and sought out the company of an American-born teacher, Swami Rudrananda, who instructed him in Indian kundalini yoga.

> He then entered a Lutheran seminary at Swami's instruction. At 28 while at the seminary, he underwent another religious experience, and came up with a new insight, that his whole search had been founded on the avoidance of relationships and the recoil from reality in its many forms. The next year he sought out Swami Muktananda in India, and stayed briefly with him there, and during that time the Swami acknowledged that Franklin had reached "yogic liberation."

> At 30 he entered the permanent condition of Sahaj Samadhi, essential to transcendental being-consciousness. After this, he

---

[497] https://www.astro.com/astro-databank/Friedman,_Hank_(1950)

was moved to teach others the condition of "the Heart" or the reality in which everything inheres. He spent three years of struggle with students who were not prepared for his teaching, which weakened his physical body.

He returned to India to clarify his teaching, changed his name to "Bubba Free John," as Bubba was his childhood nickname and "Free John" a rendering of Franklin Jones. When he returned to America, he began to teach differently.

At 37 he ceased to have frequent contact with his many followers and lived in seclusion for the next three years. When he was 43, now known as Adi Da, he moved with a group of about 40 followers to the Fijian island of Naitaba, which had been purchased by a wealthy follower. It was his primary residence until the end of his life.

However, accusations that he abused his power as a spiritual leader attracted international attention a couple of years later. In investigative reports and dozens of interviews, both named and anonymous ex-members made numerous specific allegations of Adi Da forcing members to engage in psychologically, sexually, and physically abusive and humiliating behaviour, as well as accusing the church of committing tax fraud.

Two lawsuits were filed against Adi Da and the church in California. One was dismissed the next year, however the other lawsuit and several threatened suits in subsequent years were settled with payments and confidentiality agreements, negatively impacting member morale and bleeding the organisation financially.[498]

Dane Rudhyar was a French-American astrologer, one of most noted and respected astrologers of the 20th century. He had Sedna in the third house of ideas and communication, square his Ceres in the first house of identity.

He was called a modern renaissance man for his ability to express himself in many fields: music, painting, poetry, philosophy and metaphysics. He wrote for national magazines since the '30s and was the author of many books.

---

[498] https://en.wikipedia.org/wiki/Adi_Da

He had poor health as a child, a distraction that continued through his life. At 12, he had life-threatening surgery to remove his left kidney and adrenal gland. A bright youth, he passed his baccalaureate at the Sorbonne at 16, majoring in philosophy. Becoming involved in the artistic and musical climate of Paris, he was heavily influenced by the radical ideas of Nietzsche.

At this time, he had a mystical experience or realisation in which he "became intuitively aware of the cyclic nature of all existence and of the fact that our Western civilisation was coming to an autumnal conclusion." He later wrote that it was from this time that he sought to gain a clearer understanding of the cyclic patterns and basic meaning of human existence.

At the age of 21, he left his native France and traveled to the U.S., reinventing himself with the name of Dane Rudhyar. Believing in the necessity of a fundamental transformation of our civilisation, his change of name was a symbolic reflection of his contribution to that change. The name "Rudhyar" is derived from the Sanskrit God Rudra, the Destroyer and Regenerator.

Attaining a position in the avant-garde art community of the West, he also studied and wrote. His seminal book in which he emphasised integration, *The Astrology of Personality*, was first published when he was 41.[499]

In-conjunct

With the evolutionary inconjunct between Sedna and Ceres the esoteric spiritual energy of Sedna bursts into our potency, our nurturing nature and our ability to deal with change in an evolutionary way and we have a fated role to play.

Ceres is associated with prosperity and abundance. She represents the actual bounty – the foods, the flowers, the birds and plants, and the desperation that results when the bounty is withdrawn. It shows how well we go with the flow… the universal one, that is. The unification of both giving and receiving through ourselves as an exchange of energy.

The inconjunct sometimes acts as a flow and at other times as a stress, so we have to learn to actively manage the process as the rarified spiritual energy sometimes reinforces our potency, our nurturing nature

---

[499] https://en.wikipedia.org/wiki/Dane_Rudhyar

and our ability to deal with change and, at other times, isn't there to back us up. By adjusting to this, we gain a deeper understanding of ourselves and how to play our role.

I have this aspect and Ceres is conjunct my Venus, the planet of values and relationships, in the eleventh house of ideals. I've made a practice of going with the flow, it's been a catch phrase, particularly in my work as a clown, which was improvised interactive play, all process and no product.

We also associate Ceres with loss, compromise, rage and grief, so unfortunately, along with our abundance, Ceres will also deliver some pretty dramatic episodes when we must give up and give in – likely triggering deep emotion.

This I can also attest to and so the other practice I have developed is acceptance. With all Sedna Ceres contacts things happen which we have no control over, but particularly with this aspect. We could rage against it or accept and make the most of the situation. Rage breeds illness and victimization and the negative sides of Sedna, so acceptance is a better strategy.

At the unconscious level, however, we might well lash out, rather than accept and we might well struggle with going with the flow, because we are so involved in our own soap opera, as we see in the following examples.

William Jewett Jr. is an American who was accused of sexual assault and murder. He had Sedna in the eighth house of shared resources, inconjunct Ceres, which is together with Neptune, the planet of delusions and lies, both in the third house of ideas and communication. He was seen leaving a party in the early hours with a girl who was later found raped and then strangled to death. He was arrested nearly five years later on suspicion of her murder and was convicted and sentenced to life in prison.

Abraham Kasparian is a former American politician who stabbed his wife three times in a public restaurant. He had been arrested previously and received sentences for welfare fraud and larceny. He has Sedna in the fifth house of romance and children, inconjunct Ceres in the tenth house of profession.

His wife had filed for a divorce but agreed to meet him for lunch. She survived the attack. Earlier that same day, a former tenant sued the couple, charging them with negligence in connection with an apartment fire that killed two children.[500]

And Paula Yates was a Welsh TV personality in the UK, a tarted-up presenter of the TV series *The Tube*, who loved to use shock as an attention-getter and whose approach took her from flirtatious celebrity interviewer, to celebrity in her own right. She had Sedna in the fourth house of home, inconjunct Ceres in the eleventh house of collective consciousness.

Engagingly ebullient and flirtatious, her irreverent approach to the rich-and-famous won her industry awards twice. As a provocative columnist and author, her subjects ranged from baby care, to sexual turn-ons. However, it was her notably frank autobiography that made her best known.

As a child, she had an uncomfortable relationship with her dad, TV star Jess Yates, who was known as "the Bishop" for his presentation of the religious show *Stars on Sunday*. It was an unconventional childhood in a unique family. Her dad was 16-years-older than her mom, who was a former showgirl, actress and writer of erotic novels. From age eight, the girl lived mostly with her mom, at times in Malta and Majorca.

It was a revelation to discover when she was 38, via DNA testing, that Yates was not her father at all, but rather, her dad was Hughie Green, TV host of several popular shows. When she found this out, it added further strain to her relationship with her mom, which was already tenuous.

She started a relationship with Bob Geldof at 18 and produced her first book, *Rockstars In Their Underpants,* consisting of semi-clad photographs of everyone she and Geldof knew. They finally married in Las Vegas when she was 27. They had three daughters and she wrote two books about parenting, in which she urged women to stay at home to look after their children and to breast-feed their babies for as long as possible.

---

[500] https://www.astro.com/astro-databank/Kasparian,_Abraham

Her big break came when she was recruited as co-presenter of *The Tube*, an anarchic TV pop show which swiftly developed cult status. She stayed with the show for five years, winning the best documentary award at the New York Film Festival two years running for her interviews with Tina Turner and Elton John. She graduated to Channel Four's early morning program, *The Big Breakfast,* where she interviewed stars while everyone reclined on a large bed.

However, at 36, she was fired from her TV hostess job and her tangled life began its most turbulent period. She began an impassioned affair with the Michael Hutchence, singer with the rock group INXS, whom she called "a sexy love god." They had met the year before and began a three-year affair. She was linked to alcohol and drugs and Geldof secured custody of their three daughters. She had her breasts enlarged and trilled that the first time she and Michael went to bed, "he did six things within the first hour I was sure were illegal."

Pregnant, she divorced Geldof and gave birth to Michael's daughter, Heavenly Tiger Lily. She and Michael were planning to marry and move to Australia and were negotiating the purchase of a house overlooking Sydney Harbour. Michael's drug days were allegedly over and they both were filled with promise when mysteriously and tragically Michael was found dead in a hotel room.

Paula insisted that it was an accident rather than a suicide but was nonetheless treated several times for depression and made a suicide attempt herself the next year. She was found dead at her home in London two years later. Her body was found by a friend after repeated phone calls went unanswered. Tiger Lily was playing by herself when Mummy would not wake up, and an empty vodka bottle and half-empty one of barbiturates left mute testimony.[501]

As we tire of density and the grief it creates, and we start a spiritual journey to get out of the swamp, Sedna rewards us with transcendent crises, experiences which force us to let go and rise above them, resulting in a huge growth to a new level of consciousness. There is no

---

[501] https://en.wikipedia.org/wiki/Paula_Yates

choice with these crises, and the more we try and solve them, the more we will get hurt.

Werner Erhard is an American entrepreneurial guru, a multi-million dollar merchandiser of enlightenment, the founder of 'est', Erhard Seminar Training. He has Sedna in twelfth house of the unconscious, inconjunct Ceres, which is conjunct Quaoar, the planet of new perspectives and Venus, the planet of values, all in the fifth house of creativity.

His high-energy brand of instant salvation flourished in the mid-'70s, making him an equally instant multimillionaire. His organisation spawned a network centred on the principles of transformation. A onetime used-car salesman, he studied the consciousness disciplines of east and west to integrate his own brand of group therapy workshops. It is reported that est attracted 500,000 people and much of the jargon of est became part of the culture of the "me generation," such as "getting it" and "creating your own space."

At 25 he left his first wife and four children in Philadelphia and changed his name so they could not find him. He slipped into the California subcultures of human potential movements, pop psychology and eastern metaphysics. The story goes that he "got it" one day in an instant while stuck on a crowded freeway, the awareness that he was not his emotions and beliefs and intellect, but he was the creator and source of his experience.

He married again that year and the couple was together for 22 years and had a son. His second wife later said in an interview that Werner's ego and public image were the most important things in the world to him, and that "children, money or whatever, are so far down it doesn't matter."

When he was 37, enrolment in est began dropping and the IRS claimed that he owed $2 million in back taxes. The following year, his ex-wife sued for half of everything. When he retired est when he was 49, he came up with another program called "The Forum," which was pitched to people who wanted to "make it happen' and 'get a decisive edge in your ability to achieve'.

A handsome man with a raspy voice thickened by cigars, he is an executive in a sleek European jacket, with power that extends well past his original est weekends. Werner Erhard and

Associates projects grossed revenues of $39 million when he was 53. From the age of 49, he also ran Transformational Technologies Inc, a management consultant firm that brings in an annual $25 million.

In spite of his many critics who deride his quick-fix approach, his followers swear that his system works. However, when he was 56, a memo from his Bay Area company recommended bankruptcy and his children, in interviews, were telling the press horror stories of abuse. His daughter telling a San Jose paper: 'You never knew when he was going to go off and throw things or smack mom'.[502]

D. H. Lawrence was a British novelist and poet, the author of novels which include *Sons and Lovers, Women in Love, The Virgin and the Gypsy* and the *classic Lady Chatterley's Lover.*

He had Sedna in the fifth house of creativity, inconjunct Ceres, which is conjunct Juno, the asteroid of partnership, in the first house of identity.

He was one of the most controversial writers of the twentieth century, who believed in the concept that man should bring his instinct into balance with his intellect. His explicit treatment of sexual fulfilment led to over three decades of censorship and ultimately to the Supreme Court.

He was the fourth child of an abusive coal miner and a refined mother whom he idolised. After surviving bronchitis at the age of two weeks, which left him in permanently delicate health, he grew to be a frail and hypersensitive child, who was often in tears and was overly dominated by his unhappy mother. She was a refined schoolteacher, who met his father at a local dance and after the wedding, found that he did not own his own house and did not work in the mining office, as she had been led to believe, but instead laboured as a miner himself. Her misery is reflected in Lawrence's persistent theme in his novels of the elegant, well-bred woman under the influence of a common, low-bred man.

At 26, with two novels in progress, he accepted a luncheon invitation from his favourite teacher and his aristocratic wife.

---

[502] https://en.wikipedia.org/wiki/Werner_Erhard

According to legend, she had him in her bed within 20 minutes of meeting him. Two months later they eloped to Germany, marrying a couple of years later when her divorce became final. When they returned to England at the outbreak of WWI however, they were forbidden to travel outside of it, because his outspoken opposition to the war and her German birth aroused the suspicion that they were spies.

They left England at the end of the war, returning only for short visits thereafter, and led a peripatetic life through France, Italy, Sri Lanka, Australia, California and Mexico, where he was diagnosed with tuberculosis at 40. Despite his illness, he wrote voraciously during these years, introducing Freudian theory into the modern novel and especially writing openly about sexual passion and its necessary and explicit incorporation into human expression.

His theory of "blood consciousness" was a constant emphasis on humanity basing its decisions on instinct rather reason. His best-known work, *Lady Chatterley's Lover,* was published when he was 43, but it was banned in England and the U.S. for describing the sexual act in minute detail. However, thirty two years later the United States Supreme Court overruled the censorship and the book was published again.[503]

Jorge Luis Borges was an Argentinean writer, a literary giant with short stories, essays, poetry and all shades and types of books. He had Sedna in the ninth house of philosophy, inconjunct Ceres in the fourth house of home.

He had a razor-sharp wit and a self-depreciating style and a powerful imagination, but was a shy, retiring man who had a strong bond with his mother, living with her until her death at 99, when he was 75. Acclaimed as one of the greatest modern writers, he was compared to Edgar Allan Poe and Frank Kafka, and was a perennial candidate for the Nobel Prize in literature. His works were translated into more than 20 languages, and he

---

[503] https://en.wikipedia.org/wiki/D._H._Lawrence

won scores of literary prizes for his production of more than 35 volumes of writing.[504]

Humour can be one path to transcend the quicksand of Sedna, giving us the objectivity to step back from the edge, but also with the inconjunct to Ceres the ability to accept what is happening and make the most of each moment.

Jacques Tati is a French actor, writer and director. He has Sedna in the eighth house of shared resources, inconjunct his Ceres, which is conjunct his ascendent, the cusp of the first house of identity.

> He was noted for his wonderful talents of wit, humour and humanity. He started in the theatre, turning music and cabaret into a mime comedy work of art, which became an immediate success. He turned several of his show pieces into short films, by writing and producing them himself.[505]

His Sedna is also quintile Mars, the planet of action in the fifth house of creativity and bi-quintile Ixion, the planet of lawlessness, in the twelfth house of the unconscious.

> His first milestone film, *Jour de Fete,* had a comic style and visual humour which proved very successful. As a director, he was devoted to painstaking preparation of all of his films. Despite being troubled by financial problems and large debts, he produced six films throughout his career spanning three decades, two of the most successful being *Mon Oracle* and *Playtime*[506].

At this juncture in human evolution, few of us use our planets at the spiritual level, but many of us are striving to, and such people are wonderful to be around. As with the other planets, the spiritual level of evolution is vastly different with Sedna from the two previous levels. Here, the inconjunct with Ceres to husband the spiritual destiny of life on the planet, at this crucial point in the evolutionary cycle.

Once we embrace the Sedna energy, which is the oneness of everything, our nurturing becomes an expression of Sedna consciousness and it becomes devotional in nature. The struggle of the

---

[504] https://en.wikipedia.org/wiki/Jorge_Luis_Borges
[505] https://en.wikipedia.org/wiki/Jacques_Tati
[506] Ibid.

beginner's level is gone, as are the transcendental crises of the intermediate level. At this level everything Saturnian is meaningless and yet everything Sednian has its place.

Interestingly, it doesn't matter whether our spiritual vision is an illusion, our endeavours will still promote the spiritual growth of the planet, as is beautifully illustrated in the following example of a key figure in the Theosophical Society, whose spiritual vision was rejected by the Avatar she anointed and yet the ideas of both have formed the basis of what has come to be called New Age consciousness.

Annie Besant was a British-Indian social reformer and feminist at the forefront of liberal movements for 60 years. She had Sedna conjunct Chariklo, the centaur of foresight, in the twelfth house of the unconscious, inconjunct Ceres in the sixth house of service.

> Her family background was genteel, though her father was from an impoverished branch and died when Annie was only five. Deeply religious as a child, she longed to serve humanity with some sort of glorious martyrdom.
>
> She was married to a dour Anglican clergyman at 21, which was apparently a type of martyrdom in itself; the marriage lasted for six years. Leaving him at age 27, she had an alimony income of 110 pounds per annum, a comfortable if not extreme fortune. Taking up the worthy cause of birth control, she was arrested and tried at 30 on a morals charge for her publication written with Charles Bradlaugh, "The Fruits of Philosophy." The litigation cost her the custody of her two children and her alimony. An attractive, feminine woman, she held a fiery sword in her public demonstrations.
>
> She met Mme Blavatsky when she was 42 and was greatly taken with her and with the doctrine of Theosophy. From the age of 60 until her death, she served as the President of the Theosophical Society in India. She took the young Krishnamurti under her wing a couple of years later and nurtured him as the New Avatar, the Messiah. She founded the Order of the Star in the East with the 16-year-old Krishnamurti as the official head.
>
> However, the society was fraught with intrigue, spiritual competition, power-struggles and scandals. When Krishna finally broke with the Theosophical society when Anne was 82, she was

nearly completely senile and never realized that her cultivation of the Matreya had been denied by the embodiment himself. When he visited her for the last time, she hardly knew who he was.[507]

Lisa Williams is a British psychic, medium and healer. She has Sedna in the fifth house of creativity, inconjunct Ceres in the first house of identity.

> he starred in two shows on Lifetime Television: *Lisa Williams: Life Among the Dead* and *Lisa Williams: Voices From the Other Side*. The shows followed Williams on a typical day, as she communicated with spirits, investigated haunted houses, and conducted other spirit-seeking activities.[508]

Her Sedna is also at the tip of a finger of fate, inconjunct with Pluto, the planet of life and death, in the tenth house of profession and inconjunct Neptune, the planet of sensitivity to the spirit world in the first house of identity.

> She came out as a lesbian at 37 and said: 'For many years, speaking to dead people was hard enough for people to accept me, but then on top of that to then say 'by the way, I'm gay', I didn't want to acknowledge it'. Asked by a reporter, because of her unique insight into life after death, where she thought gay people were headed, she said: 'In my experience with those who have crossed, it is a place of love. It isn't a place of 'you didn't live this way so we'll punish you', it is a place where all your loved ones accept you for who you are'.[509]

Ramana Maharishi was an Indian mystic of the Hindu religion. who, after a mystical experience at age 17 and left his parents to become an aesetic. He has Sedna in the sixth house of service, inconjunct Ceres in the eleventh house of collective consciousness.

> The second of three sons of a farmer, he was raised in a religious family who gave ritual offerings and visited the temple. A disinterested student, he was more concerned with seeking his own identity and meaning.

> At 17 he went into an altered state of consciousness which had a profound effect on him. He experienced what he understood to

---

[507] https://en.wikipedia.org/wiki/Annie_Besant
[508] https://en.wikipedia.org/wiki/Lisa_Williams_(psychic)
[509] Ibid.

be his own death, and later returned to life. He also felt himself as being outside of his own body, an entity of light. He spent the next ten years in silence and meditation, living in temples and hillside caves as an aesetic. It is the custom in India to regard such holy men, seeking non-attachment, with respect and he was called The Sage of Anarchala.

Devotees brought him a bit of food and books of religious tradition, and when he began to teach, disciples came. After his decade of discipline, he lived a more normal life in an ashram that his disciplines built and taught student and supplicants. When he was finally diagnosed with cancer, he accepted this with the same equanimity that he had for mundane goods, and died sitting in the lotus position with his last word, the sacred syllable OM.[510]

Quintile, Bi-quintile

The evolutionary quintile or bi-quintile aspect between Sedna and Ceres infuses our potency, our nurturing nature and our ability to deal with change with the all-encompassing spiritual energy of Sedna to the point where we can push the boundaries of human development.

Quintiles and bi-quintiles point to talent, the desire to create order and to categorize, a fascination with patterns and structures, perfectionist tendencies, and the desire to build or make things. These aspects have the characteristics of both the trine and opposition. They point to awareness of conflicts, or problems and finding solutions for them; however, they do not automatically kick into action and must be cultivated over time.

Ceres is associated with prosperity and abundance. She represents the actual bounty – the foods, the flowers, the birds and plants, and the desperation that results when the bounty is withdrawn. It shows how well we go with the flow... the universal one, that is. The unification of both giving and receiving through ourselves as an exchange of energy.

Ceres is the planet of prosperity and abundance, but we also associate her with loss, compromise, rage and grief, so unfortunately, along with our bounty, Ceres will also deliver some pretty dramatic episodes when we must give up and give in – triggering deep emotion.

---

[510] https://en.wikipedia.org/wiki/Ramana_Maharshi

At the unconscious level, however, we might well struggle with both going with the flow and with giving in, because we are so involved in our own soap opera, as we can see in the following examples.

Mata Hari was a Dutch prostitute and exotic dancer who also served as a spy. She had Sedna in the fifth house of creativity, bi-quintile Ceres in the twelfth house of the unconscious.

> The daughter of a merchant, in her younger years she was expelled from convent school for sleeping with a priest and, at the age of 18, moved to Java with her 40-year-old husband. The couple had a violent marriage and one of their two children died. She left her husband and returned to Europe at 29 where, as a nude belly dancer, she went to Paris to work in a brothel.
>
> She also attended German espionage school and at the outbreak of WW I, she was offered cash up-front for a German mission, but turned out to be not a very good spy. With the codename of H21, she returned to Paris, spent the money and did precious little else. However, she was arrested as a double agent when she delivered a message on German submarine activity to the French embassy. She was 40 when she was arrested and placed on trial for treason. Convicted, she was executed by firing squad.
>
> On the morning of her execution, she put on her stockings, dressed in a pearl-gray frock, slung a coat over her shoulders, buttoned her boots, put on a dark tri-corned hat with a veil and glove. "This lady knows how to die," said the sergeant major who helped her. "After the shots were fired, she crumpled in a heap of petticoats." After her death documents were revealed which showed French falsification of the records and that instead of being a major spy for the Germans, she was an elegant but naive adventuress, essentially the first strip-tease dancer.[511]

Cameron Hooker is an American kidnapper, murderer and sadist who, despite no history of family abuse, was into S/M and B&D fantasies from his youth. He has Sedna in the seventh house of relationships, bi-quintile Ceres in the eleventh house of collective consciousness.

---

[511] https://en.wikipedia.org/wiki/Mata_Hari

He grew up in a small California town and got a job in a lumber mill following high school. At age 19, he started going with a 15-year-old girl, playing bondage-sex games with her. They married a couple of years later and had two daughters. Neither of the girls knew anything about what was happening in their home.

A year later he kidnapped, tortured and killed a woman, whose body was never found. He was never charged. When he was 23, he picked up a hitchhiker and kept her nude in a box under his bed for seven years. She was whipped, strangled, dunked in water, burned, electrically shocked, raped, humiliated and systematically brainwashed. After three years she had a year out of her box, doing housework, yard work and sleeping on the floor. However, she was put back into near total confinement for another three years, before she was brought out again.

She and Cameron's wife gradually became friends, as both were caught in the same web of terror. They fled together when Cameron was 30, but his wife returned home within a week. Three months later she broke down and told her pastor of her personal hell, and then the police. He was arrested and was found guilty on ten counts of kidnapping and other charges and given life in prison.[512]

Diane Luciferia was a French Wiccan high priestess who descended into black masses and orgies, until she herself became a homicide victim. She had Sedna in the tenth house of profession, quintile Ceres in the seventh house of relationships.

She was born Nicole Martin and she met her partner at 24 on the Isle of Man, where the Wicca International Witchcraft movement originated. They lived together and represented the sect in France with Nicole taking the name of Diane Luciferia.

He was an author of pornographic film scripts and he met a girl on the set of a film shoot and adopted her as his daughter, ignoring the fact that she had personality disorders and a history of time spent in psychiatric hospitals. She grew up in the movement and became a witch. The Wiccan chapter began

---

[512] https://en.wikipedia.org/wiki/Kidnapping_of_Colleen_Stan

conducting black masses which ended up in sexual orgies. Eventually many members left, following a dissident.

When she was 49, Diane and her partner's adopted daughter, who were both witches, appeared on a French TV show to air their grievances. However, when they were not allowed to voice their opinions, they furiously stormed off the set. Their rivalry escalated and later that year, the daughter murdered Diane with a shotgun, staging the scene to make it look like a suicide. She then took her place as high priestess. A few weeks later, crazed with grief, her adopted father murdered her by hanging her and then, hung himself.[513]

As we tire of density and the grief it creates, and we start a spiritual journey to get out of the swamp, Sedna rewards us with transcendent crises, experiences which force us to let go and rise above them, resulting in a huge growth to a new level of consciousness. There is no choice with these crises, and the more we try and solve them, the more we will get hurt.

Betty Friedan was an American feminist pioneer and organizer, lecturer and writer, the author of *The Feminine Mystique*, which became a best-seller, translated into 13 languages. She had Sedna in the third house of communication, quintile Ceres in the seventh house of relationships.

Her mother quit her job as editor of the local newspaper's women's pages to become a housewife. She was aware of the toll this took, and the impact it had on her family. And as an adult, after becoming pregnant, she was herself fired from a job.

During her 20s and 30s she was a deeply committed radical activist. A brilliant, energetic reporter for union newspapers, she was intensely engaged in the leftist politics of the time. By the time she stopped working at 31, pregnant with her second child, McCarthyism had chased underground much of this visionary women's movement. The rest was smothered by anti-female union policies and longstanding misogyny among male leaders on the left.

She retreated to the suburbs and began writing about family and work for women's magazines, doing what her mother had not

---

[513] https://www.astro.com/astro-databank/Luciferia,_Diane

done. And she came out swinging. Women in labor unions were fighting for equal pay, maternity leave and higher minimum wages, while other progressive women agitated for government-sponsored day care, national health insurance and an end to racial discrimination.

She later said: "I decided I was going to be fulfilled as a housewife, but I could not suppress the itch to write, and I did it in the morning, like secret drinking." She authored *The Feminine Mystique* at 42, which became a best-seller and was translated into 13 languages. This book exposed the "desperate housewives" of 1950s America, women imprisoned in suburbia with little to do. She came to believe that "the only way for a woman, as for a man, to find herself, to know herself as a person, is by creative work of her own."

On the heels of the Civil Rights Movement, she helped to found the National Organization for Women when she was 45, the largest and most effective group for women's rights, and served as its first president.[514]

Dan Rather was an American news broadcaster, one of the top in his competitive field. He had Sedna conjunct Uranus, the planet of intuition, in the twelfth house of the unconscious,

bi-quintile Ceres, which is conjunct Venus, the planet of values, in the seventh house of relationships.

He was anchor of the CBS Evening News for 24 years and he made a name for himself in journalism for his refusal to play "nice" with political leaders during his hard-hitting interviews. However, at the end of his career he became embroiled in controversy about a disputed news report involving President George W. Bush's Vietnam-era service in the National Guard. He was 73 when he reported on 60 Minutes that a series of memos critical of President George W. Bush's Texas Air National Guard service record had been discovered in the personal files of his former commanding officer.

Once copies of the documents were made available on the Internet, their authenticity was quickly called into question. Much

---

[514] https://en.wikipedia.org/wiki/Betty_Friedan

of this was based on the fact that the documents were proportionally printed and displayed using other modern typographic conventions usually unavailable on military typewriters of the 1970s. The font used on the documents has characteristics that exactly match standard font features of Microsoft Word. This led to claims that the memos were forgeries. The accusations then spread over the following days into mainstream media outlets.

Rather and CBS initially defended the story, insisting that the documents had been authenticated by experts; however, this was contradicted by some of the experts it originally cited, and later reported that its source for the documents had misled the network about how he had obtained them. CBS retracted the story and Rather stated, "If I knew then what I know now, I would not have gone ahead with the story as it was aired, and I certainly would not have used the documents in question."

Following an investigation commissioned by CBS, which many believe was the result of political pressure on the board, they fired the story producer and asked three other producers connected with the story to resign and many believe Rather's retirement was also hastened by this incident. Five years later he was interviewed on Larry King Live, commenting "Nobody has proved that they were fraudulent, much less a forgery... The truth of this story stands up to this day."[515]

US congressman, John McCain, has a close bi-quintile between Ceres and Sedna. His Sedna is in his second house of material reality and his Ceres is in his ninth house of knowledge.

While on a bombing mission over Hanoi when he was 31, he was shot down, seriously injured, and captured by the North Vietnamese. He was a prisoner of war for six years, during which he experienced episodes of torture, which have left him with lifelong physical limitations.

His personal character has been a dominant feature of his public image. This image includes the military service of both himself and his family, the circumstances and tensions surrounding the

[515] https://en.wikipedia.org/wiki/Dan_Rather

end of his first marriage and beginning of second, his maverick political persona, his temper, his admitted problem of occasional ill-considered remarks, and his close ties to his children from both his marriages.

His political appeal has been more nonpartisan and less ideological compared to many other national politicians. His stature and reputation stem partly from his service in the Vietnam War. He also carries physical vestiges of his war wounds, as well as his melanoma surgery. When campaigning, he quips: "I am older than dirt and have more scars than Frankenstein."[516]

And William Butler Yeats, the famous Irish writer, a poet and dramatist who won a Nobel Prize for Literature, has Sedna in his first house of identity, quintile Ceres in the fourth house of home.

He was first published at age 21 with elaborate early work. As he became noted as a poet and novelist, his works became more simplified, while his own philosophy developed in complexity. This complex man was at once courteous and self-centred, gregarious, and spiritually and intellectually questing. He was a hobby astrologer with a very active interest in mysticism. His somewhat astrological work, A Vision, resulted from a collaboration with his wife, who worked for many years with automatic writing, penning messages from the spirit masters. Her automatic writings fuelled the book that involves a unique approach to the twenty-eight phases of the Moon.

He also had a finger of fate with Sedna at the apex. One of the inconjunct aspects forming the finger is with the Node in eighth house of the occult and the other with Nessus, the centaur of 'sweeping way the old', in the seventh house of relationships. He believed that "the sexual principle lies at the heart of all behaviour as well as history." His lovers were a spur to his poetry, taking him and his readers to a brink "beyond human notes, nor words, to dwell upon the soul's destiny".[517]

---

[516] https://en.wikipedia.org/wiki/John_McCain
[517] https://en.wikipedia.org/wiki/W._B._Yeats

Humour can be one path to transcend the quicksand of Sedna, giving us the objectivity to step back from the edge, but also with the quintile and bi-quintike aspects to Ceres the ability to accept and make the most of the chaos of each moment.

Richard Pryor is an American comedian and actor. He has Sedna in the first house of identity, bi-quintile Ceres, which is conjunct his Mercury in the eighth house of shared resources.

> A sharp, brash star of nightclubs, TV and films who thrived on chaos, he was elected to the Comedy Hall of Fame. His earthy, profane humour and low-life characterisations brought him great popularity and he went on to win two Grammy's for his comedy albums, appear in movies and TV specials and in guest shots. He was also a writer and film director.

> In the middle of his career he progressed heavily into booze and drugs. He set himself on fire while free-basing cocaine at 40 and was badly burned over 50% of his body. After recovery, he toned down both his act and his incendiary personal life. He had five marriages and paid child support for the son of an actress. When he was 46 he began to lose weight and was diagnosed with multiple sclerosis. By 53 he was confined to a life of wheelchairs, canes and physical therapy and just nine days after his 65th birthday, he suffered a heart attack.[518]

At this juncture in human evolution, few of us use our planets at the spiritual level, but many of us are striving to and such people are wonderful to be around. As with the other planets, the spiritual level of evolution is vastly different with Sedna from the two previous levels. Here, the quintile and bi-quintile aspects with Ceres give us the ability to husband the spiritual destiny of life on the planet, at this crucial point in the evolutionary cycle.

Once we embrace the Sedna energy, which is the oneness of everything, our nurturing becomes an expression of Sedna consciousness and it becomes devotional in nature. The struggle of the beginner's level is gone, as are the transcendental crises of the intermediate level. At this level everything Saturnian is meaningless and yet everything Sednian has its place.

---

[518] https://en.wikipedia.org/wiki/Richard_Pryor

Alan Oken is an American astrologer. He has Sedna conjunct Mercury and also Varuna, the planet of notability, in the fifth house of creativity, quintile Ceres in the eighth house of the occult.

> He is a translator, teacher, global traveler and international tour guide, who lectures in five languages and does natal horoscope readings in seven. He is a member of the New Group of World Servers and a life-long student of the Work and Teachings of the Tibetan Master, Djwhal Khul and legacy of the Ancient Wisdom.[519]

His Sedna is also sextile Saturn, the planet of structure, and semi-square Uranus, the planet of intuition, both in the seventh house of relationships, and square Pholus, the centaur of illumination, in the second house of material resources.

> He is the author of a dozen titles, including *Soul-Centered Astrology*, *Rulers of the Horoscope*, and *Alan Oken's Complete Astrology*. In addition, he has written hundreds of articles for Dell Horoscope Magazine and many other national and international reviews and journals. Alan was the Director of The Wisdom School in Santa Fe, is co-founder of the Australian Institute for the Development of Consciousness and was Director of Esoteric Studies in Lisbon.[520]

Zoe Wells was an American artist and psychic who worked with Marc Edmund Jones and Elsie Wheeler on the 360 degree meanings that became known as the Sabian Symbols. She had Sedna on the cusp of the eleventh house of collective consciousness, quintile Ceres, which is conjunct Nessus, the centaur of radical change, and Varuna, the planet of notability, all in the eighth house of the occult.

> When she was 40 she was a recognised commercial artist and student of Marc's and she possessed remarkable psychic skills. In an experimental session she brought through fifty-two symbols for a pack of ordinary playing cards. Marc described this event, in his book *The Sabian Symbols in Astrology*, as the 'beginning

---

[519] https://www.alanoken.com/about/
[520] Ibid.

of a conscious recognition of the ancient sources as a self-contained and living integrity available for use'.[521]

Jeff Green is an American astrologer and the author of *Pluto: The Evolutionary Journey of the Soul* and *Uranus: Freedom From the Known,* books that have been translated into ten languages. He has Sedna in the fifth house of creativity, quintile Ceres in the third house of ideas and communication.

> His early family life was brutal. He experienced severe psychological and physical abuse from his mother and he and his brother were sent for a time to an orphanage, before being later returned to family. Always the "black sheep", at an early age, he recounts overhearing his parents say that they didn't care for him. Feeling a strong sense of alienation from both his family and his overall environment, he spent most of his school days at the ocean, where he could "escape" with the accompaniment of the ocean sounds and a surfboard.
>
> He became an alcoholic. One drunken evening, he reached a fatal turning point when he got into a car accident and came to an intense altercation with the other driver. Arrested before a near violent ending, he was offered one of two sentences - go to jail or go to Vietnam. He had already experienced a life of abuse, devastation and trauma, but it was nothing in comparison to the violence and insanity of the war he was about to experience.
>
> "Life made no sense to me; even the idea of God made no sense. I had a very close friend during the war. One day we were bombed and he was reading the Bible when this happened. He got a direct hit, and all that was left when I returned was pieces of flesh and a blood covered Bible. I too had the shared illusion that God is perfect, and did not understand how he allowed such a thing to happen, especially when someone was reading His book... At the age of eighteen this is completely senseless. And so, I erased God from my life."
>
> As did many of the soldiers at the time, drugs became his form of emotional survival. One month before being evacuated from Vietnam, another life altering experience occurred. Searching for

---

[521] https://www.astro.com/astro-databank/Wells,_Zoe

drugs in a nearby village, he stumbled upon a hill with steps. Climbing to the top, he found a Buddhist monastery. One of the monks approached him, but although the language barrier prevented his ability to converse directly with the monk, he experienced a telepathic communion.

At the end of military service, he continued to experience trauma and his roaming eventually took him to Mexico, where he had another extraordinary mystical experience. This time he encountered a Shaman of the Navaho tribe. Like the experience with the Buddist monk, the language barrier was again surpassed through telepathic communication. He spent six months here, during which time the Shaman initiated him in the sacred peyote experience. While undergoing this time of initiation, which created a lasting shift and expansion of consciousness, he encountered a pack of wolves and developed the ability to communicate telepathically with them. He spent three weeks living as a member of the pack.

The incredible experiences of his life eventually brought him to his true path as teacher and he has lectured throughout the U.S, Canada, Europe and has been a participant in almost all of the major astrological conferences in the world. He is founder and director of the School of Evolutionary Astrology. His pioneering work has expanded the concepts of astrology to encompass a broader vision and greater understanding of the soul's purpose, necessity and desire for evolution.[522]

He is called the founder of Evolutionary Astrology because he first started to lecture on the revolutionary astrological paradigm at 31, after receiving a dream from the spiritual master Swami Sri Yukteswar, who was Yogananda's guru. In that dream the entire paradigm of Evolutionary Astrology was conveyed to Jeffrey.

This was the first time in astrology's long history that a specific paradigm was realized that allowed for an understanding of the evolutionary progression of a Soul from life to life. Jeffrey lectured all over the world on Evolutionary Astrology for 25 years from his early thirties. He established Evolutionary Astrology

---

[522] Ibid.

schools in a number of countries and wrote books on Evolutionary Astrology.

The first of these, Pluto: The Evolutionary Journey of the Soul, Volume I was published at 38. It has been in continuous print ever since and has become one of the all-time best-selling astrology books. Translations have been made into French, German, Dutch, Chinese, Bulgarian, Spanish, Portuguese, Italian, Serbian and other languages. Volume II, Pluto: The Soul's Evolution through Relationships was published when he was 52 and has been in continuous print.

Since starting his original Pluto School at 48, he had many students, a number of whom are now professional Evolutionary Astrologers. He personally counseled over 30,000 clients in his lengthy career. This exposure to so many Souls from so many different backgrounds and orientations allowed him to come to the deepest possible understandings of the nature of the Soul. He communicated these insights through all of his teachings.[523]

---

[523] http://schoolofevolutionaryastrology.com/about

34: Sedna / Jupiter

Conjunction

With the conjunction of Sedna and Jupiter, the all-encompassing spiritual energy of Sedna infuses our growth and optimism, our ability to seek insight through knowledge and express our generosity and tolerance.

Jupiter has generally been associated with good luck and bounty. Optimism and growth, including mental and spiritual growth, come under its rule. On the positive side, Jupiter is associated with a sense of humour, good will, and mercy.

If we are unconscious of the Sedna energy, however, or there are other stressful aspects to the conjunction, we are likely to call the more negative manifestations of Jupiter into our lives, including blind optimism, excess, overindulgence, intolerance and the irresponsibility that results from blind optimism.

Like Anthony Magnoni, who was a French teenager, known as Hades, age 19 when he and three other local teens desecrated the Toulon cemetery. He has Sedna conjunct Jupiter in the eleventh house of collective consciousness.

> In the early hours the four kids brought up a body of someone who had been buried twenty years earlier. With ideology that is somewhat vague and borders around Satanism and Hitlerism, they performed satanic rituals on the cadaver, including necrophilia. They all admitted a ferocious hatred for human beings. They went before the courts and Anthony was given four years prison with one year suspended.[524]

Or Juan Belmonte, who was a Spanish bullfighter, considered by many to have been the greatest matador of all time. He had Sedna conjunct Jupiter and also Vesta, the asteroid of regeneration, all in the twelfth house of the unconscious. He is began his bullfighting career at 16, touring around Spain in a children's bullfighting group called Los Niños Sevillanos. He killed his first bull when he was 18.

> As an adult, his technique was unlike that of previous matadors; he stood erect and nearly motionless, and always stayed within

---

[524] https://www.astro.com/astro-databank/Magnoni,_Anthony

inches of the bull, unlike previous matadors, who stayed far from the animal to avoid the horns. As a result of this daring technique, Belmonte was frequently gored, sustaining many serious wounds. One such incident occurred in a bullfight in Barcelona, when he was 35. He was gored through his chest and pinned against a wall.

His rivalry with Joselito, another contender for the appellation "greatest matador of all time", from when he was 22 through to 28, during what is known as the Golden Age of Bullfighting, was cut short when Joselito was fatally gored at a bullfight in a small town near Madrid. Belmonte then had to carry alone the weight of the whole bullfighting establishment, which proved to be unbearable, and which led to the first of his three temporary retirements when he was 30. His final retirement was in at 43. During his career he received 24 serious wounds and 'countless minor ones'. He committed suicide aged 69.[525]

Helene Demuth was a German domestic worker who served as the housekeeper of Jenny and Karl Marx. She had Sedna conjunct Jupiter in the fifth house of children.

At the age of 30 she gave birth to a boy believed by most scholars to have been fathered by Marx. Marx's closest personal friend, Frederick Engels, a bachelor living in Manchester, claimed fatherhood of the boy. After Marx's death when she was 63, Helene moved to Engels's home, where she ran the household. The pair worked together organizing and arranging the publication of Marx's literary remains.[526]

As we tire of density and the grief it creates, and we start a spiritual journey to get out of the swamp, Sedna rewards us with transcendent crises, experiences which force us to let go and rise above them, resulting in a huge growth to a new level of consciousness. There is no choice with these crises. and the more we try and solve them, the more we will get hurt.

[525] https://en.wikipedia.org/wiki/Juan_Belmonte
[526] https://en.wikipedia.org/wiki/Helene_Demuth

Ethel Kennedy was an American news figure and the wife of Robert Kennedy. She has been her family's beacon of faith, whose life work has been her children.

She has Sedna conjunct Jupiter, and also Nessus, the centaur of radical change, in the first house of identity. A wonderful sense of humour sustains her and she likes to tease and be teased. Born into a large Catholic family with more money than the Kennedy's, she loved her parents, who were both alcoholics. Ethel and her siblings grew up wild and she developed the habit of lashing out at anyone that was critical of her family and has remained fierce when provoked. Both of her parents and her brother were killed in separate plane crashes.

She married Bobby Kennedy when she was 22 and they had 11 children, the youngest of which was born after Bobby's assassination when she was 40. She takes her widowhood very seriously and never remarried because no other man could be as good as Bobby. Through all of the problems over the years she has been the glue that holds the family together in every crisis. Her children see her as a 'doer' who is filled with love, supports causes and makes people feel special.

Through many family tragedies, she has relied on her religious faith. Crises have included not only the death of her senator husband, but drug rehab for her sons, the death of son David when she was 56, due to a drug overdose, reckless driving of son Joe that left a girl paralysed for life, and the death of son Michael in a skiing accident when she was 70. However, her daughter, Kathleen Kennedy Townsend, was elected lieutenant governor of Virginia and all of her children now are committed to public service.

At 64 she toured Eastern Europe, donating medical equipment and at 69 toured Kenya to promote democratic reforms. She attends mass every day, prays often and has softened over time. At 96 she was awarded a Presidential Medal of Freedom by President Obama for her dedication to "advancing the cause of social justice, human rights, environmental protection, and poverty reduction by creating countless ripples of hope to effect change around the world".[527]

Friedrich Nietzsche was a German philosopher who is considered one of the most influential voices of modern times. He had Sedna conjunct Jupiter in the fourth house of home.

He came from a long line of Lutheran pastors and was destined to follow in the footsteps of his clergyman dad, who died after 11 months of suffering from a serious illness, when he was age five. Shortly after his father's death, his younger brother died, leaving him to live with his mother, younger sister, grandmother and two aunts. He received a strict Christian upbringing as his mother was also the child of a Protestant minister. He suffered continually from severe headaches, sore throats, and rheumatic ailments as a child, especially during his school days.

At age 23, recognised for his brilliant work, he was appointed to the chair of philology at the University of Basel, and later was granted to Doctorate without examination. However, at the age of 35 he resigned his post and began a decade of travels across Europe, during which he wrote his greatest books, including *Thus Spoke Zarathustra* and *Twilight of the Idols.*

His dealings with the opposite sex were consistently awkward. He made a precipitous and impulsive proposal to a woman at 32, just two hours after meeting her. His late 30's was probably among the loneliest and most desperate periods in his life, the time when he began his *Thus Spoke Zarathustra.*

He had a desire to define himself as a European and looked forward to a time when the peoples of Europe would define themselves as Europeans rather than as citizens of particular countries. He believed that history is a genealogy of geniuses, in which each genius created the mental world in which his successors live.

His mental degeneration, apparently caused by syphilis, began with megalomania. He started to call himself a genius, the leading person of all millenniums and he claimed that all women loved him. He took on different identities - the Buddha,

[527] https://en.wikipedia.org/wiki/Ethel_Kennedy

Alexander the Great, Caesar, Voltaire, Napoleon, Wagner - and danced naked in his room. In January 1889 he broke down in the street and tearfully embraced a horse which had been beaten. He was declared insane by doctors and taken back to Germany where he sat in a vegetative state until his death eleven years later.[528]

Willem De Kooning was a Dutch-American abstract experimental painter. His swirls and colors helped define abstract expressionism and made him one of the 20th century's greatest painters. He had Sedna conjunct Jupiter in the second house of material reality.

The son of a wine and beer distributor and a barmaid, he emigrated to the U.S. at 22 as a stowaway on a ship. He learned English while working as a house painter and commercial artist. His first one-man show was at age 44. When his canvas "Excavation" won the major prize at the Art Institute of Chicago's 1951 exhibition, it was viewed as a vindication for abstract expressionism, the movement that stresses the depiction of emotion through shapes and colours.

In his late 40s, he returned to the figure. He worked for three years on "Woman I," which was bought by the Museum of Modern Art. He never considered the work finished, or even a success, but it became the most frequently reproduced work of art of the 1950s.

He married fellow painter Elaine Fried at 39. They separated later and when he was 52. He had a daughter with Joan Ward. He never divorced Elaine and she returned when he was 74, helping him to stop his heavy drinking and handling his affairs for the next ten years until her death.

He painted daily through his 80s, despite an advancing handicap of Alzheimer's. However, after a bitter court fight when he was 85, he was declared mentally incompetent and control of his $150 million estate was given to his attorney and his daughter Lisa. He died in his studio at 93.[529]

---

[528] https://en.wikipedia.org/wiki/Friedrich_Nietzsche
[529] https://en.wikipedia.org/wiki/Willem_de_Kooning

Charles Darwin was an English naturalist, geologist and biologist, best known for his contributions to the science of evolution and as author of *Origin of the Species*. He had Sedna conjunct Jupiter and also with Juno the asteroid of partnership, in the third house of ideas. This is the root of his theory of evolution which describes how animals develop their abilities over time in relation to one another and their environment.

He established that all species of life have descended over time from common ancestors and introduced his scientific theory that this branching pattern of evolution resulted from a process that he called natural selection, in which the struggle for existence has a similar effect to the artificial selection involved in selective breeding. His theories of evolution through natural selection instigated a revolution in biological science.

He published his theory with compelling evidence in his book *On the Origin of Species* when he was 50. Within a decade or two the scientific community and much of the general public had accepted evolution as a fact. However, many favoured competing explanations and it was not until the emergence of the modern evolutionary synthesis, some 50 to 70 years after his death, that a broad consensus developed in which natural selection was the basic mechanism of evolution. His scientific discovery is the unifying theory of the life sciences, explaining the diversity of life.

His father was a freethinker, believing that positions regarding truth should be formed on the basis of logic, reason, and empiricism, rather than authority, tradition, revelation, or other dogma, but he was brought up by his mother within the Unitarian Christian Church. He later said, "I never gave up Christianity until I was forty years of age." He then agreed that Christianity was "not supported by the evidence", but he had reached this conclusion only slowly.

However, his Theory of Evolution is recognised as having impacted massively on human societies across the World, not least in the areas of faith and religious beliefs. These diverse impacts on so many aspects of human lives have been so far-reaching that a "Darwinian Revolution" has been accepted as having taken place. He hesitated about making his theory - which he had crafted into a 'publishable' sketch by his early 30's

- widely known in his own lifetime. His wife was sincerely religious and he also seems to have feared for his own and his family's perceived respectability if he made his potentially massively controversial evolutionary views public.[530]

At this juncture in human evolution, few of us use our planets at the spiritual level, but many of us are striving to, and such people are wonderful to be around. As with the other planets, the spiritual level of evolution is vastly different with Sedna from the two previous levels. Here, the conjunction with Jupiter brings the ability to tune into people at a deep level across all walks of life, to see both the potential and the blocks and the ability to use this insight to encourage the evolutionary benefits of optimism.

Once we embrace the Sedna energy, which is the oneness of everything, our nurturing becomes an expression of Sedna consciousness and it becomes devotional in nature. The struggle of the beginner's level is gone, as are the transcendental crises of the intermediate level. At this level everything Saturnian is meaningless and yet everything Sednian has its place.

Florence Nightingale was an English social reformer and statistician and the founder of modern nursing. She had Sedna conjunct Jupiter in her seventh house of one to one relationships.

> Though she did not think herself deeply religious, when she was scarcely 17 years old she felt that God spoke to her, calling her to a future of service. From that time on her life was changed. Not knowing the nature of the service, she feared making herself unworthy of whatever it was by leading the frivolous life that her mother and her social set demanded of her and instead was given to periods of preoccupation, or to what she called "dreams" of how to fulfil her mission.

> She came to prominence in her mid-thirties, serving as a teacher and manager of nurses during the Crimean War, where she organised the care of wounded soldiers. She gave nursing a highly favourable reputation and became an icon of Victorian culture, as "The Lady with the Lamp" making rounds of wounded soldiers at night.

---

[530] https://en.wikipedia.org/wiki/Charles_Darwin

At 40, she laid the foundation of professional nursing with the establishment of her nursing school at St Thomas' Hospital in London. It was the first secular nursing school in the world. Her social reforms include improving healthcare for all sections of British society, advocating better hunger relief in India, helping to abolish prostitution laws that were over-harsh to women, and expanding the acceptable forms of female participation in the workforce.

Although much of her work improved the lot of women everywhere, she was of the opinion that women craved sympathy and were not as capable as men. She preferred the friendship of powerful men, insisting they had done more than women to help her attain her goals. She often referred to herself in the masculine, as 'a man of action' and 'a man of business'. Some scholars believe that she remained chaste for her entire life, perhaps because she felt a religious calling to her career.

However, during the Crimean War she contracted a fever that left her so weakened that she spent the last 50 years of her life as an invalid. From the age of 37 onwards, she was intermittently bedridden and suffered from depression. Despite her symptoms, she remained phenomenally productive in social reform.

She was a prodigious and versatile writer. In her lifetime, much of her published work was concerned with spreading medical knowledge. Some of her tracts were written in simple English so that they could easily be understood by those with poor literary skills. She also helped popularise the graphical presentation of statistical data. Much of her writing, including her extensive work on religion and mysticism, has only been published posthumously.[531]

Corrie ten Boom was a Dutch heroine and Christian evangelist, famous for the book and the deeds of her noted family in *The Hiding Place*. She had Sedna conjunct Jupiter and also Vesta, the asteroid of regeneration, in the seventh house of relationships.

During the Second World War her father sheltered Jewish people, who were trying to escape from the Nazi Holocaust at

---

[531] https://en.wikipedia.org/wiki/Florence_Nightingale

their home. Some thirty-eight Jewish people were saved, but she was the only one in her family to survive the Holocaust.

Her father believed that all people were equal before God and when a desperate Jewish women appealed to him, he gave her shelter for the Holocaust in his house. Many persecuted Jews and Nazi resisters would follow. Corrie at first had trouble with the necessity of keeping these activities secret. She suffered a moral crisis over the lying, theft, forgery, and bribery that was necessary to keep the Jews her family was hiding alive.

With help of the Dutch underground, they built a secret room in the top of the building, where the refugees could hide in case of a a raid. She was 52 when the house was raided after a tip of an unknown person. That day some 27 persons were in the house, including six Jews that slipped in the hiding place. Twenty-one persons were arrested, including Corrie, her sister and father.

Her father's health was weakened by age and tuberculosis and he was sent to a medical clinic where he died ten days after the arrest of the family. Corrie and her sister were interrogated by the Gestapo, but not tortured. They took all the blame for hiding the Jews, and after four months in prison, they were sentenced to forced labour. Through their confession, the other arrested guests in their father's house were released.

After the war, she became an evangelist, motivational speaker and social critic, protesting against the Vietnam War. She visited more than 60 countries, not preaching for any particular belief, but believing in a Universal Holy Spirit that asks for peace and forgiveness.[532]

Joseph Campbell was an American mythologist, writer, and lecturer, best known for his work in comparative mythology and comparative religion. He had Sedna conjunct Jupiter in the sixth house of service.

His magnum opus is his book, *The Hero with a Thousand Faces*, published when he was 45, in which he discusses his theory of the journey of the archetypal hero found in world mythologies.

---

[532] https://en.wikipedia.org/wiki/Corrie_ten_Boom

As a strong believer in the psychic unity of mankind and its poetic expression through mythology, he used this concept to express the idea that the whole of the human race can be seen as engaged in the effort of making the world "transparent to transcendence", by showing that underneath the world of phenomena lies an eternal source which is constantly pouring its energies into this world of time, suffering, and ultimately death.

To achieve this task, one needs to speak about things that existed before and beyond words, a seemingly impossible task, the solution to which lies in the metaphors found in myths. These metaphors are statements that point beyond themselves into the transcendent. *The Hero's Journey* was the story of the man or woman who, through great suffering, reached an experience of the eternal source and returned with gifts powerful enough to set their society free.

Since the book's publication, his theory has been consciously applied by a wide variety of modern writers and artists. His philosophy has been summarised by his own often-repeated phrase: "Follow your bliss." He thought of God as a metaphor for a mystery that absolutely transcends all human categories of thought, even the categories of being and non-being. Saying, "It depends on how much you want to think about it. Whether it is putting you in touch with the mystery that's the ground of your own being. If it isn't, well, it's a lie."[533]

Opposition

With the opposition of Sedna and Jupiter, the all-encompassing spiritual energy of Sedna challenges our growth and optimism, our ability to seek insight through knowledge and express our generosity and tolerance.

The opposition challenges us to explore our growth and optimism from a vastly larger and yet still uniquely personal perspective. This might bring us into conflict with others and even the authorities, who feel threatened by our growth.

If we are unconscious of the Sedna energy, or there are other stressful aspects to Jupiter, we are likely to call the more negative manifestations of Jupiter into our lives, including blind optimism, excess,

---

[533] https://en.wikipedia.org/wiki/Joseph_Campbell

overindulgence, intolerance and the irresponsibility that results from blind optimism.

Richard Kameese was an American drug fatality at age 21, an addiction that began at high school. He had Sedna in the ninth house of knowledge, conjunct Saturn, the planet of rules and restrictions, opposite Jupiter in the third house of ideas and communication.

> He was living with his parents, when his folks went to a wake, leaving him home alone because he was using drugs. When they returned they saw his shoeless footprints in the snow and knew he was on another rampage. He went to the home of a couple who lived a couple hundred yards away and burst in, staggering and in a drug-crazed state saying "They're going to get me." He grabbed a kitchen mop and began swinging at his imaginary enemies and at the couple, who then called the police, as Richard drew a knife. It took four men to subdue him; however, while in a jail cell, he stopped breathing and died a few hours later.[534]

Lucky Luciano was a Sicilian-American gangster, who rose from grubby street urchin, through the ranks of organized crime, to became director of a crime syndicate. He had Sedna in the second house of material resources, opposite Jupiter in the eighth house of shared resources.

> By the age of ten he had embarked on his life of crime. At nineteen he spent six months in jail for selling heroin. By 23, ruthless and upwardly mobile, he began working for the crime boss, Joe Masseria and within five years he became his chief lieutenant.

> At 32, he survived a "one-way ride," which is a rare feat. He was abducted, beaten, stabbed repeatedly, had his throat cut and was left for dead; he never named his abductors, and soon afterward he changed his name to Luciano. He earned the nickname "Lucky" because he successfully evaded arrest on a number of occasions and eventually became famous for racketeering in narcotics, prostitution, slot machines, loan sharking and 'protection'.

---

[534] https://www.astro.com/astro-databank/Kameese,_Richard

However, at 39 he was indicted, tried and convicted on charges of extortion and prostitution and sentenced to 30 to 50 years in prison. Nevertheless, his power continued to grow, even while he was incarcerated, as he issued orders and ruled from his cell. Near the end of his life, however, a reporter asked him if he would do it all again, and he replied, "I'd do it legal. I learned too late that you need just as good a brain to make a crooked million, as an honest million.[535]

William Shockley was an American physicist who co-invented the transistor, the forerunner of the microchip, an invention that changed the course of history for computers and electronics. He had Sedna conjunct Orcus, the planet of delving down and speaking out, in the twelfth house of the unconscious, opposite Jupiter in the sixth house of service. He was an ardent proponent of Eugenics, a movement to improve the gene pool by killing or sterilizing stupid people. This intolerance obviously put him at odds with most people and he died a lonely, grumpy old man.

However, his drive to develop and commercially apply the transistor has been a huge service to the evolutionary needs of humanity and even his abrasive personality served this end, by alienating key employees so they left and started their own businesses, spawning Silicon Valley.

His parents were eccentric and they kept him out of school until the 8th grade, so he lacked socialisation and grew up not knowing how to handle and deal with other people. At 46 he started Shockley Semiconductor Laboratory, the first establishment working on silicon semiconductor devices in what came to be known as Silicon Valley. His management style could generally be summed up as domineering and paranoid. And after he received the Nobel Prize his demeanour became increasingly autocratic, erratic and hard-to-please.

Late the next year, eight of his researchers resigned after he decided not to continue research into silicon-based semiconductors. They went on to form Fairchild Semiconductor, a loss from which Shockley Semiconductor never recovered and which would eventually spawn Silicon Valley. Over the course of the next 20 years, more than 65 new enterprises would end up having employee connections back to Fairchild.

---

[535] https://en.wikipedia.org/wiki/Lucky_Luciano

The biography, *Broken Genius: The rise and fall of William Shockley, Creator of the Electronic Age* describes Shockley as: "A nasty old man. One of his friends actually described him as having reverse charisma; he would walk into a room and you instantly took a disliking to him. He was extraordinarily bright and he knew it. He was a bit arrogant about it."

In his later years he slipped into Eugenics, the belief that humanity would be better served by only allowing the smart and healthy to breed. He was attacked for this in print, on television and in scientific journals and by the time of his death he was almost completely estranged from most of his friends and family, except for his second wife. His last years were very sad. His children are reported to have only learned of his death through the print media.[536]

As we tire of density and the grief it creates, and we start a spiritual journey to get out of the swamp, Sedna rewards us with transcendent crises, experiences which force us to let go and rise above them, resulting in a huge growth to a new level of consciousness. There is no choice with these crises, and the more we try and solve them, the more we will get hurt.

Bertold Brecht was a German playwright and poet, one of the leaders of the "epic theatre movement." He had Sedna in the third house of ideas and communication, opposite Jupiter in the ninth house of publishing.

He wrote his first prize-winning play while at Munich University in his early twenties, and directed his first play at 26. As a poet, he showed great mastery and forceful simplicity. His operas and plays champion alienation the way that Kafka epitomises anxiety. He combines text, balladry, stagecraft, imagery, movement and spoken word in a way now associated with performance art. His "Three-penny Opera" is familiar to every patron who has ever recognised theater as an art form.

A Marxist, a vegetarian, a genius and a contradictory figure, he was also considered an opportunist with an all-too-convenient ability to temporise. Despite his purposely shabby dress, unwashed stench, rotting teeth and icy persona, Brecht was

---

[536] https://en.wikipedia.org/wiki/William_Shockley

some sort of modern Mesmer, able to hypnotise almost everyone he met into doing his bidding. He was considered a virtuoso in the bedroom, keeping regular revolving mistresses. When he fled Nazi Germany, he had not only his family but two other women, both of whom wrote large amounts of his work according to his specifications. Some of his major works may contain as little as 10% of his actual writing, but he served as a brilliant editor.

The saddest case - and most revealing of his character - is the story of Margaret Steffin, a young German writer from the provinces who had the misfortune to fall under his spell at an early age. She was almost single-handedly responsible for *Courage* and *Stezuan*, as well as *Galileo* and at least four other major plays, a novel, and countless poems and stories, all published under Brecht's name. He was not able to read the source material in French for the works, and the manuscripts are all in her handwriting. Suffering from TB, she died alone in a Moscow hospital ward after arranging for his safe passage to America. He mourned for four days, then promptly swindled her family out of her royalties and took her inheritance. While he became a millionaire, secretly depositing thousands of gold marks in a Swiss bank account, her family was left to subside on their meagre income.

He wrote most of his best work in exile: *The Good Woman of Szechwan, Galileo, Putila*, and *Mother Courage*. Along the way, he seduced everyone he met with his charisma, for fame, attention, favors, money, sex, all the while that he unscrupulously rode roughshod over everyone, cheating and using them. He once said, "What I don't like to admit is that I myself have contempt for the unfortunate".[537]

Françoise Gilot is a French artist and writer of a candid, humorous and intelligent memoir, *Life with Picasso*. She has Sedna in the seventh house of relationships, opposite Jupiter which is conjunct both Mars, the planet of fighting, and Ceres, the planet of nurturing, all in the first house of identity.

---

[537] https://en.wikipedia.org/wiki/Bertolt_Brecht

An only child, she had a cold father who beat her in fury when she dropped out of the Sorbonne to be an artist. She painted from the time she was 17 and was an insomniac and voracious reader.

She met Pablo Picasso when she was 21 and he was 63. As she had recently left both school and her childhood home, she was living with her grandmother. She and Picasso developed an easy, close camaraderie, involved in the same social group of artists and intellectuals. They became lovers and she moved in with him soon after. She shared his life for nearly a decade, giving her life to him, taking care of his needs and putting up with his moods, modelling for him as she painted steadily herself.

During their ten years together, she was often harassed on the streets of Paris by Picasso's legal wife, a former Russian ballet dancer. As well, Picasso himself physically abused her. He chafed under the domesticity, had affairs with other women and they began to pull apart. Following a period of calm, she took the kids and left him when she was 32. It is believed by some art historians that this is what cut short her artistic career. When she left him, he told all art dealers he knew not to purchase her art.

Eleven years after their separation she co-wrote *Life with Picasso*, a book that sold over one million copies in dozens of languages, despite an unsuccessful legal challenge from Picasso attempting to stop its publication. From then on, he refused to see his children, Claude or Paloma, ever again. She never saw Picasso again, but now lives in New York City and Paris and continues to exhibit her work internationally.[538]

Jack Kerouac was an American writer and poet, the author of 21 books. He had Sedna, conjunct Chiron, the centaur of wounding and healing, in the eighth house of shared resources, opposite Jupiter in the second house of material resources. He is perhaps best known for his books, *On The Road*, published when he was 35 and *The Dharma Bums*, published the following year. These classic novels established him as a hero who epitomised the style of living and writing associated with the 'Beat Movement' and served as the Bible for Beatniks.

---

[538] https://en.wikipedia.org/wiki/Françoise_Gilot

When he was 23 he met the charismatic and bisexual Neal Cassady, a Denver reform school graduate and car thief who eventually became Kerouac's lover and buddy. During a three-week binge of creativity in the following April and May, he wrote *On The Road* on a single ream of paper. Following Neal's marriage to Caroline, Kerouac moved into the attic of their San Francisco home, where they made up a ménage atrois. He was hospitalised at 29 with thrombophlebitis as a result of heavy Benzedrine use.

In his early thirties, he roamed the US and Mexico taking odd jobs to support himself while studying Buddhism. However, at 38 he suffered alcohol withdrawal, coupled with a nervous breakdown. During the next four years he lived with his mother. At 44 he made his third and final marriage, to the sister of a childhood friend. This marriage was probably celibate, and he was often arrested for public drunkenness as a means of taking out his frustration.

While he hit the road for in search of direct experience and spontaneity, his acute wanderlust left him homeless in his soul, even when he owned a home. Despite the chaos in every area of his life however, he meticulously kept an archive of every sexual experience he had with a woman. One of these bore him a daughter, a girl whom he met twice, but never acknowledged. His daughter Jan states, "I wish I had known him better. He could spout all kinds of things on paper, but in person, he was non-communicative."

He was unable to cope with fame, fatherhood and his bi-sexuality. "He wanted to be seen as the voice of America, but instead he was seen as a voice of juvenile delinquents, and that hurt him a lot...He couldn't take the easy bullet because he was a Catholic. But he rationalised that it was not a sin if he drank himself to death." So that is what he did. His final years were marked by virulent alcohol rages and fierce anti-Semitism.[539]

Helen Duncan was a Scottish medium taken to trial at the Old Bailey in London during WW2 for fraud, charged under the 1735 Witchcraft Act of "pretending to raise the spirits of the dead." She had Sedna in the sixth

---

[539] https://en.wikipedia.org/wiki/Jack_Kerouac

house of service, opposite Jupiter in the the twelfth house of the unconscious. She had inadvertently revealed the wartime sinking of HMS Barham by summoning up one of its dead sailors at a séance.

> During the war, she would "raise" the spirits of dead soldiers and sailors at séances across the country, claiming that she brought comfort to grieving family members. At a séance in Portsmouth a dead sailor appeared and allegedly told his mother, "My ship has sunk." Anxious for confirmation, the woman wrote the War Office to ask for details. This alerted the authorities to Duncan's activities, at the same time alarming them inasmuch as the sinking of the ship had been kept secret and she was in danger of becoming a national security risk.
>
> She was a pleasant looking, overweight woman, married to a cabinet-maker and the mother of seven children. A well-known spiritualist, she had given séances all over Britain for twenty years, however, the Government argued that she was guilty of fraud and of preying on the bereaved. She was convicted and was jailed at 47 for nine months.
>
> She had a prior conviction at 36 of "pretending to be a medium" at a séance in Edinburgh and may have been imprisoned then as well. After the 1944 conviction, she was disowned by her peers and had her diploma withdrawn by the Spiritualists' National Union. She emerged from prison a broken woman and died 11 years after her release and five years after the law which convicted her was repealed as archaic.[540]

At this juncture in human evolution, few of us use our planets at the spiritual level, but many of us are striving to and such people are wonderful to be around. As with the other planets, the spiritual level of evolution is vastly different with Sedna from the two previous levels. Here, the opposition with Jupiter brings the ability to tune into people at a deep level across all walks of life, to see both the potential and the blocks and the ability to use this insight to encourage the evolutionary benefits of optimism.

Once we embrace the Sedna energy, which is the oneness of everything, our nurturing becomes an expression of Sedna

---

[540] https://en.wikipedia.org/wiki/Helen_Duncan

consciousness and it becomes devotional in nature. The struggle of the beginner's level is gone, as are the transcendental crises of the intermediate level. At this level everything Saturnian is meaningless and yet everything Sednian has its place.

Hugo Ball was a German author, poet and one of the leading Dada artists. He has Sedna in the ninth house of publishing, opposite Jupiter conjunct Uranus, the planet of intuition, in the third house of ideas and communication.

> When he was 24 he moved to Berlin in order to become an actor and collaborated with Max Reinhardt. At the beginning of the First World War he tried joining the army as a volunteer but was denied enlistment for medical issues. After witnessing the invasion of Belgium, he was disillusioned saying: "The war is founded on a glaring mistake; men have been confused with machines."

> "Considered a traitor in his country, he crossed the frontier with his wife and settled in Zürich. Here, he continued his interest in anarchism, rejecting its militant aspects and viewing it as only a means to his personal goal of enlightenment.

> He was 30 when he created the Dada Manifesto, making a political statement about his views on the terrible state of society and acknowledging his dislike for philosophies in the past claiming to possess the ultimate Truth. The same year as the Manifesto, he wrote his poem "Karawane," which is a German poem consisting of nonsensical words. The meaning, however, resides in its meaninglessness, reflecting the chief principle behind Dadaism.

> As co-founder of the Cabaret Voltaire in Zürich, he led the Dada movement in Zürich, and is one of the people credited with naming the movement "Dada", by allegedly choosing the word at random from a dictionary. His involvement with the Dada movement lasted less than two years. He then worked for a short period as a journalist for Freie Zeitung in Bern. After returning to Catholicism at 34, he retired and lived a religious and relatively poor life, dying at 41.[541]

[541] https://en.wikipedia.org/wiki/Hugo_Ball

Margot Adler is an American leader in the Goddess and Pagan Spirituality Movement. She has Sedna in the first house of identity, opposite Jupiter in the seventh house of relationships.

> A Wicca priestess for 18 years, she was an Elder in the Covenant of the Goddess, and is author of *Drawing Down the Moon*, a classic study of contemporary Paganism. The book is considered a watershed in American Neopagan circles, as it provided the first comprehensive look at modern nature-based religions in the US. For many years it was the only introductory work about American Neopagan communities. Her second book, *Heretic's Heart: A Journey Through Spirit and Revolution*, was published when she was 51. In her mundane life she is a correspondent for National Public Radio.[542]

Liz Greene is an American-British professional astrologer and author, Jungian analyst and lecturer; one of the most highly respected astrologers of the 20th century. She has Sedna in the fifth house of creativity, opposite Jupiter in the eleventh house of collective consciousness.

> With Howard Sasportas, she co-founded the Centre for Psychological Astrology in London when she was 34 and was co-director for 20 years, before becoming the sole director. She continues directing the organisation. In addition, she also directs CPA Press, a publishing company that focuses on specialist astrological works.

> At 39 she started co-operating with Alois Treindl, founder of Swiss-based Astrodienst, on the development of computer-generated horoscopes, which would present a person with a chart synthesis, simulating Greene's own method of horoscope interpretation during a personal reading.

> Two years later, in 1987, they presented the Psychological Horoscope Analysis, which was followed by several other interpretations. Greene remains Astrodienst's most popular author.

> She was awarded the Regulus Award for Theory and Understanding when she was 43, recognising the work with

---

[542] https://en.wikipedia.org/wiki/Margot_Adler

other disciplines and philosophical models. She has been one of the most consistently popular astrologers of the 20th century. Almost all of her many books remain in print. Her books include *Saturn: A New Look at an Old Devil, Star Signs for Lovers,* and *The Outer Planets and Their Cycles.*[543]

Semi-sextile, Sextile, Trine

With the flowing aspects between Sedna and Jupiter, the all-encompassing spiritual energy of Sedna aligns with our growth and optimism, our ability to seek insight through knowledge and express our generosity and tolerance.

Jupiter is associated with good luck and bounty, with a sense of humour, good will, and mercy, and with optimism and growth, including mental and spiritual growth. And the flowing aspects with Jupiter likely give us an evolutionary drive to succeed, together with a sensitivity to the bigger picture to see how others are also working.

If we are unconscious of the Sedna energy, however, or there are other stressful aspects to the conjunction, we are likely to call the more negative manifestations of Jupiter into our lives, including blind optimism, excess, overindulgence, intolerance and the irresponsibility that results from blind optimism.

Rudolf Hess was a German politician, the Deputy Leader of the Nazi party and number three in power after Hitler and Goering. He had Sedna in the tenth house of profession,

sextile Jupiter in the eleventh house of collective consciousness.

> Believing that he was obeying supernatural powers and had a mission to end the war, Hess flew from Germany to Scotland early in WW2, bailing out of the plane and taking it on his own to attempt negotiations with England on behalf of Germany. Unfortunately, Hitler denied his authority, calling him insane and he was imprisoned, tried and given a life sentence. After 21 months in a Nuremberg prison, he spent 41 years at Spandau.[544]

His Sedna is bi-quintile Uranus in the fifth house of creativity, and he wrote prodigiously in prison about the Nazis and the war, convinced that

---

[543] https://en.wikipedia.org/wiki/Liz_Greene
[544] https://en.wikipedia.org/wiki/Rudolf_Hess

he would play a leading role in the "Fourth Reich." He initially goose-stepped down the corridors of Spandeau, snapping the Nazi salute. His Sedna was also in a stressful sesquiquadrate with Pallas, the asteroid of wisdom, in the second house of material restrictions, inconjunct Vesta, the asteroid of regeneration, in the third house of communication, and semi-square Mars, the planet of war, in the eighth house of shared resources.

> However, after an initial period of rages and bouts of persecution mania, he settled into a routine of numbing regularity. His days started with an hour of calisthenics, breakfast, a walk in the prison garden, lunch, an afternoon of reading and television (he was banned from news programs). For a half hour each month, he was allowed a visit from his wife and son; no touching was permitted. For the last 21 years, he was the sole inmate of Spandeau and after four suicide attempts, he strangled himself with an electric cord age 93.[545]

Abraham Kasparian is a former American politician who stabbed his wife three times in a public restaurant. He has Sedna in the fifth house of romance and children, sextile Jupiter in the seventh house of relationships.

> His wife had filed for a divorce but agreed to meet him for lunch. She survived the attack. He had been arrested previously for welfare fraud and larceny. Earlier that same day, a former tenant sued the couple, charging them with negligence in connection with an apartment fire that killed two children.[546]

Alan Turing, was a British mathematician, logician, scientist and the technical genius behind Britain's successful efforts to break German codes in WW2. He had Sedna in the 12th house of the unconscious, trine his Jupiter, which is together with Juno, the asteroid of partnership, in the seventh house of relationships. He was an eccentric who was not easy to relate to, but he was able to form close collaborative working relationships with people who supported his research.

> He made inestimable contributions to cybernetics. His 'Computable Numbers', published when he was 25, is

---

[545] Ibid.
[546] https://www.astro.com/astro-databank/Kasparian,_Abraham

considered one of the outstanding scientific papers of the 20th century, a blueprint for what would become the electronic digital computer. His 'Universal Turing Machine' was an ancestor for the entire information age.

He was accustomed to being a non-conformist. At boarding school, he refused to adapt and ignored subjects that did not interest him. He was an atheist and felt marginalised because of his homosexuality. From the age if 13 he formed a significant friendship with another boy who has been described as his 'first love'. Their relationship provided inspiration in his future endeavours, but it was cut short by his friend's death when Alan was 17, from drinking infected cow's milk some years previously. The event caused him great sorrow and he coped with this by working that much harder on the topics of science and mathematics that he had shared with his friend.[547]

His Sedna is also conjunct Chariklo, the centaur of foresight and bi-quintile Ixion, the planet of lawlessness.

Though he envisioned a time when "ladies will take their computers for walks in the park," his own reality was not quite so whimsical. When a robbery occurred at his house in Manchester, he frankly told the police that the robber probably knew the man with whom he was having an affair. As homosexual relations were still a felony in Britain, he was tried and convicted of gross indecency. He was spared prison but was given a year probation with the condition that he take oestrogen to diminish his sex drive.[548]

As we tire of density and the grief it creates, and we start a spiritual journey to get out of the swamp, Sedna rewards us with transcendent crises, experiences which force us to let go and rise above them, resulting in a huge growth to a new level of consciousness. There is no choice with these crises, and the more we try and solve them, the more we will get hurt.

Simone de Beauvoir was a French writer and existentialist teacher who fashioned an impressive literary career as a novelist, philosopher,

---

[547] https://en.wikipedia.org/wiki/Alan_Turing
[548] Ibid.

essayist and writer of memoirs. She had Sedna in the fourth house of home, trine Jupiter in the eighth house of the deals we do in our relationships.

> She looked on marriage as an obscene, bourgeois institution that put women in an inferior position. In rejecting marriage, she also rejected children, noting that she had escaped most of women's bondages.

> She was a prominent member of the young avant-garde Parisian intelligentsia in the '40s, she was the presiding celebrity of the Existentialist movement along with Jean Paul Sartre, who was her life companion in an open relationship. They never lived in the same residence, nor did they require sexual fidelity of each other, but they did keep a close and steady relationship, seeing each other daily from the time they met at the Sorbonne when she was 21, until Sartre died 50 years later.[549]

Her Sedna was also closely bi-quintile Ixion, the planet of lawlessness in the ninth house of higher education.

> She had a very turbulent, often scandalous life. Although she had a long time relationship with Sartre, she was known to have a number of female lovers. The nature of some of these relationships, some of which she began with underage students while working as a professor, later led to a controversy.

> A former student wrote in her book that, while she was a student at Lycée Molière, she had been sexually exploited by her teacher de Beauvoir, who was in her 30s at the time. She and Jean-Paul Sartre developed a pattern, which they called the "trio", in which de Beauvoir would seduce her students and then pass them on to Sartre. Finally, she was suspended from her teaching job, when she was accused of seducing a 17-year-old pupil. The girl's parents laid formal charges against her for debauching a minor and she had her license to teach in France permanently revoked.[550]

> Katherine Mansfield was a prominent New Zealand modernist short story writer who was born and brought up in colonial New

---

[549] https://en.wikipedia.org/wiki/Simone_de_Beauvoir
[550] Ibid.

Zealand. She had Sedna conjunct Vesta, the asteroid of regeneration, in the fifth house of creativity, trine Jupiter in the twelfth house of the unconscious.

She was first published at 23 with her novel, *In A German Pension,* but didn't receive much notice. However, in the next five years she became an important contributor to European magazines. She was the daughter of a successful businessman, schooled in New Zealand and sent to London at 15 to attend Queen's College. Grief stricken by the loss over her brother's death during WW I, she also learned at that time that she had incurable tuberculosis.

When she was 22 she married to give her unborn child a name and left her husband almost immediately, but unfortunately, the child was stillborn. Two years later she met an editor, and they married when she was 30. She died of tuberculosis at 35 in Fontainebleau, France. Her most noted book, *The Garden Party* was released just before she died and two of her books were published after her death.[551]

Our case study, the father of the Singularity theory, Ray Kurzweil, has a trine to Jupiter, which is in the second house of material possessions. Ray is an author, computer scientist, inventor and futurist. Ray is pushing the envelope with his inventive expansion of the technological frontier with the Jupiter in the second.

He was the principal inventor of the first flatbed scanner, the first omni-font optical character recognition, the first print-to-speech reading machine for the blind, the first commercial text-to-speech synthesizer, the first music synthesizer capable of simulating the sound of the grand piano and other orchestral instruments.

He has written books on health, artificial intelligence (AI), transhumanism, the technological singularity, and futurism. Kurzweil is a public advocate for the futurist and transhumanist movements and gives public talks to share his optimistic outlook on life extension technologies and the future of nanotechnology, robotics, and biotechnology.[552]

---

[551] https://en.wikipedia.org/wiki/Katherine_Mansfield
[552] https://en.wikipedia.org/wiki/Ray_Kurzweil

Humour can be one path to transcend the quicksand of Sedna, giving us the objectivity to step back from the edge and also with the flowing aspects to Jupiter the optimism and drive to make it big.

Paula Prentiss is an American actress, a leading lady in Hollywood films, adept at urbane screwball comedy roles. She has Sedna conjunct her moon in the eighth house of shared resources and partnership agreements, sextile Jupiter in the sixth house of service.

> At 20, while studying drama at Northwestern University, she met her future husband Richard Benjamin, who impressed her with his sophistication. She married him when she was 23 and the marriage has been solid, standing the test of time for over fifty years.
>
> While attending university she was discovered by the Metro-Goldwyn-Mayer Studio and was offered a film contract, which in those days was a fulltime job, moving from one film to another. A highly sensitive performer, having acted in a string of films back to back, she had a nervous breakdown on the set of *What's New Pussycat?* in Paris when she was 27. She was hospitalised for nine months and the breakdown kept her out of film work for the next five years.
>
> She returned to work with her husband in the television series *He & She*. The couple also appeared together in a number of films, like *Catch-22,* when she was 32, as well as in various plays. Except for brief cameo roles, she had not appeared in a feature film for more than 30 years until she played in a horror film, *I Am the Pretty Thing That Lives in the House*, when she was 79. The film premiered at the 2016 Toronto International Film Festival.[553]

David Shiner is an American actor and clown. He has Sedna in tenth house of profession, sextile Jupiter in the twelfth house of the unconscious. He built an early reputation working regularly in the streets at the Avignon Festival in France, drawing huge crowds to watch his antics on the castle walls of the old city and making a fortune in the hat.

> He performed in the 2000 Broadway musical Seussical and has movie appearances as a clown and as an actor, including

---

[553] https://en.wikipedia.org/wiki/Paula_Prentiss

Lorenzo's Oil, which was released when he was 39. He has also toured solo shows in Europe and America and mentored and guest directed for a German youth circus program. At 37 he was featured in Cirque du Soleil's production Nouvelle Expérience, touring for 19 months through Canada and the USA and playing for another year in Las Vegas. With his antics, including stepping through, on and over much of the crowd and the staging of a mock silent-movie melodrama with four members of the audience, he may be the best remembered of the Cirque's clowns. At 53 he wrote and directed Cirque du Soleil's touring production, Koozå.[554]

At this juncture in human evolution, few of us use our planets at the spiritual level, but many of us are striving to and such people are wonderful to be around. As with the other planets, the spiritual level of evolution is vastly different with Sedna from the two previous levels. Here, the flowing aspects with Jupiter the ability to tune into people at a deep level across all walks of life, to see both the potential and the blocks and the ability to use this insight to encourage the evolutionary benefits of optimism.

Once we embrace the Sedna energy, which is the oneness of everything, our nurturing becomes an expression of Sedna consciousness and it becomes devotional in nature. The struggle of the beginner's level is gone, as are the transcendental crises of the intermediate level. At this level everything Saturnian is meaningless and yet everything Sednian has its place.

Maria Quattrocchi was an Italian saint, who was beatified after her death along with her husband, the first time in church history that a woman and her husband were given that honour together, as exemplars of the Christian life. She had Sedna in the second house of material resources, trine Jupiter in the sixth house of service.

She was a member of the noble Corsini family. She was a professor and writer on educational topics, writing several books and also served as a Voluntary Nurse in the Italian Red Cross during World War II. They were made saints because they opened their home to refugees during WWII, at great risk to the

---

[554] https://en.wikipedia.org/wiki/David_Shiner_(clown)

family. According to Pope John Paul II, they lived "an ordinary life in an extraordinary way".[555]

German writer, teacher and philosopher, Immanuel Kant, also had this aspect. He was the foremost thinker of the Enlightenment and is considered one of the greatest philosophers of all time. He had Sedna in 12th house of the unconscious, semi-sextile Jupiter in the eleventh house of collective consciousness.

> He was a short man, scarcely five feet tall, and he had a deformed chest. He suffered from poor health throughout his life, and because of this, he maintained a strict regimen of walking.

> His systematic and comprehensive work on ethics and aesthetics inaugurated a new era in the development of philosophical thought and thus greatly influenced all subsequent philosophy, particularly in the various schools of Idealism. His works included *The Critique of Pure Reason*, and *The Critique of Practical Reason*.

> He taught at Königsberg University for 14 years, and his reputation brought large numbers of students to the university. He lectured on many subjects including logic, metaphysics and moral philosophy. His style was humorous and vivid, and he used many examples from his reading to enliven his subjects.

> He was made a professor of logic and metaphysics, a position he held until he retired from the university. Though often charged with attacking metaphysics, he believed in the existence of God and in a future life, and he is often described as an ethical Rationalist. However, his unorthodox religious teachings eventually brought him into conflict with the King of Prussia, who finally forbade him to teach or write on religious subjects, an order he obeyed until the King died five years later.[556]

Marthe Robin was a French mystic and stigmatic. She had Sedna conjunct Pallas, the asteroid of wisdom, in the eighth house of the occult, sextile Jupiter in the fifth house of creativity.

> Serious illness marked her adult life and from her twenties she was confined to bed, crippled, and gradually paralysed. She ate

---

[555] https://en.wikipedia.org/wiki/Luigi_Beltrame_Quattrocchi_and_Maria_Corsini
[556] https://en.wikipedia.org/wiki/Immanuel_Kant

only wafers and neither drank nor slept but lived for seven decades and carried on a busy apostolate.

From the age of 28 she was completely paralysed and bedridden. Although she still could move the thumb and forefinger of one hand, she became motionless apart from her head which she could move slightly. Since the previous year, at the age of 25, she could not eat anything at all. And from the age of 26 she couldn't even take a sip of water. When doctors tried to force some water down her throat, it merely came out her nostrils.

For the next 53 years her only food was the holy Eucharist, a wafer of bread which Catholics believe is the body of Christ. They also believe that they become his body on ingesting it. Once a week she was given the sacred host. Once she had received it she went immediately into ecstasy and began her weekly re-living of Christ's crucifixion. Every Friday wounds appeared in the palms of her hands and the stigmata, the scourging and crowning with thorns appeared on her body, and she appeared to be dead.

For 53 years she also carried on a busy apostolate, which is a Christian organisation directed to serving and evangelising the world. She was directed to found two schools in her native village, one for girls and one for boys. All this she directed down to the smallest detail from her bed in her darkened little room. Later on she was told to found a community which would welcome people looking for a retreat and which would be a home of "light, charity and love." It became known as the Foyer de Charité and there are now some 70 affiliated houses and communities throughout the world.[557]

Marc Edmund Jones was an American astrologer, a popular professional and author whose books include, *Guide To Horoscope Interpretation*. Prior to becoming a professional, he was a Hollywood scriptwriter in his youth. He had Sedna in the fifth house of creativity, conjunct Vesta, the asteroid of regeneration, trine Jupiter in the first house of identity.

---

[557] https://en.wikipedia.org/wiki/Marthe_Robin

Greatly interested in metaphysics, he and the gifted clairvoyant Elsie Wheeler set about to find a set of symbols for every degree of the zodiac that was an improvement on existing degree symbology. One day when he was 37 he took a series of 360 small blank cards on each of which was noted a sign and degree on the back and held them up for Wheeler to describe her vision. The cards were shuffled continually to keep the selection random.

The images did not seem entirely appropriate, or some were exaggerated, so the cards were put aside for six years, before the definitions were revised, This process was repeated some 17 years later and the results were first published when Marc was 63 as the Sabian Symbols. Two years before his death, he was given a respectful and affectionate 90th birthday party by 200 colleagues while planning his next book. He died aged 91.[558]

Semi-square, Square, Sesquiquadrate,

With the stressful aspects between Sedna and Jupiter, the all-encompassing spiritual energy of Sedna challenges our growth and optimism, our ability to seek insight through knowledge and express our generosity and tolerance.

Jupiter is associated with good luck and bounty, with a sense of humour, good will and mercy, and with optimism and growth, including mental and spiritual growth.

The stressful aspects with Jupiter can give us an evolutionary drive to succeed, without the sensitivity to the bigger picture to see how others are also working. As we develop the Sedna energy, we can learn to dovetail our efforts with others and then we can move mountains.

If we are unconscious of the Sedna energy, however, or there are other stressful aspects to Jupiter, we are likely to call the more negative manifestations of Jupiter into our lives, including blind optimism, excess, overindulgence and the irresponsibility that results from blind optimism.

Sharon Tate was an American actress, sex symbol and model, who was murdered by members of Charles Manson's 'family'. She had Sedna conjunct Varuna, the planet of notability, in the tenth house of profession, square Jupiter in the twelfth house of the unconscious.

---

[558] https://en.wikipedia.org/wiki/Marc_Edmund_Jones

In her early twenties she played small television roles, before appearing in several motion pictures. She also appeared regularly in fashion magazines as a model and cover girl. After receiving positive reviews for her comedic and dramatic performances, she was hailed as one of Hollywood's most promising newcomers, making her film debut at 23.

A year later she co-stared in *The Fearless Vampire Killers* with Roman Polanski, who also directed the film. The following year she and Polanski got married in London and at the time of her death, she was eight-and-a-half months pregnant with their son and was two weeks from giving birth. That day she entertained two friends, for lunch at her home, confiding in them her disappointment at her husband's delay in returning from London.

That evening she dined at her favourite restaurant with three other friends, returning with them to her home. Shortly after midnight, they were all murdered by members of Manson's "family" and their bodies were discovered the following morning by her housekeeper. Police arrived at the scene to find her body and that of one of her friends in the living room; a long rope tied around each of their necks connected them. On the front lawn lay the bodies of the other two. All of the victims had been stabbed numerous times.[559]

John Hinckley is an American attempted assassin who shot and wounded President Reagan when he was 25. He has Sedna in the second house of material reality, square Jupiter in the sixth house of service.

The year before he shot Reagan, he went to Ted Kennedy's office and waited for three hours with a loaded gun to see the Senator, before he gave up on the assassination attempt and left. He was found not guilty of attempting to assassinate Reagan by reason of insanity and sentenced to an asylum for the mentally ill in Washington, DC.

Prior to the assassination attempt he wrote a string of love letters to actress Jodie Foster. Then at 27, he met a woman who was a patient in the same facility for the shotgun murder of her ten-

---

[559] https://en.wikipedia.org/wiki/Sharon_Tate

year-old daughter, followed by her own suicide attempt. She was 12 years older. They were both in the hell of their mental illness, anguish and despair and their growing friendship led to improvement for both of them. Their long hours of talks led to love and he asked her to marry him.

A couple of years later she was able to function responsibly in society and was released. His progress was slower however they were able to see each other on weekends and kiss goodbye, feeling like a couple of teenagers. During the Christmas holidays, the young lovers spent time alone for the first time when he was allowed to spend a day with his family. His sexual experience was limited to a few encounters with prostitutes shortly before the assassination attempt. They were not able to consummate their relationship, but the promise of a future together was a strong incentive to healthy responsibility.

During the next five years, his progress was interspersed with unsettling relapses. His psychological evaluations took a turn for the worse. A report from this period read, "The issues of poor judgment, need for ego-gratification through the media, isolation from others at all but a superficial level, grandiosity, suspiciousness, defiance in the face of narcissistic injury, refusal to accept responsibility for his actions other than in a fleeting way, emotional volatility, tendency to lie, lack of empathy for others, sense of entitlement - all remain as unresolved therapeutic issues." His ability to maintain a stable relationship with his fiancé was a plus.

At 35, he was living in a medium-security ward and was working four hours a day in a clerical position. The next year he was allowed to walk with his fiancé without an escort around the hospital grounds. Not long after this, they had sexual relations for the first time and he was moved to a minimum-security ward. A divided appeals court finally ruled when he was 43 that he could make supervised day trips away from the mental hospital where he has lived for the past 18 years to visit his family and friends, a process of gradual re-entry into society. Four years later he was granted unsupervised visits with his parents, but it would be 14 more years before he was released from institutional psychiatric care at 61.[560]

Virginia Woolf was a British writer, a novelist and essayist who used the English language superbly. She had Sedna in the eleventh house of collective consciousness, semi-square Jupiter in the twelfth house of the unconscious.

After the death of her father in 1904, she and her siblings moved to Bloomsbury where their home becoming the center for the avant-garde literary salon, the Bloomsbury Group. She married Leonard Woolf when she was 30. They were true companions, though it was a sexless marriage and she later fell in love with another woman.

She received income from a small trust fund but it was insufficient to meet her needs. In 1917, she and her husband founded the Hogarth Press. With a small, kitchen-table model printing press, they taught themselves to set type and print. They were both budding novelists, reviewers and essayists. Their first publication, a 32-page pamphlet, sold 134 copies of the 150 printed. Within several years, they developed a commercially successful publishing company that produced 25 to 35 books per year. They were prolific writers and managed the publishing company as a part time enterprise.

She suffered from a mental breakdown during WW I, followed by subsequent periods of physical, mental and emotional breakdowns, which doctors treated with psychiatric drugs. Her early childhood experience of sexual abuse by her half-brothers, Gerald and George Dunkworth, was thought to be the cause. Gerald later became her publisher. Virginia had a complicated and stormy relationship with her sister, Vanessa Bell, which biographers reveal was also physical. She is also reported to have an early love interest with a close friend, Violet Dickinson.

Her writing expressed the themes that troubled her the most; life, death, suicide, madness and past memories. She was hypersensitive to criticism. She was a noted biographer and critic and used writing as a distraction from realty. When she realised

---

[560] https://en.wikipedia.org/wiki/John_Hinckley_Jr.

she could not write any longer, she chose not to live and drowned herself, fearing the recurrence of a mental breakdown.[561]

As we tire of density and the grief it creates, and we start a spiritual journey to get out of the swamp, Sedna rewards us with transcendent crises, experiences which force us to let go and rise above them, resulting in a huge growth to a new level of consciousness. There is no choice with these crises, and the more we try and solve them, the more we will get hurt.

Swami Bhaktipada was a highly controversial, charismatic American Hare Krishna guru. He had Sedna in the first house of identity, square Jupiter in the eleventh house of collective consciousness.

A victim of childhood polio, who walked with the assistance of canes, he was the son of a conservative Baptist minister, who inherited his father's missionary spirit and attempted to convert school classmates to his family's faith.

As a student at the University of North Carolina, he met an undergraduate English major who became his homosexual lover and lifelong friend. The two resigned from the university when he was 23, after being threatened with an investigation over a sex scandal. He moved to New York City, started promoting LSD use and became an LSD guru. Then he worked as an unemployment claims reviewer and enrolled at Columbia University to study religious history but quit after several years to travel to India at 28 in search of a guru, only to return to New York after six months, unsuccessful.

After returning from India however, he met the Bengali guru who was know simply as Swamiji to his disciples, who was the founder of the Hare Krishnas. After attending Bhagavad-gita classes at the modest storefront temple in the Lower East Side of Manhattan, he accepted Swamiji as his spiritual master, receiving initiation at 29. A couple of years later he co-founded a 4,000 acre Hare Krishna community in West Virginia, which eventually housed over 300 faithful followers, and where he served as spiritual leader for 26 years.

---

[561] https://en.wikipedia.org/wiki/Virginia_Woolf

When he was 40, he and ten other high-ranking Hare Krishna leaders assumed the position of initiating gurus, because of Swamiji's death; however, at 49 the Krishna Governing Body Commission expelled him because he had started claiming to be the sole spiritual heir to the Hare Krishna movement. They cited his ruthless tactics, an overly independent nature and general callousness to the spiritual well-being of the movement.

He then established his own organization, taking several properties with him. A couple of years later his New Vrindaban had 13 satellite centers in the United States and Canada. However, when he was 53 the US federal government indicted him on five counts of racketeering, six counts of mail fraud, and conspiracy to murder two of his opponents in the Hare Krishna movement when he was 48. The government charged that he ordered the killings because the victims had threatened to reveal his sexual abuse of minors. They also claimed that he had illegally amassed a profit of more than $10.5 million over four years.

At 53 he was convicted on nine of the 11 charges, but the jury failed to reach a verdict on the murder charges. However, the Court of Appeals threw out all the convictions, saying that child molestation evidence had unfairly prejudiced the jury against him and he was not charged with those crimes. A retrial was ordered and at 55, he was released from house arrest where he had lived for nearly two years and returned triumphantly to his community.

He lost his iron grip on the community a month later however when he was accidentally discovered in a compromising position with a young male Malaysian disciple in the back of a Winnebago van. The community split into two camps and the challengers eventually ousted him and his supporters completely and most of his followers moved to the temple in New York, which remained under his control.

However, before his retrial was completed, he pleaded guilty to one count of racketeering for mail fraud and was sentenced to 20 years in prison. While he was in prison the Hare Krishna Child Protection Office concluded a 17-month investigation and determined that he had molested two boys. He was released from prison after serving eight years of a 12-year sentence and moved to India at 70 where he still had a significant number of loyal disciples, who worshiped him as a guru, dying there three years later.[562]

Petra Kelly was a Bavarian political human rights activist, ecologist and co-founder of the Green Party. She had Sedna conjunct Ceres in the eleventh house of collective consciousness, sesquiquadrate Jupiter in the sixth house of service.

> She studied World Politics and International Relations and worked at the European Communities in Brussels, continuing her development of social consciousness and political awareness. When she was 32 she helped found a political party that was dedicated to human rights and ecology which was officially named the Green Party six years later; she was one of 27 Greens elected to the Bundestag.

> Abandoned by her dad at the age of six, she was educated by Catholic nuns and raised largely by her grandmother, while her mom worked to support the family. When she was 11, her mom married an American Army officer who moved the family to the U.S., to Ft. Bening, Georgia. Petra became a classic overachiever; cheerleader, member of the student senate, scholarship winner. Despite physical pain from lifelong kidney ailments and the emotional trauma associated with the death of her younger half-sister Grace, she was able to maintain an almost maniacal focus on achievement. She returned to Europe for post grad study and her beginning involvement in European Federalist politics.

> She began an affair with the 65-year-old married EC president Sicco Mansholt, the first of a number of affairs with politically powerful older men. She had a long-term companionship with 25-year older Gert Bastian, a former NATO General who had done under-cover spy work. As brilliant, romantic and mercurial as Petra was, Bastian in contrast was plodding methodical and obsessive. To all evidence, their love was compelling and uncompromising. When she was 45, they were both found dead in their Bonn home with a gunshot to the head. Whether their

---

[562] https://en.wikipedia.org/wiki/Kirtanananda_Swami

deaths were suicide or murder was unresolved and the case remained a mystery.[563]

Our case study, Rachel Carson, the mother of the environmental movement, has Sedna in the first house of identity, square Jupiter, which is conjunct Ceres, the planet of nurture, Neptune, the planet associated with chemicals and lies, and Haumea, the planet of rebirth, all in the fourth house of home. Jupiter relates to publishing and her seminal book, *Silent Spring,* chronicled the devastating effects of the overuse of pesticides. The book was startling for its rigorous scientific assessment of how, by spraying for one issue, to get rid of a bug or a weed, without considering how the chemicals would impact everything else, people were often doing more harm than good.

> As a child she loved the outdoors, the birds and plants around her family's rural property sparking her imagination. She found fossilised fish and inspired by her expeditions wrote a book at age 8 and was published in a literary magazine at 13.

> At age eight she wrote a book and a few years later joined an underage literary elite with published works in a children's magazine which also published early writings by William Faulkner, F. Scott Fitzgerald, E. E. Cummings, and E. B. White. Carson was fond of noting that she had become a professional writer at age eleven.

> She entered the Pennsylvania College for Women on a senatorial district scholarship, earning an English degree, as preparation to become a writer. However it was biology that she found most thrilling during her undergraduate years. Biology gave her the tools to learn what had happened to that fossilised fish she found as a child.

> After earning a master's in zoology from Johns Hopkins, she found part-time work at the US Bureau of Fisheries. Though she'd chosen science over prose, her former specialty proved useful in her new occupation. Carson's first assignment for the bureau was to write a fifty-two-episode radio program called 'Romance Under the Waters.' "I had given up writing forever, I

[563] https://en.wikipedia.org/wiki/Petra_Kelly

thought. It never occurred to me that I was merely getting something to write about."

Her first book, *Under the Sea-Wind*, was a commercial failure, selling only two thousand copies. She needed a couple of years to recover from the blow, but both driven and strapped for cash, she wrote another book. *The Sea Around Us* was published when she was 44 and it won the National Book Award for nonfiction and solidified her position as a literary heavyweight. To this day, it's credited as being one of the most successful books ever written about nature.

In her fifties she turned her attention to conservation, especially some problems that she believed were caused by synthetic pesticides. The result was the book *Silent Spring*, published when she was 55, which brought environmental concerns to an unprecedented share of the American people. Although it was met with fierce opposition by chemical companies, it spurred a reversal in national pesticide policy, which led to a nationwide ban on DDT and other pesticides. It also inspired a grassroots environmental movement that led to the creation of the U.S. Environmental Protection Agency.[564]

Our case study, Steve Jobs, was an American entrepreneur, one of the originators of the computer revolution, co-founder of Apple Computers and Pixar Animation Studios. He had Sedna conjunct Mars in the eighth house of power and control, square to Jupiter, which is in the tenth house of profession, together with Uranus, the planet relating to electronics, and Makemake, the planet of extreme talent, just across the cusp in the eleventh house of ideals.

He and his friend, Steve Wozniak, made their first circuit board in their garage and they called it the Apple. By the time he was 24, his Apple Corporation was worth $10 million. A year later, its value had grown to $100 million. Its graphical user interface, business applications and word processing won kudos, and millions cheered while Apple took on IBM and its personal computer.[565]

---

[564] https://en.wikipedia.org/wiki/Rachel_Carson
[565] https://en.wikipedia.org/wiki/Steve_Jobs

However, he was called a haunted house by Chrisann Brennan, a high school sweetheart who lived with him and was an early Apple employee. She said he became a threatening monster and their relationship fell apart amid wild recriminations when she became pregnant with his first child. He denied he was the father, despite a positive paternity test and he paid a pittance in child support, while living the life of a millionaire. In her memoir she says:

"I've truly hated Steve at times, but never for very long. Sharing a daughter with him has forced me to think about things more deeply. Steve the saint, the alien, the despot, the punishing masculine god, the liar, the obsessed narcissist, the cult hero, the ID of the iEverything, the genius and the motherless boy."[566]

> As the Apple empire grew, Steve became a tyrant, subject to moody outbursts and gloomy silences. Hard feelings arose and power struggles with other executives ensued. He resigned and the following year co-founded NeXt, in an attempt to do for the hardware industry, what he had down for software. He also bought a company which he renamed Pixar Animation Studios and negotiated a deal with Disney to distribute Pixar's films and became a Disney partner. Under Jobs' leadership, Pixar won 20 Academy awards for successful animated feature films and was acquired by Disney.[567]

With a twist of fate and a large amount of Sednian transcendence, he then convinced Apple to buy NeXt and was invited back to Apple as interim CEO and a few years later was made permanent CEO once again. Under his renewed leadership Apple computer became a major player in the computer industry once more and his team created visually aesthetic computers in bright colours that appealed to younger buyers.

Helen Crawfurd was a Scottish suffragette and communist activist. She had Sedna in the twelfth house of the unconscious, square Jupiter, which is conjunct Venus, the planet of values in the ninth house of knowledge.

> Her father was a Catholic but converted to the Church of Scotland, and was a conservative trade unionist. Initially religious

---

[566] Brennan, Chrisann. *The Bite In The Apple: A Memoir Of My Life With Steve Jobs*
[567] https://en.wikipedia.org/wiki/Steve_Jobs

herself, she married the Reverend Alexander Crawfurd at 21, but became increasingly radical.

She first became active in the women's suffrage movement in her early twenties, then at 32 she switched her support to the more radical Women's Social and Political Union. Two years later she smashed the windows of the Minister for Education and received one month in prison. The following year, she was twice arrested for protesting in Glasgow, received another month in prison, and went on a five-day hunger strike. Following one more arrest, she left the Women's Political Union in protest at its support of WWI and joined the Independent Labour Party.

During the war, she was involved with the Red Clydeside movement, including rent strikes and became secretary of the Women's Peace Crusade. When she was 40 her husband died, and she was also elected as vice-chair of the Scottish division of the ILP. Shortly after, she was a founder member of the ILP's left-wing faction, which campaigned for it to affiliate to the Communist International. When this policy was defeated, she joined the new Communist Party of Great Britain, within which she served on the Central Committee, and was involved with various journalistic projects. She also became secretary of Workers' International Relief.[568]

Barack Obama, the first African American president, has Sedna in the second house of material resources, square Jupiter which is conjunct Saturn, the planet of structure, in the twelfth house of government institutions.

A self-described "skinny kid with a funny name," he is the child of a Kenyan man and an American woman. His parents met at the University of Hawaii where they were both students. When Barack was two, his father returned to Africa, and the young boy lived in Hawaii with his mom and grandparents. After his mother married an Indonesian, she took him with her when she moved to her new husband's native country. Young Barack was sent back to Hawaii at age 10 to live with his grandparents.

---

[568] https://en.wikipedia.org/wiki/Helen_Crawfurd

He graduated in 1983 from Columbia University with a degree in political science and international relations. He worked in Chicago's inner city, helping church groups improve job-training, education and city services to the poor and then went on to law school at Harvard. At 35 he was elected to the Illinois General Assembly as a state senator. At 43 he burst onto the national scene when he delivered a rousing keynote address at the Democratic National Convention in Boston. That year he won election to the U.S. Senate by a wide margin.

He announced his candidacy for the Democratic Party's nomination for President at 46. On the campaign trail he racked up an impressive number of primary and caucus wins. Exhibiting composure, thoughtfulness, a quick mind and self-deprecating humour, his debate performance earns kudos, while his powerful oratory evoked comparisons to Martin Luther King, Jr. and John F. Kennedy. Along with his life story, which he touts as a representation of the American dream, his emphasis on unity, hope and civility captured media and public attention.

His religious background is more diverse than that of most prominent politicians. But it may prove to be more representative of an increasingly diverse America. His mother was raised by non-practicing Christians; his father was raised a Muslim but was an atheist by the time he had married Obama's mother. His step-father was also Muslim, but of an eclectic kind who could make room for animist and Hindu beliefs.

In his book, *The Audacity of Hope*, published when he was 45, he writes, 'I was not raised in a religious household. For my mother, organised religion was too often dressed up closed-mindedness in the garb of piety, cruelty and oppression in the cloak of righteousness. However, in her mind, a working knowledge of the world's great religions was a necessary part of any well-rounded education. In our house the Bible, the Koran, sat on the shelf alongside books of Greek and Norse and African mythology.'

As a child in Indonesia, he studied for two years at one Muslim school and then two years at a Catholic school. Eventually however, he abandoned this non-conformism and skepticism as an adult to be baptised in the Trinity United Church of Christ, a denomination which emphasises the freedom of the individual conscience over adherence to creeds or hierarchical authority.[569]

Humour can be one path to transcend the quicksand of Sedna, giving us the objectivity to step back from the edge and also with the stressful aspects to Jupiter the optimism and drive to make it big.

I have a square to Jupiter, which is together with Makemake, the spiritual trickster planet, and Uranus, the planet of intuition, in my seventh house of relationships. This is the other half of my tenth house Juno/Ixion clown work, but this is my clown adventure, throwing myself out into the world, working mostly in an improvised way and seeing what happens. This has been a big research into people.

The 'throwing myself out there' is the square to Jupiter and the blind optimism of that definitely got me into tricky situations. But I have also felt the square in all my creative work, self-publishing my books and producing my own movies. My moto has been 'ask no-one's permission, so they can't say no and 'just do it'.

Red Skelton was an American film, nightclub and Emmy-award-winning TV comedian. He had Sedna in the fifth house of creativity, square Jupiter in the third house of communication.

> He was the youngest of four sons of a circus clown, who died two months before he was born. Left destitute, his mother worked as a cleaning woman. He began selling newspapers at age seven. He dropped out of school at 14 to entertain in a traveling minstrel show, making ten dollars a week. After working as a minstrel man on a showboat that cruised the Ohio and Missouri rivers, and as a clown with his late father's circus, he turned to burlesque in his late teens.

> At 17 he met a 15-year-old usherette and they were married two years later. Soon she was writing his material and managing his career. She negotiated a $1,500-a-week movie contract for him with MGM when he was 25 and he went on to appear in over 40 movies. CBS then offered him his own variety show, which premiered when he was 40 and was an instant hit. By 58, he had won three Emmy awards with shows that included his irreverent and hilarious alter ego characters. However, CBS eventually

---

[569] https://en.wikipedia.org/wiki/Barack_Obama

canceled the show despite high ratings, saying it wasn't hip with the times.

After the cancellation, he hit the stage playing to sold-out audiences well into his 70s with his stock characters. He had divorced amicably from his first wife at 30 and she continued to manage his career and write for him. Two years after his divorce, he married a model and four years later their daughter was born, followed by a son the next year. Tragedy occurred at the height of his career, when his son died of leukemia at age nine. He divorced his second wife at 60 and, that same year, he married his third wife, a secretary 25 years his junior.

He sustained a second lucrative career as an author of children's books and an artist of clown paintings that sold for as much as $20,000. Toward the end of his life he estimated that he earned $2.5 million a year with his lithographs. He was inducted into the Comedy Hall of Fame at 80 and retired to a Californian ranch. At a frail 84, he still wrote every morning, still together with his third wife of the previous 24 years, who was by then a 59-year-old horse breeder.[570]

At this juncture in human evolution, few of us use our planets at the spiritual level, but many of us are striving to, and such people are wonderful to be around. As with the other planets, the spiritual level of evolution is vastly different with Sedna from the two previous levels. Here, the stressful aspects with Jupiter the challenge to tune into people at a deep level across all walks of life, to see both the potential and the blocks and the ability to use this insight to encourage the evolutionary benefits of optimism.

Once we embrace the Sedna energy, which is the oneness of everything, our nurturing becomes an expression of Sedna consciousness and it becomes devotional in nature. The struggle of the beginner's level is gone, as are the transcendental crises of the intermediate level. At this level everything Saturnian is meaningless and yet everything Sednian has its place.

Anne Frank was a Dutch-Jewish writer of a diary from age 14 -15, while she and her family lived in total confinement, hiding in an attic from the

[570] https://en.wikipedia.org/wiki/Red_Skelton

Nazis, where non-Jewish friends had sheltered them. She had Sedna in the tenth house of profession, semi-square Jupiter in the eleventh house of collective consciousness.

> She began scrawling in her diary in 1942, writing as a typical teen in many ways, childish and profound, thoughtful and painful, writing, "In spite of everything, I still believe that people are really good at heart."
>
> Her last entry was three days before their hiding place was discovered and they were arrested. She died of typhus at the Bergen-Belsen concentration camp in March 1945. Her father, who survived, returned after the war and found his daughter's diary. At the turn of the century a new edition of her diary was released with five previously secret pages that described her conflict with her mother, whom she wrote, "had cold eyes," and with whom she could not talk to unburden herself, and her lament that her parents had a loveless marriage of convenience.
>
> Her diary remains as a poignant symbol of the millions whose lives and homes were lost during a tragic page in history. Translated into 54 languages with sales hovering around 25 million copies worldwide, her book is an established part of most high school educations. Putting a single face on the vast horror of the Holocaust, she served as a reminder of the quiet acts of heroism that were part of that high-water mark of evil.[571]

Hank Friedman is an American astrologer who began to study the field at 34 to disprove it, but became convinced of its validity. He had Sedna in the ninth house of spirituality and knowledge, semi-square Jupiter in the sixth house of service.

> He was trained for five years in Ericksonian Hypnotherapy and also as an advisor in parental deprogramming. He also studied Sufism for 20 years. He moved into a synthesis of Vedic with Western astrology and is a world expert in astrological software. He has beta-tested, designed and reviewed software from the age of 34 and is the author of *Astrology for Your PC* and review articles for astrology magazines. He is considered one of the

---

[571] https://en.wikipedia.org/wiki/Anne_Frank

San Francisco Bay's foremost psychics and psychic therapists.[572]

And finally, we have our case study, Edgar Cayce, the father of wholistic medicine. He is an American mystic who is known as the Sleeping Prophet, because, while in a sleep state he could discuss history, geology, metaphysics, philosophy and medicine. He had Sedna in the eighth house of life and death and inherited health issues, square Jupiter, which is together with Nessus, the centaur which provides a guide to deep energies of regeneration, both in the fifth house of creativity.

He prayed to be able to help others, especially children, and had a spiritual vision at age 13, that told him he would be able to accomplish this dream of service. A lady bathed in light told him to sleep with his head on his books and then he would be able to remember what was in them. This was at a time when he was having trouble in school, and his father was beating him for not being able to spell the words in his lessons correctly. Soon after, he showed signs of special abilities when he found that he could sleep on his schoolbooks and have photographic recall of every page.

Two years after his first vision he was pronounced dead from drowning, but recovered. At 23 he developed a severe case of laryngitis which stopped him working as an insurance salesman, a job he hated. Doctors couldn't cure it. In desperation he tried hypnosis from a traveling practitioner and was cured after several treatments. Under hypnosis, he gave his first psychic reading at 24 and learned that he could give accurate medical diagnoses and healing recommendations for himself and for other people.

He gave approximately 30,000 life-readings and medical diagnosis to people during his lifetime. He founded a hospital, a university and the Association for Research and Enlightenment that promotes research on his readings and continues his work. Throughout his life, he claimed no special abilities and did not capitalise financially or otherwise on his gifts. The readings never offered a set of beliefs or "religion" to be embraced, but instead

---

[572] https://www.astro.com/astro-databank/Friedman,_Hank_(1950)

focused on the idea that every person should test in his or her own life the principles presented.

Though he was a devout Christian who read the Bible through once for every year of his life, his work emphasised the importance of comparative study of belief systems from around the world. In fact, some of the metaphysical material that came through the sleeping Cayce was at first confusing and distressing to him in his waking state. However, he overcame his doubts, as have others, by observing the amazing accuracy and unfailing helpfulness of the readings in other areas, such as healing. The underlying principle of the readings is the oneness of all life, acceptance of all people, and a compassion and understanding for every major religion.[573]

In-conjunct

With the evolutionary inconjunct between Sedna and Jupiter the esoteric spiritual energy of Sedna bursts into our growth and optimism, our ability to seek insight through knowledge and express our generosity and tolerance in an evolutionary way and we have a fated role to play.

Jupiter is associated with good luck and bounty, with a sense of humour, good will and mercy, and with optimism and growth, including mental and spiritual growth.

However, the inconjunct sometimes acts as a flow and at other times as a stress, so we have to learn to actively manage the process as the rarified spiritual energy sometimes reinforces our growth and, at other times, isn't there to back us up. By adjusting to this, we gain a deeper understanding of ourselves and how to play our role.

If we are unconscious of the Sedna energy however, or there are other stressful aspects to Jupiter, we are still likely to call the more negative manifestations of Jupiter into our lives, including blind optimism, excess, overindulgence and the irresponsibility that results from blind optimism.

Polly Klaas was an American homicide victim. While hosting a slumber party for girlfriends at her home when she was 12, a stranger entered her window and kidnapped her at knifepoint. She had Sedna in the second house of material reality, inconjunct Jupiter, which is conjunct Saturn the planet of structure, in the seventh house of relationships.

---

[573] https://en.wikipedia.org/wiki/Edgar_Cayce

She was two and a half when her parents divorced. Her mother remarried and the family relocated frequently due to her new husband's uneven success in his career. So, she spent her formative years living all over northern California, but when her mother and step-father separated when she was 11, life with her mother became stable and productive. Mom was employed full-time as a manager in a clothing store and Polly was looking forward to spending a second year in the same school where she flourished. After taking up the clarinet, she was accepted into the advanced band in junior high school and was pursuing her talents by acting in local community theatre and singing in a children's choir.

Then news came of a possible reconciliation between her mother and stepfather, meaning the family would be uprooted again and move to Idaho. Mom, now eager to reunite with her husband, relied heavily on Polly to help care for her baby half-sister Annie, a job which Polly dutifully undertook. "Polly was just trying to help, to hold things together. That's what she did. I mean the last words anyone ever heard Polly say were what she said to the man who was kidnapping her, as he led her out of the house. "Please don't wake up my mother." Her body was found in a wooded area, 35 miles north of her home.[574]

Josef Mengele was a German doctor and member of the Nazi party who was known as the 'Angel of Death' at the Auschwitz concentration camp during World War II for his grisly genetic research on twins and other subjects. He had Sedna conjunct Orcus, the planet of delving down and speaking out, in the tenth house of profession, inconjunct Jupiter, which is together with Pholus, the centaur of illumination, in the fifth house of creativity. He was the subject of a 40-year international hunt in the postwar years, known for being the butcher who had supervised the torture and death of as many as 400,000 Jews in a maniacal quest for racial purity.

Joseph McCarthy was an American politician who, as a Senator, was the chairman of various investigating committees commonly known as 'The Red Witch Hunts'. He had Sedna, conjunct Orcus, the planet of

---

[574] https://en.wikipedia.org/wiki/Murder_of_Polly_Klaas

delving down and speaking out, in the twelfth house of the unconscious, inconjunct Jupiter in the sixth house of service.

He was an inflammatory speaker and insidious interrogator, with a tendency to fabricate evidence, which ruined many lives. He was elected to the Senate in a Republican landslide at the age of 38, where he was known mainly for being a genial drinking companion and a soft touch for the real estate lobby. He burst into prominence at 42 when he announced, "I have in my hand a list of 205 names, known to the Secretary of State as being members of the Communist Party, who are nevertheless still working and shaping policy in the State Department."

The numbers began to change in a matter of days, to "207 bad risks", then "57 card-carrying Communists," and finally, "81 loyalty risks." In the end not one was a card-carrying Communist in the State Department and all those listed were from outdated files on government employees who had been investigated for offences ranging from alleged communist and fascist sympathies to drinking problems and homosexuality.

However, the bluff worked and the polls showed that half of the American public applauded, while only 29 percent disapproved. Then he announced he'd uncovered the top Soviet espionage agent in the US; however, the spy turned out to be a bespectacled university professor and East Asia expert whose only crime was predicting the fall of the Chinese Nationalist government and urging the U.S. to deal rationally with Mao Tse Tung.

TV was still in its infancy at that time and when the McCarthy hearings began with 36 days of live TV exposure, it had the whole nation intensely watching. He was 46. His fatal moment came when the chief attorney for his sub-committee, was being questioned by the Army's special counsel. McCarthy interrupted, as was his irritating habit, and announced that a young lawyer from counsel's firm had once belonged to a leftist lawyer's group. The stunned lawyer responded slowly and emotionally, "Have you no sense of decency, sir? At long last, have you no sense of decency?"

The lawyer received a standing ovation and the subsequent polls showed McCarthy's popularity plummeting. Two days later a motion was introduced to censure him in the Senate for conduct 'contrary to senatorial traditions'. His strange and stormy career was ended at 46 when he was censured in a 67-22 vote. After the censure his health started failing and he began drinking more and holding it less well. He died of acute hepatitis as a result of alcohol abuse a couple of years later.[575]

As we tire of density and the grief it creates, and we start a spiritual journey to get out of the swamp, Sedna rewards us with transcendent crises, experiences which force us to let go and rise above them, resulting in a huge growth to a new level of consciousness. There is no choice with these crises, and the more we try and solve them, the more we will get hurt.

Jessica Lynch was an American Marine assigned to the Iraq War. An adorable 19-year-old honey-blonde, Jessica was captured in an Iraqi raid. She has Sedna conjunct the Sun in the twelfth house of the unconscious, inconjunct Jupiter, which is together with Uranus, the planet of the unusual, in the seventh house of relationships.

> In a Special Ops raid, US soldiers wearing night goggles brought helicopters into the southern Iraqi city to carry out a daring rescue raid. The petite soldier was held in a second-floor room with fractures in both legs, her right arm, ankle and foot. Intelligent briefings relate that some of her wounds were the results of extensive torture.

> She came up missing after Iraqi forces ambushed an Army supply convoy near four days before her 20th birthday. The details of her imprisonment and her rescue were subsequently much discussed in the news with reports that the U.S. military exaggerated the rescue. There was also a question about whether she was tortured, or whether all her injuries were sustained in the fighting just before her capture.

> A book written by Rick Bragg with her help, *I'm a Soldier Too*, was released and a TV biopic was produced and televised. The book alleges that she was raped while in captivity and that she

---

[575] https://en.wikipedia.org/wiki/Joseph_McCarthy

does not remember this mistreatment. Iranian doctors dispute that she was raped, but she underwent rigorous physical therapy and treatment for her serious injuries and emotional trauma.

Nevertheless, at 24 she appeared before a House Committee on Oversight and Government Reform and testified that the tales about her capture in Iraq were not true, that they were embellished to make her seem like a hero. She said, "The bottom line is the American people are capable of determining their own ideals for heroes and they don't need to be told elaborate tales.[576]

Betty Friedan was an American feminist pioneer and organizer, lecturer and writer, the author of *The Feminine Mystique*, which became a best-seller, translated into 13 languages. She had Sedna in the third house of communication, inconjunct Jupiter, which is conjunct Ixion, the planet of lawlessness, in the ninth house of knowledge.

"Her mother quit her job as editor of the local newspaper's women's pages to become a housewife. She was aware of the toll this took, and the impact it had on her family. And as an adult, after becoming pregnant, she was herself fired from a job.

During her 20s and 30s she was a deeply committed radical activist. A brilliant, energetic reporter for union newspapers, she was intensely engaged in the leftist politics of the time. By the time she stopped working at 31, pregnant with her second child, McCarthyism had chased underground much of this visionary women's movement. The rest was smothered by anti-female union policies and longstanding misogyny among male leaders on the left.

She retreated to the suburbs and began writing about family and work for women's magazines, doing what her mother had not done. And she came out swinging. Women in labor unions were fighting for equal pay, maternity leave and higher minimum wages, while other progressive women agitated for government-sponsored day care, national health insurance and an end to racial discrimination.

---

[576] https://en.wikipedia.org/wiki/Jessica_Lynch

She later said, "I decided I was going to be fulfilled as a housewife, but I could not suppress the itch to write, and I did it in the morning, like secret drinking." She authored *The Feminine Mystique* at 42, which became a best-seller and was translated into 13 languages. This book exposed the "desperate housewives" of 1950s America, women imprisoned in suburbia with little to do. She came to believe that "the only way for a woman, as for a man, to find herself, to know herself as a person, is by creative work of her own."

On the heels of the Civil Rights Movement, she helped to found the National Organization for Women when she was 45, the largest and most effective group for women's rights, and served as its first president.[577]

Thomas Piketty is a French economist who is professor at the Paris School of Economics and Centennial professor at the London School of Economics. He has Sedna in the eleventh house of ideals, inconjunct Jupiter which is conjunct Neptune, the planet of inspiration, both in the sixth house of service. His work has focussed on wealth and income inequality and when he was 43 he refused to receive the French legion of honour.

He is the author of the best-selling book, *Capital in the Twenty-First Century*, which emphasises the themes of his work on wealth concentrations and distribution over the past 250 years. His Sedna is also square the conjunction of Vesta, the asteroid of regeneration, and Mars, the planet of action, in the eighth house of shared resources and bi-quintile Pluto, the planet of transformation, in the fourth house of home.

The book argues that the rate of capital return in developed countries is persistently greater than the rate of economic growth, and that this will cause wealth inequality to increase in the future. He considers that to be a problem, and to address it, he proposes redistribution through a progressive global tax on wealth.[578]

---

[577] https://en.wikipedia.org/wiki/Betty_Friedan
[578] https://en.wikipedia.org/wiki/Thomas_Piketty

Ken Kesey was an American actor and novelist who worked at various times as a logger, a mental-hospital attendant, a farmer and musician in a band. He had Sedna in the second house of material resources, inconjunct Jupiter in the ninth house of knowledge.

> He volunteered for drug experiments run by the government, prior to the time that Timothy Leary started his experiments in psychedelics. His job as a psychiatric attendant for the Veteran's Administration Hospital in California when he was 26, provided background for his most famous work, *One Flew Over the Cuckoo's Nest*. The next year he sold the movie rights for $28,000. The film won five Oscars and reportedly made $50 million in gross earnings.
>
> A major counter culture figure in the 1960's, he and his band, The Merry Pranksters, made a cross-country drug-fuelled trip in a psychedelic painted bus called "Further" that was chronicled by Tom Wolfe in his book *The Electric Kool-Aid Acid Test*. When he was 30 he purchased a farm in Pleasant Hill, Oregon, converting the barn into living quarters. Many of the outbuildings on the farm were built by The Merry Pranksters. He married his high school sweetheart, Faye, and they had four children. He has always been close to family.
>
> He was an inspiration for many young people. With an ear for dialog and the ability to create characters that live on the page, all of his works are about prisoners, some who realise their position and rail against it, others who are just doing their time. An old-fashioned kind of writer, he is a moral critic. He won the Robert Kirsch Award given by the Los Angeles Times in 1991 for his body of work.[579]

Humour can be one path to transcend the quicksand of Sedna, giving us the objectivity to step back from the edge, and also with the inconjunct to Jupiter the optimism and drive to make it big.

Joan Rivers was an American comedienne, thought by many to be the funniest lady on the planet. She had Sedna in the first house of identity, inconjunct Jupiter, which is conjunct Quaoar, the planet of new

---

[579] https://en.wikipedia.org/wiki/Ken_Kesey

perspectives, and Mars, the planet of action, all in the sixth house of service.

> She certainly was one of the fastest, most agile minds in show biz. Her rapid-fire mix of gossip, insults, flaunting of taboos and ridicule of flaws and neurosis is written 90% by her. She also wrote comedy for Candid Camera, scripts and material for Phyllis Diller and Zsa Zsa Gabor and humorous books.

> The younger of two daughters of Russian-Jewish refugees, she learned from her doctor dad to crack a joke and was making people laugh by the time she was 11. She learned from her mom that rich was better than poor and was raised with privilege and a good education. She married at 24 and had it annulled the following year when she decided she wanted to be an actress, not a housewife. While doing off-Broadway, she worked in offices and turned to comedy at 27 to supplement her income.

> At the age of 32 she was told that she was too old and passed over, however a week later she was booked on Johnny Carson's *Tonight Show*. They clicked. Their immediate rapport was a hit with the audience and she appeared for years with Carson before hosting her own *Late Show Starring Joan Rivers*, with a contract for $10 million over three years. She moved into the stratosphere as America's top comedienne, the darling of the circuit with tours, magazine covers, nightclub and Las Vegas gigs, TV projects, books and records.[580]

At this juncture in human evolution, few of us use our planets at the spiritual level, but many of us are striving to and such people are wonderful to be around. As with the other planets, the spiritual level of evolution is vastly different with Sedna from the two previous levels. Here the inconjunct aspect with Jupiter the fate to tune into people at a deep level across all walks of life, to see both the potential and the blocks and the ability to use this insight to encourage the evolutionary benefits of optimism.

Once we embrace the Sedna energy, which is the oneness of everything, our nurturing becomes an expression of Sedna consciousness and it becomes devotional in nature. The struggle of the

---

[580] https://en.wikipedia.org/wiki/Joan_Rivers

beginner's level is gone, as are the transcendental crises of the intermediate level. At this level everything Saturnian is meaningless and yet everything Sednian has its place.

Swami Vivekananda, was an Indian religious leader, a disciple of Sri Ramakrishna, who became inspired by his teacher to serve men as a visible manifestation of God. His Sedna was on the cusp of the third house of communication, inconjunct Jupiter in the ninth house of knowledge.

> Highly intelligent with a retentive memory, he had stories of the scripture memorised by the time he was six. An illumined being of the highest order, he was the forerunner who brought the spiritual teachings of India to the West, greatly influencing the last hundred years of spiritual growth in Europe and America.
>
> He became one of the most beloved disciples of Sri Ramakrishna and, as the master spent his last years teaching his disciples and streams of visitors, he recorded his instruction. He then brought the spiritual teachings of India to the West in 1893 at the convening of the Parliament of Religions in Chicago. During his three-year stay in American, he founded Hindu philosophy schools, many of which acknowledge him as a modern Buddha and an emanation of Lord Shiva.
>
> When he took the universal teachings to the West, he broke with the Indian caste tradition and lost his caste as a result. His Sedna was also quintile Chariklo, the centaur of foresight, in the the fifth house of creativity, square Orcus, the planet of speaking out in the twelfth house of the unconscious, and sesquiquadrate Nessus, the centaur of radical transformation, in the seventh house of relationships. His denial of the rigid system brought him severe censure from Indian traditionalists.[581]

Elsie Wheeler was an American spiritualist and psychic who worked with Marc Edmund Jones and Zoe Wells on the Sabian Symbols and was noted for being the primary contributor. She had Sedna in the eleventh house of collective consciousness, inconjunct Jupiter in the sixth house of service.

---

[581] https://en.wikipedia.org/wiki/Swami_Vivekananda

The experiment was conducted when she was 38. Crippled with arthritis, she had to be carried to the session. 360 cards had been prepared, one for each degree of the zodiac, which were presented to her at random and were shuffled continuously. One at a time the cards were placed face down in front of her and she pictured an image and reported it.

At first the images did not seem entirely appropriate, or some were exaggerated, so the cards were put aside for six years, when they were revised. She died seven years after that, but the revision process was repeated after her death and the results were first published thirteen years later. Today the Sabian symbols are one of the tools widely used by astrologers to understand the meaning behind the placements of the planets.[582]

Shivabalayogi was a meditation guru in the tradition of the ancient and modern yogis of India. He had Sedna in the eleventh house of collective consciousness, inconjunct Jupiter on the cusp of the sixth house of service.

He attained self-realisation through twelve years of arduous tapas, meditating in samādhi, a state of total thoughtlessness, for an average of twenty hours a day. Tapas is the most advanced stage of meditation in which one remains absorbed for long periods in this non-dualistic state of consciousness.

After he completed tapas, he assumed the name Shivabalayogi, meaning Yogi devoted to Shiva and Parvati. The name reflects that he is a manifestation of both the male and female aspects of the divine. The female aspect represents the invisible energy of the divine through which the entire creation operates, while the male aspect represents the pure consciousness of existence beyond all imaginations. Generally, devotees called him simply Swamiji, meaning respected Master.

For three decades he traveled extensively in India and Sri Lanka, initiating over ten million people into dhyana meditation. In his early fifties he traveled for four years in England and the United

---

[582] https://www.astro.com/astro-databank/Wheeler,_Elsie

States. His teaching is consistent with the Vedanta, emphasising the need for spiritual practice to achieve self-realisation.[583]

The man we know as the Dalai Lama, Tenzin Gyatso, has Sedna in the tenth house, with a close inconjunct to Jupiter in the third house of ideas. He is actually the 14th Dalai Lama, a title given to spiritual leaders of the Tibetan people.

Despite his humble beginnings, being born on a straw mat in a cowshed to a farmer's family in a remote part of Tibet, he had become the joint most popular world leader by 2013, according to a poll which sampled public opinion in the USA and six major European countries.

He was not formally enthroned until he was 15, during the Battle of Chamdo with the People's Republic of China. The following year, he and the Tibetan government were pressured into accepting the Seventeen Point Agreement for the Peaceful Liberation of Tibet, by which it became formally incorporated into the People's Republic of China. Fearing for his life in the wake of a revolt in Tibet when he was 24, he fled to India, from where he led a government in exile.

With the aim of launching guerrilla operations against the Chinese, the Central Intelligence Agency funded his administration with US $1.7 million a year in the 1960s. At 66 he ceded his partial power over the government to an elected parliament of selected Tibetan exiles. His original goal was full independence for Tibet, but by the late 1980s he was seeking high-level autonomy instead.[584]

Quintile, Bi-quintile

The evolutionary quintile or bi-quintile aspect between Sedna and Jupiter infuses our growth and optimism, our ability to seek insight through knowledge and express our generosity and tolerance with the all-encompassing spiritual energy of Sedna to the point where we can push the boundaries of human development.

---

[583] https://en.wikipedia.org/wiki/Shivabalayogi
[584] https://en.wikipedia.org/wiki/Dalai_Lama

Jupiter is associated with good luck and bounty, with a sense of humour, good will and mercy, and with optimism and growth, including mental and spiritual growth.

Quintiles and bi-quintiles point to talent, the desire to create order and to categorize, a fascination with patterns and structures, perfectionist tendencies, and the desire to build or make things. These aspects have the characteristics of both the trine and opposition. They point to awareness of conflicts, or problems and finding solutions for them, however they do not automatically kick into action and must be cultivated over time.

If we are unconscious of the Sedna energy, however, or there are other stressful aspects to Jupiter, we are still likely to call the more negative manifestations of Jupiter into our lives, including blind optimism, excess, overindulgence and the irresponsibility that results from blind optimism.

Arthur Shawcross was an American sexual deviant and a serial killer of 13 prostitutes in upper New York. Like Dawn, he also had Sedna conjunct the Moon in the twelfth house of the unconscious, bi-quintile Jupiter in the fifth house of creativity.

> He was a weird child, unusually quiet and baby-talked up to the time he was five or six. He was a bed-wetter who played with imaginary playmates and tried to run away from home frequently. He was violently and painfully raped by an older man when he was a child. And as a youth, he claimed that he had sex with girls and as a teen, that he began a relationship with an older woman who taught him all the tricks including oral sex.

> He learned to please the older women whom he saw and also had sex with younger boys and farm animals. He found that torturing and killing an animal was a great rush, especially during bestiality. During military duty in Viet Nam, he witnessed and participated in sadistic acts. He said that he killed and butchered victims, and sex-tortured and cannibalised Vietnamese women, but by this time he was unable to tell the difference between truth and fantasy, because records show that he was never in combat, or on jungle patrol.

> After Vietnam, he returned home to a cold welcome from his mom and resumed residence with the third woman whom he married and then began a spree of felony, arson, rape, murder,

and cannibalisation of the genitalia of both male and female victims. At 26, he strangled an 11-year-old boy, then sexually molested and killed a little girl. Caught, he was sentenced to 17 years prison; however, he was paroled early under a plea bargain after 12 years.

He was 42 when he was released, he worked as a manual labor, working with food packaging, however soon local prostitutes started going missing, their bodies later found. He was caught and convicted again at 46. And his original parole was called one of the most egregious examples of the unwarranted release of a prisoner in American history. Later resonance imaging showed brain lesions and right-brain formations resulting from childhood injuries, apparently from being brutally abused. He also had an XYY chromosome pattern, lead poisoning and a weak ability to deal with stress.[585]

Paula Yates was a Welsh TV personality in the UK, a tarted-up presenter of the TV series The Tube, who loved to use shock as an attention-getter and who's approach took her from flirtatious celebrity interviewer, to celebrity in her own right. She had Sedna in the fourth house of home, bi-quintile Jupiter on the cusp of the twelfth house of the unconscious.

Engagingly ebullient and flirtatious, her irreverent approach to the rich-and-famous won her industry awards twice. As a provocative columnist and author, her subjects ranged from baby care, to sexual turn-ons. However, it was her notably frank autobiography that made her best known.

As a child, she had an uncomfortable relationship with her dad, TV star Jess Yates, who was known as "the Bishop" for his presentation of the religious show *Stars on Sunday*. It was an unconventional childhood in a unique family. Her dad was 16-years-older than her mom, who was a former showgirl, actress and writer of erotic novels. From age eight, the girl lived mostly with her mom, at times in Malta and Majorca.

It was a revelation to discover when she was 38, via DNA testing, that Yates was not her father at all, but rather, her dad

---

[585] https://en.wikipedia.org/wiki/Arthur_Shawcross

was Hughie Green, TV host of several popular shows. When she found this out, it added further strain to her relationship with her mom, which was already tenuous.

She started a relationship with Bob Geldof at 18 and produced her first book *Rockstars In Their Underpants,* consisting of semi-clad photographs of everyone she and Geldof knew. They finally married in Las Vegas when she was 27. They had three daughters and she wrote two books about parenting, in which she urged women to stay at home to look after their children and to breast-feed their babies for as long as possible.

Her big break came when she was recruited as co-presenter of *The Tube*, an anarchic TV pop show which swiftly developed cult status. She stayed with the show for five years, winning the best documentary award at the New York Film Festival two years running for her interviews with Tina Turner and Elton John. She graduated to Channel Four's early morning program, *The Big Breakfast*, where she interviewed stars while everyone reclined on a large bed.

However, at 36, she was fired from her TV hostess job and her tangled life began its most turbulent period. She began an impassioned affair with the Michael Hutchence, singer with the rock group INXS, whom she called "a sexy love god." They had met the year before and began a three-year affair. She was linked to alcohol and drugs and Geldof secured custody of their three daughters. She had her breasts enlarged and trilled that the first time she and Michael went to bed, "he did six things within the first hour I was sure were illegal."

Pregnant, she divorced Geldof and gave birth to Michael's daughter, Heavenly Tiger Lily. She and Michael were planning to marry and move to Australia and were negotiating the purchase of a house overlooking Sydney Harbour. Michael's drug days were allegedly over and they both were filled with promise when mysteriously and tragically Michael was found dead in a hotel room.

Paula insisted that it was an accident rather than a suicide but was nonetheless treated several times for depression and made a suicide attempt herself the next year. She was found dead at her home in London two years later. Her body was found by a friend after repeated phone calls went unanswered. Tiger Lily was playing by herself when Mummy would not wake up, and an empty vodka bottle and half-empty one of barbiturates left mute testimony.[586]

Amy Grossberg is an American teenager who gave birth to a baby and discarded it in a trash bag. She has Sedna in the twelfth house of the unconscious, quintile Jupiter, which is conjunct her Sun, the planet of willpower, in the third house of ideas and communication.

She and her boyfriend were in love. They were both 18, from good homes and an affluent, caring background. When Amy got pregnant, they kept it a secret. When she went into labor they drove to a motel where they delivered a baby boy, put it in a plastic bag and left it in a dumpster.

The bloody sheets were discovered by a cleaning woman, who immediately contacted police. After returning to school, Amy began to have severe seizures as a result of not having expelled the placenta. She was taken to a hospital, and it was clear to the doctors that she had just given birth. Not long after, police officials and the hospital put the two incidents together. The baby was found and diagnosed as a live, healthy birth; however, it had died from multiple skull fractures and from having been shaken.

At first the pair seemed to remain a loving couple, but they turned on each other and each began blaming the other. By the time they came to trial, the two former lovers sat in a courtroom for sentencing, not looking across the room at each other. Despite initially denying her pregnancy, then denying giving birth and then blaming Peterson for killing the baby, at her sentencing she pleaded for leniency and told the judge, "I want to help others. I want to make a difference."

She was given two and a half years prison, and her boyfriend, two years. It was the day before her 20th birthday. She was released from prison after serving only 17 months and returned to live with her parents, who, from the time of their daughter's arrest and through her sentencing, maintained she did nothing

---

[586] https://en.wikipedia.org/wiki/Paula_Yates

wrong. An artist, she started her own company, called Just Because Invitations, several years later at 26.[587]

As we tire of density and the grief it creates, and we start a spiritual journey to get out of the swamp, Sedna rewards us with transcendent crises, experiences which force us to let go and rise above them, resulting in a huge growth to a new level of consciousness. There is no choice with these crises, and the more we try and solve them, the more we will get hurt.

L. Ron Hubbard was an American entrepreneur, engineer, and prolific writer of science fiction, who established the Church of Scientology. He had Sedna in the third house of ideas, bi-quintile Jupiter, which is conjunct Pholus, the centaur of enlightenment, in the eleventh house of collective consciousness.

> Imaginative, intelligent, and with a mind that was a factory of ideas, he was also broke and in debt in the late 1940s and was forced to sell his typewriter for $28.50 to pay alimony to his first wife. Troubled, restless and adrift he became an expert hypnotist, and shared an ageing mansion in Pasadena, CA with writers, artists, Bohemians and occultists in the late 1940s. Neighbours complained when their rituals of sexual magic got out of hand in the back yard. Hubbard's best friend at the time was a lover of Hubbard's second wife and they all followed the black magic practices of Aleister Crowley.

> His Sedna was also conjunct Orcus, the planet of delving down and speaking out in the fourth house of home, and bi-quintile Ixion, the planet of lawlessness, in the nineth house of knowledge. He wrote a book, *Dianetics: The Modern Science of Mental Health,* which was written in one draft in 30 days and became an instant bestseller. He became an overnight celebrity. His system became known as "the poor man's psychotherapy." However, by the following year profits were beginning to fall and Dianetics became Scientology, as he turned from pop therapist to religious leader.

> Skillfully transforming himself from a pulp fiction writer to a writer of "sacred scriptures," Hubbard made a fortune and achieved his

---

[587] https://en.wikipedia.org/wiki/Amy_Grossberg_and_Brian_Peterson

dream of fame. Starting as a collection of mental therapy centers it grew into one of the world's most controversial and secretive religions. The courses included instruction of how to help kick drug habits, improve communication skills, build confidence and help people take control of their lives.

However, by preying on the anxieties and the loneliness of his converts and by using hypnotherapy, Pavlovian conditioning and twisted psychotherapy, he was able to establish himself as the leader of a movement of millions, less than 900 of which ever reached the highest levels of his imparted wisdom. Australian courts have since revoked the status of Scientology as a religion, and France convicted Hubbard in absentia of fraud. However, in spite of all the exposure, he still ignited the fire of self-improvement in many sincere people.[588]

Timothy Leary was an American professor, guru of the 1960's drug culture who coined the phrase, "Turn on, tune in, drop out." He had Sedna in the fourth house of home, bi-quintile Jupiter in the ninth house of knowledge. Well ahead of his time, he was fired from Harvard for his controlled experiments with psychedelic drugs.

He began experimenting with psylocybin, mescaline and LSD when he became a lecturer at Harvard. Although the experiments were controlled and scholarly papers on the experiments were published in prestigious journals, he and fellow Harvard researcher Richard Alpert (later known as Ram Dass) were fired. A patron set them up in a Millbrook, NY estate where they could continue their research. Instead, it became a kind of Bohemian salon where Leary dropped acid with the likes of Jack Kerouac, Allen Ginsberg and Thelonius Monk.

Arrested 29 times, President Richard Nixon once called him "the most dangerous man in America." When he was 45 he was sentenced to 30 years and $30,000 for smuggling a small amount of marijuana into the U.S. from Mexico. The following year his estate mansion was raided and he was again arrested on drug charges. After appeals and more arrests he was sent to the state prison at 50, to face up to 20 years for two possession convictions.

---

[588] https://en.wikipedia.org/wiki/L._Ron_Hubbard

Later that year he escaped prison with the help of the radical Weathermen underground movement and was smuggled out of the country. However, three years later he was detained while trying to enter Afghanistan, and was sent back to the U.S. He was returned to Folsom prison, where he at one point had a cell across from Charles Manson. He was released on parole when he was 56.

His life was marked by tragedy and broken relationships. When he was 35 his first of five wives, Marianne, committed suicide. At 70, his daughter Susan, who was 42, was found mentally unfit to stand trial for shooting her sleeping boyfriend. Later that year she used shoelaces to hang herself from the bars of her cell. His son Jack also felt his father had deserted him at a critical time in his life and was not close to him.

At 75 he called his closest friends to tell them he had prostate cancer. He turned his death into a cyber-happening by chronicling his illness on a personal Web site. Two days before he died, his request to have his ashes launched into space was approved. With videotape rolling, he died at his home, whispering his last word, "beautiful".[589]

Jimmy Swaggart was an American charismatic maestro of hi-tech salvation, television evangelist of Pentecostal Christianity blessed with the ability to spellbind audiences to the tune of $150 million a year. He had Sedna in the fourth house of home, bi-quintile Jupiter in the eleventh house of collective consciousness. His Sedna is also at the focal point of a bi-quintiles to Neptune, the planet of dreams and visions, in the ninth house of spirituality.

He conducted a vast yet dubious ministry secluded behind the walls of his $30 milliondollar compound in Louisiana. Known as a frequent hell-raiser as a teen, he dropped out of high school and played honky tonk piano with his notoriously carousing cousin Jerry Lee Lewis. At age 17, he married a 15-year old farm girl who lived down the road, both successfully lying about their ages. Soon after his marriage, he preached his first sermon in front of a grocery store interspersed with playing the accordion, 'knowing we get crowds with the music'.

---

[589] https://en.wikipedia.org/wiki/Timothy_Leary

By his late 20s, he was itinerant preacher traveling the Southeastern US and began to cut gospel records, of which he eventually sold over 150 million. After another message from God, he began a radio show, and from that point onward TV became his manifest destiny. The ministry probably quadrupled with radio. With TV it exploded. In front of the TV camera, he became more outspoken than ever, verbally attacking Roman Catholicism, Jews and homosexuals while soliciting money from his viewers. During each sermon, the impassioned preacher ranted and raved, coercing his followers and himself into a feeding frenzy of devotion.[590]

His Sedna is also closely semi-square Orcus, the planet of delving down and speaking out, in the fifth house of creativity.

His antics backfired and in his late 40s he became a target of investigations. His Sedna is also square Ceres, the planet of nurture, in the seventh house of relationships and semi-square Saturn, the planet of structure, in the second house of material resources. A wealthy California widow left almost her entire estate to Swaggart Ministries. The Evangelistic Association and its agents were charged by family lawyers with 'preying upon her loneliness and illness for the purpose of securing donations from her.'" By now Swaggart was flush with 3 palatial estates and a private jet.

Further allegations of misallocations of monies, death threats, handsome payoffs and the exploitation of prostitutes led to private investigation. When confronted by photos of himself with prostitutes he reportedly admitted he had a fascination with pornography from childhood. This incident earned him a three-month suspension from his US pulpit and a two-year rehabilitation period, which proved unsuccessful. Further confirmed encounters with prostitutes sent him reeling into a tortured, televised public confession for which he may be best known. However, he was back to preaching once more against sin within three months.[591]

---

[590] https://en.wikipedia.org/wiki/Jimmy_Swaggart
[591] Ibid.

Humour can be one path to transcend the quicksand of Sedna, giving us the objectivity to step back from the edge, and also with the quintile and bi-quintile aspects to Jupiter the optimism and drive to make it big.

Carol Burnett is an American comedienne on stage, in films and on TV. An outstanding performer, she has won many Emmys and other awards. She had Sedna in the first house of identity, bi-quintile Jupiter in the sixth house of service.

> Her father died when she was 21 and her mother 12 years later. She became the primary caretaker of her 12-year-old sister from the age of 22. Her sister later said, "She always seemed to have a great inner strength and discipline. Her grades were good because she applied herself. Fate may have stepped in here and there, but she was ready for opportunity."

> In college, she headed toward journalism and cartooning, that is, until she was bitten by the stage-bug. When she took a college role on stage and heard the first laugh, her path was set. She acted, she sang, she tried comedy, and for the first time in her life, had a measure of popularity. It was heady stuff after being a wallpaper nerd. With every bit of approval, her confidence grew. The doors opened when she was given a thousand-dollars to go to New York, on the stipulation that she would pay it back, keep the donor anonymous and help others who were starting out.

> She reached New York at 21, working as a hatcheck girl while organising a show. On opening night, she came onstage in a housedress and curlers to sing and skewer "Monotonous," a sexy Eartha Kitt number. She got three bows and a lot of bravos. The *Carol Burnett Show* made its debut when she was 34, bringing into her lexicon of characters her singing charwoman, dimwitted secretary Mrs. Wiggins and raging Eunice's dysfunctional family. Mostly she pillaged the movies she loved. None of the old movies was safe from her relentless hilarity and she got to be all the magical characters she had watched on the screen while growing up - with a little something extra.

> The show became the longest running on the air when it hit 11 years. It closed when she was 44, after reaping a total of 22 Emmy awards. Many of the people she's worked with have become part of her extended family, and they return her loyalty

and devotion. Some have remarked on how generous she was as a performer, giving away great punch lines, and others say she extends generosity in her look, her humour and everything she does.[592]

At this juncture in human evolution, few of us use our planets at the spiritual level, but many of us are striving to and such people are wonderful to be around. As with the other planets, the spiritual level of evolution is vastly different with Sedna from the two previous levels. Here, the inconjunct aspect with Jupiter the potential to tune into people at a deep level across all walks of life, to see both the potential and the blocks and the ability to use this insight to encourage the evolutionary benefits of optimism.

Once we embrace the Sedna energy, which is the oneness of everything, our nurturing becomes an expression of Sedna consciousness and it becomes devotional in nature. The struggle of the beginner's level is gone, as are the transcendental crises of the intermediate level. At this level everything Saturnian is meaningless and yet everything Sednian has its place.

English occultist, Aleister Crowley, has a close bi-quintile with Jupiter, which is in the fourth house of home.

> In addition to an occultist, Crowley was also a ceremonial magician, poet, painter, novelist, and mountaineer. He founded the religion of Thelema, identifying himself as the prophet entrusted with guiding humanity into the Æon of Horus in the early 20th century. A prolific writer, he published widely over the course of his life.

> When he was 45 he established the Abbey of Thelema, a religious commune in Cefalù, Sicily where he lived with various followers. His libertine lifestyle led to denunciations in the British press, and the Italian government evicted him three years later. He divided the following two decades between France, Germany, and England, and continued to promote Thelema until his death.

> Crowley gained widespread notoriety during his lifetime, being a recreational drug experimenter, bisexual and an individualist

---

[592] https://en.wikipedia.org/wiki/Carol_Burnett

social critic. He was denounced in the popular press as "the wickedest man in the world" and a Satanist. However, Crowley has remained a highly influential figure over Western esotericism and the counter-culture.[593]

Karl Marx was a German-Jewish communist and philosopher who developed the theory of socialism and was the father of modern social science. He had Sedna in the first house of identity, quintile Jupiter, which is conjunct Makemake, the planet of extreme talent, in the eleventh house of collective consciousness. He pushed the boundaries of human development with his ideas on society.

His Sedna is also quintile Mercury in the third house of communication and bi-quintile to Pholus, the centaur of catalysing change, in the eighth house of shared resources. This explains how his ideas and writing about social ideals involving a change in the distribution of social resources made him the powerful evolutionary change agent that he was.

> For him social change was about conflict between opposing interests, driven, in the background, by economic forces. This became the inspiration for the body of works known as the conflict theory. In his evolutionary model of history, he argued that human history began with free, productive and creative work that was over time coerced and dehumanised, a trend most apparent under capitalism. Fundamentally, he assumed that human history involves transforming human nature, which he saw, in a very Sednian way, as encompassing both human beings and material objects.

> He believed, like the philosopher Hegel, that humans recognise that they possess both actual and potential selves and that self-development begins with an experience of internal alienation, which Marx argued was because of 'the despotism of capital'. This leads to a realisation that the actual self, as a subjective agent, renders its potential self as an object to be apprehended by capitalism. Marx further argued that by moulding nature in desired ways, the subject takes the object as its own, and thus permits the individual to be actualised as fully human.

---

[593] https://en.wikipedia.org/wiki/Aleister_Crowley

In the new society that would emerge, he reasoned that the self-alienation would end, and humans would be free to act without being bound by the labour market. It would be a democratic society, enfranchising the entire population. In such a utopian world there would also be little if any need for a state, the goal of which was only to enforce the alienation.[594]

Nirmala Srivastava was an Indian spiritual teacher and writer, also known as Shri Mataji Nirmala Devi. She had Sedna conjunct Chiron, the centaur of wounding and healing, and Nessus, the centaur representing 'a guide to deep energies of regeneration' in the tenth house of profession, bi-quintile Jupiter in the fifth house of creativity.

She was the founder of Sahaja Yoga, a meditation technique and new religious movement. She claimed to have been born in a fully realised state and spent her life working for peace by developing and promoting a simple technique through which people can achieve their own self-realization. Shri Mataji never charged for her instruction in Sahaja Yoga, which is now practiced and taught for free in over 140 countries. She died at 88, in Genoa, Italy.[595]

---

[594] https://en.wikipedia.org/wiki/Karl_Marx
[595] https://en.wikipedia.org/wiki/Nirmala_Srivastava

35: Sedna / Saturn

Conjunction

With the conjunction of Sedna and Saturn, the all-encompassing spiritual energy of Sedna infuses our limitations, our sense of structure and meaning, our fears and responsibilities and also our sense of commitment.

Saturn brings structure and meaning to our world. Saturn knows the limits of time and matter and it reminds us of our boundaries. It brings definition to our lives. Saturn makes us aware of the need for self-control and of our limits.

With the conjunction, the bigger context of Sedna can allow us to push the bubble and expand our Saturnian boundaries, if other aspects concur, or it may present us with the challenge to define ourselves and maintain appropriate boundaries in the midst of this vastly bigger context.

At the unconscious level it is more likely to manifest as a boundary issue, like Barabara Plekker, a Dutch prostitute and homicide victim. Her Sedna was conjunct Saturn, in the seventh house of relationships. She was working out of a small, apartment-like room with a single window in the red-light district of Amsterdam, when she was strangled. It was a copycat crime, as four years prior, another prostitute had been killed in the same room, the same way.

Or as an addiction, like Richard Kameese, who was an American drug fatality at age 21. He had Sedna conjunct Saturn in the ninth house of knowledge.

> His addiction began at high school and he was living with his parents. His folks went to a wake, leaving him home alone, because he was using drugs. When they returned they saw his shoeless footprints in the snow and knew he was on another rampage. He went to the home of a couple who lived a couple hundred yards away and burst in, staggering and in a drug-crazed state saying, "They're going to get me." He grabbed a kitchen mop and began swinging at his imaginary enemies and at the couple, who then called the police, as Richard drew a

knife. It took four men to subdue him; however, while in a jail cell, he stopped breathing and died a few hours later.[596]

With this placement there can also be father issues, as exemplified in the extreme by American murderer, Sean Richard Sellers. He had Sedna conjunct Saturn in the eighth house of life and death.

> He robbed a convenience store and shot the clerk to death when he was 16. Then six months later he shot his father and step-mother to death. He claimed that he heard voices and was possessed by demons.
>
> He became a Christian while in prison. His friends started a website on his behalf, and he campaigned for clemency based on his religious conversion, age and involvement in Satanism. While on death row, he made numerous appearances in the mass media, appearing on *The Oprah Winfrey Show* and on a notorious segment of *Geraldo* about Satanism.
>
> His imminent execution brought condemnation from a wide variety of sources, including the European Union, Archbishop Desmond Tutu, the American Bar Association and Bianca Jagger. Nearly all raised issues about his age at the time of the crimes, and many argued that his religious work from prison outweighed the state's need to execute him. Nevertheless, he was executed by lethal injection at 29.[597]

And because Saturn relates to the body here can also be physical issues and illnesses. Like Francisco Marto, who was a Portuguese child noted for the Miracle of Fatima, during which the sun appeared to spin and fall from the sky, witnessed by 70,000 people. He had Sedna conjunct Saturn and also Orcus, the planet of delving down and speaking out, in the twelfth house of the unconscious.

> On a spring day when he was six he was tending sheep with his cousin and sister, who were nine and eight, when they first began to see visions of the Virgin Mary. Later that year a large crowd gathered near Fátima, Portugal, in response to their prophecy that the Virgin Mary, referred to as Our Lady of Fatima, would appear and perform miracles on that date.

---

[596] https://www.astro.com/astro-databank/Kameese,_Richard
[597] https://en.wikipedia.org/wiki/Sean_Sellers

Newspapers published testimony from reporters and other people who claimed to have witnessed extraordinary solar activity, such as the sun appearing to "dance" or zig-zag in the sky, careen towards the earth, or emit multi-coloured light and radiant colours. According to these reports, the event lasted approximately ten minutes.

During a second apparition the Virgin Mary had said to his cousin, "In a short time I will take Francisco and his sister up to heaven with me. You, on the other hand, will remain on earth for a great many years to spread the devotion to my Immaculate Heart." The two Marto children were both stricken by the Spanish flu and Francisco died at Fatima, age ten.[598]

As we tire of density and the grief it creates, and we start a spiritual journey to get out of the swamp, Sedna rewards us with transcendent crises, experiences which force us to let go and rise above them, resulting in a huge growth to a new level of consciousness. There is no choice with these crises, and the more we try and solve them, the more we will get hurt.

Paul Ryan is an American politician, a Republican congressman for Wisconsin and at time of writing the 54th Speaker of the United States House of Representatives. He has Sedna conjunct Saturn, the planet of structure, in the fifth house of creativity.

When he was 16, he found his 55-year-old father lying dead in bed of a heart attack. Following the death of his father, his grandmother moved in with the family. As she had Alzheimer's, Ryan helped care for her while his mother commuted to college.[599]

His Sedna is also semi-square Chariklo, the centaur of foresight, and sextile Ceres, the planet of nurturing, both in the third house of ideas and in a fateful inconjunct with Neptune, the planet of inspiration, which is exactly conjunct his ascendent, the cusp of the first house of identity.

He has a bachelor's degree in economics and political science and at University he often visited the office of libertarian professor Richard Hart to discuss the theories of these

---

[598] https://en.wikipedia.org/wiki/Francisco_and_Jacinta_Marto
[599] https://en.wikipedia.org/wiki/Paul_Ryan

economists and of Ayn Rand. He has credited Rand with having inspired him to get involved in public service. In a speech that same year at the Atlas Society, he said he grew up reading Rand, and that her books taught him about his value system and beliefs. He required staffers and interns in his congressional office to read Rand and gave copies of her novel, *Atlas Shrugged*, as gifts to his staff for Christmas. In his Atlas Society speech, he also described Social Security as a socialist-based system.

When he was 39, he said, "What's unique about what's happening today in government, in the world, in America, is that it's as if we're living in an Ayn Rand novel right now. I think Ayn Rand did the best job of anybody to build a moral case for capitalism, and that morality of capitalism is under assault."

However, at 42 after receiving criticism from Georgetown University faculty members on his budget plan, he rejected Rand's philosophy as an atheistic one, saying it "reduces human interactions down to mere contracts." He also called the reports of his adherence to Rand's views an "urban legend" and stated that he was deeply influenced by his Roman Catholic faith and by Thomas Aquinas.[600]

Rita Levi-Montalcini was an Italian neurologist. She had Sedna conjunct Saturn and also Orcus, the planet of delving down and speaking out, in the fourth house of home.

For years she worked with the researcher Stanley Cohen, searching for "causes of growth", during which time she discovered Nerve Growth Factor (NGF), which is responsible for the development and distribution of nerve cells. She won several prizes throughout the world for her significant research, including the Nobel Prize in Medicine when she was 77 for her discovery of NGF. The following year she was awarded the National Medal of Science, and at 92 she was appointed as Senator-for-Life for her outstanding contributions to science. She never married and died at 103 having worked well into her final years.[601]

---

[600] Ibid.
[601] https://en.wikipedia.org/wiki/Rita_Levi-Montalcini

Albert Einstein was a German-Swiss-American scientist, a physicist who developed the theory of relativity and the general theory, laying the groundwork for 20th century physics and providing the essential structure of the cosmos. He had Sedna conjunct Saturn, and Mercury, the planet of ideas and communication, all in the tenth house of profession.

His name is synonymous with genius and the scientific definitions of the modern age from the atomic bomb, to space travel, electronics and quantum physics. However, he was born with a misshapen head and abnormally large body. He learned to talk so late that his parents feared that he was mentally retarded, not until he was three, and was not fluent until he was nine. For a while, he was considered subnormal because of his slow development, and his teachers were continually saying that he would never amount to anything.

His youth seemed to be one of deliberate rebellion against the establishment of his times. At age 16 he quit school, joined his parents in Milan, Italy, where they had moved, and renounced his German citizenship. At 17, he entered the Zurich Polytechnic Institute after having failed on the first try and graduated with a mathematics teaching degree. The next year he took Swiss citizenship, and the year after that, a post at the Swiss patent office. It was while at the Swiss patent office, in a clerical position, that Einstein began the work that would make him a legend.

At 26 he published three seminal papers on theoretical physics in a single volume of a German scientific journal and two years later he came up with the immortal e=mc2, better known as the Special Theory of Relativity, encapsulating energy and matter as aspects of a single phenomenon. A year later, while still at the patent office, he began work on his major achievement, the general theory of relativity, which he officially proposed eight years later.

These theories were the greatest challenge to Newtonian mechanics that the modern world had ever known, but Einstein had a way of conceptualising and communicating them. He described relativity thus: 'Put your hand on a hot stove for a minute and it seems like an hour. Sit with a pretty girl for an hour and it seems like a minute.'

Experiencing the universe as a harmonious whole, he encouraged the use of intuition to solve problems, marvelled at the the mystery of God in nature, and applauded the ideals of great spiritual teachers such as Buddha and Jesus. Here's how he put it: 'I like to experience the universe as one harmonious whole. Every cell has life. Matter, too, has life; it is energy solidified. Our bodies are like prisons, and I look forward to be free, but I don't speculate on what will happen to me. I live here now, and my responsibility is in this world now. I deal with natural laws. This is my work here on earth.

'If we want to improve the world we cannot do it with scientific knowledge but with ideals. Confucius, Buddha, Jesus and Gandhi have done more for humanity than science has done. We must begin with the heart of man, with his conscience, and the values of conscience can only be manifested by selfless service to mankind. Religion and science go together. Science without religion is lame and religion without science is blind. They are interdependent and have a common goal, the search for truth.'

'Without religion there is no charity. The soul given to each of us is moved by the same living spirit that moves the universe. I am not a mystic. Trying to find out the laws of nature has nothing to do with mysticism, though in the face of creation I feel very humble. It is as if a spirit is manifest that is infinitely superior to man's spirit. Through my pursuit in science I have known cosmic religious feelings. But I don't care to be called a mystic.'[602]

Humour can be one path to transcend the quicksand of Sedna, giving us the objectivity to step back from the edge, and also with the conjunction to Saturn a natural business sense and a talent for physical comedy.

Milton Berle was an American comedian whose most successful medium was TV, which he practically dominated from 1948-1956, gaining the nickname, Mr. Television. His Sedna is the ninth house of

---

[602] https://en.wikipedia.org/wiki/Albert_Einstein

broadcasting, conjunct Saturn and also Orcus, the planet of delving down and speaking out.

At six he took part in "Charlie Chaplin contests," wearing his dad's suits and shoes, usually winning prizes. Charlie Chaplin was a main part of Berle's comedic upbringing, as he appeared in the first full-length movie comedy, *Tillie's Punctured Romance,* which starred Chaplin. At his standup opening at the Palace Theater in New York, he "took the theatre by storm," and in the following two years set attendance records.

But Berle came into his own in when he inaugurated the *Texaco Star Theatre*, which has been described as TV's number-one show and was the first real smash hit in the new medium. The show made network TV popular and sold more TV sets than any other ad campaign, with an estimated 80 percent of all TV sets in the US tuning in every Tuesday night. Enormously funny, with great energy and versatility, he laid out rapid gags and broad clowning, and was named "the television star of the year." His income was over $700,000 for the year.

"Berle's holding company, Milton Berle Enterprises Inc., now manages a machine tool company, a furniture company and real estate. Separate corporations control his songs, literature, theatre work, nightclub, TV, producing and radio acting interests. It also handles his extensive charity activities. He has toured Army hospitals and has been credited with presenting 10,000 benefits. He has raised more than a million dollars for cancer research and treatment and is Honorary Mayor of the National Children's Cardiac Home in Florida.[603]

At this juncture in human evolution, few of us use our planets at the spiritual level, but many of us are striving to and such people are wonderful to be around. As with the other planets, the spiritual level of evolution is vastly different with Sedna from the two previous levels. Here, the conjunction with Saturn brings a direct connection between the the physical and spiritual worlds that can set us on a mission to nurture the collective spiritual consciousness.

---

[603] https://en.wikipedia.org/wiki/Milton_Berle

Once we embrace the Sedna energy, which is the oneness of everything, our nurturing becomes an expression of Sedna consciousness and it becomes devotional in nature. The struggle of the beginner's level is gone, as are the transcendental crises of the intermediate level. At this level everything Saturnian is meaningless and yet everything Sednian has its place.

Rudi Schneider is an Austrian medium known with his older brother, Willy, for trance phenomena involving materialisation and telekinesis. He also has Sedna conjunct Saturn and Orcus, but this time in the second house of material reality.

> As a teenager, a German physician and psychic researcher heard of the home services held by the Schneider family, during which objects reportedly moved without physical cause and small hands and even phantoms were said to materialise.
>
> The researcher launched a series of experiments in the laboratory under rigid test conditions, first with Willy and then Rudi, who became the better known. During trance, objects moved and small materialisations occurred. Rudi was studied by researchers in France, England and Germany. There was much lively debate and skepticism. He was an auto mechanic by trade and opened a driving school; however, in his 40s, he gave up all psychic activities.[604]

Ralph Houston was an American guru. He also had Sedna conjunct Saturn and also Orcus, in the twelfth house of the unconscious.

> He was raised in Europe and met his spiritual teacher, Nicholas Roerich, a Russian painter, philanthropist and writer when he was 24 and was initiated as his student two days later. He became a metaphysical teacher and fourth initiate chelae and founded an Agni Yoga group in San Francisco when he was 46, another in Los Angeles the following year, and in upper New York State in his early 50s. He had a gift for lighting the fires of inspiration, though his advice was often questionable.[605]

Elizabeth Clare Prophet was an American spiritual leader and guru, leader of the Church Universal and Triumphant based on Gnostic

---

[604] https://en.wikipedia.org/wiki/Rudi_Schneider
[605] https://www.astro.com/astro-databank/Houston,_Ralph

Christianity, Buddhism, New Age mysticism and masonry. She had Sedna conjunct Saturn and also her Sun, her willpower, in the tenth house of profession.

With intense and, it seems, utterly sincere belief in her own righteousness, Prophet convinced her followers that she was able to foretell the end of time. And, although she prepared for the apocalypse at least six times, her church continued to draw followers. She had visions from the time she was a kid. By the age of nine she had visited every church and synagogue in her hometown, seeking spiritual enlightenment.

When she was a student at Boston University she met Mark Prophet, who claimed to be a reincarnation of Sir Lancelot. A former insurance and vacuum cleaner salesman, he had founded a church which he was operating out of a Washington, DC storefront. Both were married to other people, but with divine guidance, they shed their respective mates and wed. She was 24. They soon moved their burgeoning flock to Colorado Springs and produced four children.

Ten years later Mark died suddenly of a stroke and, becoming an ascended Master, she found herself the keeper of a sprawling spiritual empire worth by then about $50 million, funded by the tithing of members. They headed for California to settle on a 257-acre estate in the hills above Malibu. The church continued to grow despite major controversy, including the defection of a former husband. After divorcing her, he accused her of slavery and sued her and the church for $23 million. She settled out of court.

When she was 42 she married a much younger follower and he soon became business manager of the Church. She received a message from St. Germain that it was time to move on, and the cult moved their headquarters from Malibu, California, to a 12,000 acre ranch in Montana. The ranch was operated on strict guidelines seven days a week, with the day beginning at 5 am with two hours prayer and meditation and hard labor in between communal meal breaks. The diet was low protein and all stimulants were banned. Sex between married couples was allowed, but for no more than 30 minutes, twice a week.

Once probation has been passed, devotees signed away all their property irrevocably to the Church. Mrs. Prophet and her young husband had luxurious private quarters and she made her appearances dressed in spotless white satin with the occasional pink and gold sari, wearing diamonds and looking like a queen, being treated like a goddess. However, as head of the church, they each drew a modest salary of $1,900 a month plus expenses.[606]

Opposition

With the opposition of Sedna and Saturn, the all-encompassing spiritual energy of Sedna challenges our limitations, our sense of structure and meaning, our fears and responsibilities and also our sense of commitment.

Saturn is often associated with our fathers or authority figures. In childhood, the discipline, rules, and regulations imposed on us by our authority figures, from parents, teachers, and the like, were not always pleasant, but they actually helped us to understand the world around us. Similarly, Saturn's lessons help us to grow.

With the opposition our sense of structure stands in relief against the vast backdrop of Sedna and if we are unconscious of the Sedna energy, or there are other stressful aspects to Saturn, we are likely to call the more negative manifestations into our lives, such as limitations and constriction, rules and regulations, and authoritarian tendencies, or projections.

As we grow in consciousness and embrace the Sedna energy, the canvas is so vast that our sense of structure can embrace a much bigger playing field and bring a higher compassion to the responsibilities and commitment of Saturn.

At the unconscious level, however, this aspect can manifest as a kind of blind spot, which can leave us open to danger from areas which we don't expect. Like Holly Piirainen, who was a American homicide victim at the age of ten. She had Sedna in the first house of identity, opposite Saturn in the seventh house of relationships. Her Saturn is also conjunct Pluto, the planet of life and death.

---

[606] https://en.wikipedia.org/wiki/Elizabeth_Clare_Prophet

She was visiting her grandparents when she disappeared after she and her five-year-old brother walked up the road to see some new puppies at a neighbour's house. When the dogs began to bark, her brother ran home. Holly's mom sent the other two brothers to bring her home, but they could not find her. One of her sneakers was found near the dog pen. The country mobilised with an immediate search but there was no sign of the girl. Her body was found by hunters in the woods five months later, about five miles from where she had disappeared.[607]

Or it might put us in a helpless position, like Allison Darling, who was an American teenager killed in a car accident at 14. She had Sedna in the tenth house of social standing, opposite Saturn, which is conjunct Mars, the planet of action, both in the fourth house of home. Her sister was driving her to school when she lost control of the car on a wet road and hit a pick up truck, killing Allison.

Drug use can also play into this potential blind spot, as it did with Ethan Morgan, an American perpetrator of vehicular homicide. He had Sedna in the twelfth house of the unconscious, opposite Saturn in the sixth house of daily routine, with Saturn again conjunct Pluto, the planet of life and death. He stopped at a liquor store on his way to a party and one of his passengers bought a six pack of beer. On his way home, he sped through a stop sign and crashed into a camper van, killing the driver.

Or we might get completely swallowed by the blind spot, like Henri Jean Jacomet, a French homicide suspect who was in prison for seven years for a triple murder he didn't commit. He had Sedna in the third house of communication, opposite Saturn in the eleventh house of collective consciousness.

Or we could have a blind faith which leads nowhere, like Joachim Von Ribbentrop, the top German diplomatic agent for Hitler. He had Sedna in the first house of identity, opposite Saturn in the seventh house of relationships.

He was foreign minister for seven years from the age of 45, during which time he helped engineer the seizure of Austria, the partition of Czechoslovakia and the alliances with Italy and Japan. Everyone in the Nazi party, except Hitler, thought him

---

[607] https://www.astro.com/astro-databank/Piirainen,_Holly

stupid, a boor and an ass, making one faux pas after another. He was reportedly described as, "Such an imbecile, he is a freak of nature." Goering called him "Germany's No.1 parrot." The French Ambassador said, "I cannot speak to him, he listens only to himself." After the Allied victory he was tried in Nuremberg for war crimes, was convicted and hanged.[608]

As we tire of density and the grief it creates, and we start a spiritual journey to get out of the swamp, Sedna rewards us with transcendent crises, experiences which force us to let go and rise above them, resulting in a huge growth to a new level of consciousness. There is no choice with these crises, and the more we try and solve them, the more we will get hurt.

The founder of Facebook, Mark Zuckerberg, has Sedna in the eighth house of shared resources, opposite Saturn in the second house of material resources.

He launched Facebook from his Harvard University dormitory room when he was 20, assisted by his college roommates and fellow Harvard students. The group then introduced Facebook to other college campuses and it expanded rapidly, reaching one billion users by the time he was 28.

Meanwhile, he was involved in various legal disputes brought by others in the group, who claimed a share of the company based upon their involvement during the development phase of Facebook. Another suit was thrown out and the person who filed it arrested for fabricating evidence in a scheme to defraud the company.

When he was 28, Zuckerberg and his wife Priscilla Chan announced that over the course of their lives they would give the majority of their wealth to "advancing human potential and promoting equality" in the spirit of The Giving Pledge. Three years later they announced they would eventually give 99 percent of their Facebook shares to the Chan Zuckerberg Initiative.[609]

---

[608] https://en.wikipedia.org/wiki/Joachim_von_Ribbentrop
[609] https://en.wikipedia.org/wiki/Mark_Zuckerberg

With this placement our father is likely to play a significant role in shaping our lives. Like Louisa May Alcott, who was an American writer. She had Sedna in the seventh house of relationships, opposite Saturn in the first house of identity.

> She was the dutiful daughter of an idealistic, influential but mostly impoverished Transcendentalist philosopher, Bronson Alcott. She became an assertive and self-contained woman, an early and ardent feminist who set out to win fortune and fame and was utterly unsurprised when she did so. She was a nurse during the American Civil War and she became one of America's most famous and beloved writers of children's stories.

> Tired of "providing moral pap for the young," she wrote *A Modern Mephistopheles* when she was 45. Once secret, her novel is surprisingly erotic. This perception is reinforced by her letters, published as *The Selected Letters of Louisa May Alcott*. She was a self-described "literary spinster," and wrote, "I was born with a boy's nature and have always fought my fight . . . with a boy's spirit." Literature took the place of love, marriage and children. She published her first book at 22 and called it her "firstborn".

> She suffered from vertigo and other maladies for many years. About two years before her death she entered a homeopathic nursing home in Boston, complaining of insomnia and lack of appetite. Despite a permanent writer's cramp in her thumb, she was able to complete the final book in the March family saga at 54 and to write the last book of all, *A Garland for Girls*, when she was 56. She went to see her dying father in Boston and caught a chill. A day or so later she suffered a violent headache, and sinking rapidly, died the day of her father's funeral.[610]

We see the father's influence again with Marcel Marceau, a French pantomime artist, actor, author, and creator of the internationally acclaimed white-faced clown, Bip. He had Sedna conjunct Nessus, the centaur of radical change, and Chiron, the centaur of wounding and healing, all in the twelfth house of the unconscious, opposite Saturn in the sixth house of service.

---

[610] https://en.wikipedia.org/wiki/Louisa_May_Alcott

He was encouraged by his parents to pursue a career in theatre but was unable to complete his training due to the outbreak out of WW II. Tragedy struck when his father was seized by the Nazis and died in Auschwitz. Marceau, in his zeal to help his fellow Jews escape the horror of the Nazi regime, assisted his brother Alain, a leader in the Limoges underground, in falsifying identification documents so young men could avoid the German labor camps, citizens could get fake ration cards and Jewish children could be safely smuggled into Switzerland.

When police raids became imminent, he fled to Paris, where he was saved from further persecution by having a cousin place him in an orphanage. There he taught dramatics and entertained the children with mime. In his spare time, he began studying with under the tutelage of the master of mime, Etienne Decroux. "He was a kind of Christ.... In his class we dedicated our bodies to the discipline of silence." Setting up his own company in "The Pocket Theatre," at 24, he created the white-faced clown with the top hat (a la Chaplin) called Bip. His first performance as Bip occurred on his 24th birthday.

He founded the Compagnie de Mime Marcel Marceau that year and couple of years later took his company on tour to Israel and Holland. Two years later they toured to Berlin, but it was not until he was 29 that the performance could sell 1,200 seats. Two years after that his U.S. and Canada tour, which was originally scheduled for two weeks, was so successful it was extended for three months. "When I got back to Paris after being a hit on Broadway, everything changed for me. It was a new, almost frightening experience."

An international talent, by his late 30s he had given over 18,000 performances in over 100 countries, extending his acting ability onto the screen. He set up the 'Ecole de Mimodrame Marcel Marceau' in Paris when he was 55, having made 17 tours of the US by that time. He worked on the international stage into his 80s.

While fluent in five languages offstage, onstage he perfected his silent, subtle art. "The art of mime is an art of metamorphosis. You cannot say in mime what you can say better in words. You have to make a choice. It is the art of the essential. And you cannot lie. You have to show the truth. Why am I popular? Because I brought silence to the stage, because I made the invisible visible. I create abstract worlds and make them complete."[611]

As we see humour can be one path to transcend the quicksand of Sedna, giving us the objectivity to step back from the edge, and also with the opposition to Saturn the perseverance and practical understanding of how to achieve this. Those of us struggling with the opposition would be well advised to develop our sense of humour.

Roseanne Barr has Sedna in the second house of material resources, opposite Saturn in the eighth house of shared resources. She is an American actress, comedian, writer, and television producer. She was also the 2012 presidential nominee of the California-based Peace and Freedom Party.

She began her career in stand-up comedy at clubs before gaining fame for her role in the hit television sitcom, *Roseanne.* The show ran for nine seasons and she won both an Emmy and a Golden Globe Award for Best Actress for her work. She had crafted a "fierce working-class domestic goddess" persona in the eight years preceding her sitcom and wanted to do a realistic show about a strong mother who was not a victim of patriarchal consumerism.

The granddaughter of immigrants from Europe and Russia, she was the oldest of four children in a working-class Jewish Salt Lake City family. She was active in The Church of Jesus Christ of Latter-day Saints, yet courted controversy by stunts like singing the national anthem off-key at a nationally aired baseball game, followed by grabbing her crotch and spitting.

After her sitcom ended, she launched her own talk show, *The Roseanne Show*, and returned to stand-up comedy with a world tour. Then she announced she was running for the presidential nomination of the Green Party, which she lost, before getting the nomination of the Peace and Freedom Party. She received

---

[611] https://en.wikipedia.org/wiki/Marcel_Marceau

61,971 votes in the general election which brought Trump to power, placing sixth overall.[612]

David Shiner is an American actor and clown. He has Sedna in tenth house of profession,

opposite Saturn in the fourth house of home. He built an early reputation working regularly in the streets at the Avignon Festival in France, drawing huge crowds to watch his antics on the castle walls of the old city and making a fortune in the hat.

> He performed in the 2000 Broadway musical 'Seussical' and has movie appearances as a clown and as an actor, including *Lorenzo's Oil*, which was released when he was 39. He has also toured solo shows in Europe and America and mentored and guest directed for a German youth circus program. At 37 he was featured in Cirque du Soleil's production Nouvelle Expérience, touring for 19 months through Canada and the USA and playing for another year in Las Vegas. With his antics, including stepping through, on and over much of the crowd and the staging of a mock silent-movie melodrama with four members of the audience, he may be the best remembered of the Cirque's clowns.[613]

At this juncture in human evolution, few of us use our planets at the spiritual level, but many of us are striving to, and such people are wonderful to be around. As with the other planets, the spiritual level of evolution is vastly different with Sedna from the two previous levels. Here the opposition brings a higher compassion to the responsibilities and commitment of Saturn.

Once we embrace the Sedna energy, which is the oneness of everything, our nurturing becomes an expression of Sedna consciousness and it becomes devotional in nature. The struggle of the beginner's level is gone, as are the transcendental crises of the intermediate level. At this level everything Saturnian is meaningless and yet everything Sednian has its place.

Sam Francis is an American Abstract Expressionist Painter and Muralist, with a career spanning half a century that brought him international

---

[612] https://en.wikipedia.org/wiki/Roseanne_Barr
[613] https://en.wikipedia.org/wiki/David_Shiner_(clown)

acclaim. He has Sedna conjunct Nessus, the centaur of making huge changes, in the tenth house of profession, opposite Saturn in the fourth house of home.

> Called California's answer to Matisse, Francis' eclectic and prodigious output placed him front and centre in the second generation of Abstract Expressionists. He was raised by avant-garde parents who encouraged his artistic talent. He began his career at 20 while hospitalised for spinal tuberculosis, which he contracted as a result of a plane crash. He never fully recovered and the illness left him with a delicate bill of health and in a state of almost constant pain.

> After earning a master's degree in art from Berkeley at 26, he moved to Paris the following year and had his first solo show a year later, maintain strong ties to Europe for the rest of his life. Moving to California at 38, he survived a second bout of TB and subsequently established himself as an artistic guru in the Santa Monica community. His creative drive was fuelled by Far Eastern philosophy, most notably Buddhism, combined with Jungian archetypes and his own homespun superstition.[614]

Willy Blaas is a German psychologist, a family and reincarnation therapist, and a professional astrologer. He has Sedna conjunct Venus, the planet of values, and Juno, the asteroid of partnership, in the twelfth house of the unconscious, opposite Saturn, which is together with Neptune, the planet of sensitivity to the beyond, in the sixth house of service. With a background in psychological astrology, specialising in the influence of the family history, he conducted scientific research on the Gauquelin findings, which is considered the most significant body of statistical research into astrology to date. He was 30 years old.

> The preliminary profession findings involved two studies: the one comprised of a group of 576 birth charts revealing a correlation of Mars and Saturn with physicians, at a chance level in the millions to one. The second study involving 508 births revealing the same results for other professions, correlating them with their traditionally related planets: Mars with athletes, Saturn with scientists, the Moon with writers, and Jupiter with actors and

[614] https://en.wikipedia.org/wiki/Sam_Francis

politicians. The significance level for some of these correlations was also in the millions to one chance level.[615]

Nirmala Srivastava was an Indian spiritual teacher and writer, also known as Shri Mataji Nirmala Devi. She was the founder of Sahaja Yoga, a meditation technique and new religious movement. She had Sedna conjunct Chiron, the centaur of wounding and healing, and Nessus, the centaur representing 'a guide to deep energies of regeneration', in the tenth house of profession, opposite Saturn in the fourth house of home.

> She claimed to have been born in a fully realised state and spent her life working for peace by developing and promoting a simple technique through which people can achieve their own self-realisation. Shri Mataji never charged for her instruction in Sahaja Yoga, which is now practiced and taught for free in over 140 countries. She died at 88, in Genoa, Italy.[616]

Semi-sextile, Sextile, Trine

With the flowing aspects between Sedna and Saturn, the all-encompassing spiritual energy of Sedna aligns with our limitations, our sense of structure and meaning, with our fears and responsibilities and also our sense of commitment.

Saturn brings structure and meaning to our world. Saturn knows the limits of time and matter and it reminds us of our boundaries. It brings definition to our lives. Saturn makes us aware of our limits and the lessons that it brings help us to grow.

With the flowing aspects we understand the alignment of Saturn's lessons with the bigger context that we sense around us; however, at the unconscious level we might well play beyond the boundaries without realizing the risk we are potentially facing in the process.

Like Juliana McCourt, who was an American fatality at the age of 4 on board an aircraft that struck the World Trade Centre in New York, killing all on board instantly. She had Sedna conjunct the Sun in the seventh house of relationships, semi-sextile Saturn in the fifth house of children. She was on her way to Disneyland with her mother and then onto a

---

[615] http://astrologynewsservice.com/articles/the-gauquelin-controversy/
[616] https://en.wikipedia.org/wiki/Nirmala_Srivastava

spiritual conference at the Deepak Chopra Centre for WellBeing when the plane was hijacked by terrorists and crashed into the building.

Or like Pebbles Santiago, an American, Hispanic-Puerto Rican missing child, who disappeared when she was 12. She had Sedna in the ninth house of knowledge, trine Saturn in the first house of identity.

> She was last seen by her mother that morning. She was leaving for school at the time. She called her mother at work at midday and said that she had missed the school bus and would remain at home for the day. Her mother returned to their residence during the evening and realized that she had disappeared. She has never been heard from again. Her mother waited until over eight hours, before reporting her as a missing child. She believed that the police department would not accept a report unless she had been missing for an extended period of time. As a result, the investigation was stalled and many possible leads had vanished by the time law enforcement became involved.
>
> An adult male acquaintance admitted that he had taken her to the State University campus five days before her presumed abduction. The man stated to police that he did not have permission from her mother to drive her to the school. He said that he had seen her in a parking lot and felt sorry for her. He purchased snacks for her at the school cafeteria and allegedly admitted that he secretly masturbated while she waited in line. He was questioned less than 48 hours after her disappearance and signed a statement but was never charged due to a lack of evidence. Foul play is possible in the case and it remains unsolved.[617]

Or like Julian Assange, who is an Australian whistleblower, with a background is in physics, math and computer programming, currently living in political asylum in the embassy of Ecuador in London. He has Sedna in the sixth house of service, semi-sextile Saturn on the cusp of the seventh house of relationships.

> He is best known for his work with WikiLeaks, which is supposedly an investigative journalism Internet-based organization, with a mission to make public otherwise secret

---

[617] http://missingchildren.wikia.com/wiki/Monique_Santiago

information, but which is designated by the US government as a hostile non-state intelligence service.

He is spokesperson and editor-in-chief of the organization. His name became nearly a household word when at 39 he leaked over 250,000 classified diplomatic cables of the US government and therefore caused an uproar in government circles. Prior to that he had published many classified documents and a video from the Iraq and Afghanistan Wars.

That same year the Swedish government posted a warrant for his arrest on rape and molestation charges. The warrant cited one count of unlawful coercion, two counts of sexual molestation and one count of rape. He denied the charges, but refused to face the courts, fighting his extradition. Two years later he walked into the embassy of Ecuador in London to ask for political asylum and five years on he is still living there in virtual house arrest, unable to leave without being arrested.[618]

With this placement our father is likely to play a significant role in shaping our lives. Like Petra Kelly, who was a Bavarian political human rights activist, ecologist and co-founder of the Green Party. She had Sedna conjunct Ceres in the eleventh house of collective consciousness, trine her Saturn in the third house of ideas and communication.

She was abandoned by her dad at the age of six and was educated by Catholic nuns and raised largely by her grandmother, while her mom worked to support the family. When she was 11, her mom married an American Army officer who moved the family to the U.S. Petra became a classic overachiever, cheerleader, member of the student senate, and scholarship winner. Despite physical pain from lifelong kidney ailments and the emotional trauma associated with the death of her younger half-sister Grace, she was able to maintain an almost maniacal focus on achievement.

She returned to Europe for post grad study and her beginning involvement in European Federalist politics. She studied World Politics and International Relations and worked at the European

---

[618] https://en.wikipedia.org/wiki/Julian_Assange

Communities in Brussels, continuing her development of social consciousness and political awareness. When she was 32 she helped found a political party that was dedicated to human rights and ecology which was officially named the Green Party six years later; she was one of 27 Greens elected to the Bundestag.

She began an affair with the 65-year-old married EC president Sicco Mansholt, the first of a number of affairs with politically powerful older men. She had a long-term companionship with 25-year older Gert Bastian, a former NATO General who had done under-cover spy work. As brilliant, romantic and mercurial as Petra was, Bastian in contrast was plodding methodical and obsessive. To all evidence, their love was compelling and uncompromising. However, when she was 45, they were both found dead in their Bonn home with a gunshot to the head. Whether their deaths were suicide, or murder was unresolved and the case remains a mystery.[619]

As we tire of density and the grief it creates, and we start a spiritual journey to get out of the swamp, Sedna rewards us with transcendent crises, experiences which force us to let go and rise above them, resulting in a huge growth to a new level of consciousness. There is no choice with these crises, and the more we try and solve them, the more we will get hurt.

Paul Keating is an Australian politician and was Prime Minister representing the Labour Party. He has Sedna conjunct Varuna in the first house of identity, sextile Saturn in the third house of ideas and communication.

Born into a working class Catholic family, he left school at 14 to work as a clerk, while managing the rock group, the Ramrods, on the side. He entered local politics at age 24. He was appointed Treasurer by newly elected Prime Minister Hawke at 39. Although lacking any formal education in economics, he went on to become one of the most reforming Treasurers in Australian history; floating the Australian dollar, deregulating the financial sector, privatising state sector industries, introducing a capital gains tax, and a Prices and Incomes Accord.

---

[619] https://en.wikipedia.org/wiki/Petra_Kelly

Seven years after becoming treasurer he became Deputy Prime Minister. He later challenged Hawke for the leadership and resigned from the ministry following his defeat. Six months later he challenged again, this time successfully, and subsequently became Prime Minister. He would go on to deliver the Labor government a record fifth consecutive victory and a record 13 years in government at the next election, defeating the opposition despite consistently poor government opinion polls.[620]

His Sedna is also opposite his Moon, the planet of emotions, in the seventh house of relationships

semisquare the conjunction of Mars, the planet of action, and Uranus, the planet of revolution, in the second house of material resources.

His government introduced native title to Aborigines, greatly increased the social wage and the family benefits system, saw increased bilateral relations between Australia and countries in Asia, and vehemently promoted a vision of Australia as a republic.[621]

Heinrich Boll was a German author who was awarded the Nobel Prize for Literature. He has Sedna in the third house of communications, trine Saturn in the ninth house of publishing.

He was a leader of the German writers who tried to come to grips with the memory of World War II, the Nazis, and the Holocaust and the guilt that came with them. Because of his refusal to avoid writing about the complexities and problems of the past, he was the leading critic of West German society.

His disillusionment with postwar Germany was also apparent through his strong sense of ethical responsibility of authorship and critical attitude toward social institutions. His writing style was plain and accessible, and his books were translated into many languages. He was particularly successful in Eastern Europe, as he seemed to portray the dark side of capitalism in his books, which were sold by the millions in the Soviet Union alone.

---

[620] https://en.wikipedia.org/wiki/Paul_Keating
[621] Ibid.

Despite the variety of themes and content in his work, there are certain recurring patterns: many of his novels and stories describe intimate and personal life struggling to sustain itself against the wider background of war, terrorism, political divisions, and profound economic and social transition.

In a number of his books there are protagonists who are stubborn and eccentric individualists opposed to the mechanisms of the state or of public institutions. His villains are the figures of authority in government, business, the mainstream media, and in the Church, whom he castigates, sometimes humorously, sometimes acidly, for what he perceived as their conformism, lack of courage, self-satisfied attitude and abuse of power.[622]

And our case study, futurist, Ray Kurzweil, has Sedna in the 6th house, trine Saturn, which is conjunct Haumea, the planet of rebirth, and Pluto, the planet of transformation, and the MC, the cusp of the tenth house of occupation. This is a powerful picture of Ray's evolutionary influence.

He is an author and computer scientist who for over three decades has been one of the most respected and provocative advocates of the role of technology in our future. In his classic book, *The Age of Spiritual Machines*, he presented the daring argument that with the ever-accelerating rate of technological change, computers would rival the full range of human intelligence at its best.

Then, in *The Singularity Is Near*, he examined the next step in this inexorable evolutionary process: the union of human and machine, in which the knowledge and skills embedded in our brains will be combined with the vastly greater capacity, speed, and knowledge-sharing ability of our own creations.

He has written books on health, artificial intelligence, trans-humanism, the technological singularity, and futurism. He is a public advocate for the futurist and trans-humanist movements and gives public talks to share his optimistic outlook on life

---

[622] https://en.wikipedia.org/wiki/Heinrich_Böll

extension technologies and the future of nanotechnology, robotics, and biotechnology.[623]

Humour can be one path to transcend the quicksand of Sedna, giving us the objectivity to step back from the edge, and also with the flowing aspects to Saturn a tenacity of purpose and a talent for physical comedy.

Joan Rivers was an American comedienne, thought by many to be the funniest lady on the planet. She had Sedna in the first house of identity, sextile Saturn in the eleventh house of collective consciousness.

> She had one of the fastest, most agile minds in show biz. Her rapid-fire mix of gossip, insults, flaunting of taboos and ridicule of flaws and neurosis is written 90% by her. She also wrote comedy for *Candid Camera,* scripts and material for Phyllis Diller and Zsa Zsa Gabor and humorous books.

> The younger of two daughters of Russian-Jewish refugees, she learned from her doctor dad to crack a joke and was making people laugh by the time she was 11. She learned from her mom that rich was better than poor and was raised with privilege and a good education. She married at 24 and had it annulled the following year when she decided she wanted to be an actress, not a housewife. While doing off-Broadway, she worked in offices and turned to comedy at 27 to supplement her income.

> At the age of 32 she was told that she was too old and passed over; however, a week later she was booked on Johnny Carson's *Tonight Show.* They clicked. Their immediate rapport was a hit with the audience and she appeared for years with Carson before hosting her own *Late Show Starring Joan Rivers*, with a contract for $10 million over three years. She moved into the stratosphere as America's top comedienne, the darling of the circuit with tours, magazine covers, nightclub and Las Vegas gigs, TV projects, books and records.[624]

At this juncture in human evolution, few of us use our planets at the spiritual level, but many of us are striving to, and such people are wonderful to be around. As with the other planets, the spiritual level of

[623] https://en.wikipedia.org/wiki/Ray_Kurzweil
[624] https://en.wikipedia.org/wiki/Joan_Rivers

evolution is vastly different with Sedna from the two previous levels. Here, the flowing aspects with Saturn brings the ability to transcend the physical challenges we face and sets us on a mission to nurture the collective spiritual consciousness.

Once we embrace the Sedna energy, which is the oneness of everything, our nurturing becomes an expression of Sedna consciousness and it becomes devotional in nature. The struggle of the beginner's level is gone, as are the transcendental crises of the intermediate level. At this level everything Saturnian is meaningless and yet everything Sednian has its place.

Immanuel Kant was a German writer, teacher and philosopher. He had Sedna in the twelfth house of the unconscious, sextile Saturn in the ninth house of Spirituality and knowledge.

> He was the foremost thinker of the Enlightenment and is considered one of the greatest philosophers of all time. He was a short man, scarcely five feet tall, and he had a deformed chest. He suffered from poor health throughout his life, and because of this, he maintained a strict regimen of walking.

> His systematic and comprehensive work on ethics and aesthetics inaugurated a new era in the development of philosophical thought and thus greatly influenced all subsequent philosophy, particularly in the various schools of Idealism. His works included *The Critique of Pure Reason*, and *The Critique of Practical Reason*.

> He taught at Königsberg University for 14 years, and his reputation brought large numbers of students to the university. He lectured on many subjects including logic, metaphysics and moral philosophy. His style was humorous and vivid, and he used many examples from his reading to enliven his subjects.

> He was made a professor of logic and metaphysics, a position he held until he retired from the university. Though often charged with attacking metaphysics, he believed in the existence of God and in a future life, and he is often described as an ethical Rationalist. However, his unorthodox religious teachings eventually brought him into conflict with the King of Prussia, who

finally forbade him to teach or write on religious subjects, an order he obeyed until the King died five years later.[625]

Walden Welch was a California Astrologer and Psychic. He had Sedna in the eighth house of sensitivity to the spirit world, sextile Saturn in the tenth house of profession.

> His career began at the age of 17 when he moved to San Francisco and started doing psychic readings. At 18 he began using astrological charts for more accuracy in the timing of his predictions. He moved to San Francisco the following year and studied under spiritual teachers and started following the writings of the 'sleeping prophet', Edgar Cayce. He credited the teachings of Cayce as his greatest influence.
>
> When he was 24 he moved to Sonoma, where he and his homosexual partner opened an antique shop. While his partner operated the successful antique business, Walden did readings for many years from his spacious office in the back of the building. They married when he was 64, after 45 years of relationship, as soon as California law allowed it. His career also included lecturing and appearing on radio and television shows and for five years he hosted his own television shows, *Walden Welch, Astrologer*, and *Star Talk*.[626]

Alan Oken is an American astrologer and a student of the works and teachings of the Tibetan Master Djwahl Khul. He has Sedna conjunct Mercury and also Varuna, the planet of notability, in the fifth house of creativity, sextile Saturn in the seventh house of relationships.

> He is a translator, teacher, global traveler and international tour guide, who lectures in five languages and does natal horoscope readings in seven. He is the author of a dozen titles, including *Soul-Centered Astrology*, *Rulers of the Horoscope*, and *Alan Oken's Complete Astrology*. In addition, he has written hundreds of articles for Dell Horoscope Magazine and many other national and international reviews and journals. Alan was the Director of The Wisdom School in Santa Fe, is co-founder of the Australian

---

[625] https://en.wikipedia.org/wiki/Immanuel_Kant
[626] https://www.astro.com/astro-databank/Welch,_Walden

Institute for the Development of Consciousness and was Director of Esoteric Studies in Lisbon.[627]

Semi-square, Square, Sesquiquadrate,

With the stressful aspects between Sedna and Saturn the all-encompassing spiritual energy of Sedna challenges our limitations, our sense of structure and meaning, our fears and also our responsibilities and commitment.

Saturn is often associated with our father, or with authority figures. In childhood, we may not have found that the discipline, rules, and regulations imposed on us by authority figures, from parents, teachers and the like, were always pleasant, but they actually helped us to understand the world around us. Similarly, Saturn's lessons help us to grow.

If we are unconscious of the Sedna energy, however, or if there are other stressful aspects to Saturn, we are likely to call the more negative manifestations of the planet into our lives, including limitations and constriction, excess rules and regulations, and authoritarian tendencies, or projections.

So, this placement, in the extreme, can indicate the danger of abuse, as we see with Sharon Tate, an American actress, sex symbol and model, who was murdered by members of Charles Manson's 'family'. She had Sedna conjunct Varuna, the planet of notability, in the tenth house of profession, semi-square Saturn in the eleventh house of collective consciousness.

> In her early twenties she played small television roles, before appearing in several motion pictures. She also appeared regularly in fashion magazines as a model and cover girl. After receiving positive reviews for her comedic and dramatic performances, she was hailed as one of Hollywood's most promising newcomers, making her film debut at 23.

> A year later she co-stared in *The Fearless Vampire Killers* with Roman Polanski, who also directed the film. The following year she and Polanski got married in London and at the time of her death, she was eight-and-a-half months pregnant with their son and was two weeks from giving birth.

---

[627] https://www.alanoken.com/about/

> That day she entertained two friends, for lunch at her home, confiding in them her disappointment at her husband's delay in returning from London. In the evening she dined at her favourite restaurant with three other friends, returning with them to her home. However shortly after midnight, they were all murdered by members of Manson's "family" and their bodies were discovered the following morning by her housekeeper.[628]

It can also indicate an abusing attitude and it's interesting to see here a repeat of stressful aspects between these planets in both one of the victims and one of the perpetrators of the Manson killings.

Leslie Van Houten is an American convicted murderer and former member of the Manson Family. She has Sedna in the eighth house of life and death, sesquiquadrate Saturn, which is conjunct Pallas, the asteroid of wisdom, in the first house of identity.

> She wasn't selected by Manson for the Tate killings, but she asked to participate a couple of days later when he selected followers for the killings of another couple. She was 20 years old. She was arrested and charged, then convicted and sentenced to death. Despite this ruling, a California Supreme Court subsequently ruled that the death penalty was unconstitutional, resulting in her sentence being commuted to life in prison.

> This conviction was then overturned when she was 27 on a technicality and she was granted a retrial. Her second trial ended with a deadlocked jury and a mistrial. However, at her third trial when she was 29, she was convicted on two counts of murder and one count of conspiracy and sentenced to between 7 years and life in prison.

> In relation to her case, high courts, parole boards, and the state governor have said that an inexplicable, or racial motive for murder could merit exemplary punishment and outweigh any evidence of subsequent reform, so she has been denied parole 19 times and is still in jail 48 years later, at time of writing.[629]

At the unconscious level these aspects can also manifest as a lack of resources and problems with the legal system. Like Laren Sims, an

---

[628] https://en.wikipedia.org/wiki/Sharon_Tate
[629] https://en.wikipedia.org/wiki/Leslie_Van_Houten

American murderer, who killed her husband, a 53-year-old California lawyer.

> He was last seen being pushed in a wheel chair by her, at a Los Angeles horse show. Authorities claimed that the following day, she began clearing out his office and sold his $110,000 horse trailer and truck. She shut down the law practice in January 2002 and disappeared with $500,000 of his assets. She was 36.

> Assisted by a 21-year-old secretary in her husband's office, she administered horse tranquillisers to her husband in a Los Angeles hotel and the two women drove him to Yosemite National Park to bury him. However, they discovered that he was still alive so they took him back home, where he died shortly after. She said that she kept his body in a refrigerator for several months before burying it in a vineyard, where farm workers found the body.

> After her arrest, she was held in the Hernando County jail in Florida, awaiting extradition to California. The cool-looking, attractive brunette hanged herself with a braided bed sheet. She was found to have a 113-page criminal record and was wanted in Florida and Washington for credit card and grand theft charges.[630]

It can also manifest as health issues. Like Katherine Mansfield, who was a prominent modern short story writer who was born and brought up in colonial New Zealand. She had Sedna conjunct Vesta, the asteroid of regeneration, in the fifth house of creativity, sesquiquadrate Saturn in the ninth house of publishing.

> She was the daughter of a successful businessman, schooled in New Zealand and sent to London at the age of 15 to attend Queen's College. When she was 22, she married to give her unborn child a name and left her husband almost immediately, but unfortunately the child was stillborn. Two years later she met an editor, and they married when she was 30.

> She was first published at 23 with her novel, *In A German Pension,* but didn't receive much notice. However, in the next five years she became an important contributor to European

---

[630] https://en.wikipedia.org/wiki/Murder_of_Larry_McNabney

magazines. Grief stricken by the loss over her brother's death during WW I, she also learned at that time that she had incurable tuberculosis. She died at 35 in France. Her most noted book, *The Garden Party* was released just before she died and two of her books were published after her death.[631]

As we tire of density and the grief it creates, and we start a spiritual journey to get out of the swamp, Sedna rewards us with transcendent crises, experiences which force us to let go and rise above them, resulting in a huge growth to a new level of consciousness. There is no choice with these crises, and the more we try and solve them, the more we will get hurt.

Susan Boyle is a Scottish singer who rose to fame on a British talent show. She has Sedna conjunct Venus in the eleventh house of collective consciousness, square her Saturn in the ninth house of knowledge.

> She is the youngest of nine children and reportedly suffered some oxygen deprivation at birth, resulting in learning disabilities. Never married, she lived with her parents, working in low-level jobs and volunteering in the church. Her father died when she was 36 and her mother died when she was 46, after which she became distraught.
>
> Her music gave her great comfort and she auditioned for "Britain's Got Talent" in the hopes of launching a music career in her mother's memory. When she appeared on stage at 48 her appearance belied her talent, but she wowed the audiences with her rendition of "I Dreamed a Dream" from the musical "Les Miserables." The clip of her performance is one of the most-viewed on YouTube.
>
> News reports made much of this plain-looking middle-aged woman. For subsequent performances on the show she underwent a slight makeover. She made it all the way to the finals based on judges' and viewers' votes. However, the ensuing publicity was a lot for her to handle. Although she sang well on the last evening of the competition and came in second, she was rushed to a London health care facility that night,

---

[631] https://en.wikipedia.org/wiki/Katherine_Mansfield

reportedly suffering from an anxiety attack. She was released within the week.

Her album was released later that year and it quickly shot to the top of the charts. The success was continued with her second album the following year, and her third album the year after that. The following year her net worth was estimated at £22 million.[632]

The most powerful media tycoon in the world, Rupert Murdoch also has a square to Saturn, which is in his first house of identity. His Sedna is just in the fifth house of creativity, conjunct the north node, the point of dharma and Uranus, the planet of revolution, which are both just across the cusp in the fourth house of home. Despite his success he has faced many legal disputes.

At 55, keen to adopt newer electronic publishing technologies, Murdoch consolidated his UK printing operations in Wapping, causing bitter industrial disputes. And at 80 he faced allegations that his companies had been regularly hacking the phones of celebrities, royalty, and public citizens. He faced police and government investigations into bribery and corruption by the British government and FBI investigations in the U.S.

Our case study, James lovelock, the father of Gaia Theory, has Sedna sesquiquadrate to Saturn, which is conjunct Mercury, the planet of communication, and Quaoar, the planet of new perspectives, in the tenth house of profession. Quaoar is the Californian Indian creation god, which has to do with new perspectives and new realities, so together with the planet of the existing reality structure, Saturn, and that of ideas and communication, Mercury, we can see the evolutionary focus on communicating a new perspective on the nature of the eco-system.

James is a British independent scientist, environmentalist and futurologist who lives in Devon, England. A lifelong inventor, he has created and developed many scientific instruments, some of which were designed for NASA in its program of planetary exploration. It was while working as a consultant for NASA, when he was in his forties, that he developed the Gaia Hypothesis for which he is best known. Gaia hypothesis postulates that the biosphere of the Earth is a self-regulating entity with the capacity

---

[632] https://en.wikipedia.org/wiki/Susan_Boyle

to keep our planet healthy by controlling the chemical and physical environment.

However, in his book, the *The Revenge of Gaia,* published when he was 87, he argues that the lack of respect humans have had for Gaia, through the damage done to rainforests and the reduction in planetary biodiversity, is testing Gaia's capacity to minimise the effects of the addition of greenhouse gases in the atmosphere. This eliminates the planet's negative feedbacks and increases the likelihood of runaway global warming.

Three years later he published *The Vanishing Face of Gaia,* rejecting scientific modelling that disagreed with the scientific findings that sea levels are rising faster, and Arctic ice is melting faster than the models predict. And suggesting that we may already be beyond the tipping point of terrestrial climate resilience into a permanently hot state. Given these conditions, he expects human civilisation will be hard pressed to survive in the coming years.

At that point he expected the change to be similar to the Paleocene-Eocene period when atmospheric concentration of CO_2 was high and at that point the Arctic Ocean was 23 °C and had crocodiles in it, with the rest of the world mostly scrub and desert. Seven years later however, at 97 his position on climate change had changed dramatically, saying, 'Anyone who tries to predict more than five to 10 years is a bit of an idiot, because so many things can change unexpectedly.' He now believes that "CO_2 is going up, but nowhere near as fast as they thought it would."

There are various possible explanations for his change of heart. One is that he is right, and the models on which his former predictions were based were fatally flawed. Another is that his iconoclastic sensibility made revision irresistible. An incorrigible subversive, Lovelock was warning the world about climate change for decades before it began to pay attention, and just when the scientific consensus began to call for intervention to prevent it, he decided we were already too late.

But there is a third explanation for why he has shifted his position again, he expects that before the consequences of global warming can impact on us significantly, something else will have made our world unrecognisable and threaten the human race, the rise of Artificial Intelligence. 'Before we've reach the end of this century, I think what people call robots will have taken over. They will be in charge of us, if we're still here.

'It is possible that human beings may fuse with robots to become a blend of robotic and human tissue, but the likelier scenario will be pure robots, because that will probably be their preference. The implications for climate change are obvious. The world that they're going to be comfortable in is wildly different from the one that we feel comfortable in. So once they really get established, they will, with regret, start losing organic life.'[633]

Authoritarianism, a la Donald Trump, the oldest US president, can also be a feature of these aspects, yet interestingly while both Trump and Obama, the first African American president, have squares to Saturn, Barack doesn't display the authoritarian tendencies of Donald, showing how much each has worked with their Sedna energies.

Barack Obama has Sedna in the second house of material resources, square Saturn, which is conjunct Jupiter, the planet of expansion, in the twelfth house of government institutions.

A self-described "skinny kid with a funny name," he is the child of a Kenyan man and an American woman. When he was two, his father returned to Africa, and he lived in Hawaii with his mom and grandparents. After his mother married an Indonesian, she took him with her when she moved to her new husband's native country. However, he was sent back to Hawaii at age 10 to live with his grandparents.

He graduated at 22 from Columbia University with a degree in political science and international relations. He worked in Chicago's inner city, helping church groups improve job-training, education and city services to the poor and then went on to law school at Harvard. At 35 he was elected to the Illinois General Assembly as a state senator. At 43 he burst onto the national scene when he delivered a rousing keynote address at the

[633] Aitkenhead, Decca. *Guardian.*
https://www.theguardian.com/environment/2016/sep/30/james-lovelock-interview-by-end-of-century-robots-will-have-taken-over) September 30 2016

Democratic National Convention in Boston. That year he won election to the U.S. Senate by a wide margin.

He announced his candidacy for the Democratic Party's nomination for President at 46. On the campaign trail he racked up an impressive number of primary and caucus wins. Exhibiting composure, thoughtfulness, a quick mind and self-deprecating humour, his debate performance earns kudos, while his powerful oratory. Along with his life story, which he touted as a representation of the American dream, his emphasis on unity, hope and civility captured media and public attention.

His presidency was culturally evolutionary for America, but the square brought with it strong opposition who tried to impose constriction on his power by denying to make resources available or pass legislation.

His religious background is more diverse than that of most prominent politicians. But it may prove to be more representative of an increasingly diverse America. His mother was raised by non-practicing Christians; his father was raised a Muslim but was an atheist by the time he had married Obama's mother. His step-father was also Muslim, but of an eclectic kind who could make room for animist and Hindu beliefs.

In his book, *The Audacity of Hope*, published when he was 45, he writes: 'I was not raised in a religious household. For my mother, organised religion was too often dressed up closed-mindedness in the garb of piety, cruelty and oppression in the cloak of righteousness. However, in her mind, a working knowledge of the world's great religions was a necessary part of any well-rounded education. In our house the Bible, the Koran, sat on the shelf alongside books of Greek and Norse and African mythology.'

As a child in Indonesia, he studied for two years at one Muslim school and then two years at a Catholic school. Eventually, however, he abandoned this non-conformism and skepticism as an adult to be baptised in the Trinity United Church of Christ, a denomination which emphasises the freedom of the individual conscience over adherence to creeds or hierarchical authority.[634]

Humour can be one path to transcend the quicksand of Sedna, giving us the objectivity to step back from the edge, and also with the stressful aspects to Saturn a pressure to deliver, together with a talent for physical comedy. Any of us who are struggling with these stressful aspects would be well advised to develop our sense of humour.

Harpo Marx was an American comedian, actor, mime artist, and musician, and the second oldest of the Marx Brothers. He had Sedna in the sixth house of service, sesquiquadrate Saturn in the eleventh house of collective consciousness.

> In contrast to the mainly verbal comedy of his brothers, Harpo's comic style was visual, being an example of both clown and pantomime traditions. He wore a curly reddish blonde wig, and never spoke during performances, rather he blew a horn or whistled to communicate. He frequently used props such as a horn cane, made up of a lead pipe, tape, and a bulb horn, and he played the harp in most of his films.

> He received little formal education and left grade school at age eight due to bullying, during his second attempt to pass the second grade. He began to work in odd jobs alongside his brother Chico to contribute to the family income, including selling newspapers, working in a butcher shop, and as an errand office boy.

> At 21 he joined two of his brothers to form "The Three Nightingales", later changed to "The Marx Brothers". Multiple stories exist to explain Harpo's evolution as the silent character in the brothers' act. In his memoir, Groucho wrote that Harpo simply wasn't very good at memorising dialogue, and thus was ideal for the role of the "dunce who couldn't speak", a common character in vaudeville acts of the time.

> In their films he was often cast as Chico's eccentric partner-in-crime, whom he would often help by playing charades to tell of Groucho's problem, and/or annoy by giving Chico his leg, either to give it a rest, or as an alternative to a handshake. He became

---

[634] https://en.wikipedia.org/wiki/Barack_Obama

known for prop-laden sight gags, in particular the seemingly infinite number of odd things stored in his topcoat's oversized pockets. He often used facial expressions and mime to get his point across. In later films, he was put into situations where he would repeatedly attempt to convey a vital message to another person, but only did so through nonverbal means, usually by whistling or pantomime.

He married at 47 and the marriage was lifelong. The couple adopted four children and when he was asked how many children he planned to adopt, he answered, "I'd like to adopt as many children as I have windows in my house. So when I leave for work, I want a kid in every window, waving goodbye".[635]

At this juncture in human evolution, few of us use our planets at the spiritual level, but many of us are striving to, and such people are wonderful to be around. As with the other planets, the spiritual level of evolution is vastly different with Sedna from the two previous levels. Here, the stressful aspects with Saturn bring the challenge to transcend the physical challenges we face and sets us on a mission to nurture the collective spiritual consciousness.

Once we embrace the Sedna energy, which is the oneness of everything, our nurturing becomes an expression of Sedna consciousness and it becomes devotional in nature. The struggle of the beginner's level is gone, as are the transcendental crises of the intermediate level. At this level everything Saturnian is meaningless and yet everything Sednian has its place.

However, even in a more evolved Sedna consciousness the stressful aspects still bring temptations to abuse power and deviate from the spiritual path, as we see with Jimmy Swaggart, who was an American charismatic maestro of hi-tech salvation, a television evangelist of Pentecostal Christianity blessed with the ability to spellbind audiences to the tune of $150 million a year. He had Sedna in the fourth house of home, semi-square Saturn in the second house of material resources.

He conducted a vast yet dubious ministry secluded behind the walls of his $30 million dollar compound in Louisiana. Known as a frequent hell-raiser as a teen, he dropped out of high school

---

[635] https://en.wikipedia.org/wiki/Harpo_Marx

and played honky tonk piano with his notoriously carousing cousin Jerry Lee Lewis. At age 17, he married a 15-year old farm girl who lived down the road, both successfully lying about their ages. Soon after his marriage, he preached his first sermon in front of a grocery store interspersed with playing the accordion, 'knowing we get crowds with the music'.

By his late 20s, he was itinerant preacher traveling the Southeastern US and began to cut gospel records, of which he eventually sold over 150 million. After another message from God, he began a radio show and from that point onward TV became his manifest destiny. The ministry probably quadrupled with radio. With TV it exploded.[636]

His Sedna is also at the focal point of two evolutionary bi-quintiles, one to Neptune, the planet of dreams and visions, in the ninth house of spirituality, and the other to Jupiter, the planet of expansion, in the eleventh house of collective consciousness.

In front of the TV camera, he became more outspoken than ever, verbally attacking Roman Catholicism, Jews and homosexuals while soliciting money from his viewers. His Sedna is also closely semi-square Orcus, the planet of delving down and speaking out, in the fifth house of creativity. During each sermon, the impassioned preacher ranted and raved, coercing his followers and himself into a feeding frenzy of devotion. His antics backfired and in his late 40s he became a target of investigations.[637]

His Sedna is also square Ceres, the planet of nurture, in the seventh house of relationships and semi-square Saturn, the planet of structure, in the second house of material resources.

A wealthy California widow left almost her entire estate to Swaggart Ministries. The Evangelistic Association and its agents were charged by family lawyers with 'preying upon her loneliness and illness for the purpose of securing donations from her.' By now Swaggart was flush with 3 palatial estates and a private jet.

Further allegations of misallocations of monies, death threats, handsome payoffs and the exploitation of prostitutes led to

---

[636] https://en.wikipedia.org/wiki/Jimmy_Swaggart
[637] Ibid.

private investigation. When confronted by photos of himself with prostitutes he reportedly admitted he had a fascination with pornography from childhood. This incident earned him a three-month suspension from his US pulpit and a two-year rehabilitation period, which proved unsuccessful. Further confirmed encounters with prostitutes sent him reeling into a tortured, televised public confession for which he may be best known. However, he was back to preaching once more against sin within three months.[638]

Although the Saturnian reality appears meaningless at this level, it still exists, so we are still likely to fall into spiritual traps if we conflate our ego needs with our spiritual mission. Like our case study, new age guru, Bhagwan Shree Rajneesh, who has Sedna is in the eleventh house of ideals, square Saturn, which is conjunct his Moon, the planet of emotions, and Venus, the planet of values and relationships, all in the eighth house of shared resources.

> He was an Indian guru and author of more than a hundred books. He built a community in Oregon on ideals which included shared resources, which he then abused by manipulating followers and buying 93 Rolls-Royces with their money. To this day however, those same followers will tell you that this was just his way of teaching, his spiritual joke on American capitalism, and still support him because they learned something valuable in the process.

> He was not only intimately familiar with the world's great religions and philosophies, but also the modern psychologies of Jung, Freud, Maslow, and the rest of the West's best thinkers in modern psychology and psychiatry. His syncretic teachings emphasise the importance of meditation, awareness, love, celebration, courage, creativity, and humour — qualities that he viewed as being suppressed by adherence to static belief systems and religious tradition.

> When he was 50, he founded a commune in Oregon of 1,700 disciples, a sprawling religious community of a hundred square miles. The ashram was an attempt to build a self-sufficient commune based on ecological and organic farming principles,

---

[638] https://en.wikipedia.org/wiki/Jimmy_Swaggart

turning the desert into a garden, which they achieved in part. The devotees who joined came from all walks of life, devoting their money and labor to create a utopia. These years saw an increased emphasis on his prediction that the world might be destroyed by nuclear war. He predicted that "the third and last war is now on the way" and frequently spoke of the need to create a 'new humanity' to avoid global suicide.

A key facet of his charismatic ability was that he was a brilliant manipulator of the unquestioning disciple. While his followers might be at a mere subsistence level, having severed ties with outside friends and family and donated all, or most of their money and possessions to the commune, he was seen to live in ostentation and offensive opulence, famously buying 93 Rolls-Royces as a so-called spiritual challenge to the commercial culture in America. Called the "sex-guru" because of his popular talks about tantric sex, his ashram became known as one big love fest during celebrations.

The task of running the commune fell to his personal secretary and the assets of the organization were all in her name. Almost immediately it ran into conflict with county residents and the state government and a succession of legal battles ensued, concerning the ashram's construction and continued development, which curtailed its success. In response he gave her power of attorney and she mounted a campaign of harassment and terrorism against the county. He was 50. Two years later she announced that he would henceforth speak only with her.

He had coached her in using media coverage to her advantage and during his period of public silence he privately stated that when she spoke, she was speaking on his behalf. However, he later alleged she committed crimes, included the attempted murder of his personal physician, poisonings of public officials, wiretapping and bugging within the commune and within his own home, and a bio-terror attack on the citizens of the Dalles, using salmonella to impact the county elections.

At 53, a few days after his secretary and her entire management team had suddenly left the commune for Europe, he held a press conference in which he labelled her and her associates a gang of fascists. He accused them of having committed a number of serious crimes and invited the authorities to investigate. He claimed that she was trying to establish the Rajneeshees as a religion, and that her quest for personal power led to her paranoia, which eventually spread throughout the commune. He spoke often of how organised religion is an obstacle to enlightenment and he blamed his secretary for her ambition of wanting to be the first Popess.

While his allegations were initially greeted with scepticism by outside observers, the subsequent investigation by the US authorities confirmed them and resulted in her conviction, along with several of her lieutenants. However, difficulties accumulated with the National Immigration Service and Inland Revenue Service, who were trying to deport him and he was arrested as he fled his strife-torn utopia at 53, on 35 counts of conspiracy and fraud. He was released and on his return to India, he changed his name to Osho to signal a change in his consciousness.[639]

And finally, Billy Graham is an American evangelist, a Southern Baptist preacher who was "born again" as a teen, accepting Jesus as his personal saviour. He has Sedna in the first house of identity, sesquiquadrate Mercury in the eighth house of life and death.

He spread the good word of God by way of 900 radio stations and many TV crusades. He published a magazine, *Decision,* with circulation of more than four million, and gradually moved into the TV ministry. World- traveled, he became internationally known as the spiritual leader of presidents and noted people in many walks of life.

The author of 24 books, many of them best-sellers, Graham is the recipient of several awards. He is never unctuous or pious; rather, he is earnest, quietly confident and, despite his iconic status, ministers from a personal level. It is estimated that he has preached to more people in live audiences than anyone else in history: some 210 million in more than 185 countries and

---

[639] https://en.wikipedia.org/wiki/Rajneesh

territories. Hundreds of millions more have been reached through his TV, film, radio, video and print projects.[640]

In-conjunct

With the evolutionary inconjunct between Sedna and Saturn, the esoteric spiritual energy of Sedna bursts into our limitations, our sense of structure and meaning, our fears and responsibilities and also our sense of commitment, in an evolutionary way and we have a fated role to play.

Saturn brings structure and meaning to our world. It teaches us about the limits of time and matter and reminds us of our boundaries. It brings definition to our lives. Saturn makes us aware of the need for self-control and of our limits and the lessons that it brings help us to grow.

The inconjunct sometimes acts as a flow and at other times as a stress, so we have to learn to actively manage the process as the rarified spiritual energy sometimes reinforces our sense of structure and meaning and, at other times, isn't there to back us up. By adjusting to this, we gain a deeper understanding of ourselves and how to play our role.

If we are unconscious of the Sedna energy however, or if there are other stressful aspects to Saturn, we are likely to call the more negative manifestations of the planet into our lives, including limitations and constriction, excess rules and regulations, and authoritarian tendencies, or projections.

So, at the unconscious level this aspect can indicate abuse, or an abusing attitude, but it can also manifest as a kind of blind spot, which can leave us open to danger from fateful changes in the conditions around us.

Like Erin Darling, an American teenager who was killed in a car accident when she was 17. She had Sedna in the third house of communication, inconjunct Saturn, which was conjunct Jupiter, the planet of expansion, in the eighth house of life and death. She was driving three other girls to school on a wet road, when she lost control and crashed into an oncoming pick-up truck. All four attended the same Catholic high school, were good students, active in the community and well regarded.

---

[640] https://en.wikipedia.org/wiki/Billy_Graham

Father figures may play a significant or karmic role in our lives with this aspect. Polly Klaas was an American homicide victim. While hosting a slumber party for girlfriends at her home when she was 12, a stranger entered her window and kidnapped her at knifepoint. She had Sedna in the second house of material reality, inconjunct Saturn, which is conjunct Jupiter the planet of expansion, in the seventh house of relationships.

> She was two and a half when her parents divorced. Her mother remarried and the family relocated frequently due to her new husband's uneven success in his career. So, she spent her formative years living all over northern California, but her mother and step-father separated when she was 11 and then her life with her mother became more stable and productive. Her mother was employed full-time as a manager in a clothing store and Polly was looking forward to spending a second year in the same school where she flourished. After taking up the clarinet, she was accepted into the advanced band in junior high school and was pursuing her talents by acting in local community theatre and singing in a children's choir.

> Then news came of a possible reconciliation between her mother and step-father, meaning the family would be uprooted again and move to Idaho. Mom, now eager to reunite with her husband, relied heavily on Polly to help care for her baby half-sister Annie, a job which Polly dutifully undertook. A friend of the family said: "Polly was just trying to help, to hold things together. That's what she did. I mean the last words anyone ever heard her say were what she said to the man who was kidnapping her, as he led her out of the house. "Please don't wake up my mother." Her body was found in a wooded area, 35 miles north of her home.[641]

At this level the inconjunct can also manifest as problems with the legal system and while we might feel a sense of fate in our actions, we will learn that that does not change the rules. Like Mark Quinn Denton, an American criminal charged with rape, robbery and aggravated assault at the age of 23. He had Sedna in the second house of material reality, inconjunct Saturn in the ninth house of knowledge. He tried to use his horoscope in his legal defence, citing "inevitable actions", testifying that

---

[641] https://en.wikipedia.org/wiki/Murder_of_Polly_Klaas

he did it because the stars predicted that he would go berserk. His attorney said, "It was the law of Karma." The judge decided that it was his Karma to be found guilty and appointed another lawyer to defend him.

Or like Caryl Chessman, who was an American robber and rapist called the 'Red Light Bandit' because he would flash a red light on his car to stop people, pretending to be a cop, rape the woman and rob the man. He had Sedna conjunct Chiron, the centaur of wounding, and Nessus the centaur of righteousness, all in the eighth house of life and death, inconjunct Saturn, which is together with Ixion, the planet of lawlessness, in the first house of identity. We can see this aspect acting throughout his life, right through to his fated execution.

> He was born to an alcoholic dad and a mother paralysed from an auto accident when he was nine, he was a sickly, asthmatic child. He joined a gang, and married a 16-year-old girl when he was 19. Then in a binge of rape, robbery and kidnapping, he shot a man to death, and was convicted at 26.[642]

His Sedna is also square Juno, the asteroid of partnership, in the fifth house of creativity and sextile Mars, the planet of male sexuality and war, in the tenth house of profession.

> While in San Quentin prison he studied law, wrote appeals and a book. However, after 12 years on death row, he was finally executed in the gas chamber. A last-minute stay and ninth reprieve had been ordered by State Supreme Court, but it was too late. A wrong number was dialed to the prison and then quickly redialed, but when the judge listened on the other end he reported back, 'It's too late. The pellets have already been dropped'.[643]

As we tire of density and the grief it creates, and we start a spiritual journey to get out of the swamp, Sedna rewards us with transcendent crises, experiences which force us to let go and rise above them, resulting in a huge growth to a new level of consciousness. There is no choice with these crises, and the more we try and solve them, the more we will get hurt.

---

[642] https://en.wikipedia.org/wiki/Caryl_Chessman
[643] Ibid.

Agatha Christie was a British writer of some 67 detective mystery books that are universally popular. She had Sedna in the third house of communication, inconjunct Saturn in the eighth house of mystery. Her Sedna was also opposite her Moon, the planet of emotions, in the ninth house of publishing.

> Her novels have sold more than a billion copies in English and another billion translated in more than 100 languages. However, with a solitary childhood, she was so painfully shy that she never did get accustomed to public appearance and seldom gave interviews. Her mother was not keen on education but in spite of her, five-year-old Agatha taught herself to read. On a dare from her sister, she wrote her first book in two weeks, introducing for the first time her protagonist, Hercule Poirot.[644]

Her Sedna is sextile Neptune, the planet of imagination, in the fifth house of creativity, which is together with Pluto, the planet of life and death, just across the cusp in the sixth house of service.

> The book was uniformly rejected by publishers; however, later someone inadvertently opened the book and recommended it for publication. Agatha was given a five-book contract and her central character went on to solve crime in 33 more novels. Her popularity was close to immediate. By the time she was 40, she was a plain and matronly woman with hair forever locked in a wave, wearing dowdy housedresses; a deeply religious teetotaller who loved to putter in her garden.

> Around this time her mother died however, and soon after that her husband announced that he loved another. She fell apart and disappeared, checking into a hotel under an alias, while an all-out search turned up her abandoned car on a deserted road and a discarded fur coat. Police dragged the pond for her body while the plot thickened. Some bizarre letters turned up or were rumoured.

> When she was found at the hotel, she never really explained the episode and it was accounted for by stating that she had stress-related amnesia, or a secret affair was also considered as another possibility. However, while recovering from the divorce,

---

[644] https://en.wikipedia.org/wiki/Agatha_Christie

she took the Orient Express to Baghdad and met her second husband, an archeologist who was fourteen years her junior. Though she gave every possible reason to not marry him, she nonetheless did so, and the "most unsuitable match" lasted very happily for 45 years until her death.[645]

Johnny Carson was an American TV personality who began as the host of *The Tonight Show* at 37, reportedly for $100,000 a year, retiring at 67 on a $25 million per year. He had Sedna in the sixth house of service, inconjunct Saturn in the first house of identity.

When he was 54 he bought into 17% of NBC's earnings, which insured his billionaire status. With his nonchalant, inventive wit, he was one of the most popular and enduring figures on American TV, a household icon for millions of Americans. He was reliable, respected, reassuring - and funny, a familiar figure who was part of many lives. Keeping his finger on the common pulse, he instinctively knew when to pull back to avoid hurting anyone.

As host of *The Tonight Show* for over 30 years, he interviewed thousands of guests from royalty to the ordinary, introduced dozens of new personalities to the public, and will always be known as America's humorous late-night friend, a mid-Western boy not afraid to poke fun at himself as well as the powerful. He easily outlasted an array of competition. Dubbed the "naughty but good-natured son," Middle America liked him.

He married his first wife during his senior year at university when he was 23. The relationship was difficult and they separated after 10 years and divorced 4 years later. His early marriages were reputed to have suffered from his abuse, alcoholism, and neglect. His second marriage at 38 lasted nine years. and his third at 47 lasted eleven years. His fourth marriage lasted 17 years from the age of 62 to his death at 79. His divorces were always fuel for his late-night humour and he commented, "If I had given as much to marriage as I gave to *The Tonight Show*, I'd probably have a hell of a marriage".[646]

[645] Ibid.
[646] https://en.wikipedia.org/wiki/Johnny_Carson

And case study, Sally Ride, the first American woman in space and the mother of NASA's Planet Earth study, has Sedna in the tenth house of profession, inconjunct Saturn in the fourth house of home. Before becoming the first American woman in space and the first known LGBT astronaut, she got a PhD in astrophysics from Stanford and subjected herself to five years of astronaut training at NASA. Navy test pilots took her on gut-dropping, 600-mile-per-hour flights 39,000 feet in the air. Her flight instructor called her the best student he'd ever had.

> When Space Shuttle Challenger exploded seventy-three seconds after liftoff, seven of Ride's colleagues died in the accident. She had a total of more than 343 hours in space at that stage and had completed eight months of training for her third space flight when the disaster occurred. She was named to the presidential commission investigating the accident and headed its subcommittee on operations, revealing crucial information that revealed that NASA's push for rapid-fire missions, had come at the expense of safety and sacrificed lives.
>
> Following the investigation, she was assigned to NASA headquarters in Washington, D.C., where she led their first strategic planning effort, authored a visionary report titled "NASA Leadership and America's Future in Space" and founded NASA's Office of Exploration with the Mission to Planet Earth to study our planet.
>
> The goal of the Mission to Planet Earth was to use space technology to understand Earth as a total system, to learn how man-made and natural shifts affect the environment. When NASA adopted the Mission to Planet Earth, she had an answer to the questions that arose in her on seeing Earth from space. The astrophysicist in her saw a fragile planet and her greatest legacy is convincing NASA that Earth is worth trying to protect.[647]

Humour can be one path to transcend the quicksand of Sedna, giving us the objectivity to step back from the edge, and also with the inconjunct aspect to Saturn a fated life path and a talent for physical comedy.

Buster Keaton was a famous American comedian, considered one of the greats of silent pictures for his physical humour and pantomime. He had

---

[647] https://en.wikipedia.org/wiki/Sally_Ride

Sedna in the eighth house of shared resources, inconjunct Saturn, which is exactly conjunct his Mercury, the planet of communication, in the third house of communication.

He was born into a vaudeville family, his father owned a traveling show with Harry Houdini called the Mohawk Indian Medicine Company, which performed on stage and sold patent medicine on the side. And at the age of three, he began performing with his parents in 'The Three Keatons.'

His mother played the saxophone, while on stage Buster would goad his father by disobeying him, and the elder Keaton would respond by throwing him against the scenery, or into the orchestra pit, or even into the audience. A suitcase handle was sewn into Keaton's clothing to aid with the constant tossing. The act evolved as he learned to take trick falls safely; he was rarely injured or bruised on stage; however, this knockabout style of comedy led to accusations of child abuse, and occasionally, arrest.

Decades later, Keaton said that he was never hurt by his father and that the falls and physical comedy were a matter of proper technical execution. He told the Detroit News: "The secret is in landing limp and breaking the fall with a foot or a hand. It's a knack. I started so young that landing right is second nature with me.

By the time he was 21, his father's alcoholism threatened the reputation of the family act however, so Keaton and his mother left for New York, where his career swiftly moved from vaudeville to film. He is best known for his silent films, in which his trademark was physical comedy, with a consistently stoic, deadpan expression, earning him the nickname "The Great Stone Face." He had an extraordinary period from when he was 25 to 34, when he worked without interruption on a series of films that make him, arguably, the greatest actor–director in the history of the movies.

His career declined afterward, with a dispiriting loss of his artistic independence, when he was hired by Metro-Goldwyn-Mayer and he descended into alcoholism, ruining his family life. Then he recovered in his late 40s, remarried, and revived his career as an honoured comic performer for the rest of his life, earning an Academy Honorary Award at 64.[648]

At this juncture in human evolution, few of us use our planets at the spiritual level, but many of us are striving to and such people are wonderful to be around. As with the other planets, the spiritual level of evolution is vastly different with Sedna from the two previous levels. Here, the inconjunct aspect with Saturn brings an ability to transcend the physical challenges we face and sets us on a fated mission to nurture the collective spiritual consciousness.

Once we embrace the Sedna energy, which is the oneness of everything, our nurturing becomes an expression of Sedna consciousness and it becomes devotional in nature. The struggle of the beginner's level is gone, as are the transcendental crises of the intermediate level. At this level everything Saturnian is meaningless and yet everything Sednian has its place.

Linda Goodman was an American astrologer and poet who wrote a top selling book, *Sun Signs,* published when she was 43, which sold over five million copies, bringing astrology into the everyday market. Her Sedna is conjunct Venus, the planet of values and also Nessus, the centaur of radical change, and Pallas, the asteroid of wisdom, all in the twelfth house of the unconscious, and inconjunct Saturn in the seventh house of relationships. The paperback rights for her second book, *Love Signs*, sold for a record $2.25 million ten years later.

> She began her career as a local newspaper writer, and married her first husband, also a writer. They had five kids, three of whom died in infancy. With a divorce, she took a job as a radio announcer in Pittsburgh where she took the name Linda and married her second husband, also a radio announcer. Her interest in astrology blossomed when she moved to New York City at 38 and she totally immersed herself in the study to the exclusion of everything else.

> Determined and intense, with an explosive temper, she was also generous, often giving gifts to friends of cars or jewellery, a habit that led to bankruptcy in her early 60s. Then she moved to the remote mining town of Cripple Creek, Colorado at 45, where she

---

[648] https://en.wikipedia.org/wiki/Buster_Keaton

could write with less distraction. She had an affair with a 26-year-old marine biologist, who left her a year later.

When she was 48, her 21-year-old daughter, who was an aspiring actress, committed suicide by overdosing on Demerol in New York. Linda refused to believe that she was dead and said it was a government conspiracy, a cover-up, and spent a half milliondollars searching for her daughter, eventually claiming that Marilyn Monroe, Howard Hughes and Elvis Presley were also alive and in hiding.

Diagnosed diabetic in her early 60s, she distrusted traditional medicine and sometimes refused to take medication, or treatment. She had a toe removed and then part of her leg amputated. She became a virtual recluse. However, she continued to write and completed her *Linda Goodman's Love Signs Relationship Report* to go on the internet before her death.[649]

Tracy Marks is an American psychotherapist, astrologer, lecturer and teacher who is the author of 15 books and pamphlets which have been translated into nearly a dozen languages. She has Sedna in the fourth house of home, inconjunct Saturn in the ninth house of spirituality and knowledge.

She has a Master's Degree in psycho-synthesis and is acclaimed for her in-depth integration of psychological, spiritual and astrological concepts. She is skilled at leading dream work, women's empowerment, and the art of friendship groups. Some of her more notable books include *How To Handle Your T-Square, The Astrology of Self Discovery,* and *The Art Of Chart Interpretation.*[650]

And Dane Rudhyar was a French-American astrologer, one of most noted and respected astrologers of the 20th century. He had Sedna in the third house of ideas and communication, inconjunct Saturn in the tenth house of profession.

He was called a modern renaissance man for his ability to express himself in many fields; music, painting, poetry,

---

[649] https://en.wikipedia.org/wiki/Linda_Goodman
[650] https://www.astro.com/astro-databank/Marks,_Tracy

philosophy and metaphysics. He wrote for national magazines since his late '30s and was the author of many books.

He had poor health as a child, a distraction that continued through his life. At 12, he had life-threatening surgery to remove his left kidney and adrenal gland. A bright youth, he passed his baccalaureate at the Sorbonne at 16, majoring in philosophy. Becoming involved in the artistic and musical climate of Paris, he was heavily influenced by the radical ideas of Nietzsche.

At this time, he had a mystical experience or realisation in which he "became intuitively aware of the cyclic nature of all existence and of the fact that our Western civilisation was coming to an autumnal conclusion." He later wrote that it was from this time that he sought to gain a clearer understanding of the cyclic patterns and basic meaning of human existence.

At the age of 21, he left his native France and traveled to the U.S., reinventing himself with the name of Dane Rudhyar. Believing in the necessity of a fundamental transformation of our civilisation, his change of name was a symbolic reflection of his contribution to that change. The name "Rudhyar" is derived from the Sanskrit God Rudra, the Destroyer and Regenerator.

Attaining a position in the avant-garde art community of the West, he also studied and wrote. His seminal book in which he emphasised integration, *The Astrology of Personality*, was first published when he was 41.[651]

Quintile, Bi-quintile

The evolutionary quintile or bi-quintile aspect between Sedna and Saturn infuses our limitations, our sense of structure and meaning, our fears and our responsibilities and commitment with the all-encompassing spiritual energy of Sedna to the point where we can push the boundaries of human development.

Saturn brings structure and meaning to our world. Saturn knows the limits of time and matter and it reminds us of our boundaries. It brings definition to our lives. Saturn makes us aware of the need for self-control and of our limits, and Saturn's lessons help us to grow

---

[651] https://en.wikipedia.org/wiki/Dane_Rudhyar

Quintiles and bi-quintiles point to talent, the desire to create order and to categorize, a fascination with patterns and structures, perfectionist tendencies, and the desire to build or make things. These aspects have the characteristics of both the trine and opposition. They point to awareness of conflicts, or problems and finding solutions for them, however they do not automatically kick into action and must be cultivated over time.

With these aspects we can learn to understand the alignment of Saturn's lessons with the bigger context that we sense around us, however at the unconscious level we might well play beyond the boundaries without realizing the risk we are potentially facing in the process.

Like Ryan O'Rourke, who was an American car crash victim at the age of 17. He had Sedna in the eighth house of life and death, bi-quintile Saturn in the third house of communication. Just prior to his death he obtained his driver's license. He was driving his teen-age buddies illegally, apparently speeding, when he skidded on wet pavement into a tree. He and one of his friends died immediately. The teens had been inseparable.

Father figures are also likely to play a significant role in our lives. Like Amy Fisher, who was an American teenager, in the news for adolescent prostitution and the attempted murder of her lover's wife. She has Sedna in the first house of identity, quintile Saturn in the fourth house of home.

> She first ran away from home at 11 to go to Disneyland and claimed that she had been sexually assaulted at 13 by a workman at home. By 16, she was sporting new clothes and having fun, spending some $400 to $500 a week, telling her classmates and others that she was working for an escort service and that having sex for money was no big deal.[652]

Her Sedna is also in a fateful inconjunct with Pluto, the planet of life and death, in the sixth house of service.

> She began a sexual relationship with a 35-year-old mechanic after damaging the car her parents had given her for her 16th birthday and appealing to the owner of the body shop to which she took it, to make the repairs without her family knowing of the damage.

---

[652] https://en.wikipedia.org/wiki/Amy_Fisher

Fisher gradually fell in love with him and became increasingly jealous of his wife. Eventually, the then 17-year-old shared her idea of murdering his wife. Less than a year after she first had sex with him, she rang the doorbell of his home and when his wife answered the door, shot her in the face, wounding her severely. She was picked up by the police three days later, pled guilty to charges of assault with a deadly weapon and was sentenced to 5-15 years in prison.[653]

Her Sedna is also trine to Mercury, the planet of communication, in the fourth house of home.

She received $8,000 from a magazine for a first-person piece on her experience and after her release from prison, she became a columnist for the Long Island Press and dictated a book about her experiences titled *If I Knew Then...* indicating she had grown through the crises.

She met her husband, a physical-fitness fanatic and wedding-photographer, some 25 years older than her, who has two kids from a former marriage. They married and, although the relationship was tempestuous, the couple have three children. And she reunited a few years later with the wife she had shot, in sessions televised for *Entertainment Tonight* and its spin-off, *The Insider,* saying she wanted to heal and move on with her life. However, two years later, she said she felt no sympathy for the woman, without giving an explanation.

Then the *New York Post* published allegations that her husband had sold a sex tape of the couple to Red Light District Video of Los Angeles. Nude pictures from the video were posted at various internet sites, and a teaser clip was released that showed her nude showering and sunbathing. But a year later Fisher announced that she had settled with Red Light and agreed to do a related promotional appearance. The same announcement indicated that she and her husband had reconciled.

The following year she released a pay-per-view adult film titled *Amy Fisher: Totally Nude & Exposed* and signed a deal with Lee

---

[653] Ibid.

Entertainment to become a stripper doing club shows at least once a month. And her struggles to assert herself and deal with her alcohol problems were documented during her time as a cast member in the fifth season of the reality television series, *Celebrity Rehab with Dr. Drew*. In her time as one of his patients, Fisher revealed intimate details of her personal life and experiences, and remarked that the media had "ruined her life".[654]

At the unconscious level these aspects can also manifest as problems with the legal system. Amanda Knox is an American involved in famous criminal case, she was initially convicted of homicide by an Italian court and later cleared of murder charges on appeal. She has Sedna in the twelfth house of the unconscious, bi-quintile Saturn in the seventh house of relationships.

She was 20 and a student in Italy, when her roommate, a girl from the UK, was killed. As the dramatic investigation unfolded, she was accused of being responsible for the brutal stabbing death. The prosecutors painted a grim picture of her as a party girl who wanted the UK girl to be involved in sex games at a party. She reportedly enlisted the help of her boyfriend and another man. Both men were also convicted.

Her trial was covered extensively by US, British and Italian media for the nearly full year that it took to obtain a verdict. The jury handed down its guilty verdict when she was 22 and she was sentenced to 26 years in prison for murder and sexual assault. However she and her parents protested that she did not receive a fair trial and steadily maintained her innocence.

A year later she was granted the right to an appeal. The case captured media and public attention in both the US, Italy and elsewhere. When she was 24 she was cleared of murder and assault charges. The court upheld a charge of slander since she had initially accused her former boss of the murder, but the three-year sentence for that charge was deemed already served.

---

[654] Ibid.

She was immediately released from custody and able to return to the US with her joyful family.[655]

As we tire of density and the grief it creates, and we start a spiritual journey to get out of the swamp, Sedna rewards us with transcendent crises, experiences which force us to let go and rise above them, resulting in a huge growth to a new level of consciousness. There is no choice with these crises, and the more we try and solve them, the more we will get hurt.

Mia Farrow is an American actress and activist, who has appeared in more than 50 films and won numerous awards, including a Golden Globe. She has Sedna in the twelfth house of the unconscious, quintile Saturn in the third house of communication. She is known for her extensive work as a UNICEF Goodwill Ambassador in Africa.

> She had a bout with polio when she was nine, an experience that shaped her life from then on. Exiled to a ward in Los Angeles General Hospital, she lay on a bed among the suffering and dying. She recovered from the illness, but tragedy struck again four years later when her brother Michael died in a plane crash. Her parent's marriage suffered under that blow and, while her mother revived her stage career on Broadway, her father quit working and drank heavily, dying of a heart attack 4 years later, when Mia was 17 and in a convent school in England.

> The following year she left the school for New York where she began drama training. With one off-Broadway play under her belt, she took the role of a teenager in the TV series *Peyton Place.* The show became a major hit of the season, and made the 19-year-old Mia, a star. Her third film, *Rosemary's Baby,* was a mega success.

> Before she had turned 20 she began an affair with 29-year-older Frank Sinatra. When the press picked up on the unlikely romance between the sophisticated and debonair Sinatra and the skinny, awkward teenager, they documented every move. The couple married when she was 21, but their odds were not great, with a difference in age, style and custom, conflicting

---

[655] https://en.wikipedia.org/wiki/Amanda_Knox

careers and diametrically opposed temperaments, and they split up after a year.

At 23, she took off on a spiritual quest to India, where she spent part of the year at the ashram of Maharishi Mahesh Yogi, studying Transcendental Meditation. Her visit received worldwide media attention because of the presence of all four members of The Beatles but was cut short when the guru wrapped her in his hairy arms one day during a private meditation.

Not long after, she began a dalliance with the married conductor Andre Previn and had their twin sons at 25. When his divorce came final six months later, they married. It was the time of the Vietnam war and she and Previn decided to adopt a Vietnamese war orphan. While filming *The Great Gatsby* at 28, Farrow became pregnant with her third son, Fletcher. A second daughter, Daisy, arrived from Saigon when she was 29. Three years later, the Previn's adopted an older child who had been abandoned on the streets of Seoul, a girl named Soon-Yi.

By 33, the marriage had reached critical mass. her husband was steadily on tour, and she was involved with the six kids. Separating from him, she took the children to Manhattan and the following year played in a Broadway production of 'Romantic Comedy'. One night after a performance, her friend Michael Caine introduced her to Woody Allen. Allen lived in a penthouse on Fifth Avenue directly across Central Park from her apartment. She felt confident and happy in the beginning about the affair they began.

They began to spend weekends at each other's apartment, though he was uncomfortable parenting material and they never lived together as a full-time family couple, however they both adopted a boy when she was 40. They also worked together fruitfully with 13 movies in their 12-year-relationship, but things began to fall apart by the time she was 45, and they had a huge, explosive break-up when she found porno pictures in his apartment of her daughter Soon-Yi. Two years later their split was official, complete with bitter accusations and legal volleys.

By the age of 52, she had a total of 14 children, ten of whom were adopted. The family was centred in an eight-bedroom house in Connecticut. Her autobiography, *What Falls Away* was published that year and in it she reveals much of her life, writing candidly about the traumas and joys.[656]

Steve Wozniak is an American entrepreneur, a self-taught computer engineer who designed virtually the entire product line that enabled Apple Corporation to go from a two-man garage operation to a half-billion dollar a year business in six years. He had Sedna in the seventh house of relationships, bi-quintile Saturn in the twelfth house of the unconscious.

He built his first computer at the age of 13 and as an adult, co-founded Apple corporation and single-handedly developed the Apple I when he was 26, which was the computer that launched Apple. He primarily designed the Apple II which was launched the following year, known as one of the first highly successful mass-produced microcomputers.

He has been married three times. His first marriage was brief with no kids; with his second marriage he had three kids. At a party when he was 38 he met a lawyer and found they had known each other in the seventh grade; they married a couple of years later. They have six kids altogether, aged 5 to 18, three from his previous marriage and three from her previous marriage.

After stepping away from Apple when he was 35, he founded CL 9 and created the first universal remote. He then became involved in several other business and philanthropic ventures, focusing primarily on tech in K–12 schools. He is currently Chief Scientist at the data virtualization company, Primary Data.[657]

Jane Austen was a British writer, the first renowned female novelist of England. She had Sedna in the sixth house of service, bi-quintile Saturn in the second house of material resources.

She was the seventh of eight kids born to a scholarly village rector. She wrote from age 12, with her first novel at 15. For family entertainment, the entire family would tell stories, stimulating her young imagination. Her father was a kindly,

---

[656] https://en.wikipedia.org/wiki/Mia_Farrow
[657] https://en.wikipedia.org/wiki/Steve_Wozniak

reserved cleric and her mother, witty. There were few opportunities available to a young woman in that time and place; women were not even allowed into the universities and she only had two years of formal education.

As a young girl she was as high-spirited and silly. She had several suitors. She had a flirtation with the attractive but poor young man, which set neighbourhood tongues wagging. Later, she suffered a deeper embarrassment in first accepting, then rejecting the very next morning, the proposal of someone who was suitable from a social viewpoint, but not to her heart. She remained a lifelong spinster, later becoming somewhat tight-lipped with chastity.

She had six novels published from the age of 36, a remarkable accomplishment for a woman in that era, including her most famous, *Pride and Prejudice*. Her use of biting irony, along with her realism and social commentary have earned her great and historical importance to critics and scholars. Her novels have rarely been out of print, although they were published anonymously and brought her little fame during her lifetime.

A significant transition in her reputation occurred 15 years after her death, when her novels were illustrated and republished in the Standard Novels series and sold as a set. They gradually gained wider acclaim and popular readership. Fifty-two years after her death, her nephew's publication of *A Memoir of Jane Austen* introduced a compelling version of her writing career and 'supposedly uneventful life' to an eager audience.[658]

Jean Piaget was a Swiss psychologist, educator and author, known for his studies of children's learning patterns. He had Sedna conjunct Ceres in the eleventh house of collective consciousness, bi-quintile Saturn, which is in his sixth house of service.

He was a leading investigator and writer of thought processes among children. He received numerous prizes and honorary degrees from all over the world and is considered the father of developmental psychology.

---

[658] https://en.wikipedia.org/wiki/Jane_Austen

His life work was learning how children learn, as their thought process is not that of adults. The conjunction with Ceres gave him the insight to see the relationship between his children's growth and the nurturing they received, which was the basis of his theories. This seems obvious now, but prior to this, children's growth was thought simply to be due to hereditary factors.

His four developmental steps are studied by educators the world over. He developed several new fields of science, developmental psychology, cognitive theory and what came to be called genetic epistemology, the theory of knowledge. His 'constructivist theory of knowing' enabled researchers in a wide variety of fields and provided the basis for early computer programming languages.[659]

Martin Heidegger was an German existentialist philosopher who was one of the most influential voices and foremost thinkers and writers of the 20th century. He had Sedna in the fourth house of home, bi-quintile Saturn, which is conjunct Venus, the planet of values and Mars, the planet of action, in the ninth house of knowledge.

With the publication of his first book, *Being and Time,* when he was 38, he achieved instant fame as one of the spokesmen of 20th century existentialism. Though unfinished, *Being and Time* is one of the central philosophical works of the 20th century. In the first division of the work, He attempted to turn away from "ontic" questions about beings to ontological questions about Being and recover the most fundamental philosophical question: the question of Being, of what it means for something to be.

He argued that being human is defined by care, that it's practically engaged and is a concernfull mode of being-in-the-world. This was in opposition to rationalist thinkers like René Descartes who located the essence of man in our thinking abilities. For Heidegger thinking is thinking about things originally discovered in our everyday practical engagements. The consequence of this is that our capacity to think cannot be the most central quality of our being, because thinking is a reflecting upon this more original way of discovering the world.

---

[659] https://en.wikipedia.org/wiki/Jean_Piaget

In the second section, he argues that human being is even more fundamentally structured by its temporality, or its concern with, and relationship to time, existing as a structurally open 'possibility-for-being'. He emphasised the importance of authenticity in human existence, involving a truthful relationship to our being thrown into a world, and to our being-towards-death, the finitude of the time and being that we are given, and the closing down of our various possibilities for being through time.

He also made critical contributions to philosophical conceptions of truth, arguing that its original meaning was un-concealment, to philosophical analyses of art as a site of the revelation of truth, and to philosophical understanding of language as the 'house of being'.[660]

At this juncture in human evolution, few of us use our planets at the spiritual level, but many of us are striving to and such people are wonderful to be around. As with the other planets, the spiritual level of evolution is vastly different with Sedna from the two previous levels. Here, the quintile and bi-quintile aspects with Saturn bring an ability to transcend the physical challenges we face and set us on a mission to nurture the collective spiritual consciousness.

Once we embrace the Sedna energy, which is the oneness of everything, our nurturing becomes an expression of Sedna consciousness and it becomes devotional in nature. The struggle of the beginner's level is gone, as are the transcendental crises of the intermediate level. At this level everything Saturnian is meaningless and yet everything Sednian has its place.

Marthe Robin was a French mystic and stigmatic. She had Sedna conjunct Pallas, the asteroid of wisdom, in the eighth house of the occult, quintile Saturn in the fifth house of creativity.

Serious illness marked her adult life and from her twenties she was confined to bed, crippled, and gradually paralysed. She ate only wafers and neither drank nor slept, but lived for seven decades and carried on a busy apostolate.

From the age of 28 she was completely paralysed and bedridden. Although she still could move the thumb and

---

[660] https://en.wikipedia.org/wiki/Martin_Heidegger

forefinger of one hand, she became motionless apart from her head which she could move slightly. Since the previous year, at the age of 25, she could not eat anything at all. And from the age of 26 she couldn't even take a sip of water. When doctors tried to force some water down her throat, it merely came out her nostrils.

For the next 53 years her only food was the holy Eucharist, a wafer of bread which Catholics believe is the body of Christ. They also believe that they become his body on ingesting it. Once a week she was given the sacred host. Once she had received it she went immediately into ecstasy and began her weekly re-living of Christ's crucifixion. Every Friday wounds appeared in the palms of her hands and the stigmata, the scourging and crowning with thorns appeared on her body, and she appeared to be dead.

For 53 years she also carried on a busy apostolate, which is a Christian organisation directed to serving and evangelising the world. She was directed to found two schools in her native village, one for girls and one for boys. All this she directed down to the smallest detail from her bed in her darkened little room. Later on she was told to found a community which would welcome people looking for a retreat and which would be a home of "light, charity and love." It became known as the Foyer de Charité and there are now some 70 affiliated houses and communities throughout the world.[661]

Or traumatic external circumstances beyond our control may overwhelm us and push us into a greater spiritual mission, like Maria Quattrocchi, an Italian saint, who was beatified after her death along with her husband, the first time in church history that a woman and her husband were given that honour together as exemplars of the Christian life. She had Sedna in the second house of material resources, quintile Saturn in the fourth house of home.

She was a member of the noble Corsini family. She was a professor and writer on educational topics, writing several books and also served as a Voluntary Nurse in the Italian Red Cross during World War II. They were made saints because they

---

[661] https://en.wikipedia.org/wiki/Marthe_Robin

opened their home to refugees during WWII, at great risk to the family. According to Pope John Paul II, they lived "an ordinary life in an extraordinary way".[662]

Although the Saturnian reality appears meaningless at this level, it still exists, so we may fall into spiritual traps if we conflate our ego needs with our spiritual mission. Swami Kriyananda was an American writer, composer, playwright, photographer and singer, who is best known as a disciple of Paramhansa Yogananda, the first Master from India to live and teach in the West. He had Sedna conjunct Nessus, the centaur of radical change, and Venus, the planet of values and relationships, on the cusp of the eleventh house of collective consciousness, bi-quintile Saturn in the fifth house of creativity.

After reading Yogananda's autobiography at age 22, he headed for Los Angeles, where he was accepted as a disciple in the Self-Realization Fellowship. Eventually he was initiated into the order, taking life vows of poverty, chastity, obedience and loyalty. From that point on, Donald Walters became Swami Kriyananda. He spent 3 years in close contact with Yogananda and, as his disciple, was accorded great respect. He eventually became vice-president of the Fellowship, but at 42 he left to found Ananda, a worldwide movement dedicated to sharing with others the teachings of Yogananda.

From its meagre beginnings in the Sierra Nevada foothills, tirelessly promoted by its charismatic founder, Ananda flourished, expanding into a collection of churches, meditation centres, stores and other enterprises. The members describe their leader as thoroughly honest, kind and loving, and in New Age circles, Ananda is referred to as the poster child of cooperative spiritual communities. Others disagree, however, saying that the organisation is a cult and the beliefs seem based on self-delusion.

At 68 he was named in a sexual harassment lawsuit on behalf of a former member. She charged that he took advantage of her sexually throughout her years with the church, and that as a result, she became depressed and suicidal. Other ex-Ananda members supported her case, saying that Kriyananda would

---

[662] https://en.wikipedia.org/wiki/Luigi_Beltrame_Quattrocchi_and_Maria_Corsini

request massages from the impressionable young females who flocked to the community, and that these massages turned into sexual events.

When they questioned their leaders about this practice, the women were told that they were "extremely blessed to provide energy to him." Although Kriyananda admitted the sexual contacts, he denied they were sexual abuse. The presiding judge however noted the arrogant and uncaring attitude that the defendant exhibited throughout the trial, and the jury found him liable on all counts and returned a million-plus-dollar judgment. During the trial, he retired as spiritual director of Ananda.

However, from the age of 70 he lived and taught for seven years at the Ananda Italy center, near Assisi. And when he was 77 he moved to India, where he began an Ananda center in Gurgaon, near Delhi. For five years he appeared on television channels that were broadcast throughout India, Asia, Europe, and the United States. Since his move to India, Ananda teachers have been giving classes on meditation and Kriyā Yoga in many major Indian cities. At age 83 he moved to Pune to start a new community, where he died four years later.[663]

---

[663] https://en.wikipedia.org/wiki/Kriyananda

36: Sedna / Uranus

Conjunction

With the conjunction of Sedna and Uranus, the all-encompassing spiritual energy of Sedna infuses our rebelliousness, our individuality, our sense of discovery and our intuition.

Uranus represents the spark of intuition that spurs invention. The energies of Uranus are electric and filled with change. Uranus is forward-looking. It balks at tradition, celebrates originality and is associated with technology, innovation, discovery, and all that is progressive.

The conjunction places this forward-looking energy in a much bigger spiritual context and gives us a vastly larger playing field on which our sense of discovery can play. When Uranus is not developed, it reacts; but when we are truly in tune with its energies, it is highly intuitive and is associated with enlightenment, objectivity, novelty, and ingenuity.

At the unconscious level, with a reactive Uranus together with a deep-diving Sedna, we have to be careful of becoming the victim of unexpected vulnerabilities and risks that seem to come from nowhere, or from our blind side. Generally, these come because we have been ignoring the warning signs and our intuition in the buildup, but we may also be a helpless victim.

Like Charles Lindbergh Jr, who was the first son of a noted American family, aviator Charles and pilot-writer Anne Morrow Lindbergh. He was abducted from his home when he was 20 months old. He had Sedna in the seventh house of relationships, conjunct Uranus, the planet of revolution, which was right on his descendant.

> The family nurse put 20-month-old Charles in his crib and later discovered it empty. A ransom note in an envelope was found on the windowsill and a ladder outside. An extensive investigation by police followed, together with extended ransom negotiations, which resulted in a 70,000 ransom being paid. However, the boy was not returned.
>
> Two months later, a delivery truck driver pulled to the side of a road about 7 kms south of the Lindbergh home. Going into a grove of trees he discovered the body of the toddler. His skull was badly fractured and there were indications of an attempt at a

hasty burial. It appeared the child had been killed by a blow to the head. The culprit was eventually convicted through tracing the spending of the ransom money, the numbers of which had been recorded. And the case led to the Lindbergh law that made kidnapping a federal offence.[664]

Because of the enormity and depth of Sedna, together with the intuitive sensitivity of Uranus, we might have an ever-present sense of the fragility of life and of our psyches, and if we grow depressed, we might contemplate suicide. The key, if we are struggling with this, is to foster the positive side of Uranus, particularly focusing on developing our ingenuity and enlightenment.

Sylvia Plath was an American poet and novelist known for her exquisite poetry and her autobiographical novel, *The Bell Jar,* published when she was 31. The novel centers on a young woman with a fragile hold on life, and she committed suicide shortly after its publication. She had Sedna in the first house of identity, conjunct Uranus just across in the second house of material resources.

> She was a sensitive, studious child, born to a college professor and his educated, cultured wife. When she was just 8 years old, her father died from complications of diabetes. An intense student, she worked hard to achieve good grades. By age 18, she had won awards for her poetry and, with her excellent grades and obvious talent, she won a scholarship to Smith College. However, while still a student at Smith, she had a nervous breakdown, attempted suicide by swallowing sleeping pills and was given shock treatments. Despite such upheaval, she graduated at 23 and went to Cambridge, England on a Fulbright scholarship.

> One night at a party in Cambridge, she met the poet, Ted Hughes. Their romance began in a blaze of passion and the handsome, gifted pair married four months later. The couple had two children, the first when she was 28 and the second at 30. During their time together, the brilliant and tortured Plath mined her own anguish, writing obsessively of her depression, her jealousy, her marriage and her father, the strict, formal professor who had abandoned her by his premature death.

---

[664] https://en.wikipedia.org/wiki/Lindbergh_kidnapping

During the course of her marriage, her behaviour became increasingly more erratic and obsessive. Beset by worry over money, insecurity over her worth as a writer, jealousy over her husband's friendships with other women, she wrote furiously in her torment. Their relationship suffered tremendously from her fragility and his inability to deal with her roller-coaster emotions. Suspecting her husband of an affair, she gathered all of his papers she could find and burned them in the garden. He finally left her for another woman when she was 29.

A year later and just one month after the publication of *The Bell Jar*, on a frigid wintry day in England, she tucked her two small children safely away in their room, set out milk and cookies for them, and put her head in their London flat's gas oven, ending her life. Her last-written poems appeared two years later in *Ariel*. In a twist of irony, the poems established her as a fiercely original poet who exceeded her husband as an icon in the world of literature. Other collections of her poetry followed.[665]

Or we might become a pawn in a larger game, like Tom Sutherland, the Scottish-American Dean of Agriculture at the American University at Beirut, who was taken hostage by terrorists in one of the mid-East hostage crises. He has Sedna conjunct Uranus in the twelfth house of the unconscious.

He studied agriculture in Scotland before immigrating to the U.S., where he taught courses at the Colorado State University in livestock. He was recruited years later by the American University at Beirut, but did not accept the position for three years, using the time to weigh the singularly risky career decision. However, eventually he did move to Beirut with his family.[666]

His Sedna is also square Pluto however, the planet of transformation, which is on the cusp of the fourth house of home.

En route back from his daughter's graduation in America, he was stopped by gunmen on his way from the airport to his on-campus home. They sprayed his car with automatic rifle fire and took him

---

[665] https://en.wikipedia.org/wiki/Sylvia_Plath

[666] https://en.wikipedia.org/wiki/Thomas_Sutherland_(academic)

as a hostage. He was held by Muslim fundamentalists and kept in a Lebanese prison for over six years, incognito and chained by the ankle to a wall.

While in captivity he maintained Scottish traditions, including a celebration of the birthday of poet Robert Burns. When one liberated American hostage delivered a letter to the Tom's family, it contained questions regarding the brakes on his daughter's car. On his release, he returned home to a national celebration of his freedom.[667]

With this aspect we can have an electrifying effect on our followers, but at the unconscious level, if the conjunction to Sedna encourages us to go to any length to maintain this position, we will still have to face the results of any betrayal of trust and irresponsibility that we undertake.

Like Jim Jones, who was an American cult figure, the Leader of The People's Temple. He had Sedna conjunct Uranus in the third house of communication.

When he was 46, he led his followers from San Francisco to Guyana. He was known as a manic-depressive who suffered from paranoia and delusions. However, he held an incredible power of persuasion and led nearly 1000 people, including himself, to a mass suicide a year later.

His mother was convinced that her child was a messiah. His father was a member of the Ku Klux Klan and died when Jim was young. His high-school classmates recall that he was popular but not a leader, noticing his growing interest in religion.

After graduating from high school, he become a pastor of a Methodist church in Indianapolis, where his strong views on integration made him a target of bigots. Disenchanted with the Methodist faith, he created his own church, the Community National Church. At 25, he opened the first Peoples Temple in Indianapolis. The Temple formed a soup kitchen, an employment desk to help people find jobs, and a nursing home.

He moved the Temple to northern California, near Ukiah when he was 34. There he built a new flock using fraudulent "healing"

---

[667] Ibid.

performances to win worshipers and encouraged members to inform on spouses or children who transgressed his rules of loyalty. A hierarchy of trusted members formed, ones who would eventually help carry out his last order for mass suicide.

Members' money and possessions were to be freely given to Jones at his command, along with sexual favours. At 40, he purchased new temples in San Francisco's Fillmore district and in Los Angeles. His public relations talents brought him political clout four years later, but it also brought the attention of newspaper reporters who amassed enough data to devastate The People's Temple.

When his strong-arm tactics to squelch the story failed, he prepared to move to a leased tract of land in Guyana. Black followers were told they would be placed in concentration camps if they remained behind and Whites were informed they were on a CIA "enemies" list along with threats of blackmail and reprisals against defectors. Jones managed to be in Guyana when the edition of "New West" appeared. Incredibly, in light of the cruelty, stealing and sexual pervasion revealed in the article, 800 people were ready to follow him to Guyana.

When Congressman Leo Ryan became concerned enough about the affairs of The People's Temple to embark on a fact-finding trip with Temple lawyers and a team of reporters, Jones' paranoia was at an all-time high. After a day and night at the Jones compound, Ryan and the reporters had ferreted out enough information to take home a negative report despite the Herculean attempts by Jones' followers to keep the compound an appearance of utopia.

Ryan and his entourage were at the small airport an hour away from Jonestown preparing to return home when a tractor-trailer pulled onto the runway with armed People's Temple gunmen. They fired on the party, killing Ryan, several newsmen and Temple members attempting to leave with the congressional party.

At the same time, the camp doctor was ordered to prepare a vat of strawberry flavor-aide, dumping in a quantity of painkillers and tranquilizers as well as jugs of cyanide. The members of

Jonestown drank the poison as ordered and Jones put a bullet through his head. Over 900 bodies were counted. A box of over 800 passports were found, Social Security checks of elderly members and a million dollars in cash.[668]

As we tire of density and the grief it creates, and we start a spiritual journey to get out of the swamp, Sedna rewards us with transcendent crises, experiences which force us to let go and rise above them, resulting in a huge growth to a new level of consciousness. There is no choice with these crises, and the more we try and solve them, the more we will get hurt.

Like Skeeter Davis, who is an American musician with a career that has always been eventful. She has Sedna conjunct Uranus in the third house of communication.

> The eldest of seven kids, she formed a harmony group with her friend, Betty Jack Davis, and they called themselves The Davis Sisters. They began to play regular gigs on the radio in Lexington and on other shows in Detroit and Cincinnati before they signed a record contract. When she was 22 their first RCA release went to number one on the charts in 26 weeks.

> However, a car accident on the highway to Cincinnati killed Betty Jack and critically injured Skeeter, leading to a long rehabilitation period of recovery. She worked with Betty's sister for a while before going solo. At 28 she had a big breakthrough with 'Set Him Free', which established her as a star. And three years later 'The End of The World' went gold and put her in the world-class. Her heart is in country, though she does a variety of styles.[669]

Or like Dan Rather, who was an American news broadcaster, one of the top in his competitive field. He had Sedna conjunct Uranus, the planet of intuition, in the twelfth house of the unconscious.

> As a kid in Texas, he dreamed of becoming a reporter and at 14, he worked as a gofer fetching coffee for the local newspaper office. He was anchor of the CBS Evening News for 24 years and made a name for himself in journalism for his refusal to play "nice" with political leaders during his hard-hitting interviews on

---

[668] https://en.wikipedia.org/wiki/Jim_Jones
[669] https://en.wikipedia.org/wiki/Skeeter_Davis

the network. He had a furious temper and has been known to unleash his anger on people who misjudge his character.

At the end of his career he became embroiled in controversy about a disputed news report involving President George W. Bush's Vietnam-era service in the National Guard. He was 73 when he reported on 60 Minutes that a series of memos critical of President George W. Bush's Texas Air National Guard service record had been discovered in the personal files of his former commanding officer.

Once copies of the documents were made available on the Internet, their authenticity was quickly called into question. Much of this was based on the fact that the documents were proportionally printed and displayed using other modern typographic conventions usually unavailable on military typewriters of the 1970s. The font used on the documents has characteristics that exactly match standard font features of Microsoft Word. This led to claims that the memos were forgeries. The accusations then spread over the following days into mainstream media outlets.

Rather and CBS initially defended the story, insisting that the documents had been authenticated by experts, however this was contradicted by some of the experts it originally cited, and later reported that its source for the documents had misled the network about how he had obtained them. CBS retracted the story and Rather stated, "If I knew then what I know now, I would not have gone ahead with the story as it was aired, and I certainly would not have used the documents in question."

Following an investigation commissioned by CBS, which many believe was the result of political pressure on the board, they fired the story producer and asked three other producers connected with the story to resign and many believe Rather's retirement was also hastened by this incident. Five years later he was interviewed on Larry King Live, commenting "Nobody has proved that they were fraudulent, much less a forgery... The truth of this story stands up to this day."[670]

---

[670] https://en.wikipedia.org/wiki/Dan_Rather

Gunter Sachs was a German photographer, author, industrialist, and head of an institute that researched astrology. He first became a sportsman, then gained international fame as a documentary film-maker and photographer. He had Sedna conjunct Uranus in the seventh house of relationships. In his younger years his public image was that of the archetypal rich playboy.

He married three times. His first wife died during surgery. He courted his second wife, Brigitte Bardot, by flying over her villa on the French Riviera in a helicopter and dropping hundreds of roses. The couple was married for three years before divorcing. His final marriage was to Swedish former model, when he was 37. She was 26 at the time and this relationship lasted 42 years until his death.

At 40 he started working professionally as a photographer and the following year caused a stir with the first nude photograph for French Vogue. The focus of his photography was surreal nudes and landscapes, which were published in no less than seven image volumes. Early on, he also experimented with digital photography.

He was also interested in astrology and its connection with mathematics and statistics. His Sedna is also in an evolutionary bi-quintile Neptune, the planet of dreams and visions, in the eleventh house of collective consciousness. He published a book on the *Scientific Proof of the Link Between Star Signs and Human Behaviour* and is quoted as saying of his astrological research: 'In every case, there were significant results, way beyond what is explicable through mere coincidence'. Three years after his death, his family published posthumously his second astrology book, *My Astrological Legacy: The Secret of Love, Happiness and Death.*

He committed suicide at 77, with a gunshot wound to the head, at his home in Switzerland. His Sedna was also semi-square Vesta, the asteroid of regeneration, conjunct his Moon, his emotional nature, in the eighth house of life and death. The suicide note stated that he acted because of what he defined as 'hopeless illness A', which some have speculated to be Alzheimer's. He added that "The loss of mental control over my life was an undignified condition, which I decided to counter decisively.[671]

At this juncture in human evolution, few of us use our planets at the spiritual level, but many of us are striving to, and such people are wonderful to be around. As with the other planets, the spiritual level of evolution is vastly different with Sedna from the two previous levels. Here, the conjunction brings an inventive, open-minded approach to life.

Once we embrace the Sedna energy, which is the oneness of everything, our nurturing becomes an expression of Sedna consciousness and it becomes devotional in nature. The struggle of the beginner's level is gone, as are the transcendental crises of the intermediate level. At this level everything Saturnian is meaningless and yet everything Sednian has its place.

Ian Channel is a British-born New Zealand eccentric, known as 'The Wizard of New Zealand,' famous as the country's only official Wizard. He has Sedna conjunct Uranus in the first house of identity.

> At 28 he enrolled in a degree in psychology and sociology, and on graduation he moved to Australia and worked as a lecturer and organiser of community arts. At 35 he landed an assignment as college instructor and began his Ph.D. work at the School of Sociology at the University of New South Wales.[672]

His Sedna is also inconjunct Quaoar in the sixth house of service and in a close evolutionary bi-quintile with Neptune, the planet of dreams and visions, which is also in the sixth. The combination of these aspects often signifies a unique evolutionary contribution.

> During the student upheavals, which began at this time, he created a direct action reform movement called 'Action for Love and Freedom' and implemented this with what he announced to be 'The Fun Revolution'. The result was a revitalisation of the university referred to in the Sydney Morning Herald as 'the university that swings'.

> His head of department, convinced he was mad, dismissed him without consultation for insufficient progress in his thesis in the sociology of art. However, he wanted to stay on campus and

---

[671] https://en.wikipedia.org/wiki/Gunter_Sachs
[672] https://en.wikipedia.org/wiki/Wizard_of_New_Zealand

continue his social experiments and he was able to persuade the Vice Chancellor to appoint him official University Wizard, with a small honorarium paid jointly by the University Administration and the Student Union.[673]

With Sedna in the first house, he began to experiment with his own identity and allowed his driving licence, social security ID, passport and other important documents to lapse.

After travelling to the World University Service headquarters in Geneva, he received their backing to travel round Australian universities to promote his new revitalisation movement.

In a condition of considerable financial hardship, he persuaded Melbourne University Union Activities Department to appoint him their unpaid 'Cosmologer, Living Work of Art and Shaman'. The vice chancellor gave him the use of a lecture theatre for his classes in synthetic cosmology and the director of the National Gallery accepted the offer of his live body as a living work of art.

Becoming increasingly eccentric, he developed a unique world view blending magic, mysticism and sociology. A tall man with long beard and robes, he began giving performances as a Wizard. At 42 he moved to Christchurch in New Zealand and began to speak on a ladder in Cathedral Square. The city council attempted to have him arrested, but he became so popular that they made the square a public speaking area.

Wearing his costume as a false prophet of the Church of England or his wizard's pointy hat, he has been speaking there at lunchtimes in the summer months for over 40 years, becoming a beloved, if controversial, figure, performing rain dances and other wizardry as necessary to fans and tourists.

At 50 the New Zealand Art Gallery Directors Association issued a statement that in their opinion the Wizard was an authentic living work of art and the City Council appointed him Wizard of Christchurch. Eight years later the Prime Minister of New Zealand appointed him the official Wizard of New Zealand.[674]

---

[673] Ibid.
[674] Ibid.

Ram Dass is an American educator and author, who was fired as a Harvard professor for early experiments with LSD and other hallucinogenic drugs and who later became a follower of the path of Eastern philosophy. He has Sedna conjunct Uranus and also conjunct the Sun, the planet of willpower, all in the tenth house of profession.

He became a psychology professor at Harvard and was immersed in sports cars, antiques and even an air plane, pursuing the "middle-class bachelor" life until his early 30s, when hallucinogens changed his world view.

With his friend, Timothy Leary, he allowed undergraduates to participate in drug experiments, for which both he and Leary were fired from Harvard when he was 32. He traveled to India where he met a guru who changed his life and eventually, his name. Ram Dass means "servant of God" in Hindi. He began to see hallucinogens as shallow and artificial. He became a Guru himself, a leader to those on the spiritual quest. He reportedly struggled with relationship issues, including sex, alternating between celibacy and bisexuality.

In his 50s he urged people to engage in selfless service and he worked with the homeless, setting up a hospice for dying people and helping to start a foundation to treat the blind in third-world countries that has funded cataract operations and training for local doctors. He raised half a million dollars for this work during a 60-city lecture tour. His books included, *Be Here Now,* published when he was 40, *How Can I Help,* published at 54, and *Journey of Awakening*, at 59.

At 66 he had a stroke, leaving his left side partly paralysed. It was ironic that a master at speaking, a brilliant teacher and hilarious raconteur who could hold thousands rapt now could not speak, that he had been silenced by illness. He embarked on a long course of rehabilitation. He said the stroke had taught him to appreciate silence. After the stroke, his friends said 'He became much sweeter and softer'.[675]

Bhagwan Shree Rajneesh's conjunction is in the 11th house of ideals, very appropriate for the rebellious spiritual ideals he espoused. He

---

[675] https://en.wikipedia.org/wiki/Ram_Dass

combined western self-development techniques with eastern spiritualism in a way that drew many followers to him, and also deeply challenged the traditional spiritual systems. However, while controversial at the time, much of his 'follow your own spiritual path' philosophy is central in New Age thinking today.

A number of commentators have also remarked upon Rajneesh's charisma, noting that many of those who visited him for the first time felt that their most intimate feelings were instantly understood, that they were accepted and unequivocally welcomed, rather than judged. He seemed to radiate energy and to awaken hidden possibilities in those who came into contact with him.

Opposition

With the opposition of Sedna and Uranus, the all-encompassing spiritual energy of Sedna challenges our rebelliousness, our individuality, our sense of discovery and our intuition.

Uranus represents the spark of intuition that spurs invention. The energies of Uranus are electric and filled with change. Uranus is forward-looking. It balks at tradition, and celebrates originality and individuality. Uranus is associated with technology, innovation, discovery, and all that is progressive.

The opposition sets this forward-looking energy up in relief against the much bigger spiritual context of Sedna, so with this aspect we will likely be thrown out into the world to experience new discoveries from an early age. This process of revolutionary energies entering the life to push us out into the big wide Sedna world is likely to encourage the development our consciousness, so we are likely to mature early.

When Uranus is not developed, it reacts; but when we are truly in tune with its energies, Uranus is highly intuitive. The responsibility here is to foster our unique self, as it is being thrust out into the world and this, in turn, will enable us to foster the wider eco-system.

If we don't and we remain unconscious of our Sedna, or there are other stressful aspects to either planet, we can encourage the negative expression of Uranus into our lives, which is rebelliousness without a cause and irresponsibility.

Like Anthony Magnoni, who was a French teenager, known as Hades, age 19 when he and three other local teens desecrated the Toulon cemetery. He has Sedna conjunct Jupiter in the eleventh house of collective consciousness, opposite Uranus in the fifth house of romance.

> In the early hours the four kids brought up a body of someone who had been buried twenty years earlier. With ideology that is somewhat vague and borders around Satanism and Hitlerism, they performed satanic rituals on the cadaver, including necrophilia. They all admitted a ferocious hatred for human beings. They went before the courts and Anthony was given four years in prison.[676]

Or like Monica Mullaly, who is an American woman who has been at the wheel during two fatal car accidents. She has Sedna in the fifth house of romance, opposite Uranus in the eleventh house of collective consciousness.

> She was a 17-year-old high school junior driving her boyfriend home the morning after the prom. She fell asleep at the wheel, veered into oncoming traffic and collided with another vehicle. He boyfriend was killed and she was convicted of motor vehicle homicide. That verdict was later overturned by a jury on appeal. Records show her license was suspended when she was 23 following three speeding citations. Her license was also suspended for short periods of time for non-payment issues, records indicate.

> Then when she was 24 she drove her Volkswagen Jetta into the back of a family car, which pushed the vehicle into oncoming traffic, where it was hit broadside. The two parents in the car were killed, but two children survived. She said her brakes failed but pleaded guilty to motor vehicle homicide charges in 2001 and was sentenced to 2½ years in jail, with 90 days to serve. Her license was also revoked, according to records from the state Registry of Motor Vehicles.

> A decade later she said she needed her license back because she has been diagnosed with a degenerative spinal disease, which requires her to travel to Boston for four or five doctor appointments per week. Earlier that month she told the Times

---

[676] https://www.astro.com/astro-databank/Magnoni,_Anthony

that she wanted her license reinstated so she could do volunteer work. The application was refused.[677]

In the extreme this rebelliousness and irresponsibility can lead to abuse, where we may be the victim of a sudden accident, but this comes because we have been ignoring the warning signs and our intuition in the buildup.

Like Melissa Herlihy, who was an American homicide victim, age 17. She had Sedna conjunct Vesta, the asteroid of 'curing pain from the past', in the seventh house of relationships, but just a degree away from the cusp of the eighth house of life and death, opposite Uranus, which is also conjunct Quaoar, the planet of new perspectives, and Ixion, the planet of lawlessness, this time in the second house of material reality.

> During the early-morning hours her boyfriend intentionally shot her in the face, at close range with a rifle while she in lay in bed sleeping with the couple's infant daughter a few feet from the bed. He met her, then 15, at age 18 and she became pregnant a year later. During their turbulent relationship, he later told the parole board he cheated on her and stole money from one of two jobs to feed his cocaine habit. He was "terrified" of becoming a father and didn't want the responsibility. Prosecutors allege that the couple argued twice before the shooting and that he spent the day before drinking alcohol and using cocaine.[678]

Or it may give us an abusing attitude and a sense of entitlement. Like Elia Del Grande, who is an Italian murderer, who was aged 22 when he killed his family. He had Sedna in the ninth house of higher education, opposite Uranus, which is conjunct Quaoar, the planet of new perspectives, and Ixion, the planet of lawlessness, all in the third house of communication.

> The youngest son of a wealthy family, his father and mother were always away on business and when at home would vent their frustrations with fighting and screaming, which were often severe and violent. His mother beat him and his brother with household utensils. Through these frequent episodes during his childhood, he develops a love-hate relationship towards the

---

[677] http://www.capecodtimes.com/article/20010613/news01/306139992
[678] https://patch.com/massachusetts/medford/medford-man-denied-parole-1994-brutal-murder-his-teenage-girlfriend

mother. During his adolescent years dramatic personality traits emerge, resulting in violent behavior. When he was about seven years old, he experienced a very dramatic and destabilizing episode when his mother attempted suicide by ingesting various tablets. He found her, lying on the bed and foaming at the mouth.

As a young man he was sent to manage a nightclub owned by the family. He became head of the premises, noted for the beautiful girls and sexual services in private rooms. He fell in love with a girl with whom he began a sexual relationship. Together they consume cocaine and he discovered a new world, far away from Moscow, where he was nothing. For his partner but he is everything: she is very poor and it is not long before that he decides to deposit all money earned at the club in her personal account.

He felt like an important part of another family. He felt tied to his birth family only because of the money he needed to buy a house and to pamper his girl. So, he called his parents to give him his share of heritage that would allow him to break away forever. However, on his return to Italy he learned that his father had decided to go to a notary in order to strip him of his share of the estate. He went to their house and shot his father, who he met first. The mother, awakened by gunfire, was struck in the chest and finally his brother, who was seriously injured and died on the way to the hospital after he managed to call for help. He was arrested later that day as he attempted to flee.[679]

Our rebelliousness and irresponsibility might lead us into situations where we become a victim of the wider social context. Like Florence Cassez, who is a French woman, convicted in Mexico of belonging to the kidnapping gang, The Zodiacs. She has Sedna in the twelfth house of the unconscious, opposite Uranus, which is conjunct, Quaoar, the planet of new perspectives, and Mercury, the planet of communication, and also Ixion, the planet of lawlessness, all in the sixth house of daily routine.

She received a 60-year sentence for the crimes of kidnapping, organized crime, and illegal possession of firearms. The sentence and a possible extradition to her home country created

---

[679] http://www.misteriemisfatti.it/00160/elia-del-grande/

diplomatic tensions between France and Mexico. She denied all charges. When she was 28 she arrived in Mexico legally as tourist, to live and work with her brother, who was there with his Mexican wife. She met the kidnapper, Israel Vallarta, the following year, through her brother, and the pair began a difficult relationship that alienated her friends, who sensed that he was trouble.

Her arrest took place when she was 31, on the highway as she rode with Vallarta. She had been living with him, and they were always seen together. She was detained overnight, then moved to Vallarta's house in the early morning hours of the next morning. The Mexican Federal Police, which had tipped off several journalists, staged a fake arrest that TV crews from the Mexican networks reported live. Three kidnapped victims were freed and four persons, including Cassez, were arrested.

A few weeks later, during a live television show, she called and confronted the head of Mexican Federal Police with the truth about the staged arrest. In the weeks that followed the Attorney General of Mexico was forced to admit that the arrest seen on TV was staged.

The following year an official probe was launched by the Mexican police against the federal agents who arrested her. When she was 38, three Ministers of the Mexican Supreme Court, concluded that many of her fundamental rights were violated in her arrest and they started an investigation to search for those responsible for violating her rights and for staging the arrest. A year later the Supreme Court of Justice of Mexico ordered her immediate release, due to the police simulating her arrest for the cameras the day after her real arrest. She was repatriated to France at 39.[680]

As we tire of density and the grief it creates, and we start a spiritual journey to get out of the swamp, Sedna rewards us with transcendent crises, experiences which force us to let go and rise above them, resulting in a huge growth to a new level of consciousness. There is no choice with these crises, and the more we try and solve them, the more we will get hurt.

---

[680] https://en.wikipedia.org/wiki/Florence_Cassez

D. H. Lawrence was a British novelist and poet, the author of novels which include *Sons and Lovers, Women in Love, The Virgin and the Gypsy* and the classic *Lady Chatterley's Lover*. He had Sedna in the fifth house of creativity, opposite Uranus in the eleventh house of collective consciousness.

He was one of the most controversial writers of the twentieth century, who believed in the concept that man should bring his instinct into balance with his intellect. His explicit treatment of sexual fulfilment led to over three decades of censorship and ultimately to the Supreme Court.

He was the fourth child of an abusive coal miner and a refined mother whom he idolised. After surviving bronchitis at the age of two weeks, which left him in permanently delicate health, he grew to be a frail and hypersensitive child, who was often in tears and was overly dominated by his unhappy mother. She was a refined schoolteacher, who met his father at a local dance and after the wedding, found that he did not own his own house and did not work in the mining office, as she had been led to believe, but instead laboured as a miner himself. Her misery is reflected in Lawrence's persistent theme in his novels of the elegant, well-bred woman under the influence of a common, lowbred man.

At 26, with two novels in progress, he accepted a luncheon invitation from his favourite teacher and his aristocratic wife. According to legend, she had him in her bed within 20 minutes of meeting him. Two months later they eloped to Germany, marrying a couple of years later when her divorce became final. When they returned to England at the outbreak of WWI however, they were forbidden to travel outside of it, because his outspoken opposition to the war and her German birth aroused the suspicion that they were spies.

They left England at the end of the war, returning only for short visits thereafter, and led a peripatetic life through France, Italy, Sri Lanka, Australia, California and Mexico, where he was diagnosed with tuberculosis at 40. Despite his illness, he wrote voraciously during these years, introducing Freudian theory into the modern novel and especially writing openly about sexual passion and its necessary and explicit incorporation into human expression.

His theory of "blood consciousness" was a constant emphasis on humanity basing its decisions on instinct rather reason. His best-known work, *Lady Chatterley's Lover* was published when he was 43, but it was banned in England and the U.S. for describing the sexual act in minute detail. However thirty two years later the United States Supreme Court overruled the censorship and the book was published again.[681]

We can see the forward-looking revolutionary energies of this aspect in the work of Janet Chance, who was a British feminist writer, sex education advocate and birth control and abortion law reformer. She had Sedna in the third house of ideas and communication, opposite Uranus, which is conjunct Jupiter, the planet of expansion, in the ninth house of knowledge.

She married a successful chemical firm owner and stockbroker when she was 26. The couple soon moved to London, where they both became enthusiastic advocate and financial supporters of the English Malthusian League and the efforts of American reformer Margaret Sanger and the birth control movement.

Despite suffering from intermittent bouts of depression, Janet threw herself into work becoming a member of the Workers' Birth Control Group, founded when she was 38 by birth control advocates to give women wider access to birth control information. Chance was so moved by the plight of poor and working-class women who had no knowledge of sex and reproduction and no access to the latest available contraceptive methods that she helped run a sex education centre in the East End of London. She presented a report, "A Marriage Education Centre in London," at the Third Congress of the World League for Sexual Reform when she was 43.

Convinced that a large part of the problem lay in the repressed, provincial British view of sex and reproduction, Chance wrote several books on the importance of acknowledging women's sexuality and educating them about it, reflecting, albeit in modest

---

[681] https://en.wikipedia.org/wiki/D._H._Lawrence

terms, the views of the sex reform movement. These included *The Cost of English Morals, Intellectual Crime,* and *The Romance of Reality.*

She was increasingly convinced that a large part of the problem lay in the fact that birth control options for poor women especially were limited and in many cases their only option was abortion. But abortion was illegal in all cases in Great Britain. To this end, at the age of 50 she helped found and support the Abortion Law Reform Association. Working through Women's Co-operative Guilds and the Labour Party, this association sought to pressure politicians to support the notion that women should have the power to decide if their own pregnancies would be terminated.

During her late 40s, she also worked to help get refugees out of Germany, Austria and other Nazi-occupied nations. She also continued to chair the ALRA through World War II, helping to keep the organisation alive and ready for a post-war resurgence. But after the war, the ALRA shifted from pressuring Labour Party members, to campaigning more generally for a new parliamentary law by pushing for a private member's bill.

When she was 67 her husband died and her battle with depression intensified. She had to be hospitalised and, four months after her husband's death, she threw herself from a window at London's University College Hospital and died. Fourteen years after her death an abortion bill was finally passed by the British parliament.[682]

And, on a more creative level in the work of Hans Arp, who was a German-French poet, abstract painter and sculptor known as a great innovator and founder of the dada movement. He had Sedna in the seventh house of relationships, opposite Uranus, which is conjunct Jupiter, the planet of expansion, in the first house of identity.

To avoid the German draft in WW I, he fled Alsace for Switzerland where he became a leading member of the original dada group centred around Zurich's Cafe Voltaire, protesting the idiocy of the war and bourgeois values in general. As a dadaist in Zurich in his early thirties, he and his wife made geometrical

---

[682] https://en.wikipedia.org/wiki/Janet_Chance

abstract art, always allowing a happy relaxation, a formal gaiety into the composition.

He was denied Swiss citizenship when officials decided that his poetry proved him mentally deranged, and he left staid Switzerland for Paris. Eventually, he became part of a cutting edge that included Kandinsky, Picasso and Mondrian, an acknowledged bulwark of modernism and a founder of dadaism. His exceptional collages were widely imitated and he also wrote experimental poetry.

He and his wife, Sophie Taeuber, married when he was 35 and were co-founders of the Abstraction-Creation group ten years later. She became known as a formidable talent in her own right. In life, she was completely subservient to his career, his major inspiration and deepest human love. She died when he was 57, suffocated by fumes from a gas heater while visiting a friend's house. Her death depressed him profoundly and his work became more conventional and less magical. However, in his later years, he was an icon, revered and covered with honours.[683]

At this juncture in human evolution, few of us use our planets at the spiritual level, but many of us are striving to, and such people are wonderful to be around. As with the other planets, the spiritual level of evolution is vastly different with Sedna from the two previous levels. Here, the opposition brings an inventive, open-minded approach to the challenges we perceive.

Once we embrace the Sedna energy, which is the oneness of everything, our nurturing becomes an expression of Sedna consciousness and it becomes devotional in nature. The struggle of the beginner's level is gone, as are the transcendental crises of the intermediate level. At this level everything Saturnian is meaningless and yet everything Sednian has its place.

Like Hugo Ball, who was a German author, poet and another of the leading Dada artists. He has Sedna in the ninth house of publishing, opposite Uranus conjunct Jupiter, the planet of expansion, in the third house of ideas and communication.

---

[683] https://en.wikipedia.org/wiki/Jean_Arp

When he was 24 he moved to Berlin in order to become an actor and collaborated with Max Reinhardt. At the beginning of the First World War he tried joining the army as a volunteer but was denied enlistment for medical issues.

After witnessing the invasion of Belgium, he was disillusioned saying: "The war is founded on a glaring mistake, men have been confused with machines." Considered a traitor in his country, he crossed the frontier with his wife and settled in Zürich. Here, he continued his interest in anarchism, rejecting its militant aspects and viewing it as only a means to his personal goal of enlightenment.

He was 30 when he created the Dada Manifesto, making a political statement about his views on the terrible state of society and acknowledging his dislike for philosophies in the past claiming to possess the ultimate Truth. The same year as the Manifesto, he wrote his poem "Karawane," which is a German poem consisting of nonsensical words. The meaning, however, resides in its meaninglessness, reflecting the chief principle behind Dadaism.

As co-founder of the Cabaret Voltaire in Zürich, he led the Dada movement in Zürich, and is one of the people credited with naming the movement "Dada", by allegedly choosing the word at random from a dictionary. His involvement with the Dada movement lasted less than two years. He then worked for a short period as a journalist, for Freie Zeitung in Bern. After returning to Catholicism at 34, he retired and lived a religious and relatively poor life, dying at 41.[684]

Or Peter Kentenuch, who was a German priest of the Society of the Catholic Apostolate and founder of the Schoenstatt Movement, which attempted to teach Christians how to live out their faith. He had Sedna conjunct his Moon in the fourth house of home, opposite Uranus, which is conjunct Jupiter, the planet of expansion, in the tenth house of profession.

He saw the movement as a means of spiritual renewal within the Catholic Church. The group focuses on education and spiritual

---

[684] https://en.wikipedia.org/wiki/Hugo_Ball

development. 'We seek to grow as free, dedicated, and active witnesses of Christ in modern life by uniting our faith with our everyday lives. We look to Mary to educate us in this task and to guide us in becoming better followers of Christ'.

His teachings underwent a series of challenges from political and ecclesiastical powers. During WW2 the Nazis were quick to classify him as one of their main opponents and, after endless vexations, he was summoned by Gestapo. An informer had reported him as saying: "My mission is to reveal the inner emptiness of National Socialism, and there by to defeat it."

As a result, at 56 he was imprisoned for a month in a cell without ventilation to break his resistance; however, he left physically debilitated, but calm and peaceful, as at the entry. After 5 months in prison he was sent to the Dachau concentration camp, at a time when the living conditions there were worsening. Of the 12,000 prisoners, 2,600 were priests. The Germans were grouped in one block and he gave a spiritual conference each night to his fellow inmates.

He founded two new branches of his movement that year at Dachau. When he was transferred into a new block, he restarted his apostleship every time, despite the personal risk he incurred. Over the last three months of 1944, the tightening of the Nazi regime and epidemics caused the death of 10,000 prisoners. It is at this point, in a surprising act of faith, full of hope in the middle of that hellish place, he founded the international arm of his Movement which extended his teachings to the world. Under these unimaginable material conditions and at the peril of his life, he wrote treaties of spirituality, prayers and a didactic poem of over 20,000 verses.

On the arrival of the American troops at the end of the war, he was released and returned to his community at Schoenstatt. He immediately restarted his work, the experience of deportation helping him to teach his disciples on how to maintain inner freedom. Considered by many of those who came into contact with him to have been a saint, his cause for sainthood is currently under consideration by the church, pending the compilation of his writings and correspondences.[685]

And finally, Padre Pio was an Italian healer, a Capuchin monk and stigmatic. He had Sedna conjunct Ceres, the planet of nurturing, in the fifth house of children, opposite Uranus in the eleventh house of collective consciousness.

He was a special, unique case as he was the first priest "marked by God" in two thousand years. Nuns, monks and even lay persons have experienced the stigmata but never a consecrated priest. His phenomena was witnessed and reported by tens of thousands of people.

Francesco Forgione was the eighth child in a poor family. He followed his vocation at 16 by joining the Capuchins, the most austere order of Franciscans, and he studied with them for eight years before being ordained at 23. Conscripted when he was 29, he attracted the attention of military doctors when he went on "sick call." He fell gravely ill with a temperature that climbed to 118 degrees, leaving the doctors gasping. He was given leave, sent home to die. His father superior sent him to a monastery. Once there, he recovered suddenly.

His stigmata first appeared when he was 31 when one of the brothers found him with his hands bleeding copiously. He was taken immediately to his cell. When the doctor arrived, he insisted that photographs be taken. There was no reason for the wounds and the blood did not coagulate and left a pleasant odour. These stigmata remaining visible for his lifetime.

The church did not welcome the phenomena and they restricted him to his quarters, not allowing him to give the Mass or sacraments, while conducting examinations and inquiries, both by medical specialists and church dignitaries. He was kept under tight watch to see that he was not physically mutilating himself, with his hands in tight dressings and sealed with wax. No fraud could be found; indeed, the bloody bandages remained sweet smelling. The Vatican forbade him to show his hands to anyone

---

[685] https://en.wikipedia.org/wiki/Joseph_Kentenich

other than his inquisitors. From the age of 44 to 47 he was literally sentenced to remain incognito.

When he was 36 the Vatican had published an apostolic act officially informing the public that the phenomena associated with the Capuchin brother Padre Pio had not been authenticated by Rome as supernatural. Ten years later, to silence him, his superiors ordered him to another monastery. When word got out, the people revolted. Peasants, businessmen, hotelkeepers and even the mayor blocked all the exits from the monastery, armed with hatchets, scythes and rifles, ready to stop any attempt to take their priest away. Business was booming in the town due to the rumours and declarations of evidence, and the good Italians wed their sense of devotion with their sense of commerce. Never again did he receive orders of transfer.

While the priest was in solitary confinement, people reported that he was seen at different bedsides of the ill and stricken. At times he was seen hundreds of miles away, comforting and healing, at the same time that he was known to be at prayers in the chapel. Then he was allowed once more to celebrate the Mass, but only at 5 am. The people were not deterred by the hour but flocked to the church to see the man whose hands bled when he lifted them in blessing, as had those of Christ.

No mystic was ever victim of so many attacks by his peers or faced such hostility in the bosom of the church. It was the sheer weight of the mass of people who sustained him. During WW II, soldiers from Europe and as far away as American made the rugged trek up to the mountainous village and carried the awesome story home with them of the priest who bore the wounds of Christ. One day in 1947, a Polish priest, just ordained, came to the monastery to make his confession and heard Pio say, "One day you will be Pope." Later, John Paul II prayed before the tomb of Padre Pio.

His miracles numbered in the thousands. In the tradition of stigmatics, he had the graces of bilocation (being seen in more than one place simultaneously); distant vision; knowledge of the past, present and future life of the faithful; reading of souls; and healing. He suffered continually, with the wounds also on his feet, and it was witnessed that on occasion, while saying the

Mass, he levitated. While in the state of mystical ecstasy, he appeared to be catatonic, though at times he was heard conversing with unseen angels. Known as a great healer, he was visited by multitudes, whose donations helped build and support a hospital. He died at 81 and on the day of his death, the stigmata disappeared, leaving a clear and immaculate skin.[686]

Semi-sextile, Sextile, Trine

With the flowing aspects between Sedna and Uranus, the all-encompassing spiritual energy of Sedna aligns with our rebelliousness, our individuality, our sense of discovery and our intuition.

Uranus represents the spark of intuition that spurs invention. The energies of Uranus are electric and filled with change. Uranus is forward-looking. It balks at tradition, celebrates originality and is associated with technology, innovation, discovery, and all that is progressive.

The flowing aspects aligns this forward looking energy in a much bigger spiritual context and gives us a vastly larger playing field on which our sense of discovery can play. When Uranus is not developed, it reacts; but when we are truly in tune with its energies, it is highly intuitive and is associated with enlightenment, objectivity, novelty, and ingenuity.

At the unconscious level, with a reactive Uranus together with a deep-diving Sedna, we have to be careful of becoming the victim of unexpected vulnerabilities and risks that seem to come from nowhere, or from our blind side. Generally, these come because we have been ignoring the warning signs and our intuition in the buildup, but we may also be a helpless victim.

An example is Maria, a blond 4 year old, who was born to a Bulgarian Roma woman in Greece, and illegally adopted by another Roma family. She has Sedna on the cusp of the seventh house of relationships, sextile Uranus in the fourth house of home.

> The fake parents were under suspicion of having bought her, with the intention to use her for professional begging. The couple who appeared to be Maria's parents had fraudulently registered

---

[686] https://en.wikipedia.org/wiki/Padre_Pio

14 children in three different municipalities and had faced charges for robbery and forging official documents in the past.[687]

The negative side of Uranus is rebelliousness and irresponsibility and at the unconscious level, even with the flows, the depth of Sedna can lead us in extreme circumstances into abusive areas, in which we could either be the victim, or the perpetrator.

Like Susan Atkins, who was an American homicide perpetrator. A hippie dropout product of the drug culture, she met and loved cult leader, Charles Manson, joining his camp on the old Spahn ranch in Death Valley. She had Sedna conjunct Pallas, the asteroid of wisdom and together with the Moon, her emotional nature, in the second house of material reality and restrictions, sextile Uranus conjunct Orcus, the planet of 'delving down and speaking out' in the fifth house of love affairs.

> She had a child, Zee Zo Zeze Zedfrack, father unknown, when she was 20. A year later she joined in the ritualistic killing of five people, holding eight-month pregnant Sharon Tate while she was stabbed her to death. While in prison, she later had a "religious conversion" at 26, which she described in her memoir, written at 29. She later began a prison ministry. When she was 33 she was married for a few months to a Texan who claimed he was a millionaire. She married again at 39. While in prison her health deteriorated. At 60 she was diagnosed with brain cancer and also underwent a leg amputation. She died at age 61 at a women's prison in California.[688]

Or like Gaetano Badalementi, who was an Italian mafia boss involved in drug trafficking, the black market and smuggling. He had Sedna conjunct Nessus, the centaur of extremism, in the seventh house of relationships, semi-sextile Uranus in the sixth house of daily routine.

> Drafted into the Italian army at 18, he deserted before the Allies invaded Sicily. When he was 23 he was named in an arrest warrant on charges of conspiracy and kidnapping and a year later he was charged with murder as well. He fled to his brother

---

[687] https://www.astro.com/astro-databank/Adopted_illegally:_Maria
[688] https://en.wikipedia.org/wiki/Susan_Atkins

in the US, but was arrested three years later and deported back to Italy.

By 28 he was living in Detroit as an illegal immigrant and the American police identified him as the recipient of a 50kg shipment of heroin. He became the Godfather, chief of the Sicilian Mafia's supreme "commission" from the age of 48 to 55. And by his late 50's he was involved with the "Pizza Connection" case, where the mafia smuggled millions worth of heroin and cocaine to USA using mafia-owned pizzerias as distribution points.

When the FBI began to close in he fled to Spain but was arrested in Madrid. He was 60. He was imprisoned in Massachusetts and sentenced to 45 years in prison, where he died of a heart attack aged 80.[689]

Or Lee Harvey Oswald, who was the assassin of US President John F. Kennedy when he was 24. He had Sedna in the tenth house of profession, semi-sextile Uranus in the eleventh house of collective consciousness.

A habitual truant at school, he underwent psychiatric study in New York at the age of 12 and was diagnosed as emotionally disturbed as early as 1952. His mom denied that her teenager had any problems and refused to allow treatment.

At 17, while in the U.S. Marine Corps, he was rated as a sharpshooter. After serving in the Marines, where he became a Marxist, he defected to Russia at 20, but returned to the US three years later, after becoming disillusioned with Russian life. He became an ardent supporter of Cuba's Marxist president, Fidel Castro and talked to his Russian wife of killing Richard Nixon and other public figures. When he was 24, using a mail-order rifle, he shot at and barely missed hitting a retired Major General.

After the assassination of President Kennedy, he was arrested and charged with the murder of a police patrolman then later that day with the murder of the president. He was never brought to trial. While leaving his holding cell, being escorted through the

[689] https://en.wikipedia.org/wiki/Gaetano_Badalamenti

basement of the Dallas police headquarters to a vehicle, he was shot to death by the operator of a local nightclub, who pushed forward through the crowd and shot him once in the chest.[690]

As we tire of density and the grief it creates, and we start a spiritual journey to get out of the swamp, Sedna rewards us with transcendent crises, experiences which force us to let go and rise above them, resulting in a huge growth to a new level of consciousness. There is no choice with these crises, and the more we try and solve them, the more we will get hurt.

Al Gore was an American politician and environmentalist who served as the 45th Vice President of the United States. His Sedna is conjunct the MC, the cusp of the tenth house of profession, sextile Uranus, which is conjunct Orcus, the planet of 'delving down and speaking out', in the eleventh house of ideals.

> He served as an elected official for 24 years. He was a Congressman from Tennessee and served as one of the State's senators. He is a devout Baptist as he has made that clear in many interviews: 'Faith is the centre of my life. I don't wear it on my sleeve, but I'm happy to respond to your question by affirming my faith.' Despite his devotion to one particular brand of Christianity, Gore has stated that he supports religious tolerance, the First Amendment, freedom of religion, expression, etc. and the strict separation of church and state.
>
> He was initially hesitant to accept a position as Bill Clinton's running mate, but after clashing with the George H. W. Bush administration over global warming issues, he decided to accept the offer. Clinton's choice was criticised as unconventional because, rather than picking a running mate who would diversify the ticket, Clinton chose a fellow Southerner who shared his political ideologies and who was nearly the same age as Clinton. Yet, Gore has come to be regarded by strategists in both parties as the best vice-presidential pick in at least 20 years.
>
> In the 2000 presidential election, in what was one of the closest presidential races in history, he won the popular vote by half a

---

[690] https://en.wikipedia.org/wiki/Lee_Harvey_Oswald

million, but lost in the Electoral College to Republican George W. Bush by 537 votes in the key state of Florida.

After his term as vice-president ended, Gore remained prominent as an author and activist and returned his focus to his environmental agenda. He edited and adapted a slide show he had compiled years earlier and began featuring the slide show in presentations on global warming across the U.S. and around the world. By the time the documentary about his work, *An Inconvenient Truth* was made, he estimated that he had shown the presentation more than one thousand times.

Premiering at the 2006 Sundance Film Festival and opening in New York City and Los Angeles his film, *An Inconvenient Truth* was a critical and box office success, winning two Academy Awards for Best Documentary Feature and Best Original Song. The film grossed $24 million in the U.S. and $26 million in the foreign box office, becoming the tenth highest grossing documentary film to date in the United States. Since the film's release, it has been credited for raising international public awareness of global warming and reenergising the environmental movement.[691]

His work in climate change activism earned him the Nobel Peace Prize in 2007 and we now know the evolutionary results of his work with the Paris Climate Change Agreement, which has been far more valuable for society than his being president.

Our case study, futurist, Ray Kurzweil also has Sedna sextile his conjunction of Uranus and Orcus, but his conjunction is in the eighth house of transformation and shared resources. He is an author and computer scientist. His prediction is that we will merge with a superconscious AI around 2045 is called the Singularity Theory, because we can't know how life will change after that. The conjunction to Orcus in the eighth gives him the role of a modern prophet.

The progressiveness and sense of discovery of these aspects can be seen in the work of Margaret Atwood, who is a Canadian poet, novelist, literary critic, essayist, inventor, and environmental activist. She had

---

[691] https://en.wikipedia.org/wiki/Al_Gore

Sedna in the twelfth house of the unconscious, semi-sextile Uranus, also in the twelfth.

Many of her poems have been inspired by myths and fairy tales, which have been interests of hers from an early age. Her themes are mainly the emotional interdependence of the sexes and their search for self-discovery.

This theme is exemplified in her book, *The Handsmaid's Tale*, published when she was 46, in which the sole function of the heroine is to breed. She often portrays female characters dominated by patriarchy in her novels. She also sheds light on women's social oppression as a result from patriarchal ideology. Still, she denies that her books are feminist and believes that the feminist label can only be applied to writers who consciously work within the framework of the feminist movement.

She is a winner of the Arthur C. Clarke Award and has been shortlisted for the Booker Prize five times, winning once. But she has also resisted the suggestion that her books, like *The Handmaid's Tale*, are science fiction, suggesting that they are speculative fiction instead, explaining that 'science fiction has monsters and spaceships, whereas speculative fiction takes place on Planet Earth and could really happen'.[692]

And Barack Obama, the first African American president, has Sedna in the second house of material resources, trine Uranus which is together with his Node, the point of his dhama and Haumea, the planet of rebirth, all in the seventh house of relationships. He enjoys relating to people of all walks of life and is credited with helping to birth Rainbow America, a cultural identity which celebrates the diverse makeup of the people across the country.

A self-described "skinny kid with a funny name," he is the child of a Kenyan man and an American woman. His parents met at the University of Hawaii where they were both students. When Barack was two, his father returned to Africa, and the young boy lived in Hawaii with his mom and grandparents. After his mother married an Indonesian, she took him with her when she moved

---

[692] https://en.wikipedia.org/wiki/Margaret_Atwood

to her new husband's native country. Young Barack was sent back to Hawaii at age 10 to live with his grandparents.

He graduated in 1983 from Columbia University with a degree in political science and international relations. He worked in Chicago's inner city, helping church groups improve job-training, education and city services to the poor and then went on to law school at Harvard. At 35 he was elected to the Illinois General Assembly as a state senator. At 43 he burst onto the national scene when he delivered a rousing keynote address at the Democratic National Convention in Boston. That year he won election to the U.S. Senate by a wide margin.

He announced his candidacy for the Democratic Party's nomination for President at 46. On the campaign trail he racked up an impressive number of primary and caucus wins. Exhibiting composure, thoughtfulness, a quick mind and self-deprecating humour, his debate performance earns kudos, while his powerful oratory evoked comparisons to Martin Luther King, Jr. and John F. Kennedy. Along with his life story, which he touts as a representation of the American dream, his emphasis on unity, hope and civility captured media and public attention.

His religious background is more diverse than that of most prominent politicians. But it may prove to be more representative of an increasingly diverse America. His mother was raised by non-practicing Christians; his father was raised a Muslim but was an atheist by the time he had married Obama's mother. His step-father was also Muslim, but of an eclectic kind who could make room for animist and Hindu beliefs.

In his book, *The Audacity of Hope,* published when he was 45, he writes: 'I was not raised in a religious household. For my mother, organised religion was too often dressed up closed-mindedness in the garb of piety, cruelty and oppression in the cloak of righteousness. However, in her mind, a working knowledge of the world's great religions was a necessary part of any well-rounded education. In our house the Bible, the Koran, sat on the shelf alongside books of Greek and Norse and African mythology.'

> As a child in Indonesia, he studied for two years at one Muslim school and then two years at a Catholic school. Eventually however, he abandoned this non-conformism and skepticism as an adult to be baptised in the Trinity United Church of Christ, a denomination which emphasises the freedom of the individual conscience over adherence to creeds or hierarchical authority.[693]

Humour can be one path to transcend the quicksand of Sedna, giving us the objectivity to step back from the edge, but also with the flowing aspects to Uranus, an embrace of the unique, the bizarre and the unusual.

John Cleese is an English actor, screenwriter, producer, and comedian who has made the bizarre and unusual his stock and trade, with films like the Monty Python series. He has Sedna conjunct his Moon in the eighth house of shared resources, semi-sextile Uranus in the ninth house of knowledge.

> When he got a scholarship to an English public high school, he allegedly defaced the school grounds as a prank, by painting footprints to suggest that the statue of Field Marshal Earl Haig had got down from his plinth and gone to the toilet.

> In his autobiography, *So, Anyway*, he says that discovering, aged 17, he had not been made a house prefect by his housemaster affected his outlook: 'It was not fair and therefore it was unworthy of my respect... I believe that this moment changed my perspective on the world'. Handsome and hyperactive, he wrote and played in humorous sketches and radio comedy while at Cambridge University.

> He achieved success at the Edinburgh Festival Fringe and as a scriptwriter and performer on The Frost Report. And he was in his late twenties, when he co-founded Monty Python, the comedy troupe responsible for the TV sketch show *Monty Python's Flying Circus* and the four Monty Python films. He also played in a hilarious sit-com *Fawlty Towers* for 12 episodes, and in 1972 he started Video Arts, writing and producing more than 70 business training films that use humour to make the point.[694]

---

[693] https://en.wikipedia.org/wiki/Barack_Obama
[694] https://en.wikipedia.org/wiki/John_Cleese

At this juncture in human evolution, few of us use our planets at the spiritual level, but many of us are striving to and such people are wonderful to be around. As with the other planets, the spiritual level of evolution is vastly different with Sedna from the two previous levels. Here, the flowing aspects bring an inventive, open-minded approach to life.

Once we embrace the Sedna energy, which is the oneness of everything, our nurturing becomes an expression of Sedna consciousness and it becomes devotional in nature. The struggle of the beginner's level is gone, as are the transcendental crises of the intermediate level. At this level everything Saturnian is meaningless and yet everything Sednian has its place.

The Saturnian rules still apply in the material world in which we live however, so even at this level the impulsiveness of Uranus and depth of field of Sedna can present us with spiritual challenges to detach from our ego center and rise above them.

Like Franklin Jones, who was an American siddha-guru known as Bubba Free John and later Adi Da. He had Sedna in the third house of ideas and communication, semi-sextile Uranus in the fourth house of home.

> He was a handsome, ample and happy mystic with an ashram called Horse House Commune in California. His teachings deal with various forms to harmonize and purify action in life. *The Method of the Disshas* and *Garbage and the Goddess* are among his works, which include books and recorded talks.

> It is said of Jones that he lived in a world of sheer light and joy known as "the Bright" until his second or third year. This condition would assert itself in the form of uncommon psychic and mystical experiences, as well as physical symptoms such as sudden attacks of fever or skin rashes with no diagnosable medical cause. These signs subsided in his eighth year and didn't return until he was 17.

> At 21 he went through a despair that yielded two insights which would be crucial to his philosophy. The first was that there is only one reality or transcendental consciousness; the second is that this reality is man's true identity and anything else is a product of an un-enlightened mind. For the next few years he sequestered himself in spiritual disciplines, and sought out the company of an

American-born teacher, Swami Rudrananda, who instructed him in Indian kundalini yoga. He then entered a Lutheran seminary at Swami's instruction. At 28 while at the seminary, he underwent another religious experience, and came up with a new insight, that his whole search had been founded on the avoidance of relationships and the recoil from reality in its many forms. The next year he sought out Swami Muktananda in India, and stayed briefly with him there, and during that time the Swami acknowledged that Franklin had reached "yogic liberation."

At 30 he entered the permanent condition of Sahaj Samadhi, essential to transcendental being-consciousness. After this, he was moved to teach others the condition of "the Heart" or the reality in which everything inheres. He spent three years of struggle with students who were not prepared for his teaching, which weakened his physical body.

He returned to India to clarify his teaching, changed his name to "Bubba Free John," as Bubba was his childhood nickname and "Free John" a rendering of Franklin Jones. When he returned to America, he began to teach differently.

At 37 he ceased to have frequent contact with his many followers and lived in seclusion for the next three years. When he was 43, now known as Adi Da, he moved with a group of about 40 followers to the Fijian island of Naitaba, which had been purchased by a wealthy follower. It was his primary residence until the end of his life.

However, accusations that he abused his power as a spiritual leader attracted international attention a couple of years later. In investigative reports and dozens of interviews, both named and anonymous ex-members made numerous specific allegations of Adi Da forcing members to engage in psychologically, sexually, and physically abusive and humiliating behaviour, as well as accusing the church of committing tax fraud.

Two lawsuits were filed against Adi Da and the church in California. One was dismissed the next year; however, the other lawsuit and several threatened suits in subsequent years were settled with payments and confidentiality agreements, negatively impacting member morale and bleeding the organisation financially.[695]

A more positive example is Liz Greene, who is an American-British professional astrologer and author, in addition to being a Jungian analyst and lecturer. She has Sedna in the fifth house of creativity, sextile Uranus, which is conjunct Orcus, the planet of delving down and speaking out, in the seventh house of relationships.

> She is one of the most highly respected astrologers of the 20th century. She co-founded the Centre for Psychological Astrology in London when she was 34 and was co-director for 20 years, before becoming the sole director, a position she continues to hold. In addition she also directs CPA Press, a publishing company that focuses on specialist astrological works.

> At 39 she started co-operating with Alois Treindl, founder of Swiss-based Astrodienst, on the development of computer-generated horoscopes, which would present a person with a chart synthesis, simulating Greene's own method of horoscope interpretation during a personal reading.

> Two years later they presented the Psychological Horoscope Analysis, which was followed by several other interpretations. Greene remains Astrodienst's most popular author.

> She was awarded the Regulus Award for Theory and Understanding when she was 43, recognising the work with other disciplines and philosophical models. Almost all of her many books remain in print, including: *Saturn: A New Look at an Old Devil, Star Signs for Lovers,* and *The Outer Planets and Their Cycles.*[696]

Another is Jeff Green, who is an American astrologer and the author of *Pluto: The Evolutionary Journey of the Soul* and *Uranus: Freedom From the Known,* books that have been translated into ten languages. He has Sedna in the fifth house of creativity, sextile Uranus, which is conjunct Orcus, the planet of delving down and speaking out, in the eighth house of the occult.

---

[695] https://en.wikipedia.org/wiki/Adi_Da
[696] https://en.wikipedia.org/wiki/Liz_Greene

His early family life was brutal. He experienced severe psychological and physical abuse from his mother and he and his brother were sent for a time to an orphanage, before being later returned to family. Always the "black sheep", at an early age, he recounts overhearing his parents say that they didn't care for him. Feeling a strong sense of alienation from both his family and his overall environment, he spent most of his school days at the ocean, where he could "escape" with the accompaniment of the ocean sounds and a surfboard.

He became an alcoholic. One drunken evening, he reached a fatal turning point when he got into a car accident and came to an intense altercation with the other driver. Arrested before a near violent ending, he was offered one of two sentences - go to jail or go to Vietnam. He had already experienced a life of abuse, devastation and trauma, but it was nothing in comparison to the violence and insanity of the war he was about to experience.

"Life made no sense to me; even the idea of God made no sense. I had a very close friend during the war. One day we were bombed and he was reading the Bible when this happened. He got a direct hit, and all that was left when I returned was pieces of flesh and a blood covered Bible. I too had the shared illusion that God is perfect, and did not understand how he allowed such a thing to happen, especially when someone was reading his book... At the age of eighteen this is completely senseless. And so I erased God from my life."

As did many of the soldiers at the time, drugs became his form of emotional survival. One month before being evacuated from Vietnam, another life altering experience occurred. Searching for drugs in a nearby village, he stumbled upon a hill with steps. Climbing to the top, he found a Buddhist monastery. One of the monks approached him, but although the language barrier prevented his ability to converse directly with the monk, he experienced a telepathic communion.

At the end of military service he continued to experience trauma and his roaming eventually took him to Mexico, where he had another extraordinary mystical experience. This time he encountered a Shaman of the Navaho tribe. Like the experience with the Buddhist monk, the language barrier was again surpassed through telepathic communication. He spent six months here, during which time the Shaman initiated him in the sacred peyote experience. While undergoing this time of initiation, which created a lasting shift and expansion of consciousness, he encountered a pack of wolves and developed the ability to communicate telepathically with them. He spent three weeks living as a member of the pack.

The incredible experiences of his life eventually brought him to his true path as teacher and he has lectured throughout the U.S, Canada, Europe and has been a participant in almost all of the major astrological conferences in the world. He is founder and director of the School of Evolutionary Astrology. His pioneering work has expanded the concepts of astrology to encompass a broader vision and greater understanding of the soul's purpose, necessity and desire for evolution.[697]

He is called the founder of Evolutionary Astrology because he first started to lecture on the revolutionary astrological paradigm at 31, after receiving a dream from the spiritual master Swami Sri Yukteswar, who was Yogananda's guru. In that dream the entire paradigm of Evolutionary Astrology was conveyed to Jeffrey.

This was the first time in astrology's long history that a specific paradigm was realized that allowed for an understanding of the evolutionary progression of a Soul from life to life. Jeffrey lectured all over the world on Evolutionary Astrology for 25 years from his early thirties. He established Evolutionary Astrology schools in a number of countries and wrote books on Evolutionary Astrology.

The first of these, Pluto: The Evolutionary Journey of the Soul, Volume I was published at 38. It has been in continuous print ever since and has become one of the all-time best-selling astrology books. Translations have been made into French, German, Dutch, Chinese, Bulgarian, Spanish, Portuguese, Italian, Serbian and other languages. Volume II, Pluto: The Soul's Evolution through Relationships was published when he was 52 and has been in continuous print.

---

[697] Ibid.

Since starting his original Pluto School at 48, he had many students, a number of whom are now professional Evolutionary Astrologers. He personally counseled over 30,000 clients in his lengthy career. This exposure to so many Souls from so many different backgrounds and orientations allowed him to come to the deepest possible understandings of the nature of the Soul. He communicated these insights through all of his teachings.[698]

Semi-square, Square, Sesquiquadrate,

With the stressful aspects between Sedna and Uranus, the all-encompassing spiritual energy of Sedna challenges our rebelliousness, our individuality, our sense of discovery and our intuition.

Uranus represents the spark of intuition that spurs invention. The energies of Uranus are electric and filled with change. Uranus is forward-looking. It balks at tradition and celebrates originality and individuality. Uranus is associated with technology, innovation, discovery, and all that is progressive.

When Uranus is not developed, it reacts; but when we are truly in tune with its energies, Uranus is highly intuitive. The responsibility here is to foster our unique self, as it is challenged and, in turn, challenges the wider eco-system.

With the stressful aspects, if we are unconscious of our Sedna, or there are other stressful aspects to either planet, we can encourage the negative expression of Uranus into our lives, which is rebelliousness without a cause and irresponsibility.

Like Abraham Kasparian, who is a former American politician who stabbed his wife three times in a public restaurant. He has Sedna in the fifth house of romance and children, square Uranus, which is conjunct Makemake, the planet of devotion, in the eighth house of life and death.

> His wife had filed for a divorce but agreed to meet him for lunch. She survived the attack. He had been arrested previously for welfare fraud and larceny. Earlier that same day, a former tenant sued the couple, charging them with negligence in connection with an apartment fire that killed two children.[699]

---

[698] http://schoolofevolutionaryastrology.com/about
[699] https://www.astro.com/astro-databank/Kasparian,_Abraham

With the stressful aspects at the unconscious level there is a chance we might be the victim of abuse and, unfortunately, we may play along with this, encouraging the behaviour in our efforts to deal with it. Like Elizabeth Smart, who is an American who went missing at age fourteen, abducted from her home as her family slept. Her Sedna is in the third house of communication, sesquiquadrate Uranus in the eleventh house of collective consciousness.

> She was the second of six kids and grew up in a close-knit Mormon family, reading scripture and praying morning and evening. On the evening just before her disappearance, she and her family had attended an award ceremony at her middle school, where she was recognised for various school accomplishments. The family prayed together and kissed goodnight; however, sometime in the early morning hours, a man entered the bedroom she shared with her younger sister and spirited her away.[700]

Her Sedna is also closely opposite her conjunction of Pluto, the planet of transformation, and the Sun, the planet of willpower, in the ninth house of knowledge.

> No ransom note was found and no trace of her was reported, until she was spotted walking in a suburb of the same city with a shaggy-haired vagabond nine months later. During her ordeal, she spent a great deal of the time near her home wearing disguises and veils in public. The Smart family believes she was brainwashed, citing that she did not call out for help, or apparently try to escape, even when she heard rescuers call out her name.

> However, nearly two years after her rescue, her father said that she is "just a normal teenager who likes shopping and going to the movies with friends". A self-assured young woman and college graduate, she confronted her kidnapper at his trial and then accepted a job as a contributor for a television network in its coverage of missing persons.[701]

---

[700] https://en.wikipedia.org/wiki/Elizabeth_Smart
[701] Ibid.

Or like Carla Flanagan, who is an American battered wife, whose history of abuse began nine weeks before her wedding. Her Sedna is in the fourth house of home, square Uranus, which is conjunct Makemake the planet of devotion and Jupiter the planet of expansion, all in the eighth house of life and death.

> In what prosecutors called one of the worst cases of domestic abuse her husband admitted to ritualistically beating her, his son and two daughters with bats, chair legs and sticks in an attempt to control their every move. He lacked self-esteem, self-worth and self-dignity after losing six jobs and was affected by the pressure of his wife, a nurse, being the sole "bread winner" of the family. She now suffers chronic headaches and other stress-related ailments.[702]

Sedna is also in a fateful inconjunct with Juno, the asteroid of partnership, in the ninth house of knowledge, and opposite Venus, the planet of relationships, and Ceres, the planet of nurturing, and Neptune, the planet of deception, all in the tenth house of social standing.

> He threatened to kill his three children if they told anybody of the frequent beatings they received, which were administered in areas where he hoped bruises wouldn't be noticeable, authorities said. And the judge said Flanagan only permitted his children to use the bathroom with his permission, beating them if they failed to comply with his authority.

> A Department of Social Services investigation that found he beat his three children, between the ages of 7 and 15, with a variety of weapons, including sticks and baseball bats. He also threatened to kill his wife of 18 years, on multiple occasions and has been accused of two counts of attempted murder, for twice attempting to strangle her.

> His daily activity included keeping a detailed journal, lists or notes of every minute observation he made inside and outside the house, every car that passed, every person he saw. He obsessively compiled these notes for hours and, all the while,

---

[702] Flanagan gets 9-11 years; Apologizes to family for abuse by David Linton, Sun Chronicle, Mar 30, 2000

demanded complete silence from his family under penalty of violent beatings."[703]

Fortunately, her Sedna is also in an evolutionary bi-quintile with Mercury, the planet of communication. She still limps and the kids are learning not to wince. And they still have nightmares and are all in counselling. However, she now counsels other women trying to leave untenable situations and she is working on a book to help women recognise and reject the victim syndrome.

Or we could develop an abusing attitude ourselves. Like John Hinckley, an American attempted assassin, who shot and wounded President Reagan when he was 25. He has Sedna in the second house of material reality, square Uranus, which is conjunct Jupiter, the planet of expansion, and Makemake, the planet of devotion, all in the sixth house of daily routine.

> The year before he shot Reagan, he went to Ted Kennedy's office and waited for three hours with a loaded gun to see the Senator, before he gave up on the assassination attempt and left. He was found not guilty by reason of insanity and sentenced to an asylum for the mentally ill in Washington, DC.

> Prior to the assassination attempt upon President Reagan, he wrote a string of love letters to actress Jodie Foster. Then at 27, he met a woman who was a patient in the same facility for the shotgun murder of her ten-year-old daughter, followed by her own suicide attempt. She was 12 years older. They were both in the hell of their mental illness, anguish and despair and their growing friendship led to improvement for both of them. Their long hours of talks led to love and he asked her to marry him.

> A couple of years later she was able to function responsibly in society and was released. His progress was slower however they were able to see each other on weekends and kiss goodbye, feeling like a couple of teenagers. During the Christmas holidays, the young lovers spent time alone for the first time when he was allowed to spend a day with his family. His sexual experience was limited to a few encounters with prostitutes shortly before the assassination attempt. They were

---

[703] http://www.southcoasttoday.com/article/19990924/news/309249958

not able to consummate their relationship, but the promise of a future together was a strong incentive to healthy responsibility.

During the next five years, his progress was interspersed with unsettling relapses. His psychological evaluations took a turn for the worse. A report from this period read, "The issues of poor judgment, need for ego-gratification through the media, isolation from others at all but a superficial level, grandiosity, suspiciousness, defiance in the face of narcissistic injury, refusal to accept responsibility for his actions other than in a fleeting way, emotional volatility, tendency to lie, lack of empathy for others, sense of entitlement - all remain as unresolved therapeutic issues." His ability to maintain a stable relationship with his fiancé was a plus.

At 35, he was living in a medium-security ward and was working four hours a day in a clerical position. The next year he was allowed to walk with his fiancé without an escort around the hospital grounds. Not long after this, they had sexual relations for the first time and he was moved to a minimum-security ward. A divided appeals court finally ruled when he was 43 that he could make supervised day trips away from the mental hospital where he has lived for the past 18 years to visit his family and friends, a process of gradual re-entry into society. Four years later he was granted unsupervised visits with his parents, but it would be 14 more years before he was released from institutional psychiatric care at 61.[704]

As we tire of density and the grief it creates, and we start a spiritual journey to get out of the swamp, Sedna rewards us with transcendent crises, experiences which force us to let go and rise above them, resulting in a huge growth to a new level of consciousness. There is no choice with these crises, and the more we try and solve them, the more we will get hurt.

The responsibility here is to foster our unique self, as it is being challenged and, in turn, challenge the wider eco-system. And the key is to solving any tensions we are experiencing is to focus on the positive Uranian traits, which are enlightenment, progressiveness, objectivity, novelty, and ingenuity.

---

[704] https://en.wikipedia.org/wiki/John_Hinckley_Jr.

Like our case study, Steve Jobs, who was an American entrepreneur, one of the originators of the computer revolution, co-founder of Apple Computers and Pixar Animation Studios. He had Sedna conjunct Mars in the eighth house of power and control, square to Uranus, which is in the tenth house of profession, together with Jupiter, the planet of expansion, and Makemake, the planet of extreme talent, just across the cusp in the eleventh house of ideals. So this represents ideals based technology and talent together with professional expansion.

He and his friend, Steve Wozniak, made their first circuit board in their garage and they called it the Apple. By the time he was 24, his Apple Corporation was worth $10 million. A year later, its value had grown to $100 million. Its graphical user interface, business applications and word processing won kudos, and millions cheered while Apple took on IBM and its personal computer.

However, he was called a 'haunted house' by Chrisann Brennan, a high school sweetheart who lived with him and was an early Apple employee. She said he became a threatening monster and their relationship fell apart amid wild recriminations when she became pregnant with his first child. He denied he was the father, despite a positive paternity test and he paid a pittance in child support, while living the life of a millionaire. In her memoir she says:

"I've truly hated Steve at times, but never for very long. Sharing a daughter with him has forced me to think about things more deeply. Steve the saint, the alien, the despot, the punishing masculine god, the liar, the obsessed narcissist, the cult hero, the ID of the iEverything, the genius and the motherless boy."[705]

> As the Apple empire grew, Steve became a tyrant, subject to moody outbursts and gloomy silences. Hard feelings arose and power struggles with other executives ensued. He resigned and the following year co-founded NeXt, in an attempt to do for the hardware industry, what he had down for software. He also bought a company which he renamed Pixar Animation Studios and negotiated a deal with Disney to distribute Pixar's films and became a Disney partner. Under Jobs' leadership, Pixar won 20

---

[705] Brennan, Chrisann. *The Bite In The Apple: A Memoir Of My Life With Steve Jobs*

Academy awards for successful animated feature films and was acquired by Disney.[706]

With a twist of fate and a large amount of Sednian transcendence, he then convinced Apple to buy NeXt and was invited back to Apple as interim CEO and a few years later was made permanent CEO once again. Under his renewed leadership Apple computer became a major player in the computer industry once more and his team created visually aesthetic computers in bright colours that appealed to younger buyers.

Or like our case study, Rachel Carson, who was the mother of the environmental movement. She had Sedna in the first house of identity, square Uranus, which was in her tenth house of profession. Uranus represents an awakening, and through her work exposing the danger of pesticides on the environment, particularly through her book, *Silent Spring*, this is what she achieved.

> *Silent Spring* chronicled the devastating effects of the overuse of pesticides. The book was startling for its rigorous scientific assessment of how, by spraying for one issue, to get rid of a bug or a weed, without considering how the chemicals would impact everything else, people were often doing more harm than good. It was a beautifully written treatise of horrors aimed at a general audience.

> As a child she loved the outdoors, the birds and plants around her family's rural property sparking her imagination. She found fossilised fish and inspired by her expeditions wrote a book at age 8 and was published in a literary magazine at 13.

> At age eight she wrote a book and a few years later joined an underage literary elite with published works in a children's magazine which also published early writings by William Faulkner, F. Scott Fitzgerald, E. E. Cummings, and E. B. White. Carson was fond of noting that she had become a professional writer at age eleven.

> She entered the Pennsylvania College for Women on a senatorial district scholarship, earning an English degree, as preparation to become a writer. However it was biology that she found most thrilling during her undergraduate years. Biology

---

[706] https://en.wikipedia.org/wiki/Steve_Jobs

gave her the tools to learn what had happened to that fossilised fish she found as a child.

After earning a master's in zoology from Johns Hopkins, she found part-time work at the US Bureau of Fisheries. Though she'd chosen science over prose, her former specialty proved useful in her new occupation. Carson's first assignment for the bureau was to write a fifty-two-episode radio program called 'Romance Under the Waters'. "I had given up writing forever, I thought. It never occurred to me that I was merely getting something to write about."

Her first book, *Under the Sea-Wind*, was a commercial failure, selling only two thousand copies. She needed a couple of years to recover from the blow, but both driven and strapped for cash, she wrote another book. *The Sea Around Us* was published when she was 44 and it won the National Book Award for nonfiction and solidified her position as a literary heavyweight. To this day, it's credited as being one of the most successful books ever written about nature.

In her fifties she turned her attention to conservation, especially some problems that she believed were caused by synthetic pesticides. The result was the book, *Silent Spring*, published when she was 55, which brought environmental concerns to an unprecedented share of the American people. Although it was met with fierce opposition by chemical companies, it spurred a reversal in national pesticide policy, which led to a nationwide ban on DDT and other pesticides. It also inspired a grassroots environmental movement that led to the creation of the U.S. Environmental Protection Agency.[707]

Or like Spike Milligan was a British director and writer best known for "The Goon Show," which began as a radio series when he was 33. He had Sedna in the second house of material resources, semi-square Uranus in the first house of identity.

The son of a British military man, he was raised in India, Burma and Ceylon, arriving in England at 15. He started his career as a singer, trumpet player and guitar player. His big break came in

---

[707] https://en.wikipedia.org/wiki/Rachel_Carson

his 30s in a show called "Crazy People," which eventually became the legendary "Goon Show." He wrote much of his own comedy material for the show as well as many TV vehicles.

In addition to radio and TV scripts, he also wrote several comedy novels and a book of nonsense and verse, in spite of his own lifetime battle with depression. Diagnosed as being bi-polar, he was noted for being difficult and demanding to work with. His career on screen never matched his success on radio and TV but his books and comedy recordings maintained their popularity long after the end of the Goons and he received a Lifetime Achievement Award given at the British Comedy Awards in at the age of 76.[708]

As we see, humour can be one path to transcend the quicksand of Sedna, giving us the objectivity to step back from the edge, but also with the stressful aspects to Uranus an embrace of the unique, the bizarre and the unusual. Those of us struggling with the tensions of these aspects would be well advised to develop our sense of humour.

I also have a square to Uranus, which is in my seventh house of relationships, but it is exactly conjunct Makemake, the trickster dwarf planet signifying intense focus and talent, so, until Makemake was discovered, I couldn't understand why others didn't find Uranus to be as much fun as I did. Both planets are also conjunct my Jupiter, the planet of expansion, so this is the other half of my tenth house Juno/Ixion clown work, but this is my clown adventure, throwing myself out into the world, working mostly in an improvised way and seeing what happens. This has been a big research into people.

Sandra Bernhard also has a square. She is an American comedienne, tall, skinny, aggressive, ultra-hip and manic. She has Sedna in the tenth house of profession, square to Uranus, which is together with Jupiter, the planet of expansion, and Makemake, the planet of extreme talent, in the twelfth house of the unconscious.

She was born in Flint, Michigan, to a proctologist father and an abstract-artist mother. After she graduated she spent eight months in Israel on a kibbutz. She then moved to Los Angeles where she lived with an aunt and uncle and went to beauty

---

[708] https://en.wikipedia.org/wiki/Spike_Milligan

school to learn how to be a manicurist, while pursuing her comedy career. Her early stand-up comedy acts were not major successes initially.

She became hot property in her late 20s, after working for five years as a manicurist and stand-up comic prior to landing a lead role in *The King of Comedy* with Robert de Niro, released when she was 28. She did nightclubs, TV and films. She is most remembered for playing lesbian Nancy Bartlett on the television show *Roseanne* for six years from the age of 36. She has one daughter, Cicely, born when she was 43. She has never said who the father is, nor how the child was conceived, but she is openly bisexual and is a strong supporter of gay rights.[709]

And so does David Shiner, who is an American actor and clown. He has Sedna in tenth house of profession, square Uranus, which is conjunct Juno, the asteroid of partnership, and Makemake, the planet of extreme talent, all in the twelfth house of the unconscious and right on his Ascendant. He built an early reputation working regularly in the streets at the Avignon Festival in France, drawing huge crowds to watch his antics on the castle walls of the old city and making a fortune in the hat.

He performed in the 2000 Broadway musical, 'Seussical' and has movie appearances as a clown and as an actor, including *Lorenzo's Oil*, which was released when he was 39. He has also toured solo shows in Europe and America and at 37 was featured in Cirque du Soleil's production Nouvelle Expérience, touring for 19 months through Canada and the USA and playing for another year in Las Vegas. With his antics, including stepping through, on and over much of the crowd and the staging of a mock silent-movie melodrama with four members of the audience, he may be the best-remembered of the Cirque's clowns.[710]

At this juncture in human evolution, few of us use our planets at the spiritual level, but many of us are striving to, and such people are wonderful to be around. As with the other planets, the spiritual level of evolution is vastly different with Sedna from the two previous levels.

---

[709] https://en.wikipedia.org/wiki/Sandra_Bernhard
[710] https://en.wikipedia.org/wiki/David_Shiner_(clown)

Here, the stressful aspects bring an inventive, open minded approach to the challenges we perceive.

Once we embrace the Sedna energy, which is the oneness of everything, our nurturing becomes an expression of Sedna consciousness and it becomes devotional in nature. The struggle of the beginner's level is gone, as are the transcendental crises of the intermediate level. At this level everything Saturnian is meaningless and yet everything Sednian has its place.

Karl Marx was a German-Jewish communist and philosopher who developed the theory of socialism and was the father of modern social science. He had Sedna in the first house of identity, square Uranus in the tenth house of profession. He pushed the boundaries of human development with his ideas on society.

His Sedna is also quintile Mercury in the third house of communication and bi-quintile to Pholus, the centaur of catalyzing change, in the eighth house of shared resources. This explains how his ideas and writing about social ideals involving a change in the distribution of social resources made him the powerful evolutionary change agent that he was.

> For him social change was about conflict between opposing interests, driven, in the background, by economic forces. This became the inspiration for the body of works known as the conflict theory. In his evolutionary model of history, he argued that human history began with free, productive and creative work that was over time coerced and dehumanised, a trend most apparent under capitalism. Fundamentally, he assumed that human history involves transforming human nature, which he saw, in a very Sednian way, as encompassing both human beings and material objects.
>
> He believed, like the philosopher Hegel, that humans recognise that they possess both actual and potential selves and that self-development begins with an experience of internal alienation. In the new society that would emerge, he reasoned that the self-alienation would end, and humans would be free to act without being bound by the labour market. It would be a democratic society, enfranchising the entire population. In such a utopian

world there would also be little if any need for a state, the goal of which was only to enforce the alienation.[711]

Walden Welch was a California astrologer and psychic. He had Sedna in the eighth house of sensitivity to the spirit world, semi-square Uranus, which is conjunct Mars, the planet of action, and Vesta, the asteroid of regeneration, in the tenth house of profession.

> His career began at the age of 17 when he moved to San Francisco and started doing psychic readings. At 18 he began using astrological charts for more accuracy in the timing of his predictions. He moved to San Francisco the following year and studied under spiritual teachers and started following the writings of the 'sleeping prophet', Edgar Cayce. He credited the teachings of Cayce as his greatest influence.

> When he was 24 he moved to Sonoma, where he and his homosexual partner opened an antique shop. While his partner operated the successful antique business, Walden did readings for many years from his spacious office in the back of the building. They married when he was 64, after 45 years of relationship, as soon as California law allowed it. His career also included lecturing and appearing on radio and television shows and for five years he hosted his own television shows, *Walden Welch, Astrologer*, and *Star Talk*.[712]

Chidvilasananda is a female Indian guru known as Gurumayi. She has Sedna in the eighth house of metaphysical studies, square Uranus, which is conjunct Makemake, the planet of devotion, and Vesta, the asteroid of regeneration, in the eleventh house of collective consciousness. She became one of the guru Muktananda's two successors at the time of his death when she was 27. She had formerly been his translator. She and her followers practice Siddha Yoga. The group is based in India but maintains centres throughout the world.

> As a Siddha Guru she carries out her mission of awakening seekers to their own potential for enlightenment and describes the essence of her vision for all human beings like this: In truth the gift of life must always be recognised and never be taken for

---

[711] https://en.wikipedia.org/wiki/Karl_Marx
[712] https://www.astro.com/astro-databank/Welch,_Walden

granted. Why is life so precious? In Siddha Yoga philosophy we recognise that in this human life we have a rate opportunity. We can transform an ordinary perception of this universe, into an extraordinary vision. To be on this planet and to behold the universe from the divine perspective is a sign of an illuminated heart. To put this vision to use in the best way possible is a human being's highest duty.[713]

Alan Oken is an American astrologer and a student of the works and teachings of the Tibetan Master Djwahl Khul. He has Sedna conjunct Mercury, the planet of communication, and also Varuna, the planet of notability, in the fifth house of creativity, semi-square Uranus in the seventh house of relationships.

> He is a translator, teacher, global traveler and international tour guide, who lectures in five languages and does natal horoscope readings in seven. He is the author of a dozen titles, including *Soul-Centered Astrology*, *Rulers of the Horoscope*, and *Alan Oken's Complete Astrology*. In addition, he has written hundreds of articles for Dell Horoscope Magazine and many other national and international reviews and journals. Alan was the Director of The Wisdom School in Santa Fe, is co-founder of the Australian Institute for the Development of Consciousness and was Director of Esoteric Studies in Lisbon.[714]

And finally, Pope Pius XII was an Italian ecclesiastic and Pope of the Roman Catholic Church. He wrote many encyclicals making it easier for Catholics to participate in the church. His Sedna is in his fifth house of creativity, sesquiquadrate Uranus conjunct the MC in the tenth house of profession.

> Born into a family devoted to the papal service, he worked so hard at the Seminary that his health gave way and he was forced to leave, however Pope Leo XIII allowed him to live at home while completing his courses, until he was ordained. During World War I he was involved in humane efforts and was sent to Berlin to be its first nuncio, papal ambassador. He left Germany

---

[713] http://www.siddhayoga.org/gurumayi-chidvilasananda
[714] https://www.alanoken.com/about/

to be made cardinal and then became secretary of state for the Vatican, before being crowned Pope.[715]

His Sedna is also in a fateful inconjunct with Pallas, the asteroid of wisdom, in the twelfth house of the unconscious.

At the beginning of World War II he spoke out against the Nazis, helping Jews with false baptismal certificates and allowing thousands to stay in Vatican City, convents and cloisters.[716]

In-conjunct

With the evolutionary inconjunct between Sedna and Uranus the esoteric spiritual energy of Sedna bursts into our rebelliousness, our individuality, our sense of discovery and our intuition in an evolutionary way and we have a fated role to play.

The inconjunct sometimes acts as a flow and at other times as a stress, so we have to learn to actively manage the process as the rarified spiritual energy sometimes reinforces our sense of discovery and, at other times, isn't there to back us up. By adjusting to this, we gain a deeper understanding of ourselves and how to play our role.

Uranus represents the spark of intuition that spurs invention. The energies of Uranus are electric and filled with change. Uranus is forward-looking. It balks at tradition and celebrates originality and individuality. Uranus is associated with technology, innovation, discovery, and all that is progressive.

When we are truly in tune with our Uranus energy it is highly intuitive. It represents the spark of intuition that spurs invention, further studies, or investigation and the bursts of Sedna energy from the inconjunct deepen this process. As we develop this aspect, we will be able to explore our intuitive investigations so deeply, that people may call it genius.

At the unconscious level however, we might call the negative expression of Uranus into our lives, which is rebelliousness without a cause and irresponsibility. With the inconjunct aspect at this level there is a chance we might be the victim of abuse which might come from an unexpected quarter.

---

[715] https://en.wikipedia.org/wiki/Pope_Pius_XII
[716] Ibid.

Like Holly Piirainen, who was an American homicide victim at the age of ten. She had Sedna in the first house of identity, inconjunct Uranus, which is conjunct Jupiter, the planet of expansion, in the eighth house of life and death.

> She was visiting her grandparents when she disappeared, after she and her five-year-old brother walked up the road to see some new puppies at a neighbour's house. When the dogs began to bark, her brother ran home. Holly's mom sent the other two brothers to bring her home, but they could not find her. One of her sneakers was found near the dog pen. The country mobilised with an immediate search but there was no sign of the girl. Her body was found by hunters in the woods five months later, about five miles from where she had disappeared.[717]

Or we might just be fated to be in the wrong place at the wrong time, like Mark Benton, who was an American murder victim at 22. He had Sedna in the twelfth house of the unconscious, inconjunct Uranus, which was conjunct Jupiter, the planet of expansion, in the sixth house of daily routine.

> A judge decided that a 43-year-old unemployed auto mechanic was insane when he opened fire with a rifle from the third-story attic of his family's Brockton home, killing Mark who was walking down the street and wounding two others who came to his aid. The killer was committed to Bridgewater State Hospital. Five years later he was released to a civil commitment, which means a state medical official successfully petitioned for him to remain hospitalized because, due to his mental illness, he would pose a threat to others if released.[718]

Or it might put us in a helpless fateful position, like Allison Darling, who was an American teenager killed in a car accident at 14. She had Sedna in the tenth house of social standing, inconjunct Uranus, which is conjunct the Moon, representing her feelings, in the fifth house of creativity. She and three other girls were on their way to school in a car driven by her sister, when the car hit a patch of rain-filmed road and hydroplaned. Her sister lost control and they careened across the dividing line into the path of an oncoming pick-up truck, killing Allison.

---

[717] https://www.astro.com/astro-databank/Piirainen,_Holly
[718] http://www.enterprisenews.com/article/20121014/News/310149877

Unfortunately, we may play along with abusive ideas, turning it into a game and encouraging the behaviour in our efforts to deal with it. Like Melissa Poirier and Melody Maillet, who were American teenage suicides. Melissa had Sedna conjunct Saturn, the planet of physical reality, in the ninth house of belief, inconjunct Uranus in the second house of material reality. Melody also had Sedna inconjunct Uranus, but her Sedna was in the eleventh house of ideals and her Uranus in the fourth house of home. Both were popular students with many friends. However, consumed with adolescent angst and listening to morbid punk music, "Sick as a Dog" by Arrowsmith, they killed themselves with a 12-gauge shotgun in the bathroom of Melissa's home. They were 15. Both girls left loving notes behind.

Or we may develop abusive tendencies ourselves. Like Francisco Franco, who was a Spanish military general, long-time ruler and dictator who commanded his country for 36 years with an iron hand. He had Sedna in the seventh house of relationships, inconjunct Uranus, which is conjunct Venus, the planet of values, in the second house of material resources.

> A man of tremendous determination, he led rebel forces during the Spanish Civil War and went on to become Chief of State. He maintained a strong anti-communist policy, though many disapproved of his methods. The son of a naval paymaster, he entered a military academy at age 15, graduating at 18 and rising rapidly through the ranks.

> By the time he was 33, he was the youngest general in Europe. At 44, he began a revolt against the republic and three years later, became dictator of Spain. Called "El Caudillo," he joined Hitler and Mussolini in an alliance of the Axis powers as both Germany and Italy had supported him during his take-over of the government. He refused Hitler's request to be part of World War II. At 81 he relinquished his position as premier, but continued to be Head of State.[719]

If we are unconscious of our Sedna, or there are other stressful aspects to either planet, we can encourage the negative expression of Uranus into our lives, which is rebelliousness and drug abuse. Like Dorothy Parker, who was an American humorist, one of the most famous for her

---

[719] https://en.wikipedia.org/wiki/Francisco_Franco

exceptional wit and corrosive style. She had Sedna in the twelfth house of the unconscious, inconjunct Uranus in the sixth house of daily routine.

She authored short stories, plays, a handful of poems and a slight amount of bitchy journalism. By the time she was in her 20s, she was the most quoted woman in America. Her mother died when she was four. She adored her dad but loathed the woman he re-married. The reviled step-mother died when she was nine.

Awaking to politics at a Boston demonstration at 34, she became concerned with race relations, the support of Spanish loyalists and the championing of the writer's guild and other political causes. She helped form an Anti-Nazi league at 43, but her flirtation with the Communist Party brought her to McCarthy's attention, and she later said she'd been blackballed. Friends tended to be mystified by her radicalism, as her luxurious Hollywood home and lavish life style furnished an unlikely backdrop for left-wing fund-raisers.

She had two broken marriages and a number of unhappy love affairs; both husbands were alcoholics. Her first mate came back from WWI addicted to morphine. She married and divorced Alan Campbell twice during their 30-year relationship, with the second marriage to him at 57. Their strain was primarily due to his homosexuality, fuelled by an easy flow of alcohol. Of the many men in her life, not one could be called a healthy relationship. As a result, she drank to excess for decades and made four suicide attempts. She had appeal, style, brains and celebrity but did not find happiness or peace. With no kids, she devoted love to her many dogs.[720]

As we tire of density and the grief it creates, and we start a spiritual journey to get out of the swamp, Sedna rewards us with transcendent crises, experiences which force us to let go and rise above them, resulting in a huge growth to a new level of consciousness. There is no choice with these crises, and the more we try and solve them, the more we will get hurt.

---

[720] https://en.wikipedia.org/wiki/Dorothy_Parker

Jessica Lynch was an American Marine assigned to the Iraq War. An adorable 19-year-old honey-blonde, Jessica was captured in an Iraqi raid. She has Sedna conjunct the Sun in the twelfth house of karma and the unconscious, inconjunct Uranus, which is together with Jupiter, the planet of justice, in the seventh house of relationships.

> In a Special Ops raid, US soldiers wearing night goggles brought helicopters into the southern Iraqi city to carry out a daring rescue raid. The petite soldier was held in a second-floor room with fractures in both legs, her right arm, ankle and foot. Intelligent briefings relate that some of her wounds were the results of extensive torture.
>
> She came up missing after Iraqi forces ambushed an Army supply convoy near four days before her 20th birthday. The details of her imprisonment and her rescue were subsequently much discussed in the news with reports that the U.S. military exaggerated the rescue. There was also a question about whether she was tortured, or whether all her injuries were sustained in the fighting just before her capture.
>
> A book written by Rick Bragg with her help, *I'm a Soldier Too*, was released and a TV biopic was produced and televised. The book alleges that she was raped while in captivity and that she does not remember this mistreatment. Iranian doctors dispute that she was raped, but she underwent rigorous physical therapy and treatment for her serious injuries and emotional trauma.
>
> Nevertheless at 24 she appeared before a House Committee on Oversight and Government Reform and testified that the tales about her capture in Iraq were not true, that they were embellished to make her seem like a hero. She said, "The bottom line is the American people are capable of determining their own ideals for heroes and they don't need to be told elaborate tales.[721]

J. Paul Getty was an American entrepreneur in real estate and the oil business whose estate was valued at $2 to $4 billion. He had Sedna in the second house of material resources, inconjunct Uranus, which is conjunct his Moon and the MC in the tenth house of profession.

---

[721] https://en.wikipedia.org/wiki/Jessica_Lynch

At 61 he became the world's richest man by striking oil in the Middle East, but he was notoriously cheap, at one time putting a pay phone in his English castle for house guests to use. He was also vain and had periodic facial cosmetic surgery.

An only child, he was raised by a mother who was deaf and dour and he grew indifferent toward her. His dad was a strong influence, a hard-working Christian Scientist who amassed considerable wealth in the oil business. He worked in his dad's oil fields for a year when he was 22, after which he bought an interest in an Oklahoma field where he began his own production. On his dad's death, he inheriting $15 million that he then parlayed into an empire.

With a strong sex drive, he was a lifelong philanderer noted for his prowess and it was reported in a biography that he had a penis close to 9" long. He married five times to women who gave him five sons. The family was too dysfunctional to be called a dynasty, but splintered into generations of divorce, drug abuse and suicide.

When his oldest grandson was kidnapped by Italian gangsters when he was 81, he responded with the same hard edge that made him the world's wealthiest man. He refused to pay the demanded $3.2 million, afraid that doing so would jeopardise the lives of all of his kin. The kidnappers hacked off 16-year-old Jean Paul III's right ear and mailed it to a Rome newspaper. The boy was released when Getty reluctantly loaned the boy's dad part of the money at 4% interest.

He was afraid of flying. He wrote three autobiographies. His primary hobby was that of filling his country estate with mistresses - as many as five at a time in residence. He made a parlour game out of revising his will, manipulating the obsequious by promising reward. Finally, he left half of his estate to his museum.

He died of cancer of the prostate at 84. After his death there were a series of lawsuits generated over his money. Twenty years later the $1 billion Getty Center opened in Los Angles with a world-class collection of classical art. He was an avid art collector and left $700 million for the creation of the extraordinary museum.[722]

Helen Crawfurd was a Scottish suffragette and communist activist. She had Sedna in the twelfth house of the unconscious, inconjunct Uranus in the fifth house of creativity.

Her father was a Catholic but converted to the Church of Scotland, and was a conservative trade unionist. Initially religious herself, she married the Reverend Alexander Crawfurd at 21, but became increasingly radical.

She first became active in the women's suffrage movement in her early twenties, then at 32 she switched her support to the more radical Women's Social and Political Union. Two years later she smashed the windows of the Minister for Education and received one month in prison. The following year, she was twice arrested for protesting in Glasgow, received another month in prison, and went on a five-day hunger strike. Following one more arrest, she left the Women's Political Union in protest at its support of WWI and joined the Independent Labour Party.

During the war, she was involved with the Red Clydeside movement, including rent strikes and became secretary of the Women's Peace Crusade. When she was 40 her husband died, and she was also elected as vice-chair of the Scottish division of the ILP. Shortly after, she was a founder member of the ILP's left-wing faction, which campaigned for it to affiliate to the Communist International. When this policy was defeated, she joined the new Communist Party of Great Britain, within which she served on the Central Committee, and was involved with various journalistic projects. She also became secretary of Workers' International Relief.[723]

At this juncture in human evolution, few of us use our planets at the spiritual level, but many of us are striving to, and such people are wonderful to be around. As with the other planets, the spiritual level of evolution is vastly different with Sedna from the two previous levels. Here, the inconjunct brings an inventive, open-minded approach to the

---

[722] https://en.wikipedia.org/wiki/J._Paul_Getty
[723] https://en.wikipedia.org/wiki/Helen_Crawfurd

fated challenges in our lives enabling us to explore them so deeply, that people may call it genius.

Once we embrace the Sedna energy, which is the oneness of everything, our nurturing becomes an expression of Sedna consciousness and it becomes devotional in nature. The struggle of the beginner's level is gone, as are the transcendental crises of the intermediate level. At this level everything Saturnian is meaningless and yet everything Sednian has its place.

Albert Einstein was a German-Swiss-American scientist, a physicist who developed the theory of relativity and the general theory, laying the groundwork for 20th century physics and providing the essential structure of the cosmos. He had Sedna conjunct Saturn, and Mercury, the planet of ideas and communication, all in the tenth house of profession, inconjunct Uranus in the third house of ideas. If there is a mark of genius, this could be it. His name is synonymous with genius and the scientific definitions of the modern age from the atomic bomb, to space travel, electronics and quantum physics.

And if we look closer, we see that his Uranus is actually at the tip of a Finger of Fate, which is two inconjuncts with the same planet at the tip. The second inconjunct is from the Node, which represents Einstein's point of dharma, that's the karma he created as he lived. The Node is in the eighth house of shared resources, and so the Finger of Fate illustrates how his destiny in his profession and the influence of his dhama on our shared resources would generate a revolution in our way of thinking.

> He was born with a misshapen head and abnormally large body. He learned to talk so late that his parents feared that he was mentally retarded, not until he was three, and was not fluent until he was nine. For a while, he was considered subnormal because of his slow development, and his teachers were continually saying that he would never amount to anything.
>
> His youth seemed to be one of deliberate rebellion against the establishment of his times. At age 16 he quit school, joined his parents in Milan, Italy, where they had moved, and renounced his German citizenship. At 17, he entered the Zurich Polytechnic Institute after having failed on the first try, and graduated with a mathematics teaching degree. The next year he took Swiss

citizenship, and the year after that, a post at the Swiss patent office. It was while at the Swiss patent office, in a clerical position, that Einstein began the work that would make him a legend.

At 26 he published three seminal papers on theoretical physics in a single volume of a German scientific journal and two years later he came up with the immortal e=mc2, better known as the Special Theory of Relativity, encapsulating energy and matter as aspects of a single phenomenon. A year later, while still at the patent office, he began work on his major achievement, the general theory of relativity, which he officially proposed eight years later.

These theories were the greatest challenge to Newtonian mechanics that the modern world had ever known, but Einstein had a way of conceptualising and communicating them. He described relativity thus: 'Put your hand on a hot stove for a minute and it seems like an hour. Sit with a pretty girl for an hour and it seems like a minute.'

Experiencing the universe as a harmonious whole, he encouraged the use of intuition to solve problems, marvelled at the the mystery of God in nature, and applauded the ideals of great spiritual teachers such as Buddha and Jesus. Here's how he put it: 'I like to experience the universe as one harmonious whole. Every cell has life. Matter, too, has life; it is energy solidified. Our bodies are like prisons, and I look forward to be free, but I don't speculate on what will happen to me. I live here now, and my responsibility is in this world now. I deal with natural laws. This is my work here on earth.

'If we want to improve the world we cannot do it with scientific knowledge but with ideals. Confucius, Buddha, Jesus and Gandhi have done more for humanity than science has done.

We must begin with the heart of man, with his conscience, and the values of conscience can only be manifested by selfless service to mankind. Religion and science go together. Science without religion is lame and religion without science is blind. They are interdependent and have a common goal, the search for truth.'

'Without religion there is no charity. The soul given to each of us is moved by the same living spirit that moves the universe. I am not a mystic. Trying to find out the laws of nature has nothing to do with mysticism, though in the face of creation I feel very humble. It is as if a spirit is manifest that is infinitely superior to man's spirit. Through my pursuit in science I have known cosmic religious feelings. But I don't care to be called a mystic.'[724]

Corrie ten Boom was a Dutch heroine and Christian evangelist, famous for the book and the deeds of her noted family in *The Hiding Place*. She had Sedna conjunct Jupiter and also Vesta, the asteroid of regeneration, in the seventh house of relationships, inconjunct Uranus on the cusp of the third house of communication.

During the Second World War her father sheltered Jewish people, who were trying to escape from the Nazi Holocaust at their home. Some thirty-eight Jewish people were saved, but she was the only one in her family to survive the Holocaust.

Her father believed that all people were equal before God and when a desperate Jewish woman appealed to him, he gave her shelter for the Holocaust in his house. Many persecuted Jews and Nazi resisters would follow. Corrie at first had trouble with the necessity of keeping these activities secret. She suffered a moral crisis over the lying, theft, forgery, and bribery that was necessary to keep the Jews that her family was hiding alive.

With help of the Dutch underground, they built a secret room in the top of the building, where the refugees could hide in case of a raid. She was 52 when the house was raided after a tip of an unknown person. That day some 27 persons were in the house, including six Jews that slipped in the hiding place. Twenty-one persons were arrested, including Corrie, her sister and father.

Her father's health was weakened by age and tuberculosis and he was sent to a medical clinic where he died ten days after the arrest of the family. Corrie and her sister were interrogated by the Gestapo, but not tortured. They took all the blame for hiding the Jews, and after four months in prison, they were sentenced

---

[724] https://en.wikipedia.org/wiki/Albert_Einstein

to forced labour. Through their confession, the other arrested guests in their father's house were released.

After the war, she became an evangelist, motivational speaker and social critic, protesting against the Vietnam War. She visited more than 60 countries, not preaching for any particular belief, but believing in a Universal Holy Spirit that asks for peace and forgiveness.[725]

Saint Catherine was a French ecclesiastic, a Roman Catholic nun and visionary. She had Sedna in the fifth house of creativity, inconjunct Uranus, which is conjunct Saturn, the planet of structure, in the twelfth house of institutions and the unconscious. She was born to a successful farming family, and was the ninth of eleven children When she was nine, her mother died and she was raised by aunts until she was eleven. As a child, she attended morning mass several times a week, getting up to walk three kilometres for the 5:30 AM service.

When she was 22 her dad sent her to Paris to work as a maid in his brother's home. She longed to become a nun and a couple of years later she was admitted as a novice at the Seminary of the Charity Nuns of Paris; she had frequent visions of the Lord and of St. Vincent while there. Simple, quiet and unassuming, the other Sisters sometimes teased and ridiculed her about her submissiveness.

A couple of months after her admission to the Seminary, an angel came to wake her and guided her to the Chapel where she had her first apparition of the Blessed Virgin. In this, the most famous of her visions, she was shown the medal of Immaculate Conception and was told to spread devotion. She told no one of her miraculous experience besides her spiritual director, Father Aladel.

Fully convinced of her sincerity, he went to the archbishop and received sanction to strike the medal. Now known as the "Miraculous Medal," it is inscribed with "O Mary conceived without sin, pray for us who have recourse to you!" and is well known throughout the Catholic world. Around this time she also

[725] https://en.wikipedia.org/wiki/Corrie_ten_Boom

foresaw a revelation of the death of the Archbishop during the riots of 1848 and of the Commune of 1870.

Self-effacing and humble, her life was very ordinary aside from these experiences, and she was a woman of high virtue. She spent the next forty-five years keeping mute about her visions, and Father Aladel kept her secret as well. She spent her last years at a convent on the outskirts of Paris, where she tended the poultry. Just prior to her death, however, she spoke of her visions to one of her superiors while attempting to fulfil the Virgin Mary's last request and have a statue made.[726]

Quintile, Bi-quintile

The evolutionary quintile or bi-quintile aspect between Sedna and Uranus infuses our rebelliousness, our individuality, our sense of discovery and our intuition with the all-encompassing spiritual energy of Sedna, to the point where we can push the boundaries of human development.

Quintiles and bi-quintiles point to talent, the desire to create order and to categorize, a fascination with patterns and structures, perfectionist tendencies, and the desire to build or make things. These aspects have the characteristics of both the trine and opposition. They point to awareness of conflicts, or problems and finding solutions for them; however, they do not automatically kick into action and must be cultivated over time.

The energies of Uranus are electric and filled with change. Uranus is forward-looking. It balks at tradition, celebrates originality and is associated with technology, innovation, discovery, and all that is progressive.

When we are truly in tune with our Uranus energy it is highly intuitive. It represents the spark of intuition that spurs invention, further studies, or investigation and, as we develop the quintile and bi-quintile aspects with Sedna, we can see the problems and solutions to those intuitive sparks from the wholistic spiritual perspective and so explore them very deeply and develop an intuitive understanding of the big picture of life.

---

[726] https://en.wikipedia.org/wiki/Catherine_Labouré

At the unconscious level, however, we might still call the Uranian rebelliousness and irresponsibility into our lives, even with these evolutionary aspects.

Like Kurt Cobain, who was the lead singer of Nirvana. He took Ritalin as child, married former actress and strip joint dancer, Courtney Love when she was forming her own punk band, "Hole." The couple easily bonded over their mutual drug habit. Cobain's addiction to heroin fuelled fights between him and his wife and he suffered chronic undiagnosed stomach pains that he believed were relieved by his heroin use.

He had Sedna in the eighth house of life and death, bi-quintile Uranus, which is conjunct Pluto, the planet of life and death, in the twelfth house of the unconscious. He shot himself and left a one-page note written with a red ballpoint pen addressing his unhappiness, "I have felt guilty for so many years...the worst crime is faking it. I don't have any passion any more."

And, even with these aspects, at this level there is still a chance we might be the victim of abuse which might come from an unexpected quarter, or that we play the abuser ourselves. Like Leslie Van Houten, who is an American convicted murderer and former member of the Manson cult Family. She has Sedna in the eighth house of life and death, quintile Uranus in the tenth house of profession.

> She wasn't selected by Manson for the Sharon Tate killings, but she asked to participate a couple of days later when he selected followers for the killings of another couple. She was 20 years old. She was arrested and charged, then convicted and sentenced to death. Despite this ruling, a California Supreme Court subsequently ruled that the death penalty was unconstitutional, resulting in her sentence being commuted to life in prison.

> This conviction was then overturned when she was 27 on a technicality and she was granted a retrial. Her second trial ended with a deadlocked jury and a mistrial. However, at her third trial when she was 29, she was convicted of two counts of murder and one count of conspiracy and sentenced to between 7 years and life in prison. In relation to her case, high courts, parole boards, and the state governor have said that an inexplicable, or racial motive for murder could merit exemplary punishment and outweigh any evidence of subsequent reform, so she has been

denied parole 19 times and is still in jail 48 years later at time of writing.[727]

Or in an extreme case, like Josef Mengele, who was a German doctor and member of the Nazi party. He had Sedna conjunct Orcus, the planet of delving down and speaking out, in the tenth house of profession, quintile Uranus on the cusp of the eighth house of life and death.

> He was known as the 'Angel of Death' at the Auschwitz concentration camp during World War II for his grisly genetic research on twins and other subjects. He was the subject of a 40-year international hunt in the postwar years, known for being the butcher who had supervised the torture and death of as many as 400,000 Jews in a maniacal quest for racial purity.[728]

With these aspects we might seize on some hair brained scheme as the answer to everything, whereas in reality the whole project is simply an antidepressant, giving us a reason to live. Like Timothy McVeigh, who was an American terrorist convicted of committing the largest act of terrorism on American soil. He was 27. He had Sedna conjunct Mercury and also his Sun, his will and sense of self, all in the eleventh house of collective consciousness, bi-quintile Uranus in the fourth house of home.

> He grew up in a small upstate New York town. He had a happy childhood, swimming in his family's pool, hiking and playing with the neighbourhood kids. He enjoyed organising casino games for local kids on the block. His father and mother divorced when he was ten-years-old. He grew closer to his dad, helping him cultivate his vegetable garden. His mom remarried and moved to Florida with his younger sister.

> Looking for excitement, he signed up for the U.S. Army when he was twenty. He took to military life and the comradeship with his fellow troops, becoming a straight-arrow soldier. He was promoted to corporal and then to sergeant. During the Persian Gulf War, he was sent to Iraq as a gunner on a Bradley fighting vehicle. On returning to the States, he sensed a major shift in the U.S. Army. The post-cold-war army downsizing changed his life

---

[727] https://en.wikipedia.org/wiki/Leslie_Van_Houten
[728] https://en.wikipedia.org/wiki/Josef_Mengele

as he watched his companions leave military service. Discharged from the army, he tried to adjust to civilian life.

At 25, he arrived in Waco to watch the standoff between the Branch Davidians cult and federal agents. He wandered around the country as a militant drifter visiting gun shows and selling guns and ammunition from his car. His political views became more racist and far-right as he kept company with political militia groups harbouring anger against the U.S. government. He returned to Waco and declared himself a "non-resident alien." He claimed the U.S. Army had implanted a computer chip in his derriere during his active duty.

Together with accomplices he carried out an ammonium nitrate bombing of a federal building when he was 27, claimed 168 victims between the ages of four months old to 73 years old. The building was the main office for the federal agents who were involved in the Branch Davidian standoff in Waco. Two hours after the bombing, he was stopped by a policeman for a traffic violation 70 miles away. He was almost released until they recognised him as one of the possible suspects in the terrorist act.

His stubborn refusal to express any remorse tormented the families of his victims. His psychiatrist felt that he was committed to the ideal that he must object to a federal government that had become excessively oppressive and deceitful. He was able to rationally make the decision to bomb the building and "fully understood the consequences. He had an underlying depression, but he was not anti-social. It simply became easier to act because he had nothing and he needed an enemy. This whole project was his antidepressant. He intellectualises to avoid emotion, to avoid pain." He was found guilty of conspiracy, use of a weapon of mass destruction, destruction by explosive, and eight counts of first degree murder and was sentenced to death.[729]

Or we might be the victim or the beneficiary of some hair-brained scheme, like the Gosselin Sextuplets, who were American children who were featured in a cable TV reality program *Jon and Kate plus 8*. The

---

[729] https://en.wikipedia.org/wiki/Timothy_McVeigh

three girls and three boys were all born within three minutes. Sedna is conjunct each of their Suns in the twelfth house of karma, quintile Uranus, which is conjunct Vesta, the asteroid of regeneration and the Part of Fortune, all in the tenth house of social standing. This shows their unique karmic experience, growing up in the social spotlight of the tenth house.

> After the success of two one-hour specials on the Discovery Health Channel, chronicling their lives with their mother Kate and her then husband Jon, the series was moved to The Learning Channel. During its run, it was one of the network's highest-rated programs, with the fifth season premiere seen by a record 9.8 million viewers, the most watched show of that evening including broadcast television, twice as many viewers as the show's previous series high.

> The parents had a messy public split up when the children were 5 years old and the series was later renamed *Kate Plus 8*, focusing on Kate as a divorced mother raising the children, with Jon appearing less frequently. However, filming was later suspended due to Jon's lawyers delivering letters demanding that they cease and desist production and barred production crews from the couple's Pennsylvania property. Despite this a second season of *Kate Plus 8* premiered as the children were turning seven and ran for 150 episodes that year, with more seasons following when they were 11 and 12 years.[730]

As we tire of density and the grief it creates, and we start a spiritual journey to get out of the swamp, Sedna rewards us with transcendent crises, experiences which force us to let go and rise above them, resulting in a huge growth to a new level of consciousness. There is no choice with these crises, and the more we try and solve them, the more we will get hurt.

Richard Branson is a British entrepreneur, investor and philanthropist, who is the founder of Virgin Records. He has Sedna in the ninth house of knowledge, quintile Uranus in the eleventh house of collective consciousness.

---

[730] https://en.wikipedia.org/wiki/Kate_Plus_8#Family

His mother was a strong influence on his success, emphasising independence and self-reliance. Basically shy, his public persona is one of bravado, but the private man remains an enigma. At the age of sixteen his first business venture was a magazine called *Student*. He started his record business from the church where he ran the magazine. He started advertising popular records in the magazine and selling them by mail order. It was an overnight success, as he sold records for considerably less than the High Street outlets.

He started a record shop in Oxford Street in London at 20, and the following year, earning enough money from his record store, he launched the record label Virgin Records. By the age of 20, he had a thriving business and 40 employees. Twelve years later, his empire consisted of 50 companies that were giving him a turnover of 50 million pounds and he was ready to expand into the software, film, video and property markets.

His Virgin brand grew rapidly during the 1980s, as he set up Virgin Atlantic airline at 34 and expanded the Virgin Records music label. He launched Virgin Mobile in 1999 and Virgin Blue in Australia (now named Virgin Australia) in 2000. His Virgin Group now controls more than 400 companies, but he has also been involved in many failed business ventures, such as Virgin Cola, Virgin Cars, Virgin Clothing and Virgin Brides.

He wrote in his autobiography of the decision to start an airline: "My interest in life comes from setting myself huge, apparently unachievable challenges and trying to rise above them ... from the perspective of wanting to live life to the full, I felt that I had to attempt it."

He has also made several world record-breaking attempts. His first attempt at the fastest Atlantic Ocean crossing when he was 35, led to the boat capsizing in British waters and a rescue by RAF helicopter, which received wide media coverage. A year later he beat the record by two hours. The following year his hot air balloon "Virgin Atlantic Flyer" crossed the Atlantic. And at 40 he crossed the Pacific from Japan to Arctic Canada, in a balloon. This broke the record, with a speed of 394 km/h.

In his late 40s, he and musician, Peter Gabriel, discussed with the former president of South Africa, Nelson Mandela, their idea of a small group of leaders working to solve difficult global conflicts and Mandela announced the formation of a new group, The Elders which is funded by a group of donors, including Branson and Gabriel. Through the Carbon War Room, founded when he was 59, the entrepreneur is seeking solutions for global warming and the energy crisis.[731]

Julia Child was an American chef and writer of over nine cookbooks, appearing in more than three hundred television shows. She had Sedna in the eleventh house of collective consciousness, quintile Uranus in the ninth hose of publishing.

She achieved celebrity status with her book, *Mastering the Art of French Cooking*, at 50; however, she was raised in a well-to-do family that hired a professional cook to prepare elaborate family meals as her mother couldn't cook. As a 15-year-old student in California, she was a history major with a "C" average and a reputation as a prankster.

She married a member of the Foreign Service and he was assigned to the American embassy in Paris, so from the age of 24 she lived in France for the six years. Her first meal there was a lunch of oysters on a half shell, and this introduction to French food led her to an epiphany and she enrolled in Cordon Bleu, the world-renowned school of French cooking. She then began teaching classes at a cooking school she founded with two Frenchwomen. They became her collaborators on the famous cookbook, *Mastering the Art of French cooking*. Ten years in preparation, it was finished when she was 46 and published three years later.

The year her book was published, she settled in Massachusetts, after her husband's retirement from his job. A year later she began filming her own TV show, *The French Chef*. The popular series began when she was 51 and continued for 206 episodes. A natural clown on camera, she often improvised and joked, charming viewers with her relaxed spontaneity and warbling voice. Unpretentious and outspoken, even in her 80s she

---

[731] https://en.wikipedia.org/wiki/Richard_Branson

continued to lecture and write articles and create new TV cooking shows.[732]

John Cage was an American avant-garde musician and composer, writer, photographer, reporter, and critic. He had Sedna conjunct Chariklo, the centaur of foresight, in the eighth house of shared resources, quintile Uranus in the eleventh house of collective consciousness.

Eclectically talented and endlessly enchanted by the mystery and beauty of the commonplace, he wrote essays and reviews, scores and sketches. He was also a photographer and journalist noted for raucous multimedia works.

The son of an inventor, he was raised in Los Angeles and attended Pomona college before dropping out to go to Europe. While in Europe, he began to write music, much of which he threw away. Back in Los Angeles, he began to compose, a period in which he was very enthusiastic about both modern painting and music. It was at the time of the Depression, and he worked as a gardener in exchange for housing.

When he wrote a solo for clarinet, one of his piano teachers arranged to have it played at a small concert in San Francisco. He hitchhiked to the concert from LA and when the musician said it was too difficult for him to play; he played the piece himself on the piano for the audience.

He spent the last 50 years of his life in New York City, often in the company of his lifelong companion, dancer Merce Cunningham, for whom he wrote many pieces. As his creativity developed, he moved into the role as an extraordinarily important American composer. A documentary, *Cage/Cunningham*, about the long collaboration between the composer and the choreographer was filmed, featuring interviews, archival dance footage and music from the various project the two artist created.[733]

L. Ron Hubbard was an American entrepreneur, engineer, and prolific writer of science fiction, who established the Church of Scientology. He

---

[732] https://en.wikipedia.org/wiki/Julia_Child
[733] https://en.wikipedia.org/wiki/John_Cage

had Sedna in the third house of ideas, quintile Uranus, which is conjunct Mars, the planet of action in the second house of material resources.

> Imaginative, intelligent, and with a mind that was a factory of ideas, he was also broke and in debt in the late 1940s and was forced to sell his typewriter for $28.50 to pay alimony to his first wife. Troubled, restless and adrift he became an expert hypnotist, and shared an ageing mansion in Pasadena, CA with writers, artists, Bohemians and occultists in the late 1940s. Neighbours complained when their rituals of sexual magic got out of hand in the back yard.[734]

His Sedna was also conjunct Orcus, the planet of delving down and speaking out in the fourth house of home, and bi-quintile Ixion, the planet of lawlessness, in the nineth house of knowledge.

> He wrote a book, *Dianetics: The Modern Science of Mental Health,* which was written in one draft in 30 days and became an instant bestseller. He became an overnight celebrity. His system became known as "the poor man's psychotherapy." However, by the following year profits were beginning to fall and Dianetics became Scientology, as he turned from pop therapist to religious leader.

> Skillfully transforming himself from a pulp fiction writer to a writer of "sacred scriptures," Hubbard made a fortune and achieved his dream of fame. Starting as a collection of mental therapy centers it grew into one of the world's most controversial and secretive religions. The courses included instruction of how to help kick drug habits, improve communication skills, build confidence and help people take control of their lives.

> However, by preying on the anxieties and the loneliness of his converts and by using hypnotherapy, Pavlovian conditioning and twisted psychotherapy, he was able to establish himself as the leader of a movement of millions, less than 900 of which ever reached the highest levels of his imparted wisdom. Australian courts have since revoked the status of Scientology as a religion, and France convicted Hubbard in absentia of fraud. However, in

---

[734] https://en.wikipedia.org/wiki/L._Ron_Hubbard

spite of all the exposure, he still ignited the fire of self-improvement in many sincere people.[735]

And finally, case study, Sally Ride, the first American woman in space and the mother of NASA's Planet Earth study, has Sedna in the tenth house of profession, quintile Uranus, which is conjunct the Ascendent in the twelfth house of the unconscious.

Before becoming the first American woman in space and the first known LGBT astronaut, she got a PhD in astrophysics from Stanford and subjected herself to five years of astronaut training at NASA. Navy test pilots took her on gut-dropping, 600-mile-per-hour flights 39,000 feet in the air. Her flight instructor called her the best student he'd ever had.

When Space Shuttle Challenger exploded seventy-three seconds after liftoff, seven of Ride's colleagues died in the accident. She had a total of more than 343 hours in space at that stage and had completed eight months of training for her third space flight when the disaster occurred. She was named to the presidential commission investigating the accident and headed its subcommittee on operations, revealing crucial information that revealed that NASA's push for rapid-fire missions had come at the expense of safety and sacrificed lives.

Following the investigation, she was assigned to NASA headquarters in Washington, D.C., where she led their first strategic planning effort, authored a visionary report titled "NASA Leadership and America's Future in Space" and founded NASA's Office of Exploration with the Mission to Planet Earth to study our planet.

The goal of the Mission to Planet Earth was to use space technology to understand Earth as a total system, to learn how man-made and natural shifts affect the environment. When NASA adopted the Mission to Planet Earth, she had an answer to the questions that arose in her on seeing Earth from space. The astrophysicist in her saw a fragile planet and her greatest legacy is convincing NASA that Earth is worth trying to protect.[736]

---

[735] Ibid.
[736] https://en.wikipedia.org/wiki/Sally_Ride

At this juncture in human evolution, few of us use our planets at the spiritual level, but many of us are striving to and such people are wonderful to be around. As with the other planets, the spiritual level of evolution is vastly different with Sedna from the two previous levels. Here the quintile and bi-quintile aspects bring an inventive, open=minded approach to our lives enabling us to explore them deeply.

Once we embrace the Sedna energy, which is the oneness of everything, our nurturing becomes an expression of Sedna consciousness and it becomes devotional in nature. The struggle of the beginner's level is gone, as are the transcendental crises of the intermediate level. At this level everything Saturnian is meaningless and yet everything Sednian has its place.

Peter Hurkos is a Dutch psychic who gained ESP abilities after a blow to his head, which left him unconscious for three days. He has Sedna in the eleventh house of collective consciousness, quintile Uranus in the ninth house of spirituality. His Sedna is also bi-quintile Ixion, the planet of lawlessness, in the fourth house of home.

> His psychic abilities were tested psychometrically with a claimed 87% accuracy. As a boy, he was a poor student, dropping out of school when he entered his teens. He was a loner who spent much time in the woods or in solitude, dreaming and exploring, prone to fantasies and visions. After his accident, he became religious and also became afflicted with blinding headaches and his temperament became volatile and moody.[737]

Sedna is also in a fateful inconjunct with Pholus, the centaur of enlightenment in the sixth house of service.

> In addition to using his new-found abilities to do professional work, he also did TV guest spots and wrote an autobiography, titled *Psychic*. He tuned in to some of his subjects while in a sleep state, when he could speak in tongues, or in foreign languages, but he also did psychic work while awake.[738]

Tracy Marks is an American psychotherapist, astrologer, lecturer and teacher and author of 15 books and pamphlets which have been translated into nearly a dozen languages. She has Sedna in the fourth

---

[737] https://en.wikipedia.org/wiki/Peter_Hurkos
[738] Ibid.

house of home, quintile Uranus in the seventh house of relationships. She is skilled at leading dream work, women's empowerment, and the art of friendship groups. She has a master's degree in psycho-synthesis and is acclaimed for her in-depth integration of psychological, spiritual and astrological concepts. Some of her more notable books include *How To Handle Your T-Square, The Astrology of Self Discovery,* and *The Art Of Chart Interpretation.*

Paramahansa Yogananda was an East Indian author, mystic and founder of the Self-Realisation Fellowship. He had Sedna conjunct Mars the planet of action, in the eighth house of shared resources, bi-quintile Uranus in the third house of ideas and communication.

World traveled and a world teacher, he carried Eastern philosophy to the West. At 27 he was invited to serve as India's delegate to an international congress of religious leaders convening in Boston. His address to the congress, on 'The Science of Religion', was enthusiastically received. When he arrived in America, the "New World" was ready to receive the advanced teachings that had previously been reserved for monastics and chelas in ashrams. Science, literacy, communication, and new spiritual insights had just begun breaking down the dark ages of theology and dogma.

He founded his fellowship to disseminate worldwide his teachings on India's ancient science and philosophy of Yoga and its time honoured tradition of meditation, introducing the Bhagavad Gita and other scriptures to help raise the consciousness of humanity. He lectured and taught on the East coast of American for several years and at 31 began a speaking tour across the country. His lectures, in which he spoke of the underlying unity of the world's great religions, were attended by thousands drawn to his message. His personal students were taught the ancient soul-awakening techniques of Kriya Yoga.

His articulate and sincere introduction to the disciplines of the East opened the door for many other Indian teachers and gurus, as a serious interest in yoga and meditation made great inroads in the West. His main mission was to build a lasting bridge of

World Brotherhood based on raising the spiritual awareness between the East and West.[739]

Sri Meher Baba was an Indian religious figure who was known as "The Silent Guru." He was born in India to Irani Zoroastrian parents. He had Sedna in the second house of material resources, bi-quintile Uranus conjunct the MC, the cusp of the tenth house of profession.

> At the age of 19, he began a seven-year spiritual transformation and during this time he contacted five spiritual masters before beginning his own mission and gathering his own disciples at the age of 27. His early followers gave him the name Meher Baba, meaning "Compassionate Father".[740]

His Sedna is also inconjunct his Moon, the planet of emotions, in the ninth house of spirituality.

> He moved into silence at 31 and did not speak until his death. To communicate, he spelled words on an alphabet board with quick fingers, such as "I am the Supreme Spirit." And from the age of 60 he used a unique sign language of gestures, rather than the alphabet board. With his circle of disciples, he spent long periods in seclusion, during which time he often fasted. He also traveled widely, held public gatherings and engaged in works of charity with lepers, the poor and the mentally ill.[741]

His Sedna is also quintile Haumea, the planet of rebirth, in the fifth house of creativity, semi-square Venus, the planet of values in the first house of identity, and sesquiquadrate Juno, the asteroid of partnership, in the tenth house of profession.

> He gave numerous teachings on the cause and purpose of life, including teaching reincarnation and that the phenomenal world is an illusion. He taught that the Universe is imagination, that God is what really exists, and that each soul is really God passing through imagination to realise individually his own divinity.

> In addition, he gave practical advice for the aspirant who wishes to attain self-realisation and thereby escape the wheel of birth

---

[739] https://en.wikipedia.org/wiki/Paramahansa_Yogananda
[740] https://en.wikipedia.org/wiki/Meher_Baba
[741] Ibid.

and death. He also taught about the concept of Perfect Masters, the Avatar, and those on the various stages of the spiritual path that he called involution. His teachings are most importantly recorded in his principal books, *Discourses* and *God Speaks*. And his legacy includes an influence on pop-culture artists and the introduction of common expressions such as 'Don't Worry, Be Happy'.[742]

---

[742] Ibid.

37: Sedna / Neptune

Conjunction

There is no one alive today with this aspect and no one will be born with this aspect in the next 50 years, so it is not interpreted here.

Opposition

With the opposition between Sedna and Neptune, the all-encompassing spiritual energy of Sedna challenges our inspiration, our dreams and our psychic receptivity, and also our tendency towards illusion and confusion.

Neptune rules spirituality and all things subtle and a youthful, and the sometimes naive, spirit that characterizes those of us with a strong placement of Neptune in our natal charts. It is the bridge to the mysterious and to the knowing that we're all somehow connected, especially those in our family, friend circle, or ancestral lineage.

With the opposition to Sedna our psychic sensitivity stands in relief against the big spiritual picture and we will likely feel challenged by this larger framework from an early age. As we get older and if Neptune is prominent in our chart, we could be naturally drawn toward the spiritual path and mysticism.

If we remain unconscious of our Sedna energy however, the opposition can call the more negative manifestations of Neptune into our lives, including delusion, deception, trickery, deceit, guilt, self-sacrifice, escapism and addiction.

The biggest problem here is self-delusion, because we all have a personal dream world and the potential for creativity, which is represented by the placement of Neptune in our charts and it is essential with the opposition to enact these dreams to discover which are real.

Like John Hinckley, an American attempted assassin who shot and wounded President Reagan when he was 25. He has Sedna in the second house of material reality, opposite Neptune in the eighth house of shared resources.

> The year before he shot Reagan, he went to Ted Kennedy's office and waited for three hours with a loaded gun to see the Senator, before he gave up on the assassination attempt and

left. He was found not guilty by reason of insanity and sentenced to an asylum for the mentally ill in Washington, DC.

Prior to the assassination attempt upon President Reagan, he wrote a string of love letters to actress Jodie Foster. Then at 27, he met a woman who was a patient in the same facility for the shotgun murder of her ten-year-old daughter, followed by her own suicide attempt. She was 12 years older. They were both in the hell of their mental illness, anguish and despair and their growing friendship led to improvement for both of them. Their long hours of talks led to love and he asked her to marry him.

A couple of years later she was able to function responsibly in society and was released. His progress was slower however they were able to see each other on weekends and kiss goodbye, feeling like a couple of teenagers. During the Christmas holidays, the young lovers spent time alone for the first time when he was allowed to spend a day with his family. His sexual experience was limited to a few encounters with prostitutes shortly before the assassination attempt. They were not able to consummate their relationship, but the promise of a future together was a strong incentive to healthy responsibility.

During the next five years, his progress was interspersed with unsettling relapses. His psychological evaluations took a turn for the worse. A report from this period read, "The issues of poor judgment, need for ego-gratification through the media, isolation from others at all but a superficial level, grandiosity, suspiciousness, defiance in the face of narcissistic injury, refusal to accept responsibility for his actions other than in a fleeting way, emotional volatility, tendency to lie, lack of empathy for others, sense of entitlement - all remain as unresolved therapeutic issues." His ability to maintain a stable relationship with his fiancé was a plus.

At 35, he was living in a medium-security ward and was working four hours a day in a clerical position. The next year he was allowed to walk with his fiancé without an escort around the hospital grounds. Not long after this, they had sexual relations for the first time and he was moved to a minimum-security ward. A divided appeals court finally ruled when he was 43 that he could make supervised day trips away from the mental hospital where he has lived for the past 18 years to visit his family and friends, a process of gradual re-entry into society. Four years later he was granted unsupervised visits with his parents, but it would be 14 more years before he was released from institutional psychiatric care at 61.[743]

Or we could also get caught in someone else's delusion. Like Janice Hagerty, who was an American office manager at Edgewater Technology. She had Sedna in the second house of material reality, opposite Neptune in the eighth house of life and death. One morning when she was 46, a mentally unstable software tester at the institute went berserk, shooting and killing seven people, including her. Transiting Saturn, the planet of structure, was in a fateful inconjunct aspect with her Neptune that day and transiting Mars, the planet of war, was opposite her Sedna and conjunct Venus, the planet of relationships, and Ceres, the planet of nurturing.

Or like Patricia Gilmore, who was an American homicide victim, murdered at age 24 by her lover. She had Sedna in the tenth house of profession, opposite Neptune in the fourth house of home.

> Her boyfriend was so possessive and jealous he would not take her out where other men might see and admire her, and so controlling, that when she broke it off, he went to the place where she worked, slashed his wrists and smeared her and her car with his blood. He stalked her and made repeated phone calls, ignoring the Restraining Order that she had requested. Later that year he was convicted of threats and sent to State Mental Hospital for observation, and from there to jail.
>
> She worked at the bank as a teller and customarily went home for lunch. Out of jail on a 24-hour leave, he kidnapped her at gunpoint. He fled with her, evading helicopters, squad cars and police cruisers on search, with her mom and eight brothers and sisters on alert. He stabbed her 29 times and pushed her out of the car, where her body was found. Six months later, he was convicted of first-degree murder and given life in prison.[744]

---

[743] https://en.wikipedia.org/wiki/John_Hinckley_Jr.
[744] https://www.astro.com/astro-databank/Gilmore,_Patricia

At the unconscious level this aspect can also lead us down a path of deception and trickery. Like Jonathan Pollard, who was an American who passed classified information to Israel while working as an American civilian intelligence analyst. He has Sedna in the tenth house of profession, opposite Neptune in the fourth house of home.

> He started passing classified information from when he was 29, until he was finally arrested a year and a half later at the gates of the Israeli Embassy in Washington. He pleaded guilty and received a life sentence.[745]

Or we might become involved in deceit, which might lead to a build-up of guilt, that leads us into deluded action. Like Abraham Kasparian, who is a former American politician who stabbed his wife three times in a public restaurant. He has Sedna in the fifth house of romance and children, opposite Neptune in the eleventh house of collective consciousness.

> She had filed for a divorce but agreed to meet him for lunch. She survived the attack. He had been arrested previously for welfare fraud and larceny. Earlier that same day, a former tenant sued the couple, charging them with negligence in connection with an apartment fire that killed two children.[746]

At the unconscious level this aspect can also encourage a life of escapism and addiction. Like Althea Flynt, who was an American publisher of the *Hustler* magazine, together with her husband, Larry Flynt. She had Sedna in the twelfth house of the unconscious, opposite Neptune, which is conjunct Venus, the planet of relationships, in the sixth house of daily routine.

> At the age eight, her dad went on a homicidal rampage, killed his wife and two others, and then shot himself. She ran away from an orphanage at 17, blowing her $10,000 inheritance on clothes and drugs. She got a job as a go-go dancer at one of Larry Flynt's Ohio clubs. They were both renegades with bawdy dreams. *Hustler* began as a newsletter to promote Larry's clubs when she was 20.

> It was an inventively obscene celebration of debauchery and carnality, a porn magazine that made them millionaires by the

---

[745] https://en.wikipedia.org/wiki/Jonathan_Pollard

[746] https://www.astro.com/astro-databank/Kasparian,_Abraham

time she was 23. They moved into a two million Bel Aire mansion. However, when she was 25, Larry was shot by a sniper, shattering his spine. She stayed loyal to him, never leaving his side. However, her heroin addiction escalated after he was shot. She died at the age of 33, her body found in a filled bathtub. She had AIDS-related complex.[747]

Or in a more managed way like Katherine Ippolito, who is an American nursery school teacher and big-time slot machine winner. She has Sedna conjunct Juno, the asteroid of partnership, and Venus, the planet of values, in the fourth house of home, opposite Neptune, which is conjunct Saturn, the planet of wealth, in the tenth house of profession. She put $3.00 into a slot machine at the Taj Mahal Casino Resort late on a Sunday night when she was 38 and on vacation with her husband. She won 1.7 million and broke the world's record for a 50-cent slot machine win. This was her second big win. Four years earlier she won 37 thousand from a slot machine. She only gambles twice a year when on vacation.

As we tire of density and the grief it creates, and we start a spiritual journey to get out of the swamp, Sedna rewards us with transcendent crises, experiences which force us to let go and rise above them, resulting in a huge growth to a new level of consciousness. There is no choice with these crises, and the more we try and solve them, the more we will get hurt.

Christopher Boyce was an American spy, the son of a former FBI agent who had an affluent upbringing and an IQ tested at 142. He had Sedna in the tenth house of profession, opposite Neptune, which is conjunct Saturn, the planet of responsibility, and Ixion, the planet of lawlessness, in the fourth house of home.

> He had a job at a top-secret CIA code room, where he had access to America's most sensitive satellite system's documents. In his early twenties he stole and sold information to Russian agents in Mexico along with his pal, Dalton Lee. Arrested, he went to trial and was given a prison term of 40 years. He hated prison and escaped when he was 27. To survive, he hid out, robbing banks. After one of the country's greatest manhunts, he

---

[747] https://en.wikipedia.org/wiki/Althea_Flynt

was captured 19 months later and given an extra 28 years in prison.

He was called "the Falcon" for his hobby of hunting with his birds, with which he identified for their wild freedom. His story was told by Robert Lindsay in *The Falcon and the Snowman*. While at Leavenworth, he was beaten by the prison's Aryan Brotherhood gang after telling Australian TV that espionage was "high adventure" and that he had "no problem with the label "traitor."

He was moved to maximum security where he lived in solitary confinement at the end of a corridor underneath the prison hospital, a dismal sequence of days that consisted of cockroaches, ants and flies for the next six years. Every day was a repeat of the previous and he wrote that he felt "submerged, alone, in a submarine." He rescued himself with books, devouring histories.

When he was 32, he testified before a Senate panel looking for ways to prevent future spys, and he worked with the FBI to produce Army recruit programs on the dangers of espionage. Four years later he was moved to a state lock-up. He took courses in art and history and earned a B.A., consistently getting A's and earning the praise of his instructors. He began work on his master's.

When he was 44, he broke down in tears at his review board under the weight of so much of life's time lost. The following year he showed himself to be such a model prisoner that he was scheduled to enter a halfway house in 4 years with full release the year after that. Heartened and invigorated, he continued to write for the Minneapolis newspaper, with many pieces addressing prison reform.

He was released from prison on parole after serving a little over 25 years, accounting for his time spent outside from the escape. Shortly thereafter he married a woman he had met when she was working as a paralegal, spearheading efforts to obtain parole for Lee. After her success with Lee, she turned her attention to securing parole for Boyce as well, and the two developed a personal relationship. The couple moved to Oregon, and Boyce's own parole ended when he was 54.

At 60 he published a book titled *American Sons: The Untold Story of the Falcon and the Snowman*, which mainly discusses his time in prison and relationship with Cait. At that time, he was living a relatively quiet life with Cait in central Oregon, where he had resumed his participation in falconry as a frequent pastime. When interviewed at the time his book was released, Boyce expressed support for the actions of Edward Snowden in exposing information about the United States government's surveillance programs.[748]

Bernard Stiegler is a French philosopher who came to the profession through personal crisis. He has Sedna conjunct Jupiter, the planet of expansion, on the cusp of the third house of communication, opposite Neptune, which is conjunct Ixion, the planet of lawlessness, in the eighth house of shared resources.

He is currently head of the Institute of Research and Innovation, which he founded at the age of 54 at the Centre Georges-Pompidou in Paris. However, when he was 26 he was incarcerated for five years for armed robbery. It was during this period that he became interested in philosophy, studying it by correspondence. His transformation in prison is recounted in his book, *Passer à l'acte*. Key themes in his work are technology, time, individuation, consumerism, consumer capitalism, technological convergence, digitization, Americanization, education and the future of politics and human society.

His best known work is *Technics and Time*, published when he was 46. The thesis of the book is that the genesis of technology corresponds not only to the genesis of what is called "human" but of temporality as such, and that this is the clue toward understanding the future of the dynamic process in which the human and technology consists.

This book conducts a reading of approaches to the history of technology and the origin of humanisation. The outcome of this is the conjecture that history cannot be thought according to the

---

[748] https://en.wikipedia.org/wiki/Christopher_John_Boyce

idea that we are the "subject" of this history and technology simply the object. When it comes to the relation between the human and the technical, the "who" and the "what" are in an undecidable relation.

At 53 he founded the political and cultural group, Ars Industrialis, the manifesto of which calls for an "industrial politics of spirit." And at 58 he founded the philosophy school, Ecole de Philosophie d'Épineuil-le-Fleuriel. The context and themes of the school lie in his argument that we are entering a period of post-consumerism and post-globalization.[749]

And our case study, Steve Jobs, was an American entrepreneur and one of the originators of the computer revolution, co-founder of Apple Computers and Pixar Animation Studios. He had Sedna conjunct Mars in the eighth house of shared resources, opposite Neptune in the second house of material reality. His High School sweetheart and mother of his first child, who he initially disowned, called him 'a haunted house' and yet his creative visions have revolutionized our lives.

He and his friend, Steve Wozniak, made their first circuit board in their garage and they called it the Apple. By the time he was 24, his Apple Corporation was worth $10 million. A year later, its value had grown to $100 million. Its graphical user interface, business applications and word processing won kudos, and millions cheered while Apple took on IBM and its personal computer.

However, he was called 'a haunted house' by Chrisann Brennan, a high school sweetheart who lived with him and was an early Apple employee. She said he became a threatening monster and their relationship fell apart amid wild recriminations when she became pregnant with his first child. He denied he was the father, despite a positive paternity test and he paid a pittance in child support, while living the life of a millionaire. In her memoir she says:

> I've truly hated Steve at times, but never for very long. Sharing a daughter with him has forced me to think about things more deeply. Steve the saint, the alien, the despot, the punishing

---

[749] https://en.wikipedia.org/wiki/Bernard_Stiegler

masculine god, the liar, the obsessed narcissist, the cult hero, the ID of the iEverything, the genius and the motherless boy.[750]

As the Apple empire grew, Steve became a tyrant, subject to moody outbursts and gloomy silences. Hard feelings arose and power struggles with other executives ensued. He resigned and the following year co-founded NeXt, in an attempt to do for the hardware industry, what he had down for software. He also bought a company which he renamed Pixar Animation Studios and negotiated a deal with Disney to distribute Pixar's films and became a Disney partner. Under Jobs' leadership, Pixar won 20 Academy awards for successful animated feature films and was acquired by Disney.[751]

With a twist of fate and a large amount of Sednian transcendence, he then convinced Apple to buy NeXt and was invited back to Apple as interim CEO and a few years later was made permanent CEO once again. Under his renewed leadership Apple computer became a major player in the computer industry once more and his team created visually aesthetic computers in bright colours that appealed to younger buyers.

Humour can be one path to transcend the quicksand of Sedna, giving us the objectivity to step back from the edge, but also with the opposition to Neptune a psychic sensitivity to people and good audience rapport.

Like Sandra Bernhard, who is an American comedienne, tall, skinny, aggressive, ultra-hip and manic. She has Sedna in the tenth house of profession, opposite Neptune in the fourth house of home.

She was born in Flint, Michigan, to a proctologist father and an abstract-artist mother. After she graduated she spent eight months in Israel on a kibbutz. She then moved to Los Angeles where she lived with an aunt and uncle and went to beauty school to learn how to be a manicurist, while pursuing her comedy career. Her early stand-up comedy acts were not major successes initially.

She became hot property in her late 20s, after working for five years as a manicurist and stand-up comic prior to landing a lead role in *The King of Comedy* with Robert de Niro, released when

---

[750] Brennan, Chrisann. *The Bite In The Apple: A Memoir Of My Life With Steve Jobs*
[751] https://en.wikipedia.org/wiki/Steve_Jobs

she was 28. She did nightclubs, TV and films. She is most remembered for playing lesbian Nancy Bartlett on the television show *Roseanne* for six years from the age of 36. She has one daughter, Cicely, born when she was 43. She has never said who the father is, nor how the child was conceived, but she is openly bisexual and is a strong supporter of gay rights.[752]

And Roseanne Barr, who is an American actress, comedian, writer, and television producer. She was also the 2012 presidential nominee of the California-based Peace and Freedom Party. She has Sedna in the second house of material resources, opposite Neptune, which is conjunct Saturn, the planet of responsibility, in the eighth house of shared resources.

She began her career in stand-up comedy at clubs before gaining fame for her role in the hit television sitcom, *Roseanne*. The show ran for nine seasons and she won both an Emmy and a Golden Globe Award for Best Actress for her work. She had crafted a "fierce working-class domestic goddess" persona in the eight years preceding her sitcom and wanted to do a realistic show about a strong mother who was not a victim of patriarchal consumerism.

The granddaughter of immigrants from Europe and Russia, she was the oldest of four children in a working-class Jewish Salt Lake City family. She was active in The Church of Jesus Christ of Latter-day Saints, yet courted controversy by stunts like singing the national anthem off-key at a nationally aired baseball game, followed by grabbing her crotch and spitting.

After her sitcom ended, she launched her own talk show, *The Roseanne Show*, and returned to stand-up comedy with a world tour. Then she announced she was running for the presidential nomination of the Green Party, which she lost, before getting the nomination of the Peace and Freedom Party. She received 61,971 votes in the general election which brought Trump to power, placing sixth overall.[753]

---

[752] https://en.wikipedia.org/wiki/Sandra_Bernhard
[753] https://en.wikipedia.org/wiki/Roseanne_Barr

At this juncture in human evolution, few of us use our planets at the spiritual level, but many of us are striving to, and such people are wonderful to be around. As with the other planets, the spiritual level of evolution is vastly different with Sedna from the two previous levels. Here, the opposition brings spiritual enlightenment into our lives and sets us on a mystical, or spiritual mission.

Once we embrace the Sedna energy, which is the oneness of everything, our nurturing becomes an expression of Sedna consciousness and it becomes devotional in nature. The struggle of the beginner's level is gone, as are the transcendental crises of the intermediate level. At this level everything Saturnian is meaningless and yet everything Sednian has its place.

With work over time, the opposition with Sedna can give us psychic abilities. I have Sedna in the fourth house of home, opposite Neptune, which is conjunct Mercury, the planet of ideas and communication, in the tenth house of profession. This is my writing point. I've written four books (this is the fifth) and four film scripts, two of which I've directed and produced into award winning movies. But obviously this aspect comes most into focus with this book, which has certainly challenged my psychic receptivity, but in a very satisfying way.

Karen Hamaker-Zondag is a Dutch professional astrologer, one of the most highly respected and well-regarded astrologers of the 20th century. She has Sedna in the first house of identity, opposite Neptune, which is conjunct Saturn, the planet of structure, in the seventh house of relationships.

> She studied social geography and planning at the University of Amsterdam but has become known as an astrologer. She was editor of the astrological magazine Spica, and founder of the astrology program Achernar and the astrological magazine Symbolon. She has written a large number of books, which have been translated into several languages. Although not psychologically educated, she is considered a representative of psychological astrology, a movement that focuses mainly on the psychologist, Carl Gustav Jung. She is also interested in forms of traditional astrology. In addition to astrology, Hamaker also practices other techniques that fall under the New Age movement. She published, among other things, I Ching, Tarot and medical subjects. At 46 she received an international award

for her work in the field of astrological education and the dissemination of astrology, the American Regulus Award for Astrological Education.[754]

teve Hill was an American Christian clergyman and evangelist. He had Sedna in the seventh house of relationships, opposite Neptune in the first house of identity.

As a teenager, he got heavily into alcohol and illicit drugs. At the age of twenty-one due to the effects of drug abuse, he spent three days suffering extreme convulsions, and turned to Christianity. A few weeks after his conversion experience, he was arrested and faced 25 years in prison for drug trafficking. Instead of jail, he was remanded to the Teen Challenge drug rehabilitation program, from which he graduated.

He is best known as the evangelist who preached in what became known as the Brownsville Revival. The Brownsville Revival was a series of meetings at Brownsville Assembly of God in Pensacola, Florida that began on Father's Day, when he was 41 and continued for five years. At 46 he moved to Texas to resume traveling evangelism. And at 49 he founded Heartland World Ministries Church in a suburb of Dallas.[755]

Chidvilasananda is a female Indian guru known as Gurumayi. She has Sedna in the eighth house of metaphysical studies, opposite Neptune in the second house of material reality. She became one of the guru Muktananda's two successors at the time of his death when she was 27. She had formerly been his translator. She and her followers practice Siddha Yoga. The group is based in India, but maintains centres throughout the world.

As a Siddha Guru she carries out her mission of awakening seekers to their own potential for enlightenment and describes the essence of her vision for all human beings like this: In truth the gift of life must always be recognised and never be taken for granted. Why is life so precious? In Siddha Yoga philosophy we recognise that in this human life we have a rate opportunity. We can transform an ordinary perception of this universe, into an

---

[754] https://nl.wikipedia.org/wiki/Karen_Hamaker
[755] https://en.wikipedia.org/wiki/Steve_Hill_(evangelist)

extraordinary vision. To be on this planet and to behold the universe from the divine perspective is a sign of an illuminated heart. To put this vision to use in the best way possible is a human being's highest duty.[756]

Semi-sextile, Sextile, Trine

With the flowing aspects between Sedna and Neptune, the all-encompassing spiritual energy of Sedna aligns with our inspiration, our dreams and our psychic receptivity, but also with our tendencies to illusion, or confusion.

Neptune is a bridge to the mysterious and to that knowing that many of us have that we're all somehow connected, especially those in our family, friend circle or ancestral lineage and with the flowing aspects to Sedna this circle can be enlarged to include all of humanity.

Our nightly dreams can be a portal through which we find meaning in life. And dreams, as well as the visions of waking life, can also be expressed through art, dance, movies, music, etc, reflecting back to us a vision of that inner world, which is the personal dream world of Neptune.

At the unconscious level however, we could still be a victim of karma and abuse, which my brought about by delusions, deception or confusion, or come out of nowhere, depending on other factors in the chart.

Like Julia Ann Deneau, who was an American homicide victim at the age of two. She had Sedna conjunct Jupiter, the planet of expansion, and Juno, the asteroid of partnership, in the tenth house of public standing, trine Neptune in the sixth house of daily routine. Her parents divorced bitterly. On his custody day Julia and her mother arrived at her father's home one morning. An hour later he called his attorney to say he had shot them and was going to shoot himself. He shot them both in the heart. All three bodies were found together in the closet, with a Bible laid over Julia's heart.

And if we experience abuse, we may also develop abusive tendencies. Like John Odgren, who was an American youth, suffering from Asberger's Syndrome, hyperactivity, and perhaps other emotional challenges, who allegedly killed a high school boy by stabbing him in the

---

[756] http://www.siddhayoga.org/gurumayi-chidvilasananda

school bathroom. He had Sedna in the tenth house of public standing, trine Neptune in the sixth house of daily routine.

> He was charged with fatally stabbing another student at Lincoln-Sudbury Regional High School. He was portrayed by a prosecutor as a calculating killer who often talked about committing "the perfect murder." Described as a "geeky, uncoordinated, awkward 16-year-old," allegedly brought a carving knife to school, picked a victim at random in a boys' bathroom, then stabbed him eight times.

> The teen's defense attorney told jurors that he was mentally ill when he killed the 15-year-old. His attorney said he was struggling with a form of autism, attention deficit hyperactivity disorder, depression, anxiety and possibly bipolar disorder when he attacked the freshman, whom he had never met. The defense portrayed him as a troubled teenager who had suffered from mental illness and developmental disabilities since he was a young child.

> Bipolar disorder runs in his family. His mother has the disorder and four of her relatives committed suicide. He became obsessed with Stephen King novels, violence, crime and forensics. He also developed an "irrational fear that something was going to happen to him". He started bringing weapons to school, once a knife and another time a toy gun. By January 2009, he was "consumed by his delusions," his lawyer said. After he stabbed his victim, a student who had been in the bathroom heard him blurt out, "Oh, my God. What have I done? What have I done?"[757]

Or we may develop a deluded world view, like Howard Unruh, who was an American killer, who was judged insane and incapable of standing trial. He had Sedna conjunct the cusp of the seventh house of relationships, trine Neptune in the tenth house of social standing.

> One day when he was 28 he left the home where he lived with his mother at 9:00 AM and in the following twenty minutes shot and killed 13 men, women and children, and wounded three

---

[757] https://www.cbsnews.com/news/did-teen-john-odgren-commit-perfect-murder-or-is-mental-disorder-to-blame-for-high-school-killing/

others because "people have made derogatory remarks about my character." The young white male, slender, attractive and clean-cut, was a gun collector but had sold most of his collection prior to the carnage.

During his stint in the U.S. army, when he spent two years in the European theater of WW II, he had qualified as a sharpshooter. He was working as a sheet metal worker at the Philadelphia Naval Base when he joined up when he was 21. After he was discharged from the army at 24 he started a pharmacy course but dropped out in three months. He was described as a "quiet" student. He was a born-again Christian who attended church on Sundays and Bible class on Monday evenings.

He told his psychiatrist that he had contemplated killing several specific people for the last two years, and expressed no remorse, except for the children he shot. He had grievances with several of the neighbors, the Cohen's because "they made many remarks about me," the barber because the location of his building caused flooding in the Unruh cellar and the local shoemaker because he had thrown garbage over the fence into their yard. The tailor and his son had "circulated a story about me that was false." Other victims were passersby in automobiles, a two-year-old in an apartment window and a six-year-old boy sitting in the barber shop.

Confined to the New Jersey State Hospital, by the age of 60 he was a stoop-shouldered man who walked in circles, feared contamination from books and believed that doctors were treating him through the television.[758]

Or we might develop perversions, like Donald Kinman, who was an American murderer who liked to strangle his women while making love. He had Sedna in the seventh house of relationships, trine Neptune in the eleventh house of collective consciousness. He choked his first victim to death at 35 and his second victim a year later, at which time he gave himself up to authorities. He also choked his wife more than a dozen times in their four years together, then suffered from remorse and shame. He moved from state to state and had more than 80 felonies on his record in five states for theft, armed robbery, and forgery.

---

[758] https://en.wikipedia.org/wiki/Howard_Unruh

Or we could be inspired by Neptune to write and create art, but the flowing aspects can also indicate possible issues with drugs and addictions. Like Jack Kerouac, who was an American writer and poet, the author of 21 books. He had Sedna, conjunct Chiron, the centaur of wounding and healing, in the eighth house of shared resources, trine Neptune in the eleventh house of collective consciousness.

He is perhaps best known for his books *On The Road*, published when he was 35 and *The Dharma Bums*, published the following year. These classic novels established him as a hero who epitomised the style of living and writing associated with the 'Beat Movement' and served as the bible for Beatniks.

When he was 23 he met the charismatic and bisexual Neal Cassady, a Denver reform school graduate and car thief who eventually became Kerouac's lover and buddy. During a three-week binge of creativity in the following April and May, he wrote 'On The Road' on a single ream of paper. Following Neal's marriage to Caroline, Kerouac moved into the attic of their San Francisco home, where they made up a ménage a trois. He was hospitalised at 29 with thrombophlebitis as a result of heavy Benzedrine use.

In his early thirties, he roamed the US and Mexico taking odd jobs to support himself while studying Buddhism. However, at 38 he suffered alcohol withdrawal, coupled with a nervous breakdown. During the next four years he lived with his mother. At 44 he made his third and final marriage, to the sister of a childhood friend. This marriage was probably celibate, and he was often arrested for public drunkenness as a means of taking out his frustration.

While he hit the road for in search of direct experience and spontaneity, his acute wanderlust left him homeless in his soul, even when he owned a home. Despite the chaos in every area of his life however, he meticulously kept an archive of every sexual experience he had with a woman. One of these bore him a daughter, a girl whom he met twice, but never acknowledged. His daughter Jan states, "I wish I had known him better. He could spout all kinds of things on paper, but in person, he was non-communicative."

He was unable to cope with fame, fatherhood and his bi-sexuality. "He wanted to be seen as the voice of America, but instead he was seen as a voice of juvenile delinquents, and that hurt him a lot...He couldn't take the easy bullet because he was a Catholic. But he rationalised that it was not a sin if he drank himself to death." So that is what he did. His final years were marked by virulent alcohol rages and fierce anti-Semitism.[759]

Or in an effort to nurture our creative imagination we might become withdrawn. Like Emily Dickinson, who was an American writer, acclaimed as the greatest woman poet of the English language. During her lifetime she had seven poems published anonymously; since her death she has been revered as a literary treasure. She had Sedna in the fourth house of home, sextile Neptune, which is conjunct Jupiter, the planet of publishing, and Makemake, the planet of devotion in the third house of ideas and communication.

With poor health, shy and fastidious, she had a reclusive and uneventful life with her domineering dad, an attorney, and a mom who "did not care for thought." She was one of three children, an older brother and a younger sister who were her closest companions through her lifetime. Her parents sent her to seminary school at 17, where she was cramped, curbed and repressed into a tight Victorian mold.

Becoming increasingly withdrawn and mystical, dressed always in white, she ventured outside only at dusk to water the garden. She never married and some biographers conclude that she was gay. By the early 1860s, she had created a wall of isolation around herself, which she believed critical to artistic expression. The major relationships in her life were with Susan Dickinson, her brother Austin's wife and with Bowles, a married man and the editor of the Springfield republican. She and Sue met when they were both 17. Through the 40 years of their correspondence, Bowles was her closest personal friend until his death. He was vigorous, earthy and dashing; however, Dickinson's biographer writes that with neither relationship was physical union possible.

---

[759] https://en.wikipedia.org/wiki/Jack_Kerouac

In her last two decades, she became even more reclusive, seldom going far from her brother's house in Amherst. At 54 her health was set back by the death of a friend and by late the following year she was often too ill to leave her room. Stricken by Bright's disease, a type of kidney inflammation, she lost consciousness and died in the house where she was born. After her death her sister found a manuscript of almost 900 poems, a legacy of glorious words to show the blazing wondrous genius that was hidden inside her.[760]

As we tire of density and the grief it creates, and we start a spiritual journey to get out of the swamp, Sedna rewards us with transcendent crises, experiences which force us to let go and rise above them, resulting in a huge growth to a new level of consciousness. There is no choice with these crises, and the more we try and solve them, the more we will get hurt.

Like Timothy Leary, who was an American professor, guru of the 1960's drug culture who coined the phrase, "Turn on, tune in, drop out." He had Sedna in the fourth house of home, trine Neptune in the eighth house of shared resources.

Well ahead of his time, he was fired from Harvard for his controlled experiments with psychedelic drugs. He began experimenting with psylocybin, mescaline and LSD when he became a lecturer at Harvard. Although the experiments were controlled and scholarly papers on the experiments were published in prestigious journals, he and fellow Harvard researcher Richard Alpert (later known as Ram Dass) were fired. A patron set them up in a New York estate where they could continue their research. Instead, it became a kind of Bohemian salon where Leary dropped acid with the likes of Jack Kerouac, Allen Ginsberg and Thelonius Monk.

Arrested 29 times, President Richard Nixon once called him "the most dangerous man in America." When he was 45 he was sentenced to 30 years and $30,000 for smuggling a small amount of marijuana into the U.S. from Mexico. The following year his estate mansion was raided and he was again arrested on drug charges. After appeals and more arrests he was sent to

[760] https://en.wikipedia.org/wiki/Emily_Dickinson

the state prison at 50, to face up to 20 years for two possession convictions.

Later that year he escaped prison with the help of the radical Weathermen underground movement and was smuggled out of the country. However three years later he was detained while trying to enter Afghanistan, and was sent back to the U.S. He was returned to Folsom prison, where he at one point had a cell across from Charles Manson. He was released on parole when he was 56.

His life was marked by tragedy and broken relationships. When he was 35 his first of five wives, Marianne, committed suicide. At 70 his daughter Susan, who was 42, was found mentally unfit to stand trial for shooting her sleeping boyfriend. Later that year she used shoelaces to hang herself from the bars of her cell. His son Jack also felt his father had deserted him at a critical time in his life and was not close to him.

At 75 he called his closest friends to tell them he had prostate cancer. He turned his death into a cyber-happening by chronicling his illness on a personal Web site. Two days before he died, his request to have his ashes launched into space was approved. With videotape rolling, he died at his home, whispering his last word, "beautiful".[761]

Or Agatha Christie, who was a British writer of some 67 detective mystery books that are universally popular. She had Sedna in the third house of communication, sextile Neptune in the fifth house of creativity, which is together with Pluto, the planet of life and death, just across the cusp in the sixth house of service. Sedna was also opposite her Moon, the planet of emotions, in the ninth house of publishing.

Her novels have sold more than a billion copies in English and another billion translated in more than 100 languages. However, with a solitary childhood, Agatha was so painfully shy that she never did get accustomed to public appearance and seldom gave interviews.

Her mother was not keen on education but in spite of her, five-year-old Agatha taught herself to read. On a dare from her sister,

[761] https://en.wikipedia.org/wiki/Timothy_Leary

she wrote her first book in two weeks, introducing for the first time her protagonist, Hercule Poirot. The book was uniformly rejected by publishers, however later someone inadvertently opened the book and recommended it for publication. She was given a five-book contract and her central character went on to solve crime in 33 more novels.

Her popularity was close to immediate. By the time she was 40, she was a plain and matronly woman with hair forever locked in a wave, wearing dowdy housedresses; a deeply religious teetotaller who loved to putter in her garden.

Around this time her mother died however, and soon after that her husband announced that he loved another. She fell apart and disappeared, checking into a hotel under an alias, while an all-out search turned up her abandoned car on a deserted road and a discarded fur coat. Police dragged the pond for her body while the plot thickened. Some bizarre letters turned up or were rumoured.

When she was found at the hotel, she never really explained the episode and it was accounted for by stating that she had stress-related amnesia, or a secret affair was also considered as another possibility. However, while recovering from the divorce, she took the Orient Express to Baghdad and met her second husband, an archeologist who was fourteen years her junior. Though she gave every possible reason to not marry him, she nonetheless did so, and the "most unsuitable match" lasted very happily for 45 years until her death.[762]

And Betty Friedan, who was an American feminist pioneer and organizer, lecturer and writer, the author of *The Feminine Mystique*, which became a best-seller, translated into 13 languages. She had Sedna in the third house of communication, trine Neptune in the eighth house of shared resources.

Her mother quit her job as editor of the local newspaper's women's pages to become a housewife. She was aware of the toll this took, and the impact it had on her family. And as an adult, after becoming pregnant, she was herself fired from a job.

---

[762] https://en.wikipedia.org/wiki/Agatha_Christie

During her 20s and 30s she was a deeply committed radical activist. A brilliant, energetic reporter for union newspapers, she was intensely engaged in the leftist politics of the time. By the time she stopped working at 31, pregnant with her second child, McCarthyism had chased underground much of this visionary women's movement. The rest was smothered by anti-female union policies and longstanding misogyny among male leaders on the left.

She retreated to the suburbs and began writing about family and work for women's magazines, doing what her mother had not done. And she came out swinging. Women in labor unions were fighting for equal pay, maternity leave and higher minimum wages, while other progressive women agitated for government-sponsored day care, national health insurance and an end to racial discrimination.

She later said: "I decided I was going to be fulfilled as a housewife, but I could not suppress the itch to write, and I did it in the morning, like secret drinking." She authored *The Feminine Mystique* at 42, which became a best-seller and was translated into 13 languages. This book exposed the "desperate housewives" of 1950s America, women imprisoned in suburbia with little to do. She came to believe that "the only way for a woman, as for a man, to find herself, to know herself as a person, is by creative work of her own."

On the heels of the Civil Rights Movement, she helped to found the National Organization for Women when she was 45, the largest and most effective group for women's rights, and served as its first president.[763]

With the flowing aspects we could be a natural inventor. Like our case study, Thomas Edison, the inventor of the light bulb, the telegraph and the phonograph, and the father of our modern electronic media world. He has Sedna in the fourth house of the laboratory home, semi-sextile Neptune, which is in his third house of ideas. This Neptune placement fed his imagination and, together with the flow with Sedna in the fourth house of home, accounts for the 1093 patents in his name for inventions of electrical home appliances which connected the home to the world.

---

[763] https://en.wikipedia.org/wiki/Betty_Friedan

His Sedna is also in a close quintile with Jupiter, the planet of expansion, also in the seventh house.

A characteristic of his personality contributing strongly to his achievements is an intense, not to say courageous, optimism in which no thought of failure can enter, an optimism born of self-confidence, and becoming, after forty or fifty years of experience, more and more a sense of certainty in the accomplishment of success.

In the overcoming of difficulties, he had the same intellectual pleasure as the chess-master when confronted with a problem requiring all the efforts of his skill and experience to solve. To advance along smooth and pleasant paths, to encounter no obstacles, to wrestle with no difficulties and hardships--such has absolutely no fascination to him.

At the conclusion of his ore-milling experiments, practically his entire fortune was sunk in an enterprise that had to be considered an impossibility. At the age of fifty he looked back upon five or six years of intense activity expended apparently for naught and the financial clouds were quickly gathering on the horizon. However, for him the main experiment had succeeded, he had accomplished what he sought for. Nature at another point had outstripped him, yet he had broadened his own sum of knowledge to a prodigious extent.

Twelve years later a friend accompanied him on a Sunday drive in New Jersey and Edison in the highest spirits, pointing out with the keenest enjoyment the many beautiful views of valley and wood. The wanderings led to the old ore-milling plant, by then practically a mass of deserted buildings all going to decay. It was a depressing sight, marking such titanic but futile struggles with nature.

To Edison, however, no trace of sentiment or regret occurred, and the whole ruins were apparently as much a matter of unconcern as if he were viewing the remains of Pompeii. Sitting on the porch of the house where he lived during that period, in the light of the setting sun, his fine face in repose, he looked as placidly over the scene as a happy farmer over a field of ripening corn. 'I never felt better in my life than during the five years I worked here' he said. 'Hard work, nothing to divert my thought, clear air and simple food made my life very pleasant. We learned a great deal. It will be of benefit to some one some time'.[764]

Or we might be a natural philosopher. Like Martin Heidegger, who was a German existentialist philosopher and one of the most influential voices and foremost thinkers and writers of the 20th century. He had Sedna in the fourth house of home, sextile Neptune which is just in the sixth house of daily routine but closely conjunct the descendent, the cusp of the seventh house of relationships.

With the publication of his first book, *Being and Time*, when he was 38, he achieved instant fame as one of the spokesmen of 20th century existentialism. Though unfinished, Being and Time is one of the central philosophical works of the 20th century. In the first division of the work, He attempted to turn away from "ontic" questions about beings to ontological questions about Being, and recover the most fundamental philosophical question: the question of Being, of what it means for something to be.

He argued that being human is defined by care, that it's practically engaged and is a concernfull mode of being-in-the-world. This was in opposition to rationalist thinkers like René Descartes who located the essence of man in our thinking abilities. For Heidegger thinking is thinking about things originally discovered in our everyday practical engagements. The consequence of this is that our capacity to think cannot be the most central quality of our being, because thinking is a reflecting upon this more original way of discovering the world.

In the second section, he argues that human being is even more fundamentally structured by its temporality, or its concern with, and relationship to time, existing as a structurally open 'possibility-for-being'. He emphasised the importance of authenticity in human existence, involving a truthful relationship to our being thrown into a world, and to our being-towards-death, the finitude of the time and being that we are given, and the closing down of our various possibilities for being through time.

---

[764] Dyer, Frank Lewis, and Martin, Thomas Commerford. *Edison, His Life and Inventions,* 1910

He also made critical contributions to philosophical conceptions of truth, arguing that its original meaning was un-concealment, to philosophical analyses of art as a site of the revelation of truth, and to philosophical understanding of language as the 'house of being'.[765]

Or like Carl Jung, who was a Swiss psychiatrist and author, noted as being an outstanding influence in the development of the theory and practice of analytical psychiatry. He had Sedna in the second house of material reality, semi-sextile Neptune which is also in the second house. With this placement he saw dreams as a practical process, believing that they do the work of integrating our conscious and unconscious lives and he called this the process of individuation.

At age 12, he developed fainting spells which kept him out of school. He spent hours out in the nature, dreaming. Overhearing his father's talk of financial concerns around his illness, he realised on some level he could overcome the fainting spells and was able to return to school. Shortly after this, on a long walk to school, he experienced an intense moment of knowing himself: "Previously, I had existed…everything had merely happened to me. Now, I happened to myself. Now I knew: I am myself now… now I exist."

When he was 23 he decided to pursue a career in psychiatry. His career began in earnest five years later when he picked up Sigmund Freud's book, the Interpretation of Dreams, realising how his work linked up with his own ideas. The initial correspondence and friendship between them began three years later and they collaborated on some work, but when he was 34 he broke from Freud to place greater emphasis on the growth of mankind by archetypal vital forces in the individual. His theories of synchronicity, introvert-extrovert types, individuation and the personal-collective unconscious come from this work.

During this period he had a decisive dream of being in a two-story house. As he explored it, each floor and room reflected historical eras, or from the collective unconscious. When he was 38, he had numerous visions. He said in his autobiography, *Memories, Dreams, and Reflections*, that all of his creative work

---

[765] https://en.wikipedia.org/wiki/Martin_Heidegger

came from these initial visions. He built a successful psychological practice and was much sought after as a mentor to countless devotees of his work.

An advocate of the use of astrology, he said 'Astrology would be a large scale example of synchronism if it had at its disposal thoroughly tested findings… In other words, whatever is born or done this moment of time has the qualities of this moment of time'. In his book, *Synchronicity*, he published a study of 483 pairs of couples, seeking to prove the validity that there is a causal connection between the planets and psycho-physiological disposition.[766]

Humour can be one path to transcend the quicksand of Sedna, giving us the objectivity to step back from the edge, but also with the flowing aspects to Neptune a psychic sensitivity to people and good audience rapport.

Groucho Marx was an American writer, comedian, stage, film and television star. His Sedna is in the fifth house of creativity, sextile Varuna, which is conjunct Jupiter, the planet of success, both in the third house of communication.

He was known as a master of quick wit and is widely considered one of the best comedians of the modern era. He made 13 feature films with his siblings the Marx Brothers, Harpo Marx and Chico Marx, of whom he was the third-born.

His distinctive appearance, carried over from his days in vaudeville, included quirks such as an exaggerated stooped posture, glasses, cigar, and a thick greasepaint moustache and eyebrows. Among Groucho's many contributions to film comedy were his rapier wit, illogical chain of deductive reasoning and the visual pun. His standard persona of eyes rolled upward under wiggled brows with painted moustache and poised cigar created an classic comic insouciance.

Towards the end of his long career, after a decade of semi-retirement, Marx began appearing in one-night solo concert performances, culminating in a sold-out performance in New York's Carnegie Hall. This outstanding comeback created a

---

[766] https://en.wikipedia.org/wiki/Carl_Jung

sensation that revived an international interest in his films, and the Cannes Film Festival made him a Commander of the French Order of Arts and Letters.[767]

At this juncture in human evolution, few of us use our planets at the spiritual level, but many of us are striving to, and such people are wonderful to be around. As with the other planets, the spiritual level of evolution is vastly different with Sedna from the two previous levels. Here, the flowing aspects likely brings spiritual enlightenment into our lives and sets us on a mystical, or spiritual mission.

Once we embrace the Sedna energy, which is the oneness of everything, our nurturing becomes an expression of Sedna consciousness and it becomes devotional in nature. The struggle of the beginner's level is gone, as are the transcendental crises of the intermediate level. At this level everything Saturnian is meaningless and yet everything Sednian has its place.

Jeff Mayo was a British astrologer, author and teacher who was the director and principal of the Mayo School of Astrology, established when he was 52. He had Sedna in the sixth house of service, trine Neptune in the tenth house of profession.

> After leaving the faculty he started a correspondence course aimed at students all over the world. The Mayo School still continues to provide world-wide tuition. He opened the doors of astrology to literally thousands of students at the same time as he demonstrated his organisational and administrative abilities. His books include *Teach Yourself Astrology, How to Read the Ephemeris, How to Cast a Natal Chart, "he Astrologer's Astronomical Handbook, The Planets and Human Behaviour,* and *Astrology, a Key to Personality*. A modest and sensitive man, he was also fun to be with. He went into farming in Devon with his brother. He loved the outdoors, the wilderness and wildlife.[768]

Eleanor Bach was an American astrologer. She has Sedna conjunct Nessus, the centaur of radical change, and Chiron, the centaur of

---

[767] https://en.wikipedia.org/wiki/Groucho_Marx

[768] https://en.wikipedia.org/wiki/Jeff_Mayo

wounding and healing in the sixth house of service, trine Neptune in the tenth house of profession.

> She has been called "Mother of the Asteroids." She was among the first to devote serious research to this subject. She received the Matrix Pioneer Award for, "high standards of professionalism in educating the astrological community in the application and value of the asteroids (Goddesses) through chart interpretations." With her magnificent work on the Big Four asteroids – Ceres, Pallas, Vesta, and Juno – she showed us how these feminine goddesses had relevance in every chart, male and female.

> Writing and lecturing took up most of her time, but her reasons were not self-aggrandizement but rather a need to disseminate her information. She published a long-running monthly newsletter, Planet Watch, and her contribution to astrology was recognized when she was named a winner of the Marc Edmund Jones Award for Research.[769]

Corrie ten Boom was a Dutch heroine and Christian evangelist, famous for the book and the deeds of her noted family in "The hiding place". She had Sedna conjunct Jupiter, the planet of expansion, and also Vesta, the asteroid of regeneration, in the seventh house of relationships, sextile Neptune in the ninth house of spirituality.

> During the Second World War her father sheltered Jewish people, who were trying to escape from the Nazi Holocaust at their home. Some thirty-eight Jewish people were saved, but she was the only one in her family to survive the Holocaust.

> Her father believed that all people were equal before God and when a desperate Jewish woman appealed to him, he gave her shelter for the Holocaust in his house. Many persecuted Jews and Nazi resisters would follow. Corrie at first had trouble with the necessity of keeping these activities secret. She suffered a moral crisis over the lying, theft, forgery, and bribery that was necessary to keep the Jews her family was hiding alive.

> With help of the Dutch underground, they built a secret room in the top of the building, where the refugees could hide in case of

---

[769] http://www.astrologersmemorial.org/home/bach/

a a raid. She was 52 when the house was raided after a tip of an unknown person. That day some 27 persons were in the house, including six Jews that slipped in the hiding place. Twenty-one persons were arrested, including Corrie, her father and sister. Her father's health was weakened by age and tuberculosis and he was sent to a medical clinic where he died ten days after the arrest of the family.

Corrie and her sister were interrogated by the Gestapo, but not tortured. They took all the blame for hiding the Jews, and after four months in prison, they were sentenced to forced labour. Through their confession, the other arrested guests in their father's house were released. After the war, she became an evangelist, motivational speaker and social critic, protesting against the Vietnam War. She visited more than 60 countries, not preaching for any particular belief, but believing in an Universal Holy Spirit that asks for peace and forgiveness.[770]

And finally, Nirmala Srivastava was an Indian spiritual teacher and writer, also known as Shri Mataji Nirmala Devi. She was the founder of Sahaja Yoga, a meditation technique and new religious movement. She had Sedna conjunct Chiron, the centaur of wounding and healing, and Nessus, the centaur representing 'a guide to deep energies of regeneration', in the tenth house of profession, trine Neptune in the second house of material reality.

She claimed to have been born in a fully realised state and spent her life working for peace by developing and promoting a simple technique through which people can achieve their own self-realisation. She never charged for her instruction in Sahaja Yoga, which is now practiced and taught for free in over 140 countries.[771]

Semi-square, Square, Sesquiquadrate,

With the stressful aspects between Sedna and Neptune, the all-encompassing spiritual energy of Sedna challenges our inspiration, our dreams and our psychic receptivity, and also our tendency towards illusion, or confusion.

---

[770] https://en.wikipedia.org/wiki/Corrie_ten_Boom
[771] https://en.wikipedia.org/wiki/Nirmala_Srivastava

Neptune takes us beyond the known, to what's alive only in our wildest dreams. It is a bridge to the mysterious and that knowing many of us have that we're all somehow connected, especially those in our family, friend circle or ancestral lineage.

If we remain unconscious of our Sedna energy however the stressful aspects can call the more negative manifestations of Neptune into our lives, including delusion, deception, trickery, deceit, guilt, self-sacrifice, escapism and addiction.

Here again, the biggest problem can be self-delusion, because we all have a personal dream world and the potential for creativity, which is represented by the placement of Neptune in our charts and it is essential with the stressful aspects to test these dreams in reality, to discover which are real.

At the unconscious level this aspect can manifest as a kind of blind spot, which can leave us open to danger from fateful changes in the conditions around us. Like Erin Darling, an American teenager who was killed in a car accident when she was 17. She had Sedna in the third house of communication, sesquiquadrate Neptune in the eleventh house of collective consciousness. She was driving three other girls to school when she lost control on a wet road and crashed into a pick-up truck. All four attended the same Catholic high school, were good students, active in the community and well regarded.

It can also indicate that there is a chance of becoming a victim of someone else's delusion. Like Charles Lindbergh Jr, who was the first son of a noted American family, aviator Charles and pilot-writer Anne Morrow Lindbergh. He was abducted from his home in New Jersey when he was 20 months. He had Sedna in the seventh house of relationships, conjunct Uranus, the planet of revolution, which was right on his descendant, and sesquiquadrate Neptune in the eleventh house of collective consciousness.

> The family nurse put 20-month-old Charles in his crib and later discovered it empty. A ransom note in an envelope was found on the windowsill and a ladder outside. An extensive investigation by police followed, together with extended ransom negotiations which resulted in a 70,000 ransom being paid, however the boy was not returned.

Two months later, a delivery truck driver pulled to the side of a road about 7 kms south of the Lindbergh home. Going into a grove of trees he discovered the body of the toddler. His skull was badly fractured and there were indications of an attempt at a hasty burial. It appeared the child had been killed by a blow to the head. The culprit was eventually convicted through tracing the spending of the ransom money, the numbers of which had been recorded. And the case led to the Lindbergh law that made kidnapping a federal offence.[772]

Or as a victim of the illusions or deceit of others. Like Rachel Entwistle, who was an American homicide victim. She had Sedna conjunct Chiron, the centaur of wounding and healing, on the cusp of her 4th house of home, sesquiquadrate Neptune in the tenth house of profession. She and her 9-month daughter were found dead in their home, murdered by her supposedly successful husband, as she slept with their child, because he had created a fantasy world which was all about to collapse and he couldn't face telling her.

According to one of her teachers, she was adept at understanding concepts and complex situations. Rachel had genuine intellectual curiosity," he said. She was the kind of kid who loved learning. She wasn't just interested in getting good grades, but in understanding the material. The quality of her writing in the papers she did for the class was excellent. Rachel had tremendous potential and a positive and upbeat personality to go along with her intellectual ability.[773]

Or we might develop an abusing attitude. Like Wilhelm Keitel, who was a German Nazi Field Marshall and Chief of Staff of the High Command of the German Armed Forces, Hitler's closest military advisor and second only to him. He had Sedna in the ninth house of belief, semi-square Neptune in the tenth house of profession.

At the age of 58 he took over the Axis African Command, where he condoned measures leading to mass murder in Poland and Russia. Described as hard, unsmiling and mysterious, he was tried by the International Military Tribunal, found guilty of war

[772] https://en.wikipedia.org/wiki/Lindbergh_kidnapping

[773] https://en.wikipedia.org/wiki/Murders_of_Rachel_and_Lillian_Entwistle

crimes and crimes against humanity, and hanged when he was 64 in Nuremberg Prison.[774]

With this aspect we might have the ability to entrance people with our visions, or illusions, but at the unconscious level we may still be abusing their trust in the process. Like Marshall Applewhite, who was the American cult leader who led 39 members of "Heaven's Gate" to their death by suicide. He had Sedna conjunct Uranus, the planet of bohemian tendencies, in the first house of identity, sesquiquadrate Neptune, which is conjunct Pallas, the asteroid of wisdom, in the sixth house of service.

> He was married with two kids, when he left both his wife and the University of Alabama after a gay affair. His divorce after 16 years of marriage was a painful experience. Troubled by depression and sex demons, he checked into a hospital asking to be "cured" of his homosexual desires. When he met his new love, he was adrift, in debt, without his former social connections. With his career as a professional in doubt, he had found himself in a spiritual wasteland.

> Everything came together for them both. They felt connected as soul mates and beings from another dimension. Their relationship was chaste, but their minds were complementary and their passions the same. They wanted to escape mankind's eternal predicament, to get out of life alive. They formed their own theology out of scripture and the occult.

> They began an odyssey across America, recruiting members who were 'their people'. At first, they found their vision of eternity a hard sell and their bleak doctrine underwent a long gestation. It took nearly a year and a half to find their first disciple. She folded $25 into her pocket and left notes for her husband and daughters, the youngest of whom was a two-year-old, to follow her personal messiahs.

> Only four weeks into the mission however, she began to have doubts about the divinity of their sojourn. The three were running up bills on her credit card, and Applewhite had rented a car that he neglected to return. When they reached Houston, her family

---

[774] https://en.wikipedia.org/wiki/Wilhelm_Keitel

was waiting for them. She reunited with sanity, and Applewhite was arrested for car theft, spending six months in jail.

He used the time to polish his manifesto and when released in early 1975, unveiled his new, improved revelation. They would not take their bodies with them in death, but death would provide them with new bodies within the sacred furnace of space, as they were to be resurrected in a "cloud of light," a spaceship!

He carried his new doctrine to the fertile ground for Guru-UFO-revelation religions, California and had a meeting in Los Angeles with some 80 prospective devotees. Two dozen people joined, their first flock and they set up their center in a Wyoming campground and sent their followers out to canvass and recruit. The press began to catch wind of the story and the new cult soon reached the proportions of some 200.

At a gathering of the faithful in Medicine Bow National Forest in Wyoming, they were told that smoking grass and having sex was forbidden, stop it or leave, which left 70 people for instructions on The Next Level. One of these had a convenient trust fund and though strict living arrangements and spiritual disciplines were observed faithfully, the group also laughed and played together. They had a cheerful and highly regulated social life with total repression of sexuality.

However, the Next Level, that of leaving the earth in a space ship, remained elusive. Then when astronomers sighted the comet Halle-Bopp, Applewhite told them it was their message. A spaceship was scheduled to be traveling in the wake of the comet that would pick up the cultists to go to the Next Level and he suggested that it would be necessary to take things into their own hands.

By then the group was running a computer-consulting business and living in a gated estate in California in an elegant house. Applewhite was 65. The group had settled to a small core of true believers who felt that it was time to get on with it. Farewell videos were bequeathed to the world. Happy prospects were written across photos and letters. The cult had gone on for 24 years when they left the earthly habitat for the eternity of their dreams.

Their bodies were found in the mansion near San Diego, where their macabre ritual had been carried out over the prior three days, as they took Phenobarbital in apple sauce and vodka. They were all wearing new Nike shoes, had pockets full of quarters and were draped in purple cloths.[775]

Or like Jim Jones, who was an American cult figure, the Leader of The People's Temple. He had Sedna conjunct Uranus in the third house of communication, also sesquiquadrate with Neptune, which is also conjunct Pallas, the asteroid of wisdom, this time in the eighth house of shared resources.

When he was 46, he led his followers from San Francisco to Guyana. He was known as a manic-depressive who suffered from paranoia and delusions. However, he held an incredible power of persuasion and led nearly 1000 people, including himself, to a mass suicide a year later. His mother was convinced that her child was a messiah. His father, James Thurmond Jones, was a member of the Ku Klux Klan and died when Jim was young. His high-school classmates recall that he was popular but not a leader, noticing his growing interest in religion.

After graduating from High School, he become a pastor of a Methodist church in Indianapolis, where his strong views on integration made him a target of bigots. Disenchanted with the Methodist faith, he created his own church, the Community National Church. At 25, he opened the first Peoples Temple in Indianapolis. The Temple formed a soup kitchen, an employment desk to help people find jobs, and a nursing home.

He moved the Temple to northern California, near Ukiah when he was 34. There he built a new flock using fraudulent "healing" performances to win worshipers and encouraged members to inform on spouses or children who transgressed his rules of loyalty. A hierarchy of trusted members formed, ones who would eventually help carry out his last order for mass suicide. "Members' money and possessions were to be freely given to Jones at his command, along with sexual favours. At 40, he purchased new temples in San Francisco's Fillmore district and

---

[775] https://en.wikipedia.org/wiki/Marshall_Applewhite

in Los Angeles. His public relations talents brought him political clout four years later, but it also brought the attention of newspaper reporters who amassed enough data to devastate The People's Temple.

When his strong-arm tactics to squelch the story failed, he prepared to move to a leased tract of 27,000 acres in Guyana. Black followers were told they would be placed in concentration camps if they remained behind and Whites were informed they were on a CIA "enemies" list along with threats of blackmail and reprisals against defectors. Jones managed to be in Guyana when the edition of "New West" appeared. Incredibly, in light of the cruelty, stealing and sexual pervasion revealed in the article, 800 people were ready to follow him to Guyana.

When Congressman Leo Ryan became concerned enough about the affairs of The People's Temple to embark on a fact-finding trip with Temple lawyers and a team of reporters, Jones' paranoia was at an all-time high. After a day and night at Jonestown, the Jones compound, Ryan and the reporters had ferreted out enough information to take home a negative report despite the Herculean attempts by Jones' followers to keep the compound an appearance of utopia. Ryan and his entourage were at the small airport an hour away from Jonestown preparing to return home when a tractor trailer pulled onto the runway with armed People's Temple gunmen.

They fired on the party, killing Ryan, several newsmen and Temple members attempting to leave with the congressional party. At the same time, the camp doctor was ordered to prepare a vat of strawberry flavor-aide, dumping in a quantity of painkillers and tranquilizers as well as jugs of cyanide. The members of Jonestown drank the poison as ordered and Jones put a bullet through his head. Over 900 bodies were counted. A box of over 800 passports were found, Social Security checks of elderly members and a million dollars in cash.[776]

As we tire of density and the grief it creates, and we start a spiritual journey to get out of the swamp, Sedna rewards us with transcendent crises, experiences which force us to let go and rise above them,

---

[776] https://en.wikipedia.org/wiki/Jim_Jones

resulting in a huge growth to a new level of consciousness. There is no choice with these crises, and the more we try and solve them, the more we will get hurt.

Philip K. Dick was an American writer notable for publishing works of science fiction. He explored philosophical, social, and political themes in novels, with plots dominated by monopolistic corporations, authoritarian governments, alternate universes, and altered states of consciousness.

He had Sedna in the first house of identity, sesquiquadrate Neptune in the sixth house of service.

His work reflected his personal interest in metaphysics and theology, and often drew upon his life experiences in addressing the nature of reality, identity, drug abuse, schizophrenia, and transcendental experiences. His stories typically focus on the fragile nature of what is real and the construction of personal identity. They often become surreal fantasies, as the main characters slowly discover that their everyday world is actually an illusion assembled by powerful external entities, vast political conspiracies, or the vicissitudes of an unreliable narrator.

"All of his work starts with the basic assumption that there cannot be one, single, objective reality", writes science fiction author Charles Platt. "Everything is a matter of perception. The ground is liable to shift under your feet. A protagonist may find himself living out another person's dream, or he may enter a drug-induced state that actually makes better sense than the real world, or he may cross into a different universe completely."

Alternate universes and simulacra are common plot devices, with fictional worlds inhabited by common, working people, rather than galactic elites. Dick's thinking and work was heavily influenced by the writings of Carl Jung. The Jungian constructs and models that most concerned Dick seem to be the archetypes of the collective unconscious, group projection/hallucination, synchronicities, and personality theory.

In the Seventies, while recovering from the effects of sodium pentothal administered for the extraction of an impacted wisdom tooth, he began experiencing strange hallucinations. Although initially attributing them to side effects from medication, he considered this explanation implausible after they continued. He came to believe they imparted wisdom and clairvoyance. On one occasion the hallucinations imparted the information to him that his infant son was ill. The Dicks rushed the child to the hospital, where his suspicion was confirmed by professional diagnosis.

""I experienced an invasion of my mind by a transcendentally rational mind, as if I had been insane all my life and suddenly I had become sane," Dick told Charles Platt. As the hallucinations increased in length and frequency, Dick claimed he began to live two parallel lives, one as himself, and one as "Thomas", a Christian persecuted by Romans in the first century AD. He referred to the "transcendentally rational mind" as "Zebra", "God" and "VALIS" and wrote about these experiences in his VALIS trilogy.[777]

As we develop our Sedna energy and test our visions, we will likely be able to confront social issues and present visions which have the power to change the world.

Like our case study, Rachel Carson, the mother of the environmental movement, has Sedna in the first house of identity, square Neptune, which is together with Ceres, the dwarf planet of nurture and Jupiter, the planet of publishing, and Haumea, the dwarf planet of rebirth, all in the fourth house of home. Her book, *Silent Spring*, chronicled the devastating effects of the overuse of pesticide.

The book was startling for its rigorous scientific assessment of how, by spraying for one issue, to get rid of a bug or a weed, without considering how the chemicals would impact everything else, people were often doing more harm than good. It was a beautifully written treatise of horrors aimed at a general audience, which launched the environmental movement.

As a child she loved the outdoors, the birds and plants around her family's rural property sparking her imagination. She found fossilised fish and inspired by her expeditions wrote a book at age 8 and was published in a literary magazine at 13.

At age eight she wrote a book and a few years later joined an underage literary elite with published works in a children's magazine which also published early writings by William

---

[777] https://en.wikipedia.org/wiki/Philip_K._Dick

Faulkner, F. Scott Fitzgerald, E. E. Cummings, and E. B. White. Carson was fond of noting that she had become a professional writer at age eleven.

She entered the Pennsylvania College for Women on a senatorial district scholarship, earning an English degree, as preparation to become a writer. However, it was biology that she found most thrilling during her undergraduate years. Biology gave her the tools to learn what had happened to that fossilised fish she found as a child.

After earning a master's in zoology from Johns Hopkins, she found part-time work at the US Bureau of Fisheries. Though she'd chosen science over prose, her former specialty proved useful in her new occupation. Carson's first assignment for the bureau was to write a fifty-two-episode radio program called 'Romance Under the Waters'. "I had given up writing forever, I thought. It never occurred to me that I was merely getting something to write about."

Her first book, *Under the Sea-Wind,* was a commercial failure, selling only two thousand copies. She needed a couple of years to recover from the blow, but both driven and strapped for cash, she wrote another book. *The Sea Around Us* was published when she was 44 and it won the National Book Award for nonfiction and solidified her position as a literary heavyweight. To this day, it's credited as being one of the most successful books ever written about nature.

In her fifties she turned her attention to conservation, especially some problems that she believed were caused by synthetic pesticides. The result was the book, *Silent Spring*, published when she was 55, which brought environmental concerns to an unprecedented share of the American people. Although it was met with fierce opposition by chemical companies, it spurred a reversal in national pesticide policy, which led to a nationwide ban on DDT and other pesticides. It also inspired a grassroots environmental movement that led to the creation of the U.S. Environmental Protection Agency.[778]

---

[778] https://en.wikipedia.org/wiki/Rachel_Carson

Or like Karl Marx, who was a German-Jewish communist and philosopher who developed the theory of socialism and was the father of modern social science. He had Sedna in the first house of identity, square Neptune, which is conjunct Uranus, the planet of revolution, in the tenth house of profession. He was a revolutionary philosopher, who predicted that, like previous socioeconomic systems, capitalism would produce internal tensions, which would lead to its self-destruction and replacement by a new system: socialism.

His Sedna is also quintile Mercury in the third house of communication and bi-quintile to Pholus, the centaur of catalyzing change, in the eighth house of shared resources. This explains how his ideas and writing about social ideals involving a change in the distribution of social resources, made him the powerful evolutionary change agent that he was.

For him social change was about conflict between opposing interests, driven, in the background, by economic forces. This became the inspiration for the body of works known as the conflict theory. In his evolutionary model of history, he argued that human history began with free, productive and creative work that was over time coerced and dehumanised, a trend most apparent under capitalism. Fundamentally, he assumed that human history involves transforming human nature, which he saw, in a very Sednian way, as encompassing both human beings and material objects.

> He believed, like the philosopher Hegel, that humans recognise that they possess both actual and potential selves and that self-development begins with an experience of internal alienation, which Marx argued was because of 'the despotism of capital'. This leads to a realisation that the actual self, as a subjective agent, renders its potential self as an object to be apprehended by capitalism. Marx further argued that by moulding nature in desired ways, the subject takes the object as its own, and thus permits the individual to be actualised as fully human.

> In the new society that would emerge, he reasoned that the self-alienation would end, and humans would be free to act without being bound by the labour market. It would be a democratic society, enfranchising the entire population. In such a utopian

world there would also be little if any need for a state, the goal of which was only to enforce the alienation.[779]

Humour can be one path to transcend the quicksand of Sedna, giving us the objectivity to step back from the edge and also the challenge and ability with the stressful aspects to Neptune, to push the boundaries while staying sensitive and responsive to the audience.

Bob Newhart is an American actor, comedian, recording artist, and TV series star. He has Sedna in the sixth house of service, sesquiquadrate Neptune in the tenth house of profession. His Sedna is also sextile Jupiter, the planet of expansion, in the eighth house of shared resources.

> He is known for his deadpan double-takes and cautious stammer, a master of the well-timed pause. His humour as a child was dry and low-key and he was, for the most part, shy and introspective. Comedy became his way of looking at life. He studied business and became an accountant and, to relieve the monotony, started doing comic improv with a friend at parties.
>
> The duo became so popular that everyone encouraged them to play a pro venue. After a brief try, Bob's friend dropped out, but Bob continued to do the stand-up routine himself. One night a Warner Brothers Record scout caught Bob's act, and it led to his first recording. He was the first comedian in history to break into fame through LP records, "The Button-Down Mind Strikes Back," won a Grammy Award.[780]

At this juncture in human evolution, few of us use our planets at the spiritual level, but many of us are striving to, and such people are wonderful to be around. As with the other planets, the spiritual level of evolution is vastly different with Sedna from the two previous levels. Here the stressful aspects challenge us to bring spiritual enlightenment into our lives and sets us on a mystical, or spiritual mission.

Once we embrace the Sedna energy, which is the oneness of everything, our nurturing becomes an expression of Sedna consciousness and it becomes devotional in nature. The struggle of the beginner's level is gone, as are the transcendental crises of the

---

[779] https://en.wikipedia.org/wiki/Karl_Marx
[780] https://en.wikipedia.org/wiki/Bob_Newhart

intermediate level. At this level everything Saturnian is meaningless and yet everything Sednian has its place.

Jan Foudraine was a Dutch psychiatrist, psychotherapist and publicist, also known as Swami Deva Amrito, meaning immortality. He had Sedna conjunct Nessus, the centaur of radical change, in the sixth house of service, sesquiquadrate Neptune in the tenth house of profession.

He worked for five years in the psychotherapeutic centre and studied the art of interpersonal and transpersonal psychiatry. This is an interpersonal discipline, in which the patient is not seen an an object with an objective disease that had an illness to be cured, as in the strict medical model, but as a feeling soma-mind holistic (body/ego and soul) subject, who just like the human observer, wants to be mirrored and reflected by the therapist as a Higher Self. He thought of this higher insight and cure as "dis-identification". "It happened to me, but what seemingly happens to me, is seen from another perspective, as not me. It is just stuff I have to deal with."

When he was 39 he worked in a then "first in field" Dutch psychotherapeutic community, where psychiatric nurse's became socio-therapists, that had to reflect in their communication with patients, the values of society and the principles of good mothering. The supposed to be, all- or better-knowing psychiatrists and psychologists had to monitor, to reflect on and to steer the ongoing social process as if it was community theatre. This seldom worked, but the feedback could lead to more self-knowledge of the participants.

At 42 he published the Dutch best-seller *Not Made of Wood: A Psychiatrist Discovers His Own Profession*, of which 200,000 copies were sold in the Netherlands and many more abroad. As the first representative of anti-psychiatry in Holland, he became a "Messiah of the schizophrenics". With the LSD prophets of the Hippy generation, he believed that psychosis could be a way of "metanoia", a Dante like spiritual voyage through the inferno of the mind that might lead to more self-knowledge and greater inner stability.

However, he personally got involved into dualistic "for or against his views" conflicts, and could therefore not stay unattached in any job for long, got tired of the rhetorical Maya confusion about his spiritual message and used tranquillisers to deal with the stress.

Disappointed and confused, he travelled to Poona at 47 to seek rest and to visit Bhagwan Shree Rajneesh. He became a modest "silent" disciple of the Indian guru and the Bhagwan changed his mind set. He came back as another person in an orange dress and with another name: Swami Devi Amrito. His "conversion" to an Indian philosophy again received a lot of media attention in the Dutch press and he was now seen by some as a saint, but by most as a typical fool.[781]

Martin Luther King was an American clergyman and inspirational leader of the civil rights movement. He had Sedna conjunct Nessus, the centaur of radical change, and Vesta, the asteroid of regeneration, in the twelfth house of the unconscious, sesquiquadrate Neptune in the fifth house of creativity.

A symbol of the struggle against black segregation in the American South, he galvanized black Americans into action through his electrifying oratory skills and rose to become a legend and national hero in his own time.

Growing up in a pious, proud and progressive black community in segregated Atlanta, King was the son of a Baptist minister. Living in a family of black Brahmins he never experienced poverty, yet he continuously heard his father preach from his pulpit, "I don't care how long I have to live with this system. I will never accept it."

At age 26, after refusing to be heir apparent to his father's pulpit, his first position was at the prestigious Dexter Baptist Church at Montgomery, Alabama. When seamstress Rose Parks refused to move to the back of the bus on December 1st of that same year, King began his sermon to a church full of agitated supporters of her cause, four days after her courageous act. "You know my friends, there comes a time when people get tired of being trampled over by the iron feet of oppression." Individual cheers gave way to a resounding din within the church walls and King

---

[781] https://nl.wikipedia.org/wiki/Jan_Foudraine

walked into history that day as the delegated spokesman for the Montgomery Bus Boycott.

When the Montgomery buses finally began to operate on a non-segregated basis 381 days later, King formed the Southern Christian Leadership Conference, giving him a sound base from which to operate his vast congregation of everyday soldiers for civil rights.

His philosophy of passive resistance led to his frequent arrests and tours through the Bible Belt, where he became known as "Alabama's Modern Moses." The Southern student lunch counter sit-in when he was 31, the Freedom Riders a year later, marches in Birmingham two years after that, St. Augustine the following year and Selma the year after that, all put him in the national headlines as a civil rights activist. His greatest coup was the march on Washington, where 200,000 people gathered to demand their civil rights and hear him make his famous speech, "I have a dream...."

For upholding his allegedly radical views he was stoned, physically attacked and his house was bombed. As society grew more militant in the mid '60s, his interests widened to the Viet Nam War and those living in poverty. His plans for a Poor People's March on Washington in 1968 were interrupted by a sanitation workers' strike in Memphis, Tennessee. At 39, he delivered his legendary speech to supporters at the Mason Street Temple: "I have been to the mountaintop...I see the Promised Land. I may not get there with you, but mine eyes have seen the glory." The following evening, he was shot to death by an allegedly lone assassin.[782]

And finally, Oonagh Shanley-Toffolo was an Irish former nun, a midwife and acupuncturist. She has Sedna in the sixth house of service, sesquiquadrate Neptune in the tenth house of profession.

In her inspiring memoir, *The Voice of Silence*, published when she was 73, she tells of her childhood in Ireland, her training in Chinese medicine, her own brush with death, miraculous recovery, leaving the convent, getting married, and her work with

---

[782] https://en.wikipedia.org/wiki/Martin_Luther_King_Jr.

Princess Diana. She is a born healer, who has lived life on her own terms. She speaks confidently with an engaging Irish brogue and has always known that her role was to serve and to heal. After an acupuncture session, clients report that they feel like they could levitate off the table. Her philosophy is that 'the secret of unhappiness lies in trying to please everybody. It is a moral impossibility and compromises our true selves'.[783]

In-conjunct

With the evolutionary inconjunct between Sedna and Neptune, the esoteric spiritual energy of Sedna bursts into our inspiration, our dreams and our psychic receptivity, in an evolutionary way and we have a fated role to play.

The inconjunct sometimes acts as a flow and at other times as a stress, so we have to learn to actively manage the process as the rarified spiritual energy sometimes reinforces our inspiration and, at other times, isn't there to back us up. By adjusting to this, we gain a deeper understanding of ourselves and how to play our role.

Neptune takes us beyond the known, to what's alive only in our wildest dreams. It's a bridge to the mysterious and to that knowing that many of us have that we're all somehow connected, especially those in our family, friend circle, or ancestral lineage.

Neptune is associated with inspiration and spiritual enlightenment, it's the planet of mercy and compassion and its placement shows the areas of life where we find spiritual meaning. With this aspect with Sedna we could be naturally drawn over time toward the spiritual path and mysticism.

However, at the unconscious level we may have to deal with the more negative manifestations of Neptune, which include deception, trickery, deceit, guilt, and addiction.

At this level we might simply be in the wrong place at the wrong time, when suddenly something 'comes out of nowhere'. Like Douglas Neff, who was an American accident victim, who was killed when a car slammed into the back of his family vehicle and pushed them into oncoming traffic. He had Sedna on the descendent, the cusp of the seventh house of relationships, inconjunct Neptune on the cusp of the

---

[783] https://www.astro.com/astro-databank/Shanley-Toffolo,_Oonagh

second house of material reality. His wife was also killed and their two young children, seated in the back seat, were injured.

Or we might provoke abuse by teasing and disrespecting others. Like Jody Driscoll, who was an American homicide victim who was assaulted with an automobile. She had Sedna in the ninth house of knowledge, inconjunct Neptune in the fourth house of home.

> She approached a boy making a telephone call in a supermarket parking lot. Appearing annoyed, he shouted at her and pushed her forcefully away. When a friend of hers questioned him about his pushing her, the friend was told in foul language to move away. Jody left, but shortly thereafter, accompanied by two friends, she started to return by foot to the scene of the confrontation. While she was crossing the street, approaching the curb near the supermarket, he drove his automobile out of the parking lot, the car screeching as it turned the corner into the street that she and her two friends were crossing.He aimed the car first at one of her friends, struck her and then swerved toward Jody, hit her, ran over her body with the car, then swiftly left the scene without stopping.[784]

At the unconscious level we might also get caught up in a delusion, ours or someone else's. Like Barabara Plekker, who was a Dutch prostitute and homicide victim. Her Sedna was conjunct Saturn, the planet of limits and boundaries, in the seventh house of relationships, inconjunct Neptune, which is conjunct Mercury, the planet of communication, and Quaoar, the planet of new perspectives, all in the twelfth house of the unconscious. She was working out of a small, apartment-like room with a single window in the red-light district of Amsterdam, when she was strangled. It was a copycat crime, as four years prior, another prostitute had been killed in the same room, the same way.

Or to live a lie in an attempt to hide abusive behaviour. Like William Jewett Jr, an American who was accused of sexual assault and murder. He had Sedna in the eighth house of life and death, inconjunct Neptune, which is together with Ceres, the planet of nurturing, in the third house of ideas and communication. He was seen leaving a party late at night with a girl who was later found raped and then strangled to death. He was

---

[784] https://law.justia.com/cases/massachusetts/court-of-appeals/volumes/35/35massappct919.html

arrested nearly five years later on suspicion of her murder and was convicted and sentenced to life in prison.

Or we might hatch deluded schemes and get involved in the criminal underworld. Like Amy Fisher, who was an American teenager in the news for adolescent prostitution and the attempted murder of her lover's wife. She has Sedna in the first house of identity, inconjunct Neptune in the eighth house of life and death.

> She first ran away from home at 11 to go to Disneyland and claimed that she had been sexually assaulted at 13 by a workman at home. By 16, she was sporting new clothes and having fun, spending some $400 to $500 a week, telling her classmates and others that she was working for an escort service and that having sex for money was no big deal.[785]

Her Sedna is also in a fateful inconjunct with Pluto, the planet of life and death, in the sixth house of service.

> She began a sexual relationship with a 35-year-old mechanic after damaging the car her parents had given her for her 16th birthday and appealing to the owner of the body shop to which she took it, to make the repairs without her family knowing of the damage.
>
> Fisher gradually fell in love with him and became increasingly jealous of his wife. Eventually the then 17-year-old shared her idea of murdering his wife. Less than a year after she first had sex with him, she rang the doorbell of his home and when his wife answered the door, shot her in the face, wounding her severely. She was picked up by the police three days later, pled guilty to charges of assault with a deadly weapon and was sentenced to 5-15 years in prison.[786]

Her Sedna is also trine to Mercury, the planet of communication, in the fourth house of home.

> She received $8,000 from a magazine for a first-person piece on her experience and after her release from prison, she became a columnist for the *Long Island Press* and dictated a book about

---

[785] https://en.wikipedia.org/wiki/Amy_Fisher
[786] Ibid.

her experiences titled *If I Knew Then...* indicating she had grown through the crises.

She met her husband, a physical-fitness fanatic and wedding-photographer, some 25 years older than her, who has two kids from a former marriage. They married and, although the relationship was tempestuous, the couple had three children. And she reunited a few years later with the wife she had shot, in sessions televised for *Entertainment Tonight* and its spin-off, The Insider, saying she wanted to heal and move on with her life. However, two years later, she said she felt no sympathy for the woman, without giving an explanation.

Then the *New York Post* published allegations that her husband had sold a sex tape of the couple to Red Light District Video of Los Angeles. Nude pictures from the video were posted at various internet sites, and a teaser clip was released that showed her nude showering and sunbathing. But a year later Fisher announced that she had settled with Red Light and agreed to do a related promotional appearance. The same announcement indicated that she and her husband had reconciled.

The following year she released a pay-per-view adult film titled *Amy Fisher: Totally Nude & Exposed* and signed a deal with Lee Entertainment to become a stripper doing club shows at least once a month. And her struggles to assert herself and deal with her alcohol problems were documented during her time as a cast member in the fifth season of the reality television series, *Celebrity Rehab with Dr. Drew.* In her time as one of his patients, Fisher revealed intimate details of her personal life and experiences and remarked that the media had "ruined her life".[787]

Or we might delude ourselves and others into believing that we can act in an underhand way. Like Julian Assange, who is an Australian whistleblower, with a background in physics, math and computer programming, currently living in political asylum in the embassy of Ecuador in London. He has Sedna in the sixth house of daily routine,

---

[787] Ibid.

inconjunct Neptune in the twelfth house of the unconscious and conjunct his Ascendent.

> He is spokesperson and editor-in-chief of WikiLeaks, which is supposedly an investigative journalism internet-based organisation, with a mission to make public otherwise secret information, but which is designated by the US government as a hostile non-state intelligence service. His name became nearly a household word when at 39 he leaked over 250,000 classified diplomatic cables of the US government and therefore caused an uproar in government circles. Prior to that he had published many classified documents and a video from the Iraq and Afghanistan Wars.

> That same year the Swedish government posted a warrant for his arrest on rape and molestation charges. The warrant cited one count of unlawful coercion, two counts of sexual molestation and one count of rape. He denied the charges, but refused to face the courts, fighting his extradition from England. Two years later he walked into the embassy of Ecuador in London to ask for political asylum and five years on he is still living there in virtual house arrest, unable to leave without being arrested.[788]

Or we could live an illusion, which unfortunately will likely defraud other people. Like Bernie Madoff, who is a former American businessman, stockbroker, investment advisor, and financier. He has Sedna conjunct Ceres, the planet of nurture, in the eighth house of shared resources, inconjunct Neptune, which is conjunct Quaoar, the planet of new perspectives in the first house of identity.

> He is the former non-executive chairman of the NASDAQ stock market, and the admitted operator of a Ponzi scheme that is considered to be the largest financial fraud in U.S. history. He aroused the suspicion of his two sons when they learned that he intended to pay out bonuses two months early. When they confronted him, he confessed that his entire career was a fraud. He was 70. Arrested the following morning at his Manhattan home, he was sentenced to 150 years in federal prison.[789]

---

[788] https://en.wikipedia.org/wiki/Julian_Assange
[789] https://en.wikipedia.org/wiki/Bernard_Madoff

Or we could be visionary but might still run afoul of the Sedna tendency to harbor a blind spot. Like Adam Sedgwick, who was an English geologist and one of the founders of modern geology. He had Sedna conjunct Mercury, the planet of ideas and communication, in the second house of material reality, inconjunct Neptune in the ninth house of knowledge.

> He was the first to propose the Devonian period of the geological timescale. And later he proposed the Cambrian period, based on work which he did on Welsh rock strata. However, though he had guided the young Charles Darwin in his early study of geology and continued to be on friendly terms, he was an outspoken opponent of Darwin's theory of evolution by means of natural selection.[790]

As we tire of density and the grief it creates, and we start a spiritual journey to get out of the swamp, Sedna rewards us with transcendent crises, experiences which force us to let go and rise above them, resulting in a huge growth to a new level of consciousness. There is no choice with these crises, and the more we try and solve them, the more we will get hurt.

Swami Bhaktipada was a highly controversial, charismatic American Hare Krishna guru. He had Sedna in the first house of identity, inconjunct Neptune, which is conjunct Quaoar, the planet of new perspectives, in the seventh house of relationships.

> A victim of childhood polio, who walked with the assistance of canes, he was the son of a conservative Baptist minister, who inherited his father's missionary spirit and attempted to convert school classmates to his family's faith. As a student at the University of North Carolina, he met an undergraduate English major who became his homosexual lover and lifelong friend. The two resigned from the university when he was 23, after being threatened with an investigation over a sex scandal.
>
> He moved to New York City, started promoting LSD use and became an LSD guru. Then he worked as an unemployment claims reviewer and enrolled at Columbia University to study religious history, but quit after several years to travel to India at

---

[790] https://en.wikipedia.org/wiki/Adam_Sedgwick

28 in search of a guru, only to return to New York after six months, unsuccessful.

After returning from India however, he met the Bengali guru who was known simply as Swamiji to his disciples, who was the founder of the Hare Krishnas. After attending Bhagavad-gita classes at the modest storefront temple in the Lower East Side of Manhattan, he accepted Swamiji as his spiritual master, receiving initiation at 29. A couple of years later he co-founded a 4,000 acre Hare Krishna community in West Virginia, which eventually housed over 300 faithful followers, and where he served as spiritual leader for 26 years.

When he was 40, he and ten other high-ranking Hare Krishna leaders assumed the position of initiating gurus, because of Swamiji's death; however, at 49 the Krishna Governing Body Commission expelled him because he had started claiming to be the sole spiritual heir to the Hare Krishna movement. They cited his ruthless tactics, an overly independent nature and general callousness to the spiritual well-being of the movement.

He then established his own organization, taking several properties with him. A couple of years later his New Vrindaban had 13 satellite centers in the United States and Canada. However when he was 53 the US federal government indicted him on five counts of racketeering, six counts of mail fraud, and conspiracy to murder two of his opponents in the Hare Krishna movement when he was 48. The government charged that he ordered the killings because the victims had threatened to reveal his sexual abuse of minors. They also claimed that he had illegally amassed a profit of more than $10.5 million over four years.

At 53 he was convicted on nine of the 11 charges, but the jury failed to reach a verdict on the murder charges. However, the Court of Appeals threw out all the convictions, saying that child molestation evidence had unfairly prejudiced the jury against him and he was not charged with those crimes. A retrial was ordered and at 55, he was released from house arrest where he had lived for nearly two years and returned triumphantly to his community.

However, he lost his iron grip on the community a month later when he was accidentally discovered in a compromising position with a young male Malaysian disciple in the back of a Winnebago van. The community split into two camps and the challengers eventually ousted him and his supporters completely and most of his followers moved to the temple in New York, which remained under his control.

However, before his retrial was completed, he pleaded guilty to one count of racketeering for mail fraud and was sentenced to 20 years in prison. While he was in prison the Hare Krishna Child Protection Office concluded a 17-month investigation and determined that he had molested two boys. He was released from prison after serving eight years of a 12-year sentence and moved to India at 70 where he still had a significant number of loyal disciples, who worshiped him as a guru, dying there three years later.[791]

Paula Prentiss is an American actress, a leading lady in Hollywood films, adept at urbane screwball comedy roles. She has Sedna conjunct her moon in the eighth house of shared resources and partnership agreements, inconjunct her Neptune in the first house of identity.

At 20, while studying drama at Northwestern University, she met her future husband Richard Benjamin, who impressed her with his sophistication. She married him when she was 23 and the marriage has been solid, standing the test of time for over fifty years.

While attending university she was discovered by the Metro-Goldwyn-Mayer Studio and was offered a film contract, which in those days was a full-time job, moving from one film to another. A highly sensitive performer, having acted in a string of films back to back, she had a nervous breakdown on the set of *What's New Pussycat?* in Paris when she was 27. She was hospitalised for nine months and the breakdown kept her out of film work for the next five years.

She returned to work with her husband in the television series He & She. The couple also appeared together in a number of

---

[791] https://en.wikipedia.org/wiki/Kirtanananda_Swami

films, like Catch-22, when she was 32, as well as in various plays. Except for brief cameo roles, she had not appeared in a feature film for more than 30 years until she played in a horror film, *I Am the Pretty Thing That Lives in the House*, when she was 79. The film premiered at the 2016 Toronto International Film Festival.[792]

With this aspect our creative imagination may be may be strengthened through karmic experience, giving us faith in ourselves. Like Pina Bausch, who was a German dancer, choreographer and ballet director, mastermind of the company that changed the face of post-modern dance. She had Sedna conjunct Varuna, the planet of notability, in the ninth house of knowledge, inconjunct Neptune, which is together with Quaoar, the planet of new perspectives, on the cusp of her third house of communication.

She was the leading contemporary exponent of dance theatre in Germany, directing the Wuppertal Dance Theatre from the age of 33. She was a shy and fearful child, raised by parents who ran a modest hotel cafe in Solingen. She remembers speaking seldom. Taken to an exercise dance class, she was singled out for praise and filled with pride; all her dreams from then on were of the theater. She began with ballet classes and then studied under Kurt Joos, the great German choreographer. At 19, she went to Juilliard in New York. She studied at the Essen Folkwang School, and danced with the New American Ballet and the Met Opera House Ballet.

Gaunt and 5'7, with a pale, angular face, she tends to wear men's trousers and an oversized coat in her signature black. Her productions are distinctive, bold and vital, with highly original signatures. When she was 44 her company made its U.S. debut at the Los Angeles Olympic Arts Festival. She lived in her art and demanded that her people do so as well. Her scripts spring from close collaboration with the dancers, who went through group mind exercises in order to dredge up material that gave depth to the movement. The sets and music were given as precise attention, and the completed production became transformed into something greater than the sum of its parts.

---

[792] https://en.wikipedia.org/wiki/Paula_Prentiss

Her first set designer, the brilliant Rolf Borzik, was her great love and mentor and she lived with him until he died of cancer when she was 40. Reclusive and anxious, when she began her state-supported company, she confessed to terror at the challenge. What emerged was a strange, dream-like, violent, disturbing form of dance theatre that eventually influenced her generation.[793]

Or we may chart an imaginative course which is so avant-garde that we will have to have faith in ourselves to persevere. Like William Blake, who was a British artist, writer, engraver, painter and poet; a master in each field. His works are marked by genius, mysticism and compassion. He had Sedna in the ninth house of knowledge and belief, inconjunct Neptune which is on the cusp of the second house of material reality.

His "Prophetic" books are so complex and obscure, that few profess to understand them. He left Soho, the district of his birth, only once, and most of his life was spent in the same small area. His father was a hosier, and both his parents were stout adherents of a dissenting sect, the precise nature of which is not known. His formal education was limited, which may have been partly by choice. He wrote, *I must Create a System, or be enslaved by another Man's.*

At age 15, he was apprenticed to an engraver and over the years of his training he became more than a craftsman, but a universal artist. Plying his craft, he was a lower-middle-class tradesman, a mystic intimately involved in the world of commerce and craft. He lived with the smell of nut oil, varnish and lampblack as well as that of ink. It was a dirty work place, but one that always gave him stability and comfort.

After his seven years apprenticeship, he went into his own small business, hiring a shop to sell his own prints and offering himself as an illustrator of books. He had little success, and in worldly terms his life must be considered a failure. He felt this keenly and in later years grew embittered and resentful of the success of lesser artists of his acquaintance.

---

[793] https://en.wikipedia.org/wiki/Pina_Bausch

His wife, Catherine, sustained him in that her belief never faltered in his genius and his vision. When he might explain to a visitor the nature of his second sight, she would look at her husband with reverential awe, then look to their guest to ascertain that he comprehended the remarkable thing that he had just heard. Catherine was without reservation in her devotion to him.

His art, his poetry and paintings, and his books which he engraved and published himself, were a melding of word and image that must be considered all together to understand him. His visionary system is intricate, outlandish, hermetic and at times, preposterous. He held fast to certain precepts, such as "everything that lives is holy," and that sexual energy is one of the prime moving forces of the world and that its repression leads to conflict and spiritual death. In his *Marriage of Heaven and Hell*, he wrote, "... men forgot that All deities reside in the human breast."

He died at 70, at his home in London. A friend wrote that he died "in a most glorious manner." He hoped for salvation through Jesus Christ and just before he died, "his countenance became fair, his eyes brightened and he burst out into singing of the things he saw in heaven." His work never faded from the public view; however, it took time before the true nature of his genius was recognised. Like all true artists, he never lost faith in himself.[794]

Humour can be one path to transcend the quicksand of Sedna, giving us the objectivity to step back from the edge and also, with the inconjunct to Neptune, the challenge to push the boundaries while staying grounded and not getting lost in addictions.

George Carlin was an American comedian who began doing TV variety shows at 29, and nightclubs. He had Sedna conjunct Venus, the planet of aesthetics and art in the ninth house of knowledge, inconjunct Neptune in the second house of material reality.

He quit high school after his freshman year and joined the air force, leaving a year early with an honourable discharge. He had

---

[794] https://en.wikipedia.org/wiki/William_Blake

a short radio disk jockey career, which led to stand up work, and by the late sixties he was in Las Vegas doing network television talk shows.

He teamed with comedian Jack Burns before his solo act when he was 25. His film debut was at 31, although he only gained minimal popularity. He was fired from a big Las Vegas hotel a couple of years later, for saying a four-letter word. His notorious comedy act, called "The Seven Word's you can never say on Television," became a legal matter when he was 35, and was not resolved for six years, which was good promotion.

In his 30s he was the hottest act in the country, a whacked-out hippie whose LPs routinely went gold. By 36 he was heavily into self-destruct with his use of drugs and alcohol, favoring cocaine. His records sold liked crazy in the next couple of years, and he was a natural when he hosted *Saturday Night Live*. After a serious car accident and a heart attack at 41 he put his life back in order over the next few years, but it was not until his starring role in *Outrageous Fortune* at 50, which co-starred Better Midler, that he regained popularity.

The comedian and social critic entered a drug rehabilitation program at 67. In a statement he acknowledged that he had been using "too much wine and Vicodin." The decision to admit himself to the rehab facility was his own. "No one told me I needed this. I recognised the problem and took the step myself.[795]

At this juncture in human evolution, few of us use our planets at the spiritual level, but many of us are striving to and such people are wonderful to be around. As with the other planets, the spiritual level of evolution is vastly different with Sedna from the two previous levels. Here, the inconjunct aspect likely brings fated spiritual enlightenment into our lives and sets us on a mystical, or spiritual mission.

Once we embrace the Sedna energy, which is the oneness of everything, our nurturing becomes an expression of Sedna consciousness and it becomes devotional in nature. The struggle of the beginner's level is gone, as are the transcendental crises of the

---

[795] https://en.wikipedia.org/wiki/George_Carlin

intermediate level. At this level everything Saturnian is meaningless and yet everything Sednian has its place.

Elizabeth Clare Prophet was an American spiritual leader and guru, leader of the Church Universal and Triumphant based on Gnostic Christianity, Buddhism, New Age mysticism and masonry. She had Sedna conjunct Saturn, the planet of structure, and also her Sun, her willpower, in the tenth house of profession, inconjunct Neptune, which is conjunct Quaoar, the planet of new perspectives, in the third house of ideas and communication.

With intense and, it seems, utterly sincere belief in her own righteousness, she convinced her followers that she was able to foretell the end of time. And, although she prepared for the apocalypse at least six times, her church continued to draw followers. She had visions from the time she was a child. By the age of nine she had visited every church and synagogue in her hometown, seeking spiritual enlightenment.

When she was a student of Boston University she met Mark Prophet, who claimed to be a reincarnation of Sir Lancelot. A former insurance and vacuum cleaner salesman, he had founded a church which he was operating out of a Washington, DC storefront. Both were married to other people, but with divine guidance, they shed their respective mates and wed when she was 24. They soon moved their burgeoning flock to Colorado Springs and produced four children.

When she was 34 Mark died suddenly of a stroke and, becoming an ascended Master, she found herself the keeper of a sprawling spiritual empire worth by then about $50 million, funded by the tithing of members. They headed for California to settle on a 257-acre estate in the hills above Malibu. The church continued to grow despite major controversy, including the defection of a former husband. After divorcing her, he accused her of slavery and sued her and the church for $23 million. She settled out of court.

When she was 42 she married a much younger follower and he soon became business manager of the Church. She received a message from St. Germain that it was time to move on, and the cult moved their headquarters from Malibu, California, to a

12,000-acre ranch in Montana. The ranch was operated on strict guidelines seven days a week, with the day beginning at 5 am with two hours prayer and meditation and hard labor in between communal meal breaks. The diet was low protein and all stimulants were banned. Sex between married couples was allowed, but for no more than 30 minutes, twice a week.

Once probation has been passed, devotees signed away all their property irrevocably to the Church. Mrs. Prophet and her young husband had luxurious private quarters and she made her appearances dressed in spotless white satin with the occasional pink and gold sari, wearing diamonds and looking like a queen, being treated like a goddess. However, as head of the church, they each drew a modest salary of $1,900 a month plus expenses.[796]

Pope Francis is the 266th and current Pope of the Catholic Church. He has Sedna in the ninth house of spirituality in a close inconjunct with Neptune in the second house of material reality.

He chose Francis as his papal name in honour of Saint Francis of Assisi. Francis is the first Jesuit pope, the first from the Americas, the first from the Southern Hemisphere, and the first pope from outside Europe since the Syrian Gregory III, who reigned in the 8th century. Born in Buenos Aires, Argentina, he worked briefly as a chemical technologist and nightclub bouncer before beginning seminary studies. He became the Archbishop of Buenos Aires at 62 and was created a cardinal at 65. Following the resignation of Pope Benedict XVI a papal conclave elected Francis as his successor at the age of 76.

Throughout his public life, Pope Francis has been noted for his humility, emphasis on God's mercy, concern for the poor and commitment to interfaith dialogue. He is credited with having a less formal approach to the papacy than his predecessors, choosing to reside in the guesthouse rather than in the papal apartments of the Apostolic Palace used by his predecessors. In addition, due to both his Jesuit and Ignatian aesthetic, he is known for favouring simpler vestments void of ornamentation. He maintains that the Church should be more open and welcoming

[796] https://en.wikipedia.org/wiki/Elizabeth_Clare_Prophet

and has been freeing up some of the doctrinaire issues which have pushed people away, like divorce.[797]

This aspect can also give us a sensitivity to the spirit world. Like Lisa Williams, who is a British psychic, medium and healer. She has Sedna in the fifth house of creativity, inconjunct Neptune, which is conjunct Ceres, the planet of nurturing, in the first house of identity.

> She starred in two shows on Lifetime Television: *Lisa Williams: Life Among the Dead* and *Lisa Williams: Voices From the Other Side*. The shows followed Williams on a typical day, as she communicated with spirits, investigated haunted houses, and conducted other spirit-seeking activities.

> She came out as a lesbian at 37 and said: 'For many years, speaking to dead people was hard enough for people to accept me, but then on top of that to then say 'by the way, I'm gay', I didn't want to acknowledge it'. Asked by a reporter, because of her unique insight into life after death, where she thought gay people were headed, she said: 'In my experience with those who have crossed, it is a place of love. It isn't a place of 'you didn't live this way so we'll punish you', it is a place where all your loved ones accept you for who you are'.[798]

Quintile, Bi-quintile

The evolutionary quintile or bi-quintile aspect between Sedna and Neptune infuses our inspiration, our dreams and our psychic receptivity, with the all-encompassing spiritual energy of Sedna to the point where we can push the boundaries of human development.

These aspects point to talent, the desire to create order and to categorize, a fascination with patterns and structures, perfectionist tendencies, and the desire to build, or make things. These aspects have the characteristics of both the trine and opposition. They point to awareness of conflicts, or problems and finding solutions for them, however, they do not automatically kick into action and must be cultivated over time.

Neptune takes us beyond the known, to what's alive only in our wildest dreams. It's a bridge to the mysterious and to that knowing that many of

---

[797] https://en.wikipedia.org/wiki/Pope_Francis
[798] https://en.wikipedia.org/wiki/Lisa_Williams_(psychic)

us have that we're all somehow connected, especially those in our family, friend circle, or ancestral lineage.

Neptune is associated with inspiration and spiritual enlightenment, it's the planet of mercy and compassion and its placement shows the areas of life where we find spiritual meaning. With these aspects with Sedna we could be naturally drawn over time toward the spiritual path and mysticism.

However, at the unconscious level we may still have to deal with the more negative manifestations of Neptune, which include deception, trickery, deceit, guilt, and addiction. These can manifest in our own actions, or in the actions of others that affect us.

So, we could be the victim of a sudden freak accident, like Laetitia Laurain and Marie-Celine Grandjean, who were both killed at 20 years of age, when a crane collapsed on their high school. Both had Sedna bi-quintile Neptune. Laetitia had her Sedna conjunct the IC, the cusp of the fourth house of home, bi-quintile Neptune in the eleventh house of collective consciousness and Marie-Celine had it reversed, with Sedna in the eleventh and Neptune in the fourth.

Or we might have a blindspot, like Jennifer Mullin, who was an American homicide victim, who was raped and then strangled to death at the age of 18. She had Sedna in the fifth house of romance, bi-quintile Neptune in the twelfth house of the unconscious. She was last seen alive leaving a party in the early hours with an acquaintance who was arrested nearly five years later on suspicion of her murder.

We could also have the ability to mesmerize our friends, but at this level our visions might still be deluded and come more from a sense of victimhood, or alienation created by events, or abuse in our childhood.

An extreme example of this is Charles Manson, who is an American ritual cult leader, a psychopath who had a band of drug-numbed followers. He had Sedna in the twelfth house of the unconscious, bi-quintile Neptune, which is conjunct Mars, the planet of sex and war, in the fifth house of romance.

> He mesmerised his gang with liberal sex and drugs, while living on a ranch in the desert of southern California. He was the illegitimate son of a teenage prostitute and an army colonel. He was raised by an aunt and uncle and by the age of 11, he

developed into a delinquent, shuffling from foster parent to foster parent. He spent his youth and adulthood in and out of prison, spending 19 of his first 32 years behind bars.

In his mid-30s, while on parole he went to San Francisco to be a part of the hippie counter-culture in the Height-Ashbury district. He gathered adoring women around him by giving out LSD. Soon he was able to attract young men to his group by promising sex with his 'young loves'. They enjoyed long group LSD sessions, listening to the Beatles' "Helter Skelter" song on the White Album. However, unable to keep his friendships, He began to prophesy chaos to his followers.

When he was 34, he directed the ritual grisly killings of a Hollywood socialite and her house guests who were stabbed to death by his followers and their blood was smeared along the walls of the kitchen. A few days later, an older couple were tied up and carved and stabbed by forks and kitchen knives by Manson's followers.

The deaths frightened the Hollywood community and in the nine months of the trial, when he was 35, the jury found him guilty of first degree murder and conspiracy. He was convicted and given the death penalty, but the following year the California Supreme Court invalidated the capital punishment stature, and he became a life-termer. He has been continually refused parole by the California parole board.

He was denied parole for the ninth time at 63 and at his hearing he rambled for an hour, insisting that he did not kill seven people, saying, "I've killed a lot of people in my life, but I was convicted for those I did not kill." His behaviour in prison has been vicious and demented and yet, inexplicably, every year he receives letters and gifts from young people, Satanists, neo-Nazis and skinheads who view him as their role model, hoping for one day when he will be released.[799]

Or like Candy Barr, who was an American exotic dancer. She had Sedna conjunct Juno, the asteroid of partnership, in the eleventh house of collective consciousness, bi-quintile Neptune, which is conjunct her

---

[799] https://en.wikipedia.org/wiki/Charles_Manson

Moon, her feelings, in the fourth house of home. Her mother died when she was nine, and her dad married a woman with four children to add to his existing five. Sexually abused as a child by a neighbour and the baby sitter, she grew up to be a small Texas town bad girl. She ran away from home and became a prostitute before she was 16. She became one of the first superstars of the porno genre, starring in her first film, *Smart Aleck*, at 16.

> She was also one of the most famous and highly paid strippers, as well as a playmate to gangster Mickey Cohan. She made national news at 22 when she was arrested for drug possession. She began a 15-year jail term, but was paroled four years later and pardoned four years after that. In her late 30s, she emerged as a serious poet with her book, *A Gentle Mind - Confused*. Married four times, she had one daughter.[800]

As we tire of density and the grief it creates, and we start a spiritual journey to get out of the swamp, Sedna rewards us with transcendent crises, experiences which force us to let go and rise above them, resulting in a huge growth to a new level of consciousness. There is no choice with these crises, and the more we try and solve them, the more we will get hurt.

Skeeter Davis is an American musician with a career that was always eventful. She has Sedna conjunct Uranus in the third house of communication, bi-quintile Neptune in the eighth house of life and death.

> The eldest of seven kids, she formed a harmony group with her friend Betty Jack Davis and they called themselves The Davis Sisters. They began to play regular gigs on the radio in Lexington and on other shows in Detroit and Cincinnati before they signed a record contract. When she was 22 their first RCA release went to number one on the charts in 26 weeks.
>
> However, a car accident on the highway to Cincinnati killed Betty Jack and critically injured Skeeter, leading to a long rehabilitation period of recovery. She worked with Betty's sister for a while before going solo. At 28 she had a big breakthrough with 'Set Him Free', which established her as a star. And three years later

---

[800] https://en.wikipedia.org/wiki/Candy_Barr

'The End of The World', went gold and put her in the world-class. Her heart is in country, though she does a variety of styles.[801]

Neptune can inspire us to make great art, but as we struggle with our ego, we might still suffer from deceitful behaviour designed to bolster our own standing at the expense of others, which really amounts to abuse.

Like Bertold Brecht, who was a German playwright and poet, one of the leaders of the "epic theatre movement." He had Sedna in the third house of ideas and communication, quintile Neptune in the sixth house of daily routine.

He wrote his first prize-winning play while at Munich University in his early twenties, and directed his first play at 26. As a poet, he showed great mastery and forceful simplicity. His operas and plays champion alienation the way that Kafka epitomises anxiety. He combines text, balladry, stagecraft, imagery, movement and spoken word in a way now associated with performance art. His "Three-penny Opera" is familiar to every patron who has ever recognised theater as an art form.

A Marxist, a vegetarian, a genius and a contradictory figure, he was also considered an opportunist with an all-too-convenient ability to temporise. Despite his purposely shabby dress, unwashed stench, rotting teeth and icy persona, Brecht was some sort of modern Mesmer, able to hypnotise almost everyone he met into doing his bidding. He was considered a virtuoso in the bedroom, keeping regular revolving mistresses. When he fled Nazi Germany, he had not only his family but two other women, both of whom wrote large amounts of his work according to his specifications. Some of his major works may contain as little as 10% of his actual writing, but he served as a brilliant editor.

The saddest case - and most revealing of his character - is the story of Margaret Steffin, a young German writer from the provinces who had the misfortune to fall under his spell at an early age. She was almost single-handedly responsible for "Courage" and "Stezuan," as well as "Galileo" and at least four other major plays, a novel, and countless poems and stories, all

---

[801] https://en.wikipedia.org/wiki/Skeeter_Davis

published under Brecht's name. He was not able to read the source material in French for the works, and the manuscripts are all in her handwriting.

Suffering from TB, she died alone in a Moscow hospital ward after arranging for his safe passage to America. He mourned for four days, then promptly swindled her family out of her royalties and took her inheritance. While he became a millionaire, secretly depositing thousands of gold marks in a Swiss bank account, her family was left to subside on their meagre income.

He wrote most of his best work in exile: *The Good Woman of Szechwan, Galileo, Putila, and Mother Courage*. Along the way, he seduced everyone he met with his charisma, for fame, attention, favors, money, sex, all the while that he unscrupulously rode roughshod over everyone, cheating and using them. He once said, "What I don't like to admit is that I myself have contempt for the unfortunate.[802]

Ken Kesey was an American actor and novelist who worked at various times as a logger, a mental-hospital attendant, a farmer and musician in a band. He had Sedna in the second house of material resources, bi-quintile Neptune in the seventh house of relationships.

He volunteered for drug experiments run by the government, prior to the time that Timothy Leary started his experiments in psychedelics. His job as a psychiatric attendant for the Veteran's Administration Hospital in California when he was 26, provided background for his most famous work, "One Flew Over the Cuckoo's Nest." The next year he sold the movie rights for $28,000. The film won five Oscars and reportedly made $50 million in gross earnings.

A major counter culture figure in the 1960s, he and his band, The Merry Pranksters, made a cross-country drug-fuelled trip in a psychedelic painted bus called "Further" that was chronicled by Tom Wolfe in his book 'The Electric Kool-Aid Acid Test'. When he was 30 he purchased a farm in Pleasant Hill, Oregon, converting the barn into living quarters. Many of the outbuildings on the farm were built by The Merry Pranksters. He married his

[802] https://en.wikipedia.org/wiki/Bertolt_Brecht

high school sweetheart, Faye, and they had four children. He has always been close to family.

He was an inspiration for many young people. With an ear for dialog and the ability to create characters that live on the page, all of his works are about prisoners, some who realise their position and rail against it, others who are just doing their time. An old-fashioned kind of writer, he is a moral critic.[803]

Even once we are on a spiritual path, because of the ease these aspects introduce into our lives, there can be the temptation to take advantage of others, or of a situation, to abuse power and deviate from the spiritual path.

Like Jimmy Swaggart, who was an American charismatic maestro of hi-tech salvation, a television evangelist of Pentecostal Christianity blessed with the ability to spellbind audiences to the tune of $150 million a year. He had Sedna in the fourth house of home, bi-quintile Neptune in the ninth house of belief. His Sedna is also at the focal point of another bi-quintile to Jupiter, the planet of expansion, in the eleventh house of collective consciousness.

He conducted a vast yet dubious ministry secluded behind the walls of his $30-million-dollar compound in Louisiana. Known as a frequent hell-raiser as a teen, he dropped out of high school and played honky-tonk piano with his notoriously carousing cousin Jerry Lee Lewis. At age 17, he married a 15-year old farm girl who lived down the road, both successfully lying about their ages. Soon after his marriage, he preached his first sermon in front of a grocery store interspersed with playing the accordion, 'knowing we get crowds with the music'.

By his late 20s, he was itinerant preacher traveling the Southeastern US and began to cut gospel records, of which he eventually sold over 150 million. After another message from God, he began a radio show and from that point onward TV became his manifest destiny. The ministry probably quadrupled with radio. With TV it exploded.

In front of the TV camera, he became more outspoken than ever, verbally attacking Roman Catholicism, Jews and homosexuals

---

[803] https://en.wikipedia.org/wiki/Ken_Kesey

while soliciting money from his viewers. His Sedna is also closely semi-square Orcus, the planet of delving down and speaking out, in the fifth house of creativity. During each sermon, the impassioned preacher ranted and raved, coercing his followers and himself into a feeding frenzy of devotion. His antics backfired and in his late 40s he became a target of investigations.[804]

His Sedna is also square Ceres, the planet of nurture, in the seventh house of relationships.

A wealthy California widow left almost her entire estate to Swaggart Ministries. The Evangelistic Association and its agents were charged by family lawyers with 'preying upon her loneliness and illness for the purpose of securing donations from her.'" By now Swaggart was flush with 3 palatial estates and a private jet.

Further allegations of misallocations of monies, death threats, handsome payoffs and the exploitation of prostitutes led to private investigation. When confronted by photos of himself with prostitutes he reportedly admitted he had a fascination with pornography from childhood. This incident earned him a three-month suspension from his US pulpit and a two-year rehabilitation period, which proved unsuccessful. Further confirmed encounters with prostitutes sent him reeling into a tortured, televised public confession for which he may be best known. However, he was back to preaching once more against sin within three months.[805]

We may also be a natural philosopher and a deep thinker with these aspects. Like Arthur Schopenhauer, who was a German philosopher and writer known for his fine prose style and pessimistic philosophies. He had Sedna in the tenth house of profession, bi-quintile Neptune in the fifth house of creativity.

He led a solitary life and became deeply involved in the study of Buddhist and Hindu philosophies and mysticism. He was also a misogynist, never marrying and discouraging any friendships. His main work was, *The World as Will and Idea*, published when he was 31, in which he characterises the phenomenal world as

---

[804] https://en.wikipedia.org/wiki/Jimmy_Swaggart
[805] Ibid.

the product of a blind and insatiable metaphysical will. Coming from the transcendental idealism of Immanuel Kant, he developed an atheistic metaphysical and ethical system that has been described as an exemplary manifestation of philosophical pessimism, rejecting the post-Kantian philosophies of German idealism.

He was among the first thinkers in Western philosophy to share and affirm significant tenets of Eastern philosophy, like asceticism and 'the world-as-appearance', having initially arrived at similar conclusions, as the result of his own philosophical work. Though his work failed to garner substantial attention during his life, he has had a posthumous impact across various disciplines, including philosophy, literature, and science. His writing on aesthetics, morality, and psychology exerting important influence on thinkers and artists throughout the 19th and 20th centuries.[806]

Or like Jean Piaget, who was a Swiss psychologist, educator and author, known for his studies of children's learning patterns and the father of modern developmental psychology. He had Sedna conjunct Ceres in the eleventh house of collective consciousness, quintile Neptune, which is conjunct Vesta, the asteroid of regeneration, and the Ascendent, just inside the first house of identity.

His life work was learning how children learn, as their thought process is not that of adults. The conjunction with Ceres gave him the insight to see the relationship between his children's growth and the nurturing they received, which was the basis of his theories. This seems obvious now, but prior to this, children's growth was thought simply to be due to hereditary factors.

And this Neptune aspect gave him a sensitivity to his own natural reactions and how they were shaping his sense of self and the quintile gave him the ability to see this process in his children as they grew. From these personal observations of behaviour, he develop his understanding of a child's growth into the developmental psychology theories that have revolutionised early childhood education today.

---

[806] https://en.wikipedia.org/wiki/Arthur_Schopenhauer

His four developmental steps are studied by educators the world over. He developed several new fields of science, developmental psychology, cognitive theory and what came to be called genetic epistemology, the theory of knowledge. His 'constructivist theory of knowing' enabled researchers in a wide variety of fields and provided the basis for early computer programming languages.[807]

Humour can be one path to transcend the quicksand of Sedna, giving us the objectivity to step back from the edge and also, with the inconjunct to Neptune, the challenge to push the boundaries while staying grounded and not getting lost in addictions.

Buster Keaton was an American comedian, considered one of the greats of silent pictures for his physical humour and pantomime. He had Sedna in the eighth house of collective energies, quintile Neptune in the tenth house of profession.

He was born into a vaudeville family, his father owned a traveling show with Harry Houdini called the Mohawk Indian Medicine Company, which performed on stage and sold patent medicine on the side. And at the age of three, he began performing with his parents in The Three Keatons.

His mother played the saxophone, while on stage Buster would goad his father by disobeying him, and the elder Keaton would respond by throwing him against the scenery, or into the orchestra pit, or even into the audience. A suitcase handle was sewn into Keaton's clothing to aid with the constant tossing. The act evolved as he learned to take trick falls safely; he was rarely injured or bruised on stage; however, this knockabout style of comedy led to accusations of child abuse, and occasionally, arrest.

Decades later, Keaton said that he was never hurt by his father and that the falls and physical comedy were a matter of proper technical execution. He told the Detroit News: "The secret is in landing limp and breaking the fall with a foot or a hand. It's a knack. I started so young that landing right is second nature with me."

---

[807] https://en.wikipedia.org/wiki/Jean_Piaget

By the time he was 21, his father's alcoholism threatened the reputation of the family act however, so Keaton and his mother left for New York, where his career swiftly moved from vaudeville to film. He is best known for his silent films, in which his trademark was physical comedy, with a consistently stoic, deadpan expression, earning him the nickname "The Great Stone Face." He had an extraordinary period from when he was 25 to 34, when he worked without interruption on a series of films that make him, arguably, the greatest actor–director in the history of the movies.

His career declined afterward, with a dispiriting loss of his artistic independence, when he was hired by Metro-Goldwyn-Mayer and he descended into alcoholism, ruining his family life. Then he recovered in his late 40s, remarried, and revived his career as an honoured comic performer for the rest of his life, earning an Academy Honorary Award at 64.[808]

At this juncture in human evolution, few of us use our planets at the spiritual level, but many of us are striving to, and such people are wonderful to be around. As with the other planets, the spiritual level of evolution is vastly different with Sedna from the two previous levels. Here, the quintile and bi-quintile aspects brings spiritual enlightenment into our lives and sets us on a mystical, or spiritual mission.

Once we embrace the Sedna energy, which is the oneness of everything, our nurturing becomes an expression of Sedna consciousness and it becomes devotional in nature. The struggle of the beginner's level is gone, as are the transcendental crises of the intermediate level. At this level everything Saturnian is meaningless and yet everything Sednian has its place.

Ian Channel is a British-born New Zealander eccentric, known as 'The Wizard of New Zealand,' famous as the country's only official Wizard. He has Sedna conjunct Uranus in the first house of identity, bi-quintile Neptune, which is conjunct Mars, the planet of action, in the sixth house of service.

At 28 he enrolled in a degree in psychology and sociology, and on graduation he moved to Australia and worked as a lecturer

---

[808] https://en.wikipedia.org/wiki/Buster_Keaton

and organiser of community arts. At 35 he landed an assignment as college instructor and began his Ph.D. work at the School of Sociology at the University of New South Wales.[809]

His Sedna is also inconjunct Quaoar in the sixth house of service, and in a close evolutionary bi-quintile with Neptune, the planet of dreams and visions, which is also in the sixth. The combination of these aspects often signifies a unique evolutionary contribution.

During the student upheavals, which began at this time, he created a direct-action reform movement called 'Action for Love and Freedom' and implemented this with what he announced to be 'The Fun Revolution'. The result was a revitalisation of the university referred to in the Sydney Morning Herald as 'the university that swings'.

His head of department, convinced he was mad, dismissed him without consultation for insufficient progress in his thesis in the sociology of art. However, he wanted to stay on campus and continue his social experiments and he was able to persuade the Vice Chancellor to appoint him official University Wizard, with a small honorarium paid jointly by the University Administration and the Student Union.[810]

With Sedna in the first house, he began to experiment with his own identity and allowed his driving licence, social security ID, passport and other important documents to lapse.

After travelling to the World University Service headquarters in Geneva, he received their backing to travel round Australian universities to promote his new revitalisation movement. In a condition of considerable financial hardship, he persuaded Melbourne University Union Activities Department to appoint him their unpaid 'Cosmologer, Living Work of Art and Shaman'. The vice chancellor gave him the use of a lecture theatre for his classes in synthetic cosmology and the director of the National Gallery accepted the offer of his live body as a living work of art.

Becoming increasingly eccentric, he developed a unique world view blending magic, mysticism and sociology. A tall man with

---

[809] https://en.wikipedia.org/wiki/Wizard_of_New_Zealand
[810] Ibid.

long beard and robes, he began giving performances as a Wizard. At 42 he moved to Christchurch in New Zealand and began to speak on a ladder in Cathedral Square. The city council attempted to have him arrested, but he became so popular that they made the square a public speaking area.

Wearing his costume as a false prophet of the Church of England or his wizard's pointy hat, he has been speaking there at lunchtimes in the summer months for over 40 years, becoming a beloved, if controversial, figure, performing rain dances and other wizardry as necessary to fans and tourists.

At 50 the New Zealand Art Gallery Directors Association issued a statement that in their opinion the Wizard was an authentic living work of art and the City Council appointed him Wizard of Christchurch. Eight years later the Prime Minister of New Zealand appointed him the official Wizard of New Zealand.[811]

The man we know as the Dalai Lama, Tenzin Gyatso, has Sedna in the tenth house, bi-quintile Neptune in the third house of communication. He is actually the 14th Dalai Lama, which is a title given to spiritual leaders of the Tibetan people.

Despite his humble beginnings, being born on a straw mat in a cowshed to a farmer's family in a remote part of Tibet, he had become the joint most popular world leader by 2013, according to a poll which sampled public opinion in the USA and six major European countries.

He was not formally enthroned until he was 15, during the Battle of Chamdo with the People's Republic of China. The following year, he and the Tibetan government were pressured into accepting the Seventeen Point Agreement for the Peaceful Liberation of Tibet, by which it became formally incorporated into the People's Republic of China. Fearing for his life in the wake of a revolt in Tibet when he was 24, he fled to India, from where he led a government in exile.

With the aim of launching guerrilla operations against the Chinese, the Central Intelligence Agency funded his administration with US$ 1.7 million a year in the 1960s. At 66 he

---

[811] Ibid.

ceded his partial power over the government to an elected parliament of selected Tibetan exiles. His original goal was full independence for Tibet, but by the late 1980s he was seeking high-level autonomy instead.[812]

And Shivabalayogi was a meditation guru in the tradition of the ancient and modern yogis of India. He had Sedna in the eleventh house of collective consciousness, bi-quintile Neptune in the fourth house of home.

He attained self-realization through twelve years of arduous tapas, meditating in samādhi, a state of total thoughtlessness, for an average of twenty hours a day. Tapas is the most advanced stage of meditation in which one remains absorbed for long periods in this non-dualistic state of consciousness.

After he completed tapas, he assumed the name Shivabalayogi, meaning Yogi devoted to Shiva and Parvati. The name reflects that he is a manifestation of both the male and female aspects of the divine. The female aspect represents the invisible energy of the divine through which the entire creation operates, while the male aspect represents the pure consciousness of existence beyond all imaginations. Generally, devotees called him simply Swamiji, meaning respected Master.

For three decades he traveled extensively in India and Sri Lanka, initiating over ten million people into dhyana meditation. In his early fifties he traveled for four years in England and the United States. His teaching is consistent with the Vedanta, emphasising the need for spiritual practice to achieve self-realisation.[813]

---

[812] https://en.wikipedia.org/wiki/Dalai_Lama
[813] https://en.wikipedia.org/wiki/Shivabalayogi

38: Sedna / Pluto

Conjunction

There is no one alive today with this aspect and no one will be born with this aspect in the next 100 years, so it is not interpreted here.

Opposition

With the opposition of Sedna and Pluto, the all-encompassing spiritual energy of Sedna challenges our spiritual growth, our desire for change and our urge to let go and surrender so as to become a new person.

The energies of Pluto are transforming. Pluto represents subconscious forces, ruling all that is below the surface. On the up side, Pluto is associated with renewal and rebirth. It represents endings and new beginnings, as well as spiritual growth.

The opposition pits the transformative energies of Pluto against the transcendent energies of Sedna and brings existential transformative experiences into our lives from an early age that encourage, or force, the process of becoming what we have to be.

Pluto governs power itself, including struggles between people for domination, and of course, personal power. With the opposition we may find ourselves under the thumb of someone else's control. Facing down the manipulation of others, especially parents, will probably be part of the early maturing process likely with this aspect.

In the extreme this can unfortunately lead to a violent confrontation. Like it did with the American homicide victims, Amy and Daniel Seguin. Amy had Sedna conjunct Vesta, the asteroid of regeneration, opposite Pluto in the ninth house of knowledge. She was age five when her dad, in a fit of insanity, killed her mom. Her mom's body was found in a river near their home, but Amy and her brother Daniel were missing. Daniel also had Sedna opposite Pluto, with his Sedna in the eighth house of life and death and Pluto in the second house of material reality. Their bodies were found in a Franklin pond with their throats were cut.

Or it might put us in the path of violent forces beyond our control. Like Patrick Murphy, who was an American accident victim. He had Sedna in the third house of communication, opposite Pluto, which is conjunct Venus, the planet of relationships, in the ninth house of knowledge. He and a friend died in a fiery car crash when a drunk driver, speeding on the wrong side of the highway, collided into the car in which Murphy was driving. He had turned 18 just the month before his death.

The more negative expression of Pluto is an obsessive desire for power and control and general destructiveness and, until we develop our Sedna energy, the opposition can lend to a sense of righteousness in our use of these transformative energies, which may make it hard for us to tell that we are manifesting them negatively until it is too late.

Like Oscar Pistorius, who is a South African sprint runner and convicted murderer. He has Sedna conjunct the IC and both of his legs were amputated below the knee when he was eleven months old. The opposition puts Pluto on his MC, his point of social standing.

He was the tenth athlete to compete at both the Paralympic Games and Olympic Games, competing in sprint events for below-knee amputees in Paralympic events, and in non-disabled sprint events. After becoming a Paralympic champion, he attempted to enter non-disabled international competition, over persistent objections of the IAAF and charges that his artificial limbs gave an unfair advantage. He eventually prevailed in this legal dispute and at the 2012 Summer Olympics he became the first double-leg amputee to participate in the Olympics.

However, his Sedna opposition placed Pluto on his MC, together with Venus, the planet of relationships and he fatally shot his girlfriend in a fit of rage on Valentine's Day in 2013. He claimed he had mistaken her for an intruder hiding in the bathroom, but he was arrested and charged with murder. At his trial the following year, he was found guilty of culpable homicide. He received a five-year prison sentence and a concurrent three-year suspended prison sentence for a separate reckless endangerment conviction.

However, later that year the prosecutors asked the sentencing judge for permission to appeal the verdict. Permission was granted and the case was presented to a five-person panel at the Supreme Court of Appeal, which overturned the culpable homicide verdict and convicted him of murder. On Appeal by the state for a longer prison sentence, the Supreme Court of Appeal more than doubled Pistorius's prison term to 13 years and five months.[814]

At the unconscious level there is a chance with this aspect that we might be the victim of abuse or become an abuser ourselves. At this level these aspects can also manifest as problems with the legal system.

Like Amanda Knox, who is an American involved in famous criminal case, she was initially convicted of homicide by an Italian court and later cleared of murder charges on appeal. She has Sedna in the twelfth house of the unconscious, opposite Pluto in the sixth house of daily routine.

> She was 20 and a student in Italy, when her roommate, a girl from the UK, was killed. As the dramatic investigation unfolded, she was accused of being responsible for the brutal stabbing death. The prosecutors painted a grim picture of her as a party girl who wanted the UK girl to be involved in sex games at a party. She reportedly enlisted the help of her boyfriend and another man. Both men were also convicted.
>
> Her trial was covered extensively by US, British and Italian media for the nearly full year that it took to obtain a verdict. The jury handed down its guilty verdict when she was 22 and she was sentenced to 26 years in prison for murder and sexual assault. However, she and her parents protested that she did not receive a fair trial and steadily maintained her innocence.
>
> A year later she was granted the right to an appeal. The case captured media and public attention in both the US, Italy and elsewhere. When she was 24 she was cleared of murder and assault charges. The court upheld a charge of slander since she had initially accused her former boss of the murder, but the three-year sentence for that charge was deemed already served. She was immediately released from custody and able to return to the US with her joyful family.[815]

As we tire of density and the grief it creates, and we start a spiritual journey to get out of the swamp, Sedna rewards us with transcendent crises, experiences which force us to let go and rise above them,

---

[814] https://en.wikipedia.org/wiki/Oscar_Pistorius
[815] https://en.wikipedia.org/wiki/Amanda_Knox

resulting in a huge growth to a new level of consciousness. There is no choice with these crises, and the more we try and solve them, the more we will get hurt.

Like Elizabeth Smart, who is an American who went missing at age fourteen, abducted from her home as her family slept. Her Sedna is in the third house of communication, opposite Pluto, which is conjunct her Sun, the planet of willpower, in the ninth house of knowledge.

> She was the second of six kids and grew up in a close-knit Mormon family, reading scripture and praying morning and evening. On the evening just before her disappearance, she and her family had attended an award ceremony at her middle school, where she was recognised for various school accomplishments. The family prayed together and kissed goodnight, however sometime in the early morning hours, a man entered the bedroom she shared with her younger sister and spirited her away.

> No ransom note was found and no trace of her was reported, until she was spotted walking in a suburb of the same city with a shaggy-haired vagabond nine months later. During her ordeal, she spent a great deal of the time near her home wearing disguises and veils in public. The Smart family believes she was brainwashed, citing that she did not call out for help, or apparently try to escape, even when she heard rescuers call out her name.

> However, nearly two years after her rescue, her father said that she is "just a normal teenager who likes shopping and going to the movies with friends". A self-assured young woman and college graduate, she confronted her kidnapper at his trial and then accepted a job as a contributor for a television network in its coverage of missing persons.[816]

Or like Kesha, who is an American singer-songwriter. She has Sedna conjunct Mars, the planet of sex, in the fifth house of creativity and romance, opposite Pluto in the eleventh house of collective consciousness.

---

[816] https://en.wikipedia.org/wiki/Elizabeth_Smart

Her mother is also a singer-songwriter and when Keesha was young they relied on welfare payments and food stamps to get by. Her mother frequently brought Kesha and her brothers along to recording studios and encouraged her to sing when she noticed her vocal talent.

At 18, she was signed to Dr. Luke's label, Kemosabe Entertainment, and his music publishing company, Prescription Songs. Her breakthrough came four years later after appearing on rapper Flo Rida's number-one single "Right Round". Her debut album, Animal, and her first extended play, Cannibal, were released iwhen she was 23. Her music and image propelled her to immediate commercial success, with Animal debuting as the number-one album in the United States.

She also achieved two number-one singles and a string of top-ten hits singles from the album and its re-release, including one of the best-selling digital singles in history, selling over 14 million units internationally. Thematically, her music generally revolves around escapism, partying, individuality, supernatural moments, rebellion, and grief. She has been involved with animal rights and LGBT activism.

Then at 27 she sued producer Dr. Luke for alleged sexual assault and battery, sexual harassment, gender violence, emotional abuse, and violation of California business practices which had occurred over 10 years working together. She claimed that he repeatedly drugged her, had sexual contact with her, with and without her consent, and that his abuse caused her eating disorder. She asked the court to break her contract with Dr. Luke.

However, the court ruled against her request for a preliminary injunction that would release her from her contract with Kemosabe Records, under the umbrella of Sony Music Entertainment. The decision was made after the judge told her lawyer that he was essentially "asking the court to decimate a contract that was heavily negotiated and typical for the industry". The judge also cited what she felt was vagueness in Kesha's counterclaims, referring to the lack of documentation or hospital records supporting the alleged attack.[817]

As we get the power and control side of Pluto working within the rich sweep of Sedna's bounty, we can become an effective leader and this aspect shows up in the carts of several powerful rulers.

Like Henry VII, who was the King of England. He had Sedna conjunct his Sun in the second house of material resources, opposite Pluto, which is conjunct Uranus, the planet of innovation, and Chiron, the centaur of wounding and healing, in the eighth house of shared resources.

> He was considered tough, cold, shrewd and sly, ruling with strategy, intrigue and negotiation. At the age of 40 he sent explorers to North America.[818]

And like Friedrich II, King of Prussia, known as Frederick the Great, who ruled for 46 years. He had Sedna in the eleventh house of collective consciousness, opposite Pluto, which is conjunct Uranus, the planet of innovation, in the fifth house of romance and creativity.

> He suffered grave disapproval early on for his homosexuality and his dad had his male lover executed. He began his reign at 28 by invading Silesia, Austria, causing the War of the Austrian Succession and the Seven-Years War. He ranks as one of history's most innovative military strategists. Building a strong government and an efficient army, he encouraged industry and agriculture, making Prussia a strong rival to Austria for power.

> He was also an enlightened despot, he was a strong king and a military hero, yet he wrote verse in French and corresponded with Voltaire. Thirty volumes of his writings were published some hundred years after his death.[819]

At this juncture in human evolution, few of us use our planets at the spiritual level, but many of us are striving to and such people are wonderful to be around. As with the other planets, the spiritual level of evolution is vastly different with Sedna from the two previous levels. Here the opposition challenges us to bring the power of spiritual transformation into each moment.

---

[817] https://en.wikipedia.org/wiki/Kesha
[818] https://en.wikipedia.org/wiki/Henry_VII_of_England
[819] https://en.wikipedia.org/wiki/Frederick_the_Great

Once we embrace the Sedna energy, which is the oneness of everything, our nurturing becomes an expression of Sedna consciousness and it becomes devotional in nature. The struggle of the beginner's level is gone, as are the transcendental crises of the intermediate level. At this level everything Saturnian is meaningless and yet everything Sednian has its place.

We can see this in the life of Jean Jacques Rousseau, who was a Swiss philosopher, one of the most influential of the 18th century in political and social theory and in literature. He had Sedna in the sixth house of service, opposite Pluto, which is conjunct Uranus, the planet of intuition, in the twelfth house of the unconscious.

> He dreamed of the small, simple equalitarian state and thought that man and God are inherently good. However, his domestic partner Thérèse Levasseur, a seamstress, bore him a son and as many as four other children, all of whom he abandoned. He was essentially the founder of progressive education. His novel, *Emile*, or *On Education*, is a treatise on the education of the whole person for citizenship. His sentimental novel, *Julie*, or the *New Heloise*, was of importance to the development of pre-romanticism and romanticism in fiction.

> "His autobiographical writings exemplified the late 18th-century movement known as the Age of Sensibility and featured an increased focus on subjectivity and introspection that later characterized modern writing. His *Discourse on Inequality* and *The Social Contract* are cornerstones in modern political and social thought.[820]

Or like Christian Gellert, who was a German poet and novelist, a prominent representative of the German Enlightenment and whose works were, for a time, second in popularity only to the Bible. He had Sedna in the fifth house of creativity, opposite Pluto on the cusp of the eleventh house of collective consciousness.

> He was esteemed and venerated by his students, and others who knew him, due in great part to his personal character; he was known to be unflaggingly amiable and generous, and of unaffected piety and humility. His lectures in the Leipzig

---

[820] https://en.wikipedia.org/wiki/Jean-Jacques_Rousseau

university on poetry, rhetoric, and ethics were exceptionally well attended.

Owing to shyness and weak health he gave up all idea of entering the ministry, but he wrote in order to raise the religious and moral character of the people, and to this end he employed language which, though at times long-winded, was always correct and clear. He thus became one of the most popular German authors. He was best known for his *"Fables and Tales*, a collection of naïvely realistic fables and moralizing stories charming for their directness and simplicity.[821]

Semi-sextile, Sextile, Trine

With the flowing aspects between Sedna and Pluto, the all-encompassing spiritual energy of Sedna aligns with our spiritual growth, our desire for change and our urge to let go and surrender to become a new person.

The energies of Pluto are transforming. Pluto represents subconscious forces, ruling all that is "below the surface". On the up side, it is associated with renewal and rebirth, representing endings and new beginnings, as well as spiritual growth.

The more negative expression of Pluto however, is an obsessive desire for power and control and general destructiveness and while the flows don't encourage this side of Pluto, it can give us a sense of righteousness in our use of these transformative energies, which may make it hard for us to tell that we are manifesting them negatively.

There might be a buildup of guilt that leads us into abusive action. Like Abraham Kasparian, who is a former American politician who stabbed his wife three times in a public restaurant. He has Sedna in the fifth house of romance and children, trine Pluto and trine Haumea, the planet of rebirth, conjunct in the ninth house of the law.

> She had filed for a divorce but agreed to meet him for lunch. She survived the attack. He had been arrested previously for welfare fraud and larceny. Earlier that same day, a former tenant sued

---

[821] https://en.wikipedia.org/wiki/Christian_Fürchtegott_Gellert

the couple, charging them with negligence in connection with an apartment fire that killed two children.[822]

With any contact between Sedna and Pluto at the unconscious level there is a chance of a debilitating illness and physical problems. Like Katherine Mansfield, who was a prominent modern short story writer who was born and brought up in colonial New Zealand. She had Sedna conjunct Vesta, the asteroid of regeneration, in the fifth house of creativity, sextile Pluto in the sixth house of daily routine.

> She was the daughter of a successful businessman, schooled in New Zealand and sent to London at the age of 15 to attend Queen's College. When she was 22, she married to give her unborn child a name and left her husband almost immediately, but unfortunately the child was stillborn. Two years later she met an editor, and they married when she was 30.

> She was first published at 23 with her novel, *In A German Pension*, but didn't receive much notice. However, in the next five years she became an important contributor to European magazines. Grief stricken by the loss over her brother's death during WW I, she also learned at that time that she had incurable tuberculosis. She died at 35 in France. Her most noted book, *The Garden Party* was released just before she died and two of her books were published after her death.[823]

The drive for power and control that Pluto wants to exert can still lead to abuse, or abusive tendencies with the flows at the unconscious level, only on a far vaster scale, but it still comes with the same inevitable karmic kickback.

As it did with Adolf Hitler, the Austrian-German politician who became the Dictator of Germany and was responsible for WW2. He had Sedna on the cusp of the sixth house of service, sextile Pluto in the eighth house of life and death. His infamous dictatorship, lasted for only thirteen years, but it created a permanent shift in world politics and was directly responsible for the death of over 30 million people.

> He joined the German Workers' party at 31 and turned the tiny, ineffective group into a formidable paramilitary organisation.

---

[822] https://www.astro.com/astro-databank/Kasparian,_Abraham
[823] https://en.wikipedia.org/wiki/Katherine_Mansfield

Three years later he tried to force the Bavarian government into a full-scale revolution against the Weimar Republic, but his beer hall putsch failed. He spent nine months in prison, where he wrote the first volume of his book, *Mein Kampf,* which means My Struggle, his plan for Germany's dominion over the world.

Aided by Germany's internal chaos and worsening economic condition, he schemed his way into authority at 44 and was named Chancellor. It was a time of economic depression in Germany with a third of the country out of work. His speaking power was awesome, winning him the support of the masses. He built a private army of 100,000 men, the brown-shirted Storm Troopers and purged potential threats to his leadership, murdering or jailing political rivals on the infamous 'Night of the Long Knives'.

He re-armed Germany, re-occupied the Rhineland, took over Austria and seized Czechoslovakia, as his first steps toward conquering Europe, then the world. He ordered a huge pogrom with Jewish arrests all over Germany to achieve his demonic vision of Aryan dominion, a policy which sent over six million European Jews, Gypsies and political dissidents to the gas chambers. He had 'immoral books' burned in his police state, but he offered national pride and jobs, offering hope for an economic recovery.

He was 50 when his armoured columns rolled across the Polish border, triggering WW2. When battlefield casualties numbering in the millions provoked an unsuccessful assassination plot on his life towards the end of the war, he condemned the men responsible to death. They were hung on meat hooks and strangled with piano wire, but just short of death. They were then revived and rehanged, repeatedly, with the episodes filmed for his later enjoyment. Toward the last days, he and his long time mistress were married in the bunker under the chancellery and then they committed suicide.

The women in his life had uniformly tragic fates. His 20-year-younger half-niece and first romantic obsession, was found dead in her bed in the Berlin apartment that she shared with him, when he was 42. He had persuaded her and her mother to serve as his live-in housekeepers. The nature of their relationship has been debated ever since, with theories that Hitler was entirely asexual, to the belief that he led a normal sexual life, to stories of perversions and phobias. It has been established that he had had a huge pornographic collection. Whatever the explicit form his affections took, it seemed evident that his young half-niece was increasingly confined and resistant to her position.

She was found with a bullet through her chest and his gun by her side. Whether the death was a murder or suicide has never been resolved. There was a hasty attempt to cover it up with the announcement that she was nervous about an upcoming recital, but there were also news reports that they had yet another fierce quarrel because the 23-year old wanted to go to Vienna, where she intended to become engaged. He met a 29-year-old German movie star a few years later, a petite, blue-eyed blonde, who accepted a command invitation to the private quarters of the Fuhrer. However, by the time he was 48, the meetings ended abruptly, when she either jumped from her Berlin apartment window, or was thrown out by the Gestapo, after being charged with having a Jewish lover.[824]

And as it did for Osama bin Laden, who was the founder of al-Qaeda, the organization that claimed responsibility for the September 11 attacks on the United States, along with numerous other mass-casualty attacks worldwide. He had Sedna in the eleventh house of collective consciousness, trine with Pluto, which is in the third house of ideas. This gave him a sense of righteousness in his cause and shows how transformative his ideas would be; however, unfortunately, his Pluto is square Mars, so they also provoked endless conflict.

He was a Saudi Arabian and a member of the wealthy bin Laden family. His mother was his father's tenth wife, but she was Syrian and was called the slave by the rest of the family. Osama was called the son of a slave. His father divorced his mother soon after he was born, recommending her to an associate, who married her and they are still together. The couple had four children, and Osama lived in the new household with three half-brothers and one half-sister.

---

[824] https://en.wikipedia.org/wiki/Adolf_Hitler

This early sense of victimisation was formative in shaping his perspective. He projected his victimisation onto his fellow Muslims and set out to save them from, as he saw it, the decadent Saudi Arabian leadership in cahoots with the infidels. At 22 he joined the Mujahideen forces in Pakistan fighting against the Soviet Union in Afghanistan. He helped to fund the Mujahideen by funnelling arms, money and fighters from the Arab world into Afghanistan, and gained popularity among many Arabs.

At 31 he formed al-Qaeda. He was banished from Saudi Arabia four years later, and shifted his base to Sudan, until U.S. pressure forced him to leave four years after that. His Sedna was also opposite Ixion, the planet of lawlessness, in the fifth house of 'what is produced in the home', which gives the signature of his style of terrorism: A major component of his ideology was the concept that civilians from enemy countries, including women and children, were legitimate targets for jihadists to kill.

After establishing a new base in Afghanistan, he declared a war against the United States, initiating a series of bombings and related attacks. He was on the American FBI's lists of Ten Most Wanted Fugitives and Most Wanted Terrorists for ten years from the age of 44. The FBI placed a $25 million bounty on him. He was finally shot and killed inside a private residential compound in Parkistan, where he lived with a local family, during a covert operation conducted by members of the US Naval Special Warfare Development Group.[825]

As we tire of density and the grief it creates, and we start a spiritual journey to get out of the swamp, Sedna rewards us with transcendent crises, experiences which force us to let go and rise above them, resulting in a huge growth to a new level of consciousness. There is no choice with these crises, and the more we try and solve them, the more we will get hurt.

Like our case study, Steve Jobs, the founder of Apple computers, who had Sedna conjunct Mars, the planet of action, in the eighth house of shared resources, trine to Pluto, which is together with Haumea, the planet of rebirth, on the cusp of his twelfth house of karmic results.

---

[825] https://en.wikipedia.org/wiki/Osama_bin_Laden

He and his friend, Steve Wozniak, made their first circuit board in their garage and they called it the Apple. By the time he was 24, his Apple Corporation was worth $10 million. A year later, its value had grown to $100 million. Its graphical user interface, business applications and word processing won kudos, and millions cheered while Apple took on IBM and its personal computer.

However, his high school sweetheart, who lived with him and was an early Apple employee, said he became a threatening monster and their relationship fell apart amid wild recriminations when she became pregnant with his first child. He denied he was the father, despite a positive paternity test and he paid a pittance in child support, while living the life of a millionaire.[826]

In her memoir, *The Bite In The Apple: A Memoir Of My Life With Steve Jobs* she says: "I've truly hated Steve at times, but never for very long. Sharing a daughter with him has forced me to think about things more deeply. Steve the saint, the alien, the despot, the punishing masculine god, the liar, the obsessed narcissist, the cult hero, the ID of the iEverything, the genius and the motherless boy.[827]

As the Apple empire grew, Steve became a tyrant, subject to moody outbursts and gloomy silences. Hard feelings arose and power struggles with other executives ensued. He resigned and the following year co-founded NeXt, in an attempt to do for the hardware industry, what he had down for software. He also bought a company which he renamed Pixar Animation Studios and negotiated a deal with Disney to distribute Pixar's films and became a Disney partner. Under Jobs' leadership, Pixar won 20 Academy awards for successful animated feature films and was acquired by Disney.[828]

With a twist of fate and a large amount of Sednian transcendence, he then convinced Apple to buy NeXt and was invited back to Apple as interim CEO and a few years later was made permanent CEO once again. Under his renewed leadership Apple computer became a major

---

[826] https://en.wikipedia.org/wiki/Steve_Jobs
[827] Brennan, Chrisann. *The Bite In The Apple: A Memoir Of My Life With Steve Jobs*
[828] https://en.wikipedia.org/wiki/Steve_Jobs

player in the computer industry once more and his team created visually aesthetic computers in bright colors that appealed to younger buyers.

The trine with Pluto gave him the ambition to change the world. "What is Apple, after all?" he mused to Time. "Apple is about people who think 'outside the box,' people who want to use computers to help them change the world, to help them create things that make a difference, and not just to get a job done." And when Jobs was luring John Sculley away from Pepsi in order to apply his marketing skills to the personal computer market, he famously said: "Do you want to sell sugared water for the rest of your life? Or do you want to come with me and change the world?"

T.S. Eliot was an American-British poet, playwright, literary critic and editor; he was a leader of the modernistic movement in poetry. Eliot was awarded both the British Order of Merit and the Nobel Prize for Literature. He had Sedna conjunct Vesta, the asteroid of regeneration, in the sixth house of service, sextile Pluto in the eighth house of shared resources.

> From private high schools he went on to Harvard University, where he received his Bachelor of Arts degree. He went to France, attending philosophy lectures at the Sorbonne and reading poetry. These studies helped him find his own voice and style. For three years from the age of 23 he studied Sanskrit and read Indian philosophy back at Harvard.

> At 26 he established residence in London and at 39 he was confirmed in the Church of England and became a British subject. At 31 he published *Poems* which included "Gerontion," a meditative interior monologue in blank verse like nothing before published in English. His career as an editor was always secondary to his main interests. From 34 to 51 he edited his own quarterly, the *Criterion*, which was the most distinguished international critical journal of its time.

> At 37 he started working for the publishing house of Faber and Faber, where he eventually became a director. Probably one of the most erudite English poets of his time, his first important published work and the first masterpiece of modernism in English was "The Love Song of J. Alfred Prufrock." With the

publication of his most famous poem about the disenchantment and disgust after World War I,

"The Waste Land," at the age of 34 he earned an international reputation.[829]

Edith Sitwell was a British writer, the first poet to be named a Commander of the British Empire and at 67 she was made a Dame. She had Sedna in the third house of communication, sextile Pluto in the sixth house of daily routine.

> As a poet she is experimental and eccentric. She also edited *Wheels*, an annual magazine during WWI. As she hated physical exercise, she wrote in bed. Her early work was lightly imagistic, macabre and wistful and exhibited a spectrum of colour. Later, her work became more tightly knit, infusing simple matters with reverence and an aura of great significance. At 67 she converted to Catholicism, for which she held a deep religious passion. And three years later, she became a visiting professor at the Institute of Contemporary Arts.[830]

We may also be a deep thinker with these aspects. Like Arthur Schopenhauer, who was a German philosopher and writer known for his fine prose style and pessimistic philosophies. He had Sedna in the tenth house of profession, semi-sextile Pluto in the ninth house of philosophy.

> He led a solitary life and became deeply involved in the study of Buddhist and Hindu philosophies and mysticism. He was also a misogynist, never marrying and discouraging any friendships.

> His main work was, *The World as Will and Idea*, published when he was 31, in which he characterises the phenomenal world as the product of a blind and insatiable metaphysical will. Coming from the transcendental idealism of Immanuel Kant, he developed an atheistic metaphysical and ethical system that has been described as an exemplary manifestation of philosophical pessimism, rejecting the post-Kantian philosophies of German idealism.

> He was among the first thinkers in Western philosophy to share and affirm significant tenets of Eastern philosophy, like

---

[829] https://en.wikipedia.org/wiki/T._S._Eliot
[830] https://en.wikipedia.org/wiki/Edith_Sitwell

asceticism and 'the world-as-appearance', having initially arrived at similar conclusions, as the result of his own philosophical work. Though his work failed to garner substantial attention during his life, he has had a posthumous impact across various disciplines, including philosophy, literature, and science. His writing on aesthetics, morality, and psychology exerting important influence on thinkers and artists throughout the 19th and 20th centuries.[831]

The flows can also give us a sense of humour, allowing the release of the existential challenge that inherently exists between Sedna and Pluto, because of the transformative nature of both their energies. Humour can be one path to transcend the quicksand of Sedna, giving us the objectivity to step back from the edge and also, with the flowing aspects, enjoy the transformation process itself.

Clown is an art form that teases us to release the stuff below the surface and, by laughing at ourselves we can release the hang-ups and allow the transformation. A number of famous clowns have flows to Pluto, including Charlie Chaplin and Harpo Marx, who have sextiles and David Shiner, Rowan Atkinson and Roseanne Barr and Sandra Bernhard, who share the trine.

I also have a trine with Pluto, which is conjunct my Haumea, the planet of re-birth, in my eighth house of shared resources. This aspect definitely talks about my 30 years of clown teaching work. And, despite the public perception, clowning is not an easy art to learn, and teaching it is one of the most difficult jobs on the planet, because it is totally person centered and each person is unique.

Harpo Marx was an American comedian, actor, mime artist, and musician, and the second-oldest of the Marx Brothers. He had Sedna in the sixth house of daily routine, sextile Pluto in the eighth house of shared resources.

> He received little formal education and left grade school at age eight due to bullying, during his second attempt to pass the second grade. He began to work in odd jobs alongside his brother Chico to contribute to the family income, including selling

---

[831] https://en.wikipedia.org/wiki/Arthur_Schopenhauer

newspapers, working in a butcher shop, and as an errand office boy.

At 21 he joined two of his brothers to form "The Three Nightingales", later changed to "The Marx Brothers". In contrast to the mainly verbal comedy of his brothers, Harpo's comic style was visual, being an example of both clown and pantomime traditions. He wore a curly reddish blonde wig, and never spoke during performances; rather, he blew a horn or whistled to communicate. He frequently used props such as a horn cane, made up of a lead pipe, tape, and a bulb-horn, and he played the harp in most of his films.

In their films he was often cast as Chico's eccentric partner-in-crime, whom he would often help by playing charades to tell of Groucho's problem, and/or annoy by giving Chico his leg, either to give it a rest, or as an alternative to a handshake. He became known for prop-laden sight gags, in particular the seemingly infinite number of odd things stored in his topcoat's oversized pockets. He often used facial expressions and mime to get his point across. In later films, he was put into situations where he would repeatedly attempt to convey a vital message to another person, but only did so through nonverbal means, usually by whistling or pantomime.

He married at 47 and the marriage was lifelong. The couple adopted four children and when he was asked how many children he planned to adopt, he answered, "I'd like to adopt as many children as I have windows in my house. So when I leave for work, I want a kid in every window, waving goodbye.[832]

Roseanne Barr is an American actress, comedian, writer, and television producer. She was also the 2012 presidential nominee of the California-based Peace and Freedom Party. She has Sedna in the second house of material resources, trine Pluto, which is conjunct Haumea, the planet of rebirth, in the seventh house of relationships.

She began her career in stand-up comedy at clubs before gaining fame for her role in the hit television sitcom, *Roseanne.* The show ran for nine seasons and she won both an Emmy and

---

[832] https://en.wikipedia.org/wiki/Harpo_Marx

a Golden Globe Award for Best Actress for her work. She had crafted a "fierce working-class domestic goddess" persona in the eight years preceding her sitcom and wanted to do a realistic show about a strong mother who was not a victim of patriarchal consumerism.

The granddaughter of immigrants from Europe and Russia, she was the oldest of four children in a working-class Jewish Salt Lake City family. She was active in The Church of Jesus Christ of Latter-day Saints, yet courted controversy by stunts like singing the national anthem off-key at a nationally aired baseball game, followed by grabbing her crotch and spitting.

After her sitcom ended, she launched her own talk show, *The Roseanne Show*, and returned to stand-up comedy with a world tour. Then she announced she was running for the presidential nomination of the Green Party, which she lost, before getting the nomination of the Peace and Freedom Party. She received 61,971 votes in the general election which brought Trump to power, placing sixth overall[833]

Sandra Bernhard is an American comedienne, tall, skinny, aggressive, ultra-hip and manic. She has Sedna in the tenth house of profession, trine Pluto, which is conjunct Haumea, the planet of rebirth, in the first house of identity.

She was born in Flint, Michigan, to a proctologist father and an abstract-artist mother. After she graduated she spent eight months in Israel on a kibbutz. She then moved to Los Angeles where she lived with an aunt and uncle and went to beauty school to learn how to be a manicurist, while pursuing her comedy career. Her early stand-up comedy acts were not major successes initially.

She became hot property in her late 20s, after working for five years as a manicurist and stand-up comic prior to landing a lead role in *The King of Comedy* with Robert de Niro, released when she was 28. She did nightclubs, TV and films. She is most remembered for playing lesbian Nancy Bartlett on the television show *Roseanne* for six years from the age of 36. She has one

---

[833] https://en.wikipedia.org/wiki/Roseanne_Barr

daughter, Cicely, born when she was 43. She has never said who the father is, nor how the child was conceived, but she is openly bisexual and is a strong supporter of gay rights.[834]

At this juncture in human evolution, few of us use our planets at the spiritual level, but many of us are striving to, and such people are wonderful to be around. As with the other planets, the spiritual level of evolution is vastly different with Sedna from the two previous levels. Here, the flowing aspects bring the power of spiritual transformation into each moment.

Once we embrace the Sedna energy, which is the oneness of everything, our nurturing becomes an expression of Sedna consciousness and it becomes devotional in nature. The struggle of the beginner's level is gone, as are the transcendental crises of the intermediate level. At this level everything Saturnian is meaningless and yet everything Sednian has its place.

Corrie ten Boom was a Dutch heroine and Christian evangelist, famous for the book and the deeds of her noted family in *The Hiding Place*. She had Sedna conjunct Jupiter, the planet of expansion, and also Vesta, the asteroid of regeneration, in the seventh house of relationships, but on the cusp of the eighth house of life and death.

> During the Second World War her father sheltered Jewish people, who were trying to escape from the Nazi Holocaust at their home. Some thirty-eight Jewish people were saved, but she was the only one in her family to survive the Holocaust.

> Her father believed that all people were equal before God and when a desperate Jewish woman appealed to him, he gave her shelter for the Holocaust in his house. Many persecuted Jews and Nazi resisters would follow. Corrie at first had trouble with the necessity of keeping these activities secret. She suffered a moral crisis over the lying, theft, forgery, and bribery that was necessary to keep the Jews her family was hiding alive.

> With help of the Dutch underground, they built a secret room in the top of the building, where the refugees could hide in case of a a raid. She was 52 when the house was raided after a tip of an unknown person. That day some 27 persons were in the house,

---

[834] https://en.wikipedia.org/wiki/Sandra_Bernhard

including six Jews that slipped in the hiding place. Twenty-one persons were arrested, including Corrie, her father and sister. Her father's health was weakened by age and tuberculosis and he was sent to a medical clinic where he died ten days after the arrest of the family.

Corrie and her sister were interrogated by the Gestapo, but not tortured. They took all the blame for hiding the Jews, and after four months in prison, they were sentenced to forced labour. Through their confession, the other arrested guests in their father's house were released. After the war, she became an evangelist, motivational speaker and social critic, protesting against the Vietnam War. She visited more than 60 countries, not preaching for any particular belief, but believing in an Universal Holy Spirit that asks for peace and forgiveness.[835]

Or like Steve Hill, who was an American Christian clergyman and evangelist. He had Sedna in the seventh house of relationships, trine Pluto, which is conjunct Juno, the asteroid of partnership, and Haumea, the planet of rebirth, all in the eleventh house of collective consciousness.

As a teenager, he got heavily into alcohol and illicit drugs. At the age of twenty-one due to the effects of drug abuse, he spent three days suffering extreme convulsions, and turned to Christianity. A few weeks after his conversion experience, he was arrested and faced 25 years in prison for drug trafficking. Instead of jail, he was remanded to the Teen Challenge drug rehabilitation program, from which he graduated.

He is best known as the evangelist who preached in what became known as the Brownsville Revival. The Brownsville Revival was a series of meetings at Brownsville Assembly of God in Pensacola, Florida that began on Father's Day, when he was 41 and continued for five years. At 46 he moved to Texas to resume traveling evangelism. And at 49 he founded Heartland World Ministries Church in a suburb of Dallas.[836]

---

[835] https://en.wikipedia.org/wiki/Corrie_ten_Boom
[836] https://en.wikipedia.org/wiki/Steve_Hill_(evangelist)

As we engage with the spiritual growth side of Pluto, these aspects become some of the most powerful agents for growth in the chart, combining the transformation powers of Pluto with the transcendent powers of Sedna.

Like Martin Heidegger, who was an German existentialist philosopher and one of the most influential voices and foremost thinkers and writers of the 20th century. He had Sedna in the fourth house of home, sextile Pluto, which is conjunct Neptune, the planet of philosophy, on the cusp pf the seventh house of relationships.

> With the publication of his first book, *Being and Time*, when he was 38, he achieved instant fame as one of the spokesmen of 20th century existentialism. Though unfinished, Being and Time is one of the central philosophical works of the 20th century. In the first division of the work, He attempted to turn away from "ontic" questions about beings to ontological questions about Being and recover the most fundamental philosophical question: the question of Being, of what it means for something to be.

> He argued that being human is defined by care, that it's practically engaged and is a concernfull mode of being-in-the-world. This was in opposition to rationalist thinkers like René Descartes who located the essence of man in our thinking abilities. For Heidegger thinking is thinking about things originally discovered in our everyday practical engagements. The consequence of this is that our capacity to think cannot be the most central quality of our being, because thinking is a reflecting upon this more original way of discovering the world.

> In the second section, he argues that human being is even more fundamentally structured by its temporality, or its concern with, and relationship to time, existing as a structurally open 'possibility-for-being'. He emphasised the importance of authenticity in human existence, involving a truthful relationship to our being thrown into a world, and to our being-towards-death, the finitude of the time and being that we are given, and the closing down of our various possibilities for being through time.

> He also made critical contributions to philosophical conceptions of truth, arguing that its original meaning was un-concealment, to philosophical analyses of art as a site of the revelation of truth,

and to philosophical understanding of language as the 'house of being'.[837]

Or like Elsie Wheeler, the American spiritualist and psychic who worked with Marc Edmund Jones and Zoe Wells on the Sabian Symbols and who was noted for being the primary contributor. She had Sedna in the eleventh house of collective consciousness, sextile Pluto in the first house of identity. She shares the aspect with her collaborator Marc Edmund Jones.

Marc Edmund Jones was an American astrologer, a popular professional and author, whose books include, *Guide to Horoscope Interpretation*. He had Sedna in the fifth house of creativity, conjunct Vesta, the asteroid of regeneration, sextile Pluto in the seventh house of relationships.

> As a child Marc Edmund Jones was interested in complex patterns observable in the environment, and he gradually developed a distinctive personal system of thought that later produced notable perspectives on occultism and the cabalistic world-view in general.

> He has been called the dean of American astrology and was a major leader in the twentieth century of a movement to reformulate the study of astrology. He developed the seven categories of horoscopic patterns or distributions of the astrological planets around the zodiac, which are called the Splay, Splash, Bundle, Bowl, Locomotive, Bucket, and Seesaw shapes or patterns.

> Greatly interested in metaphysics, he and the gifted clairvoyant Elsie Wheeler set about to find a set of symbols for every degree of the zodiac that was an improvement on existing degree symbology. One day when he was 37 he took a series of 360 small blank cards on each of which was noted a sign and degree on the back and held them up for Wheeler to describe her vision. The cards were shuffled continually to keep the selection random.

> The images did not seem entirely appropriate, or some were exaggerated, so the cards were put aside for six years, before

---

[837] https://en.wikipedia.org/wiki/Martin_Heidegger

the definitions were revised. This process was repeated some 17 years later and the results were first published when Marc was 63 as *The Sabian Symbols in Astrology*, a book that renders a specific symbol and interpretive character for each of the 360° of the zodiac that are found on the astronomical ecliptic.[838]

Semi-square, Square, Sesquiquadrate,

With the stressful aspects between Sedna and Pluto, the all-encompassing spiritual energy of Sedna challenges our spiritual growth, our desire for change and our urge to let go and surrender to become a new person.

Where we find Pluto in the chart is where we either seek change and transformation, or have it thrust upon us, if we refuse to accept our deepest needs. If we fear Pluto's energies, or our dark side, then destructiveness is likely, both directed at ourselves and at others.

With the stressful aspects the transformative energies of Pluto challenge the transcendent energies of Sedna. Pluto governs power itself, including struggles between people for domination, and of course, personal power.

At the unconscious level we may find ourselves under the thumb of someone else's control. Facing down the manipulation of others, especially parents, will probably be part of the early maturing process likely with these aspects. And in the process, we are likely to learn some manipulative skills ourselves, which may be expressed later in life at this level as an obsessive desire for power and control, or general destructiveness.

Like Klaus Kinski, who was a German actor famed for his wide-eyed, histrionic performances, as seen in hundreds of roles in movies which he chose for their commercial possibilities. He had Sedna conjunct Nessus, the centaur likened to a sympathetic monster, in the tenth house pf profession, square Pluto in the twelfth house of the unconscious.

> Described as unpredictable, rebellious and whimsical, he refused to work under such famous directors as Fellini, Pasolini or Visconti as "they don't pay me enough." He was the author of a highly readable and bigger-than-life autobiography, *I Need Love*, which is largely centred on his miserable youth, his countless

---

[838] https://en.wikipedia.org/wiki/Marc_Edmund_Jones

love affairs, his obsessive adoration of his son and his unrelenting hatred of cops and film makers. He also fathered two daughters, the youngest being famed actress, Nastassja Kinski. However, twenty years after his death, his oldest daughter published an autobiography in which she reported about years of sexual abuse by her father.[839]

Or it might put us in the path of violent forces beyond our control. Like Margaret Eden, who was an American worker whose car stalled on the railroad tracks as she was driving to work when she was 24. Her Sedna was conjunct Nessus, the centaur of sudden change, in the sixth house of daily routine, square Pluto, which is conjunct the North Node in the ninth house of knowledge. Her passenger jumped out before the train hit the car, dragging it 116 ft. and killing Margaret.

It can also indicate a chance of becoming a victim of abuse. Like Charles Lindbergh Jr, who was the first son of a noted American family, aviator Charles and pilot-writer Anne Morrow Lindbergh. He was abducted from his home in New Jersey when he was 20 months. He had Sedna in the seventh house of relationships, conjunct Uranus, the planet of revolution, which was right on his descendant, and square Pluto, which is conjunct Ceres, the planet of nurturing, and the MC in the tenth house of social standing.

> The family nurse put 20-month-old Charles in his crib and later discovered it empty. A ransom note in an envelope was found on the windowsill and a ladder outside. An extensive investigation by police followed, together with extended ransom negotiations which resulted in a 70,000 ransom being paid, however the boy was not returned.

> Two months later, a delivery truck driver pulled to the side of a road about 7 kms south of the Lindbergh home. Going into a grove of trees he discovered the body of the toddler. His skull was badly fractured and there were indications of an attempt at a hasty burial. It appeared the child had been killed by a blow to the head. The culprit was eventually convicted through tracing the spending of the ransom money, the numbers of which had

---

[839] https://en.wikipedia.org/wiki/Klaus_Kinski

been recorded. And the case led to the Lindbergh law that made kidnapping a federal offence.[840]

Or we could find ourselves to be both victim and abuser at the same time. Like Tommaso Buscetta, who was a Sicilian Mafiosa, the first major figure in the Sicilian Mafia to break the code of omerta, the traditional vow of silence. His Sedna is also in the ninth house of knowledge, square Pluto, which is conjunct his Sun, his willpower, in the twelfth house of institutions and the unconscious.

His criminal record began at 21, with bootlegged cigarettes. He soon began traveling to Brazil and America where at one time he opened a chain of pizza parlors that reportedly served as a cover for drug dealing. Arrested in New York at 42, he fled to Brazil.

Up till that time, a hundred top Mafia families had controlled organised crime in Italy, focusing on their traditional areas of agriculture, construction, extortion, prostitution and some drug smuggling. They had their codes; politicians and police were "cultivated," not murdered and women and children were off-limits. All that changed when the French Connection was broken in the 1970s and Sicily succeeded Marseilles as the world's heroin capital.

The heroin traffic became immense and new groups began fighting for a piece of the action. Wives and children were massacred, along with their Mafia husbands and troublesome officials. Unfortunately, Buscetta aligned himself with one of the loosing clans, two of his sons disappeared and his brother and nephew were gunned down at work. In all, at least 14 members of his family were slain. When he was extradited to Italy, he sought assurance that he would be protected, should he talk and, when he did, authorities were amazed at the amount and detail of his accounts.

He provided a comprehensive description of the Mafia's internal structure and precise information on 122 recent murders. He explained the command structure and how each clan had its territorial base. Though each clan was autonomous, a supreme commission, composed of representatives from a dozen major

---

[840] https://en.wikipedia.org/wiki/Lindbergh_kidnapping

families, made all decisions on crimes and investments and arbitrated disputes. He also provided previously unknown information about the mob operation in the U.S.

His lengthy confession, at 57, precipitated the most determined crack-down on organised crime that has ever been instigated. Following his testimony 66 suspected Mafiosa were arrested, with warrants for another 140. He then effectively disappeared into the witness protection program, assuming a new name and identity somewhere in the U.S.[841]

Interesting to note here that these aspects can go either way, with a possibility of becoming a victim, or an abuser. As an example, we find both the perpetrator and the victim of one of the most famous assassinations in history have the same aspect between Sedna and Pluto. We'll look first at the perpetrator here at the unconscious level.

James Earl Ray was an American assassin who shot civil rights leader Dr. Martin Luther King to death. He had Sedna, conjunct Nessus, the centaur of radical change, both in the ninth house of knowledge, square Pluto in the twelfth house of institutions and the unconscious.

He had a long criminal record and had previously served prison terms. He was born into an extremely poor family with an extensive history of run-ins with the law. He grew up in rough and tumble river towns along the Illinois and Missouri, which doubled as spawning grounds for the KKK. His father abandoned the family when Ray was young, his mother, an alcoholic, eventually had all of her eight children removed to foster care.

One positive relationship grew out of Ray's chaotic childhood, the bond between him and his brothers, Jerry and John. They grew very close through their horrible childhoods and trusted and relied on one another. As the years progressed, Ray was convicted of increasingly severe crimes. A racist, he refused to work with blacks on a prison honour farm.

After an escape from prison when he was 39, he caught up with his brothers and they discussed ways to earn money, including kidnapping the governor of Illinois or a local star radio host. They also flirted with the idea of going into the porn business. Ray

---

[841] https://en.wikipedia.org/wiki/Tommaso_Buscetta

shocked even his brothers when he told them that he was, "going to kill that n----- King. That's something that's been on my mind. That's something I've been working on."

The following year he arrived in Memphis, the exact same day as Dr. Martin Luther King Jr. Newspaper publicity revealed the hotel at which King was staying, as well as the room number. The next day, Ray reconnoitered the hotel from a rundown rooming house across the street and when King stepped outside the door to his room, he fired the single shot that killed him.

After the shooting, he panicked and threw the murder weapon, which was wrapped in a bundle, against a storefront. The quick discovery of this by police was the critical piece of evidence that helped police identify him as the shooter. An accustomed international traveler however, he was able to flee to Canada and return to England. But he ran low on money, which caused him to rob a bank, and just as he was about to board a plane for Brussels, he was arrested at Heathrow International Airport.[842]

As we tire of density and the grief it creates, and we start a spiritual journey to get out of the swamp, Sedna rewards us with transcendent crises, experiences which force us to let go and rise above them, resulting in a huge growth to a new level of consciousness. There is no choice with these crises, and the more we try and solve them, the more we will get hurt.

Marie Curie was a Polish-French scientist, a physicist and chemist, winning Nobel Prizes for both, but not allowed in the French Academy of Science as she was female. She had Sedna in the second house of material reality, semi-square Pluto in the third house of ideas and communication.

At 24 she joined her sister in Paris to study math, physics and chemistry at the Sorbonne. She proved a brilliant student with an early interest in the magnetic properties of steel. Within two years she received her license in science with the highest marks of her class. She later held a chair in physics at the Sorbonne, the first female professor at the university.

---

[842] https://en.wikipedia.org/wiki/James_Earl_Ray

She was drawn to fellow scientist, Pierre Curie by their mutual interest in magnetism and devotion to science. They married when she was 28 and in Pierre, she found a new love, a partner, and a scientific collaborator on whom she could depend. However their early years were very hard. In 1898, after they discovered radium, Marie had a struggle of four years of toil which finally resulted in the extraction of one-tenth of a gram of radium from one ton of uranium mine waste, one of the epic stories of science.

The Curies worked together for 11 harmonious years, isolating radium and polonium. As well as being one of history's outstanding scientists, Marie lived the normal life of a wife and mother; a month after discovering radium, she carefully notes having made 14 pots of gooseberry jelly. Her letters show her very close and affectionate relationships with her father, brother and sisters, her daughters and many friends.

When she was 36 the Royal Swedish Academy of Sciences awarded them the Nobel Prize in Physics, together with another male physicist, "in recognition of the extraordinary services they have rendered by their joint researches on the radiation phenomena." At first, the Committee intended just to honour the two men, but one of the committee members alerted Pierre to the situation, and after his complaint, Marie's name was added to the nomination. She was the first woman to be awarded a Nobel Prize.

She was devastated when Pierre was killed in a road accident when she was 39. The physics department of the University of Paris had offered him a professorship the year before and was preparing his laboratory when he died. The university decided to retain the chair that had been created for him and to offer it to her. She accepted it, hoping to create a world-class laboratory as a tribute to Pierre. She was the first woman to become a professor at the University of Paris.

She received a second Nobel Prize in her own right at 44, this time for Chemistry, for the discovery of the elements radium and polonium, but was never allowed to join the French Society of Scientists because she was a woman. A biography by her daughter stresses her parent's unworldliness and the idealism that made them refuse to patent the process they developed of isolating radium, which could have made them wealthy.[843]

One of our case studies, new age guru, Bhagwan Shree Rajneesh's Sedna is in his eleventh house of ideals, square his Pluto in the second house of material resources. Despite his evolved spirituality, the square to Pluto is reflected in what his bodyguard observed was another key facet of Rajneesh's charismatic ability. He was "a brilliant manipulator of the unquestioning disciple."

Bhagwan's Saturn is in his 8th house of the occult and of shared resources, conjunct his Moon, representing his emotions, and Venus, the planet of values and relationships. The opposition with Pluto and the squares to Sedna are the engine of his teaching approach, sharing 'transformational tools' in return for his followers donating all, or most of their money and possessions to the commune, to live at a mere subsistence level, while he bought 97 Rolls Royce cars.

The manipulative nature of these Pluto, Sedna aspects is also evident with media tycoon, Rupert Murdoch. His Sedna is in his fifth house of creativity, square his Pluto in the seventh house of one-to-one relationships. He is notorious for micro managing his media empire and for being a hugely successful businessman. Business is all about one-to-one relationships and selling and buying. Often manipulation is a tactic used in business.

His Saturn, the planet of structure and wealth, is in his first house of identity and, because of the righteousness of the Sedna squares he is breaking rules and crossing boundaries in his quest to build his business empire. In 2011 there were allegations that his companies had been regularly hacking the phones of celebrities, royalty, and public citizens and Murdoch faced police and government investigations into bribery and corruption by the British government and the FBI.

As our Sedna consciousness evolves however, these aspects give us the power and scope to achieve great things. Like H.G. Wells, who was a British writer, historian, prognosticator, economist and novelist who was known for his sci-fi predictions of the future. He had Sedna in the first house of identity, semi-square Pluto in the second house of material resources.

---

[843] https://en.wikipedia.org/wiki/Marie_Curie

After a sketchy education, he went on to graduate from London University with a BS at 22. He taught biology and wrote educational articles, writing his first novel at 29 and went on to write many other works. His book, *The War of the Worlds*, which was read on radio by Orson Wells, caused the famous Mars invasion panic when he was 72. He was an enormously prolific and popular writer, capturing the early twentieth century's need to rebel and overthrow the oppressive Victorian conventions.[844]

Or like Indian lawyer and civil rights champion, Mohandas Gandhi, the spiritual and political leader of India through the tempestuous birth of independence. He has Sedna in the sixth house of service, semi-square Pluto, conjunct Jupiter, the planet of expansion, in the seventh house of relationships.

Known as Mahatma, which means 'great soul', he began the freedom movement at the age of 50 with nonviolent disobedience. Fond of the simple life, eating primarily fresh fruits and nuts, he often fasted, as he had done in his youth. He spent much time experimenting with fasting as a form of self-restraint. He was a self-confessed quack as far as his medical views were concerned, and fully believed that a light diet, lots of exercise and a mudpack were all that anyone needed to be healed.

At 57, having grown weary from periods in prison and periods of fasting, he retired to his ashram for a year of silence. Refreshed, he toured India the following year, and expanded his principles of nonviolence, homespun unity and equality for untouchables, by adding equality for women and abstinence from drugs and alcohol.

India broke from England when he was 78, assuring his rank as a saint and holy man. His assassination during the Hindu-Moslem riots a year later shook the world but left it with a message greater than the humble man himself; the power of peaceful protest and the reassurance that justice has its place.[845]

At this juncture in human evolution, few of us use our planets at the spiritual level, but many of us are striving to, and such people are

---

[844] https://en.wikipedia.org/wiki/H._G._Wells
[845] https://en.wikipedia.org/wiki/Mahatma_Gandhi

wonderful to be around. As with the other planets, the spiritual level of evolution is vastly different with Sedna from the two previous levels. Here, the stressful aspects challenge us to bring the power of spiritual transformation into each moment.

Once we embrace the Sedna energy, which is the oneness of everything, our nurturing becomes an expression of Sedna consciousness and it becomes devotional in nature. The struggle of the beginner's level is gone, as are the transcendental crises of the intermediate level. At this level everything Saturnian is meaningless and yet everything Sednian has its place.

We see this exemplified in Anne Frank, who was a Dutch-Jewish writer of a diary from age 14 to 15, while she and her family lived in total confinement, hiding in an attic from the Nazis during WW2. She had Sedna in the tenth house of social standing, square Pluto in the twelfth house of the unconscious.

> She began scrawling in her diary in 1942, writing as a typical teen in many ways, childish and profound, thoughtful and painful, writing, "In spite of everything, I still believe that people are really good at heart.
>
> Her last entry was three days before their hiding place was discovered and they were arrested. She died of typhus at the Bergen-Belsen concentration camp in March 1945. Her father, who survived, returned after the war and found his daughter's diary. At the turn of the century a new edition was published with five previously secret pages that described her conflict with her mother, whom she wrote, "had cold eyes," and with whom she could not talk to unburden herself, and her lament that her parents had a loveless marriage of convenience.
>
> Her diary remains as a poignant symbol of the millions whose lives and homes were lost during a tragic page in history. Translated into 54 languages with sales hovering around 25 million copies worldwide, her book is an established part of most high school educations. Putting a single face on the vast horror of the Holocaust, she served as a reminder of the quiet acts of heroism that were part of that high-water mark of evil.[846]

---

[846] https://en.wikipedia.org/wiki/Anne_Frank

Or like Emanuel Swedenborg, who was a Swedish scientist, philosopher, theologian and mystic. He had Sedna conjunct Neptune, the planet of dreams and visions, in the second house of material reality, sequiquadrate Pluto in the seventh house of relationships.

> He had a prolific career as an inventor and scientist, establishing Sweden's first scientific journal and anticipating a number of modern inventions, including prototype submarines and aeroplanes.

> He also published treatises on cosmology, lunar measurements, chemistry, physics, the circulation of the blood and sensory perception, and developed a theory of atomic structure with anticipates our own by describing matter as a system of indefinitely divisible particles grouped in swirling vortices.

> Then, in his search to locate the human soul and prove its immortality, he began to have transcendent religious experiences at 54, experiencing dreams and visions. This culminated in a 'spiritual awakening' in which Jesus appeared to him again with a commission to present a new revelation based on the premise that Heaven and Hell are not places, but states of being.

> He wrote a series of 30 volumes describing Heaven and Hell and the New Jerusalem. His visions were frequent and he himself visited heaven and hell, conversing with angels and spirits, and even with God Himself. His basic conclusion was that the universe is a harmonious whole, temporarily disturbed by sin.[847]

And finally, we come to Martin Luther King, who was an American clergyman and inspirational leader of the civil rights movement. He had Sedna conjunct Nessus, the centaur of radical change, and Vesta, the asteroid of regeneration, in the twelfth house of the unconscious, square Pluto in the third house of ideas and communication.

He was a symbol of the struggle against black segregation in the American South and he galvanized black Americans into action through his electrifying oratory skills and rose to become a legend and national hero in his own time. Then was assassinated by James Earl Ray, who

---

[847] https://en.wikipedia.org/wiki/Emanuel_Swedenborg

also has a square, showing how the same aspect can manifest differently at each level.

King grew up in a pious, proud and progressive black community in segregated Atlanta, the son of a Baptist minister. Living in a family of black Brahmins he never experienced poverty, yet he continuously heard his father preach from his pulpit, "I don't care how long I have to live with this system. I will never accept it."

At age 26, after refusing to be heir apparent to his father's pulpit, his first position was at the prestigious Dexter Baptist Church at Montgomery, Alabama. When seamstress Rose Parks refused to move to the back of the bus on December 1st of that same year, King began his sermon to a church full of agitated supporters of her cause, four days after her courageous act. "You know my friends, there comes a time when people get tired of being trampled over by the iron feet of oppression." Individual cheers gave way to a resounding din within the church walls and King walked into history that day as the delegated spokesman for the Montgomery Bus Boycott.

When the Montgomery buses finally began to operate on a non-segregated basis 381 days later, King formed the Southern Christian Leadership Conference, giving him a sound base from which to operate his vast congregation of everyday soldiers for civil rights.

His philosophy of passive resistance led to his frequent arrests and tours through the Bible Belt, where he became known as "Alabama's Modern Moses." The Southern student lunch counter sit-in when he was 31, the Freedom Riders a year later, marches in Birmingham two years after that, St. Augustine the following year and Selma the year after that, all put him in the national headlines as a civil rights activist. His greatest coup was the march on Washington, where 200,000 people gathered to demand their civil rights and hear him make his famous speech, "I have a dream...."

For upholding his allegedly radical views he was stoned, physically attacked and his house was bombed. As society grew more militant in the mid '60s, his interests widened to the Viet Nam War and those living in poverty. His plans for a Poor

People's March on Washington in 1968 were interrupted by a sanitation workers' strike in Memphis, Tennessee. At 39, he delivered his legendary speech to supporters at the Mason Street Temple: "I have been to the mountaintop....I see the Promised Land. I may not get there with you, but mine eyes have seen the glory." The following evening he was shot to death by an allegedly lone assassin.[848]

In-conjunct

With the evolutionary inconjunct between Sedna and Pluto the esoteric spiritual energy of Sedna bursts into our spiritual growth, our desire for change and our urge to let go and surrender to become a new person in an evolutionary way and we have a fated role to play.

The inconjunct sometimes acts as a flow and at other times as a stress, so we have to learn to actively manage the process as the rarified spiritual energy sometimes reinforces our spiritual growth, our desire for change and our urge to let go and surrender to become a new person and, at other times, isn't there to back us up. By adjusting to this, we gain a deeper understanding of ourselves and how to play our role.

The energies of Pluto are transforming. Pluto represents subconscious forces, ruling all that is below the surface. It is associated with renewal. It represents endings and new beginnings, as well as spiritual growth.

The inconjunct with Pluto points to a fated interest in investigating the hidden realms and understanding ourselves and our world at a deeper level, however while we are unconscious of the Sedna energy we might act on deeply buried impulses, in an effort to transform our lives, feeling it to be totally natural and yet these actions are often violent, or are perceived as violent by others.

Like Amy Fisher, who was an American teenager in the news for adolescent prostitution and the attempted murder of her lover's wife. She has Sedna in the first house of identity, inconjunct Pluto in the sixth house of daily routine.

> She first ran away from home at 11 to go to Disneyland and claimed that she had been sexually assaulted at 13 by a workman at home. By 16, she was sporting new clothes and having fun, spending some $400 to $500 a week, telling her

---

[848] https://en.wikipedia.org/wiki/Martin_Luther_King_Jr.

classmates and others that she was working for an escort service and that having sex for money was no big deal.

Her Sedna is also in a fateful inconjunct with Pluto, the planet of life and death, in the sixth house of daily routine. She began a sexual relationship with a 35-year-old mechanic after damaging the car her parents had given her for her 16th birthday and appealing to the owner of the body shop to which she took it, to make the repairs without her family knowing of the damage.

She gradually fell in love with him and became increasingly jealous of his wife. Eventually the then 17-year-old shared with him her idea of murdering his wife. Less than a year after she first had sex with him, she rang the doorbell of his home and when his wife answered, shot her in the face, wounding her severely. She was picked up by the police three days later, pled guilty to charges of assault with a deadly weapon and was sentenced to 5-15 years in prison.[849]

Her Sedna is also trine to Mercury, the planet of communication, in the fourth house of home, and she received $8,000 from a magazine for a first-person piece on her experience and after her release from prison, she became a columnist for the Long Island Press and dictated a book about her experiences titled *If I Knew Then…,* indicating she had grown through the crises.

She met her husband, a physical-fitness fanatic and wedding-photographer, some 25 years older than her, who has two kids from a former marriage. They married and, although the relationship was tempestuous, the couple had three children. And she reunited a few years later with the wife she had shot, in sessions televised for Entertainment Tonight and its spin-off, The Insider, saying she wanted to heal and move on with her life. However, two years later, she said she felt no sympathy for the woman, without giving an explanation.

Then the *New York Post* published allegations that her husband had sold a sex tape of the couple to Red Light District Video of Los Angeles. Nude pictures from the video were posted at various internet sites, and a teaser clip was released that

---

[849] https://en.wikipedia.org/wiki/Amy_Fisher

showed her nude showering and sunbathing. But a year later Fisher announced that she had settled with Red Light and agreed to do a related promotional appearance. The same announcement indicated that she and her husband had reconciled.

The following year she released a pay-per-view adult film titled *Amy Fisher: Totally Nude & Exposed* and signed a deal with Lee Entertainment to become a stripper doing club shows at least once a month. And her struggles to assert herself and deal with her alcohol problems were documented during her time as a cast member in the fifth season of the reality television series, Celebrity Rehab with Dr. Drew. In her time as one of his patients, Fisher revealed intimate details of her personal life and experiences, and remarked that the media had "ruined her life".[850]

We may also be the helpless victim of forces greater than us and are particularly vulnerable as children. Like Rebecca Riley, who was an American victim of prescription drug overdose at age 4. She had Sedna in the ninth house of knowledge, inconjunct Pluto in the fourth house of home.

The parents were unemployed and the family relied on Social Security Benefits. From the age of two she was diagnosed with ADHD and bipolar disorder by a licensed psychiatrist at a reputable hospital, mainly on the basis of information given by her mother.

However, her heart and lungs were damaged due to prolonged use of the prescription drugs and two years later, she died and her parents were accused of first degree murder. Prosecutors argued that they had her declared mentally unstable so they could collect social security disability benefits and purposely fed her the overdose. They were convicted and sentenced to life in prison.[851]

Or like Douglas Neff, who was an American accident victim, who was killed when his car was struck on Easter Sunday. He had Sedna on the

---

[850] Ibid.
[851] https://en.wikipedia.org/wiki/Death_of_Rebecca_Riley

cusp of the seventh house of relationships, inconjunct Pluto in the eleventh house of the collective unconscious, and opposite Ixion, the planet of lawlessness, which is conjunct his Ascendent, the point where he 'meets the world'. The accident occurred when another car slammed into the back of the family vehicle and pushed them into oncoming traffic. His wife was also killed and their two young kids, seated in the back seat, were injured.

There is a danger we may become overwhelmed by our experiences at times and take it all too seriously, which may mean that we snap suddenly from the tension, feeling that we can't handle it any more.

Like Nicholas Teague, who was an American murderer who shot and killed his mother and seriously wounded his father before killing himself. He also had Sedna in the eleventh house of collective consciousness, inconjunct Pluto in the fourth house of home.

> By the age of 23, he was taking medication for serious psychological problems and had just lost his job as a refrigerator repair apprentice. He had gotten the job through his dad who was an employee with the refrigerator firm as well as a volunteer firefighter. His mom was a cook at the local school. He shot her in the chest and side and when his dad ran upstairs, shot him in the torso. His dad staggered back downstairs and Nick shot himself in the head.[852]

The more negative expression of Pluto is an obsessive desire for power and control and general destructiveness and, until we develop our Sedna energy, the inconjunct can lend to a sense of righteousness in our use of these transformative energies, opening us to abuse, or abusive tendencies.

Like William Jewett Jr, who is an American who was convicted of sexual assault and murder. He had Sedna in the eighth house of shared resources, inconjunct Pluto in his fist house of identity. He also has an inconjunct with Neptune, the planet of delusions and lies, which is conjunct Ceres, the planet of nurturing, both in the third house of ideas and communication. He was seen leaving a party late at night with a girl who was later found raped and then strangled to death. He was arrested

---

[852] https://www.astro.com/astro-databank/Teague,_Nicholas

nearly five years later on suspicion of her murder and was convicted and sentenced to life in prison.

As we tire of density and the grief it creates, and we start a spiritual journey to get out of the swamp, Sedna rewards us with transcendent crises, experiences which force us to let go and rise above them, resulting in a huge growth to a new level of consciousness. There is no choice with these crises, and the more we try and solve them, the more we will get hurt.

Captain James Cook was a British explorer, navigator, cartographer, and captain in the Royal Navy. He had Sedna in the second house of material resources, inconjunct Pluto in the eighth house of life and death.

> He made detailed maps of Newfoundland prior to making three voyages to the Pacific Ocean, during which he achieved the first recorded European contact with the eastern coastline of Australia and the Hawaiian Islands, and the first recorded circumnavigation of New Zealand.

> In three voyages Cook sailed thousands of miles across largely uncharted areas of the globe. He mapped lands from New Zealand to Hawaii in the Pacific Ocean in greater detail and on a scale not previously achieved. As he progressed on his voyages of discovery he surveyed and named features and recorded islands and coastlines on European maps for the first time. He displayed a combination of seamanship, superior surveying and cartographic skills, physical courage and an ability to lead men in adverse conditions.[853]

However, his Sedna was also square Neptune, the planet of illusions, in the fifth house of creativity and a stressful semi-square with Chariklo, the centaur of foresight, in the third house of communication.

> On his third voyage, after a month's stay in Hawaii, he had attempted to resume his exploration of the Northern Pacific; however, shortly after leaving his ship's foremast broke, so they returned for repairs. Tensions rose, and a number of quarrels broke out between the Europeans and Hawaiians and an unknown group took one of Cook's small boats. That evening the

---

[853] https://en.wikipedia.org/wiki/James_Cook

Hawaiians had become "insolent", even under threats to fire upon them and Cook determined to kidnap and ransom the King of Hawaii, to get the boat back.

The following day he marched through the village to retrieve him, taking the King by his hand and leading him willingly away. One of the King's favourite wives and two chiefs approached the group as they were heading to boats and pleaded with the King not to go, until he stopped and sat where he stood. An old priest, chanting rapidly, while holding out a coconut, attempted to distract Cook and his men as a large crowd began to form at the shore. The king began to understand that Cook was his enemy. And as Cook turned his back to help launch the boats, he was struck on the head by the villagers and then stabbed to death as he fell on his face in the surf.[854]

Catherine the Great was a Prussian-Russian Empress, one of the most powerful and memorable in history. She had Sedna conjunct Saturn, the planet of structure, in the first house of identity, inconjunct Pluto in the seventh house of relationships.

She married Karl Ulrich at 16; he was the grandson of Peter the Great and heir to the throne. He was weak, neurotic and paranoid; she took over by 33, having him assassinated. Short and handsome but no beauty, she was ambitious, cruel, egotistical and domineering. However, she was also cultured, intelligent, studious and charming and she made powerful friends and won the loyalty of the Russian court.

When Empress Elizabeth died, Peter ascended to the throne. Within six months, Catherine undermined him and had herself proclaimed Empress. Peter III abdicated but was killed eight days later. She had a son who succeeded her, Paul I, who very possibly was not Peter's son at all, but the son of one of the guards. A passionate woman, she had a series of young lovers, 22 at least that were known and historically tallied.[855]

---

[854] https://en.wikipedia.org/wiki/James_Cook

[855] https://en.wikipedia.org/wiki/Catherine_the_Great

American radio and television personality, Rachel Maddow, also has an inconjunct, this time with Sedna in tenth house of profession and Pluto in the third house of communication.

> She is the host of cable program, *The Rachel Maddow Show* and the first openly gay anchor for a major prime-time news and commentary television show. Maddow is an intelligent and popular commentator for MSNBC's primarily liberal audiences.

> She also has Sedna semi-sextile Chariklo, the centaur of foresight, sesquiquadrate Ceres, the planet of nurturing and bi-quintile Neptune, the planet of broadcasting. A graduate of Stanford University and a Rhodes scholar concentrating on public policy, she earned a doctorate in philosophy from Oxford University.

> She began her talk show career on radio and in 2004 joined "Air America." She began appearing on television talk shows. Her articulate and thoughtful analysis and engaging style earned her spots as guest hosts on other MSNBC's television shows. In August 2008 the cable news network gave her the opportunity to host her own show, *The Rachel Maddow Show.* It soon zoomed to the top of the network's lineup in popularity.[856]

Justin Trudeau is a Canadian politician, the 23rd Prime Minister of Canada, as well as the Leader of the Liberal Party of Canada. He comes from a Canadian noted political family and is the first- born son of Pierre and Margaret Trudeau.

He has Sedna in the ninth house of philosophy and higher education, inconjunct Pluto in the second house of material resources. He also has a trine with his Sun, the planet of will, a square with Venus, the planet of values, a semi-sextile with Saturn, the planet of structure, a sexitile with Pholus, the centaur of practical transformation, and an opposition with Quaoar, the planet of new perspectives. So, he has a lot going for him.

> Trudeau, then 28, emerged as a prominent figure at the turn of the century, after delivering a eulogy at his father's state funeral. The Canadian Broadcasting Corporation received numerous calls to rebroadcast the speech after its initial transmission, and leading Quebec politician Claude Ryan described it as "perhaps

---

[856] https://en.wikipedia.org/wiki/Rachel_Maddow

the first manifestation of a dynasty." A book issued by the broadcaster three years later included the speech in its list of significant Canadian events from the past fifty years.

Eight years after his father's death, Trudeau entered politics. In the 2008 federal election, he was elected to the House of Commons. The next year he was appointed the Liberal Party's critic for youth and multiculturalism, and the following year for citizenship and immigration. He won the leadership of the Liberal Party in 2013 and went on to lead his party to a huge victory in the 2015 federal election, moving the 3rd-placed Liberals from 36 seats to 184 seats, the largest-ever numerical increase by a party in a Canadian election.[857]

At this juncture in human evolution, few of us use our planets at the spiritual level, but many of us are striving to, and such people are wonderful to be around. As with the other planets, the spiritual level of evolution is vastly different with Sedna from the two previous levels. Here, the inconjunct with Pluto brings the power of spiritual transformation into each moment.

Once we embrace the Sedna energy, which is the oneness of everything, our nurturing becomes an expression of Sedna consciousness and it becomes devotional in nature. The struggle of the beginner's level is gone, as are the transcendental crises of the intermediate level. At this level everything Saturnian is meaningless and yet everything Sednian has its place.

This is exemplified by the life of Georges Vandenbeusch, who was a French Catholic priest, who was held hostage by the terrorist group Boko Haram, before escaping. His Sedna is in his first house of identity, inconjunct Pluto in the sixth house of daily routine. Sedna is also opposite his Quaoar, the planet of new perspectives and inconjunct Neptune, the planet named after the god of the sea, but thankfully bi-quintile Jupiter, the planet of success.

When he was 7 years old, the family was on a boat tour of Corsica at night, when the propeller stalled and everyone was thrown into the water. Only Georges survived, helped to the

---

shore by his lifejacket. Once orphaned, he was raised by his grandparents.

He studied to be a priest and was ordained and held various vicarage positions in Paris, before deciding to become a priest in the extreme north of Cameroon, on the Nigerian border, in order to carry the faith in remote and unstable areas.

When he was 42 he was kidnapped by some fifteen armed men claiming to be Boko Haram and escaped seven weeks later. Boko Haram then said that, "The leadership decided to release the priest out of compassion. The priest offered his medical services to members during his period of captivity. Management felt that there was no need to keep it.

These remarks, however, are contested by Georges Vandenbeusch, who states: "I am neither a nurse nor a doctor. If they had brought me somebody to take care with a hemorrhage, I would have done what I could, but they did not. They have no compassion for anyone ".

The following year he was part of the delegation of President François Hollande during his visit to Pope Francis. The meeting was marked by the warm embrace of the Pope. Very soon, he resumed his ministry in the church of Saint-Pierre-Saint-Paul of Courbevoie, of which he was officially appointed parish priest.[858]

Or like Antoine Court, who named himself Antoine Court de Gébelin, a former Protestant pastor, who initiated the interpretation of the Tarot as an arcane repository of timeless esoteric wisdom. He had Sedna in the second house of material reality, inconjunct Pluto conjunct his Moon, his sensitivity, in the eighth house of the occult.

> His goal was to reconstruct what he believed to be the high primeval civilisation. Reinterpreting Classical and Renaissance evocation of the Golden Age into mankind's early history, he asserted that the primitive worldwide civilisation had been advanced and enlightened. He is the intellectual grandfather of much of modern occultism.

---

[858] https://fr.wikipedia.org/wiki/Georges_Vandenbeusch

His centres of focus are the familiar ones of universal origins of languages in deep time and the hermeneutics of symbolism. While his views on hermeneutics and religious matters were largely conservative, his original ideas and research on the origin of language earn him a place among pioneers of linguistics.

He presented dictionaries of etymology, what he called a universal grammar, and discourses on the origins of language. His volumes were so popular he republished them separately. With regard to mythology and symbology, he discussed the origins of allegory in antiquity and recreated a history of the calendar from civil, religious, and mythological perspectives.

It was his immediate perception, the first time he saw the Tarot deck, that it held the secrets of the Egyptians. Writing without the benefit of deciphering of the Egyptian language, he developed a reconstruction of Tarot history, without producing any historical evidence, which was that Egyptian priests had distilled the ancient Book of Thoth into these images. These they brought to Rome, where they were secretly known to the popes, who brought them to Avignon in the 14th century, whence they were introduced into France.[859]

And Lisa Williams, who is a British psychic, medium and healer. She has Sedna in the fifth house of creativity, inconjunct Pluto in the tenth house of profession.

She starred in two shows on Lifetime Television: *Lisa Williams: Life Among the Dead* and *Lisa Williams: Voices From the Other Side.* The shows followed Williams on a typical day, as she communicated with spirits, investigated haunted houses, and conducted other spirit-seeking activities.

She came out as a lesbian at 37 and said: 'For many years, speaking to dead people was hard enough for people to accept me, but then on top of that to then say 'by the way, I'm gay', I didn't want to acknowledge it'. Asked by a reporter, because of her unique insight into life after death, where she thought gay people were headed, she said: 'In my experience with those who have crossed, it is a place of love. It isn't a place of 'you didn't

[859] https://en.wikipedia.org/wiki/Antoine_Court_de_Gébelin

live this way so we'll punish you', it is a place where all your loved ones accept you for who you are'.[860]

Quintile, Bi-quintile

The evolutionary quintile or bi-quintile aspect between Sedna and Pluto infuses our spiritual growth, our desire for change and our urge to let go and surrender to become a new person, with the all-encompassing spiritual energy of Sedna to the point where we can push the boundaries of human development.

Quintiles and bi-quintiles point to talent, the desire to create order and to categorize, a fascination with patterns and structures, perfectionist tendencies, and the desire to build or make things. These aspects have the characteristics of both the trine and opposition. They point to awareness of conflicts, or problems and finding solutions for them; however, they do not automatically kick into action and must be cultivated over time.

The energies of Pluto are transforming. Pluto represents subconscious forces, ruling all that is below the surface. It is associated with renewal. It represents endings and new beginnings, as well as spiritual growth. The more negative expression however is an obsessive desire for power and control and general destructiveness and, until we develop our Sedna energy, these aspects can lead to a sense of righteousness, which may make it hard for us to tell that we are manifesting the energy negatively.

Like Richard Kameese, who was an American drug fatality at age 21. He had Sedna conjunct Saturn in the ninth house of knowledge, inconjunct Pluto on the cusp of the second house of material reality.

> His addiction began at high school and he was living with his parents. His folks went to a wake, leaving him home alone, because he was using drugs. When they returned they saw his shoeless footprints in the snow and knew he was on another rampage.
>
> He went to the home of a couple who lived a couple hundred yards away and burst in, staggering and in a drug-crazed state saying "They're going to get me." He grabbed a kitchen mop and began swinging at his imaginary enemies and at the couple, who then called the police, as Richard drew a knife. It took four men

---

[860] https://en.wikipedia.org/wiki/Lisa_Williams_(psychic)

to subdue him; however, while in a jail cell, he stopped breathing and died a few hours later.[861]

At this unconscious level there is a chance with these aspects that we might be the victim of abuse, or we may play along with abusive ideas. Like Melody Maillet, who was an American teenage suicide. She had Sedna in the in the eleventh house of ideals, bi-quintile Pluto, which is conjunct Mercury, the planet of communication in the fourth house of home. She was hanging out at a friend's home; both were popular students with many friends. However, consumed with adolescent angst and listening to morbid punk music, they killed themselves with a 12-gauge shotgun in the bathroom. They were 15. Both girls left loving notes behind.

Facing down the manipulation of others, especially parents, may be part of the early maturing process with these aspects. In the process however, we will likely learn some manipulative skills ourselves, which may be expressed later in life as an obsessive desire for power and control, or general destructiveness.

Like Stephane Delabriere, who was a French serial killer. He had Sedna in the sixth house of daily routine, bi-quintile Pluto in the tenth house of social standing.

> The eldest of five children, he was tortured by his violent and alcoholic father. At age 13 he was put in a foster home. Calling himself the Prince of Darkness, he dedicated to Satan his performance of ritual sacrifices on animals. When he was 20, during a robbery he strangled, raped and slit the throat of a 63-year-old woman. A year later he beheaded his best friend using an ax and carried the head in his knapsack for the rest of the day.

> Apprehended and awaiting trial, he murdered a prison guard using a knife. Of 14 psychiatric experts who were assigned to his case, none came to the same conclusion, beyond their agreement that he was beyond redemption. His murders were premeditated and he declared that he had a goal of 5,000 victims. He was sentenced to life in prison at 25.[862]

---

[861] https://www.astro.com/astro-databank/Kameese,_Richard
[862] https://www.astro.com/astro-databank/Delabriere,_Stephane

As we see, the drive for power and control that Pluto wants to exert can still lead to abusive tendencies with these aspects at the unconscious level, only on a far vaster scale, but it still comes with the same inevitable karmic kickback.

Like Julian Assange, who is an Australian whistleblower, with a background in physics, math and computer programming, currently living in political asylum in the embassy of Ecuador in London. He has Sedna in the sixth house of daily routine, bi-quintile Pluto in the eleventh house of collective consciousness.

> He is spokesperson and editor-in-chief of WikiLeaks, which is supposedly an investigative journalism internet-based organisation, with a mission to make public otherwise secret information, but which is designated by the US government as a hostile non-state intelligence service. His name became nearly a household word when at 39 he leaked over 250,000 classified diplomatic cables of the US government and therefore caused an uproar in government circles. Prior to that he had published many classified documents and a video from the Iraq and Afghanistan Wars.

> That same year the Swedish government posted a warrant for his arrest on rape and molestation charges. The warrant cited one count of unlawful coercion, two counts of sexual molestation and one count of rape. He denied the charges, but refused to face the courts, fighting his extradition from England. Two years later he walked into the embassy of Ecuador in London to ask for political asylum and five years on he is still living there in virtual house arrest, unable to leave without being arrested.[863]

With these aspects it is possible for the spiritual energy to manifest even at the unconscious level. Like it did with Francisco Marto, who was a Portuguese child noted for the Miracle of Fatima, during which the sun appeared to spin and fall from the sky, witnessed by 70,000 people. He had Sedna conjunct Saturn and also Orcus, the planet of delving down and speaking out, in the twelfth house of the unconscious, quintile Pluto in the second hose of material reality.

---

[863] https://en.wikipedia.org/wiki/Julian_Assange

On a spring day when he was six he was tending sheep with his cousin and sister, who were nine and eight, when they first began to see visions of the Virgin Mary. Later that year a large crowd gathered near Fátima, Portugal, in response to their prophecy that the Virgin Mary, referred to as Our Lady of Fatima, would appear and perform miracles on that date.

Newspapers published testimony from reporters and other people who claimed to have witnessed extraordinary solar activity, such as the sun appearing to "dance" or zig-zag in the sky, careen towards the earth, or emit multicoloured light and radiant colours. According to these reports, the event lasted approximately ten minutes.

During a second apparition the Virgin Mary had said to his cousin, "In a short time I will take Francisco and his sister up to heaven with me. You, on the other hand, will remain on earth for a great many years to spread the devotion to my Immaculate Heart." The two Marto children were both stricken by the Spanish flu and Francisco died at Fatima, age ten.[864]

As we tire of density and the grief it creates, and we start a spiritual journey to get out of the swamp, Sedna rewards us with transcendent crises, experiences which force us to let go and rise above them, resulting in a huge growth to a new level of consciousness. There is no choice with these crises and the more we try and solve them, the more we will get hurt.

Like our case study, Rachel Carson, the mother of the environmental movement, who has Sedna in the first house of identity, quintile Pluto, which is in her third house of ideas and communication. Her book, *Silent Spring*, chronicled the devastating effects of the overuse of pesticide.

The book was startling for its rigorous scientific assessment of how, by spraying for one issue, to get rid of a bug or a weed, without considering how the chemicals would impact everything else, people were often doing more harm than good. It was a beautifully written treatise of horrors aimed at a general audience, which launched the environmental movement.

---

[864] https://en.wikipedia.org/wiki/Francisco_and_Jacinta_Marto

She entered the Pennsylvania College for Women on a senatorial district scholarship, earning an English degree, as preparation to become a writer. However it was biology that she found most thrilling during her undergraduate years. After earning a master's in zoology, she found part-time work at the US Bureau of Fisheries.

Though she'd chosen science over prose, her former specialty proved useful in her new occupation. Carson's first assignment for the bureau was to write a fifty-two-episode radio program called 'Romance Under the Waters'. "I had given up writing forever, I thought. It never occurred to me that I was merely getting something to write about."

Her first book, *Under the Sea Wind,* was a commercial failure, selling only two thousand copies. She needed a couple of years to recover from the blow, but both driven and strapped for cash, she wrote another book. *The Sea Around Us* was published when she was 44 and it won the National Book Award for nonfiction and solidified her position as a literary heavyweight. To this day, it's credited as being one of the most successful books ever written about nature.

In her fifties she turned her attention to conservation, especially some problems that she believed were caused by synthetic pesticides. The result was the book, *Silent Spring*, published when she was 55, which brought environmental concerns to an unprecedented share of the American people. Although it was met with fierce opposition by chemical companies, it spurred a reversal in national pesticide policy, which led to a nationwide ban on DDT and other pesticides. It also inspired a grassroots environmental movement that led to the creation of the U.S. Environmental Protection Agency.[865]

Or like Simone de Beauvoir, who was a French writer and existentialist teacher who fashioned an impressive literary career as a novelist, philosopher, essayist and writer of memoirs. She had Sedna in the fourth house of home, quintile Pluto in the seventh house of relationships.

---

[865] https://en.wikipedia.org/wiki/Rachel_Carson

She looked on marriage as an obscene, bourgeois institution that put women in an inferior position. In rejecting marriage, she also rejected children, noting that she had escaped most of women's bondages.

She was a prominent member of the young avant-garde Parisian intelligentsia in the '40s, she was the presiding celebrity of the Existentialist movement along with Jean Paul Sartre, who was her life companion in an open relationship. They never lived in the same residence, nor did they require sexual fidelity of each other, but they did keep a close and steady relationship, seeing each other daily from the time they met at the Sorbonne when she was 21, until Sartre died 50 years later.[866]

Her Sedna was also closely bi-quintile Ixion, the planet of lawlessness in the ninth house of higher education. She had a very turbulent, often scandalous life. Although she had a long time relationship with Sartre, she was known to have a number of female lovers. The nature of some of these relationships, some of which she began with underage students while working as a professor, later led to a controversy.

A former student wrote in her book that, while she was a student at Lycée Molière, she had been sexually exploited by her teacher de Beauvoir, who was in her 30s at the time. She and Jean-Paul Sartre developed a pattern, which they called the "trio", in which de Beauvoir would seduce her students and then pass them on to Sartre. Finally she was suspended from her teaching job, when she was accused of seducing a 17-year-old pupil. The girl's parents laid formal charges against her for debauching a minor and she had her license to teach in France permanently revoked.[867]

Her life companion, Jean-Paul Sartre, who was a French writer, existentialist philosopher, novelist, essayist and playwright, also had this aspect. His Sedna is in the third house of ideas and communication, with Pluto in the seventh house of relationships.

With a vindictive and angry personality, he was self-confident, knowing he was smarter than other children. His philosophy of

---

[866] https://en.wikipedia.org/wiki/Simone_de_Beauvoir
[867] Ibid.

existentialism stated that the world had no meaning for mankind, but instead proposed that the individual is responsible for his or her own purpose.

From the age of 34 he served as the leader of the French intelligentsia. One of his most famous essays, "Being and Nothingness" was published when he was 38. His fame grew over the next two years, as he rejected God and external values, touting existentialism as the philosophy to study. He became co-editor of the magazine, *Les Temps Modernes*. His politics moved to the left when he was in his early 50's. He was awarded the Nobel Prize for Literature at 59 but declined on political grounds.[868]

Humour can be one path to transcend the quicksand of Sedna, giving us the objectivity to step back from the edge and also, with the quintile and bi-quintile aspects to Pluto, enjoy the transformation process itself.

Fernandel was a French actor and mime comedian with a long, sorrowful, equine face and a radiant and toothy smile. He had Sedna in the eleventh house of collective consciousness, quintile Pluto in the twelfth house of the unconscious.

One of France's leading box-office draws, he built a four-decade career from the age of 27. His films included the four great "Don Camillo" political comedies. His father was an accountant but also an amateur comedian-singer and his mother was also an amateur actress, and they quickly noticed the talent of the young Fernand. He often accompanied his father during the concerts he organised in the Marseilles suburbs. It was during a contest for amateur singers that he won the first prize for children prodigies at the theatre of Châtelet de Marseille. He made his debut on stage at five years singing the military repertory with his elder brother.

He had his first great success at the age of seven, a day when, paralyzed by stage-fright, he was propelled on the stage by his father, with a great kick to the rear; He fell into his sabre, and stretched his whole length under a storm of laughter. Later, he was never afraid to face the public.

---

[868] https://en.wikipedia.org/wiki/Jean-Paul_Sartre

In 1930, he appeared in his first motion picture and for more than forty years he would be France's top comic actor. He was perhaps best loved for his portrayal of the irascible Italian village priest at war with the town's Communist mayor in the Don Camillo series of motion pictures which he also directed. His horse-like teeth became part of his trademark.[869]

Milton Berle was an American comedian whose most successful medium was TV, which he practically dominated in his 40's, gaining the nickname, Mr. Television. His Sedna is the ninth house of broadcasting, conjunct Saturn and also Orcus, the planet of delving down and speaking out, and quintile Pluto, which is conjunct the North Node, in the eleventh house of collective consciousness.

At six he took part in "Charlie Chaplin contests," wearing his dad's suits and shoes, usually winning prizes. His mom was always in the audience, setting the pace with her piercing laugh. Charlie Chaplin was a main part of Berle's comedic upbringing, as he appeared in the first full-length movie comedy, *Tillie's Punctured Romance*, which starred Chaplin.

At his standup opening at the Palace Theater in New York, he "took the theatre by storm," and in the following two years set attendance records. But Berle came into his own in when he inaugurated the "Texaco Star Theatre," which has been described as TV's number-one show and was the first real smash hit in the new medium.

The show made network TV popular and sold more TV sets than any other ad campaign, with an estimated 80 percent of all TV sets in the US tuning in every Tuesday night. Enormously funny, with great energy and versatility, he laid out rapid gags and broad clowning, and was named "the television star of the year." His income was over $700,000 for the year.

Berle's holding company, Milton Berle Enterprises Inc., now manages a machine tool company, a furniture company and real estate. Separate corporations control his songs, literature, theatre work, night club, TV, producing and radio acting interests. It also handles his extensive charity activities. He had

---

[869] https://en.wikipedia.org/wiki/Fernandel

toured Army hospitals and has been credited with presenting 10,000 benefits. He has raised more than a million dollars for cancer research and treatment and is Honorary Mayor of the National Children's Cardiac Home in Florida.[870]

At this juncture in human evolution, few of us use our planets at the spiritual level, but many of us are striving to, and such people are wonderful to be around. As with the other planets, the spiritual level of evolution is vastly different with Sedna from the two previous levels. Here, the quintile and bi-quintile aspects bring the power of spiritual transformation into each moment.

Once we embrace the Sedna energy, which is the oneness of everything, our nurturing becomes an expression of Sedna consciousness and it becomes devotional in nature. The struggle of the beginner's level is gone, as are the transcendental crises of the intermediate level. At this level everything Saturnian is meaningless and yet everything Sednian has its place.

Jeanne Dixon was an American psychic called "The Seeress of Washington" who claimed that her psychic gift was revealed to her through dreams, visions and the crystal ball. She had Sedna in the eleventh house of collective consciousness, quintile Pluto in the first house of identity.

> She grew up in California and married an auto dealer at 35. Later, when they moved to Washington, D.C. she became a real estate executive. Her reputation began to grow from the readings she gave people and she gained national attention with her prediction of J. F. Kennedy's assassination. Her famed clients were said to include Ronald Reagan, whom she told that he would one day be President.

> She was the author of seven books, including an autobiography, an astrology cookbook and a horoscope book for dogs. Ruth Montgomery's book about her, *A Gift of Prophecy: the Phenomenal Jeanne Dixon* was published when she was 61, selling over three million copies and putting her in demand on the lecture circuit. Though she was not actually an astrologer,

---

[870] https://en.wikipedia.org/wiki/Milton_Berle

she had enough knowledge to add sun-sign delineation to her repertory and had a syndicated horoscope column.[871]

Lanza Del Vasto was a philosopher, poet, artist, catholic and nonviolent activist. He had Sedna in the third house of communication, quintile Pluto in the sixth house of service.

> He was a western disciple of Mohandas K. Gandhi; he worked for inter-religious dialogue, spiritual renewal, ecological activism and nonviolence. At 35 he went to India and joining the movement for Indian independence led by Gandhi. He spent six months with the Mahatma, then went to the source of the Ganges river in the Himalayas, a famous pilgrimage site. There he saw a vision who told him "Go back and found!" He then left India and went back to Europe. Six years later he published the story of his trip to India, Return to the Source, which became a huge success.

> He founded the Community of the Ark when he was 47, which first met a lot of difficulties. By the time he was 60, the Community of the Ark settled in Haut-Languedoc, in the south of France, in a deserted village. He remained a leading figure in many non-violent movements until his death. He was criticised for the traditional role of women in his movement, and for his expressed opposition to homosexuality.[872]

And Joseph Campbell was an American mythologist, writer, and lecturer, best known for his work in comparative mythology and comparative religion. He had Sedna conjunct Jupiter in the sixth house of service, quintile Pluto in the eighth house of the occult.

> His magnum opus is his book, *The Hero with a Thousand Faces*, published when he was 45, in which he discusses his theory of the journey of the archetypal hero found in world mythologies.

> As a strong believer in the psychic unity of mankind and its poetic expression through mythology, he used this concept to express the idea that the whole of the human race can be seen as engaged in the effort of making the world "transparent to transcendence", by showing that underneath the world of

---

[871] https://en.wikipedia.org/wiki/Jeanne_Dixon
[872] https://en.wikipedia.org/wiki/Lanza_del_Vasto

phenomena lies an eternal source which is constantly pouring its energies into this world of time, suffering, and ultimately death.

To achieve this task one needs to speak about things that existed before and beyond words, a seemingly impossible task, the solution to which lies in the metaphors found in myths. These metaphors are statements that point beyond themselves into the transcendent. The Hero's Journey was the story of the man or woman who, through great suffering, reached an experience of the eternal source and returned with gifts powerful enough to set their society free.

Since the book's publication, his theory has been consciously applied by a wide variety of modern writers and artists. His philosophy has been summarised by his own often-repeated phrase: "Follow your bliss." He thought of God as a metaphor for a mystery that absolutely transcends all human categories of thought, even the categories of being and non-being, saying, "It depends on how much you want to think about it. Whether it is putting you in touch with the mystery that's the ground of your own being. If it isn't, well, it's a lie".[873]

---

[873] https://en.wikipedia.org/wiki/Joseph_Campbell

39: Sedna / Ixion

Conjunction

There is no one alive today with this aspect and no one will be born with this aspect in the next 100 years, so it is not interpreted here.

Opposition

With the opposition of Sedna and Ixion, the all-encompassing spiritual energy of Sedna challenges our lawlessness, our lust for life, our sense of entitlement, our ability to create trouble, to have no regrets and to forgive ourselves.

The predominant trait of Ixion is utter lawlessness, not being held back by rules and by doing what we want, when we want. This Plutino also represents our deepest fears about who and what we may really be, and what we may be capable of.

With the opposition to Sedna our lust for life stands in relief against the big spiritual picture and we will likely feel the awesome challenge of this larger framework from an early age. As we get older and if Ixion is prominent in our chart, we could be naturally drawn toward playing a provocateur role in relation to existing social rules.

Until we develop the Sedna energy however the opposition can lead to a sense of righteousness in our rebellious behaviour and can bring out the negative side of Ixion, which is ingratitude, wasting second chances, not keeping our word and problems with the law.

Like Melissa Poirier and Melody Maillet, who were American teenage suicides. Melissa had Sedna conjunct Saturn, the planet of physical reality, in the ninth house of belief, opposite Ixion in the third house of communication. Melody also had Sedna opposite Ixion, but her Sedna was in the eleventh house of ideals and her Ixion in the fifth house of romance. Both were popular students with many friends. However, consumed with adolescent angst and listening to morbid punk music, they killed themselves with a 12-gauge shotgun in the bathroom of Melissa's home. They were 15. Both girls left loving notes behind.

Or like Amy Fisher, who was an American teenager in the news for adolescent prostitution and the attempted murder of her lover's wife. She has Sedna in the first house of identity, opposite Ixion in the seventh house of relationships.

She first ran away from home at 11 to go to Disneyland and claimed that she had been sexually assaulted at 13 by a workman at home. By 16, she was sporting new clothes and having fun, spending some $400 to $500 a week, telling her classmates and others that she was working for an escort service and that having sex for money was no big deal.[874]

Her Sedna is also in a fateful inconjunct with Pluto, the planet of life and death, in the sixth house of daily routine.

She began a sexual relationship with a 35-year-old mechanic after damaging the car her parents had given her for her 16th birthday and appealing to the owner of the body shop to which she took it, to make the repairs without her family knowing of the damage.

She gradually fell in love with him and became increasingly jealous of his wife. Eventually the then 17-year-old shared with him her idea of murdering his wife. Less than a year after she first had sex with him, she rang the doorbell of his home and when his wife answered, shot her in the face, wounding her severely. She was picked up by the police three days later, pled guilty to charges of assault with a deadly weapon and was sentenced to 5-15 years in prison.[875]

Her Sedna is also trine to Mercury, the planet of communication, in the fourth house of home,

She received $8,000 from a magazine for a first-person piece on her experience and after her release from prison, she became a columnist for the *Long Island Press* and dictated a book about her experiences titled *If I Knew Then...*, indicating she had grown through the crises.

She met her husband, a physical-fitness fanatic and wedding-photographer, some 25 years older than her, who has two kids from a former marriage. They married and, although the relationship was tempestuous, the couple had three children. And she reunited a few years later with the wife she had shot, in sessions televised for *Entertainment Tonight* and its spin-off, *The*

---

[874] https://en.wikipedia.org/wiki/Amy_Fisher
[875] Ibid.

Insider, saying she wanted to heal and move on with her life. However, two years later, she said she felt no sympathy for the woman, without giving an explanation.

Then the *New York Post* published allegations that her husband had sold a sex tape of the couple to Red Light District Video of Los Angeles. Nude pictures from the video were posted at various internet sites, and a teaser clip was released that showed her nude showering and sunbathing. But a year later Fisher announced that she had settled with Red Light and agreed to do a related promotional appearance. The same announcement indicated that she and her husband had reconciled.

The following year she released a pay-per-view adult film titled *Amy Fisher: Totally Nude & Exposed* and signed a deal with Lee Entertainment to become a stripper doing club shows at least once a month. And her struggles to assert herself and deal with her alcohol problems were documented during her time as a cast member in the fifth season of the reality television series, *Celebrity Rehab with Dr. Drew*. In her time as one of his patients, Fisher revealed intimate details of her personal life and experiences, and remarked that the media had "ruined her life".[876]

Or like Stephane Delabriere, who was a French serial killer. He had Sedna in the sixth house of daily routine, opposite Ixion in the twelfth house of the unconscious.

The eldest of five children, he was tortured by his violent and alcoholic father. At age 13 he was put in a foster home. Calling himself the Prince of Darkness, he dedicated to Satan his performance of ritual sacrifices on animals. When he was 20, during a robbery he strangled, raped and slit the throat of a 63-year-old woman. A year later he beheaded his best friend using an ax and carried the head in his knapsack for the rest of the day.

Apprehended and awaiting trial, he murdered a prison guard using a knife. Of 14 psychiatric experts who were assigned to his

---

[876] Ibid.

case, none came to the same conclusion, beyond their agreement that he was beyond redemption. His murders were premeditated and he declared that he had a goal of 5,000 victims. He was sentenced to life in prison at 25.[877]

Or Timothy McVeigh, who was an American terrorist convicted of committing the largest act of terrorism on American soil. He was 27. He had Sedna conjunct Mercury and also his Sun, his will and sense of self, all in the eleventh house of collective consciousness, opposite Ixion in the fifth house of creativity.

He grew up in a small upstate New York town. He had a happy childhood swimming in his family's pool, hiking and playing with the neighbourhood kids. He enjoyed organising casino games for local kids on the block. His father and mother divorced when he was ten years old. He grew closer to his dad, helping him cultivate his vegetable garden. His mom remarried and moved to Florida with his younger sister.

Looking for excitement, he signed up for the U.S. Army when he was twenty. He took to military life and the comradeship with his fellow troops, becoming a straight-arrow soldier. He was promoted to corporal and then to sergeant. During the Persian Gulf War, he was sent to Iraq as a gunner on a Bradley fighting vehicle. On returning to the States, he sensed a major shift in the U.S. Army. The post-cold-war army downsizing changed his life as he watched his companions leave military service. Discharged from the army, he tried to adjust to civilian life.

At 25, he arrived in Waco to watch the standoff between the Branch Davidians cult and federal agents. He wandered around the country as a militant drifter visiting gun shows and selling guns and ammunition from his car. His political views became more racist and far right as he kept company with political militia groups harbouring anger against the U.S. government. He returned to Waco and declared himself a "non-resident alien." He claimed the U.S. Army had implanted a computer chip in his derriere during his active duty.

---

[877] https://www.astro.com/astro-databank/Delabriere,_Stephane

Together with accomplices he carried out an ammonium nitrate bombing of a federal building when he was 27, claimed 168 victims between the ages of four months old to 73 years old. The building was the main office for the federal agents who were involved in the Branch Davidian standoff in Waco. Two hours after the bombing, he was stopped by a policeman for a traffic violation, 70 miles away. He was almost released until they recognised him as one of the possible suspects in the terrorist act.

His stubborn refusal to express any remorse tormented the families of his victims. His psychiatrist felt that he was committed to the ideal that he must object to a federal government that had become excessively oppressive and deceitful. He was able to rationally make the decision to bomb the building and "fully understood the consequences. He had an underlying depression, but he was not anti-social. It simply became easier to act because he had nothing and he needed an enemy. This whole project was his antidepressant. He intellectualises to avoid emotion, to avoid pain." He was found guilty of conspiracy, use of a weapon of mass destruction, destruction by explosive, and eight counts of first degree murder and was sentenced to death.[878]

As we tire of density and the grief it creates, and we start a spiritual journey to get out of the swamp, Sedna rewards us with transcendent crises, experiences which force us to let go and rise above them, resulting in a huge growth to a new level of consciousness. There is no choice with these crises, and the more we try and solve them, the more we will get hurt.

Susan Boyle is a Scottish singer who rose to fame on a British talent show. She has Sedna conjunct Venus in the eleventh house of collective consciousness, opposite Ixion in the fifth house of creativity.

She is the youngest of nine children and reportedly suffered some oxygen deprivation at birth, resulting in learning disabilities. Never married, she lived with her parents, working in low-level jobs and volunteering in the church. Her father died

---

[878] https://en.wikipedia.org/wiki/Timothy_McVeigh

when she was 36 and her mother died when she was 46, after which she became distraught.

Her music gave her great comfort and she auditioned for "Britain's Got Talent" in the hopes of launching a music career in her mother's memory. When she appeared on stage at 48 her appearance belied her talent, but she wowed the audiences with her rendition of "I Dreamed a Dream" from the musical "Les Miserables." The clip of her performance is one of the most-viewed on YouTube.

News reports made much of this plain-looking middle-aged woman. For subsequent performances on the show she underwent a slight makeover. She made it all the way to the finals based on judges' and viewers' votes. However, the ensuing publicity was a lot for her to handle. Although she sang well on the last evening of the competition and came in second, she was rushed to a London health care facility that night, reportedly suffering from an anxiety attack. She was released within the week.

Her album was released later that year and it quickly shot to the top of the charts. The success was continued with her second album the following year, and her third album the year after that. The following year her net worth was estimated at £22 million.[879]

As we evolve and develop our Sedna consciousness, the opposition with Ixion allows us to play with the normal rules and not take them so seriously and, in doing so, so chart new paths that are evolutionary and point to new rules that need to be set in place.

The founder of Apple computers, Steve Jobs's has Sedna in the eighth house, opposite Ixion, which is together with his Neptune, the planet of psychic receptivity, in the second house of material resources. His creative visions of technological tools revolutionised our lives. But, more than this, he believed that these were tools to change the world, by giving everyone the power to be creative and disrupting the control of existing monopolies.

We see the same energy, although in a less evolved form, in the Al-Qaeda terrorist leader, Osama bin Laden. He had Sedna in the eleventh

---

[879] https://en.wikipedia.org/wiki/Susan_Boyle

house, opposite Ixion in his fifth house of 'what is produced in the home'. This is the signature of his style of terrorism. A major part of his ideology was the concept that civilians from enemy countries, including women and children, were legitimate targets for jihadists to kill.

And we find it in a more evolved form with Barack Obama, the first African American president, who has Sedna in the second house of material resources, opposite Ixion in the eighth house of shared resources. The opposition drove him into government to impose more lawful order and his Healthcare bill saved millions of Americans from lawlessness in the health sector.

> A self-described "skinny kid with a funny name," he is the child of a Kenyan man and an American woman. His parents met at the University of Hawaii where they were both students. When Barack was two, his father returned to Africa, and the young boy lived in Hawaii with his mom and grandparents. After his mother married an Indonesian, she took him with her when she moved to her new husband's native country. Young Barack was sent back to Hawaii at age 10 to live with his grandparents.

> He graduated from Columbia University with a degree in political science and international relations. He worked in Chicago's inner city, helping church groups improve job-training, education and city services to the poor and then went on to law school at Harvard. At 35 he was elected to the Illinois General Assembly as a state senator. At 43 he burst onto the national scene when he delivered a rousing keynote address at the Democratic National Convention in Boston. That year he won election to the U.S. Senate by a wide margin.

> He announced his candidacy for the Democratic Party's nomination for President at 46. On the campaign trail he racked up an impressive number of primary and caucus wins. Exhibiting composure, thoughtfulness, a quick mind and self-deprecating humour, his debate performance earns kudos, while his powerful oratory evoked comparisons to Martin Luther King, Jr. and John F. Kennedy. Along with his life story, which he touts as a representation of the American dream, his emphasis on unity, hope and civility captured media and public attention.

His religious background is more diverse than that of most prominent politicians. But it may prove to be more representative of an increasingly diverse America. His mother was raised by non-practicing Christians; his father was raised a Muslim but was an atheist by the time he had married Obama's mother. His step-father was also Muslim, but of an eclectic kind who could make room for animist and Hindu beliefs.

In his book, *The Audacity of Hope*, published when he was 45, he writes, 'I was not raised in a religious household. For my mother, organised religion was too often dressed up closed-mindedness in the garb of piety, cruelty and oppression in the cloak of righteousness. However, in her mind, a working knowledge of the world's great religions was a necessary part of any well-rounded education. In our house the Bible, the Koran, sat on the shelf alongside books of Greek and Norse and African mythology.'

As a child in Indonesia, he studied for two years at one Muslim school and then two years at a Catholic school. Eventually however, he abandoned this non-conformism and skepticism as an adult to be baptised in the Trinity United Church of Christ, a denomination which emphasises the freedom of the individual conscience over adherence to creeds or hierarchical authority.[880]

Judith Butler is an American philosopher and gender theorist, considered by many as "one of the most influential voices in contemporary political theory," and as the most widely read and influential gender theorist in the world. She has Sedna in the first house of identity, opposite Ixion in the seventh house of relationships.

Her work has had a significant influence on the fields of feminist, queer, and literary theory, philosophy, political philosophy, and ethics. She is perhaps best known for her works, *Gender Trouble: Feminism and the Subversion of Identity* (1990, 2007) and *Bodies That Matter: On the Discursive Limits of "Sex"* (1993, 2011), where she challenges the sex/gender distinction and develops her theory of gender performativity. Indeed, Butler's conception of gender performativity has shaped the scholarship of an entire generation in feminist and queer studies.

---

[880] https://en.wikipedia.org/wiki/Barack_Obama

All of her books have been translated into numerous languages; *Gender Trouble*, alone, has been translated into twenty-seven different languages. She has also been outspoken on many contemporary political issues. She has been active in lesbian and gay human rights, and, more recently, she has engaged with the question of Palestine/Israel. She is a vocal critic of Israeli politics and has repeatedly emphasized that Israel does not represent all Jews.[881]

Humour can be one path to transcend the quicksand of Sedna, giving us the objectivity to step back from the edge and also to play with the rules with impunity and the opposition with Ixion can bring this out.

I have this aspect and so do two of my long-term clown and life partners. My Ixion is in my tenth house conjunct Juno, the asteroid of partnership. What I loved most about the clown work was the utter freedom it gives to act and interact as you choose. Anything is possible in clown; there are no rules. This is the wonderful freedom of Ixion.

I have Sedna in the fourth house of home, opposite Ixion in the tenth house of profession. Now there are not many professions in which you can be lawless without ending up in trouble and I would recommend the clown art form to anyone with a tenth house Ixion.

At this juncture in human evolution, few of us use our planets at the spiritual level, but many of us are striving to and such people are wonderful to be around. As with the other planets, the spiritual level of evolution is vastly different with Sedna from the two previous levels. Here the opposition with Ixion brings the challenge to be irreverent to religious traditions and strike out spiritually on our own.

Once we embrace the Sedna energy, which is the oneness of everything, our nurturing becomes an expression of Sedna consciousness and it becomes devotional in nature. The struggle of the beginner's level is gone, as are the transcendental crises of the intermediate level. At this level everything Saturnian is meaningless and yet everything Sednian has its place.

This is exemplified by the life of Georges Vandenbeusch, who was a French Catholic priest, who was held hostage by the terrorist group Boko Haram, before escaping. His Sedna is in his first house of identity,

---

[881] https://en.wikipedia.org/wiki/Judith_Butler

opposite Ixion, which is conjunct Mercury, the planet of communication, and Quaoar, the planet of new perspectives, all in the seventh house of relationships. Sedna is also inconjunct Neptune, the planet named after the god of the sea, but thankfully bi-quintile Jupiter, the planet of success.

> When he was 7 years old, the family was on a boat tour of Corsica at night, when the propeller stalled and everyone was thrown into the water. Only Georges survived, helped to the shore by his lifejacket. Once orphaned, he was raised by his grandparents.
>
> He studied to be a priest and was ordained and held various vicarage positions in Paris, before deciding to become a priest in the extreme north of Cameroon, on the Nigerian border, in order to carry the faith in remote and unstable areas.
>
> When he was 42 he was kidnapped by some fifteen armed men claiming to be Boko Haram and escaped seven weeks later. Boko Haram then said that, "The leadership decided to release the priest out of compassion. The priest offered his medical services to members during his period of captivity. Management felt that there was no need to keep it."
>
> These remarks, however, are contested by Georges Vandenbeusch, who states: "I am neither a nurse nor a doctor. If they had brought me somebody to take care with a hemorrhage, I would have done what I could, but they did not. They have no compassion for anyone."
>
> The following year he was part of the delegation of President François Hollande during his visit to Pope Francis. The meeting was marked by the warm embrace of the Pope. Very soon, he resumed his ministry in the church of Saint-Pierre-Saint-Paul of Courbevoie, of which he was officially appointed parish priest.[882]

And Lisa Williams, who is a British psychic, medium and healer. She has Sedna in the fifth house of creativity, opposition Ixion in the eleventh house of collective consciousness.

---

[882] https://fr.wikipedia.org/wiki/Georges_Vandenbeusch

She starred in two shows on Lifetime Television: *Lisa Williams: Life Among the Dead* and *Lisa Williams: Voices From the Other Side.* The shows followed Williams on a typical day, as she communicated with spirits, investigated haunted houses, and conducted other spirit-seeking activities.

She came out as a lesbian at 37 and said: 'For many years, speaking to dead people was hard enough for people to accept me, but then on top of that to then say 'by the way, I'm gay', I didn't want to acknowledge it'. Asked by a reporter, because of her unique insight into life after death, where she thought gay people were headed, she said: 'In my experience with those who have crossed, it is a place of love. It isn't a place of 'you didn't live this way so we'll punish you', it is a place where all your loved ones accept you for who you are'.[883]

Semi-sextile, Sextile, Trine

With the flowing aspects between Sedna and Ixion, the all-encompassing spiritual energy of Sedna aligns with our lawlessness, our lust for life, our sense of entitlement, our ability to create trouble with no regrets and to forgive ourselves.

The predominant trait of Ixion is utter lawlessness, not being held back by rules and by doing what we want, when we want. It also represents our deepest fears about who and what we may really be, and what we may be capable of.

With the larger frame of reference provided by the flowing aspects with Sedna, we also inherently feel that the normal rules are just artificial framework which don't really serve the common good and so always need to be changed.

If we haven't developed our Sedna energy however, the flowing aspects can still lead to a sense of righteousness in our rebellious behaviour and can bring out the more negative side of Ixion, which is ingratitude, wasting second chances, not keeping our word and problems with the law.

An extreme example is Peter Kürten, who was a German serial murderer, who for over 16 years murdered, mutilated and dismembered

---

[883] https://en.wikipedia.org/wiki/Lisa_Williams_(psychic)

some 68 female victims. He had Sedna in the twelfth house of the unconscious, trine Ixion in the fourth house of home.

> Perverted and sadistic from childhood, his outer mannerisms were so mild and courteous that it seemed incredible that he was the Monster of Dusseldorf. He was raised by an abusive, alcoholic father. By age nine his first homicide was in drowning another child. He masturbated excessively and learned to experience pleasure while torturing animals. By 14 he was having sex with sheep and goats, reaching orgasm while stabbing the animal.

> Arrested for theft, he served two years in prison. When released, he committed his first sex-murder at 30, with the victim a 13-year-old girl whom he strangled, cutting her throat. He established a pattern of reaching orgasm at the sight of blood and he even drank the blood of his victims. He was apprehended when a victim, whose life he had spared, led police to him and he was beheaded.[884]

Another is Fritz Haarmann, who was a German homicidal manic and a homosexual epileptic. He has Sedna in the eleventh house of collective consciousness, trine Ixion, which was in his third house of communication, but closely conjunct his IC, the cusp of his fourth house of home.

> From youth he served several prison terms for indecency and was committed several times to an insane asylum. He primarily lived as a petty thief, burglar and con artist. Although he did occasionally obtain legitimate employment, he invariably stole from his employers, or their customers.

> Despite police knowledge that he was both a criminal and a homosexual, which was then illegal and punishable by imprisonment in Germany, he gradually began to establish a relationship with Hanover police as an informer, largely as a means of redirecting their attention from himself in his own criminal activities, and to facilitate his access to young males.

> He is known to have committed at least 24 murders, although he is suspected of murdering a minimum of 27. All of his victims

---

[884] https://en.wikipedia.org/wiki/Peter_Kürten

were males between the ages of 10 and 22, the majority of whom were in their mid- to late-teens. They would be lured back to one of three addresses in which he is known to have lived, on the promise of assistance, accommodation, work, or under the pretence of citizen's arrest.[885]

Pablo Picasso was a Spanish artist who lived most of his life in France, Picasso is world-renowned as one of the inventors of the Cubist movement. He has Sedna in the ninth house of knowledge, trine Ixion in the twelfth house of the unconscious.

Considered to be the most original, influential and dominant presence in the visual arts of the early 20th century, his works are on display in the most prestigious museums and galleries of the world. His enormous output, including 14,000 canvases and thousands of prints, engravings, book illustrations, ceramics and sculptures, made him a billionaire at his death.[886]

His Sedna was also trine Juno, the asteroid of partnership, in the fifth house of creativity and his sexual appetite led him into many relationships and two marriages.

Beauty and relative youth were the only consistent qualities he desired in women. He used almost all of his women as models, both before and after relationships. A jealous man, he locked his first partner in their Paris apartment when he went out.

He met his first wife, the daughter of a Russian colonel of good family and upper class tastes, while he was designing for the Ballet Russe during their tour in Italy. He took her to Spain to introduce her to friends and relatives, painted her in a mantilla. They had a child, but she was soon out of the picture romantically, but they remained married due to their faith.

His next mistress whom he met at 45, eventually committed suicide by hanging herself. The one after that was Dora Maar. They met when he was 54 and she became increasingly deranged as their relationship progressed. Matching his ferocious temperament and depressions with her own, she

---

[885] https://en.wikipedia.org/wiki/Fritz_Haarmann
[886] https://en.wikipedia.org/wiki/Pablo_Picasso

ultimately had electro-shock treatments. All his paintings of crying women were of Dora.

In his 60s his sexual gluttony was becoming obsessive. He met Françoise Gilot, 40 years his junior. They had a son and a daughter, but after seven years she took the children and left. Shortly afterwards, Jacqueline Roque moved in.

His first wife died of natural causes when he was 73, clearing the way for another marriage. When he was 79 the children he had with Françoise officially received his name, however, while telling her he would marry her, he instead married Jacqueline in secrecy.[887]

As we tire of density and the grief it creates, and we start a spiritual journey to get out of the swamp, Sedna rewards us with transcendent crises, experiences which force us to let go and rise above them, resulting in a huge growth to a new level of consciousness. There is no choice with these crises, and the more we try and solve them, the more we will get hurt.

Like Janet Chance, who was a British feminist writer, sex education advocate and birth control and abortion law reformer. She had Sedna in the third house of ideas and communication, trine Ixion in the eighth house of shared resources.

She married a successful chemical firm owner and stockbroker when she was 26. The couple soon moved to London, where they both became enthusiastic advocate and financial supporters of the English Malthusian League and the efforts of American reformer Margaret Sanger and the birth control movement.

Despite suffering from intermittent bouts of depression, she threw herself into work becoming a member of the Workers' Birth Control Group, founded when she was 38 by birth control advocates to give women wider access to birth control information. She was so moved by the plight of poor and working-class women who had no knowledge of sex and reproduction and no access to the latest available contraceptive methods that she helped run a sex education centre in the East End of London.

---

[887] Ibid.

She presented a report, "A Marriage Education Centre in London," at the Third Congress of the World League for Sexual Reform when she was 43. Convinced that a large part of the problem lay in the repressed, provincial British view of sex and reproduction, she wrote several books on the importance of acknowledging women's sexuality and educating them about it, reflecting, albeit in modest terms, the views of the sex reform movement.

She was increasingly convinced that the problem lay in the fact that birth control options for poor women, especially were limited and in many cases their only option was abortion, but abortion was illegal in all cases in Great Britain. To this end, at the age of 50, she helped found and support the Abortion Law Reform Association. Working through Women's Co-operative Guilds and the Labour Party, this association sought to pressure politicians to support the notion that women should have the power to decide if their own pregnancies would be terminated.

During her late 40s, she also worked to help get refugees out of Germany, Austria and other Nazi-occupied nations. She also continued to chair the ALRA through World War II, helping to keep the organisation alive and ready for a post-war resurgence. But after the war, the ALRA shifted from pressuring Labour Party members, to campaigning more generally for a new parliamentary law by pushing for a private member's bill.

When she was 67 her husband died and her battle with depression intensified. She had to be hospitalised and, four months after her husband's death, she threw herself from a window at London's University College Hospital and died. Fourteen years after her death an abortion bill was finally passed by the British parliament.[888]

Jules Verne was a French writer widely popular for his science fiction novels and amazing anticipation of future discoveries. He had Sedna semi-sextile Ixion, with both in the eleventh house of collective consciousness.

---

[888] https://en.wikipedia.org/wiki/Janet_Chance

Regarded as the father of science fiction, he predicted the use of submarines, helicopters, air conditioning, guided missiles, trips to outer space and motion pictures long before they were developed. The son of a magistrate, he went to Paris to study law, however became interested in the theatre and began writing plays and opera librettos.

"He achieved success with his first short fantasy, *Five Weeks in a Balloon*, released when he was 35. His books have been translated into many languages and plays and films have been made from a number of them. His last years were marked with enormous popularity and numerous honours. By the time of his death, he had written over 50 books.

"Though he was raised Catholic, he became a deist from his early forties. Deism is a philosophical position that posits that a god does not interfere directly with the world. It also rejects revelation as a source of religious knowledge and asserts that reason and observation of the natural world are sufficient to determine the existence of a single creator of the universe. Some scholars believe his deist philosophy is reflected in his novels, as they often involve the notion of God, or divine providence, but rarely mention the concept of Christ.[889]

And on a different note, German novelist, Franz Kafka, had Sedna in the ninth house of knowledge, in a close trine with Ixion in the twelfth house of the unconscious.

He is widely regarded as one of the major figures of 20th-century literature. His work, which fuses elements of realism and the fantastic, typically features isolated protagonists faced by bizarre or surrealistic predicaments and incomprehensible social-bureaucratic powers, and has been interpreted as exploring themes of alienation, existential anxiety, guilt, and absurdity.

Few of his works were published during his lifetime and he ordered his unfinished books be destroyed on his death, but his friend ignored his direction and published them anyway. His books went on to influence a vast range of writers, artists, and philosophers during the 20th century and the term Kafkaesque

---

[889] https://en.wikipedia.org/wiki/Jules_Verne

entered the English language to describe situations like those in his writing.[890]

Humour can be one path to transcend the quicksand of Sedna, giving us the objectivity to step back from the edge and also the opportunity to play with the rules with impunity and the flowing aspects with Ixion can bring this out.

The English comic actor, filmmaker, and composer, Charlie Chaplin, who rose to fame during the era of silent film, has Sedna in the fifth house of creativity, trine Ixion in the ninth house of knowledge.

> Chaplin became a worldwide icon through his screen persona "the Tramp" and is considered one of the most important figures in the history of the film industry. His career spanned more than 75 years, from childhood in the Victorian era, until a year before his death at 88, and encompassed both adulation and controversy.
>
> Chaplin wrote, directed, produced, edited, starred in, and composed the music for most of his films. He was a perfectionist, and his financial independence enabled him to spend years on the development and production of a picture. His films are characterised by slapstick, combined with pathos, typified in the Tramp's struggles against adversity. Many contain social and political themes, as well as autobiographical elements.[891]

And the famous Swiss clown, Grock, a composer and musician, who is often called "the king of clowns" also has a trine. This time Sedna is in the first house of identity and Ixion is in the sixth house of daily routine.

> He was once the most highly paid entertainer in the world. He started early as a performer, learning musicianship and acrobatic skills from his father and later became a clown, working with the famous clown, Antonet. They developed an act with the aim of making the transition from circus, to music hall stages, which were more lucrative. Refining their performances according to audience response, Grock came to dominate the act, and they eventually split up. By then Grock's fame had spread, his act

---

[890] https://en.wikipedia.org/wiki/Franz_Kafka
[891] https://en.wikipedia.org/wiki/Charlie_Chaplin

having developed into the mixture of pantomime and musical blunders for which he is now remembered.[892]

At this juncture in human evolution, few of us use our planets at the spiritual level, but many of us are striving to, and such people are wonderful to be around. As with the other planets, the spiritual level of evolution is vastly different with Sedna from the two previous levels. Here, the flowing aspects with Ixion brings the ability to be irreverent to religious traditions and enables us to strike out spiritually on our own.

Once we embrace the Sedna energy, which is the oneness of everything, our nurturing becomes an expression of Sedna consciousness and it becomes devotional in nature. The struggle of the beginner's level is gone, as are the transcendental crises of the intermediate level. At this level everything Saturnian is meaningless and yet everything Sednian has its place.

Maria Quattrocchi, an Italian saint, who was beatified after her death along with her husband, the first time in church history that a woman and her husband were given that honour together as exemplars of the Christian life. She had Sedna in the second house of material resources, trine Ixion in the sixth house of service.

> She was a member of the noble Corsini family. She was a professor and writer on educational topics, writing several books and also served as a Voluntary Nurse in the Italian Red Cross during World War II. They were made saints because they opened their home to refugees during WWII, at great risk to the family. According to Pope John Paul II, they lived "an ordinary life in an extraordinary way".[893]

Hugo Ball was a German author, poet and another of the leading Dada artists. He had Sedna in the ninth house of publishing, trine Ixion in the first house of identity. When he was 24 he moved to Berlin in order to become an actor and collaborated with Max Reinhardt. At the beginning of the First World War he tried joining the army as a volunteer but was denied enlistment for medical issues.

> After witnessing the invasion of Belgium, he was disillusioned saying, "The war is founded on a glaring mistake, men have

---

[892] https://en.wikipedia.org/wiki/Grock
[893] https://en.wikipedia.org/wiki/Luigi_Beltrame_Quattrocchi_and_Maria_Corsini

been confused with machines". Considered a traitor in his country, he crossed the frontier with his wife and settled in Zürich. Here, he continued his interest in anarchism, rejecting its militant aspects and viewing it as only a means to his personal goal of enlightenment.

He was 30 when he created the Dada Manifesto, making a political statement about his views on the terrible state of society and acknowledging his dislike for philosophies in the past claiming to possess the ultimate Truth. The same year as the Manifesto, he wrote his poem "Karawane," which is a German poem consisting of nonsensical words. The meaning however resides in its meaninglessness, reflecting the chief principle behind Dadaism.

As co-founder of the Cabaret Voltaire in Zürich, he led the Dada movement in Zürich, and is one of the people credited with naming the movement "Dada", by allegedly choosing the word at random from a dictionary. His involvement with the Dada movement lasted less than two years. He then worked for a short period as a journalist, for Freie Zeitung in Bern. After returning to Catholicism at 34, he retired and lived a religious and relatively poor life, dying at 41.[894]

As we evolve and develop our Sedna consciousness, the flows allow us to step outside the normal rules and so chart new paths that are evolutionary and thereby point to new rules that need to be set in place.

Like Zoe Wells was an American artist and psychic who worked with Marc Edmund Jones and Elsie Wheeler on the 360-degree meanings that became known as the Sabian Symbols. She had Sedna on the cusp of the eleventh house of collective consciousness, trine Ixion in the second house of material reality.

When she was 40 she was a recognised commercial artist and student of Marc's and she possessed remarkable psychic skills. In an experimental session she brought through fifty-two symbols for a pack of ordinary playing cards. Marc described this event, in his book, The Sabian Symbols in Astrology, as the 'beginning

---

[894] https://en.wikipedia.org/wiki/Hugo_Ball

of a conscious recognition of the ancient sources as a self-contained and living integrity available for use'.[895]

Or like Antoine Court, who named himself Antoine Court de Gébelin, a former Protestant pastor, who initiated the interpretation of the Tarot as an arcane repository of timeless esoteric wisdom. He had Sedna in the second house of material reality, trine Ixion, which is also conjunct Mars, the planet of action, in the ninth house of spirituality.

His goal was to reconstruct what he believed to be the high primeval civilisation. Reinterpreting Classical and Renaissance evocation of the Golden Age into mankind's early history, he asserted that the primitive worldwide civilisation had been advanced and enlightened. He is the intellectual grandfather of much of modern occultism.

His centres of focus are the familiar ones of universal origins of languages in deep time and the hermeneutics of symbolism. While his views on hermeneutics and religious matters were largely conservative, his original ideas and research on the origin of language earn him a place among pioneers of linguistics.

He presented dictionaries of etymology, what he called a universal grammar, and discourses on the origins of language. His volumes were so popular he republished them separately. With regard to mythology and symbology, he discussed the origins of allegory in antiquity and recreated a history of the calendar from civil, religious, and mythological perspectives.

It was his immediate perception, the first time he saw the Tarot deck, that it held the secrets of the Egyptians. Writing without the benefit of deciphering of the Egyptian language, he developed a reconstruction of Tarot history, without producing any historical evidence, which was that Egyptian priests had distilled the ancient Book of Thoth into these images. These they brought to Rome, where they were secretly known to the popes, who brought them to Avignon in the 14th century, whence they were introduced into France.[896]

---

[895] https://www.astro.com/astro-databank/Wells,_Zoe
[896] https://en.wikipedia.org/wiki/Antoine_Court_de_Gébelin

Semi-square, Square, Sesquiquadrate,

With the stressful aspects between Sedna and Ixion, the all-encompassing spiritual energy of Sedna challenges our lawlessness, our lust for life, our sense of entitlement, our ability to create trouble with no regrets and to forgive ourselves.

The predominant trait of Ixion is utter lawlessness, not being held back by rules and by doing what we want, when we want. This Plutino also represents our deepest fears about who and what we may really be, and what we may be capable of.

Ixion has no sense of right or wrong, he lacks boundaries and he squanders his second chance, but he has a joy in life and an inventiveness which carries him through. So in our charts it can give us the strength to take the tiger by the tail and create change, secure in the knowledge that we have to break some eggs in order to make an omelet.

These aspects with Ixion can give us the strength to pursue our spiritual passion, which is what we need to pursue a personal spiritual path in this world, a path which will likely start by accepting ourselves and possibly involve forgiving ourselves.

Until we develop the Sedna energy however, the stressful aspects can lead to a sense of righteousness in our rebellious behaviour and can bring out the more negative side of Ixion, which is ingratitude, wasting second chances, not keeping our word and problems with the law.

Like Lizzie Borden, who was an American homicide suspect in the brutal murders of her parents after their bodies were found hacked beyond recognition when she was 31. She had Sedna conjunct Neptune, the planet of deception, in the seventh house of relationships, closely square Ixion, which is conjunct Vesta, the asteroid of 'hearth and home', in the tenth house of social standing.

> She spent almost a year in jail before her trial, which lasted for 13 days before her acquittal. Much of the evidence was inadmissible and there was a general public opinion that an upper class, respectable Christian woman and Sunday school teacher could never have committed an act of such brutality.
>
> She was two and her sister Emma was 11 when their mother died and their father later remarried a disliked step-mother. After

the acquittal, Lizzie and Emma moved out of their home to a bigger one in a wealthier area that they purchased with their inheritance. However, despite initial support, the community generally shunned her for the rest of her life.

The sisters lived together in the mansion until they experienced a rift over Lizzie's friendship with an actress, a relationship which was suspected to be lesbian. When Lizzie was 45, Emmy moved to her own home.

She had a history of irrational fits during her menses, which only occurred four times a year. A theory was later proposed that she suffered from temporal epilepsy. She died alone and friendless at 67, reportedly from complications of gall bladder surgery. Emma died 11 days later and the two were buried together in the family plot. She left the bulk of her fortune to a fund for animals.[897]

Or we might experience these issues in projected form, like Margherita Pezzoni, who was an Italian octogenarian who married a 23-year-old when she was 93. She had Sedna in the fifth house of romance, sesquiquadrate Ixion in the tenth house of social standing.

Sprightly and lucid of mind, she explained that she wanted to protect him with her estate as she was fond of him. She wanted to adopt him, but it would take too long, so she married him instead. The media got hold of the story and made it highly public, covering the wedding. When she died mysteriously two years later, her young husband was left the small inheritance of her pension, not the fortune he anticipated. He was arrested later that year on suspicion of killing another women and confessed to the murder of both women.[898]

Another example is Lucky Luciano, who was a Sicilian-American gangster, who rose from grubby street urchin, through the ranks of organized crime to became director of a crime syndicate. He had Sedna in the second house of material resources, sesquiquadrate Ixion in the seventh house of relationships.

---

[897] https://en.wikipedia.org/wiki/Lizzie_Borden

[898] https://www.astro.com/astro-databank/Pezzoni,_Margherita

By the age of ten he had embarked on his life of crime. At nineteen he spent six months in jail for selling heroin. By 23, ruthless and upwardly mobile, he began working for the crime boss, Joe Masseria and within five years he became his chief lieutenant.

At 32, he survived a "one-way ride," which is a rare feat. He was abducted, beaten, stabbed repeatedly, had his throat cut and was left for dead; he never named his abductors, and soon afterward he changed his name to Luciano. He earned the nickname "Lucky" because he successfully evaded arrest on a number of occasions and eventually became famous for racketeering in narcotics, prostitution, slot machines, loan sharking and 'protection'.

However, at 39 he was indicted, tried and convicted on charges of extortion and prostitution and sentenced to 30 to 50 years in prison. Nevertheless his power continued to grow, even while he was incarcerated, as he issued orders and ruled from his cell. Near the end of his life however, a reporter asked him if he would do it all again, and he replied, "I'd do it legal. I learned too late that you need just as good a brain to make a crooked million, as an honest million".[899]

The lawless energy of these aspects can also be expressed through social structures and roles. Like Douglas Haig, who was a senior officer of the British Army, appointed Commander-in-Chief of the British army in France and Belgium during WW1. He had Sedna conjunct Neptune, the planet of vision, in the second house of material reality, square Ixion, which is conjunct Pallas, the asteroid of wisdom, and the Sun, his willpower, all in the sixth house of service.

A year and a half after he was appointed, he began the Battle of Passchendaele in Flanders. Over the next three months there were 300,000 British and 200,000 German casualties. The following year his attack broke Germany's Hindenburg line.

Although he had gained a favourable reputation during the immediate post-war years, with his funeral becoming a day of national mourning, he has since become an object of criticism for

---

[899] https://en.wikipedia.org/wiki/Lucky_Luciano

his leadership during the First World War. He was nicknamed "Butcher Haig" for the two million British casualties endured under his command.

One of his biographers praised his leadership and some historians have argued that the public hatred in which his name had come to be held failed to recognise the adoption of new tactics and technologies by forces under his command, the important role played by British forces in the Allied victory and that high casualties were a consequence of the tactical and strategic realities of the time.[900]

As we tire of density and the grief it creates, and we start a spiritual journey to get out of the swamp, Sedna rewards us with transcendent crises, experiences which force us to let go and rise above them, resulting in a huge growth to a new level of consciousness. There is no choice with these crises, and the more we try and solve them, the more we will get hurt.

Emmeline Pankhurst was a British feminine social activist who founded the "Women's Franchise League" at 31, working for her lifetime for women's rights. She had Sedna in the first house of identity, square Ixion in the fourth house of home.

Educated in Paris, she married Richard Marsden Pankhurst when she was 21, a barrister and advocate of suffrage. After helping to found the League at 31, she became a member of the Independent Labour Party. She was widowed at 40, leaving her with three daughters; her one son died when she was 52.

She took the post of Registrar of Births and Deaths but later had to resign due to her propaganda activities. She established headquarters in London. As she became more deeply passionate and involved with her cause, she was imprisoned several times for Breach of the Peace.

She and her daughter Christabel became more militant by her mid 40's and when she was 53 they directed a window-breaking campaign for which she was sentenced to nine months jail. Their suffrage efforts led to arson and destruction of property. She was sentenced to three years prison but fled to Paris, then to the U.S.

---

[900] https://en.wikipedia.org/wiki/Douglas_Haig,_1st_Earl_Haig

During WWI, she became involved in public service, which took some of the pressure off her reputation as a trouble-maker. An able and ardent public speaker, she ran as candidate for various political posts. When she was 60, due in large part to her conviction, the Suffrage Act was passed.[901]

Arthur Conan Doyle was a British writer best known for his detective fiction featuring the character Sherlock Holmes. He has Sedna conjunct Neptune, the planet of inspiration, and also Vesta, the asteroid of regeneration, in the eleventh house of collective consciousness, square Ixion, which is conjunct Jupiter, the planet of expansion, in the first house of identity.

The Sherlock Holmes stories are generally considered milestones in the field of crime fiction and Doyle was a prolific writer, whose other works include fantasy and science fiction stories, plays, romances, poetry, non-fiction and historical novels.

He had a longstanding interest in mystical subjects. He was initiated as a Freemason at 28 and, influenced by a member of the Portsmouth Literary and Philosophical Society, he began a series of psychic investigations. These included attending around 20 seances, experiments in telepathy and sittings with mediums. Writing to Spiritualist journal Light, that year, he declared himself to be a Spiritualist and spoke of one particular psychic event that had convinced him.

He was a founding member of the Hampshire Society for Psychical Research at 30 and joined the London-based Society for Psychical Research five years later. Though he later wavered, resigning from the Freemasons at 30, but returned to it at 43, only to resign again when he was 52, he remained fascinated by the paranormal[902]

As we evolve and develop our Sedna consciousness however, the stressful aspects challenge us to confront the normal rules and to step outside the boundary of the known and so chart new paths that are evolutionary and point to new rules that need to be set in place.

---

[901] https://en.wikipedia.org/wiki/Emmeline_Pankhurst
[902] https://en.wikipedia.org/wiki/Arthur_Conan_Doyle

Jan Hendrik Oort, a Dutch astronomer and pioneer in the field of radio astronomy has a sesquiquadrate with Ixion. His New York Times obituary called him "one of the century's foremost explorers of the universe;" the European Space Agency website describes him as, "one of the greatest astronomers of the 20th century," and states that he "revolutionised astronomy through his ground-breaking discoveries."

> Oort determined that the Milky Way rotates and overturned the idea that the Sun was at its center. He also postulated the existence of the mysterious invisible dark matter in 1932, which is believed to make up roughly 84.5% of the total matter in the Universe and whose gravitational pull causes "the clustering of stars into galaxies and galaxies into connecting strings of galaxies." He also discovered the galactic halo, a group of stars orbiting the Milky Way but outside the main disk.

> Additionally, Oort is responsible for a number of important insights about comets, including the realisation that their orbits "implied there was a lot more solar system than the region occupied by the planets." The Oort Cloud, an extended shell of icy objects that exist in the outermost reaches of the solar system, roughly spherical in shape and thought to be the origin of most of the long-period comets. was named after him. Sedna is said to be the first of the Oort Cloud planets.[903]

Humour can be one path to transcend the quicksand of Sedna, giving us the objectivity to step back from the edge and also, with the stressful aspects to Ixion, the challenge to play with the rules with impunity.

Fernandel was a French actor and mime comedian with a long, sorrowful, equine face and a radiant and toothy smile. He had Sedna in the eleventh house of collective consciousness, sesquiquadrate Ixion in the third house of communication.

> One of France's leading box-office draws, he built a four-decade career from the age of 27. His films included the four great "Don Camillo" political comedies. His father was an accountant but also an amateur comedian-singer and his mother was also an amateur actress, quickly noticed the talent of the young Fernand. He often accompanied his father during the concerts he

---

[903] https://en.wikipedia.org/wiki/Jan_Oort

organised in the Marseilles suburbs. It was during a contest for amateur singers that he won the first prize for children prodigies at the theatre of Châtelet de Marseille.

He made his debut on stage at five years singing the military repertory with his elder brother. He had his first great success at the age of seven, a day when, paralyzed by stage fright, he was propelled on the stage by his father, with a great kick to the rear. He fell into his sabre and stretched his whole length under a storm of laughter. Later, he was never afraid to face the public.

In 1930, he appeared in his first motion picture and for more than forty years he would be France's top comic actor. He was perhaps best loved for his portrayal of the irascible Italian village priest at war with the town's Communist mayor in the Don Camillo series of motion pictures which he also directed. His horse-like teeth became part of his trademark.[904]

At this juncture in human evolution, few of us use our planets at the spiritual level, but many of us are striving to, and such people are wonderful to be around. As with the other planets, the spiritual level of evolution is vastly different with Sedna from the two previous levels. Here, the stressful aspects with Ixion bring the challenge to be irreverent to religious traditions and to strike out spiritually on our own.

Once we embrace the Sedna energy, which is the oneness of everything, our nurturing becomes an expression of Sedna consciousness and it becomes devotional in nature. The struggle of the beginner's level is gone, as are the transcendental crises of the intermediate level. At this level everything Saturnian is meaningless and yet everything Sednian has its place.

Swami Vivekananda, was an Indian religious leader, a disciple of Sri Ramakrishna, who became inspired by his teacher to serve men as a visible manifestation of God. His Sedna is conjunct Neptune, the planet of spiritual inspiration, on the cusp of the third house of communication, square Ixion in the sixth house of service.

An illumined being of the highest order, he was the forerunner who brought the spiritual teachings of India to the West, greatly influencing the last hundred years of spiritual growth in Europe

---

[904] https://en.wikipedia.org/wiki/Fernandel

and America. Highly intelligent with a retentive memory, he had stories of the scripture memorised by the time he was six.

He became one of the most beloved disciples of Sri Ramakrishna and, as the master spent his last years teaching his disciples and streams of visitors, he recorded his instruction. He then brought the spiritual teachings of India to the West in 1893 at the convening of the Parliament of Religions in Chicago. During his three-year stay in American, he founded Hindu philosophy schools, many of which acknowledge him as a modern Buddha and an emanation of Lord Shiva.

When he took the universal teachings to the West, he broke with the Indian caste tradition and lost his caste as a result. His Sedna was also quintile Chariklo, the centaur of foresight, in the the fifth house of creativity, square Orcus, the planet of speaking out in the twelfth house of the unconscious, and sesquiquadrate Nessus, the centaur of radical transformation, in the seventh house of relationships. His denial of the rigid system brought him severe censure from Indian traditionalists.[905]

Reinhold Ebertin was a German astrologer, and an exponent and developer of Cosmobiology. He had Sedna conjunct the cusp of the third house of communication, sesquiquadrate Ixion in the eighth house of psychic sensitivity.

He wrote over 60 astrological textbooks, and his work included 21 volumes that were translated into other languages and 40 annuals of Cosmobiology Yearbooks.

When he was five, Reinhold's parents divorced and he was placed in a foster home. During childhood and adolescence, his contacts with his mother, Elsbeth, were sporadic, made more difficult by interference from his father and paternal grandfather. When he was 16, Elsbeth introduced him to his chart and to astrology, which proved to be a turning point in his life.

At 21, he and his mother were finally reunited and he began his extensive studies of astrology. He worked at the time as a schoolteacher. At 22 he began his practice and at 27, he

---

[905] https://en.wikipedia.org/wiki/Swami_Vivekananda

founded the Ebertin Publishing House with the assistance and encouragement of his mother. He turned to Cosmobiology at 37.

He developed many interesting methods such as midpoint-structure, psychograms and the 90 degree-wheel, and was also interested in distance values, heliocentric, mundane and prognostic astrology, primary directions and Pluto research.

He met his future wife at the Astrologers Convention at Nuremberg when he was 28. They had a close and supportive marriage for 53 years until her death. Totally dedicated to a vegetarian diet, he also practiced yoga. He finished a new book after his 85th birthday.[906]

Marthe Robin was a French mystic and stigmatic. She had Sedna conjunct Pallas, the asteroid of wisdom, in the eighth house of the occult, sesquiquadrate Ixion in the twelfth house of the unconscious.

Serious illness marked her adult life and from her twenties she was confined to bed, crippled, and gradually paralysed. She ate only wafers and neither drank nor slept, but lived for seven decades and carried on a busy apostolate.

From the age of 28 she was completely paralysed and bedridden. Although she still could move the thumb and forefinger of one hand, she became motionless apart from her head which she could move slightly. Since the previous year, at the age of 25, she could not eat anything at all. And from the age of 26 she couldn't even take a sip of water. When doctors tried to force some water down her throat, it merely came out her nostrils.

For the next 53 years her only food was the holy Eucharist, a wafer of bread which Catholics believe is the body of Christ. They also believe that they become his body on ingesting it. Once a week she was given the sacred host. Once she had received it she went immediately into ecstasy and began her weekly re-living of Christ's crucifixion. Every Friday wounds appeared in the palms of her hands and the stigmata, the scourging and crowning with thorns appeared on her body, and she appeared to be dead.

---

[906] https://en.wikipedia.org/wiki/Reinhold_Ebertin

For 53 years she also carried on a busy apostolate, which is a Christian organisation directed to serving and evangelising the world. She was directed to found two schools in her native village, one for girls and one for boys. All this she directed down to the smallest detail from her bed in her darkened little room. Later on she was told to found a community which would welcome people looking for a retreat and which would be a home of "light, charity and love." It became known as the Foyer de Charité and there are now some 70 affiliated houses and communities throughout the world.[907]

In-conjunct

With the evolutionary inconjunct between Sedna and Ixion the esoteric spiritual energy of Sedna bursts into our lawlessness, our lust for life, our sense of entitlement, our ability to create trouble, to have no regrets and to forgive ourselves in an evolutionary way and we have a fated role to play.

The predominant trait of Ixion is utter lawlessness, not being held back by rules and by doing what we want, when we want. This Plutino also represents our deepest fears about who and what we may really be, and what we may be capable of.

This aspect sometimes acts as a flow and at other times as a stress, so we have to learn to actively manage the process as the rarified spiritual energy sometimes reinforces our lust for life and, at other times, isn't there to back us up. By adjusting to this, we gain a deeper understanding of ourselves and how to play our role.

Ixion has no sense of right or wrong, he lacks boundaries and he squanders his second chance, but he has a joy in life and an inventiveness which carries him through. So, in our charts it can give us the strength to take the tiger by the tail and create change, secure in the knowledge that we have to break some eggs in order to make an omelet.

As we develop our Sedna consciousness, we may well take on the role of social provocateur, however until we do this aspect can lead to a sense of righteousness, or rebellious behaviour, likely to bring out the

---

[907] https://en.wikipedia.org/wiki/Marthe_Robin

negative side of Ixion, which is ingratitude, wasting second chances, not keeping our word and problems with the law.

This can happen even if we are the law. Like Nicolae Ceausescu, who was a Romanian politician, an indestructible dictator for 24 years and one of history's mass murderers. He had Sedna in the eleventh house of ideals, inconjunct Ixion in the fifth house of creativity.

> The son of a shoemaker, he had a limited education before he joined the Communist army fighting against fascists. He was captured and spent several years in prison before assembling a coup that won him the nation's highest office. His rule was marked by an extensive cult of personality, and by nepotism.

> However, after a brief period of relatively moderate rule, he became increasingly brutal and repressive. He maintained controls over speech and the media that were very strict even by Soviet-bloc standards. Internal dissent was not tolerated under his rule. His secret police, the Securitate, was one of the most ubiquitous and brutal secret police forces in the world.

> Seventeen years after ceasing power, he ordered the export of much of the country's agricultural and industrial production, with the goal of paying off Romania's large foreign debt. The resulting extreme shortages of food, fuel, energy, medicines, and other basic necessities drastically lowered living standards and intensified unrest. Four years later, on the week before Christmas, he ordered a massacre of protesters and the country erupted in a furious revolution, the only violent removal of a Communist government. He was tried in secret and swiftly executed.[908]

Or like Ian Douglas Smith, who served as Prime Minister of Rhodesia, now Zimbabwe, when it declared independence from the United Kingdom. He has Sedna in the fifth house of creativity, inconjunct Ixion in the tenth house of profession.

> He was the country's first premier not born abroad and led a predominantly white government. He unilaterally declared independence from the United Kingdom, following prolonged

---

[908] https://en.wikipedia.org/wiki/Nicolae_Ceaușescu

dispute over the terms and remained Prime Minister for almost all of the 14 years of international isolation that followed.

In that role he also oversaw Rhodesia's security forces during most of the guerrilla war during that time, which pitted the unrecognised administration against communist-backed black nationalist guerrilla groups. He has been described as personifying white Rhodesia; however, he remains a highly controversial figure, with supporters venerating him as a man of integrity and vision, while critics describe an unrepentant racist, whose policies and actions caused the deaths of thousands and contributed to Zimbabwe's later crises.[909]

We can see the fatalistic nature of this aspect in the the life and particularly the death of Caryl Chessman. He was an American robber and rapist called the 'Red Light Bandit' because he would flash a red light on his car to stop people, pretending to be a cop, then rape the woman and rob the man. He had Sedna conjunct Chiron, the centaur of wounding, and Nessus the centaur of righteousness, all in the eighth house of life and death, inconjunct Ixion, which is together with Saturn, the planet of rules, in the first house of identity.

He was born to an alcoholic dad and a mother paralysed from an auto accident when he was nine, he was a sickly, asthmatic child. He joined a gang and married a 16-year-old girl when he was 19. Then in a binge of rape, robbery and kidnapping, he shot a man to death, and was convicted at 26.

While in San Quentin prison he studied law, wrote appeals and a book. However, after 12 years on death row, he was finally executed in the gas chamber. A last-minute stay and ninth reprieve had been ordered by state Supreme Court, but it was too late. A wrong number was dialed to the prison and then quickly redialed, but when the judge listened on the other end he reported back, 'It's too late. The pellets have already been dropped'.[910]

And on a more redemptive note, Violette Nozière, was a French homicide perpetrator. Violette murdered her father with poison and

---

[909] https://en.wikipedia.org/wiki/Ian_Smith
[910] https://en.wikipedia.org/wiki/Caryl_Chessman

attempted the murder of her mom when she was 18. She had Sedna in the fourth house of home, inconjunct Ixion in the ninth house of spirituality.

> Her motive was to gain their savings as an inheritance. She was initially sentenced to death, but the sentence was commuted to life in prison. A renewed passion for Catholicism served in securing her release at the age of 30, and the following year she married the son of the prison bursar, whom she had met during her time in incarceration. The couple had four sons and a daughter.[911]

As we tire of density and the grief it creates, and we start a spiritual journey to get out of the swamp, Sedna rewards us with transcendent crises, experiences which force us to let go and rise above them, resulting in a huge growth to a new level of consciousness. There is no choice with these crises, and the more we try and solve them, the more we will get hurt.

Betty Ford was an American First Lady when her husband, Gerald Ford, was sworn in as the nation's 38th president, minutes after Richard Nixon resigned, when she was 56. She had Sedna in the eighth house of shared resources, inconjunct Ixion in the first house of identity.

> A tomboy in her early years, she grew up among the privileges of middle class life with dancing lessons and a summer cottage on a lake. After her father's death when she was 16, she moved to New York City, modeling on Seventh Avenue and dancing with the Martha Graham Company.

> At 30, she married local football hero Jerry Ford, who was elected to House of Representatives eight months later. Moving to Washington she assumed the social role of a politician's wife and gave birth to four children in the next seven years.

> Medication for a pinched nerve at 46, coupled with alcohol abuse, led to a nervous breakdown and psychiatric care the following year, a turning point for Ford, which spiralled her downward to drug and alcohol dependency. The addiction pattern of closet pill popper and alcoholic housewife had the accompanying ripple effects in her family, marriage and social

---

[911] https://fr.wikipedia.org/wiki/Violette_Nozière

life, yet her actions were overlooked due to her social position and status.

After husband Gerald was elected to the Presidency when she was 56, she proved herself an honest and outspoken First Lady with her comments on pre-marital sex, marijuana, and her marital relationship. Further public candor followed with her announcement of breast cancer and mastectomy surgery.

A timely warning from secret service agent Chuck Vance to his girlfriend Susan Ford blew the whistle for help, and daughter Susan followed through with intervention and counseling on when she was 60, resulting in Ford's admission to rehab. "My family saved my life," she later said appreciatively.

Six months later she emerged a new woman with a clean bill of health. Her experience in rehab prompted her to spread the healing process to others and three years later she and several colleagues raised three million dollars to build a rehab clinic of their own, naming it the Betty Ford Center.[912]

Our case study, James Lovelock, the father of Gaia theory, has Sedna in the sixth house of service, inconcjunct Ixion, which is in his tenth house of profession, conjunct Venus, the planet of Values. Gaia theory holds that we form a symbiotic relationship with our environment on Earth, creating a living planet that works together to maintain a liveable environment. With the inconjunct to Ixion, James has been the consumate subversive provocateur, calling for climate change action before there was any and calling it too late when the world did finally come together to address the problem.

Spike Milligan was a British director and writer best known for "The Goon Show," which began as a radio series when he was 33. He had Sedna in the second house of material resources, inconjunct Ixion, which is conjunct Mars, the planet of action, in the seventh house of relationships.

The son of a British military man, he was raised in India, Burma and Ceylon, arriving in England at 15. He started his career as a singer, trumpet player and guitar player. His big break came in his 30s in a show called "Crazy People," which eventually

---

[912] https://en.wikipedia.org/wiki/Betty_Ford

became the legendary "Goon Show." He wrote much of his own comedy material for the show as well as many TV vehicles.

In addition to radio and TV scripts, he also wrote several comedy novels and a book of nonsense and verse, in spite of his own lifetime battle with depression. Diagnosed as being bi-polar, he was noted for being difficult and demanding to work with. His career on screen never matched his success on radio and TV but his books and comedy recordings maintained their popularity long after the end of the Goons and he received a Lifetime Achievement Award given at the British Comedy Awards in at the age of 76.[913]

As we see, humour can be one path to transcend the quicksand of Sedna, giving us the objectivity to step back from the edge and also the opportunity to play with the rules with impunity and these aspects can bring this out.

Phyllis Diller was an American comedienne. She had Sedna in the eleventh house of the collective consciousness, inconjunct Ixion which is conjunct Pallas, the asteroid of wisdom, on the fifth house cusp.

The only child of strict, older parents, she remembers being a nerd and a misfit, a shy, scrawny and plain kid who spent much of her time alone with her dolls and her cat. At school she used humour as a defence and began to discover the perks of being the class clown; laughter, attention and admiration.

She wisecracked her way from the local laundromat, to community events, then exploded on stage in San Francisco, wearing a sequined mini-dress and an orange fright-wig, gold ankle-high boots and black satin opera gloves. A married housewife until she was 37, she buried the ironing in the backyard and took her show on the road, complaining about her husband, "Fang," and keeping an audience howling.

She made her debut as a stand-up comic at the Purple Onion, a popular San Francisco nightspot, and stayed for 89 weeks. Soon everyone wanted her as their guest speaker. In the following

---

[913] https://en.wikipedia.org/wiki/Spike_Milligan

years she went from $60 a week to $75,000 a week as an international star, writing most of her own material.[914]

At this juncture in human evolution, few of us use our planets at the spiritual level, but many of us are striving to, and such people are wonderful to be around. As with the other planets, the spiritual level of evolution is vastly different with Sedna from the two previous levels. Here, the inconjunct with Ixion brings a fated ability to strike out spiritually in an innovative way.

Once we embrace the Sedna energy, which is the oneness of everything, our nurturing becomes an expression of Sedna consciousness and it becomes devotional in nature. The struggle of the beginner's level is gone, as are the transcendental crises of the intermediate level. At this level everything Saturnian is meaningless and yet everything Sednian has its place.

Like Doris Conway Battle, who was an American astrologer who was the first American woman to be certified by the Faculty of Astrological Studies in London. She had Sedna in the eleventh house of collective consciousness, inconjunct Ixion in the fourth, but right on the fifth house cusp, and together with Mars, the planet of action, in the fifth house of creativity. At 36, she became the first American woman to be certified by the Faculty of Astrological Studies headed by Margaret Hone and founded under the auspices of the Astrological Lodge of London.

And Maxine Bell, who was an American trance medium, pianist and composer. She had Sedna in the tenth house of profession, inconjunct Ixion in the third house of communication. She played the works of dead masters while in trance and was able to play 3,000 notes per minute. She also worked with the Los Angeles Police Department on murder cases, as a psychic.

And like Billy Graham, who was an American evangelist, a Southern Baptist preacher who was "born again" as a teen, accepting Jesus as his personal saviour. He has Sedna in the first house of identity, inconjunct Ixion in the sixth house of service.

> He spread the good word of God by way of 900 radio stations and many TV crusades. He published a magazine, *Decision*, with circulation of more than four million, and gradually moved

---

[914] https://en.wikipedia.org/wiki/Phyllis_Diller

into the TV ministry. World- traveled, he became internationally known as the spiritual leader of presidents and noted people in many walks of life.

The author of 24 books, many of them best-sellers, Graham is the recipient of several awards. He is never unctuous or pious; rather, he is earnest, quietly confident and, despite his iconic status, ministers from a personal level. It is estimated that he has preached to more people in live audiences than anyone else in history: some 210 million in more than 185 countries and territories. Hundreds of millions more have been reached through his TV, film, radio, video and print projects.[915]

Quintile, Bi-quintile

The evolutionary quintile or bi-quintile aspect between Sedna and Ixion infuses our lawlessness, our lust for life, our sense of entitlement, our ability to create trouble with no regrets and ability to forgive ourselves with the all-encompassing spiritual energy of Sedna to the point where we can push the boundaries of human development.

Quintiles and bi-quintiles point to talent, the desire to create order and to categorize, a fascination with patterns and structures, perfectionist tendencies, and the desire to build or make things. These aspects have the characteristics of both the trine and opposition. They point to awareness of conflicts, or problems and finding solutions for them, however they do not automatically kick into action and must be cultivated over time.

Ixion has no sense of right or wrong, he lacks boundaries and he squanders his second chance, but he has a joy in life and an inventiveness which carries him through. So in our charts it can give us the strength to take the tiger by the tail and create change, secure in the knowledge that we have to break some eggs in order to make an omelet.

With these aspects, Ixion can give us the strength to pursue our spiritual passion, which is what we need to pursue a personal spiritual path in this world, a path which will likely start by accepting ourselves and possibly involve forgiving ourselves.

---

[915] https://en.wikipedia.org/wiki/Billy_Graham

Until we develop our Sedna energy however, these aspects can still lead to a sense of righteousness, or rebellious behaviour, which can bring out the more negative side of Ixion, which is ingratitude, wasting second chances, not keeping our word and problems with the law.

An extreme example is Josef Mengele, who was a German doctor and member of the Nazi party. He had Sedna conjunct Orcus, the planet of delving down and speaking out, in the tenth house of profession, bi-quintile Ixion in the third house of ideas and communication.

> He was known as the 'Angel of Death' at the Auschwitz concentration camp during World War II for his grisly genetic research on twins and other subjects. He was the subject of a 40-year international hunt in the postwar years, known for being the butcher who had supervised the torture and death of as many as 400,000 Jews in a maniacal quest for racial purity.[916]

The father of Silicon Valley, William Shockley's Sedna is in the twelfth house of the unconscious, bi-quintile Ixion in the fifth house of creativity, indicating how his research would unleash a technology, computers, which would disrupt existing business models and empower personal creativity. However, he held some controversial views as a supporter of Eugenics, believing that humanity would be better served by not allowing the less intelligent amongst us to have children. This placed him at odds with public attitudes and led to him, later in life, being called a nasty old man, even by his friends.

And the father of modern computers, Alan Turing's Sedna is also in the twelfth house, bi-quintile his Ixion in the fifth house of personal creativity and this found direct expression in his creation of a machine to break coded communication. But the aspect also prefigures how disruptive the digital technology that would come from his research would be to existing ways of working. However, Turing did run afoul of the law for being a homosexual, which was illegal in England at the time. He complained to the police about a robbery by a friend of his lover, revealing the relationship and leading to his conviction. The bi-quintile to Ixion is shown in the passing of the Alan Turing law, which is an informal term for a 2017 law in the United Kingdom that retroactively pardoned all men cautioned or convicted under historical legislation that outlawed homosexual acts.

---

[916] https://en.wikipedia.org/wiki/Josef_Mengele

With these aspects it is possible for the spiritual energy to manifest even at the unconscious level. Like it did with Francisco Marto, who was a Portuguese child noted for the Miracle of Fatima, during which the sun appeared to spin and fall from the sky, witnessed by 70,000 people. He had Sedna conjunct Saturn and also Orcus, the planet of delving down and speaking out, in the twelfth house of the unconscious, bi-quintile Ixion in the fifth house of children.

> On a spring day when he was six he was tending sheep with his cousin and sister, who were nine and eight, when they first began to see visions of the Virgin Mary. Later that year a large crowd gathered near Fátima, Portugal, in response to their prophecy that the Virgin Mary, referred to as Our Lady of Fatima, would appear and perform miracles on that date.
>
> Newspapers published testimony from reporters and other people who claimed to have witnessed extraordinary solar activity, such as the sun appearing to "dance" or zig-zag in the sky, careen towards the earth, or emit multicoloured light and radiant colours. According to these reports, the event lasted approximately ten minutes.
>
> During the second apparition the Virgin Mary had said to his cousin, "In a short time I will take Francisco and his sister up to heaven with me. You, on the other hand, will remain on earth for a great many years to spread the devotion to my Immaculate Heart." The two Marto children were both stricken by the Spanish flu and Francisco died at Fatima, age ten.[917]

As we tire of density and the grief it creates, and we start a spiritual journey to get out of the swamp, Sedna rewards us with transcendent crises, experiences which force us to let go and rise above them, resulting in a huge growth to a new level of consciousness. There is no choice with these crises, and the more we try and solve them, the more we will get hurt.

Simone de Beauvoir was a French writer and existentialist teacher who fashioned an impressive literary career as a novelist, philosopher, essayist and writer of memoirs. She had Sedna in the fourth house of home, bi-quintile Ixion in the ninth house of knowledge.

---

[917] https://en.wikipedia.org/wiki/Francisco_and_Jacinta_Marto

She looked on marriage as an obscene, bourgeois institution that put women in an inferior position. In rejecting marriage, she also rejected children, noting that she had escaped most of women's bondages.

She was a prominent member of the young avant-garde Parisian intelligentsia in the '40s, she was the presiding celebrity of the Existentialist movement along with Jean Paul Sartre, who was her life companion in an open relationship. They never lived in the same residence, nor did they require sexual fidelity of each other, but they did keep a close and steady relationship, seeing each other daily from the time they met at the Sorbonne when she was 21, until Sartre died 50 years later.[918]

Her Sedna was also closely bi-quintile Ixion, the planet of lawlessness in the ninth house of higher education.

She had a very turbulent, often scandalous life. Although she had a longtime relationship with Sartre, she was known to have a number of female lovers. The nature of some of these relationships, some of which she began with underage students while working as a professor, later led to a controversy.

A former student wrote in her book that, while she was a student at Lycée Molière, she had been sexually exploited by her teacher de Beauvoir, who was in her 30s at the time. She and Jean-Paul Sartre developed a pattern, which they called the "trio", in which de Beauvoir would seduce her students and then pass them on to Sartre. Finally, she was suspended from her teaching job, when she was accused of seducing a 17-year-old pupil. The girl's parents laid formal charges against her for debauching a minor and she had her license to teach in France permanently revoked.[919]

Jane Austen was a British writer, the first renowned female novelist of England. She had Sedna in the sixth house of daily routine, quintile Ixion in the fourth house of home.

She was the seventh of eight kids born to a scholarly village rector. She wrote from age 12, with her first novel at 15. For

---

[918] https://en.wikipedia.org/wiki/Simone_de_Beauvoir
[919] Ibid.

family entertainment, the entire family would tell stories, stimulating her young imagination. Her father was a kindly, reserved cleric and her mother, witty. There were few opportunities available to a young woman in that time and place; women were not even allowed into the universities and she only had two years of formal education.

As a young girl she was as high-spirited and silly. She had several suitors. She had a flirtation with the attractive but poor young man, which set neighbourhood tongues wagging. Later, she suffered a deeper embarrassment in first accepting, then rejecting the very next morning, the proposal of someone who was suitable from a social viewpoint, but not to her heart. She remained a lifelong spinster, later becoming somewhat tight-lipped with chastity.

She had six novels published from the age of 36, a remarkable accomplishment for a woman in that era, including her most famous, *Pride and Prejudice*. Her use of biting irony, along with her realism and social commentary have earned her great and historical importance to critics and scholars. Her novels have rarely been out of print, although they were published anonymously and brought her little fame during her lifetime.

A significant transition in her reputation occurred 15 years after her death, when her novels were illustrated and republished in the Standard Novels series and sold as a set. They gradually gained wider acclaim and popular readership. Fifty-two years after her death, her nephew's publication of *A Memoir of Jane Austen* introduced a compelling version of her writing career and 'supposedly uneventful life' to an eager audience.[920]

L. Ron Hubbard was an American entrepreneur, engineer, and prolific writer of science fiction, who established the Church of Scientology. He had Sedna in the third house of ideas, bi-quintile Ixion in the ninth house of spirituality.

Imaginative, intelligent, and with a mind that was a factory of ideas, he was also broke and in debt in the late 1940s and was forced to sell his typewriter for $28.50 to pay alimony to his first

---

[920] https://en.wikipedia.org/wiki/Jane_Austen

wife. Troubled, restless and adrift he became an expert hypnotist, and shared an ageing mansion in Pasadena, CA with writers, artists, Bohemians and occultists in the late 1940s. Neighbours complained when their rituals of sexual magic got out of hand in the back yard.[921]

His Sedna was also conjunct Orcus, the planet of delving down and speaking out in the fourth house of home.

He wrote a book, *Dianetics: The Modern Science of Mental Health*, which was written in one draft in 30 days and became an instant bestseller. He became an overnight celebrity. His system became known as "the poor man's psychotherapy." However, by the following year profits were beginning to fall and Dianetics became Scientology, as he turned from pop therapist to religious leader.

Skillfully transforming himself from a pulp fiction writer to a writer of "sacred scriptures," Hubbard made a fortune and achieved his dream of fame. Starting as a collection of mental therapy centers it grew into one of the world's most controversial and secretive religions. The courses included instruction of how to help kick drug habits, improve communication skills, build confidence and help people take control of their lives.

However, by preying on the anxieties and the loneliness of his converts and by using hypnotherapy, Pavlovian conditioning and twisted psychotherapy, he was able to establish himself as the leader of a movement of millions, less than 900 of which ever reached the highest levels of his imparted wisdom. Australian courts have since revoked the status of Scientology as a religion, and France convicted Hubbard in absentia of fraud. However, in spite of all the exposure, he still ignited the fire of self-improvement in many sincere people.[922]

Humour can be one path to transcend the quicksand of Sedna, giving us the objectivity to step back from the edge and also the opportunity to play with the rules with impunity. These aspects can bring this out.

[921] https://en.wikipedia.org/wiki/L._Ron_Hubbard
[922] Ibid.

Lucille Ball is an an American actress, comedienne, model, film-studio executive, and producer. She has Sedna in the third house of communication, bi-quintile Ixion in the eighth house of shared resources.

> She was best known as the star of the self-produced sitcoms, *I Love Lucy, The Lucy Show, Here's Lucy,* and *Life with Lucy*. In the 1950s she ventured into television, creating the sitcom *I Love Lucy* In 1951, a series that became one of the most beloved programs in television history. In 1962, Ball became the first woman to run a major television studio, Desilu Productions, which produced many popular television series, including *Mission: Impossible* and *Star Trek*.[923]

At this juncture in human evolution, few of us use our planets at the spiritual level, but many of us are striving to, and such people are wonderful to be around. As with the other planets, the spiritual level of evolution is vastly different with Sedna from the two previous levels. Here, the quintile and bi-quintile aspects with Ixion bring the ability to be irreverent to religious traditions and enables us to strike out spiritually on our own.

Once we embrace the Sedna energy, which is the oneness of everything, our nurturing becomes an expression of Sedna consciousness and it becomes devotional in nature. The struggle of the beginner's level is gone, as are the transcendental crises of the intermediate level. At this level everything Saturnian is meaningless and yet everything Sednian has its place.

Annie Besant was a British-Indian social reformer and feminist at the forefront of liberal movements for 60 years. She had Sedna conjunct Chariklo, the centaur of foresight, in the twelfth house of the unconscious, quintile Ixion in the second house of material reality.

> Her family background was genteel, though her father was from an impoverished branch and died when Annie was only five. Deeply religious as a child, she longed to serve humanity with some sort of glorious martyrdom. She was married to a dour Anglican clergyman at 21, which was apparently a type of martyrdom in itself; the marriage lasted for six years. Leaving

---

[923] https://en.wikipedia.org/wiki/Lucille_Ball

him at age 27, she had an alimony income of 110 pounds per annum, a comfortable if not extreme fortune.

Taking up the worthy cause of birth control, she was arrested and tried at 30 on a morals charge for her publication written with Charles Bradlaugh, *The Fruits of Philosophy*. The litigation cost her the custody of her two children and her alimony. An attractive, feminine woman, she held a fiery sword in her public demonstrations.

She met Mme Blavatsky when she was 42 and was greatly taken with her and with the doctrine of Theosophy. From the age of 60 until her death, she served as the President of the Theosophical Society in India. She took the young Krishnamurti under her wing a couple of years later and nurtured him as the New Avatar, the Messiah. She founded the Order of the Star in the East with the 16-year-old Krishnamurti as the official head.

However, the society was fraught with intrigue, spiritual competition, power-struggles and scandals. When Krishna finally broke with the Theosophical society when Anne was 82, she was nearly completely senile and never realized that her cultivation of the Matreya had been denied by the embodiment himself. When he visited her for the last time, she hardly knew who he was.[924]

Ralph Houston was an American guru. He also had Sedna conjunct Saturn and also Orcus, in the twelfth house of the unconscious, bi-quintile Ixion in the fifth house of creativity.

He was raised in Europe and met his spiritual teacher, Nicholas Roerich, a Russian painter, philanthropist and writer, when he was 24 and was initiated as his student two days later. He became a metaphysical teacher and fourth initiate chelae, and founded an Agni Yoga group in San Francisco when he was 46, another in Los Angeles the following year, and in upper New York State in his early 50s. He had a gift for lighting the fires of inspiration, though his advice was often questionable.[925]

Peter Hurkos is a Dutch psychic who gained ESP abilities after a blow to his head, which left him unconscious for three days. His psychic abilities

[924] https://en.wikipedia.org/wiki/Annie_Besant
[925] https://www.astro.com/astro-databank/Houston,_Ralph

were tested psychometrically with a claimed 87% accuracy. He has Sedna in the eleventh house of collective consciousness, bi-quintile Ixion in the fourth house of home.

> As a boy, he was a poor student, dropping out of school when he entered his teens. He was a loner who spent much time in the woods or in solitude, dreaming and exploring, prone to fantasies and visions. After his accident, he became religious and also became afflicted with blinding headaches and his temperament became volatile and moody.[926]

Sedna is also in a fateful inconjunct with Pholus, the centaur of enlightenment in the sixth house of service.

> In addition to using his new-found abilities to do professional work, he also did TV guest spots and wrote an autobiography, titled *Psychic*. He tuned in to some of his subjects while in a sleep state, when he could speak in tongues, or in foreign languages, but he also did psychic work while awake.[927]

---

[926] https://en.wikipedia.org/wiki/Peter_Hurkos
[927] Ibid.

40: Sedna / Orcus

Conjunction

There is no one alive today with this aspect and no one will be born with this aspect in the next 100 years, so it is not interpreted here.

Opposition

There is no one alive today with this aspect and no one will be born with this aspect in the next 100 years, so it is not interpreted here.

Semi-sextile, Sextile, Trine

With the flowing aspects between Sedna and Orcus, the all-encompassing spiritual energy of Sedna aligns with our curiosity, our search for hidden truth, our intellectual independence, and ability to challenge established thought and speak out.

Orcus works with the theme of exploration, of uncovering a blueprint, or map that leads to a new picture, to delve below the constructs of mind that are merely based upon the convenience of our collective consensus and gain a deeper understanding of life.

With the larger frame of reference provided by the flowing aspects with Sedna, we also inherently want to tear apart the distinctions and categories that are established in order to reach a novel and innovative understanding beyond the established categories of thought and action.

If we haven't developed the Sedna energy however the flows can still lead to a sense of righteousness in our intellectual independence and bring out the more negative side of Orcus, such as lustfulness, inconsiderateness, and not learning from experience.

Like Pauline Dubuisson, who was a French murderer and suicide victim. She had Sedna in the fourth house of home, semi-sextile Orcus in the sixth house of daily routine.

> She was the mistress of a German Colonel at 17 and kept a notebook of his and other lover's performances. She was listed by the Resistance as a Nazi collaborator. She enrolled as a medical student at 20 and began a stormy three-year affair with fellow student before they parted. She attempted a reconciliation but he had plans to marry another. She was 25 when she shot and killed him and gassed herself. She was revived and given a

sentence of life in prison; finally managing to kill herself 12 years later.[928]

Or like Jeannie Donald, who was a Scottish murderer. She had Sedna semi-sextile Orcus, with both in the second house of material resources.

She was tried at the age of 39 for the murder of her eight-year-old neighbour, who had left the first-floor tenement, where her family lived, to fetch a loaf of bread from the local Co-op bakery and had not returned. Her body was found the next day in a lavatory of the tenement. The cause of death was determined to be asphyxiation and there appeared to be signs of rape.

Further forensic tests determined that the child had not been raped but had been injured to make it appear as though she had been sexually assaulted. Suspicion fell upon Jeannie Donald. The two families refused to talk after Mrs Donald had hit the girl when she had been cheeky to her. When the Donald home was examined stains were found and Jeannie Donald was charged with Helen's murder.

At the trial the defence contended that the child's injuries were consistent with rape that, of course, would have cleared Mrs Donald. The most damning evidence came from Jeannie's daughter who testified that the Co-op loaf, that had been found in the Donald house, was not theirs. Jeannie Donald did not testify, was found guilty and sentenced to death. This was commuted to penal servitude for life and she was released ten years later and disappeared from the public eye, dying at 81.

It was speculated that what actually happened was that the girl had been ringing the Donald's doorbell and running away. Jeannie Donald had hidden under the stairs and when the child did it again, she had leapt out and frightened the child so much she had caused the child to choke on her own vomit. The girl had suffered from an enlarged thymus gland and this would have made her more prone to fainting. A frightened Jeannie then molested the child to make it look like a rape killing.[929]

---

[928] https://fr.wikipedia.org/wiki/Pauline_Dubuisson
[929] http://murderpedia.org/female.D/d/donald-jeannie.htm

Or like Patricia Krenwinkel, an American homicide perpetrator and a member of the Charles Manson family. She had Sedna in the sixth house of daily routine, sextile Orcus in the eighth house of life and death.

> Formerly a Sunday School teacher, she was fond of animals. Her folks divorced when she was 17. Her direction changed when she joined Manson at 20, abandoning her job and car. She was arrested for possession of drugs at 21 and was in and out of jail several times. The next year she took part in the Manson massacre in Los Angeles in which five people were killed. She was arrested at the Manson Ranch and released into her dad's custody.

> She was found guilty at 24 of one count of conspiracy to commit murder and seven counts of first degree murder. She was given the death sentence; however, it was later commuted to life imprisonment. During a parole hearing at 57, when asked who she would place at the top of the list of people she has harmed, she responded, "Myself".[930]

At time of writing she has been denied parole fourteen times and is now the longest-incarcerated female inmate in the California penal system.

As we tire of density and the grief it creates, and we start a spiritual journey to get out of the swamp, Sedna rewards us with transcendent crises, experiences which force us to let go and rise above them, resulting in a huge growth to a new level of consciousness. There is no choice with these crises, and the more we try and solve them, the more we will get hurt.

Like Virginia Woolf, who was a British writer, a novelist and essayist who used the English language superbly. She had Sedna in the eleventh house of collective consciousness, sextile Orcus in the ninth house of knowledge.

> After the death of her father when she was 22, she and her siblings moved to Bloomsbury, where their home became the center for the avant-garde literary salon, the Bloomsbury Group. She married Leonard Woolf when she was 30. They were true

---

[930] https://en.wikipedia.org/wiki/Patricia_Krenwinkel

companions, though it was a sexless marriage and she later fell in love with another woman.

She received income from a small trust fund but it was insufficient to meet her needs. So when she was 35, she and her husband founded the Hogarth Press. With a small, kitchen-table model printing press, they taught themselves to set type and print. They were both budding novelists, reviewers and essayists. Their first publication, a 32-page pamphlet, sold 134 copies of the 150 printed. Within several years, they developed a commercially successful publishing company that produced 25 to 35 books per year. They were prolific writers and managed the publishing company as a part time enterprise.

She suffered from a mental breakdown during WW I, followed by subsequent periods of physical, mental and emotional breakdowns, which doctors treated with psychiatric drugs. Her early childhood experience of sexual abuse by her half-brothers, Gerald and George Dunkworth, was thought to be the cause. Gerald later became her publisher. Virginia had a complicated and stormy relationship with her sister, Vanessa Bell, which biographers reveal was also physical. She is also reported to have an early love interest with a close friend, Violet Dickinson.

Her writing expressed the themes that troubled her the most; life, death, suicide, madness and past memories. She was hypersensitive to criticism. She was a noted biographer and critic and used writing as a distraction from realty. When she realised she could not write any longer, she chose not to live and drowned herself, fearing the recurrence of a mental breakdown.[931]

Or like Petra Kelly, who was a Bavarian political human rights activist, ecologist and co-founder of the Green Party. She had Sedna conjunct Ceres in the eleventh house of collective consciousness, sextile Orcus in the twelfth house of institutions and the unconscious.

She was abandoned by her dad at the age of six and was educated by Catholic nuns and raised largely by her grandmother, while her mom worked to support the family. When

---

[931] https://en.wikipedia.org/wiki/Virginia_Woolf

she was 11, her mom married an American Army officer who moved the family to the U.S. Petra became a classic overachiever; cheerleader, member of the student senate, scholarship winner.

Despite physical pain from lifelong kidney ailments and the emotional trauma associated with the death of her younger half-sister, Grace, she was able to maintain an almost maniacal focus on achievement. She returned to Europe for post grad study and her beginning involvement in European Federalist politics.

She studied World Politics and International Relations and worked at the European Communities in Brussels, continuing her development of social consciousness and political awareness. When she was 32 she helped found a political party that was dedicated to human rights and ecology which was officially named the Green Party six years later; she was one of 27 Greens elected to the Bundestag.

She began an affair with the 65-year-old married EC president Sicco Mansholt, the first of a number of affairs with politically powerful older men. She had a long-term companionship with 25-year older Gert Bastian, a former NATO General who had done under-cover spy work. As brilliant, romantic and mercurial as Petra was, Bastian in contrast was plodding methodical and obsessive. To all evidence, their love was compelling and uncompromising. However, when she was 45, they were both found dead in their Bonn home with a gunshot to the head. Whether their deaths were suicide, or murder was unresolved and the case remains a mystery.[932]

Futurist Ray Kurzweil has Sedna in the sixth house of service, sextile a conjunction of Orcus and Uranus, the planet of intuition, in the eighth house of transformation, which gives him the role of a modern prophet. Ray has correctly predicted all the technology changes of the last 25 years and he predicts in the 2040s humanity will merge with superconscious Artificial Intelligence, in what he calls a point of singularity, beyond which we can't know what reality will be like.

---

[932] https://en.wikipedia.org/wiki/Petra_Kelly

The first American woman in space, Sally Ride, has Sedna in the tenth house of profession, sextile to Orcus, which is conjunct Vesta the asteroid of regeneration in the twelfth house of institutions. Ride was the only current NASA representative on the presidential commission to review the Challenger space shuttle accident. She was responsible for gathering some of the most shocking information regarding the agency's missteps and helped hold her employer accountable.

And blind-deaf linguist, Helen Keller, has Sedna in the fourth house of home, sextile to Orcus in the third house of ideas. This aspect tells of her research into language and communication, growing from a blind, deaf baby who had no words and could only communicate by touch, to a woman who wrote 12 books and toured the world extensively speaking of her research. Yes, she taught herself to talk, even though she couldn't hear the words, or read others lips.

Richard Branson is a British entrepreneur, investor and philanthropist, who is the founder of Virgin Records. He has Sedna in the ninth house of knowledge, sextile Orcus, which is conjunct Venus, the planet of values, in the eleventh house of collective consciousness.

> His mother was a strong influence on his success, emphasising independence and self-reliance. Basically shy, his public persona is one of bravado, but the private man remains an enigma.

> At the age of sixteen his first business venture was a magazine called *Student*. He started his record business from the church where he ran the magazine. He started advertising popular records in the magazine and selling them by mail order. It was an overnight success, as he sold records for considerably less than the High Street outlets.

> He started a record shop in Oxford Street in London at 20, and the following year, earning enough money from his record store, he launched the record label Virgin Records. By the age of 20, he had a thriving business and 40 employees. Twelve years later, his empire consisted of 50 companies that were giving him a turnover of 50 million pounds and he was ready to expand into the software, film, video and property markets.

> His Virgin brand grew rapidly during the 1980s, as he set up Virgin Atlantic airline at 34 and expanded the Virgin Records

music label. He launched Virgin Mobile in 1999, and Virgin Blue in Australia (now named Virgin Australia) in 2000. His Virgin Group now controls more than 400 companies, but he has also been involved in many failed business ventures, such as Virgin Cola, Virgin Cars, Virgin Clothing and Virgin Brides.

He wrote in his autobiography of the decision to start an airline: "My interest in life comes from setting myself huge, apparently unachievable challenges and trying to rise above them ... from the perspective of wanting to live life to the full, I felt that I had to attempt it."

He has also made several world record-breaking attempts. His first attempt at the fastest Atlantic Ocean crossing when he was 35, led to the boat capsizing in British waters and a rescue by RAF helicopter, which received wide media coverage. A year later he beat the record by two hours. The following year his hot air balloon "Virgin Atlantic Flyer" crossed the Atlantic. And at 40 he crossed the Pacific from Japan to Arctic Canada, in a balloon. This broke the record, with a speed of 394 km/h.

In his late 40s, he and musician, Peter Gabriel, discussed with the former president of South Africa, Nelson Mandela, their idea of a small group of leaders working to solve difficult global conflicts and Mandela announced the formation of a new group, The Elders which is funded by a group of donors, including Branson and Gabriel. Through the Carbon War Room, founded when he was 59, the entrepreneur is seeking solutions for global warming and the energy crisis.[933]

However, with the flowing aspects we can see the comedy theme coming out again as a way to transcend the Sedna induced stresses with the famous Swiss clown, Grock, a composer and musician, who is often called "the king of clowns", having Sedna in the first house of identity, sextile Orcus in the twelfth house of the unconscious.

He was once the most highly paid entertainer in the world. He started early as a performer, learning musicianship and acrobatic skills from his father and later became a clown, working with the famous clown, Antonet. They developed an act with the aim of

---

[933] https://en.wikipedia.org/wiki/Richard_Branson

making the transition from circus, to music hall stages, which were more lucrative.

Refining their performances according to audience response, Grock came to dominate the act, and they eventually split up. By then Grock's fame had spread, his act having developed into the mixture of pantomime and musical blunders for which he is now remembered.[934]

At this juncture in human evolution, few of us use our planets at the spiritual level, but many of us are striving to, and such people are wonderful to be around. As with the other planets, the spiritual level of evolution is vastly different with Sedna from the two previous levels. Here, the flowing aspects with Orcus brings an accountability for personal thought, word and deed and an alignment with a spiritual creed, which likely generates a strong independent spiritual voice.

Once we embrace the Sedna energy, which is the oneness of everything, our nurturing becomes an expression of Sedna consciousness and it becomes devotional in nature. The struggle of the beginner's level is gone, as are the transcendental crises of the intermediate level. At this level everything Saturnian is meaningless and yet everything Sednian has its place.

Liz Greene is an American-British professional astrologer and author, Jungian analyst and lecturer; one of the most highly respected astrologers of the 20th century. She has Sedna in the fifth house of creativity, sextile Orcus, which is conjunct Uranus, the plant of intuiyion, in the sevenh house of relationships.

> With Howard Sasportas, she co-founded the Centre for Psychological Astrology in London when she was 34 and was co-director for 20 years, before becoming the sole director. She continues directing the organisation. In addition, she also directs CPA Press, a publishing company that focuses on specialist astrological works.

> At 39 she started co-operating with Alois Treindl, founder of Swiss-based Astrodienst, on the development of computer-generated horoscopes, which would present a person with a chart synthesis, simulating Greene's own method of horoscope

---

[934] https://en.wikipedia.org/wiki/Grock

interpretation during a personal reading. Two years later they presented the Psychological Horoscope Analysis, which was followed by several other interpretations. Greene remains Astrodienst's most popular author.

She was awarded the Regulus Award for Theory and Understanding when she was 43, recognising the work with other disciplines and philosophical models. She has been one of the most consistently popular astrologers of the 20th century. Almost all of her many books remain in print. Her books include *Saturn: A New Look at an Old Devil, Star Signs for Lovers,* and *The Outer Planets and Their Cycles.*[935]

Linda Goodman was an American astrologer and poet who wrote a top selling book, *Sun Signs,* published when she was 43, which sold over five million copies, bringing astrology into the everyday market. Her Sedna is conjunct Venus, the planet of values and also Nessus, the centaur of radical change, and Pallas, the asteroid of wisdom, all in the twelfth house of the unconscious, semi-sextile Orcus in the first house of identity. The paperback rights for her second book, *Love Signs,* sold for a record $2.25 million ten years later.

She began her career as a local newspaper writer and married her first husband, also a writer. They had five kids, three of whom died in infancy. With a divorce, she took a job as a radio announcer in Pittsburgh where she took the name Linda and married her second husband, also a radio announcer. Her interest in astrology blossomed when she moved to New York City at 38, and she totally immersed herself in the study to the exclusion of everything else.

Determined and intense, with an explosive temper, she was also generous, often giving gifts to friends of cars or jewellery, a habit that led to bankruptcy in her early 60s. Then she moved to the remote mining town of Cripple Creek, Colorado at 45, where she could write with less distraction. She had an affair with a 26-year-old marine biologist, who left her a year later.

When she was 48, her 21-year-old daughter, who was an aspiring actress, committed suicide by overdosing on Demerol in

---

[935] https://en.wikipedia.org/wiki/Liz_Greene

New York. Linda refused to believe that she was dead and said it was a government conspiracy, a cover-up, and spent a half million dollars searching for her daughter, eventually claiming that Marilyn Monroe, Howard Hughes and Elvis Presley were also alive and in hiding.

Diagnosed diabetic in her early 60s, she distrusted traditional medicine and sometimes refused to take medication, or treatment. She had a toe removed and then part of her leg amputated. She became a virtual recluse. However, she continued to write and completed her "Linda Goodman's Love Signs Relationship Report" to go on the internet before her death.[936]

And Dane Rudhyar was a French-American astrologer, one of most noted and respected astrologers of the 20th century. He had Sedna in the third house of ideas and communication, semi-sextile Orcus conjunct Mercury, the planet of communication on the cusp of the third house.

He was called a modern renaissance man for his ability to express himself in many fields; music, painting, poetry, philosophy and metaphysics. He wrote for national magazines since his late 30s and was the author of many books.

He had poor health as a child, a distraction that continued through his life. At 12, he had life-threatening surgery to remove his left kidney and adrenal gland. A bright youth, he passed his baccalaureate at the Sorbonne at 16, majoring in philosophy. Becoming involved in the artistic and musical climate of Paris, he was heavily influenced by the radical ideas of Nietzsche.

At this time, he had a mystical experience or realisation in which he "became intuitively aware of the cyclic nature of all existence and of the fact that our Western civilisation was coming to an autumnal conclusion." He later wrote that it was from this time that he sought to gain a clearer understanding of the cyclic patterns and basic meaning of human existence.

At the age of 21, he left his native France and traveled to the U.S., reinventing himself with the name of Dane Rudhyar. Believing in the necessity of a fundamental transformation of our

---

[936] https://en.wikipedia.org/wiki/Linda_Goodman

civilisation, his change of name was a symbolic reflection of his contribution to that change. The name "Rudhyar" is derived from the Sanskrit God Rudra, the Destroyer and Regenerator.

Attaining a position in the avant-garde art community of the West, he also studied and wrote. His seminal book in which he emphasised integration, *The Astrology of Personality,* was first published when he was 41.[937]

Semi-square, Square, Sesquiquadrate

With the stressful aspects between Sedna and Orcus, the all-encompassing spiritual energy of Sedna challenges our curiosity, our search for hidden truth, our intellectual independence, and ability to challenge established thought and speak out.

Orcus works with the theme of exploration, of uncovering a blueprint or map that leads to a new picture, to delve below the constructs of mind that are merely based upon the convenience of our collective consensus to gain a deeper understanding of life.

If we haven't developed the Sedna energy however the stressful aspects likely lead to a sense of righteousness in our intellectual independence and can bring out the more negative side of Orcus, such as lustfulness, inconsiderateness, and not learning from experience.

Like Candy Barr, who was an American exotic dancer. She had Sedna conjunct Juno, the asteroid of partnership, in the eleventh house of collective consciousness, semi-square Orcus in the twelfth house of the unconscious.

Her mother died when she was nine, and her dad married a woman with four children to add to his existing five. Sexually abused as a child by a neighbour and the baby sitter, she grew up to be a small Texas town bad girl. She ran away from home and became a prostitute before she was 16.

She became one of the first superstars of the porno genre, starring in her first film, *Smart Aleck*, at 16. She was also one of the most famous and highly paid strippers, as well as a playmate to gangster Mickey Cohan. She made national news at 22 when she was arrested for drug possession. She began a 15-year jail

[937] https://en.wikipedia.org/wiki/Dane_Rudhyar

term but was paroled four years later and pardoned four years after that. In her late 30s, she emerged as a serious poet with her book, *A Gentle Mind - Confused.* Married four times, she had one daughter.[938]

Orcus demands intellectual independence and challenges established thought, however at the unconscious level it talks about blind minds and their consequences and, in the extreme, these aspects can make us susceptible to brainwashing.

Like Elizabeth Smart, who is an American who went missing at age fourteen, abducted from her home as her family slept. Her Sedna is in the third house of communication, square Orcus in the seventh house of relationships.

> She was the second of six kids and grew up in a close-knit Mormon family, reading scripture and praying morning and evening. On the evening just before her disappearance, she and her family had attended an award ceremony at her middle school, where she was recognised for various school accomplishments. The family prayed together and kissed goodnight, however sometime in the early morning hours, a man entered the bedroom she shared with her younger sister and spirited her away.

> No ransom note was found and no trace of her was reported, until she was spotted walking in a suburb of the same city with a shaggy-haired vagabond nine months later. During her ordeal, she spent a great deal of the time near her home wearing disguises and veils in public. The Smart family believes she was brainwashed, citing that she did not call out for help, or apparently try to escape, even when she heard rescuers call out her name.

> However, nearly two years after her rescue, her father said that she is "just a normal teenager who likes shopping and going to the movies with friends". A self-assured young woman and college graduate, she confronted her kidnapper at his trial and

---

[938] https://en.wikipedia.org/wiki/Candy_Barr

then accepted a job as a contributor for a television network in its coverage of missing persons.[939]

Or we may attempt to brainwash others. Like Charles Manson, who is an American ritual cult leader, a psychopath who had a band of drug-numbed followers. He has Sedna in the twelfth house of the unconscious, semi-square Orcus in the first house of identity. He mesmerised his gang with liberal sex and drugs, while living on a ranch in the desert of southern California.

He was the illegitimate son of a teenage prostitute and an army colonel. He was raised by an aunt and uncle and by the age of 11, he developed into a delinquent, shuffling from foster parent to foster parent. He spent his youth and adulthood in and out of prison, spending 19 of his first 32 years behind bars.

In his mid-30s, while on parole he went to San Francisco to be a part of the hippie counter-culture in the Height-Ashbury district. He gathered adoring women around him by giving out LSD. Soon he was able to attract young men to his group by promising sex with his 'young loves'. They enjoyed long group LSD sessions, listening to the Beatles' "Helter Skelter" song on the White Album. However, unable to keep his friendships, He began to prophesy chaos to his followers.

When he was 34, he directed the ritual grisly killings of a Hollywood socialite and her house guests who were stabbed to death by his followers and their blood was smeared along the walls of the kitchen. A few days later, an older couple were tied up and carved and stabbed by forks and kitchen knives by Manson's followers.

The deaths frightened the Hollywood community and in the nine months of the trial, when he was 35, the jury found him guilty of first degree murder and conspiracy. He was convicted and given the death penalty, but the following year the California Supreme Court invalidated the capital punishment stature, and he became a life-termer. He has been continually refused parole by the California parole board.

---

[939] https://en.wikipedia.org/wiki/Elizabeth_Smart

He was denied parole for the ninth time at 63 and at his hearing he rambled for an hour, insisting that he did not kill seven people, saying, "I've killed a lot of people in my life, but I was convicted for those I did not kill." His behaviour in prison has been vicious and demented and yet, inexplicably, every year he receives letters and gifts from young people, Satanists, neo-Nazis and skinheads who view him as their role model, hoping for one day when he will be released.[940]

At this level these aspects may also make us hypocritical and encourage us to find fault in the ways of others, or blame others, rather than take responsibility for our own words and actions.

Like Jimmy Swaggart, who was an American charismatic maestro of hi-tech salvation, a television evangelist who conducted a vast yet dubious ministry earning $150 million a year. He had Sedna in the fourth house of home, semi-square Orcus in the fifth house of creativity.

Known as a frequent hell-raiser as a teen, he dropped out of high school and played honky tonk piano with his notoriously carousing cousin Jerry Lee Lewis. At age 17, he married a 15-year old farm girl who lived down the road, both successfully lying about their ages. Soon after his marriage, he preached his first sermon in front of a grocery store interspersed with playing the accordion, 'knowing we get crowds with the music'.

By his late 20s, he was itinerant preacher traveling the Southeastern US and began to cut gospel records, of which he eventually sold over 150 million. After another message from God, he began a radio show and from that point onward TV became his manifest destiny. The ministry probably quadrupled with radio. With TV it exploded.[941]

His Sedna is also at the focal point of two evolutionary bi-quintiles, one to Neptune, the planet of dreams and visions, in the ninth house of spirituality, and the other to Jupiter, the planet of expansion, in the eleventh house of collective consciousness.

In front of the TV camera, he became more outspoken than ever, verbally attacking Roman Catholicism, Jews and homosexuals

---

[940] https://en.wikipedia.org/wiki/Charles_Manson
[941] https://en.wikipedia.org/wiki/Jimmy_Swaggart

while soliciting money from his viewers. During each sermon, the impassioned preacher ranted and raved, coercing his followers and himself into a feeding frenzy of devotion.

His antics backfired and in his late 40s he became a target of investigations. His Sedna is also square Ceres, the planet of nurture, in the seventh house of relationships. A wealthy California widow left almost her entire estate to Swaggart Ministries. The Evangelistic Association and its agents were charged by family lawyers with 'preying upon her loneliness and illness for the purpose of securing donations from her.'" By now Swaggart was flush with 3 palatial estates and a private jet.

Further allegations of misallocations of monies, death threats, handsome payoffs and the exploitation of prostitutes led to private investigation. When confronted by photos of himself with prostitutes he reportedly admitted he had a fascination with pornography from childhood. This incident earned him a three-month suspension from his US pulpit and a two-year rehabilitation period, which proved unsuccessful. Further confirmed encounters with prostitutes sent him reeling into a tortured, televised public confession for which he may be best known. However, he was back to preaching once more against sin within three months.[942]

As we tire of density and the grief it creates, and we start a spiritual journey to get out of the swamp, Sedna rewards us with transcendent crises, experiences which force us to let go and rise above them, resulting in a huge growth to a new level of consciousness. There is no choice with these crises, and the more we try and solve them, the more we will get hurt.

The challenges to established thought encouraged by these aspects can lead to intellectual persecution. Like Pakistani activist for female education, Malala Yousafzai, who has Sedna in the ninth house of knowledge, square Orcus in the twelfth house of the unconscious.

She is known for human rights advocacy, especially education of women in her native Swat Valley in northwest Pakistan, where the local Taliban had at times banned girls from attending

---

[942] Ibid.

school. When she was 11–12, she wrote a blog under a pseudonym for the BBC Urdu detailing her life during the Taliban occupation of Swat. The following summer there was a *New York Times* documentary about her life as the Pakistani military intervened in the region. She rose in prominence, giving interviews in print and on television, and she was nominated for the International Children's Peace Prize by activist Desmond Tutu.

However, at 15, she was injured after a Taliban gunman attempted to murder her on her way to school. Since recovering however, she has become a prominent education activist and her advocacy has since grown into an international movement. In 2014, when she was 17, she was a co-recipient of the Nobel Peace Prize for her struggle against the suppression of children and young people and for the right of all children to education. Aged 17 at the time, she became the youngest-ever Nobel Prize laureate.[943]

Or we may embrace the challenge of the unknown, like existential German philosopher, Martin Heidegger, one of the most influential voices and foremost thinkers and writers of the 20th century. He had Sedna in the fourth house of home, in a close semi-square with Orcus on the cusp of the third house of ideas and communication. He is widely acknowledged to be one of the most original and important philosophers of the 20th century, best known for his contributions to phenomenology and existentialism. The publication of his first book, *Being and Time*, when he was 38, he achieved instant fame as one of the spokesmen of 20th century existentialism. Though unfinished, Being and Time is one of the central philosophical works of the 20th century. In the first division of the work, He attempted to turn away from "ontic" questions about beings to ontological questions about Being and recover the most fundamental philosophical question: the question of Being, of what it means for something to be.

He argued that being human is defined by care, that it's practically engaged and is a concernfull mode of being-in-the-world. This was in opposition to rationalist thinkers like René Descartes who located the essence of man in our thinking

---

[943] https://en.wikipedia.org/wiki/Malala_Yousafzai

abilities. For Heidegger thinking is thinking about things originally discovered in our everyday practical engagements. The consequence of this is that our capacity to think cannot be the most central quality of our being, because thinking is a reflecting upon this more original way of discovering the world.

In the second section, he argues that human being is even more fundamentally structured by its temporality, or its concern with, and relationship to time, existing as a structurally open 'possibility-for-being'. He emphasised the importance of authenticity in human existence, involving a truthful relationship to our being thrown into a world, and to our being-towards-death, the finitude of the time and being that we are given, and the closing down of our various possibilities for being through time.

He also made critical contributions to philosophical conceptions of truth, arguing that its original meaning was un-concealment, to philosophical analyses of art as a site of the revelation of truth, and to philosophical understanding of language as the 'house of being'.[944]

Or the challenge of outer space, like Carl Sagan, an American astronomer, astrophysicist, exobiologist, educator, and popular celebrity, who has Sedna in the twelfth house of the unconscious, in a close semi-square to Orcus in the first house of identity.

As host of the TV series and the author of the book, *Cosmos*, he inspired a generation with his enthusiastic lectures, books and documentaries about space and life. As a child he is said to have gazed with awe at the heavens and speculated on the existence of life beyond earth. At age 12 he told his grandfather he wanted to be an astronomer and vowed to be on a university faculty so he could support himself in his chosen field, which he did. Charming, brilliant and successful, he was not above smoking marijuana and advocating its use for both 'brainstorming and great sex'.[945]

And finally, at this level we have two of the fathers of science fiction. Jules Verne was a French writer widely popular for his science fiction

---

[944] https://en.wikipedia.org/wiki/Martin_Heidegger
[945] https://en.wikipedia.org/wiki/Carl_Sagan

novels and amazing anticipation of future discoveries. The author of *Journey to the Center of the Earth, Twenty Thousand Leagues Under the Sea,* and *Around the World in Eighty Days,* he had Sedna in the eleventh house of collective consciousness, in a close sesquiquadrate with Orcus, in the sixth house of service.

> Regarded as the father of science fiction, he predicted the use of submarines, helicopters, air conditioning, guided missiles, trips to outer space and motion pictures long before they were developed.
>
> The son of a magistrate, he went to Paris to study law; however, he became interested in the theatre and began writing plays and opera librettos. He achieved success with his first short fantasy, *Five Weeks in a Balloon*, released when he was 35. His books have been translated into many languages and plays and films have been made from a number of them. His last years were marked with enormous popularity and numerous honours. By the time of his death, he had written over 50 books.
>
> Though he was raised Catholic, he became a deist from his early forties. Deism is a philosophical position that posits that a god does not interfere directly with the world. It also rejects revelation as a source of religious knowledge and asserts that reason and observation of the natural world are sufficient to determine the existence of a single creator of the universe. Some scholars believe his deist philosophy is reflected in his novels, as they often involve the notion of God, or divine providence, but rarely mention the concept of Christ.[946]

And H.G. Wells, who was a British writer, historian, prognosticator, economist and novelist, known for his sci-fi predictions of the future. He is the author of *The Time Machine* and *The War of the Worlds*. He had Sedna in the first house of identity, square Orcus, which is conjunct Varuna, the planet of notability, in the eleventh house of collective consciousness.

> He was also an outspoken socialist from an early date, often sympathising with pacifist views and his later works became increasingly political and didactic. After a sketchy education, he

---

[946] https://en.wikipedia.org/wiki/Jules_Verne

went on to graduate from London University with a BS at 22. He taught biology and wrote educational articles, writing his first novel at 29 and went on to write many other works. His book, *The War of the Worlds,* which was read on radio by Orson Wells, caused the famous Mars invasion panic when he was 72. He was an enormously prolific and popular writer, capturing the early twentieth century's need to rebel and overthrow the oppressive Victorian conventions.[947]

With the stressful aspects with Sedna we can again see the comedy theme coming out as a way to transcend the Sedna stresses, with both the famous clown and filmmaker, Charlie Chaplin and the famous filmmaker and comedian, Woody Allen, having close semi-squares with Orcus.

Another example is George Carlin, who was an American comedian who began doing TV variety shows at 29, and nightclubs. He had Sedna conjunct Venus in the ninth house of knowledge, semi-square Orcus in the tenth house of profession.

He quit high school after his freshman year and joined the air force, leaving a year early with an honourable discharge. He had a short radio disk jockey career, which led to stand up work, and by the late sixties he was in Las Vegas doing network television talk shows.

He teamed with comedian Jack Burns before his solo act when he was 25. His film debut was at 31, although he only gained minimal popularity. He was fired from a big Las Vegas hotel a couple of years later for saying a four-letter word. His notorious comedy act, called "The Seven Word's you can never say on Television," became a legal matter when he was 35, and was not resolved for six years, which was good promotion.

In his 30s he was the hottest act in the country, a whacked-out hippie whose LPs routinely went gold. By 36 he was heavily into self-destruct with his use of drugs and alcohol, favoring cocaine. His records sold liked crazy in the next couple of years, and he was a natural when he hosted *Saturday Night Live*. After a serious car accident and a heart attack at 41 he put his life back

---

[947] https://en.wikipedia.org/wiki/H._G._Wells

in order over the next few years, but it was not until his starring role in *Outrageous Fortune* at 50, which co-starred Better Midler, that he regained popularity.

The comedian and social critic entered a drug rehabilitation program at 67. In a statement he acknowledged that he had been using "too much wine and Vicodin." The decision to admit himself to the rehab facility was his own. "No one told me I needed this. I recognised the problem and took the step myself.[948]

At this juncture in human evolution, few of us use our planets at the spiritual level, but many of us are striving to, and such people are wonderful to be around. As with the other planets, the spiritual level of evolution is vastly different with Sedna from the two previous levels. Here, the stressful aspects with Orcus brings an accountability for personal thought, word and deed and an alignment with a spiritual creed, which likely generates a strong independent spiritual voice.

Once we embrace the Sedna energy, which is the oneness of everything, our nurturing becomes an expression of Sedna consciousness and it becomes devotional in nature. The struggle of the beginner's level is gone, as are the transcendental crises of the intermediate level. At this level everything Saturnian is meaningless and yet everything Sednian has its place.

The man we know as the Dalai Lama, Tenzin Gyatso, has Sedna in the tenth house of profession, semi-square Orcus, which is conjunct Chiron, the centaur of wounding and healing, in the eleventh house of collective consciousness and right in the cusp of the twelfth house of the unconscious.

He is actually the 14th Dalai Lama, which is a title given to spiritual leaders of the Tibetan people. Despite his humble beginnings, being born on a straw mat in a cowshed to a farmer's family in a remote part of Tibet, he had become the joint most popular world leader by 2013, according to a poll which sampled public opinion in the USA and six major European countries.

---

[948] https://en.wikipedia.org/wiki/George_Carlin

He was not formally enthroned until he was 15, during the Battle of Chamdo with the People's Republic of China. The following year, he and the Tibetan government were pressured into accepting the Seventeen Point Agreement for the Peaceful Liberation of Tibet, by which it became formally incorporated into the People's Republic of China. Fearing for his life in the wake of a revolt in Tibet when he was 24, he fled to India, from where he led a government in exile.

With the aim of launching guerrilla operations against the Chinese, the Central Intelligence Agency funded his administration with US $1.7 million a year in the 1960s. At 66 he ceded his partial power over the government to an elected parliament of selected Tibetan exiles. His original goal was full independence for Tibet, but by the late 1980s he was seeking high-level autonomy instead.[949]

And Shivabalayogi was a meditation guru in the tradition of the ancient and modern yogis of India. He had Sedna in the eleventh house of collective consciousness, bi-quintile Neptune in the fourth house of home.

He attained self-realisation through twelve years of arduous tapas, meditating in samādhi, a state of total thoughtlessness, for an average of twenty hours a day. Tapas is the most advanced stage of meditation in which one remains absorbed for long periods in this non-dualistic state of consciousness.

After he completed tapas, he assumed the name Shivabalayogi, meaning Yogi devoted to Shiva and Parvati. The name reflects that he is a manifestation of both the male and female aspects of the divine. The female aspect represents the invisible energy of the divine through which the entire creation operates, while the male aspect represents the pure consciousness of existence beyond all imaginations. Generally, devotees called him simply Swamiji, meaning respected Master.

For three decades he traveled extensively in India and Sri Lanka, initiating over ten million people into dhyana meditation. In his early fifties he traveled for four years in England and the United

States. His teaching is consistent with the Vedanta, emphasising the need for spiritual practice to achieve self-realisation.[950]

Swami Vivekananda, was an Indian religious leader, a disciple of Sri Ramakrishna, who became inspired by his teacher to serve men as a visible manifestation of God. His Sedna is conjunct Neptune, the planet of inspiration, on the cusp of the third house of communication, square Orcus, which is conjunct Ceres, the planet of nurturing, in the twelfth house of the unconscious.

An illumined being of the highest order, he was the forerunner who brought the spiritual teachings of India to the West, greatly influencing the last hundred years of spiritual growth in Europe and America. Highly intelligent with a retentive memory, he had stories of the scripture memorised by the time he was six.

He became one of the most beloved disciples of Sri Ramakrishna and, as the master spent his last years teaching his disciples and streams of visitors, he recorded his instruction. He then brought the spiritual teachings of India to the West in 1893 at the convening of the Parliament of Religions in Chicago. During his three-year stay in American, he founded Hindu philosophy schools, many of which acknowledge him as a modern Buddha and an emanation of Lord Shiva.

When he took the universal teachings to the West, he broke with the Indian caste tradition and lost his caste as a result. His Sedna was also quintile Chariklo, the centaur of foresight, in the the fifth house of creativity, square Orcus, the planet of speaking out in the twelfth house of the unconscious, and sesquiquadrate Nessus, the centaur of radical transformation, in the seventh house of relationships. His denial of the rigid system brought him severe censure from Indian traditionalists.[951]

Pope Francis is the 266th and current Pope of the Catholic Church. He has Sedna in the ninth house of spirituality, semi-square Orcus in the eleventh house of collective consciousness.

Born in Buenos Aires, Argentina, he worked briefly as a chemical technologist and nightclub bouncer before beginning seminary

---

[950] https://en.wikipedia.org/wiki/Shivabalayogi
[951] https://en.wikipedia.org/wiki/Swami_Vivekananda

studies. He became the Archbishop of Buenos Aires at 62 and was created a cardinal at 65. Following the resignation of Pope Benedict XVI a papal conclave elected Francis as his successor at the age of 76. He chose Francis as his papal name in honour of Saint Francis of Assisi. Francis is the first Jesuit pope, the first from the Americas, the first from the Southern Hemisphere, and the first pope from outside Europe since the Syrian Gregory III, who reigned in the 8th century.

Throughout his public life, Pope Francis has been noted for his humility, emphasis on God's mercy, concern for the poor and commitment to interfaith dialogue. He is credited with having a less formal approach to the papacy than his predecessors, choosing to reside in the guesthouse rather than in the papal apartments of the Apostolic Palace used by his predecessors. In addition, due to both his Jesuit and Ignatian aesthetic, he is known for favouring simpler vestments void of ornamentation. He maintains that the Church should be more open and welcoming and has been freeing up some of the doctrinaire issues which have pushed people away, like divorce.[952]

In-conjunct

There is no one alive today with this aspect and no one will be born with this aspect in the next 100 years, so it is not interpreted here.

Quintile, Bi-quintile

The evolutionary quintile or bi-quintile aspect between Sedna and Orcus infuses our curiosity, our search for hidden truth, our intellectual independence, and ability to challenge established thought and speak out, with the all-encompassing spiritual energy of Sedna to the point where we can push the boundaries of human development.

Quintiles and bi-quintiles point to talent, the desire to create order and to categorize, a fascination with patterns and structures, perfectionist tendencies, and the desire to build or make things. These aspects have the characteristics of both the trine and opposition. They point to awareness of conflicts, or problems and finding solutions for them; however, they do not automatically kick into action and must be cultivated over time.

---

[952] https://en.wikipedia.org/wiki/Pope_Francis

Orcus works with the theme of exploration, of uncovering a blueprint or map that leads to a new picture, to delve below the constructs of mind that are merely based upon the convenience of our collective consensus to gain a deeper understanding of life.

It demands intellectual independence and challenges established thought, so there can be a resulting sense of intellectual persecution, however at the unconscious level it talks more of blind minds and their consequences.

Like Brenda Spencer, an American murderer who killed a custodian and principal and wounded eight children and a policeman when she was 17. She had Sedna conjunct Venus in the twelfth house of the unconscious, quintile Orcus on the cusp of the third house of ideas and communication.

> She had said the prior week that she was going to do something to get herself on TV. A tiny girl, under 5 ft. with red hair and an epileptic, she had lived with her father since her parents had divorced. She claimed to have gone on her rampage because, "I hate Mondays." Who was she trying to kill? "No one in particular. I kinda like the red and blue jackets." After hours of futile attempts to get her to surrender, she finally decided it was time to end what she had called "fun." Found sane, she was sentenced to 25 years to life in prison.[953]

Or like Kathleen Dempsey, who was an American homicide victim who died of massive stab wounds to her abdomen, diaphragm, liver and kidneys at 41. The killer was not known and was never apprehended. She had Sedna in the third house of communication, quintile Orcus in the sixth house of daily routine.

> Fatally wounded, she called 911 for help and was unable to get through. Reaching a telephone operator instead, her call was transferred to the fire department. Her family sued the telephone company because the operator failed to identify herself to the fire department dispatcher and failed to give him the phone number from which Kathleen had called, which would have enabled them to find the address where she lay bleeding. It took the fire

---

[953]

https://en.wikipedia.org/wiki/Cleveland_Elementary_School_shooting_(San_Diego)

department hours to decipher the call, by which time it was too late.[954]

Or like Mata Hari, who was a Dutch prostitute and exotic dancer who also served as a spy. She had Sedna in the fifth house of creativity, quintile Orcs in the third house of communication.

> The daughter of a merchant, in her younger years she was expelled from convent school for sleeping with a priest and, at the age of 18, moved to Java with her 40-year-old husband. The couple had a violent marriage and one of their two children died. She left her husband and returned to Europe at 29 where, as a nude belly dancer, she went to Paris to work in a brothel.
>
> She also attended German espionage school and at the outbreak of WW I, she was offered cash up-front for a German mission, but turned out to be not a very good spy. With the codename of H21, she returned to Paris, spent the money and did precious little else. However, she was arrested as a double agent when she delivered a message on German submarine activity to the French embassy. She was 40 when she was arrested and placed on trial for treason. Convicted, she was executed by firing squad.
>
> On the morning of her execution, she put on her stockings, dressed in a pearl-gray frock, slung a coat over her shoulders, buttoned her boots, put on a dark tri-corned hat with a veil and glove. "This lady knows how to die," said the sergeant major who helped her. "After the shots were fired, she crumpled in a heap of petticoats." After her death documents were revealed which showed French falsification of the records and that instead of being a major spy for the Germans, she was an elegant but naive adventuress, essentially the first strip-tease dancer.[955]

Or we might devise vast schemes to prey on those with blank minds. Like Miss Cleo, who was an American spokeswoman for a psychic hot line, claiming Jamaica as her birthplace to feint more glamour and mystery than California County Hospital. She had Sedna in the eighth

[954] https://www.astro.com/astro-databank/Dempsey,_Kathleen
[955] https://en.wikipedia.org/wiki/Mata_Hari

house of sensitivity to the spirit world, quintile Orcus in the tenth house of profession.

> Acting on more than 2,000 complaints, state authorities have sued Access Resource Services Inc. and Psychic Readers Network for fraud, alleging they misrepresented costs, billed for services never purchased, harassed consumers with unwanted telemarketing calls and responded to consumer complaints with abusive, threatening language.

> Harris has been challenged to prove she really is a renowned shaman from Jamaica. Her national television commercials promise insights into love, money and other personal matters, designed to bilk the gullible. Florida was the eighth state to move against Feder and Stolz, who launched the Mind and Spirit psychic network when she was 37, but had been running other telephone psychic operations for six years.

> Then an investigation found that many of the psychics who staff the psychic hotline, which charged just under $5 per minute, used scripts, instead of performing actual tarot card readings. Eventually Access Resource Services and Psychic Readers Network, the two companies behind the Caribbean-inflected phone-in psychic, agreed to disconnect their service and pay $5 million to settle charges that it misled customers looking for a supposedly free glimpse into their futures.

> I'm no psychic, but I can see this: If you make deceptive claims there will be a Federal Trade Commission action in your future," said the head of the agency's consumer-protection division. However, Miss Cleo came up with a $5 million fine to settle the federal charges that her Pyschic Hot Line was fraudulent and deceptive.[956]

Or like Jeanne Weber, who was a French homicidal maniac, guilty of infanticide and drug addiction. She had Sedna conjunct her IC, the cusp of the fourth house of home, quintile Orcus in the second house of material reality.

> Short, fat and lethargic herself, she was a heavy drinker along with her alcoholic husband.

---

[956] https://en.wikipedia.org/wiki/Miss_Cleo

She was available to watch her sister-in-law's kids when a grim series of events began to plague the family for a terrifying month. One of the kids died from a sudden illness, then a second child died when Jeanne was baby-sitting and the doctor said it was from convulsions. A third death on was attributed to diphtheria and then Jeanne's own seven-year-old son died and the doctor again said it was from diphtheria.

When she was 31, the mother came home to find Jeanne strangling one of the boys. He recovered and told of her attack. There was a nine-day trial. Two of Jeanne's kids had died from supposed illnesses, as well as two others for whom she had cared. As there was no witness, she was acquitted. She was shunned by neighbors who gathered in the streets to revile her. Her husband left her and she fled the hostile environment, disappearing for 15 months.

Assuming an alias, she took up with a man who took her into his home and bed. When his nine-year-old son died suddenly, she was again arrested on 5/04/1907. She was again acquitted when the doctor testified that the boy's death was from an illness. Released when she was 33, she vanished. Reports surfaced that she had been seen working as an orderly in a children's hospital, and also in a children's home. When caught choking a sick child, she was fired. On the streets of Paris, she was arrested as a vagrant and sent to a mental asylum, but later released.

She became a street whore until she found a man who took her in as a housekeeper. When she was caught in the act of strangling to death a ten-year-old boy, she was declared insane on 10/25/1908 and locked in a mental hospital. The doctor who had been responsible for declaring her innocence admitted his responsibility in the deaths of the children. Credited with eight murders, she may have killed 20 or more children. While in the asylum, she would have insane fits of imaginary strangulations and during such an attack, at the age of 44, she hanged herself.[957]

As we tire of density and the grief it creates, and we start a spiritual journey to get out of the swamp, Sedna rewards us with transcendent

---

[957] https://en.wikipedia.org/wiki/Jeanne_Weber

crises, experiences which force us to let go and rise above them, resulting in a huge growth to a new level of consciousness. There is no choice with these crises, and the more we try and solve them, the more we will get hurt.

Like Susan Boyle, who is a Scottish singer who rose to fame on a British talent show. She has Sedna conjunct Venus in the eleventh house of collective consciousness.

> She is the youngest of nine children and reportedly suffered some oxygen deprivation at birth, resulting in learning disabilities. Never married, she lived with her parents, working in low-level jobs and volunteering in the church. Her father died when she was 36 and her mother died when she was 46, after which she became distraught.

> Her music gave her great comfort and she auditioned for *Britain's Got Talent* in the hopes of launching a music career in her mother's memory. When she appeared on stage at 48 her appearance belied her talent, but she wowed the audiences with her rendition of "I Dreamed a Dream" from the musical "Les Miserables." The clip of her performance is one of the most-viewed on YouTube.

> News reports made much of this plain-looking middle-aged woman. For subsequent performances on the show she underwent a slight makeover. She made it all the way to the finals based on judges' and viewers' votes. However, the ensuing publicity was a lot for her to handle. Although she sang well on the last evening of the competition and came in second, she was rushed to a London health care facility that night, reportedly suffering from an anxiety attack. She was released within the week.

> Her album was released later that year and it quickly shot to the top of the charts. The success was continued with her second album the following year, and her third album the year after that. The following year her net worth was estimated at £22 million.[958]

---

[958] https://en.wikipedia.org/wiki/Susan_Boyle

Mary Anne Evans was a British writer, given the name George Eliot by her lover, writer George Henry Lewes, because as a woman writer she would not have been given any credence.

She had Sedna in the fifth house of creativity, bi-quintile Orcus in the twelfth house of the unconscious.

One of the most intellectually rigorous writers of the 19th century, her books include the classics *The Mill on the Floss, Silas Marner* and *Middlemarch*, which is considered her masterpiece. She was the fifth child of an ambitious farmer and was intelligent and gifted, though remarkably unattractive. She was brought up in a constricting conventional religious atmosphere. After her mom died when she was 17, she cared for her beloved dad until his death.

At the age of 22 she declared herself an atheist, which alienated her from her father. She moved to London to work where she learned editorial work as an assistant on the *Westminster Review*; her first book was published when she was 40. Though she longed to settle down with an understanding husband and start a family, she was thwarted by her growing notoriety as well by a difficult and high-strung personality prone to depression. She settled for a series of love affairs with married men who were attracted to her vast intelligence.

At 31, while working as a journalist, she met her match, the married writer, George Henry Lewes. Three years later they began to openly live together, an act which severed for good any chance she might have of being accepted into Victorian society. With Lewes, however, she found the kind of peace that allowed her to produce her novels. As he was a preeminent writer, people overlooked the unconventional status of his living arrangement in order to meet him and enlarged her social and intellectual milieu.[959]

Karl Marx was a German-Jewish communist and philosopher who developed the theory of socialism and was the father of modern social science. He had Sedna in the first house of identity, bi-quintile to Orcus,

---

[959] https://en.wikipedia.org/wiki/George_Eliot

which is conjunct Pholus, the centaur of catalyzing change, in the eighth house of shared resources.

This is complimented by a quintile to Mercury, the planet of communication in the third house of ideas and communication, and a quintile to Makemake, the planet of extreme talent, conjunct Jupiter, the planet of philosophy, both in the eleventh house of ideals. These aspects explain how his ideas and writing about social ideals involving a change in the distribution of social resources made him the powerful evolutionary change agent that he was.

> For him social change was about conflict between opposing interests, driven, in the background, by economic forces. This became the inspiration for the body of works known as the conflict theory. In his evolutionary model of history, he argued that human history began with free, productive and creative work that was over time coerced and dehumanised, a trend most apparent under capitalism. Fundamentally, he assumed that human history involves transforming human nature, which he saw, in a very Sednian way, as encompassing both human beings and material objects.

> He believed, like the philosopher Hegel, that humans recognise that they possess both actual and potential selves and that self-development begins with an experience of internal alienation, which Marx argued was because of 'the despotism of capital'. This leads to a realisation that the actual self, as a subjective agent, renders its potential self as an object to be apprehended by capitalism.

> Marx further argued that by moulding nature in desired ways, the subject takes the object as its own, and thus permits the individual to be actualised as fully human. In the new society that would emerge, he reasoned that the self-alienation would end, and humans would be free to act without being bound by the labour market. It would be a democratic society, enfranchising the entire population. In such a utopian world there would also be little if any need for a state, the goal of which was only to enforce the alienation.[960]

---

[960] https://en.wikipedia.org/wiki/Karl_Marx

Florence Nightingale, the English social reformer and statistician, and the founder of modern nursing, has Sedna in the seventh house of relationships, in a close bi-quintile with Orcus is in the second house of material resources.

> She laid the foundation of professional nursing with the establishment of her nursing school at St Thomas' Hospital in London. It was the first secular nursing school in the world. She was also a prodigious and versatile writer. In her lifetime, much of her published work was concerned with spreading medical knowledge. Some of her tracts were written in simple English so that they could easily be understood by those with poor literary skills. She also helped popularize the graphical presentation of statistical data. Much of her writing, including her extensive work on religion and mysticism, has only been published posthumously.[961]

Tracey Ullman is an English-born actress, comedian, singer, dancer, screenwriter, producer, director, author, and businesswoman. She has Sedna in the sixth house of service, quitile Orcus in the eighth house of shared resources.

> Her father died when she was 6 and, in the aftermath, her mother slipped into a deep depression and spent a lot of time in bed. In an effort to cheer her up, Ullman, along with her sister, created and performed a nightly variety show on the windowsill in their mother's bedroom. In the show, Ullman would mimic neighbours, teachers, family members, and celebrities such as Julie Andrews and Édith Piaf.

> "Some kids can play the piano or kick a football; I could just impersonate everyone." She would also perform alone for herself after everyone had gone to bed. "I'd stand in front of the mirror and talk to myself until I fell asleep. I'd interview myself as women with problems. Women in documentaries who had three kids and chain-smoked and husbands in prison that hit them."

> Her mother would eventually remarry to a man who Ullman has described as a maniac who drove a London taxi and had a son who stole. The marriage brought an end to the children's

---

[961] https://en.wikipedia.org/wiki/Florence_Nightingale

latenight antics. "There was a new person in her bed now and I couldn't do my nightly performance anymore. I was nine years old and my show had been cancelled."

Alcoholism and domestic violence became a common occurrence in the household. The marriage also resulted in the family moving around the country, with Ullman attending numerous state schools. Her flair for mimicry helped with the transitions as her new classmates didn't take to her upper crust accent. "I had to talk like them to avoid being beaten up."

Her earliest appearances were on British television sketch comedy shows and she emigrated from the United Kingdom to the United States where she starred in her own network television comedy series, *The Tracey Ullman Show*, when she was 27. It ran for three years. She later produced programmes for HBO for which she garnered numerous awards. Her sketch comedy series, *Tracey Ullman's State of the Union*, ran for two years on *Showtime* in her late 40's. She has also appeared in several feature films.

She was the first British woman to be offered her own television sketch show in both the United Kingdom and the United States. At 56, she returned to British television with the BBC sketch comedy show *Tracey Ullman's Show*, her first project for the broadcaster in over thirty years. This led to the creation of the topical comedy series *Tracey Breaks the News* in 2017. She is currently the richest British actress and female comedian and the third richest British comedian overall.[962]

At this juncture in human evolution, few of us use our planets at the spiritual level, but many of us are striving to, and such people are wonderful to be around. As with the other planets, the spiritual level of evolution is vastly different with Sedna from the two previous levels. Here, the brings an accountability for personal thought, word and deed and an alignment with a spiritual creed, which likely generates a strong independent spiritual voice.

Once we embrace the Sedna energy, which is the oneness of everything, our nurturing becomes an expression of Sedna

---

[962] https://en.wikipedia.org/wiki/Tracey_Ullman

consciousness and it becomes devotional in nature. The struggle of the beginner's level is gone, as are the transcendental crises of the intermediate level. At this level everything Saturnian is meaningless and yet everything Sednian has its place.

Pope Pius XII was an Italian ecclesiastic and Pope of the Roman Catholic Church. He wrote many encyclicals making it easier for Catholics to participate in the church. His Sedna is in his fifth house of creativity, quintile Orcus in the third house of ideas and communication.

> Born into a family devoted to the papal service, he worked so hard at the Seminary that his health gave way and he was forced to leave, however Pope Leo XIII allowed him to live at home while completing his courses, until he was ordained.

> During World War I he was involved in humane efforts and was sent to Berlin to be its first nuncio, papal ambassador. He left Germany to be made cardinal and then became secretary of state for the Vatican, before being crowned Pope. At the beginning of World War II he spoke out against the Nazis, helping Jews with false baptismal certificates and allowing thousands to stay in Vatican City, convents and cloisters.[963]

Carl Jung was a Swiss psychiatrist and author, noted as being an outstanding influence in the development of the theory and practice of analytical psychiatry. He had Sedna in the second house of material reality, in a close quintile to Orcus, in the twelfth house of the unconscious. This placement is so apt for the creator of the psychological concept of the collective unconscious. Among the central concepts of his analytical psychology is individuation—the lifelong psychological process of differentiation of the self, out of each individual's conscious and unconscious elements.

> At age 12, he developed fainting spells which kept him out of school. He spent hours out in nature, dreaming. Overhearing his father's talk of financial concerns around his illness, he realised on some level he could overcome the fainting spells and was able to return to school. Shortly after this, on a long walk to school, he experienced an intense moment of knowing himself: "Previously, I had existed...everything had merely happened to

---

[963] https://en.wikipedia.org/wiki/Pope_Pius_XII

me. Now, I happened to myself. Now I knew: I am myself now… now I exist."

When he was 23 he decided to pursue a career in psychiatry. His career began in earnest five years later when he picked up Sigmund Freud's book, the Interpretation of Dreams, realising how his work linked up with his own ideas. The initial correspondence and friendship between them began three years later and they collaborated on some work, but when he was 34 he broke from Freud to place greater emphasis on the growth of mankind by archetypal vital forces in the individual. His theories of synchronicity, introvert-extrovert types, individuation and the personal-collective unconscious come from this work.

During this period, he had a decisive dream of being in a two-story house. As he explored it, each floor and room reflected historical eras, or from the collective unconscious. When he was 38, he had numerous visions. He said in his autobiography, *Memories, Dreams, and Reflections*, that all of his creative work came from these initial visions. He built a successful psychological practice and was much sought after as a mentor to countless devotees of his work.

An advocate of the use of astrology, he said 'Astrology would be a large-scale example of synchronism if it had at its disposal thoroughly tested findings… In other words, whatever is born or done this moment of time, has the qualities of this moment of time'. In his book, *Synchronicity*, he published a study of 483 pairs of couples, seeking to prove the validity that there is a causal connection between the planets and psycho-physiological disposition.[964]

Rawat Prem is an Indian American spiritual leader, also known as Maharaji and formerly known as Guru Maharaj Ji and Balyogeshwar, who teaches a meditation practice he calls Knowledge. He has Sedna in the seventh house of relationships, quintile Orcus in the ninth house of knowledge.

At the age of eight, Rawat succeeded his father Hans Ji Maharaj as leader of the Divine Light Mission and as the new Perfect

---

[964] https://en.wikipedia.org/wiki/Carl_Jung

Master to millions of Indian followers. He gained further prominence when he traveled to the West at age 13 to spread his message. His claimed ability to impart direct knowledge of God attracted a great deal of interest from young adults but he was ridiculed by the media for his youth and his supposed divine status.

By the time he was 16 the Divine Light Mission was active in 55 countries and tens of thousands of followers had been initiated. In his mid-twenties, he began to discard direct references to religion in his speeches and closed the ashrams. The name of the movement was changed to Elan Vital. From that period through to the present, he has continued to travel extensively.

When he was 44 he established "The Prem Rawat Foundation" to fund his work and humanitarian efforts. He continues to speak for large and/or select audiences worldwide, and on several occasions has received significant recognition for his work and message of peace. The core of his teaching is that the individual's need for fulfilment can be satisfied by turning within to contact a constant source of peace and joy. Rather than a body of dogma, he emphasizes a direct experience of transcendence that is accessible through the meditation techniques he teaches.

He claims that light, love, wisdom and clarity exist within each individual, and that the meditation techniques which he teaches, and which he learned from his teacher, are a way of accessing them. These techniques are known as the 'Knowledge'. In his public talks he quotes from Hindu, Muslim and Christian scriptures, but he relies on this inner experience for his inspiration and guidance.[965]

---

[965] https://en.wikipedia.org/wiki/Prem_Rawat

41: Sedna / Makemake

Conjunction

There is no one alive today with this aspect and none occurs during the next century, so it is not interpreted here.

Opposition

There is no one alive today with this aspect and none occurs during the next century, so it is not interpreted here.

Semi-sextile, Sextile, Trine

With the flowing aspects between Sedna and Makemake, the all-encompassing spiritual energy of Sedna aligns with our sense of being part of a community and our ability to playfully devote ourselves to the utmost towards something we see as valuable.

Makemake is the Devine trickster, allowing us to experiment with the area of life signified by its position in the chart and bringing a narrowness of focus which permits extreme talent in that area, a talent that can come however at the expense of neglecting other areas.

At the unconscious level, even the flows between these two planets can be challenging, just because the energies of the two planets are so ethereal that we have no practical way of dealing with it and may fall victim to what someone else sees as valuable, however deluded that might be.

Like Rebecca Riley, who was an American victim of prescription drug overdose at age 4. She had Sedna in the ninth house of knowledge, trine Makemake in the first house of identity.

> "The Riley parents were unemployed and the family relied on Social Security Benefits. From the age of two she was diagnosed with ADHD and bipolar disorder by a licensed psychiatrist at a reputable hospital, mainly on the basis of information given by her mother. Her heart and lungs were damaged due to prolonged use of the prescription drugs and two years later, she died and her parents were accused of first-degree murder. Prosecutors argued that they had her declared mentally unstable so they could collect social security disability benefits and

purposely fed her the overdose. They were convicted and sentenced to life in prison.[966]

Or like Shane Lambert, who was a 4-year-old American accidental death/homicide victim, who was killed along with his sister and his aunt, while attempting to cross a busy multi-lane highway. He had Sedna in the fourth house of home, trine Makemake in the eighth house of life and death.

His aunt, a married mom with two teenagers, had inexplicably crossed the median on the Interstate highway. After stopping her car in the wrong direction, she then undressed herself, Shane and his sister and walked the children into oncoming traffic. All three of them were killed when two cars hit them head-on.

Although she had suffered from depression and bipolar disorder in recent years, "we thought she was taking medication and everything was under control," says the children's mother, who was the aunt's twin. "She seemed perfectly normal when she picked up the kids at our house that night. But somewhere on the way to her house for the party, she suffered a psychotic breakdown."

After Shane's funeral, she had been shocked to discover that her sister had received a citation from a state trooper for failing to stay within striped lines while on the way to their home that evening. "She had stopped in the highway median, and when a good Samaritan tried to help her, she hit him and kept calling him 'Harry,'" his mon recalls. "Then she sat down in a puddle of water and started splashing around."

Passing drivers called the police, and three officers debated whether to take the aunt involuntarily to the hospital. But they ultimately decided to allow her sister to drive on, even though she told them she was on her way to pick up her niece and nephew.[967]

Or we may try to strive against the odds to maintain our sense of community at the expense of everyone else. Like Nicolae Ceausescu,

---

[966] https://en.wikipedia.org/wiki/Death_of_Rebecca_Riley
[967] https://www.womansday.com/relationships/family-friends/news/a50713/her-sister-killed-her-kids-and-she-forgave-her/

who was a Romanian politician, an indestructible dictator for 24 years and one of history's mass murderers. He has Sedna in the eleventh house of ideals, sextile Makemake in the first house of identity.

> The son of a shoemaker, he had a limited education before he joined the Communist army fighting against fascists. He was captured and spent several years in prison before assembling a coup that won him the nation's highest office. His rule was marked by an extensive cult of personality, and by nepotism.
>
> However, after a brief period of relatively moderate rule, he became increasingly brutal and repressive. He maintained controls over speech and the media that were very strict even by Soviet-bloc standards. Internal dissent was not tolerated under his rule. His secret police, the Securitate, was one of the most ubiquitous and brutal secret police forces in the world.
>
> Seventeen years after ceasing power, he ordered the export of much of the country's agricultural and industrial production, with the goal of paying off Romania's large foreign debt. The resulting extreme shortages of food, fuel, energy, medicines, and other basic necessities drastically lowered living standards and intensified unrest. Four years later, on the week before Christmas, he ordered a massacre of protesters and the country erupted in a furious revolution, the only violent removal of a Communist government. He was tried in secret and swiftly executed.[968]

Another example is Ian Douglas Smith, who served as Prime Minister of Rhodesia, now Zimbabwe, when it declared independence from the United Kingdom. He had Sedna in the fifth house of creativity, sextile Makemake in the seventh house of relationships. He was the country's first premier not born abroad and led a predominantly white government.

His Sedna is also sesquiquadrate Quaoar however, the planet of new perspectives, which is on his MC, his place in society, and inconjunct Ixion, the planet of lawlessness, in the tenth house of profession.

> He unilaterally declared independence from the United Kingdom in 1965, following prolonged dispute over the terms and remained Prime Minister for almost all of the 14 years of

---

[968] https://en.wikipedia.org/wiki/Nicolae_Ceauşescu

international isolation that followed. In that role he also oversaw Rhodesia's security forces during most of the guerrilla war during that time, which pitted the unrecognised administration against communist-backed black nationalist guerrilla groups.

He has been described as personifying white Rhodesia; however, he remains a highly controversial figure, with supporters venerating him as a man of integrity and vision "who understood the uncomfortable truths of Africa", while critics describe an unrepentant racist, whose policies and actions caused the deaths of thousands and contributed to Zimbabwe's later crises.[969]

As we tire of density and the grief it creates, and we start a spiritual journey to get out of the swamp, Sedna rewards us with transcendent crises, experiences which force us to let go and rise above them, resulting in a huge growth to a new level of consciousness. There is no choice with these crises, and the more we try and solve them, the more we will get hurt.

Like Agatha Christie, who was a British writer of some 67 detective mystery books that are universally popular. Her novels have sold more than a billion copies in English and another billion translated in more than 100 languages. She had Sedna in the third house of communication, semi-sextile Makemake in the fourth house of home. Sedna was also opposite her Moon, the planet of emotions, in the ninth house of publishing.

With a solitary childhood, Agatha was so painfully shy that she never did get accustomed to public appearance and seldom gave interviews. Her mother was not keen on education but in spite of her, five-year-old Agatha taught herself to read. On a dare from her sister, she wrote her first book in two weeks, introducing for the first time her protagonist, Hercule Poirot.[970]

Her Sedna was also sextile Neptune, the planet of imagination, in the fifth house of creativity, together with Pluto, the planet of life and death, just across the cusp in the sixth house of service.

---

[969] https://en.wikipedia.org/wiki/Ian_Smith
[970] https://en.wikipedia.org/wiki/Agatha_Christie

The book was uniformly rejected by publishers, however later someone inadvertently opened the book and recommended it for publication. Agatha was given a five-book contract and her central character went on to solve crime in 33 more novels. Her popularity was close to immediate. By the time she was 40, she was a plain and matronly woman with hair forever locked in a wave, wearing dowdy housedresses; a deeply religious teetotaller who loved to putter in her garden.

Around this time her mother died however and soon after that her husband announced that he loved another. She fell apart and disappeared, checking into a hotel under an alias, while an all-out search turned up her abandoned car on a deserted road and a discarded fur coat. Police dragged the pond for her body while the plot thickened. Some bizarre letters turned up or were rumoured.

When she was found at the hotel, she never really explained the episode and it was accounted for by stating that she had stress-related amnesia, or a secret affair was also considered as another possibility. However, while recovering from the divorce, she took the Orient Express to Baghdad and met her second husband, an archeologist who was fourteen years her junior. Though she gave every possible reason to not marry him, she nonetheless did so, and the "most unsuitable match" lasted very happily for 45 years until her death.[971]

Or like Vincent Van Gogh, who was a Dutch artist, a legend for his brilliant work, who lived his brief life in misery and poverty. He had Sedna conjunct Mars, the planet of action, and also Venus, the planet of values, all in the tenth house of profession, semi-sextile Makemake in the ninth house of knowledge.

Disappointed in love and religion, he was intense, difficult and unhappy. He seemed to lack a psychological shield to protect him from the pain of everything and every moment. Washed out as a preacher to impoverished coal miners, he turned to full time art when he was 27. At 33 he went to Paris to immerse himself in the vanguard styles of the day. He began using the impressionist's choppy brush strokes of pastel color. Within two

---

[971] Ibid.

years, he was disillusioned by what he saw in the Parisian scene, and living with his brother upon whom he was financially dependent. proved to be a strain for both of them.

He fled south to Arles, where, intoxicated by the countryside, he painted with thicker impasto in blazing yellows, piercing reds and icy greens. His work still did not make him happy; in fact, he was frequently in despair. When his friend, Paul Gauquin, arrived he welcomed him. However, they began to quarrel, drink absinthe, a potent alcohol, and partake in debauchery. When Gauquin left Vincent followed him with a razor, and then locked himself in his room and cut off the lobe of his left ear. He was 35.

The following year he went quite mad, to the point where he was considered dangerous. He was put in an asylum near Paris early the next year. His doctor encouraged him to keep painting, and flying into a creative frenzy, he completed 70 canvases in 70 days. Six months later while painting in a wheat field, he became suddenly, intolerably despondent and shot himself in the chest. He died two days later.

At the time of his death he was a failure, a misfit who had sold only two paintings in his lifetime, an artist who was later known as one of the most famous painters of all time. Two years after his death, a Dutch museum gave him a retrospective. And a hundred years later a collector paid close to $54 million for his "Irises," now in the Getty Museum in Los Angeles.[972]

Or Emily Dickinson, who was an American writer, acclaimed as the greatest woman poet of the English language. During her lifetime she had seven poems published anonymously; since her death she has been revered as a literary treasure. She had Sedna in the fourth house of home, sextile Makemake in the third house of communication.

With poor health, shy and fastidious, she had a reclusive and uneventful life with her domineering dad, an attorney, and a mom who "did not care for thought." She was one of three children, an older brother and a younger sister who were her closest companions through her lifetime. Her parents sent her to

---

[972] https://en.wikipedia.org/wiki/Vincent_van_Gogh

seminary school at 17, where she was cramped, curbed and repressed into a tight Victorian mold.

Becoming increasingly withdrawn and mystical, dressed always in white, she ventured outside only at dusk to water the garden. She never married and some biographers conclude that she was gay. By the early 1860s, she had created a wall of isolation around herself, which she believed critical to artistic expression. The major relationships in her life were with Susan Dickinson, her brother Austin's wife and with Bowles, a married man and the editor of the Springfield republican. She and Sue met when they were both 17. Through the 40 years of their correspondence, Bowles was her closest personal friend until his death. He was vigorous, earthy and dashing, however Dickinson's biographer writes that with neither relationship was physical union possible.

In her last two decades, she became even more reclusive, seldom going far from her brother's house in Amherst. At 54 her health was set back by the death of a friend and by late the following year she was often too ill to leave her room. Stricken by Bright's disease, a type of kidney inflammation, she lost consciousness and died in the house where she was born. After her death her sister found a manuscript of almost 900 poems, a legacy of glorious words to show the blazing wondrous genius that was hidden inside her.[973]

As we see, the flowing aspects with Makemake can make us articulate and communicative. Self-assuredness, especially by verbal means, characterizes this planet. Its energy is clever, quick-witted and interested in invoking insight and inspiration.

Heinrich Boll was a German author who was awarded the Nobel Prize for Literature. He has Sedna in the third house of communications, sextile Makemake in the sixth house of service.

He was a leader of the German writers who tried to come to grips with the memory of World War II, the Nazis, and the Holocaust and the guilt that came with them. Because of his

---

[973] https://en.wikipedia.org/wiki/Emily_Dickinson

refusal to avoid writing about the complexities and problems of the past, he was the leading critic of West German society.

His disillusionment with postwar Germany was also apparent through his strong sense of ethical responsibility of authorship and critical attitude toward social institutions. His writing style was plain and accessible, and his books were translated into many languages. He was particularly successful in Eastern Europe, as he seemed to portray the dark side of capitalism in his books, which were sold by the millions in the Soviet Union alone.

Despite the variety of themes and content in his work, there are certain recurring patterns: many of his novels and stories describe intimate and personal life struggling to sustain itself against the wider background of war, terrorism, political divisions, and profound economic and social transition.

In a number of his books there are protagonists who are stubborn and eccentric individualists opposed to the mechanisms of the state or of public institutions. His villains are the figures of authority in government, business, the mainstream media, and in the Church, whom he castigates, sometimes humorously, sometimes acidly, for what he perceived as their conformism, lack of courage, self-satisfied attitude and abuse of power.[974]

And our case study, James Lovelock, the father of Gaia theory, also has a sextile to Makemake. His Sedna is in the sixth house of service, sextile Makemake in the eighth house of shared resources. Gaia theory proposes that organisms interact with their inorganic surroundings on Earth to form a synergistic self-regulating, complex system that helps to maintain and perpetuate the conditions for life on the planet. This is a very Makemake in the eighth observation.

Humour can be one path to transcend the quicksand of Sedna, giving us the objectivity to step back from the edge and also the opportunity to adopt a more playful approach to our particular area of devotion.

---

[974] https://en.wikipedia.org/wiki/Heinrich_Böll

Phyllis Diller was an American comedienne. She had Sedna in the eleventh house of the collective consciousness, sextile Makemake in the first house of identity.

> The only child of strict, older parents, she remembers being a nerd and a misfit, a shy, scrawny and plain kid who spent much of her time alone with her dolls and her cat. At school she used humour as a defence and began to discover the perks of being the class clown; laughter, attention and admiration.

> She wisecracked her way from the local Laundromat, to community events, then exploded on stage in San Francisco, wearing a sequined mini-dress and an orange fright-wig, gold ankle-high boots and black satin opera gloves. A married housewife until she was 37, she buried the ironing in the backyard and took her show on the road, complaining about her husband, "Fang," and keeping an audience howling.

> She made her debut as a stand-up comic at the Purple Onion, a popular San Francisco nightspot, and stayed for 89 weeks. Soon everyone wanted her as their guest speaker. In the following years she went from $60 a week to $75,000 a week as an international star, writing most of her own material.[975]

At this juncture in human evolution, few of us use our planets at the spiritual level, but many of us are striving to, and such people are wonderful to be around. As with the other planets, the spiritual level of evolution is vastly different with Sedna from the two previous levels.

Here, the flowing aspects with Makemake bring a courageous approach to life, giving us the willfulness to confront the peril required for discovery or spiritual evolution. The struggle of the beginner's level is gone, as are the transcendental crises of the intermediate level. At this level everything Saturnian is meaningless and yet everything has its place.

Corrie ten Boom was a Dutch heroine and Christian evangelist, famous for the book and the deeds of her noted family in *The Hiding Place*. She had Sedna conjunct Jupiter, the planet of expansion, and also Vesta, the asteroid of regeneration, in the seventh house of relationships, but on the cusp of the eighth house of sensitivity to the spirit world, semi-sextile Makemake in the ninth house of spirituality.

---

[975] https://en.wikipedia.org/wiki/Phyllis_Diller

During the Second World War her father sheltered Jewish people, who were trying to escape from the Nazi Holocaust at their home. Some thirty-eight Jewish people were saved, but she was the only one in her family to survive the Holocaust.

Her father believed that all people were equal before God and when a desperate Jewish woman appealed to him, he gave her shelter for the Holocaust in his house. Many persecuted Jews and Nazi resisters would follow. Corrie at first had trouble with the necessity of keeping these activities secret. She suffered a moral crisis over the lying, theft, forgery, and bribery that was necessary to keep the Jews her family was hiding alive.

With help of the Dutch underground, they built a secret room in the top of the building, where the refugees could hide in case of a a raid. She was 52 when the house was raided after a tip of an unknown person. That day some 27 persons were in the house, including six Jews that slipped in the hiding place. Twenty-one persons were arrested, including Corrie, her father and sister. Her father's health was weakened by age and tuberculosis and he was sent to a medical clinic where he died ten days after the arrest of the family.

Corrie and her sister were interrogated by the Gestapo, but not tortured. They took all the blame for hiding the Jews, and after four months in prison, they were sentenced to forced labour. Through their confession, the other arrested guests in their father's house were released. After the war, she became an evangelist, motivational speaker and social critic, protesting against the Vietnam War. She visited more than 60 countries, not preaching for any particular belief, but believing in an Universal Holy Spirit that asks for peace and forgiveness.[976]

Maxine Bell was an American trance medium, pianist and composer. She had Sedna in the tenth house of profession, sextile Makemake in the eleventh house of collective consciousness. She played the works of dead masters while in trance and was able to play 3,000 notes per minute. She also worked with the Los Angeles Police Department on murder cases, as a psychic.

---

[976] https://en.wikipedia.org/wiki/Corrie_ten_Boom

Sri Meher Baba was an Indian religious figure who was known as "The Silent Guru." He was born in India to Irani Zoroastrian parents. He had Sedna in the second house of material resources, semi-sextile Makemake in the third house of communication.

> At the age of 19, he began a seven-year spiritual transformation and during this time he contacted five spiritual masters before beginning his own mission and gathering his own disciples at the age of 27. His early followers gave him the name Meher Baba, meaning "Compassionate Father".[977]

His Sedna is also inconjunct the Moon, the planet of emotions, in the ninth house of spirituality.

> He moved into silence at 31 and did not speak until his death. To communicate, he spelled words on the alphabet board with quick fingers, such as "I am the Supreme Spirit." From the age of 60 he used unique sign language of gestures, rather than the alphabet board. With his circle of disciples, he spent long periods in seclusion, during which time he often fasted. He also traveled widely, held public gatherings and engaged in works of charity with lepers, the poor and the mentally ill.[978]

His Sedna is also quintile Haumea, the planet of rebirth, in the fifth house of creativity, semi-square Venus, the planet of values in the first house of identity, and sesquiquadrate Juno, the asteroid of partnership, in the tenth house of profession.

> He gave numerous teachings on the cause and purpose of life, including teaching reincarnation and that the phenomenal world is an illusion. He taught that the Universe is imagination, that God is what really exists, and that each soul is really God passing through imagination to realise individually His own divinity.

> In addition, he gave practical advice for the aspirant who wishes to attain Self-realization and thereby escape the wheel of birth and death. He also taught about the concept of Perfect Masters, the Avatar, and those on the various stages of the spiritual path that he called involution. His teachings are most importantly

---

[977] https://en.wikipedia.org/wiki/Meher_Baba
[978] Ibid.

recorded in his principal books, *Discourses* and *God Speaks*. And his legacy includes an influence on pop-culture artists and the introduction of common expressions such as 'Don't Worry, Be Happy'.[979]

Semi-square, Square, Sesquiquadrate,

With the stressful aspects between Sedna and Makemake, the all-encompassing spiritual energy of Sedna challenges our cleverness, our sense of being part of a community and our ability to playfully devote ourselves to the utmost towards something we see as valuable.

Makemake is the Devine trickster, allowing us to experiment with the area of life signified by its position in the chart and bringing a narrowness of focus which permits extreme talent in that area, a talent that can come however at the expense of neglecting other areas.

If we haven't developed our Sedna energy however the stressful aspects likely lead to a sense of righteousness in our devotion that can bring out the more negative side of Makemake, which is being reckless and self-serving, being verbally manipulative, engaging in double talk and diversion of facts, and taking flight to avoid consequence, or hiding as a coping skill.

At the unconscious level the stressful aspects between these two planets can be challenging, because the energies are so ethereal that we have no practical way of dealing with it and may fall victim to what someone else sees as valuable, however deluded that might be.

Like Leslie Van Houten, who is an American convicted murderer and former member of the Manson Family. She has Sedna in the eighth house of life and death, square Makemake, which is conjunct Mars, the planet of war, in the eleventh house of collective consciousness.

> She wasn't selected by Manson for the Tate killings, but she asked to participate a couple of days later when he selected followers for the killings of another couple. She was 20 years old. She was arrested and charged, then convicted and sentenced to death. Despite this ruling, a California Supreme Court subsequently ruled that the death penalty was unconstitutional, resulting in her sentence being commuted to life in prison.

---

[979] Ibid.

This conviction was then overturned when she was 27 on a technicality and she was granted a retrial. Her second trial ended with a deadlocked jury and a mistrial. However at her third trial when she was 29, she was convicted on two counts of murder and one count of conspiracy and sentenced to between 7 years and life in prison.

In relation to her case, high courts, parole boards, and the state governor have said that an inexplicable, or racial motive for murder could merit exemplary punishment and outweigh any evidence of subsequent reform, so she has been denied parole 19 times and is still in jail 48 years later, at time of writing.[980]

At this level these aspects can send us on a life mission, something to give our lives meaning, but it may be a delusion. Interestingly we have two failed assassins as examples of this.

The first is Squeaky Fromme, who is an American who was in the news for the attempted assassination of President Gerald Ford when she was 26. She has Sedna in the seventh house of relationships, square Makemake in the tenth house of social standing.

She was a worshipful follower of ritual cult leader and psychopath, Charles Manson, and she had begun a correspondence with a newscaster on NBC to get him on TV with his message of enlightenment. NBC would not agree, so she decided to stalk and shoot Ford to get the publicity that would put her on TV.

She watched as Ford and his entourage left a hotel one morning. Petite and childlike, in a red gown and red turban, she followed the crowd and angled in to meet Ford face to face. She fumbled in her robe for her pistol and aimed at his genitals. A secret service man grabbed the gun and everyone piled on her. The attempt got her the publicity she wanted; she was on TV, but she also was sent to prison, and she never did get Manson, or his message across. She was released from jail on parole at the age of 60.[981]

---

[980] https://en.wikipedia.org/wiki/Leslie_Van_Houten
[981] https://en.wikipedia.org/wiki/Lynette_Fromme

And the second is John Hinckley, who is an American attempted assassin who shot and wounded President Reagan when he was 25. He has Sedna in the second house of material reality, square Makemake in the sixth house of daily routine.

> The year before he shot Reagan, he went to Ted Kennedy's office and waited for three hours with a loaded gun to see the Senator, before he gave up on the assassination attempt and left. He was found not guilty of attempting to assassinate Reagan by reason of insanity and sentenced to an asylum for the mentally ill in Washington, DC.

> Prior to the assassination attempt he wrote a string of love letters to actress Jodie Foster. Then at 27, he met a woman who was a patient in the same facility for the shotgun murder of her ten-year-old daughter, followed by her own suicide attempt. She was 12 years older. They were both in the hell of their mental illness, anguish and despair and their growing friendship led to improvement for both of them. Their long hours of talks led to love and he asked her to marry him.

> A couple of years later she was able to function responsibly in society and was released. His progress was slower however they were able to see each other on weekends and kiss goodbye, feeling like a couple of teenagers. During the Christmas holidays, the young lovers spent time alone for the first time when he was allowed to spend a day with his family. His sexual experience was limited to a few encounters with prostitutes shortly before the assassination attempt. They were not able to consummate their relationship, but the promise of a future together was a strong incentive to healthy responsibility.

> During the next five years, his progress was interspersed with unsettling relapses. His psychological evaluations took a turn for the worse. A report from this period read, "The issues of poor judgment, need for ego-gratification through the media, isolation from others at all but a superficial level, grandiosity, suspiciousness, defiance in the face of narcissistic injury, refusal to accept responsibility for his actions other than in a fleeting way, emotional volatility, tendency to lie, lack of empathy for others, sense of entitlement - all remain as unresolved

therapeutic issues." His ability to maintain a stable relationship with his fiancé was a plus.

At 35, he was living in a medium-security ward and was working four hours a day in a clerical position. The next year he was allowed to walk with his fiancé without an escort around the hospital grounds. Not long after this, they had sexual relations for the first time and he was moved to a minimum-security ward. A divided appeals court finally ruled when he was 43 that he could make supervised day trips away from the mental hospital where he has lived for the past 18 years to visit his family and friends, a process of gradual re-entry into society. Four years later he was granted unsupervised visits with his parents, but it would be 14 more years before he was released from institutional psychiatric care at 61.[982]

And finally, at this level we have our case study, Osama bin Laden, the Al Qaeda terrorist leader, had Sedna in the eleventh house of ideals, also square to Makemake, this time in the second house of material resources. His obsessional devotion represented by Makemake, motivated him to bankroll the Taliban insurgency against Russia in Afghanistan and the aspect is also epitomized in the Al Qaeda plane attacks on the World Trade Centre in New York, bringing down the financial hub of the world. And bin Laden famously hid as a coping skill for the last ten years of his life, until the American's found and assassinated him.

As we tire of density and the grief it creates, and we start a spiritual journey to get out of the swamp, Sedna rewards us with transcendent crises, experiences which force us to let go and rise above them, resulting in a huge growth to a new level of consciousness. There is no choice with these crises, and the more we try and 'solve them', the more we will just get hurt.

Like American politician and environmentalist, Al Gore, whose Sedna is conjunct the MC, the cusp of the tenth house of profession and the square to Makemake, in the twelfth house of institutions.

Gore was an elected official for 24 years. He was a Congressman from Tennessee and served as one of the state's

---

[982] https://en.wikipedia.org/wiki/John_Hinckley_Jr.

Senators. He also served as Vice President during the Clinton administration. He was initially hesitant to accept a position as Bill Clinton's running mate, but after clashing with the George H. W. Bush administration over global warming issues, he decided to accept the offer.

Clinton's choice was criticized as unconventional because, rather than picking a running mate who would diversify the ticket, Clinton chose a fellow Southerner who shared his political ideologies and who was nearly the same age as Clinton. Yet, Gore has come to be regarded by strategists in both parties as the best vice presidential pick in at least 20 years.

In the 2000 presidential election, in what was one of the closest presidential races in history, Gore won the popular vote by half a million, but lost in the Electoral College to Republican George W. Bush by 537 votes in the key state of Florida.

After his term as vice-president ended, Gore remained prominent as an author and activist and returned his focus to his environmental agenda. He edited and adapted a slide show he had compiled years earlier, and began featuring the slide show in presentations on global warming across the U.S. and around the world. By the time the documentary about his work, *An Inconvenient Truth*, was made, he estimated that he had shown the presentation more than one thousand times[983]

His work in climate change activism earned him the Nobel Peace Prize in 2007 and we now know the evolutionary results of his work with the Paris Climate Change Agreement, which has been far more valuable for society than his being president. So here we note that both with the politics and the environmental activism, it was his extreme focus, despite the setbacks the square produces, and the transcendent challenges presented by Sedna that helped change the world.

And like our case study, Steve Jobs, who had Sedna in the eighth house of shared resources, square Makemake conjunct Uranus, the planet of electronics, in his eleventh house of ideals and also square Jupiter, the planet of expansion just across the house cusp in the tenth house of profession.

---

[983] https://en.wikipedia.org/wiki/Al_Gore

Jobs and his pal Steve Wozniak made their first circuit board in their garage and they called it the Apple. By the time he was 24, Job's Apple Corporation was worth $10 million. A year later, its value had grown to $100 million. Its graphical user interface, business applications and word processing won kudos, and millions cheered while Apple took on IBM and its personal computer.

As the Apple empire grew, Steve became a tyrant, subject to moody outbursts and gloomy silences. Hard feelings arose and power struggles with other executives ensued. Jobs resigned and the following year co-founded NeXt in an attempt to do for the hardware industry, what he had down for software.

With ever-broadening vision, he also bought a company which he renamed Pixar Animation Studios and negotiated a deal with Disney to distribute Pixar's films and became a Disney partner. Under Jobs' leadership, Pixar won 20 Academy awards for successful animated feature films and was acquired by Disney, leaving Jobs with a very large share of Disney stock and a seat on the Board of Directors.

With a twist of fate and a large amount of Sednian transcendence, he then convinced Apple to buy NeXt and was invited back to Apple as interim CEO and a few years later was made permanent CEO once again. Under his renewed leadership Apple computer became a player in the computer industry once more and his team created visually aesthetic computers in bright colours that appealed to younger buyers.[984]

We might also become caught up in transcendent crises on a social level, like our case study, Sally Ride, the mother of NASA's Planet Earth study. She has Sedna in the tenth house of profession, square Makemake in the first house of identity.

Before becoming the first American woman in space and the first known LGBT astronaut, she got a PhD in astrophysics from Stanford and subjected herself to five years of astronaut training at NASA. Navy test pilots took her on gut-dropping, 600-mile-

---

[984] https://en.wikipedia.org/wiki/Steve_Jobs

per-hour flights 39,000 feet in the air. Her flight instructor called her the best student he'd ever had.

When Space Shuttle Challenger exploded seventy-three seconds after liftoff, seven of Ride's colleagues died in the accident. She had a total of more than 343 hours in space at that stage and had completed eight months of training for her third space flight when the disaster occurred. She was named to the presidential commission investigating the accident and headed its subcommittee on operations, revealing crucial information that revealed that NASA's push for rapid-fire missions had come at the expense of safety and sacrificed lives.

Following the investigation, she was assigned to NASA headquarters in Washington, D.C., where she led their first strategic planning effort, authored a visionary report titled "NASA Leadership and America's Future in Space" and founded NASA's Office of Exploration with the Mission to Planet Earth to study our planet.[985]

As we see, the stressful aspects with Makemake can make us articulate and communicative. Self-assuredness, especially by verbal means, characterizes this planet. Its energy is clever, quick-witted and interested in invoking insight and inspiration.

Bernard Stiegler is a French philosopher who came to the profession through personal crisis. He has Sedna conjunct Jupiter, the planet of expansion, on the cusp of the third house of communication, quintile Makemake in the seventh house of relationships.

He is currently head of the Institute of Research and Innovation, which he founded at the age of 54 at the Centre Georges-Pompidou in Paris. However, when he was 26 he was incarcerated for five years for armed robbery. It was during this period that he became interested in philosophy, studying it by correspondence. His transformation in prison is recounted in his book, *Passer à l'acte*.

Key themes in his work are technology, time, individuation, consumerism, consumer capitalism, technological convergence, digitization, Americanization, education and the future of politics

---

[985] https://en.wikipedia.org/wiki/Sally_Ride

and human society. His best-known work is *Technics and Time*, published when he was 46. The thesis of the book is that the genesis of technology corresponds not only to the genesis of what is called "human" but of temporality as such, and that this is the clue toward understanding the future of the dynamic process in which the human and technology consists.

This book conducts a reading of approaches to the history of technology and the origin of humanisation. The outcome of this is the conjecture that history cannot be thought according to the idea that we are the "subject" of this history and technology simply the object. When it comes to the relation between the human and the technical, the "who" and the "what" are in an undecidable relation.

At 53 he founded the political and cultural group, Ars Industrialis, the manifesto of which calls for an "industrial politics of spirit." And at 58 he founded the philosophy school, Ecole de Philosophie d'Épineuil-le-Fleuriel. The context and themes of the school lie in his argument that we are entering a period of post-consumerism and post-globalization.[986]

And case study, Ray Kurzweil, scientist, inventor, futurist, has Sedna in the sixth house of service, square Makemake, in the ninth house of philosophy.

He was born to secular Jewish parents who had emigrated from Austria just before the onset of World War II. He was exposed via Unitarian Universalism to a diversity of religious faiths during his upbringing. His Unitarian church had the philosophy of many paths to the truth – the religious education consisted of spending six months on a single religion before moving onto the next. As an adult, Kurzweil is agnostic about the existence of a soul. On the possibility of divine intelligence, he is quoted as saying, "Does God exist? I would say, 'Not yet.'

His singularity is a hypothesised time in the future, approximately 2045, when the capabilities of non-living electronic machines will supersede human capabilities. Un-dismissible contemporary thinkers like Elon Musk and Stephen Hawking warn us that it will

---

[986] https://en.wikipedia.org/wiki/Bernard_Stiegler

change everything. Hawking likens it to receiving a message from aliens announcing their arrival in "a few decades," saying this is "more or less" what's happening with artificial intelligence.

Talk of the singularity ripples with religious undertones: It's obsessed with the unknown future and assumes the arrival of a superior entity down the road. It has its naysayers and true believers alike, each eager to tell you why, or why not, such an entity will actually show up. Some believe Artificial Spiritual Intelligence is the new God and that Kurzweil is his prophet.

Others see him as evidence for the post-secularisation hypothesis that religion is not at all dying but is merely continuing to evolve. They argue that he is probably by far the most influential Singularitarian in the world and perhaps the most influential living futurist, and he got there by directly engaging in post-secular rhetoric.

The most obvious example can be found in the title of his book, *The Age of Spiritual Machines,* that made him a thought leader and no longer only an inventor or entrepreneur. Furthermore, although an atheist or agnostic, he chooses explicitly to leverage references to "God" inside his books, as at least a literary device, if not a vision for the future of humanity. They argue his success in doing these things speaks to the persisting power of religion.[987]

Humour can also be one path to transcend the quicksand of Sedna, giving us the objectivity to step back from the edge and also, with the stressful aspects to the Devine trickster, to treat our lives as more of a game. If we're struggling with these stressful aspects, we would be well advised to develop our sense of humour.

Roseanne Barr is an American actress, comedian, writer, and television producer. She was also the 2012 presidential nominee of the California-based Peace and Freedom Party. She has Sedna in the second house of material resources, trine Pluto, which is conjunct Haumea, the planet of rebirth, in the seventh house of relationships, square Makemake in the sixth house of service.

---

[987] https://en.wikipedia.org/wiki/Ray_Kurzweil

She began her career in stand-up comedy at clubs before gaining fame for her role in the hit television sitcom, *Roseanne*. The show ran for nine seasons and she won both an Emmy and a Golden Globe Award for Best Actress for her work. She had crafted a "fierce working-class domestic goddess" persona in the eight years preceding her sitcom and wanted to do a realistic show about a strong mother who was not a victim of patriarchal consumerism.

The granddaughter of immigrants from Europe and Russia, she was the oldest of four children in a working-class Jewish Salt Lake City family. She was active in The Church of Jesus Christ of Latter-day Saints, yet courted controversy by stunts like singing the national anthem off-key at a nationally aired baseball game, followed by grabbing her crotch and spitting.

After her sitcom ended, she launched her own talk show, *The Roseanne Show,* and returned to stand-up comedy with a world tour. Then she announced she was running for the presidential nomination of the Green Party, which she lost, before getting the nomination of the Peace and Freedom Party. She received 61,971 votes in the general election which brought Trump to power, placing sixth overall.[988]

At this juncture in human evolution, few of us use our planets at the spiritual level, but many of us are striving to, and such people are wonderful to be around. As with the other planets, the spiritual level of evolution is vastly different with Sedna from the two previous levels.

Here even the stressful aspects with Makemake bring a courageous approach to life, giving us the willfulness to confront the peril required for discovery, or spiritual evolution. The struggle of the beginner's level is gone, as are the transcendental crises of the intermediate level. At this level everything Saturnian is meaningless and yet everything Sednian has its place.

Like Steve Hill, who was an American Christian clergyman and evangelist. He had Sedna in the seventh house of relationships, square Makemake in the tenth house of profession.

---

[988] https://en.wikipedia.org/wiki/Roseanne_Barr

As a teenager, he got heavily into alcohol and illicit drugs. At the age of twenty-one due to the effects of drug abuse, he spent three days suffering extreme convulsions, and turned to Christianity. A few weeks after his conversion experience, he was arrested and faced 25 years in prison for drug trafficking. Instead of jail, he was remanded to the Teen Challenge drug rehabilitation program, from which he graduated.

He is best known as the evangelist who preached in what became known as the Brownsville Revival. The Brownsville Revival was a series of meetings at Brownsville Assembly of God in Pensacola, Florida that began on Father's Day, when he was 41 and continued for five years. At 46 he moved to Texas to resume traveling evangelism. And at 49 he founded Heartland World Ministries Church in a suburb of Dallas.[989]

I have a square with Makemake. My Sedna is in my fourth house of home, square Makemake in the seventh house of relationships, together with Jupiter, the planet of expansion and Uranus, the planet of intuition. The Devine trickster in my house of relationships is the other half of my tenth house Juno/Ixion clown work, but this is my clown adventure, throwing myself out into the world, working mostly in an improvised way and seeing what happens.

This has been a big research into people, and one of my big discoveries is we all take it far too seriously. When I was young and had just starting clowning, I realized it was all a game. That if we don't take our experiences seriously, we won't get caught up in the Sedna quicksand and we will be able to rise above the experience. That doesn't mean we don't participate deeply in the experience, but Makemake teaches us that, by adopting a playful approach, any apparent failures just become valuable learning experiences. Failures are in fact the best learning experiences, so there is no failure at this level.

Marthe Robin was a French mystic and stigmatic. She had Sedna conjunct Pallas, the asteroid of wisdom, in the eighth house of the occult, semi-square Makemake in the ninth house of spirituality.

Serious illness marked her adult life and from her twenties she was confined to bed, crippled, and gradually paralysed. She ate

---

[989] https://en.wikipedia.org/wiki/Steve_Hill_(evangelist)

only wafers and neither drank nor slept, but lived for seven decades and carried on a busy apostolate.

From the age of 28 she was completely paralysed and bedridden. Although she still could move the thumb and forefinger of one hand, she became motionless apart from her head which she could move slightly. Since the previous year, at the age of 25, she could not eat anything at all. And from the age of 26 she couldn't even take a sip of water. When doctors tried to force some water down her throat, it merely came out her nostrils.

For the next 53 years her only food was the holy Eucharist, a wafer of bread which Catholics believe is the body of Christ. They also believe that they become his body on ingesting it. Once a week she was given the sacred host. Once she had received it she went immediately into ecstasy and began her weekly re-living of Christ's crucifixion. Every Friday wounds appeared in the palms of her hands and the stigmata, the scourging and crowning with thorns appeared on her body, and she appeared to be dead.

For 53 years she also carried on a busy apostolate, which is a Christian organisation directed to serving and evangelising the world. She was directed to found two schools in her native village, one for girls and one for boys. All this she directed down to the smallest detail from her bed in her darkened little room. Later on she was told to found a community which would welcome people looking for a retreat and which would be a home of "light, charity and love." It became known as the Foyer de Charité and there are now some 70 affiliated houses and communities throughout the world.[990]

Pakh Subuh is an Dutch Indonesian spiritual leader with an Islamic background, who was given a spiritual vision and a Messianic message as his Call. He has Sedna in the tenth house of profession, semi-square Makemake in the eleventh house of collective consciousness.

He founded a form of Islamic mysticism in which the supplicant is initiated by means of a kind of meditative communal submission

---

[990] https://en.wikipedia.org/wiki/Marthe_Robin

to divine understanding, a method of communion that involves surrender. During this the devotee is 'opened', an experience which may be expressed in silent meditation, in dancing and movement, in speaking in tongues, or whatever form the applicant wishes to employ.[991]

Tracy Marks is an American psychotherapist, astrologer, lecturer and teacher who is the author of 15 books and pamphlets which have been translated into nearly a dozen languages. She has Sedna in the fourth house of home, square Makemake in the seventh house of relationships.

She has a master's degree in psycho-synthesis and is acclaimed for her in-depth integration of psychological, spiritual and astrological concepts. She is skilled at leading dream work, women's empowerment, and the art of friendship groups. Some of her more notable books include *How To Handle Your T-Square, The Astrology of Self Discovery,* and *The Art Of Chart Interpretation.*[992]

In-conjunct

There is no-one alive today with this aspect and none occurs during the next century, so it is not interpreted here.

Quintile, Bi-quintile

The evolutionary quintile or bi-quintile aspect between Sedna and Makemake infuses our cleverness, our sense of being part of a community and our ability to playfully devote ourselves to the utmost towards something we see as valuable, with the all-encompassing spiritual energy of Sedna to the point where we can push the boundaries of human development.

Quintiles and bi-quintiles point to talent, the desire to create order and to categorize, a fascination with patterns and structures, perfectionist tendencies, and the desire to build or make things. These aspects have the characteristics of both the trine and opposition. They point to awareness of conflicts, or problems and finding solutions for them, however they do not automatically kick into action and must be cultivated over time.

---

[991] https://www.astro.com/astro-databank/Subuh,_Pakh
[992] https://www.astro.com/astro-databank/Marks,_Tracy

Makemake is the Devine trickster, allowing us to experiment with the area of life signified by its position in the chart and bringing a narrowness of focus which permits extreme talent in that area, a talent that can come however at the expense of neglecting other areas.

Until we develop our Sedna energy however, any aspects with Makemake can lead to a sense of righteousness in our devotion that can bring out the more negative side of Makemake, which is being reckless and self-serving, being verbally manipulative, engaging in double talk and diversion of facts, and taking flight to avoid consequence, or hiding as a coping skill.

At the unconscious level, even the quintile and bi-quintile aspects between these two planets can be challenging, because the energies are so ethereal that we have no practical way of dealing with it and may fall victim to what someone else sees as valuable, however deluded that might be.

Like Charles Lindbergh Jr, who was the first son of a noted American family, aviator Charles and pilot-writer Anne Morrow Lindbergh. He was abducted from his home in New Jersey when he was 20 months. He had Sedna in the seventh house of relationships, conjunct Uranus, the planet of revolution, which was right on his descendant, quintile Makemake in the ninth house of knowledge.

> The family nurse put 20-month-old Charles in his crib and later discovered it empty. A ransom note in an envelope was found on the windowsill and a ladder outside. An extensive investigation by police followed, together with extended ransom negotiations which resulted in a 70,000 ransom being paid, however the boy was not returned.

> Two months later, a delivery truck driver pulled to the side of a road about 7 kms south of the Lindbergh home. Going into a grove of trees he discovered the body of the toddler. His skull was badly fractured and there were indications of an attempt at a hasty burial. It appeared the child had been killed by a blow to the head. The culprit was eventually convicted through tracing the spending of the ransom money, the numbers of which had

been recorded. And the case led to the Lindbergh law that made kidnapping a federal offence.[993]

Or like Tom Sutherland, the Scottish-American Dean of Agriculture at the American University at Beirut, who was taken hostage by terrorists in one of the mid-East hostage crises. He has Sedna in the twelfth house of karma, conjunct Uranus, the planet of revolution, both closely quintile Makemake in the second house of material resources.

> He studied agriculture in Scotland before immigrating to the U.S. where he taught courses at the Colorado State University in livestock. He was recruited years later by the American University at Beirut, but did not accept the position for three years, using the time to weigh the singularly risky career decision. However eventually he did move to Beirut with his family.
>
> Then en route back from his daughter's graduation in America, he was stopped by gunmen on his way from the airport to his on-campus home. They sprayed his car with automatic rifle fire and took him as a hostage. He was held by Muslim fundamentalists and kept in a Lebanese prison for over six years, incognito and chained by the ankle to a wall.
>
> While in captivity he maintained Scottish traditions, including a celebration of the birthday of poet Robert Burns. When one liberated American hostage delivered a letter to the Tom's family, it contained questions regarding the brakes on his daughter's car. On his release, he returned home to a national celebration of his freedom.[994]

At this level these aspects can send us on a life mission, something to give our lives meaning, but it may be a delusion.

Like James Earl Ray, who was an American assassin who shot civil rights leader Dr. Martin Luther King to death. He had Sedna, conjunct Nessus, the centaur of radical change, both in the ninth house of knowledge, quintile Makemake in the eleventh house of collective consciousness.

---

[993] https://en.wikipedia.org/wiki/Lindbergh_kidnapping
[994] https://en.wikipedia.org/wiki/Thomas_Sutherland_(academic)

He had a long criminal record and had previously served prison terms. He was born into an extremely poor family with an extensive history of run-ins with the law. He grew up in rough and tumble river towns along the Illinois and Missouri, which doubled as spawning grounds for the KKK. His father abandoned the family when Ray was young, his mother, an alcoholic, eventually had all of her eight children removed to foster care.

One positive relationship grew out of Ray's chaotic childhood, the bond between him and his brothers, Jerry and John. They grew very close through their horrible childhoods and trusted and relied on one another. As the years progressed, Ray was convicted of increasingly severe crimes. A racist, he refused to work with blacks on a prison honour farm.

After an escape from prison when he was 39, he caught up with his brothers and they discussed ways to earn money, including kidnapping the governor of Illinois or a local star radio host. They also flirted with the idea of going into the porn business. Ray shocked even his brothers when he told them that he was, "going to kill that n----- King. That's something that's been on my mind. That's something I've been working on."

The following year he arrived in Memphis, the exact same day as Dr. Martin Luther King Jr. Newspaper publicity revealed the hotel at which King was staying, as well as the room number. The next day, Ray reconnoitred the hotel from a rundown rooming house across the street and when King stepped outside the door to his room, he fired the single shot that killed him.

After the shooting, he panicked and threw the murder weapon, which was wrapped in a bundle, against a store front. The quick discovery of this by police was the critical piece of evidence that helped police identify him as the shooter. An accustomed international traveler however, he was able to flee to Canada and return to England. But he ran low on money, which caused him to rob a bank, and just as he was about to board a plane for Brussels, he was arrested at Heathrow International Airport.[995]

---

[995] https://en.wikipedia.org/wiki/James_Earl_Ray

Or we could construct an elaborate criminal enterprise, like Tommaso Buscetta, who was a Sicilian Mafiosa, the first major figure in the Sicilian Mafia to break the code of omerta, the traditional vow of silence. His Sedna is also in the ninth house of knowledge, quintile Makemake in the eleventh house of collective consciousness.

His criminal record began at 21, with bootlegged cigarettes. He soon began traveling to Brazil and America where at one time he opened a chain of pizza parlors that reportedly served as a cover for drug dealing. Arrested in New York at 42, he fled to Brazil.

Up till that time, a hundred top Mafia families had controlled organised crime in Italy, focusing on their traditional areas of agriculture, construction, extortion, prostitution and some drug smuggling. They had their codes; politicians and police were "cultivated," not murdered and women and children were off-limits. All that changed when the French Connection was broken in the 1970s and Sicily succeeded Marseilles as the world's heroin capital.

The heroin traffic became immense and new groups began fighting for a piece of the action. Wives and children were massacred, along with their Mafia husbands and troublesome officials. Unfortunately, Buscetta aligned himself with one of the loosing clans, two of his sons disappeared and his brother and nephew were gunned down at work. In all, at least 14 members of his family were slain. When he was extradited to Italy, he sought assurance that he would be protected, should he talk and, when he did, authorities were amazed at the amount and detail of his accounts.

He provided a comprehensive description of the Mafia's internal structure and precise information on 122 recent murders. He explained the command structure and how each clan had its territorial base. Though each clan was autonomous, a supreme commission, composed of representatives from a dozen major families, made all decisions on crimes and investments and arbitrated disputes. He also provided previously unknown information about the mob operation in the U.S.

His lengthy confession, at 57, precipitated the most determined crack-down on organised crime that has ever been instigated.

Following his testimony 66 suspected Mafiosa were arrested, with warrants for another 140. He then effectively disappeared into the witness protection program, assuming a new name and identity somewhere in the U.S.[996]

These aspects can be found in the charts of cult leaders and I've included three here, two at the unconscious level and one at the spiritual level.

The first is Jim Jones, who was an American cult figure, the Leader of The People's Temple. He had Sedna conjunct Uranus in the third house of communication, quintile Makemake in the sixth house of daily routine.

When he was 46, he led his followers from San Francisco to Guyana. He was known as a manic-depressive who suffered from paranoia and delusions. However, he held an incredible power of persuasion and led nearly 1000 people, including himself, to a mass suicide a year later.

His mother was convinced that he was a messiah. His father, James Thurmond Jones, was a member of the Ku Klux Klan and died when Jim was young. His high-school classmates recall that he was popular but not a leader, noticing his growing interest in religion. After graduating from High School, he become a pastor of a Methodist church in Indianapolis, where his strong views on integration made him a target of bigots. Disenchanted with the Methodist faith, he created his own church, the Community National Church. At 25, he opened the first Peoples Temple in Indianapolis. The Temple formed a soup kitchen, an employment desk to help people find jobs, and a nursing home.

He moved the Temple to northern California, near Ukiah when he was 34. There he built a new flock using fraudulent "healing" performances to win worshipers and encouraged members to inform on spouses or children who transgressed his rules of loyalty. A hierarchy of trusted members formed, ones who would eventually help carry out his last order for mass suicide. Members' money and possessions were to be freely given to Jones at his command, along with sexual favours. At 40, he purchased new temples in San Francisco's Fillmore district and

---

[996] https://en.wikipedia.org/wiki/Tommaso_Buscetta

in Los Angeles. His public relations talents brought him political clout four years later, but it also brought the attention of newspaper reporters who amassed enough data to devastate The People's Temple.

When his strong-arm tactics to squelch the story failed, he prepared to move to a leased tract of 27,000 acres in Guyana. Black followers were told they would be placed in concentration camps if they remained behind and Whites were informed they were on a CIA "enemies" list along with threats of blackmail and reprisals against defectors. Jones managed to be in Guyana when the edition of "New West" appeared. Incredibly, in light of the cruelty, stealing and sexual pervasion revealed in the article, 800 people were ready to follow him to Guyana.

When Congressman Leo Ryan became concerned enough about the affairs of The People's Temple to embark on a fact-finding trip with Temple lawyers and a team of reporters, Jones' paranoia was at an all-time high. After a day and night at Jonestown, the Jones compound, Ryan and the reporters had ferreted out enough information to take home a negative report despite the Herculean attempts by Jones' followers to keep the compound an appearance of utopia. Ryan and his entourage were at the small airport an hour away from Jonestown preparing to return home when a tractor trailer pulled onto the runway with armed People's Temple gunmen.

They fired on the party, killing Ryan, several newsmen and Temple members attempting to leave with the congressional party. At the same time, the camp doctor was ordered to prepare a vat of strawberry flavor-aide, dumping in a quantity of painkillers and tranquilizers as well as jugs of cyanide. The members of Jonestown drank the poison as ordered and Jones put a bullet through his head. Over 900 bodies were counted. A box of over 800 passports was found, Social Security checks of elderly members and a million dollars in cash.[997]

Or like Marshall Applewhite, who was an American cult leader who led 39 members of "Heaven's Gate" to their death by suicide. He had Sedna

---

[997] https://en.wikipedia.org/wiki/Jim_Jones

in the first house of identity, conjunct Uranus and quintile Markemake, the planet of devotion, in the third house of communication.

He was married with two kids, when he left both his wife and the University of Alabama after a gay affair and his divorce after 16 years of marriage was a painful experience. Troubled by depression and sex demons, he checked into a hospital asking to be "cured" of his homosexual desires. When he met his new love, he was adrift, in debt, without his former social connections. With his career as a professional in doubt, he had found himself in a spiritual wasteland.

Everything came together for them both. They felt connected as soul mates and beings from another dimension. Their relationship was chaste, but their minds were complementary and their passions the same. They wanted to escape mankind's eternal predicament, to get out of life alive. They formed their own theology out of scripture and the occult.

They began an odyssey across America, recruiting members who were 'their people'. At first, they found their vision of eternity a hard sell and their bleak doctrine underwent a long gestation. It took nearly a year and a half to find their first disciple. She folded $25 into her pocket and left notes for her husband and daughters, the youngest of whom was a two-year-old, to follow her personal messiahs.

Only four weeks into the mission however, she began to have doubts about the divinity of their sojourn. The three were running up bills on her credit card, and Appelwhite had rented a car that he neglected to return. When they reached Houston, her family was waiting for them. She reunited with sanity, and Applewhite was arrested for car theft, spending six months in jail.

He used the time to polish his manifesto and when released in early 1975, unveiled his new, improved revelation. They would not take their bodies with them in death, but death would provide them with new bodies within the sacred furnace of space, as they were to be resurrected in a "cloud of light," a spaceship!

He carried his new doctrine to the fertile ground for Guru-UFO-revelation religions, California and had a meeting in Los Angeles with some 80 prospective devotees. Two dozen people joined, their first flock and they set up their center in a Wyoming campground and sent their followers out to canvass and recruit. The press began to catch wind of the story and the new cult soon reached the proportions of some 200.

At a gathering of the faithful in Medicine Bow National Forest in Wyoming, they were told that smoking grass and having sex was forbidden, stop it or leave, which left 70 people for instructions on The Next Level. One of these had a convenient trust fund and though strict living arrangements and spiritual disciplines were observed faithfully, the group also laughed and played together. They had a cheerful and highly regulated social life with total repression of sexuality.

However, the Next Level, that of leaving the earth in a space ship, remained elusive. Then when astronomers sighted the comet Halle-Bopp, Applewhite told them it was their message. A space ship was scheduled to be traveling in the wake of the comet that would pick up the cultists to go to the Next Level and he suggested that it would be necessary to take things into their own hands.

By then the group was running a computer-consulting business and living in a gated estate in California in an elegant house. Applewhite was 65. The group had settled to a small core of true believers who felt that it was time to get on with it. Farewell videos were bequeathed to the world. Happy prospects were written across photos and letters. The cult had gone on for 24 years when they left the earthly habitat for an eternity of their dreams.

Their bodies were found in the mansion near San Diego, where their macabre ritual had been carried out over the prior three days, as they took Phenobarbital in applesauce and vodka. They were all wearing new Nike shoes, had pockets full of quarters and were draped in purple cloths.[998]

As we tire of density and the grief it creates, and we start a spiritual journey to get out of the swamp, Sedna rewards us with transcendent crises, experiences which force us to let go and rise above them,

---

[998] https://en.wikipedia.org/wiki/Marshall_Applewhite

resulting in a huge growth to a new level of consciousness. There is no choice with these crises, and the more we try and 'solve them', the more we will just get hurt.

Like Skeeter Davis, who is an American musician with a career that was always eventful. She has Sedna conjunct Uranus in the third house of communication, quintile Makemake in the sixth house of daily routine.

> The eldest of seven kids, she formed a harmony group with her friend Betty Jack Davis and they called themselves The Davis Sisters. They began to play regular gigs on the radio in Lexington and on other shows in Detroit and Cincinnati before they signed a record contract. When she was 22 their first RCA release went to number one on the charts in 26 weeks.
>
> However, a car accident on the highway to Cincinnati killed Betty Jack and critically injured Skeeter, leading to a long rehabilitation period of recovery. She worked with Betty's sister for a while before going solo. At 28 she had a big breakthrough with 'Set Him Free', which established her as a star. And three years later 'The End of The World', went gold and put her in the world-class. Her heart is in country, though she does a variety of styles.[999]

Or like Debbie Reynolds, who was an American actress, dancer, stage entertainer and durable star, had Sedna conjunct Uranus, the planet of intuition, and Nessus, the centaur of 'making huge changes', and the Sun, the planet of will, all in the seventh house of relationships, quintile Makemake in the ninth house of new horizons and spirituality.

> As a young actress she had the adorable image of the all-American girl-next-door. She entered films in 1948 after winning the Miss Burbank beauty contest and played bouncy, wholesome parts through the '50s and '60s. In the early '70s as her film career ebbed, she starred on Broadway in a hit revival of "Irene," then in an extravagant revue, "The Debbie Reynolds Show."
>
> Her Sedna is also square the conjunction of Juno, the asteroid of partnership and Chariklo, the centaur of foresight, and Pluto, the planet of transformation, all in the tenth house of profession.

---

[999] https://en.wikipedia.org/wiki/Skeeter_Davis

She was married to singer Eddie Fisher for four years until he left her with two babies for Liz Taylor, eliciting a wave of sympathy from the public. Then she married 20-year-older wealthy shoe baron Harry Karl. A decade later his business failed and she became responsible for some $2 million of his debts. They divorced and she married real estate developer Richard Hamlett, who encouraged her to buy a run-down Las Vegas property for $3 million. She turned it into the Debbie Reynolds Hollywood Hotel Casino, putting about $5 million into the renovation. However, the club had continual business and money woes.

Early 1997, she and her ex-husband, Hamlett were sued for fraud and misrepresentation by a Colorado investment company and, with her Las Vegas hotel more than $7 million in debt, she filed for bankruptcy. The property went to auction and was sold for $9 million. Because the bid fell short of the $11.5 million that she owed, she became liable for the shortfall plus facing personal debts up to $100 million. Instead of facing a comfortable retirement, Reynolds, who made three movies the next year and worked weekends performing in clubs, faced having to start over again at 66.

'Life is both faith and love.' she once said. 'Without faith, love is only one dimensional and incomplete. Faith helps you to overlook other people's shortcomings and love them as they are. If you ask too much of any relationship, you can't help but be disappointed. But if you ask nothing, you can't be hurt or disappointed'.[1000]

As we see, the stressful aspects with Makemake can make us articulate and communicative. Self-assuredness, especially by verbal means, characterizes this planet. Its energy is clever, quick-witted and interested in invoking insight and inspiration.

Andy Warhol was an American underground artist and filmmaker who had a genius for creating attention. He had Sedna in the ninth house of knowledge, quintile Makemake in the eleventh house of collective consciousness.

[1000] https://en.wikipedia.org/wiki/Debbie_Reynolds

An androgyne and voyeur himself, his salon became the New York centre of the freak scene in the 1960s. When the pop-art movement exploded at the end of 1962, his drawings of soup cans and screens of the famous became hot property. He started film making in 1963, hovering in the twilight zone between reality and fantasy.

He designed ads for women's shoes before bursting upon the cultural scene in the early '60s. When he was 40 he was shot by a demented fan; after his recovery he was somewhat subdued, but still newsworthy in the '80s for his personal outrage of convention and aberrative entourage. He founded *Interview* magazine in the early forties and remained a pop-culture figure into his 50s.

On his death at 58 his estate was estimated to be worth $220 million. The year after his death the posthumous publication of *The Andy Warhol Diaries* hit the best seller list with their litany of limo's, dinners, tips, encounters, all the trivia of life among the 'beautiful people'. The book contained gossip on almost every star from Warhol's experience as a party fixture.[1001]

And Karl Marx, has Sedna in the first house, quintile with Makemake, conjunct Jupiter, the planet of philosophy, in the eleventh house of ideals. Social change, for Marx, was about conflict between opposing interests, driven, in the background, by economic forces. This became the inspiration for the body of works known as the conflict theory.

In his evolutionary model of history, he argued that human history began with free, productive and creative work that was over time coerced and dehumanised, a trend most apparent under capitalism. Fundamentally, he assumed that human history involves transforming human nature, which he saw, in a very Sednian way, as encompassing both human beings and material objects.

He believed, like the philosopher Hegel, that humans recognise that they possess both actual and potential selves and that self-development begins with an experience of internal alienation, which Marx argued was because of 'the despotism of capital'.

[1001] https://en.wikipedia.org/wiki/Andy_Warhol

This leads to a realisation that the actual self, as a subjective agent, renders its potential self as an object to be apprehended by capitalism. Marx further argued that by moulding nature in desired ways, the subject takes the object as its own, and thus permits the individual to be actualised as fully human.

In the new society that would emerge, he reasoned that the self-alienation would end, and humans would be free to act without being bound by the labour market. It would be a democratic society, enfranchising the entire population. In such a utopian world there would also be little if any need for a state, the goal of which was only to enforce the alienation.[1002]

Humour can be one path to transcend the quicksand of Sedna, giving us the objectivity to step back from the edge and also the opportunity with the inconjunct to Makemake to adopt a more playful approach to our particular area of devotion.

Bob Newhart is an American actor, comedian, recording artist, and TV series star. He has Sedna in the sixth house of daily routine, quintile Makemake in the ninth house of knowledge. His Sedna is also sextile Jupiter, the planet of expansion, in the eighth house of shared resources, and sesquiquadrate Neptune, the planet of imagination, in the tenth house of profession.

He is known for his deadpan double takes and cautious stammer, a master of the well-timed pause. His humour as a child was dry and low-key and he was, for the most part, shy and introspective. Comedy became his way of looking at life. He studied business and became an accountant and, to relieve the monotony, started doing comic improv with a friend at parties.

The duo became so popular that everyone encouraged them to play a pro venue. After a brief try, Bob's friend dropped out, but Bob continued to do the stand-up routine himself. One night a Warner Brothers Record scout caught Bob's act, and it led to his first recording. He was the first comedian in history to break into fame through LP records, "The Button-Down Mind Strikes Back," won a Grammy Award.[1003]

[1002] https://en.wikipedia.org/wiki/Karl_Marx
[1003] https://en.wikipedia.org/wiki/Bob_Newhart

At this juncture in human evolution, few of us use our planets at the spiritual level, but many of us are striving to, and such people are wonderful to be around. As with the other planets, the spiritual level of evolution is vastly different with Sedna from the two previous levels.

Here, the quintile and bi-quintile aspects with Makemake bring a courageous approach to life, giving us the willfulness to confront the peril required for discovery or spiritual evolution. The struggle of the beginner's level is gone, as are the transcendental crises of the intermediate level. At this level everything Saturnian is meaningless and yet everything has its place.

Philip K. Dick was an American writer notable for publishing works of science fiction. Dick explored philosophical, social, and political themes in novels with plots dominated by monopolistic corporations, authoritarian governments, alternate universes, and altered states of consciousness. His work reflected his personal interest in metaphysics and theology, and often drew upon his life experiences in addressing the nature of reality, identity, drug abuse, schizophrenia, and transcendental experiences.

He has Sedna in the first house of identity, square Makemake in the third house of communication. His stories typically focus on the fragile nature of what is real and the construction of personal identity. His stories often become surreal fantasies, as the main characters slowly discover that their everyday world is actually an illusion assembled by powerful external entities, vast political conspiracies or the vicissitudes of an unreliable narrator.

> All of his work starts with the basic assumption that there cannot be one, single, objective reality", writes science fiction author Charles Platt. "Everything is a matter of perception. The ground is liable to shift under your feet. A protagonist may find himself living out another person's dream, or he may enter a drug-induced state that actually makes better sense than the real world, or he may cross into a different universe completely.
>
> Alternate universes and simulacra are common plot devices, with fictional worlds inhabited by common, working people, rather than galactic elites. Dick's thinking and work was heavily influenced by the writings of Carl Jung. The Jungian constructs and models that most concerned Dick seem to be the archetypes

of the collective unconscious, group projection/hallucination, synchronicities, and personality theory

In the seventies, while recovering from the effects of sodium pentothal administered for the extraction of an impacted wisdom tooth, he began experiencing strange hallucinations. Although initially attributing them to side effects from medication, he considered this explanation implausible after they continued. He came to believe they imparted wisdom and clairvoyance. On one occasion the hallucinations imparted the information to him that his infant son was ill. The Dicks rushed the child to the hospital, where his suspicion was confirmed by professional diagnosis.

I experienced an invasion of my mind by a transcendentally rational mind, as if I had been insane all my life and suddenly I had become sane," Dick told Charles Platt. As the hallucinations increased in length and frequency, Dick claimed he began to live two parallel lives, one as himself, and one as "Thomas", a Christian persecuted by Romans in the first century AD. He referred to the "transcendentally rational mind" as "Zebra", "God" and "VALIS" and wrote about these experiences in his VALIS trilogy.[1004]

Although the Saturnian reality appears meaningless at this level, it still exists, so we are still likely to fall into spiritual traps if we conflate our ego needs with our spiritual mission. Like our third cult leader example with these aspects, our case study of new age guru, Bhagwan Shree Rajneesh, who has Sedna is in the eleventh house of collective consciousness, quintile Makemake in the first house of identity.

He was an Indian guru and author of more than a hundred books. He built a community in Oregon on ideals which included shared resources, which he then abused by manipulating followers and buying 93 Rolls-Royces with their money. To this day however, those same followers will tell you that this was just his way of teaching, his spiritual joke on American capitalism, and still support him because they learned something valuable in the process.

[1004] https://en.wikipedia.org/wiki/Philip_K._Dick

He was not only intimately familiar with the world's great religions and philosophies, but also the modern psychologies of Jung, Freud, Maslow, and the rest of the West's best thinkers in modern psychology and psychiatry. His syncretic teachings emphasise the importance of meditation, awareness, love, celebration, courage, creativity, and humour — qualities that he viewed as being suppressed by adherence to static belief systems and religious tradition.

When he was 50, he founded a commune in Oregon of 1,700 disciples, a sprawling religious community of a hundred square miles. The ashram was an attempt to build a self-sufficient commune based on ecological and organic farming principles, turning the desert into a garden, which they achieved in part. The devotees who joined came from all walks of life, devoting their money and labor to create a utopia. These years saw an increased emphasis on his prediction that the world might be destroyed by nuclear war. He predicted that, "the third and last war is now on the way" and frequently spoke of the need to create a 'new humanity' to avoid global suicide.

A key facet of his charismatic ability was that he was a brilliant manipulator of the unquestioning disciple. While his followers might be at a mere subsistence level, having severed ties with outside friends and family and donated all, or most of their money and possessions to the commune, he was seen to live in ostentation and offensive opulence, famously buying 93 Rolls-Royces as a so-called spiritual challenge to the commercial culture in America. Called the "sex-guru" because of his popular talks about tantric sex, his ashram became known as one big love fest during celebrations.

The task of running the commune fell to his personal secretary and the assets of the organization were all in her name. Almost immediately it ran into conflict with county residents and the state government and a succession of legal battles ensued, concerning the ashram's construction and continued development, which curtailed its success. In response he gave her power of attorney and she mounted a campaign of harassment and terrorism against the county. He was 50. Two years later she announced that he would henceforth speak only with her.

He had coached her in using media coverage to her advantage and during his period of public silence he privately stated that when she spoke, she was speaking on his behalf. However, he later alleged she committed crimes, included the attempted murder of his personal physician, poisonings of public officials, wiretapping and bugging within the commune and within his own home, and a bio-terror attack on the citizens of the Dalles, using salmonella to impact the county elections.

At 53, a few days after his secretary and her entire management team had suddenly left the commune for Europe, he held a press conference in which he labelled her and her associates a gang of fascists. He accused them of having committed a number of serious crimes and invited the authorities to investigate. He claimed that she was trying to establish the Rajneeshees as a religion, and that her quest for personal power led to her paranoia, which eventually spread throughout the commune. He spoke often of how organised religion is an obstacle to enlightenment and he blamed his secretary for her ambition of wanting to be the first Popess.

While his allegations were initially greeted with scepticism by outside observers, the subsequent investigation by the US authorities confirmed them and resulted in her conviction, along with several of her lieutenants. However, difficulties accumulated with the National Immigration Service and Inland Revenue Service, who were trying to deport him and he was arrested as he fled his strife-torn utopia at 53, on 35 counts of conspiracy and fraud. He was released and on his return to India, he changed his name to Osho to signal a change in his consciousness.[1005]

Antoine Court, who named himself Antoine Court de Gébelin, a former Protestant pastor, who initiated the interpretation of the Tarot as an arcane repository of timeless esoteric wisdom. He had Sedna in the second house of material reality, bi-quintile Makemake in the eighth house of the occult.

[1005] https://en.wikipedia.org/wiki/Rajneesh

His goal was to reconstruct what he believed to be the high primeval civilisation. Reinterpreting Classical and Renaissance evocation of the Golden Age into mankind's early history, he asserted that the primitive worldwide civilisation had been advanced and enlightened. He is the intellectual grandfather of much of modern occultism.

His centres of focus are the familiar ones of universal origins of languages in deep time and the hermeneutics of symbolism. While his views on hermeneutics and religious matters were largely conservative, his original ideas and research on the origin of language earn him a place among pioneers of linguistics.

He presented dictionaries of etymology, what he called a universal grammar, and discourses on the origins of language. His volumes were so popular he republished them separately. With regard to mythology and symbology, he discussed the origins of allegory in antiquity and recreated a history of the calendar from civil, religious, and mythological perspectives.

It was his immediate perception, the first time he saw the Tarot deck, that it held the secrets of the Egyptians. Writing without the benefit of deciphering of the Egyptian language, he developed a reconstruction of Tarot history, without producing any historical evidence, which was that Egyptian priests had distilled the ancient Book of Thoth into these images. These they brought to Rome, where they were secretly known to the popes, who brought them to Avignon in the 14th century, whence they were introduced into France.[1006]

[1006] https://en.wikipedia.org/wiki/Antoine_Court_de_Gébelin

42: Sedna / Haumea

Conjunction

There is no one alive today with this aspect and none occurs during the next century, so it is not interpreted here.

Opposition

There is no one alive today with this aspect and none occurs till much later this century, so it is not interpreted here.

Semi-sextile, Sextile, Trine

With the flowing aspects between Sedna and Haumea, the all-encompassing spiritual energy of Sedna aligns with our ability to make breakthroughs, to overcome fears and try new adaptive strategies, to extract the true essence of life from the dross of the world.

The energy of Haumea is earnest, vivid, alive with spirit and in touch with a transcendental magic of being. Haumea is always searching for spiritual answers, so can indicate mystical awareness and spiritual wealth and bring us the insight to see the divinity of human beings and the oneness of existence.

At the unconscious level, even the flows between these two planets can be challenging, as we'll see in the following examples, just because their energies are so ethereal that we have no practical way of dealing with it and may fall victim to a constant and idle daydreaming or engage in a spiritual deception.

Like Maria Silbert, who was an Austrian trance medium who channeled her spirits but was exposed for a slight of hand artist. She had Sedna in the sixth house of service, semi-sextile Haumea in the seventh house of relationships.

> She claimed the power to teleport inanimate objects and also move them by thought, as well as the ability to produce "spirit raps". Her famous trick was to engrave cigarette cases under the table during her séances. She allowed some lighting in her séances but did not allow investigators to look under the table where most of her phenomena was said to occur.[1007]

[1007] https://en.wikipedia.org/wiki/Maria_Silbert

Her Sedna was in an evolutionary bi-quintile to Pallas, the asteroid of wisdom, but it was also semi-square Pluto, the planet of transformation, in the eighth house of the occult and sesquiquadrate the Moon, the planet of empathy, in the eleventh house of collective consciousness.

> A psychical researcher caught her using her feet and toes to move objects in the séance room. And another discovered how she performed the cigarette trick. She had developed the ability to manoeuvre a stiletto using only her feet and was thus able to write names on the cigarette cases when they were held under the table. It was also observed that the "spirit raps" only occurred when she had her legs under the table, or in front of the chair, which suggested that she tapped the furniture herself with her feet to makes the sounds.[1008]

Or we might become trapped in someone else's spiritual deception, which unfortunately can lead to physical abuse. Like Carla Flanagan, who is an American battered wife whose history of abuse began nine weeks before her wedding. Her Sedna is in the fourth house of home, trine the conjunction of Haumea and of Pluto, the planet of transformation, in her ninth house of knowledge. Sedna is also in a stressful sesquiquadrate to her Sun, the planet of willpower, again in the ninth house and in a fateful inconjunct with Juno, the asteroid of partnership, also in the ninth.

> In what prosecutors called one of the worst cases of domestic abuse her husband admitted to ritualistically beating her, his son and two daughters with bats, chair legs and sticks in an attempt to control their every move. He lacked self-esteem, self-worth and self-dignity after losing six jobs and was affected by the pressure of his wife, a nurse, being the sole "bread winner" of the family. She now suffers chronic headaches and other stress-related ailments.[1009]

Her Sedna is also opposite Venus, the planet of relationships, and Ceres, the planet of nurturing, and Neptune, the planet of deception, all in the tenth house of social standing.

[1008] Ibid.

[1009] Flanagan gets 9-11 years; Apologizes to family for abuse by David Linton, Sun Chronicle, Mar 30, 2000

He threatened to kill his three children if they told anybody of the frequent beatings they received, which were administered in areas where he hoped bruises wouldn't be noticeable, authorities said. And the judge said Flanagan only permitted his children to use the bathroom with his permission, beating them if they failed to comply with his authority.

A Department of Social Services investigation that found he beat his three children, between the ages of 7 and 15, with a variety of weapons, including sticks and baseball bats. He also threatened to kill his wife of 18 years, on multiple occasions and has been accused of two counts of attempted murder, for twice attempting to strangle her.

His daily activity included keeping a detailed journal, lists or notes of every minute observation he made inside and outside the house, every car that passed, every person he saw. He obsessively compiled these notes for hours and, all the while, demanded complete silence from his family under penalty of violent beatings.[1010]

Fortunately, Carla's Sedna is also in an evolutionary bi-quintile with Mercury, the planet of communication. She still limps and the kids are learning not to wince. And they still have nightmares and are all in counselling. However, she now counsels other women trying to leave untenable situations and she is working on a book to help women recognize and reject the victim syndrome.

Or we might abuse others, or condone abuse, because of our deluded beliefs. Like Wilhelm Keitel, who was a German Nazi Field Marshall and Chief of Staff of the High Command of the German Armed Forces under Hitler. He has Sedna in the ninth house of knowledge, sextile Haumea in the tenth house of profession. His Sedna is also trine Ixion, the planet of lawlessness, in the twelfth house of the unconscious and semi-square Neptune, the planet of delusions, in the tenth house of profession.

He was Hitler's closest military advisor and second only to him. At the start of the war he took over the Axis African Command. He condoned measures leading to mass murder in Poland and Russia. Described as hard, unsmiling and mysterious, he was

---

[1010] http://www.southcoasttoday.com/article/19990924/news/309249958

tried by the International Military Tribunal, found guilty of war crimes and crimes against humanity, and hanged in Nuremberg Prison.[1011]

Christopher Boyce is an American spy, the son of a former FBI agent who had an affluent upbringing and a high IQ. Boyce had a job at a top-secret CIA code room, where he had access to America's most sensitive satellite system's documents. He has Sedna conjunct the eleventh house cusp, the house of ideals, trine Haumea in his second house of material resources. His Haumea is conjunct Pluto however, the planet of the underworld and his Sedna is opposite Saturn, the planet of authority.

> He stole and sold information to Russian agents in Mexico and was arrested and tried and given a prison term of 40 years. However, he hated prison and escaped, hiding out and robbing banks for 19 months, before being captured again and given an extra 28 years.

> In jail he was beaten by the prison's Aryan Brotherhood gang after telling Australian TV that espionage was "high adventure" and that he had "no problem with the label "traitor." He was then moved to maximum security, where he lived in solitary confinement at the end of a corridor underneath the prison hospital. This was a dismal sequence of days that consisted of cockroaches, ants and flies for the next six years. Every day was a repeat of the previous and he wrote that he felt "submerged, alone, in a submarine."

> However, he took courses in art and history and earned a BA, consistently getting A's and earning the praise of his instructors. And he started to write for the Minneapolis newspaper with many pieces addressing prison reform. He broke down in tears at his review board hearing under the weight of so much of life's time lost. Sentenced to be in prison until 2046, he showed himself such a model prisoner that he was released in 2003.[1012]

As we tire of density and the grief it creates, and we start a spiritual journey to get out of the swamp, Sedna rewards us with transcendent crises, experiences which force us to let go and rise above them,

---

[1011] https://en.wikipedia.org/wiki/Wilhelm_Keitel

[1012] https://en.wikipedia.org/wiki/Christopher_John_Boyce

resulting in a huge growth to a new level of consciousness. There is no choice with these crises, and the more we try and solve them, the more we will get hurt.

With Haumea there is often a profound idealism, a passionate belief in the humanizing and social function of art and a sense of freedom as the highest principle and these themes may be evident in the crises we face.

Like Hugo Ball, who was a German author, poet and one of the leading Dada artists. He had Sedna in the ninth house of publishing, sextile Haumea in the eleventh house of collective consciousness.

When he was 24 he moved to Berlin in order to become an actor and collaborated with Max Reinhardt. At the beginning of the First World War he tried joining the army as a volunteer but was denied enlistment for medical issues. After witnessing the invasion of Belgium, he was disillusioned saying: "The war is founded on a glaring mistake; men have been confused with machines".

Considered a traitor in his country, he crossed the frontier with his wife and settled in Zürich. Here, he continued his interest in anarchism, rejecting its militant aspects and viewing it as only a means to his personal goal of enlightenment.

He was 30 when he created the Dada Manifesto, making a political statement about his views on the terrible state of society and acknowledging his dislike for philosophies in the past claiming to possess the ultimate Truth. The same year as the Manifesto, he wrote his poem "Karawane," which is a German poem consisting of nonsensical words. The meaning however resides in its meaninglessness, reflecting the chief principle behind Dadaism.

As co-founder of the Cabaret Voltaire in Zürich, he led the Dada movement in Zürich, and is one of the people credited with naming the movement "Dada", by allegedly choosing the word at random from a dictionary. His involvement with the Dada movement lasted less than two years. He then worked for a short period as a journalist, for Freie Zeitung in Bern. After returning to

Catholicism at 34, he retired and lived a religious and relatively poor life, dying at 41.[1013]

Our case study, Osama bin Laden, has Sedna in the eleventh house of ideals, trine Haumea in the third house of ideas. A psychology paper 'characterizing the evolution, meaning-making, and cognitive complexity of Osama bin Laden using the developmental framework of Robert Kegan's Theory of Self-Evolution' argues:

> There is evidence of bin Laden functioning at different developmental stages varying by life domain. He was simultaneously simple and complex, both constructing and operating within a world that was, in his perspective, absolute in some domains and relative in others.
>
> Ideologically, he adhered to one simple, absolute reality rooted in his interpretation of fundamentalist Islam, reflecting a lack of perspective-taking ability and systematic thinking. But what made bin Laden exceedingly dangerous and particularly interesting from a developmental perspective is the fact that this low-stage ideological orientation was complemented by an extremely complex leadership style and administrative disposition that encouraged members to contribute uniquely to, and take ownership of the process.
>
> As a leader, and for purposes of furthering the goals of the institution, bin Laden's ability to organize both his experience and that of others is indicative of a higher-order understanding. His ability to lead is equivalent of a "first-rate innovator" and a "hugely successful" and "out-of-the-box-thinking CEO" in this regard. In leading al Qaeda, bin Laden operates as a businessman and ideologue, soliciting creative ideas from those around him for purposes of furthering the larger institution.
>
> Bin Laden's understanding of how al Qaeda, as a meta-system comprised of a myriad of terrorist sub- organisations, has the potential to impact another system, like the United States, itself comprised of many sub-systems, such as economic and social domains, is evidence of a more complex, systematic ability to think.

[1013] https://en.wikipedia.org/wiki/Hugo_Ball

This ability is reflected in how bin Laden and his organisation go about picking targets, and the extent to which they commit themselves to the task - to the point where operatives train for years, in their enemies' own homeland, to learn how to fly airplanes, for example. Not only does this reflect an ability to both integrate and synthesise multiple competing perspectives, it also evidences a propensity towards systematic and dialectic understanding.

His evolution in consciousness was also evidenced by bin Laden shifting from actively fighting as one of the mujahideen towards directing them in the jihad against the Soviets. That a multi-millionaire would relegate himself to these sorts of duties was inspiring to those fighting with him. As a result, many began to look to him as a leader, another external factor fuelling his transformation.[1014]

Interestingly, the man who brought him down, Barack Obama, also has a trine. Barack's Sedna is in the second house of material resources, trine the conjunction of Haumea together with Uranus, the planet of diversity, in the seventh house of relationships. His religious background is more diverse than that of most prominent politicians, but it may prove to be more representative of an increasingly diverse America.

His mother was raised by non-practicing Christians; his father was raised a Muslim but was an atheist by the time he had married Obama's mother. His step-father was also Muslim, but of an eclectic kind who could make room for animist and Hindu beliefs.

In his book, *The Audacity of Hope*, he writes, 'I was not raised in a religious household. For my mother, organised religion was too often dressed up closed-mindedness in the garb of piety, cruelty and oppression in the cloak of righteousness. However, in her mind, a working knowledge of the world's great religions was a necessary part of any well-rounded education. In our house the Bible, the Koran, sat on the shelf alongside books of Greek and Norse and African mythology.'

[1014] Sinclair, Samuel and LoCicero, Alice. "Osama bin Laden: A Developmental Perspective" Volume 5, No. 1, 2007.

As a child in Indonesia, he studied for two years at one Muslim school and then two years at a Catholic school. Eventually however, he abandoned this non-conformism and skepticism as an adult to be baptised in the Trinity United Church of Christ, a denomination which emphasises the freedom of the individual conscience over adherence to creeds or hierarchical authority.[1015]

In the next three examples we see how with these aspects the rebirth energy of Haumea can encourage us to play a leading role in the evolutionary process. And we also see the link between evolution and climate change.

The father of the Theory of Evolution, Charles Darwin, had Sedna in the third house of ideas, sextile Haumea, which is together with his Moon, the planet of emotions, in the second house of material resources. This placement is very appropriate for the person who integrated emotions into the traditional philosophical categories of mind and body.

He examined human evolution and emotions in his book, *The Expression of the Emotions in Man and Animals*, which looks at genetically determined aspects of behaviour. In this book, Darwin seeks to trace the origins of such human characteristics as the pursing of the lips in moments of concentration and the mental confusion which typically accompanies blushing.

Before Darwin, human emotional life had posed problems to the traditional philosophical categories of mind and body. Darwin's biological approach links mental states to the neurological organization of movement and the book forms his main contribution to psychology.

Darwin said, "I never gave up Christianity until I was forty years of age." He then agreed that Christianity was "not supported by the evidence", but he had reached this conclusion only slowly. However, his Theory of Evolution is recognised as having impacted massively on human societies across the World, not least in the areas of faith and religious beliefs. These diverse impacts on so many aspects of human lives have been so far-

---

[1015] https://en.wikipedia.org/wiki/Barack_Obama

reaching that a "Darwinian Revolution" has been accepted as having taken place.[1016]

Interestingly, Darwin hesitated about making his theory widely known in his own lifetime. His wife was sincerely religious and he also seems to have feared for his own and his family's perceived respectability if he made his potentially massively controversial evolutionary views public.

Our case study, Sally Ride, the first American woman in space, has Sedna in the tenth house of profession, trine Haumea in the second house of material resources. This aspect is part of a grand trine with Chariklo, the centaur of foresight, in the sixth house of service.

> Sally's parents were both Presbyterian elders in California, where she grew up with her sister, who, as an adult is leading her own Presbyterian congregation. Sally, however, announced in junior high school that she was done with church.

> "There are a lot of people who have asked me since I've come back whether I found religion in space," she said in a TV interview, "or whether I had any mystical experiences up there. And no!"

> Another TV interviewer asked: "Was it spiritual as you kissed the heavens?" Sally responded smoothly, "You know, what was absolutely amazing to me was the feeling I had looking back at earth . . . it's remarkable how beautiful our planet is, and how fragile it looks".[1017]

She was charged with coming up with new directions for NASA after the Challenger Shuttle disaster and this trine is strongly evident in her final report to NASA, recommending the Mission to Planet Earth.

> In the report, she weighed four recommendations: sending humans to Mars, exploring the solar system, creating a space station on the moon, and the one she was most passionate about, organising a mission to Planet Earth. Internally, NASA favoured big projects that ignited the imagination and the longtime heavyweights wanted a mission to Mars; Ride argued for an approach more beneficial to the planet.

[1016] https://en.wikipedia.org/wiki/Charles_Darwin
[1017] https://en.wikipedia.org/wiki/Sally_Ride

Mission to Planet Earth's goal was to use space technology to understand Earth as a total system, to learn how man-made and natural shifts affect the environment. "This initiative," she wrote, "directly addresses the problems that will be facing humanity in the coming decades, and its continuous scientific return will produce results which are of major significance to all the residents of the planet." Finally, with the Mission to Planet Earth, she had an answer to those questions she had about seeing Earth from space. The astrophysicist in her saw a fragile planet and her greatest legacy is convincing NASA that Earth is worth trying to protect.[1018]

And climate change activist, Al Gore, also has Sedna in the tenth in a trine to the conjunction of Haumea and Mars, the planet of action, in the first house of identity, showing how he has been able to reenergize the environmental movement by his actions.

Premiering at the 2006 Sundance Film Festival and opening in New York City and Los Angeles his film, *An Inconvenient Truth* was a critical and box office success, winning two Academy Awards for Best Documentary Feature and Best Original Song. The film grossed $24 million in the U.S. and $26 million in the foreign box office, becoming the tenth highest grossing documentary film to date in the United States. Since the film's release, it has been credited for raising international public awareness of global warming and reenergising the environmental movement.[1019]

At this juncture in human evolution, few of us use our planets at the spiritual level, but many of us are striving to, and such people are wonderful to be around. As with the other planets, the spiritual level of evolution is vastly different with Sedna from the two previous levels.

Here, the flowing aspects with Haumea bring a real connection with the transcendental magic of being, a spiritual wealth and an understanding of the divinity of human beings and the oneness of existence. The struggle of the beginner's level is gone, as are the transcendental crises of the intermediate level. At this level everything Saturnian is meaningless and yet everything Sednian has its place.

[1018] Ibid.
[1019] https://en.wikipedia.org/wiki/Al_Gore

Case study, Ray Kurzweil, scientist, inventor, futurist, has Sedna in the sixth house of service, part of a grand trine with Haumea conjunct Saturn, the planet of structure, in the tenth house of occupation. These planets are also conjunct both the MC and Pluto. the planet of transformation, which is in the ninth, the house of philosophy and ideas. This is a powerful picture of Ray's evolutionary influence.

He was born to secular Jewish parents who had emigrated from Austria just before the onset of World War II. He was exposed via Unitarian Universalism to a diversity of religious faiths during his upbringing. His Unitarian church had the philosophy of many paths to the truth – the religious education consisted of spending six months on a single religion before moving onto the next. As an adult Kurzweil is agnostic about the existence of a soul. On the possibility of divine intelligence, he is quoted as saying, "Does God exist? I would say, 'Not yet.'

His singularity is a hypothesised time in the future, approximately 2045, when the capabilities of non-living electronic machines will supersede human capabilities. Undismissible contemporary thinkers like Elon Musk and Stephen Hawking warn us that it will change everything. Hawking likens it to receiving a message from aliens announcing their arrival in "a few decades," saying this is "more or less" what's happening with artificial intelligence software.

Talk of the singularity ripples with religious undertones: It's obsessed with the unknown future and assumes the arrival of a superior entity down the road. It has its naysayers and true believers alike, each eager to tell you why, or why not, such an entity will actually show up. Some believe Artificial Spiritual Intelligence is the new God and that Kurzweil is his prophet.

Others see him as evidence for the post-secularisation hypothesis that religion is not at all dying but is merely continuing to evolve. They argue that he is probably by far the most influential Singularitarian in the world and perhaps the most influential living futurist, and he got there by directly engaging in post-secular rhetoric.

The most obvious example can be found in the title of the book, *The Age of Spiritual Machines*, that made him a thought leader and no longer only an inventor or entrepreneur. Furthermore, although an atheist or agnostic, he chooses explicitly to leverage references to "God" inside his books, as at least a literary device, if not a vision for the future of humanity. They argue his success in doing these things speaks to the persisting power of religion.[1020]

William Butler Yeats, the famous Irish writer, a poet and dramatist who won a Nobel Prize for Literature, has Sedna in his first house of identity, semi-sextile Haumea in his second house of material resources.

He was first published at age 21 with elaborate early work. As he became noted as a poet and novelist, his works became more simplified, while his own philosophy developed in complexity. The complex man was at once courteous and self-centred, gregarious, and spiritually and intellectually questing. He was a hobby astrologer with a very active interest in mysticism.[1021]

He had a finger of fate pointing to Sedna, with one inconjunct with the Node in eighth house of the occult and the other with Nessus, the centaur of 'sweeping way the old' in the seventh house of relationships. His Sedna is also in an evolutionary quintile with Ceres, the planet of nurturing in fourth house of home.

He believed that "the sexual principle lies at the heart of all behaviour as well as history." His lovers were a spur to his poetry, taking him and his readers to a brink "beyond human notes nor words to dwell upon the soul's destiny. His somewhat astrological work, *A Vision*, resulted from a collaboration with his wife, who worked for many years with automatic writing, penning messages from the spirit masters. Her automatic writings fuelled the book that involves a unique approach to the twenty-eight phases of the Moon.[1022]

And Tracy Marks is an American psychotherapist, astrologer, lecturer and teacher who is the author of 15 books and pamphlets which have been translated into nearly a dozen languages. She has Sedna in the

---

[1020] Love, Dylan. 'Artificial intelligence will make religion obsolete within our lifetime,' dailydot.com, Aug 5, 2015
[1021] https://en.wikipedia.org/wiki/W._B._Yeats
[1022] Ibid.

fourth house of home, trine Haumea in the eighth house of sensitivity to the spirit world.

> She has a master's degree in psycho-synthesis and is acclaimed for her in-depth integration of psychological, spiritual and astrological concepts. She is skilled at leading dream work, women's empowerment, and the art of friendship groups. Some of her more notable books include *How To Handle Your T-Square, The Astrology of Self Discovery*, and *The Art Of Chart Interpretation*.[1023]

Semi-square, Square, Sesquiquadrate

With the stressful aspects between Sedna and Haumea, the all-encompassing spiritual energy of Sedna challenges our ability to make breakthroughs, to overcome fears and try new adaptive strategies in our attempts to extract the true essence of life from the dross of the world.

The energy of Haumea is earnest, vivid, alive with spirit and in touch with a transcendental magic of being. Haumea is always searching for spiritual answers, so can indicate mystical awareness and spiritual wealth and bring us the insight to see the divinity of human beings and the oneness of existence.

The stressful aspects between these two planets can be very challenging at the unconscious level because the energies of these planets are so ethereal that we have no practical way of dealing with it and may fall victim to a constant and idle daydreaming or engage in a spiritual deception.

Like Henri Girard, who was a French sociopath, murderer and suicide victim. He had Sedna in the third house of communication, semi-square the conjunction of Haumea and Pallas, the asteroid of wisdom, in the fifth house of creativity.

> Well educated, he began what might have been a successful military career by joining the French regiment of the 4th Hussars. However, at 22 he was dishonorably discharged. He continued to make a living as a petty swindler including illegal gambling and insurance fraud. During this time, he had an interest in bacteriology and poisons was experimenting with cultures of

---

[1023] https://www.astro.com/astro-databank/Marks,_Tracy

typhoid bacilli, both at his home and at a secret laboratory in the home of his mistress.

He moved to Paris where he founded a bogus insurance company and was then banned and fined for deceptive practices. Undeterred, when he was 34 he befriended a wealthy insurance broker, who seemed willing to go along with his scams. It may have been a business arrangement or part of an elaborate plan to defraud; whatever, they signed into a joint life insurance policy payable to each-other upon the death of the other.

Cause of death was diagnosed as typhoid, which was not unusual in the early 19th century. Hence, he received a sizable sum of money upon the insurance payout. He tried infecting two more people who did not die and, aware that using cultures of typhoid as a poison could not be relied upon to kill his victims he began experimenting with poisonous mushrooms.

When he was confident that he had developed a poison that would kill. He was also desperate for money and decided to go for a multiple insurance payout against his next victim. This was family friend Madam Monin. His mistress, claiming to be Madam Monin, insured herself with three different companies that would payout substantial sums of money upon her death, payable to him.

Shortly after; Madame Monin accepted an invitation to dine with him and his wife at their home. During her return home Madame Monin fell ill in the street and died. Two of the insurance companies paid out on the policies but the third became skeptical in that the deceased was a young healthy woman. They also believed that the woman who had taken the original medical examination prior to granting the insurance policy was an impostor; thus they refused to pay out, and instigated an investigation by the police.[1024]

Or Josef Mengele, the Nazi angel of death. He had Sedna conjunct Orcus in the tenth house of profession, square Haumea on ASC, and opposite the Moon in the fourth house of home. His Sedna is also bi-

---

[1024] https://owlcation.com/humanities/Criminal-Law-Murder-by-Poison

quintile Ixion, the planet of lawlessness, in the third house of communication and quintile Uranus on the eighth house cusp.

> He was a German physician and member of the Nazi party who was known as the "Angel of Death" at the Auschwitz concentration camp during World War II for his grisly genetic research on twins and other subjects. He was the subject of a 40-year international hunt in the postwar years, known for being the butcher who had supervised the torture and death of as many as 400,000 Jews in a maniacal quest for racial purity.[1025]

Another example is Charles Baudelaire, who was a French poet tormented by religion and the struggle between good and evil in man, suffused with his deeply Catholic sense of sin and remorse. His Sedna is in the seventh house of relationships, semi-square Haumea in the fifth house of creativity. It was also trine the conjunction of the Moon, the planet of emotions and Vesta, the asteroid of home, in the eleventh house of collective consciousness.

> He was a Catholic and a Satanist, a debauchee and mystic, cynical sensualist and yearner for purity. Sexually morbid and a sadist, he sought the unbathed women "of the streets." In his extraordinarily complicated life, he had a suffocatingly intimate relationship with his bewildered mother, who lovingly nurtured and then callously ignored his lifelong dependence on her which reached classically Oedipal proportions.

> After his dad died his mom remarried a dour career diplomat who, disgusted by his high-strung stepson's eccentricities, tried to impose military standards of discipline and conduct, values that Baudelaire disavowed in a rebellion that lasted the rest of his life. By the time he came into his inheritance from his birth father, he was already exorbitantly precocious and foppish, squandering over a half of his considerable fortune in 18 months.

> His taste ran to elegant fashion, and he would have gone through the entire amount had not his stepfather brought the spending spree to a halt with legal intervention. Much to his humiliation, Baudelaire was then forced to petition an attorney for his funds, cap in hand, living on a meagre monthly allowance.

[1025] https://en.wikipedia.org/wiki/Josef_Mengele

His spending spree was the only time in his short and miserable life that he was ever without financial stress.

He lived in dilapidated fleabag hotels, eking out a precarious existence as a poet, art critic and translator of Edgar Allan Poe. He changed his address in Paris about 30 times during his adult life, once moving six times in a single month to evade creditors.[1026]

His Sedna is also bi-quintile Orcus, the planet of delving down and speaking out, which is on the cusp of his third house of communication.

His writings were not only scandalous, but paid poorly, and he once remarked that his income for years was the equivalent of the price of two cigars a day. His *Flowers of Evil* was condemned as immoral and confiscated by authorities for offending public morals.[1027]

Or we could become a victim to believing what we want to about people and so overlooking someone else's psychic deception. Like George Van Tassel, who was an American UFO enthusiast who, at one time, held a yearly UFO conference at his private airport in California. He has Sedna in the sixth house of service, square Haumea in the ninth house of knowledge and opposite Jupiter, the planet of expansion, in the twelfth house of the unconscious.

He stated that after his first sighting he contacted outer-space beings repeatedly in person and in trance. The beings reportedly instructed him to build a machine to heal and bring the dead back to life. For many years he collected funds for his project, until he died. His Sedna was conjunct Orcus, the planet of speaking out and conjunct the Moon, the planet of the emotions. It was also and bi-quintile Ixion, the planet of lawlessness. He died of an "apparent heart attack" in his Pasadena, CA hotel room according to his second wife who was with him at the time.

However, others in his family did not buy this explanation and they believed he had been poisoned. According to his mother and others, he had been very healthy with no history of heart problems. Furthermore, they claimed, his wife at the time of his

---

[1026] https://en.wikipedia.org/wiki/Charles_Baudelaire
[1027] Ibid.

death was a chiropractor whose two previous husbands had died under mysterious circumstances. In addition, they cited the fact that she had the body cremated immediately after his death and before the rest of the family had been notified.[1028]

Or, like William Shockley, the American physicist and father of Silicon Valley, we might imprison ourselves in our own delusions. He had Sedna in the twelfth house of the unconscious, square Haumea in the third house of ideas. His Sedna is also bi-quintile Ixion, the planet of lawlessness and conjunct Orcus, the planet of delving down and speaking out.

> He co-invented the transistor, an invention that changed the course of history for computers and electronics in a big way and he was awarded many prizes and received many honours culminating in the Nobel Prize for Physics. His contributions during the WWII were numerous. He worked in Bell Labs but his abrasive management style caused him to run his own company. He became increasing paranoid and because of that his team broke up, spawning Silicon Valley.

> In his later years he slipped into eugenics, the belief that humanity would be better served by only allowing the smart and healthy to breed. He was attacked for this in print, on television and in scientific journals, became estranged from all his friends and his last years were a very sad.[1029]

As we tire of density and the grief it creates, and we start a spiritual journey to get out of the swamp, Sedna rewards us with transcendent crises, experiences which force us to let go and rise above them, resulting in a huge growth to a new level of consciousness. There is no choice with these crises and the more we try and solve them, the more we will get hurt.

With Haumea there is often a profound idealism, a passionate belief in the humanizing and social function of art and a sense of freedom as the highest principle and these themes may be evident in the crises we face.

Simone de Beauvoir was a French writer and existentialist teacher who fashioned an impressive literary career as a novelist, philosopher,

---

[1028] https://en.wikipedia.org/wiki/George_Van_Tassel
[1029] https://en.wikipedia.org/wiki/William_Shockley

essayist and writer of memoirs. She had Sedna in the fourth house of home, square Haumea in the eighth house of shared resources.

> She was the eldest daughter of a middle-class lawyer, raised Catholic with a convent education. She was deeply religious as a child, at one point intending to become a nun, but experienced a crisis of faith at age 14 and sided with her dad as an atheist, and remaining an atheist for the rest of her life. She looked on marriage as an obscene, bourgeois institution that put women in an inferior position. In rejecting marriage, she also rejected children, noting that she had escaped most of women's bondages.

> She was a prominent member of the young avant-garde Parisian intelligentsia in the '40s, she was the presiding celebrity of the Existentialist movement along with Jean Paul Sartre, who was her life companion in an open relationship. They never lived in the same residence, nor did they require sexual fidelity of each other, but they did keep a close and steady relationship, seeing each other daily from the time they met at the Sorbonne when she was 21, until Sartre died 50 years later.[1030]

Her Sedna was also closely bi-quintile Ixion, the planet of lawlessness in the ninth house of higher education.

> She had a very turbulent, often scandalous life. Although she had a longtime relationship with Sartre, she was known to have a number of female lovers. The nature of some of these relationships, some of which she began with underage students while working as a professor, later led to a controversy.

> A former student wrote in her book that, while she was a student at Lycée Molière, she had been sexually exploited by her teacher de Beauvoir, who was in her 30s at the time. She and Jean-Paul Sartre developed a pattern, which they called the "trio", in which de Beauvoir would seduce her students and then pass them on to Sartre. Finally, she was suspended from her teaching job, when she was accused of seducing a 17-year-old pupil. The girl's parents laid formal charges against her for debauching a

---

[1030] https://en.wikipedia.org/wiki/Simone_de_Beauvoir

minor and she had her license to teach in France permanently revoked.[1031]

The esoteric energies of the newly discovered dwarf planets like Haumea permeate our lives at all levels and make the distinctions of 'unconscious', 'on the path' and 'spiritually developed' are harder to make.

A good example is L. Ron Hubbard, an American entrepreneur, engineer, and prolific writer of science fiction, who established the Church of Scientology. He has Sedna in the third house of ideas, square Haumea in the seventh house of relationships.

> Imaginative, intelligent, and with a mind that was a factory of ideas, he was also broke and in debt in the late 1940s and was forced to sell his typewriter for $28.50 to pay alimony to his first wife. Troubled, restless and adrift he became an expert hypnotist, and shared an ageing mansion in Pasadena, CA with writers, artists, Bohemians and occultists in the late 1940s. Neighbours complained when their rituals of sexual magic got out of hand in the back yard.[1032]

His Sedna was also conjunct Orcus, the planet of delving down and speaking out in the fourth house of home.

> He wrote a book, *Dianetics: The Modern Science of Mental Health*, which was written in one draft in 30 days and became an instant bestseller. He became an overnight celebrity. His system became known as "the poor man's psychotherapy." However, by the following year profits were beginning to fall and Dianetics became Scientology, as he turned from pop therapist to religious leader.

> Skillfully transforming himself from a pulp fiction writer to a writer of "sacred scriptures," Hubbard made a fortune and achieved his dream of fame. Starting as a collection of mental therapy centers it grew into one of the world's most controversial and secretive religions. The courses included instruction of how to help kick drug habits, improve communication skills, build confidence and help people take control of their lives.

[1031] Ibid.
[1032] https://en.wikipedia.org/wiki/L._Ron_Hubbard

However, by preying on the anxieties and the loneliness of his converts and by using hypnotherapy, Pavlovian conditioning and twisted psychotherapy, he was able to establish himself as the leader of a movement of millions, less than 900 of which ever reached the highest levels of his imparted wisdom. Australian courts have since revoked the status of Scientology as a religion, and France convicted Hubbard in absentia of fraud. However, in spite of all the exposure, he still ignited the fire of self-improvement in many sincere people.[1033]

Alan Turing, a British mathematician, logician, scientist and the technical genius behind Britain's successful efforts to break German codes in World War II, has Sedna in the 12th house of the unconscious, square to Haumea, which is right on the cusp of the third house of communication.

He made inestimable contributions to cybernetics. His 'Computable Numbers', published when he was 25, is considered one of the outstanding scientific papers of the 20th century, a blueprint for what would become the electronic digital computer. His 'Universal Turing Machine' was an ancestor for the entire information age.

He was accustomed to being a non-conformist. At boarding school, he refused to adapt and ignored subjects that did not interest him. He was an atheist, and felt marginalised because of his homosexuality. From the age if 13 he formed a significant friendship with another boy who has been described as his 'first love'. Their relationship provided inspiration in his future endeavours, but it was cut short by his friend's death when Alan was 17, from drinking infected cow's milk some years previously. The event caused him great sorrow and he coped with this by working that much harder on the topics of science and mathematics that he had shared with his friend.[1034]

His Sedna is also conjunct Chariklo, the centaur of foresight and bi-quintile Ixion, the planet of lawlessness.

Though he envisioned a time when "ladies will take their computers for walks in the park," his own reality was not quite so

---

[1033] Ibid.

[1034] https://en.wikipedia.org/wiki/Alan_Turing

whimsical. When a robbery occurred at his house in Manchester, he frankly told the police that the robber probably knew the man with whom he was having an affair. As homosexual relations were still a felony in Britain, he was tried and convicted of gross indecency. He was spared prison but was given a year's probation with the condition that he take oestrogen to diminish his sex drive.[1035]

Humour can be one path to transcend the quicksand of Sedna, giving us the objectivity to step back from the edge, and also with Haumea, a sensitivity to the transcendental magic of being and an ability to extract the true essence of life from the dross of the world, which is the essence of good comedy. Developing our sense of humour will definitely help if we're struggling with these stressful aspects.

Jacques Tati is a French actor, writer and director. He has Sedna in the eighth house of shared resources, square Haumea, which right on the cusp of the eleventh house of collective consciousness.

He was noted for his wonderful talents of wit, humour and humanity. He started in the theatre, turning music and cabaret into a mime comedy work of art, which became an immediate success. He turned several of his showpieces into short films, by writing and producing them himself. His Sedna is also quintile Mars, the planet of action in the fifth house of creativity and bi-quintile Ixion, the planet of lawlessness, in the twelfth house of the unconscious. His first milestone film "Jour de Fete" had a comic style and visual humour which proved very successful.

As a director, he was devoted to painstaking preparation of all of his films. His Sedna is also in a fateful inconjunct with Ceres, the planet of nurturing, which is conjunct his Ascendent, the cusp of his first house of identity. Despite being troubled by financial problems and large debts, he produced six films throughout his career spanning three decades, two of the most successful being *Mon Oracle* and *Playtime*.[1036]

At this juncture in human evolution, few of us use our planets at the spiritual level, but many of us are striving to, and such people are

---

[1035] Ibid.
[1036] https://en.wikipedia.org/wiki/Jacques_Tati

wonderful to be around. As with the other planets, the spiritual level of evolution is vastly different with Sedna from the two previous levels.

Here, the stressful aspects with Haumea bring a strong connection with the transcendental magic of being, a spiritual wealth and an understanding of the divinity of human beings and the oneness of existence. The struggle of the beginner's level is gone, as are the transcendental crises of the intermediate level. At this level everything Saturnian is meaningless and yet everything Sednian has its place.

Reverend Robert Taylor, was an early 19th-century English Radical, a clergyman turned freethinker. He had Sedna in the third house of communication, square Haumea in the first house of identity.

> He studied at St John's College, Cambridge to qualify as a clergyman, but five years after ordination gave up on orthodox Christianity and turned from evangelism to eccentric anti-clericalism.

> He set up a Christian Evidence Society and lectured in London pubs dressed in elaborate vestments, attacking the Anglican liturgy and the barbarities of the Establishment for what he called its "Pagan creed". At this time blasphemy was a criminal offence and he spent a year in jail. In his cell he wrote *The Diegesis*, attacking Christianity on the basis of comparative mythology and attempting to expound it as a scheme of solar myths. On his release he joined up with the Radical Richard Carlile and, with his book newly published, set out on an "infidel home missionary tour".

> Several times a week in his mid-40's, he dressed in "canonicals", staged infidel melodramas, preaching bombastic sermons to artisans. Two Sunday sermons on "The Devil" caused particular outrage when he pronounced "God and the Devil... to be but one and the self-same being... Hell and Hell-fire... are, in the original, nothing more than names and titles of the Supreme God."

> He was then dubbed "The Devil's Chaplain", and thousands of copies of his ceremonies were circulated in a seditious publication, The Devil's Pulpit. At 47 he was indicted for blasphemy over two Easter sermons in the last days of The

Rotunda and he was sentenced to a further two years' imprisonment.[1037]

Peter Hurkos is a Dutch psychic who gained ESP abilities after a blow to the head, which left him unconscious for three days. He has Sedna in the eleventh house of collective consciousness, square Haumea in the second house of material reality. Sedna is also bi-quintile Ixion, the planet of lawlessness, in the fourth house of home.

> As a boy, he was a poor student, dropping out of school when he entered his teens. He was a loner who spent much time in the woods or in solitude, dreaming and exploring, prone to fantasies and visions. After his accident, he became religious and also became afflicted with blinding headaches and his temperament became volatile and moody.

> His psychic abilities were tested psychometrically with a claimed 87% accuracy. His Sedna is also bi-quintile Uranus, the planet of intuition, in the ninth house of knowledge and in a fateful inconjunct with Pholus, the centaur of enlightenment in the sixth house of service. In addition to using his new-found abilities to do professional work, he also did TV guest spots and wrote an autobiography, titled *Psychic*. He tuned in to some of his subjects while in a sleep state, when he could speak in tongues, or in foreign languages, but he also did psychic work while awake.[1038]

And Pope Pius XII was an Italian ecclesiastic and Pope of the Roman Catholic Church. He wrote many encyclicals making it easier for Catholics to participate in the church. His Sedna is in his fifth house of creativity, semi-square Haumea in the seventh house of relationships.

> Born into a family devoted to the papal service, he worked so hard at the Seminary that his health gave way and he was forced to leave. His Sedna is also semi-square Mercury, the planet of communication, in the fourth house of home. Pope Leo XIII allowed him to live at home while completing his courses, until he was ordained.

[1037] https://en.wikipedia.org/wiki/Robert_Taylor_(Radical)
[1038] https://en.wikipedia.org/wiki/Peter_Hurkos

During World War I he was involved in humane efforts and was sent to Berlin to be its first nuncio, papal ambassador. He left Germany to be made cardinal and then became secretary of state for the Vatican, before being crowned Pope. His Sedna is also in a fateful inconjunct Pallas, the asteroid of wisdom, in the twelfth house of karma, and at the beginning of World War II he spoke out against the Nazis, helping Jews with false baptismal certificates and allowing thousands to stay in Vatican City, convents and cloisters.[1039]

In-conjunct

With the evolutionary inconjunct between Sedna and Haumea the esoteric spiritual energy of Sedna bursts into our ability to make breakthroughs, to overcome fears and try new adaptive strategies, our ability to extract the true essence of life from the dross of the world, and we have a fated role to play.

The energy of Haumea is earnest, vivid, alive with spirit and in touch with a transcendental magic of being. Haumea is always searching for spiritual answers, so can indicate mystical awareness and spiritual wealth and bring us the insight to see the divinity of human beings and the oneness of existence.

The inconjunct sometimes acts as a flow and at other times as a stress, so we have to learn to actively manage the process as the rarified spiritual energy sometimes reinforces our search for spiritual answers and, at other times, isn't there to back us up. By adjusting to this, we gain a deeper understanding of ourselves and how to play our role.

We all start life unconscious of the spiritual energies in our chart and have to develop them, but even if we don't bother to do the work to become conscious of the energies, they still act on us anyway and we may fall victim to a constant and idle daydreaming, or engage in a spiritual deception, as we see in the following examples.

A new generation was born with this aspect early this century, but this generation is still young at time of writing and the last generation with this aspect was in the 1700s, so most our examples are drawn from this period.

[1039] https://en.wikipedia.org/wiki/Pope_Pius_XII

One example of the current generation at the unconscious level is Maria, is a blond 4-year-old, who was born to a Bulgarian Roma woman in Greece, and illegally adopted by another Roma family. She has Sedna on the cusp of the seventh house of relationships, inconjunct Haumea in the eleventh house of collective consciousness.

> The fake parents were under suspicion of having bought her with the intention to use her for professional begging. The couple who appeared to be Maria's parents had fraudulently registered 14 children in three different municipalities and had faced charges for robbery and forging official documents in the past.[1040]

A young example from the former generation is Christian Heinrich Heineken, a German child prodigy known as 'the infant scholar of Lübeck'. He had Sedna in the second house of material resources, inconjunct Haumea, which was together with Makemake, the planet of extreme talent, both in the eighth house of sensitivity to the spirit world. His Sedna is also quintile Neptune, the planet of connection with spiritual world, in the fourth house of home.

> When he was eight weeks old, he could speak German. He read the Pentateuch at age one, and between the ages of two and three, he read the Old and New Testament in Latin. When he was three years old, he was said to have authored *A History of Denmark* and recited it when visiting the King of Denmark later the same year. Unfortunately, he died at age four of coeliac disease.[1041]

The fated nature of our psychic mission with this aspect can be seen in the life of Charles Eisen, who was a French painter and engraver. He had Sedna in the fifth house of creativity, inconjunct Haumea, which is together with Jupiter, the planet of expansion and Makemake, the planet of devotion, all in twelfth house of the unconscious.

> At 21 he went to Paris, and the following year entered the studio of Le Bas. His talent and his sparkling wit gained him admission to the court, where he became painter and draftsman to the King, and drawing-master to Madame de Pompadour. However, afterwards he fell into disgrace, and retired to Brussels, where he

---

[1040] https://www.astro.com/astro-databank/Adopted_illegally:_Maria
[1041] https://en.wikipedia.org/wiki/Christian_Heinrich_Heineken

died in poverty. His pictures are not without merit, but it is as a designer of illustrations and vignettes for books that he is best known.[1042]

Or in that of Samuel Adams, who was an American statesman, political philosopher, and one of the Founding Fathers of the United States. He had Sedna in the third house of communication, inconjunct Haumea, which is conjunct Makemake, the planet of devotion, Mercury, the planet of communication and Mars, the planet of action, all in the tenth house of profession.

> He was a politician in colonial Massachusetts, a leader of the movement that became the American Revolution, and one of the architects of the principles of American republicanism that shaped the political culture of the United States. He was brought up in a religious and politically active family. A graduate of Harvard College, he was an unsuccessful businessman and tax collector before concentrating on politics.

> He was an influential official of the Massachusetts House of Representatives and the Boston Town Meeting in his 40s, and he became a part of a movement opposed to the British Parliament's efforts to tax the British American colonies without their consent. His Massachusetts Circular Letter calling for colonial non-cooperation prompted the occupation of Boston by British soldiers, eventually resulting in the Boston Massacre of 1770.

> Adams and his colleagues devised a committee of correspondence system to help coordinate resistance to what he saw as the British government's attempts to violate the British Constitution at the expense of the colonies, which linked like-minded Patriots throughout the Thirteen Colonies. Continued resistance to British policy resulted in the 1773 Boston Tea Party and the coming of the American Revolution.

> The following year Parliament passed the Coercive Acts, at which time Adams attended the Continental Congress in Philadelphia, which was convened to coordinate a colonial response. He helped guide the Congress towards issuing the

---

[1042] https://en.wikipedia.org/wiki/Charles-Dominique-Joseph_Eisen

Continental Association that year and the Declaration of Independence two years later.

He later became a controversial figure in American history. Accounts written in the 19th century praised him as someone who had been steering his fellow colonists towards independence long before the outbreak of the Revolutionary War. This view gave way to negative assessments of "Adams in the first half of the 20th century, in which he was portrayed as a master of propaganda who provoked mob violence to achieve his goals.[1043]

As we tire of density and the grief it creates, and we start a spiritual journey to get out of the swamp, Sedna rewards us with transcendent crises, experiences which force us to let go and rise above them, resulting in a huge growth to a new level of consciousness. There is no choice with these crises, and the more we try and solve them, the more we will get hurt.

With Haumea there is often a profound idealism, a passionate belief in the humanizing and social function of art and a sense of freedom as the highest principle and these themes may be evident in the crises we face.

In this next example we see the sacrifice required when fate steps into our lives and blesses us with a serving role. Leopold Mozart was a German composer, conductor, teacher, and violinist, who is best known as the father and teacher of Wolfgang Amadeus Mozart. He had Sedna in the sixth house of service, inconjunct Haumea on the cusp of the second house of material resources.

Leopold discovered that his two children were musically gifted in about the time he was 40, when he began with keyboard lessons for the seven-year-old Nannerl. The toddler Wolfgang immediately began imitating his sister, at first picking out thirds on the keyboard and then making rapid progress under Leopold's instruction.

Three years later, the children were ready to work as concert performers, and Leopold began taking the family on extensive concert tours, performing for both aristocracy and public, throughout central and western Europe. The discovery of his

---

[1043] https://en.wikipedia.org/wiki/Samuel_Adams

children's talent is considered to have been a life-transforming event for Leopold. He once referred to his son as the "miracle which God let be born in Salzburg".

Of Leopold's attitude, the Grove Dictionary says: 'The recognition of this 'miracle' must have struck Leopold with the force of a divine revelation and he felt his responsibility to be not merely a father's and teacher's but a missionary's as well.' By "missionary", the Grove Dictionary refers to the family's concert tours.

The children performed before large audiences and took in large sums, but the expenses of travel were also very high, and no money at all was made during the various times that Leopold and the children suffered serious illnesses. The touring continued for more than ten years. The last three trips were to Italy, with only Leopold accompanying Wolfgang.

Wolfgang left home for good when Leopold was 62, when instead of returning from a stay in Vienna with his employer Archbishop Colloredo he remained in the city to pursue a freelance career. This effort was to a fair degree successful; Wolfgang achieved great fame and was for a time quite prosperous. The move almost certainly aided Wolfgang's musical development; the great majority of his most celebrated works were composed in Vienna.

Leopold was strongly opposed to the Vienna move; however, he visited Wolfgang and his wife in Vienna later that year, at a time when his son's career success was at its peak. He witnessed firsthand his son's success as a performer. The visit was the last time that he saw his son, though they continued to correspond, and Wolfgang sometimes sent copies of his piano concertos and string quartets. Leopold's music is inevitably overshadowed by the work of his son Wolfgang, and in any case the father willingly sacrificed his own career to promote his son's.[1044]

Elisabeth Christine, Queen of Prussia, was the spouse of King Frederick the Great. She had Sedna in the third house of communication,

---

[1044] https://en.wikipedia.org/wiki/Leopold_Mozart

inconjunct Haumea, together with Saturn, the planet of structure, and Makemake, the planet of devotion, all in the tenth house of profession.

When Crown Prince Frederick of Prussia failed in his attempt to flee from his father's tyrannical regime, he was ordered to marry Elizabeth, in a match arranged by the Austrian court in the hopes of securing influence over Prussia for another generation.

On their wedding night, Frederick spent a reluctant hour with his new wife and then walked about outside for the rest of the night. It was well known that he resented the marriage from the very beginning and only submitted to his father's will in order to regain his freedom. Elisabeth-Christine was only seventeen when she was married, so her position at the Berlin Court was difficult from the beginning, as the only support that she could count on was the King's, who remained attached to his daughter-in-law until his death and was particularly fond of her piety.

This did nothing to endear her husband to her; however, Frederick was shrewd enough to recognise the opportunity his wife provided to improve his own relationship with his father, and systematically used her to gain favours from him.[1045]

Her Sedna is trine Orcus, the planet of 'understanding the karmic wheel', in the eighth house of shared resources and square Mercury, the planet of communication, in the first house of identity.

When he succeeded to the throne of Prussia however, he initiated the separation between the two, and she began living separately from him, taking up her residence at Schönhausen Palace, which is nowadays in the north of Berlin, while Frederick resided in Potsdam. It should be mentioned that throughout his life, he did not show any sexual interest in women. He had no known affairs and presided over a very spartan, almost military court, where women never held any influence.

Despite his personal contempt for representational court life, however, he realized its importance in the system of state, and therefore did not abolish court life in Prussia, but rather left virtually all representational duties to his wife, so she had a very

---

[1045] https://en.wikipedia.org/wiki/Elisabeth_Christine_of_Brunswick-Wolfenbüttel-Bevern

visible and official role as queen of Prussia. She spent her winters in the Royal Palace in Berlin, receiving foreign princes, ambassadors and generals and hosting official court events such as royal birthdays and weddings.

Her summers were spent at Schönhausen, where she entertained the royal family and the Prussian aristocracy with concerts and dinners in a circle of Lutheran theologians. She is noted to have regularly spent more than half her income on charity and particularly supported the French emigrée community in Berlin. Upon her death, it was said: "her memory will always be blessed as a touching example of the noblest mental qualities, the most enlightened and lively piety, and the most wonderfully active benevolence.[1046]

Frederick V was King of Denmark. He had Sedna in the fourth house of home, inconjunct Haumea, together with Makemake, the planet of devotion, in the eleventh house of collective consciousness.

His parents were deeply devoted to Pietism, and Frederick was given a strictly religious upbringing. Despite this he grew into a hedonist who enjoyed the pleasures of life, such as wine and women.[1047]

Her Sedna is also semi-sextile the Sun in the fifth house of creativity and semi-sextile Moon in the third house of ideas. It is also sextile Jupiter, the planet of expansion, in the second house of material resources.

Art and science prospered under his reign, and although he wasn't personally interested in cultural affairs, the public entertainment and freedom of expression that had been banned under the pietistic hypocrisy characterised during his father's reign, was again permitted. He became an active Freemason and set up the first Masonic lodge in Norway. His last words were reportedly: "It is a great consolation to me in my last hour that I have never willfully offended anyone, and that there is not a drop of blood on my hands.[1048]

[1046] Ibid.

[1047] https://en.wikipedia.org/wiki/Frederick_V_of_Denmark

[1048] Ibid.

At this juncture in human evolution, few of us use our planets at the spiritual level, but many of us are striving to, and such people are wonderful to be around. As with the other planets, the spiritual level of evolution is vastly different with Sedna from the two previous levels.

Here, the inconjunct with Haumea bring a real connection with the transcendental magic of being, a spiritual wealth and an understanding of the divinity of human beings and the oneness of existence. The struggle of the beginner's level is gone, as are the transcendental crises of the intermediate level. At this level everything Saturnian is meaningless and yet everything Sednian has its place.

Like Antoine Court, who was a former Protestant pastor, born at Nîmes, who initiated the interpretation of the Tarot as an arcane repository of timeless esoteric wisdom. He has Sedna in the second house of material resources, inconjunct Haumea in the eighth house of shared resources.

> He wrote a series of books on The Primeval World, Analyzed and Compared to the Modern World', and he published these in series form, to a distinguished list of subscribers, headed by Louis XVI of France. His fame, however, is associated is a single section in his vast compendium, the chapter on tarot cards. It was his immediate perception, the first time he saw the Tarot deck, that it held the secrets of the Egyptians.[1049]

His Sedna is also bi-quintile with Makemake, the planet of devotion, also in the eighth house and a semi-square with Chariklo, the centaur of foresight in the third house of ideas.

> Writing without the benefit of Champollion's deciphering of the Egyptian language, he developed a reconstruction of Tarot history, without producing any historical evidence, which was that Egyptian priests had distilled the ancient Book of Thoth into these images. These they brought to Rome, where they were secretly known to the popes, who brought them to Avignon in the 14th century, whence they were introduced into France.

> An essay appended to this gave suggestions for cartomancy and within two years the fortune-teller known as "Etteilla" published a

---

[1049] https://en.wikipedia.org/wiki/Antoine_Court_de_Gébelin

technique for reading the tarot, and the practice of tarot reading was born.[1050]

And Immanuel Kant, who was a German writer, teacher and philosopher, also had this aspect. Kant was the foremost thinker of the Enlightenment and is considered one of the greatest philosophers of all time. He had Sedna in twelfth house of the unconscious, inconjunct Haumea together with Makemake, the planet of intense focus and talent, in the sixth house of service.

He was a short man, scarcely five feet tall, and he had a deformed chest. He suffered from poor health throughout his life, and because of this, he maintained a strict regimen of walking.

His systematic and comprehensive work on ethics and aesthetics inaugurated a new era in the development of philosophical thought and thus greatly influenced all subsequent philosophy, particularly in the various schools of Idealism. His works included *Kant's Critique of Pure Reason*, and *Critique of Practical Reason*.

He taught at Königsberg University for 14 years, and his reputation brought large numbers of students to the university. He lectured on many subjects including logic, metaphysics and moral philosophy. His style was humorous and vivid, and he used many examples from his reading to enliven his subjects.

He was made a professor of logic and metaphysics, a position he held until he retired from the university. Though often charged with attacking metaphysics, he believed in the existence of God and in a future life, and he is often described as an ethical Rationalist. However, his unorthodox religious teachings eventually brought him into conflict with the King of Prussia, who finally forbade him to teach or write on religious subjects, an order he obeyed until the King died five years later.[1051]

Quintile, Bi-quintile

The evolutionary quintile or bi-quintile aspect between Sedna and Haumea infuses our ability to make breakthroughs, to overcome fears and try new adaptive strategies in our mission to extract the true

---

[1050] Ibid.
[1051] https://en.wikipedia.org/wiki/Immanuel_Kant

essence of life from the dross of the world, with the all-encompassing spiritual energy of Sedna to the point where we can push the boundaries of human development.

The energy of Haumea is earnest, vivid, alive with spirit and in touch with a transcendental magic of being. Haumea is always searching for spiritual answers, so can indicate mystical awareness and spiritual wealth and bring us the insight to see the divinity of human beings and the oneness of existence.

Quintiles and bi-quintiles point to talent, the desire to create order and to categorize, a fascination with patterns and structures, perfectionist tendencies, and the desire to build or make things. These aspects have the characteristics of both the trine and opposition. They point to awareness of conflicts, or problems and finding solutions for them.

These aspects do not automatically kick into action however, and must be cultivated over time, so at the unconscious level we may not notice them, but they are likely still shaping our spiritual mission, or our delusionary mission, like the character Don Quixote, jousting with windmills.

Like Leonarda Cianciulli, who was an Italian homicidal maniac. She had Sedna, conjunct Mercury, the planet of ideas, both in the sixth house of daily routine, quintile Haumea in the eighth house of life and death.

> Afflicted with epilepsy from the time she was a kid, she attempted suicide twice. At 17, she married Raffaele Pansardi with whom she managed to become pregnant 18 times. She lost 14 of the babies in a row; four children survived birth. She began to read cards, working as a fortune-teller and a few years later separated from her husband. When her first-born son was called into military service in WW2, her anxiety over the possibility of losing him tipped her over the edge into madness.[1052]

Unfortunately, Sedna is also sextile her Pluto, the planet of life and death, in the eighth house of life and death, and opposite her Moon, the planet of emotions, in her twelfth house of the unconscious.

> She became convinced that she needed to make a spell with a human sacrifice to defend her children. Over an eight-month

---

[1052] https://en.wikipedia.org/wiki/Leonarda_Cianciulli

period she killed three women, boiling the body of each and making them into soap. Apprehended, she was found to be mentally impaired and was condemned to 30 years in an institution for the criminally insane, where she died of an apoplectic fit.[1053]

Rudolf Hess was a German politician, the Deputy Leader of the Nazi party and number three in power after Hitler and Goering. He had Sedna in the tenth house of profession, quintile Haumea in the twelfth house of the unconscious.

Believing that he was obeying supernatural powers and had a mission to end the war, Hess flew from Germany to Scotland early in WW2, bailing out of the plane and taking it on his own to attempt negotiations with England on behalf of Germany. Unfortunately, Hitler denied his authority, calling him insane and he was imprisoned, tried and given a life sentence. After 21 months in a Nuremberg prison, he spent 41 years at Spandau.

He wrote prodigiously in prison about the Nazis and the war, convinced that he would play a leading role in the "Fourth Reich." He initially goose-stepped down the corridors of Spandeau, snapping the Nazi salute.[1054]

His Sedna was also in a stressful sesquiquadrate with Pallas, the asteroid of wisdom, in the second house of material restrictions, inconjunct Vesta, the asteroid of regeneration, in the third house of communication, and semi-square Mars, the planet of war, in the eighth house of shared resources.

However, after an initial period of rages and bouts of persecution mania, he settled into a routine of numbing regularity. His days started with an hour of calisthenics, breakfast, a walk in the prison garden, lunch, an afternoon of reading and television (he was banned from news programs). For a half hour each month, he was allowed a visit from his wife and son; no touching was permitted. For the last 21 years, he was the sole inmate of

---

[1053] Ibid.

[1054] https://en.wikipedia.org/wiki/Rudolf_Hess

Spandeau and after four suicide attempts, he strangled himself with an electric cord age 93.[1055]

Or we could become a victim of someone else's deluded mission, like Rebecca Riley, who was an American victim of prescription drug overdose at age 4. She had Sedna in the ninth house of knowledge, bi-quintile Haumea in the second house of material resources.

> The Riley parents were unemployed and the family relied on Social Security Benefits. From the age of two she was diagnosed with ADHD and bipolar disorder by a licensed psychiatrist at a reputable hospital, mainly on the basis of information given by her mother. Her heart and lungs were damaged due to prolonged use of the prescription drugs and two years later, she died and her parents were accused of first-degree murder. Prosecutors argued that they had her declared mentally unstable so they could collect social security disability benefits and purposely fed her the overdose. They were convicted and sentenced to life in prison.[1056]

Or like Shane Lambert, who was a 4-year-old American accidental death/homicide victim, who was killed along with his sister and his aunt, while attempting to cross a busy multi-lane highway. He had Sedna in the fourth house of home, bi-quintile Haumea in the ninth house of knowledge.

> His aunt, a married mom with two teenagers, had inexplicably crossed the median on the Interstate highway. After stopping her car in the wrong direction, she then undressed herself, Shane and his sister and walked the children into oncoming traffic. All three of them were killed when two cars hit them head-on.

> Although she had suffered from depression and bipolar disorder in recent years, "we thought Marci was taking medication and everything was under control," says the children's mother, who was the aunt's twin. "She seemed perfectly normal when she picked up the kids at our house that night. But somewhere on the way to her house for the party, she suffered a psychotic breakdown."

[1055] Ibid.
[1056] https://en.wikipedia.org/wiki/Death_of_Rebecca_Riley

> After Shane's funeral, she had been shocked to discover that her sister had received a citation from a state trooper for failing to stay within striped lines while on the way to their home that evening. "She had stopped in the highway median, and when a good Samaritan tried to help her, she hit him and kept calling him 'Harry,'" his mon recalls. "Then she sat down in a puddle of water and started splashing around."

> Passing drivers called the police, and three officers debated whether to take the aunt involuntarily to the hospital. But they ultimately decided to allow her sister to drive on, even though she told them she was on her way to pick up her niece and nephew.[1057]

As we tire of density and the grief it creates, and we start a spiritual journey to get out of the swamp, Sedna rewards us with transcendent crises, experiences which force us to let go and rise above them, resulting in a huge growth to a new level of consciousness. There is no choice with these crises, and the more we try and solve them, the more we will get hurt.

With Haumea there is often a profound idealism, a passionate belief in the humanizing and social function of art and a sense of freedom as the highest principle and these themes may be evident in the crises we face.

Like Dorothy Parker, who was an American humorist, famous for her exceptional wit and corrosive style. She had Sedna in the twelfth house of the unconscious, quintile Haumea in the second house of material resources.

> She authored short stories, plays, a handful of poems and a slight amount of bitchy journalism. By the time she was in her 20s, she was the most quoted woman in America. Her mother died when she was four. She adored her dad but loathed the woman he re-married. The reviled step-mother died when she was nine.

> Awaking to politics at a Boston demonstration at 34, she became concerned with race relations, the support of Spanish loyalists and the championing of the writer's guild and other political

---

[1057] https://www.womansday.com/relationships/family-friends/news/a50713/her-sister-killed-her-kids-and-she-forgave-her/

causes. She helped form an Anti-Nazi league at 43, but her flirtation with the Communist Party brought her to McCarthy's attention, and she later said she'd been blackballed. Friends tended to be mystified by her radicalism, as her luxurious Hollywood home and lavish life style furnished an unlikely backdrop for left-wing fund-raisers.

She had two broken marriages and a number of unhappy love affairs; both husbands were alcoholics. Her first mate came back from WWI addicted to morphine. She married and divorced Alan Campbell twice during their 30-year relationship, with the second marriage to him at 57. Their strain was primarily due to his homosexuality, fuelled by an easy flow of alcohol. Of the many men in her life, not one could be called a healthy relationship. As a result, she drank to excess for decades and made four suicide attempts. She had appeal, style, brains and celebrity but did not find happiness or peace. With no kids, she devoted her love to her many dogs.[1058]

Or like Captain James Cook, who was a British explorer, navigator, cartographer, and captain in the Royal Navy. He has Sedna in the second house of material resources, bi-quintile Haumea in the ninth house of knowledge.

Cook made detailed maps of Newfoundland prior to making three voyages to the Pacific Ocean, during which he achieved the first recorded European contact with the eastern coastline of Australia and the Hawaiian Islands, and the first recorded circumnavigation of New Zealand.

In three voyages Cook sailed thousands of miles across largely uncharted areas of the globe. He mapped lands from New Zealand to Hawaii in the Pacific Ocean in greater detail and on a scale not previously achieved. As he progressed on his voyages of discovery he surveyed and named features and recorded islands and coastlines on European maps for the first time. He displayed a combination of seamanship, superior surveying and

---

[1058] https://en.wikipedia.org/wiki/Dorothy_Parker

cartographic skills, physical courage and an ability to lead men in adverse conditions.[1059]

However, his Sedna was also square Neptune, the planet of illusions, in the fifth house of creativity and in a fateful inconjunct with Pluto, the planet of life and death, in the eighth house of shared resources, and a stressful semi-square with Chariklo, the centaur of foresight, in the third house of communication.

> On his third voyage, after a month's stay in Hawaii, he had attempted to resume his exploration of the Northern Pacific, however shortly after leaving his ship's foremast broke, so they returned for repairs. Tensions rose, and a number of quarrels broke out between the Europeans and Hawaiians and an unknown group took one of Cook's small boats. That evening the Hawaiians had become "insolent", even under threats to fire upon them and Cook determined to kidnap and ransom the King of Hawaii, to get the boat back.

> The following day he marched through the village to retrieve him, taking the King by his hand and leading him willingly away. One of the King's favourite wives and two chiefs approached the group as they were heading to boats and pleaded with the King not to go, until he stopped and sat where he stood. An old priest, chanting rapidly, while holding out a coconut, attempted to distract Cook and his men as a large crowd began to form at the shore. The king began to understand that Cook was his enemy. And as Cook turned his back to help launch the boats, he was struck on the head by the villagers and then stabbed to death as he fell on his face in the surf.[1060]

Agatha Christie was a British writer of some 67 detective mystery books that are universally popular. She had Sedna in the third house of communication, quintile Haumea in the sixth house of daily routine.

> Her novels have sold more than a billion copies in English and another billion translated in more than 100 languages. However, with a solitary childhood, she was so painfully shy that she never did get accustomed to public appearance and seldom gave

---

[1059] https://en.wikipedia.org/wiki/James_Cook
[1060] Ibid.

interviews. Her mother was not keen on education but in spite of her, five-year-old Agatha taught herself to read. On a dare from her sister, she wrote her first book in two weeks, introducing for the first time her protagonist, Hercule Poirot.[1061]

Her Sedna was also sextile Neptune, the planet of imagination, in the fifth house of creativity, which is together with Pluto, the planet of life and death, just across the cusp in the sixth house of daily routine. Sedna was also opposite her Moon, the planet of emotions, in the ninth house of publishing, and semi-square Nessus, the centaur representing the fragility of life in the second house of material resources.

The book was uniformly rejected by publishers, however later someone inadvertently opened the book and recommended it for publication. Agatha was given a five-book contract and her central character went on to solve crime in 33 more novels. Her popularity was close to immediate. By the time she was 40, she was a plain and matronly woman with hair forever locked in a wave, wearing dowdy housedresses, a deeply religious teetotaller who loved to putter in her garden.

Around this time her mother died however, and soon after that her husband announced that he loved another. She fell apart and disappeared, checking into a hotel under an alias, while an all-out search turned up her abandoned car on a deserted road and a discarded fur coat. Police dragged the pond for her body while the plot thickened. Some bizarre letters turned up or were rumoured.

When she was found at the hotel, she never really explained the episode and it was accounted for by stating that she had stress-related amnesia, or a secret affair was also considered as another possibility. However, while recovering from the divorce, she took the Orient Express to Baghdad and met her second husband, an archeologist who was fourteen years her junior. Though she gave every possible reason to not marry him, she nonetheless did so, and the "most unsuitable match" lasted very happily for 45 years until her death.[1062]

[1061] https://en.wikipedia.org/wiki/Agatha_Christie
[1062] Ibid.

Humour can be one path to transcend the quicksand of Sedna, giving us the objectivity to step back from the edge and also with Haumea a sensitivity to the transcendental magic of being and an ability to extract the true essence of life from the dross of the world, which is the essence of good comedy.

Like Groucho Marx, who was an American writer, comedian, stage, film and television star. His Sedna is in the fifth house of creativity, quintile Haumea in the eighth house of shared resources.

He was known as a master of quick wit and is widely considered one of the best comedians of the modern era. He made 13 feature films with his siblings the Marx Brothers (Harpo Marx and Chico Marx), of whom he was the third-born. He also had a successful solo career, most notably as the host of the radio and television game show *You Bet Your Life*.

His distinctive appearance, carried over from his days in vaudeville, included quirks such as an exaggerated stooped posture, glasses, cigar, and a thick greasepaint moustache and eyebrows. These exaggerated features resulted in the creation of one of the world's most ubiquitous and recognisable novelty disguises, known as Groucho glasses: a one-piece mask consisting of horn-rimmed glasses, large plastic nose, bushy eyebrows and moustache.

Among Groucho's many contributions to film comedy were his rapier wit, illogical chain of deductive reasoning and the visual pun. His standard persona of eyes rolled upward under wiggled brows with painted moustache and poised cigar created a classic comic insouciance.

After a decade of semi-retirement, Marx began appearing in one-night solo concert performances, culminating in a sold-out performance in New York's Carnegie Hall entitled "An Evening with Groucho". This outstanding comeback created a sensation that revived an international interest in his films, and the Cannes Film Festival made him a Commander of the French Order of Arts and Letters.

But from the time that he broke up with his brothers, his wit continued but not his humour. He became a crabby miser as he grew older, shamefully manipulative of his three former wives and three children and, toward the end of his life, had dreadful battles over his property in a sad diminishing of capacity.[1063]

At this juncture in human evolution, few of us use our planets at the spiritual level, but many of us are striving to, and such people are wonderful to be around. As with the other planets, the spiritual level of evolution is vastly different with Sedna from the two previous levels.

Here, the quintile and bi-quintile aspects with Haumea bring a real connection with the transcendental magic of being, a spiritual wealth and an understanding of the divinity of human beings and the oneness of existence. The struggle of the beginner's level is gone, as are the transcendental crises of the intermediate level. At this level everything Saturnian is meaningless and yet everything Sednian has its place.

Like Sri Meher Baba, who was an Indian religious figure who was known as "The Silent Guru." He was born in India to Irani Zoroastrian parents. He had Sedna in the second house of material resources, quintile Haumea in the fifth house of offspring and creativity.

> At the age of 19, he began a seven-year spiritual transformation and during this time he contacted five spiritual masters before beginning his own mission and gathering his own disciples at the age of 27. His early followers gave him the name Meher Baba, meaning "Compassionate Father".[1064]

His Sedna is also inconjunct the Moon, the planet of emotions, in the ninth house of spirituality.

> He moved into silence at 31 and did not speak until his death. To communicate, he spelled words on the alphabet board with quick fingers, such as "I am the Supreme Spirit." From the age of 60 he used unique sign language of gestures, rather than the alphabet board. With his circle of disciples, he spent long periods in seclusion, during which time he often fasted. He also traveled widely, held public gatherings and engaged in works of charity with lepers, the poor and the mentally ill.[1065]

His Sedna is also quintile Haumea, the planet of rebirth, in the fifth house of creativity, semi-square Venus, the planet of values in the first

---

[1063] https://en.wikipedia.org/wiki/Groucho_Marx
[1064] https://en.wikipedia.org/wiki/Meher_Baba
[1065] Ibid.

house of identity, and sesquiquadrate Juno, the asteroid of partnership, in the tenth house of profession.

> He gave numerous teachings on the cause and purpose of life, including teaching reincarnation and that the phenomenal world is an illusion. He taught that the Universe is imagination, that God is what really exists, and that each soul is really God passing through imagination to realise individually His own divinity.
>
> In addition, he gave practical advice for the aspirant who wishes to attain Self-realization and thereby escape the wheel of birth and death. He also taught about the concept of Perfect Masters, the Avatar, and those on the various stages of the spiritual path that he called involution. His teachings are most importantly recorded in his principal books, *Discourses* and *God Speaks*. And his legacy includes an influence on pop-culture artists and the introduction of common expressions such as 'Don't Worry, Be Happy'.[1066]

Or like Dane Rudhyar, who was a French-American astrologer, one of most noted and respected astrologers of the 20th century. He had Sedna in the third house of ideas and communication, quintile Haumea in the seventh house of relationships.

> He was called a modern renaissance man for his ability to express himself in many fields; music, painting, poetry, philosophy and metaphysics. He wrote for national magazines since his late '30s and was the author of many books.
>
> He had poor health as a child, a distraction that continued through his life. At 12, he had life-threatening surgery to remove his left kidney and adrenal gland. A bright youth, he passed his baccalaureate at the Sorbonne at 16, majoring in philosophy. Becoming involved in the artistic and musical climate of Paris, he was heavily influenced by the radical ideas of Nietzsche.
>
> At this time, he had a mystical experience or realisation in which he "became intuitively aware of the cyclic nature of all existence and of the fact that our Western civilisation was coming to an autumnal conclusion." He later wrote that it was from this time

---

[1066] Ibid.

that he sought to gain a clearer understanding of the cyclic patterns and basic meaning of human existence.

At the age of 21, he left his native France and traveled to the U.S., reinventing himself with the name of Dane Rudhyar. Believing in the necessity of a fundamental transformation of our civilisation, his change of name was a symbolic reflection of his contribution to that change. The name "Rudhyar" is derived from the Sanskrit God Rudra, the Destroyer and Regenerator.

Attaining a position in the avant-garde art community of the West, he also studied and wrote. His seminal book in which he emphasised integration, *The Astrology of Personality*, was first published when he was 41.[1067]

And finally, at this level we have Paramahansa Yogananda, who was an East Indian author, mystic and founder of the Self-Realisation Fellowship. World traveled and a world teacher, he carried Eastern philosophy to the West. He had Sedna conjunct Mars the planet of action, in the eighth house of shared resources, quintile Haumea in the twelfth house of profession.

At 27 he was invited to serve as India's delegate to an international congress of religious leaders convening in Boston. His address to the congress, on 'The Science of Religion', was enthusiastically received. When he arrived in America, the "New World" was ready to receive the advanced teachings that had previously been reserved for monastics and chelas in ashrams. Science, literacy, communication, and new spiritual insights had just begun breaking down the dark ages of theology and dogma.

He founded his fellowship to disseminate worldwide his teachings on India's ancient science and philosophy of Yoga and its time-honoured tradition of meditation, introducing the Bhagavad Gita and other scriptures to help raise the consciousness of humanity. He lectured and taught on the East coast of American for several years and at 31 began a speaking tour across the country. His lectures, in which he spoke of the underlying unity of the world's great religions, were attended by

---

[1067] https://en.wikipedia.org/wiki/Dane_Rudhyar

thousands drawn to his message. His personal students were taught the ancient soul-awakening techniques of Kriya Yoga.

His articulate and sincere introduction to the disciplines of the East opened the door for many other Indian teachers and gurus, as a serious interest in yoga and meditation made great inroads in the West. His main mission was to build a lasting bridge of World Brotherhood based on raising the spiritual awareness between the East and West.[1068]

[1068] https://en.wikipedia.org/wiki/Paramahansa_Yogananda

43: Sedna / Varuna

Conjunction

With the conjunction between Sedna and Varuna, the all-encompassing spiritual energy of Sedna infuses our sense of competence and mastery, our ability to let go of losses and resentments, and to accept and delegate authority.

Varuna deals with questions of the gain and loss of reputation and the issue of immortality through fame. It represents that which is beyond the real and also beyond visions and aspirations, something that is quite literally behind everything. Varuna's energy seems closest to what we in the West think of as God, the all-knowing cosmic entity that exists silently behind consciousness and events.

At the unconscious level however, the spiritual power of the conjunction can give us a somewhat distorted world view, which lends a sense of righteousness to the way we live our lives and a personal blindness to the problems we create.

Like Ronald Paquin, who was an American ecclesiastic, a Reverend father in the Roman Catholic church, who was removed from his parish for molesting children. He had Sedna conjunct Varuna in the fifth house of children.

> Over six years there were 13 complaints to the archdiocese alleging sexual misbehavior by Paquin over the previous two decades. The accusations were filled with grim detail about how he allegedly plied boys with gifts and liquor before molesting and orally raping them - charges that prompted the church to make payments to his victims. The behavior was found to be so repugnant and the pattern of abuse so clear that a church review board urged that he be dismissed from the priesthood, though they later changed their minds and said he should be given a second chance. Before he was reassigned as a chaplain, the archdiocese had already settled six of the 13 reported molestation cases for more than half a million.[1069]

[1069]

http://archive.boston.com/globe/spotlight/abuse/stories2/053002_paquin_spotlight.htm

His Sedna is also opposite his Sun, the planet of will, together with Mars, the planet of male sexuality, both in the eleventh house of collective consciousness.

> It was not for another four years that he was permanently removed from service, after the archdiocese received several more complaints of past abuse against him, including one from a man who expressed dismay that he was still working as a priest, and threatened to go to the press.[1070]

Or like Ratko Mladic, who was a former Bosnian Serb military leader accused of committing war crimes, crimes against humanity and genocide in the Bosnian war in the former Yugoslavia. He has Sedna exactly conjunct Varuna, and almost exactly conjunct Ceres, the planet of nurturing, with a little wider orb to Venus, the planet of values and relationships. Unfortunately, we don't know the house placement, because his time of birth is not known.

> A long-time member of the League of Communists of Yugoslavia, Mladić began his career in the Yugoslav People's Army and came to prominence in the Yugoslav Wars, initially as a high-ranking officer of the army and subsequently as the Chief of Staff of the Army of Serbian republic in the Bosnian War.[1071]

His Sedna is also semi-square his Moon, the planet of empathy, and also semi-square Saturn, the planet of rules and authority.

> His daughter committed suicide, reportedly to protest his brutal behaviour to others, because she she knew he loved her and nothing else would touch him. Some media said that her body was found in her blood-splattered bedroom, while others claim it was found in a nearby park, or in the woods near the cemetery.

> Mladić himself said she had been killed by his enemies. Some people who knew him claimed his daughter's death had transformed him into a bloodthirsty maniac. One of his former commanders told *Newsweek* magazine: "Some people think he went mad. Mladić's life had two phases – before and after the death of his daughter. He never recovered. He was a broken man.

[1070] Ibid.
[1071] https://en.wikipedia.org/wiki/Ratko_Mladić

Eventually he was indicted by the International Criminal Tribunal for the former Yugoslavia for genocide, war crimes and crimes against humanity. As the top military general with command responsibility, he was accused of being responsible for the Siege of Sarajevo and the Srebrenica massacre. He was extradited to The Hague where, at time of writing, his trial is in its closing phases.[1072]

Another example is Ted Kaczynski, who was an American terrorist, called the Unabomber. He has Sedna conjunct Varuna in the ninth house of knowledge.

He was a gifted child but was shy and aloof. As an infant, he was hospitalized for several weeks and the hospital staff discouraged the parents from visiting their child and prevented them from holding him in their rare visits. He reportedly was never the same.

He excelled in school, skipping two grades and graduating at age 16. He obtained his bachelor's degree from Harvard University and landed an assistant professor's position with the University of California at Berkeley, but resigned suddenly some years later without explanation, moving to a remote shack and living on very little.

Then he sent a bomb to a professor at Northwestern University and a security guard opened it and sustained minor injuries. His Sedna is also at the tip of a T square, between Pholus, the centaur of illumination, in the sixth house of service, opposite Mars, the planet of war, in the twelfth house of the unconscious. Several more bombs were sent by mail to others, but did not cause much injury, until a computer store owner was killed and a Yale University computer science professor with a distinguished reputation was injured.[1073]

His Sedna is also sextile Mercury, the planet of communication, in the eleventh house of ideals.

He demanded that if a 35,000-word manifesto was printed in newspapers, he would quit his bombing campaign. The

---

[1072] Ibid.
[1073] https://en.wikipedia.org/wiki/Ted_Kaczynski

document, arguing that technological progress was harmful and must be stopped, was published in the *New York Times* and *Washington Post*.

Kaczynski's younger brother recognised the writing style and ideas and after an anguished debate with himself, reported his brother to the police. The Unabomber was arrested at his cabin in a remote part of Montana. Lawyers tried to convince him to use the insanity plea, and a psychologist diagnosed paranoid schizophrenia, but he refused to plead insanity. He pled guilty to avoid the death penalty. Although he later retracted his guilty plea, he was found guilty and sentenced to life imprisonment with no hope of appeal.[1074]

As we tire of density and the grief it creates, and we start a spiritual journey to get out of the swamp, Sedna rewards us with transcendent crises, experiences which force us to let go and rise above them, resulting in a huge growth to a new level of consciousness. There is no choice with these crises, and the more we try and solve them, the more we will get hurt.

Paul Keating is an Australian politician and was Prime Minister representing the Labour Party. He has Sedna conjunct Varuna in the first house of identity.

Born into a working class Catholic family, he left school at 14 to work as a clerk, while managing the rock group, the Ramrods, on the side. He entered local politics at age 24. He was appointed Treasurer by newly elected Prime Minister Hawke in 1983. Although lacking any formal education in economics, he went on to become one of the most reforming Treasurers in Australian history; floating the Australian dollar, deregulating the financial sector, privatising state sector industries, introducing a capital gains tax, and a Prices and Incomes Accord.

"Seven years after becoming treasurer he became Deputy Prime Minister. He later challenged Hawke for the leadership and resigned from the ministry following his defeat. Six months later

---

[1074] Ibid.

he challenged again, this time successfully, and subsequently became Prime Minister.[1075]

His Sedna is square Pholus, the centaur of practical change, in the tenth house of profession.

> He would go on to deliver the Labor government a record fifth consecutive victory and a record 13 year's in government at the next election, defeating the opposition despite consistently poor government opinion polls.[1076]

His Sedna is also opposite his Moon, the planet of emotions, in the seventh house of relationships

Semi-square the conjunction of Mars, the planet of action, and Uranus, the planet of revolution, in the second house of material resources.

> His government introduced native title to Aborigines, greatly increased the social wage and the family benefits system, saw increased bilateral relations between Australia and countries in Asia, and vehemently promoted a vision of Australia as a republic.[1077]

Patch Adams is an American physician, famed throughout the medical community for charging no fees, carrying no malpractice insurance and living with his patients in a country farm setting. He has always maintained that humour and joy are more important than any drug or therapy. He has Sedna conjunct Varuna and Venus, the planet of Values, in the fifth house of creativity.

> He grew up as an Army brat in Japan, Germany and the U.S. and has been described as an iconoclast, a pattern-breaker and professional clown. He was deeply shaken by his dad's death, but it was his uncle's suicide that pushed him into despair. He dropped out of school and made the first of several suicide attempts.[1078]

His Sedna is semi-square his Sun, the planet of willpower, on the cusp of the seventh house of relationships and in a fateful inconjunct with Pallas, the asteroid of wisdom, in the ninth house of knowledge.

[1075] https://en.wikipedia.org/wiki/Paul_Keating
[1076] Ibid.
[1077] Ibid.
[1078] https://en.wikipedia.org/wiki/Patch_Adams

He was 18 when his mom checked him into a mental ward at Fairfax Hospital in Virginia, where he turned his own emotional corner by helping his roommate conquer hallucinations and fear. A few weeks later he left the ward and enrolled at University to become a doctor.

His Gesundheit Institute began as an experiment. For the first 12 years, 20 adults lived in a large home and used it as a crude hospital, open 24 hours a day. Three physicians and others did what they could for whoever came. They never charged money and their work was supported by part-time jobs of the live-in staff. For staff and patients, medicine was integrated with the performing arts, arts and crafts, agriculture, nature, recreation and social service. During those first 12 years, 15,000 people came through the home/facility for everything from profound illnesses to simple curiosity and play.[1079]

As we see, humour can be one path to transcend the quicksand of Sedna, giving us the objectivity to step back from the edge and also with the conjunction to Varuna a sensitivity to the freeing effect of humour on our lives.

Eric Idle was a British member of the Monty Python group. He has Sedna conjunct Varuna in the tenth house of profession.

During college, he wrote and acted in many comedyshows and skits, moving into TV and film as an actor, screenwriter and songwriter. He wrote for several TV series, and, later, was the only one of the five Pythons who wrote alone. As he went to Cambridge later than Cleese and Chapman, he met and joined the troupe later than the other members.[1080]

His Sedna is also square the conjunction of Pholus, the centaur of illumination, and Juno, the asteroid of partnership, in the sixth house of service.

An only child whose RAF pilot dad was killed in a car crash when he was two years old, Idle was sent to boarding school at seven. It was a semi-orphanage where he had a miserable 12 years. At

---

[1079] Ibid.
[1080] https://en.wikipedia.org/wiki/Eric_Idle

19, he won admission to Cambridge, a change from a grim and unhappy world to a storybook existence.

He considered the Monty Python crew his family and the five Pythons reached critical mass together as writers on David Frost's satirical weekly comedy show, before creating Monty Python. The Python shows were composed of surreality, risqué or innuendo-laden humour, sight gags and observational sketches without punchlines. Their comedy is often pointedly intellectual, with numerous erudite references to philosophers and literary figures.

The series followed and elaborated upon the style used by Spike Milligan in his groundbreaking series Q5, rather than the traditional sketch show format. They intended their humour to be impossible to categorise and succeeded so completely that the adjective "Pythonesque" was invented to define it and, later, similar material. However, after 4 seasons, 4 books, 4 films and 11 albums with the Flying Circus, Eric moved on to work as writer and host of other BBC series and American television specials.[1081]

At this juncture in human evolution, few of us use our planets at the spiritual level, but many of us are striving to, and such people are wonderful to be around. As with the other planets, the spiritual level of evolution is vastly different with Sedna from the two previous levels.

Here, the conjunction with Varuna brings a moral authority born of a deeply spiritual understanding of our lives, which is what we call wisdom. The struggle of the beginner's level is gone, as are the transcendental crises of the intermediate level. At this level everything Saturnian is meaningless and yet everything Sednian has its place.

Like Judith Richardson, who is a world famous American psychic. She has Sedna conjunct Varuna, the planet of notability, in the second house of material resources, sextile Venus in the twelfth house of the unconscious.

She brought a medical malpractice action after a CT scan allegedly caused her chronic and disabling headaches and

---

[1081] Ibid.

prevented her from practicing her occupation as a psychic. A jury awarded her $600,000 after a four-day trial.

The most interesting part of the case was the testimony pertaining to her psychic abilities. She presented several police officers as witnesses who testified that her psychic abilities had helped them solve cases. One special agent testified that he sought plaintiff's advice in solving five to seven homicide cases and that information provided by plaintiff proved to be 80-90 percent accurate. The opinion describes detailed information plaintiff provided to help solve a variety of cases.[1082]

Alan Oken is an American astrologer, author and a student of the works and teachings of the Tibetan Master Djwahl Khul. He has Sedna is conjunct Varuna and also Mercury, the planet of communication, in the fifth house of creativity.

He is a translator, teacher, global traveler and international tour guide, who lectures in five languages and does natal horoscope readings in seven. He is the author of a dozen titles, including *Soul-Centered Astrology*, *Rulers of the Horoscope*, and *Alan Oken's Complete Astrology*. In addition, he has written hundreds of articles for Dell Horoscope Magazine and many other national and international reviews and journals. Alan was the Director of The Wisdom School in Santa Fe, is co-founder of the Australian Institute for the Development of Consciousness and was Director of Esoteric Studies in Lisbon.[1083]

Barbara Hand Clow has been an astrologer and writer for 30 years. She has Sedna conjunct Varuna on the cusp of the ninth house of knowledge.

She is an international lecturer and workshop teacher and writer. She majored in philosophy at Seattle University, then behavioral psychology at the University of Washington, Seattle, and then began extensive reading and study of Reichian, Freudian and Jungian Psychology. At 26, she discovered that astrology was an exceedingly accurate diagnostic tool, and she began her study and practice of astrology. In her late thirties, she earned a

---

[1082] lawhaha.com/plaintiff-sues-for-loss-of-psychic-powers/
[1083] https://www.alanoken.com/about/

Master's degree in theology and healing with Matthew Fox in Chicago, and her thesis compared Jungian psychoanalytic technique and past life regression therapy.[1084]

Her Chiron is conjunct her North Node, in the twelfth house of karma, in a wide trine to her Sedna and at 51 she published a groundbreaking book on Chiron.

> The early attempts to define Chiron were the most rapid planetary research in the history of astrology. In this book we discover the inner secrets of Chiron, the most recently discovered planet, and see how it is interpreted in astrological charts by renowned astrologer Barbara Hand Clow. Based on over 700 charts from the author's personal files, Chiron is the first book to explore in depth the astrological meanings of this planet. Learn how you can incorporate Chironic wisdom in your astrological readings and your life with this groundbreaking work. Most important is Clow's revelation that Chiron is the bridge between the inner and outer planets.[1085]

Her Sedna is also closely square Pholus, the centaur of illumination in the fifth house of creativity, and semi-square Pallas, the asteroid of wisdom, in the seventh house of relationships.

> She is also a ceremonial teacher and visionary leader in Mayan calendar research, having taught at sacred sites throughout the world. She believes that with the completion of the 2012 Mayan Calendar, we are in the midst of a critical evolutionary leap that inspires us to heal our bodies and commune with our souls. As we awaken the Universe, we are being flooded with advanced spiritual knowledge that leaves many of us feeling ungrounded and disoriented. Through her numerous books, including *The Mayan Code*, *The Pleiadian Agenda*, and *Alchemy of Nine Dimensions*, she aims to help people transmute their emotional blocks and clarify their minds.[1086]

[1084] https://www.amazon.co.uk/Chiron-Rainbow-Between-Llewellyns-Astrology-ebook/dp/B00292BHW2

[1085] Ibid.

[1086] https://www.gaia.com/person/barbara-hand-clow

Opposition

There is no one alive today with this aspect and none occurs during the next century, so it is not interpreted here.

Semi-sextile, Sextile, Trine

With the flowing aspects between Sedna and Varuna, the all-encompassing spiritual energy of Sedna aligns with our sense of competence and mastery, our ability to let go of losses and resentments, and to accept and delegate authority.

Varuna deals with questions of the gain and loss of reputation, and the issue of immortality through fame. It seems to represent that which is beyond the real and also beyond visions and aspirations, something that is quite literally behind everything. Of all the planets named after deities, Varuna's energy seems closest to what we in the west think of as God, the all-knowing cosmic entity that exists silently behind consciousness and events.

At the unconscious level however, even the flows between these two planets can be challenging, as the spiritual power of the aspect can give us a rosier perspective on our lives than is realistic, and a personal blindness to the existential nature of our actions.

Like Jody Driscoll, who was an American homicide victim who was assaulted with an automobile. She had Sedna in the ninth house of knowledge, semi-sextile Varuna, which is conjunct her MC, her place in society.

> She approached a boy making a telephone call in a supermarket parking lot. Appearing annoyed, he shouted at her and pushed her forcefully away. When a friend of hers questioned him about his pushing her, the friend was told in foul language to move away. Jody left, but shortly thereafter, accompanied by two friends, she started to return by foot to the scene of the confrontation.

> While she was crossing the street, approaching the curb near the supermarket, he drove his automobile out of the parking lot, the car screeching as it turned the corner into the street that she and her two friends were crossing.He aimed the car first at one of her friends, struck her and then swerved toward Jody, hit her, ran

over her body with the car, then swiftly left the scene without stopping.[1087]

Or like Audry Maupin, who was a French homicide perpetrator. Of middle-class descent, he entered a political group of "ultra-left" extremists. He had Sedna in the twelfth house of the unconscious, conjunct his sun, the planet of will, semi-sextile Varuna in the first house of identity.

At 22 he was a philosophy sophomore at the University of Nanterre and was living together with his 19-year-old girlfriend in a squat in an abandoned bourgeoise house. The pair was already under observation by the French intelligence services prior to the incident, due to their involvement with an underground political group.

The pair climbed a perimeter fence with the intention of stealing the service firearms of the two policemen on night duty inside and neutralising them with their own handcuffs. They discovered that the two officers did not carry handcuffs, so they sprayed them with tear gas before making their escape. Outside they boarded a taxi waiting at a red light, with a passenger already on board. Ten minutes after hijacking the taxi, the driver decided to provoke an accident, ran a red light and slammed into a patrol car. Three officers jumped out and Maupin and his girlfriend opened fire, killing two of them. After a further chase he himself was shot and died a day later.

When the police searched their squat after the killings they found revolutionary and anarchist literature, such as *The Society Of The Spectacle.* And they found the couple's writings, which echoed surrealism, radicalism and situationism. This criminal case remains as one of the most important in France at the end of the 20th Century.[1088]

As we tire of density and the grief it creates, and we start a spiritual journey to get out of the swamp, Sedna rewards us with transcendent crises, experiences which force us to let go and rise above them, resulting in a huge growth to a new level of consciousness. There is no

---

[1087] https://law.justia.com/cases/massachusetts/court-of-appeals/volumes/35/35massappct919.html
[1088] https://en.wikipedia.org/wiki/Rey-Maupin_affair

choice with these crises, and the more we try and solve them, the more we will get hurt.

Edwin Hubble was an American astronomer, one of the major figures in 20th century science. He had Sedna in the eighth house of shared resources, sextile Varuna on the cusp of the sixth house of service.

> Working with the 100-inch Hooker telescope at California's Mount Wilson observatory, he made a series of discoveries that revolutionised humanity's vision of the cosmos. He was the first astronomer who provided reliable evidence that the universe is homogenous, the same in all directions as far as the telescope can see.

> During the '20s and '30s, as his stature increased, he became part of Hollywood society. A character in his tweed jackets, knickers and English briar pipes, he and his witty wife mingled with the Huxleys, Walt Disney, Charlie Chaplin and Helen Hayes. His friend Albert Einstein called Hubble's work "beautiful," and modified his equations on relativity to account for the discovery that the cosmos is expanding.[1089]

Arthur C Clarke was a British science fiction writer, science writer, inventor, undersea explorer, and television series host. He has Sedna in the fourth house of home, semi-sextile Varuna in the third house of communication.

> He is perhaps most famous for being co-writer of the screenplay for the movie *2001: A Space Odyssey*, considered by the American Film Institute to be one of the most influential films of all time. His other science fiction writings earned him a number of Hugo and Nebula awards, along with a large readership.

> He was a lifelong proponent of space travel. While still a teenager, he joined the British Interplanetary Society. At 28 he proposed a satellite communication system, an idea that, eighteen years later, won him the Franklin Institute's Stuart Ballantine Medal. Later he was the longtime chairman of the British Interplanetary Society. He was also a science writer, who was both an avid populariser of space travel and a futurist of

---

[1089] https://en.wikipedia.org/wiki/Edwin_Hubble

uncanny ability. These all together eventually earned him the moniker "prophet of the space age".[1090]

Humour can be one path to transcend the quicksand of Sedna, giving us the objectivity to step back from the edge and also with the flowing aspects to Varuna, a sensitivity to the freeing effect of humour on our lives.

Oliver Hardy was an American comic actor and one half of Laurel and Hardy, the classic double act that began in the era of silent films and lasted 25 years. He had Sedna conjunct Pholus, the centaur of enlightenment, in the first house of identity, sextile Varuna in the twelfth house of the unconscious. He appeared with his comedy partner Stan Laurel in 107 short films, feature films, and cameo roles.

And Groucho Marx was an American writer, comedian, stage, film and television star. His Sedna is in the fifth house of creativity, sextile Varuna, which is conjunct Jupiter, the planet of success, both in the third house of communication.

> He was known as a master of quick wit and is widely considered one of the best comedians of the modern era. He made 13 feature films with his siblings the Marx Brothers, Harpo Marx and Chico Marx, of whom he was the third-born.

> His distinctive appearance, carried over from his days in vaudeville, included quirks such as an exaggerated stooped posture, glasses, cigar, and a thick greasepaint moustache and eyebrows. Among Groucho's many contributions to film comedy were his rapier wit, illogical chain of deductive reasoning and the visual pun. His standard persona of eyes rolled upward under wiggled brows with painted moustache and poised cigar created an classic comic insouciance. Towards the end of his long career, after a decade of semi-retirement, he began appearing in one-night solo concert performances, culminating in a sold-out performance in New York's Carnegie Hall. This outstanding comeback created a sensation that revived an international interest in his films and the Cannes Film Festival made him a Commander of the French Order of Arts and Letters.[1091]

[1090] https://en.wikipedia.org/wiki/Arthur_C._Clarke
[1091] https://en.wikipedia.org/wiki/Groucho_Marx

At this juncture in human evolution, few of us use our planets at the spiritual level, but many of us are striving to, and such people are wonderful to be around. As with the other planets, the spiritual level of evolution is vastly different with Sedna from the two previous levels.

Here, the flowing aspects with Varuna bring a moral authority which is able to mediate between the the incomprehensible cosmic order and the order of society. The struggle of the beginner's level is gone, as are the transcendental crises of the intermediate level. At this level everything Saturnian is meaningless and yet everything Sednian has its place.

Billy Graham was an American evangelist, a Southern Baptist preacher who was "born again" as a teen, accepting Jesus as his personal saviour. He has Sedna in the first house of identity semi-sextile Varuna in the 12th house of the unconscious.

> He spread the good word of God by way of 900 radio stations and many TV crusades. He published a magazine, *Decision,* with circulation of more than four million, and gradually moved into the TV ministry. World- traveled, he became internationally known as the spiritual leader of presidents and noted people in many walks of life.[1092]

His Sedna is also in a fateful inconjunct with his sun, the planet of will, in the eighth house of shared resources and sits at the tip of two stressful sesquiquadrates, one to Mercury, the planet of communication, also in the eighth house, and the other with Saturn, the planet of structure, in the sixth house of service.

> The author of 24 books, many of them best-sellers, Graham is the recipient of several awards. He is never unctuous or pious; rather, he is earnest, quietly confident and, despite his iconic status, ministers from a personal level. It is estimated that he has preached to more people in live audiences than anyone else in history: some 210 million in more than 185 countries and territories. Hundreds of millions more have been reached through his TV, film, radio, video and print projects.[1093]

And Paramahansa Yogananda was an East Indian author, mystic and founder of the Self-Realization Fellowship. World traveled and a world

---

[1092] https://en.wikipedia.org/wiki/Billy_Graham
[1093] Ibid.

teacher, he carried Eastern philosophy to the West. He has Sedna conjunct Mars the planet of action, in the eighth house of shared resources, sextile Varuna in the sixth house of service.

In 1920, he was invited to serve as India's delegate to an international congress of religious leaders convening in Boston. His address to the congress, on "The Science of Religion," was enthusiastically received. When Yogananda arrived in America on 9/20/1920, the "New World" was ready to receive the advanced teachings that had previously been reserved for monastics and chelas in ashrams. Science, literacy, communication, and new spiritual insights had just begun breaking down the dark ages of theology and dogma.

He founded his fellowship to disseminate worldwide his teachings on India's ancient science and philosophy of Yoga and its time-honored tradition of meditation, introducing the Bhagavad Gita and other scriptures to help raise the consciousness of humanity. He lectured and taught on the East coast of American for several years and in 1924 began a speaking tour across the country. His lectures, in which he spoke of the underlying unity of the world's great religions, were attended by thousands drawn to his message. His personal students were taught the ancient soul-awakening techniques of Kriya Yoga.

Yogananda's articulate and sincere introduction to the disciplines of the East opened the door for many other Indian teachers and gurus, as a serious interest in yoga and meditation made great inroads in the West. His main mission was to build a lasting bridge of World Brotherhood based on raising the spiritual awareness between the East and West.[1094]

Semi-square, Square, Sesquiquadrate,

With the stressful aspects between Sedna and Varuna, the all-encompassing spiritual energy of Sedna challenges our sense of competence and mastery, our ability to let go of losses and resentments, and accept and delegate authority.

[1094] https://en.wikipedia.org/wiki/Paramahansa_Yogananda

Varuna deals with questions of the gain and loss of reputation, and the issue of immortality through fame. It seems to represent that which is beyond the real and also beyond visions and aspirations, something that is quite literally behind everything. Varuna's energy seems closest to what we in the West think of as God, the all-knowing cosmic entity that exists silently behind consciousness and events.

At the unconscious level however, the stressful aspects between these two planets can be challenging, as they can bring out the more negative side of Varuna, which is incompetence and casting blame, rather than taking responsibility, and lamenting losses and holding resentments.

Like Winnie Ruth Judd, who was an American secretary and homicide perpetrator. She had Sedna in the sixth house of daily routine, semi-square Varuna in the fourth house of home.

> A tiny, sweet-faced, redheaded young woman with enigmatic blue eyes, she married at 18, quitting nursing school to wed Dr. William Judd, a widower, more than 20 years her senior. Seeking the desert climate for her health, she moved to Phoenix by herself at 25 and lived with two other female flatmates, who had some good times together, aided by prohibition hooch and a number of free-spending gentleman callers.
>
> When Judd and one of the other girls started up dating the same man, Judd moved out. Then one night when her beau did not call, she went to her friend's apartment, but he was not there. According to prosecutors, she then killed her two ex flatmates in cold blood as they slept in their beds.
>
> Her story is that they argued. One of the others brought out a pistol that Judd had left there when she moved out. As the two struggled, the gun went off twice, killing the girl. The second girl swung an ironing board at her and Judd shot her. A gunshot wound on her hand and 147 bruises lent credence to her story, however she never told this story of self-defence in court, but kept silent to protect her married lover, whom she said had assured her that he would "take care of things."
>
> Evading the gallows by declaring insanity, she escaped seven times from an asylum for the criminally insane, until her parole and release 38 years later. During one of her periods on the outside, she worked for a wealthy blind woman as a companion;

it was to this family in northern California that she went when she was released. After her employer died, she wound up suing the family for keeping her in in virtual slavery and won a $50,000 settlement and a lifetime monthly income of $1,250. Then lived out her years quietly under an assumed name.[1095]

Or like Elizabeth Smart, who is an American who went missing at age fourteen, abducted from her home as her family slept. Her Sedna is in the third house of communication, semi-square Varuna in the fifth house of creativity.

The second of six kids, she grew up in a close-knit Mormon family, reading scripture and praying morning and evening. On the evening just before her disappearance, she and her family had attended an award ceremony at Elizabeth's middle school, where she was recognised for various school accomplishments. The family prayed together and kissed goodnight, however sometime in the early morning hours, a man entered the bedroom she shared with her younger sister and spirited her away.[1096]

Her Sedna is also closely opposite her conjunction of Pluto, the planet of transformation, and the Sun, the planet of willpower, in the ninth house of knowledge.

No ransom note was found and no trace of her was reported until she was spotted walking in a suburb of the same city with a shaggy-haired vagabond nine months later. During her ordeal, she spent a great deal of the time near her home wearing disguises and veils in public. The Smart family believes she was brainwashed, citing that she did not call out for help, or apparently try to escape, even when she heard rescuers call out her name.

However, nearly two years after her rescue, her father said that she is "just a normal teenager who likes shopping and going to the movies with friends". A self-assured young woman and college graduate, she confronted her kidnapper at his trial and

[1095] https://en.wikipedia.org/wiki/Winnie_Ruth_Judd
[1096] https://en.wikipedia.org/wiki/Elizabeth_Smart

then accepted a job as a contributor for a television network in its coverage of missing persons.[1097]

As we tire of density and the grief it creates, and we start a spiritual journey to get out of the swamp, Sedna rewards us with transcendent crises, experiences which force us to let go and rise above them, resulting in a huge growth to a new level of consciousness. There is no choice with these crises, and the more we try and solve them, the more we will get hurt.

Gustavo Rol was an Italian psychic whose skills were studied by many parapsychologists and who has also been studied in many books dealing with psychic or paranormal phenomena. His Sedna was in the seventh house of relationships, semi-square Varuna in the fifth house of creativity.

> While in Marseille he encountered a person, who showed him some card tricks, triggering an interest in magical and paranormal phenomena. He pursued deeper spiritual studies and had an experience in Paris of which he wrote in his diary: "I discovered a tremendous law that links the colour green, the musical fifth, and heat. I have lost my will to live. I am frightened by power. I shall write no more!" As a result of this crisis, he briefly retreated to a convent.

> He engaged in various demonstrations of his supposed mystical powers, including telepathy, clairvoyance, and other psychic or magical feats, however toward the later part of his life, and after his death, he was a focal point of debate in Italy between skeptics and advocates of parapsychology. His followers felt his refusal to be the subject of a serious study was proof of the existence of his powers, while skeptics felt this refusal was proof that it was all a fraud.

> Although his followers felt he was possessed of sometimes dangerous supernatural powers and there were others who classified him a great thinker, yet others considered him to be a clever exploiter, this despite the fact that he never asked his

---

[1097] Ibid.

followers for money and he continually discouraged everyone from an interest in the occult and supernatural.[1098]

B.F. Skinner was an American psychologist who believed human behaviour could be engineered to build a better world, one of the most influential and controversial psychologists of the 20th Century. He was both adored as a messiah and abhorred as a menace. He had Sedna in the second house of material resources, semi-square Varuna in the first house of identity.

A Harvard psychology professor, he made behavioural modification studies with rats and pigeons, applying the observation methods to working with the modification of human response. His principle of "operant behaviour" holds that even seemingly spontaneous action is a response to rewards and punishment. People do not shape the world, he believed, the world shapes them. He fathered the experimental analysis of behaviour in which an organism's behaviour was studied in a controlled laboratory environment. Skinner's work came in a series of scholarly books, including *The Behaviour of Organisms*, and *Science and Human Behavior.*

He also wrote a novel, *Walden Two*, in which he described a tightly controlled utopia in which people were motivated by positive and negative reinforcements, by rewards and punishment. In his image of a better world, people don't know the meaning of envy and jealousy, buildings are communally owned and everyone helps out with chores. There is time for reading and painting, song and friendship. And the key to this community's success is child rearing. Youngsters are raised together. Discipline is strict, and children are taught to rein in their desires through self-control exercises.

The book didn't do well initially, critics decried his model society as tyrannical and others thought a world populated by such happy and well-behaved people would be bland, but during the 1960s the book attracted a kind of cult following and hundreds of thousands of copies were sold.[1099]

[1098] https://en.wikipedia.org/wiki/Gustavo_Rol
[1099] https://en.wikipedia.org/wiki/B._F._Skinner

George Orwell was a British novelist and essayist whose work is marked by lucid prose, awareness of social injustice, opposition to totalitarianism, and outspoken support of democratic socialism. He has Sedna in the sixth house of service, semi-square Varuna in the fourth house of home.

> He won his greatest success with his amusing and witty anti-communist satire, *Animal Farm*, and with his shocking and insightful futuristic novel, *1984*. His work continues to influence popular and political culture, and the term Orwellian – descriptive of totalitarian or authoritarian social practices – has entered the language together with many of his neologisms, including cold war, Big Brother, Thought Police, Room 101, memory hole, newspeak, doublethink, and thoughtcrime.[1100]

Humour can be one path to transcend the quicksand of Sedna, giving us the objectivity to step back from the edge and also with the stressful aspects to Varuna, a sensitivity to the freeing effect of humour on our lives.

Fernandel was a French actor and mime comedian with a long, sorrowful, equine face and a radiant and toothy smile. He had Sedna in the eleventh house of collective consciousness, semi-square Varuna in the ninth house of knowledge.

> One of France's leading box-office draws, he built a four-decade career from the age of 27. His films included the four great "Don Camillo" political comedies. His father was an accountant but also an amateur comedian-singer and his mother was also an amateur actress, quickly noticed the talent of the young Fernand. He often accompanied his father during the concerts he organised in the Marseilles suburbs.

> He made his debut on stage at five years singing the military repertory with his elder brother. He had his first great success at the age of seven, a day when, paralyzed by stage fright, he was propelled on the stage by his father, with a great kick to the rear; He fell into his sabre, and stretched his whole length under a storm of laughter. Later, he was never afraid to face the public.

[1100] https://en.wikipedia.org/wiki/George_Orwell

In 1930, he appeared in his first motion picture and for more than forty years he would be France's top comic actor. He was perhaps best loved for his portrayal of the irascible Italian village priest at war with the town's Communist mayor in the Don Camillo series of motion pictures which he also directed. His horse-like teeth became part of his trademark.[1101]

At this juncture in human evolution, few of us use our planets at the spiritual level, but many of us are striving to, and such people are wonderful to be around. As with the other planets, the spiritual level of evolution is vastly different with Sedna from the two previous levels.

Here, even the stressful aspects with Varuna bring a moral authority born of a deeply spiritual understanding of our lives and a transcendence of restrictions. The struggle of the beginner's level is gone, as are the transcendental crises of the intermediate level. At this level everything Saturnian is meaningless and yet everything Sednian has its place.

Few of us are born enlightened however, and most of us have to work to grow out of the unconscious state. Marthe Robin was a French mystic and stigmatic. She had Sedna conjunct Pallas, the asteroid of wisdom, in the eighth house of the occult, semi-square Varuna in the sixth house of service.

> Serious illness marked her adult life and from her twenties she was confined to bed, crippled, and gradually paralyzed. She ate only wafers and neither drank nor slept, but lived for seven decades and carried on a busy apostolate. From the age of 28 she was completely paralysed and bedridden. Although she still could move the thumb and forefinger of one hand, she became motionless apart from her head which she could move slightly. Since the previous year, at the age of 25, she could not eat anything at all. And from the age of 26 she couldn't even take a sip of water. When doctors tried to force some water down her throat, it merely came out her nostrils.
>
> For the next 53 years Marthe's only food was the holy Eucharist. Once a week she was given the sacred host. Once she had received it she went immediately into ecstasy and began her

---

[1101] https://en.wikipedia.org/wiki/Fernandel

weekly re-living of Christ's Passion and crucifixion. Every Friday wounds appeared in the palms of her hands and the stigmata, the scourging and crowning with thorns appeared on her body, and she appeared to be dead.

She was directed to found two schools in her native village, one for girls and one for boys. All this she directed down to the smallest detail from her bed in her darkened little room. Later she was told to found a community which would welcome people looking for a retreat and which would be a home of "light, charity and love." It became known as the Foyer de Charité and there are now some 70 affiliated houses and communities throughout the world.[1102]

Some however, are born enlightened. Swami Vivekananda was an Indian religious leader, a disciple of Sri Ramakrishna, who became inspired by his teacher to serve men as a visible manifestation of God. His Sedna was on the cusp of the third house of communication, square Varuna in the twelfth house of karma.

An illumined being of the highest order, he was the forerunner who brought the spiritual teachings of India to the West, greatly influencing the last hundred years of spiritual growth in Europe and America. Highly intelligent with a retentive memory, he had stories of the scripture memorised by the time he was six.

He became one of the most beloved disciples of Sri Ramakrishna and, as the master spent his last years teaching his disciples and streams of visitors, Vivekananda recorded his instruction. He then brought the spiritual teachings of India to the West at the convening of the Parliament of Religions in Chicago. During his three-year stay in American, he founded Hindu philosophy schools, many of which acknowledge him as a modern Buddha and an emanation of Lord Shiva.[1103]

In-conjunct

There is no one alive today with this aspect and none occurs during the next century, so it is not interpreted here.

[1102] https://en.wikipedia.org/wiki/Marthe_Robin
[1103] https://en.wikipedia.org/wiki/Swami_Vivekananda

Quintile, Bi-quintile

The evolutionary quintile or bi-quintile aspect between Sedna and Varuna infuses our sense of competence and mastery, our ability to let go of losses and resentments, and accept and delegate authority, with the all-encompassing spiritual energy of Sedna to the point where we can push the boundaries of human development.

Quintiles and bi-quintiles point to talent, the desire to create order and to categorize, a fascination with patterns and structures, perfectionist tendencies, and the desire to build or make things. These aspects have the characteristics of both the trine and opposition. They point to awareness of conflicts, or problems and finding solutions for them; however, they do not automatically kick into action and must be cultivated over time.

Varuna deals with questions of the gain and loss of reputation, and the issue of immortality through fame. It seems to represent that which is beyond the real and also beyond visions and aspirations, something that is quite literally 'behind everything'. Varuna's energy seems closest to what we in the West think of as God, the all-knowing cosmic entity that exists silently behind consciousness and events.

At the unconscious level the quintiles and bi-quintiles with Varuna can give us brilliant ideas and insight, but this is likely to come with a distorted world view which accepts no boundaries to our behaviour and which lends a sense of righteousness to the way we live our lives

Like Fritz Haarmann, who was a German homicidal manic and a homosexual epileptic. He had Sedna in the eleventh house of ideals in a fateful inconjunct with his Sun, the planet of willpower, in the sixth house of service and in a stressful sesquiquadrate with Ceres, the planet of nurturing, in the fourth house of home.

> From youth, he served several prison terms for indecency and was committed several times to an insane asylum. He primarily lived as a petty thief, burglar and con artist. Although he did occasionally obtain legitimate employment, he invariably stole from his employers or their customers.

> Despite police knowledge that he was both a criminal and a homosexual, which was then illegal and punishable by imprisonment in Germany, he gradually began to establish a

relationship with Hanover police as an informer, largely as a means of redirecting their attention from himself in his own criminal activities, and to facilitate his access to young males.

He is known to have committed at least 24 murders, although he is suspected of murdering a minimum of 27. All of his victims were males between the ages of 10 and 22, the majority of whom were in their mid- to late-teens. They would be lured back to one of three addresses in which he is known to have lived, on the promise of assistance, accommodation, work, or under the pretence of citizen's arrest. Following his arrest, rumours circulated that he had eaten the flesh of his victims and sold it on the black market as pork, or horsemeat. Although no physical evidence was ever produced to confirm these theories, he was known to be an active trader in contraband meat, which was invariably boneless, diced and often sold as mince.[1104]

Or like Pietro Vincenzo Peruggia, who was an Italian thief who first moved to France as a house painter, decorator and labourer. He has Sedna in the fourth house of home, quintile Varuna in the second house of material resources.

He was an Italian decorator, who became famous for having stolen the Mona Lisa from the Louvre Museum. He had hidden himself in a dark room in the Louvre and at the closing he took the Mona Lisa from the frame and then escaped from a back door that he opened with a small knife. The next day the employees thought at first that the picture was with the official photographer, but then they had to inform the police.

After about two years he tried to sell the Mona Lisa to a gallery for a few million lire, if the buyer would "return it to its homeland, Italy." He met the gallery director in a hotel in Florence, who, after seeing the painting, took it into his possession to examine it. He was arrested the following day by the carabinieri, who took him directly from his hotel room.[1105]

Or, without appropriate boundaries, but with the venire of notability, we might get mired in the depths of Sedna, like Edgar Allan Poe, who was

---

[1104] https://en.wikipedia.org/wiki/Fritz_Haarmann
[1105] https://it.wikipedia.org/wiki/Vincenzo_Peruggia

an American writer known for his poetry and short stories in the early 1800s, most famous for his macabre and mysterious works. He had Sedna in the fifth house of creativity, bi-quintile Varuna in the twelfth house of the unconscious. His Sedna is also semi-square Eris, the planet of 'consciousness through discord', and sextile Haumea, the planet of rebirth, both in the third house of ideas and communication.

> His first publication was at the age of eighteen and all of his works, including poetry and short stories were widely translated. The second of three kids, his dad disappeared when he was two and his mom died when he was four. His brother Henry drank himself to an early death and his sister Rosalie died homeless and destitute. He himself lived a life of grinding poverty and a series of calamities and had periods of insanity from alcohol, heroin and opium dementia.

> He married his 13-year-old first cousin when he was 27 and they delayed intimacy for at least two years. He was widowed at 38 and died a couple of years later, allegedly from alcoholism though one historian relates that it could have been from rabies. He had twice made serious suicide attempts and had period of psychotic episodes, however he was inducted into the Hall of Fame for Great Americans early last century.[1106]

As we tire of density and the grief it creates, and we start a spiritual journey to get out of the swamp, Sedna rewards us with transcendent crises, experiences which force us to let go and rise above them, resulting in a huge growth to a new level of consciousness. There is no choice with these crises, and the more we try and solve them, the more we will get hurt.

Like Guillaume Seznec, who was a French citizen unjustly accused of a homicide. His Sedna is in a wide conjunction to his Saturn, the planet of restrictions, in the seventh hose of relationships, and in a wide square to Mars, the planet of action, in the tenth house of social standing. It is also closely square Nessus, the centaur of sudden transformation, in the fourth house of home.

> He left for Paris with a friend to sell a Cadillac and when his friend's family did not hear from him, they reported that he was

---

[1106] https://en.wikipedia.org/wiki/Edgar_Allan_Poe

missing. Guillaume was arrested and accused of the murder. He was sentenced to hard labour for life and was sent to Guyana, the French penal colony.[1107]

His Sedna is also semi-square the conjunction of Venus, the planet of values, and Vesta, the asteroid of hearth and home, both in the ninth house of law and this, together with his Quintile with Varuna in the fourth house of home, enabled his release.

> The case was reopened seven years later when six of the jurors who had condemned him said they regretted their verdict and asked for a review of the trial. The Inspector who had been involved in the original investigation concluded that he had sent an innocent man to jail, a presidential pardon was made and Seznec returned to France.[1108]

Charles Darwin was an English naturalist and author of *Origin of the Species*, a book which caused a storm of debate by proposing the theory of evolution. He had Sedna conjunct Juno, the asteroid of partnership, in the third house of ideas, bi-quintile Varuna, which is conjunct Mars, the planet of action, in the tenth house of profession.

> He is described as one of the most influential figures in human history. The son of a famed doctor, he was raised in a free-thinking family and studied medicine at Edinburgh, which he soon abandoned to become a fanatical naturalist. Frail in health, he spent a lifetime with a chronic intestinal disorder that caused bouts of vomiting. His Sedna is also semi-square Eris, the planet of 'consciousness through discord' in the second house of material resources and his theories of evolution through natural selection instigated a revolution in biological science.[1109]

Pablo Picasso was a Spanish artist who lived most of his life in France, Picasso is world-renowned as one of the inventors of the Cubist movement. He has Sedna in the ninth house of knowledge, quintile Varuna in the sixth house of service.

> Considered to be the most original, influential and dominant presence in the visual arts of the early 20th century, his works

---

[1107] https://en.wikipedia.org/wiki/Seznec_affair
[1108] Ibid.
[1109] https://en.wikipedia.org/wiki/Charles_Darwin

are on display in the most prestigious museums and galleries of the world. His enormous output, including 14,000 canvases and thousands of prints, engravings, book illustrations, ceramics and sculptures, made him a billionaire at his death. His various studios and houses contained not only his own work, but also other works and collections that he had amassed over the years.[1110]

His Sedna was also closely opposite Venus, the planet of values and relationships, in the third house of ideas and communication, and trine Juno, the asteroid of partnership, in the fifth house of romance.

His sexual appetite led him into many relationships and two marriages. Beauty and relative youth were the only consistent qualities he desired in women and he used almost all of his women as models, both before and after relationships.[1111]

Humour can be one path to transcend the quicksand of Sedna, giving us the objectivity to step back from the edge and also with Varuna both an authority and a sensitivity to the freeing effect of humour on our lives.

Famous Swiss clown, Grock, is a composer and musician, who is often called 'the king of clowns'. He has Sedna in the first house of identity, quintile with Varuna in the twelfth house of the unconscious.

He was a great success from both the financial and entertainment point of view and was once the most highly paid entertainer in the world. He started early, learning musicianship and acrobatic skills from his father and later became a clown, working with the famous clown, Antonet. Their act was developed with the aim of making the transition from circus, to music hall stages, which were more lucrative.

Refining their performances according to audience response, Grock came to dominate the act, and they eventually split up. By then Grock's fame had spread, his act having developed into the mixture of pantomime and musical blunders for which he is now remembered. He was also the author of the book, *I Love Life*.[1112]

[1110] https://en.wikipedia.org/wiki/Pablo_Picasso
[1111] Ibid.
[1112] https://en.wikipedia.org/wiki/Grock

At this juncture in human evolution, few of us use our planets at the spiritual level, but many of us are striving to, and such people are wonderful to be around. As with the other planets, the spiritual level of evolution is vastly different with Sedna from the two previous levels.

Here, the quintile and bi-quintile aspects with Varuna bring a moral authority born of a deeply spiritual understanding of our lives, which can reshape the world for generations. The struggle of the beginner's level is gone, as are the transcendental crises of the intermediate level. At this level everything Saturnian is meaningless and yet everything Sednian has its place.

Like Albert Einstein, who was a German-Swiss-American scientist, a physicist who developed the theory of relativity and the general theory, laying the groundwork for 20th century physics and providing the essential structure of the cosmos. He has Sedna conjunct Mercury, the planet of ideas, and Saturn the planet of Structure, all in the tenth house of profession, quintile Varuna in the seventh house of relationships.

> He was born with a misshapen head and abnormally large body. He learned to talk so late that his parents feared that he was mentally retarded, not until he was three, and was not fluent until he was nine. For a while, he was considered subnormal because of his slow development, and his teachers were continually saying that he would never amount to anything.

> His youth seemed to be one of deliberate rebellion against the establishment of his times. At age 16 he quit school, joined his parents in Milan, Italy, where they had moved, and renounced his German citizenship. At 17, he entered the Zurich Polytechnic Institute after having failed on the first try and graduated with a mathematics teaching degree. The next year he took Swiss citizenship, and the year after that, a post at the Swiss patent office. It was while at the Swiss patent office, in a clerical position, that Einstein began the work that would make him a legend.

> At 26 he published three seminal papers on theoretical physics in a single volume of a German scientific journal and two years later he came up with the immortal e=mc2, better known as the Special Theory of Relativity, encapsulating energy and matter as aspects of a single phenomenon. A year later, while still at the

patent office, he began work on his major achievement, the general theory of relativity, which he officially proposed eight years later. These theories were the greatest challenge to Newtonian mechanics that the modern world had ever known, but Einstein had a way of conceptualising and communicating them. He described relativity thus: 'Put your hand on a hot stove for a minute and it seems like an hour. Sit with a pretty girl for an hour and it seems like a minute.'

Experiencing the universe as a harmonious whole, he encouraged the use of intuition to solve problems, marvelled at the the mystery of God in nature, and applauded the ideals of great spiritual teachers such as Buddha and Jesus. Here's how he put it: 'I like to experience the universe as one harmonious whole. Every cell has life. Matter, too, has life; it is energy solidified. Our bodies are like prisons, and I look forward to be free, but I don't speculate on what will happen to me. I live here now, and my responsibility is in this world now. I deal with natural laws. This is my work here on earth. If we want to improve the world we cannot do it with scientific knowledge but with ideals. Confucius, Buddha, Jesus and Gandhi have done more for humanity than science has done. We must begin with the heart of man, with his conscience, and the values of conscience can only be manifested by selfless service to mankind. Religion and science go together. Science without religion is lame and religion without science is blind. They are interdependent and have a common goal, the search for truth.'

'Without religion there is no charity. The soul given to each of us is moved by the same living spirit that moves the universe. I am not a mystic. Trying to find out the laws of nature has nothing to do with mysticism, though in the face of creation I feel very humble. It is as if a spirit is manifest that is infinitely superior to man's spirit. Through my pursuit in science I have known cosmic religious feelings. But I don't care to be called a mystic.'[1113]

By contrast Ramana Maharishi was an Indian mystic of the Hindu religion. who, after a mystical experience at age 17, left his parents to

---

[1113] https://en.wikipedia.org/wiki/Albert_Einstein

become an aesetic. He has Sedna in the sixth house of service, quintile Varuna on the IC, the cusp of the fourth house of home.

> The second of three sons of a farmer, he was raised in a religious family who gave ritual offerings and visited the temple. A disinterested student, he was more concerned with seeking his own identity and meaning. At 17 he went into an altered state of consciousness which had a profound effect on him. He experienced what he understood to be his own death, and later returned to life. He also felt himself as being outside of his own body, an entity of light.
>
> He spent the next ten years in silence and meditation, living in temples and hillside caves as an aesetic. It is the custom in India to regard such holy men, seeking non-attachment, with respect and he was called The Sage of Anarchala. Devotees brought him a bit of food and books of religious tradition, and when he began to teach, disciples came. After his decade of discipline, he lived a more normal life in an ashram that his disciplines built and taught student and supplicants. When he was finally diagnosed with cancer, he accepted this with the same equanimity that he had for mundane goods, and died sitting in the lotus position with his last word, the sacred syllable OM.[1114]

And finally, Alice A Bailey was an American theosophist, esoteric astrologer and author. She had Sedna in the ninth house of knowledge, quintile Varuna in the sixth house of service.

> Unhappy in youth, she broke away from her early environment when she was 22. While studying the occult, she became an evangelist and social worker. Then at 39 she made contact with 'the Tibetan' and two years later founded her Arcane School. Together with her second husband, she organised the International Goodwill Movement, which had centres in 19 countries and she wrote 30 metaphysical books on ancient teachings.[1115]

[1114] https://en.wikipedia.org/wiki/Ramana_Maharshi
[1115] https://en.wikipedia.org/wiki/Alice_Bailey

44: Sedna / Quaoar

Conjunction

There is no one alive today with this aspect and none occurs during the next century, so it is not interpreted here.

Opposition

With the opposition between Sedna and Quaoar, the all-encompassing spiritual energy of Sedna challenges our ability to see the big picture, flaws and all, to understand the sacredness of life, to set out in a spirit of discovery and gain new perspectives and thereby create a harmonious revolution.

Quaoar is that glorious metaphysical process wherein material form is created out of chaos. It urges us to question, construct, clarify and reveal and gives us the potential to ground the sacred energy, to take the cosmic chaos and bring it into form, thereby creating a new reality.

With the opposition to Sedna this ability to bring form out of chaos stands in relief against the big spiritual picture and at the unconscious level will likely result in ego-based attempts to hijack the energy rather than surrendering to the cosmic order. If we are misusing the Quaoar energy we will see how ego can bungle chaos and snarl us up in a personal soap opera.

Like Richard Kameese, who was an American drug fatality at age 21, after drug addiction that began when he was in high school. He had Sedna in the ninth house of knowledge, conjunct Saturn, the planet of restrictions, opposite Quaoar and the Moon, the planet of emotions, and Jupiter, the planet of expansion, in the third house of ideas and communication. To top it off his Sedna is also in a fateful inconjunct with Neptune, the planet of delusions, which is conjunct his IC, the cusp of his fourth house of home.

> Richard was living with his parents when his folks went to a wake, leaving him home alone because he was using drugs. When they returned they saw his shoeless footprints in the snow and knew he was on another rampage. He went to the home of a couple who lived a couple hundred yards away and burst in, staggering and in a drug-crazed state saying "They're going to get me." He grabbed a kitchen mop and began swinging at his imaginary enemies and at the couple, who then called the police,

as Richard drew a knife. It took four men to subdue him; however, while in a jail cell, he stopped breathing and died a few hours later.[1116]

Or like Amy Fisher, who was an American teenager who was in the news for adolescent prostitution and the attempted murder of her lover's wife. She has Sedna in the first house of identity, opposite Quaoar in the seventh house of relationships.

> She first ran away from home at 11 to go to Disneyland and claimed that she had been sexually assaulted at 13 by a workman at home. By 16, she was sporting new clothes and having fun, spending some $400 to $500 a week, telling her classmates and others that she was working for an escort service and that having sex for money was no big deal.[1117]

Her Sedna is also in a fateful inconjunct with Pluto, the planet of life and death, in the sixth house of service, quintile Saturn, the planet of restrictions, in the fourth house of home.

> She began a sexual relationship with a 35-year-old mechanic after damaging the car her parents had given her for her 16th birthday and appealing to the owner of the body shop to which she took it, to make the repairs without her family knowing of the damage.
>
> She gradually fell in love with him and became increasingly jealous of his wife. Eventually, the then 17-year-old shared her idea of murdering his wife. Less than a year after she first had sex with him, she rang the doorbell of his home and when his wife answered the door, Amy shot her in the face, wounding her severely. She was picked up by the police three days later, pled guilty to charges of assault with a deadly weapon and was sentenced to 5-15 years in prison.[1118]

Her Sedna is also trine to Mercury, the planet of communication, in the fourth house of home and she received $8,000 from a magazine for a first-person piece on her experience. After her release from prison, she became a columnist for the *Long Island Press* and dictated a book about

---

[1116] https://www.astro.com/astro-databank/Kameese,_Richard
[1117] https://en.wikipedia.org/wiki/Amy_Fisher
[1118] Ibid.

her experiences titled *If I Knew Then...*, indicating she had grown through the crises.

> She met her husband, a physical-fitness fanatic and wedding-photographer, some 25 years older than her, who has two kids from a former marriage. They married and, although the relationship was tempestuous, the couple had three children. And she reunited a few years later with the wife she had shot, in sessions televised for *Entertainment Tonight* and its spin-off, *The Insider*, saying she wanted to heal and move on with her life. However, two years later, she said she felt no sympathy for the woman, without giving an explanation.
>
> Then the *New York Post* published allegations that her husband had sold a sex tape of the couple to Red Light District Video of Los Angeles. Nude pictures from the video were posted at various internet sites, and a teaser clip was released that showed her nude showering and sunbathing. But a year later Fisher announced that she had settled with Red Light and agreed to do a related promotional appearance. The same announcement indicated that she and her husband had reconciled.
>
> The following year she released a pay-per-view adult film titled *Amy Fisher: Totally Nude & Exposed* and signed a deal with Lee Entertainment to become a stripper doing club shows at least once a month. And her struggles to assert herself and deal with her alcohol problems were documented during her time as a cast member in the fifth season of the reality television series, *Celebrity Rehab with Dr. Drew*. In her time as one of his patients, Fisher revealed intimate details of her personal life and experiences, and remarked that the media had "ruined her life".[1119]

The soap opera morphed into spectacle with Marilyn Manson, who was an American shock-rocker, rising to the top of the charts on a platform of drag, nudity, arson, drugs and Satanism. He has Sedna in the ninth house of knowledge, opposite Quaoar in the third house of communication.

[1119] Ibid.

The self-proclaimed Antichrist superstar, carved out a goal for himself of becoming the most controversial entertainer of the '90s, whose show has at times included skinned goats heads and a fluorescent "Kill God" sign, all under the umbrella of free speech with the express intention of "exploring the limits of censorship." Though widely dismissed by critics, his brand of metal nevertheless struck a major chord with the youth market, comprised almost entirely of disaffected white suburban teens - primarily through the same sort of marketing that Madonna does so well, in-your-face performance spectacle.[1120]

His Sedna is also square Mercury, the planet of communication, in the sixth house of service, and bi-quintile Pluto, the planet of the occult, in the second house of material resources.

His father had a very violent temper and was never home, so he was a mama's boy. He tells us: 'I had a weird relationship with my mom as a kid, because I was kind of abusive. I wish I could go back and change the way I treated my mom because I used to be really rude to her, and she didn't really have any kind of control over me." One of the Manson T-shirts reads, Kill Your Parents.

I first started having really vivid dreams as a kid around the same time when I was spying on my grandfather masturbating,' he goes on, "I used to take pictures of naked women, and I would cut out just their sex organs. And I started having really violent dreams that I was going that to real people. It freaked me out as a kid." He was fascinated with the devil, with abortion, with sex, and terrified of scorpions.[1121]

His Sedna is also sextile Venus, the planet of values, in the seventh house of relationships, trine Ceres, the planet of nurturing, in the fifth house of creativity and semi-sextile Chiron, the centaur of shamanistic processes, in the eighth house of shared resources.

Manson craves spectacle, success and attention. When it comes to the traditional rock-star lifestyle, he can outdo most of his contemporaries with an ostentatious lifestyle, and his occasional

---

[1120] https://en.wikipedia.org/wiki/Marilyn_Manson
[1121] Ibid.

temper tantrums have left dressing rooms destroyed and a band member hospitalised. He takes his name and himself very seriously. He has the repulsion-fascination of a car-wreck where we may see blood, gore and death. He is quoted as having the viewpoint that "the opposite of love is apathy, and hate is really the same as love.[1122]

As we tire of density and the grief it creates, and we start a spiritual journey to get out of the swamp, Sedna rewards us with transcendent crises, experiences which force us to let go and rise above them, resulting in a huge growth to a new level of consciousness. There is no choice with these crises, and the more we try and solve them, the more we will get hurt.

Michelle Mone is a Scottish entrepreneur, designer of the Ultimo, a bra that has taken engineering to a new front as it has tiny pockets filled with silicone gel to imitate the natural movement of a real breast. She has Sedna in the second house of material resources, opposite Quaoar in the eighth house of shared resources.

> For her financial backing, one businessman took a 25% stake in the company when his wife tried on a model and promptly announced from Michelle's bedroom that he must do so. She was an ambitious kid from the time she was ten, reading business magazines instead of comic books. She is restless, active, full of ideas outside of her busy family with a husband and three kids.

> She released her Ultimo bra when she was 31 and it became very popular. She spent two years working on it before marketing it to manufacturers, while retaining sole distributorship rights to the UK and Europe. Her first goal from profits was to build a wheelchair-friendly bungalow for her dad, who has a rare spinal disease.

> At 43 she was nominated by the British Prime Minister as a Life Peer. Her inclusion drew criticism from other business leaders and some Conservatives questioned her suitability for the House of Lords. Senior Scottish Conservatives also criticised Cameron's action, describing Mone as 'a public relations

---

[1122] Ibid.

creation, a personal brand rather than a serious businesswoman'.[1123]

Thomas Piketty is a French economist who is professor at the Paris School of Economics and Centennial professor at the London School of Economics. He has Sedna in the eleventh house of ideals, opposite Quaoar in the fifth house of creativity.

His work has focussed on wealth and income inequality and when he was 43 he refused to receive the French legion of honour. His Sedna is also in a fateful inconjunct with the conjunction of Neptune, the planet of inspiration, and Jupiter, the planet of expansion, both in the sixth house of service.

He is the author of the best-selling book, *Capital in the Twenty-First Century,* which emphasises the themes of his work on wealth concentrations and distribution over the past 250 years. His Sedna is also square the conjunction of Vesta, the asteroid of regeneration, and Mars, the planet of action, in the eighth house of shared resources and bi-quintile Pluto, the planet of transformation, in the fourth house of home.

The book argues that the rate of capital return in developed countries is persistently greater than the rate of economic growth, and that this will cause wealth inequality to increase in the future. He considers that to be a problem, and to address it, he proposes redistribution through a progressive global tax on wealth.[1124]

Paul Ryan is an American politician, a Republican congressman for Wisconsin and at time of writing the 54th Speaker of the United States House of Representatives. He has Sedna conjunct Saturn, the planet of structure, in the fifth house of creativity, opposite Quaoar in the eleventh house of ideals.

When he was 16, Ryan found his 55-year-old father lying dead in bed of a heart attack. Following the death of his father, Ryan's grandmother moved in with the family. As she had Alzheimer's, Ryan helped care for her while his mother commuted to college.

[1123] https://en.wikipedia.org/wiki/Michelle_Mone,_Baroness_Mone
[1124] https://en.wikipedia.org/wiki/Thomas_Piketty

He has a bachelor's degree in economics and political science from Miami University in Oxford, Ohio, where he became interested in the writings of economists like Milton Friedman. He often visited the office of libertarian professor Richard Hart to discuss the theories of these economists and of Ayn Rand.

He has credited Rand with having inspired him to get involved in public service. In a speech that same year at the Atlas Society, he said he grew up reading Rand, and that her books taught him about his value system and beliefs. He required staffers and interns in his congressional office to read Rand and gave copies of her novel, *Atlas Shrugged*, as gifts to his staff for Christmas. In his Atlas Society speech, he also described Social Security as a "socialist-based system".

In 2009, he said, "What's unique about what's happening today in government, in the world, in America, is that it's as if we're living in an Ayn Rand novel right now. I think Ayn Rand did the best job of anybody to build a moral case for capitalism, and that morality of capitalism is under assault."

However, in 2012, after receiving criticism from Georgetown University faculty members on his budget plan, he rejected Rand's philosophy as an atheistic one, saying it "reduces human interactions down to mere contracts". He also called the reports of his adherence to Rand's views an "urban legend" and stated that he was deeply influenced by his Roman Catholic faith and by Thomas Aquinas.[1125]

At this juncture in human evolution, few of us use our planets at the spiritual level, but many of us are striving to, and such people are wonderful to be around. As with the other planets, the spiritual level of evolution is vastly different with Sedna from the two previous levels.

Here, the opposition with Quaoar brings a sensitivity to esoteric guides and the spirit world and the ability to see things from a fresh perspective, to see the big picture and then take the cosmic chaos and bring it into new form. The struggle of the beginner's level is gone, as are the transcendental crises of the intermediate level. At this level everything Saturnian is meaningless and yet everything Sednian has its place.

[1125] https://en.wikipedia.org/wiki/Paul_Ryan

At this level we have shed our ego-based attempts to hijack cosmic intention and are able to surrender to the cosmic order, because we see that the universe manifests through us, rather than from us, and we'll be at peace with that.

Like Georges Vandenbeusch, who is a French Catholic priest, who was held hostage by the terrorist group Boko Haram and escaped. His Sedna is in his first house of identity, opposite Quaoar in his seventh house of relationships.

> When he was 7 years old, the family was on a boat tour of Corsica at night, when the propeller stalled and everyone was thrown into the water. Only Georges survived, helped to the shore by his lifejacket. Once orphaned, he was raised by his grandparents.[1126]

His Sedna is also at the tip of a finger of fate, in an inconjunct with Pluto, the planet of transformation, in the sixth house of service, and another with Neptune, the planet of inspiration, in the eighth house of life and death.

> He studied to be a priest, was ordained and then held various vicarage positions in Paris, before deciding to become a priest in the extreme north of Cameroon, on the Nigerian border, in order to carry the faith in remote and unstable areas.
>
> He was kidnapped by armed men claiming to be Boko Haram and escaped seven weeks later. Boko Haram then said: "The leadership decided to release the priest out of compassion. The priest offered his medical services to members during his period of captivity. Management felt that there was no need to keep him'.
>
> These remarks, however, are contested by Georges, who stated: "I am neither a nurse nor a doctor. If they had brought me somebody to take care with a hemorrhage, I would have done what I could, but they did not. They have no compassion for anyone ."[1127]

His Sedna is is also thankfully bi-quintile Jupiter, the planet of success, in the eighth house of shared resources.

[1126] https://fr.wikipedia.org/wiki/Georges_Vandenbeusch
[1127] Ibid.

The following year he was part of the delegation of President François Hollande during his visit to Pope Francis. The meeting was marked by the warm embrace of the Pope. And he resumed his ministry in the church of Saint-Pierre-Saint-Paul of Courbevoie, of which he was officially appointed parish priest.[1128]

Mu'Min Bey is a Western and Vedic Astrologer of African American descent. He has Sedna in the third house of ideas, opposite Quaoar in the ninth house of knowledge.

He does Astrology from an African American perspective. He tends to write about social issues. His writing has caused controversy and he has been accused of stirring stuff up. He has many interests in Astrology, primarily in the political, predictive, and counseling areas and he has been a volunteer instructor of Astrological Studies at Temple University, which has been very popular.

He has been a regular contributor to many of the Internet's most popular astrological forums. He founded his own astrological discussion forum, known as The Pan Astrological Forum and at 37 he also founded his blog, the Mu'Min Bey Astroblog. Known for his incisive, and insightful writing, his posts, letters and articles are considered welcome additions to the many forums he frequents; his approach, particularly in the area of Vedic Astrology, is considered fresh, modern and innovative.[1129]

Lisa Williams is a British psychic, medium and healer. She has Sedna in the fifth house of creativity, opposite Quaoar in the eleventh house of collective consciousness.

She starred in two shows on Lifetime Television: *Lisa Williams: Life Among the Dead* and *Lisa Williams: Voices From the Other Side*. The shows followed Williams on a typical day, as she communicated with spirits, investigate haunted houses, and conducted other spirit-seeking activities.[1130]

Her Sedna is also at the tip of a finger of fate, inconjunct with Pluto, the planet of life and death, in the tenth house of profession and inconjunct

---

[1128] Ibid.

[1129] http://www.linda-goodman.com/ubb/Forum1/HTML/016811.html

[1130] https://en.wikipedia.org/wiki/Lisa_Williams_(psychic)

Neptune, the planet of sensitivity to the spirit world in the first house of identity.

> She came out as a lesbian at 37 and said: 'For many years, speaking to dead people was hard enough for people to accept me, but then on top of that to then say 'by the way, I'm gay', I didn't want to acknowledge it'. Asked by a reporter, because of her unique insight into life after death, where she thought gay people were headed, she said: 'In my experience with those who have crossed, it is a place of love. It isn't a place of 'you didn't live this way so we'll punish you'. it is a place where all your loved ones accept you for who you are'.[1131]

Semi-sextile, Sextile, Trine

With the flowing aspects between Sedna and Quaoar, the all-encompassing spiritual energy of Sedna aligns with our ability to see the big picture, flaws and all, to understand the sacredness of life, to set out in a spirit of discovery and gain new perspectives and thereby create a harmonious revolution.

Quaoar is that glorious metaphysical process wherein material form is created out of chaos. It urges us to question, construct, clarify and reveal and gives us the potential to ground sacred energy, to take the cosmic chaos and bring it into form, thereby creating a new reality.

At the unconscious level, even the flows between these two planets can be challenging, as we'll see in the following examples, because the energies of the two planets are so ethereal that we have no practical way of dealing with it and may fall victim to our own delusions, or cut corners and take the easy way, just because we see we can.

Like Margherita Pezzoni, who was an Italian octogenarian who married a 23-year-old when she was 93. She has Sedna in the fifth house of romance, trine Quaoar in the ninth house of knowledge.

> Sprightly and lucid of mind, she explained that she wanted to protect him with her estate as she was fond of him. She wanted to adopt him, but it would take too long, so she married him instead. The media got hold of the story and made it highly public, covering the wedding. When she died mysteriously two years later, her young husband was left the small inheritance of

---

[1131] Ibid.

her pension, not the fortune he anticipated. He was arrested later that year on suspicion of killing another woman and confessed to the murder of both women.[1132]

Or like Bruno Hauptmann, who was a German-born carpenter who was convicted of the abduction and murder of the 20-month-old son of aviator Charles Lindbergh in America. He had Sedna in the first house of identity, trine Quaoar in the sixth house of service.

On the evening the child disappeared, a homemade ladder was found under the window of the child's room and a $50,000 ransom note was delivered, but the infant's body was found in woods 6 kilometres from the family home. The death was ascribed to a blow to the head, which some have theorised occurred accidentally during the abduction

When he was arrested, evidence against him included: $20,000 of the ransom money found in his garage; testimony alleging handwriting and spelling similarities to that found on the ransom notes; testimony that lumber used in constructing the ladder probably originated in his house; and what appeared to be a hand-drawn sketch of a ladder was found in one of his notebooks.

He was also seen near the Lindbergh home on the day of the kidnapping, had been absent from work on the day of the ransom payment and had quit his job two days later. The defence argued that the evidence against him was entirely circumstantial, as his fingerprints were not found on the ladder, the ransom notes, or anywhere in the nursery. Despite this he was convicted and sentenced to death. His case, however, led to the Lindbergh law that made kidnapping a federal offence in America.[1133]

Lucky Luciano was a Sicilian-American gangster. From grubby street urchin, Luciano rose through the ranks of organised crime and became director of a crime syndicate. He had Sedna in the second house of material resources, trine Quaoar in the sixth house of service.

[1132] https://www.astro.com/astro-databank/Pezzoni,_Margherita
[1133] https://en.wikipedia.org/wiki/Richard_Hauptmann

By the age of ten he had embarked on his life of crime. At nineteen he spent six months in jail for selling heroin. By 23, ruthless and upwardly mobile, he began working for the crime boss, Joe Masseria, and within five years, he became his chief lieutenant.

At 32, he survived a "one-way ride," a rare feat. He was abducted, beaten, stabbed repeatedly, had his throat cut and was left for dead; he never named his abductors, and soon afterward he changed his name to Luciano. He earned the nickname "Lucky" because he successfully evaded arrest on a number of occasions and eventually became famous for racketeering in narcotics, prostitution, slot machines, loan sharking and 'protection'.

However, at 39 he was indicted, tried and convicted on charges of extortion and prostitution and sentenced to 30 to 50 years in prison. Nevertheless, his power continued to grow, even while he was incarcerated, as he issued orders and ruled from his cell. Near the end of his life however, a reporter asked him if he would do it all again, and he replied, "I'd do it legal. I learned too late that you need just as good a brain to make a crooked million, as an honest million".[1134]

And the British writer, Charlotte Bronte, had Sedna in the seventh house of relationships, semi-sextile Quaoar in the eighth house of shared resources.

One of three sisters who became published authors, together they opened a school in 1841. Six years later, Charlotte shocked the Victorian world with her *Jane Eyre*, a passionate tale of repressed sexual longing on the moors. Charlotte was the bossy, controlling older sister, capable of ruthlessness, fury and sarcasm, a hypochondriac who suffered from migraines. She was only 4' 9" tall. Fascinated and intimidated by that which lay outside of Haworth, she made trips to London to meet the intelligentsia, but always as a freakish outsider, improperly

---

[1134] https://en.wikipedia.org/wiki/Lucky_Luciano

dressed, awkward and ambivalent about the very people with whom she longed to mingle.[1135]

As we tire of density and the grief it creates, and we start a spiritual journey to get out of the swamp, Sedna rewards us with transcendent crises, experiences which force us to let go and rise above them, resulting in a huge growth to a new level of consciousness. There is no choice with these crises, and the more we try and solve them, the more we will get hurt.

Like our case study, Rachel Carson, the mother of the environmental movement, who had Sedna in the first house of identity, trine Quaoar in the fifth house of creativity. This pulled the developing writer in new directions.

> As a child she loved the outdoors, the birds and plants around her family's rural property sparking her imagination. She found fossilised fish and inspired by her expeditions wrote a book at age 8 and was published in a literary magazine at 13.
>
> She entered the Pennsylvania College for Women on a senatorial district scholarship, earning an English degree, as preparation to become a writer. However it was biology that she found most thrilling during her undergraduate years. Biology gave her the tools to learn what had happened to that fossilised fish she found as a child.
>
> After earning a master's in zoology from Johns Hopkins, Carson found part-time work at the US Bureau of Fisheries. Though she'd chosen science over prose, her former specialty proved useful in her new occupation. Carson's first assignment for the bureau was to write a fifty-two-episode radio program called 'Romance Under the Waters'. "I had given up writing forever, I thought. It never occurred to me that I was merely getting something to write about.
>
> Her first book, *Under the Sea-Wind*, although it would be Carson's favourite, was a commercial failure, selling only two thousand copies. Carson needed a couple of years to recover from the blow, but both driven and strapped for cash, she pushed forward. Carson wrote another book. When *The Sea*

[1135] https://en.wikipedia.org/wiki/Charlotte_Brontë

Around Us arrived she was 44, it won the National Book Award for nonfiction and solidified her position as a literary heavyweight. To this day, it's credited as being one of the most successful books ever written about nature.

At 50, she turned her attention to conservation, especially some problems that she believed were caused by synthetic pesticides. The result was the book, *Silent Spring,* published when she was 55, which brought environmental concerns to an unprecedented share of the American people. Although *Silent Spring* was met with fierce opposition by chemical companies, it spurred a reversal in national pesticide policy, which led to a nationwide ban on DDT and other pesticides. It also inspired a grassroots environmental movement that led to the creation of the U.S. Environmental Protection Agency.[1136]

Louis Armstrong was an American jazz trumpeter, a raspy voiced singer and band leader who was known as the great "Satchmo" for Satchelmouth, the size of his mouth. His infectious huge grin made him lovable to people everywhere and he was known for his sense of humor and vivid energy. He had Sedna in the twelfth house of the unconscious, trine Quaoar in the fifth house of creativity.

Armstrong was the most important improviser of jazz of his day with his perfect pitch and immaculate timing and he taught the world to swing. Innovation and excitement marked his style of the music that is distinctly American, born in the black quarters of New Orleans.

He grew up poor among prostitutes and lowlifes in New Orleans, working from the time, he was a kid to help his family. He sang on the street corners in the Old Quarter and taught himself to play the cornet, quickly becoming acquainted with the culture of music that could be heard on every street. He rose from a rough and tumble childhood to become one of the first black men in America who had the courage and clout to say, "I wouldn't play no place I couldn't stay."

At age 21, he was the talk of South Side Chicago, playing in his mentor's band, Joe "King" Oliver's Creole Jazz Band. So popular

---

[1136] https://en.wikipedia.org/wiki/Rachel_Carson

were the trademark two-cornet breaks he and Oliver worked out, that they would perform with handkerchiefs over their hands to hide their fingering from imitators. At 41, his records and movie appearances had made him world famous. He had a rigorous schedule of touring, recording and performing, gradually adding films and TV.

Somehow, he stayed down to earth, never moving any further into drugs than his daily hits of marijuana, which never seemed to hurt his playing. He was, however, known as a world-class eccentric, his own man, brash and irreverent. His talents as a virtuoso trumpet player and irrepressible stage personality were inseparable, as was his mugging, teeth baring and eye-rolling. With a record of top-ten hits in every decade for half a century, he is memorable for "Hello, Dolly," and "When The Saints go Marchin' In," as well as his classic, "What a Wonderful World".[1137]

Joris Ivens was a Dutch documentary film-maker ever, a cosmopolitan, anarchist and communist. He had Sedna in the fifth house of creativity, trine Quaoar conjunct Mars, in the ninth house of knowledge.

He was a socially and culturally active driven man. At home he played Schubert and took his family to the cinema, theatre and concerts. Outside he was active in Liberal local politics and in professional and amateur societies. Unlike his more traditional wife, he seldom visited the Roman Catholic Church.

He was the second of the five children of a successful merchant in photographic articles, who was the director of a photo shop chain. He called his Liberal Catholic father "a man with a heavy sense of morality" and learned from him to work for the good of all. He believed in the Idea of Progress of the 19th century, but of course he and his children had to study and work hard to reach it.

He studied in Berlin and worked in camera factories in Germany. At 26 he returned to Holland and got a leading position in Amsterdam is his father's firm. He enjoyed the leftwing Amsterdam cultural scene. At 28 he enabled the exhibition of the

---

[1137] https://en.wikipedia.org/wiki/Louis_Armstrong

the forbidden Dutch film *Mother* by Vsevolod Pudovkin, through the artists society De Kring.

This resulted in the establishment of the Dutch Filmliga, which showed European and Russsian avant garde films instead of the American Hollywood productions that flooded the continent. The "arthouses" as an alternative for the popular Cinema became a platform for the European avant garde and Ivens became the talent of this scene.

Unlike other filmmakers, he had the great advantage that he did not have to rely on the capital of producers. The actors of his documentary films were found in real life on the street and the then expensive film material was provided by his father's firm. This enabled him to film social matters, for which typically no capitalistic investors were found.[1138]

And case study, Thomas Edison, the father of the light bulb, has Sedna in the fourth house of the laboratory home, sextile Quaoar in the seventh house of relationships. His Sedna is also in a close quintile with Jupiter, the planet of expansion, also in the seventh house.

A characteristic of his personality contributing strongly to his achievements is an intense, not to say courageous, optimism in which no thought of failure can enter, an optimism born of self-confidence, and becoming--after forty or fifty years of experience more and more a sense of certainty in the accomplishment of success.

In the overcoming of difficulties, he had the same intellectual pleasure as the chess-master when confronted with a problem requiring all the efforts of his skill and experience to solve. To advance along smooth and pleasant paths, to encounter no obstacles, to wrestle with no difficulties and hardships--such has absolutely no fascination to him.

At the conclusion of his ore-milling experiments, practically his entire fortune was sunk in an enterprise that had to be considered an impossibility. At the age of fifty he looked back upon five or six years of intense activity expended apparently for naught and the financial clouds were quickly gathering on the

---

[1138] https://en.wikipedia.org/wiki/Joris_Ivens

horizon. However, for him the main experiment had succeeded, he had accomplished what he sought for. Nature at another point had outstripped him, yet he had broadened his own sum of knowledge to a prodigious extent.

Twelve years later a friend accompanied him on a Sunday drive in New Jersey and Edison in the highest spirits, pointing out with the keenest enjoyment the many beautiful views of valley and wood. The wanderings led to the old ore-milling plant, by then practically a mass of deserted buildings all going to decay. It was a depressing sight, marking such titanic but futile struggles with nature.

To Edison, however, no trace of sentiment or regret occurred, and the whole ruins were apparently as much a matter of unconcern as if he were viewing the remains of Pompeii. Sitting on the porch of the house where he lived during that period, in the light of the setting sun, his fine face in repose, he looked as placidly over the scene as a happy farmer over a field of ripening corn. 'I never felt better in my life than during the five years I worked here' he said. 'Hard work, nothing to divert my thought, clear air and simple food made my life very pleasant. We learned a great deal. It will be of benefit to some one some time'.[1139]

Humour can be one path to transcend the quicksand of Sedna, giving us the objectivity to step back from the edge and also with the flowing aspects to Quaoar the opportunity to present a new perspective.

Fernandel was a French actor and mime comedian with a long, sorrowful, equine face and a radiant and toothy smile. He had Sedna in the eleventh house of collective consciousness, trine Quaoar in the third house of communication.

One of France's leading box-office draws, he built a four-decade career from the age of 27. His films included the four great "Don Camillo" political comedies. His father was an accountant but also an amateur comedian-singer and his mother was also an amateur actress, quickly noticed the talent of the young Fernand.

[1139] Dyer, Frank Lewis and Martin, Thomas Commerford. *Edison, His Life and Inventions* 1910.

He often accompanied his father during the concerts he organised in the Marseilles suburbs.

He made his debut on stage at five years singing the military repertory with his elder brother. He had his first great success at the age of seven, a day when, paralyzed by stage fright, he was propelled on the stage by his father, with a great kick to the rear; He fell into his sabre, and stretched his whole length under a storm of laughter. Later, he was never afraid to face the public.

In 1930, he appeared in his first motion picture and for more than forty years he would be France's top comic actor. He was perhaps best loved for his portrayal of the irascible Italian village priest at war with the town's Communist mayor in the Don Camillo series of motion pictures which he also directed. His horse-like teeth became part of his trademark.[1140]

At this juncture in human evolution, few of us use our planets at the spiritual level, but many of us are striving to, and such people are wonderful to be around. As with the other planets, the spiritual level of evolution is vastly different with Sedna from the two previous levels.

Here, the flowing aspects with Quaoar brings a sensitivity to esoteric guides and the spirit world

and the ability to see things from a fresh perspective, to see the big picture and then take the cosmic chaos and bring it into new form. The struggle of the beginner's level is gone, as are the transcendental crises of the intermediate level. At this level everything Saturnian is meaningless and yet everything Sednian has its place.

Like Marthe Robin, who was a French mystic and stigmatic. She had Sedna conjunct Pallas, the asteroid of wisdom, in the eighth house of the occult, trine Quaoar in the eleventh house of collective consciousness. Her Sedna is also square Vesta, the asteroid of regeneration, in the fourth house of home.

Serious illness marked her adult life and from her twenties she was confined to bed, crippled, and gradually paralyzed. She ate only wafers and neither drank nor slept, but lived for seven decades and carried on a busy apostolate.

[1140] https://en.wikipedia.org/wiki/Fernandel

From the age of 28 she was completely paralysed and bedridden. Although she still could move the thumb and forefinger of one hand, she became motionless apart from her head which she could move slightly. Since the previous year, at the age of 25, she could not eat anything at all. And from the age of 26 she couldn't even take a sip of water. When doctors tried to force some water down her throat, it merely came out her nostrils.

For the next 53 years Marthe's only food was the holy Eucharist. Once a week she was given the sacred host. Once she had received it she went immediately into ecstasy and began her weekly re-living of Christ's Passion and crucifixion. Every Friday wounds appeared in the palms of her hands and the stigmata, the scourging and crowning with thorns appeared on her body, and she appeared to be dead.

She was directed to found two schools in her native village, one for girls and one for boys. All this she directed down to the smallest detail from her bed in her darkened little room. Her Sedna is also semi-square Mercury, the planet of ideas in the sixth house of service, and quintile Saturn, the planet of structure, in the fifth house of creativity. Later on she was told to found a community which would welcome people looking for a retreat and which would be a home of "light, charity and love." It became known as the Foyer de Charité and there are now some 70 affiliated houses and communities throughout the world.[1141]

Lanza Del Vasto was a philosopher, poet, artist, catholic and nonviolent activist. A western disciple of Mohandas K. Gandhi, he worked for inter-religious dialogue, spiritual renewal, ecological activism and nonviolence. He had Sedna in the third house of communication, trine Quaoar in the eighth house of shared resources.

At 35 he went to India and joining the movement for Indian independence led by Gandhi. He spent six months with the Mahatma, then went to the source of the Ganges river in the Himalayas, a famous pilgrimage site. There he saw a vision who told him "Go back and found!" He then left India and went back

---

[1141] https://en.wikipedia.org/wiki/Marthe_Robin

to Europe. Six years later he published the story of his trip to India, *Return to the Source*, which became a huge success.

He founded the Community of the Ark when he was 47, which first met a lot of difficulties. By the time he was 60, the Community of the Ark settled in Haut-Languedoc, in the south of France, in a deserted village. He remained a leading figure in many non-violent movements until his death, however he was criticised for the traditional role of women in his movement, and for his expressed opposition to homosexuality.[1142]

Reinhold Ebertin was a German astrologer, and an exponent and developer of Cosmobiology. He had Sedna conjunct the cusp of the third house of communication, trine Quaoar in the seventh house of relationships.

When he was five, his parents divorced and he was placed in a foster home. During childhood and adolescence, his contacts with his mother, Elsbeth, were sporadic, made more difficult by interference from his father and paternal grandfather. When he was 16, Elsbeth introduced him to his chart and to astrology, which proved to be a turning point in his life.

At 21, he and his mother were finally reunited and he began his extensive studies of astrology. He worked at the time as a schoolteacher. At 22 he began his practice and at 27, he founded the Ebertin Publishing House with the assistance and encouragement of his mother. He turned to Cosmobiology at 37.

He developed many interesting methods such as midpoint-structure, psychograms and the 90 degree-wheel, and was also interested in distance values, heliocentric, mundane and prognostic astrology, primary directions and Pluto research. He wrote over 60 astrological textbooks, and his work included 21 volumes that were translated into other languages and 40 annuals of Cosmobiology Yearbooks

He met his future wife at the Astrologers Convention at Nuremberg when he was 28. They had a close and supportive marriage for 53 years until her death. Totally dedicated to a

---

[1142] https://en.wikipedia.org/wiki/Lanza_del_Vasto

vegetarian diet, he also practiced yoga. He finished a new book after his 85th birthday.[1143]

Semi-square, Square, Sesquiquadrate

With the stressful aspects between Sedna and Quaoar, the all-encompassing spiritual energy of Sedna aligns with our ability to see the big picture, flaws and all, to understand the sacredness of life, to set out in a spirit of discovery and gain new perspectives and thereby create a harmonious revolution.

Quaoar is that glorious metaphysical process wherein material form is created out of chaos. It urges us to question, construct, clarify and reveal and gives us the potential to ground sacred energy, to take the cosmic chaos and bring it into form, thereby creating a new reality.

With the stressful aspects to Sedna this ability to bring form out of chaos is challenged by the big spiritual picture and at the unconscious level this will likely result in ego-based attempts to hijack the energy rather than surrendering to the cosmic order. If we are misusing the Quaoar energy we will see how ego can bungle chaos and snarl us up in a personal soap opera.

Like Caryl Chessman, who was an American robber and rapist called the 'Red Light Bandit' as he would flash a red light on his car to stop people, pretending to be a cop, rape the woman and rob the man. He had Sedna conjunct Chiron, the centaur of wounding and Nessus the centaur of righteousness, all in the eighth house of life and death, sesquiquadrate Quaoar in the twelfth house of the unconscious.

> Born to an alcoholic dad and a mom paralyzed from an auto accident when he was nine, he was a sickly, asthmatic kid. He joined a gang and married a 16-year-old girl when he was 19. In a binge of rape, robbery and kidnapping, he shot a man to death, and was convicted at 26.[1144]

His Sedna is also in a fateful inconjunct with Ixion, the planet of lawlessness, in the first house of identity, square Juno, the asteroid of partnership, in the fifth house of creativity and sextile mars, the planet of male sexuality and war, in the tenth house of profession.

[1143] https://en.wikipedia.org/wiki/Reinhold_Ebertin
[1144] https://en.wikipedia.org/wiki/Caryl_Chessman

While in San Quentin prison, CA, he studied law, wrote appeals and a book. After 12 years on death row, he finally was executed in the gas chamber. A last-minute stay and ninth reprieve had been ordered by state Supreme Court but it was too late. A wrong number was dialed to the prison and then quickly redialed, but when the judge listened on the other end he reported back, 'It's too late. The pellets have already been dropped'.[1145]

Or like Nicolae Ceausescu, who was a Romanian politician, an indestructible dictator for 24 years and one of history's mass murderers. He has Sedna in the eleventh house of ideals, sesquiquadrate Quaoar in the fourth house of home.

The son of a shoemaker, he had a limited education before he joined the Communist army fighting against fascists. He was captured and spent several years in prison before assembling a coup that won him the nation's highest office. His rule was marked by an extensive cult of personality, and by nepotism. However, after a brief period of relatively moderate rule, he became increasingly brutal and repressive. He maintained controls over speech and the media that were very strict even by Soviet-bloc standards.[1146]

He also has a fateful inconjunct with Ixion, the planet of lawlessness in the fifth house of children, and another sesquiquadrate with his Moon, the planet of emotions, in the sixth house of service.

Internal dissent was not tolerated under his rule. His secret police, the Securitate, was one of the most ubiquitous and brutal secret police forces in the world. Seventeen years after ceasing power, he ordered the export of much of the country's agricultural and industrial production, with the goal of paying off Romania's large foreign debt.

The resulting extreme shortages of food, fuel, energy, medicines, and other basic necessities drastically lowered living standards and intensified unrest. Four years later, on the week before Christmas, he ordered a massacre of protesters and the country erupted in a furious revolution, the only violent removal of a

---

[1145] Ibid.
[1146] https://en.wikipedia.org/wiki/Nicolae_Ceaușescu

Communist government. He was tried in secret and swiftly executed.[1147]

Or Ian Douglas Smith, who served as Prime Minister of Rhodesia, now Zimbabwe, when it declared independence from the United Kingdom. He has Sedna in the fifth house of creativity, sesquiquadrate Quaoar on the MC, the cusp of the tenth house of profession. His Sedna is also inconjunct Ixion, the planet of lawlessness, in the tenth house of profession.

> He was the country's first premier not born abroad and led a predominantly white government. He unilaterally declared independence from the United Kingdom in 1965, following prolonged dispute over the terms and remained Prime Minister for almost all of the 14 years of international isolation that followed.
>
> In that role he also oversaw Rhodesia's security forces during most of the guerrilla war during that time, which pitted the unrecognised administration against communist-backed black nationalist guerrilla groups. He has been described as personifying white Rhodesia, however he remains a highly controversial figure, with supporters venerating him as a man of integrity and vision "who understood the uncomfortable truths of Africa", while critics describe an unrepentant racist, whose policies and actions caused the deaths of thousands and contributed to Zimbabwe's later crises.[1148]

As we tire of density and the grief it creates, and we start a spiritual journey to get out of the swamp, Sedna rewards us with transcendent crises, experiences which force us to let go and rise above them, resulting in a huge growth to a new level of consciousness. There is no choice with these crises, and the more we try and solve them, the more we will get hurt.

Guglielmo Marconi was an Italian scientist and physicist who invented wireless telegraph and radio signal transmission. He has Sedna in the tenth house of profession, square Quaoar in the twelfth house of the unconscious.

[1147] Ibid.

[1148] https://en.wikipedia.org/wiki/Ian_Smith

From the time he was a small boy he was extraordinarily interested in physics. Spurred on by the work of Benjamin Franklin, at 18 he designed and installed on his house a rooftop mechanism that set off a bell whenever there was an electrical storm nearby. This was the first example of the aerial-to-earth system that later became essential to radio-telegraphy.

At twenty, while on a summer holiday, he read a detailed description of Heinrich Hertz's experiments, demonstrating the production and detection of electromagnetic radiation, now generally referred to as radio waves. Marconi began working on radio telegraphy, the idea of using the radio waves to transmit telegraph messages without connecting wires. This was not a new idea; numerous investigators and inventors had been exploring wireless telegraph technologies and even building systems using electric conduction, electromagnetic induction and optical signalling for over 50 years, but none had proven technically and commercially successful.

Eager to develop and apply his work on a large scale, he went to England, accompanied by his mother. The Chief Engineer of the Post Office, made enthusiastic mention of his experiments in a postal conference, thus clearing the way for experiments in Post Office laboratories. The first aerial transmissions were done between the Post Office building and the Savings Bank, a distance of some hundreds of meters.

Soon after, the first demonstration of overseas radio transmission took place. Obsessed with the idea of sending messages across the Atlantic, at 27 he built a powerful transmitter and receiver and succeeded in receiving signals from across the ocean. This opened up the possibility of regular communications between land and sea. News of this achievement spread around the world, and his work was applauded by outstanding scientists, including Thomas Edison. He received many honours including the Nobel Prize for Physics.[1149]

Our case study James Lovelock is a British independent scientist, environmentalist and futurologist who lives in Devon, England. He has

---

[1149] https://en.wikipedia.org/wiki/Guglielmo_Marconi

Sedna on the cusp of the sixth house, sesquiquadrate the conjunction of Quaoar with Saturn, the planet of structure, and Mercury, the planet of communication, all in the tenth house of profession.

A lifelong inventor, he has created and developed many scientific instruments, some of which were designed for NASA in its program of planetary exploration. It was while working as a consultant for NASA, when he was in his forties, that he developed the Gaia Hypothesis for which he is best known. Gaia hypothesis postulates that the biosphere of the Earth is a self-regulating entity with the capacity to keep our planet healthy by controlling the chemical and physical environment.

However, in his book, *The Revenge of Gaia*, published when he was 87, he argues that the lack of respect humans have had for Gaia, through the damage done to rainforests and the reduction in planetary biodiversity, is testing Gaia's capacity to minimise the effects of the addition of greenhouse gases in the atmosphere. This eliminates the planet's negative feedbacks and increases the likelihood of runaway global warming.

Three years later he published *The Vanishing Face of Gaia*, rejecting scientific modelling that disagreed with the scientific findings that sea levels are rising faster, and Arctic ice is melting faster than the models predict. And suggesting that we may already be beyond the tipping point of terrestrial climate resilience into a permanently hot state. Given these conditions, he expects human civilisation will be hard pressed to survive in the coming years.

> At that point he expected the change to be similar to the Paleocene-Eocene period when atmospheric concentration of CO_2 was high and at that point the Arctic Ocean was 23 °C and had crocodiles in it, with the rest of the world mostly scrub and desert. Seven years later however, at 97 his position on climate change had changed dramatically, saying: 'Anyone who tries to predict more than five to 10 years is a bit of an idiot, because so many things can change unexpectedly.' He now believes that "CO_2 is going up, but nowhere near as fast as they thought it would.
>
> There are various possible explanations for his change of heart. One is that he is right, and the models on which his former predictions were based were fatally flawed. Another is that his

iconoclastic sensibility made revision irresistible. An incorrigible subversive, Lovelock was warning the world about climate change for decades before it began to pay attention, and just when the scientific consensus began to call for intervention to prevent it, he decided we were already too late.

But there is a third explanation for why he has shifted his position again, he expects that before the consequences of global warming can impact on us significantly, something else will have made our world unrecognisable, and threaten the human race, the rise of Artificial Intelligence. 'Before we've reach the end of this century, I think what people call robots will have taken over. They will be in charge of us, if we're still here.'

'It is possible that human beings may fuse with robots to become a blend of robotic and human tissue, but the likelier scenario will be pure robots, because that will probably be their preference. The implications for climate change are obvious. The world that they're going to be comfortable in is wildly different from the one that we feel comfortable in. So once they really get established, they will, with regret, start losing organic life'.[1150]

Anthony Burgess is a British novelist noted for his comic imagination and skillful use of language. His book, *A Clockwork Orange*, published when he was 45, was a thriller set in a classless and futurist society. He has Sedna in the eleventh house of collective consciousness, sesquiduadrate Quaoar in the third house of communication.

> *A Clockwork Orange* is a dystopian novel set in a near future English society featuring a subculture of extreme youth violence. The teenage protagonist narrates his violent exploits and his experiences with state authorities, intent on reforming him. The book is partially written in a Russian-influenced argot called Nadsat and according to Burgess it was a 'jeu d'esprit' (a play of the spirit) written in just three weeks. *A Clockwork Orange* was included on *Time* magazine's list of the 100 best English-language novels written since 1923, and it was named by Modern Library and its readers as one of the 100 best English-

---

[1150] Aitkenhead, Decca. Guardian, September 30 2016.
https://www.theguardian.com/environment/2016/sep/30/james-lovelock-interview-by-end-of-century-robots-will-have-taken-over

language novels of the 20th century. The book was later made into a film.[1151]

Humour can be one path to transcend the quicksand of Sedna, giving us the objectivity to step back from the edge, but also with the stressful aspects to Quaoar the challenge to see the big picture and bring new form out of the cosmic chaos and not get lost in our personal soap opera.

Martha Raye was an American entertainer, a zestful, boisterous comedienne with a huge, elastic mouth and zany antics. She had Sedna in the eleventh house of collective consciousness, sesquiquadrate Quaoar in the fourth house of home.

> She was born in a charity ward, the daughter of touring vaudeville parents. She joined the family vaudeville act by the time she was three. By 13 she was a specialty singer with a band. She was a veteran of stage and nightclubs by 19 when she made her first film, after which she played in many minor roles. Her greatest acclaim always came from live entertainment, stage, Broadway, clubs and wartime tours with variety shows. She married seven times, the last time when she was 75 to a 30-year-younger man after a three-week courtship in Las Vegas.[1152]

Her Sedna is also in a stressful sesquiquadrate to the Moon, the planet of emotions, and in a fateful inconjunct with Ixion, the planet of lawlessness, both also in the fourth house of home.

> She was in a wheelchair after a stroke, drinking a lot, lonely since being widowed two years before and estranged from her only child. She said that she was in love with him as he made her feel young and a woman, with sex for the first time in years. In her last few years she had eight strokes and both legs amputated, Parkinson's and cataracts. Her daughter said she had dementia in contesting the will, in which she left one million to her daughter and the rest to her younger husband.[1153]

At this juncture in human evolution, few of us use our planets at the spiritual level, but many of us are striving to, and such people are

[1151] https://en.wikipedia.org/wiki/Anthony_Burgess
[1152] https://en.wikipedia.org/wiki/Martha_Raye
[1153] Ibid.

wonderful to be around. As with the other planets, the spiritual level of evolution is vastly different with Sedna from the two previous levels.

Here, the stressful aspects with Quaoar brings a sensitivity to esoteric guides and the spirit world

and the ability to see things from a fresh perspective, to see the big picture and bring new form out of the cosmic chaos. The struggle of the beginner's level is gone, as are the transcendental crises of the intermediate level. At this level everything Saturnian is meaningless and yet everything Sednian has its place.

Carl Jung was a Swiss psychiatrist and author, noted as being an outstanding influence in the development of the theory and practice of analytical psychiatry. He had Sedna in the second house of material reality, square to Quaoar in the fifth house of creativity. His Sedna is also in an evolutionary quintile with Orcus, the planet of delving down and speaking out in the twelfth house of the unconscious, and semi-sextile Neptune, the planet of dreams and visions in the second house of material reality.

> At age 12, he developed fainting spells which kept him out of school. He dreamt for hours, was out in nature, drew, "but above all...was able to plunge into the world of the mysterious." Overhearing his father's talk of financial concerns around his illness, Jung realised on some level he could overcome the fainting spells and was able to return to school.

> Shortly after this, on a long walk to school, he experienced an intense moment of knowing himself: "Previously, I had existed...everything had merely happened to me. Now, I happened to myself. Now I knew: I am myself now, now I exist."

> When he was 23 he decided to pursue a career in psychiatry. His career began in earnest five years later when he picked up Sigmund Freud's book, *The Interpretation of Dreams*, realising how Freud's work linked up with his own ideas.

> The initial correspondence and friendship with Freud began three years later and they collaborated on some work, but when he was 34 he broke from Freud to place greater emphasis on the growth of mankind by archetypal vital forces in the individual. His

theories of synchronicity, introvert-extrovert types, individuation and the personal-collective unconscious all come from this work.

During this period, he had a decisive dream of being in a two-story house. As he explored it, each floor and room reflected historical eras or from the collective unconscious. When he was 38, he had numerous visions. He stated in his autobiography, *Memories, Dreams, and Reflections* that all of his creative work came from these initial visions, fantasies and dreams. He had a successful practice and was a much soughtafter mentor to countless devotees of his work.

An advocate of the use of astrology, he said 'Astrology would be a largescale example of synchronism, if it had at its disposal thoroughly tested findings… In other words, whatever is born or done this moment of time, has the qualities of this moment of time'. In his book, *Synchronicity*, he published a study of 483 pairs of couples, seeking to show that there is a causal connection between the planets and psycho-physiological disposition.[1154]

One of the devotees of Jung's work was Marie-Louise Von Franz, a Swiss Jungian psychologist, researcher and author. She had Sedna in the fifth house of creativity, sesquiquadrate Quaoar in the eleventh house of collective consciousness.

The daughter of a colonel in the Austrian army, born in Munich, after World War I, her family moved to Switzerland, where she met Jung during a school trip when she was 18 and knew until his death 46 years later. She subsequently did translation work for him in order to pay him for her analysis. Jung believed in the unity of the psychic and material worlds, meaning that they are one and the same, just different manifestations. He also believed that this concept of the unus mundus could be investigated by means of researching archetypes. Due to his advanced age, he turned the problem over to von Franz and two of her books, Number and Time, and Psyche and Matter, deal with this research.[1155]

[1154] https://en.wikipedia.org/wiki/Carl_Jung
[1155] https://en.wikipedia.org/wiki/Marie-Louise_von_Franz

Indian lawyer and civil rights champion, Mohandas Gandhi, the spiritual and political leader of India through the tempestuous birth of independence, has Sedna in the sixth house of service, square Quaoar in the ninth house of spirituality.

> Known as Mahatma, which means 'great soul', he began the freedom movement in 1919 with nonviolent disobedience. Fond of the simple life, eating primarily fresh fruits and nuts, He often fasted, as he had done in his youth. He spent much time experimenting with fasting as a form of self-restraint. He was a self-confessed quack as far as his medical views were concerned, and fully believed that a light diet, lots of exercise and a mud pack were all that anyone needed to be healed.

> At 57, having grown weary from periods in prison and periods of fasting, he retired to his ashram for a year of silence. Then, refreshed, he toured India the following year, and expanded his principles of nonviolence, homespun unity and equality for untouchables, by adding equality for women and abstinence from drugs and alcohol.

> India broke from England in 1947, assuring Gandhi's rank as a saint and holy man. His assassination during the Hindu-Moslem riots the following year, shook the world, but left it with a message greater than the humble man himself; the power of peaceful protest and the reassurance that justice has its place.[1156]

And our case study, Edgar Cayce, an American mystic and the father of modern wholistic medicine, has Sedna in the eighth house of the occult, square Quaoar in the eleventh house of collective consciousness.

> He was known as 'The Sleeping Prophet'' because while in a sleep state he could discuss history, geology, metaphysics, philosophy and medicine. He gave approximately 30,000 life-readings and medical diagnosis to people during his lifetime and founded a hospital and a university.

> He was born to uneducated farming parents and attended country school only as far as the eighth grade. As a child he had a strong desire to become a preacher, which he never formally

---

[1156] https://en.wikipedia.org/wiki/Mahatma_Gandhi

realised. He prayed to be able to help others, especially children, and had a spiritual vision at age 13, that told him he would be able to accomplish this dream of service.

A lady bathed in light told Cayce to sleep with his head on his books, and then he would be able to remember what was in them. This was at a time when he was having trouble in school, and his father was apparently beating him for not being able to spell the words in his lessons correctly. Soon after, he showed signs of special abilities when he found that he could sleep on his school books and have photographic recall of every page.

Throughout his life, he claimed no special abilities and did not capitalise financially or otherwise on his gifts. The readings never offered a set of beliefs or religion to be embraced, but instead focused on the idea that every person should test in his or her own life, the principles presented. Though Cayce was a devout Christian who read the Bible through once for every year of his life, his work emphasized the importance of comparative study of belief systems from around the world.

In fact, some of the metaphysical material that came through the sleeping Cayce was at first confusing and distressing to him in his waking state. However, he overcame his doubts, as have others, by observing the amazing accuracy and unfailing helpfulness of the readings in other areas, such as healing. For some, the Christian language of the readings is at first an obstacle. Yet, the underlying principle of the readings is the oneness of all life, acceptance of all people, and a compassion and understanding for every major religion in the world.[1157]

In-conjunct

With the fateful inconjunct between Sedna and Quaoar, the esoteric spiritual energy of Sedna bursts into our ability to see the big picture, flaws and all, to understand the sacredness of life, to set out in a spirit of discovery and gain new perspectives, in an evolutionary way and we have a fated role to play.

The inconjunct sometimes acts as a flow and at other times as a stress, so we have to learn to actively manage the process as the rarified

---

[1157] https://en.wikipedia.org/wiki/Edgar_Cayce

spiritual energy sometimes reinforces our spirit of discovery and, at other times, isn't there to back us up. By adjusting to this, we gain a deeper understanding of ourselves and how to play our role.

Quaoar is that glorious metaphysical process wherein material form is created out of chaos. It urges us to question, construct, clarify and reveal and gives us the potential to ground sacred energy, to take the cosmic chaos and bring it into form, thereby creating a new reality.

With the inconjunct to Sedna this ability to bring form out of chaos has a fated relationship with the big spiritual picture and at the unconscious level this will likely result in ego-based attempts to control the energy, which is likely to snarl us up in a personal soap opera. And we are all unconscious of the energy at birth and must develop it as we grow.

Like Alberta Elaine Schambert, who is an American missing person, seen on the television program *Unsolved Mysteries*. She has Sedna in the eighth house of shared resources, inconjunct Quaoar which is exactly conjunct her ascendent, the cusp of the first house of identity. She was born a healthy baby girl, delivered at home, but her mom died a few hours later. Dad joined the military and left her in the care of neighbours, who later gave her up for adoption without his knowledge. He has not seen her since and still searches for her.

Another young example is Maria, a blond 4-year-old, who was born to a Bulgarian Roma woman in Greece, and illegally adopted by another Roma family. She has Sedna on the cusp of the seventh house of relationships, inconjunct Quaoar, which is conjunct Ixion, the planet of lawlessness, with both in the first house of identity.

> The fake parents were under suspicion of having bought her, with the intention to use her for professional begging. The couple who appeared to be Maria's parents had fraudulently registered 14 children in three different municipalities and had faced charges for robbery and forging official documents in the past.[1158]

Luigi Fasulo was a 67-year-old Swiss private pilot, who flew his light aircraft into the Pirelli skyscraper in Milano. He also has Sedna in the eighth house of life and death, inconjunct Quaoar in the first house of identity.

[1158] https://www.astro.com/astro-databank/Adopted_illegally:_Maria

He took off in a Rockwell Commander from the Locarno airport in Switzerland and according to the flight plan presented at the time of departure, his destination was Milan and he intended to return to Locarno that evening.

When he arrived at the Milan airport, he asked permission to land on the runway usually reserved for general aviation, but on that day, it was closed to fixed-wing aircraft traffic so his request was refused and he was given instructions to approach another runway. Probably inexperienced with this runway, he did not succeed in following the correct alignment path and this was complicated by the unclear indications provided by the tower.

A few minutes later, he signalled he had an anomaly in the landing gear. The Milanese air traffic control then ordered him to circuit on an elliptical waiting route that runs along the outskirts of Milan, pending a solution to the problem. Probably involved in controlling the various commands in order to solve the malfunction, he took the wrong route and instead of going to the waiting circuit went to the city centre, pointing directly towards the Pirelli skyscraper. The low sun on the horizon probably further confused him and, in his effort to remedy the anomaly, he began to give non-standard and outdated responses to radio communications.

Witnesses reported that when the plane was a few meters from the building, the engine was pushed to the maximum and he radioed he was making a corrective turn but could not avoid the accident. His plane crashed into the 26th floor of the Pirelli skyscraper, instantly releasing a vast fire, which was only tamed after a few hours. Two people in the building also died and 70 were injured.

Investigators quickly dismissed the theory of terrorism, which was suggested by the proximity of the incident with the events of September 11, 2001 in America the year before. At first, there was conjecture he committed suicide, because of his long-time financial problems, which sometimes led to legal problems, or that it was simply human error, as he had a history of small plane incidents. In the accident report, the National Flight Safety Agency said the probable cause was the inability of the pilot to adequately handle the conduct of the final stage of the flight, in the presence of technical, operational and environmental problems.[1159]

Johannes Van Damme was a Dutch engineer, arrested in Singapore when 4.5 kg of heroin was found in his luggage. He had Sedna in the seventh house of relationships, inconjunct Quaoar in the twelfth house of the unconscious.

He denied guilt, saying that it was a plot organised by a businessman who was his competitor. He had lived in Nigeria for a while and was married to a Nigerian woman at the time of his arrest. He was arrested at Singapore Changi Airport when 4.32 kilograms of heroin was found in a secret compartment of his trunk. He claimed he had been framed by his Nigerian engineer partner, but this claim was rejected by the court, as was his appeal. A plea for clemency from the Dutch government was rejected by the President of Singapore, nor could a letter from Queen Beatrix prevent him from being executed.

His hanging prompted science fiction author, William Gibson, to describe Singapore as 'Disneyland with the Death Penalty', the title of in his first major non-fiction piece, which was first published by *Wired* magazine. The article had an immediate and lasting impact. The Singapore government banned *Wired* upon the publication of the issue, and the phrase "Disneyland with the death penalty" became a byword for bland authoritarianism that the city-state could not easily discard.[1160]

Bernardo Provenzano was an Italian mob boss, a member of the Sicilian Mafia suspected of having been the head of the Corleonesi, a Mafia faction that originated in the town of Corleone, and the de facto boss of bosses of the entire Sicilian Mafia until his arrest. He had Sedna in the fourth house of home, inconjunct Quaoar, which is conjunct Mars, the planet of war, in the ninth house of knowledge.

One of his nicknames is 'Binnie the tractor' because, in the words of one informant, 'he mows people down'. However, another nickname is the Accountant, due to his apparently subtle and low-key approach to running his crime empire, at least in

---

[1159] https://en.wikipedia.org/wiki/2002_Pirelli_Tower_airplane_crash
[1160] https://en.wikipedia.org/wiki/Johannes_van_Damme

contrast to some of his more violent predecessors. In 1993 the Mafia had been engaged in a terrorist bombing campaign against the state to get them to back off in their crackdown against the Mafia after the murders of two prosecutors. There were a series of bombings by the Corleonesi against several tourist spots on the Italian mainland, which left 10 people dead and 93 injured, as well as severe damage to centres of cultural heritage.

Provenzano proposed a new, less violent strategy, one of patience, compartmentalisation, coexistence with state institutions, and systematic infiltration of public finance. And he tried to stem the flow of mafia members who, following their arrests, decide to repent and collaborate with the judiciary to help further investigations, by not targeting their families, only using violence in case of absolute necessity.[1161]

As we become more aware of our Quaoar energy, we can get our ego out of the way and learn to surrender more to the cosmic order. And as we tire of density and the grief it creates, and we start a spiritual journey to get out of the swamp, Sedna rewards us with transcendent crises, experiences which force us to let go and rise above them, resulting in a huge growth to a new level of consciousness. There is no choice with these crises, and the more we try and solve them, the more we will get hurt.

Hannelore Kohl is the wife of former German Chancellor Helmut Kohl. She met him for the first time at a prom in Ludwigshafen, Germany, when she was 15 years old. She has Sedna in the eleventh house of ideals, inconjunct Quaoar in the fourth house of home.

> In the days following Germany's defeat in World War II, at the age of 12, she was raped by Red Army soldiers and subsequently "thrown out of a window like a sack of potatoes by the Russians." In addition to the obvious psychological impact, the attacks left her with a fractured vertebra and back pain for the rest of her life. However, in order to help others with similar injuries, she established a foundation that helps those with

---

[1161] https://en.wikipedia.org/wiki/Bernardo_Provenzano

trauma-induced injuries to the central nervous system and became its president.[1162]

Skeeter Davis is an American musician with a career that was always eventful. She has Sedna in the third house of communication, inconjunct Quaoar in the eighth house of life and death.

> The eldest of seven kids, she formed a harmony group with her friend Betty Jack Davis and they called themselves The Davis Sisters. They began to play regular gigs on the radio in Lexington and on other shows in Detroit and Cincinnati before they signed a record contract. When she was 22 their first RCA release went to number one on the charts in 26 weeks.

> However, a car accident on the highway to Cincinnati killed Betty Jack and critically injured Skeeter, leading to a long rehabilitation period of recovery. She worked with Betty's sister for a while before going solo. At 28 she had a big breakthrough with 'Set Him Free', which established her as a star. And three years later 'The End of The World', went gold and put her in the world-class. Her heart is in country, though she does a variety of styles.[1163]

Dan Rather was an American news broadcaster, one of the top in his competitive field. He had Sedna conjunct Uranus, the planet of revolution, in the twelfth house of the unconscious, inconjunct Quaoar in the eighth house of shared resources.

> As a kid in Texas, he dreamed of becoming a reporter and at 14, he worked as a gofer, fetching coffee for the local newspaper office. He was anchor of the *CBS Evening News* for 24 years and he made a name for himself in journalism for his refusal to play "nice" with political leaders during his hard-hitting interviews.

> He became embroiled in controversy about a disputed news report involving President George W. Bush's Vietnam-era service in the National Guard. He was 73 when he reported on *60 Minutes* that a series of memos critical of President George W. Bush's Texas Air National Guard service record had been discovered in the personal files of Lt. Bush's former commanding officer.

[1162] https://en.wikipedia.org/wiki/Hannelore_Kohl
[1163] https://en.wikipedia.org/wiki/Skeeter_Davis

Once copies of the documents were made available on the Internet, their authenticity was quickly called into question. Much of this was based on the fact that the documents were proportionally printed and displayed using other modern typographic conventions usually unavailable on military typewriters of the 1970s. The font used on the documents has characteristics that exactly match standard font features of Microsoft Word. This led to claims that the memos were forgeries. The accusations then spread over the following days into mainstream media outlets including *The Washington Post, The New York Times*, and the *Chicago Sun-Times*.

Rather and CBS initially defended the story, insisting that the documents had been authenticated by experts. CBS was contradicted by some of the experts it originally cited, and later reported that its source for the documents, former Texas Army National Guard officer Lt. Col. Bill Burkett, had misled the network about how he had obtained them. CBS retracted the story and Rather stated, "If I knew then what I know now, I would not have gone ahead with the story as it was aired, and I certainly would not have used the documents in question."

Following an investigation commissioned by CBS, which many believe was the result of political pressure on the Board, they fired the story producer and asked three other producers connected with the story to resign and many believe Rather's retirement was hastened by this incident. Five years later he was interviewed on *Larry King Live*, commenting, "Nobody has proved that they were fraudulent, much less a forgery... The truth of this story stands up to this day".[1164]

Gunter Sachs was a German photographer, author, industrialist, and head of an institute that researched astrology. He had Sedna in the seventh house of relationships, inconjunct Quaoar, which is together with Jupiter, the planet of expansion, in the eleventh house of collective consciousness.

In his younger years his public image was that of the archetypal rich playboy. He first became a sportsman, then gained international fame as a documentary film-maker and

---

[1164] https://en.wikipedia.org/wiki/Dan_Rather

photographer. He married three times. His first wife died during surgery. He courted his second wife, Brigitte Bardot, by flying over her villa on the French Riviera in a helicopter and dropping hundreds of roses. The couple was married for three years, before divorcing. His final marriage was to Swedish former model, when he was 37. She was 26 at the time and this relationship lasted 42 years until his death.

At 40 he started working professionally as a photographer and the following year caused a stir with the first nude photograph for French Vogue. The focus of his photography was surreal nudes and landscapes, which were published in no less than seven image volumes. Early on, he also experimented with digital photography.

He was also interested in astrology and its connection with mathematics and statistics. His Sedna is also in an evolutionary bi-quintile Neptune, the planet of dreams and visions, in the eleventh house of collective consciousness. He published a book on the *Scientific Proof of the Link Between Star Signs and Human Behaviour* and is quoted as saying of his astrological research: 'In every case, there were significant results, way beyond what is explicable through mere coincidence'. Three years after his death, his family published posthumously his second astrology book, *My Astrological Legacy: The Secret of Love, Happiness and Death.*[1165]

His Sedna was also semi-square Vesta, the asteroid of regeneration, conjunct his Moon, his emotional nature, in the eighth house of life and death.

He committed suicide at 77, with a gunshot wound to the head, at his home in Switzerland. The suicide note stated that he acted because of what he defined as 'hopeless illness A', which some have speculated to be Alzheimer's. He added that "The loss of mental control over my life was an undignified condition, which I decided to counter decisively".[1166]

[1165] https://en.wikipedia.org/wiki/Gunter_Sachs
[1166] Ibid.

Jimmy Swaggart was an American charismatic maestro of hi-tech salvation, television evangelist of Pentecostal Christianity blessed with the ability to spellbind audiences to the tune of $150 million a year. He had Sedna in the fourth house of home, inconjunct Quaoar in the ninth house of spirituality.

> He conducted a vast yet dubious ministry secluded behind the walls of his $30 million dollar compound in Louisiana. Known as a frequent hell-raiser as a teen, he dropped out of high school and played honky tonk piano with his notoriously carousing cousin Jerry Lee Lewis. At age 17, he married a 15-year old farm girl who lived down the road, both successfully lying about their ages. Soon after his marriage, he preached his first sermon in front of a grocery store interspersed with playing the accordion, 'knowing we get crowds with the music'. By his late 20s, he was itinerant preacher traveling the Southeastern US and began to cut gospel records, of which he eventually sold over 150 million.[1167]

His Sedna is also at the focal point of two evolutionary bi-quintiles, one to Neptune, the planet of dreams and visions, in the ninth house of spirituality, and the other to Jupiter, the planet of expansion, in the eleventh house of collective consciousness.

> After another message from God, he began a radio show and from that point onward TV became his manifest destiny. The ministry probably quadrupled with radio. With TV it exploded. In front of the TV camera, he became more outspoken than ever, verbally attacking Roman Catholicism, Jews and homosexuals while soliciting money from his viewers.[1168]

His Sedna is also closely semi-square Orcus, the planet of delving down and speaking out, in the fifth house of creativity.

> During each sermon, the impassioned preacher ranted and raved, coercing his followers and himself into a feeding frenzy of devotion. His antics backfired and in his late 40s he became a target of investigations. His Sedna is also square Ceres, the planet of nurture, in the seventh house of relationships and semi-

---

[1167] https://en.wikipedia.org/wiki/Jimmy_Swaggart
[1168] Ibid.

square Saturn, the planet of structure, in the second house of material resources. A wealthy California widow left almost her entire estate to Swaggart Ministries. The Evangelistic Association and its agents were charged by family lawyers with 'preying upon her loneliness and illness for the purpose of securing donations from her. By now Swaggart was flush with 3 palatial estates and a private jet.

Further allegations of misallocations of monies, death threats, handsome payoffs and the exploitation of prostitutes led to private investigation. When confronted by photos of himself with prostitutes he reportedly admitted he had a fascination with pornography from childhood. This incident earned him a three-month suspension from his US pulpit and a two-year rehabilitation period, which proved unsuccessful. Further confirmed encounters with prostitutes sent him reeling into a tortured, televised public confession for which he may be best known. However, he was back to preaching once more against sin within three months.[1169]

At this juncture in human evolution, few of us use our planets at the spiritual level, but many of us are striving to, and such people are wonderful to be around. As with the other planets, the spiritual level of evolution is vastly different with Sedna from the two previous levels.

Here, the inconjunct with Quaoar brings an ability to see things from a fresh perspective, to see the big picture and bring new form out of the cosmic chaos. The struggle of the beginner's level is gone, as are the transcendental crises of the intermediate level. At this level everything Saturnian is meaningless and yet everything Sednian has its place.

Ian Channel is a British-born New Zealander eccentric, known as 'The Wizard of New Zealand,' famous as the country's only official Wizard. He has Sedna in the first house of identity, inconjunct Quaoar in the sixth house of service, and also in a close evolutionary bi-quintile with Neptune, the planet of dreams and visions, which is also in the sixth, and the combination of these aspects often signifies a unique evolutionary contribution.

[1169] Ibid.

As a young adult he drifted, serving a stint in the Royal Air Force, and teaching in the Middle East. At 28 he enrolled in a degree in psychology and sociology, and on graduation he moved to Australia and worked as a lecturer and organizer for the community and for the arts. At 35 he landed an assignment as college instructor and began his Ph.D. work at the School of Sociology at the University of New South Wales.

During the student upheavals, which began at this time, he created a direct-action reform movement called 'Action for Love and Freedom' and implemented this with what he announced to be 'The Fun Revolution'. The result was a revitalisation of the university referred to in the Sydney Morning Herald as 'the university that swings'.

His head of department, convinced he was mad, dismissed him without consultation for insufficient progress in his thesis in the sociology of art. However, Channell wanted to stay on campus and continue his social experiments and he was able to persuade the Vice Chancellor to appoint him official University Wizard, with a small honorarium paid jointly by the University Administration and the Student Union.[1170]

With Sedna in the first house, he began to experiment with his own identity and allowed his driving licence, social security ID, passport and other important documents to lapse.

After travelling to the World University Service headquarters in Geneva he received their backing to travel round Australian universities to promote his new revitalisation movement. In a condition of considerable financial hardship, he persuaded Melbourne University Union Activities Department to appoint him their unpaid 'Cosmologer, Living Work of Art and Shaman'. The vice chancellor gave him the use of a lecture theatre for his classes in synthetic cosmology and the director of the National Gallery accepted the offer of his live body as a living work of art.

Becoming increasingly eccentric he developed a unique world view blending magic, mysticism and sociology. A tall man with long beard and robes, he began giving performances as a

[1170] https://en.wikipedia.org/wiki/Wizard_of_New_Zealand

Wizard. At 42 he moved to Christchurch in New Zealand and began to speak on a ladder in Cathedral Square. The city council attempted to have him arrested, but he became so popular that they made the square a public speaking area.

Wearing his costume as a false prophet of the Church of England or his wizard's pointy hat, he has been speaking there at lunchtimes in the summer months ever since, becoming a beloved, if controversial, figure, giving audience to fans and tourists, performing rain dances and other wizardry as necessary.

At 50 the New Zealand Art Gallery Directors Association issued a statement that in their opinion the Wizard was an authentic living work of art and the City Council appointed him Wizard of Christchurch. Eight years later the Prime Minister of New Zealand appointed him the official Wizard of New Zealand.[1171]

Bhagwan Shree Rajneesh was an Indian guru and author of more than a hundred books, which are sold through his organisation. He has Sedna in the eleventh house of collective consciousness, inconjunct Quaoar in the fourth house of home. He was not only intimately familiar with the world's great religions and philosophies, but the modern psychologies of Jung, Freud, Maslow, and the rest of the West's best thinkers in modern psychology and psychiatry.

His syncretic teachings emphasise the importance of meditation, awareness, love, celebration, courage, creativity, and humour — qualities that he viewed as being suppressed by adherence to static belief systems and religious tradition.

When he was 50, the guru founded a commune in Oregon of 1,700 disciples, a sprawling religious community of a hundred square miles. He had continual problems with the local government over land development along with bad press and controversy over his string of pricey Rolls Royce automobiles and fat bankroll. Called the "sex-guru" because of his popular talks about tantric sex, Rajneesh's ashram became known as one big love fest during celebrations.

[1171] Ibid.

"he ashram was an attempt to build a self-sufficient commune based on ecological and organic farming principles, turning the desert into a garden, which they achieved in part. The devotees who joined the ashram came from all walks of life, devoting their money and labor to create a utopia.

The task of running the commune fell to Ma Anand Sheela and the assets of the organization were all in her name. She took full charge of the daily running of the commune and internal strife between her and Rajneesh added to the mix. He claimed that she was trying to establish the Rajneeshees as a religion, and that her quest for personal power led to her paranoia, which eventually spread throughout the commune. He spoke often of how organized religion is an obstacle to enlightenment and he blamed Ma for her ambition of wanting to be the first Popess.

Difficulties accumulated with not only the local citizens but with the National Immigration Service and Revenue Service and Rajneesh was arrested as he fled his strife-torn utopia 4 years later to the tune on 35 counts of conspiracy and fraud, indicted by a Grand Jury in Oregon. On his return to India, he changed his name to Osho to signal a change in his consciousness.[1172]

Shivabalayogi was a meditation guru in the tradition of the ancient and modern yogis of India. He had Sedna in the eleventh house of collective consciousness, inconjuct Quaoar in the fourth house of home.

He attained self-realisation through twelve years of arduous tapas, meditating in samādhi, a state of total thoughtlessness, for an average of twenty hours a day. Tapas is the most advanced stage of meditation in which one remains absorbed for long periods in this non-dualistic state of consciousness.

After he completed tapas, he assumed the name Shivabalayogi, meaning Yogi devoted to Shiva and Parvati. The name reflects that he is a manifestation of both the male and female aspects of the divine. The female aspect represents the invisible energy of the divine through which the entire creation operates, while the male aspect represents the pure consciousness of existence

[1172] https://en.wikipedia.org/wiki/Rajneesh

beyond all imaginations. Generally, devotees called him simply Swamiji, meaning respected Master.

For three decades he traveled extensively in India and Sri Lanka, initiating over ten million people into dhyana meditation. In his early fifties he traveled for four years in England and the United States. His teaching is consistent with the Vedanta, emphasising the need for spiritual practice to achieve self-realisation.[1173]

Quintile, Bi-quintile

The evolutionary quintile or bi-quintile aspect between Sedna and Quaoar infuses our ability to see the big picture, flaws and all, to understand the sacredness of life, to set out in a spirit of discovery and gain new perspectives, with the all-encompassing spiritual energy of Sedna to the point where we can push the boundaries of human development.

Quaoar is that glorious metaphysical process wherein material form is created out of chaos. It urges us to question, construct, clarify and reveal and gives us the potential to ground sacred energy, to take the cosmic chaos and bring it into form, thereby creating a new reality.

Quintiles and bi-quintiles point to talent, the desire to create order and to categorize, a fascination with patterns and structures, perfectionist tendencies, and the desire to build or make things.

These aspects have the characteristics of both the trine and opposition. They point to awareness of conflicts, or problems and finding solutions for them; however, they do not automatically kick into action and must be cultivated over time.

At the unconscious level therefore, these aspects can be challenging, as we'll see in the following examples, because the energies of the two planets are so ethereal that we have no practical way of dealing with it and may fall victim to somebody's deluded perspective.

Like Charles Lindbergh Jr, who was the first son of a noted American family, aviator Charles and pilot-writer Anne Morrow Lindbergh. He was abducted from his home in New Jersey when he was 20 months. He had Sedna in the seventh house of relationships, conjunct Uranus, the planet

---

[1173] https://en.wikipedia.org/wiki/Shivabalayogi

of revolution, which was right on his descendant, inconjunct Quaoar in the eleventh house of collective consciousness.

> The family nurse put 20-month-old Charles in his crib and later discovered it empty. A ransom note in an envelope was found on the windowsill and a ladder outside. An extensive investigation by police followed, together with extended ransom negotiations which resulted in a 70,000 ransom being paid, however the boy was not returned.

> Two months later, a delivery truck driver pulled to the side of a road about 7 kms south of the Lindbergh home. Going into a grove of trees he discovered the body of the toddler. His skull was badly fractured and there were indications of an attempt at a hasty burial. It appeared the child had been killed by a blow to the head. The culprit was eventually convicted through tracing the spending of the ransom money, the numbers of which had been recorded. And the case led to the Lindbergh law, that made kidnapping a federal offence.[1174]

Or like Sybille Niemans, who was a Dutch prostitute, model, and murder victim, known as "Blond Dolly". She had Sedna in the eighth house of shared resources, bi-quintile Quaoar, conjunct Venus, the planet of asthetics and relationships in the twelfth house of the unconscious.

> She was born in Amsterdam as the daughter of a shoemaker. Her first job was that of a fortune teller, but after her divorce somewhere in the mid-1950s, she became a lady of company for rich businessmen. She led a double life, in the evening, she received customers behind the window, but during the day moved in better circles as a model.

> She was emancipated in her prostitution, working without a pimp and and from her own house, which she bought, followed by more real estate. However, she was found dead in her house at the age of 32. Her murderer was never caught; however, she was reportedly afraid of her blue book, which contained a handful of names of high-end regular customers. And the police

---

[1174] https://en.wikipedia.org/wiki/Lindbergh_kidnapping

refused to release the details in the book, leading to rumours that one of these high-ranking people was involved in her murder.[1175]

Or we might develop a deluded perspective ourselves, like James Earl Ray, who was an American assassin who shot civil rights leader Dr. Martin Luther King to death. He had Sedna, conjunct Nessus, the centaur of radical change, both in the ninth house of knowledge, bi-quintile Quaoar in the second house of material resources.

He had a long criminal record and had previously served prison terms. He was born into an extremely poor family with an extensive history of run-ins with the law. He grew up in rough and tumble river towns along the Illinois and Missouri, which doubled as spawning grounds for the KKK. His father abandoned the family when Ray was young, his mother, an alcoholic, eventually had all of her eight children removed to foster care.

One positive relationship grew out of Ray's chaotic childhood, the bond between him and his brothers, Jerry and John. They grew very close through their horrible childhoods and trusted and relied on one another. As the years progressed, Ray was convicted of increasingly severe crimes. A racist, he refused to work with blacks on a prison honour farm.

After an escape from prison when he was 39, he caught up with his brothers and they discussed ways to earn money, including kidnapping the governor of Illinois, or a local star radio host. They also flirted with the idea of going into the porn business. Ray shocked even his brothers when he told them that he was, "going to kill that n----- King. That's something that's been on my mind. That's something I've been working on."

The following year he arrived in Memphis, the exact same day as Dr. Martin Luther King Jr. Newspaper publicity revealed the hotel at which King was staying, as well as the room number. The next day, Ray reconnoitred the hotel from a rundown rooming house across the street and when King stepped outside the door to his room, he fired the single shot that killed him.

After the shooting, he panicked and threw the murder weapon, which was wrapped in a bundle, against a store front. The quick

---

[1175] https://en.wikipedia.org/wiki/Blonde_Dolly

discovery of this by police was the critical piece of evidence that helped police identify him as the shooter. An accustomed international traveler however, he was able to flee to Canada and return to England. But he ran low on money, which caused him to rob a bank, and just as he was about to board a plane for Brussels, he was arrested at Heathrow International Airport.[1176]

Or we might cut corners and take the easy way, just because we see we can. Like Tommaso Buscetta, who was a Sicilian Mafiosa, the first major figure in the Sicilian Mafia to break the code of omerta, the traditional vow of silence. His Sedna is also in the ninth house of knowledge, bi-quintile Quaoar in the second house of material resources.

His criminal record began at 21, with bootlegged cigarettes. He soon began traveling to Brazil and America where at one time he opened a chain of pizza parlors that reportedly served as a cover for drug dealing. Arrested in New York at 42, he fled to Brazil.

Up till that time, a hundred top Mafia families had controlled organised crime in Italy, focusing on their traditional areas of agriculture, construction, extortion, prostitution and some drug smuggling. They had their codes; politicians and police were "cultivated," not murdered and women and children were off-limits. All that changed when the French Connection was broken in the 1970's and Sicily succeeded Marseilles as the world's heroin capital.

The heroin traffic became immense and new groups began fighting for a piece of the action. Wives and children were massacred, along with their Mafia husbands and troublesome officials. Unfortunately, Buscetta aligned himself with one of the loosing clans, two of his sons disappeared and his brother and nephew were gunned down at work. In all, at least 14 members of his family were slain. When he was extradited to Italy, he sought assurance that he would be protected, should he talk and, when he did, authorities were amazed at the amount and detail of his accounts.

He provided a comprehensive description of the Mafia's internal structure and precise information on 122 recent murders. He

[1176] https://en.wikipedia.org/wiki/James_Earl_Ray

explained the command structure and how each clan had its territorial base. Though each clan was autonomous, a supreme commission, composed of representatives from a dozen major families, made all decisions on crimes and investments and arbitrated disputes. He also provided previously unknown information about the mob operation in the U.S.

His lengthy confession, at 57, precipitated the most determined crack-down on organized crime that has ever been instigated. Following his testimony 66 suspected Mafiosa were arrested, with warrants for another 140. He then effectively disappeared into the witness protection program, assuming a new name and identity somewhere in the U.S.[1177]

As we tire of density and the grief it creates, and we start a spiritual journey to get out of the swamp, Sedna rewards us with transcendent crises, experiences which force us to let go and rise above them, resulting in a huge growth to a new level of consciousness. There is no choice with these crises, and the more we try and solve them, the more we will get hurt.

We are all unconscious of our Sedna energy at times, particularly as children, and must grow to understand it, so our lives are likely to represent different stages of the Sedna journey at different times. In the last example Buscetta did have a transcendent crisis at 57, through which he rose above the density and the grief in his life to achieve a more peaceful state. So, my placement of him in the unconscious section is rather arbitrary.

Gwen Verdon was an American dancer, a Tony-award winning performer, who took lessons at age two to strengthen her crippled legs. She had Sedna conjunct Mars, the planet of action, in the first house of identity, bi-quintile Quaoar in the sixth house of service.

As an infant, her legs were so badly bent that medical advisors recommended they be broken and reset. Her mother, who was a former vaudeville dancer, refused, put her in corrective shoes, and started her on dance lessons. She had a first recital at age four and was in her first theatre show at six. During childhood, she wore corrective boots designed to support her legs.

[1177] https://en.wikipedia.org/wiki/Tommaso_Buscetta

After taking dancing lessons, she appeared with her mother in a dance recital in Los Angeles, and at six was billed as "the world's fastest tapper" at local theatres. When she became a teenager, she modelled for bathing suit pictures, and danced in chorus lines in night clubs. She also appeared in a revival of Showboat in Los Angeles and was a pro before she ever studied ballet.

In her early 20s, she went to work as an assistant to a dance director, had a few small parts, but mostly worked behind the scenes, teaching and directing. At 28, she tried out for the Broadway show "Can-Can." She got the part and won a Tony award for her work. In her early thirties, she appeared on Broadway as Lola in "Damn Yankees" and won her second Tony. Throughout the rest of her career she appeared in movies, plays and more television performances and a long list of hit musical comedies.[1178]

Gerald Wasserburg is an American geophysicist who serves as a professor of geology and geophysics at the California Institute of Technology and heads a division of the Institute's Laboratory of Geological Sciences. His Sedna is conjunct Nessus, the centaur of radical change, in the third house of ideas, bi-quintile Quaoar in the eighth house of shared resources.

At the lab, he has produced some of the most critical measurements in the history of geophysics, significantly influencing theories about the creation of the solar system. He is pugnacious, hyper and a high school dropout. He also forged a birth certificate, enlisted in the army when he was 16 and was decorated for bravery under fire. At 27, he received his Ph.D.

He was deeply involved in the Apollo Program with the returned Lunar samples, including pioneering the precise measurement of ultra-small samples under strict clean room conditions with minimal contamination. His research led to a better understanding of the origins and history of the solar system and its component bodies and the precursor stellar sources contributing to the solar system; this research established a time scale for the development of the early solar system, including the processes of nucleosynthesis and the formation and evolution of

---

[1178] https://en.wikipedia.org/wiki/Gwen_Verdon

the planets, the Moon and the meteorites. More recently, he investigated models of the chemical evolution of the Galaxy. He is noted as an egomaniac and scientific compulsive.[1179]

Francis Clark Howell was an American anthropologist. His Sedna is also conjunct Nessus, the centaur of radical change, but in almost the opposite house placement to Wasserberg. Howel has both conjunct the MC, the cusp of the tenth house of profession, bi-quintile Quaoar in the second house of material resources.

He altered the landscape of his discipline irrevocably by adding a broad spectrum of modern sciences to the traditional "stones and bones" approach of the past and is considered the father of modern paleo-anthropology.

His early work focused on Homo neanderthalensis for which he made trips to Europe beginning when he was 28. His later work brought him to Africa, the cradle of mankind. In his early thirties he worked in Tanzania, where he recovered enormous 260,000-year-old hand-axes. Continuing his study of this period, he excavated in Spain in his late 30's at the sites which are 300,000 to 400,000 years old. At none of these sites did he find skeletal material however.

"That had to wait until he worked on lower Pleistocene deposits in southern Ethiopia. There he found vertebrate fossils of monkeys as well as hominids. It was here that he also pioneered new dating methods based on potassium-argon radioisotope techniques. Finally, he wrote a popular mainstream book on human evolution, *Early Man*, which was published when he was 40 as part of the *Time-Life's LIFE Nature Library* series.[1180]

Ethel Kennedy was an American news figure and the wife of Robert Kennedy. She has Sedna conjunct Jupiter, the planet of expansion, and Nessus, the centaur of radical change, in the first house of identity, bi-quintile Quaoar in the seventh house of relationships.

A wonderful sense of humour sustains her and she likes to tease and be teased. She has been her family's beacon of faith, whose life work has been her children. Born into a large Catholic family

---

[1179] https://en.wikipedia.org/wiki/Gerald_J._Wasserburg
[1180] https://en.wikipedia.org/wiki/Francis_Clark_Howell

with more money than the Kennedy's, she loved her parents, who were both alcoholics. Ethel and her siblings grew up wild and she developed the habit of lashing out at anyone that was critical of her family and has remained fierce when provoked. Both of her parents and her brother were killed in separate plane crashes.

She married Bobby Kennedy when she was 22 and they had 11 children, the youngest of which was born after Bobby's assassination when she was 40. She takes her widowhood very seriously and never remarried because no other man could be as good as Bobby. Through all of the problems over the years she has been the glue that holds the family together in every crisis. Her children see her as a 'doer' who is filled with love, supports causes and makes people feel special.

Through many family tragedies, she has relied on her religious faith. Crises have included not only the death of her Senator husband, but drug rehab for her sons, the death of son David when she was 56, due to a drug overdose, reckless driving of son Joe that left a girl paralysed for life, and the death of son Michael in a skiing accident when she was 70. Her daughter, Kathleen Kennedy Townsend, was elected lieutenant governor of Virginia however, and all of her children now are committed to public service.

At 64 she toured Eastern Europe, donating medical equipment and at 69 toured Kenya to promote democratic reforms. She attends mass every day, prays often and has softened over time. At 96 she was awarded a Presidential Medal of Freedom by President Obama for her dedication to "advancing the cause of social justice, human rights, environmental protection, and poverty reduction by creating countless ripples of hope to effect change around the world".[1181]

At this juncture in human evolution, few of us use our planets at the spiritual level, but many of us are striving to, and such people are wonderful to be around. As with the other planets, the spiritual level of evolution is vastly different with Sedna from the two previous levels.

[1181] https://en.wikipedia.org/wiki/Ethel_Kennedy

Here, the quintile and bi-quintile aspects with Quaoar brings a sensitivity to esoteric guides and the spirit world and the ability to see things from a fresh perspective, to see the big picture and bring new form out of the cosmic chaos. The struggle of the beginner's level is gone, as are the transcendental crises of the intermediate level. At this level everything Saturnian is meaningless and yet everything Sednian has its place.

Dolores Ashcroft-Nowicki is a British author of occult books and director of an organisation called Servants of Light, located on Jersey Island. She has Sedna in the fifth house of creativity, bi-quintile Quaoar in the tenth house of profession.

> She is a third-generation psychic, who has working with magic since childhood. She studied under the late W. E. Butler and, with him, was a founding member of the Servants of the Light School of Occult Science, of which she was Director of Studies. She travels the world lecturing on all aspects of the occult and is the author of many successful books, including *The Ritual Magic Workbook, A Practical Course of Self-Initiation*, designed to take a student of the occult through a full year of magical training, published when she was 62; *The Tree of Ecstasy*, published at 69 and *The New Book of the Dead*, published at 82.[1182]

Marion Woodman is a Canadian Jungian analyst, a renowned speaker and author of several books; she is an expert on eating disorders. She has Sedna in the fourth house of home, bi-quintile Quaoar in the ninth house of knowledge.

> The daughter of a minister with two younger brothers, Woodman completed her education to become a teacher. Beginning her inward journey, she began reading Jung. She traveled to India and to Zurich to study and became a practicing Jungian analyst at 51. She is regarded internationally as an expert on the spiritual causes of addictions and well respected for her work helping women escape the traps of patriarchal culture. Her intensive workshops are well attended and her books have sold well over 200,000 copies worldwide. Her books include; *Addiction to Perfection*, published when she was 54; *The*

[1182] https://en.wikipedia.org/wiki/Dolores_Ashcroft-Nowicki

Pregnant Virgin, published at 57 and *The Ravaged Bridegroom*, published at 62.[1183]

Irwyn Greif is a practicing American psychic from the age of 25, specialising in reincarnation readings. He has Sedna in the twelfth house of the unconscious, bi-quintile Quaoar in the fifth house of creativity. He also reads photographs and can spot cancer, schizophrenia and suicidal tendencies. He has developed motivational counselling and also does dream analysis. He has written a number of books, notably *The Soul Is a Traveler in Time*, published when he was 65.

> This book describes psychic experiences and Angel contacts made by the author. It is designed for New Age readers, to help them to raise their consciousness levels and to give them understanding of what lies beyond our five senses, beyond our earthly plane, and even beyond our comprehension.[1184]

Another titled, *Other Dimensions*, was published when he was 78.

> This book is the culmination of a lifetime of psychic experiences and revelations and communications with Angels and UFOs. In order to achieve this the author's consciousness had to be "raised" to an angelic level. Although there are many books written on these subjects, the author dares to reveal the true definition of the Creator and explains why the Creator has the need to create.

> This book contradicts and challenges the existing religions and scientific beliefs and explains in simple language the existence and mysteries of other dimensional worlds and the role that UFOs play in the evolution and preservation of the human race. Some of the material in this book is based upon "contactee" reports and observations. This book attempts to reveal and explain the "big picture" of existence. This book is the most controversial, challenging and mindexpanding writing of our times.[1185]

[1183] https://en.wikipedia.org/wiki/Marion_Woodman
[1184] Greif, Irwyn. *The Soul Is a Traveler in Time*, 1985
[1185] Greif, Irwyn. *Other Dimensions*, 2008

Oonagh Shanley-Toffolo was an Irish former nun, a midwife and acupuncturist. She has Sedna in the sixth house of service, bi-quintile Quaoar in the eleventh house of collective consciousness.

In her inspiring memoir, *The Voice of Silence*, published when she was 73, she tells of her childhood in Ireland, her training in Chinese medicine, her own brush with death, miraculous recovery, leaving the convent, getting married, and her work with Princess Diana. She is a born healer, who has lived life on her own terms. She speaks confidently with an engaging Irish brogue and has always known that her role was to serve and to heal. After an acupuncture session, clients report that they feel like they could levitate off the table. Her philosophy is that 'the secret of unhappiness lies in trying to please everybody. It is a moral impossibility and compromises our true selves'.[1186]

[1186] https://www.astro.com/astro-databank/Shanley-Toffolo,_Oonagh

45: Sedna / Eris

There is no one alive today with any aspect between Sedna and Eris except the flows and no other aspect occurs during the next century, so only the flows are interpreted here.

Semi-sextile, Sextile, Trine

With the flowing aspects between Sedna and Eris, the all-encompassing spiritual energy of Sedna aligns with our personal sense of emergence, our no-holds-barred fight for continued existence and our ability to embrace new ideas and new concepts that challenge us to grow and to make a stand for what we believe.

Eris provokes change by upsetting our limiting and antiquated structures of consciousness, opening us to see beyond the finite bounds of our current perception, beyond the bounds we place on ourselves, arousing and challenging us in the process and catalysing significant shifts in our lives that we would not otherwise initiate on our own.

At the unconscious level, even the flows between these two planets can be challenging, because the energies are so ethereal that we have no practical way of dealing with it and so may fall victim to the more negative side of Eris, which is greed and workaholism, a general lack of spiritual regard for life, or being forsaken, condemned or abandoned. And we are all unconscious of our Sedna energy at times, particularly as children, and must grow to understand it.

Like Shane Lambert, who was a 4-year-old American accidental death/homicide victim, who was killed along with his sister and his aunt, while attempting to cross a busy multi-lane highway. He had Sedna in the fourth house of home, semi-sextile Eris in the third house of ideas.

> His aunt, a married mom with two teenagers, had inexplicably crossed the median on the Interstate highway. After stopping her car in the wrong direction, she then undressed herself, Shane and his sister and walked the children into oncoming traffic. All three of them were killed when two cars hit them head-on.[1187]

Shane's Sedna however was also in a fateful inconjunct with Pluto, the planet of life and death, in the twelfth house of the unconscious, and

---

[1187] https://www.womansday.com/relationships/family-friends/news/a50713/her-sister-killed-her-kids-and-she-forgave-her/

opposite the conjunction of Juno, the asteroid of partnership, and Phollus, the centaur of reality meltdown, in the tenth house of social standing.

> Although the aunt had suffered from depression and bipolar disorder in recent years, "we thought she was taking medication and everything was under control," says the children's mother, who was the aunt's twin. "She seemed perfectly normal when she picked up the kids at our house that night. But somewhere on the way to her house for the party, she suffered a psychotic breakdown."

> After Shane's funeral, she had been shocked to discover that her sister had received a citation from a state trooper for failing to stay within striped lines while on the way to their home that evening. "She had stopped in the highway median, and when a good Samaritan tried to help her, she hit him and kept calling him 'Harry,'" his mon recalls. "Then she sat down in a puddle of water and started splashing around."

> Passing drivers called the police, and three officers debated whether to take the aunt involuntarily to the hospital. But they ultimately decided to allow her sister to drive on, even though she told them she was on her way to pick up her niece and nephew.[1188]

Or like Maria Swanenburg, who was a Dutch care provider known as "Good Natured Mie" for her cheerful attitude of taking care of people. She had Sedna in the eleventh house of collective consciousness, semi-sextile Eris in the tenth house of profession. She professionally cared for kin and friends who were ill or needy. However, her Sedna is also semi-square Neptune, the planet of lies and deceit, in the ninth house of knowledge, and square Pholus, the centaur for which nothing is sacred, in the seventh house of relationships.

> She poisoned at least 102 people with arsenic, of whom 27 died and 16 of those were her relatives. The investigation included more than ninety suspicious deaths. Forty-five of the survivors sustained chronic health problems after ingesting the poison. Her motive was the money she would receive either through the

---

[1188] Ibid.

victims' insurance, or their inheritance. She had secured most of the insurance policies herself. Her first victim was her own mother when she was 41; shortly after this, she killed her father too. She was sentenced to life in prison at 46, dying in jail 30 years later.[1189]

Herculine Barbin was a French hermaphrodite, born in the eighteenth century with ambiguous genitalia and was consigned the female sex. She had Sedna in the eighth house of shared resources, semi-sextile Eris in the sixth house of daily routine.

Her father died sometime early in her life and when she was age seven her destitute mother accepted the offer of a Mother Superior in a convent. Barbin was moved from the hospital where she had lived since birth into a Catholic orphanage where she lived as a pious girl till she was 15. From 15 to 18 she lived as a boarding student and completed her teaching certificate at a normal school and at the top of her class. During this time she cut away with scissors the light down growing on her upper lips and cheeks and kept her body concealed when the female trainee teachers went swimming.[1190]

Her Sedna is also opposite the conjunction of Pallas, the asteroid of wisdom, and Ceres, the planet of nurturing, in the second house of physical reality and the body.

From 20 to 22 she became schoolmistress at a nearby town, falling passionately in love with Sara, another schoolmistress. They moved from bedmates to lovers. At 22 she confided her predicaments to a bishop who sent her to a doctor. The doctor's reports revealed that she was androgynous when dressed, but with a man's chest, slightly brown and hairy upper arms, hips and pelvis of a man, and buttocks and thighs covered in abundant black hair. She had never menstruated. A sort of clitoris-penis of about 5cm and below this was a urethral opening that was "completely feminine" through which she would urinate and apparently pass sperm.

[1189] https://en.wikipedia.org/wiki/Maria_Swanenburg
[1190] https://en.wikipedia.org/wiki/Herculine_Barbin

Barbin was subsequently renamed Abel, with the changes made on her birth certificate to officially reclassify her as a man. Abel's story was reported in the press. Moving to Paris, he became an employee of the railroad administration, continuing his correspondence with Sara.[1191]

However, his Sedna is also semi-square Neptune, which, like Eris, is in the sixth house of daily routine.

He committed suicide close to age 30, asphyxiating himself with carbon dioxide by means of a charcoal stove in a miserable attic in Paris. He was alone and left a letter saying he had killed himself in order to escape the sufferings that constantly obsessed him.[1192]

As we tire of density and the grief it creates, and we start a spiritual journey to get out of the swamp, Sedna rewards us with transcendent crises, experiences which force us to let go and rise above them, resulting in a huge growth to a new level of consciousness. There is no choice with these crises, and the more we try and solve them, the more we will get hurt.

Nicchia Oldoini was an Italian Countess, said to be the most beautiful woman of her time and who, as a courtesan, also worked as a political operative. She had Sedna in the third house of communication, semi-sextile Eris, also in the third house.

She had married the Count of Castiglione, who was twelve years her senior, at the age of 17, but her cousin was a minister to the king of Sardinia and she traveled to Paris with him, under instruction to plead the cause of Italian unity with Napoleon III of France.[1193]

Her Sedna was also bi-quintile Juno, the asteroid of partnership, in the eleventh house of collective consciousness.

She achieved notoriety by becoming the French Emperor's mistress, a scandal that led her husband to demand a marital separation. During her relationship with Napoleon when she was

---

[1191] Ibid.

[1192] Ibid.

[1193] https://en.wikipedia.org/wiki/Virginia_Oldoini,_Countess_of_Castiglione

Alan Clay

19 and 20, she entered the social circle of European royalty and then returned to Italy when her affair was over.

Four years later, the Kingdom of Italy was proclaimed, conceivably in part due to her influence on Napoleon. That same year, she returned to France. At the age of 34, just after the defeat of France in the Franco-Prussian War, she was called to a secret meeting with Otto von Bismarck to explain to him how the German occupation of Paris could be fatal to his interests. She may have been very persuasive, because Paris was spared Prussian occupation.[1194]

Her Sedna is also sesquiquadrate the conjunction of Mars, the planet of action and Jupiter, the planet of expansion, in the eighth house of shared resources.

She was also a significant figure in the early history of photography. She began sitting for the photographers at the imperial court and over the next four decades she directed one of these to help her produce 700 different photographs in which she re-created the signature moments of her life for the camera. She spent a large part of her personal fortune and even went into debt to execute this project; however, a large part of this collection is now in the Metropolitan Museum of Art in New York.[1195]

Lewis Carroll was an English logician, mathematician, clergyman, photographer and novelist, who was considered a master in the genre of nonsense literature. He had Sedna in the third house of ideas and communication, semi-sextile Eris, which is conjunct Haumea, the dwarf planet of rebirth, and Pallas, the asteroid of feminine wisdom, all in the second house of material resources.

Inherently shy, he disliked public school. Additionally, he suffered from a bad stammer, and was often the target of bullies. He received a Bachelor of Arts degree at 22 and the next year was appointed as a lecturer in mathematics, a post he held until he was 49. He was ordained a deacon in the Church of England and could have continued on to become a priest, a position that

[1194] Ibid.
[1195] Ibid.

would have allowed him to marry, but he was content to remain single and was frequently described as a 'shy, fussy bachelor'. Often regarded as a crank, he nevertheless enjoyed good health throughout his life.[1196]

His Sedna is also square Venus, the planet of relationships in the first house of identity.

> His love of children seemed natural and innocent in nature. He had grown up in a large family and his stammer disappeared completely when he was speaking with children. He began to entertain the children of the families in the community and he would keep them amused with what seemed like an endless store of fantastical tales.[1197]

With a semi-square to Quaoar, the planet of new perspectives, in the fifth house of creativity, and an evolutionary quintile with Mercury, the planet of communication, in the second house of material resources.

> As he made up the stories, drawing on incidents in his life, he would sketch his characters on a sheet of paper; his tales holding the children spellbound. Prompted to publish his stories, he wrote the children's books he would be particularly remembered for. *Alice's Adventures in Wonderland*, published when he was 33, and its sequel, *Alice Through the Looking Glass*, became the most popular children's books in England, perhaps the most famous in the world. He also authored several books on mathematics, with *Euclid and His Modern Rivals*, being the most well known. Early in his life he wanted to become an artist, however, failing in this pursuit, he instead became a photographer, specialising in studies of children in every possible situation and costume, including nudes. However, at 48, he abandoned his photographic work, apparently amid much speculation about his motives, as suspicions remained that his pleasure in children had sexual overtones.[1198]

Frances Willard was an American educator and writer, a temperance activist who helped found the Women's Christian Temperance Union, an organisation with the stated purpose of creating a "sober and pure world"

[1196] https://en.wikipedia.org/wiki/Lewis_Carroll
[1197] Ibid.
[1198] Ibid.

by abstinence, purity, and evangelical Christianity. She had Sedna in the fourth house of home, semi-sextile Eris in the third house of communication.

She was an avid promoter of women's rights and heartily campaigned for equal pay for equal work, as well as for the eight-hour workday. The middle child of three, she spent most of her childhood on a farm in Wisconsin. Even as a child, it was evident that she was a leader, whether at play or at school. After graduation, she taught briefly before becoming president of Evanston College for Ladies at 32. Two years later, she became the first Dean of Women at Northwestern.

However, a year later, she left her promising career in education to devote herself fully to the temperance crusade. At 40 she became the second National President of the Temperance Union, a post she held for the next 19 years until she died. Her tireless efforts for the temperance cause included a 50-day speaking tour in 1874, an average of 30,000 miles of travel a year, and an average of 400 lectures a year for a 10-year period. She proved to be an expert lobbyist and was a popular speaker who was seen as both magnetic and sympathetic.

She made a strong argument for female voting rights, based on the platform of Home Protection, 'the object of which was to secure for all women above the age of twenty-one years the ballot, as one means for the protection of their homes from the devastation caused by the legalised traffic in strong drink'. The devastation she was referencing was the prevalence of violent acts against women committed by intoxicated men, both in and outside the home. She argued that it was too easy for men to get away with their crimes if women couldn't vote.

The Home Protection argument was used to garner the support of the average woman, who had been told to be suspicious of female suffragists by the patriarchal press, religious authorities, and society as a whole. The desire for home protection gave the average woman a socially appropriate avenue to seek enfranchisement. However, the goal of the suffrage movement for Willard was to construct an "ideal of womanhood" that allowed women to fulfil their potential as the companions and counsellors of men, as opposed to the "incumbrance and toy of man."

Her suffrage argument also hinged on her feminist interpretation of Scripture. She claimed that natural and divine laws called for equality in the American household, with the mother and father sharing leadership. She expanded this notion of the home, arguing that men and women should lead side by side in matters of education, church, and government, just as "God sets male and female side by side throughout his realm of law".[1199]

Nicolaus Copernicus was a Renaissance-era Polish astronomer, author and mathematician, who is considered the founder of modern astronomy. He formulated a model of the universe that placed the Sun, rather than the Earth, at the centre and was the first to propose that the Earth revolves once on its axis each day. He had Sedna in the sixth house of service, sextile Eris in the eighth house of shared resources.

His expertise spanned a significant number of different subject areas, so he was able to draw on complex bodies of knowledge to solve specific problems. He obtained a doctorate in canon law, the body of laws and regulations made by church leadership for the governance of Christian organisations, churches and their members. And he was also a mathematician, astronomer, physician, classics scholar, translator, governor, diplomat, and economist.

Sometime before he was 41 Copernicus made available to friends a forty-page manuscript describing his ideas about the heliocentric hypothesis. Thereafter he continued gathering data for a more detailed work. By the age of 59 he had basically completed his work on the book manuscript, but despite the urging by his closest friends, he resisted openly publishing his views, not wishing to risk the scorn to which he would expose himself on account of the novelty and incomprehensibility of his theses.

A year later however, a friend delivered a series of lectures in Rome outlining Copernicus's theory and the Pope and several Catholic cardinals heard the lectures and were interested in the

---

[1199] https://en.wikipedia.org/wiki/Frances_Willard

theory. By then Copernicus's work was nearing its definitive form, and rumours about it had reached educated people all over Europe. Despite urgings from many quarters, Copernicus still delayed publication of his book. Scholars disagree on whether his concern was limited to possible astronomical and philosophical objections, or whether he was also concerned about religious objections.

He was still working on the book, even if not certain that he wanted to publish it, when at 66 a mathematician arrived and became Copernicus's pupil, staying with him for two years. He wrote a book, *First Account*, outlining the essence of Copernicus's theory and, having seen the favourable first general reception of his work, Copernicus finally agreed to publish his signature work, *On the Revolutions of the Celestial Spheres*, just before his death at 70. This was a major event in the history of science, triggering the Copernican Revolution and making an important contribution to the Scientific Revolution.[1200]

At this juncture in human evolution, few of us use our planets at the spiritual level, but many of us are striving to, and such people are wonderful to be around. As with the other planets, the spiritual level of evolution is vastly different with Sedna from the two previous levels.

Here, the flowing aspects with Eris brings the awareness that we can't take it with us, which gives us the ability to apply our full resourcefulness in this life. The struggle of the beginner's level is gone, as are the transcendental crises of the intermediate level. At this level everything Saturnian is meaningless and yet everything Sednian has its place.

Isaac Newton was a British astronomer, physicist, mathematician and astrologer who showed how the universe is held together. He had Sedna in the fourth house of home, trine Eris, conjunct his Moon, which are both either in the eighth, or the ninth house, as his time of birth is disputed.

He evidently had a difficult childhood. His father died before he was born; his mother remarried when he was young and left him in the care of his grandparents. He is often described as one of the greatest names in the history of human thought. Biographers

---

[1200] https://en.wikipedia.org/wiki/Nicolaus_Copernicus

speak of his 'year of wonder' when he was 23, when he began his studies into light and color. The mythic story of the apple falling and his discovery of gravity, was said to have happened during this time.

At the age of 30, after presenting his reflecting telescope to the Royal Society, he sent them his paper on the theory of light, which met with uncommon applause and assuring his place in history. He completed his book III of the "Principia" when he was 45. His close collaborator and benefactor was Edmond Halley, who encouraged him with the book, proofread the manuscript and paid for the printing.

Known as an absentminded professor, a reclusive scholar in academia, Newton was suddenly a public figure. He was appointed Master of the Mint at 58 and spent the rest of his life involved in politics. In the early 21st century Newton's cryptic notes were translated and this new review revealed that he was interested in the occult and had very likely carried out secret experiments in alchemy. He "sought to combine a scientific and spiritual understanding of the Universe".[1201]

Reverend Robert Taylor is an early 19th-century English Radical, who was a clergyman turned freethinker. His Sedna was in the third house of communication, sextile Eris in the first house of identity.

He studied at Cambridge to qualify as a clergyman, but five years after ordination gave up on orthodox Christianity and turned to eccentric anti-clericalism. He set up a Christian Evidence Society and lectured in London pubs dressed in elaborate vestments, attacking the Anglican liturgy and the barbarities of the Establishment for what he called its "Pagan creed". At this time blasphemy was a criminal offence and he spent a year in jail, during which time he wrote *The Diegesis*, attacking Christianity on the basis of comparative mythology and attempting to expound it as a scheme of solar myths. On his release he joined up with the radical Richard Carlile and, with his book newly published, they set out on an "infidel home missionary tour". Several times a week when he was 46, he dressed in "canonicals", staged infidel melodramas, preaching

---

[1201] https://en.wikipedia.org/wiki/Isaac_Newton

bombastic sermons to artisans. Two Sunday sermons on "The Devil" caused particular outrage when he pronounced "God and the Devil... to be but one and the self-same being... Hell and Hell-fire... are, in the original, nothing more than names and titles of the Supreme God." He was then dubbed "The Devil's Chaplain", and thousands of copies of his ceremonies were circulated in a seditious publication, *The Devil's Pulpit*.

The following year he was indicted for blasphemy over two Easter sermons was sentenced to a further two years' imprisonment. Charles Darwin was studying at Cambridge at this time and Taylor would be remembered by Darwin as a warning example of an outcast from society who had challenged Christianity and had been imprisoned for blasphemy. This was one of many warnings that gave Darwin a well-founded fear of revealing his theory of evolution.[1202]

Ramakrishna was an Indian saint and mystic, renowned as the founder of the Ramakrishna Mission, better known in the west as the Vedanta Society. He had Sedna in the second house of material resources, semi-sextile Eris in the first house of identity.

An assistant in the temple of the goddess Kali from the age of 19, he devoted his life to his religious ideals. He was a pantheist, believing that all religious paths lead to God-consciousness. To many Hindus he represented a "supremely realized self" and an incarnation of the divine.

Born into a Brahman family, his striking characteristic in childhood was his emotional and aesthetic sensitivity and power. When overwhelmed by beauty and emotion, he would lose consciousness in an ecstatic trance. His early spiritual experiences included going into a state of rapture while watching a flight of cranes and losing consciousness of the outer world while playing the role of the god Shiva in a school play.

His brother became the adviser of a wealthy widow who was building a temple to the Divine Mother Kali, and was appointed the temple's chief priest, and Ramakrishna also became a priest. When his brother died a year later, Ramakrishna took on his role

---

[1202] https://en.wikipedia.org/wiki/Robert_Taylor_(Radical)

as a priest to the Divine Mother, however bereft and desolate by his loss, it drove him to the edge of suicide. After this he experienced his first "God intoxicated state," losing consciousness in a vision of the Divine Mother and submerged in waves of bliss and light. When he regained consciousness, he craved more of the experience. Years later, he would attest that he became "positively insane," spending several years in a state of "divine madness or inebriation" during which visions of various deities appeared repeatedly.

When he was 25, a renunciant mendicant woman arrived at the temple. A master of Tantric discipline, she became Krishna's first guru and guided him through a remarkable transformation over a four-year period that overcame his sense of separation from the world. Altering his continuous visionary state to instead make it his "mansion of mirth," Krishna again returned to the Hindu practices of his childhood.

Four years later another renunciant named Totapuri came to the temple, giving Krishna instruction in the state of the Absolute, a state of consciousness devoid of all conceptual forms. The result was another trance-like state which allegedly lasted nearly a year, almost causing Krishna's physical death. After recovering from this experience, he returned to his "mansion of mirth" and began to expand his religious awareness by studying Islam and Christianity. Both teachings brought visionary realisations, which he recognised were similar to those he experienced of his own Hindu deities. These brief but no less intense visions became the experiential basis for his claim that all religions can lead to the same realisation of the divine.

By the age of 43 he was attracting disciples among the intellectual circles in Calcutta, many of whom had been previously been adopting European and Christian customs. He spent his last years teaching these disciples and streams of visitors. One of these disciples, Vivekananda, recorded his instruction for four years, starting when Krishna was 46 and then spread his message to the world.[1203]

[1203] https://en.wikipedia.org/wiki/Ramakrishna

CPSIA information can be obtained
at www.ICGtesting.com
Printed in the USA
BVHW040937220519
548309BV00012B/7/P